Fodor's 07

P9-AOV-077

CALIFORNIA

Where to Stay and Eat
for All Budgets

Must-See Sights
and Local Secrets

Ratings You Can Trust

Fodor's Travel Publications   New York, Toronto, London, Sydney, Auckland
www.fodors.com

FODOR'S CALIFORNIA 2007

Editors: Carissa Bluestone, Amanda Theunissen, Paul Eisenberg, Michael Nalepa, William Travis

Editorial Production: Eric B. Wechter

Editorial Contributors: Kristina Brooks, Kathy Bryant, Andrew Collins, Cheryl Crabtree, Matthew Flynn, Lenore Greiner, Roger J. Grody, Lisa M. Hamilton, Jim Harrington, Veronica Hill, Kate Hurwitz, Constance Jones, Lina Lecaro, Denise M. Leto, Kathy A. McDonald, Andy Moore, David Nelson, Reed Parsell, Laura Randall, Sharon Silva, John A. Vlahides, Christine Vovakes, Kastle Waserman, Sharron Wood, Bobbi Zane

Maps: David Lindroth, *cartographer;* Rebecca Baer and Bob Blake, *map editors*

Design: Fabrizio La Rocca, *creative director;* Guido Caroti, *art director;* Melanie Marin, *senior picture editor*

Production/Manufacturing: Angela L. McLean

Cover Photo (Coastline, Crescent City): Gary Crabbe/Alamy Images

ISBN: 978–1–4000–1732–4

ISSN: 0192–9925

SPECIAL SALES

This book is available for special discounts for bulk purchases for sales promotions or premiums. Special editions, including personalized covers, excerpts of existing books, and corporate imprints, can be created in large quantities for special needs. For more information, write to Special Markets/Premium Sales, 1745 Broadway, MD 6-2, New York, NY 10019, or e-mail specialmarkets@randomhouse.com.

AN IMPORTANT TIP & AN INVITATION

Although all prices, opening times, and other details in this book are based on information supplied to us at time of writing, changes occur all the time in the travel world, and Fodor's cannot accept responsibility for facts that become outdated or for inadvertent errors or omissions. So **always confirm information when it matters,** especially if you're making a detour to visit a specific place. Your experiences—positive and negative—matter to us. If we have missed or misstated something, **please write to us.** We follow up on all suggestions. Contact the California editor at editors@fodors.com or c/o Fodor's at 1745 Broadway, New York, NY 10019.

PRINTED IN THE UNITED STATES OF AMERICA

10 9 8 7 6 5 4 3 2 1

Be a Fodor's Correspondent

Your opinion matters. It matters to us. It matters to your fellow Fodor's travelers, too. And we'd like to hear it. In fact, we *need* to hear it.

When you share your experiences and opinions, you become an active member of the Fodor's community. That means we'll not only use your feedback to make our books better, but we'll publish your names and comments whenever possible. Throughout our guides, look for "Word of Mouth," excerpts of your unvarnished feedback.

Here's how you can help improve Fodor's for all of us.

Tell us when we're right. We rely on local writers to give you an insider's perspective. But our writers and staff editors—who are the best in the business—depend on you. Your positive feedback is a vote to renew our recommendations for the next edition.

Tell us when we're wrong. We're proud that we update most of our guides every year. But we're not perfect. Things change. Hotels cut services. Museums change hours. Charming cafés lose charm. If our writer didn't quite capture the essence of a place, tell us how you'd do it differently. If any of our descriptions are inaccurate or inadequate, we'll incorporate your changes in the next edition and correct factual errors at fodors.com *immediately.*

Tell us what to include. You probably have had fantastic travel experiences that aren't yet in Fodor's. Why not share them with a community of like-minded travelers? Maybe you chanced upon a beach or bistro or B&B that you don't want to keep to yourself. Tell us why we should include it. And share your discoveries and experiences with everyone directly at fodors.com. Your input may lead us to add a new listing or highlight a place we cover with a "Highly Recommended" star or with our highest rating, "Fodor's Choice."

Give us your opinion instantly at our feedback center at www.fodors.com/feedback. You may also e-mail editors@fodors.com with the subject line "California Editor." Or send your nominations, comments, and complaints by mail to California Editor, Fodor's, 1745 Broadway, New York, NY 10019.

You and travelers like you are the heart of the Fodor's community. Make our community richer by sharing your experiences. Be a Fodor's correspondent.

Happy traveling!

Tim Jarrell, Publisher

CONTENTS

CONTENTS

ABOUT THIS BOOK

Our Ratings

Sometimes you find terrific travel experiences, and sometimes they just find you. But usually the burden is on you to select the right combination of experiences. That's where our ratings come in.

As travelers we've all discovered a place so wonderful that its worthiness is obvious. And sometimes that place is so unique that superlatives don't do it justice: you just have to be there to know. These sights, properties, and experiences get our highest rating, **Fodor's Choice,** indicated by orange stars throughout this book.

Black stars highlight sights and properties we deem **Highly Recommended**, places that our writers, editors, and readers praise again and again for consistency and excellence.

By default, there's another category: any place we include in this book is by definition worth your time, unless we say otherwise. And we will.

Disagree with any of our choices? Care to nominate a place or suggest that we rate one more highly? Visit our feedback center at www.fodors.com/feedback.

Budget Well

Hotel and restaurant price categories from ¢ to $$$$ are defined in the opening pages of each chapter. For attractions, we always give standard adult admission fees; reductions are usually available for children, students, and senior citizens. Want to pay with plastic? **AE, D, DC, MC, V** following restaurant and hotel listings indicate whether American Express, Discover, Diners Club, MasterCard, and Visa are accepted.

Restaurants

Unless we state otherwise, restaurants are open for lunch and dinner daily. We mention dress only when there's a specific requirement and reservations only when they're essential or not accepted—it's always best to book ahead.

Hotels

Hotels have private bath, phone, TV, and air-conditioning and operate on the European Plan (aka EP, meaning without meals), unless we specify that they use the Continental Plan (CP, with a continental breakfast), Breakfast Plan (BP, with a full breakfast), or Modified American Plan (MAP, with breakfast and dinner) or are all-inclusive (including all meals and most activities). We always

list facilities but not whether you'll be charged an extra fee to use them, so when pricing accommodations, find out what's included.

Many Listings
- ★ Fodor's Choice
- ★ Highly recommended
- ✉ Physical address
- ✛ Directions
- ⌂ Mailing address
- ☎ Telephone
- 🖷 Fax
- ⊕ On the Web
- ✆ E-mail
- 🎟 Admission fee
- ☉ Open/closed times
- ► Start of walk/itinerary
- Ⓜ Metro stations
- ▭ Credit cards

Hotels & Restaurants
- 🏨 Hotel
- ⤴ Number of rooms
- ⚲ Facilities
- ⏍⃝ Meal plans
- ✕ Restaurant
- 🖎 Reservations
- 🛆 Dress code
- ↘ Smoking
- ⛏ BYOB
- ✕🏨 Hotel with restaurant that warrants a visit

Outdoors
- ⅄ Golf
- ⛺ Camping

Other
- ☾ Family-friendly
- 🆔 Contact information
- ⇨ See also
- ✉ Branch address
- ☞ Take note

WHAT'S
WHERE

SAN DIEGO 	One of America's favorite tourist destinations, San Diego draws families, retirees, and overseas visitors in droves to mega-attractions such as SeaWorld, the San Diego Zoo, and the Gaslamp Quarter. The nearly constant sunshine helps (though in summer, a marine overcast called "June gloom" is likely to descend), beckoning Boogie-boarders and golfers to the beaches and links. Cruise through the surfer neighborhoods of Pacific, Mission, and Ocean beaches, the stylish gay district of Hillcrest, or well-heeled La Jolla and you'll get an eyeful of the mythical, buff Southern California blond in its natural habitat. But in the faces of many locals you'll also see the legacy of San Diego's Spanish history and the strength of its bond with neighboring Mexico—which you'll also taste almost anywhere you eat.
ORANGE COUNTY 	To some, it's just a sprawling suburb of a sprawling city, an impossible tangle of freeways and shopping centers. To many, however, Orange County is a dreamland of sunny oceanfront communities, premium golf and spa resorts, first-rate restaurants, and kid-friendly attractions. The Pacific Coast Highway winds past strollable stops such as arty downtown Laguna Beach and the yacht harbor at Newport Beach; head inland for big-time family fun at Disneyland and Knott's Berry Farm. Off the coast, Catalina Island offers refreshment in the form of mountains, coves, and two tiny harbor towns.
LOS ANGELES 	Love it or hate it, you have to admit that Los Angeles is a world-class metropolis on a par with New York, London, or Tokyo. A vibrant mix of arts and cultural institutions, from the Geffen Contemporary to the Museum of Tolerance, thrive. In a mosaic of neighborhoods, inventive restaurants serve some truly fine food and fashionable shops peddle urban style. Along the Sunset Strip the club scene sizzles—until last call at 2 AM. You can take an up-close look at still-mighty Hollywood on one of the studio tours, and the colorful beach scene awaits in Venice and Santa Monica. Just don't expect to go anywhere on foot, on public transportation, or quickly: addicted to the automobile, spread-out L.A. is a prisoner of its clogged freeway system.

THE INLAND EMPIRE 	The bedroom communities east of Los Angeles get a bad (and not undeserved) rap for traffic congestion and suburban monotony, but lift your eyes to the hills and you'll see the area's appeal. In the year-round alpine retreats of Wrightwood and Idyllwild, galleries, inns, and hiking trails provide welcome respite from cookie-cutter living. Los Angelenos come to the San Bernardino Mountains for Big Bear's skiing and Lake Arrowhead's water sports. Much farther south, the wineries of the Temecula Valley are starting to mature.
PALM SPRINGS & THE SOUTHERN DESERT 	What are several hundred thousand people doing in the middle of the California desert, where temperatures top 100° for four straight months and only a few inches of rain fall each year? When they're not playing golf on some of the West's finest courses, they're likely enjoying spa treatments, doing some high-end shopping, or dining at swanky—though perhaps not very good and probably overpriced—restaurants. You can join the ranks of the pampered at one of the fabulous resorts, or slip away to commune with the desert's purity at Joshua Tree National Park, Anza-Borrego Desert State Park, or the Salton Sea.
THE MOJAVE DESERT & DEATH VALLEY 	If you allow it to, the stark, sun-blasted beauty of the desert can strip your mind of its everyday clutter. Sparsely settled, the vast landscapes of southeastern California are hardly empty: the colors, craters, and dunes of Death Valley rank among the most spectacular scenery in the national park system. Canyons and ridges break the blistering terrain of the Mojave Desert, where the thread of human history stretches from Petroglyph Canyons to Calico Ghost Town to the California Route 66 Museum. In this hardscrabble country, bland chains or simple mom-and-pops provide basic food and shelter. Worldly pleasures may be in short supply, but nature makes up the difference.
THE SOUTHERN SIERRA 	People from around the world travel to California to see Yosemite National Park's towering granite monoliths, verdant glacial valleys, and lofty waterfalls. The park's natural attributes do live up to the hype, but if you come May through September, you're likely to see more visitors than vistas. The same holds true for neighboring Sequoia and Kings Canyon national parks, which share Yosemite's jaw-dropping Sierra Nevada backdrop, thick with giant sequoias. If you can take the road less traveled by the motor coaches, miles of hiking trails await in all three parks. In winter the Sierra's magically

WHAT'S
WHERE

	powdery snow drifts high, bestowing the state's best skiing on the resorts around Mammoth Lakes.
THE CENTRAL VALLEY 	On the arid plain between the Sierra Nevada and the Coast Ranges the incredibly fertile land works. Mile after mile of irrigated fields, vineyards, and pastureland produce fruits, vegetables, and livestock. Farm equipment often lifts a haze of soil and agricultural chemicals into the brutal summer heat; dense tule fog shuts out the sun for much of the winter. Built for function rather than form, the valley's towns and cities are less destinations than stopovers off Interstate 5, the fastest route between Los Angeles and the San Francisco Bay Area. Fresno serves as the major gateway to the Southern Sierra, and about 50 wineries operate around Lodi.
THE CENTRAL COAST 	Stretched along the coast between the L.A. metroplex and the San Francisco Bay Area lies a miracle: a 200-plus-mi swath of virtually undeveloped oceanfront real estate. It's as if the densely populated corridor between New York City and Washington, D.C., were replaced by an estimable yet untrammeled wine country, picture-perfect ranches and farms, and a scattering of laid-back beach towns. Driving the famously scenic Pacific Coast Highway, most tourists make only three stops: in pricey Santa Barbara, nestled in the hills behind a crescent bay; at lavish, remote Hearst Castle, perched high above San Simeon; and around the nontown of Big Sur, where the mountains crowd up against the sea along ragged cliffs. Stop anywhere else along the way to see how California's regular Joes catch their R&R.
MONTEREY BAY 	Monterey well deserves its popularity as a vacation destination. The city has carefully preserved history, an outstanding aquarium, souvenir and gift shops galore, and a setting on a broad bay. Herds of tour buses stampede daily in season, but to the south, on either end of 17-Mile Drive, Victorian-flavored Pacific Grove and the exclusive mission town of Carmel are incrementally quieter. On the northern edge of the bay Santa Cruz occupies several wrinkles in time, with its old-school beach boardwalk, ethnic clothing shops, surfer dudes, and pierced college students. All around Monterey Bay you can spend a lot to dine very well or badly, and you'll probably pay dearly for your room.

THE PENINSULA & SOUTH BAY 	South of San Francisco, Silicon Valley occupies the eastern shore of the peninsula that sequesters the bay from the Pacific Ocean. In this prosperous land of corporate parks, technology eclipses tourism, though the twain do meet in places such as Stanford University and San Jose's Tech Museum of Innovation. The bump and hustle of dot-com business, which can make for heavy traffic along the many freeways, imparts an energetic buzz to the restaurants and bars of downtown Palo Alto and San Jose. A world away across a mountain range, nature still reigns on the often foggy coastal peninsula. Highway 1 threads up rugged shoreline past the elephant seal rookery at Año Nuevo State Reserve and beach getaways such as Half Moon Bay.
SAN FRANCISCO 	It's possible that no city in America outranks San Francisco in recognizable landmarks per square mile: the Golden Gate Bridge, Fisherman's Wharf, cable cars, Alcatraz, Chinatown—the list goes on and on. But if you look beyond all that, you'll see something even better: the real San Francisco. Dump the car, hop on the great public transport, and use your feet to get out into the diverse neighborhoods, from exclusive Pacific Heights to the Hispanic Mission to the gay Castro. That's where the city's personality—an amalgam of gold-rush history, immigrant traditions, counterculture proclivities, and millennial materialism—looms large in a population only around the size of Indianapolis. This character also manifests itself in spirited dining, arts, and shopping scenes packed into a small and very manageable footprint. Remember to carry a thick wallet, and dress in layers for the weird and changeable weather.
THE WINE COUNTRY 	No longer the state's only wine-producing region, Napa and Sonoma counties nonetheless retain their title as *the* California wine country famed around the country and the world. Along Highway 29 in the Napa Valley and Highway 12 in the Sonoma Valley the wineries stand cheek by jowl, as do the cars and buses in high season. Come when the crowds have thinned, though, and avoid the dumbed-down category of tasting rooms with tiny plastic cups, and you will find your reward. An orgy of impossible-to-find-elsewhere bottles awaits you, as well as restaurants that stand among California's best, indulgent spas, and extravagant inns and hotels. Throw in the velvety green hills and the gentle climate, and you can almost forgive the steep tasting fees.

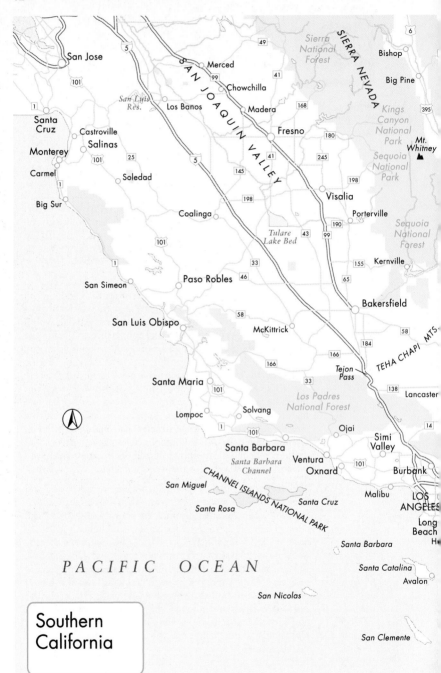

Southern
California

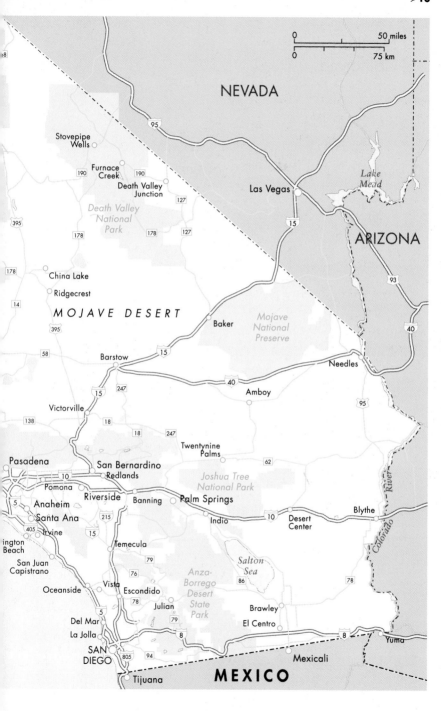

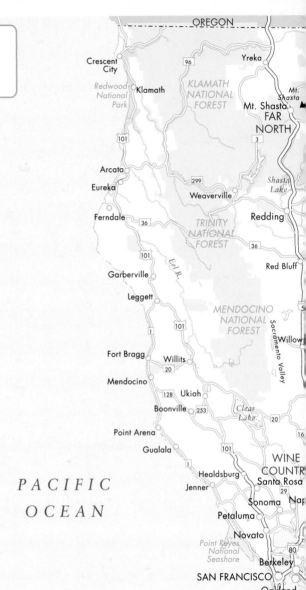

Northern
California

OREGON

Crescent
City

96

Yreka

Redwood
National
Park

Klamath

KLAMATH
NATIONAL
FOREST

Mt.
Shasta

Mt. Shasta

FAR
NORTH

3

Arcata

Eureka

299

Shasta
Lake

Weaverville

Redding

Ferndale

36

TRINITY
NATIONAL
FOREST

36

101

Eel R.

Red Bluff

Garberville

Leggett

MENDOCINO
NATIONAL
FOREST

5

1

101

Sacramento Valley

Willows

Fort Bragg

Willits

20

Mendocino

128

Ukiah

Boonville

253

Clear
Lake

20

Point Arena

16

Gualala

101

WINE
COUNTR

1

Healdsburg

Santa Rosa

Jenner

29

Sonoma

Nap

PACIFIC

Petaluma

OCEAN

Novato

Point Reyes
National
Seashore

80

Berkeley

SAN FRANCISCO

Oakland

San Mateo

Palo Alto

1

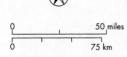

0   50 miles

0   75 km

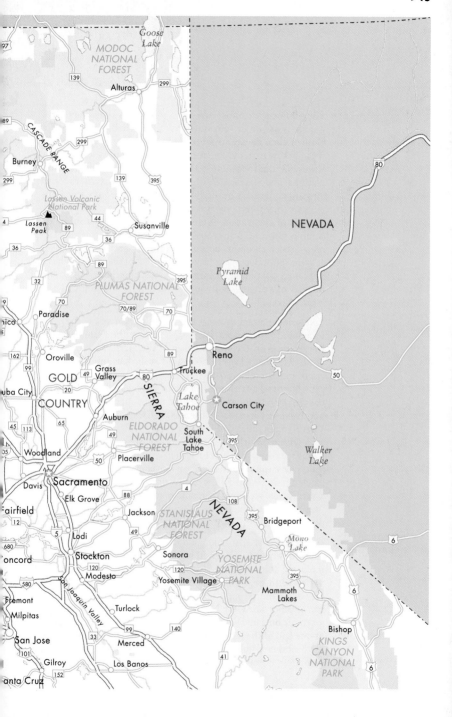

WHAT'S WHERE

THE NORTH COAST 	The 400 northernmost miles of California's coastline unfurl gradually as you drive winding, two-lane Highway 1 from the Golden Gate Bridge to the Oregon state line. Indeed, slowly is the best way to experience natural knockouts such as Point Reyes National Seashore, Salt Point State Park, and Redwood National and State Parks. Even when rain or fog turns the land lonesome, nature's beauty is the main attraction, with shopping and nightlife a novelty and inspired cuisine a rarity. A few pockets of civilization—sophisticated southern Marin, unassuming Gualala, Yankee-ish Mendocino, gingerbready Eureka—serve as oases, as do several noteworthy lodgings in isolated spots. But if your heart doesn't race at the sight of whales migrating past craggy bluffs or of mist filtering through the boughs of colossal redwoods, you'll miss the point of the North Coast.
THE GOLD COUNTRY 	Like some mammoth historical theme park that's been dynamited and blown across several counties, the Gold Country freezes time on the western face of the Sierra Nevada, circa 1848–98. The delirious 1849 gold rush that built San Francisco and Sacramento started here, and the former mining camps strung out along 185 mi of Highway 49 replay their past to the hilt. In family-oriented towns such as Sutter Creek and Nevada City small museums, galleries, and cafés occupy Victorian buildings on Old West main streets; most of Coloma falls within Marshall Gold Discovery State Historic Park. It seems appropriate that gold-rush history saturates Sacramento, the state capital, otherwise an unremarkable place. You'll catch unmistakable whiffs of cheesiness along the Gold Country trail, as well another, much lovelier, scent: the Sierra Foothills wine country is booming, especially in the Shenandoah Valley north of Amador City.
LAKE TAHOE 	When you first visit Lake Tahoe, especially if you arrive on a sunny day, you will be awed by the sight of miles of crystalline, intensely blue water against the peaks of the High Sierra. A perfect setting for outdoor activities from hiking to golf in summer and from skiing to snowmobiling in winter, the lake also has another side—the Nevada side. Casinos in all their tacky splendor butt up to the state line bordering South Lake Tahoe at one end of the lake and delimiting Nevada's Incline Village at the other. Whether for the sightseeing, the exercise, the gambling, or all three, the throngs overrun Tahoe in summer.

California's far northeast corner has a backwoods character that appeals to hard-core outdoorsy types. Hiking in thermally active Lassen Volcanic National Park, mountaineering on Mt. Shasta, and rock climbing in Castle Crags State Park number among the ways you can enjoy the cool air and the alpine scenery. All summer, anglers fish the Far North's trout-rich lakes and streams while houseboats and Jet-Skis buzz around Lake Shasta. Many of the humble—and humbly priced—visitor services shut down in winter, though not those near Mt. Shasta's ski resort.

QUINTESSENTIAL CALIFORNIA

The Automobile

If America has a love affair with the car, California has an out-and-out obsession. Even when gasoline prices go through the roof and freeway traffic slows to a crawl, their passion burns as hot as ever. Witness this ardor any summer weekend at huge classic- and custom-car shows throughout the state. An even better place to feel the love is behind the wheel. Drive through a canyon to the sea on Laguna Canyon Road to Laguna Beach; trace an old stagecoach route through the mountains above Santa Barbara on Highway 154; follow 17-Mile Drive along the precipitous edge of the Monterey Peninsula. Gorgeous for the most part, but authentically congested in some areas down south, Highway 1 runs almost the entire length of the California coast. Wherever you go on the road, you'll see California the way many locals prefer to: from inside a car.

The Beach

California's beach culture is, in a word, legendary. It only makes sense that a state with 1,264 mi of coastline, a hefty portion of which sees the sun upward of 300 days a year, would perfect the art of beach-going. It starts with year-round maintenance of a reasonably beach-ready physique and a wardrobe of stylish flip-flops, bikinis, and wet suits. Mastery of at least one beach skill—surfing, Boogie-boarding, kayaking, Frisbee-tossing, power-walking—is essential, as is having the right gear. As a visitor, you need only one bathing suit and some rented equipment. You can go to the beach almost anywhere, thanks to the Californian belief in coastal access as a birthright. The farther south you go, the wider, sandier, and sunnier the beaches; the farther north, the rockier and foggier, with colder and rougher surf. Each offers a little something different: just find any beach and spend an afternoon.

Californians live in such a large and splashy state that they seem sometimes to forget about the rest of the country. They have a distinctive culture all their own, which you can delve into by doing as the natives do.

The Wine

If California were a country, it would rank as the world's fourth-largest wine producer, after Italy, France, and Spain. In those countries, which hardly think of it as an alcoholic beverage, wine represents delicious nourishment to be shared with friends and family. A modern, American-ized version of that mentality integrates wine into daily life in California. In the Napa and Sonoma valleys, Mendocino County, the Central Coast, the Sierra Foothills, and the Temecula Valley are respected appellations where numerous wineries offer tours and tastings. Simply driving through vineyard-blanketed countryside lets you feel the Wine Country vibe. Better restaurants and wineshops anywhere in the state will do the same if you take the time to ask their friendly experts which California bottles you might like.

The Outdoors

One of the great attractions of living in California—the mild year-round weather enjoyed by most of the state—inspires the people here to live outdoors as much as they can. To be sure, they have tremendous enthusiasm for every conceivable outdoor sport and wilderness activity, but the open-air life, California-style, has much greater scope. Alfresco dining on patios, decks, and wharves; open-air shopping malls with walkways through landscaped grounds; jazz, classical, and contemporary concert series held under the stars; street markets specializing in food, crafts, imported wares, antiques, or junk; major art museums with sculpture installed in extensive gardens; theater festivals in outdoor amphitheaters; fiestas and fairs celebrating everything from gay pride to garlic. Remember your sunscreen or sweater.

IF YOU LIKE

Food

Some of the world's best chefs prefer to work in California, which grows more varieties of fruits and vegetables than any other state. Dairies and ranches also thrive here, and fleets take fish and shellfish offshore. The organic-foods movement began in California, sparking an appreciation for seasonal ingredients.

Many of California's chefs take inspiration from the state's dynamic immigrant communities, bringing flavors and techniques from Mexico, China, the Philippines, Korea, Vietnam, India, and elsewhere into their kitchens. You'll find the finest restaurants and the greatest abundance of high-quality dining in and around San Francisco and Los Angeles, and in the Napa and Sonoma Wine Country.

- **Bastide,** West Hollywood. Provençal warmth and gracious, unfussy service enhance *fantastique* cooking.

- **French Laundry,** Yountville. At this contemporary American restaurant you'll spend lots of time and money on your meal—and it'll be worth it.

- **Gary Danko,** San Francisco. Foodies flock to Fisherman's Wharf to see what's on the French menu and to mine the prodigious wine list.

- **Jardinière,** San Francisco. The superb contemporary cooking of chef Traci Des Jardins packs patrons into one of the city's sexiest restaurants.

- **Mustard's Grill,** Yountville. Not an ounce of pretension weighs down the solid service or hearty American fare here.

- **Patina,** Los Angeles. The setting—Frank Gehry's Walt Disney Concert Hall—provides a dramatic backdrop to show-stopping French cuisine.

Nature

Fog-shrouded redwood groves and sunbaked golden hills, sheltered coastal coves and snowy mountain ranges, canyon-slashed deserts and lake-pocked forests: California's geographical diversity is staggering. You can easily explore tide pools, chapparal, lava beds, woodlands, estuaries, and just about any other kind of ecological zone.

California has eight national parks, five national monuments, three national recreation areas, one national preserve, and one national seashore. With more than 270 sites, the state park system extends your reach to underwater preserves, wildlife reserves, dune systems, and other environmentally sensitive habitats.

- **Channel Islands National Park,** Ventura. Some 2,000 species of plants and animals, including 35 kinds of marine mammals, live on and around this cluster of five islands.

- **Death Valley National Park,** Death Valley. Deep canyons, colorful volcanic formations, and other geological wonders mark the hottest spot in the Western Hemisphere.

- **La Jolla Cove,** La Jolla. Peek into tide pools and cliff caves at low tide, or dive and snorkel in the San Diego–La Jolla Underwater Park.

- **Monterey Bay Aquarium,** Monterey. Commune with creatures native to California's shores: sardines in a circular tank swim around your head; otters backstroke at eye level.

- **Point Reyes National Seashore,** Marin County. Elephant seals, 225 bird species, and purple urchins thrive along this untamed shoreline.

History

In 1769 Spanish missionaries and soldiers established California's first European settlement, at San Diego. From its origins as a Mexican outpost of missions and ranchos, California grew into a kind of perpetual promised land that has represented many things to many people.

The state has given American history some of its most recognizable characters: indigenous peoples victimized by Euro-American hubris, forty-niners who rushed here in search of gold, Chinese workers who helped build the West's railroads, Great Depression farmers fleeing the Dust Bowl, Hollywood tycoons and stars, Haight-Ashbury hippies, Silicon Valley dot-commers. Their human drama echoes at museums and historic sites throughout the state.

- **Bodie Ghost Town,** Bodie State Historic Park. Preserved in a state of "arrested decay," this remote place in the eastern Sierra was once a wild mining town.

- **Columbia State Historic Park,** Columbia. Pan for gold in a restored gold-rush town where history lives in shops, forges, and newspaper offices.

- **Maritime Museum,** San Diego. Five rehabilitated sail- and steam-powered ships recall the seaport's turn-of-the-20th-century heyday.

- **Mission San Juan Capistrano,** San Juan Capistrano. The adobe buildings and workers' implements give an evocative picture of early mission life.

- **Petroglyph Canyons,** Ridgecrest. Two canyons hold the largest concentration of ancient rock art in the Northern Hemisphere.

Fun

Hey, you're on vacation, so why not cut yourself some slack and enjoy California's lighter-weight pleasures?

If you want concentrated doses of fun, head for the southern half of the state, between San Diego and Silicon Valley, for slick theme parks and creaky old oceanfront arcades and roller-coasters. To get a little exercise, try spectacular skiing in the Sierra Nevada, sybaritic golfing in the desert, or surfing along much of the coast. Cheer a frog-jumping competition in Gold Country. Tour a brewery (and taste the product) way up north. Drop some quarters at a Native American casino. Ride the cable cars in San Francisco. Best of all, watch the people wherever you go. You can't help but have a good time at these attractions.

- **Disneyland,** Anaheim. The original and still the best, it rocks even if you don't have kids in tow.

- **Grauman's Chinese Theatre,** Los Angeles. See the footprints of Marilyn Monroe and the nose print of Jimmy Durante in the sidewalk out front.

- **Heavenly Gondola,** South Lake Tahoe. Ride up the mountain with the skiers for stunning views of cobalt-blue Lake Tahoe.

- **SeaWorld of California,** San Diego. Walk through a world of sharks and walruses and see killer whales, sea lions, and otters perform.

- **Venice Boardwalk,** Los Angeles. Five blocks of beachfront exhibitionism—magicians, bodybuilders, fortune-tellers, you name it—is pure eye candy.

WHEN TO GO

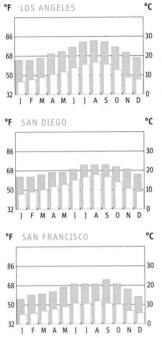

The climate varies amazingly in California, sometimes within an hour's drive. A foggy, cool August day in San Francisco makes you grateful for a sweater, but head north 50 mi to the Napa Valley, and you'll probably need no more than short sleeves. Similarly, nighttime temperatures may differ greatly from daytime temperatures.

Because the weather is so varied throughout the state, it's hard to generalize much about it. Rain comes in the winter, summers are dry. As a rule, compared with the coastal areas, which are relatively cool year-round, inland regions are hot in summer and cool in winter. As you climb into the mountains, the climate changes more distinctly with the seasons: winter brings snow (at elevations above 3,000 feet), autumn is crisp, spring can go either way, and summer is sunny and warm, with only an occasional thunder-shower.

⛅ Forecasts **National Weather Service** (⊕ www.wrh.noaa.gov). **Weather Channel** (⊕ www.weather.com).

GREAT ITINERARIES

ROAD TRIP OF A LIFETIME
HIGHWAY 1 FROM END TO END

Day 1: Arrival/Los Angeles

Pick up your rental car at LAX and shoot down the San Diego Freeway (Interstate 405) to Dana Point, the official starting point of Highway 1, which in southern California is called the Pacific Coast Highway, or PCH. At Doheny State Park, a great surf spot, you should see some action. Gallery-glutted Laguna Beach makes a good lunch stop before a walk on the pristine beach of Crystal Cove State Park. Feel like a million bucks on a gondola cruise of Newport Beach's yacht harbor or go surf-crazy in Huntington Beach, then get a waterfront room in either town.

Day 2: Los Angeles & Santa Monica

Play tourist in Hollywood and Beverly Hills in the morning, or raise your cultural bar with a few hours amid the masterpieces and gardens of the Getty Center. Sunset Boulevard takes you through tony neighborhoods back to the coast, where the boardwalk at Venice Beach is kinetic with jugglers and daredevil bladers. Balance the tacky pleasures of Santa Monica's amusement pier with a stylish dinner in the neighborhood.

Day 3: Malibu to Santa Barbara

You've seen Malibu's stretch of the PCH countless times on TV and film: mountains on one side, ocean on the other, and mile after mile of beaches. Then, after skirting an ugly port, Highway 1 merges with U.S. 101 for about 70 mi. Spread out behind a beach-rimmed harbor, Santa Barbara goes in big for red tile–topped white-stucco architecture. A real Mexican lunch at La Super-Rica, a visit to the magnificent Spanish mission, and a stroll down hopping State Street (before dark) to Stearns Wharf, and you've done the minitour.

Day 4: San Luis Obispo & Hearst Castle

A couple of hours' drive (during which Highway 1 morphs into the Cabrillo Highway, separating from and then rejoining U.S. 101) takes you through rolling vineyards and rangeland to San Luis Obispo, where any legit road trip includes a photo stop at the wacky, pink Madonna Inn. Downtown, the Spanish mission stands by a tree-shaded creek edged with shops and cafés. Here, U.S. 101 heads inland and Highway 1 continues up the coast to splendidly solitary Hearst Castle, the art-filled extravaganza at San Simeon. Forsake the depressing motels and scary food nearby and backtrack to hospitality-rich Cambria for the evening.

Day 5: Big Sur & Carmel

Today's 100-mi drive, which for much of its distance twists up and down bluffs above the ocean, could easily take four hours—without stops to gawk at the vistas. This part of Highway 1 is famously scenic, but rain-induced mudslides sometimes shut it down in winter. At Julia Pfeiffer Burns State Park one easy but rewarding hike leads to a waterfall off a beachfront cliff. Lunch on Nepenthe's terrace comes with a mind-blowing Big Sur view. History, beautifully preserved at Carmel's mission, is turned on its head in the ersatz old-world-ish architecture of the town's myriad galleries and restaurants.

Day 6: Monterey to San Francisco

Between Carmel and Monterey, the Cabrillo Highway cuts across the base of the Mon-

GREAT
ITINERARIES

terey Peninsula. If you're determined to maximize your ocean-view mileage, pony up the toll and take the long way around: 17-Mile Drive, which traverses a surf-pounded landscape of cypress trees, sea lions, gargantuan estates, and the Pebble Beach Golf Links. You might forget the tourist hordes when surrounded by the kelp forests and bat rays of the Monterey Bay Aquarium or the adobes and artifacts of Monterey State Historic Park. Northward past a string of secluded beaches and small towns, Highway 1 reaches San Francisco. Check into the lighthearted Hotel Monaco near Union Square and request a goldfish for your room.

Day 7: San Francisco

The best way to do San Francisco is on foot and public transport. A Union Square stroll packs a wallop of people-watching, window-shopping, and architecture-viewing. In Chinatown, department stores give way to dim-sum shops, storefront temples, and open-air markets. Catch a Powell Street cable car to the end of the line and get off to see the bay views and the antique arcade games at Musée Mécanique, the gem of otherwise mindless Fisherman's Wharf. Head to cosmopolitan North Beach for cocktail hour, dinner, and live music.

Day 8: Marin County

If fog hasn't socked in the bay, a drive across the Golden Gate Bridge and a stop at a Marin Headlands overlook yield memorable city prospects. Hike beyond the crowded trails at Muir Woods National Monument to feel the power of the giant redwoods. Highway 1 (now called Shoreline Highway) runs straight through the center of Stinson Beach, whose cafés cater to surfers; reclusive hippie-types hide out at the end of a side road in tiny Bolinas. Put down roots in Inverness or Olema for two nights.

Day 9: Point Reyes National Seashore

You can take a deep breath on this wild and sometimes gray piece of seashore, where you might claim an unspoiled beach for yourself. Expect company around the lighthouse at the tip of Point Reyes, though, for the great view and for elephant seal- and whale-watching in season. Cap a day of fresh air with the best meal of your vacation: dinner cooked over a wood fire at Manka's Inverness Lodge.

Day 10: The Sonoma Coast

Passing only a few minuscule towns, this stretch of Highway 1 shows off the northern coast in all its ragged glory—when the fog stays away. Fort Ross State Historic Park's reconstructed compound of eerily foreign buildings recalls the era of Russian fur trading in California. Pull into Gualala for an espresso, a sandwich, and a little human contact before rolling onward. After another 50 mi of tranquil state beaches and parks you'll return to civilization in Mendocino, a clapboard village of shops, inns, and restaurants.

Day 11: Mendocino & Fort Bragg

A profusion of flowers, cypress groves, and meadows overlooks the ocean in the Mendocino Coast Botanical Gardens. Traveling back in time, the Skunk Train follows an old logging route from Fort Bragg deep into the redwood forest. A little timbering history and a lot of artsy retail fill the restored 19th-century homes and storefronts of downtown Mendocino.

Day 12: Departure/San Francisco

The last 53 mi of your trip take you through wilderness to Highway 1's northern terminus, at U.S. 101 in Leggett. From here, you've got a 3½-hour (181-mi) drive down the 101 to San Francisco, a 4-hour (193 mi) haul sans stops straight to SFO.

TIPS

❶ If you can, spare yourself some hassle up front by flying into John Wayne/ Orange County Airport. You'll bypass insane LAX and land 40 mi closer to Dana Point.

❷ Don't ruin the end of your vacation by driving back to L.A. Many rental-car agencies will waive the drop-off fee for your one-way rental. Even if yours won't, is it worth an extra six-plus hours of driving and all that expensive California gas to avoid paying the typical $99 charge?

❸ If you see traffic backed up behind you on a long two-lane, no-passing stretch, do everyone a favor and use the first available pull-out. Without someone on your tail, you can enjoy the drive.

❹ Prone to motion sickness? Do the driving on the especially tortuous sections of road; focusing on the landscape out- side should make you feel less queasy. Opening a window and letting fresh air blow on your face may also help.

GREAT ITINERARIES

SOUTHERN CALIFORNIA DREAMING
LOS ANGELES, PALM SPRINGS & SAN DIEGO

Day 1: Arrival/Los Angeles

As soon as you land at LAX, make like a local and get on the freeway. Downtown's hodgepodge of art-deco, beaux-arts, and futuristic architecture begs at least a drive-by, if the top-notch art, history, and science museums don't tempt you. Headed west, Wilshire Boulevard cuts through a historical and cultural cross-section of the city. Two stellar sights on its Miracle Mile are the encyclopedic Los Angeles County Museum of Art and the fossil-filled La Brea Tar Pits; parking requires tenacity. Come dinner time, the open-air Farmers Market and its many eateries hum. Your Beverly Hills or West Hollywood hotel beckons only a few minutes away.

Day 2: Hollywood & the Movie Studios

Every L.A. tourist must devote at least one day to the movies and take at least one studio tour. For thrills and laughs choose the special-effects theme park at Universal Studios Hollywood; for the nitty-gritty choose Warner Bros. Studios. Nostalgic musts in half-seedy, half-preening Hollywood include the star-studded Walk of Fame along Hollywood Boulevard, the celebrity concrete footprints outside Grauman's Chinese Theater, and a glimpse of the Hollywood sign. West Hollywood's restaurants sizzle, and the Sunset Strip club scene could not get any hotter—the parking nightmare proves it.

Day 3: Beverly Hills & Santa Monica

Even without its extensive art collection, the hilltop Getty Center dazzles with its pavilion architecture, gardens, and views of L.A. Descend to the sea via Sunset Boulevard for lunch along Santa Monica's Third Street Promenade, followed by some cheap amusement on the pier. The buff and the bizarre meet on the boardwalk at Venice Beach; strap on some Rollerblades if you dare. Rodeo Drive specializes in exhibitionism with a heftier price tag, voyeurs welcome.

Day 4: Los Angeles to Palm Springs

Freeway traffic permitting, you can make it from the middle of L.A. to the middle of the desert in a couple of hours. Somehow in harmony with the harsh land, mid-century modern homes and businesses with clean, low-slung lines define the Palm Springs style. The city seems far away when you go hiking in hushed Tahquitz or Indian canyons, where cliffs and palm trees shelter rock art, irrigation works, and other remnants of Agua Caliente culture. Words cannot do justice to the very senior, very limber showgirls who sell out 10 shows a week at the Fabulous Palm Springs Follies.

Day 5: The Desert

If riding a tram to the top of an 8,516-foot mountain for a hike or even a snowball fight above a desert panorama sounds like fun to you, show up at the Palm Springs Aerial Tramway before the first morning tram leaves: the line can get discouragingly long. Along trails through naturalistic habitats, Living Desert Zoo and Gardens in Palm Desert provides an up-close view of flora and fauna from wolves to warthogs. Everywhere, championship golf courses and plush spas sing their Siren song.

Day 6: Palm Springs to San Diego

South through desert and mountains on your way to San Diego, you might pause in the Temecula Valley for lunch at a winery. Go straight for San Diego's nautical heart in the waterfront downtown, with an exploration of the restored ships at the Maritime Museum and a boat tour of the harbor. Victorian-era buildings—and plenty of other tourists—surround you on a stroll through the Gaslamp Quarter, but the 21st century is in full swing at the leviathan Horton Plaza retail and entertainment complex. Plant yourself at a downtown hotel and graze the neighborhood's many restaurants and nightspots.

Day 7: San Diego Zoo & Coronado

Malayan tapirs in a simulated Asian rain forest, Siberian reindeer in an imitation Arctic: the San Diego Zoo maintains a vast and varied collection of creatures in a world-renowned complex of painstakingly designed habitats. Come early, wear comfy shoes, and stay as long as you can stand the droves of children. Grown-up, boutiquey Coronado, anchored by the grand Victorian Hotel Del Coronado, offers an antidote. Tea, cocktails, or perhaps dinner at the Del makes a civilized end to an untamed day.

Day 8: SeaWorld & Old Town

Resistance is futile: you're going to SeaWorld. So what if it screams "commercial" and "touristy": this humongous theme park of walk-through shark tanks and peppy killer-whale shows also screams "fun." Surrender to the experience and try not to sit in anything sticky. Also touristy, but with genuine historical significance, Old Town drips with Spanish and Mexican heritage. Soak it up in the plaza at Old Town San Diego State Historic Park, then browse the stalls and shops of Bazaar del Mundo and San Diego Avenue.

Day 9: La Jolla to Laguna Beach

Above a jewel of a cove, posh La Jolla invites lingering along its shop-lined streets, on its sheltered beaches, and at cultural institutions such as the huge Birch Aquarium at Scripps and the well-curated Museum of Contemporary Art. At Mission San Luis Rey, in Oceanside, and Mission San Juan Capistrano you can glimpse life as it was during California's Spanish colonial days. Once a haven for artists, Laguna Beach still abounds with galleries; its strollable downtown streets would abut always-busy Main Beach Park if the Pacific Coast Highway didn't run through the middle of town.

GREAT ITINERARIES

Day 10: Disneyland

With your advance-purchased ticket in hand, skirt the lines at the box office and storm the gates of the Magic Kingdom at opening time. Whatever your fancy, from Adventureland to Fantasyland, from Mickey's Toontown to New Orleans Square, hitting it all in one day will be impossible. Map out a strategy before you arrive.

Day 11: Departure/Los Angeles

Pack up your mouse gear and give yourself an ample head start for the airport. Without traffic the 35-mi drive from Anaheim to LAX would take 45 minutes, but by now you know all about Southern California's traffic.

TIPS

❶ If you don't have 11 days of vacation, or if really hot weather bothers you, cut this itinerary down to 9 days. Skip the Palm Springs segment and head directly to San Diego from Los Angeles; it's a 120-mi drive on Interstate 5.

❷ Don't get shut out of any of the sights you really want to see, and don't waste precious vacation time standing in line: for all the big attractions, museums, tours, and rides that offer them, make reservations and purchase tickets in advance.

❸ No matter how carefully you plan your movements to avoid busy routes at peak hours—and you should do so—you will inevitably encounter heavy traffic in L.A. and San Diego. Relax, remain alert, and go with the flow, whether fast or slow.

❹ On departure day, allow yourself twice as much time as you think you need to negotiate LAX. At this sprawling, high-volume, tightly controlled airport, returning your rental car, making your way to the terminal, checking in, and passing through the heavy layers of security will take time—lots of time.

ON THE CALENDAR

Hundreds of festivals and special events take place annually in California. Here are a few of the favorites. If you plan to visit during a big festival, book your accommodations and event tickets well in advance.

WINTER December	For the Newport Harbor Christmas Boat Parade, in Newport Beach, more than 200 festooned boats glide through the harbor nightly the week before Christmas (call for exact dates).
	Over the first two weekends in December the Miners' Christmas Celebration in Columbia is an extravaganza of costumed carolers and children's piñatas. Related events include a Victorian Christmas feast at the City Hotel, lamplight tours, an equestrian parade, and Las Posados Nativity Procession.
January	Palm Springs' annual Palm Springs International Film Festival showcases the best of international cinema, with more than 100 screenings, lectures, and workshops.
	In Pasadena the annual Tournament of Roses Parade takes place on New Year's Day, with lavish flower-decked floats, marching bands, and equestrian teams, followed by the Rose Bowl game.
February	The legendary AT&T Pebble Beach National Pro-Am golf tournament begins in late January and ends in early February.
	San Francisco's Chinatown is the scene of parades and noisy fireworks, all part of a several-day Chinese New Year celebration. Los Angeles also has a Chinese New Year Parade.
	From early February through March, the Napa Valley Mustard Festival highlights the art, culture, cooking, and—of course—the wines of Napa.
	Indio's Riverside County Fair and National Date Festival is an exotic event with an *Arabian Nights* theme; camel and ostrich races, date exhibits, and tastings are among the draws.
SPRING March	The finest female golfers in the world compete for the richest purse on the LPGA circuit at the Kraft Nabisco Championship, in Rancho Mirage.
	The North Tahoe Snow Festival celebrates the region's winter sports, with everything from slope-side parties to kids' events at venues all around North Tahoe.

ON THE CALENDAR

		The Mendocino/Fort Bragg Whale Festival includes whale-watching excursions, marine-art exhibits, wine and beer tastings, crafts displays, and a chowder contest.
	April	The Cherry Blossom Festival, an elaborate presentation of Japanese culture and customs, winds up with a colorful parade through San Francisco's Japantown.
		The Toyota Grand Prix, in Long Beach, the largest street race in North America, draws top competitors from all over the world.
	May	Oxnard celebrates its big cash crop at the California Strawberry Festival, with exhibitors preparing the fruit in every imaginable form—shortcake, jam, tarts, and pizza.
		California's largest outdoor tasting anchors the mid-May Paso Robles Wine Festival, a weekend of winery and winemaker events.
		Inspired by Mark Twain's story "The Notorious Jumping Frog of Calaveras County," the Jumping Frog Jubilee, in Angels Camp, is for frogs and trainers who take their competition seriously.
		Sacramento is host to the four-day Sacramento Jazz Jubilee; the late-May event is the world's largest Dixieland festival, with 125 bands from around the world.
		Thousands sign up to run the San Francisco Bay to Breakers Race, a 7½-mi route from the Bay side to the ocean side that's a hallowed San Francisco tradition.
		The Santa Ysabel Art Festival is a mountain art celebration with works by 50 San Diego–area painters, sculptors, and fiber artists, plus a poetry fair and jazz and classical music.
SUMMER	June	In early June, Ojai hosts the Ojai Music Festival, a noted outdoor classical-music celebration.
		The Christopher Street West Gay & Lesbian Pride Festival celebrates the diversity of the gay and lesbian community in West Hollywood with a parade, music, dancing, food, and merchandise.
		The last week in June, the San Francisco Lesbian, Gay, Bisexual, and Transgender Pride Celebration culminates on Sunday, with a giant parade and festival, one of the largest of its kind in the world.
		The Napa Valley Wine Auction, in St. Helena, is accompanied by open houses and a wine tasting.

	During the last weekend of June or the first weekend of July Pasadena City Hall Plaza is host to the Absolut Chalk Festival, the world's largest chalk-painting festival. Artists use the pavement as their canvas to create masterpieces that wash away once festivities have come to a close.
July	During the three weeks of the Carmel Bach Festival, the works of Johann Sebastian Bach and 18th-century contemporaries are performed; events include concerts, recitals, and seminars.
	Most performances during Shakespeare Santa Cruz, a six-week festival in July and August take place outdoors in the striking Redwood Glen.
	Late July through early August the California Mid-State Fair takes place in Paso Robles. Nearly a quarter-million people show up for carnival fun, agricultural exhibits, live music, and barbecue.
	The San Luis Obispo Mozart Festival takes place in late July and early August at venues around the county. Along with Mozart, Haydn and others are performed.
August	The California State Fair showcases the state's agricultural side, with a rodeo, horse racing, a carnival, and big-name entertainment. It runs 18 days from August to early September in Sacramento.
	Santa Barbara's Old Spanish Days Fiesta is held the first Wednesday through Sunday in August, sometimes beginning in the last days of July. There are two Mexican marketplaces, a carnival, a rodeo, and the nation's largest all-equestrian parade.
FALL September	On Catalina Island the Pottery & Tile Extravaganza showcases unique tile and pottery from private collections. There are displays, walking tours, demonstrations, and lectures.
	The longest-running event of its kind, the Monterey Jazz Festival attracts big names for three days of music in mid-September.
	The San Francisco Blues Festival is held at Fort Mason in late September.
	The Los Angeles County Fair, in Pomona, is the largest county fair in the world. It includes entertainment, exhibits, livestock, horse racing, food, and more.
October	The Grand National Rodeo, Horse, and Stock Show, at San Francisco's Cow Palace, is a 10-day competition straddling the end of October and the beginning of November.

ON THE
CALENDAR

November	The Death Valley '49er Encampment, at Furnace Creek, commemorates the historic crossing of Death Valley in 1849, with a fiddlers' contest, trail rides, and an art show.
	On the Sunday before Thanksgiving, Pasadena's Doo Dah Parade, a spoof of the annual Rose Parade, brings out partyers such as the Lounge Lizards, who dress as reptiles and lip-synch to Frank Sinatra favorites.

San Diego

WITH NORTH COUNTY

WORD OF MOUTH

"We spent a long weekend in San Diego and the best thing about our trip was the Maritime Museum. We took the ½ day sail on the *Californian*, a must!"

—marymccord

"You can't visit San Diego and miss the experience of seeing one of the best zoos in the world. The San Diego Zoo is top-notch—beautiful and fascinating. We visited with 2 adults and 3 teens and it was hit with everyone."

—Jill2

Updated by
Lenore Greiner,
David Nelson,
Andrew
Collins, and
Bobbi Zane

SAN DIEGO IS A BIG CITY, where locals take pride in its small-town feel. With more than 1 million people, San Diego is second only to Los Angeles in population among California cities. It also covers a lot of territory, roughly 400 square mi of land and sea. To the north and south of the city are 70 mi of beaches. Inland, a succession of chaparral-covered mesas are punctuated with deep-cut canyons that step up to savannalike hills, separating the verdant coast from the arid Anza-Borrego Desert. Unusually clear skies make the inland countryside ideal for stargazing.

The San Diego area, the birthplace of California, was claimed for Spain by explorer Juan Rodríguez Cabrillo in 1542 and eventually came under Mexican rule. You'll find reminders of San Diego's Spanish and Mexican heritage throughout the region—in architecture and place-names, in distinctive Mexican cuisine, and in the historic buildings of Old Town.

In 1867 developer Alonzo Horton, who called the town's bayfront "the prettiest place for a city I ever saw," began building a hotel, a plaza, and prefab homes on 960 downtown acres. The city's fate was sealed in 1908, when President Theodore Roosevelt's Great White Fleet sailed into the bay. The U.S. Navy, impressed by the city's excellent harbor and temperate climate, decided to build a destroyer base on San Diego Bay in the 1920s. The newly developed aircraft industry soon followed (Charles Lindbergh's plane *Spirit of St. Louis* was built here). The military, which operates many bases and installations throughout the county, continues to contribute to the local economy.

EXPLORING SAN DIEGO

Although many attractions in San Diego are separated by some distance, the downtown area is delightfully urban and accessible. You can walk around the Gaslamp Quarter and the harbor, then catch a trolley or bus to the Balboa Park museums and zoo, the funky neighborhood of Hillcrest, the Old Town historic sites, and Mission Bay marine park and SeaWorld. After that, a car is the quickest way to get to the Coronado, Point Loma, and the beachside communities, though public transportation is available and reliable.

Numbers in the text correspond to numbers in the margin and on the neighborhood maps.

Balboa Park

★ Overlooking downtown and the Pacific Ocean, 1,200-acre Balboa Park is the cultural heart of San Diego, where you'll find most of the city's museums, the San Diego Zoo, restaurants, performance venues, and picnic areas. Cultivated and wild gardens are an integral part of Balboa Park, thanks to the "Mother of Balboa Park," Kate Sessions, who made sure the park was planted with thousands of palms, purple-blossoming jacarandas, and other trees.

Many of the park's Spanish colonial–revival buildings were meant to be temporary exhibit halls for the Panama–California International Ex-

GREAT ITINERARIES

1

IF YOU HAVE 3 DAYS

Start your first day early with a morning visit to the San Diego Zoo in Balboa Park. In the afternoon stroll along El Prado, and stop into the museum of your choice. On your second day, head downtown to Seaport Village. After browsing the shops, catch a ferry from the Broadway Pier to Coronado, and board a bus going down Orange Avenue to see the Hotel Del Coronado. Back in San Diego after lunch, walk north on the Embarcadero to Ash Street; if you have time, you can explore the Maritime Museum. Spend the morning of your third day shopping in the Gaslamp Quarter, and in the afternoon head to La Jolla for a walk on the beach, dinner, and a sunset.

IF YOU HAVE 5 DAYS

Follow the three-day itinerary above, then begin your fourth day with a morning visit to Cabrillo National Monument on Point Loma. Have lunch at one of the seafood restaurants on Scott Street, then drive to Old Town (Rosecrans Street north to San Diego Avenue). If low tide is in the afternoon, reverse the order to catch the tide pools at Cabrillo. Spend your fifth day at Legoland California in Carlsbad if you have children. En route to North County, stop off for a picnic at Torrey Pines State Park. If you're not going to Legoland, take Interstate 5 north to Del Mar for lunch, shopping, and sea views. A visit to Mission San Luis Rey, slightly inland from Oceanside on Highway 76, will infuse some history and culture into the tour.

position of 1915, which celebrated the opening of the Panama Canal. Fortunately, city leaders realized the value of the buildings and incorporated them into their plans for Balboa Park's acreage, which had been set aside by the city founders in 1868.

Parking near Balboa Park's museums is no small accomplishment. If you end up parking a bit far from your destination, consider the stroll back through the greenery part of the day's recreational activities. Alternatively, you can park at Inspiration Point on the east side of the park, off Presidents Way. Free trams run from there to the museums every 8 to 10 minutes, 9:30 to 5:30 daily.

TIMING Unless you're pressed for time, you'll want to devote an entire day to the perpetually expanding zoo; there are more than enough exhibits to keep you occupied for five or more hours.

Although some of the park's museums are open on Monday, most are open Tuesday through Sunday 10 to 4; in summer a number have extended hours—phone ahead to ask. On Tuesday the museums have free admission to their permanent exhibits on a rotating basis; call the Balboa Park Visitors Center for a schedule. Free architectural, historical, or nature tours depart from the visitor center every Saturday at 10, while park ranger–led tours start out from the visitor center at 1 PM every Wednesday and Sunday.

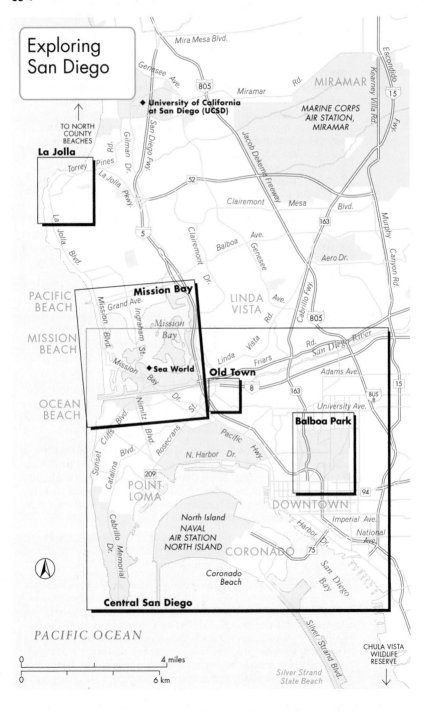

Exploring San Diego

TO NORTH COUNTY BEACHES

La Jolla

Mira Mesa Blvd.

Genesee Ave.

805

Miramar

Rd.

MIRAMAR

Escondido

Kearney Villa Rd.

15

◆ **University of California at San Diego (UCSD)**

MARINE CORPS AIR STATION, MIRAMAR

Gilman Dr.

San Diego Fwy.

Torrey Pines Rd.

La Jolla Pkwy.

52

Jacob Dekema Freeway

Clairemont Mesa Blvd.

163

La Jolla Blvd.

5

Clairemont Dr.

Balboa Ave.

Genesee

Aero Dr.

Murphy Canyon Rd.

PACIFIC BEACH

Mission Bay

Mission Blvd.

Grand Ave.

Ingraham St.

LINDA VISTA

Ave.

Cabrillo Fwy.

805

MISSION BEACH

Mission Bay

◆ **Sea World**

Vista Rd.

Linda

San Diego River

Rd.

Old Town

Friars

Adams Ave.

15

OCEAN BEACH

Mission Bay Dr.

Nimitz Blvd.

8

163

BUS 8

University Ave.

Balboa Park

Sunset Cliffs Blvd.

Rosecrans Blvd.

N. Harbor Dr.

Pacific Hwy.

Catalina Blvd.

209

POINT LOMA

94

DOWNTOWN

Cabrillo Memorial Dr.

North Island NAVAL AIR STATION NORTH ISLAND

CORONADO

Imperial Ave.

National Ave.

Harbor Dr.

75

San Diego Bay

Coronado Beach

Central San Diego

PACIFIC OCEAN

Silver Strand Blvd.

CHULA VISTA WILDLIFE RESERVE

Silver Strand State Beach

0 ———— 4 miles

0 ———— 6 km

IF YOU LIKE

BEACHES

San Diego's coastline shimmers with crystalline Pacific waters rolling up to some of the prettiest beaches on the West Coast. Some, like the Silver Strand on Coronado, are wide and sandy; others, like Sunset Cliffs on Point Loma, are narrow and rocky. You can join the athletes and sun-worshippers on Mission Bay, or wander the tiny, little-known coves of Point Loma and the North County community of Encinitas. Families with children love to explore the tidal pools at La Jolla Cove. Check the weather page of a local newspaper for information about tides and pollution before you head out.

EATING WELL

Striving to become one of the nation's premier "food cities" of the 21st century, sun-drenched San Diego has abandoned its former laissez-faire attitude toward serious cooking and adopted the point of view that a region this blessed with gorgeous vegetables, fruits, herbs, and seafood should make a culinary statement. The result is a generation of chefs that like to surprise, dazzle, and delight diners with inventive, California-colorful creations. A stroll down the 5th Avenue restaurant row (which now extends to both 4th and 6th avenues) reveals San Diego's preference for Italian cuisine above all others, but you'll also find casual burgers-and-fries fare, Spanish tapas and paellas, traditional and nuevo Mexican cuisine, elegant seafood, and all-American steaks. Seafood, of course, abounds, and there's a whole lot of "fusion" going on, which is to say that many chefs borrow idiosyncratically from a mixture of culinary traditions.

HISTORY

As the site of California's earliest European settlement, San Diego occupies a special place in U.S. history. Well-preserved and reconstructed historic sites, such as Cabrillo National Monument, Old Town State Historic Park, and Mission San Luis Rey in Oceanside help you to imagine what the San Diego area was like when Spanish and Portuguese explorers and missionaries arrived, usually by sea, in the 16th and 17th centuries. You can see evidence in *Star of India* and along the Prado in Balboa Park.

SHOPPING

Horton Plaza, in the heart of downtown, is the place to go for department stores, mall shops, and one-of-a-kind boutiques; the adjoining Gaslamp Quarter is chock-full of art galleries, antiques shops, and specialty stores. Seaport Village on the waterfront is thick with theme shops and arts-and-crafts galleries. Coronado has a few blocks of fancy boutiques and galleries as well as Ferry Landing Marketplace, a waterfront shopping and dining center. Bazaar del Mundo in the historic Old Town district resembles a colorful Mexican marketplace, where you can browse in shops selling international goods, toys, souvenirs, and arts and crafts. Hillcrest is the place to go for vintage clothing, furnishings, and accessories. La Jolla has a collection of trendy designer boutiques and galleries along Prospect Street and Girard Avenue. Discounted designer fashions can also be found at the popular Carlsbad Company Stores.

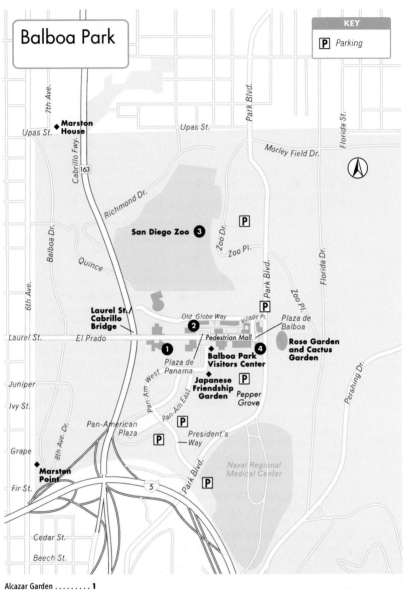

Balboa Park

KEY

P Parking

Sights to See

❶ Alcazar Garden. The gardens surrounding the Alcazar Castle in Seville, Spain, inspired the landscaping here; you'll feel like royalty resting on the benches by the exquisitely tiled fountains. The flower beds are ever-changing horticultural exhibits featuring more than 6,000 annuals for a nearly perpetual bloom. ⊠ *Off El Prado, Balboa Park.*

OFF THE BEATEN PATH

HILLCREST – Northwest of Balboa Park, Hillcrest is San Diego's center for the gay community and artists of all types. University, 4th, and 5th Avenues are filled with cafés, a superb collection of restaurants (including many outstanding ethnic eateries), and boutiques (among which are several indie bookstores). The self-contained residential-commercial Uptown District, on University Avenue at 8th Avenue, was built to resemble an inner-city neighborhood, with shops and restaurants within easy walking distance of high-price town houses. To the northeast, Adams Avenue, reached via Park Boulevard heading north off Washington Street, has many antiques stores. Adams Avenue leads east into Kensington, a handsome old neighborhood that overlooks Mission Valley.

❹ Reuben H. Fleet Science Center. The Fleet Center's clever interactive exhibits are artfully educational. You can reconfigure your face to have two left sides, or, by replaying an instant video clip, watch yourself coming and going at different speeds. The IMAX Dome Theater, the world's first, screens exhilarating nature and science films. The SciTours simulator is designed to take you on virtual voyages—stomach lurches and all. The Meteor Storm lets up to six players at a time have an interactive virtual-reality experience, this one sans motion-sickness potential. A big hit is the Nierman Challenger Learning Center—a realistic mock mission-control and futuristic space station. ⊠ *1875 El Prado, Balboa Park* ☎ *619/238–1233* ⊕ *www.rhfleet.org* ☑ *Gallery exhibits $6.75, gallery exhibits and 1 IMAX film $11.75* ☉ *Daily 9:30; closing hrs vary from 5 to 9, call ahead.*

NEED A BREAK

You'll find a tranquil oasis at the **Japanese Friendship Garden** (⊠ 2215 Pan American Rd., Balboa Park ☎ 619/232–2721 ⊕ www.niwa.org ☉ Tues.–Sun. 10–4), where you can meander under a wisteria arbor, sip green tea, and watch koi cruising in a pond.

★ ❷ San Diego Museum of Art. Known primarily for its Spanish baroque and Renaissance paintings, including works by El Greco, Goya, Rubens, and van Ruisdael, San Diego's most comprehensive art museum also has strong holdings of South Asian art, Indian miniatures, and contemporary California paintings. The Baldwin M. Baldwin collection includes more than 100 pieces by Toulouse-Lautrec. An outdoor Sculpture Court and Garden exhibits both traditional and modern pieces. Free docent tours are offered throughout the day. ⊠ *Casa de Balboa, 1450 El Prado, Balboa Park* ☎ *619/232–7931* ⊕ *www.sdmart.org* ☑ *$10, $12 for special exhibits* ☉ *Tues.–Sun. 10–6, open until 9 Thurs.*

❸ San Diego Zoo. Balboa Park's—and perhaps the city's—most famous attraction is its 100-acre zoo, and it deserves all the press it gets. Nearly 4,000 animals of some 800 diverse species roam in hospitable, expertly crafted habitats that replicate natural environments as closely as possible. Walkways wind over bridges and past waterfalls ringed with tropical ferns; elephants in a sandy plateau roam so close you're tempted to pet them.

Open-air double-decker buses let you zip through three-quarters of the exhibits, and the Skyfari Aerial Tram gives a good overview of the zoo's layout. However, the zoo is at its best when you wander its paths, such as the one that climbs through the huge, enclosed **Scripps Aviary**, where brightly colored tropical birds swoop between branches just inches from your face, and into the neighboring **Gorilla Tropics**, one of the zoo's bioclimatic zone exhibits, where animals live in enclosed environments modeled on their native habitats.

The zoo's simulated Asian rain forest, **Tiger River**, has 10 exhibits with more than 35 species of animals; tigers, Malayan tapirs, and Argus pheasants wander among the exotic trees and plants. **Ituri Forest**—a 4-acre African rain forest at the base of Tiger River—lets you glimpse huge but surprisingly graceful hippos frolicking underwater, and buffalo cavorting with monkeys. At the popular **Polar Bear Plunge**, where you can watch the featured animals take a chilly dive, Siberian reindeer, white foxes, and other Arctic creatures are separated from their predatory neighbors by a series of camouflaged moats.

The zoo's most famous residents are a family of giant pandas: Bai Yun, mother of Hua Mei, the first giant panda cub born in the United States to survive to adulthood; her mate Gao Gao; and their cubs Mei Sheng and Su Lin (born in August 2005). Su Lin, Mei Sheng, and their parents are generally available for viewing from 9:00 to 4:15 each day at the Giant Panda Research Station; call the panda hotline for up-to-date information. Note that all pandas in the United States are on loan from China, and even babies born here pass to China's control after their third birthday (Mei Sheng turned three in August 2006, but was still at the San Diego Zoo at this writing.)

The zoo's newest exhibit, opened in mid-2005, is **Monkey Trails and Forest Tales.** Spanning three acres representing African and Asian forests, this is the largest and most elaborate animal habitat in the zoo's history. ⊠ *2920 Zoo Dr., Balboa Park* ☎ *619/234–3153, 888/697–2632 Giant panda hotline* ⊕ *www.sandiegozoo.org* ✐ *$22 includes zoo, Children's Zoo, and animal shows; $32 includes above, plus guided bus tour, unlimited express bus rides, and round-trip Skyfari Aerial Tram rides; zoo free for children under 12 in Oct.; $54.45 pass good for admission to zoo and San Diego Wild Animal Park within 5 days* ▤ *AE, D, MC, V* ☻ *June–Sept., daily 9–9; Sept.–June, daily 9–4; Children's Zoo and Skyfari ride generally close 1 hr earlier.*

Downtown

Downtown is San Diego's Lazarus. Written off as moribund by the 1970s, when few people willingly stayed in the area after dark, downtown is now one of the city's prime draws. The turnaround began in the late 1970s with the revitalization of the Gaslamp Quarter Historic District and massive redevelopment that gave rise to the Horton Plaza shopping center and the San Diego Convention Center, as well as to elegant hotels, upscale condominium complexes, and swank, trendy restaurants and cafés. Now people linger downtown well into the night—and also wake up there the next morning.

Of the newest downtown projects—there are more than 100 in the works—the most ambitious is the 26-block Ballpark District, which occupies the East Village area extending between the railroad tracks up to J Street, and from 6th Avenue east to around 10th Street. It includes Petco Park, a new 42,000-seat baseball stadium for the San Diego Padres, opened in 2004; a distinctively San Diego–style, 8-acre "Park at the Park" from which fans watch games while picnicking; a sports-related retail complex; at least 850 hotel rooms; and several apartment and condominium complexes. Trendy shops and good eateries are sprinkled throughout this booming neighborhood.

There are reasonably priced ($4 to $7 per day) parking lots along Harbor Drive, Pacific Highway, and lower Broadway and Market Street. The price of many downtown parking meters is $1 per hour, with a maximum stay of two hours (meters are in effect Monday through Saturday [except holidays], 8 to 6); unless you know for sure that your stay in the area will be short, you're better off in a lot.

What to See

Embarcadero. The bustle here comes less these days from the activities of fishing folk than from the throngs of tourists, but this waterfront walkway along San Diego Bay remains the nautical soul of the city. There are several seafood restaurants, as well as sea vessels of every variety—cruise ships, ferries, tour boats, and naval destroyers.

On the north end of the Embarcadero, at Ash Street, you'll find the Maritime Museum. South of it, the **B Street Pier** is used by ships from major cruise lines—San Diego has become a major cruise-ship port, both a port of call and a departure point. The cavernous pier building has a cruise-information center as well as a small bar (nice for cooling off on a hot day) and gift shop.

Day-trippers getting ready to set sail gather at the **Broadway Pier,** also known as the excursion pier. Tickets for the harbor tours and whale-watching trips are sold here. The terminal for the Coronado Ferry lies just beyond the Broadway pier.

The next few waterfront blocks to the south are under the control of the U.S. Navy, and here, at the Navy pier, is the decommissioned USS *Midway,* now the home of the San Diego Aircraft Carrier Museum. The pleasant Tuna Harbor Park offers a great view of boating on the bay and across to any aircraft carriers docked at the North Island naval base.

The next bit of seafront greenery is a few blocks south at **Embarcadero Marina Park North,** an 8-acre extension into the harbor from the center of Seaport Village. It's usually full of kite fliers, in-line skaters, and picnickers. Seasonal celebrations are held here and at the similar **Embarcadero Marina Park South.**

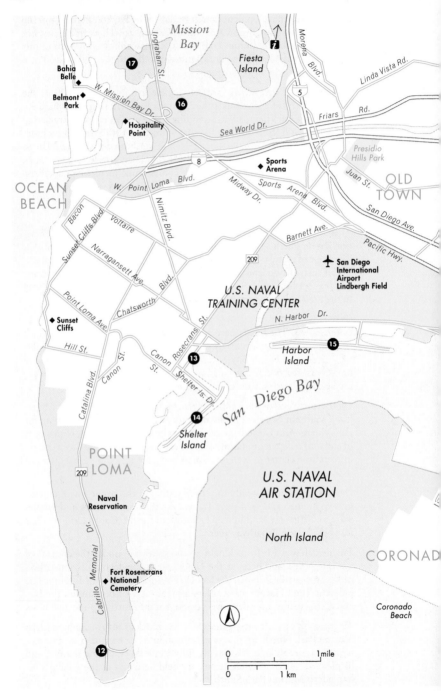

Central San Diego & Mission Bay

KEY

🚢 *Ferry*

▶ *Start of walk*

ℹ *Tourist information*

The **San Diego Convention Center,** on Harbor Drive between 1st and 5th avenues, is a waterfront landmark designed by Canadian architect Arthur Erickson. The center often holds trade shows that are open to the public, and tours of the building are available.

❽ Gaslamp Quarter Historic District. The 16½-block national historic district contains most of the Victorian-style buildings that rose in San Diego after Alonzo Horton arrived in 1867. Business boomed here in the late 1800s, when Market Street was the center of the downtown commercial district, but at the turn of the 20th century commerce moved west toward Broadway, and many of San Diego's first buildings fell into disrepair. During the early 1900s, prostitutes picked up sailors in lively area taverns and dance halls, and crime flourished.

History buffs, developers, architects, and artists formed the Gaslamp Quarter Council in 1974. They gathered funds from the government and private benefactors to clean up and preserve the quarter, restoring the finest old buildings, and attracting businesses and the public back to its heart. Today former flophouses are choice office buildings, and the area is filled with trendy shops, restaurants and nightclubs.

William Heath Davis House (⊠ 410 Island Ave., at 4th Ave., Gaslamp Quarter ☎ 619/233–4692), one of the first residences in town, houses the Gaslamp Quarter Historical Foundation, the district's curator. Before Alonzo Horton came to town, Davis, a prominent San Franciscan, had made an unsuccessful attempt to develop the waterfront area. Two-hour walking tours of the historic district leave from the house on Saturday at 11 and cost $8. The museum also sells detailed self-guided tour maps of the district for $2.

The Victorian **Horton Grand Hotel** (⊠ 311 Island Ave., Gaslamp Quarter ☎ 619/544–1886) was created in the mid-1980s by joining together two historic hotels, the Kahle Saddlery and the Grand Hotel, built in the boom days of the 1880s; Wyatt Earp stayed at the Kahle Saddlery—then called the Brooklyn Hotel—while he was in town speculating on real-estate ventures and opening gambling halls. The two hotels were once located about four blocks away, but were dismantled and reconstructed to make way for Horton Plaza. A small Chinese Museum behind the lobby serves as a tribute to the surrounding Chinatown district, a collection of modest structures that once housed Chinese laborers and their families.

The majority of the quarter's landmark buildings are on 4th and 5th avenues, between Island Avenue and Broadway. If you don't have much time, stroll down 5th Avenue, where highlights include the Backesto Building (No. 614), the Mercantile Building (No. 822), the Louis Bank of Commerce (No. 835), and the Watts-Robinson Building (No. 903). The Romanesque-revival **Keating Building** (⊠ 432 F St., at 5th Ave., Gaslamp Quarter) was designed by the same firm that created the famous Hotel Del Coronado. The section of G Street between 6th and 9th avenues has become a haven for galleries; stop in one of them to pick up a map of the downtown arts district. For additional information about the historic area, call the **Gaslamp Quarter Association** (☎ 619/233–5227) or log on to their Web site (⊕ www.gaslamp.org).

★ ❼ **Horton Plaza.** Downtown's centerpiece is the shopping, dining, and entertainment mall that fronts Broadway and G Street from 1st to 4th avenues and covers more than six city blocks. A collage of pastels with elaborate, colorful tile work on benches and stairways, banners waving in the air, and modern sculptures marking the entrances, Horton Plaza rises in uneven, staggered levels to six floors; great views of downtown from the harbor to Balboa Park and beyond can be had here.

Macy's and Nordstrom department stores anchor the plaza, and more than 140 clothing, sporting-goods, jewelry, book, and gift shops flank them. Other attractions include a movie complex, restaurants, and a long row of take-out ethnic food shops and dining patios on the uppermost tier—and the respected San Diego Repertory Theatre below ground level. Most stores are open 10 to 9 weekdays, 10 to 6 Saturday, and 11 to 7 Sunday, but during the winter holidays and in summer many places stay open longer. The **International Visitor Information Center** (✉ 1040⅓ W. Broadway, at Harbor Dr. ☎ 619/236–1212 ⊕ www.sandiego.org ☉ June–Aug., daily 9–5; Sept.–May, Thurs.–Tues. 9–4), at street level on the corner of 1st Avenue and F Street, is the best resource for information on San Diego.

Horton Plaza has a multilevel parking garage; even so, lines to find a space can be long. The first three hours of parking are free with validation; after that it's $1 for every 20 minutes. If you use this notoriously confusing fruit-and-vegetable–themed garage, be sure to remember at which produce level you've left your car. If you're staying downtown, inquire at your hotel about the complimentary Horton Plaza shopping shuttle, which stops at the cruise-ship terminal and the convention center in addition to several downtown lodgings. ☎ *619/238–1596 ⊕ www. westfield.com/hortonplaza.*

☾ ❺ **Maritime Museum.** A must for anyone with an interest in nautical history, this collection of restored and replica ships affords a fascinating glimpse of San Diego during its heyday as a commercial seaport. The museum's headquarters are the *Berkeley,* an 1898 ferryboat moored at the foot of Ash Street. The steam-driven ship, which served the Southern Pacific Railroad in San Francisco until 1958, played its most important role during the great earthquake of 1906, when it saved thousands of people from the fires that had engulfed San Francisco by carrying them across San Francisco Bay to Oakland. Its ornate carved-wood paneling, stained-glass windows, and plate-glass mirrors have been restored, and its main deck serves as a floating museum, with permanent exhibits on West Coast maritime history and complementary rotating exhibits.

Fodor'sChoice
★

A large number of visitors are drawn to the museum's sailing ships. The newest is a replica of an 18th-century British Royal Navy frigate, HMS *Surprise,* used in the Academy Award-winning *Master and Commander: The Far Side of the World.* Another, the *Star of India,* is often considered a symbol of the city. An iron windjammer built in 1863, the *Star of India* made 21 trips around the world in the late 1800s and is the oldest active iron sailing ship in the world. If you crave more than a dockside experience, you can take to the water in the museum's other sailing ship, the *Californian*. Designated the state's official tall ship, it can be boarded for a variety of half- and full-day sails (weather permitting) on weekends. Tickets may be purchased only at the museum on the day of sail. ✉ *1492 N. Harbor Dr., Embarcadero* ☎ *619/234–9153* ⊕ *www.sdmaritime.org* ✉ *$12 includes entry to all ships* ☉ *Daily 9–8, until 9 PM in summer.*

Museum of Contemporary Art, San Diego. The downtown branch of the city's modern art museum has taken on its own personality. Its postmodern, cutting-edge exhibitions are perfectly complemented by the steel-and-glass transportation complex of which it's a part. Four small galleries in the two-story building host rotating shows, some from the permanent collection in the older La Jolla branch, others loaned from far-flung international museums. ✉ *1001 Kettner Blvd., Downtown* ☎ *619/234–1001* ✉ *Free* ☉ *Daily 11–5. Closed Wed.*

★ ☾ ❻ **Seaport Village.** On a prime stretch of waterfront that spreads out across 14 acres connecting the harbor with hotel towers and the convention center, the village's three bustling shopping plazas are designed to reflect the architectural styles of early California, especially New England clapboard and Spanish mission. A ¼-mi wooden boardwalk that runs along the bay, and 4 mi of paths lead to specialty shops, snack bars, and restaurants. Seaport Village's shops are open daily 10 to 9 (10 to 10 in summer). The **Seaport Village Carousel** has 54 animals, hand-carved and hand-painted by Charles Looff in 1895. Tickets are $2. Strolling clowns, balloon sculptors, mimes, musicians, and magicians are also on hand throughout the village to entertain kids; those not impressed by such pretechnological displays can duck into the Time Out entertainment center near the carousel and play video games. ✉ *Downtown* ☎ *619/235–4014, 619/235–4013 events hotline, 888/387–3879 carousel information* ⊕ *www.seaportvillage.com.*

Coronado

Although it's actually an isthmus, easily reached from the mainland if you head north from Imperial Beach, Coronado has always seemed like an island and is often referred to as such. The streets of Coronado are wide, quiet, and friendly, with lots of neighborhood parks and grand old homes. Naval Air Station North Island, established in 1911, was the site of Charles Lindbergh's departure on the transcontinental flight that preceded his famous solo flight across the Atlantic

Coronado is visible from downtown and Point Loma and accessible via the arching blue 2¹⁄₁₀-mi-long San Diego–Coronado Bridge. Until the bridge was completed in 1969, visitors and residents relied on the Coronado Ferry. San Diego's Metropolitan Transit System runs a shuttle bus, No. 904, around Coronado; you can pick it up where you disembark the ferry and ride it out as far as Silver Strand State Beach. Buses start leaving from the ferry landing at 10:30 AM and run once an hour on the half hour until 6:30 PM.

You can board the ferry, operated by **San Diego Harbor Excursion** (☎ 619/234–4111, 800/442–7847 in CA ⊕ www.sdhe.com), at the Broadway

Pier on the Embarcadero in downtown San Diego; you'll arrive at the Ferry Landing Marketplace in Coronado. Boats depart every hour on the hour from the Embarcadero and every hour on the half hour from Coronado, daily 9 to 9 from San Diego (9 to 10 Friday and Saturday), 9:30 to 9:30 from Coronado (9:30 to 10:30 Friday and Saturday); the fare is $3 each way, 50¢ extra for bicycles. Buy tickets at the Broadway Pier or the Ferry Landing Marketplace. San Diego Harbor Excursion also offers water-taxi service weekdays 2 PM to 10 PM, and weekends 11 AM to 11 PM, later hours can be arranged. The taxi can run between any two points in San Diego Bay. The fare is $6 per person. Call ☎ 619/235–8294 to book.

What to See

Coronado Museum of History and Art. The neoclassical First Bank of Commerce building, constructed in 1910, holds the headquarters and archives of the Coronado Historical Association and a museum. The collection celebrates Coronado's history with photographs and displays of its formative events and major sights. For information on the town's historic houses, pick up a copy of the inexpensive *Coronado California Centennial History & Tour Guide* at the gift shop. There's also a café and lecture hall. The museum sponsors a 60-minute walking tour of the architecturally and historically significant buildings that surround it. The tour departs from the museum lobby on Wednesday at 2 PM and Friday at 10:30 AM and costs $8. ⊠ *1100 Orange Ave., Coronado* ☎ *619/435–7242* ⌸ *Donations accepted* ☉ *Weekdays 9–5, Sat. 10–5, Sun. 11–4.*

★ ☺ **Ferry Landing Marketplace.** This collection of shops at the ferry landing is on a smaller—and generally less interesting—scale than Seaport Village, but you do get a great view of the downtown San Diego skyline from here. If you want to rent a bike or in-line skates, stop in at **Bikes and Beyond** (⊠ No. 122 ☎ 619/435–7180). ⊠ *1201 1st St., at B Ave., Coronado* ☎ *619/435–8895.*

⑩ **Hotel Del Coronado.** One of San Diego's best-known sites, this 1888 hotel

Fodor'sChoice has been a national historic landmark since 1977. It has a colorful his-

★ tory, integrally connected with that of Coronado itself. The Hotel Del, as natives call it, was the brainchild of financiers Elisha Spurr Babcock Jr. and H. L. Story, who saw the potential of Coronado's virgin beaches and its view of San Diego's emerging harbor. The Del's distinctive red-tile peaks and Victorian gingerbread architecture has served as a set for many movies, political meetings, and extravagant social happenings. Fourteen presidents have been guests of the Del, and the film *Some Like It Hot*—starring Marilyn Monroe, Jack Lemmon, and Tony Curtis—was filmed here. The patio surrounding the swimming pool is a great place to sit back and imagine what the bathers looked like during the 1920s, when the hotel rocked with the good times. To its right, the new Windsor Lawn provides a green oasis between the hotel and the beach. ⊠ *1500 Orange Ave., Coronado* ☎ *619/435–6611* ⊕ *www.hoteldel.com.*

⑨ **Orange Avenue.** Coronado's business district and its village-like heart, this is surely one of the most charming spots in Southern California. Slow-paced and very "local" (the city fights against chain stores), it's a blast from the past, although entirely up-to-date in other respects.

⟳ ⓫ **Silver Strand State Beach.** The stretch of sand that runs along Silver
Fodor'sChoice Strand Boulevard from the Hotel Del Coronado to Imperial Beach is a
★ perfect family gathering spot, with restrooms and lifeguards. Don't be surprised if you see groups exercising in military style along the beach; this is a training area for the U.S. Navy's SEAL teams.

Harbor Island, Point Loma & Shelter Island

Point Loma protects the center city from the Pacific's tides and waves. It's shared by military installations, funky motels and fast-food shacks, stately family homes, huge estates, and private marinas packed with sailboats and yachts. Created out of sand dredged from the San Diego Bay in the second half of the past century, Harbor and Shelter islands have become tourist hubs with high-rise hotels, seafood restaurants, and boat-rental centers.

What to See

★ ⟳ ⓬ **Cabrillo National Monument.** This 144-acre preserve marks the site of the first European visit to San Diego, made by 16th-century explorer Juan Rodríguez Cabrillo (circa 1498–1543). Cabrillo landed at this spot, which he called San Miguel, in 1542. Government grounds were set aside to commemorate his discovery in 1913, and today the site, with its rugged cliffs and shores and outstanding overlooks, is one of the most frequently visited of all the national monuments.

The **visitor center** presents films and lectures about Cabrillo's voyage, the sea-level tide pools, and migrating gray whales. **Interpretive stations** with recorded information have been installed along the walkways that edge the cliffs. The moderately steep **Bayside Trail**, 2½ mi round-trip, winds through coastal sage scrub, curving under the cliff-top lookouts and taking you ever closer to the bayfront scenery. You cannot reach the beach from this trail and must stick to the path to protect the cliffs from erosion and yourself from thorny plants and snakes—including rattlers. The climb back is long but gradual, leading up to the **Old Point Loma Lighthouse.**

The western and southern cliffs of Cabrillo National Monument are prime whale-watching territory. A sheltered **viewing station** has a tape-recorded lecture describing the great gray whales' yearly migration from the Bering and Chukchi seas near Alaska to Baja California, and high-powered telescopes help you focus on the whales' water spouts. Sea creatures can also be seen in the **tide pools** at the foot of the monument's western cliffs. Drive north from the visitor center to the first road on the left, which winds down to the coast guard station and the shore. ⊠ *1800 Cabrillo Memorial Dr., Point Loma* ☎ *619/557–5450* ⊕ *www. nps.gov/cabr* ⊠ *$5 per car, $3 per person entering on foot or by bicycle, entrance pass allows unlimited admissions for 1 wk from date of purchase; free for Golden Age and Golden Access passport and National Parks Pass holders* ⊙ *Park buildings daily 9–5:15, to 6:15 in summer; park grounds 9–dusk.*

⑮ Harbor Island. Following the success of nearby Shelter Island, the U.S. Navy decided to use the residue that resulted from digging berths deep enough to accommodate aircraft carriers to build another recreational island. Thus in 1961 some 12-million-cubic yards of sand and mud dredged from the bay were deposited adjacent to San Diego International Airport and became the 1½-mi-long peninsula known as Harbor Island. Restaurants and high-rise hotels now line its inner shore. The bay shore has pathways, gardens, and picnic spots for sightseeing or working off the calories from the various indoor or outdoor food fests held here. On the west point, Tom Ham's Lighthouse restaurant has a U.S. Coast Guard–approved beacon shining from its tower.

⑬ Scott Street. Running along Point Loma's waterfront from Shelter Island to the old Naval Training Center on Harbor Drive, this thoroughfare is lined with deep-sea fishing charters and whale-watching boats. It's a good spot from which to watch fishermen (and women) haul marlin, tuna, and puny mackerel off their boats.

⑭ Shelter Island. In 1950 San Diego's port director thought there should be some use for the sand and mud the Works Project Administration dredged up during the course of deepening a ship channel in the 1930s and '40s. He decided it might be a good idea to raise the shoal that lay off the eastern shore of Point Loma above sea level, landscape it, and add a 2,000-foot causeway to make it accessible. His hunch paid off. Shelter Island—actually a peninsula—now supports towering mature palms, a cluster of resorts, restaurants, and side-by-side marinas. It's the center of San Diego's yacht-building industry, and boats in every stage of construction are visible in the yacht yards. On the bay side, fishermen launch their boats or simply stand on shore and cast. Families relax at picnic tables along the grass, where there are fire rings and permanent barbecue grills.

Mission Bay & the Beaches

Mission Bay Park is San Diego's monument to sports and fitness. This 4,600-acre aquatic park has 27 mi of shoreline including 19 of sandy beach. Admission is free. Playgrounds and picnic areas abound on the beach and low grassy hills of the park. In the daytime, swimmers, water-skiers, anglers, and boaters—some in single-person kayaks, others in crowded powerboats—vie for space in the water. On weekday evenings, joggers, bikers, and skaters take over. Mission Boulevard runs along a two-block-wide strip embraced by the Pacific Ocean on the west and the bay on the east. The pathways in this area are lined with vacation homes, many for rent by the week or month.

⚠ One Mission Bay caveat: swimmers should note signs warning about water pollution; on occasions when heavy rains or other events cause pollution, swimming is strongly discouraged.

What to See

☺ **⑯ SeaWorld San Diego.** One of the world's largest marine-life amusement
Fodor'sChoice parks, SeaWorld is spread over 100 tropically landscaped bayfront
★ acres—and it seems to be expanding into every available square inch of

space with new exhibits, shows, and activities. The majority of SeaWorld's exhibits are walk-through marine environments. Kids get a particular kick out of the **Shark Encounter,** where they come face-to-face with sandtiger, nurse, bonnethead, black-tipped, and white-tipped reef sharks by walking through a 57-foot clear acrylic tube that passes through the 280,000-gallon shark habitat. At **Wild Arctic,** which starts out with a simulated helicopter ride to a research post at the North Pole, beluga whales, walruses, and polar bears can be viewed in areas decked out like the wrecked hulls of two 19th-century sailing ships.

SeaWorld's highlights are its large-arena entertainments. You can get front-row seats if you arrive 10 or 15 minutes in advance, and the stadiums are large enough for everyone to get a seat even at the busiest times. Introduced in 2006 and starring the ever-beloved Shamu the Killer Whale, **Believe** features synchronized whales and brings down the house. Another favorite is the 3-D movie *R.L. Stine's Haunted Lighthouse,* which has special effects like sprays of water, blasts of air, and other wild surprises designed to bring you into the scene. A new sea lion and otter production, **Clyde and Seamore in Deep, Deep Trouble,** also is widely popular. **Shipwreck Rapids,** SeaWorld of California's first adventure ride, offers plenty of excitement—but you may end up getting soaked. ✉ *1720 South Shores Rd., near west end of I–8, Mission Bay* ☎ *619/226–3815, 619/226–3901 recorded information* ⊕ *www.seaworld.com* 🖅 *$50.95; parking $8 cars, $4 motorcycles, $9 RVs and campers; 1-hr behind-the-scenes walking tours $11 extra* ▭ *AE, D, MC, V* ☉ *Daily 10–dusk; extended hrs in summer.*

⑰ Vacation Isle. Ingraham Street bisects this island, providing two distinct experiences for visitors. The west side is taken up by the Paradise Point Resort & Spa, but you don't have to be a guest to enjoy the hotel's lushly landscaped grounds and bayfront restaurants. The water-ski clubs congregate at **Ski Beach** on the east side of the island, where there's a parking lot as well as picnic areas and restrooms. At a pond on the south side of the island, children and young-at-heart adults take part year-round in motorized miniature boat races. ✉ *Mission Bay.*

Old Town

San Diego's Spanish and Mexican roots are most evident in Old Town, the area north of downtown at Juan Street, near the intersection of Interstates 5 and 8, that was the first European settlement in Southern California. Although Old Town was largely a 19th-century phenomenon, the pueblo's true beginnings took place much earlier and on a hill overlooking it, where soldiers from New Spain established a military outpost in May 1769 and two months later Father Junípero Serra established the first of California's missions, San Diego de Alcalá.

On San Diego Avenue, the district's main drag, art galleries and expensive gift shops are interspersed with tacky curio shops, restaurants, and open-air stands selling inexpensive Mexican pottery, jewelry, and blankets. The Old Town Esplanade on San Diego Avenue between Harney and Conde streets is the best of several mall-like affairs constructed in

1

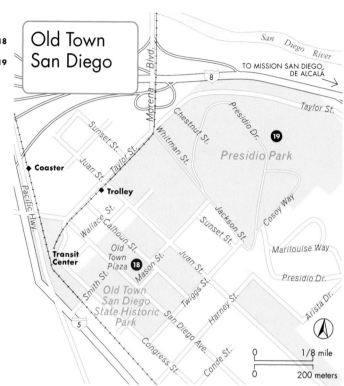

Old Town San Diego

San Diego River

TO MISSION SAN DIEGO,
DE ALCALÁ

Taylor St.

Presidio Park

19

Coaster

Trolley

Transit
Center

Old
Town
Plaza **18**

Old Town
San Diego
State Historic
Park

0   1/8 mile
0   200 meters

mock Mexican-plaza style. Shops and restaurants also line Juan and Congress streets.

Access to Old Town is easy thanks to the nearby Transit Center. Ten bus lines stop here, as do the San Diego Trolley and the Coaster commuter rail line. Two large parking lots linked to the park by an underground pedestrian walkway ease some of the parking congestion, and signage leading from Interstate 8 to the Transit Center is easy to follow.

What to See

★ **18** **Old Town San Diego State Historic Park.** The six square blocks on the site of San Diego's original pueblo are the heart of Old Town. Most of the 20 historic buildings preserved or re-created by the park cluster around **Old Town Plaza** and San Diego Avenue, which is closed to vehicle traffic here. Worth exploring in the plaza area are the Cosmopolitan Hotel/ Casa de Bandini, Casa de Estudillo, Seeley Stable, Dental Museum, Mason Street School, Wells Fargo History Museum, First San Diego Courthouse, Casa de Machado y Silvas Commercial Restaurant Museum, and the Casa de Machado Y Stewart. The **Robinson-Rose House** (☏ 619/ 220–5422), on Wallace Street facing Old Town Plaza, was the original commercial center of old San Diego, housing railroad offices, law offices, and the first newspaper press. It now serves as the park's visitor center and administrative headquarters, and contains a model of Old Town as it looked in 1872.

On San Diego Avenue at Arista Street, you'll find **El Campo Santo,** the cemetery that served San Diego between 1849 and 1880. The adobe-walled cemetery was the burial place for many members of Old Town's founding families—as well as for some gamblers and bandits. Most of the markers give only approximations of where the people named on them are buried; some of the early settlers laid to rest at El Campo Santo really reside under San Diego Avenue.

The **Thomas Whaley Museum** (✉ 2482 San Diego Ave., Old Town ☎ 619/297–7511 💲 $5) commemorates a New York entrepreneur who came to California during the gold rush and built Southern California's first two-story brick structure. The house, which served as the county courthouse and government seat during the 1870s, stands in strong contrast to the Spanish-style adobe residences that surround the nearby historic plaza and marks an early stage of San Diego's "Americanization." Among the historical artifacts in the reconstructed courtroom is one of the six life-size masks of Abraham Lincoln. It's also one of the few houses authenticated by the U.S. Department of Commerce as being haunted. The museum is open from Tuesday to Thursday, 10 to 4:30.

🔟 **Presidio Park.** The hillsides of the 40-acre green space overlooking Old Town from the north end of Taylor Street are popular with picnickers. It's a nice walk from Old Town to the summit if you're in good shape and wearing the right shoes—it should take about half an hour. You can also drive to the top of the park via Presidio Drive, off Taylor Street.

If you do decide to walk, look in at the Presidio Hills Golf Course on Mason Street. It has an unusual clubhouse that incorporates the ruins of Casa de Carrillo, the town's oldest adobe, constructed in 1820. At the end of Mason Street, veer left on Jackson Street to reach the **Presidio Ruins,** where adobe walls and a bastion have been built above the foundations of the original fortress and chapel. Also on-site are the 28-foot-high Serra Cross, built in 1913 out of brick tiles found in the ruins, and a bronze statue of Father Serra. Before you do much poking around here, however, it's a good idea to get some historical perspective at the **Junípero Serra Museum** (✉ 2727 Presidio Dr., Old Town ☎ 619/297–3258 💲 $5) just to the east. It's open daily 10 to 5. Take Presidio Drive southeast of the museum and you'll come to the site of Fort Stockton, built to protect Old Town and abandoned by the United States in 1848. ✉ *1 block north of Old Town.*

La Jolla

La Jollans have long considered their village to be the Monte Carlo of California, and with good cause. Its coastline curves into natural coves backed by verdant hillsides covered with homes worth millions. Although La Jolla is a neighborhood of the city of San Diego, it has its own postal zone and a coveted sense of class; the ultrarich from around the globe own second homes here (the seaside zone between the neighborhood's bustling downtown and the cliffs above the Pacific has a distinctly European flavor).

The Native Americans called the site La Hoya, meaning "the cave," referring to the grottoes that dot the shoreline. The Spaniards changed the name to La Jolla (same pronunciation as La Hoya), "the jewel," and its residents have cherished the name and its allusions ever since.

To reach La Jolla from Interstate 5, if you're traveling north, take the La Jolla Parkway (formerly known as Ardath Road) exit, which veers into Torrey Pines Road, and turn right onto Prospect Street. If you're heading south, get off at the La Jolla Village Drive exit, which also leads into Torrey Pines Road. For those who enjoy meandering, the best way to approach La Jolla from the south is to drive on Mission Boulevard through Mission and Pacific beaches, past the crowds of in-line skaters, bicyclists, and sunbathers. The clutter and congestion ease up as the street becomes La Jolla Boulevard; road signs direct drivers and bicyclists past homes designed by such respected architects as Frank Lloyd Wright and Irving Gill. As you approach the village, La Jolla Boulevard turns into Prospect Street. Prospect Street and Girard Avenue, the village's main drags, are lined with expensive shops and office buildings.

What to See

C **Birch Aquarium at Scripps.** The largest oceanographic exhibit in the United States, maintained by the Scripps Institution of Oceanography, sits at the end of a signposted drive leading off North Torrey Pines Road just north of La Jolla Village Drive. More than 60 tanks are filled with colorful saltwater fish, and a 70,000-gallon tank simulates a La Jolla kelp forest. Besides the fish themselves, attractions include a gallery with exhibits based on the institution's ocean-related research, other interactive educational exhibits, a simulated submarine ride, and supermarket shelves stocked with products derived from the sea (including some surprisingly common ones). A concession sells food, and there are outdoor picnic tables. ⊠ *2300 Expedition Way, La Jolla* ☎ *858/534–3474* ⊕ *www.aquarium.ucsd.edu* ⊡ *$11, parking free for 3 hrs* ☉ *Daily 9–5, last ticket sold at 4:30.*

Golden Triangle. La Jolla's newest enclave, spreading east of Interstate 5, is perhaps of little interest to visitors, but it's an important neighborhood. In places formerly populated solely by coyotes and jays, high-tech research-and-development companies, attracted by the proximity of the University of California at San Diego, the Scripps Institution of Oceanography, and the Salk Institute, have developed huge state-of-the-art compounds. The area along La Jolla Village Drive and Genesee Avenue has become a proving ground for futuristic buildings, including the striking Michael Graves–designed Aventine office complex and the huge, white Mormon Temple, as eye-catching as a psychedelic castle. Completed in 1993, it still startles drivers heading up the freeway. ⊠ *La Jolla.*

C **㉒** **La Jolla Caves.** It's a walk of 145 sometimes slippery steps down a tunnel to Sunny Jim, the largest of the caves in La Jolla Cove and the only one reachable by land. The tunnel, man-made, took two years to dig, beginning in 1902; later, a shop was built at its entrance. Today, La Jolla

La Jolla

PACIFIC OCEAN

Torrey Pines State Beach and Reserve **23**

Torrey Pines State Park

◆ **Salk Institute**

University of California at San Diego

La Jolla Village Dr.

Torrey Pines Rd.

Scripps Pier

◆ **Birch Aquarium at Scripps**

La Jolla Scenic Dr. N.

Gilman Dr.

La Jolla Shores

La Jolla Shores Dr.

Point La Jolla

La Jolla Cove

Shell Beach

21

Museum of Contemporary Art, San Diego

22 **La Jolla Caves**

Torrey Pines Rd.

La Jolla Pkwy.

20

Children's Pool

Prospect St.

Torrey Pines

Virginia Way

Girard Ave.

Pearl St.

La Jolla Country Club

Mt. Soledad ◆

TO GOLDEN TRIANGLE

5

Marine St. Beach

0 ——— 1 mile
0 ——— 1 km

Cave Store, a throwback to that early shop, is still the entrance to the cave. ⊠ *1325 Cave St., La Jolla* ☎ *858/459–0746* ☒ *$4* ☼ *Daily 9–5.*

★ ☙ **21** **La Jolla Cove.** This shimmering blue inlet is what first attracted everyone to La Jolla, from Native Americans to the glitterati; it's the secret to the village's enduring cachet. You'll find the cove—as locals always refer to it—beyond where Girard Avenue dead-ends into Coast Boulevard, marked by towering palms that line a promenade. An underwater preserve at the north end of La Jolla Cove makes the adjoining beach the most popular one in the area. On summer days, the sea seems to disappear under the mass of bodies floating face down, snorkels poking up out of the water. The **Children's Pool,** at the south end of the park, has a curving beach protected by a seawall from strong currents and waves. Since the pool and its beach have become home to an ever-growing colony of Harbor seals, it's no longer open to swimmers; however it's the best place on the coast to view these engaging creatures. Make sure to walk through **Ellen Browning Scripps Park,** past the groves of twisted junipers to the cliff's edge. You can spread your picnic out on a table and enjoy the scenery.

Mount Soledad. La Jolla's highest spot can be reached by taking Nautilus Street to La Jolla Scenic Drive South, and then turning left. Proceed a few blocks to the park, where parking is plentiful and the views are astounding, unless the day is hazy, as it can be along the coast. The top of the mountain is an excellent vantage point from which to get a sense of San Diego's geography: looking down from here you can see the coast from the county's northern border to the south far beyond downtown. ⊠ *La Jolla.*

★ ⑳ **Museum of Contemporary Art, San Diego.** The oldest section of La Jolla's branch of San Diego's modern art museum was originally a residence, designed by Irving Gill for philanthropist Ellen Browning Scripps in 1916. In the mid-1990s, the compound was updated and expanded by architect Robert Venturi and his colleagues at Venturi, Scott Brown and Associates. The museum's permanent collection of post-1950s includes examples of every major art movement since that time—works by Andy Warhol, Robert Rauschenberg, Frank Stella, Joseph Cornell, and Jenny Holzer, to name a few. The museum's artwork gets major competition from the setting: you can look out from the top of a grand stairway onto a landscaped garden that contains permanent and temporary sculpture exhibits as well as rare 100-year-old California plant specimens and, beyond that, to the Pacific Ocean. ⊠ *700 Prospect St., La Jolla* ☎ *858/ 454–3541* ⊕ *www.mcasd.org* ☑ *$6, free 1st Sun. and 3rd Tues. of month* ☉ *Thurs. 11–7, Fri.–Tues. 11–5.*

Salk Institute. The world-famous biological-research facility founded by polio-vaccine developer Jonas Salk sits on 26 cliff-top acres. The twin structures that modernist architect Louis I. Kahn designed in the 1960s in consultation with Dr. Salk used poured concrete and other low-maintenance materials to clever effect. The thrust of the laboratory–office complex is outward toward the Pacific Ocean, an orientation that is accentuated by a foot-wide "Stream of Life" that flows through the center of a travertine marble courtyard between the buildings. Architects-to-be and building buffs enjoy the free tours of the property; call ahead to book, because the tours take place only when enough people express interest. ⊠ *10010 N. Torrey Pines Rd., La Jolla* ☎ *858/453–4100 Ext. 1200* ⊕ *www.salk.edu* ☑ *Free* ☉ *Grounds weekdays 9–5; architectural tours Mon., Wed., and Fri. at noon, Thurs. at 12:30 and every other Tues. at 11.* ⌂ *Reservations are required, so call ahead.*

㉓ **Torrey Pines State Beach and Reserve.** *Pinus torreyana,* the rarest native pine tree in the United States, enjoys a 1,750-acre sanctuary at the northern edge of La Jolla. The reserve has several hiking trails leading to the cliffs, 300 feet above the ocean; trail maps are available at the park station. Wildflowers grow profusely in spring, and the ocean panoramas are always spectacular. When the tide is out, it's possible to walk south all the way past the lifeguard towers to Black's Beach over rocky promontories carved by the waves (avoid the bluffs, however; they're unstable). **Los Peñasquitos Lagoon** at the north end of the reserve is one of the many natural estuaries that flow inland between Del Mar and Oceanside. It's a good place to watch shorebirds. Volunteers lead guided nature walks at 11:30 and 1:30 on most weekends. ⊠ *N. Torrey Pines Rd., Old Hwy. 101, La Jolla, exit I–5 onto Carmel Valley Rd. going west, then turn left (south) on Old Hwy. 101* ☎ *858/755–2063* ☑ *Parking $6* ☉ *Daily 8–dusk.*

WHERE TO EAT

San Diego's status as a vacationer's paradise and its growth into the seventh-largest city in the United States have made it a magnet for restaurateurs and chefs from around the globe. Few other American cities yield so many dining options, indoors and out. Downtown, the dramatically restored Gaslamp Quarter offers vigorous nightlife and some 100 restaurants. The 5th Avenue restaurant row has many cosmopolitan choices, and the uptown neighborhoods centered by Hillcrest are marked by increasing culinary sophistication. Convoy Street—the commercial spine of the busy Kearny Mesa area—is the unofficial Asian Restaurant Row of San Diego, and presents a comprehensive selection of Chinese, Korean, and Vietnamese restaurants. And rich, elegant La Jolla, with many of San Diego's most expensive restaurants, offers some of the best dining in the city.

WHAT IT COSTS				
$$$$	**$$$**	**$$**	**$**	**¢**
AT DINNER over $30	$23–$30	$16–$22	$10–$15	under $10

Prices are for a main course, excluding 7.75% tax.

Coronado & South Bay

French

$$–$$$$ ✕ **Chez Loma.** This is widely considered one of the most romantic restaurants in Southern California, and it's a favorite with guests at nearby Hotel Del Coronado. Lots of windows, soft lighting, and an upstairs Victorian parlor for coffee and dessert are some of the charms. The more elaborate dishes among the carefully prepared meals are boeuf bourguignon, pan-roasted lamb loin with vanilla-merlot sauce, and New York steak au poivre. There's sidewalk dining and Sunday brunch, and new proprietor Lars Sjostrand vows to keep the menu, service, and mood precisely the way they were under founding chef/owner Ken Irvine. ⊠ *1132 Loma Ave., Coronado* ☎ *619/435–0661* ▤ *AE, MC, V* ☻ *No lunch.*

Seafood

$$–$$$$ ✕ **Azzura Point.** Decorated in a romantic 1930s style, Azzura Point is ideal for a leisurely and memorable meal. The view up San Diego Bay to the Coronado Bridge and the downtown skyline is unbeatable. Expect first-class seasonal produce and thoroughly contemporary preparations such as pan-braised baby chicken with chorizo-langoustine broth, an elaborately garnished veal porterhouse, and grilled escolar with a Portuguese-style seafood sauce. Five-course tasting menus change with the season. The herbs often come from the restaurant's extensive garden. Several choice, artisanal cheeses are an alternative to the deftly executed desserts, and the wine list is written and served with particular skill. ⊠ *Loews Coronado Bay Resort, 4000 Coronado Bay Rd., Coronado* ☎ *619/424–4477* ▤ *AE, MC, V* ☻ *Closed Mon. No lunch.*

¢–$$$$ ✕ **Baja Lobster.** To experience something akin to dining in Puerto Nuevo,
Fodor'sChoice Baja California—the famed lobstering village south of the border—
★ head to this excellent but quite informal eatery, easily reached from Interstate 5. Local lobsters are split and lightly fried, served with family-style
portions of fresh flour tortillas, creamy beans crammed with flavor, and
well-seasoned rice. Although lobsters are the big catch, steak and chicken
options are on the menu, too, and there's full bar service. A pair of high-
quality shrimp tacos costs just $5.95. Note that a similarly named
chain, Rockin' Baja Lobster, is not related to Baja Lobster. ✉ *1060 Broadway, Chula Vista* ☎ *619/425–2512* ▭ *MC, V.*

Downtown

Contemporary

★ ¢ ✕ **Bread on Market.** The baguettes at this artisanal bakery near the Petco
Park baseball stadium are every bit as good as the ones you'd buy in
Paris. Baguettes, focaccia, and other superior loaves are the building
blocks for solid, sometimes creative sandwiches, which range from the
simple goodness of Genoa salami and sweet butter, to a vegan sandwich that includes locally grown avocado. The menu extends to a daily
soup, a fruit-garnished cheese plate, and an appetizing Mediterranean
salad. Snackers gravitate here for fudge-textured brownies, orange-al-
mond biscotti, and other irresistible sweets. During baseball season, the
"take-me-out-to-the-ballgame" box lunch offers a choice of sandwich,
chips, a freshly baked cookie, and a bottle of water for $10.75. ✉ *730
Market St., Downtown* ☎ *619/795–2730* ▭ *MC, V* ☺ *Closed Sun.
No dinner.*

French

★ $$$–$$$$ ✕ **Bertrand at Mister A's.** Restaurateur Bertrand Hug's sumptuous 12th-
floor dining room has vanilla walls, contemporary paintings, and a
view that stretches to Mexico and San Diego Bay. (It used to be an even
greater view, before a building rose to the east, but you can still watch
the aerial ballet of jets descending upon nearby Lindbergh Field.) Ideal
for a special occasion, Bertrand at Mister A's serves luxurious seasonal
dishes such as sautéed foie gras with caramelized fruit and Dover sole
in lemon butter. The dessert list encompasses a galaxy of sweets every
bit as memorable as the view. ✉ *2550 5th Ave., Middletown* ☎ *619/
239–1377* ⌔ *Reservations essential* ⌂ *Jacket required* ▭ *AE, MC, V*
☺ *No lunch weekends.*

★ $$$–$$$$ ✕ **Le Fontainebleau.** On the second floor of the elegant Westgate Hotel,
this restaurant is worthy of the famous chateau for which it is named.
Normandy-born chef Fabrice Hardel writes seasonal menus, but usu-
ally offers classics like French pepper steak (dramatically flambéed at
your table), along with contemporary creations like pepper-crusted
Hudson Valley duck breast with a "pancake" of wild mushrooms and
country ham. Pairing the multicourse tasting menu with specially selected
wines costs in excess of $100 per person, a price that seems not unrea-
sonable when read to the accompaniment of the harp or piano music
that is a Le Fontainebleau staple. ✉ *1055 2nd Ave., Downtown* ☎ *619/
557–3655* ⌂ *Jacket required* ▭ *AE, D, DC, MC, V.*

Where to Eat
in San Diego

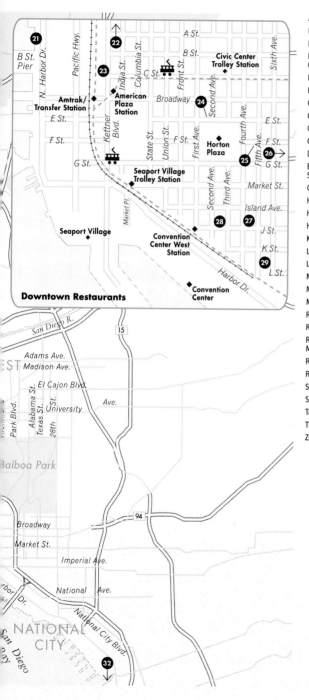

Downtown Restaurants

Indian

★ **$–$$** ✕ **Monsoon.** An exceptionally attractive restaurant, Monsoon delights with features such as a room-centering waterfall that splashes like a cloudburst from a bower of hanging plants. Folding doors allow some tables to share the outdoor atmosphere of the terrace, but at a distance from the sidewalk. The menu offers many dishes not easily found at local Indian eateries, including a sweetly spiced mango soup, and "balti"-style pan-sautéed lamb. The dozens of curries and similar dishes are spiced to taste, and baked-to-order breads should not be missed. ✉ *729–733 4th Ave., Gaslamp Quarter* ☎ *619/234–5555* ▭ *AE, DC, MC, V.*

Mexican

$$$–$$$$ ✕ **Candelas.** The scents and flavors of imaginative Mexican cuisine permeate this handsome, romantic little hideaway in the shadow of San Diego's tallest residential towers. Candles glow everywhere around the small, comfortable dining room. There isn't a burrito or taco in sight. Fine openers such as cream of black-bean and beer soup, and salad of watercress with bacon and pistachios warm diners up for local lobster stuffed with mushrooms, jalapeño peppers, and aged tequila; or tequila-flamed jumbo prawns over creamy, seasoned goat cheese. The new, adjacent bar pours many elegant tequilas and has become a popular, often jam-packed nightspot. ✉ *416 3rd Ave., Gaslamp Quarter* ☎ *619/702–4455* ▭ *MC, V* ☉ *Closed Sun. No lunch weekends.*

Seafood

$$$–$$$$ ✕ **Star of the Sea.** This is the flagship of the Anthony's chain of seafood restaurants, its most formal dining room (although dress is quite casual), and long an all-around favorite for location (the setting is exceptional), cuisine, and design. The menu changes seasonally, and the food and service, which had declined of late, seem to have improved since the arrival of young chef Paul McCabe. Best bets when ordering are choices like the potato-beer bisque, sparklingly fresh oysters on the half-shell, diver scallops with braised pork belly, and grilled swordfish with lobster "bolognese" sauce. To be sure, have one of the baked-to-order soufflés, which are puffy, fragrant, and lovely on the palate. The outdoor patio takes full advantage of the choice waterfront location. ✉ *1360 N. Harbor Dr., Downtown* ☎ *619/232–7408* ▭ *AE, D, DC, MC, V* ☉ *No lunch.*

★ **¢–$** ✕ **The Tin Fish.** On the rare rainy day, the staff takes it easy at this eatery less than 100 yards from the Petco Park baseball stadium (its 100-odd seats are all outdoors). Musicians entertain some evenings, making this a lively spot for dinners of grilled and fried fish and shellfish, as well as Mexican-style seafood burritos and tacos. The quality here routinely surpasses that at grander establishments—for instance, the bread used for sandwiches stuffed with fried oysters and the like is baked on the premises. For kids (or unadventurous grown-ups) there's an inexpensive peanut butter and jelly sandwich. Service hours vary with the day of the week, the weather, and whether it's baseball season or not, but generally, Tin Fish closes at 3 PM Sunday through Wednesday and at 8 PM Thursday through Saturday. ✉ *170 6th Ave., Gaslamp Quarter* ☎ *619/238–8100* ▱ *Reservations not accepted* ▭ *MC, V.*

Steak Houses

★ **$$$–$$$$** ✕ **Rainwater's on Kettner.** San Diego's premier homegrown steak house also ranks as the longest running of the pack, not least because it has the luxurious look and mood of an old-fashioned Eastern men's club. The cuisine is excellent: open with the signature black-bean soup with Madeira. Continue with the tender, expertly roasted prime rib, superb calves' liver with onions and bacon, broiled free-range chicken, fresh seafood, or the amazingly succulent pork chops, all served in vast portions with plenty of hot-from-the-oven cornsticks on the side. The prime steaks sizzle, as does the bill. The well-chosen wine list has pricey but superior selections. ✉ *1202 Kettner Blvd., Downtown* ☎ *619/233–5757* ▤ *AE, D, MC, V* ⊗ *No lunch weekends.*

Thai

¢–$$ ✕ **Rama.** Gauzy draperies and a rock wall flowing with water create a dreamy rain-forest effect in the back room of this excellent newcomer to the Gaslamp Quarter's booming restaurant row. Without question the best Thai restaurant in San Diego, Rama combines professional service with a kitchen that understands the subtle demands of spicing the myriad dishes. The tart, pungent, spiced-to-order (as everything can be) *talay* (seafood soup—it literally means "ocean") pairs well with a crispy duck salad as a light meal for two. Dozens of curries and stir-fries take the tastebuds on exciting adventures in flavor. Reservations are advised. ✉ *327 4th Ave., Gaslamp Quarter* ☎ *619/501–8424* ▤ *AE, D, DC, MC, V.*

FodorsChoice ★

Little Italy

Italian

★ **$–$$$** ✕ **Buon Appetito.** The booming Little Italy restaurant scene includes this charmer serving old world–style cooking in a casual but decidedly sophisticated environment. The young Italian waiters' good humor makes the experience fun. Choose a table on the breezy sidewalk or in an indoor room jammed with art and fellow diners. Baked eggplant *all'amalfitana*, in a mozzarella-topped tomato sauce, is a dream of a dish, and in San Diego, tomato sauce doesn't get better than this. Consider also veal with tuna sauce, a hot chicken-liver salad, fusilli pasta in savory duck ragout, and hearty seafood cioppino. ✉ *1609 India St., Little Italy* ☎ *619/238–9880* ▤ *MC, V.*

Uptown

American

★ **¢–$$** ✕ **Hob Nob Hill.** That Hob Nob never seems to change suits San Diego just fine; this is the type of place where regulars have been ordering the same meal for 20 years. With its dark-wood booths and patterned carpets, the restaurant seems suspended in the 1950s, but you don't need to be a nostalgia buff to appreciate the bargain-price American home cooking—dishes such as oat-raisin French toast, fried chicken, and corned beef like your mother never really made. The crowds line up morning, noon, and night. Reservations are suggested for Sunday breakfast. ✉ *2271 1st Ave., Middletown* ☎ *619/239–8176* ▤ *AE, D, MC, V.*

Contemporary

$$–$$$$ ✕ **Laurel.** New proprietor Tracy Borkum has returned this old favorite to top-tier status by installing a fresh "Swinging London" look and a creative, French-inspired cuisine. The menu changes seasonally and features items such as roast chicken stuffed with Gouda and arugula, and a grilled pork chop with fennel confit and a brandied fig glaze. The oysters on the half-shell with a frozen ginger-cilantro-lime relish always open the meal well. Borkum wisely retained the chocolate pot de crème from the original menu, and Laurel remains especially popular with guests attending theatrical events in nearby Balboa Park. ⊠ *505 Laurel St., Middletown* ☎ *619/239–2222* ▱ *AE, D, DC, MC, V* ⊘ *No lunch.*

$–$$$ ✕ **Region.** Rich in talented owner-chefs who use the finest local produce
Fodor'sChoice to create traditional recipes, Region is one of the most intriguing restau-
★ rants in San Diego. The kitchen's approach nears perfection with dishes like veal osso buco, roast pork with onion-olive dressing, and pan-gilded skate (a type of ray) that flakes at the touch of a fork. The menu changes daily, but count on fine sweets like a molten-centered chocolate "fondant" cake with raisins and caramel ice cream. A chalkboard not only lists the evening's special fruits and vegetables and their provenance but also illustrates some of them. The food and prices at this purposely informal place (the waiters wear jeans) mean value for the money, making it competitive with more formal establishments. Reservations are strongly advised. ⊠ *3671 5th Ave., Hillcrest* ☎ *619/299–6499* ▱ *AE, D, DC, MC, V* ⊘ *No lunch. No dinner Mon.*

Indian

★ **$–$$$** ✕ **Bombay Exotic Cuisine of India.** Notable for its elegant dining room, Bombay employs a chef whose generous hand with raw and cooked vegetables gives each course a colorful freshness reminiscent of California cuisine, though the flavors definitely hail from India. Try the tandoori lettuce-wrap appetizer and any of the stuffed *nan* (a delectably chewy tandoori bread). The unusually large selection of curries may be ordered with meat, chicken, fish, or tofu. The curious should try the *dizzy noo shakk*, a sweet and spicy banana curry. Try a *thali*, a plate that includes an entrée, traditional sides, nan, dessert, and tea. ⊠ *Hillcrest Center, 3975 5th Ave., Suite 100, Hillcrest* ☎ *619/298–3155* ▱ *AE, D, DC, MC, V.*

Thai

★ **¢–$$** ✕ **Celadon Fine Thai Cuisine.** Talk to young proprietor Alex Thao if you want to try some of the specialties not listed on the menu, like the spicy, stir-fried cashew appetizer or the tart, invigorating stir-fry of shredded dried beef and citrus sauce. These dishes are superb, but the everyday menu is good enough to keep the small, well-furnished dining room jumping, even on Monday nights. Start with "Celadon squares," small toasts covered with a paste of shrimp and pork, and move along to refreshing, if spicy, papaya salad, the excellent *tom kha* (chicken soup), and such entrées as deep-fried whole striped bass with green mangoes. Note that Celadon is under the same ownership as downtown's Rama, which is San Diego's best Thai eatery. ⊠ *540 University Ave., Hillcrest* ☎ *619/ 297–8424* ▱ *MC, V.*

Kearny Mesa

Chinese

★ **$-$$$$** ✕ **Emerald Chinese Seafood Restaurant.** Emerald holds pride of place among fanciers of elaborate, carefully prepared, and sometimes costly seafood dishes. Even when the restaurant is full to capacity with 300 diners, the noise level is moderate and conversation flows easily between bites of the best Chinese cuisine in the area. Market-priced—and that can be high—shrimp, prawns, lobsters, clams, and fish reside in tanks until the moment of cooking. Simple preparations flavored with scallions, black beans, and ginger are among the most worthy. Other recommended dishes include beef with Singapore-style satay sauce, honey-walnut shrimp, baked chicken in five spices, Peking duck served in two savory courses, and, at lunch, the dim sum. ✉ *3709 Convoy St., Kearny Mesa* ☎ *858/565–6888* ▤ *AE, DC, MC, V.*

★ **¢-$** ✕ **Dumpling Inn.** Modest, family-style, and absolutely wonderful, Dumpling Inn is in some ways the most likable of Convoy Street's Asian restaurants. The tiny establishment loads its tables with bottles of aromatic and spicy condiments for the boiled, steamed, and fried dumplings that are the house specialty. These delicately flavored, hefty mouthfuls preface a meal that may continue simply, with hearty pork and pickled cabbage soup, or elaborately, with Shanghai-style braised pork shank. Ask about the daily specials, such as shredded pork in plum sauce served on a sea of crispy noodles. You may bring your own wine or beer; the house serves only tea and soft drinks. ✉ *4619 Convoy St., #F, Kearny Mesa* ☎ *858/268–9638* ⌔ *Reservations not accepted* ▤ *MC, V* ⊘ *Closed Mon.*

Beaches

American

★ **¢-$** ✕ **Hodad's.** No, it's not a flashback. The 1960s live on at this fabulously funky burger joint founded in that era: an unrepentant hippy crowd sees to it. Walls are covered with license plates, and the amiable servers with tattoos. Still, this is very much a family place, and Hodad's clientele often includes toddlers and octogenarians. Burgers are the thing, loaded with onions, pickles, tomatoes, lettuce, and condiments, and so gloriously messy that you might wear a swimsuit so you can stroll to the beach for a bath afterwards. The mini-hamburger is good, the double bacon cheeseburger absolutely awesome. ✉ *5010 Newport Ave., Ocean Beach* ☎ *619/224–4623* ▤ *AE, DC, MC, V.*

German

★ **$$-$$$$** ✕ **Kaiserhof.** Without question this is the best German restaurant in San Diego County, and the lively bar and beer garden work to inspire a sense of *Gemütlichkeit* (happy well-being). Tourist board–style posters of Germany's romantic destinations hang on the wall and Warsteiner and St. Pauli Girl flow from the tap. Gigantic portions are accompanied by such side dishes as potato pancakes, bread dumplings, red cabbage, and spaetzle noodles. Entrées include sauerbraten, Wiener schnitzel, goulash, and smoked pork chops, plus excellent daily specials such as crisp pork schnitzel with tart red cabbage. Reservations are a good idea. ✉ *2253 Sunset Cliffs Blvd., Ocean Beach* ☎ *619/224–0606* 🗖 *MC, V* ⊗ *Closed Mon. No lunch Tues.–Thurs.*

Italian

$–$$$ ✕ **Caffe Bella Italia.** Contemporary Italian cooking as prepared in Italy— an important point in fusion-mad San Diego—is the rule at this simple restaurant near one of the principal intersections in Pacific Beach. The menu presents Neapolitan-style macaroni with sausage and artichoke hearts in spicy tomato sauce, pappardelle with a creamy Gorgonzola and walnut sauce, plus formal entrées like chicken breast sautéed with balsamic vinegar, and slices of rare filet mignon tossed with herbs and topped with arugula and Parmesan shavings. Impressive daily specials include beet-stuffed ravioli in creamy saffron sauce. ✉ *1525 Garnet Ave., Pacific Beach* ☎ *858/273–1224* 🗖 *MC, V* ⊗ *Closed Mon. No lunch Sun.*

Japanese

★ **¢–$$$** ✕ **Sushi Ota.** Wedged into a minimall between a convenience store and a looming medical building, Sushi Ota initially seems less than prepossessing. Still, San Diego–bound Japanese business people frequently call for reservations before boarding their trans-Pacific flights. Look closely at the expressions on customers' faces as they stream in and out of the doors, and you can see the eager anticipation and satisfied glows that are products of San Diego's best sushi. Besides the usual California roll and tuna and shrimp sushi, sample the sea urchin or surf clam sushi, and the soft-shell crab roll. Sushi Ota offers the cooked as well as the raw. There's additional parking behind the mall. Servers can be curt, to say the least. ✉ *4529 Mission Bay Dr., Pacific Beach* ☎ *858/270–5670* ⌕ *Reservations essential* 🗖 *AE, D, MC, V* ⊗ *No lunch Sat.–Mon.*

Seafood

★ **¢–$** ✕ **Hudson Bay Seafood.** Part of the pleasure in this small, friendly, waterside fish house is watching the day-charter boats arrive at the adjacent dock and discharge their passengers, some seasoned fishermen and some first-timers grateful to be back on dry land. More than a few march up the wooden walkway to Hudson Bay, which bakes the sourdough rolls in which it places delicately fried fish fillets or shellfish. The french fries are freshly cut, the fish tacos taste of Mexico, and even the tartar sauce is homemade. There are salads and excellent breakfasts, too, and even the burgers are exceptional. ✉ *1403 Scott St., Shelter Island* ☎ *619/222–8787* 🗖 *MC, V.*

La Jolla

Contemporary

★ **$$$–$$$$** ✕ **Marine Room.** Gaze at the ocean from this venerable La Jolla Shores mainstay and, if you're lucky, watch the grunion run or the waves race across the sand and beat against the glass. Long-running chef Bernard Guillas, now an internationally known celebrity, takes a bold approach to combining ingredients. Creative seasonal menus score with "trilogy" plates that combine three meats, sometimes including game, in distinct preparations. Disparate elements like Korean-style barbecue sauce and

Dungeness crab risotto contribute to the success of such entrées as glazed cobia (another name for this critter is "lemonfish"), lemon thyme and sea salt–rubbed free-range veal loin with a truffled corn cake, and Maine lobster tail basted in fennel pollen butter with Maltese orange emulsion. ⊠ *2000 Spindrift Dr., La Jolla* ☎ *858/459–7222* ▭ *AE, D, DC, MC, V* ☉ *No lunch.*

★ **$$–$$$$** ✕ **Roppongi.** A hit from the moment it opened, Roppongi serves global cuisine with strong Asian notes. The contemporary dining room done in wood tones and accented with Asian statuary has a row of comfortable booths along one wall. It can get noisy when crowded; tables near the bar are generally quieter. Order the imaginative Euro–Asian tapas as appetizers or combine them for a full meal. Try the teriyaki portobello mushroom with breaded goat cheese and the Mongolian chopped duck salad with crisp won tons. Good entrées are filet mignon with Thai basil-flavored hollandaise sauce, and miso-marinated black cod in balsamic vinegar sauce. The creative sushi bar rocks. ⊠ *875 Prospect St., La Jolla* ☎ *858/551–5252* ▭ *AE, D, DC, MC, V.*

French

$$$–$$$$ ✕ **Tapenade.** Named after the delicious Provençal black olive–and–anchovy
Fodor'sChoice paste that accompanies the bread here, Tapenade specializes in the cui-
★ sine of the south of France—although that cuisine has lost some of its weight in the trip across the Atlantic. It now matches the unpretentious, light, and airy room, lined with 1960s French movie posters, in which it is served. Very fresh ingredients, a delicate touch with sauces, and an emphasis on seafood characterize the menu, which changes frequently. If you're lucky, it may include boar stewed in red wine (possibly the single best entrée in San Diego), lobster in a lobster-corn sauce flavored with Tahitian vanilla, pan-gilded sea scallops in fragrant curry sauce, and desserts like fried *bugnes,* dumplings with pistachio ice cream, chocolate sauce and, believe it or not, tomato marmalade. The two-course "Riviera Menu" served at lunch for $19.95 is a fabulous steal. No lunch weekends. ⊠ *7612 Fay Ave., La Jolla* ☎ *858/551–7500* ▭ *AE, D, DC, MC, V.*

★ **¢–$$$** ✕ **Michele Coulon Dessertier.** A "dessertier" confects desserts, a job that Michele Coulon does exceedingly well in the back of a small, charming shop in the heart of La Jolla. The colorful raspberry pinwheel *bombe* (a molded dessert of cake, jam, and creamy filling), the cherry torte, and a tricolor mousse of chocolate and coffee creams are a few treats. This is not just a place for dessert, however. Lunch is served Monday through Saturday (the store is open 9 to 4), and chef Don Ramsdell cooks a menu that includes French onion soup, quiche Lorraine (baked fresh daily), and a bubbling gratin of baby spinach, prosciutto, cream, and Pecorino cheese. ⊠ *7556 Fay Ave., La Jolla* ☎ *858/456–5098* ▭ *AE, D, MC, V* ☉ *Closed Sun. No dinner.*

Seafood

$$$–$$$$ ✕ **George's at the Cove.** Hollywood types and other visiting celebrities
Fodor'sChoice can be spotted in the elegant main dining room, where a wall-length win-
★ dow overlooks La Jolla Cove. Renowned for fresh seafood and fine preparations of beef and lamb, this also is the place to taste the wonders chef Trey Foshee works with seasonal produce from local specialty growers.

Give special consideration to imaginatively garnished, wild Scottish salmon, a combination of roast lamb loin and braised lamb shoulder with spicy couscous, or choice cuts of beef and pork from the state's celebrated Niman Ranch. For more informal dining and a sweeping view of the coast try the rooftop Ocean Terrace ($–$$). The main dining room now serves dinner only (no lunch). ⊠ *1250 Prospect St., La Jolla* ☎ *858/454–4244* ⌦ *Reservations essential* ▭ *AE, D, DC, MC, V.*

Old Town

Mexican

★ **$–$$$** ✕ **Zocalo Grill.** Try for a table by the fireplace on the covered terrace, but the contemporary cuisine tastes just as good anywhere in the spacious and handsome eatery. Instead of cooking the carnitas (in this case, chunks of pork) the traditional way, simmering them in well-seasoned lard, Zocalo braises them in a mixture of honey and Porter beer and serves the dish with mango salsa and avocado salad. Recommended starters include artichoke fritters and crisp shrimp skewers with pineapple-mango relish. The Seattle surf and turf roasts wild salmon and forest mushrooms on a cedar plank. This is one of the best bets in Old Town. ⊠ *2444 San Diego Ave., Old Town* ☎ *619/298–9840* ▭ *AE, D, DC, MC, V.*

★ **¢–$$** ✕ **Rancho Corona Mexican Restaurant.** A vast veranda wraps around a small-ish dining room, and heaters keep the outdoor space enjoyable in virtually all kinds of weather. A best bet in Old Town, Rancho Corona captures authentic Mexican flavors better than most and offers an education in the variety of tacos found in Mexico by serving a half-dozen, including crisp, Texcoco-style lamb tacos. Tortilla soup opens a meal well, as does the bubbling "queso fundido," or melted cheese, and either can be followed by Oaxaca-style marinated chicken, Puebla chicken enchiladas in dark mole sauce, and deliciously flavored pork rib carnitas. ⊠*2543 Congress St., Old Town* ☎ *619/683–9220* ▭ *AE, D, DC, MC, V.*

WHERE TO STAY

San Diego is spread out, so the first thing to consider when selecting lodging is location. If you choose a hotel with a waterfront setting and extensive outdoor sports facilities, you may decide never to leave. But if you plan to sightsee, be sure to look into a hotel's proximity to attractions. There are plenty of hotel-resorts for families in Mission Valley and Mission Bay, which are convenient to the San Diego Zoo, SeaWorld, or nearby beaches. The downtown center has hip boutique hotels and preserved Victorian-era hostelries in the Gaslamp Quarter.

Prices

The lodgings we list run from bare-bones basic to lavishly upscale. Note that even in the most expensive areas, you can find some more affordable rooms. High season is summer, and rates are lowest in the fall. If an ocean view is important, request it when booking, but be aware that it will cost significantly more than a nonocean view room.

WHAT IT COSTS				
	$$$$	**$$$**	**$$**	**$**	**¢**
FOR 2 PEOPLE	over $250	$176–$250	$121–$175	$90–$120	under $90

Prices are for a standard double room in high (summer) season, excluding 10.5% tax.

Coronado

$$$$ **Hotel Del Coronado.** "The Hotel Del" stands as a social and historic
FodorśChoice landmark, its whimsical red turrets and balconied walkways taking you
★ as far back as 1888, the year it was built. U.S. presidents, European royalty, and movie stars have enjoyed its Victorian rooms and suites, which
are as grand today as ever, fresh from a $10 million renovation completed
in summer 2005. Public areas always bustle with activity; for quieter quarters, stay in the Ocean Towers or California Cabanas. In all, rates are
defined largely by size of room and views. ☒ *1500 Orange Ave., 92118*
☎ *619/435–6611 or 800/468–3533* 🖷 *619/522–8262* ⊕ *www.hoteldel.
com* ⤳ *618 rooms, 70 suites ♿ 2 restaurants, coffee shop, room service, in-room safes, cable TV with movies and video games, in-room data
ports, 3 tennis courts, 2 pools, gym, hair salon, outdoor hot tub, massage, sauna, spa, steam room, beach, bicycles, 4 bars, piano bar, shops,
children's programs (ages 3–17), dry cleaning, laundry service, concierge,
business services, meeting rooms, convention center, airport shuttle, car
rental, parking (fee); no smoking* ⊟ *AE, D, DC, MC, V.*

$$$–$$$$ **Coronado Island Marriott Resort.** Near San Diego Bay, this snazzy
hotel has many rooms with great views of the downtown skyline. Large
rooms and suites in low-slung buildings are done in a cheerful
California–country French fashion, with colorful impressionist prints;
all rooms have separate showers and tubs and come with plush robes.
The resort is a short walk away from a $5 water taxi that'll take you
right downtown. ☒ *2000 2nd St., 92118* ☎ *619/435–3000 or 800/543–
4300* 🖷 *619/435–3032* ⊕ *www.marriotthotels.com/sanci* ⤳ *273 rooms,
27 suites ♿ 4 restaurants, room service, cable TV with movies, in-room
data ports, 6 tennis courts, 3 pools, fitness classes, health club, hair salon,
2 outdoor hot tubs, massage, sauna, spa, beach, snorkeling, windsurf-
ing, boating, jet skiing, waterskiing, bicycles, bar, shops, laundry serv-
ice, concierge, business services, meeting rooms, convention center,
parking (fee); no smoking* ⊟ *AE, D, DC, MC, V.*

$$$–$$$$ **Glorietta Bay Inn.** The main building on this property is an Edwar-
dian-style mansion built in 1908 for sugar baron John D. Spreckels, who
once owned much of downtown San Diego. Rooms in the mansion and
in the newer motel-style buildings are attractively furnished. Some
rooms have patios or balconies. The inn is adjacent to the Coronado
harbor and near many restaurants and shops, but is much smaller and
quieter than the Hotel Del across the street. Tours ($8) of the island's
historical buildings depart from the inn three mornings a week. Ginger
snaps and lemonade are served daily from 3 to 5. ☒ *1630 Glorietta Blvd.,
92118* ☎ *619/435–3101 or 800/283–9383* 🖷 *619/435–6182* ⊕ *www.
gloriettabayinn.com* ⤳ *100 rooms ♿ Dining room, some kitchenettes,*

refrigerators, cable TV with movies, in-room data ports, pool, outdoor hot tub, bicycles, library, laundry service, concierge, business services, free parking; no smoking ⊟ *AE, DC, MC, V.*

Downtown

Lively, continuously revitalizing downtown is San Diego's hotel hub, where anything from budget chains to boutique and business hotels to major high-rises flourish. You can walk to Seaport Village, the Embarcadero, the Gaslamp Quarter, theaters and nightspots, galleries and coffeehouses, and the Horton Plaza shopping center, or hop a bus to Balboa Park and the world-famous zoo. Visitors downtown can indulge in plenty of excellent restaurants and wild nightlife, especially along 4th and 5th avenues south of Broadway in the Gaslamp Quarter.

$$$$ ⊡ **Manchester Grand Hyatt San Diego.** Built primarily for business travelers, this hotel between Seaport Village and the San Diego Convention Center is the largest in San Diego, and its 40- and 33-story towers make it the West Coast's tallest waterfront hostelry. The interior combines old-world opulence with California airiness; palm trees pose next to ornate tapestry couches in the light-filled lobby. All of the British Regency–style guest rooms have water views and windows that open to catch fresh bay breezes. Stay in the newer Seaport Tower for more recently updated rooms. The hotel's Business Plan includes access to an area with desks and office supplies. A trolley station is one block away and the Gaslamp's clubs and restaurants are also within walking distance. ⊠ *1 Market Pl., Embarcadero, 92101* ☎ *619/232–1234 or 800/233–1234* ⊟ *619/233–6464* ⊕ *www.manchestergrand.hyatt.com* ⤶ *1,625 rooms, 95 suites* � *3 restaurants, room service, minibars, cable TV, in-room data ports, 4 tennis courts, pool, health club, outdoor hot tub, sauna, steam room, boating, bicycles, 2 bars, shops, dry cleaning, laundry service, concierge, concierge floor, business services, meeting rooms, airport shuttle, car rental, parking (fee); no smoking* ⊟ *AE, D, DC, MC, V.*

$$$$ ⊡ **San Diego Marriott Hotel and Marina.** This 25-story twin-tower hotel next to the convention center has everything a businessperson—or leisure traveler—could want. As a major site for conventions, the complex can be hectic and impersonal, and the hallways can be noisy. Lending some tranquillity are the lagoon-style pools nestled between cascading waterfalls. The standard rooms are smallish, but pay a bit extra for a room with a balcony overlooking the bay and you'll have a serene, sparkling world spread out before you. Seaport Village and a trolley station are nearby. ⊠ *333 W. Harbor Dr., Embarcadero, 92101* ☎ *619/234–1500 or 800/228–9290* ⊟ *619/234–8678* ⊕ *www.marriotthotels. com/sandt* ⤶ *1,300 rooms, 54 suites* ð *3 restaurants, room service, cable TV with movies, in-room data ports, 6 tennis courts, 2 pools, fitness classes, health club, hair salon, outdoor hot tub, massage, sauna, boating, bicycles, basketball, 3 bars, recreation room, video game room, shops, laundry facilities, concierge, concierge floor, business services, meeting rooms, convention center, airport shuttle, car rental, parking (fee); no smoking* ⊟ *AE, D, DC, MC, V.*

$$$$ ⊞ **Westgate Hotel.** A nondescript, modern high-rise near Horton Plaza hides
Fodor'sChoice   what must be the most opulent hotel in San Diego. The lobby, modeled
★   after the anteroom at Versailles, has hand-cut Baccarat chandeliers. Rooms
are individually furnished with antiques, Italian marble counters, and bath
fixtures with 24-karat-gold overlays. From the ninth floor up the views
of the harbor and city are breathtaking. Afternoon tea is served in the lobby
to the accompaniment of piano and harp music. The San Diego Trolley
stops right outside the door. ⊠ *1055 2nd Ave., Gaslamp Quarter, 92101*
☎ *619/238–1818 or 800/221–3802, 800/522–1564 in CA* 🖷 *619/557–
3737* ⊕ *www.westgatehotel.com* 🛏 *223 rooms* ♺ *2 restaurants, room
service, cable TV with movies, in-room data ports, health club, hair salon,
spa, bicycles, bar, concierge, business services, meeting rooms, airport shuttle, parking (fee); no smoking* ⊟ *AE, D, DC, MC, V.*

$$$–$$$$ ⊞ **Holiday Inn San Diego on the Bay.** On the Embarcadero and overlook-
ing San Diego Bay, this hotel made up of twin high-rises has unsurpris-
ing but spacious rooms and hard-to-beat views from the balconies.
Although the hotel grounds are nice if fairly sterile, the bay is just across
the street and offers boat rides, restaurants, and picturesque walking
areas. The hotel is very close to the airport and Amtrak station. The Eng-
lish-style Elephant and Castle Pub is a great place for food, drink, and
meeting people. ⊠ *1355 N. Harbor Dr., Embarcadero, 92101* ☎ *619/
232–3861 or 800/877–8920* 🖷 *619/232–4924* ⊕ *www.holiday-inn.
com* 🛏 *600 rooms, 17 suites* ♺ *3 restaurants, cable TV, in-room data
ports, 2 pools, gym, outdoor hot tub, sauna, bar, shops, laundry facil-
ities, concierge, business services, meeting rooms, airport shuttle, car rental,
parking (fee); no smoking* ⊟ *AE, D, DC, MC, V.*

★ **$$$–$$$$**   ⊞ **Omni San Diego Hotel.** The product of burgeoning downtown growth,
this modern masterpiece occupies the first 21 floors of a building that rises
32 stories above the new Petco Park baseball stadium. Though built for
the business traveler, the hotel attracts a fair share of sports fans (it's con-
nected to the stadium by a skybridge). The modern lobby is simply stun-
ning; all rooms have windows that open to the breeze, and most have views
of the ocean, bay, the downtown skyline, or the Petco outfield. Pleasantly
decorated, rooms have DVD players and soothing sound machines. The
pool terrace has a stone fireplace, outdoor dining, and a tanning area. ⊠*675
L St., Gaslamp Quarter, 92101* ☎ *619/231–6664 or 800/843–6664*
🖷 *619/645–6517* ⊕ *www.omnisandiegohotel.com* 🛏 *478 rooms, 33
suites* ♺ *3 restaurants, room service, in-room safe, minibars, cable TV
with movies, in-room DVD, in-room data ports, Wi-Fi, pool, gym, hot
tub, lounge, shop, dry cleaning, laundry service, concierge, business serv-
ices, meeting rooms, airport shuttle, parking (fee), some pets allowed (fee);
no smoking* ⊟ *AE, D, DC, MC, V.*

★ **$$$–$$$$**   ⊞ **W Hotel.** Come here for the trendy decor and neon drinks, not the
service. The W chain's urban finesse adapts to San Diego with nautical
blue-and-white rooms with beach-ball pillows and goose-down comforters
atop the beds. The Beach bar has a heated sand floor and fire pit, but
the pool is tiny by San Diego standards. The lobby doubles as the fu-
turistic Living Room lounge, a local hipster nightspot where nonhotel
guests have to wait behind a velvet rope. Be sure to get a room on an
upper floor—the leather- and black-clad crowd parties into the night.

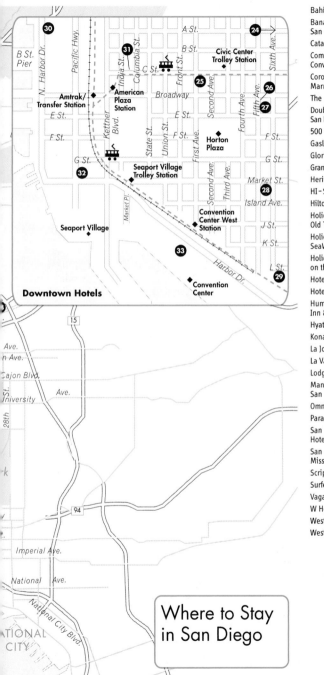

Downtown Hotels

Where to Stay
in San Diego

The hotel restaurant, Rice, serves stylish Asian and Latin cuisine, and the Anatomy Spa caters to both body and spirit. ⊠ *421 West B St., Downtown, 92101* ☎ *619/231–8220 or 877/946–8357* 🖷 *619/232–3626* ⊕ *www.whotels.com/sandiego* ➶ *277 rooms, 16 suites* ☖ *Restaurant, room service, cable TV with video games, in-room VCRs, in-room data ports, gym, spa, 3 bars, concierge, business services, meeting rooms, airport shuttle, parking (fee); no smoking* ▤ *AE, D, MC, V.*

$–$$$$ ▥ **Gaslamp Plaza Suites.** On the National Register of Historic Places, this 11-story structure a block from Horton Plaza was built in 1913 as one of San Diego's first "skyscrapers." The public areas have old marble, brass, and mosaics. Although most rooms are rather small, they are well decorated with dark-wood furnishings that give the hotel an elegant flair. You can enjoy the view and a complimentary continental breakfast on the rooftop terrace. Book ahead if you're visiting in summer. ⊠ *520 E St., Gaslamp Quarter, 92101* ☎ *619/232–9500 or 800/874–8770* 🖷 *619/238–9945* ⊕ *www.gaslampplaza.com* ➶ *12 rooms, 52 suites* ☖ *Restaurant, microwaves, refrigerators, cable TV, in-room VCRs, hot tub, bar, nightclub, parking (fee); no a/c* ▤ *AE, D, DC, MC, V* ⦿I *CP.*

$–$$ ▥ **Comfort Inn Downtown/Convention Center.** This three-story, stucco property surrounds a parking lot and courtyard. There's nothing fancy about the accommodations, but some rooms on the south side of the hotel have good views of the city skyline. It's close to downtown hot spots as well as the attractions of Balboa Park. ⊠ *719 Ash St., Downtown, 92101* ☎ *619/232–2525 or 800/404–6835* 🖷 *619/687–3024* ⊕ *www.comfortinn.com* ➶ *45 rooms* ☖ *Microwave, cable TV with movies, in-room data ports, hot tub, business services, airport shuttle, car rental, free parking; no smoking* ▤ *AE, D, DC, MC, V.*

¢–$ ▥ **500 West.** An $8 million renovation in 2004 transformed San Diego's historic 1924 Armed Services YMCA Building into this hip, urban boutique hotel. Catering to the style-conscious, the hotel has very small rooms big on quality, with flat-screen TVs, platform beds, Michael Graves–designed lighting, and a postmodern decor. It has single rooms as well as doubles, and all rooms share bathrooms. The Grand Central Café serves breakfast and lunch daily, and the whole hotel has wireless Internet. Weekly tenants can use a gourmet kitchen equipped with a Viking range and Sub-Zero fridge; there's also a common area with tables and vending machines. The YMCA is still downstairs and guests can use it for $5 a day or $15 a week. ⊠ *500 Broadway, Downtown, 92101* ☎ *619/269–9172 or 866/500–7533* 🖷 *619/234–5272* ⊕ *www.500westhotel.com* ➶ *260 rooms* ☖ *Café, cable TV, in-room data ports, Wi-Fi, pool, gym, hot tub, sauna, steam room, basketball, lounge, laundry facilities, concierge, meeting rooms, parking (fee)* ▤ *MC, V.*

¢ ▥ **HI–San Diego Downtown.** In the center of the Gaslamp, this two-story hostel has basic, modern furnishings and facilities, including a large common kitchen and a TV room. A special event—from pizza and movie parties to discussions on traveling in Mexico—is scheduled almost every evening. There are 4-, 6-, and 10-person sex-segregated bunk rooms, as well as a 10-person coed dorm and 3- and 5-person family rooms. About 20 private (double) rooms are available, with or without bath. ⊠ *521 Market St., Gaslamp Quarter, 92101* ☎ *619/525–1531 or 800/*

909–4776 ⊠ 619/338–0129 ⊕ *www.sandiegohostels.org* ⇆ *150 beds* ⟳ *Bicycles, billiards, laundry facilities; no a/c, no room phones, no room TVs, no smoking* ▭ *MC, V.*

Shelter Island & Point Loma

$$–$$$$ 🖳 **Humphrey's Half Moon Inn & Suites.** This sprawling South Seas–style resort has grassy open areas with palms and tiki torches. Rooms, some with kitchens and some with yacht-harbor or bay views, are decorated in a breezy island fashion. The Grand Marina Suite can accommodate up to eight in 1,000 square feet with a full kitchen. Locals throng to Humphrey's, the hotel's seafood restaurant, and to the jazz lounge; the hotel also hosts outdoor jazz and pop concerts from June through October. ⊠ *2303 Shelter Island Dr., Shelter Island, 92106* ☎ *619/224–3411 or 800/542–7400* ⊠ *619/224–3478* ⊕ *www.halfmooninn.com* ⇆ *128 rooms, 54 suites* ⟳ *Restaurant, room service, kitchenettes, minibars, refrigerators, cable TV with movies and video games, in-room data ports, putting green, pool, pond, health club, hot tub, boating, bicycles, croquet, Ping-Pong, bar, concert hall, laundry facilities, business services, meeting rooms, airport shuttle, free parking; no smoking* ▭ *AE, D, DC, MC, V.*

$$–$$$ 🖳 **Kona Kai Resort.** This 11-acre property (formerly known as the Shelter Pointe Hotel & Marina) blends Mexican and Mediterranean styles. The spacious and light-filled lobby, with its Mayan sculptures and terra-cotta tiles, opens onto a lush esplanade that overlooks the hotel's marina. The rooms are well appointed, if a bit small, and most look out onto either the marina or San Diego Bay. The attractive hotel is popular for business meetings. During the summer, a two-night minimum stay might be in effect. ⊠ *1551 Shelter Island Dr., Shelter Island, 92106* ☎ *619/221–8000 or 800/566–2524* ⊠ *619/221–5953* ⊕ *www.shelterpointe.com* ⇆ *206 rooms, 31 suites* ⟳ *Restaurant, room service, kitchenettes, cable TV with movies and video games, 2 tennis courts, 2 pools, health club, 2 hot tubs, 2 saunas, beach, boating, marina, bicycles, volleyball, bar, meeting rooms, airport shuttle, free parking; no smoking* ▭ *AE, D, DC, MC, V.*

★ $$ 🖳 **Holiday Inn Express–SeaWorld Area.** In Point Loma near the West Mission Bay exit off Interstate 8, this is a surprisingly quiet lodging despite proximity to bustling traffic. The three-story building is only about a ½ mi from both SeaWorld and Mission Bay. Continental breakfast is included. ⊠ *3950 Jupiter St., Sports Arena, 92110* ☎ *619/226–8000 or 800/320–0208* ⊠ *619/226–1409* ⊕ *www.hiexpress.com* ⇆ *70 rooms, 2 suites* ⟳ *Refrigerator, cable TV with movies, in-room data ports, pool, hot tub, laundry service, concierge, business services, free parking; no smoking* ▭ *AE, D, DC, MC, V* ⵔ *CP.*

$–$$ 🖳 **Vagabond Inn–Point Loma.** This two-story budget motel is safe, clean, and comfortable, close to the airport, yacht clubs, and Cabrillo National Monument—and the popular and excellent Point Loma Seafoods is next door. A daily newspaper and continental breakfast are included. ⊠ *1325 Scott St., Point Loma, 92106* ☎ *619/224–3371* ⊠ *619/223–0646* ⊕ *www.vagabondinn.com* ⇆ *40 rooms* ⟳ *Restaurant, in-room safes, some kitchens, some refrigerators, cable TV with movies, pool, bar, airport shuttle, free parking; no smoking* ▭ *AE, D, DC, MC, V* ⵔ *CP.*

Old Town & Vicinity

★ **$$–$$$** 🏨 **Holiday Inn Express–Old Town.** Already an excellent value for Old Town, this cheerful property throws in such perks as garage parking, continental breakfast, and afternoon snacks. Rooms have a European look. When you've had enough of the heated pool off the shaded courtyard, you can tackle the historic park's attractions and restaurants nearby. ⊠ *3900 Old Town Ave., Old Town, 92110* ☎ *619/299–7400 or 800/ 272–6232* 🖷 *619/299–1619* ⊕ *www.hiexpress.com* ➴ *125 rooms, 4 suites ⟐ Restaurant, room service, microwaves, refrigerators, cable TV, in-room data ports, pool, outdoor hot tub, shops, laundry service, concierge, business services, meeting rooms, airport shuttle, free parking; no smoking* 🖃 *AE, D, DC, MC, V* ⦿ *CP.*

$–$$$ 🏨 **Heritage Park Inn.** The beautifully restored mansions in Heritage Park
Fodor'sChoice include the romantic 1889 Queen Anne–style house that is the main house
★ of this B&B as well as the Italianate but plainer house of 1887 that serves as its extension. Rooms range from smallish to ample, and most are bright and cheery. A two-bedroom suite is furnished with period antiques, and there are also two junior suites. A full breakfast and afternoon tea are included. There's a two-night minimum stay on weekends, and weekly and monthly rates are available. Some rooms share a bath. Classic vintage films are shown nightly in the parlor on a small film screen. ⊠ *2470 Heritage Park Row, Old Town, 92110* ☎ *619/299–6832 or 800/995– 2470* 🖷 *619/299–9465* ⊕ *www.heritageparkinn.com* ➴ *9 rooms, 3 suites ⟐ Cable TV, in-room data ports, library, meeting rooms; no smoking* 🖃 *AE, DC, MC, V* ⦿ *BP.*

★ **¢–$** 🏨 **Western Inn–Old Town.** The three-story Western Inn is decorated in a Spanish motif and is close to shops and restaurants, but far enough away from the main tourist drag that you don't have to worry about noise and congestion. There's a free continental breakfast, and a barbecue area where you can cook for yourself. A bus, trolley, and Coaster station is a few blocks away. ⊠ *3889 Arista St., Old Town, 92110* ☎ *619/298– 6888 or 888/475–2353* 🖷 *619/692–4497* ⊕ *www.westerninn.com* ➴ *29 rooms, 6 suites ⟐ Refrigerators, cable TV, in-room data ports, airport shuttle, free parking; no smoking* 🖃 *AE, D, DC, MC, V* ⦿ *CP.*

Mission Valley & Hotel Circle

$$$ 🏨 **Doubletree Hotel San Diego Mission Valley.** Near the Fashion Valley shopping mall and adjacent to the Hazard Center—which has a seven-screen movie theater, four major restaurants, a food pavilion, and more than 20 shops—the Doubletree is also convenient to Route 163 and Interstate 8. A San Diego Trolley station is within walking distance. Public areas are bright and comfortable, well suited to this hotel's large business clientele. Spacious rooms have ample desk space; complimentary coffee, irons, and ironing boards are also provided. ⊠ *7450 Hazard Center Dr., Mission Valley, 92108* ☎ *619/297–5466 or 800/ 222–8733* 🖷 *619/297–5499* ⊕ *www.doubletree.com* ➴ *294 rooms, 6 suites ⟐ Restaurant, room service, minibars, cable TV with movies, in-room data ports, 2 tennis courts, 2 pools, gym, outdoor hot tub, sauna, 2 bars, shops, laundry facilities, laundry service, concierge, business serv-*

ices, meeting rooms, airport shuttle, free parking; no smoking ≡ *AE, D, DC, MC, V.*

★ **$$–$$$** 🏨 **San Diego Marriott Mission Valley.** This 17-floor high-rise is well equipped for business travelers—the front desk provides 24-hour fax and photocopy services, and rooms come with desks and private voice mail. The hotel is in the middle of the San Diego River valley near Qualcomm Stadium and the Rio Vista Plaza shopping center, minutes from the Mission Valley and Fashion Valley malls. There's free transportation to the malls, and the San Diego Trolley stops across the street. Rooms are comfortable (with individual balconies) and the staff is friendly. ✉ *8757 Rio San Diego Dr., Mission Valley, 92108* ☎ *619/692–3800 or 800/228–9290* 🖷 *619/692–0769* ⊕ *www.marriott.com* 🛏 *350 rooms, 5 suites* △ *Restaurant, room service, minibars, cable TV with movies, in-room data ports, tennis court, pool, gym, health club, outdoor hot tub, sauna, sports bar, nightclub, shops, laundry service, concierge, concierge floor, business services, meeting rooms, airport shuttle, parking (fee), Internet; no smoking* ≡ *AE, D, DC, MC, V.*

La Jolla

$$$$ 🏨 **Hilton La Jolla Torrey Pines.** The hotel blends discreetly into the Torrey Pines cliff top, overlooking the Pacific Ocean and the 18th hole of the Torrey Pines Golf Course, site of the 2008 U.S. Open. Oversize accommodations are simple but elegant; most have balconies or terraces. The menu at the hotel's restaurant, the Torreyana Grille, changes with the seasons; caesar salad and filet mignon are regulars, but you're likely to find lobster pot stickers and coffee-lacquered duck breast as well. ✉ *10950 N. Torrey Pines Rd., 92037* ☎ *858/558–1500 or 800/774–1500* 🖷 *858/450–4584* ⊕ *www.hilton.com* 🛏 *377 rooms, 17 suites* △ *3 restaurants, room service, in-room safes, minibars, cable TV with movies, in-room data ports, putting green, 3 tennis courts, pool, gym, outdoor hot tub, sauna, bicycles, 3 bars, babysitting, laundry service, concierge, business services, meeting rooms, airport shuttle, car rental, parking (fee); no smoking* ≡ *AE, D, DC, MC, V.*
FodorsChoice ★

★ **$$$$** 🏨 **Hotel Parisi.** A Zen-like peace welcomes you in the lobby, which has a skylighted waterfall and is filled with Asian art. The suites are decorated according to the principles of feng shui; you can order a massage, a yoga session, or the on-staff psychologist from room service. Favored by celebrities, the hushed, earth-tone suites have granite bathrooms, fluffy robes, and ergonomic tubs. The rooms are set back enough from the street noise, but in the ocean-view suites you have to look over buildings across the street to view the Pacific. Continental breakfast is served daily in a breakfast room off the lobby. ✉ *1111 Prospect St., 92037* ☎ *858/454–1511* 🖷 *858/454–1531* ⊕ *www.hotelparisi.com* 🛏 *20 suites* △ *Room service, in-room safes, minibars, cable TV with movies, in-room VCRs, in-room data ports, massage, business services, meeting rooms, parking (fee); no smoking* ≡ *AE, D, MC, V* ⧄ *CP.*

$$$$ 🏨 **La Valencia.** This pink Spanish-Mediterranean confection drew Hollywood film stars in the 1930s and '40s with its setting and views of La Jolla Cove. Many rooms, although small, have a genteel European look, with antique pieces and richly colored rugs. The personal attention pro-
FodorsChoice ★

vided by the staff, as well as the plush robes and grand bathrooms, make the stay even more pleasurable. The hotel is right in the middle of the shops and restaurants of La Jolla village. Rates are lower if you're willing to look out on the village rather than the ocean. Be sure to stroll the tiered gardens in back. ⊠ *1132 Prospect St., 92037* ☎ *858/454–0771 or 800/451–0772* 🖷 *858/456–3921* ⊕ *www.lavalencia.com* ⤳ *117 rooms, 15 villas* ⚭ *3 restaurants, room service, in-room safes, minibars, cable TV with movies and video games, in-room VCRs, pool, health club, outdoor hot tub, massage, sauna, beach, bicycles, Ping-Pong, shuffleboard, bar, lounge, laundry facilities, concierge, business services, meeting rooms, airport shuttle, parking (fee); no smoking* ⊟ *AE, D, MC, V.*

$$$$ 🏨 **Lodge at Torrey Pines.** This beautiful Craftsman-style lodge sits on a
Fodor'sChoice bluff between La Jolla and Del Mar and commands a view of miles of
★ coastline. You know you're in for a different sort of experience when you see the Scottish kilted doorman. Rooms, though dim, are roomy and furnished with antiques and reproduction turn-of-the-20th-century pieces. The service is excellent and the restaurant, A. R. Valentien (named after a San Diego artist of the early 1900s), serves fine California cuisine. Beyond the 6-acre grounds are the Torrey Pines Golf Course and scenic trails that lead to the Torrey Pines State Beach and Reserve. The village of La Jolla is a 10-minute drive away. ⊠ *11480 N. Torrey Pines Rd., 92037* ☎ *858/453–4420 or 800/995–4507* 🖷 *858/453– 7464* ⊕ *www.lodgetorreypines.com* ⤳ *175 rooms* ⚭ *2 restaurants, in-room safes, kitchenettes, cable TV, in-room data ports, 18-hole golf course, pool, gym, hot tub, massage, spa, 2 bars, meeting rooms, free parking, Internet; no smoking* ⊟ *AE, D, DC, MC, V.*

$$$–$$$$ 🏨 **Grande Colonial.** This white wedding cake–style hotel has ocean views
Fodor'sChoice and is in the heart of La Jolla village. Built in 1913 and expanded and
★ redesigned in 1925–26, the Colonial is graced with charming European details: chandeliers, a marble hearth, mahogany railings, oak furnishings, and French doors. The hotel's restaurant, Nine-ten, run by chef Jason Knibb, is well liked by locals for its fresh, seasonal California cuisine. ⊠ *910 Prospect St., 92037* ☎ *858/454–2181 or 800/826–1278* 🖷 *858/454–5679* ⊕ *www.thegrandecolonial.com* ⤳ *58 rooms, 17 suites* ⚭ *Restaurant, room service, cable TV with movies and video games, in-room data ports, pool, bar, meeting rooms, parking (fee); no smoking* ⊟ *AE, D, DC, MC, V.*

$$$–$$$$ 🏨 **Scripps Inn.** You'd be wise to make reservations well in advance for this small, quiet inn tucked away on Coast Boulevard; its popularity with repeat visitors ensures that it's booked year-round. Lower weekly and monthly rates (not available in summer) make it attractive to long-term guests. Rooms are done in Mexican and Spanish style, with wood floors, and all have ocean views; some have fireplaces. Continental breakfast is served in the lobby each morning. ⊠ *555 S. Coast Blvd., 92037* ☎ *858/454–3391 or 800/439–7529* 🖷 *858/456–0389* ⊕ *www.jcresorts. com* ⤳ *14 rooms* ⚭ *In-room safes, some kitchens, cable TV, free parking; no smoking* ⊟ *AE, D, MC, V* ⦿ *CP.*

★ $$–$$$$ 🏨 **Hyatt Regency La Jolla.** The Hyatt is in the Golden Triangle area, about 10 minutes from the beach and the village of La Jolla. The postmodern design of architect Michael Graves' striking lobby continues in the spacious rooms, where warm cherrywood furnishings contrast with austere gray closets. Fluffy down comforters and cushy chairs and couches make you feel right at home, though, and business travelers appreciate the endless array of office and in-room services. The hotel's four trendy restaurants include Cafe Japengo. Rates are lowest on weekends. ⊠ *Aventine Center, 3777 La Jolla Village Dr., 92122 ☎ 858/552–1234 or 800/233–1234 ⊟ 858/552–6066 ⊕ www.hyatt.com ➽ 419 rooms, 20 suites ⟁ 4 restaurants, room service, minibars, cable TV with movies, 2 tennis courts, pool, health club, hair salon, outdoor hot tub, massage, basketball, bar, dry cleaning, laundry service, concierge, business services, meeting rooms, parking (fee); no smoking ⊟ AE, D, DC, MC, V.*

$$–$$$ 🖾 **La Jolla Inn.** One block from the beach and near some of the best shops and restaurants, this European-style inn with a delightful staff sits in a prime spot in the village of La Jolla. Many rooms have sweeping ocean views from their balconies; one spectacular penthouse suite faces the ocean, the other the village. Enjoy the delicious complimentary continental breakfast on the upstairs sundeck. ⊠ *1110 Prospect St., 92037 ☎ 858/454–0133 or 800/433–1609 ⊟ 858/454–2056 ⊕ www.lajollainn.com ➽ 21 rooms, 2 suites ⟁ Room service, some kitchenettes, some refrigerators, cable TV with movies, in-room data ports, library, shop, dry cleaning, laundry facilities, concierge, business services, free parking; no smoking ⊟ AE, D, DC, MC, V* ⦿| CP.

Mission Bay & the Beaches

$$$$ 🖾 **Paradise Point Resort & Spa.** The beautiful landscape at this 44-acre resort on Vacation Isle has been the setting for a number of movies. The botanical gardens have ponds, waterfalls, footbridges, waterfowl, and more than 600 varieties of tropical plants, a convincing backdrop for the Balinese spa. Many recreation activities are offered and there's access to a marina. The rooms' bright fabrics and plush carpets are cheery; unfortunately, the walls here are motel-thin. ⊠ *1404 W. Vacation Rd., Mission Bay, 92109 ☎ 858/274–4630 or 800/344–2626 ⊟ 858/581–5929 ⊕ www.paradisepoint.com ➽ 462 cottages ⟁ 3 restaurants, room service, refrigerators, cable TV with movies, in-room data ports, putting green, 6 tennis courts, 6 pools, pond, fitness classes, gym, outdoor hot tub, massage, sauna, spa, beach, boating, jet skiing, bicycles, croquet, shuffleboard, volleyball, 2 bars, concierge, business services, meeting rooms, airport shuttle, free parking; no smoking ⊟ AE, D, DC, MC, V.*

$$$–$$$$ 🖾 **Bahia Resort Hotel.** This huge complex on a 14-acre peninsula in Mission Bay Park has studios and suites with kitchens; many have wood-beam ceilings and a tropical theme. The hotel's Victorian-style sternwheeler, the *Bahia Belle*, offers guests complimentary cruises on the bay at sunset. Room rates are reasonable for a place so well located—within walking distance of the ocean—and with so many amenities, including use of the facilities at its sister hotel, the nearby Catamaran. ⊠ *998 W. Mission Bay Dr., Mission Bay, 92109 ☎ 858/488–0551 or 800/576–4229 ⊟ 858/488–1387 ⊕ www.bahiahotel.com ➽ 321 rooms ⟁ Restaurant, room service, kitchenettes, cable TV with movies, in-room data ports, 2 tennis courts, pool, gym, outdoor hot tub, boating, bicycles, 2 bars, shops, business services, meeting rooms, free parking; no smoking ⊟ AE, D, DC, MC, V.*

$$$–$$$$ ▢ **Catamaran Resort Hotel.** Exotic macaw parrots perch in the lush lobby
Fodor'sChoice of this appealing hotel on Mission Bay. Tiki torches light the way through
★ grounds thick with tropical foliage to the six two-story buildings and the
14-story high-rise. The South Seas theme continues in the room design
and also in the brand-new Catamaran Spa, where the almost 10,000-
square-feet facilities are devoted to treatments such as Lomi Lomi mas-
sage and seaweed body wraps. The fitness center has sweeping views of
Mission Bay's beach; yoga and Pilates take place outside on the secluded
lawn. A classical or jazz pianist tickles the ivories nightly at the Moray
Bar; the Atoll Restaurant serves up five-star cuisine that includes dishes
such as Shrimp Martini. Among the resort's many water-oriented activ-
ities are free cruises on Mission Bay aboard the *Bahia Belle* stern-wheeler.
⊠ *3999 Mission Blvd., Mission Beach, 92109* ☎ *858/488–1081 or 800/
422–8386* 🖷 *858/488–1387* ⊕ *www.catamaranresort.com* ⌑ *313 rooms*
⌂ *Restaurant, room service, kitchenettes, refrigerators, cable TV with
movies, in-room data ports, pool, gym, spa, outdoor hot tub, beach, boat-
ing, jet skiing, bicycles, volleyball, 2 bars, nightclub, shops, business serv-
ices, meeting rooms, parking (fee); no smoking* ▭ *AE, D, DC, MC, V.*

$$–$$$ ▢ **The Dana on Mission Bay.** Recently expanded and re-named (the for-
mer name was the Dana Inn and Marina), the resort's newer Water's
Edge rooms all have sofa sleeps—great for families—and bay views. The
Water's Edge suites have the same, plus wet bars with granite counters
and two TVs. All are done in calming earth tones. The older Marina
Cove rooms are fairly standard hotel fare with marina or courtyard views.
SeaWorld and the beach are within walking distance. The Marina Vil-
lage Conference Center next door offers meeting and banquet rooms
with bay views. ⊠ *1710 W. Mission Bay Dr., Mission Bay, 92109*
☎ *619/222–6440 or 800/326–2466* 🖷 *619/222–5916* ⊕ *www.thedana.
net* ⌑ *259 rooms, 12 suites* ⌂ *Restaurant, room service, cable TV
with movies, 2 tennis courts, 2 pools, 2 outdoor hot tubs, boating, wa-
terskiing, fishing, bicycles, Ping-Pong, shuffleboard, bar, laundry serv-
ice, business services, meeting rooms, airport shuttle, car rental, free
parking; no smoking* ▭ *AE, D, DC, MC, V.*

$–$$ ▢ **Surfer Motor Lodge.** This four-story building is right on the beach and
Fodor'sChoice directly behind a shopping center with restaurants and boutiques. Rooms
★ are plain, but those on the upper floors have good views. ⊠ *711 Pacific Beach Dr., Pacific Beach, 92109* ☎ *858/483–7070 or 800/787–3373*
🖷 *858/274–1670* ⊕ *www.surfermotorlodge.com* ⌑ *52 rooms* ⌂ *Restaurant, kitchenettes, pool, beach, bicycles, laundry service, free parking;
no a/c, no smoking* ▭ *AE, MC, V.*

¢ ▢ **Banana Bungalow San Diego.** Literally a few feet from the beach, this
popular hostel's location is its greatest asset. However, dampness and sand
take their toll, and some parts are in need of repair. There are a total of
70 beds and all dorm rooms are coed ($25 per bed in summer); a few pri-
vate rooms (sleeping two) are available, but they sell out fast. Barbecues
and movie-night parties are held weekly, as are various organized events.
Complimentary continental breakfast is served on the sundeck. There are
lockers and a small TV room. ⊠ *707 Reed Ave., Pacific Beach, 92109*
☎ *858/273–3060 or 800/546–7835* 🖷 *858/273–1440* ⊕ *www.
bananabungalow.com* ⌂ *Beach, bicycles, volleyball, airport shuttle, travel
services; no a/c, no room phones, no room TVs, no smoking* ▭ *MC, V.*

NIGHTLIFE & THE ARTS

Many people come to San Diego for the beach, but the city's club scene has developed an increasingly strong following in recent years. The Gaslamp, along with neighboring downtown and the emerging East Village (where the new baseball stadium opened in 2004), is where you'll find the most popular—and expensive—bars and clubs. The beach areas offer a more casual atmosphere. The dance clubs and bars of Pacific Beach and Mission Beach appeal to a casually dressed, college-age crowd. The Uptown district around Hillcrest is the heart of San Diego's gay nightlife and home to a few coffeehouses.

San Diego's music scene centers around rock. Hard rock, alternative rock, and indie rock dominate the music listings. Despite that fact, some of the county's best known musical artists play a softer style of music: Jewel got her start in the city's coffeehouses and Grammy-winning gospel group Nickel Creek calls San Diego home.

Check the *Reader, San Diego CityBeat, San Diego* magazine's "Restaurant & Nightlife Guide," and the *San Diego-Union Tribune* weekly (Thursday) entertainment insert, *Night and Day,* for the lowdown on nightlife.

Nightlife

Bars

Altitude Skybar (✉ 660 K St., Gaslamp Quarter ☎ 619/696–0234), which opened early in 2005 inside the trendy San Diego Marriott Gaslamp Quarter, occupies the hotel's 22nd-story rooftop. It's a great spot not only to people-watch but also to admire the city skyline.

★ **Bitter End** (✉ 770 5th Ave., Gaslamp Quarter ☎ 619/338–9300) is a tri-level martini bar and dance club that draws a crowd any night of the week. **'Canes Bar and Grill** (✉ 3105 Oceanfront Walk, Mission Beach ☎ 858/488–1780) is closer to the ocean than any other music venue in town. Step outside for a walk on the beach where the sounds of the national rock, reggae, and hip-hop acts onstage create a cacophony with the crashing waves.

Karl Strauss' Old Columbia Brewery & Grill (✉ 1157 Columbia St., Downtown ☎ 619/234–2739 ✉ 1044 Wall St., La Jolla ☎ 858/551–2739) was the first microbrewery in San Diego. The original locale draws an after-work downtown crowd and later fills with beer connoisseurs from all walks of life; the newer La Jolla version draws a mix of locals and tourists. **Martini Ranch** (✉ 528 F St., Gaslamp Quarter ☎ 619/235–6100) mixes more than 30 varieties of its namesake. Actually two clubs in one, the original Martini Ranch hosts jazz groups on weekdays and a DJ spinning an eclectic mix on Friday and Saturday. Next door in the larger Shaker Room, local and traveling DJs spin all-star dance beats.

Onyx Room/Thin (✉ 852 5th Ave., Gaslamp Quarter ☎ 619/235–6699) is the hippest split-level in town. Onyx is downstairs and feels like two bars in one. In front there's a mood-lighted cocktail lounge, and in the next room acid-jazz bands and DJs keep the crowds dancing. Thin, the upstairs venue, is more conducive to the conversation-minded. Weekend cover charges allow entrance to both clubs. **Pacific Beach Bar & Grill** (⊠ 860 Garnet Ave., Pacific Beach 🕾 858/272–4745) is a block away from the beach. The popular nightspot has a huge outdoor patio so you can enjoy star-filled skies as you party. The lines here on the weekends are generally the longest of any club in Pacific Beach.

★ **Side Bar** (⊠ 536 Market St., Downtown 🕾 619/696–0946) is one of several ultraposh lounges that have helped restore glamour to downtown. This stylish space with low-slung sofas and lounge chairs and mod lighting also has a pleasant patio, perfect for a breath of fresh air when

Fodor'sChoice you're tired of posing inside. The **W Hotel** (⊠ 421 West B St., Down-
★   town 🕾 619/231–8220) has three bars, and together they've become the trendiest places to be for the young bar-hopping set. Start at the ground floor Living Room, where cozy chairs and couches in alcoves give a true lounge feel. You can take your drink from bar to bar, so move on to Magnet, where you can grab a bite to eat before heading to Beach, the W's open-air rooftop with private beach cabanas, fire pits, and tons of heated sand covering the floor.

Coffeehouses

★ **Brockton Villa Restaurant** (⊠ 1235 Coast Blvd., La Jolla 🕾 858/454–7393), a palatial café overlooking La Jolla Cove, has indoor and outdoor seating, as well as scrumptious desserts and coffee drinks. It closes at 9 most nights, earlier on Sunday and Monday. **Claire de Lune** (⊠ 2906 University Ave., North Park 🕾 619/688–9845) won an award for its redesign of the historic Oddfellows building. High ceilings and huge arched windows give this wooden-floored hangout a funky charm. Local musicians and poets take the stage on various nights, and San Diego's most popular, and longest running, open-mike poetry night takes place every Tuesday.

Fodor'sChoice **Extraordinary Desserts** (⊠ 2929 5th Ave., Hillcrest 🕾 619/294–2132
★   ⊠ 1430 Union St., Middletown 🕾 619/294–7001) lives up to its name, which explains why there's a line at this café, even though it has ample seating. Paris-trained Karen Krasne turns out award-winning cakes, tortes, and pastries of exceptional beauty. **Javanican** (⊠ 4338 Cass St., Pacific Beach 🕾 858/483–8035) serves the young beach-community set. Aside from a good cup of joe, live acoustic entertainment is a draw. Adventurous musicians can sign up to play at the open mike Monday nights. Other local musicians headline throughout the week.

Comedy

★ **Comedy Store La Jolla** (⊠ 916 Pearl St., La Jolla 🕾 858/454–9176), like its sister establishment in Hollywood, hosts some of the best national touring and local talent.

Dance Clubs

Deco's (⊠ 721 5th Ave., Gaslamp Quarter 🕾 619/696–3326) is a popular, pricey martini–dance bar in the Gaslamp Quarter. The indoor room plays house while the packed open-air area in the back plays hip-hop mixes.

★ **On Broadway** (⊠ 615 Broadway, Gaslamp Quarter 🕾 619/231–0011), in a former bank building, is the most exclusive dance club in town. Even the steep cover charges do little to discourage San Diego's best-dressed young professionals from waiting hours to spend their hard-earned money inside. The huge club is only open Friday and Saturday. **Sevilla** (✉ 555 4th Ave., Gaslamp Quarter ☎ 619/233–5979) brings a Latin flavor to the Gaslamp Quarter with its mix of contemporary and traditional Spanish and Latin American music. Get fueled up at the tapas bar before venturing downstairs for dancing. **Stingaree** (✉ 6th Ave. and Island St., Gaslamp Quarter ☎ 619/544–0867), a posh Gaslamp Quarter newcomer, occupies a historic warehouse in the former Red Light District.

Gay & Lesbian Nightlife

MEN'S BARS **Bourbon Street** (✉ 4612 Park Blvd., University Heights ☎ 619/291–0173) is a popular karaoke spot. The outdoor courtyard draws crowds that gather to watch and comment on whatever is showing on the large-screen TV. Weekends, a back area known as the Stable Bar has DJs who turn the small room into a dance floor. **Flicks** (✉ 1017 University Ave., Hillcrest ☎ 619/297–2056), a hip video bar that's popular with the see-and-be-seen crowd, plays music and comedy videos on four big screens.

Fodor'sChoice Drink specials vary each night. **Kickers** (✉ 308 University Ave., Hillcrest ☎ 619/491–0400) rounds up country-music cowboys for line dancing and two-stepping on its wooden dance floor Thursday through Saturday, with free lessons from 7 to 8:30. Other days it offers disco, Latin, hip-hop, karaoke, and pop dance tunes.

WOMEN'S BARS **The Flame** (✉ 3780 Park Blvd., Hillcrest ☎ 619/295–4163) has a red neon sign resembling a torch with a flame on top. A San Diego institution, this friendly but slick dance club has a powerful sound system and draws the biggest crowds of any lesbian bar in town. There's also a gay-male party on Friday nights that is extremely popular.

Jazz

Croce's (✉ 802 5th Ave., Gaslamp Quarter ☎ 619/233–4355), the intimate jazz cave of restaurateur Ingrid Croce (widow of singer-songwriter Jim Croce), books superb acoustic-jazz musicians. **Dizzy's** (✉ 344 7th Ave., Gaslamp Quarter ☎ 858/270–7467) late-night jazz jam is your best bet on Friday after midnight. During the week you can count on the best in jazz, visual and performance-art shows, and the occasional spoken-word event. No alcohol is served. **Elario's Sky Lounge** (✉ 7955 La Jolla Shores Dr., La Jolla ☎ 858/459–0541) is perched on the top floor of the Hotel La Jolla, with an ocean view and a lineup of locally acclaimed jazz musicians Tuesday through Saturday. **Humphrey's by the Bay** (✉ 2241 Shelter Island Dr., Shelter Island ☎ 619/224–3577), surrounded by water, is the summer stomping grounds of musicians such as the Cowboy Junkies and Chris Isaak. From June through September this dining and drinking oasis hosts the city's best outdoor jazz, folk, and light-rock concert series. The rest of the year the music moves indoors for some first-rate jazz most Sunday, Monday, and Tuesday nights, with piano-bar music on other nights.

Live-Music Clubs

Belly Up Tavern (✉ 143 S. Cedros Ave., Solana Beach ☎ 858/481–8140), a fixture on local papers' "best of" lists, has been drawing crowds of all ages since it opened in the mid-'70s. **Blind Melons** (✉ 710 Garnet Ave., Pacific Beach ☎ 858/483–7844), a small, dark space, hosts well-known local and, occasionally, national bands playing rock, reggae, and espe-

Fodor'sChoice
★
cially potent blues. **Casbah** (✉ 2501 Kettner Blvd., Middletown ☎ 619/232–4355) is a small club with a national reputation for showcasing up-and-coming acts. Nirvana, Smashing Pumpkins, and Alanis Moris-

★ sette all played the Casbah on their way to stardom. **House of Blues** (✉ 1055 5th Ave., Downtown ☎ 619/299–2583), the nationally renowned chain of blues and rock clubs, opened a spectacular new space in downtown San Diego in summer 2005. Sunday's Gospel Brunch is one of the hottest events in town.

Night Bay Cruises

Bahia Belle (✉ 998 W. Mission Bay Dr., Mission Bay ☎ 858/539–7779) is a stern-wheeler offering relaxing evening cruises along Mission Bay that include cocktails, dancing, and live music. Board from the Bahia Resort Hotel. The $6 fare is less than most nightclub covers. **Hornblower Cruises** (✉ 1066 N. Harbor Dr., Downtown ☎ 800/668–4322) makes nightly dinner–dance cruises aboard the *Lord Hornblower*—pas-

★ sengers are treated to fabulous views of the San Diego skyline. **San Diego Harbor Excursion** (✉ 1050 N. Harbor Dr., Downtown ☎ 619/234–4111 or 800/442–7847) welcomes guests aboard with a glass of champagne as a prelude to nightly dinner–dance cruises.

The Arts

You can buy half-price tickets to most theater, music, and dance events on the day of performance at **Times Arts Tix** (✉ Horton Plaza, Gaslamp Quarter ☎ 619/497–5000). Advance full-price tickets are also sold here.

Dance

★ **California Ballet Company** (☎ 858/560–6741) performs high-quality contemporary and traditional works, from story ballets to Balanchine, September through May.

Film

Hillcrest Cinemas (✉ 3965 5th Ave., Hillcrest) is a posh multiplex right in the middle of uptown's action. **Ken Cinema** (✉ 4061 Adams Ave., Kensington) is considered by many to be the last bastion of true avant-garde film in San Diego. It publishes its listings in the *Ken,* a small newspaper distributed in nearly every coffeehouse and music store in the county.

In its 226-seat theater, the **Museum of Photographic Arts** (✉ 1649 El Prado, Balboa Park ☎ 619/238–7559) runs a regular film program that includes classic American and international cinema by prominent filmmakers, as well as the occasional cult film.

The 500-seat **Sherwood Auditorium** (✉ 700 Prospect St., La Jolla ☎ 858/454–3541), at the Museum of Contemporary Art, hosts foreign- and classic-film series and special cinema events, including the wildly popular Festival of Animation, from January through March.

Science, space-documentary, observation-of-motion, and sometimes psychedelic films are shown on the IMAX screen at the **Reuben H. Fleet Science Center** (✉ 1875 El Prado, Balboa Park ☎ 619/238–1233).

Music

Coors Amphitheatre (✉ 2050 Otay Valley Rd., Chula Vista ☎ 619/671–3500), the largest concert venue in town, can accommodate 20,000 concertgoers with reserved seats and lawn seating. It presents top-selling national and international acts during its late-spring to late-summer season.

East County Performing Arts Center (✉ 210 E. Main St., El Cajon ☎ 619/440–2277) hosts a variety of performing-arts events, but mostly music. Internationally touring jazz, classical, blues, and world-beat musicians have ensured its popularity among locals. **La Jolla Music Society** (☎ 858/459–3728) presents internationally acclaimed chamber ensembles, orchestras, and soloists at Sherwood Auditorium, the Civic Theatre, and the Stephen and Mary Birch North Park Theatre.

★ **San Diego Opera** (✉ Civic Theatre, 3rd Ave. and B St., Downtown ☎ 619/533–7000) draws international artists. Its season runs January through May. Past performances have included *Die Fledermaus, Faust, Idomeneo,* and *La Bohème,* plus concerts by such talents as Luciano Pavarotti.

San Diego Symphony Orchestra (✉ 750 B St., Downtown ☎ 619/235–0804) puts on special events year-round, including classical concerts and summer and winter pops. Concerts are held at Copley Symphony Hall, except the Summer Pops series, which is held on the Embarcadero.

★ **Spreckels Organ Pavilion** (✉ Balboa Park ☎ 619/702–8138) holds a giant outdoor pipe organ donated to the city in 1914 by sugar magnates John and Adolph Spreckels. The beautiful Spanish Baroque pavilion hosts concerts by civic organist Carol Williams on most Sunday afternoons and on most Monday evenings in summer. Local military bands, gospel groups, and barbershop quartets also perform here. All shows are free.

Spreckels Theatre (✉ 121 Broadway, Downtown ☎ 619/235–9500), a designated-landmark theater erected in 1912, hosts musical events—everything from mostly Mozart to small rock concerts. Ballets and theatrical productions are also held here. Its good acoustics and historical status make this a special venue.

Theater

California Center for the Arts, Escondido (✉ 340 N. Escondido Blvd., Escondido ☎ 760/839–4138) presents mainstream theatrical productions such as *Grease* and *The Odd Couple*. **Diversionary Theatre** (✉ 4545 Park Blvd., University Heights ☎ 619/220–0097) is San Diego's premier gay and lesbian company. It presents a range of original works that focus on gay and lesbian themes. **Horton Grand Theatre** (✉ Hahn Cosmopolitan Theatre, 444 4th Ave., Gaslamp Quarter ☎ 619/234–9583) stages the long-running comedy, *Triple Espresso,* in its 250-seat space.

Fodor'sChoice **La Jolla Playhouse** (✉ University of California at San Diego, 2910 La Jolla
★ Village Dr., La Jolla ☎ 858/550–1010) crafts exciting and innovative productions under the artistic direction of Dess McAnuff, May through November. Many Broadway shows, such as *Tommy* and *How to Succeed in Business Without Really Trying,* have previewed here before heading for the East Coast.

★ **Lamb's Players Theatre** (✉ 1142 Orange Ave., Coronado ☎ 619/437–0600) has a regular season of five productions from February through November and stages a musical, "Festival of Christmas," in December. **Lyceum Theatre** (✉ 79 Horton Plaza, Gaslamp Quarter ☎ 619/544–1000 or 619/231–3586) is the home of the San Diego Repertory Theatre and also presents productions by visiting theater companies.

Fodor'sChoice **Old Globe Theatre** (✉ Off El Prado, Balboa Park ☎ 619/234–5623) is
★ the oldest professional theater in California, presenting classics, contemporary dramas, and experimental works. It produces the famous summer Shakespeare Festival at the Old Globe and its sister theaters, the Cassius Carter Centre Stage and the Lowell Davies Festival Theatre.

Starlight Musical Theatre (✉ Starlight Bowl, 2005 Pan American Plaza, Balboa Park ☎ 619/544–7827), a summertime favorite, is a series of musicals performed in an outdoor amphitheater mid-June through early September. Because of the theater's proximity to the airport, actors often have to freeze mid-scene while a plane flies over.

★ **Theatre in Old Town** (✉ 4040 Twiggs St., Old Town ☎ 619/688–2494) presents punchy revues and occasional classics, usually one show for many months at a time. (As of this writing, it was *Forbidden Broadway: Special Victims Unit*. Previous shows like *Ruthless, Gilligan's Island,* and *Forbidden Hollywood* have made this a popular place.) **Welk Resort Theatre** (✉ 8860 Lawrence Welk Dr., Escondido ☎ 760/749–3448 or 800/932–4355), a famed dinner theater about a 45-minute drive northeast of downtown on Interstate 15, puts on polished Broadway-style productions.

SPORTS & THE OUTDOORS

San Diego has a reputation as an active, outdoors-oriented community, which makes perfect sense given the near perfect weather and the wealth of places to play: ocean, bay, lakes, mountains, deserts, parks, and golf courses offer a chance to practice nearly any sport conceivable. Surfers, swimmers, kayakers, divers, snorkelers, sailboarders, and even kiteboarders have 70 mi of shorefront to explore. There's also excellent hiking, mountain biking, and horseback riding in the county's eastern foothills and mountains.

Ballooning

Enjoy views of the Pacific Ocean, the mountains, and the coastline south to Mexico and north to San Clemente from a hot-air balloon at sunrise or sunset. The conditions are perfect: wide-open spaces, and just enough wind. **California Dreamin'** (✉ 33133 Vista del Monte Rd., Temecula ☎ 800/373–3359 ⊕ www.californiadreamin.com) specializes in Temecula wine country flights and Del Mar sunset coastal excursions. **Skysurfer Balloon Company** (✉ 1221 Camino del Mar, Del Mar ☎ 858/481–6800 or 800/660–6809 ⊕ www.sandiegohotairballoons.com) lifts off from several locations and will take you on one-hour flights in North County or Temecula.

Baseball

Long a favorite spectator sport in San Diego, where games are rarely rained out, baseball gained even more popularity in 2004 with the opening of Petco Park, a stunning 42,000-seat facility right in the heart of downtown. The **San Diego Padres** (⌧ 100 Park Blvd., Downtown ☎ 619/795–5000 or 877/374–2784 ⊕ www.sandiegopadres.com) slug it out for bragging rights in the National League West from April into October. Tickets are usually available on game day, but games with such rivals as the Los Angeles Dodgers and the San Francisco Giants often sell out quickly.

Fodor'sChoice ★

Beaches

Water temperatures are generally chilly, ranging from 55°F to 65°F from October through June, and 65°F to 75°F from July through September. For a surf and weather report, call ☎ 619/221–8824. For a general beach and weather report, call ☎ 619/289–1212. Pollution, which has long been a problem near the Mexican border, is inching north and is generally worse near rivermouths and storm drain outlets. The weather page of the *San Diego Union-Tribune* includes pollution reports along with listings of surfing and diving conditions.

Overnight camping is not allowed on any San Diego city beach, but there are campgrounds at some state beaches throughout the county (☎ 800/444–7275 for reservations). Lifeguards are stationed at city beaches from Sunset Cliffs up to Black's Beach in the summertime, but coverage in winter is provided by roving patrols only. Leashed dogs are permitted on most San Diego beaches and adjacent parks from 6 PM to 9 AM; they can run unleashed anytime at Dog Beach at the north end of Ocean Beach and, from Memorial Day through Labor Day, at Rivermouth in Del Mar.

Pay attention to signs listing illegal activities; undercover police often patrol the beaches, carrying their ticket books in coolers. Glass containers are prohibited on all San Diego beaches if their purpose is to carry drinks, and fires are allowed only in fire rings or elevated barbecue grills. Alcoholic beverages—including beer—are completely banned on some city beaches; on others you are allowed to partake from noon to 8 PM. Imbibing in beach parking lots, on boardwalks, and in landscaped areas is always illegal. Although it may be tempting to take a starfish or some other sea creature as a souvenir from a tide pool, it upsets the delicate ecological balance and is illegal, too.

Parking near the ocean can be hard to find in summer but is unmetered at all San Diego city beaches. Del Mar has a pay lot and metered street parking around the 15th Street Beach.

CORONADO

Silver Strand State Beach. This quiet Coronado beach is ideal for families. The water is relatively calm, lifeguards and rangers are on duty year-round, and there are places to Rollerblade or ride bikes. Four parking lots provide room for more than 1,000 cars. Sites at a campground ($15 to $26) for self-contained RVs are available on a first-come, first-served basis; stays are limited to seven nights. ⌧ *From San Diego–Coronado Bridge, turn left onto Orange Ave., which becomes Rte. 75, and follow signs, Coronado* ☎ 619/435–5184.

★ ♻ **Coronado Beach.** With the famous Hotel Del Coronado as a backdrop, this stretch of sandy beach is one of San Diego County's largest and most picturesque. It's perfect for sunbathing, people-watching, or Frisbee. Exercisers include Navy SEAL teams, as well as the occasional Marine Recon unit, who have training runs on the beaches in and around Coronado. ⊠ *From the bridge, turn left on Orange Ave. and follow signs, Coronado.*

POINT LOMA   **Sunset Cliffs.** Beneath the jagged cliffs on the west side of the Point Loma peninsula is one of the more secluded beaches in the area. A few miles long, it's popular with surfers and locals. At the south end of the peninsula, near Cabrillo Point, tide pools teeming with small sea creatures are revealed at low tide. ⊠ *Take I–8 west to Sunset Cliffs Blvd. and head west, Point Loma.*

MISSION BAY &   **Ocean Beach.** Much of this mile-long beach is a haven for volleyball play-
BEACHES   ers, sunbathers, and swimmers. The area around the municipal pier at the south end is a hangout for surfers and transients; the pier itself is open to the public 24 hours a day for fishing and walking and there's a restaurant at the middle. The beach is south of the channel entrance to Mission Bay. Limited parking is available. Swimmers should beware of unusually vicious rip currents here. ⊠ *Take I–8 west to Sunset Cliffs Blvd. and head west. Turn right on Santa Monica Ave., Ocean Beach.*

★   **Mission Beach.** San Diego's most popular beach draws huge crowds on hot summer days. The 2-mi-long stretch extends from the north entrance of Mission Bay to Pacific Beach. A wide boardwalk paralleling the beach is popular with walkers, joggers, roller skaters, bladers, and bicyclists. Surfers, swimmers, and volleyball players congregate at the south end. Toward its north end, near the Belmont Park roller coaster, the beach narrows and the water becomes rougher. The crowds grow thicker and somewhat rougher as well. ⊠ *Exit I–5 at Grand Ave. and head west to Mission Blvd. Turn south and look for parking near roller coaster at West Mission Bay Dr., Mission Beach.*

Pacific Beach/North Pacific Beach. The boardwalk of Mission Beach turns into a sidewalk here, but there are still bike paths and picnic tables along the beachfront. Pacific Beach runs from the north end of Mission Beach to Crystal Pier. North Pacific Beach extends from the pier north. The scene here is particularly lively on weekends. There are designated surfing areas, and fire rings are available. Parking can be a challenge, but there are plenty of restrooms, showers, and restaurants in the area. ⊠ *Exit I–5 at Grand Ave. and head west to Mission Blvd. Turn north and look for parking, Pacific Beach.*

LA JOLLA   **Tourmaline Surfing Park.** This is one of the area's most popular beaches for surfing and sailboarding year-round. There's a 175-space parking lot at the foot of Tourmaline Street that normally fills to capacity by midday. ⊠ *Take Mission Blvd. north (it turns into La Jolla Blvd.) and turn west on Tourmaline St., La Jolla.*

Windansea Beach. The beach's sometimes towering waves (caused by an underwater reef) are truly world-class. With its incredible views and secluded sunbathing spots set among sandstone rocks, Windansea is also one of the most romantic of West Coast beaches, especially at sunset. ⊠ *Take Mission Blvd. north (it turns into La Jolla Blvd.) and turn west on Nautilus St., La Jolla.*

Marine Street Beach. Wide and sandy, this strand of beach often teems with sunbathers, swimmers, walkers, and joggers. The water is known as a great spot for bodysurfing, although the waves break in extremely shallow water and you'll need to watch out for riptides. ☒ *Accessible from Marine St., off La Jolla Blvd., La Jolla.*

Children's Pool/Shell Beach. Though you can't swim here, these two coves offer panoramic views and the chance to observe resident sea lions sunning themselves and frolicking in the water. ☒ *Follow La Jolla Blvd. north. When it forks, stay to the left, then turn right onto Coast Blvd. Shell Beach is north of the Children's Pool along Coast Blvd.*

Fodor'sChoice
★
La Jolla Cove. This is one of the prettiest spots on the West Coast. A palm-lined park sits on top of cliffs formed by the incessant pounding of the waves. At low tide the tide pools and cliff caves provide a destination for explorers. Divers, snorkelers, and kayakers can explore the underwater delights of the San Diego–La Jolla Underwater Park Ecological Reserve. The cove is also a favorite of rough-water swimmers. ☒ *Follow Coast Blvd. north to signs, or take La Jolla Village Dr. Exit from I–5, head west to Torrey Pines Rd., turn left, and drive downhill to Girard Ave. Turn right and follow signs, La Jolla.*

★ ☺
La Jolla Shores. On summer holidays all access routes are usually closed, so get here early—this is one of San Diego's most popular beaches. The lures are an incredible view of La Jolla peninsula, a wide sandy beach, an adjoining grassy park, and the most gentle waves in San Diego. A concrete boardwalk parallels the beach. There is a parking lot at the foot of Calle Frescota. ☒ *From I–5 take La Jolla Village Dr. west and turn left onto La Jolla Shores Dr. Head west to Camino del Oro or Vallecitos St. Turn right, La Jolla.*

★
Black's Beach. The powerful waves at this beach, officially known as Torrey Pines City Park Beach, attract world-class surfers, and its relative isolation appeals to nudist nature lovers (although by law nudity is prohibited). Access to parts of the shore coincides with low tide. There are no lifeguards on duty, and strong rip currents are common—only experienced swimmers should take the plunge. The cliffs are dangerous to climb. ☒ *Take Genesee Ave. west from I–5 and follow signs to glider port; easier access, via a paved path, available on La Jolla Farms Rd., but parking is limited to 2 hrs, La Jolla.*

DEL MAR
★
Torrey Pines State Beach and Reserve. One of San Diego's best beaches encompasses 1,750 acres of bluffs and bird-filled marshes. A network of meandering trails leads to the sandy shoreline below. Along the way enjoy the rare Torrey Pine trees. The large parking lot is rarely full. Lifeguards patrol the beach occasionally, and guided tours of the nature preserve here are offered on weekends. ☒ *Take Carmel Valley Rd. Exit west from I–5, turn left on Rte. S21, Del Mar* ☎ *858/755–2063* ☒ *Parking $6.*

Del Mar Beach. The numbered streets of Del Mar, from 15th north to 29th, end at a wide beach popular with volleyball players, surfers, and sunbathers. Parking can be a problem on nice summer days. The portions of Del Mar south of 15th Street are lined with cliffs and rarely crowded. ⊠ *Take Via de la Valle Exit from I–5 west to Rte. S21 (also known as Camino del Mar in Del Mar) and turn left, Del Mar.*

ENCINITAS **Swami's.** Extreme low tides expose tide pools that harbor anemones, ★ starfish, and other sea life. Remember to look but don't touch; all sea life here is protected. The beach is also a top surfing spot; the only access is by a long stairway leading down from the cliff-top park. ⊠ *Follow Rte. S21 north from Cardiff, or exit I–5 at Encinitas Blvd., go west to Rte. S21, and turn left, Encinitas.*

Moonlight State Beach. Large parking areas and lots of facilities make this beach, tucked into a break in the cliffs, an easy getaway. To combat erosion sand is trucked in every year. The volleyball courts on the north end attract many competent players, including a few professionals who live in the area. ⊠ *Take Encinitas Blvd. Exit from I–5 and head west to 3rd St. Turn left. Parking lot is on your right at top of hill, Encinitas.*

CARLSBAD **Carlsbad State Beach/South Carlsbad State Beach.** Erosion from winter storms has made the southern Carlsbad beaches rockier than most beaches in Southern California. This is particularly true of South Carlsbad, a stretch of which is named in honor of Robert C. Frazee, a local politician and civic booster. Still, it's a good swimming spot, there are fine street- and beach-level promenades outside downtown Carlsbad, and for self-contained RVs there's **overnight camping** (☎ 800/444–7275). ⊠ *Exit I–5 at La Costa Ave. and head west to Rte. S21. Turn north and follow coastline, Carlsbad* ☎ *760/438–3143.*

Bicycling

On any given summer day **Route S21** from La Jolla to Oceanside looks like a freeway for cyclists. It's easily the most popular and scenic bike route around, never straying more than a quarter-mile from the beach. For those who want to take their biking experience to the extreme, the **Magdalena Ecke Family YMCA Skate Park** (⊠ 200 Saxony Rd., Encinitas ☎ 760/942–9622 ⊕ ecke.ymca.org/sk8parklocation.htm) has set times when BMXers can rip it up on the same wood vert ramp and street courses ★ that skateboarders use. **Hike Bike Kayak San Diego** (⊠ 2246 Ave. de la Playa, La Jolla ☎ 858/551–9510 or 866/425–2925 ⊕ www.hikebikekayak.com) offers a wide range of guided bike tours and mountain-biking tours; the company also rents bikes of all types (and can deliver them to your hotel). **Cheap Rentals Mission Beach** (⊠ 3221 and 3685 Mission Blvd., Mission Beach ☎ 858/488–9070 or 800/941–7761 ⊕ www.cheap-rentals.com) is right on the boardwalk.

Diving

Enthusiasts the world over come to San Diego to snorkel and scuba-dive ★ off La Jolla and Point Loma. At La Jolla Cove you'll find the **San Diego–La Jolla Underwater Park Ecological Preserve.** Because all sea life is protected here, it's the best place to see large lobster, sea bass, and sculpin, as well as numerous golden garibaldi, the state marine fish. It's common to see hundreds of beautiful (and harmless) leopard sharks schooling at the north end of the cove, near La Jolla Shores, especially in summer. Farther north, off the south end of Black's Beach, the rim of **Scripps Canyon** lies in about 60 feet of water. The canyon plummets to more than 900 feet in some sections. The HMCS *Yukon,* a decommissioned Canadian warship, was intentionally sunk off **Mission Beach** to create a diving destination. Beware and exercise caution: even experienced divers have become disoriented inside the wreck. Another popular diving spot is **Sunset Cliffs** in Point Loma. Strong rip currents make it an area best enjoyed by experienced divers. The *San Diego Union–Tribune* includes diving conditions on its weather page. For recorded diving information, contact the **San Diego City Lifeguard Service** (☎ 619/221–8824).

Diving Locker (✉ 6167 Balboa Ave., Balboa ☎ 858/292–0547 ⊕ www. divinglocker.com) has been a fixture in San Diego since 1959. **Scuba San Diego** (✉ 1775 E. Mission Bay Dr., Mission Bay ☎ 619/260–1880 or 800/ 586–3483 ⊕ www.scubasandiego.com) is well-regarded for its top-notch instruction and certification programs as well as for guided dive tours.

Fishing

No license is required to fish from a public pier, such as the Ocean Beach, Imperial Beach, and Oceanside piers. A fishing license from the **California Department of Fish and Game** (✉ 4949 Viewridge Ave., San Diego 92123 ☎ 858/467–4201), available at most bait-and-tackle and sporting-goods stores, is required for fishing from the shoreline. **Fisherman's Landing** (✉ 2838 Garrison St., Point Loma ☎ 619/221–8500 ⊕ www. fishermanslanding.com) has a fleet of luxury vessels from 57 feet to 124 feet long, offering long-range multiday trips in search of yellowfin tuna, yellowtail, and other deep-water fish. **H&M Landing** (✉ 2803 Emerson St., Point Loma ☎ 619/222–1144 ⊕ www.hmlanding.com) schedules fishing trips year-round. **Helgren's Sportfishing** (✉ 315 Harbor Dr. S, Oceanside ☎ 760/722–2133 ⊕ www.helgrensportfishing.com) is your best bet in North County, offering the full assortment of trips from Oceanside Harbor.

Football

The **San Diego Chargers** (✉ 9449 Friars Rd., Mission Valley ☎ 619/280– 2121 or 877/242–7437 ⊕ www.chargers.com) of the National Football League fill Qualcomm Stadium from August through December.

The **Holiday Bowl** (☎ 619/283–5808), one of college football's most watched playoff games, takes place in Qualcomm Stadium around the end of December.

Golf

On any given day, it would be difficult to find a better place to play golf than San Diego. The climate—generally sunny, without a lot of wind— is perfect for the sport, and there are some 90 courses in the area, appealing to every level of expertise. Experienced golfers can play the same greens as PGA-tournament participants, and beginners or rusty players can book a week at a golf resort and benefit from expert instruction.

Most public courses in the area provide a list of fees for all San Diego courses. The **Southern California Golf Association** (☎ 818/980–3630 ⊕ www. scga.org) publishes an annual directory ($15) with detailed and valuable information on all clubs. Another good resource for golfers is the **Public Links Golf Association of Southern California** (☎ 714/994–4747 ⊕ www.plga. org), which details the region's public courses on its Web site.

The **Balboa Park Municipal Golf Course** (⊠ 2600 Golf Course Dr., Balboa Park 🕾 619/239–1660 ⊕ www.balboaparkgolf.com) is in the heart ★ of Balboa Park. Greens fee: $36–$41. **Coronado Municipal Golf Course** (⊠2000 Visalia Row, Coronado 🕾619/435–3121 ⊕www.golfcoronado.com) has 18 holes and views of San Diego Bay and the Coronado Bridge from the back 9 holes. Greens fee: $25. **Mission Bay Golf Resort** (⊠ 2702 N. Mission Bay Dr., Mission Bay 🕾 858/581–7880) is a not-very-challenging, 18-hole executive (par 3 and 4) course; it's lighted for night play. Greens fee: $19–$23.

Fodor'sChoice **Torrey Pines Golf Course** (⊠ 11480 N. Torrey Pines Rd., La Jolla 🕾 800/ ★ 985–4653 ⊕ www.torreypinesgolfcourse.com), one of the best public golf courses in the United States, has views of the Pacific from every hole. The par-72 South Course was designed by Rees Jones; it's not easy to get a good tee time here as professional brokers buy up the best ones. Out-of-towners are better off booking the instructional Golf Playing Package, which includes cart, greens fee, and a golf-pro escort for the first three holes. Greens fee: $140–$205.

Fodor'sChoice **Four Seasons Aviara Golf Club** (⊠ 7447 Batiquitos Dr., Carlsbad 🕾 760/ ★ 603–6900 ⊕www.fourseasons.com) is a top-quality course with 18 holes (designed by Arnold Palmer) and views of the protected adjacent Batiquitos Lagoon and the Pacific Ocean.

★ **La Costa Resort and Spa** (⊠ 2100 Costa del Mar Rd., Carlsbad 🕾 760/ 438–9111 or 800/854–5000 ⊕ www.lacosta.com), one of the premier golf resorts in Southern California, has two 18-hole PGA-rated courses. Greens fee: $185–$195.

★ **Rancho Bernardo Inn and Country Club** (⊠ 17550 Bernardo Oaks Dr., Rancho Bernardo 🕾 858/675–8470 Ext. 1 ⊕ www.ranchobernardoinn.com) has an 18-hole course managed by JC Golf. Greens fee: $90–$115.

Hiking & Nature Trails

The **San Dieguito River Park** (⊠ 18372 Sycamore Creek Rd., 21 mi north of San Diego on I–5 to Lomas Santa Fe Dr., east 1 mi to Sun Valley Rd., north into park, Solana Beach 🕾 858/664–2270 ⊕ www.sdrp.org) is a 55-mi corridor that begins at the mouth of the San Dieguito River in Del Mar and heads from the riparian lagoon area through coastal sage scrub and mountain terrain to end in the desert just east of Volcan Mountain near Julian. **Mission Trails Regional Park** (⊠ 1 Father Junípero Serra Trail, Mission Valley 🕾 619/668–3281 ⊕ www.mtrp.org), which encompasses nearly 6,000 acres of mountains, wooded hillsides, lakes, and riparian streams, is only 8 mi northeast of downtown. Trails range from easy to difficult; they include one with a superb view of the city from Cowles Mountain and another along a historic missionary path.

Sailing & Boating

Coronado Boat Rentals (⊠ 1715 Strand Way, Coronado 🕾619/437–1514) has kayaks, Jet Skis, fishing skiffs, and power boats from 10 feet to 20 feet in length as well as sailboats from 14 feet to 30 feet. They also can hook you up with a skipper. **Seaforth Boat Rentals** (⊠ 1641 Quivira Rd., Mission Bay 🕾 619/223–1681 ⊕ www.seaforthboatrental.com) rents Jet Skis, paddleboats, sailboats, and skiffs. **Downtown Boat Rental** (⊠ Mar-riot Hotel & Marina, 333 W. Harbor Dr., Gate 1, Downtown ☎ 619/ 239–2628) is your downtown source for sailboats and other watercraft. **Carlsbad Paddle Sports** (✉ 2002 S. Coast Hwy., Oceanside ☎ 760/434– 8686 ⊕ www.carlsbadpaddle.com) handles kayak sales, rentals, and instruction for coastal North County.

Surfing

If you're a beginner, consider paddling in the waves off Mission Beach, Pacific Beach, Tourmaline Surfing Park, La Jolla Shores, Del Mar, or Oceanside. More experienced surfers usually head for Sunset Cliffs, the La Jolla ★ reef breaks, Black's Beach, or Swami's in Encinitas. **Surf Diva Surf School** (✉ 2160 Avenida de la Playa, La Jolla ☎ 858/454–8273 ⊕ www.surfdiva. com) offers clinics, surf camps, surf trips, and private lessons especially formulated for women. Many local surf shops rent both surf and bodyboards. **Cheap Rentals Mission Beach** (✉ 3221 and 3689 Mission Blvd., Mission Beach ☎ 858/488–9070 or 800/941–7761 ⊕ www.cheaprentals.com) is right on the boardwalk, just steps from the waves. **Star Surfing Company** (✉ 4652 Mission Blvd., Pacific Beach ☎ 858/273– 7827 ⊕ www.starsurfingco.com) can get you out surfing around the Crystal Pier. **Hansen's** (✉ 1105 S. Coast Hwy. 101, Encinitas ☎ 760/753–6595 or 800/480–4754 ⊕ www.hansensurf.com) is just a short walk from Swami's beach.

Tennis

Most of the more than 1,300 courts around the county are in private clubs, but a few are public. The **Balboa Tennis Club at Morley Field** (✉ 2221 Morley Field Dr., Balboa Park ☎ 619/295–9278 ⊕ www. balboatennis.com) has 25 courts, 19 of them lighted. Courts are available on a first-come, first-served basis for a daily $5-per-person fee. Heaviest usage is 9 AM to 11 AM and after 5 PM. **Rancho Bernardo Inn** (✉ 17550 Bernardo Oaks Dr., Rancho Bernardo ☎ 858/675–8500 ⊕ www. ranchobernardoinn.com) has 12 tennis courts; the courts were closed for renovation in 2006 but were, as of this writing, slated to reopen in Fodor'sChoice 2007. **Rancho Valencia Resort** (✉ 5921 Valencia Circle, Rancho Santa Fe ★ ☎ 858/759–6224 ⊕ www.ranchovalencia.com), which is among the top tennis resorts in the nation, has 18 hard courts and several instruction ★ programs. **La Costa Resort and Spa** (✉ Costa Del Mar Rd., Carlsbad ☎ 760/438–9111 ⊕ www.lacosta.com), where the annual Acura Tennis Classic is held, has 19 courts, 7 of them lighted, plus professional instruction, clinics, and workouts.

Windsurfing

Windsurfing is a sport best practiced on smooth waters, such as Mission Bay or the Snug Harbor Marina at the intersection of Interstate 5 and Tamarack Avenue in Carlsbad. More experienced windsurfers will enjoy taking a board out on the ocean. Wave jumping is especially popular at the Tourmaline Surfing Park in La Jolla and in the Del Mar area. Sailboard rentals and instruction are available at the **Bahia Resort Hotel** (✉ 998 W. Mission Bay Dr., Mission Bay ☎ 858/488–2582). The **Snug Harbor Marina** (✉ 4215 Harrison St., Carlsbad ☎ 760/434–3089) has rentals and instruction and can advise those looking to windsurf on Agua Hedionda lagoon.

SHOPPING

Coronado

Fodor'sChoice ★ The **Ferry Landing Marketplace** (✉ 1201 1st St., at B Ave., Coronado) has 30 boutiques and a Tuesday afternoon Farmers' Market. Friendly shopkeepers make the boutiques lining **Orange Avenue,** Coronado's main drag, a good place to browse.

Downtown

Art galleries, antiques stores, and boutiques fill the Victorian buildings and renovated warehouses of the lively **Gaslamp Quarter,** especially along 4th and 5th avenues. ✉ *Downtown.*

Westfield Horton Plaza (✉ Gaslamp Quarter ☎ 619/238–1596 ⊕ www. westfield.com/hortonplaza) is a multilevel shopping, dining, and entertainment complex with a terra-cotta color scheme and flag-draped facades. There are department stores, fast-food counters, upscale restaurants, the Lyceum Theater, cinemas, and 140 other stores.

Seaport Village (✉ W. Harbor Dr. at Kettner Blvd., Embarcadero ☎ 619/ 235–4014 ⊕ www.spvillage.com), a waterfront complex of more than 50 shops and restaurants has sweeping bay views, fresh breezes, and great strolling paths. Horse and carriage rides, an 1895 Looff carousel, and frequent public entertainment are side attractions.

Hillcrest, North Park, Uptown & Mission Hills

Although their boundaries blur, each of these four established neighborhoods north and northeast of downtown contains a distinct urban village with shops, many ethnic restaurants and cafés, and entertainment venues. Most of the activity is in Hillcrest, on **University Avenue** and **Washington Street,** and along the side streets connecting the two. Gay-popular and funky Hillcrest, northwest of Balboa Park, has many gift, book, and music stores. East of Hillcrest, in North Park, retro rules: nostalgia shops along Park Boulevard and University Avenue at 30th Street carry clothing, accessories, furnishings, wigs, and bric-a-brac of the 1920s–1960s. East of North Park, you'll find the Uptown District, an open-air shopping center on University Avenue that includes several furniture, gift, and specialty stores. Sophisticated, old monied elegance is the tone in the well-heeled Mission Hills neighborhood, west of Hillcrest.

La Jolla

This seaside village has chic boutiques, art galleries, and gift shops lining narrow twisty streets. On the east side of Interstate 5, office buildings surround **Westfield UTC** (✉ 4545 La Jolla Village Dr., between I–5 and I–805, La Jolla ☎ 858/546–8858 ⊕ www.westfield.com/utc), where you'll find 155 shops, a cinema, 25 eateries, and an ice-skating rink.

Mission Valley

The Mission Valley–Hotel Circle area, northeast of downtown near Interstate 8 and Route 163, has a few shopping centers. **Fashion Valley** (✉ 7007 Friars Rd., Mission Valley) has a contemporary Mission theme, lush landscaping, and more than 200 shops and restaurants. To

Fodor'sChoice ★

get here, you can use the San Diego Trolley; many hotels also provide complimentary shuttle service. The major department stores are Macy's, Neiman Marcus, Nordstrom (which also provides a shuttle from various hotels), Robinsons-May, and Saks Fifth Avenue; there's even a Tiffany's here. **Park Valley Center** (✉ 1750 Camino de la Reina, Mission Valley) is a U-shape mall anchored by **OFF 5th** (☎ 619/296–4896), where fashions by Ralph Lauren, Armani, and Burberry seen last season are sold at Costco prices. The discount stores at **Westfield Mission Valley** (✉ 1640 Camino del Rio N, Mission Valley), San Diego's largest outdoor mall, sometimes reward shoppers with the same merchandise as that sold in Fashion Valley, but at lower prices.

Old Town

The colorful Old Town San Diego historic district recalls a Mexican marketplace. Adobe architecture, flower-filled plazas, tiled fountains, and courtyards decorate the shopping areas of Plaza del Pasado and Old Town Esplanade, where you'll find international goods, toys, souvenirs, and arts and crafts. **Bazaar del Mundo Shops** (✉ 4133 Taylor St., Old Town ☎ 619/296–3161 ⊕ www.bazaardelmundo.com), a new arcade with a Mexican villa theme, offers a variety of riotously colorful gift shops.

SIDE TRIPS TO NORTH COUNTY

San Diego North County sprawls from the Pacific Ocean to Anza-Borrego Desert State Park on the eastern boundary. The beach communities of Del Mar, Encinitas, Carlsbad, and Oceanside draw multitudes of San Diego residents and visitors to its accessible beaches, surfable waves, and star attractions (like the Legoland theme park). Inland North County attracts animal and nature lovers to the San Diego Wild Animal Park and, in spring, a desert in full bloom.

Numbers in the margin correspond to points of interest on the San Diego North County map.

Del Mar

23 mi north of downtown San Diego on I–5; 9 mi north of La Jolla on Rte. S21.

Del Mar is best known for its racetrack, chic shops, tony restaurants, celebrity visitors, and wide beaches. Along with its collection of shops, **Del Mar Plaza** also contains outstanding restaurants and landscaped plazas and gardens with Pacific views.

❶ **Del Mar Fairgrounds** hosts the **Del Mar Thoroughbred Club** (✉ 2260 Jimmy Durante Blvd. ☎ 858/755–1141 ⊕ www.delmarracing.com). Crooner Bing Crosby and his Hollywood buddies—Pat O'Brien, Gary Cooper, and Oliver Hardy, among others—organized the club in the 1930s, and Del Mar soon developed into a regular train stop for the stars of stage and screen. Even now the racing season here (usually July through September, Wednesday to Monday, post time 2 PM) is one of the most fashionable in California. Del Mar Fairgrounds hosts more than 100 different events each year, including the Del Mar Fair and a number of

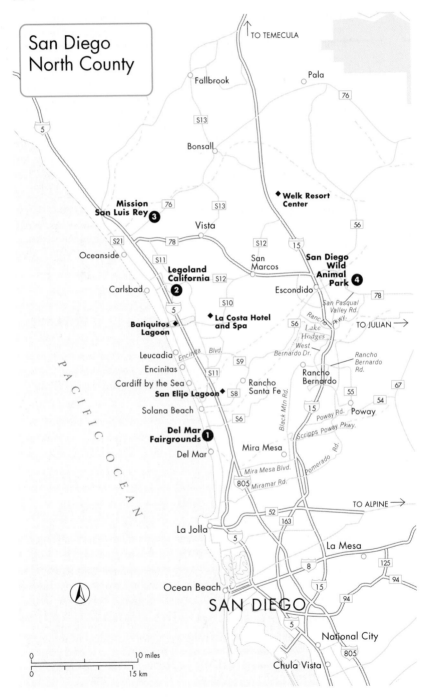

San Diego
North County

TO TEMECULA

Fallbrook

Pala

76

5

S13

Bonsall

Welk Resort
Center

**Mission
San Luis Rey** ❸

76   S13

Vista

56

S21

78

S12

15

Oceanside

S11

San
Marcos

**San Diego
Wild
Animal
Park** ❹

**Legoland
California**
❷

S12

Escondido

78

Carlsbad

5

San Pasqual
Valley Rd.

S10

Rancho

TO JULIAN →

◆ **La Costa Hotel
and Spa**

S6

Lake
Hodges

**Batiquitos
Lagoon**

West
Bernardo Dr.

Rancho
Bernardo
Rd.

Leucadia

Encinitas Blvd.

S9

Encinitas

S11

Cardiff by the Sea

San Elijo Lagoon ◆

S8

Rancho
Santa Fe

**Rancho
Bernardo**

67

55

54

Solana Beach

S6

Black Mtn Rd.

15

Poway Rd. **Poway**

**Del Mar
Fairgrounds** ❶

Scripps Poway Pkwy.

Del Mar

Mira Mesa

Mira Mesa Blvd.

Pomerado Rd.

TO ALPINE →

805 Miramar Rd.

P A C I F I C   O C E A N

52

163

La Jolla

5

La Mesa

8

125

Ocean Beach

94

SAN DIEGO

94

5

National City

805

Chula Vista

0 ——————— 10 miles
0 ——————— 15 km

horse shows. ⊠ *Head west at I–5 Via de la Valle Rd. Exit* ☎ *858/793–5555* ⊕ *www.sdfair.com.*

Where to Stay & Eat

$$-$$$$ ✕ **Jake's Del Mar.** This enormously popular oceanfront restaurant has a close-up view of the water and a menu of simple but well-prepared fare that ranges from an appetizer of mussels steamed in aromatic saffron broth to a mustard-crusted lamb rack with port-flavored garlic sauce. A menu note reminds you that the legendary, ice cream–stuffed hula pie is "what the sailors swam ashore for in Lahaina." ⊠ *1660 Coast Blvd.* ☎ *858/755–2002* ⚭ *Reservations essential* ▭ *AE, D, MC, V* ⊘ *No lunch Mon.*

$$-$$$$ ✕ **Pacifica Del Mar.** The view of the shimmering Pacific from this lovely restaurant perched atop Del Mar Plaza is one of the best along the coast, and the simply prepared, beautifully presented seafood it serves complements the scenery perfectly. The highly innovative menu is frequently rewritten to show off such creations as a barbecue sugar-spice salmon with mustard sauce and mustard catfish with Yukon Gold potato–corn succotash. The crowd ranges from young hipsters at the bar to well-dressed businesspeople on the terrace, where glass screens block any hint of a chilly breeze. ⊠ *Del Mar Plaza, 1515 Camino del Mar* ☎ *858/792–0476* ▭ *AE, D, DC, MC, V.*

★ ⊙ ✕ **Fish Market.** There's no ocean view at the North County branch of
$-$$$$ downtown's waterfront restaurant, but this eatery remains popular with residents and tourists for its simple preparations of very fresh fish and shellfish from a menu that changes daily. The oyster bar here is popular. The scene is lively, crowded, and noisy, a great place to bring the kids. ⊠ *640 Via de la Valle* ☎ *858/755–2277* ▭ *AE, D, DC, MC, V.*

$$$$ 🏨 **L'Auberge Del Mar Resort and Spa.** A boutique hotel occupying a coveted corner in Del Mar, just steps from restaurants, shopping, and the beach, the Auberge is modeled after a Tudor-style inn that welcomed the Hollywood elite for decades. The old inn is long gone, replaced by this one reeking of old-world charm: half-timbered walls, open beam ceilings, fireplaces in nooks throughout the public areas and in many rooms, year-round gardens blooming with azaleas and camellias. Rooms, wrapped around a central courtyard, have private balconies or patios with ocean or garden views, marble bathrooms, rich pink-and-green pastel fabrics, sitting areas, and workable desks. Service here is discrete and friendly. ⊠ *1540 Camino del Mar, 92014* ☎ *858/259–1515 or 866/893–4389* 🖷 *858/755–4940* ⊕ *www.laubergedelmar.com* ⇆ *112 rooms, 8 suites* ⚭ *Restaurant, room service, minibars, cable TV with movies, in-room broadband, in-room data ports, 2 tennis courts, 2 pools, gym, outdoor hot tub, massage, sauna, spa, steam room, bar, meeting room, parking (fee); no smoking* ▭ *AE, D, DC, MC, V.*

Rancho Santa Fe

4 mi east of Solana Beach on Rte. S8 (Lomas Santa Fe Dr.); 29 mi north of downtown San Diego on I–5 to Rte. S8 east.

Groves of huge, drooping eucalyptus trees cover the hills and valleys of this affluent and exclusive town east of Interstate 5. Rancho Santa Fe is horse country. It's common to see entire families riding the many trails that crisscross the hillsides. Modeled after a Spanish village, the town was designed by Lillian Rice, one of the first women to graduate with a degree in architecture from the University of California. The challenging Rancho Santa Fe Golf Course, the original site of the Bing Crosby Pro-Am and considered one of the best courses in Southern California, is open only to members of the Rancho Santa Fe community and guests of the inn.

Where to Stay & Eat

★ $$$–$$$$ ✕ **Mille Fleurs.** Mille Fleurs is a winner, from its location in the heart of wealthy, horsey Rancho Santa Fe to the warm Gallic welcome extended by proprietor Bertrand Hug and the talents of chef Martin Woesle. The quiet dining rooms are decorated like a French villa. Menus are written daily to reflect the market and Woesle's mood, but might feature a creamless soup of field greens, salad of Maine lobster (with avocado, mango, and lemon dressing), oven-roasted quail with braised cabbage, stuffed John Dory, or wiener schnitzel of milk-fed veal. ⊠ *Country Squire Courtyard, 6009 Paseo Delicias* ☎ 858/756–3085 ⌕ *Reservations essential* ▭ *AE, MC, V* ⊘ *No lunch weekends.*

$$$$ ✕▦ **Rancho Valencia Resort.** One of Southern California's hidden treasures has luxurious accommodations in Spanish-style casitas scattered
Fodor'sChoice on 40 acres of landscaped grounds. Suites have corner fireplaces, luxurious Berber carpeting, and shuttered French doors leading to private patios. Twelve suites also have steam showers, private outdoor hot tubs, and wall-mounted plasma flat-screen TVs. Rancho Valencia is one of the nation's top tennis resorts and is adjacent to three well-designed golf courses. Its first-rate restaurant ($$$–$$$$) has a seasonal menu that might include veal piccata with butternut-squash ravioli, Colorado lamb rib eye with cous cous, or goat cheese–crusted roasted *poussin.* ⊠ *5921 Valencia Circle, 92067* ☎ 858/756–1123 *or* 800/548–3664 🖷 *858/756–0165* ⊕ *www.ranchovalencia.com* ➘ *49 suites* ⌕ *Restaurant, room service, in-room safes, some in-room hot tubs, minibars, refrigerators, cable TV with movies, in-room broadband, in-room data ports, 18 tennis courts, 2 pools, fitness center, 3 outdoor hot tubs, spa, bicycles, croquet, hiking, bar, shops, business services, meeting rooms, free parking, no-smoking* ▭ *AE, MC, V.*

★ $$$–$$$$ ▦ **Inn at Rancho Santa Fe.** Understated elegance is the theme of this genteel old resort in the heart of the Spanish colonial revival–style village of Rancho Santa Fe. Guest rooms are in red-tile cottages spread around the property's 23 lushly landscaped acres. Many have private patios and wood-burning fireplaces. The inn provides guests with membership at the exclusive Rancho Santa Fe Golf Club and privileges at five other nearby, exclusive courses. ⊠ *5951 Linea del Cielo, 92067* ☎ 858/756–1131 *or* 800/843–4661 🖷 *858/759–1604* ⊕ *www.theinnatrsf.com* ➘ *73 rooms, 5 suites, 8 private 1-, 2-, and 3-bedroom cottages* ⌕ *Restaurant, room service, in-room safes, some kitchens, minibars, microwaves, cable TV with movies, in-room broadband, Wi-Fi, tennis court, pool, gym, hair salon, spa, croquet, bar, library, piano, meeting rooms, free parking, some pets allowed, no-smoking rooms* ▭ *AE, D, DC, MC, V.*

Carlsbad

15 mi north of Rancho Santa Fe via Hwy. S9 to Hwy. S21; 36 mi north of downtown San Diego on I–5.

Carlsbad has long been popular with beachgoers and sun-seekers. More recently, however, much of the attention has shifted inland, east of Interstate 5, to Legoland California and other attractions in its vicinity— resort hotels, a discount shopping mall, golf courses, and colorful flower fields. Carlsbad village owes its name to John Frazier, who dug a well for his farm here in the 1880s. When Frazier and others went into the business of luring people to the area with talk of the healing powers of the local mineral water, they changed the name of the town to Carlsbad, to emphasize the similarity with the famous Bohemian spa. Remnants from this era, including the original well and a monument to Frazier, are found at the **Carlsbad Mineral Water Spa** (⊠ 2802 Carlsbad Blvd. ☎ 760/434–1887 ⊕ www.carlsbadmineralspa.com), a stone building that houses a small day spa and the Carlsbad Water Company, a 21st-century version of Frazier's waterworks.

FodorśChoice ★

② **Legoland California** offers a full day of entertainment for pint-size fun-seekers and their parents. The mostly outdoor experience is best appreciated by kids ages 2 to 10, who often beg to ride the mechanical horses around the Royal Joust again and again or to take just one more turn through the popular Volvo Jr. Driving School. Miniland USA, an animated collection of U.S. cities and other areas constructed entirely of Lego blocks, captures the imaginations of all ages. Attractions added in a major expansion in 2006 include Splash Battle, in which kids cruise through pirate-infested waters past exploding volcanoes; Treasure Falls, a mini flume log ride with a 12-foot soaking plunge; and Pirate Shores, water-fight headquarters. ⊠ *1 Lego Dr., exit I–5 at Cannon Rd. and follow signs east ¼ mi, Carlsbad* ☎ *760/918–5346* ⊕ *www.legolandca. com* ⊡ *$53* ⊙ *Days, hrs vary.*

In spring the hillsides are abloom at **Flower Fields at Carlsbad Ranch,** the largest bulb production farm in Southern California. Here, from mid-March through mid-May, you can walk through fields planted with thousands of Giant Tecolote ranunculus—a stunning display of color against the backdrop of the blue Pacific Ocean. The walk of fame rose garden is lined with examples of every All-American Rose Selection award-winner since 1940. The unusually large and well-stocked Armstrong Garden Center at the exit carries plants, garden accessories, and ranunculus bulbs. ⊠ *5704 Paseo del Norte, east of I–5* ☎ *760/431–0352* ⊕ *www.theflowerfields.com* ⊡ *$8* ⊙ *Mar.–May, daily 9–6.*

California Surf Museum displays a large collection of surfing memorabilia, photos, vintage boards, apparel, and accessories. ⊠ *223 N. Coast Hwy.* ☎ *760/721–6876* ⊕ *www.surfmuseum.org* ⊡ *Free* ⊙ *Daily 10–4.*

FodorśChoice ★

③ **Mission San Luis Rey** was built in 1798 by Franciscan friars under the direction of Father Fermin Lasuen to help educate and convert local Native Americans. Once a location for filming Disney's *Zorro* TV series, the well-preserved mission, still owned by the Franciscans, was the 18th and largest and most prosperous of California's missions. The *sala* (parlor), the kitchen, a friar's bedroom, a weaving room, and a collection of religious art convey much about early mission life. The mission's retreat center has limited, inexpensive dormitory-style overnight accommodations. ⊠ *4050 Mission Ave.* ☎ *760/757–3651* ⊕ *www.sanluisrey. org* ☞ *$5* ☉ *Daily 10–4.*

Where to Stay

☾ **$$$$**   🏨 **Four Seasons Resort Aviara.** This hilltop resort on 30 acres overlooking Batiquitos Lagoon is one of the most luxurious in the San Diego area, with gleaming marble corridors, original artwork, crystal chandeliers, and enormous flower arrangements. Rooms have every possible amenity: oversize closets, private balconies or garden patios, and marble bathrooms with double vanities and deep soaking tubs. The resort is exceptionally family friendly, providing a wide selection of in-room amenities designed for the younger set. The kids also have their own pool, nature walks with wildlife demonstrations, and video and board games. ⊠ *7100 Four Seasons Point, 92009* ☎ *760/603–6800 or 800/332–3442* 🖷 *760/603– 6801* ⊕ *www.fourseasons.com/aviara* ☞ *285 rooms, 44 suites* ♨ *4 restaurants, room service, in-room safes, minibars, cable TV with movies and video games, in-room DVD/VCRs, in-room broadband, in-room data ports, Web TV, 18-hole golf course, 6 tennis courts, 2 pools, health club, 2 hot tubs, massage, sauna, spa, steam room, bicycles, hiking, volleyball, shops, babysitting, children's programs (ages 5–12), laundry service, concierge, business services, meeting room, airport shuttle, car rental, parking (fee), some pets allowed (fee); no smoking* ⊟ *AE, D, DC, MC, V.*

FodorsChoice
★

$$$$ 🏨 **La Costa Resort and Spa.** New owners, KSL Resorts, totally renovated this legendary resort in 2004–2006, dramatically transforming its laidback '50s look into a Spanish-colonial oasis with dark wood, open-beam ceilings and paneling, crystal chandeliers, and leather and wroughtiron furnishings. Ample guest rooms, in shades of brown and sand with oversize chairs and sofas, fill a collection of two-story buildings surrounding the lobby, Club House, and conference center. There are flower-decked gardens and fairway views throughout the resort's 400 tree-shaded acres—and the best of all fairway views may be from one of the state-of-the-art bikes in the fitness center. The resort's Blue Fire Grill attracts a local following for its coastal cuisine featuring local seafood and vegetables. There are two PGA championship golf courses, a large tennis center, and—new in 2006—a family entertainment area. ⊠ *2100 Costa del Mar Rd., 92009* ☎ *760/438–9111 or 800/854–5000* 🖷 *760/438– 3758* ⊕ *www.lacosta.com* ☞ *474 rooms, 77 suites* ♨ *2 restaurants, room service, in-room safes, minibars, some refrigerators, cable TV with movies and games, in-room broadband, driving range, 2 18-hole golf courses, 2 putting greens, 17 tennis courts, pro shop, 4 pools, health club, hair salon, 4 outdoor hot tubs, sauna, spa, steam room, bicycles, croquet, lounge, shops, babysitting, children's programs (ages 5–12), dry cleaning, laundry service, concierge, business services, meeting rooms, car rental; no-smoking* ⊟ *AE, D, DC, MC, V.*

★ **$$–$$$$**   🏨 **Oceanside Marina Suites.** Of all the oceanfront lodgings in North County towns, this motel occupies the best location—a spit of land surrounded by water and cool ocean breezes on all sides. The rooms are unusually large and have fireplaces and expansive balconies; all have either ocean or harbor views. There are barbecues for guest use. A free boat shuttles you to the beach in summer. Continental breakfast is included in the price. ⊠ *2008 Harbor Dr. N, 92054* ☎ *760/722–1561 or 800/252–2033* 🖷 *760/439–9758* ⊕ *www.omihotel.com* ⇥ *51 suites* ⚇ *Kitchens, cable TV with movies, in-room DVDs, in-room broadband, in-room data ports, pool, outdoor hot tub, sauna, fishing, Ping-Pong, volleyball, laundry facilities, meeting room, free parking; no a/c, no smoking* ⊟ *AE, DC, MC, V* ¹⁰¹ *CP.*

Escondido

8 mi north of Rancho Bernardo on I–15; 31 mi northeast of downtown San Diego on I–15.

San Diego Wild Animal Park is an extension of the San Diego Zoo, 35 mi to the south. The 1,800-acre preserve in the San Pasqual Valley is designed to protect endangered species from around the world. Exhibit areas have been carved out of the dry, dusty canyons and mesas to represent the animals' natural habitats in various parts of Africa, the Australian rain forest, the Asian swamps, and the Asian plains. The best way to see these preserves is to take the 60-minute, 5-mi monorail ride on the Wgasa Bushline Railway (included in the price of admission). The 1¼-mi-long **Kilimanjaro Safari Walk** winds through some of the park's hilliest terrain in the East Africa section, with observation decks overlooking the elephants and lions. A 70-foot suspension bridge spans a steep ravine, leading to the final observation point and a panorama of the entire park and the San Pasqual Valley. Along the trails of 32-acre **Heart of Africa** you can travel in the footsteps of an early explorer through forests and lowlands, across a floating bridge to a research station where an expert is on hand to answer questions; finally you arrive at Panorama Point for an up-close-and-personal view of cheetahs, a chance to feed the giraffes, and a distant glimpse of the expansive savanna where rhinos, impalas, wildebeest, oryx, and beautiful migrating birds reside. At **Condor Ridge,** the Wild Animal Park, which conducts captive breeding programs to save rare and endangered species, shows off one of its most successful efforts, the California condor. The exhibit occupies nearly the highest point in the park, and affords a sweeping view of the surrounding San Pasqual Valley. You can also overnight in the park in summer on a Roar and Snore Camp-Over (adults $129 to $199, kids 8 to 11 $109 to $129, plus admission), and celebrate the holidays during the annual Festival of Lights. ⊠ *15500 San Pasqual Valley Rd., take I–15 north to Via Rancho Pkwy. and follow signs, 6 mi* ☎ *760/747–8702* ⊕ *www.sandiegozoo.org/wap* 🎟 *$28.50 includes all shows and monorail tour; $54.45 combination pass grants entry, within 5 days of purchase, to San Diego Zoo and San Diego Wild Animal Park; parking $8* ⊙ *Mid-June–Labor Day, daily 9–8; early-Sept.–mid-June, daily 9–4* ⊟ *D, MC, V.*

FodorśChoice
★

Where to Stay & Eat

★ **$$–$$$$** ✕ **150 Grand Cafe.** This pretty storefront restaurant lies a block from the California Center for the Arts. It consists of a collection of individually decorated gardenlike dining rooms, and a sidewalk dining area. The seasonal menu might feature blueberry- and zinfandel-braised salmon, pecan-roasted pork with braised Swiss chard, or filet mignon with blue-cheese butter. Reservations are essential on weekends. ⊠ *150 W. Grand Ave.* ☎ *760/738–6868* ⊟ *AE, D, DC, MC, V* ⊙ *Closed Sun.*

$$–$$$$ ✕ **Vincent's Sirinos.** Here's an excellent choice for dining before attending an event at the nearby California Center for the Arts. Original paintings decorate the walls and crisp white tablecloths cover the tables, adorned with fresh flowers. The menu changes frequently; offerings might include tournedos Rossini, a grilled portobello mushroom with Parmesan, or veal prosciutto ravioli. The wine list is serious, as are the desserts. The service is friendly and attentive. ⊠ *113 W. Grand Ave.* ☎ *760/745–3835* ⊟ *AE, D, MC, V* ⊙ *Closed Mon. No lunch weekends.*

♨ **$$–$$$** ▦ **Welk Resort.** Sprawling over 600 acres of rugged, oak-studded hillside, this resort, built by bandleader Lawrence Welk in the 1960s, completed a makeover in 2005 that transformed it into a time-share property. Fully furnished and appointed, one- and two-bedroom villas are rented to nonowners when available. Amenities include fireplaces, hot tubs, original art, and balconies or patios. The resort complex is family friendly with abundant children's activities, although parents must supervise. A museum displays Welk memorabilia and the Lawrence Welk Theater presents a popular year-round season of Broadway musicals. ⊠ *8860 Lawrence Welk Dr., 92026* ☎ *760/749–3000 or 800/932–9355* ▤ *760/ 749–6182* ⊕ *www.welkresort.com/sandiego* ➬ *286 suites* �ἀ *Restaurant, kitchens, cable TV, some in-room DVD/VCRs, in-room broadband, in-room data ports, 2 18-hole golf courses, 4 tennis courts, pro shop, 6 pools, gym, 7 outdoor hot tubs, sauna, spa, basketball, billiards, horseshoes, volleyball, bar, library, theater, video game room, shops, children's programs, playground, laundry facilities, free parking, no-smoking rooms* ⊟ *AE, D, MC, V.*

SAN DIEGO ESSENTIALS

To research prices, get advice from other travelers, and book travel arrangements, visit ⊕ *www.fodors.com.*

AIRPORTS & TRANSFERS

All major and some regional U.S. carriers serve San Diego International Airport. Aero Mexico and Air Canada are the only international carriers to San Diego. All others require a connecting flight, usually in Los Angeles. Other connection points are Chicago, Dallas, and San Francisco. San Diego International Airport (SAN), called Lindbergh Field locally, is a five-minute drive from downtown. ⇨ Air Travel *in* Smart Travel Tips A to Z for airline phone numbers.

🛈 **San Diego International Airport** ☎ 619/400-2400 ⊕ www.san.org.

🛈 **Shuttles & Buses Cloud 9 Shuttle** ☎ 800/974-8885 ⊕ www.cloud9shuttle.com. **San Diego Transit** ☎ 619/233-3004, 619/234-5005 TTY, TDD ⊕ www.sdcommute.com.

BUS TRAVEL TO & FROM SAN DIEGO

🛈 **Greyhound** ⊠ 120 W. Broadway ☎ 619/239-3266 or 800/231-2222.

BUS & TROLLEY TRAVEL WITHIN SAN DIEGO COUNTY

San Diego County is served by a coordinated, efficient network of bus and rail routes that includes service to Oceanside in the north, the Mexican border at San Ysidro, and points east to the Anza-Borrego Desert. Under the umbrella of the Metropolitan Transit System, there are two major transit agencies: San Diego Transit and North County Transit District (NCTD).

North County Transit District ☎ 800/266-6883 ⊕ www.sdcommute.com. **San Diego Transit** ☎ 619/233-3004, 619/234-5005 TTY, TDD ⊕ www.sdcommute.com.

CAR TRAVEL

When traveling in the San Diego area, it pays to consider the big picture to avoid getting lost. Water lies to the west of the city. To the east and north, mountains separate the urban areas from the desert. Interstate 5, which stretches from Canada to the Mexican border, bisects San Diego. Interstate 8 provides access from Yuma, Arizona, and points east. Drivers coming from Nevada and the mountain regions beyond can reach San Diego on Interstate 15. During rush hour there are jams on Interstate 5 and on Interstate 15 between Interstate 805 and Escondido.

EMERGENCIES

In case of emergency dial 911.

Hospitals UCSD Medical Center–Hillcrest ✉ 200 West Arbor Dr., Hillcrest ☎ 619/543-6222.

TAXIS

Taxi stands are located at shopping centers and hotels; otherwise you must call and reserve a cab. The companies listed below do not serve all areas of San Diego County. If you're going someplace other than downtown, **ask if the company serves that area.**

Taxi Companies Orange Cab ☎ 619/291-3333 ⊕ www.orangecabsandiego.com. **Silver Cabs** ☎ 619/280-5555. **Yellow Cab** ☎ 619/234-6161 ⊕ www.driveu.com.

TOURS

BOAT TOURS San Diego Harbor Excursion and Hornblower Cruises & Events both operate one- and two-hour harbor cruises departing from the Broadway Pier. No reservations are necessary for the tours, which cost $15 to $20; both companies also do dinner cruises ($55 to $75) and brunch cruises. Classic Sailing Adventures, at Shelter Island Marina, has afternoon and evening cruises of the harbor and San Diego Bay aboard six-passenger sailing ships ($65 per person). These companies also operate during whale-watching season, from mid-December to mid-March.

Classic Sailing Adventures ✉ 1220 Rosecrans St., No. 137 ☎ 800/659-0141 ⊕ www.classicsailingadventures.com. **Hornblower Cruises & Events** ✉ 1066 N. Harbor Dr. ☎ 619/234-8687 or 800/668-4322 ⊕ www.hornblower.com. **San Diego Harbor Excursion** ✉ 1050 N. Harbor Dr. ☎ 619/234-4111 or 800/442-7847 ⊕ www.sdhe.com.

BUS & TROLLEY TOURS Contactours provides narrated sightseeing tours, picking up passengers at many hotels; the selection includes daily morning and afternoon city tours ($29 for adults), tours to the San Diego Zoo, Wild Animal Park, SeaWorld, and Legoland California, and trips to Tijuana, Rosarito and Ensenada. Old Town Trolley Tours take you to eight sites including Old

Town, Seaport Village, Horton Plaza and the Gaslamp Quarter, Coronado, the San Diego Zoo, and El Prado in Balboa Park. The tour is narrated, and for the price of the ticket ($27 for adults and $15 for children 4 to 12; under 4, free) you can get on and off as you please at any stop. ⛴ **Contactours** ✉ 1726 Wilson Ave., National City ☎ 619/477-8687 ⊕ www.contactours. com. **Old Town Trolley Tours** ✉ 4010 Twiggs St. ☎ 619/298-8687 ⊕ www.trolleytours. com.

TRAIN TRAVEL

Amtrak serves downtown San Diego's Santa Fe Depot with daily trains to and from Los Angeles, Santa Barbara, and San Luis Obispo. Connecting service to Oakland, Seattle, Chicago, Texas, Florida, and points beyond is available in Los Angeles. Amtrak trains stop in San Diego North County at Solana Beach and Oceanside.

Coaster commuter trains, which run between Oceanside and San Diego Monday through Saturday, stop at the same stations as Amtrak plus others.
⛴ **Amtrak** ☎ 800/872-7245 ⊕ www.amtrak.com. **Coaster** ☎ 800/266-6883 ⊕ www. sdcommute.com. **Santa Fe Depot** ✉ 1050 Kettner Blvd. ☎ 619/239-9021.

VISITOR INFORMATION

⛴ **Balboa Park Visitors Center** ✉ 1549 El Prado ☎ 619/239-0512 ⊕ www.balboapark. org, open daily 9-4. **California Welcome Center Oceanside** ✉ 928 N. Coast Hwy., 92054 ☎ 760/721-1011 or 800/350-7873 ⊕ www.oceansidechamber.com. **Carlsbad Convention & Visitors Bureau** ✉ 400 Carlsbad Village Dr., 92008 ☎ 800/227-5722 ⊕ www. visitcarlsbad.com. **Coronado Visitor Center** ✉ 1100 Orange Ave., 92118 ☎ 619/437-8788 ⊕ www.coronadovisitorcenter.com. **Del Mar Regional Chamber of Commerce** ✉ 1104 Camino del Mar, 92014 ☎ 858/793-5292 ⊕ www.delmarchamber.org. **Encinitas Chamber of Commerce** ✉ 138 Encinitas Blvd., 92024 ☎ 760/753-6041 ⊕ www. encinitaschamber.com. **San Diego Convention & Visitors Bureau International Visitor Information Center** ✉ 1040 ⅓ W. Broadway at Harbor Dr. ☎ 619/236-1212 ⊕ www. sandiego.org. **San Diego North Convention & Visitors Bureau** ✉ 360 N. Escondido Blvd., Escondido 92025 ☎ 800/848-3336 ⊕ www.sandiegonorth.com. **San Diego Visitor Information Center** ✉ 2688 E. Mission Bay Dr., off I-5 at Clairemont Dr. exit ☎ 619/ 276-8200 for recorded information ⊕ www.infosandiego.com, open daily 9-dusk.

Orange County & Catalina Island

WORD OF MOUTH

"After going to it for 38 years, I still rate the original Disneyland as the best and happiest vacation destination on earth—and I'm not that easy to please."

—Kiki

"Laguna is more interesting and picturesque than Newport, but [Newport is] easier to access and has more lodging options (although the Montage in Laguna is breathtaking—have a sunset drink upstairs there!)."

—wherenext

By Kathy
Bryant

FEW OF THE CITRUS GROVES that gave Orange County its name remain. This region south and east of Los Angeles is now ruled by tourism and high-tech business instead of farmers. Angelenos may make cracks about theme parks being the extent of culture here, but there's much more to the area than mouse ears and laid-back beach towns. With its tropical flowers and palm trees, the stretch of coast between Seal Beach and San Clemente is often called the California Riviera. Exclusive Newport Beach, artsy Laguna, and the up-and-coming surf town of Huntington Beach are the stars, but lesser-known gems on the glistening coast—such as Corona del Mar—are also worth visiting. Offshore, meanwhile, lies gorgeous Catalina Island, a terrific spot for diving, snorkeling, and hiking.

About the Hotels & Restaurants

Restaurants in Orange County are often more casual than in L.A. You'll rarely see men in jackets and ties. Of course, there's also a swath of supercasual places along the beachfronts—fish-taco takeout, taquerias, burger joints—that won't mind if you wear flip-flops. Reservations are recommended for the nicest restaurants. Many places don't serve past 11 PM, and locals tend to eat early. Remember that according to California law, smoking is prohibited in all enclosed areas.

Along the coast there's been a small flurry of luxury resort openings in the past few years; Laguna's Montage resort made a big splash in 2003, followed by Newport Beach's Balboa Bay Club and Huntington Beach's Hyatt Regency Resort and Spa. (In most cases, you can take advantage of some of the facilities of such resorts, such as restaurants or spas, without being an overnight guest.) There are also plenty of low-key hotels in the area, and those around the theme parks are very family friendly.
■ TIP➔ Prices are often lower in winter, especially near Disneyland, unless there's a convention in Anaheim, and weekend rates are often rock bottom at business hotels. It's worth calling around to search for bargains.

WHAT IT COSTS					
	$$$$	**$$$**	**$$**	**$**	**¢**
RESTAURANTS	over $32	$22–$32	$12–$22	$7–$12	under $7
HOTELS	over $325	$200–$325	$125–$200	$75–$125	under $75

Restaurant prices are per person for a main course, excluding 8.25% sales tax. Hotel prices are for two people in a standard double room in nonholiday high season on the European Plan (no meals) unless otherwise noted. Taxes (9%–14%) are extra. In listings we always name the facilities available, but we don't specify whether they cost extra. When pricing accommodations, always ask about what's included.

Exploring Orange County

Like Los Angeles, Orange County stretches over a large area, lacks a singular focal point, and has limited public transportation. You'll need a car and a sensible game plan to make the most of your visit. If you're headed to Disneyland, you'll probably want to stay in or near Anaheim and take excursions to the coast. If the Mouse's kingdom is not part of

GREAT ITINERARIES

Although you could visit Orange County as a day trip from L.A., it would mean roughly three hours, if not more, in the car. If possible, make a trip here an overnight—at least. With all the beach communities along with the theme parks, you'll have more than enough to keep you busy for a few days.

IF YOU HAVE 1 DAY

Who are we kidding? You're going to **Disneyland ❶ ▶**.

IF YOU HAVE 3 DAYS

You're still going to **Disneyland ❶ ▶** (stay overnight in 🏨 **Anaheim**), and if it's up to the kids, you could add **Disney's California Adventure** to the mix and easily devote all three days (and a considerable amount of money) to the Disneyland Resort. If

you'd prefer to escape the Magic Kingdom or avoid it altogether, get an early start and head to 🏨 **Laguna Beach ⓮** before the crowds arrive. Breakfast alfresco and then take a walk on the sand. Afterward, stroll around the local streets lined with boutiques and art galleries or go for a hike in the coastal canyons. If you'd like to splurge on a fancy dinner, this would be the town to do it in. On Day 3, visit **Newport Beach** or **Huntington Beach**; then head inland to **Costa Mesa**, where you can browse through **South Coast Plaza ❼**, one of the world's largest retail, entertainment, and dining complexes, or visit the smaller nearby shopping centers. Alternatively, catch an early boat out to **Catalina Island** for the day.

your itinerary, try staying at a midpoint location such as Irvine or Costa Mesa, both equidistant from inland tourist attractions and the coast. These towns are less crowded than Anaheim and less expensive than the beach cities. Of course, if you can afford it, staying at the beach is always recommended.

Numbers in the text correspond to numbers in the margin and on the Orange County map.

Timing

The sun shines year-round in Orange County, though in early summer there are the occasional "June gloom" days, when skies are overcast. Beat the crowds and the heat by visiting in winter, spring, or fall. Smart parents give kids their Disney fix on weekdays or during the winter months whenever possible.

INLAND ORANGE COUNTY

About a 35-minute drive from downtown Los Angeles on Interstate 5 (also known as the Santa Ana Freeway) is Anaheim, Orange County's tourist hub, which centers on the big D. The inland part of the county is often seen as an ever-spreading morass of middle- and upper-middle-class housing developments and strip malls. True, you'll see plenty of indistinguishable tract housing and may wonder how anyone finds the way home. If you get off the freeways, though, you can find diverse and

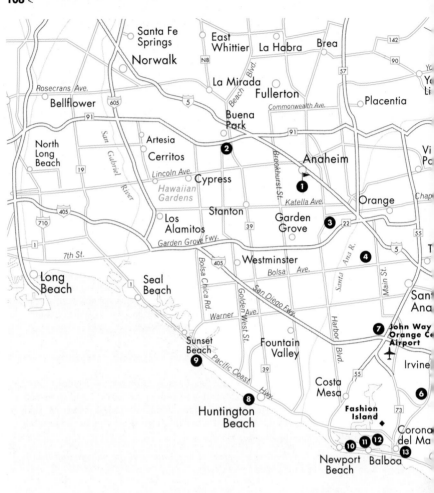

Santa Fe
Springs
East
Whittier La Habra Brea
Norwalk
La Mirada
Fullerton
Rosecrans Ave. Placentia
Bellflower
Commonwealth Ave.
North
Long
Beach
Buena
Park
Artesia
Cerritos
Anaheim
Lincoln Ave.
Cypress
Hawaiian
Gardens
Katella Ave.
Orange
Los
Alamitos
Stanton
Garden
Grove
Garden Grove Fwy.
7th St.
Westminster
Bolsa Ave.
Long
Beach
Seal
Beach
Warner
San
Ana
Sunset
Beach
Fountain
Valley
John Way
Orange C
Airport
Irvine
Costa
Mesa
Huntington
Beach
Fashion
Island
Corona
del Ma
Newport
Beach Balboa

PACIFIC
OCEAN

Orange
County

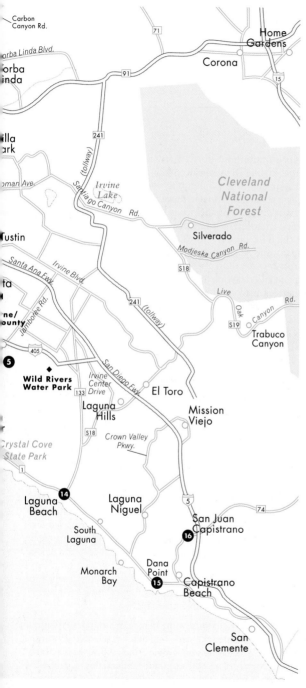

distinctive areas. In the Old Towne section of Orange, for instance, hundreds of antiques and collectibles dealers fill early-20th-century buildings. Little Saigon, a large Vietnamese community with around 3,500 businesses, is between Westminster and Garden Grove. Farther south and inland, the Santiago, Silverado, and Modjeska canyons meander toward the marvelous Cleveland National Forest, which stretches from Orange County to San Diego.

Disneyland Resort

26 mi southeast of Los Angeles, via I–5.

The snowcapped Matterhorn, the centerpiece of the Magic Kingdom, punctuates the skyline of **Anaheim.** Since 1955, when Walt Disney chose this once-quiet farming community for the site of his first amusement park, Disneyland has attracted more than 450 million visitors and thousands of workers, and Anaheim has been their host. To understand the symbiotic relationship between Disneyland and Anaheim, you need only look at the $4.2 billion spent in a combined effort by the Walt Disney Company and Anaheim, the latter to revitalize the city's tourist center and run-down areas, the former to expand and renovate the Disney properties into what is known now as **Disneyland Resort.** The resort is a sprawling complex that includes Disney's two amusement parks; three hotels; and Downtown Disney, a shopping, dining, and entertainment promenade. Anaheim's tourist center includes Angel Stadium of Anaheim, home of baseball's Los Angeles Angels of Anaheim; Arrowhead Pond, which hosts concerts and the hockey team the Anaheim Ducks; and the enormous Anaheim Convention Center.

> **KATHY'S TOP 5**
>
> **Catalina Island,** a short ferry ride and you'll feel 1,000 mi away.
>
> **Disneyland,** the first is still the best.
>
> **Huntington Beach** for surfing, even if you're just watching.
>
> **Laguna Beach,** for its beautiful cove and canyon, art galleries, and spectacular resort hotels.
>
> **Mission San Juan Capistrano** for an evocative look into Southern California's colonial history.

Fodor'sChoice ★

One of the biggest misconceptions people have about **Disneyland** is that they've "been there, done that" if they've visited either Florida's mammoth Walt Disney World or one of the Disney parks overseas. But Disneyland, opened in 1955 and the only one of the kingdoms to be overseen by Walt himself, has a genuine historic feel and occupies a unique place in the Disney legend. There's plenty here that you won't find anywhere else: for example, Storybook Land, with its miniature replicas of animated Disney scenes from classics such as *Pinocchio; Alice in Wonderland*; and the Indiana Jones Adventure ride.

The eight themed lands here comprise more than 60 major rides, 50 shops, and 30 restaurants. You enter the park through a re-created 19th-century railroad station, which opens onto **Main Street, U.S.A.** Walt's hometown of Marceline, Missouri, was the inspiration behind this romanticized image of small-town America, circa 1900. Trolleys, double-decker buses, and horse-drawn wagons travel up and down the scaled-down thoroughfare, and the sidewalks are lined with rows of shops selling everything from crystal ware to sports memorabilia to photo supplies. ■ TIP→ **Main Street opens half an hour before the rest of the park, so it's a good place to explore if you're getting an early start to beat the crowds.** If you want to save some of the walking for later, board the Disneyland Railroad at the park entrance; it tours all the lands.

Directly across from Main Street, Sleeping Beauty's Castle marks the entrance to **Fantasyland,** where you can fly on Peter Pan's Flight, take an aerial spin with Dumbo the Flying Elephant, bobsled through the **Matterhorn,** and float through It's a Small World. Fantasyland Theater has *Snow White,* a free musical that's geared to younger children. The steamboat *Mark Twain* and the sailing ship *Columbia* both set sail from **Frontierland,** where you can also raft to **Tom Sawyer Island** for an hour or so of climbing and exploring.

Inspired by some of the more exotic corners of the world, **Adventureland** is home to the popular **Jungle Cruise** and the **Indiana Jones Adventure,** which has special effects and decipherable hieroglyphics to distract you while you're standing in line. **Critter Country,** populated by animated bears, is where to find **Splash Mountain,** Disney's steepest, wettest adventure, and the Many Adventures of Winnie the Pooh. In **Tomorrowland,** you can ride on the futuristic Astro Orbitor rockets, race through **Space Mountain,** tinker with the toys of tomorrow at Innoventions, and zap your neighbors with laser beams in the interactive **Buzz Lightyear Astro Blasters.** ■ TIP→ Kids love getting soaked on rides like Splash Mountain and the Cosmic Wave. Either save these for the end of the day, bring a change of clothes, or expect to shell out for dry (and pricey) T-shirts.

Dixieland musicians play in the twisting streets of **New Orleans Square,** where you'll find theme shops selling everything from hats to gourmet foods. This is also where to catch the always-popular **Pirates of the Caribbean** and **Haunted Mansion** rides. **Mickey's Toontown** is a land where kids feel like they're actually in a cartoon. They can climb up a rope ladder on the *Miss Daisy* (Donald Duck's boat), walk through Mickey's House to meet the famous mouse, and take a spin on the **Roger Rabbit Car Toon Spin.**

Besides the eight lands, the daily live-action shows and parades are always crowd pleasers. **Fantasmic!** is a musical, fireworks, and laser show in which Mickey and friends wage a spellbinding battle against Disneyland's darker characters; and the daytime and nighttime Parade of Dreams features just about every animated Disney character ever drawn. ■ TIP→ Arrive early to secure a good view; if there are two shows scheduled for the day, the second one tends to be less crowded. A fireworks display sparks up Friday and Saturday evenings. Brochures with maps, available at the entrance, list show- and parade times.

Characters appear for autographs and photos throughout the day; guidebooks at the entrances give times and places. You can also meet some of the animated icons at one of the character meals served at the three Disney hotels (open to the public).

You can store belongings in lockers just off Main Street; purchases can also be sent to the package-pickup desk, at the front of the park. Main Street stays open an hour after the attractions close, so you may want to save your shopping for the end of your visit. ■ TIP→ **If you plan to visit for more than a day, you can save money by buying three- and four-day Park Hopper tickets that grant same-day "hopping" privileges between Disneyland and Disney's California Adventure.** ⊠ *1313 Harbor Blvd., Anaheim* ☎ *714/ 781–4565* ⊕ *www.disneyland.com* ✉ *$59* ⊘ *Daily year-round; longer hrs weekends, holidays, and summer. Call for specific times.*

★ ☺ The sprawling 55-acre **Disney's California Adventure,** right next to Disneyland (their entrances face each other), pays tribute to the Golden State with four theme areas. **Paradise Pier** re-creates the glory days of California's seaside piers. If you're looking for thrills, the **California Screamin'** roller coaster takes its riders from 0 to 55 mph in about four seconds and proceeds through scream tunnels, steeply angled drops, and a 360-degree loop. The Sun Wheel, a giant Ferris wheel, provides a good view of the grounds at a more leisurely pace.

At the **Hollywood Pictures Backlot,** Disney Animation gives you an insider's look at the work of animators and how they create characters. **Turtle Talk with Crush** lets kids have an unrehearsed talk with computer-animated Crush, a sea turtle from *Finding Nemo.* The Hyperion theater hosts **Aladdin—A Musical Spectacular,** a 45-minute live performance with terrific visual effects. ■ TIP→ **Plan on getting in line about an hour in advance: the show is well worth the wait.** On the latest film-inspired ride, **Monsters, Inc. Mike & Sulley to the Rescue,** you climb into taxis and travel the streets of Monstropolis on a mission of safely returning Boo to her bedroom. A major draw for older kids is the looming *Twilight Zone Tower of Terror,* which drops riders 13 floors.

A bug's land, inspired by the 1998 film *A Bug's Life,* skews its attractions to an insect's point of view. Kids can cool off (or get soaked) in the water jets and giant garden hose of Princess Dot Puddle Park, or hit the pill bug–shaped bumper cars. The short show *It's Tough to Be a Bug!* gives you a 3-D look at insect life.

Golden State celebrates California's history and natural beauty with six regions, including the Bay Area, Pacific Wharf, and Condor Flats, where you can enjoy Soarin' Over California, a spectacular simulated hang-glider ride over California terrain. The film *Golden Dreams* is a sentimental dash through California history with Whoopi Goldberg. There's also a working 1-acre farm and winery, a 40,000-square-foot animation exhibit, Broadway-style theater, nature trail, and tortilla factory. Like its sister park, California Adventure has a parade every day. ⊠ *1313 Harbor Blvd., Anaheim* ☎ *714/781–4565* ⊕ *www.disneyland.com* ✉ *$59* ⊘ *Daily year-round; longer hrs weekends, holidays, and summer. Call for specific times.*

Downtown Disney is a 20-acre promenade of dining, shopping, and entertainment that connects the Disneyland Resort hotels and theme parks. Restaurant-nightclubs here include the **House of Blues,** which spices up its Delta-inspired ribs and seafood with various live music acts on an intimate two-story stage. At **Ralph Brennan's Jazz Kitchen** you can dig into New Orleans–style food and music. Sports fans gravitate to **ESPN Zone,** a sports bar–restaurant–entertainment center with American grill food, interactive video games, and 175 video screens telecasting worldwide sports events. There's also an **AMC** multiplex movie theater with stadium-style seating that plays the latest blockbusters and, naturally, a couple of kids' flicks. Promenade shops sell everything from Disney goods to fine art. ⊠ *Disneyland Dr. between Ball Rd. and Katella Ave., Anaheim* ☎ *714/300–7800* ⊕ *www.disneyland.com* ⊠ *Free* ☉ *Daily 7 AM–2 AM; hrs at shops and restaurants vary.*

Where to Stay & Eat

The Anaheim area has more than 50,000 rooms in hotels, family-style inns, and RV parks. ■ **TIP→ One handy perk of staying in a Disney hotel: you can charge anything you buy in either park, such as food and souvenirs, to your room, so you don't have to carry around a lot of cash. (This doesn't hold true for Downtown Disney, though.)**

An Anaheim Resort Transit (ART) bus can take you around town for $3. The buses run every 10 minutes during peak times, 20 minutes otherwise. They go between major hotels, Disney attractions, the Anaheim Convention Center, and restaurants and shops. See the ART Web site (⊕ www.rideart.org) for more information. In addition, many hotels are within walking distance of the Disneyland Resort.

Unlike Disneyland, which is dry, Disney's California Adventure has restaurants that serve beer and wine. In addition, a small winery there has grapevines growing on the hillside and illustrations showing the transformation from grapes to wine.

$$$–$$$$ ✕ **Anaheim White House.** Several small dining rooms are set with crisp linens and candles in this flower-filled 1909 mansion. The northern Italian menu includes pasta, rack of lamb, and a large selection of fresh seafood. A three-course prix-fixe lunch, served weekdays, costs $16. ⊠ *887 S. Anaheim Blvd., Anaheim* ☎ *714/772–1381* ⊟ *AE, MC, V* ☉ *No lunch weekends.*

★ **$$$–$$$$** ✕ **Napa Rose.** In sync with its host hotel, this restaurant is done in a lovely Arts and Crafts style. The contemporary cuisine here is matched with an extensive wine list (600 bottles on display). For a look into the open kitchen, sit at the counter and watch the chefs as they whip up signature dishes such as Gulf of California rock scallops in a sauce of lemon, lobster, and vanilla and spit-roasted prime rib of pork with ranch-style black beans. A four-course prix-fixe menu ($75 without wine, $120 with wine) changes weekly. ⊠ *Grand Californian Hotel, 1600 S. Disneyland Dr.* ☎ *714/300–7170* ⊟ *AE, D, DC, MC, V.*

$$–$$$ ✕ **Catal Restaurant & Uva Bar.** Famed chef Joachim Splichal takes a more casual approach at this bilevel Mediterranean spot—with tapas breaking into the finger-food territory. At the Uva (Spanish for "grape") bar on the ground level you can graze on olives and Spanish ham, choosing from 40 wines by the glass. Upstairs, Catal's menu spans paella, rotisserie chicken, and salads. ⊠ *1580 Disneyland Dr., Suite 103, Downtown Disney* ☎ *714/774–4442* ⊟ *AE, D, DC, MC, V.*

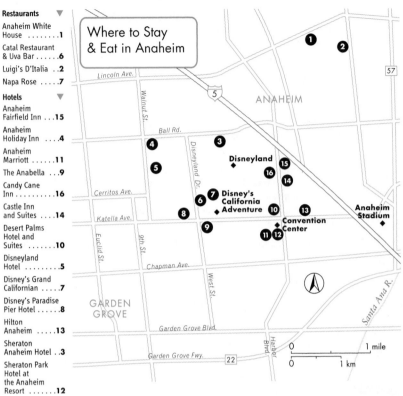

Where to Stay
& Eat in Anaheim

$–$$ ✕ **Luigi's D'Italia.** Despite the simple surroundings——red vinyl booths and
plastic checkered tablecloths——Luigi's serves outstanding Italian cuisine: spaghetti marinara, cioppino, and all the classics. Kids will feel right
at home here; there's even a children's menu. ⊠ *801 S. State College
Blvd., Anaheim* ☎ *714/490–0990* ▭ *AE, D, DC, MC, V.*

$$$–$$$$ 🏨 **Disney's Grand Californian.** The newest of Disney's Anaheim hotels,
Fodor'sChoice this Craftsman-style luxury property has guest rooms with views of the
★ California Adventure park and Downtown Disney. They don't push the
Disney brand too heavily; rooms are done in dark woods with amber-
shaded lamps and just a small Bambi image on the shower curtain. Restau-
rants include the Napa Rose dining room, Hearthstone Lounge, and
Storytellers Cafe, where Disney characters entertain children at break-
fast. Of the three pools, the one shaped like Mickey Mouse is just for
kids, and there's an evening child activity center. Room-and-ticket pack-
ages are available; the hotel has its own entry gate to California Adven-
ture. The new Mandara spa has a couple's suite with Balinese-inspired
art and textiles. ⊠ *1600 S. Disneyland Dr., Disneyland Resort, 92803*
☎ *714/956–6425* 🖷 *714/300–7701* ⊕ *www.disneyland.com* ⇌ *701
rooms, 44 suites ⚹ 2 restaurants, room service, in-room safes, minibars,
cable TV, in-room broadband, pool, health club, hot tub, 2 lounges, video
game room, shop, children's programs (ages 5–12), dry cleaning, laun-*

dry service, concierge, business services, parking (fee); no smoking 🖃 *AE, D, DC, MC, V.*

$$$–$$$$ 🏨 **Hilton Anaheim.** Next to the Anaheim Convention Center, this busy Hilton is the largest hotel in Southern California: it even has its own post office, as well as shops, restaurants, and cocktail lounges. Rooms are pleasingly bright, and a shuttle runs to Disneyland, or you can walk the few blocks. Special summer children's programs include the "Vacation Station Lending Desk," with games, toys, and books, as well as children's menus. There's a $12 fee to use the health club. ✉ *777 Convention Way, Downtown Anaheim, 92802* ☎ *714/750–4321 or 800/445–8667* 🖷 *714/740–4460* ⊕ *www.anaheim.hilton.com* 🛏 *1,492 rooms, 95 suites* 🍴 *4 restaurants, room service, cable TV with movies, Wi-Fi, pool, health club, hot tub, massage, sauna, 2 lounges, piano, children's programs (ages 3–12), laundry service, concierge, business services, meeting rooms, car rental, travel services, parking (fee), no-smoking floor* 🖃 *AE, D, DC, MC, V.*

$$$ 🏨 **Disneyland Hotel.** Not surprisingly, the first of Disney's three hotels is the one most full of Magic Kingdom magic, with Disney-theme memorabilia and Disney music. Check out the Peter Pan–theme pool, with its wooden bridge, 110-foot waterslide, and relaxing whirlpool. The cove pools' sandy shores are great for sunning and playing volleyball. East-facing rooms in the Sierra Tower have the best views of the park, whereas west-facing rooms look over gardens. At Goofy's Kitchen, kids can dine with Disney characters. Room-and-ticket packages are available. ✉ *1150 Magic Way, Disneyland Resort, 92802* ☎ *714/778–6600* 🖷 *714/956–6582* ⊕ *www.disneyland.com* 🛏 *990 rooms, 62 suites* 🍴 *5 restaurants, café, room service, in-room safes, minibars, cable TV, in-room broadband, 3 pools, health club, hot tub, massage, sauna, spa, beach, 2 bars, video game room, children's programs (ages 5–12), laundry service, concierge, business services, airport shuttle, car rental, parking (fee); no smoking* 🖃 *AE, D, DC, MC, V.*

$$$ 🏨 **Disney's Paradise Pier Hotel.** The Paradise Pier has many of the same Disney touches as the Disneyland Hotel, but it's a bit quieter and tamer. From here you can walk to Disneyland or pick up a shuttle or monorail. SoCal style manifests itself in seafoam-green guest rooms with lamps shaped like lifeguard stands, and surfboard motifs. A new wooden roller-coaster-inspired waterslide takes adventurers to a high-speed splashdown. Room-and-ticket packages are available. ✉ *1717 S. Disneyland Dr., Disneyland Resort, 92802* ☎ *714/999–0990* 🖷 *714/776–5763* ⊕ *www.disneyland.com* 🛏 *502 rooms, 38 suites* 🍴 *3 restaurants, room service, in-room safes, minibars, cable TV, in-room broadband pool, wading pool, health club, 2 lounges, video game room, children's programs (ages 5–12), dry cleaning, laundry service, concierge, business services, parking (fee); no smoking* 🖃 *AE, D, DC, MC, V.*

$$–$$$ 🏨 **Anaheim Marriott.** Rooms at this busy convention hotel are well equipped for business travelers, with desks, two phones, and data ports. Some rooms have balconies. Discounted weekend and Disneyland packages are available. ✉ *700 W. Convention Way, Anaheim 92802* ☎ *714/750–8000 or 800/228–9290* 🖷 *714/750–9100* ⊕ *www.marriott.com* 🛏 *1,031 rooms, 52 suites* 🍴 *2 restaurants, room service, in-room safes, cable TV with movies, in-room data ports, 2 pools, health club, 2 hot* *tubs, lounge, piano, video game room, laundry facilities, laundry service, concierge, meeting rooms, car rental, parking (fee), some pets allowed (fee), no-smoking floors, Internet* ⊟ *AE, D, DC, MC, V.*

★ **$$–$$$** 🏨 **Sheraton Anaheim Hotel.** If you're hoping to escape from the commercial atmosphere of the hotels near Disneyland, consider this sprawling replica of a Tudor castle. In the flower- and plant-filled lobby you're welcome to sit by the grand fireplace, watching fish swim around in a pond. Rooms are sizable; some first-floor rooms open onto interior gardens and a pool area. A shuttle to Disneyland is available. ⊠ *900 S. Disneyland Dr., Anaheim 92802* ☎ *714/778–1700 or 800/325–3535* 🖷 *714/535–3889* ⊕ *www.starwoodhotels.com* ↪ *447 rooms, 26 suites* ♿ *Restaurant, café, room service, cable TV with movies and video games, in-room data ports, pool, health club, outdoor hot tub, bar, video game room, laundry facilities, laundry service, meeting rooms, parking (fee), no-smoking rooms* ⊟ *AE, D, DC, MC, V.*

$–$$ 🏨 **The Anabella.** This Spanish Mission–style hotel is across from Disneyland Resort on the convention center campus. The hotel's Oasis, with a hot tub and pool, plus an adults-only pool, is a perfect place for relaxing. The Tangerine Grill and Patio serves a fantastic tangerine cheesecake. ⊠ *1030 W. Katella Ave., Anaheim 92802* ☎ *714/905–1050 or 800/863–4888* 🖷 *714/905–1054* ⊕ *www.anabellahotel.com* ↪ *359 rooms* ♿ *Restaurant, room service, in-room safes, refrigerators, TV with movies and video games, in-room data ports, 2 pools, health club, outdoor hot tub, lounge, laundry facilities, laundry service, concierge floor, business services, free parking* ⊟ *AE, D, DC, MC, V.*

★ **$–$$** 🏨 **Candy Cane Inn.** One of the Disneyland area's first hotels (deeds were executed Christmas Eve, hence the name), the Candy Cane is one of Anaheim's most relaxing properties. Rooms are spacious and understated, and the palm-fringed pool is especially inviting. The hotel is just steps from the Disneyland parking lot. A free Disneyland shuttle runs every half hour. ⊠ *1747 S. Harbor Blvd., Anaheim 92802* ☎ *714/774–5284 or 800/345–7057* 🖷 *714/772–5462* ⊕ *www.candycaneinn.net* ↪ *170 rooms* ♿ *Refrigerators, cable TV, pool, wading pool, outdoor hot tub, laundry facilities, laundry service, free parking, no-smoking rooms* ⊟ *AE, D, DC, MC, V* ⊺◯⊺ *CP.*

$–$$ 🏨 **Sheraton Park Hotel at the Anaheim Resort.** Sheraton took over this hotel in 2006 and freshened up the decor in guest rooms and public spaces. Rooms have balconies, and those in the tower have good views of Disneyland's summer fireworks shows. You can also relax in the nicely landscaped outdoor area or take a dip in the oversize pool. ⊠ *1855 S. Harbor Blvd., Anaheim 92802* ☎ *714/750–1811 or 800/716–6199* 🖷 *714/971–3626* ⊕ *www.sheraton.com* ↪ *490 rooms* ♿ *Restaurant, coffee shop, room service, refrigerators, cable TV with movies and video games, in-room broadband, pool, outdoor hot tub, lounge, laundry service, meeting room, car rental, parking (fee), no-smoking floor* ⊟ *AE, D, DC, MC, V.*

$ 🏨 **Anaheim Fairfield Inn by Marriott.** A chain hotel with character, the Anaheim Fairfield provides friendly, detail-oriented service and spacious rooms, most with sleeper sofas as well as beds. A five-minute walk gets you to Disneyland. In summer keep an eye out for the magician who

2

roams the premises, entertaining adults and kids alike. ⊠ *1460 S. Harbor Blvd., Anaheim 92802* ☎ *714/772–6777 or 800/228–2800* 🖷 *714/ 999–1727* ⊕ *www.marriott.com* 🖙 *467 rooms* ⚬ *Restaurant, room service, some microwaves, refrigerators, cable TV with movies, pool, outdoor hot tub, recreation room, travel services, free parking, no-smoking floor* 🖃 *AE, D, DC, MC, V.*

$ 🏨 **Castle Inn and Suites.** Faux-stone trim and towers, shield decor, and replica gas lamps dress up the Castle Inn, which is across the street from Disneyland. Suites have microwaves. ⊠ *1734 S. Harbor Blvd., Anaheim 92802* ☎ *714/774–8111* 🖷 *714/956–4736* ⊕ *www.castleinn.com* 🖙 *150 rooms, 50 suites* ⚬ *Some in-room hot tubs, some microwaves, refrigerators, cable TV, pool, wading pool, outdoor hot tub, laundry facilities, laundry service, free parking, no-smoking rooms* 🖃 *AE, D, DC, MC, V.*

$ 🏨 **Desert Palms Hotel and Suites.** This hotel midway between Disneyland and the convention center is a great value, with some $79 one-bedroom suites that can accommodate a group of four or more. Book well in advance, especially when large conventions are in town. ⊠ *631 W. Katella Ave., Anaheim 92802* ☎ *714/535–1133 or 888/788–0596* 🖷 *714/491– 7409* ⊕ *www.desertpalmshotel.com* 🖙 *50 rooms, 50 suites* ⚬ *Refrigerators, cable TV with movies, in-room broadband, pool, outdoor hot tub, video game room, laundry facilities, laundry service, free parking; no smoking* 🖃 *AE, D, DC, MC, V* ⏀❙ *CP.*

¢–$ 🏨 **Anaheim Holiday Inn.** The warmth of Old California is found in this Holiday Inn, where the walls are furnished with historic photos and water paths snake through the grounds. The residential location makes for quiet evenings. ⊠ *1240 S. Walnut Ave., Anaheim 92802* ☎ *714/535–0300 or 800/824–5459* 🖷 *714/491–8953* ⊕ *www.holidayinn-anaheim.com* 🖙 *255 rooms, 28 suites* ⚬ *Restaurant, room service, some microwaves, cable TV, pool, exercise equipment, outdoor hot tub, bar, video game room, laundry service, business services, meeting rooms, free parking, no-smoking rooms* 🖃 *AE, D, DC, MC, V.*

Nightlife

★ The little red roadhouse known as the **Doll Hut** (⊠ 107 S. Adams, Anaheim ☎ 714/533–1286) was once a truck stop between L.A. and San Diego. Southern California music booster Linda Jemison then turned it into a great place to hear about-to-break bands. In 2001 she turned it over to new owners, who are maintaining its rep for supporting up-and-comers and those below industry radar. Rockabilly, big-band, punk— no matter what kind of show is appearing, it will have a low cover.

Grove of Anaheim (⊠ 2200 E. Katella Ave. ☎ 714/712–2700 ⊕ www. thegroveofanaheim.com) is a midsize concert venue, which means nearly every seat is a good one. It books all kinds of bands and the occasional comedy act; the Gipsy Kings, Modest Mouse, Willie Nelson, and Blondie have all hit the stage here.

At the **House of Blues** (☎ 714/778–2583 ⊕ www.hob.com), in the Downtown Disney promenade, you can catch some of the best bands from the 1980s and '90s for a relatively low cover. The Southern-style restaurant has the fun Sunday Gospel Brunch. Shows often sell out.

Sports

Pro baseball's **Los Angeles Angels of Anaheim** play at Angel Stadium Anaheim (⊠ 2000 State College Blvd., East Anaheim ☎ 714/634–2000 ⊕ www.angelsbaseball.com). An "Outfield Extravaganza" celebrates great plays on the field, with fireworks and a geyser exploding over a model evoking the California coast. The National Hockey League's **Anaheim Ducks** play at Arrowhead Pond (⊠ 2695 E. Katella Ave., East Anaheim ☎ 714/704–2400 ⊕ www.mightyducks.com).

Knott's Berry Farm

25 mi south of Los Angeles, via I–5, in Buena Park

The land where the boysenberry was invented (by crossing red raspberry, blackberry, and loganberry bushes) is now occupied by Knott's Berry Farm. You can see the park in a day, but plan to start early and finish fairly late. Traffic can be heavy, so factor in time for delays. ■ TIP→ **It's a good idea to confirm the park's opening hours, which change relatively often.**

★ ☾ ❷ **Knott's Berry Farm** got its start in 1934, when Cordelia Knott began serving chicken dinners on her wedding china to supplement her family's income. Or so the story goes. The dinners and her boysenberry pies proved more profitable than husband Walter's berry farm, so the two moved first into the restaurant business and then into the entertainment business. The park is now a 150-acre complex with 100-plus rides and dozens of restaurants and shops. Although it has some good attractions for small children, the park is best known for its roster of awesome thrill rides. And, yes, you can still get that boysenberry pie (and jam, juice—you name it).

Old West Ghost Town is made up of authentic old buildings relocated from their original mining-town sites. You can stroll down the street, stop and chat with the blacksmith, pan for gold, crack open a geode, ride in an authentic 1880s passenger train, or take the **Gold Mine** ride and descend into a replica of a working gold mine. A real treasure here is the antique Dentzel carousel. **GhostRider** towers over it all; it's Orange County's first wooden roller coaster. Traveling up to 56 mph and reaching 118 feet at its highest point, the coaster is riddled with sudden dips and curves, subjecting riders to forces up to three times that of gravity. The **Timber Mountain Log Ride** is a worthwhile flume ride, especially if you're with kids who don't make the height requirements for the flumes at Disneyland.

Smaller fry will want to head straight for **Camp Snoopy,** a miniature High Sierra wonderland where the *Peanuts* gang hangs out. At nearby **Big Foot Rapids** you can ride white water in an inner tube. At the **Boardwalk,** you'll find the *Boomerang* roller coaster and the **Perilous Plunge,** billed as the world's tallest, steepest, and—thanks to its big splash—wettest thrill ride. The 1950s hot rod–theme **Xcelerator** launches you hydraulically into a supersteep U-turn, topping out at 205 feet. On the Western-theme **Silver Bullet,** riders are sent to a height of 146 feet and then back down 109 feet. Riders spiral, corkscrew, fly into a cobra roll, and experience overbanked curves. It's not for the squeamish. Over in **Fiesta**

2

Village are two more musts for adrenaline junkies: **Montezooma's Revenge,** a roller coaster that goes from 0 to 55 mph in less than five seconds, and **Jaguar!** which simulates the motions of a cat stalking its prey, twisting, spiraling, and speeding up and slowing down as it takes you on its stomach-dropping course.

Knott's Soak City Water Park is directly across from the main park and is on 13 acres in front of Independence Hall. It has 21 major water rides; the latest is **Pacific Spin,** an oversize waterslide that drops riders 75 feet into a catch pool. Soak City is only open late May through late September.

■ TIP→ **If you think you'll only need a few hours at the main park, you can save significant money by coming after 4 PM, when admission fees drop to $22.50. This deal is offered year-round.** ⊠ *8039 Beach Blvd., Buena Park, between La Palma Ave. and Crescent St., 2 blocks south of Hwy. 91* ☎ *714/220–5200* ⊕ *www.knotts.com* ☞ *$45* ⊙ *June–mid-Sept., daily 9 AM–midnight; mid-Sept.–May, weekdays 10–6, Sat. 10–10, Sun. 10–7; closed during inclement weather.*

Where to Stay & Eat

$$$$ ✕ **Pirate's Dinner Adventure.** During this interactive pirate-theme dinner show, 150 actors/singers/acrobats (some quite talented) perform on a galleon while you eat a three-course meal. Food is mediocre and seating is tight, but kids love making a lot of noise to cheer on their favorite pirate. ⊠ *7600 Beach Blvd., Buena Park* ☎ *866/439–2469* ⊟ *AE, D, MC, V.*

$$ ✕ **Mrs. Knott's Chicken Dinner Restaurant.** Cornelia Knott's fried chicken and boysenberry pies drew crowds so big that Knott's Berry Farm was built to keep the hungry customers occupied while they waited. The restaurant's current incarnation (outside the park's entrance) still serves crispy fried chicken, along with tangy coleslaw, and Mrs. Knott's signature chilled cherry-rhubarb compote. Long lines on weekends may make eating here not worth your time. ⊠ *Knott's Berry Farm, 8039 Beach Blvd., Buena Park* ☎ *714/220–5080* ⊟ *AE, D, DC, MC, V.*

$–$$ ⛆ **Knott's Berry Farm Resort Hotel.** The only hotel on the Knott's Berry Farm grounds has family-oriented "camp rooms" that are decorated in a Camp Snoopy motif. Shuttle service to Disneyland and nearby golf courses is available. Ask about packages that include entry to Knott's Berry Farm. ⊠ *7675 Crescent Ave., Buena Park 90620* ☎ *714/995–1111* ⛭ *714/828–8590* ⊕ *www.radisson.com* ↴ *320 rooms, 16 suites* ⛊ *Restaurant, room service, cable TV with movies and video games, Wi-Fi, tennis court, pool, health club, hot tub, basketball, bar, video game room, laundry facilities, concierge* ⊟ *AE, D, DC, MC, V.*

Garden Grove & Orange

South of Anaheim, via I–5 to Hwy. 22.

The city of Orange started as a legal fee; the parcel of land that became the town center was given to a pair of lawyers as payment for services back in 1871. The town square they staked out is now Orange Plaza (or Orange Circle, as locals call it), the heart of **Old Towne**

Orange, around the intersection of Glassell Street and Chapman Avenue. ■ TIP→ **The area is a must-stop for antiques browsers and architecture aficionados. You can scout out everything from antique armoires to flapper-era accessories to 1950s toys.** So vintage is this area that movies like *That Thing You Do!* (early roles for Liv Tyler and Charlize Theron) and *First Daughter* were filmed here. Locals take great pride in their many California Craftsman cottages; Christmas is a particularly lovely time to visit, when many of the area's homes are festooned with elaborate decorations.

Orange isn't all history, though. **Block at Orange** (⊠ 20 City Blvd., W. Orange ☎ 714/769–3800 ⊕ www.theblockatorange.com), a major mall complex near the Interstate 5 and Interstate 22 freeways, has a strong calling card in its **Vans Skatepark** (⊠ 1 City Blvd. ☎ 714/769–3800 ⊕www.vans.com), where skaters swoop through specially designed bowls and courses. You can rent boards, pads, and helmets to hit the ramps; there's a special area for kids and beginners.

❸ In Garden Grove the main attraction is the **Crystal Cathedral,** the domain of television evangelist Robert "*Hour of Power*" Schuller. Designed by the late architect Philip Johnson, the sparkling glass structure resembles a four-pointed star, with more than 10,000 panes of glass covering a weblike steel truss to form transparent walls. Two annual pageants, "The Glory of Christmas" and "The Glory of Easter," feature live animals, flying angels, and other special effects. ⊠ *12141 Lewis St. (take I–5 to Chapman Ave. W), Garden Grove* ☎ *714/971–4000* ⊕ *www. crystalcathedral.org* ✎ *Pageants $18–$40* ⊙ *Guided tours weekdays 9–3:30; call for schedule. Sun. services at 9:25 and 11:05.*

Where to Stay & Eat

★ **$$–$$$$** ✕ **La Brasserie.** You'll find the perennial elements of a fine French restaurant here: a warm welcome, a softly lighted dining room with oil paintings, and classic fare. You could start with vichyssoise or terrine of foie gras before sampling the chef's veal special. ⊠ *202 S. Main St., Orange* ☎ *714/978–6161* ▭ *AE, DC, MC, V* ⊙ *Closed Sun.*

$$–$$$ ✕ **Citrus City Grille.** The surroundings may be Old Towne, but the menu certainly isn't. Choices range from vegetable spring rolls to pot roast, but the roast duck and Chilean sea bass are particular standouts. The inviting half-moon bar is a surefire lively gathering place. ⊠ *122 N. Glassell St., Orange* ☎ *714/639–9600* ▭ *AE, D, DC, MC, V* ⊙ *Closed Sun.*

$$ ✕ **PJ's Abbey.** Locals come to this 1891 former Baptist church to enjoy American favorites such as pork chops with garlic-mashed potatoes, rack of lamb, and fresh-baked desserts. ⊠ *182 S. Orange St., Old Towne Orange* ☎ *714/771–8556* ▭ *AE, D, DC, MC, V* ⊙ *Closed Mon.*

$ ✕ **Felix Continental Cafe.** Facing Orange Circle's park, Felix's serves Cuban and Spanish dishes. The casual spot fills up for lunch and early dinners; try for an outdoor table and order up a chicken special with garlicky *mojo* sauce. ⊠ *36 Plaza Sq., Orange* ☎ *714/633–5842* ▭ *AE, DC, MC, V.*

¢–$ ✕ **Thanh My Restaurant.** Though frill-free, one of Little Saigon's oldest restaurants offers a deliciously wide range of Vietnamese cuisine. Try the hot pot: it comes boiling to the table, and then you add fish, vegetables, spices or the fresh egg rolls. It's also a good idea to ask your server for suggestions (and for a gauge of how spicy the dishes will be). ✉ *9553 Bolsa Ave., Westminster* ☎ *714/531–9540* ▤ *AE, MC, V.*

$–$$ ▣ **Doubletree Hotel Anaheim/Orange.** This contemporary 20-story hotel has a dramatic lobby of marble and granite, with waterfalls cascading down the walls. The hotel is near the Block, Anaheim Stadium, and the Anaheim Convention Center. ✉ *100 The City Dr., Orange 92868* ☎ *714/ 634–4500 or 800/222–8733* ☐ *714/978–3839* ⊕ *www.doubletreehotels. com* ⟿ *454 rooms, 11 suites* ⚐ *Restaurant, cable TV with movies, in-room broadband, pool, health club, bar, concierge floor, meeting rooms, parking (fee), no-smoking rooms* ▤ *AE, D, DC, MC, V.*

Santa Ana

12 mi south of Anaheim, via I–5 to Hwy. 55.

🐣 **④** The main attraction in the county seat is the **Bowers Museum of Cultural Art.** Permanent exhibits include Pacific Northwest wood carvings; bead-work of the Plains cultures; clothing, cooking utensils, and silver-adorned saddles used on early California ranches; and California impressionist paintings. Special exhibits such as a show of Egyptian mummies rotate through on a regular basis. As of this writing, a new wing was due to open in fall 2006, with a 300-seat auditorium and an Asian art gallery. The **Bowers Kidseum** (✉ 1802 N. Main St.) has interactive exhibits geared toward kids ages 6 to 12, in addition to classes, storytelling, and arts-and-crafts workshops. Admission is included in the general museum ticket. ✉ *2002 N. Main St., off I–5, Santa Ana* ☎ *714/567–3600* ⊕ *www. bowers.org* ▤ *$17; free on 2nd and 4th Tues.* ☉ *Tues.–Sun. 11–6.*

Where to Eat

★ **$–$$** ✕ **Zov's Bistro.** There's a well-worn path to both sides of Zov's. The restaurant out front prepares bistro favorites with a deft Middle Eastern spin, such as rack of lamb with pomegranate sauce or chicken *geras* (stuffed with wild rice and almonds, with sour cherry sauce). Go around back and you'll find a separate café and bakery filled with locals picking up fresh-baked pastries or deciding between the sirloin burger or mezes (appetizers) for lunch. Both sides have patio tables. The restaurant is just on the other side of the Highway 55 freeway from Santa Ana; take the 17th Street exit. ✉ *Enderle Center, 17440 E. 17th St., Tustin* ☎ *714/ 838–8855* ▤ *AE, D, DC, MC, V.*

$ ✕ **Tangata.** Inside the Bowers Museum, this eatery has a menu overseen by owner-executive chef Joachim Splichal. Choose among salads, pastas, soups, French-style roasted chicken, lamb shank over polenta, and tasty desserts. Dine on the patio or, in the main dining room, watch the "chef theater." ✉ *2002 N. Main St., Santa Ana* ☎ *714/550–0906* ▤ *AE, D, DC, MC, V* ☉ *Closed Mon. No dinner.*

Nightlife & the Arts

The 500-seat **OC Pavilion** theater opened in 2005; its performance slate ranges from comedians to Kenny G to Kool & The Gang. State-of-the-art acoustics and comfortable, wide seats are pluses. There are also a jazz lounge and a posh contemporary restaurant. ✉ *801 N. Main St., Santa Ana* ☎ *714/550–0880* ⊕ *www.ocpavilion.com.*

Toward Cleveland National Forest

4 mi east of Santa Ana.

Need a breath of nonurban air? Back in the eastern part of the county, the housing sprawl peters out into beautiful, still largely open country, a mix of parkland and privately held areas. A few two-lane, gently winding roads reach into these toast-color hills, heading toward the Cleveland National Forest. The main roads are named for the canyons they follow: Santiago, Modjeska, and Silverado. It's chaparral country, with dry grasses, hawks overhead, stands of live oak, and the smell of coastal sage. While development is creeping in, especially along Santiago Canyon Road, the canyons are known for their small, fiercely independent communities of longtime residents. ⚠ **Santiago is also a favorite for cyclists, so watch for them on the shoulder of the road.**

Driving along Santiago Canyon Road from the border of Orange, you'll pass Irvine Lake, a reservoir, on your left. The road dips and curves for a few miles before you'll reach an intersection with Silverado Canyon Road branching off to the left. Silverado Canyon Road is the usual entry point to **Cleveland National Forest** (☎ 909/736–1811 ⊕ www.fs.fed.us/ r5/cleveland). However, the road is sometimes closed due to fire risk or for environmental reasons; always call ahead. Also, check with the ranger station about any activities you may have in mind: you may need to get a day pass.

Irvine

6 mi south of Santa Ana, via Hwy. 55 to I–405, 12 mi south of Anaheim, via I–5.

Irvine—characterized by its rows of large, cream-color tract homes, tree-lined streets, uniformly manicured lawns, and pristine parks—may feel strange to people not used to such uniformity. The master-planned community has top-notch schools, a university and a community college, dozens of shopping centers, and a network of well-lighted walking and biking paths.

❺ Some of the Californian impressionist paintings on display at the small yet intriguing **Irvine Museum** depict the state's rural landscape in the years before massive freeways and sprawling housing developments. The paintings, which are displayed on the 12th floor of the cylindrical marble-and-glass Tower 17 building, were assembled by Joan Irvine Smith, granddaughter of James Irvine, who once owned a quarter of what is now Orange County. ✉ *18881 Von Karman Ave., at Martin St. north of UC Irvine campus, Irvine* ☎ *949/476–2565* ⊕ *www.irvinemuseum. org* ☑ *Free* ☉ *Tues.–Sat. 11–5.*

❻ The **University of California at Irvine** (UCI) was established on 1,000 acres of rolling ranch land donated by the Irvine family in the mid-1950s. The campus contains more than 11,000 trees from around the world and features a stellar biological science department and creative-writing program. The **Irvine Barclay Theater** (☎ 949/854–4646 ⊕ www. thebarclay.org) presents an impressive roster of music, dance, and dra-

2

matic events, and there's not a bad seat in the house. The **Art Gallery at UC Irvine** (☎ 949/824–3508 ⊕ beallcenter.uci.edu) sponsors exhibitions of student and professional art. The **Beall Center for Art & Technology** (☎ 949/824–4339 ⊕ beallcenter.uci.edu) shows the works of emerging international artists. The center and the gallery are both open from mid-September to mid-June, Tuesday and Wednesday noon to 5 and Thursday to Saturday noon to 8. ⊠ *I–405 to Jamboree Rd., west to Campus Dr. S, Irvine* ☎ *949/824–5011* ⊕ *www.uci.edu.*

Wild Rivers Water Park has more than 40 rides and attractions, including a wave pool, daring slides, and a river inner-tube ride. ⊠ *8770 Irvine Center Dr., off I–405, Irvine* ☎ *949/768–9453* ⊕ *www.wildrivers.com* ☝ *$29* ☉ *Late May–Sept.; call for hrs.*

Where to Stay & Eat

$$–$$$ ✕ **Bistango.** A sleek, art-filled bistro serves first-rate American cuisine with a European flair: salads, steak, seafood, pasta, and pizzas. Try the tuna grilled rare. An attractive group comes to savor the food, listen to live jazz, and mingle with well-dressed peers (book ahead). There's live entertainment seven nights a week and a happy hour on weekdays 5 to 7. ⊠ *19100 Von Karman Ave., Irvine, near John Wayne/ Orange County Airport* ☎ *949/752–5222* ▤ *AE, D, DC, MC, V* ☉ *No lunch weekends.*

$$–$$$ ✕ **Il Fornaio.** Two weeks a month, regional dishes from Tuscany or Puglia supplement the regular fare—house-made pastas, pizza, veal scallopine, succulent grilled eggplant with goat cheese—at this airy Italian chain eatery. ■ TIP➡ **This branch stands out by virtue of its pair of boccie courts; borrow a boccie set and play a game before your meal.** ⊠ *18051 Von Karman Ave., Irvine* ☎ *949/261–1444* ▤ *AE, D, DC, MC, V* ☉ *No lunch Sun.*

★ $$–$$$ ✕ **Prego.** Reminiscent of a Tuscan villa, this is a much larger version of the Beverly Hills Prego, with soft lighting, golden walls, and an outdoor patio. Try the spit-roasted meats and chicken, charcoal-grilled fresh fish, or pizzas from the oak-burning oven. California and Italian wines are reasonably priced. ⊠ *18420 Von Karman Ave., Irvine* ☎ *949/553– 1333* ▤ *AE, D, DC, MC, V* ☉ *No lunch weekends.*

$–$$ ✕ **Kitima Thai Cuisine.** Tucked away on the ground floor of an office building, this small, reliable Thai restaurant is a favorite with the business-lunch crowd. Try Bangkok duck and cashew chicken; the kitchen will regulate the spiciness depending on your heat tolerance. ⊠ *2010 Main St., Suite 170, Irvine* ☎ *949/261–2929* ▤ *AE, DC, MC, V* ☉ *Closed Sun.*

$$$–$$$$ ▣ **Irvine Marriott John Wayne Airport.** Towering over Koll Business Center, the Marriott offers a convenient location and amenities designed to appeal to business travelers. Despite its size, the hotel has an intimate feel, due in part to the convivial lobby and evening entertainment. There's a courtesy van to South Coast Plaza and the airport. ⊠ *18000 Von Karman Ave., Irvine 92612* ☎ *949/553–0100 or 800/228–9290* ☏ *949/261–7059* ⊕ *www.marriott.com* ⇖ *485 rooms, 10 suites ♢ 3 restaurants, cable TV with movies, Wi-Fi, 2 tennis courts, pool, health club, hot tub, business services, meeting rooms, airport shuttle* ▤ *AE, D, DC, MC, V.*

$$$ 🏨 **Fairmont Newport Beach.** An eye-catching ziggurat design is the trademark of this modern hotel in Koll Center. Bought by Fairmont in 2005, the hotel's undergone some long-needed refurbishment. Guest rooms and public spaces are now done in rich chocolate, gold, and carnation red; the heated pool is now surrounded by cabanas. Although technically in Newport Beach, the hotel is near John Wayne Airport. ⊠ *4500 MacArthur Blvd., Newport Beach 92660* 🕾 *949/476–2001 or 800/243–4141* 🖷 *949/476–0153* ⊕ *www.fairmont.com* 🛏 *444 rooms, 50 suites ⌂ 2 restaurants, cable TV with movies, in-room broadband, 2 tennis courts, pool, health club, bar, concierge, business services, airport shuttle* ▭ *AE, D, DC, MC, V.*

$–$$$ 🏨 **Hyatt Regency Irvine.** The sleek, ultramodern rooms here offer practical amenities such as coffeemakers, irons, and hair dryers. Special golf packages at nearby Oak Creek and Pelican Hills are available. In 2006 a restaurant opened, 6ix Park Grill, run by Yves Fournier, as did bar8. ⊠ *17900 Jamboree Rd., near John Wayne/Orange County Airport, Irvine 92614* 🕾 *949/975–1234 or 800/233–1234* 🖷 *949/852–1574* ⊕ *www.hyatt.com* 🛏 *536 rooms, 21 suites ⌂ 2 restaurants, cable TV with movies, Wi-Fi, 4 tennis courts, pool, health club, bicycles, babysitting, 2 bars, concierge, business services* ▭ *AE, D, DC, MC, V.*

Nightlife

It's worth checking the performance schedules at the UCI venues (*above*), as they consistently bring in interesting acts.

☾ The 32-acre **Entertainment Center at Irvine Spectrum** contains a huge, 21-theater cinema complex (with a six-story IMAX 3-D theater), several lively restaurants (including Crazy Horse Nightclub, a local bastion of country music) and cafés, and 150 shops, as well as a Giant Wheel and carousel. Other highlights are Dave and Buster's, with games for kids, and the Improv, for adult comedy. ⊠ *Exit Irvine Center Dr. at intersection of I–405, I–5, and Hwy. 133, Irvine* 🕾 *949/450–4900 film listings* ⊕ *www.irvinespectrum.com.*

The **Verizon Wireless Amphitheater** (⊠ 8808 Irvine Center Dr., Irvine 🕾 949/855–8095 or 949/855–6111), a 16,300-seat open-air venue, presents musical events April through October.

Costa Mesa

6 mi northeast of Irvine, via I–405 to Bristol St.

Though it's probably best known for its shopping malls, Costa Mesa is also the performing-arts hub of Orange County, and a formidable local business center. Patrons of the domestic and international theater, opera, and dance productions fill area restaurants and nightspots. Movie buffs have several theaters to choose from, too.

If you look at the where-to-buy listings in the bottom of couture ads in glossy magazines, you'll often see, sandwiched between listings of shops in Paris and Tokyo, the name of Costa Mesa's most famous landmark,

★ ❼ **South Coast Plaza.** This immense complex gets ritzier by the year as international designer boutiques jostle for platinum-card space. The original section has the densest concentration of shops: Gucci, Armani,

Burberry, La Perla, Hermès, Versace, Chloe, and Prada. All the familiar mall names are here, too, from Sunglass Hut to Banana Republic. One standout is the excellent bookstore Book Soup. Major department stores, including Saks and Nordstrom, flank the exterior. A pedestrian bridge crosses Bear Street to the second wing, a smaller offshoot with a huge Crate & Barrel. ✉ *3333 S. Bristol St., off I-405, Costa Mesa* ☎ *714/435-2000* ⊕ *www.southcoastplaza.com* ⊗ *Weekdays 10-9, Sat. 10-7, Sun. 11-6:30.*

South Coast Plaza has gradually become surrounded by other shopping complexes with different twists. Across Sunflower Avenue is an outdoor shopping area called South Coast Plaza Village (technically in Santa Ana), while on the other side of Bear Street is Metro Pointe, a conglomerate mass of supersize, often bargain-oriented stores. Farther down Bristol on the other side of Interstate 405 you'll find SoBeCa (short for South on Bristol Entertainment, Culture & Arts), which is a more subculture- and youth-oriented area, anchored by the **Lab** (✉ 2930 Bristol St., Costa Mesa ⊕ www.sobeca.net or www.thelab.com), also known as the antimall. After a weakish start, the Lab now has funky shops, trendy restaurants, and places to hang out. Mull it over with a coffee in the kitschy **Gypsy Den** or while browsing for hats at **Arth** (combines art and hat). For hard-to-find sneakers check out **Blends** and find cool clothes at **Carve.**

The **Camp** (✉ 2937 Bristol St. ⊕ www.thecampsite.net), another outdoor "retail community," takes a mellower, ecofriendly approach, devoting itself to sports-related stores like **Adventure 16** and **Cycle Werks.** There's **Native Foods,** a vegan restaurant, plus **Co-Op,** an art gallery. **Liburdi's Scuba Center** even has a small pool for instruction. Grab a snack from the **Village Bakery** and hang out in the grassy bowl.

Costa Mesa's role in consumer consumption is matched by its arts venues. The **Orange County Performing Arts Center** (✉ 600 Town Center Dr., east of Bristol St. ☎ 714/556-2787) houses Segerstrom Hall for opera, ballet, symphony, and musicals and the more intimate Founders Hall for chamber music. Richard Lippold's enormous *Firebird,* an angular sculpture of polished metal that resembles a bird taking flight, extends outward from the glass-enclosed lobby. A new, 2,000-square-foot concert hall and 500-seat theater is set to open in fall 2006. Across a courtyard from the original center, the new glass-fronted concert hall will host the Orange County Philharmonic, while the theater will focus on jazz and cabaret concerts. Across the way is the highly regarded South Coast Repertory Theater (⇨ Nightlife & the Arts, *below*).

★ Tucked between mirror-glass office towers near the Performing Arts Center is the **California Scenario** (✉ 611 Anton Blvd.), a 1½-acre sculpture garden designed by Isamu Noguchi, who carved this compact space into distinct areas with his abstract designs. Each represents an aspect of the state's terrain. Smooth granite boulders punctuate the sweep of flat stone paving. A pine tree–trimmed grassy slope faces a circular area planted with cacti and a sunken stream curls toward a low stone pyramid. ■ TIP→ **The garden can be hard to find—it's a block from the South Coast Repertory Theater, by the Chat Noir restaurant—but it's well worth the effort.**

Where to Stay & Eat

$$–$$$$ ╳ **Morton's of Chicago.** Hearty eaters flock to this wood-panel eatery, the quintessential steak house, for huge portions of prime aged beef and fresh seafood. During the week check out happy hour to soften the blow of the check. The soft lighting contrasts with all the noise. ⊠ *South Coast Plaza Village, 1661 W. Sunflower Ave., Santa Ana* ☎ *714/444–4834* ⊟ *AE, DC, MC, V* ⊘ *No lunch weekends.*

★ **$$–$$$**   ╳ **Troquet.** The Chanel and Hermès boutiques of South Coast Plaza's main pavilion are in good company with this burnished French bistro. Soft lighting, a low-key atmosphere, and a perch one story above the shopping fray should encourage you to take your time with the menu. Classics like steak tartare and roast duck breast get a fresh slant with accompaniments like baby bok choy with a ginger-orange reduction sauce. ■ TIP➔ The prix-fixe menus at lunch and dinner are comparative bargains here. ⊠ *South Coast Plaza, 3333 Bristol St., Costa Mesa* ☎ *714/708–6865* ⊟ *AE, MC, V.*

★ **$–$$**   ╳ **Bangkok IV.** This restaurant's elegant interior, with striking flower arrangements on every table, defies conventional mall dining. The deep-fried catfish with a chili-garlic-lemongrass sauce is exceptional. You may also want to give the Thai noodle dishes a try. ⊠ *South Coast Plaza, 3333 Bear St., Costa Mesa* ☎ *714/540–7661* ⊟ *AE, D, DC, MC, V.*

$–$$ ╳ **Habana Restaurant and Bar.** With rustic candelabras and murals in a candlelighted former industrial space, Habana serves up Cuban flavor with a hip modern flair. Chocolate lovers can't miss the Café Cubano—chocolate mousse topped with chocolate whipped cream and rum sauce. With entertainment two nights a week, this restaurant is a popular nightspot. ⊠ *The Lab, 2930 Bristol St., Costa Mesa* ☎ *714/556–0176* ⊟ *AE, D, MC, V.*

$$$ ▥ **Hilton Costa Mesa.** At this spacious hotel you can stay near John Wayne Airport without the air traffic sounding too close. In-room desks and business services make it a good stop if you're bound for the nearby office parks. ⊠ *3050 Bristol St., Costa Mesa 92626* ☎ *714/540–7000 or 800/445–8667* ⊟ *714/540–9176* ⊕ *www.hilton.com* ⊅ *486 rooms, 12 suites* � ♺ *Restaurant, cable TV with movies, Wi-Fi, pool, health club, hot tub, lobby lounge, laundry facilities, business services, meeting rooms* ⊟ *AE, D, DC, MC, V.*

$–$$$ ▥ **Country Inn and Suites.** The warm colors, art and antiques, and mahogany furniture help this hotel feel less corporate than some hotel chains. Refreshments are served in the evening Monday through Thursday. ⊠ *325 Bristol St., Costa Mesa 92626* ☎ *714/549–0300 or 800/322–9992* ⊟ *714/662–0828* ⊕ *www.ayreshotels.com* ⊅ *282 rooms* ♺ *Restaurant, some microwaves, refrigerators, cable TV with movies and video games, 2 pools, gym, 2 hot tubs, bar, laundry facilities, meeting rooms, airport shuttle* ⊟ *AE, D, DC, MC, V.*

$–$$$ ▥ **Westin South Coast Plaza.** This high-rise adjoins the South Coast Plaza complex—you can roll out of bed and hit the stores. The beds in these comfortably sized rooms come with feather duvets. The atmospheric restaurant, Pinot Provence, is a longtime local favorite, although sometimes the decor outshines the food. Tennis courts are nearby. ⊠ *686 Anton Blvd., Costa Mesa 92626* ☎ *714/540–2500 or 888/627–7213* ⊟ *714/ 662–6695* ⊕ *www.westin.com* ⊅ *391 rooms, 5 suites* ♺ *Restaurant,* *cable TV with movies, in-room broadband, pool, health club, business services, meeting rooms, some pets allowed* $\boxminus$ *AE, D, DC, MC, V.*

Nightlife & the Arts

★ The **Orange County Performing Arts Center** ($\boxtimes$ 600 Town Center Dr., Costa Mesa ☎ 714/556–2787 ⊕ www.ocpac.org) consistently presents impressively far-reaching arts performances. Companies such as the American Ballet Theater make annual appearances, as do the touring groups of major Broadway hits. Other highlights range from the Kirov Ballet to the Count Basie Orchestra to Tony Bennett. Within the Center, a jazz club in the 250-seat Founders Hall hosts performances with club-style seating on Friday and Saturday. *See above* for more details on the new performance spaces, due to open in fall 2006.

The **South Coast Repertory Theater** ($\boxtimes$ 655 Town Center Dr., Costa Mesa ☎ 714/708–5555 ⊕ www.scr.org) is a Tony Award–winning theater presenting new and traditional works on two stages.

THE COAST

Running along the Orange County coastline is scenic Pacific Coast Highway (Highway 1, known locally as PCH). Older beachfront settlements, with their modest bungalow-style homes, are joined by posh new gated communities. The pricey land between Newport Beach and Laguna Beach is where Laker Kobe Bryant, novelist Dean Koontz, and a slew of Internet and finance moguls live. Though the coastline is rapidly being filled in, there are still a few stretches of beautiful, protected open land. And at many places along the way you can catch an idealized glimpse of surfers hitting the beach, boards under their arms.

Huntington Beach

25 mi west of Anaheim, Hwy. 57 south to Hwy. 22 west to I–405; 40 mi southeast of Los Angeles, I–5 south to I–605 south to I–405 south to Beach Blvd.

Once a sleepy residential town with little more than a string of rugged surf shops, Huntington Beach has transformed itself into a resort destination. The town's appeal is its broad white-sand beaches with often-towering waves, complemented by a lively pier, shops, and restaurants on Main Street and the luxurious Hilton Waterfront Beach Resort and the Hyatt Regency. A draw for sports fans: the U.S. Open professional surf competition takes place here every July. Other top sporting events are the AVP Pro Beach Volleyball Tournament in August and the Core Tour Extreme BMX Skate Competition in September. There's even a Surfing Walk of Fame, with plaques set in the sidewalk around the intersection of the PCH and Main Street.

❽ **Huntington Pier** stretches 1,800 feet out to sea, well past the powerful waves that made Huntington Beach America's "Surf City." A farmers' market is held on Friday; an informal arts fair sets up most weekends. At the end of the pier sits **Ruby's** (☎ 714/969–7829), part of a California chain of 1940s-style burger joints. The **Pierside Pavilion** ($\boxtimes$ PCH across from Huntington Pier) has shops, restaurants, bars with live music, and a theater complex. The best surf-gear source is **Huntington Surf and Sport Pierside** (☎ 714/841–4000), staffed by true surf enthusiasts.

Just up Main Street from the pier, the **International Surfing Museum** pays tribute to the sport's greats with the Surfing Hall of Fame, which has an impressive collection of surfboards and related memorabilia. They've even got the Bolex camera used to shoot the 1966 surfing documentary *The Endless Summer.* ✉ *411 Olive Ave., Huntington Beach* ☎ *714/960–3483* ⊕ *www.surfingmuseum.org* 🎟 *$2* ⊙ *June–Sept., daily noon–5; Oct.–May, Thurs.–Mon. noon–5.*

★ **⑨ Bolsa Chica Ecological Reserve** beckons wildlife lovers and bird-watchers with an 1,180-acre salt marsh that is home to 200 species of birds, including great blue herons, snowy and great egrets, and brown pelicans. Throughout the reserve are trails for bird-watching, including a comfortable 1½-mi loop. Free guided tours depart from the walking bridge the first Saturday of each month at 9 AM. ✉ *Entrance on PCH 1 mi south of Warner Ave., opposite Bolsa Chica State Beach at traffic light* ☎ *714/840–1575* 🎟 *Free* ⊙ *Daily dawn–sunset.*

Where to Stay & Eat

$–$$$$ ✕ **Tuna Town.** Korn drummer David Silvera, a Huntington Beach resident, owns this Japanese-Hawaiian restaurant. Korn memorabilia is on the walls, which reverberate with music and chatter. Try the sushi dinner or sautéed chicken in wasabi cream sauce. The food takes center stage when the chefs chop and grill the food right before your eyes. ✉ *221 Main St.* ☎ *714/536–3194* ▤ *AE, D, MC, V* ⊙ *No dinner May–Aug.*

$–$$$ ✕ **Duke's.** A perfect people-watching spot overlooking the beach, this seafood restaurant has fish, chicken, and salads with a Hawaiian accent. Try crispy coconut shrimp or a salad of hearts of palm and papaya. The view's the thing here, although the food comes in a close second. ✉ *317 Pacific Coast Hwy.* ☎ *714/374–6446* ▤ *AE, D, MC, V.*

★ **$–$$$** ✕ **Red Pearl Kitchen.** This slim, hip, lacquer-red space near Main Street may put its bar front and center, but the pan-Asian food is no wallflower. The menu, divided into small or large servings, could include hot chili-crusted calamari, green papaya salad, or Szechuan pepper steak with sweet-and-sour eggplant. Desserts are equally strong. ■ TIP→ **DJs spin several nights a week, upping the energy but making it difficult to talk.** If you come on a weekend, you'll likely need to wait awhile; reservations are a good idea. ✉ *412 Walnut Ave., Huntington Beach* ☎ *714/969–0224* ▤ *AE, MC, V.*

¢ ✕ **Wahoo's Fish Taco.** Proximity to the ocean makes these mahimahi-filled tacos taste even better. This healthy fast-food chain brought Baja's fish tacos north of the border to quick success. Here, surf stickers cover the walls. ✉ *120 Main St., Huntington Beach* ☎ *714/536–2050* ▤ *MC, V.*

$$$–$$$$ ▥ **Hilton Waterfront Beach Resort.** Rising 12 stories above the surf, this Hilton caters to many kinds of travelers: couples, families, business types. All guest rooms have private balconies, many with panoramic ocean views. The grounds are extensive, including a sand volleyball court and a free-form pool; the staff can even arrange the fixings for a cookout on the beach. ✉ *21100 PCH, Huntington Beach 92648* ☎ *714/845–8000 or*

866/387–5760 ☐ 714/845–8425 ⊕ www.waterfrontresort.com ✆ 266 rooms, 24 suites ☐ Restaurant, some microwaves, cable TV with movies, Wi-Fi, tennis court, pool, gym, hot tub, 2 bars, children's programs; ages 5–12), concierge floor, business services, meeting rooms, airport shuttle, some pets allowed (fee) ☐ *AE, D, DC, MC, V.*

2

$ ☐ **Best Western Regency Inn.** Forgo an ocean view here, and you can save a lot of money. This moderately priced, tidy hotel is near the PCH and close to the main drag and its restaurants and shops. Rooms are cookie-cutter, but some have private whirlpools. ☒ *19360 Beach Blvd., Huntington Beach 92648* ☎ *714/962–4244* ☐ *714/963–4724* ⊕ *www. bestwestern.com* ✆ *64 rooms* ☐ *Refrigerators, cable TV, in-room broadband, pool, hot tub, laundry facilities, meeting room* ☐ *AE, D, DC, MC, V.*

Sports & the Outdoors

BEACHES **Huntington City Beach** (☎ 714/536–5281) stretches for 3 mi from the pier area. The beach is most crowded around the pier; amateur and professional surfers brave the waves daily on its north side. As you continue north, **Huntington State Beach** (☎ 714/536–1454) parallels Pacific Coast Highway. On the state and city beaches there are changing rooms, concessions, lifeguards, and ample parking; the state beach also has barbecue pits. At the northern section of the city, **Bolsa Chica State Beach** (☎ 714/846–3460) has barbecue pits and RV campsites and is usually less crowded than its southern neighbors.

SURFING **Corky Carroll's Surf School** (☎ 714/969–3959 ⊕ www.surfschool.net) organizes lessons, weeklong workshops, and surfing trips. You can rent surf- or boogie boards at **Dwight's** (☎ 714/536–8083), one block south of the pier. **HB Wahine** (☒ 301 Main St. ☎ 714/969–9399 ⊕ www. hbwahine.com) gives girls-only surf lessons, sells boards designed specially for them (narrower) and has cool surfing clothes, too. **Huntington Beach Surfing Instruction** (☎ 714/962–3515 ⊕ www.hbsurfing.com), a group of off-duty lifeguards, offers lessons by appointment only in summer and yearlong in Costa Rica.

Newport Beach

6 mi south of Huntington Beach, PCH.

Newport Beach has two distinct personalities. There's the island-dotted yacht harbor, where the wealthy play. (Newport is said to have the highest per-capita number of Mercedes-Benzs in the world.) And then there's inland Newport Beach, just southwest of John Wayne Airport, a business and commercial hub that's lined with high-rise office buildings, shopping centers, and hotels.

★ ❿ **Newport Harbor,** which shelters nearly 10,000 small boats, may seduce even those who don't own a yacht. Exploring the charming avenues and surrounding alleys can be great fun.

Within Newport Harbor are eight small islands, including Balboa and Lido. The houses lining the shore may seem modest, but this is some of the most expensive real estate in the world. Several grassy areas on primarily residential Lido Isle have views of Newport Harbor. In evidence of the upper-crust Orange County mind-set, each is marked PRIVATE COMMUNITY PARK.

Newport Pier, which juts out into the ocean near 20th Street, is the heart of Newport's beach community and a popular fishing spot. Street parking is difficult at the pier, so grab the first space you find and be prepared to walk. A stroll along West Ocean Front reveals much of the town's character. On weekday mornings, head for the beach near the pier, where you're likely to encounter dory fishermen hawking their predawn catches, as they've done for generations. On weekends the walk is alive with kids of all ages on in-line skates, skateboards, and bikes dodging pedestrians and whizzing past fast-food joints, shops, and bars.

Newport's best beaches are on **Balboa Peninsula,** whose many jetties pave the way to ideal swimming areas. The most intense body-surfing place in Orange County and arguably on the West Coast, known as the **Wedge,** is at the south end of the peninsula. Created by accident in the 1930s when the Federal Works Progress Administration built a jetty to protect Newport Harbor, the break is pure euphoria for highly skilled body surfers. ■ TIP→ Since the waves generally break very close to shore and rip currents are strong, lifeguards strongly discourage visitors from attempting it—but it sure is fun to watch an experienced local ride it.

⑪ The **Balboa Pavilion,** on the bay side of the peninsula, was built in 1905 as a bath- and boathouse. Today it houses a restaurant and shops and is a departure point for harbor and whale-watching cruises. Look for it on Main Street, off Balboa Boulevard. Adjacent to the pavilion is the three-car ferry that connects the peninsula to Balboa Island. In the blocks around the pavilion you'll find restaurants, beachside shops, and the small **Fun Zone**—a local kiddie hangout with a Ferris wheel and a nautical museum. On the other side of the narrow peninsula is **Balboa Pier.** On its end is the original branch of Ruby's, a 1940s-esque burger-and-shake joint.

★ ⑫ The **Orange County Museum of Art** gathers a collection of modernist paintings and sculpture by California artists and cutting-edge, international contemporary works. The collection includes works by such key California artists as Richard Diebenkorn, Ed Ruscha, Robert Irwin, and Chris Burden. The museum also displays some of its collection at a gallery at South Coast Plaza free of charge; it's open the same hours as the mall. Soups, salads, and daily specials are served at the Patina's Citrus Cafe. ⊠ *850 San Clemente Dr., Newport Beach* ☎ *949/759–1122* ⊕ *www.ocma.net* ⊠ *$10* ☉ *Tues., Wed., and Fri.–Sun. 11–5, Thurs. 11–8.*

Where to Stay & Eat

$–$$$ ✕ **Bluewater Grill.** On the site of an old sportfishing dock, this local spot has 15 types of fish, a bay view, and early-1900s fishing photos on the walls. Favorites include blue-nose seabass, local swordfish, and calamari steak, for those who miss the abalone that used to be common in the area. Wines are reasonably priced. ⊠ *630 Lido Park Dr.* ☎ *949/675–3474* ▤ *AE, D, DC, MC, V.*

★ $–$$$ ✕ **The Cannery.** This 1920s cannery building still teems with fish, but now they go into dishes on the Pacific Rim menu rather than being packed

2

into crates. Settle in at the sushi bar, dining room, or patio before choosing between sashimi or oven-roasted Chilean sea bass. On Tuesday night a selection of 50 wines is sold at 50% off. ⊠ *3010 Lafayette Rd., Newport Beach* ☎ *949/566-0060* ▤ *AE, D, DC, MC, V.*

$$ ✕ **Pescadou Bistro.** Owned by a French family, this casual and fun bistro serves reasonably priced Provençal fare like rabbit in mustard sauce. Try the three-course prix-fixe menu at $20, a bargain in Newport. Across the street is the Lido Marina Village, a cluster of restaurants, shops, and boating businesses at the west end of Newport Harbor. ⊠ *3325 Newport Blvd.* ☎ *949/675-6990* ▤ *AE, D, MC, V* ⊘ *Closed Mon.*

★ ¢–$ ✕ **Taco Mesa.** This extremely popular taqueria is the reason that the McDonald's parking lot next door is always empty. Other than a plastering of surf stickers and the friendliness of the staff, Taco Mesa is frill free; of the four branches in OC, this one has that intangible quality that makes it the best. Order at the counter; then grab a metal folding chair on the patio before gorging on fantastic carne asada (steak) tacos, giant burritos, and fresh salsa. Close to the end of the Highway 55 freeway, this stand is technically in Costa Mesa. ⊠ *647 W. 19th St., Costa Mesa* ☎ *949/642-0629* ▤ *MC, V.*

★ $$$$ ⌂ **The Island Hotel.** A suitably stylish hotel in a very chic neighborhood (it's across the street from the Fashion Island mall), the 20-story tower caters to luxury seekers by offering weekend golf packages in conjunction with the nearby Pelican Hill golf course. Guest rooms have outstanding views, private bars, and original art. The spa does its bit

> **VENICE IN CA**
>
> To see Newport Harbor from the water, take a one-hour gondola cruise operated by the Gondola Company of Newport (3400 Via Oporto, Suite 102B, Newport Beach ☎ 949/675-1212 ⊕ www.gondolas.com). It costs $85 for two and includes salami, cheese, bread, ice, glasses, blankets, and music—everything but the wine.

for luxury with a pearl powder facial. For gustatory richness, try the Pavilion restaurant's contemporary menu, with choices such as macadamia-crusted Chilean sea bass. ⊠ *690 Newport Center Dr., Newport Beach 92660* ☎ *949/759-0808 or 800/332-3442* ▨ *949/759-0568* ⊕ *www.theislandhotel.com* ⇱ *295 rooms, 92 suites* ♨ *2 restaurants, room service, cable TV with movies and video games, Wi-Fi, 2 tennis courts, pool, health club, sauna, spa, steam rooms, bar, concierge, business services, some pets allowed (fee),* ▤ *AE, D, DC, MC, V.*

$$$–$$$$ ⌂ **Balboa Bay Club and Resort.** Sharing the same frontage as the private Balboa Bay Club where Humphrey Bogart, Lauren Bacall, and the Reagans hung out, this hotel has one of the best bay views around. There's a yacht-club vibe in the public spaces, especially in the nautical dining room. Rooms, which have either bay or courtyard views, have a beachy decor of rattan furniture, plantation shutters, and tropical-pattern drapes. Duke's Place, a bar named for John Wayne, a former member and club governor, has photos of the star in his mariner-theme films. ⊠ *1221 W. Coast Hwy., 92663* ☎ *949/645-5000 or 888/445-7153* ▨ *949/630-4215* ⊕ *www.balboabayclub.com* ⇱ *150 rooms, 10 suites* ♨ *3 restaurants, room service, health club, spa, bar, business services, airport shuttle (fee)* ▤ *AE, D, DC, MC, V.*

$$$ ⌂ **Newport Beach Marriott Hotel and Spa.** Here you'll be smack in the monied part of town: across from Fashion Island, next to a country club, and with a view toward Newport Harbor. Rooms have that no-fuss contemporary look: dark wood, granite bathroom counters. Depending on your 'druthers, ask for a room with a balcony or patio that provides a view of the property's lush gardens or toward the Pacific. Five penthouse suites overlooking the Pacific absorb the top floors. The latest addition is the full-service Pure Blu spa, opened in 2006. ⌂ *900 Newport Center Dr., Newport Beach 92660* ☎ *949/640–4000 or 800/228–9290* 🖷 *949/640–5055* ⊕ *www.marriott.com* ⇜ *532 rooms, 20 suites* ⌂ *Restaurant, cable TV with movies, in-room broadband, Wi-Fi, 8 tennis courts, 2 pools, health club, spa, bar, concierge, business services, meeting rooms, airport shuttle* ▭ *AE, D, DC, MC, V.*

$$ ⌂ **Hyatt Regency Newport Beach.** The best aspect of this grand dame of Newport hotels is its green acres: 26 of them, overlooking the back bay. When booking your room, suite, or bungalow, let them know your preference of either bay, golf course, garden, or pool views. Each room has a balcony or veranda. ⌂ *1107 Jamboree Rd., 92660* ☎ *949/792–1234* 🖷 *949/644–1552* ⊕ *www.hyattnewporter.com* ⇜ *388 rooms, 11 suites, 4 bungalows* ⌂ *Restaurant, refrigerators, in-room broadband, 9-hole golf course, 16 tennis courts, health club, hot tub, spa, bicycles, volleyball, 3 swimming pools, 9-hole golf course, meeting rooms, complimentary shuttle, bar, business services* ▭ *AE, D, DC, MC, V.*

Sports & the Outdoors

BOAT RENTAL You can tour Lido and Balboa isles by renting kayaks ($15 an hour), sailboats ($35 an hour), small motorboats ($50 an hour), cocktail boats ($70 an hour), and ocean boats ($75–$85 an hour) at **Balboa Boat Rentals** (⌂ 510 E. Edgewater Ave., Newport Beach ☎ 949/673–7200 ⊕ www.boats4rent.com). You must have a driver's license, and some knowledge of boating is helpful; rented boats must stay in the bay.

BOAT TOURS **Catalina Passenger Service** (⌂ 400 Main St., Newport Beach ☎ 949/673–5245 ⊕ www.catalinainfo.com), at the Balboa Pavilion, operates 90-minute sightseeing tours for $10 and daily round-trip passage to Catalina Island for $44. Call first; winter service is often available only on weekends. **Hornblower Cruises & Events** (⌂ 2431 West Coast Hwy., Newport Beach ☎ 949/646–0155 or 800/668–4322 ⊕ www.hornblower.com) books three-hour weekend dinner cruises with dancing for $65 Friday, $69 Saturday; the two-hour Sunday brunch cruise is $47.

SPORTFISHING In addition to a complete tackle shop, **Davey's Locker** (⌂ Balboa Pavilion, 400 Main St., Newport Beach ☎ 949/673–1434 ⊕ www.daveyslocker.com) operates sportfishing trips starting at $29, as well as private charters and, in winter, whale-watching trips for $21.

Corona del Mar

2 mi south of Newport Beach, via Hwy. 1.

A small jewel on the Pacific Coast, Corona del Mar (known by locals as "CDM") has exceptional beaches that some say resemble their majestic northern California counterparts. **Corona del Mar Beach** (☎ 949/644–3151) is actually made up of two beaches, Little Corona and Big

2

Corona, separated by a cliff. Facilities include fire pits, volleyball courts, food stands, restrooms, and parking. ■ TIP→ **Two colorful reefs (and the fact that it's off-limits to boats) make Corona del Mar great for snorkelers and for beachcombers who prefer privacy.**

FodorsChoice
★

Midway between Corona del Mar and Laguna, stretching along both sides of Pacific Coast Highway, **Crystal Cove State Park** is a favorite of local beachgoers and wilderness trekkers. It encompasses a 3½-mi stretch of unspoiled beach and has some of the best tide-pooling in Southern California. Here you can see starfish, crabs, and other sea life on the rocks. The park's 2,400 acres of backcountry are ideal for hiking, horseback riding, and mountain biking, but stay on the trails to preserve the beauty. Environmental camping is allowed in one of the three campgrounds. Bring water, food, and other supplies; there's a pit toilet but no shower. Open fires and pets are forbidden. Parking costs $8. Rental cottages are scheduled to open in 2006. ☎ 949/494–3539 ⊕ *www. crystalcovestatepark.com* ☽ *Daily 6–sunset.*

⓭ **Sherman Library and Gardens,** a 2½-acre botanical garden and library specializing in the history of the Pacific Southwest, makes a good break from the sun and sand. You can wander among cactus gardens, rose gardens, a wheelchair-height touch-and-smell garden, and a tropical conservatory. There's a good gift shop, too. Cafe Jardin serves lunch on weekdays plus Sunday brunch. ☒ *2647 PCH, Corona del Mar* ☎ *949/ 673–2261, 949/673–0033 lunch reservations* ⊕ *www.slgardens.org* ☜ *$3* ☽ *Daily 10:30–4.*

Where to Eat

★ $$–$$$ ✕ **Oysters.** This hip but convivial seafood restaurant, which has a bustling bar and frequent live music, caters to a late-night crowd. The eclectic menu might include fire-roasted artichokes and terrific ahi tuna dishes. There's also a substantial list of outstanding desserts, cognacs, and dessert wines. ☒ *2515 E. Coast Hwy., Corona del Mar* ☎ *949/675– 7411* ▤ *AE, D, DC, MC, V* ☽ *No lunch.*

¢–$ ✕ **Pacific Whey Cafe & Baking Company.** The ovens rarely get a break here— everything is made from scratch daily. Pick up something to go here— perhaps a cinnamon-custard danish or a "B.L.T.A." (the A is for avocado)—and then venture across the street to Crystal Cove State Park for a picnic. If you stay for a hot meal, you could try lemon soufflé pancakes or a steak sandwich oozing with melted brie. ☒ *7962 E. Coast Hwy., Crystal Cove Promenade* ☎ *949/715–2200* ▤ *AE, MC, V.*

Laguna Beach

⓮ *10 mi south of Newport Beach on Hwy. 1; 60 mi south of Los Angeles, I–5 south to Hwy. 133, which turns into Laguna Canyon Rd.*

FodorsChoice
★

Even the approach tells you that Laguna Beach is exceptional. Driving in along Laguna Canyon Road from the Interstate 405 freeway gives you the chance to cruise through a gorgeous coastal canyon, large stretches of which remain undeveloped (⇨ the Laguna Coast Wilderness Park *below* in Sports & the Outdoors). After winding through the canyon, you'll arrive at a glistening wedge of ocean, at the intersection with the PCH.

Laguna's welcome mat is legendary. For decades in the mid-20th century a local booster, Eiler Larsen, greeted everyone downtown. (There's now a statue of him on the main drag.) On the corner of Forest and Park avenues you can see a 1930s gate proclaiming, THIS GATE HANGS WELL AND HINDERS NONE, REFRESH AND REST, THEN TRAVEL ON. A gay community has long been established here; until relatively recently, this was quite the exception in conservative Orange County. The Hare Krishnas run a restaurant, environmentalists rally, artists continue to gravitate here—there seems to be room for everyone.

There's a definite arty slant to this tight-knit community. The California *plein air* art movement coalesced here in the early 1900s; by the middle of the century an annual arts festival was established. Art galleries now dot the village streets, and there's usually someone daubing up in Heisler Park, overlooking the beach. The town's main street, the Pacific Coast Highway, is referred to as either South Coast or North Coast Highway, depending on the address. From this waterfront, the streets slope up steeply to the residential areas. All along the highway and side streets, you'll find dozens of fine-art and crafts galleries, clothing boutiques, and jewelry shops.

Laguna's central beach gives you a perfect slice of local life. A stocky 1920s lifeguard tower marks **Main Beach Park,** at the end of Broadway at South Coast Highway. A wooden boardwalk separates the sand from a strip of lawn. Walk along this, or hang out on one of its benches, to watch people bodysurfing, playing sand volleyball, or scrambling around one of two half-basketball courts. The beach also has children's play equipment, picnic areas, restrooms, and showers. Across the street is a lovely old movie theater.

The **Laguna Art Museum** displays American art, with an emphasis on California artists and works. Special exhibits change quarterly. ■ TIP➔ Galleries throughout the area stay open late in coordination with the museum on the first Thursday of each month (visit www.firstthursdaysartwalk.com for more information). A free shuttle service runs from the museum to galleries and studios. ✉ *307 Cliff Dr., Laguna Beach* ☎ *949/494–6531* ⊕ *www. lagunaartmuseum.org* 🎨 *$10* ⊗ *Daily 11–5.*

Where to Stay & Eat

★ **$$–$$$**   ✕ **Five Feet.** Others have attempted to mimic this restaurant's innovative blend of Chinese and French cooking styles, but Five Feet remains the leader of the pack. Among the standout dishes is the house catfish. The setting is pure Laguna: exposed ceiling, open kitchen, high noise level, and brick walls hung with works by local artists. ✉ *328 Glenneyre St., Laguna Beach* ☎ *949/497–4955* ▤ *AE, D, DC, MC, V* ⊗ *No lunch.*

$$–$$$ ✕ **French 75.** Locals love this bistro and champagne bar for its intimate, opulent feel inspired by a 1940s-style Paris supper club. It's definitely a change from the usual bright, casual restaurant look; this space has low lighting, dark-wood paneling, and a mural of cherubs spritzing bubbly. The menu focuses on bistro classics with the occasional curveball, like duck in a caramelized honey and tangerine sauce. One constant: the Callebaut chocolate soufflé. ✉ *1464 S. Coast Hwy., Laguna Beach* ☎ *949/494–8444* ▤ *AE, D, DC, MC, V* ⊗ *No lunch.*

2

$–$$$ ✕ **Mosun.** Fans of this restaurant-nightclub favor the Pacific Rim cuisine, fresh sushi, and large selection of sake. Among the entrées are teriyaki steak and pan-seared, five-spice duck breast. ⊠ *680 S. Coast Hwy., Laguna Beach* ☎ *949/497–5646* ⚠ *Reservations essential* 🚭 *AE, D, DC, MC, V* ☯ *No lunch.*

$$ ✕ **Ti Amo.** A romantic setting and creative Mediterranean cuisine have earned this place acclaim. Try the seared ahi with a sesame-seed crust. All the nooks and crannies are charming, candlelighted, and private, but to maximize romance, request a table in the enclosed garden in back. ⊠ *31727 S. Coast Hwy., Laguna Beach* ☎ *949/499–5350* 🚭 *AE, D, DC, MC, V* ☯ *No lunch.*

¢–$$ ✕ **Taco Loco.** This may look like a fast-food taco stand, and the hemp brownies on the menu may make you think the kitchen's *really* laid-back, but the quality of the food here equals that in many higher-price restaurants. Some Mexican standards get a Louisiana twist, like Cajun-spiced seafood tacos. Other favorites include blackened lobster tacos and the mushroom-and-tofu burgers. It stays open late on Friday and Saturday, till 2 AM. ⊠ *640 S. Coast Hwy.* ☎ *949/497–1635* 🚭 *AE, MC, V.*

$ ✕ **Café Zinc.** Laguna Beach cognoscenti gather at the tiny counter and plant-filled patio of this vegetarian café serving breakfast and lunch. Oatmeal is sprinkled with berries in season, poached eggs are dusted with herbs, and the orange juice is fresh squeezed. For lunch, try the spicy Thai pasta, asparagus salad with orange peel and capers, or one of the pizzettes. ⊠ *350 Ocean Ave., Laguna Beach* ☎ *949/494–6302* 🚭 *AE, MC, V* ☯ *No dinner.*

$$$$ ▥ **Montage Resort & Spa.** Laguna's connection to the Californian *plein air* artists is mined for inspiration at this head-turningly fancy hotel. The Montage uses the local Craftsman style as a touchstone. Shingled buildings ease down a bluff to the cove beaches; inside, works by contemporary and early-20th-century California artists snare your attention. Guest rooms balance ease and refinement; all have ocean views and amenities such as CD/DVD players and extra-deep tubs. Of the restaurants, Studio is the fanciest, with more sweeping Pacific views and a refined contemporary menu. At the oceanfront spa and fitness center, you can indulge in a sea-salt scrub, take a yoga class, or hit the lap pool. ⊠ *30801 S. Coast Hwy., Laguna Beach 92651* ☎ *888/715–6700* 📠 *949/715–6100* ⊕ *www.montagelagunabeach.com* ⤴ *211 rooms, 51 suites* ⚐ *3 restaurants, room service, in-room safes, minibars, in-room data ports, 3 pools, health club, outdoor hot tub, spa, beach, 4 bars, children's programs (ages 5–12), dry cleaning, laundry service, concierge, business services, meeting rooms, parking (fee)* 🚭 *AE, MC, V.*

FodorśChoice
★

★ **$$$$** ▥ **Surf & Sand Resort.** Your parents may have stayed here decades ago, but there's nothing dated about it. Guest rooms seem to hover over the beach; most have private balconies. The decor uses soft, monochromatic colors and sand-color sisal rugs. Rooms in the Towers have whirlpool tubs in the bathrooms. If you've gotten a bit too much sun, sign up for the aloe-vera wrap in the spa. ⊠ *1555 S. Coast Hwy., Laguna Beach 92651* ☎ *949/497–4477 or 888/869–7569* 📠 *949/494–2897* ⊕ *www. surfandsandresort.com* ⤴ *155 rooms, 13 suites* ⚐ *Restaurant, mini-*

bars, cable TV with movies, in-room broadband, pool, health club, spa, beach, bar, concierge, meeting rooms ⊟ *AE, D, DC, MC, V.*

★ $$–$$$$ ⊞ **Hotel Casa del Camino.** This Spanish-style hotel was built in 1927. Its ace in the hole is its large rooftop terrace, with clear ocean views—an ideal spot at sunset. Rooms have warm color schemes; beds have feather duvets to ward off the seaside chill. ⊠ *1289 S. Coast Hwy., Laguna Beach 92651* ☎ *949/497–2446 or 888/367–5232* ⊟ *949/494–5581* ⊕ *www. casacamino.com* ⊅ *42 rooms, 7 suites* ⊘ *Restaurant, cable TV, Wi-Fi, bar, free parking, some pets allowed* ⊟ *AE, D, DC, MC, V.*

$$–$$$$ ⊞ **Inn at Laguna Beach.** On a bluff overlooking the ocean, the inn is on Main Beach and steps from shops and art galleries. Location and price are the key to this good hotel. ⊠ *211 N. Coast Hwy., Laguna Beach 92651* ☎ *949/497–9722 or 800/544–4479* ⊟ *949/497–9972* ⊕ *www. innatlagunabeach.com* ⊅ *70 rooms* ⊘ *Minibars, some microwaves, refrigerators, cable TV, in-room VCRs, in-room data ports, pool, meeting rooms* ⊟ *AE, D, DC, MC, V.*

★ $$–$$$ ⊞ **Eiler's Inn.** Named for Laguna's late official greeter, this B&B is centered on a bright courtyard with a fountain. Every room is different, but all are full of antiques and travelers' journals for you to write in. Afternoon wine and cheese are served in the courtyard or in the cozy reading room, where you'll find the inn's only TV. A sundeck in back has an ocean view. ⊠ *741 S. Coast Hwy., Laguna Beach 92651* ☎ *949/ 494–3004 or 866/617–2696* ⊟ *949/497–2215* ⊅ *12 rooms* ⊘ *No room phones, no room TVs, no a/c* ⊟ *AE, D, DC, MC, V* ⧉ *BP.*

$–$$$ ⊞ **Hotel Laguna.** The oldest hotel in Laguna (opened in 1888) has manicured gardens, beach views, and an ideal location downtown. Among the perks is access to the hotel's private beach, where guests are provided with lounges, umbrellas, and towels and can order lunch or cocktails from the Beach Club menu. ⊠ *425 S. Coast Hwy., Laguna Beach 92651* ☎ *949/494–1151 or 800/524–2927* ⊟ *949/497–2163* ⊕ *www. hotellaguna.com* ⊅ *65 rooms* ⊘ *2 restaurants, in-room DVDs, Wi-Fi, beach, bar, meeting rooms, parking (fee); no a/c* ⊟ *AE, DC, MC, V* ⧉ *CP.*

Nightlife & the Arts

The **Laguna Playhouse** (⊠ 606 Laguna Canyon Rd., Laguna Beach ☎ 949/497–2787 ⊕ www.lagunaplayhouse.com), dating to the 1920s, mounts a variety of productions, from classics to youth-oriented plays. The **Sawdust Arts Festival** (☎ 949/494–3030 ⊕ www.sawdustartfestival. org), held in July and August opposite the Festival of the Arts amphitheater, always hosts musicians and entertainers.

The **Boom Boom Room** (⊠ Coast Inn, 1401 S. Coast Hwy., Laguna Beach ☎ 949/494–7588) is the town's most popular gay club. The **Sandpiper** (⊠ 1183 S. Coast Hwy., Laguna Beach ☎ 949/494–4694), a hole-in-the-wall dancing joint, attracts an eclectic crowd. **White House** (⊠ 340 S. Coast Hwy., Laguna Beach ☎ 949/494–8088), a chic club on the main strip, has nightly entertainment and dancing.

Sports & the Outdoors

BEACHES There are a handful of lovely beaches around town besides the Main Beach, (*above*). **Aliso Creek County Beach** (☎ 714/834–2400), in south La-

2

guna, has a playground, fire pits, parking, food stands, and restrooms. **1,000 Steps Beach,** off South Coast Highway at 9th Street, is a hard-to-find locals' spot with great waves. There aren't really 1,000 steps down to it, it just seems that way. **Woods Cove,** off South Coast Highway at Diamond Street, is especially quiet during the week. Big rock formations hide lurking crabs. As you climb the steps to leave, you can see a Tudor-style mansion that was once the home of Bette Davis.

BICYCLING Mountain bikes and helmets can be rented at **Rainbow Bicycles** (⊠ 485 N. Coast Hwy., Laguna Beach ☎ 949/494–5806 ⊕ www.teamrain.com).

HIKING The **Laguna Coast Wilderness Park** (☎ 949/923–2235 ⊕ www. lagunacanyon.org) is spread over 19 acres of fragile coastal territory, including the canyon. The trails are great for hiking and mountain biking and are open daily, weather permitting. Docent-led hikes are given regularly; call for information.

TENNIS Six metered courts can be found at **Laguna Beach High School.** Two courts are available at the **Irvine Bowl.** Six courts are available at **Alta Laguna Park** on a first-come, first-served basis. For more information, call the **City of Laguna Beach Recreation Department** (☎ 949/497–0716).

WATER SPORTS Because its entire beach area is a marine preserve, Laguna Beach is ideal for snorkelers. Scuba divers should head to the Marine Life Refuge area, which runs from Seal Rock to Diver's Cove. Rent bodyboards at **Hobie Sports** (⊠ 294 Forest Ave., Laguna Beach ☎ 949/497–3304).

Shopping

Forest and Ocean avenues and Glenneyre Street are full of art galleries and fine jewelry and clothing boutiques.

Artisance (⊠ 278 Beach St. ☎ 949/494–0687) pulls together posh tableware and decorative odds and ends, from shell-like porcelain by Ted Muehling to glossy coffee-table books. Get your sugar fix at the time-warped **Candy Baron** (⊠ 231 Forest Ave. ☎ 949/497–7508), filled with old-fashioned goodies like gumdrops, bull's-eyes, and more than a dozen barrels of saltwater taffy. Browse **Georgeo's Art Glass and Jewelry** (⊠ 269 Forest Ave., Laguna Beach ☎ 949/497–0907) for a large selection of etched-glass bowls, vases, and fine jewelry. The **Tung & Groov** (⊠ 950 Glenneyre St., Laguna Beach ☎ 949/494–0768) carries an eclectic mix of handcrafted and decorator items like traditional umbrellas from Bali, brass elephant bells from India, and papier-mâché boxes.

ART GALLERIES Most South Village art galleries line up along the South Coast Highway in the 900 to 2000 blocks. **DeRu'sFine Art** (⊠ 1590 S. Coast Hwy., Laguna Beach ☎ 949/376–3785) specializes in California impressionist works by artists such as Guy Rose, William Wendt, and others. The **Redfern Gallery** (⊠ 1540 S. Coast Hwy., Laguna Beach ☎ 949/497–3356) is another top source for California impressionists. You can see more of its collection at the Montage Resort. Since 1937, **Warren Imports** (⊠ 1910 S. Coast Hwy., Laguna Beach ☎ 949/494–6505) has been the place to go for Asian art and antiques—everything from Chinese porcelain to Japanese iron teapots to carved Buddhas.

Dana Point

⑮ *10 mi south of Laguna Beach, via PCH.*

Dana Point's claim to fame is its small-boat marina tucked into a dramatic natural harbor and surrounded by high bluffs. **Dana Point Harbor** (☎ 949/923–2255 ⊕ www.danapointharbor.com) was first described more than 100 years ago by its namesake, Richard Henry Dana, in his book *Two Years Before the Mast.* At the marina are docks for small boats, marine-oriented shops, restaurants, and boat and bike rentals. In early March a **whale festival** (☎ 949/472–7888 or 888/440–4309 ⊕ www. festivalofwhales.org) celebrates the passing gray whale migration with concerts, films, sports competitions, and a weekend street fair.

At the south end of Dana Point, **Doheny State Beach** (☎ 949/496–6171, 714/433–6400 water-quality information) is one of Southern California's top surfing destinations, but there's a lot more to do within this 63-acre area. Divers and anglers hang out at the beach's western end, and during low tide, the tide pools beckon both young and old. You'll also find five indoor tanks and an interpretive center devoted to the wildlife of the Doheny Marine Refuge. There are food stands and shops, picnic facilities, volleyball courts, and a pier for fishing. Camping is permitted, though there are no RV hook-ups. ⚠ **Be aware that the waters here periodically do not meet health standards established by California (warning signs are posted if that's the case).**

Two indoor tanks at the **Ocean Institute** contain touchable sea creatures, as well as the complete skeleton of a gray whale. Anchored near the institute is the *Pilgrim,* a full-size replica of the square-rigged vessel on which Richard Henry Dana sailed. You can tour the boat Sunday 10 to 3. Weekend cruises are also available. In addition, marine-mammal exploration cruises are given January through March, and cruises to explore regional tide pools set out year-round. ⊠ *24200 Dana Point Harbor Dr., Dana Point* ☎ *949/496–2274* ⊕ *www.ocean-institute.org* 🖃 *$5* ⊗ *Weekends 10–3:30.*

Where to Stay & Eat

$–$$$ ✕ **Luciana's Ristorante.** This intimate restaurant can be relied on for straightforward Italian meals. Dining rooms are small, warmed by two fireplaces; there's another fireplace on the patio. Try the freshly handmade pastas or the linguine with clams, prawns, calamari, and mussels in a light tomato sauce. ⊠ *24312 Del Prado Ave., Dana Point* ☎ *949/ 661–6500* ▤ *AE, DC, MC, V* ⊗ *No lunch.*

$–$$$ ✕ **Wind & Sea.** An unblocked ocean view makes this a great place for lunch—and looking out on the Pacific might put you in the mood for a retro cocktail like a mai tai. Of the entrées, try the macadamia-crusted mahimahi. On warm days, patio tables beckon you outside. ⊠ *34699 Golden Lantern St., Dana Point* ☎ *949/496–6500* ▤ *AE, MC, V.*

¢–$ ✕ **Proud Mary's.** On a terrace overlooking the harbor, this "Cheers" on the water serves burgers, steaks, and other American standards, and you can order breakfast all day. ⊠ *34689 Golden Lantern St., Dana Point* ☎ *949/493–5853* ▤ *AE, D, MC, V* ⊗ *No dinner.*

2

$$$$ ✕🏨 **Ritz-Carlton, Laguna Niguel.** An unrivaled setting on the edge of the
Fodor'sChoice Pacific, combined with hallmark Ritz-Carlton service, has made this re-
★ sort justly famous. The sleek, contemporary color scheme of cool blues,
silver, and cream is punctuated with magenta accents. Rooms have 42-
inch plasma TVs and DVD players, marble bathrooms, and private balconies with ocean or pool views. Restaurant 162, named for its site 162
feet above sea level, has sweeping views of the Pacific. The menu is divided into small, medium, and large plates. A small plate might be
soup; a medium plate a pizza; and a large plate oven roasted cod or maple-
chili-grilled rib-eye steak. The wood-panel former library was transformed
into a bar and meeting place. This lobby lounge has musical performances Wednesday through Saturday evenings. ⊠ *1 Ritz-Carlton Dr., Dana
Point 92629* ☎ *949/240–2000 or 800/241–3333* 🖷 *949/240–0829*
⊕ *www.ritzcarlton.com* ⇩ *363 rooms, 30 suites* ♿ *3 restaurants, in-
room safes, minibars, in-room data ports, Wi-Fi, 2 tennis courts, 2
pools, health club, hair salon, spa, lobby lounge, concierge, business services, meeting rooms* ▭ *AE, D, DC, MC, V.*

$$$$ ✕🏨 **St. Regis Monarch Beach Resort and Spa.** Exclusivity and indulgence
carry the day here; you can even have someone unpack for you. The
172-acre grounds include a private beach club, an 18-hole Robert Trent
Jones Jr.–designed golf course, and tennis courts across the street. Rooms
have views of either the coast or the lush landscaping; such amenities
as CD and DVD players and libraries are among the pluses. The best
restaurant is Stonehill Tavern, which opened in 2006 under chef Michael
Mina and serves modern American fare. Can't decide between appetizers? You can order a trio, three small plates, each focused on a key in-
gredient like lobster or duck. Entrées might include prime short rib with
braised potatoes and truffles or shellfish stew with saffron broth. ⊠ *1
Monarch Beach Resort, off Niguel Rd., Dana Point 92629* ☎ *949/234–
3200 or 800/722–1543* 🖷 *949/234–3201* ⊕ *www.stregismb.com* ⇩ *325
rooms, 75 suites* ♿ *6 restaurants, in-room safes, minibars, cable TV with
movies and video games, in-room data ports, Wi-Fi, 18-hole golf course,
3 pools, health club, hair salon, massage, spa, beach, bar, lobby lounge,
dry cleaning, laundry facilities, concierge, business services, some pets
allowed (free)* ▭ *AE, D, DC, MC, V.*

★ **$$–$$$** 🏨 **Blue Lantern Inn.** Combining New England–style architecture with a
Southern California setting, this white-clapboard B&B rests on a bluff
overlooking the harbor and ocean. A fire warms the intimate, inviting
living area, where you may enjoy complimentary snacks and play
backgammon every afternoon. The Nantucket–style guest rooms also
have fireplaces and whirlpool tubs. The top-floor Tower Suite has a 180-
degree ocean view. ⊠ *34343 St. of the Blue Lantern, Dana Point 92629*
☎ *949/661–1304 or 800/950–1236* 🖷 *949/496–1483* ⊕ *www.
bluelanterninn.com* ⇩ *29 rooms* ♿ *In-room VCRs, in-room broadband,
gym, concierge, meeting rooms; no smoking* ▭ *AE, DC, MC, V* ❢❢ *BP.*

Sports & the Outdoors

Inside Dana Point Harbor, **Swim Beach** has a fishing pier, barbecues, food
stands, parking, restrooms, and showers. Rental stands for surfboards,
Windsurfers, small powerboats, and sailboats can be found near most
of the piers.

Dana Wharf Sportfishing & Whale Watching (⊠ 34675 Golden Lantern St., Dana Point ☎ 949/496–5794 ⊕ www.danawharfsportfishing.com) runs charters and whale-watching excursions from early December to late April. Tickets cost $25; reservations are required. **Embarcadero Marina** (⊠ 34512 Embarcadero Pl., Dana Point ☎ 949/496–6177 ⊕ www.danaharbor.com) has small powerboats and sailboats for rent near the launching ramp at Dana Point Harbor. **Hobie Sports** (⊠ 24825 Del Prado, Dana Point ☎ 949/496–2366) rents surfboards and boogie boards.

San Juan Capistrano

⑯ *5 mi north of Dana Point, Hwy. 74, 60 mi north of San Diego, I–5.*

San Juan Capistrano, one of the few noteworthy historical districts in Southern California, is best known for its mission, to which the swallows traditionally return each year, migrating from their winter haven in Argentina, but these days they are more likely to choose other local sites for nesting. St. Joseph's Day, March 19, launches a week of festivities. After summering in the arches of the old stone church, the swallows head home on St. John's Day, October 23.

If you arrive by train, you'll be dropped off across from the mission at the San Juan Capistrano depot. With its appealing brick café and preserved Santa Fe cars, the depot retains much of the magic of early American railroads. If driving, park near Ortega and Camino Capistrano, the city's main streets.

FodorsChoice **Mission San Juan Capistrano,** founded in 1776 by Father Junípero Serra, ★ was the major Roman Catholic outpost between Los Angeles and San Diego. The Great Stone Church, begun in 1797, is the largest structure created by the Spanish in California. Many of the mission's adobe buildings have been preserved to illustrate mission life, with exhibits of an olive millstone, tallow ovens, tanning vats, metalworking furnaces, and the padres' living quarters. The gardens, with their fountains, are a lovely spot in which to wander. The bougainvillea-covered Serra Chapel is believed to be the oldest building standing in California. Mass takes place daily at 7 AM in the chapel and 8:30 in the new church. ⊠ *Camino Capistrano and Ortega Hwy., San Juan Capistrano* ☎ *949/234–1300* ⊕ *www.missionsjc.com* ⊡ *$6* ⊙ *Daily 8:30–5.*

Near Mission San Juan Capistrano is the **San Juan Capistrano Library,** a postmodern structure built in 1983. Architect Michael Graves combined classical and Mission styles to striking effect. Its courtyard has secluded places for reading. ⊠ *31495 El Camino Real, San Juan Capistrano* ☎ *949/493–1752* ⊙ *Mon.–Wed. 10–8, Thurs. 10–6, Sat. 10–5, Sun. noon–5.*

Where to Eat

$$–$$$ ✕ **L'Hirondelle.** Roast duck, rabbit, and Belgian dishes are the hallmark of this French and Belgian restaurant, whose name is French for—surprise—the swallow. The extensive wine list is matched by an impressive selection of Belgian beers. You can dine inside or out on the patio. Sunday brunch is superb. ⊠ *31631 Camino Capistrano, San Juan Capistrano* ☎ *949/661–0425* ▭ *AE, DC, MC, V* ⊙ *Closed Mon.*

$–$$$ ✕ **Cedar Creek Inn.** Equally suitable for family meals and romantic dinners, the inn has a children's menu as well as a secluded outdoor patio. The contemporary American menu features crowd pleasers like an ahi burger, rack of lamb, and herb-crusted halibut. ✉ *26860 Ortega Hwy., San Juan Capistrano* ☎ *949/240–2229* ▭ *AE, MC, V.*

$–$$ ✕ **The Ramos House Cafe.** Here's your chance to visit one of the historic district's simple, 19th-century homes. This café sits practically on the railroad tracks—nab a table on the patio and dig into a hearty breakfast, such as the mountainous wild-mushroom scramble. Patrons are occasionally saluted by the roar of a passing Amtrak. ✉ *31752 Los Rios St., San Juan Capistrano* ☎ *949/443–1342* ▭ *AE, D, DC, MC, V* ⊘ *Closed Mon.*

Nightlife

Coach House (✉ 33157 Camino Capistrano, San Juan Capistrano ☎ 949/ 496–8930 ⊕ www.thecoachhouse.com), a roomy, casual club with long tables and a dark-wood bar, draws crowds of varying ages for entertainment ranging from hip new bands to Dick Dale, the take-no-prisoners king of the surf guitar.

Prayer and misbehavior lie cheek by jowl; across the way from the mission you'll find a line of Harleys in front of the **Swallows Inn** (✉ 31786 Camino Capistrano, San Juan Capistrano ☎ 949/493–3188). Despite a somewhat tough look, it pulls in all kinds—bikers, college kids, Marines from San Diego, grandparents, all come for a drink, a casual bite, and some rowdy live music. There's no cover charge.

ORANGE COUNTY ESSENTIALS

To research prices, get advice from other travelers, and book travel arrangements, visit www.fodors.com.

AIRPORTS

The county's main facility is John Wayne Airport Orange County (SNA), which is served by 11 major domestic airlines and 3 commuter lines. Long Beach Airport (LGB) serves five airlines, including its major player, JetBlue. It's smaller and more low-key than John Wayne; it may not have many airport amenities, but parking is generally a snap. It's roughly 20 to 30 minutes by car from Anaheim.

🛈 Airport Information **John Wayne Airport Orange County** ✉ MacArthur Blvd. at I-405, Santa Ana ☎ 949/252–5252 ⊕ www.ocair.com. **Long Beach Airport** ✉ 4100 Donald Douglas Dr., Long Beach ☎ 562/570–6555 ⊕ www.lgb.org.

AIRPORT TRANSFERS Airport Bus, a shuttle service, carries passengers from John Wayne and LAX to Anaheim and Buena Park. The fare from John Wayne to Anaheim is $14, from LAX to Anaheim $19. Prime Time Airport Shuttle provides door-to-door service from Orange County hotels to LAX and the San Pedro cruise terminal. The fare is $13 per person and up, depending on where you're picked up and dropped off. SuperShuttle provides 24-hour door-to-door service from all the airports to all points in Orange County. The fare to the Disneyland area is $10 per person from John Wayne, $15 from LAX, and $30 from Long Beach Airport.

🚌 Shuttles **Airport Bus** ☎ 800/938-8933 ⊕ www.airportbus.com. **Prime Time Airport Shuttle** ☎ 800/262-7433 ⊕ www.primetimeshuttle.com. **SuperShuttle** ☎ 714/517-6600 ⊕ www.supershuttle.com.

BUS TRAVEL

The Los Angeles MTA has limited service to Orange County. From downtown L.A., Bus 460 goes to Knott's Berry Farm and Disneyland Resort. Greyhound serves Anaheim and Santa Ana. The Orange County Transportation Authority will take you virtually anywhere in the county, but it will take time; OCTA buses go from Knott's Berry Farm and Disneyland to Huntington Beach and Newport Beach. Bus 1 travels along the coast; Buses 701 and 721 provide express service to Los Angeles.

Fares for the OCTA local routes are $1.25 per boarding; you can also get a $3 local day pass (valid only on the date of purchase). Day passes can be purchased from bus drivers upon boarding. Express bus fare between Orange County and L.A. is $3.75 a pop, $2.50 if you have a day pass. The bus-fare boxes take coins and dollar bills, but you must use exact change.

🚌 Bus Information **Greyhound** ☎ 714/999-1256 or 800/231-2222 ⊕ www.greyhound.com. **Los Angeles MTA** ☎ 213/626-4455 ⊕ www.mta.net. **Orange County Transportation Authority (OCTA)** ☎ 714/636-7433 ⊕ www.octa.net.

CAR TRAVEL

The San Diego Freeway (Interstate 405) and the Santa Ana Freeway (Interstate 5) run north–south through Orange County. South of Laguna Interstate 405 merges into Interstate 5 (called the San Diego Freeway south from this point). A toll road, the 73 Highway, runs 15 mi from Newport Beach to San Juan Capistrano; it costs $3 and is usually less jammed than the regular freeways. Do your best to avoid freeways during rush hours (6 to 9 and 3:30 to 6:30).

Highways 55 and 91 head west to the ocean and east into the mountains. Highway 91, which goes to Garden Grove and inland points (Buena Park, Anaheim), has some express lanes for which drivers pay a toll, ostensibly to avoid the worst of rush-hour traffic. If you have three or more people in your car, though, you can use the Highway 91 express lanes most of the day for free (the exception being 4 PM to 6 PM on weekdays, when you pay half-fare). Highway 55 leads to Newport Beach. The Pacific Coast Highway (Highway 1) allows easy access to beach communities and is the most scenic route.

Laguna Canyon Road, the beautiful route that winds through a coastal canyon, is undergoing a widening project begun in 2003. The work is expected to take four years, but the road will remain open throughout. ⚠ The old road is quite narrow and used by cyclists as well as drivers, so be especially cautious and turn on your headlights even in daytime.

TRAIN TRAVEL

Amtrak makes daily stops in Orange County at Fullerton, Anaheim, Santa Ana, Irvine, San Juan Capistrano, and San Clemente. Metrolink is a weekday commuter train that runs to and from Los Angeles and Orange

County, starting as far south as Oceanside and stopping in Laguna Niguel, Tustin, San Juan Capistrano, San Clemente, Irvine, Santa Ana, Orange, Anaheim, and Fullerton. The Metrolink system is divided into a dozen zones; the fare you pay depends on how many zones you cover. Buy tickets from the vending machines at each station. Ticketing is on an honor system.

🚆 Train Information **Amtrak** ☎ 800/872-7245 ⊕ www.amtrak.com. **Metrolink** ☎ 800/ 371-5465 ⊕ www.metrolinktrains.com.

VISITOR INFORMATION

🚆 **Anaheim-Orange County Visitor and Convention Bureau** ✉ Anaheim Convention Center, 800 W. Katella Ave., Anaheim 92802 ☎ 714/765-8888 ⊕ www.anaheimoc. org. **Buena Park Convention and Visitors Office** ✉ 6601 Beach Blvd., Buena Park 90621 ☎ 800/541-3953 ⊕ www.buenapark.com. **Costa Mesa Conference and Visitors Bureau** ✍ Box 5071, Costa Mesa 92628 ☎ 714/384-0493 or 800/399-5499 ⊕ www. costamesa-ca.com. **Huntington Beach Conference and Visitors Bureau** ✉ 301 Main St., Suite 208, Huntington Beach 92648 ☎ 714/969-3492 ⊕ www.hbvisit.com. **Laguna Beach Visitors Bureau** ✉ 252 Broadway, Laguna Beach 92651 ☎ 949/376-0511 or 800/ 877-1115 ⊕ www.lagunabeachinfo.org. **Newport Beach Conference and Visitors Bureau** ✉ 3300 West Coast Hwy., Newport Beach 92663 ☎ 800/942-6278 ⊕ www. newportbeach-cvb.com. **San Juan Capistrano Chamber of Commerce and Visitors Center** ✉ 31781 Camino Capistrano, Suite 306, San Juan Capistrano 92693 ☎ 949/493-4700 ⊕ www.sanjuanchamber.com.

CATALINA ISLAND

Just 22 mi out from the L.A. coastline, across from Newport Beach and Long Beach, Catalina has virtually unspoiled mountains, canyons, coves, and beaches; best of all, it gives you a glimpse of what undeveloped Southern California once looked like.

Summer, weekends, and holidays, Catalina crawls with thousands of L.A.-area boaters, who tie their vessels at protected moorings in Avalon and other coves. Although Catalina is not known for its beaches, sunbathing and water sports are big draws; divers and snorkelers come for the exceptionally clear water surrounding the island. The main town, Avalon, is a charming, old-fashioned beach community, where yachts bob in the crescent-shape bay. Wander beyond the main drag and you'll find brightly painted little bungalows fronting the sidewalks, with the occasional golf cart purring down the street.

Cruise ships sail into Avalon twice a week and smaller boats shuttle between Avalon and Two Harbors, a small isthmus cove on the island's western end. You can also take bus excursions beyond Avalon. Roads are limited and nonresident vehicles prohibited, so hiking (by permit only) and cycling are the only other means of exploring.

In 1975 the Santa Catalina Island Conservancy, a nonprofit foundation, acquired about 86% of the island to help preserve the area's natural resources. These days the conservancy is restoring the rugged interior country with plantings of native grasses and trees. Along the coast you might spot such oddities as electric perch, saltwater goldfish, and flying fish.

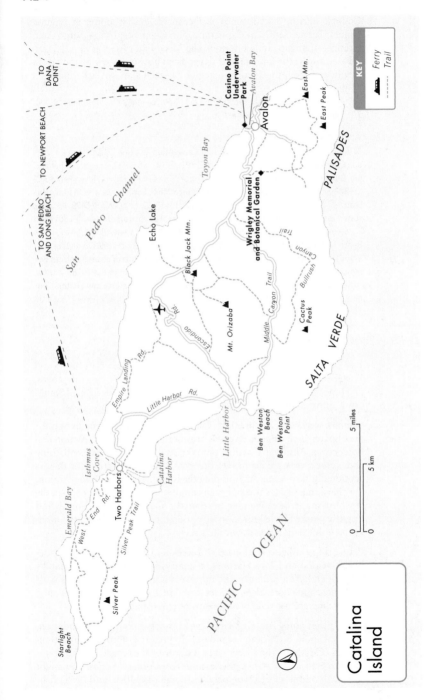

Catalina Island

Although Catalina can be seen in a day, several inviting hotels make it worth extending your stay for one or more nights. A short itinerary might include breakfast along the boardwalk, a tour of the interior, a snorkeling excursion at Casino Point, and dinner in Avalon.

Avalon

A 1- to 2-hr ferry ride from Long Beach, Newport Beach, or San Pedro; a 15-min helicopter ride from Long Beach or San Pedro.

Avalon, Catalina's only real town, extends from the shore of its natural harbor to the surrounding hillsides. Most of the city's activity, however, is centered along the pedestrian mall on Crescent Avenue, and most sights are easily reached on foot. Private cars are restricted and rental cars aren't allowed, but taxis, trams, and shuttles can take you anywhere you need to go. Bicycles and golf carts can be rented from shops along Crescent Avenue.

A walk along **Crescent Avenue** is a nice way to begin a tour of the town. Vivid art-deco tiles adorn the avenue's fountains and planters—fired on the island by the now-defunct Catalina Tile Company, the tiles are a coveted commodity. Head to the **Green Pleasure Pier,** at the center of Crescent Avenue, for a good vantage point of Avalon. At the top of the hill you'll spot a big white building, the Inn at Mt. Ada, now a top-of-the-line B&B but originally built by William Wrigley Jr. for his wife. On the pier you'll find the Catalina Island Chamber of Commerce, snack stands, the Harbor Patrol, and scads of squawking seagulls.

★ On the northwest point of Avalon Bay (looking to your right from Green Pleasure Pier) is the majestic landmark **Casino.** This circular white structure is one of the finest examples of art-deco architecture anywhere. Its Spanish-inspired floors and murals gleam with brilliant blue and green Catalina tiles. In this case, *casino,* the Italian word for "gathering place," has nothing to do with gambling. Rather, Casino life revolves around the magnificent ballroom. The same big-band dances that made the Casino famous in the 1930s and '40s still take place several times a year. The **New Year's Eve dance** (☎ 310/510–1520) is hugely popular and sells out well in advance.

Santa Catalina Island Company leads tours of the Casino, lasting about 55 minutes, for $9. You can also visit the **Catalina Island Museum,** in the lower level of the Casino, which investigates 7,000 years of island history; or stop at the **Casino Art Gallery** to see works by local artists. First-run movies are screened nightly at the **Avalon Theatre,** noteworthy for its classic 1929 theater pipe organ. ⊠ *1 Casino Way, Avalon* ☎ *310/510–2414 museum, 310/510–0808 art gallery, 310/510–0179 Avalon Theatre* 🎫 *Museum $4, art gallery free* ☉ *Museum: daily 10–4. Art gallery: mid-Mar.–Dec., daily 10:30–4; Jan.–mid-Mar, Tues. and Thurs.–Sun. 10:30–4.*

In front of the Casino are the crystal-clear waters of the **Casino Point Underwater Park,** a marine preserve protected from watercraft where moray eels, bat rays, spiny lobsters, halibut, and other sea animals cruise around kelp forests and along the sandy bottom. It's a terrific site for scuba diving, with some shallow areas suitable for snorkeling. Scuba and snorkeling equipment can be rented on and near the pier. The shallow waters of **Lover's Cove,** east of the boat landing, are also good for snorkeling.

Two miles south of the bay via Avalon Canyon Road is **Wrigley Memorial and Botanical Garden.** Here you'll find plants native to Southern California, including several that grow only on Catalina Island: Catalina ironwood, wild tomato, and rare Catalina mahogany. The Wrigley family commissioned the garden as well as the monument, which has a grand staircase and a Spanish mausoleum inlaid with colorful Catalina tile. (The mausoleum was never used by the Wrigleys, who are buried in Los Angeles.) Taxi service from Avalon is available, or you can take a tour bus from the downtown Tour Plaza or ferry landing. ✉ *Avalon Canyon Rd., Avalon* ☎ *310/510–2897* 🎟 *$5* ⏲ *Daily 8–5.*

Where to Stay & Eat

$$–$$$ ✕ **Catalina Country Club.** The spring training clubhouse built for the Chicago Cubs now does duty as a restaurant for surf-and-turf standbys. The adjacent bar is great for an after-dinner drink; it connects to the old Cubs locker room. ✉ *1 Country Club Dr., Avalon* ☎ *310/510–7404* ✍ *Reservations essential* ▭ *AE, D, MC, V.*

★ **$$–$$$** ✕ **Channel House.** A longtime Avalon family owns this restaurant, serving dishes such as Catalina swordfish, coq au vin, and pepper steak. There's a patio facing the harbor, as well as an Irish bar. ✉ *205 Crescent Ave., Avalon* ☎ *310/510–1617* ▭ *AE, D, MC, V* ⏲ *Closed Mon. mid-Oct.–Easter.*

$–$$$ ✕ **Steve's Steakhouse.** You won't lack for scenic distraction here; almost every table has a bay view. There are, of course, thick rib-eye and porterhouse steaks, but don't overlook the locally bought fish. Avalon-style shrimp from the Gulf of Mexico is also a favorite. ✉ *417 Crescent Ave., Avalon* ☎ *310/510–0333* ▭ *AE, D, MC, V* ⏲ *No lunch Dec.–Apr.*

¢–$ ✕ **Eric's on the Pier.** Stroll out on the pier to this laid-back counter spot for a buffalo burger to go or perhaps, should you snag a patio table, an order of fish-and-chips or nachos. ✉ *Green Pier No. 2, Avalon* ☎ *310/510–0894* ▭ *AE, MC, V.*

$$$$ **Fodor's Choice** ★ 🏨 **Inn on Mt. Ada.** Staying in the mansion where William Wrigley Jr. once lived gives you all the comforts of a millionaire's home—at a millionaire's prices, beginning at $360 a night in summer. Breakfast, lunch, beverages, snacks, and use of a golf cart are included. The guest rooms are traditional and elegant; some have fireplaces and all have water views. The hilltop view of the curve of the bay is spectacular, and service is discreet. ✉ *398 Wrigley Rd., Avalon 90704* ☎ *310/510–2030 or 800/608–7669* 📠 *310/510–2237* 🌐 *www.catalina.com/mtada* *6 rooms* *Dining room; no room phones, no kids under 14, no smoking, no a/c* ▭ *MC, V* 🍽 *MAP.*

$$$ 🏨 **Hotel Metropole and Market Place.** This romantic hotel evokes the former look of New Orleans's French Quarter. Some guest rooms have balconies overlooking a flower-filled courtyard of restaurants and shops; others have ocean views. Many have fireplaces. For a stunning panorama, head for the rooftop deck. ⊠ *205 Crescent Ave., Avalon 90704* ☎ *310/510–1884 or 800/541–8528* 🖷 *310/510–2534* ⊕ *www.hotel-metropole.com* ➥ *44 rooms, 4 suites* ↻ *Some in-room hot tubs, some minibars, cable TV, no-smoking rooms* ▭ *AE, MC, V* ⅋⃝ *CP.*

$$–$$$ 🏨 **Hotel Villa Portofino.** Steps from the Pleasure Pier, this hotel strikes a discreet note. Rooms are named after Italian cities, and most are decorated in deep jewel tones. Some ocean-facing rooms have open balconies, fireplaces, and marble baths. You can sunbathe on the private deck, or ask for beach towels and chairs to take to the cove. ⊠ *111 Crescent Ave., Avalon 90704* ☎ *310/510–0555 or 800/346–2326* 🖷 *310/510–0839* ⊕ *www.hotelvillaportofino.com* ➥ *34 rooms* ↻ *Restaurant, minibars, cable TV* ▭ *AE, D, DC, MC, V* ⅋⃝ *CP.*

$–$$ 🏨 **Hotel Vista del Mar.** Contemporary rooms full of rattan furniture and greenery open onto a skylighted atrium. Some rooms have fireplaces, whirlpool tubs, and wet bars. Two larger rooms have ocean views. ⊠ *417 Crescent Ave., Avalon 90704* ☎ *310/510–1452 or 800/601–3836* 🖷 *310/510–2917* ⊕ *www.hotel-vistadelmar.com* ➥ *15 rooms* ↻ *Some in-room hot tubs, minibars, refrigerators, cable TV, in-room VCRs, no-smoking rooms* ▭ *AE, D, MC, V* ⅋⃝ *CP.*

Nightlife

El Galleon (⊠ 411 Crescent Ave., Avalon ☎ 310/510–1188) has microbrews, bar nibbles, and karaoke. **Luau Larry's** (⊠ 509 Crescent Ave., Avalon ☎ 310/510–1919), famous for the potent blue Whicky Whacker cocktail, comes alive with boisterous tourists and locals on summer weekends.

Sports & the Outdoors

BICYCLING Bike rentals are widely available in Avalon for about $5 per hour and $12 per day. Look for rentals on Crescent Avenue and Pebbly Beach Road such as **Brown's Bikes** (⊠ 107 Pebbly Beach Rd., next to Island Rentals, Avalon ☎ 310/510–0986 🖷 310/510–0747 ⊕ www.catalinabiking.com). To bike beyond the paved roads of Avalon, you must buy a day-use permit from the Catalina Conservancy. There's a two-day minimum for the $10 passes, and you may not ride on hiking paths.

DIVING & SNORKELING The Casino Point Underwater Park, with its handful of wrecks, is best suited for diving. Lover's Cove is better for snorkeling (no scuba diving allowed, but you'll share the area with glass-bottom boats). Both are protected marine preserves. **Catalina Divers Supply** (⊠ Green Pleasure Pier ☎ 310/510–0330 ⊕ www.catalinadiverssupply.com) rents equipment, runs guided scuba and snorkel tours, gives certification classes, and more. It has an outpost at Casino Point.

HIKING ■ TIP➔ **If you plan to backpack overnight, you'll need a camping reservation. The interior is dry and desertlike; bring plenty of water and sunblock.**

Permits from the **Santa Catalina Island Conservancy** (⊠ 3rd and Claressa Sts., Avalon ☎ 310/510–2595) are required for hiking into Catalina Island's interior. The permits are free and can be picked up at the main house of the conservancy or at the airport. You don't need a permit for shorter hikes, such as the one from Avalon to the Botanical Garden. The conservancy has maps of the island's east-end hikes, such as Hermit's Gulch Trail. It's possible to hike between Avalon and Two Harbors, starting at the Hogsback Gate, above Avalon, though the 28-mi journey has an elevation gain of 3,000 feet and is not for the weak. ■ TIP→ **For a pleasant 4-mi hike out of Avalon, take Avalon Canyon Road to Wrigley Gardens and follow the trail to Lone Pine. At the top, you'll have an amazing view of the Palisades cliffs and, beyond them, the sea.**

Another hike option is to take the **Airport Shuttle Bus** (☏ 310/510–0143) from Avalon to the airport for $17 round-trip. The 10-mi hike back to Avalon is mostly downhill, and the bus is an inexpensive way to see the interior of the island.

HORSEBACK RIDING   Horseback riders can wrangle four-legged transportation for scenic trail rides. Reservations must be made at the **Catalina Stables** (✉ 600 Avalon Canyon Rd., Avalon ☏ 310/510–0478), which has guided rides starting at $37 for a half hour.

CATALINA ISLAND ESSENTIALS

To research prices, get advice from other travelers, and book travel arrangements, visit www.fodors.com.

AIR TRAVEL

Island Express helicopters depart hourly from San Pedro and Long Beach (8 AM to sunset). The trip takes about 15 minutes and costs $87 one-way, $165.50 round-trip. Reservations a week in advance are recommended. ✈ Airlines & Contacts **Island Express** ☏ 800/228–2566 ⊕ www.islandexpress.com.

BOAT & FERRY TRAVEL

Two companies offer ferry service to Catalina Island. The boats have both indoor and outdoor seating and snack bars. Excessive baggage is not allowed, and there are extra fees for bicycles and surfboards. The waters around Santa Catalina can get rough, so if you're prone to seasickness, come prepared.

Catalina Express makes an hourlong run from Long Beach or San Pedro to Avalon and a 90-minute run from Dana Point to Avalon. Round-trip fare for the various routes costs $54. Service from Newport Beach to Avalon is available through Catalina Passenger Service. Boats leave from Balboa Pavilion at 9 AM (in season), take 75 minutes to reach the island, and cost $44 round-trip. Return boats leave Catalina at 4:30 PM. Reservations are advised in summer and on weekends for all trips. ■ TIP→ **Keep an eye out for dolphins, which sometimes swim alongside the ferries.**

FARES & SCHEDULES   ✈ Boat & Ferry Information **Catalina Express** ☏ 310/519–1212 or 800/481–3470 🖶 800/410–9159 ⊕ www.catalinaexpress.com. **Catalina Passenger Service** ☏ 949/673–5245 or 800/830–7744 🖶 949/673–8340 ⊕ www.catalinainfo.com.

GOLF CARTS

Golf carts constitute the island's main form of transportation. You can rent them along Avalon's Crescent Avenue and Pebbly Beach Road for about $35 per hour with a $30 deposit, payable via cash or travelers checks only.

⚑ Local Agencies **Island Rentals** ✉ 125 Pebbly Beach Rd., Avalon ☎ 310/510-1456.

TOURS

Santa Catalina Island Company runs the following Discovery Tours: a summer-only coastal cruise to Seal Rocks; the *Flying Fish* boat trip (summer evenings only); a comprehensive inland motor tour (which includes an Arabian horse performance); a tour of Skyline Drive; a Casino tour; a scenic tour of Avalon; a glass-bottom-boat tour, an undersea tour on a semisubmersible vessel; and a tour of the Botanical Garden. Reservations are highly recommended for the inland tours. Tours cost $13.50 to $99. There are ticket booths on the Green Pleasure Pier, at the Casino, in the plaza, and at the boat landing. Catalina Adventure Tours, which has booths at the boat landing and on the pier, arranges similar excursions at comparable prices.

The Santa Catalina Island Conservancy organizes custom ecotours and hikes of the interior. Naturalist guides drive open Jeeps through some gorgeously untrammeled parts of island. Tours start at $98 per person for a three-hour trip (three-person minimum); you can also book half- and full-day tours. The tours run year-round.

⚑ **Catalina Adventure Tours** ☎ 310/510-2888 🖷 310/510-2797 ⊕ www.catalinaadventuretours.com. **Santa Catalina Island Company** ☎ 310/510-8687 or 800/626-1496 ⊕ www.scico.com. **Santa Catalina Island Conservancy** ✉ 3rd and Claressa Sts., Avalon 90704 ☎ 310/510-2595 ⊕ www.catalinaconservancy.org.

VISITOR INFORMATION

⚑ Tourist Information **Catalina Island Visitors' Bureau** ✉ Green Pleasure Pier, Box 217, Avalon 90704 ☎ 310/510-1520 or 714/449-3372 🖷 310/510-7606 or 714/870-0597 ⊕ www.catalina.com.

Los Angeles

WORD OF MOUTH

"The Grove is just a retail mall, but the Farmers' Market has been around since the 1930s. This is a great place to get lunch . . . unlike your typical mall food court, this is real food."

–Lisa Oh

"Bastide was the best dining experience in my life. Very different, very good, it was perfect."

–Ryne

"The architecture and gardens of the Getty Center are truly amazing. Nice way to spend a sunny afternoon."

–Alison

EXPLORING LOS ANGELES

Updated by Kathy Bryant, Matthew Flynn, Roger J. Grody, Lina LeCaro, Kathy A. McDonald, Laura Randall, Zoe Wadler, Kastle Waserman

LOOKING AT A MAP OF SPRAWLING LOS ANGELES, first-time visitors are sometimes overwhelmed. Where to begin? What to see first? And what about all those freeways? Here's some advice: relax, do your best to accept the traffic, and set your priorities. Movie and television fans should first head to Hollywood, Universal Studios, and a taping of a television show. Beach lovers and outdoorsy types might start out in Santa Monica or Venice or Malibu, or spend an afternoon in Griffith Park, one of the largest city parks in the country. Those with a cultural bent should probably make a beeline for the Getty Center, the Huntington, or the Norton Simon Museum. And architecture buffs should begin with a visit to downtown Los Angeles.

Numbers in the text correspond to numbers in the margin and on the neighborhood maps.

Downtown Los Angeles

For the past few decades, Los Angeles has continually tried to reinvent its downtown area, cultivating new businesses, attractions, and cultural landmarks in an effort to create a core for a city that is in many ways decentralized. Valiant efforts to bring the suburban-bound masses back to the city center have yielded mixed results, including the stunning Walt Disney Concert Hall, the Cathedral of Our Lady of the Angels, and the world's most expensive, but still limited, subway. The changes may not happen as quickly as the city's movers and shakers might like, but downtown L.A. is keeping its place as the cultural and historic heart of the city, and its pulse is slowly getting stronger.

What to See

★ ❷ **Bradbury Building.** Designed in 1893 by a novice architect who drew his inspiration from a science-fiction story and a conversation with his dead brother via a Ouija board, the office building is a marvelous specimen of Victorian-era commercial architecture. Originally the site of turn-of-the-20th-century sweatshops, it now houses somewhat more genteel firms beyond the pink marble staircases. The interior atrium courtyard, with its glass skylight, wrought-iron balconies, and caged elevators, is frequently used as a movie locale (*Blade Runner* was filmed here). The building is open daily 9 to 5 for a peek, as long as you don't wander beyond the first-floor landing. ⊠ *304 S. Broadway, southeast corner Broadway and 3rd St., Downtown* ☎ *213/626–1893.*

★ ❿ **California African-American Museum.** Works by 20th-century African-American artists and contemporary works of the African diaspora are the backbone of this museum's permanent collection. Its exhibits document the African-American experience from Emancipation and Reconstruction through the 20th century, especially as expressed by artists in California and elsewhere in the West. Special musical as well as educational and cultural events are offered the first Sunday of every month. ⊠ *600 State Dr., Exposition Park* ☎ *213/744–7432* ⊕ *www.caamuseum.org* ⧉ *Free, parking $6* ☉ *Wed.–Sat. 10–4.*

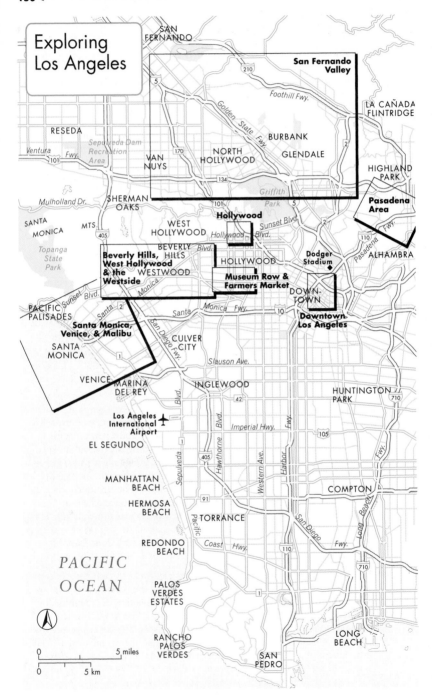

Exploring Los Angeles

SAN FERNANDO

San Fernando Valley

LA CAÑADA FLINTRIDGE

Foothill Fwy.

RESEDA

Sepulveda Dam Recreation Area

BURBANK

GLENDALE

HIGHLAND PARK

Ventura Fwy.

VAN NUYS

NORTH HOLLYWOOD

Pasadena Area

Mulholland Dr.

SHERMAN OAKS

Griffith Park

ALHAMBRA

SANTA MONICA MTS.

WEST HOLLYWOOD

Hollywood

Sunset Blvd.

Hollywood Blvd.

Topanga State Park

Beverly Hills, West Hollywood & the Westside

BEVERLY HILLS

WESTWOOD

HOLLYWOOD

Dodger Stadium

PACIFIC PALISADES

Sunset Blvd.

Santa Monica

Museum Row & Farmers Market

DOWN-TOWN

Santa Monica, Venice, & Malibu

Santa Monica Fwy.

Downtown Los Angeles

SANTA MONICA

CULVER CITY

Slauson Ave.

VENICE

MARINA DEL REY

INGLEWOOD

HUNTINGTON PARK

Los Angeles International Airport

Imperial Hwy.

EL SEGUNDO

MANHATTAN BEACH

COMPTON

HERMOSA BEACH

TORRANCE

REDONDO BEACH

Pacific Coast Hwy.

San Diego Fwy.

PACIFIC OCEAN

PALOS VERDES ESTATES

RANCHO PALOS VERDES

LONG BEACH

SAN PEDRO

0   5 miles

0   5 km

GREAT ITINERARIES

IF YOU HAVE 3 DAYS

Fortify yourself for your first whirlwind day with pancakes and coffee at the Farmers Market on Fairfax Avenue. Then drive north on Fairfax to Sunset Boulevard. Turn left onto the fabled Sunset Strip and stay on Sunset as it snakes past the lush estates of Beverly Hills and Bel Air. As you approach the San Diego freeway (Interstate 405), follow signs to the Getty Center, or if you prefer sand with your sun, skip the Getty and keep heading west on Sunset through Brentwood until the winding road gives way to breathtaking views of the Pacific Ocean. Spend the afternoon lolling on Will Rogers State Beach or farther up the coast on Malibu's Zuma Beach. As the sun sets, head south on the PCH to Santa Monica for dinner.

Start Day 2 on Hollywood Boulevard, following the pink terrazzo stars of the Walk of Fame to Grauman's Chinese Theatre. Hop on the Red Line Metro for the 20-minute ride downtown to Union Station and head over to Olvera Street and El Pueblo de Los Angeles Historical Monument. If you're an architecture buff, the Bradbury Building on Broadway (across from the market) and the Central Library's eight-story atrium a few blocks away on 5th Street are worth a look. Then head up Grand Avenue to see the swooping new Walt Disney Concert Hall and the stark Cathedral of Our Lady of the Angels. Before dark, drive or catch the Red Line Metro back to Hollywood.

On your third day get an early start and head to Universal Studios Hollywood. After the tour there, visit to the adjacent CityWalk, and finish with dinner at one of the many restaurants that line nearby Ventura Boulevard.

IF YOU HAVE 5 DAYS

Follow the three-day itinerary above, and on Day 4 hop onto the Ventura Freeway (Highway 134) and go east to Old Town Pasadena. Browse your way down Colorado Boulevard or duck into the small-but-exceptional Norton Simon Museum. Swing by the cluster of Greene and Greene Craftsman houses on Arroyo Terrace, then drive to San Marino's Huntington Library, Art Collections, and Botanical Gardens.

On your last day, cater to your cravings. Curious about the entertainment studios? Head to Burbank and take a studio tour of either NBC or Warner Bros. If you prefer urban wilderness over show business, go for a hike in Griffith Park or around the Hollywood Reservoir (with a backdrop of the HOLLYWOOD sign). If you'd rather exercise your credit cards, choose the neighborhoods that seem most up your alley—Beverly Hills, Santa Monica, and West Hollywood for luxe, Los Feliz, Silver Lake, and Echo Park for funky—and put in a few hours of shopping. Or explore the southern part of L.A. County by taking the Pacific Coast Highway to Long Beach.

3

🐾 ⑧ **California Science Center.** Clusters of interactive exhibits illustrate the relevance of science to everyday life, from bacteria to airplanes. Tess, the 50-foot animatronic star of the exhibit "Body Works," dramatically demonstrates how the body's organs work together to maintain balance. Other hands-on exhibits challenge you to construct earthquake-resistant structures and match actual brains with their animal owners. A cavernous Air and Space Gallery includes the *Gemini 11* space capsule that gave us our first view of Earth as a sphere. The latest addition: the Apollo Soyuz command module and the story behind the first joint space project between the United States and the Soviet Union. An IMAX theater shows large-format releases. ⊠ *700 State Dr., Exposition Park* ☎ *213/ 744–7400* ⊕ *www.casciencectr.org* 🖾 *Free, except for IMAX (prices vary); parking $6* ⊙ *Daily 10–5.*

⑦ **Cathedral of Our Lady of the Angels.** Controversy surrounded Spanish architect José Rafael Moneo's unconventional, costly, austere design for the seat of the Archdiocese of Los Angeles. But judging from the swarms of visitors and the standing-room-only holiday masses, the church has carved out a niche for itself in downtown's daily life. Opened in 2002, the ocher-concrete cathedral looms up by the Hollywood Freeway. The plaza in front is relatively austere, glaringly bright on sunny days; a children's play garden with bronze animals helps relieve the stark space. Imposing bronze entry doors, designed by local artist Robert Graham, are decorated with multicultural icons and New World images of the Virgin Mary. Artist John Nava used residents from his hometown of Ojai, California, as models for some of the 135 figures in the tapestries that line the nave walls. Make sure to go underground to wander the bright, somewhat incongruous, mazelike white-marble corridors of the mausoleum. Free guided tours start at the entrance fountain at 1 PM on weekdays. There's plenty of underground visitor parking; the vehicle entrance is on Hill Street. ■ TIP➡ **The café in the plaza has become one of downtown's favorite lunch spots, as you can pick up a fresh, reasonably priced meal to eat at one of the outdoor tables.** ⊠ *555 W. Temple St., Downtown* ☎ *213/ 680–5200* ⊕ *www.olacathedral.org* 🖾 *Free, parking $3 every 20 min, $14 maximum* ⊙ *Weekdays 6:30–6, Sat. 9–6, Sun. 7–6.*

FodorśChoice
★

★ ③ **The Geffen Contemporary.** Back in 1982, Disney Concert Hall architect Frank Gehry transformed a warehouse in Little Tokyo into a temporary space for the **Museum of Contemporary Art (MOCA)** while it was being built a mile away. The Temporary Contemporary—and its large, flexible space, anti-establishment character, and lively exhibits—was such a hit that it remains part of the museum facility. Now it is called the Geffen, and it houses a concise sample of MOCA's permanent collection, spanning the years from the 1940s to the present, and usually one or two temporary exhibits that evoke grins from even the most stuffy museumgoers. ⊠ *152 N. Central Ave., Downtown* ☎ *213/626–6222* ⊕ *www.moca-la.org* 🖾 *$8, free with MOCA admission on same day and on Thurs.* ⊙ *Mon. and Fri. 11–5, Thurs. 11–8, weekends 11–6.*

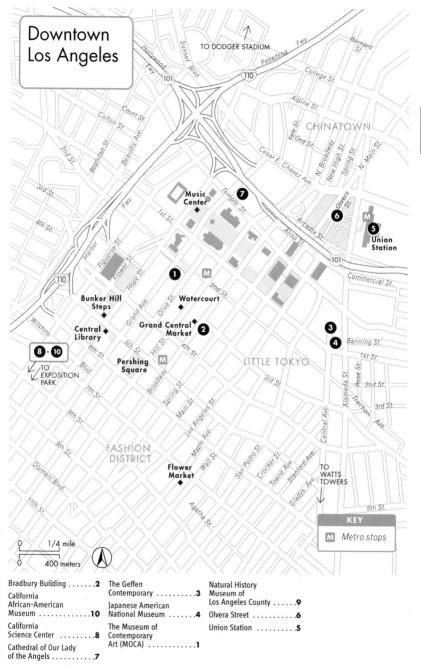

Downtown
Los Angeles

TO DODGER STADIUM

CHINATOWN

Music Center

Union Station

Bunker Hill Steps

Watercourt

Central Library

Grand Central Market

LITTLE TOKYO

Pershing Square

TO EXPOSITION PARK

FASHION DISTRICT

Flower Market

TO WATTS TOWERS

0   1/4 mile
0   400 meters

KEY
Ⓜ Metro stops

A GOOD TOUR

Weekdays are the best time to experience downtown, when the area is bustling with activity and cafés are open for lunch. Keep in mind that some museums are closed Monday. The **Los Angeles Conservancy** (☎ 213/623–2489 ⊕ www.laconservancy.org) regularly conducts Saturday morning walking tours of downtown architectural landmarks and districts. Most tours begin at 10 AM, last about 2½ hours, and are offered rain or shine. Reservations are required. Call for schedule and fees.

Begin a downtown tour by heading north on Broadway from 8th or 9th Street. At the southeast corner of Broadway and 3rd is the **Bradbury Building ② ▶**, with its fascinating interior court. (You can park behind the Bradbury Building on Spring Street for about $6.) Across the street is the Grand Central Market— once you've made your way through its tantalizing stalls you'll come out the opposite side onto Hill Street.

Cross Hill Street and climb steps up a steep hill to Watercourt, a friendly plaza with cafés and cascading fountains. Next, walk toward the glass pyramidal skylight topping the **Museum of Contemporary Art (MOCA) ①**, half a block north on Grand Avenue. Across from MOCA glimmers the swooping stainless-steel skin of the Walt Disney Concert Hall, one of the performance venues along Grand that comprises the Music Center. Heading north, you'll spot the stark concrete bell tower of the love-it-or-hate-it **Cathedral of Our Lady of the Angels ⑦**. It's well worth stepping inside the cathedral to see the delicate alabaster used instead of stained glass.

Now walk south on Grand to 5th Street, where you'll find two of downtown's historical and architectural treasures: the Millennium Biltmore Hotel and the Central Library. Take a breather behind the library in the tranquil Maguire Gardens. Across 5th Street are the Bunker Hill Steps, L.A.'s version of Rome's Spanish Steps.

Back in your car, continue north on Broadway to 1st Street. Make a right turn here and drive a few blocks to Little Tokyo and the expanded **Japanese American National Museum ④**. The Geffen **Contemporary ③** art museum, an arm of MOCA, is one block north on Central.

From Little Tokyo, turn left (north) from 1st onto Alameda Street. As you pass over the freeway, you'll come to the next stop, **Union Station ⑤**, on the right. Street parking is limited, so your best bet is to park in the pay lot at Union Station (about $5). After a look inside this grand railway terminal, cross Alameda to **Olvera Street ⑥**.

A convenient and inexpensive minibus service—DASH, or Downtown Area Short Hop—has several routes that travel past most of the sights on this tour, stopping every two blocks or so. Each ride costs 25¢, so you can hop on and off without spending a fortune. Special (limited) routes operate on weekends. Call **DASH** (☎ 808–2273 from all Los Angeles area codes) for routes and hours of operation.

4 Japanese American National Museum. What was it like to grow up on a coffee plantation in Hawaii? How difficult was life for Japanese-Americans interned in concentration camps during World War II? These questions are addressed by changing exhibits at this museum in Little Tokyo. Insightful volunteer docents are on hand to share their own stories and experiences. The museum occupies an 85,000-square-foot adjacent pavilion as well as its original site in a renovated 1925 Buddhist temple. ⊠ *369 E. 1st St., at Central Ave., next to Geffen Contemporary, Downtown* ☎ *213/625–0414* ⊕ *www.janm.org* ⊠ *$8, free Thurs. 5–8 and 3rd Thurs. of month* ☉ *Tues., Wed., and Fri.–Sun. 10–5.*

★ 1 The Museum of Contemporary Art (MOCA). The MOCA's permanent collection of American and European art from 1940 to the present divides itself between two spaces: the linear, red-sandstone building at California Plaza and the **Geffen Contemporary** in nearby Little Tokyo. Likewise, its exhibitions are split between the established and the cutting-edge. Heavy hitters such as Mark Rothko, Franz Kline, Susan Rothenberg, Diane Arbus, and Robert Frank are fixtures, and at least 20 themed shows rotate through annually. It's a good idea to check the schedule in advance, since some shows sell out, especially on weekends. The museum occasionally closes for exhibit installation. ⊠ *250 S. Grand Ave., Downtown* ☎ *213/626–6222* ⊕ *www.moca.org* ⊠ *$8, free on same day with Geffen Contemporary admission and on Thurs.* ☉ *Mon. and Fri. 11–5, Thurs. 11–8, weekends 11–6.*

☾ 9 Natural History Museum of Los Angeles County. With more than 3½ million specimens, this is the third-largest museum of its type in the United States after the Field Museum in Chicago and the American Museum of Natural History in New York. It has a rich collection of prehistoric fossils and extensive bird, insect, and marine-life exhibits. Brilliant stones shimmer in the Gem and Mineral Hall. An elaborate taxidermy exhibit shows North American and African mammals in detailed replicas of their natural habitats. Exhibits typifying various cultural groups include pre-Columbian artifacts and a display of crafts from the South Pacific. The Times-Mirror Hall of Native American Cultures delves into the history of Los Angeles's earliest inhabitants. The Ralph M. Parsons Discovery Center for children has hands-on exhibits. ⊠ *900 Exposition Blvd., Exposition Park* ☎ *213/763–3466* ⊕ *www.nhm.org* ⊠ *$9, free 1st Tues. of month* ☉ *Weekdays 9:30–5, weekends 10–5.*

★ ☾ 6 Olvera Street. This busy pedestrian block tantalizes with piñatas, mariachis, and fragrant Mexican food. As the major draw of the oldest section of the city, known as **El Pueblo deLos Angeles**, Olvera Street has come to represent the rich Mexican heritage of L.A. It had a close shave with disintegration in the early 20th century, until the socialite Christine Sterling walked through in 1926. Jolted by the historic area's decay, Sterling fought to preserve key buildings and led the transformation of the street into a Mexican-American marketplace. Today this character remains; vendors sell puppets, leather goods, sandals, serapes (woolen shawls), and handcrafts from stalls that line the center of the narrow street. On weekends, the restaurants are packed as musicians play in the central plaza. The weekends that fall around two Mexican holidays,

IF YOU LIKE

ART & ARCHITECTURE

Topping this art-loving city's museum list are the Getty Center; the Los Angeles County Museum of Art (LACMA) in the Mid-Wilshire district; the two sites of the Museum of Contemporary Art (MOCA); the Huntington Library, Art Collections, and Botanical Gardens, in San Marino; and the Norton Simon Museum in Pasadena. More than 50 other area museums house everything from medieval illuminated manuscripts to contemporary artworks. The city's art galleries have also been picking up steam, especially at Santa Monica's 5-acre Bergamot Station Art Center.

BEACHES

L.A.'s combination of sun, sand, and 72 mi of gorgeous coastline is hard to beat. It's all here: more than 30 mi of wide beaches, beach towns from the laid-back to the superchic, and plenty of sunny days to enjoy it all. Zuma Beach, north of Malibu, has always been popular with Angelenos for its pristine water and excellent facilities. Easily accessible Santa Monica beaches are always a scene, though the bay could be cleaner. Regardless of whether you like your beach rugged or serene, crowded or private, getting some sand on the floor of your car is practically a requirement here.

NIGHTLIFE

The club scene here is one of the world's best; you'll find everything from hard-hitting rock, heart-thumping techno, sophisticated jazz, and wailing blues joints to comedy clubs, dance clubs, and discos. The Sunset Strip and its environs in West Hollywood are famous for club- and bar-hopping. Though clubs on the Strip play to a young crowd, there are also plenty of venues for grown-ups, from the Troubadour to Bar Marmont. The bars of any hotels touched by hotelier André Balazs are virtually guaranteed buzz. West Hollywood's Santa Monica Boulevard is the core of the gay-and-lesbian club and coffeehouse scene. And from Echo Park to Malibu, small clubs and bars hum with local up-and-coming bands.

THE RESTAURANT SCENE

L.A.'s fantastic mix of cultures makes for a brilliant blend of cuisines. French or French-influenced cooking has been the focus at many high-profile new restaurants, but not surprisingly, Asian and Latin American elements have been sparking up menus, too. Chefs who make their mark in L.A. achieve near-celebrity status. The list includes Joachim Splichal, of Patina and the Pinot restaurants; Piero Selvaggio, of Valentino; and the king of sushi, Nobu Matsuhisa.

SHOPPING

Of course L.A. has malls, from the upscale designer-boutique variety to the mega-discount outlet type. But what Angelenos appreciate most are the city's unique shopping streets and outdoor markets. These are the places where you can not only see the sky, but also find great shops with merchandise the malls don't carry, and pop into terrific restaurants, bakeries, bookstores, and galleries. Among these places are trendy Robertson Boulevard, the Third Street Promenade in Santa Monica, elegant Rodeo Drive in Beverly Hills, and trendy Melrose Avenue.

Cinco de Mayo (May 5) and Independence Day (September 16), also draw huge crowds. To see Olvera Street at its quietest, visit late on a weekday afternoon, when long shadows heighten the romantic feeling of the passageway. For information, stop by the **Olvera Street Visitors Center** (✉ 622 N. Main St., Downtown ☎ 213/628–1274 ⊕ www.olvera-street.com), in the Sepulveda House, a Victorian built in 1887 as a hotel and boardinghouse. The center is open Monday through Saturday 10 to 3. Free 50-minute walking tours leave here at 10, 11, and noon Tuesday through Sunday.

★ ❺ **Union Station.** Built in 1939, Union Station was the key entry point into Los Angeles prior to LAX. Designed by City Hall architects John and Donald Parkinson, it combines Spanish colonial–revival and art-deco styles into a whole that's one of the country's last great rail stations and one of the most striking structures in L.A. The waiting hall's commanding scale and enormous chandeliers have provided the setting for so many films and TV shows that you may feel you've been here before. The station's restaurant, **Traxx,** is a great place for lunch, evoking a time when travel and style went hand in hand. ✉ *800 N. Alameda St., Downtown.*

Hollywood

You'll need a director's eye to find the glitter within this legendary, now largely grim locale. Still, there is some magic left, and much of it can be found on foot around the recently relocated home of the Academy Awards at the Kodak Theatre, part of the Hollywood & Highland entertainment complex. The adjacent Grauman's Chinese Theatre delivers silver-screen magic with its cinematic facade and ornate interiors from a bygone era. A shining example of a successful Hollywood revival can be seen and experienced at the 1926 El Capitan Theatre just across Hollywood Boulevard, which offers live stage shows and Wurlitzer-organ music before selected movie engagements. If you walk the renowned Hollywood Walk of Stars to find your favorite celebrities, you'll encounter derelict diversions literally screaming for your attention (and dollar), as well as numerous panhandlers and an occasional costumed superhero not sanctified by Marvel comics. A developer-interpreted vision of Schwab's Pharmacy at Sunset and Vine, across the street from the once-futuristic Cinerama Dome movie theater, draws crowds. At sundown, you can admire Hollywood's crowning jewel: the Hollywood Bowl, summer home to the Los Angeles Philharmonic.

What to See

❾ **Arclight/Cinerama Dome.** With plush stadium seating, reserved seats for some showings, state-of-the-art sound, an usher who welcomes you and introduces the film, and snack bars that cook up their own fresh caramel corn, the Arclight justifies its high ticket prices ($11 to $14, depending on the hour you go). Built next to the restored geodesic Cinerama Dome, a curved-screen architectural icon, the complex also caters to film lovers with special director's Q&A nights as well as exhibits of movie costumes and photography throughout the lobby. Even though there are 14 other theaters in the complex, many films sell out quickly. Your best chance at prime seating is to order tickets online and to choose a seat

A GOOD TOUR

Start off by driving up into the Hollywood Hills on Beachwood Drive (off Franklin Avenue, just east of Gower Street) for an up-close look at one of the world's most familiar icons: the HOLLYWOOD sign ➊ ☞. Follow the small sign pointing the way to the LAFD Helispot. Turn left onto Rodgerton Drive, which twists and turns higher into the hills. At Deronda Drive, turn right and drive to the end. The HOLLYWOOD sign looms off to the left. Turn around and retrace your route down the hill, back to Beachwood for the drive into Hollywood.

Make a right (west) at Franklin Avenue, and prepare to turn left at the next light at Gower Street. At Gower and Santa Monica Boulevard, look for the entrance to Hollywood Forever Cemetery, half a block east on Santa Monica, where you can pay your respects to Rudolph Valentino and Mel "That's all folks!" Blanc. From the cemetery, retrace your route back to Gower Street and turn left to drive along the western edge of the cemetery flanking Gower. Abutting the cemetery's southern edge is **Paramount Pictures** ➍. The famous gate Norma Desmond (Gloria Swanson in *Sunset Boulevard*) was driven through is no longer accessible to the public, but a replica marks the entrance on Melrose Avenue: turn left from Gower Street to reach the gate.

Next, drive west (right off Gower) on Melrose for three blocks to Vine Street, turn right, and continue to the world-famous intersection of Hollywood and Vine. Across the street is the **Capitol Records Tower** ➌, which resembles a stack of 45 rpm records.

Drive west along Hollywood Boulevard. Stop along the way for a look at the bronze stars that make up the **Hollywood Walk of Fame** ➎, or to visit the Lingerie Museum at the purple Frederick's of Hollywood or the Hollywood Wax Museum, Guinness World of Records, and Ripley's Believe It or Not Museum triangle.

At Hollywood Boulevard and Las Palmas Avenue is Hollywood's first movie palace, the striking Egyptian Theatre. Continue west on Hollywood Boulevard two blocks until you see the giant, Babylonian-themed, hotel-retail-entertainment complex **Hollywood & Highland** ➏, which includes the 3,300-seat Kodak Theatre, home of the Academy Awards.

Next to Hollywood & Highland is **Grauman's Chinese Theatre** ➐. The elaborate pagoda-style movie palace is still the biggest draw along Hollywood Boulevard. Also on the north side of the boulevard and west of the Chinese Theatre is the **Hollywood Entertainment Museum** ➑. From the museum, cross Hollywood Boulevard and loop back east past the Hollywood Roosevelt Hotel, a spot that's historic and newly hot.

For a spectacular Cinemascope view of the glittering city lights, from Hollywood to the ocean, head up to the Griffith Observatory, perched on a promontory in **Griffith Park** ➋. From Hollywood Boulevard, go north on Western Avenue, which becomes Los Feliz Boulevard. Take a left on Vermont Avenue and follow the signs that lead you into the park and up the hill to the observatory.

KEY

M Metro stops

▶ Start of walk

in advance. A printed receipt allows you to walk directly into the theater and avoid the lines. Weekend nights have an especially hip buzz as film enthusiasts and industry power couples linger in the soaring lobby. ✉ *6360 Sunset Blvd., at Vine St., Hollywood* ☎ *323/464–4226* ⊕ *www.arclightcinemas.com.*

★ ❸ **Capitol Records Tower.** The romantic story about the origin of this symbol of '50s chic is that singer Nat King Cole and songwriter Johnny Mercer suggested that the record company's headquarters be shaped to look like a stack of 45s. Architect Welton Becket claimed he just wanted to design a structure that economized space, and in so doing, he created the world's first cylindrical office building. On its south wall, L.A. artist Richard Wyatt's mural *Hollywood Jazz, 1945–1972* immortalizes musical greats Duke Ellington, Billie Holiday, Ella Fitzgerald, and Miles Davis. Due to tightened security, the building is not open to the public. ✉ *1750 N. Vine St., Hollywood.*

★ ❼ **Grauman's Chinese Theatre.** This fantasy of Chinese pagodas and temples is a place only Hollywood could turn out. Although you have to buy a movie ticket to appreciate the interior trappings, the courtyard is open to the public. Here you'll find those oh-so-famous cement hand- and footprints. This tradition is said to have begun at the theater's opening in 1927, with the premiere of Cecil B. DeMille's *King of Kings,* when actress Norma Talmadge accidentally stepped into wet cement. Now more than 160 celebrities have contributed imprints for posterity, including some oddball specimens, such as one of Jimmy Durante's nose. ✉ *6925 Hollywood Blvd., Hollywood* ☎ 323/461–3331, 323/463–9576 *for tours* ⊕ *www.manntheatres.com.*

❷ **Griffith Park.** L.A.'s communal backyard is the largest municipal park and urban wilderness area in the United States; its 4,100 arcres sprawl over the northwest corner of the city. The park was named after Griffith J. Griffith, a mining tycoon who donated much of the land to the city in 1896. It has been used as a filming location since the early days of motion pictures. One of the most famous filming sites is high on a hillside overlooking the city, the Griffith Observatory is one of the most celebrated icons of Los Angeles, as much for the spectacular views as for the academic astronomy shows in the planetarium theater, the free telescope viewings, and the astronomy exhibits in the Hall of Science. You might recognize the observatory and grounds from such movies as *Rebel Without a Cause* and *The Terminator.* ■ TIP➜ **At this writing, the planetarium was due to open in late 2006 after several years of renovations. Its new incarnation will double the exhibit space, double the theater size, and add a café, classroom, and bookstore.** ✉ *2800 E. Observatory Rd., Griffith Park* ☎ 323/664–1191 ⊕ *www.griffithobservatory.org.*

★ ❻ **Hollywood & Highland.** This hotel-retail-entertainment complex was a swaggering play to bring glitz and attention back to Hollywood. The design pays tribute to the city's film legacy with a grand staircase leading up to a pair of magnificent 33-foot-high elephants, a nod to the 1916 movie *Intolerance.* ■ TIP➜ **Pause at the entrance arch, Babylon Court, which frames the** HOLLYWOOD **sign in the hills above for a picture-perfect view.** There are plenty of clothing stories and eateries—and you may find yourself ducking into these for a respite from the crowds and street artists. The various stores are closed and covered with drapery come Oscar day, when Academy Awards attendees enter the plush **Kodak Theatre** through a red-carpeted portal. A Metro Red Line station provides easy access to and from other parts of the city, and there's plenty of underground parking accessible from Highland Avenue. ✉ *Hollywood Blvd. and Highland Ave., Hollywood* ⊕ *www.hollywoodandhighland.com* 🅿 *Parking $2 with validation* ⊙ *Mon.–Sat. 10–10, Sun. 10–7.*

❽ **Hollywood Entertainment Museum.** You'll get an eyeful of small- and big-screen history here; famous props are a strong suit. The entire sets of the *Cheers* bar and Mulder's office from *X-Files* have landed here; you can even sit in the *Starship Enterprise* captain's chair from *Star Trek.* Other collections focus on early television and film cameras and makeup by Max Factor, the first cosmetics designed for film. Take a docent-led tour—the enthusiastic guides give an in-depth look at costume making, storyboarding, and set design. ✉ *7021 Hollywood Blvd., Hollywood* ☎ 323/465–7900 ⊕ *www.hollywoodmuseum.com* 🅿 *$12* ⊙ *Daily 10–6.*

▶ ★ ❶ HOLLYWOOD **Sign.** With letters 50 feet tall, Hollywood's trademark sign can be spotted from miles away. The sign, which originally read HOLLYWOODLAND, was erected on Mt. Lee in the Hollywood Hills in 1923 to promote a real-estate development. In 1949 the "land" portion of the sign was taken down. Inevitably, the sign has drawn pranksters who have altered it over the years, albeit temporarily, to spell out HOLLYWEED (in the 1970s, to commemorate lenient marijuana laws), GO NAVY (before a Rose Bowl game), and PEROTWOOD (during the 1992 presidential election). A fence and surveillance equipment have since been installed to deter intruders. ⊕ *www.hollywoodsign.org.*

★ ❺ **Hollywood Walk of Fame.** Along Hollywood Boulevard runs a trail of affirmations for entertainment-industry achievers. On this mile-long stretch of sidewalk, inspired by the concrete handprints in front of Grauman's Chinese Theatre, the names are embossed in brass, each at the center of a pink star embedded in dark-gray terrazzo. The first eight stars were unveiled in 1960. Since then, more than 1,600 others have been immortalized. To aid you in spotting celebrities you're looking for, they are identified by one of five icons: a motion-picture camera, a radio microphone, a television set, a record, or a theatrical mask. Contact the **Hollywood Chamber of Commerce** (✉ 7018 Hollywood Blvd. ☎ 323/469–8311 ⊕ www.hollywoodchamber.net) for celebrity-star locations and information on future star installations.

❹ **Paramount Pictures.** With a history dating to the early 1920s, this studio Fodor'sChoice was home to some of Hollywood's most luminous stars, including ★ Rudolph Valentino, Mae West, Mary Pickford, and Lucille Ball, who filmed episodes of *I Love Lucy* here. The lot still churns out memorable movies and TV shows, including *Forrest Gump, Titanic,* and *Star Trek.* You can take a studio tour (reservations required) led by friendly guides who walk and trolley you around the back lots. As well as gleaning some gossipy history (see the lawn where Lucy and Desi broke up), you'll spot the sets of TV and film shoots in progress, including such hits as *Entertainment Tonight, Dr. Phil,* and *Everybody Hates Chris.* You can also be part of the audience for live TV tapings. Tickets are free; call for listings and times. ✉ *5555 Melrose Ave., Hollywood* ☎ *323/956–1777* ⊕ *www.paramount.com/studio* ◨ *Tours $35.*

Wilshire Boulevard, Museum Row & Farmers Market

The three-block stretch of Wilshire Boulevard known as Museum Row, east of Fairfax Avenue, racks up five intriguing museums and a prehistoric tar pit to boot. Only a few blocks away is the historic Farmers Market and the Grove shopping mall, a great place to people-watch. You can glimpse the former city center along Wilshire from Fairfax Avenue to downtown, where celebs once partied at the Coconut Grove and dined at Perino's. Finding parking along Wilshire Boulevard can present a challenge any time of the day; you'll find advice on the information phone lines of most attractions.

What to See

❶ **Farmers Market and the Grove.** In 1934 two entrepreneurs convinced oil Fodor'sChoice magnate E. B. Gilmore to open a vacant field for a bare-bones market; ★ a group of farmers simply pulled up their trucks and sold fresh produce off the back. From this seat-of-the-pants situation grew a European-style open-air market and local institution at the corner of 3rd Street and Fair-

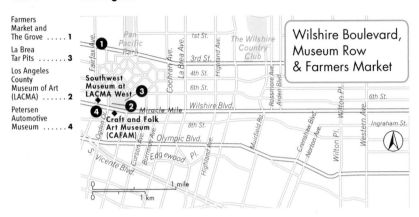

Wilshire Boulevard,
Museum Row
& Farmers Market

fax Avenue. This is the place where you can truly experience L.A.'s diversity: old and young, natives and transplants, all eating and shopping. The market includes 110 stalls and more than 20 counter-order restaurants, plus the landmark 1941 Clock Tower. The Grove, an outdoor shopping area, bulges with such chains as Banana Republic, Crate & Barrel, and J. Crew. Los Angeles history gets a nod with an electric steel-wheeled "Red Car" trolley that shuttles two blocks through the Farmers Market and the Grove. The Grove really dazzles around Christmas, with an enormous Christmas tree and a nightly faux snowfall until New Year's Day. ⊠ *Farmers Market, 6333 W. 3rd St.; The Grove, 189 The Grove Dr., Fairfax District* ☏ *Farmers Market 323/933–9211, The Grove 323/900–8080* ⊕ *www.farmersmarketla.com; www.TheGroveLA.com* ☉ *Farmers Market weekdays 9–9, Sat. 9–8, Sun. 10–9; The Grove Mon.–Thurs. 10–9, Fri. and Sat. 10–10, Sun. 11–7.*

❸ **La Brea Tar Pits.** About 40,000 years ago, deposits of oil rose to the Earth's surface, collected in shallow pools, and coagulated into sticky asphalt. In the early 20th century, geologists discovered that the sticky goo contained the largest collection of Pleistocene, or Ice Age, fossils ever found at one location: more than 600 species of birds, mammals, plants, reptiles, and insects. More than 100 tons of fossil bones have been removed in excavations over the last seven decades, making this one of the world's most famous fossil sites. You can see most of the pits through chain-link fences. Pit 91 is the site of ongoing excavation; tours are available and you can volunteer to help with the excavations in summer. Statues of a family of mammoths in the big pit near the corner of Wilshire and Curson suggest how many of them were entombed: edging down to a pond of water to drink, animals were caught in the tar and unable to extricate themselves. There are several pits scattered around Hancock Park and the surrounding neighborhood; construction in the area has often had to accommodate them and, in nearby streets and along sidewalks, little bits of tar occasionally and unstoppably ooze up. The **Page Museum at the La Brea Tar Pits** (☏ 323/934–7243) displays fossils from the tar pits. ⊠ *Hancock Park, Miracle Mile* ⊕ *www.tarpits.org* ☝ *Free.*

② Los Angeles County Museum of Art (LACMA). Since it opened in 1966, LACMA has assembled an encyclopedic collection of more than 150,000 works from around the world; its collection is widely considered the most comprehensive in the western United States. American, Latin American, Islamic, and South and Southeast Asian works are especially well represented. Other standout areas include costumes and textiles, decorative arts, European paintings and sculpture, photography, drawings, and prints. The collections are spread through five disparate buildings on the main campus, plus another building two blocks away. Most of LACMA's buildings cluster around a courtyard. The Ahmanson building is the equivalent of Art History 101, with everything from Mesoamerican artifacts to 19th-century European masters. Hit the Robert O. Anderson building for 20th-century and contemporary art. A special pavilion showcases Japanese art. LACMA West, a Streamline Moderne building a short walk from the main campus, is heavy on Mexican modern masters (Rivera, Tamayo, Orozco, Siquieros). It also contains the Experimental Gallery that, with its interactive technologies, reading room, and video stations, is geared primarily to schoolchildren and families. Plans for a renovation, set to open by 2007, were announced in 2005. ✉ *5905 Wilshire Blvd., Miracle Mile* ☎ *323/857–6000* ⊕ *www.lacma. org* ✐ *$7, free 2nd Tues. of month* ☉ *Mon., Tues., and Thurs. noon–8, Fri. noon–9, weekends 11–8.*

④ Petersen Automotive Museum. More than just a building full of antique or unusual cars, the Petersen proves highly entertaining and informative, thanks to the lifelike dioramas and street scenes that help establish a context for the history of the automobile. Rotating exhibits on the second floor may include Hollywood-celebrity and movie cars, "muscle" cars (like a 1969 Dodge Daytona 440 Magnum), motorcycles, and commemorative displays of the Ferrari. You'll also learn about the origins of our modern-day car-insurance system, as well as the history of L.A.'s formidable freeway network. A children's interactive Discovery Center illustrates the mechanics of the automobile; there's also a gift shop and research library. ✉ *6060 Wilshire Blvd., Miracle Mile* ☎ *323/930–2277* ⊕ *www.petersen.org* ✐ *$10* ☉ *Tues.–Sun. 10–6.*

Beverly Hills & West Hollywood

Although much of L.A. is fragmented and occasionally disappointing, Beverly Hills delivers big-time. In this foot-friendly district of extreme makeovers and opulent wealth, the fable of the Los Angeles lifestyle is on daily parade. World-famous Rodeo Drive—with its tony boutiques, swaying palms, and sunny skies—will make you feel you're on a movie set. Stars (along with their kids, nannies, and agents) dine, shop, and stroll here for all to see—so remember to bring your camera.

Just east of Beverly Hills is West Hollywood, which isn't so much a place to "see" things (like museums or movie studios) as it is a place to "do" things—like go nightclubbing, eat at top-notch restaurants, and attend gallery openings. Since the end of Prohibition, West Hollywood's Sunset Strip has been the city's nighttime playground, and today it's still going strong.

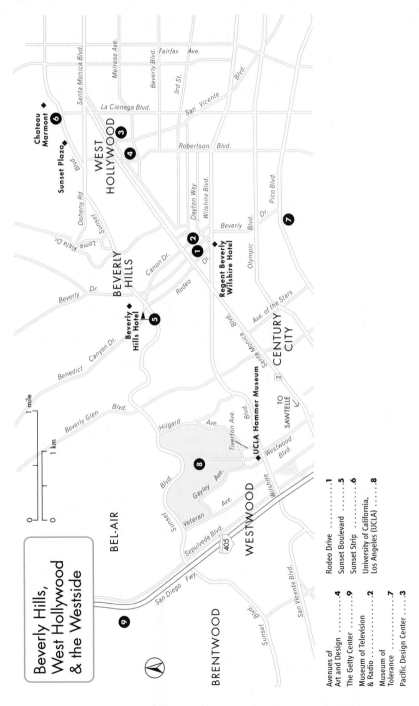

Beverly Hills,
West Hollywood
& the Westside

But hedonism isn't all that drives West Hollywood. The area attracted a particularly dedicated community and in the 1980s, a coalition of seniors, gays, and lesbians spearheaded a grassroots effort to make it an independent city. The coalition succeeded in 1984, and today West Hollywood has emerged as one of the most progressive cities in Southern California. It's also one of the most gay-friendly cities anywhere, with one third of its population estimated to be either gay or lesbian. The annual Gay Pride Parade is one of the largest in the nation, drawing tens of thousands of participants each June.

What to See

❹ Avenues of Art and Design. A concentration of design studios and art and antiques galleries along Melrose Avenue, San Vicente Boulevard, Robertson Boulevard, North Almont, and other streets around the Pacific Design Center has given rise to this catch-all designation. The galleries are very high-end, but it doesn't cost anything to look (sometimes the window is as far as you can get; many of these studios are "to the trade only"). Periodically, usually on the first Saturday evening of the month, several of the galleries host group-opening receptions, or "Gallery Walks," to premiere new exhibits and artists. Contact the **West Hollywood Convention and Visitors Bureau** for information. ☎ *310/289–2525 or 800/368–6020* ⊕ *www.visitwesthollywood.com.*

❷ Museum of Television & Radio. You can revisit your favorite *Mary Tyler Moore* episodes at this sister to the Museum of Television & Radio in New York; its collection of 100,000 programs spans eight decades. Search for your favorite commercials and television and radio shows on easy-to-use computers, and then watch or listen to them in an adjacent room. There are special exhibits of television- and radio-related art and costumes, as well as frequent seminars with television and radio cast members. ⊠ *465 N. Beverly Dr., Beverly Hills* ☎ *310/786–1000* ⊕ *www.mtr.org* 🎫 *$10 suggested donation* ⊙ *Wed.–Sun. noon–5.*

❸ Pacific Design Center. Cesar Pelli designed these two architecturally intriguing buildings, one sheathed in blue glass (the "Blue Whale"), the other in green (the "Green Whale"). Together, they house 150 design showrooms, making this the largest interior-design complex in the western United States. But the showrooms are open only to the trade; unless you've got an interior decorator in tow or you're one yourself, your browsing options are limited. The downtown Museum of Contemporary Art has opened a satellite **MOCA Gallery** (☎ 213/626–6222 ⊕ www.moca.org) here, though, which opens intermittently for shows on architecture and design. Three cafés on the premises are also open to the public. ⊠ *8687 Melrose Ave., West Hollywood* ☎ *310/657–0800* ⊕ *www.p-d-c.com* ⊙ *Weekdays 9–5.*

★ ❶ Rodeo Drive. No longer an exclusive shopping street, Rodeo Drive is one of Southern California's bona fide tourist attractions. Just as if they were at Disneyland or in Hollywood, T-shirt-and-shorts-clad tourists wander along this tony stretch of avenue, window-shopping at Tiffany & Co., Gucci, Armani, Hermès, Harry Winston, and Lladró. Several nearby restaurants have patios where you can sip a drink while watching fashionable shoppers saunter by. At the southern end of Rodeo

A GOOD DRIVE

Plan to arrive in Beverly Hills mid-morning. Most stores open by 10 or 11 AM, with limited hours on Sunday. (Some are closed on Sunday or Monday.) Park your car in one of several municipal lots (the first one or two hours are free; after that it's $6 per hour), and stroll along Rodeo Drive. There are plenty of reasonably priced cafés and restaurants for lunch. The major routes in and out of Beverly Hills—Wilshire and Santa Monica boulevards—get very congested during rush hours.

Traffic on Sunset and Santa Monica boulevards is heavy most of the day, especially at night and on weekends. Special "no-cruising" regulations are in effect at certain times on certain streets. Weekday afternoons are generally the easiest driving times. For street parking, bring plenty of quarters; parking on residential streets is by permit only.

Begin a tour of Beverly Hills on **Sunset Boulevard** ➎ ▶, at the landmark Beverly Hills Hotel, aka the Pink Palace. If you'd like to see some of the luxe estates that give the 90210 zip code its cachet, loop along a few of the streets north of Sunset. Otherwise, turn south onto **Rodeo Drive** ➊ (pronounced ro-*day*-o). You'll pass through a residential neighborhood before hitting the shopping stretch of Rodeo south of Santa Monica Boulevard. Across Wilshire, the Regent Beverly Wilshire Hotel serves as a temporary residence for the rich and famous. The **Museum of Television & Radio** ➋ stands a block east of Rodeo, on Beverly Drive at Santa Monica Boulevard. A few blocks west of Beverly Hills is the high-rise office-tower and shopping-center area known as Century City.

Head north on Beverly Drive for a few blocks to get back to Sunset Boulevard, turning right (east) toward West Hollywood. Once you pass Doheny Drive, you'll have technically left Beverly Hills and be cruising the **Sunset Strip** ➏, known for nightclubs such as the Whisky A Go-Go, the Roxy, and the Viper Room. Sunset Plaza is a good place to get out of the car and take a stroll, do some high-end window-shopping, or pass the time people-watching from a sidewalk café. Look for parking in the lot behind the shops, off Sunset Plaza Drive. A bit farther east, past La Cienega Boulevard, is the all-white ultrahip Mondrian Hotel. Back in your car, you can continue east toward Crescent Heights Boulevard if you'd like a glimpse of the famous hotel Chateau Marmont. Turning south on La Cienega will take you to Santa Monica Boulevard; from roughly La Cienega to Robertson Boulevard, Santa Monica Boulevard is the commercial core of West Hollywood's large gay and lesbian community. (It's also part of historic Route 66.) A left turn at San Vicente Boulevard will bring you to West Hollywood's most visible landmark, the **Pacific Design Center** ➌. There's public parking available at the PDC, and you can get out and walk back a block to Santa Monica Boulevard or head west on Melrose Avenue. This walkable section of town, filled with design studios and art galleries, is known as the **Avenues of Art and Design** ➍.

Drive (at Wilshire Boulevard) is **Via Rodeo,** a curvy cobblestone street designed to resemble a European shopping area. The cobblestones and flower vendor make for a pretty picture-taking spot. ⊠ *Beverly Hills.*

⑤ Sunset Boulevard. One of the most fabled avenues in the world, Sunset Boulevard began humbly enough in the 18th century as a route from El Pueblo de Los Angeles (today's downtown L.A.) to the ranches in the west and then to the Pacific Ocean. Now as it winds its way across the L.A. Basin to the ocean, it cuts through gritty urban neighborhoods and what used to be the working center of Hollywood's movie industry. In West Hollywood, it becomes the sexy and seductive Sunset Strip, then slips quietly into the tony environs of Beverly Hills and Bel-Air, twisting and winding past gated estates. Continuing on past UCLA in Westwood, through Brentwood and Pacific Palisades, Sunset finally descends to the beach, the edge of the continent, and the setting sun.

★ ⑥ Sunset Strip. For 60 years the Hollywood nighttime crowd has headed for the 1¾-mi stretch of Sunset Boulevard between Crescent Heights Boulevard and Doheny Drive, known as the Sunset Strip. In the 1930s and '40s, stars like Tyrone Power, Errol Flynn, Norma Shearer, and Rita Hayworth came for wild evenings of dancing and drinking at nightclubs like Trocadero, Ciro's, and Mocambo. By the '60s and '70s, the Strip had become the center of rock and roll: Johnny Rivers, the Byrds, the Doors, Elton John, and Bruce Springsteen gave legendary performances on stages at clubs like the Whisky A Go-Go and Roxy. Nowadays it's the Viper Room and the House of Blues, where you'll find on-the-cusp actors, rock stars, and out-of-towners all mingling over drinks and live music. Parking is tough, especially on weekends, but the time and money may be worth it if you plan on making the rounds—most clubs are within walking distance of each other.

The Westside

For some privileged Los Angelenos, the city begins west of La Cienega Boulevard, where "keeping up with the Joneses" takes place on an epic scale. Chic, attractive neighborhoods with coveted zip codes—Bel Air, Brentwood, Westwood, West Los Angeles, and Pacific Palisades—are home to power couples pushing power kids in power strollers. But the Westside is also rich in culture—and not just entertainment-industry culture. It's home to UCLA, the monumental Getty Center, and the compelling Museum of Tolerance.

What to See

⑨ The Getty Center. With its curving walls and isolated hilltop perch, the Getty Center resembles a pristine fortified city of its own. You may be lured up by the beautiful views of L.A. (on a clear day stretching all the way to the Pacific Ocean), but the architecture, the uncommon gardens, and the fascinating art collections are more than enough to hold your attention. When the sun's out, the complex's rough-cut travertine marble skin seems to soak up the light.

FodorśChoice ★

J. Paul Getty, the billionaire oil magnate and art collector, began collecting Greek and Roman antiquities and French decorative arts in the

1930s. He opened the J. Paul Getty Museum at his Malibu estate in 1954, and in the 1970s, he built a re-creation of an ancient Roman village to house his initial collection. When Getty died in 1976, the museum received an endowment of $700 million that grew to a reported $4.2 billion. The Malibu villa, reopened in 2006, is devoted to the antiquities. The Getty Center, designed by Richard Meier, opened in 1998. It pulls together the rest of the collections and museum's affiliated research, conservation, and philanthropic institutes.

The Getty's five pavilions surround a central courtyard and are bridged by walkways. Artist Robert Irwin created the Central Garden, whose focal point is an azalea maze in a pool. At almost every turn you'll spot terrific views of the city. The permanent collections include European paintings, drawings, sculpture, illuminated manuscripts, and decorative arts, as well as American and European photographs. Notable among the paintings are Rembrandt's *The Abduction of Europa*, Van Gogh's *Irises*, Monet's *Wheatstack, Snow Effects, Morning,* and James Ensor's *Christ's Entry Into Brussels*. Don't miss the exceptional collection of French furniture and decorative arts.

Parking is free and based on availability; reservations are no longer required. ⊠ *1200 Getty Center Dr., Brentwood* ☎ *310/440–7300* ⊕ *www.getty.edu* 🖃 *Free, parking $7* ⊙ *Tues.–Thurs. and Sun. 10–6, Fri. and Sat. 10–9.*

★ ❼ **Museum of Tolerance.** Using interactive technology, this important museum (part of the Simon Weisenthal Center) challenges visitors to confront bigotry and racism. One of the most affecting sections covers the Holocaust, with film footage of deportation scenes and simulated sets of concentration camps. Anne Frank artifacts are part of the museum's permanent collection. Interactive exhibits include the "Millennium Machine," which engages visitors in finding solutions to human rights abuses around the world, and the "Point of View Diner," a recreation of a 1950s diner, red booths and all, that "serves" a menu of controversial topics on video jukeboxes. To ensure a visit to this popular museum, make reservations in advance (especially for Friday, Sunday, and holidays), and plan to spend at least three hours there. In-person testimony from Holocaust survivors is offered periodically. Museum entry stops at least two hours before the actual closing time. A photo ID is required for admission. ⊠ *9786 W. Pico Blvd., just south of Beverly Hills* ☎ *310/553–8403* ⊕ *www.museumoftolerance.com* 🖃 *$10* ⊙ *Sun. 11–7:30, Mon.–Thurs. 11:30–6:30, Fri. 11:30–3 (open 'til 5 Apr.–Oct.).*

❽ **University of California, Los Angeles (UCLA).** With spectacular buildings such as a Romanesque library, the parklike UCLA campus is a wonderful place to stroll. In the heart of the north campus, the Franklin Murphy Sculpture Garden contains more than 70 works by such artists as Henry Moore and Gaston Lachaise. The Mildred Mathias Botanic Garden, which contains some 5,000 species of plants from all over the world in a 7-acre outdoor garden, is in the southeast section of the campus. West of the main campus bookstore, the Morgan Center Hall of Fame displays the sports memorabilia and trophies of the university's athletic departments.

Many visitors head straight to the **UCLA Fowler Museum of Cultural History** (☎ 310/825–4361 ⊕ www.fmch.ucla.edu), which presents changing exhibits on the world's diverse cultures and visual arts, especially those of Africa, Asia, Oceania, and Native and Latin America. Just south of the main campus area is the **UCLA Hammer Museum** (✉ 10899 Wilshire Blvd. ☎310/443–7000 ⊕www.hammer.ucla.edu), with its trove of works by old masters, French impressionists, and graphic artists.

Campus maps and information are available at drive-by kiosks at major entrances. The main entrance gate is on Westwood Boulevard. Campus parking costs $7. ✉ *Bordered by Le Conte, Hilgard, and Gayley Aves. and Sunset Blvd., Westwood* ⊕ *www.ucla.edu.*

Santa Monica, Venice & Malibu

The desirable, varied communities of Santa Monica, Venice, and Malibu curve along L.A.'s coastline. These high-rent areas hug Santa Monica Bay in an arc of diversity, from the ultracasual, ultrarich Malibu to the bohemian-seedy mix of Venice. What they have in common, however, is cleaner air, mild temperatures, often horrific traffic, and an emphasis on the beach-focused lifestyle that many people consider the hallmark of Southern California.

What to See

❹ **Malibu Lagoon State Beach.** Visitors are asked to stay on the boardwalks at this 5-acre marshy area so that the egrets, blue herons, avocets, and gulls remain undisturbed. The signs listing opening and closing hours refer only to the parking lot; the lagoon itself is open 24 hours and is particularly enjoyable in the early morning and at sunset. Streetside parking is available at those times, but not at midday. ✉ *23200 Pacific Coast Hwy., Malibu.*

▶ ☺ ❶ **Santa Monica Pier.** Eateries, souvenir shops, a psychic adviser, arcades, and **Pacific Park** are all part of this truncated pier at the foot of Colorado Boulevard below Palisades Park. The pier's trademark 46-horse Looff carousel, built in 1922, has appeared in many films, including *The Sting.* Free concerts are held on the pier in summer. ✉ *Colorado Ave. and the ocean, Santa Monica* ☎*310/458–8900* ⊕*www.santamonicapier. org* 🎟*Rides $1* ⊙ *Carousel May–Sept., Tues.–Fri. 11–9, weekends 10–9; Oct.–Apr., Thurs.–Sun., hrs vary.*

★ ❷ **Third Street Promenade.** Stretch your legs along this pedestrian-only three-block stretch of 3rd Street, just a whiff away from the Pacific, lined with jacaranda trees, ivy-topiary dinosaur fountains, strings of lights, and branches of nearly every major U.S. retail chain. Outdoor cafés, street vendors, movie theaters, and a rich nightlife make this a main gathering spot for locals, visitors, and the homeless. It's fun to watch the mix of people here, from elderly couples out for a bite to skateboarders and street musicians. ✉ *3rd St. between Wilshire Blvd. and Broadway, Santa Monica* ⊕ *www.thirdstreetpromenade.com.*

❸ **Venice Boardwalk.** "Boardwalk" may be something of a misnomer—it's really a five-block section of paved walkway—but this L.A. mainstay delivers year-round action. Bicyclists zip along and bikini-clad rollerbladers

FodorśChoice
★

A GOOD DRIVE

If you've got the time, break your coastal visit into two excursions: Santa Monica and Venice on one excursion, and Malibu on the other.

The best way to "do" L.A.'s coastal communities is to park your car and walk, cycle, or skate along the 3-mi beachside bike path. For this, of course, a sunny day is best; on all but the hottest days, when literally millions of Angelenos flock to the beaches, try to get started in the late morning. Places like Santa Monica Pier, Main Street, and the Venice Boardwalk are more interesting to observe as the day progresses. Try to avoid the boardwalk, beach, and back streets of Santa Monica and Venice at night, when the crowds dissipate. Avoid driving to Malibu during rush hour, when traffic along the PCH moves at a snail's pace.

To begin your drive, look for the arched neon sign at the foot of Colorado Avenue marking the entrance to the **Santa Monica Pier** ❶ ▶, the city's number-one landmark, built in 1906. Park on the pier and take a turn through Pacific Park, a 2-acre amusement park. The wide swath of sand on the north side of the pier is Santa Monica Beach, on hot summer weekends one of the most crowded beaches in Southern California.

From the pier, walk to Ocean Avenue, where Palisades Park, a strip of lawn and palms above the cliffs, provides panoramic ocean views. Three blocks inland is **Third Street Promenade** ❷, a popular outdoor mall.

Next stop: **Venice Boardwalk** ❸. Retrieve your car and drive two blocks inland on Colorado to Main Street. Turn right and continue until you reach Rose Avenue. You'll spot an enormous pair of binoculars, the front of the Frank Gehry–designed Chiat-Day Mojo building. Find a parking place, then head toward the sea and the boardwalk, where California beach culture is on colorful display.

For the drive to Malibu, retrace your route along Main Street. At Pico Boulevard, turn west, toward the ocean, and then right on Ocean Avenue. When you pass the pier, prepare to turn left down the California Incline (the incline is at the end of Palisades Park at Wilshire Boulevard) to the Pacific Coast Highway (Highway 1), also known as PCH. Drive roughly 11 mi north into Malibu, park in the lot adjacent to the Malibu Pier, and take a stroll out to the end for a view of the coast.

Back on land, take a walk on **Malibu Lagoon State Beach** ❹, also known as Surfrider Beach. On the highway side of the beach is the Moorish-Spanish Adamson House and Malibu Lagoon Museum, a tiled beauty with a great Pacific view. From here, you can walk along the strand of beach that fronts the famed Malibu Colony, the exclusive residential enclave of film, television, and recording stars.

TO MALIBU

4

TOPANGA
BEACH

Sunset Blvd.

Will Rogers
State Historic Park

PACIFIC
PALISADES

Pacific Coast Hwy.

Will Rogers
State Beach

Chautauqua Blvd.

Sunset Blvd.

San Vicente Blvd.

Ave.

20th St.

Montana

SANTA
MONICA

Lincoln

Ocean Ave.

Wilshire Blvd.

Broadway

Santa Monica Blvd.

Colorado Blvd.

Olympic Blvd.

Santa Monica
State Beach

1

Palisades
Park

2

Bergamot
Station

10

Santa Monica Fwy.

Pico Blvd.

Ocean Park Blvd.

National Blvd.

Nelson Way

Main St.

KEY

Start of itinerary

PACIFIC OCEAN

3

OCEAN PARK

VENICE

Abbot Kinney

Pacific

Venice Blvd.

TO
MARINA
DEL REY

0   2 miles
0   3 km

**Santa Monica,
Venice & Malibu**

3

attract crowds as they put on impromptu demonstrations, vying for attention with magicians, fortune tellers, a chain-saw juggler, and sand mermaids. At the adjacent Muscle Beach, bulging bodybuilders with an exhibitionist streak pump iron at an outdoor gym. Pick up some cheap sunglasses, grab a hot dog, and enjoy the boardwalk's show. You can rent in-line skates, roller skates, and bicycles (some with baby seats) at the south end of the boardwalk (officially known as Ocean Front Walk), along Washington Street near the Venice Pier.

The San Fernando Valley

There are some Angelenos who swear, with a sneer, that they have never set foot in "the Valley." Some even claim they have no idea of its whereabouts. But without the dreaded Valley, the world would be without Disney, Warner Bros., Universal Studios, NBC, *Seinfeld, Desperate Housewives,* and a large chunk of pornography. In fact, nearly 70% of all entertainment productions in L.A. happen here. That means that some very rich entertainment executives regularly undergo sweltering summer temperatures, smog, and bumper-to-bumper traffic on their trek from their Westside and Malibu compounds to their less glamorous workplaces.

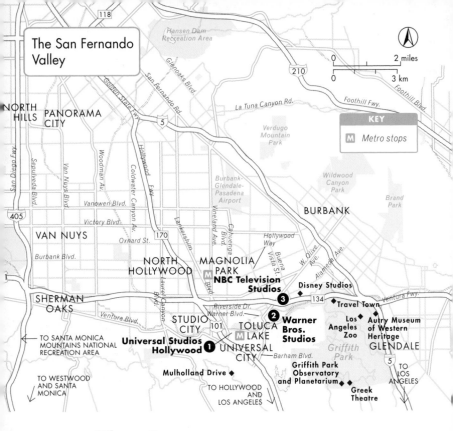

The San Fernando Valley

KEY

Ⓜ Metro stops

What to See

Santa Monica Mountains National Recreation Area. The line that forms the boundary of the San Fernando Valley is one of the most famous thoroughfares in this vast metropolis. **Mulholland Drive** cuts through the Santa Monica Mountains National Recreation Area, a vast parkland that stretches along the top and west slopes of the Santa Monica Mountains from Hollywood to the Ventura County line. Driving the length of the hilltop road is slow and can be treacherous, but the rewards are sensational views of valley and city on each side and expensive homes along the way. The park incorporates several local and state parks, including Will Rogers and Malibu Lagoon. Large scenic portions of these oak-studded hills were owned at one time by such Hollywood stars as Ronald Reagan and Bob Hope. They provided location sites for many movies; the grassy rolling hillsides continue to serve as an icon for the Wild West. Sets at the **Paramount Ranch** back lot have been preserved and continue to be used as location sites. Rangers regularly conduct tours of the Paramount Ranch, where you can see sets used by *M*A*S*H* and *Dr. Quinn, Medicine Woman*. From Hollywood reach Mulholland Drive via Outpost Drive off Franklin Avenue or Cahuenga Boulevard west via Highland Avenue north. ⊠ *401 W. Hillcrest Dr., Thousand Oaks* ☎ *805/370–2301* ☞ *Free* ☉ *Daily 9–5.*

❸ NBC Television Studios. This major network's headquarters is in Burbank, as any regular viewer of *The Tonight Show* can't help knowing. If you'd like to be part of a live studio audience, free tickets are available for tapings of the various NBC shows. ✉ *3000 W. Alameda Ave., Burbank* ☎ *818/840–3537* 🎫 *Tours $7.50.*

★ ☺ ❶ **Universal Studios Hollywood.** Worn and a bit frayed around the edges, this special-effects-laden theme park delivers a handful of thrilling experiences at a steep price. A confusing layout, long lines in summer, and subpar food service make it fall short of its main rival, Disneyland, on almost every front. Still, hard-core entertainment junkies will find a few rides worth a thumbs up. ■ TIP→ **If you get here when the park opens, you'll likely save yourself from long waits in line—arriving early pays off.**

The first-timer favorite is the tram tour, during which you can experience the parting of the Red Sea, an avalanche, a snowstorm, and a flood; meet a 30-foot-tall version of King Kong; be attacked by the ravenous killer shark of *Jaws* fame; survive an all-too-real simulation of an earthquake that measures 8.3 on the Richter scale, complete with collapsing earth; and come face to face with an evil mummy. Many attractions are based on Universal films and television shows; you can check out the 3-D effects in *Terminator 2: 3D* while *Jurassic Park—The Ride* is a short thrill ride through a jungle full of dinosaurs with an 84-foot water drop. The simulated warehouse fire in *Backdraft* is so real you can feel the heat. Aside from the park, **CityWalk** is a separate venue, where you'll find a slew of shops, restaurants, nightclubs, and movie theaters, including IMAX 3D. ✉ *100 Universal City Plaza, Universal City* ☎*818/622–3801* ⊕*www.universalstudios. com* 🎫 *$56, parking $10* ☉ *Contact park for seasonal hrs.*

❷ Warner Bros. Studios. There aren't many bells and whistles here, but you'll get a much better idea of production work than you will at Universal Studios. ■ TIP→ **The two-hour tours involve a lot of walking, so dress comfortably and bring plenty of sunscreen.** You start with a short film on Warner Bros. movies and TV shows, then hop into a tour cart for a ride to the studio museum. The archives here include costumes, props, and scripts from the studio's productions, including the sitcom *Friends* and the *Harry Potter* movies. Finally you'll visit the sets and soundstages, where you might spot a celeb or see a shoot in action—tours change from day to day depending on the productions taking place on the lot. Reservations are required. Call at least one week in advance and ask about provisions for people with disabilities; children under 8 are not admitted. Tours are given at least every hour, more frequently from May to September. ✉ *3400 W. Riverside Dr., Burbank* ☎ *818/972–8687* ⊕ *www.wbsf.com* 🎫 *$39* ☉ *Weekdays 8:30–4.*

OFF THE BEATEN PATH

SIX FLAGS MAGIC MOUNTAIN – If you're a true thrill-seeker looking for the "monster" rides and roller coasters, you'll find several of the biggest, fastest, and scariest in the world at this anti-Disney amusement park. The aptly named Scream, for instance, drops you 150 feet and tears through a 128-foot vertical loop. On X, you start with a climb of 200 feet before dropping headfirst at an 89-degree angle. Superman: The Escape is a 41-story coaster that hurtles you from 0 to 100 mph in less than seven seconds. On Riddler's Revenge, the world's tallest and fastest stand-up rollercoaster, you stand for a mile-long 65-mph total panic attack. As at other theme parks, there are shows and parades, along with rides for younger kids, to fill out a long day. Weekends are peak times here, so be prepared to stand in line for the more popular rides. (In warm weather, be sure you have sunscreen and water.) If you really need to cool down, you can hop over to its sister theme park, Six Flags Hurricane Harbor, right next door, and for $16.99, take a slippery cool trip down their massive waterslides. ⊠ *Magic Mountain Pkwy, off I–5, 25 mi northwest of Universal Studios and 36 mi outside L.A., Valencia* ☎ *661/255–4100* ⊕ *www.sixflags.com* 🎟 *$48* ⊙ *mid-Mar.–mid-Sept., daily; mid-Sept.–early Mar., weekends; call for hrs.*

Pasadena Area

Although seemingly absorbed into the general Los Angeles sprawl, Pasadena is an altogether distinct city. It's full of noteworthy sights, from its significant residential architecture to its exceptional museums, particularly the Norton Simon and the Huntington Library, Art Collections, and Botanical Gardens. Where else can you see a Chaucer manuscript and rare cacti in one place?

To reach Pasadena from downtown Los Angeles, drive north on the Pasadena Freeway (Interstate 110). From Hollywood and the San Fernando Valley use the Ventura Freeway (Highway 134, east), which cuts through Glendale, skirting the foothills, before arriving in Pasadena.

What to See

★ ❶ **Gamble House.** Built by Charles and Henry Greene in 1908, this is a spectacular example of American Arts & Crafts bungalow architecture. The term *bungalow* can be misleading, since the Gamble House is a huge three-story home. To wealthy Easterners such as the Gambles (as in Procter & Gamble), this type of vacation home seemed informal compared with their mansions back home. What makes admirers swoon is the incredible amount of hand craftsmanship, including a teak staircase and cabinetry, Greene and Greene–designed furniture, and an Emil Lange glass door. The dark exterior has broad eaves, with sleeping porches on the second floor. If you want to see more Greene and Greene homes in the neighborhood, buy a self-guided tour map in the Gamble House's bookstore. ⊠ *4 Westmoreland Pl., Pasadena* ☎ *626/793–3334* ⊕ *www.gamblehouse.org* 🎟 *$8* ⊙ *Thurs.–Sun. noon–3, tickets go on sale at 10, 1-hr tour every 20 mins.*

❺ **Huntington Library, Art Collections, and Botanical Gardens.** If you have time
Fodor'sChoice   for only one stop in the Pasadena area, it should be the Huntington, built
★   in the early 1900s as the home of railroad tycoon Henry E. Huntington. Henry and his wife Arabella (previously his aunt by marriage) voraciously collected rare books and manuscripts, botanical specimens, and 18th-century British art. The institution they established became one of the most extraordinary cultural complexes in the world.

▀ TIP➔ If you're seeking the fine art here, take note: there will be some switcheroos in 2007. The Huntington Gallery, housed in the original 1911 Georgian mansion, is closed for renovations until 2008. Its world-famous collection of British paintings will instead be shown in the Erburu Gallery. Among the

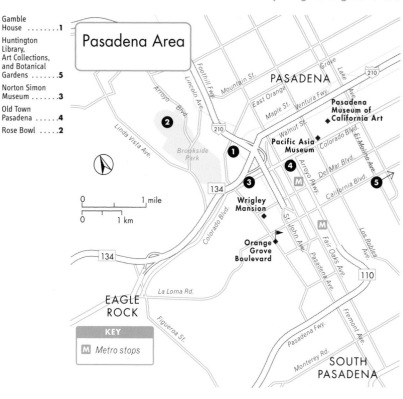

Pasadena Area

3

highlights are John Constable's intimate *View on the Stour Near Dedham* and the monumental *Sarah Siddons as the Tragic Muse,* by Joshua Reynolds. In a too-cute pairing, Gainsborough's *Blue Boy* faces *Pinkie,* by Thomas Lawrence. Once the British paintings return to the mansion, the Erburu will be filled with American artworks. Meanwhile, in the Virginia Steele Scott Gallery of American Art you can see paintings by Mary Cassatt, Frederic Remington, and more. The library contains more than 600,000 books and some 300 manuscripts, including such treasures as a Gutenberg Bible, the Ellesmere manuscript of Chaucer's *Canterbury Tales,* George Washington's genealogy in his own handwriting, scores of works by William Blake, and an unrivaled collection of early editions of Shakespeare. The estate grounds, now the Huntington Botanical Gardens, include a 12-acre Desert Garden, a Japanese Garden, a 3-acre rose garden, a Shakespeare garden, and more. ⊠ *1151 Oxford Rd., San Marino* ☏ *626/405–2100* ⊕ *www.huntington.org* ⊒ *$15, free 1st Thurs. of month* ☉ *Tues.–Fri. noon–4:30, weekends 10:30–4:30.*

❸ **Norton Simon Museum.** Long familiar to television viewers of the New Year's

Fodor'sChoice   Day Rose Parade, this brown, low-profile building is more than just a

★   background for the passing floats. It's one of the finest small museums anywhere, with an excellent collection that spans more than 2,000 years of Western and Asian art. It all began in the 1950s when Norton Simon

(Hunt-Wesson Foods, McCalls Corporation, and Canada Dry) started collecting the works of Degas, Renoir, Gauguin, and Cézanne. His collection grew to include old masters, impressionists and modern work from Europe, and Indian and Southeast Asian art. After he retired, Simon reorganized the failing Pasadena Art Institute and continued to assemble one of the world's finest collections. Today the Norton Simon Museum is richest in works by Rembrandt, Goya, Picasso, and most of all, Degas— this is one of the only two U.S. institutions to hold the complete set of the artist's model bronzes (the other is the Metropolitan Museum of Art, in New York). Renaissance, baroque, and rococo masterpieces include Raphael's profoundly spiritual *Madonna with Child with Book* (1503); Rembrandt's *Portrait of a Bearded Man in a Wide-Brimmed Hat* (1633); and a magical Tiepolo ceiling, *The Triumph of Virtue and Nobility Over Ignorance* (1740–50). The museum's collections of impressionist (Van Gogh, Matisse, Cézanne, Monet, Renoir) and cubist (Braque, Gris) work are extensive. Several Rodin sculptures are placed throughout the museum. Head down to the bottom floor to see the phenomenal Southeast Asian and Indian sculptures and artifacts, where graceful pieces like a Ban Chiang blackware vessel date to earlier than 1,000 BC. Don't miss the living artwork outdoors: the garden, conceived by noted Southern California landscape designer Nancy Goslee Power. The tranquil pond was inspired by Monet's gardens at Giverny. ☒ *411 W. Colorado Blvd., Pasadena* ☎ *626/449–6840* ⊕ *www.nortonsimon.org* ☒ *$8* ☉ *Wed., Thurs., and Sat.–Mon. noon–6, Fri. noon–9.*

★ ❹ **Old Town Pasadena.** Once the victim of decay, the area was revitalized in the 1990s as a blend of restored 19th-century brick buildings with a contemporary overlay. A phalanx of chain stores has muscled in, but there are still some less familiar shops and plenty of tempting cafés and restaurants. In the evening and on weekends, streets are packed with people, and Old Town crackles with energy. The 12-block historic district is anchored along Colorado Boulevard between Pasadena Avenue and Arroyo Parkway.

❷ **Rose Bowl.** With an enormous rose, the city of Pasadena's logo, adorned on its exterior, it's hard to miss this 100,000-seat stadium, host of many Super Bowls and home to the UCLA Bruins. Set in Brookside Park at the wide bottom of an arroyo, the facility is closed except during games and special events such as the monthly Rose Bowl Swap Meet, which is considered the granddaddy of West Coast flea markets. ☒ *Rose Bowl Dr. at Rosemont Ave., Pasadena* ☎ *626/577–3100* ⊕ *www. rosebowlstadium.com* ☒ *$7–$20* ☉ *Flea market 2nd Sun. of month 7–3.*

Long Beach

Long Beach, down at the tail end of Los Angeles County, was long stuck in limbo between Los Angeles and Orange County in the minds of visitors, but it's now rebuilding its place in the Southern California scheme. Founded as a seaside resort in the 19th century, Long Beach boomed in the early 20th century as oil discoveries drew in Midwesterners and Dust Bowlers. Bust followed boom, and for many years the city took on a somewhat raw, industrial, neglected feel. These days, however, a long-term redevelopment plan begun in the 1970s has finally come to fruition, and the city has turned back into a seaside destination.

What to See

Aquarium of the Pacific. Sea lions, nurse sharks, octopuses, and . . . parrots—this aquarium focuses primarily on ocean life from the Pacific Ocean, with a detour into Australian birds. The main exhibits include lively sea lions, a crowded tank of various sharks, and ethereal sea-dragons, which the aquarium has successfully bred in captivity. For a nonaquatic experience, head over to Lorikeet Forest, a walk-in aviary full of the friendliest parrots from down under. Buy a cup of nectar and smile as you become a human bird perch. Since these birds spend most of their day feeding, you're guaranteed a noisy—and possibly messy—encounter. (A sink, soap, and towels are strategically placed at the exhibit exit.) If you've ever wondered how an aquarium functions, book the extensive hour-long Behind the Scenes Tour ($15) at the information desk. ⊠ *100 Aquarium Way, Long Beach* ☎ *562/590–3100* ⊕ *www. aquariumofpacific.org* ⊠ *$18.95* ☉ *Daily 9–6.*

► **Queen Mary.** There's a saying among staff members that the more you get to know the *Queen Mary,* the more you realize that she has a uniquely endearing personality as well as a wealth of history. The beautifully preserved ocean liner was launched in 1934 and made 1,001 transatlantic crossings before finally berthing in Long Beach in 1967. The most substantial, informative tour is the one-hour Behind the Scenes visit, an extensive trek through the public and private areas of the ocean liner led by friendly, knowledgeable guides. The ship's neighbor, a geodesic dome originally built to house Howard Hughes's *Spruce Goose* aircraft, is now part of a terminal for Carnival Cruise Lines. ⊠ *Pier J, Long Beach* ☎ *562/435–3511* ⊕ *www.queenmary.com* ⊠ *Self-guided tours $23, Behind the Scenes tours $28* ☉ *Call for times and frequency of guided tours.*

WHERE TO EAT

Updated by
Roger J. Grody

Celebrity is big business in Los Angeles, so it's no accident that the concept of the celebrity chef—emerging from an exhibition kitchen to schmooze with an equally illustrious clientele—is a key part of the city's dining scene. Wolfgang Puck, whose culinary empire of restaurants, food products, and cooking shows has made him a household name across the nation, epitomizes this phenomenon. And L.A. keeps coming up with fresh stars to fill its ever-expanding universe of kitchens.

Although Los Angeles doesn't pretend to rival New York in terms of high-end dining rooms, its strategic location contributes to a varied and innovative local cuisine. Local produce is a linchpin; area restaurants benefit from the state's incredible agricultural yields. As one of the capitals of the Pacific Rim, L.A. also absorbs the culinary influences of its Asian communities. And the city's proximity to Latin America and its diverse Latino neighborhoods add further depth, as local chefs incorporate ingredients indigenous to El Salvador, Colombia, and the rich culinary regions of Mexico.

	WHAT IT COSTS				
	$$$$	**$$$**	**$$**	**$**	**¢**
AT DINNER	over $30	$23–$30	$16–$22	$10–$15	under $10

Prices are for a main course at dinner, excluding 8.25% sales tax.

Downtown

American/Casual

¢   ✕ **Philippe The Original.** Not only is this L.A.'s oldest restaurant (1908),
Fodor'sChoice   but it may also be where the French dip sandwich originated. Here you
★   can get one made with beef, pork, ham, lamb, or turkey on a freshly
baked roll; the house hot mustard is as famous as the sandwiches.
Philippe earns its reputation by maintaining its traditions, from saw-
dust on the floor to long, wooden tables where customers can sit and
socialize. The home cooking includes hearty breakfasts, chili, pickled
eggs, and an enormous pie selection. The best bargain: a cup of java for
only 9¢! ⊠ *1001 N. Alameda St., Downtown* ☎ *213/628–3781* ⚛ *Reservations not accepted* ⊟ *No credit cards.*

Contemporary

★ **$$–$$$**   ✕ **Traxx.** Hidden inside historic Union Station, this intimate restaurant
is an art-deco delight. Its linen-topped tables spill out onto the main concourse. Chef-owner Tara Thomas's menu gussies up popular favorites;
for example, crab cakes come with chipotle rémoulade, and striped bass
gets a hit of caramelized fennel and coriander vinaigrette. The jacaranda-
shaded courtyard is a local secret. The well-stocked bar, occupying
what was originally the station's telephone room, is just across the concourse. ⊠ *Union Station, 800 N. Alameda St., Downtown* ☎ *213/
625–1999* ⊟ *AE, D, MC, V* ⊘ *Closed Sun. No lunch Sat.*

French

$$$$ ✕ **Patina.** In a bold move, chef-owner Joachim Splichal moved his flag-
Fodor'sChoice   ship restaurant from Hollywood to downtown's striking Frank Gehry–de-
★   signed Walt Disney Concert Hall. The contemporary space, surrounded
by a rippled "curtain" of rich walnut, is an elegant, dramatic stage for
the acclaimed restaurant's contemporary French cuisine. Specialties include
seared foie gras with Pear William ice cream, wild pheasant breast with
juniper berry sauce, and a formidable *côte de boeuf* for two, carved ta-
bleside. Finish with a hard-to-match cheese tray and sensual desserts. ⊠ *Walt
Disney Concert Hall, 141 S. Grand Ave., Downtown* ☎ *213/972–3331*
⚛ *Reservations essential* ⊟ *AE, D, DC, MC, V* ⊘ *No lunch weekends.*

Italian

★ **$$–$$$$**   ✕ **Cicada.** Cicada, certainly one of the most romantic and architec-
turally dramatic dining venues in L.A., occupies the ground floor of the
1928 art-deco Oviatt Building. The glass doors are Lalique; carved
maple columns soar two stories to a gold-leaf ceiling, and from the bal-
cony, a glamorous bar overlooks the spacious dining room. "Modern
Italian" best describes the menu: shrimp ravioli in curry sauce, Maine
lobster crepes, and braised veal shank with dried-fruit risotto.

Where to Stay & Eat in Downtown Los Angeles

Restaurants ▼
Cicada **8**
Patina **4**
Philippe The Original **1**
Traxx **2**

Hotels ▼
Hilton Checkers Los Angeles **6**
Inn at 657 ......**9**
Millennium Biltmore Hotel **5**
New Otani Hotel and Garden **3**
The Standard, Downtown LA ...**7**

✉ *617 S. Olive St., Downtown* ☎ *213/488–9488* ♨ *Reservations essential* ▤ *AE, DC, MC, V* ☉ *Closed Sun. No lunch.*

Hollywood

American

$$–$$$$ ✕ **Musso & Frank Grill.** Liver and onions, lamb chops, goulash, shrimp Louis salad, gruff waiters—you'll find all the old favorites here in Hollywood's oldest restaurant. A film-industry hangout since it opened in 1919, Musso & Frank still welcomes the working studio set to its maroon faux-leather booths. Great breakfasts are served all day, but the kitchen's famous "flannel cakes" (pancakes) are served only until 3 PM. ✉ *6667 Hollywood Blvd., Hollywood* ☎ *323/467–7788* ▤ *AE, DC, MC, V* ☉ *Closed Sun. and Mon.*

Contemporary

$$–$$$$ ✕ **Vert.** Here Wolfgang Puck turns his hand to a mix of traditional brasserie and contemporary California dishes. You'll find French classics like a *tarte flambé* (a rustic onion tart from Alsace) and *moules marinières* (mussels cooked with shallots and white wine) alongside grilled tuna and a hefty Gorgonzola-topped burger. Though it's hidden in the blockbuster Hollywood & Highland center, the restaurant is always busy;

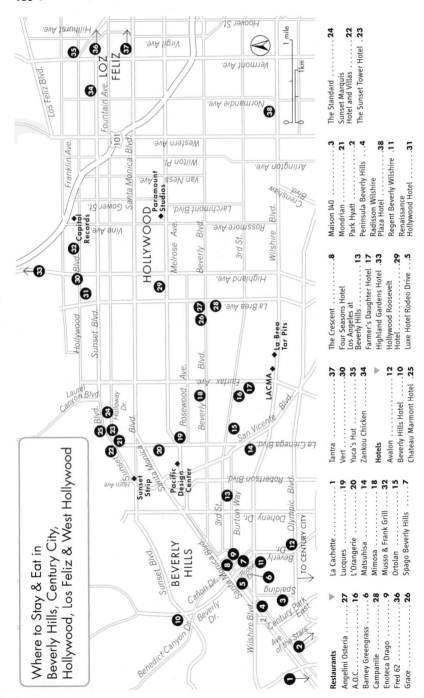

Where to Stay & Eat in
Beverly Hills, Century City,
Hollywood, Los Feliz & West Hollywood

Restaurants

Angelini Osteria	**27**
A.O.C.	**16**
Barney Greengrass	**6**
Campanile	**28**
Enoteca Drago	**9**
Fred 62	**36**
Grace	**26**
La Cachette	**1**
Lucques	**19**
L'Orangerie	**20**
Matsuhisa	**14**
Mimosa	**18**
Musso & Frank Grill	**32**
Ortolan	**15**
Spago Beverly Hills	**7**
Tantra	**37**
Vert	**30**
Yuca's Hut	**35**
Zankou Chicken	**34**

Hotels

Avalon	**12**
Beverly Hills Hotel	**10**
Chateau Marmont Hotel	**25**
The Crescent	**8**
Four Seasons Hotel Los Angeles at Beverly Hills	**13**
Farmer's Daughter Hotel	**17**
Highland Gardens Hotel	**33**
Hollywood Roosevelt Hotel	**29**
Luxe Hotel Rodeo Drive	**5**
Maison 140	**3**
Mondrian	**21**
Park Hyatt	**2**
Peninsula Beverly Hills	**4**
Radisson Wilshire Plaza Hotel	**38**
Regent Beverly Wilshire	**11**
Renaissance Hollywood Hotel	**31**
The Standard	**24**
Sunset Marquis Hotel and Villas	**22**
The Sunset Tower Hotel	**23**

the bar is back-lighted in the namesake color (green), and the walls sprout abstract sculptures. ✉ *6801 Hollywood Blvd., Hollywood* ☎ *323/491–1300* ⏳ *Reservations essential* ▤ *AE, D, DC, MC, V* ⊙ *No lunch weekends.*

Middle Eastern

¢ ✕ **Zankou Chicken.** Forget the Colonel: Zankou's aromatic, Armenian-style rotisserie chicken with perfectly crisp, golden skin—served with pita bread, veggies, hummus, and unforgettable garlic sauce—is one of L.A.'s truly great budget meals. Zankou also serves kebabs, falafel, and sensational *shawarma* (spit-roasted lamb or chicken) plates. ✉ *5065 W. Sunset Blvd., Hollywood* ☎ *323/665–7845* ⏳ *Reservations not accepted* ▤ *No credit cards.*

Los Feliz

Eclectic

¢–$$ ✕ **Fred 62.** Funky L.A. chef–restaurateur Fred Eric has created a tongue-in-cheek take on the American diner. Toasters sit on every table, and the usual burgers and shakes are joined by choices like oxtail, tofu scrambles, "cream of what you want soup," and "punk tarts." As in the neighborhood itself, nobody is out of place here, and everyone from button-down businesspeople to tattooed musicians shows up at some point during its 24/7 cycle. ✉ *1850 N. Vermont Ave., Los Feliz* ☎ *323/667–0062* ⏳ *Reservations not accepted* ▤ *AE, DC, MC, V.*

Indian

$$ ✕ **Tantra.** As the name suggests, this is a very sexy place, accented with bold colors, dramatic silk lighting fixtures, and a hanging curtain of oxidized metal. But it's not just about attitude: the regional Indian cuisine is first-rate, including mango-and-cheese samosas, *khoormani gosht* (lamb in apricot-curry sauce), tandoori monkfish, and a drink called *nimboo-paani* (sweetened lime juice with saffron). For dessert, snap up the chocolate-filled samosas. The adjoining bar-lounge has become a popular local haunt. ✉ *3705 Sunset Blvd., Silver Lake* ☎ *323/663–8268* ⏳ *Reservations essential* ▤ *AE, MC, V* ⊙ *Closed Mon. No lunch.*

Mexican

¢ ✕ **Yuca's Hut.** Blink and you might miss this place; its reputation far exceeds its size. It's known for carne asada, carnitas, and *cochinita pibil* (Yucatán-style roasted pork) tacos and burritos. There's no chance of satisfying a late-night craving, though; it closes at 6 PM. ✉ *2056 N. Hillhurst Ave., Los Feliz* ☎ *323/662–1214* ⏳ *Reservations not accepted* ▤ *No credit cards* ⊙ *Closed Sun.*

Beverly Hills

Contemporary

$$$–$$$$ ✕ **Spago Beverly Hills.** The flagship restaurant of Wolfgang Puck, the chef Fodor'sChoice who helped define California cuisine, is justifiably a modern L.A. classic. The casually elegant restaurant centers on an outdoor courtyard. There, shaded by 100-year-old olive trees, you can glimpse the exhibition kitchen and, on occasion, the affable chef-owner greeting his famous friends. (The

people-watching here is worth the price of admission.) The daily-changing menu could offer a tasting of five foie-gras preparations, *côte de boeuf* with Armagnac-peppercorn sauce, Cantonese-style duck, and some traditional Austrian specialties. Acclaimed pastry chef Sherry Yard works magic with everything from a sophisticated tart inspired by the Twix candy bar to an Austrian *kaiserschmarren* (crème fraîche pancakes with fruit). ⊠ *176 N. Cañon Dr., Beverly Hills* ☎ *310/385–0880* ⚄ *Reservations essential* ⊟ *AE, D, DC, MC, V* ☾ *No lunch Sun.*

Delicatessen

$–$$ ✕ **Barney Greengrass.** This *haute* deli on the fifth floor of Barneys department store has an appropriately high-class aesthetic: limestone floors, mahogany furniture, and a wall of windows. On the outdoor terrace, at tables shaded by large umbrellas, you can savor flawless smoked salmon, sturgeon, and whitefish flown in fresh from New York. The deli closes at 6 PM. ⊠ *Barneys, 9570 Wilshire Blvd., Beverly Hills* ☎ *310/ 777–5877* ⊟ *AE, DC, MC, V.*

Italian

★ **$$–$$$** ✕ **Enoteca Drago.** High-flying Sicilian chef Celestino Drago scores with this sleek but unpretentious version of an *enoteca* (a wine bar serving small snacks). It's an ideal spot for sampling interesting Italian wines—more than 50 available by the glass—and enjoying a menu made up of small plates such as deep-fried olives, chicken-liver pâté served in a rustic jar, and grilled baby octopus. Although the mushroom-filled ravioli bathed in foie gras–truffle sauce is a bit luxurious for an enoteca, it's one of the city's best pasta dishes. Larger portions and pizzas are also available here, but the essence of an enoteca is preserved. ⊠ *410 N. Cañon Dr., Beverly Hills* ☎ *310/786–8236* ⚄ *Reservations essential* ⊟ *AE, DC, MC, V.*

Japanese

$$$–$$$$ ✕ **Matsuhisa.** Freshness and innovation are the hallmarks of this flagship
Fodor'sChoice restaurant of superchef Nobu Matsuhisa's empire. The surprisingly modest-looking place draws crowds with its stellar menu. Here you'll encounter
★ such dishes as caviar-capped tuna stuffed with black truffles, foie-gras sushi, sea urchin wrapped in a *shiso* leaf, and monkfish-liver pâté wrapped in gold leaf. Reflecting his past stint in Peru, Matsuhisa incorporates intriguing Latin ingredients into traditional Japanese cuisine. Regulars ask for the *omakase,* (which rougly translates to "let the chef decide") to assure an amazing culinary experience, and then steel themselves for a big tab. ⊠ *129 N. La Cienega Blvd., Beverly Hills* ☎ *310/659–9639* ⚄ *Reservations essential* ⊟ *AE, DC, MC, V* ☾ *No lunch weekends.*

Century City

French

★ **$$$–$$$$** ✕ **La Cachette.** Owner-chef Jean-François Meteigner developed a following while cooking at L'Orangerie and Cicada. At his own restaurant, he combines traditional French fare—foie gras, Provençal bouillabaisse, rack of lamb—with a lighter, more modern cuisine reflected in dishes like roasted Maine cod with a passion fruit–ginger–plum sauce. A dressy (by L.A. standards) crowd makes sure that this elegant, flower-filled *ca-*

chette (little hiding place) doesn't stay hidden. ✉ *10506 Santa Monica Blvd., Century City* ☎ *310/470–4992* 🍴 *Reservations essential* 🖃 *AE, D, DC, MC, V* ☾ *No lunch weekends.*

West Hollywood

Contemporary

★ **$$$–$$$$** ✕ **Campanile.** Chef-owner Mark Peel has mastered the mix of a robust Mediterranean flavors with homey Americana. Appetizers may include sweetbread ravioli with pancetta and lobster, and grilled snapper with Meyer lemon aïoli and prime rib with tapenade appear as entrées. For dessert, consider a pecan-caramel tart or chocolate beignets. For an ultimate L.A. experience, come for weekend brunch on the enclosed patio. ✉ *624 S. La Brea Ave., Miracle Mile* ☎ *323/938–1447* 🍴 *Reservations essential* 🖃 *AE, D, DC, MC, V* ☾ *No dinner Sun.*

$$$–$$$$ ✕ **Grace.** After years of moving through the city's top kitchens, chef Neal Fraser is doing his best cooking yet in a place of his own. He mixes textures and contrasting flavors in dishes like tandoori quail with tamarind glaze, sea urchin and sweet shrimp, roasted duck with sweet-and-sour cherries, and a delightful salmon in a sweet garlic sauce. ✉ *7360 Beverly Blvd., south of West Hollywood* ☎ *323/934–4400* 🍴 *Reservations essential* 🖃 *AE, MC, V* ☾ *Closed Mon. No lunch.*

★ **$$$–$$$$** ✕ **Lucques.** Once silent-film star Harold Lloyd's carriage house, this brick building has morphed into a chic restaurant that's a big hit with the younger, well-heeled set. And the veggie-intense cooking by Suzanne Goin is smart, too: consider Italian heirloom pumpkin soup with sage and chestnut cream, pancetta-wrapped Alaskan cod with red potatoes, crushed grapes and crème fraîche, and short ribs with horseradish cream. ✉ *8474 Melrose Ave., West Hollywood* ☎ *323/655–6277* 🍴 *Reservations essential* 🖃 *AE, D, DC, MC, V* ☾ *No lunch Sun.*

French

★ **$$$$** ✕ **L'Orangerie.** Usually reserved for the most special of occasions, this is the closest L.A. gets to a fine French dining room. The regal setting channels the spirit of Versailles with soaring French doors, exquisite Louis XIV appointments, and dramatic floral arrangements. Chefs come and go, but standards are maintained at the highest levels. Current specialties include scallops with celery gelée and truffle ice cream, and walnut- and cinnamon-crusted squab with porcini marmalade. Service is attentive but not overbearing. ✉ *903 N. La Cienega Blvd., West Hollywood* ☎ *310/652–9770* 🍴 *Reservations essential* 🖃 *AE, D, DC, MC, V* ☾ *Closed Mon. No lunch.*

★ **$$$–$$$$** ✕ **Ortolan.** Despite a galaxy of crystal chandeliers, Ortolan attempts to take the pretentiousness out of haute cuisine. Here designer jeans outnumber designer suits. But ex-L'Orangerie chef Christophe Emé keeps up an impeccable standard in the kitchen with dishes such as Napa Valley escargots with lettuce emulsion and Parmesan crust, roasted squab with date puree, and what may be the silkiest foie gras in the city. Many creations are dramatically presented on stone slabs or in unique vessels. ✉ *8338 W. 3rd St., south of West Hollywood* ☎ *323/653–3300* 🍴 *Reservations essential* 🖃 *AE, MC, V* ☾ *Closed Sun. No lunch.*

$$–$$$ ✕ **Mimosa.** If you're craving a perfect Provençal meal, turn to chef Jean-
Fodor'sChoice Pierre Bosc's menu. There's *salade Lyonnaise*, served with a poached
★ egg, bouillabaisse, and fillet of sole *au pistou* (with basil-garlic paste).
The atmosphere is that of a classic bistro, with mustard walls, cozy banquettes, and jars of cornichons and olives delivered to every table on
arrival. ✉ *8009 Beverly Blvd., West Hollywood* ☎ *323/655–8895*
🖃 *AE, DC, MC, V* ☺ *Closed Sun. and Mon. No lunch.*

Italian

$–$$$$ ✕ **Angelini Osteria.** You might not guess it from the modest, rather con-
Fodor'sChoice gested dining room, but this is one of L.A.'s most celebrated Italian restau-
★ rants. The key is chef-owner Gino Angelini's thoughtful use of superb
ingredients, evident in dishes such as mussels and clams in garlic, pars-
ley, and white wine and pumpkin tortelli with butter, sage, and aspara-
gus. An awesome lasagna verde, inspired by Angelini's grandmother, is
not to be missed. Whole branzino, crusted in sea salt, and unusual spe-
cials (e.g., tender veal kidneys) consistently impress. An intelligent se-
lection of mostly Italian wines complements the menu, and desserts like
the open-face marmalade tart are baked fresh daily. ✉ *7313 Beverly Blvd.,
Beverly–La Brea* ☎ *323/297–0070* 🖃 *AE, MC, V* ☺ *Closed Mon. No
lunch weekends.*

Mediterranean

$$–$$$ ✕ **A.O.C.** Since it opened in 2002, this restaurant and wine bar has rev-
Fodor'sChoice olutionized dining in L.A., pioneering the small-plate format that has
★ now swept the city. The space is dominated by a long, candle-laden bar
serving more than 50 wines by the glass. There's also an L.A. rarity, a
charcuterie bar. The tapaslike menu is perfectly calibrated for the wine
list; you could pick duck confit, smoked trout, an indulgent slab of pork
rillettes (a sort of pâté), or just plunge into one of the city's best cheese
selections. Named for the acronym for Appellation d'Origine Con-
trôlée, the regulatory system that ensures the quality of local wines and
cheeses in France, A.O.C. upholds the standard of excellence. ✉ *8022
W. 3rd St., south of West Hollywood* ☎ *323/653–6359* 🍴 *Reservations
essential* 🖃 *AE, MC, V* ☺ *No lunch.*

West Los Angeles

American/Casual

★ ¢ ✕ **The Apple Pan.** A burger-insider haunt since 1947, this unassuming
joint with a horseshoe-shaped counter—no tables here—turns out one
heck of a good burger topped with Tillamook cheddar, plus a hickory
burger with barbecue sauce. You'll also find great fries and, of course,
an apple pie good enough to name a restaurant after (although many
regulars argue that the banana cream deserves the honor). Be prepared
to wait. ✉ *10801 W. Pico Blvd., West L.A.* ☎ *310/475–3585* 🍴 *Reser-
vations not accepted* 🖃 *No credit cards* ☺ *Closed Mon.*

Indian

¢–$$ ✕ **Bombay Cafe.** Some of the dishes here are strictly authentic, others
have been lightened up a bit to suit Southern California sensibilities, and
a few are truly innovative. Regulars (and there are many) swear by the

chile-laden lamb frankies (burritolike snacks sold by vendors on the beaches of Bombay) and *sev puri* (wafers topped with onions, potatoes, and chutneys). ☒ *12021 Pico Blvd., West L.A.* ☎ *310/473–3388* ☰ *MC, V* ☺ *No lunch weekends.*

Mexican

$–$$ ✕ **La Serenata Gourmet.** Even now that it has expanded, crowding into this Westside branch of the east L.A. original can be uncomfortable, but the restaurant scores points for its flavorful Mexican cuisine. Moles and pork dishes are delicious, but seafood is the real star—there are chubby *gorditas* (cornmeal pockets stuffed with shrimp), juicy fish enchiladas, and a soupy ceviche that sings with flavor. If your experience with Mexican food has been on the Tex-Mex end of the spectrum, come here to broaden your horizons. ☒ *10924 W. Pico Blvd., West L.A.* ☎ *310/441–9667* ⌕ *Reservations not accepted* ☰ *AE, D, MC, V.*

Santa Monica

Contemporary

$$$–$$$$ ✕ **Chinois on Main.** A once-revolutionary outpost in Wolfgang Puck's repertoire, this is still one of L.A.'s most crowded restaurants—and one of the noisiest. The jazzy interior is just as loud as the clientele. The happy marriage of Asian and French cuisines yields seasonal dishes such as grilled Mongolian lamb chops with wok-fried vegetables, Shanghai lobster with spicy ginger-curry sauce, and Cantonese duck with fresh plum sauce. ☒ *2709 Main St., Santa Monica* ☎ *310/392–9025* ⌕ *Reservations essential* ☰ *AE, D, DC, MC, V* ☺ *No lunch Sat.–Tues.*

★ $$$ ✕ **JiRaffe.** The wood-panel, two-story dining room with ceiling-high windows is as handsome as the menu is tasteful. Chef-owner Raphael Lunetta turns out seasonal appetizers such as a delicate roasted-tomato tart or a roasted-beet salad with caramelized walnuts and dried bing cherries. They're worthy preludes to such memorable main dishes as crispy-skinned salmon with parsnip puree, braised fennel, and a sweet balsamic reduction. ☒ *502 Santa Monica Blvd., Santa Monica* ☎ *310/917–6671* ⌕ *Reservations essential* ☰ *AE, DC, MC, V* ☺ *No lunch.*

$$$–$$$$ ✕ **Wilshire.** The woodsy patio at Wilshire is one of the most coveted spaces on the L.A. dining circuit—its candlelight, firelight, and gurgling fountain lure in a hip crowd beneath a cloud of canvas. The cuisine emphasizes organic market-fresh ingredients. You might try red kuri squash–Asian pear soup with cinnamon cream, a rack of lamb with farro, or roasted chicken with Swiss chard and chanterelles. There's a lively bar scene here, too. ☒ *2454 Wilshire Blvd., Santa Monica* ☎ *310/586–1707* ⌕ *Reservations essential* ☰ *AE, D, DC, MC, V* ☺ *No lunch weekends.*

French

$$$$ ✕ **Mélisse.** In a city where informality reigns, this is one of L.A.'s more Fodor'sChoice dressy—but not stuffy—restaurants. A crystal chandelier hangs in the ★ dining room, above well-spaced tables topped with flowers and Limoges china. Chef-owner Josiah Citrin enriches his modern French cooking with seasonal California produce. Consider seared foie gras with figs poached in sweet wine and huckleberry sorbet, lobster Thermidor, or seared venison in a bitter-chocolate sauce. There's also tableside cheese

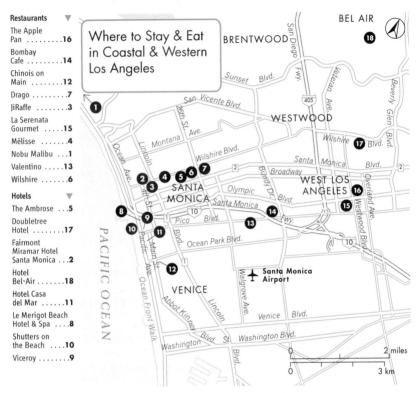

Where to Stay & Eat in Coastal & Western Los Angeles

service. ✉ *1104 Wilshire Blvd., Santa Monica* ☎ *310/395–0881* ⌂ *Reservations essential* ▤ *AE, D, DC, MC, V* ☉ *Closed Sun. and Mon. No lunch.*

Italian

★ **$$–$$$$** ✕ **Valentino.** Among the nation's best Italian restaurants, Valentino also has one of the top wine lists; its cellar contains more than 100,000 bottles. In the 1970s, suave owner Piero Selvaggio introduced L.A. to his exquisite modern Italian cuisine, and he continues to impress guests with dishes like spaghetti with garlic and *bottarga* (tuna roe), sautéed sweetbreads in a *vin santo* (sweet wine) sauce, and quails in a chardonnay–black truffle sauce. The menu recently changed to a prix-fixe format, starting at a reasonable $45. ✉ *3115 Pico Blvd., Santa Monica* ☎ *310/829– 4313* ⌂ *Reservations essential* ▤ *AE, DC, MC, V* ☉ *Closed Sun. No lunch Sat. and Mon.–Thurs.*

$–$$$ ✕ **Drago.** Native Sicilian Celestino Drago's home-style fare is carefully prepared and attentively served here in stark designer surroundings. The menu adds sophisticated finesse to rustic dishes like pappardelle with pheasant–morel mushroom sauce, squid-ink risotto, and lamb loin with garlic sauce. ✉ *2628 Wilshire Blvd., Santa Monica* ☎ *310/828–1585* ▤ *AE, DC, MC, V* ☉ *No lunch weekends.*

Malibu

Japanese

$$$–$$$$ ✕ **Nobu Malibu.** At famous chef-restaurateur Nobu Matsuhisa's coastal outpost, a casually chic clientele swarms over morsels of the world's finest fish. In addition to stellar sushi, Nobu serves many of the same ingenious specialties offered at his flagship, Matsuhisa. You'll find exotic species of fish artfully accented with equally exotic South American peppers, ultratender Kobe beef, and a broth perfumed with rare matsutake mushrooms. ⊠ *3835 Cross Creek Rd., Malibu* ☎ *310/317–9140* ✍ *Reservations essential* ▭ *AE, DC, MC, V* ⊘ *No lunch.*

Pasadena

Chinese

$$–$$$ ✕ **Yujean Kang's Gourmet Chinese Cuisine.** Forget any and all preconceived notions of what Chinese food should look and taste like—Kang's cuisine is nouvelle Chinese. Start with tender slices of veal on a bed of enoki mushrooms, topped with a tangle of quick-fried shoestring yams; or sea bass with kumquats and passion-fruit sauce. Even familiar dishes, such as the crispy sesame beef, result in nearly revelatory culinary experiences. Finish off with sweet bean-curd crepes or delicate mandarin-orange cheesecake. ⊠ *67 N. Raymond Ave., Pasadena* ☎ *626/585–0855* ▭ *AE, D, DC, MC, V.*

Fodor's Choice
★

Contemporary

★ **$$$–$$$$** ✕ **The Dining Room.** Until the arrival of charismatic chef Craig Strong, there wasn't much to say about this high-priced hotel restaurant. But Strong, a perfectionist whose bosses indulge him with the finest ingredients, put it on the map. The chef relishes the opportunity to personalize his cuisine, so consider springing for a customized tasting menu. ⊠ *Ritz-Carlton Huntington Hotel & Spa, 1401 S. Oak Knoll Ave., Pasadena* ☎ *626/577–2867* ▭ *AE, D, DC, MC, V* ⊘ *Closed Sun. and Mon. No lunch.*

Indian

$–$$ ✕ **All India Cafe.** Old Pasadena may be the last place you'd expect to find an authentic Indian restaurant, but authentic this is. Ingredients are fresh, and flavors are bold without depending on overpowering spiciness. Start with the *bhel puri,* a savory puffed rice-and-potatoes dish. In addition to meat curries and tikkas, there are many vegetarian selections and some hard-to-find items such as the burritolike frankies, a favorite Bombay street food. The prices are as palatable as the meals: a full lunch costs less than $9. ⊠ *39 Fair Oaks Ave., Pasadena* ☎ *626/440–0309* ▭ *AE, MC, V.*

Italian

★ **$$–$$$$** ✕ **Trattoria Tre Venezie.** An Italian restaurant has to be special to get noticed. This one does it by excelling in specialties from a trio of Italy's northernmost regions along the Austrian border, collectively referred to as Tre Venezie. Sparked with unusual ingredients and sauces, the menu can challenge your preconceptions about Italian food. Start with *jota* (a traditional sweet-and-sour soup) before enjoying the signature smoked pork chop with sauerkraut and a light Gorgonzola sauce. ⊠ *119 W. Green*

3

St., Pasadena ☎ *626/795–4455* ▤ *AE, DC, MC, V* ☉ *Closed Mon. No lunch Tues. or weekends.*

WHERE TO STAY

Updated by Kathy A. McDonald

Los Angeles is a town of excess, and there's no shortage of decadent palaces where you can rest your head. But whether you're going high-style or budget, make sure to consider location when selecting your hotel. Planning to hit the beach? Give some thought to Santa Monica. Want to stay out late and enjoy L.A.'s legendary nightlife? Stay in West Hollywood or the Hollywood Boulevard area. For upscale and posh, you can't do better than Beverly Hills. In Pasadena you can enjoy the charm of Old Town and some of the best public gardens in the area. If you are seeking high culture, downtown is the place to stay.

WHAT IT COSTS					
	$$$$	$$$	$$	$	¢
FOR 2 PEOPLE	over $250	$176–$250	$121–$175	$90–$120	under $90

Prices are for a standard double room in high season, excluding 9%–14% tax.

Downtown

★ **$$$** ▣ **Hilton Checkers Los Angeles.** Opened as the Mayflower Hotel in 1927, Checkers retains much of its original character; its various-size rooms all have charming period details, although they also have modern luxuries like pillow-top mattresses, coffeemakers, 24-hour room service, and cordless phones. The rooftop pool deck overlooks the L.A. library and nearby office towers. The plush lobby bar and lounge look like they belong in a private club, with comfy leather chairs and a large plasma-screen TV. In the mornings, a complimentary car service can drive you anywhere within a 2-mi radius. ⌧ *535 S. Grand Ave., Downtown, 90071* ☎ *213/624–0000 or 800/445–8667* 🖷 *213/626–9906* ⊕ *www.hiltoncheckers. com* ⌹ *188 rooms, 9 suites* ♿ *Restaurant, room service, cable TV with movies and video games, in-room broadband, pool, gym, outdoor hot tub, massage, sauna, spa, steam room, bar, library, dry cleaning, laundry service, concierge, business services, meeting room, parking (fee), some pets allowed (fee), no-smoking rooms* ▤ *AE, D, DC, MC, V.*

$$$ ▣ **Millennium Biltmore Hotel.** This elegant, gilded beaux-arts masterpiece has a storied past. The lobby (formerly the Music Room) was the headquarters of J.F.K.'s presidential campaign, and the ballroom hosted some of the earliest Academy Awards. These days, the Biltmore hosts business types drawn by its central downtown location, ample meeting spaces, and services such as a well-outfitted business center that stays open 24/7. Guest rooms are classically styled with upholstered headboards, shuttered windows, and marble bathrooms, plus up-to-date amenities like CD players and cordless phones. Stay on the Club Level for excellent views and complimentary breakfast and evening cocktails. And bring your bathing suit for the vintage tiled indoor pool and adjacent steam room. ⌧ *506 S. Grand Ave., Downtown, 90071* ☎ *213/624–1011 or 800/245–*

FodorsChoice ★

8673 🖷 *213/612–1545* ⊕ *www.millenniumhotels.com* ➷ *627 rooms, 56 suites* ⚄ *3 restaurants, 2 cafés, room service, in-room safes, minibars, cable TV with movies and video games, in-room data ports, indoor pool, health club, hot tub, massage, sauna, steam room, 3 bars, lobby lounge, sports bar, shops, babysitting, laundry service, concierge, concierge floor, Internet room, business services, convention center, car rental, parking (fee), no-smoking floors* ▭ *AE, D, DC, MC, V.*

$$$ 🖷 **New Otani Hotel and Garden.** Fittingly enough, this branch of a Japanese chain is on the edge of Little Tokyo. Its "Japanese Suites" have tatami mats, futon beds, extra-deep bathtubs, and paper screens on the windows. The American-style rooms are somewhat plain and compact. Two of the restaurants serve authentic Japanese cuisine; a third serves straightforward contemporary fare. The hotel is close to the Civic Center and state and federal courthouses. For those who seek a contemplative moment (or a scenic wedding spot), there's a ½-acre Japanese garden on the roof. ⊠ *120 S. Los Angeles St., Little Tokyo, 90012* 🖷 *213/629–1200 or 800/639–6826* 🖷 *213/622–0980* ⊕ *www.newotani.com* ➷ *414 rooms, 20 suites* ⚄ *3 restaurants, room service, in-room safes, minibars, cable TV with movies, in-room broadband, gym, hair salon, hot tub, massage, sauna, spa, 3 bars, shops, dry cleaning, laundry service, concierge, business services, meeting rooms, car rental, parking (fee), no-smoking rooms* ▭ *AE, D, DC, MC, V.*

$$ 🖷 **Inn at 657.** Proprietor Patsy Carter runs a homey, welcoming bed-and-breakfast near the University of Southern California. Rooms in this 1904-built Craftsman have down comforters, Oriental silks on the walls, and needlepoint rugs. The vintage dining room table seats 12; conversation is encouraged. You're also welcome to hang out with the hummingbirds in the private garden. All rooms include a hearty breakfast, homemade cookies, and free local phone calls. ⊠ *657 W. 23rd St., Downtown, 90007* 🖷 *213/741–2200 or 800/347–7512* ⊕ *www. patsysinn657.com* ➷ *11 rooms* ⚄ *Dining room, fans, some microwaves, refrigerators, cable TV, in-room VCRs, in-room broadband, Wi-Fi, massage, laundry service, business services, free parking; no smoking* ▭ *MC, V* ⫶⃝⫶ *BP.*

$–$$ 🖷 **The Standard, Downtown LA.** Built in 1955 as Standard Oil's company's headquarters, the building was completely revamped under the sharp eye of owner André Balazs. The large guest rooms are practical and funky: all have orange built-in couches; windows that actually open; and platform beds. (Some also have large plush toys in the shape of human feet—not practical, but definitely fun). Bathrooms have extra-large tubs. The indoor–outdoor rooftop lounge has a preening social scene and stunning setting, but be prepared for some attitude at the door. Daytime traffic and the nightly bar scene make some rooms noisy. ⊠ *550 S. Flower St., Downtown, 90071* 🖷 *213/892–8080* 🖷 *213/892–8686* ⊕ *www. standardhotel.com* ➷ *205 rooms, 2 suites* ⚄ *Restaurant, room service, in-room safes, minibars, cable TV with movies and video games, in-room broadband, in-room DVDs, pool, gym, hair salon, massage, billiards, 2 bars, lobby lounge, dry cleaning, laundry service, concierge, business services, meeting rooms, parking (fee), some pets allowed, no-smoking rooms* ▭ *AE, D, DC, MC, V.*

Fodor's Choice
★

Hollywood

$$$–$$$$ ▣ **Hollywood Roosevelt Hotel.** A renovation and a pair of hot nightspots breathed new life into the Roosevelt. The Spanish tiles, painted ceilings, arches, and other details in this hotel's Spanish colonial–revival main building are still here to evoke early Hollywood glamour. Rooms in the main building have contemporary platform beds, and those surrounding the pool have dark-wood furnishings and mirrored walls—think hip bachelor pad. The David Hockney–painted pool adds to the playful vibe. A Metro stop is one block away. ✉ *7000 Hollywood Blvd., Hollywood, 90028* 📞 *323/466–7000 or 800/950–7667* 🖷 *323/462–8056* ⊕ *www. hollywoodroosevelt.com* ➷ *305 rooms, 48 suites* ◊ *Restaurant, room service, in-room safes, minibars, cable TV with movies and video games, Wi-Fi, pool, gym, massage, 3 bars, lobby lounge, nightclub, shops, dry cleaning, laundry service, concierge, business services, meeting rooms, parking (fee), no-smoking rooms* ▭ *AE, D, DC, MC, V.*

$$$ ▣ **Radisson Wilshire Plaza Hotel.** A handy midcity location ensures a steady stream of bookings here; the bustling lobby and café give a good first impression. Guest rooms are nothing to write home about, but they have all the necessary amenities, plus oak desks and floor-to-ceiling windows with good views. Across the street from a Red Line station, the hotel gives you easy access to downtown and Hollywood. A limo-rental service is available on-site. Authentic Japanese food and sushi can be found in Sake-E, off the lobby; Korean and Japanese breakfasts are available there, too. ✉ *3515 Wilshire Blvd., Mid-Wilshire, 90010* 📞 *213/381–7411 or 800/333–3333* 🖷 *213/386–7379* ⊕ *www.radwilshire.com* ➷ *380 rooms, 13 suites* ◊ *3 restaurants, café, room service, some in-room faxes, in-room safes, minibars, cable TV with movies, in-room data ports, pool, gym, massage, lobby lounge, shop, laundry service, concierge, business services, meeting room, car rental, parking (fee), no-smoking rooms* ▭ *AE, D, DC, MC, V.*

★ $$$ ▣ **Renaissance Hollywood Hotel.** Part of the massive Hollywood & Highland shopping and entertainment complex, this 20-story Renaissance is at the center of Hollywood's action. Contemporary art (notably by L.A. favorites Charles and Ray Eames), retro '60s furniture, terrazzo floors, a Zen rock garden, and wood and aluminum accents greet you in the lobby. Rooms are vibrant: chairs are red, table lamps are molded blue plastic. Blackout shades keep the fierce sun at bay. For the ultimate party pad, book the Panorama Suite, with angled floor-to-ceiling windows, vintage Eames furniture, a grand piano, and a sunken Jacuzzi tub with a view. ✉ *1755 N. Highland Ave., Hollywood, 90028* 📞 *323/856–1200 or 800/468–3571* 🖷 *323/856–1205* ⊕ *www.renaissancehollywood.com* ➷ *604 rooms, 33 suites* ◊ *Restaurant, room service, in-room safes, minibars, cable TV with movies and video games, in-room broadband, pool, gym, 2 bars, lobby lounge, shop, babysitting, dry cleaning, laundry service, concierge, concierge floor, business services, meeting rooms, convention center, parking (fee), no-smoking rooms* ▭ *AE, D, DC, MC, V.*

★ $–$$ ▣ **Farmer's Daughter Hotel.** Tongue-in-cheek country style is the name of the game at this motel: rooms are upholstered in blue gingham with denim bedspreads, and staff members all wear overalls. A curving blue wall secludes the interior courtyard, where there's comfy patio furniture and an open-air lobby. Rooms are snug but outfitted with whimsical original art and amenities such as CD and DVD players. It's a favorite of *The Price Is Right* hopefuls; the TV show tapes at the CBS studios nearby. ■ TIP➡ **The cheap eats at the Farmers Market, as well as the Grove, L.A.'s popular outdoor shopping and entertainment mall, are directly across Fairfax Avenue.** ⊠ *115 S. Fairfax Ave., Fairfax District, 90036* ☎ *323/937–3930 or 800/334–1658* 🖷 *323/932–1608* ⊕ *www. farmersdaughterhotel.com* 🛏 *64 rooms, 2 suites* ♿ *Restaurant, room service, in-room safes, refrigerators, cable TV, in-room DVDs, in-room broadband, pool, babysitting, dry cleaning, laundry service, concierge, meeting room, car rental, parking (fee), some pets allowed (fee), no-smoking rooms.* 🖃 *AE, D, DC, MC, V.*

$ 🏨 **Highland Gardens Hotel.** A large, sparkling pool and a lush, if somewhat overgrown, tropical garden set this hotel apart from other budget lodgings. Basic but spacious units have either two queen-size beds, or a king bed with a queen-size sleeper sofa, plus a desk and sitting area with Formica tables. Rooms facing busy Franklin Avenue are noisy; ask for one facing the courtyard. The hotel is just blocks from the Walk of Fame and a few minutes' drive off the Sunset Strip. ⊠ *7047 Franklin Ave., Hollywood, 90028* ☎ *323/850–0536 or 800/404–5472* 🖷 *323/850–1712* ⊕ *www.highlandgardenshotel.com* 🛏 *70 rooms, 48 suites* ♿ *Some kitchenettes, refrigerators, pool, laundry facilities, free parking; no smoking* 🖃 *AE, MC, V* ℃ *CP.*

Beverly Hills

★ $$$$ 🏨 **Beverly Hills Hotel.** Ever since its opening in 1912, the "Pink Palace" has attracted Hollywood's elite. Celebrity guests favor the private bungalows, which come with *all* of life's little necessities (Bungalow 5, for example, has its own lap pool). Standard rooms are also well outfitted, with original artwork, butler service, Frette linens and duvets, walk-in closets, and huge marble bathrooms. Swiss skin-care company La Prairie runs the hotel's swanky day spa, which specializes in de-aging treatments. The Polo Lounge remains an iconic Hollywood meeting place. Canine guests are also pampered here; 24-hour dog-walking service is available. ⊠ *9641 Sunset Blvd., Beverly Hills 90210* ☎ *310/276–2251 or 800/283–8885* 🖷 *310/887–2887* ⊕ *www.beverlyhillshotel.com* 🛏 *204 rooms, 21 bungalows* ♿ *4 restaurants, coffee shop, room service, BBQs, in-room fax, in-room safes, some kitchenettes, minibars, cable TV with movies and video games, in-room DVDs, in-room VCRs, in-room broadband, golf privileges, 2 tennis courts, pool, gym, hair salon, hot tub, spa, 2 bars, lobby lounge, piano bar, shops, babysitting, dry cleaning, laundry service, concierge, Internet room, business services, meeting rooms, parking (fee), some pets allowed (fee), no-smoking rooms* 🖃 *AE, DC, MC, V.*

$$$$ 🏨 **Four Seasons Hotel Los Angeles at Beverly Hills.** High hedges and patio
Fodor'sChoice gardens make this hotel a secluded retreat that even the hum of traffic
★ can't permeate. It's a favorite of Hollywood's elite, so don't be surprised by a well-known face poolside or in the Windows bar. The staff here will make you feel pampered, as will the lavish guest rooms, which have beds with Frette linens, soft robes and slippers, and French doors leading to balconies. Extras include 24-hour business services, overnight shoe

shine, and a morning newspaper. Massages are available in a cabana near the pool. ⊠ *300 S. Doheny Dr., Beverly Hills 90048* ☏ *310/273–2222 or 800/332–3442* 🖷 *310/859–3824* ⊕ *www.fourseasons.com/losangeles* 🛏 *187 rooms, 98 suites* ⚐ *2 restaurants, café, room service, minibars, cable TV with movies and video games, in-room DVD/VCR, in-room broadband, pool, gym, hot tub, sauna, spa, steam room, bar, babysitting, dry cleaning, laundry service, concierge, business services, meeting rooms, car rental, parking (fee), some pets allowed (fee), no-smoking rooms.* ▤ *AE, DC, MC, V.*

$$$$ 🏨 **Luxe Hotel Rodeo Drive.** Refined design rules at this boutique hotel discreetly tucked away on Rodeo Drive between Valentino and Michael Kors boutiques. Streetside rooms look out over Gucci and the extravagant Prada Epicenter store. Dark mahogany and brushed metals fill the lobby, and the compact rooms go glam with black-and-white photography, 8-foot-high mirrors, Egyptian linens, and Frette robes and slippers. Café Rodeo, Luxe's intimate skylight restaurant, draws a well-heeled local lunch crowd with upscale comfort food and potent martinis. ⊠ *360 N. Rodeo Dr., Beverly Hills 90210* ☏ *310/273–0300 or 866/589–3411* 🖷 *310/859–8730* ⊕ *www.luxehotels.com* 🛏 *84 rooms, 4 suites* ⚐ *Restaurant, room service, in-room safes, refrigerators, cable TV with movies, in-room broadband, Wi-Fi, gym, bar, babysitting, laundry service, concierge, business services, meeting room, car rental, parking (fee), no-smoking rooms* ▤ *AE, D, DC, MC, V.*

$$$$
FodorsChoice
★

🏨 **Peninsula Beverly Hills.** They seem to think of everything at this French Riviera–style palace. It's a favorite of Hollywood bold-face names, but all kinds of visitors consistently describe their stay as near-perfect, though very expensive. Rooms overflow with antiques, artwork, and marble; high-tech room amenities are controlled by a bedside panel. Service is exemplary and always discreet. Soak up the sun by the fifth-floor pool with its fully outfitted cabanas or sip afternoon tea in the living room under ornate chandeliers. Belvedere, the hotel's flower-filled restaurant, is a lunchtime favorite for film-business types. ⊠ *9882 S. Santa Monica Blvd., Beverly Hills 90212* ☏ *310/551–2888 or 800/462–7899* 🖷 *310/788–2319* ⊕ *www.peninsula.com* 🛏 *166 rooms, 36 suites, 16 villas* ⚐ *Restaurant, room service, in-room fax, in-room safes, minibars, cable TV with movies and video games, in-room DVDs, in-room VCRs, in-room broadband, pool, gym, hair salon, outdoor hot tub, sauna, spa, steam room, bar, lobby lounge, piano, shops, babysitting, dry cleaning, laundry service, concierge, business services, meeting rooms, travel services, parking (fee), some pets allowed (fee); no smoking* ▤ *AE, D, DC, MC, V.*

$$$$ 🏨 **Regent Beverly Wilshire.** Built in 1928, the Italian Renaissance–style Wilshire wing of this fabled hotel is replete with elegant details: crystal chandeliers, oak paneling, walnut doors, crown moldings, and pink marble. Added in 1971, the Beverly wing is more contemporary. Rodeo Drive beckons outside; a complimentary limo can drive you anywhere within 3 mi of the hotel. The Boulevard is the hotel's newly posh dining room. ⊠ *9500 Wilshire Blvd., Beverly Hills 90212* ☏ *310/275–5200 or 800/427–4354* 🖷 *310/274–2851* ⊕ *www.fourseasons.com* 🛏 *262 rooms, 137 suites* ⚐ *2 restaurants, room service, in-room safes, minibars, cable TV with movies and video games, in-room DVDs, in-room broadband, Wi-Fi, pool, gym, health club, hair salon, outdoor hot tub, sauna, spa,*

2 bars, piano, shops, babysitting, dry cleaning, laundry service, concierge, business services, convention center, parking (fee), some pets allowed, no-smoking floors ⊟ *AE, DC, MC, V.*

$$$ ▦ **Avalon.** This relaxed but cosmopolitan boutique hotel combines Googie-era style with tech-savvy substance. Rooms at the three-building property incorporate '50s retro design, with classic pieces from George Nelson, Eames, and Thonet; there are also Frette linens and chenille throws, and a menu of spa treatments that can be ordered in-room. For extended stays, the Avalon also has stylish apartments that come with all hotel services, including twice-daily housekeeping. Weather permitting, things get busy poolside and in the fun private cabanas. ⊠ *9400 W. Olympic Blvd., Beverly Hills 90212* ☎ *310/277–5221 or 800/535–4715* 🖷 *310/277–4928* ⊕ *www.avalonbeverlyhills.com* ⟲ *76 rooms, 10 suites* ⌂ *Restaurant, room service, in-room fax, in-room safes, minibars, cable TV with movies and video games, in-room DVDs, in-room broadband, pool, gym, massage, bar, dry cleaning, laundry facilities, laundry service, concierge, business services, meeting room, parking (fee), some pets allowed (fee), no-smoking rooms* ⊟ *AE, DC, MC, V.*

$$$ ▦ **Maison 140.** Though the rooms are compact at this 1930s boutique hotel, they are grandly designed: antiques from France and the Far East, textured wallpaper, and colorfully painted rooms are a feast for the eyes. Refinements include down comforters, Frette linens, and bathrobes. Beverly Hills' golden triangle of shopping is within blocks. You can take advantage of the pool and restaurant at sister property the Avalon Hotel, 1 mi away. ⊠ *140 S. Lasky Dr., Beverly Hills 90212* ☎ *310/281–4000 or 800/670–6182* 🖷 *310/281–4001* ⊕ *www.maison140beverlyhills. com* ⟲ *43 rooms* ⌂ *Room service, in-room safes, minibars, cable TV with movies, in-room DVDs, in-room broadband, gym, massage, lobby lounge, dry cleaning, laundry service, concierge, parking (fee), no-smoking rooms* ⊟ *AE, DC, MC, V.*

★ $$–$$$ ▦ **The Crescent.** Built in 1926 as a dorm for silent-film actors, the Crescent is now a sleek boutique hotel within walking distance of the Beverly Hills shopping triangle. Low couches and tables, French doors that open to a streetside patio, and plenty of candlelight (at night) give the lobby and bar a sophisticated look. Rooms are small, but platform beds and built-in furniture maximize the space and create a loftlike feel. Bathrooms are finished in concrete—utilitarian but coolly cozy. High-tech amenities include flat-screen TVs, in-room iPods, and a library of the latest CDs and DVDs. ⊠ *403 N. Crescent Dr., Beverly Hills 90210* ☎ *310/247–0505* 🖷 *310/247–9053* ⊕ *www.crescentbh.com* ⟲ *40 rooms* ⌂ *Restaurant, room service, minibars, cable TV, Wi-Fi, massage, lobby lounge, dry cleaning, laundry service, parking (fee); no smoking* ⊟ *AE, D, MC, V.*

Century City

$$$ ▦ **Park Hyatt.** This hotel's proximity to 20th Century Fox Studios appeals to those in the Industry, but the central Westside location is handy for all kinds of visits. There's a decent-size balcony off every room; most have excellent views. Ask for a room facing west for brilliant sunsets over the ocean (smog permitting). Desks are computer-ready with convenient cordless phones. Bathrooms have marble vanities and separate shower and tub. Nightly turndown, complimentary shoeshine, and complimentary town-car service within Century City and Beverly Hills are nice touches. Spa treatments, offered in four spa villas with private outdoor patio and garden, are a soothing indulgence. ⊠ *2151 Ave. of the Stars, Century City, 90067* ☎ *310/277–1234 or 866/333–8881* 🖷 *310/785–9240* ⊕ *www.hyatt.com* 🛏 *185 rooms, 180 suites* ⌂ *Restaurant, room service, in-room fax, in-room safes, minibars, cable TV with movies, in-room broadband, pool, health club, outdoor hot tub, spa, steam room, bar, lobby lounge, shops, babysitting, dry cleaning, laundry service, concierge, business services, meeting rooms, parking (fee), no-smoking floors* ▭ *AE, D, DC, MC, V.*

West Hollywood

$$$$ 🖬 **Chateau Marmont Hotel.** The Chateau's swank exterior disguises its lurid place in Hollywood history—many remember it as the scene of John Belushi's fatal overdose in 1982. Actors like Johnny Depp and Keanu Reeves appreciate the hotel for its secluded cottages, bungalows, and understated suites and penthouses. The interior is 1920s-style, although some of the decor looks dated rather than vintage. The Wi-Fi throughout the hotel means that you can surf the Net while seated on the hotel's scenic, landscaped terrace with drop-dead sunset views. ⊠ *8221 Sunset Blvd., West Hollywood 90046* ☎ *323/656–1010 or 800/242–8328* 🖷 *323/655–5311* ⊕ *www.chateaumarmont.com* 🛏 *11 rooms, 63 suites* ⌂ *Restaurant, room service, in-room fax, in-room safes, minibars, cable TV with movies, in-room DVDs, in-room data ports, Wi-Fi, pool, gym, massage, bar, babysitting, dry cleaning, laundry service, concierge, business services, parking (fee), some pets allowed (fee), no-smoking rooms* ▭ *AE, DC, MC, V.*

★ **$$$$** 🖬 **Mondrian.** Ian Schrager, famed for his stylish hotels, created this all-white, high-rise, urban resort. Mod, apartment-size accommodations have floor-to-ceiling windows, slipcovered sofas, and marble coffee tables; all have kitchens. Desks and multiline phones could help you be productive, but the happening social scene in the lobby will certainly distract. The Asia de Cuba restaurant is known for its amazing views, sparkling cocktails, and scads of beautiful people. The one downside: rooms on the lower floors facing Sunset are unbearably noisy, so you should insist on a room that faces west. ⊠ *8440 Sunset Blvd., West Hollywood 90069* ☎ *323/650–8999 or 800/697–1791* 🖷 *323/650–5215* ⊕ *www.mondrianhotel.com* 🛏 *53 rooms, 185 suites* ⌂ *Restaurant, café, room service, in-room safes, kitchens, refrigerators, cable TV with movies, in-room VCRs, Web TV, Wi-Fi, pool, gym, sauna, spa, steam room, 2 bars, shop, laundry service, concierge, business services, meeting room, parking (fee), no-smoking rooms* ▭ *AE, D, DC, MC, V.*

$$$$ 🖬 **Sunset Marquis Hotel and Villas.** If you're in town to cut your new hit single, you'll appreciate the two on-site recording studios here. But even the musically challenged will appreciate this property on a quiet cul-de-sac just off the Sunset Strip. Suites and ultraprivate villas, which are set amid lush gardens, are roomy and plush, with soundproof windows and blackout curtains for total serenity. (New villas are set to open at the start of 2007.) All have stereo systems; some have grand pianos. ⊠ *1200*

N. Alta Loma Rd., West Hollywood 90069 ☎ *310/657–1333 or 800/
858–9758* 🖨 *310/652–5300* ⊕ *www.sunsetmarquishotel.com* ⮩ *102
suites, 12 villas* ⚬ *2 restaurants, room service, in-room safes, minibars,
refrigerators, cable TV with movies, in-room broadband, 2 pools, gym,
outdoor hot tub, massage, sauna, babysitting, dry cleaning, laundry service, concierge, business services, meeting room, travel services, parking
(fee); no smoking* ▭ *AE, D, DC, MC, V.*

$$$ 🏨 **The Sunset Tower Hotel.** A clubby style infuses the 1929 art-deco land-
mark formerly known as the Argyle. The lobby sets the tone with dark
wood, mauve accents, and marble floors; vintage Hollywood star pho-
tos add retro glamour. Sink into couches and cozy upholstered corners
while taking in the dramatic city views: the poolside city views are
equally impressive. Most of the Sunset Strip's clubs, bars, and hot spots
are within walking distance. ✉ *8358 Sunset Blvd., West Hollywood 90069*
☎ *323/654–7100 or 800/225–2637* 🖨 *323/654–9287* ⊕ *www.
sunsettowerhotel.com* ⮩ *20 rooms, 44 suites* ⚬ *Restaurant, room serv-
ice, in-room data ports, Wi-Fi, in-room safes, some in-room hot tubs,
minibars, cable TV with movies, pool, gym, hair salon, spa, steam
room, bar, piano bar, shop, babysitting, dry cleaning, laundry service,
concierge, Internet room, business services, parking (fee), some pets al-
lowed (fee), no smoking rooms* ▭ *AE, D, DC, MC, V.*

★ $$ 🏨 **The Standard.** Hotelier André Balazs created this affordable, hip Sunset Strip hotel from a former retirement home. The aesthetic is '70s kitsch:
pop art, shag carpets and ultrasuede sectionals fill the lobby, and the
rooms have inflatable sofas, beanbag chairs, surfboard tables, and
Warhol poppy-print curtains. DJs spin nightly and lobby socializing begins at the front desk and extends to the blue AstroTurfed pool deck
outside. ■ TIP➔ **Especially on weekends and holidays, expect a young party
scene that can drift noisily into the halls.** The 24-hour coffee shop is quite
good, more modern classic than greasy spoon. ✉ *8300 Sunset Blvd.,
West Hollywood 90069* ☎ *323/650–9090* 🖨 *323/650–2820* ⊕ *www.
standardhotel.com* ⮩ *137 rooms, 2 suites* ⚬ *Coffee shop, room service, minibars, cable TV with movies, in-room broadband, pool, hair salon,
bar, lobby lounge, shop, laundry service, concierge, meeting room, parking (fee), some pets allowed (fee)* ▭ *AE, D, DC, MC, V.*

Westwood

$$ 🏨 **Doubletree Hotel.** In the middle of the high-rise condos that predom-
inate in the mostly upscale residential Wilshire Corridor, this tastefully
appointed, 19-story hotel blends in quietly with its surroundings. It's
an ideal choice for visitors to the UCLA campus—there's a free shuttle
to take you there. Rooms have standard hotel furnishings, with two dou-
ble beds or one king; you get fresh chocolate-chip cookies at check-in.
✉ *10740 Wilshire Blvd., Westwood, 90024* ☎ *310/475–8711* 🖨 *310/
475–5220* ⊕ *www.doubletreelawestwood.com* ⮩ *281 rooms, 14 suites*
⚬ *Restaurant, room service, in-room data ports, cable TV with movies
and video games, pool, gym, outdoor hot tub, bar, shop, dry cleaning,
laundry service, concierge, Internet, business services, meeting rooms,
parking (fee), no-smoking rooms* ▭ *AE, D, DC, MC, V.*

Bel Air

$$$$ ⊡ **Hotel Bel-Air.** In a wooded canyon with lush gardens and a swan-filled
Fodor'sChoice   lake, the Hotel Bel-Air's distinctive luxury and seclusion have made it
★   a favorite of discreet celebs and royalty for decades. Bungalow-style rooms
feel like fine homes, with country-French, expensively upholstered furniture in silk or chenille; many have hardwood floors. Several rooms
have wood-burning fireplaces (the bell captain will build a fire for you).
Eight suites have private outdoor hot tubs. Complimentary tea service
greets you upon arrival; enjoy it on the terrace warmed by heated tiles.
A pianist plays nightly in the bar. The hotel's excellent restaurant spills
into the garden and a heated, vine-draped terrace. ⊠ *701 Stone Canyon
Rd., Bel Air, 90077* ☎ *310/472–1211 or 800/648–4097* 🖷 *310/476–
5890* ⊕ *www.hotelbelair.com* 🖛 *52 rooms, 39 suites* ♢ *Restaurant, room
service, in-room safes, minibars, cable TV with movies and video games,
in-room VCRs, in-room broadband, pool, gym, massage, piano bar, shop,
babysitting, dry cleaning, laundry service, concierge, business services,
meeting rooms, free parking, some pets allowed (fee), no-smoking rooms*
▭ *AE, DC, MC, V.*

Santa Monica

★ **$$$$**   ⊡ **Hotel Casa del Mar.** In the 1920s it was a posh beach club catering
to the city's elite; now the Casa del Mar is one of SoCal's most luxurious beachfront hotels, with three extravagant two-story penthouses,
a raised deck and pool, and an elegant ballroom facing the sand. Guest
rooms, designed to evoke the old days, are filled with contemporary
amenities like flat-screen TVs, CD players, and direct-dial phones.
Bathrooms are gorgeous, with sunken whirlpool tubs and glass-enclosed
showers. Spa services are top-notch. ⊠ *1910 Ocean Front Way, Santa
Monica 90405* ☎ *310/581–5533 or 800/898–6999* 🖷 *310/581–5503*
⊕ *www.hotelcasadelmar.com* 🖛 *129 rooms, 4 suites* ♢ *2 restaurants,
room service, in-room safes, minibars, cable TV with movies and video
games, in-room VCRs, in-room broadband, pool, gym, spa, bar, lobby
lounge, shop, dry cleaning, laundry service, concierge, business services, meeting room, parking (fee), some pets allowed; no smoking*
▭ *AE, D, DC, MC, V.*

★ **$$$$**   ⊡ **Le Merigot Beach Hotel & Spa.** Steps from Santa Monica's expansive
beach, Le Merigot caters to a corporate upmarket clientele (it's a JW
Marriott property). Upper floors have panoramic views of the Santa Monica Pier and the Pacific; many rooms have terraces. Contemporary
rooms have feather beds and Frette linens, and bathrooms come with
playful bath toys and votive candles. A checkerboard slate courtyard,
including a pool, cabanas, fountains, and outdoor living room, is the
center of activity. You can book a massage at the spa for a true attitude
adjustment, or dine in French country style at the comfortable Cézanne
restaurant. ⊠ *1740 Ocean Ave., Santa Monica 90405* ☎ *310/395–
9700 or 888/539–7899* 🖷 *310/395–9200* ⊕ *www.lemerigothotel.com*
🖛 *175 rooms, 15 suites* ♢ *Restaurant, room service, in-room safes, minibars, cable TV with movies and video games, in-room broadband, in-
room data ports, pool, fitness classes, gym, hair salon, sauna, spa, steam
room, beach, bicycles, bar, shop, babysitting, dry cleaning, laundry*

service, concierge, business services, meeting rooms, parking (fee), some pets allowed (fee), no-smoking rooms = *AE, D, DC, MC, V.*

$$$$ 🏨 **Fairmont Miramar Hotel Santa Monica.** A mammoth Moreton Bay fig tree dwarfs the main entrance of this sprawling place. Residential-style bungalows, built between 1920 and 1946, are extremely private and a favorite of visiting VIPs. Standard rooms in the 10-story tower have no room to spare, but they do come with beautiful ocean views, alabaster light fixtures, carved wood armoires, Bose stereo systems, and down duvets. Although you're not right on the beach, the Third Street Promenade is close by. ⊠ *101 Wilshire Blvd., Santa Monica 90401* 🕾 *310/576–7777 or 800/257–7544* 🖷 *310/458–7912* ⊕ *www.fairmont.com/santamonica* 🛏 *251 rooms, 51 suites, 32 bungalows* 🖒 *Restaurant, room service, in-room safes, minibars, cable TV with movies and video games, in-room data ports, in-room broadband, Wi-Fi (lobby only), pool, gym, hair salon, outdoor hot tub, sauna, spa, steam room, bicycles, bar, lobby lounge, shop, babysitting, dry cleaning, laundry service, concierge, business services, convention center, car rental, travel services, parking (fee), some pets allowed (fee), no-smoking rooms* = *AE, D, DC, MC, V.*

$$$$
Fodor'sChoice
★
🏨 **Shutters on the Beach.** Set right on the sand, this gray-shingle inn has become synonymous with in-town escapism. Guest rooms have those namesake shutter doors, pillow-top mattresses, and white built-in cabinets filled with art books and curios. Bathrooms are luxe, each with a whirlpool tub, a raft of bath goodies, and a three-nozzle, glass-walled shower. Although the hotel's service gets mixed reviews from some readers, the beachfront location and showhouse decor make this one of SoCal's most popular luxury hotels. ⊠ *1 Pico Blvd., Santa Monica 90405* 🕾 *310/458–0030 or 800/334–9000* 🖷 *310/458–4589* ⊕ *www.shuttersonthebeach.com* 🛏 *186 rooms, 12 suites* 🖒 *2 restaurants, room service, in-room safes, in-room hot tubs, minibars, cable TV with movies and video games, in-room DVDs, in-room broadband, Wi-Fi, pool, gym, outdoor hot tub, sauna, spa, steam room, beach, bicycles, bar, lobby lounge, piano, shop, babysitting, dry cleaning, laundry service, concierge, business services, meeting rooms, parking (fee), no-smoking rooms* = *AE, D, DC, MC, V.*

$$$ 🏨 **Viceroy.** Whimsy abounds at this stylized seaside escape—there are porcelain dogs as lamp bases and Spode china plates mounted on the walls. The compact rooms all have French balconies, and the mostly marble bathrooms have seated vanities. The glamorous socialize in the pool and cabana area amid all-white armchairs and divans. Spa services, from energizing massage to detox facials, are available in-room and poolside from nearby Fred Segal Beauty. ⊠ *1819 Ocean Ave., Santa Monica 90401* 🕾 *310/260–7500 or 800/622–8711* 🖷 *310/260–7515* ⊕ *www.viceroysantamonica.com* 🛏 *158 rooms, 5 suites* 🖒 *Restaurant, room service, in-room safes, minibars, cable TV with movies and video games, in-room DVDs, in-room broadband, 2 pools, gym, massage, bar, lobby lounge, library, dry cleaning, laundry service, concierge, meeting rooms, parking (fee), some pets allowed, no-smoking rooms* = *AE, DC, MC, V.*

$$–$$$ 🏨 **The Ambrose.** An air of tranquillity pervades the four-story Ambrose, which blends right into its mostly residential Santa Monica neighborhood. The decor incorporates many Asian accents, following the principles of feng shui. There's a Zen garden and koi pond at the entrance and Japanese wood-block prints throughout. Rooms have deluxe extras like chenille throws, Italian linens, Frette towels and robes, and a minibar with health-oriented elixirs. Windows are double-paned for quiet; upper floors have partial ocean views. Room service and the breakfast buffet includes healthy choices. A vintage London taxi is on call for free short jaunts in the area. ⊠ *1255 20th St., Santa Monica 90404* ☎ *310/ 315–1555 or 877/262–7673* 🖷 *310/315–1556* ⊕ *www.ambrosehotel. com* ⇨ *77 rooms* ⚙ *Room service, some fans, in-room data ports, in-room safes, minibars, cable TV, in-room VCRs, fitness classes, gym, massage, bicycles, library, babysitting, dry cleaning, laundry service, concierge, Internet, meeting room, car rental, free parking, some pets allowed, no-smoking rooms* ▤ *AE, D, DC, MC, V* ⦿I *CP.*

Burbank

★ **$$$** ▦ **The Graciela Burbank.** Close to Burbank's TV and movie studios, the smartly designed Graciela feels like a Beverly Hills boutique hotel. Over the years, it has become a favorite of women business travelers who like its understated look (muted beiges and greens) and residential vibe. The lobby is a welcoming living room with glass fireplace and corners for quiet conversation or cocktails. Feather beds are covered in comfy duvets; thoughtful touches include monogrammed pillowcases and plush bathrobes. Generous work spaces have state-of-the-art lighting. Bathrooms have granite vanities, make-up mirrors, and shelves for storage. The rooftop sun deck has a brightly striped cabana and view of the nearby hills. ⊠ *322 N. Pass Ave., Burbank 91505* ☎ *818/842–8887 or 888/ 956–1900* 🖷 *818/260–8999* ⊕ *www.thegraciela.com* ⇨ *91 rooms, 10 suites* ⚙ *Dining room, room service, in-room data ports, in-room safes, some kitchenettes, microwaves, refrigerators, cable TV with movies and video games, in-room DVDs, gym, outdoor hot tub, massage, sauna, bar, lobby lounge, babysitting, dry cleaning, laundry service, concierge, Internet, business services, meeting rooms, airport shuttle (Burbank), parking (fee), some pets allowed (fee), no-smoking rooms* ▤ *AE, D, DC, MC, V.*

Pasadena

$$$$ ▦ **Ritz-Carlton Huntington Hotel & Spa.** An azalea-filled Japanese garden
Fodor'sChoice and an unusual Picture Bridge whose murals celebrate California's his-
★ tory make this an especially scenic place to stay. The Mediterranean-style main building is surrounded by 23 acres of green lawns. Traditional guest rooms are handsome if a bit small. Suites and cottages, however, all have been updated in shades of gold and blue. Frette bed linens, feather beds, and thick bathrobes are standard. The hotel's restaurant, the Dining Room, serves contemporary cuisine in a formal setting. ⊠ *1401 S. Oak Knoll Ave., Pasadena 91106* ☎ *626/568–3900 or 800/241–3333* 🖷 *626/568–3700* ⊕ *www.ritzcarlton.com* ⇨ *361 rooms, 31 suites* ⚙ *2 restaurants, room service, in-room safes, minibars, cable TV with movies, in-room broadband, Wi-Fi, 3 tennis courts, pool, health club, hair salon, outdoor hot tub, sauna, spa, steam room, bicycles, bar, lobby lounge, shops, babysitting, children's programs (ages 7–12), dry cleaning, laundry service, concierge, concierge floor, business services,*

meeting rooms, convention center, car rental, travel services, parking (fee), some pets allowed (fee), no-smoking rooms ▭ *AE, D, DC, MC, V.*

$–$$$ ⊞ **Artists' Inn & Cottage.** This charming 1895 B&B is in a quiet residential neighborhood of Craftsman bungalows, not far from the antiques shops of south Pasadena. Once a chicken farm, the Artists' Inn still retains a country air with more than 100 rose bushes in the garden, wicker furniture on the front porch, and home-cooked breakfasts and afternoon tea. Some rooms have fireplaces; all have themes relating to a particular period of art (like impressionism) or famous artist (Degas, Van Gogh, O'Keeffe). Close by is a Gold Line Metro stop for easy access to downtown L.A. ✉ *1038 Magnolia St., Pasadena 91030* ☎ *626/799–5668 or 888/799–5668* 🖷 *626/799–3678* ⊕ *www.artistsinns.com* ⇨ *10 rooms* ⟠ *In-room data ports, Wi-Fi, free parking; no TV in some rooms, no smoking* ▭ *AE, MC, V* ❘◉❘ *BP.*

Los Angeles International Airport

$$$ ⊞ **Westin Los Angeles Airport.** Close to the Interstate 405 and on the airport's hotel corridor, the jumbo Westin offers reasonable park-and-ride packages. But there are strong suits here other than convenience and the long list of amenities. The guest rooms are spacious and many suites have private outdoor hot tubs. ✉ *5400 W. Century Blvd., LAX, 90045* ☎ *310/216–5858 or 800/937–8461* 🖷 *310/417–4545* ⊕ *www.westin. com* ⇨ *723 rooms, 42 suites* ⟠ *Restaurant, room service, some in-room faxes, in-room safes, minibars, refrigerators, cable TV with movies, in-room broadband, Wi-Fi, pool, gym, hot tub, sauna, billiards, bar, children's programs (ages 6–13), laundry service, concierge, business services, meeting room, airport shuttle, car rental, some pets allowed (fee), parking (fee); no smoking* ▭ *AE, D, DC, MC, V.*

$$ ⊞ **Summerfield Suites.** There's room to spread out in these extra-large one- and two-bedroom suites; there are even living-room sleeper sofas. You can cook in the fully outfitted kitchens or on the gas grills outside; the staff will stock your refrigerator with groceries (the service is free but you'll have to pay for the groceries). Weeknights, you can attend a happy hour with complimentary drinks and snacks. ✉ *810 S. Douglas Ave., El Segundo 90245* ☎ *310/725–0100 or 800/996–3426* 🖷 *310/725–0900* ⊕ *www.wyndham.com* ⇨ *122 suites* ⟠ *Dining room, BBQs, kitchens, refrigerators, cable TV, in-room VCRs, in-room data ports, pool, gym, hot tub, basketball, dry cleaning, laundry facilities, laundry service, concierge, Internet, business services, meeting rooms, free parking, some pets allowed (fee), no-smoking rooms* ▭ *AE, D, DC, MC, V* ❘◉❘ *BP.*

NIGHTLIFE & THE ARTS

Updated by
Lina Lecaro

Hollywood and West Hollywood are the chief focus of L.A. nightlife, where hip and happening nightspots liberally dot Sunset and Hollywood boulevards. L.A. is one of the best places in the world for seeing soon-to-be-famous rockers as well as top jazz, blues, and classical performers. Film emporia are naturally well represented here, but so are dance events, performance art, and an underrated theater community that might just be L.A.'s best-kept secret.

For a thorough listing of local events, ⊕ www.la.com and *Los Angeles Magazine* are both good sources. The Calendar section of the *Los Angeles Times* also lists a wide survey of Los Angeles–arts events, especially on Thursday and Sunday, as do the more alternative publications, the *LA Weekly* and the *LA Citybeat* (both free, and issued every Thursday). Call ahead to confirm that what you want to see is ongoing.

The Arts

Concert Halls

Build in 2003 as a grand addition to L.A.'s Music Center, the **Walt Disney Concert Hall** (⊠ 151 S. Grand Ave., Downtown 🕾 323/850–2000) is now the home of the Los Angeles Philharmonic and the Los Angeles Master Chorale, plus an array of eclectic, multicultural musical performers. A sculptural monument of gleaming, curved steel, the 2,265-seat theater also boasts a public park, gardens, and shops as well as two outdoor amphitheaters for children's and preconcert events. Also part of the Music Center complex, the 3,200-seat **Dorothy Chandler Pavilion** (⊠ 135 N. Grand Ave., Downtown 🕾 213/972–7211) presents an array of music programs and the L.A. Opera's classics from September through June. In Griffith Park, the open-air auditorium known as the **Greek Theater** (⊠ 2700 N. Vermont Ave., Los Feliz 🕾 323/665–1927), complete with Doric columns, presents big-name performers in its mainly pop-rock-jazz schedule from June through October.

Ever since it opened in 1920, in a park surrounded by mountains, trees, and gardens, the **Hollywood Bowl** (⊠ 2301 Highland Ave., Hollywood 🕾 323/850–2000 ⊕ www.hollywoodbowl.com) has been one of the world's largest and most atmospheric outdoor amphitheaters. Its season runs from early July through mid-September; the L.A. Philharmonic spends its summer season here. There are performances daily except Monday (and some Sundays); the program ranges from jazz to pop to classical. Concertgoers usually arrive early, bringing picnic suppers; there are plenty of picnic tables. Additionally, a moderately priced outdoor grill and a more upscale restaurant are among the dining options operated by the **Patina Group** (🕾 323/850–1885). Avoid the hassle of parking by taking one of the Park-and-Ride buses, which leave from various locations around town; call the Bowl for information.

TICKET SOURCES

In addition to contacting venues directly, try these sources to score tickets to events throughout the city. Most tickets can be bought by phone or online with a credit card.

Good Time Tickets (🕾 323/464–7383 ⊕ www.goodtime-tickets.com) sells harder-to-get tickets—and charges accordingly.

Razor Gator (🕾 800/542–4466 ⊕ www.razorgator.com) covers events at museums and small theaters, plus some stadium fare.

Theatre League Alliance L.A (⊕ www.theatrela.org) is where to score discounted theater tickets.

Ticketmaster (🕾 213/480–3232, 213/365–3500 fine arts ⊕ www.ticketmaster.com) is still the all-around top dog.

★ The jewel in the crown of Hollywood & Highland is the **Kodak Theatre** (⊠ 6801 Hollywood Blvd., Hollywood ☎ 323/308–6363 ⊕ www. kodaktheatre.com). Created to be the permanent host of the Academy Awards, the lavish 3,500-seat theater also presents music concerts and ballets. Seeing a show here is worthwhile just to witness the sparkling interior. The one-of-a-kind, 6,300-seat ersatz-Arabic **Shrine Auditorium** (⊠ 665 W. Jefferson Blvd., Downtown ☎ 213/748–5116), built in 1926 as Al Malaikah Temple, hosts touring companies from all over the world, assorted gospel and choral groups, and other musical acts as well as high-profile televised awards shows, including the Latin Grammys. It's used mainly for sporting events, but the **Staples Center** (⊠ 1111 S. Figueroa St. ☎ 213/742–7300 ⊕ www.staplescenter.com) also offers blockbuster concerts. Megaband U2 took their big-budget show to this huge arena last year. Adjacent to Universal Studios, the 6,250-seat **Gibson Amphitheater** (⊠ 100 Universal City Plaza, Universal City ☎ 818/622–4440) holds more than 100 performances a year, including the Radio City Christmas Spectacular and star-studded benefit concerts. The **Wiltern LG Theater** (⊠ 3790 Wilshire Blvd., Mid-Wilshire ☎ 213/388–1400), a green terra-cotta, art-deco masterpiece constructed in 1930, is a fine place to see pop, rock, jazz, and dance performances. The main space is standing-room-only venue, but there are still a few seats on the balcony.

Film

ART & REVIVAL HOUSES The **American Cinemathèque Independent Film Series** (⊠ 6712 Hollywood Blvd., Hollywood ☎ 323/466–3456 ⊕ americancinematheque.com) screens classics plus recent independent films, sometimes with question-and-answer sessions with the filmmakers. The main venue is the Lloyd E. Rigler Theater, within the 1922 Egyptian Theater, which combines an exterior of pharaoh sculptures and columns with a modern, high-tech design inside. The Cinemathèque also screens movies at the 1940 **Aero Theater** (⊠ 1328 Montana Ave., Santa Monica ☎ 323/466–3456).

Fodor'sChoice ★ Taking the concept of dinner and a movie to a whole new level, **Cinespace** (⊠ 6356 Hollywood Blvd., Hollywood ☎ 323/817–3456 ⊕ www.cine-space.com) screens classics and edgy indie flicks in its digital theater–restaurant. Finally, good food (gourmet comfort grub) and good film (everything from documentaries to old school faves like *Grease*) can be enjoyed at the same time, in the same place. Those looking to do more than stare at the screen can sip cocktails in the industrial-looking front bar, where hip young celluloid buffs enjoy a more clubby atmosphere with DJ-provided music and a smoking patio that hovers over bustling Hollywood Boulevard. The best of Hollywood classics and kitsch, foreign films and, occasionally, documentaries, are on tap at the **New Beverly Cinema** (⊠ 7165 Beverly Blvd., Hollywood ☎ 323/938–4038), where there's always a double bill. **Nuart** (⊠ 11272 Santa Monica Blvd., West L.A. ☎ 310/478–6379) is the best-kept of L.A.'s revival houses, with good, relatively new seats, an excellent screen, and special midnight shows. The

★ **Silent Movie Theater** (⊠ 611 N. Fairfax Ave., Fairfax District ☎ 323/655–2520 ⊕ www.silentmovietheater.com) is a treasure. Thursday through Sunday it screens exclusively the cream of the pretalkies era with live musical accompaniment, plus shorts before the films. Each show is made to seem like an event in itself, and it's the only such theater of its kind on five continents (there *is* a teensy silents-only theater in Australia). **UCLA** has two fine-film series. The program of the **Film and Television Archives at the James Bridges Theater** (✉ Hilgard Ave. near Sunset Blvd., Westwood ☎ 310/206–3456 or 310/206–8013 ⊕ www.cinema.ucla.edu) runs the gamut from documentaries to children's films. The **School of Film & Television** (⊕ www.tft.ucla.edu) also uses the Bridges Theater, but it has its own program of newer, avant-garde films.

MOVIE PALACES **The Arclight** (✉ 6360 Sunset Blvd., Hollywood ☎ 323/464–4226), which includes as its centerpiece the geodesic Cinerama Dome, the first theater in the United States designed specifically for the enormous screen and sound system that went with Cinerama, has 14 additional screens, a full restaurant, a bar, and a mall. It's the only theater in L.A. to offer greetings and background commentary about the film by theater staff before screenings.

Bridge Cinema De Lux (✉ 6081 Center Dr., in the Promenade at Howard Hughes Center, West L.A. ☎ 310/568–3375), comes by its name honestly, with superwide screens, leather recliners, and top-notch food and drink. Sip a cocktail at the bar or order a meal to take into the theater.

Fodor'sChoice **Grauman's Chinese Theatre** (✉ 6925 Hollywood Blvd., Hollywood ☎ 323/ ★ 464–6266), open since 1927, is perhaps the world's best-known theater, the home of the famous concrete walkway marked by movie stars' hand- and footprints and traditional gala premieres. There are additional, smaller screens at the Mann Chinese Six, in the adjoining Hollywood & Highland Complex.

Across the street from Grauman's is the **Pacific's El Capitan** (✉ 6838 Hollywood Blvd., Hollywood ☎ 323/467–7674), an art-deco masterpiece meticulously renovated by Disney. First-run movies alternate with Disney revivals, and the theater often presents live stage shows in conjunction with Disney's animated pictures.

Television

Audiences Unlimited (✉ 100 Universal City Plaza, Bldg. 153, Universal City, 91608 ☎ 818/506–0043 ⊕ www.tvtickets.com) helps fill seats for television programs (and sometimes for televised award shows). The free tickets are distributed on a first-come, first-served basis. Shows that may be taping or filming include *George Lopez* and *The King of Queens*. Note: you must be 16 or older to attend a television taping.

Theater

Los Angeles isn't quite the "Broadway of the West," as some have claimed—the scope of theater here doesn't compare to that in New York. Still, the theater scene's growth has been impressive. Small theaters are blossoming all over town, and the larger houses, despite price hikes to as much as $70 for a single ticket, are usually full. Even small productions might boast big names from the entertainment industry.

Now Playing (⊕ www.reviewplays.com) lists what's currently in L.A. theaters and what's coming up in the next few months. **LA Stage Alliance** (⊕ www.lastagealliance.com) also gives information on what's playing in Los Angeles, albeit with capsules that are either noncommittal or overly enthusiastic. Its LAStageTIX service allows you to buy tickets online the day of the performance at roughly half price.

MAJOR THEATERS Jason Robards and Nick Nolte got their starts at **Geffen Playhouse** (✉ 10886 Le Conte Ave., Westwood ☎ 310/208–5454 ⊕ www. geffenplayhouse.com), an acoustically superior, 498-seat theater that showcases new plays in the summer—primarily musicals and comedies. Many of the productions here are on their way to or from Broadway. In addition to theater performances, lectures, and children's programs, free summer jazz, dance, cabaret, and occasionally Latin and rock concerts

★ take place at the **John Anson Ford Amphitheater** (✉ 2580 Cahuenga Blvd. E, Hollywood ☎ 323/461–3673 ⊕ www.fordamphitheater.org), a 1,300-seat outdoor venue in the Hollywood Hills. Winter shows typically are staged at the smaller indoor theater, **Inside the Ford.**

There are three theaters in the big downtown complex known as the **Music Center** (✉ 135 N. Grand Ave., Downtown ☎ 213/972–7211 ⊕ www.musiccenter.org); the 2,140-seat **Ahmanson Theatre** (☎ 213/ 628–2772 ⊕ www.taperahmanson.com) presents both classics and new plays; the 3,200-seat **Dorothy Chandler Pavilion** shows a smattering of plays between the more prevalent musical performances; and the 760-seat **Mark Taper Forum** (☎ 213/628–2772 ⊕ www.taperahmanson.com) presents new works that often go on to Broadway, such as Tony Kushner's *Caroline, or Change.*

The home of the Academy Awards telecast from 1949 to 1959, the **Pantages Theatre** (✉ 6233 Hollywood Blvd., Hollywood ☎ 323/468–1770 ⊕ www.nederlander.com) presents large-scale Broadway musicals such as *The Lion King.* The 1,900-seat, art deco **Wilshire Theatre** (✉ 8440 Wilshire Blvd., Beverly Hills ☎ 323/468–1716 ⊕ www.nederlander. com) presents Broadway musicals and occasional concerts.

SMALLER The founders of **Actors' Gang Theater** (✉ 9070 Venice Blvd., Hollywood THEATERS ☎ 310/838–4264 ⊕ www.theactorsgang.com) include actor Tim Rob-
★ bins; the fare has included Molière, Eric Bogosian, and international works by traveling companies.

The Coronet Theatre (✉ 366 N. La Cienega Blvd., between Beverly Blvd. and Melrose Ave., West Hollywood ☎ 310/657–7377 ⊕ www.coronettheatre.com) proves good things come in small packages. It's actually three small theaters in one, with consistently funny comedy or one-person performance pieces (sometimes audience-interactive) running on all stages simultaneously. The **Edgemar Theatre for the Arts** (✉ 2437 Main St., Santa Monica ☎☎ 310/399–3666) is a nonprofit performance and rehearsal space offering dramatic performances, dance, music, and film. Its notable supporters include Neil Simon, Jason Alexander, and Kate Capshaw. The **Evidence Room** (✉ 2220 Beverly Blvd., Downtown ☎ 213/ 381–7118 ⊕ www.evidenceroom.com) is a group of actors, directors, and designers who've earned themselves a raftful of honors. It draws some of the city's best performance artists. The **Knightsbridge Theatre** (✉ 1944 Riverside Dr., Silver Lake ☎ 323/667–0955 ⊕ www. knightsbridgetheatre.com) has a reputation as one of the city's chief recyclers of classic theater, both famous (Shakespeare's *All's Well That Ends Well*) and less-so (Gilbert & Sullivan's *Ruddygore*), with results that range from solid to sensational. Founded in 1962, the nonprofit theater co-op **Theatre West** (✉ 3333 Cahuenga Blvd. W, near Universal Center Dr., North Hollywood ☎ 323/851–7977 or 818/761–2203 ⊕ www.theatrewest.org) has produced a lauded body of work. Its plays have gone on to Broadway (*Spoon River Anthology*) and been made into films (*A Bronx Tale*), and stars like Richard Dreyfuss and the late Carroll O'-Connor have acted with the company. Its interactive **Storybook Theatre** (for three- to nine-year-olds) is a long-running favorite.

THEATER ENSEMBLES

★ **Circle X** (☎ 213/804–5491 ⊕ www.circlextheatre.org) is one of the most lauded and loved acting groups in the city. The traveling troupe continues to win local theater awards thanks to its continuing quest to find and mount exciting new works on a shoestring budget.

Nightlife

Despite the high energy level of the L.A. nightlife crowd, don't expect to be partying until dawn—this is still an early-to-bed city. Liquor laws require that bars stop serving alcohol at 2 AM, and it's safe to say that by this time, with the exception of a few after-hours venues and coffeehouses, most jazz, rock, and disco clubs have closed for the night. Due to the smoking ban, most bars and clubs with a cover charge allow "in and outs"—patrons may leave the premises and return (usually with a hand stamp or paper bracelet). Some newer clubs offer outdoor smoking patios—a great way to enjoy the city's consistently warm evenings.

Although the ultimate in velvet-roped vampiness and glamour used to be the Sunset Strip, in the past couple of years the glitz has definitely shifted to Hollywood Boulevard and its surrounding streets. Foxy females, fat-walleted businessmen, and tabloid-familiar faces have no problem getting in anywhere. But there's hope for the rest us, too. Try popping in early or going on a weeknight . . . or just be very patient. If you wait in line and pay the cover, you'll get in eventually. ⚠ Note that parking, especially after 7 PM, is at a premium in West Hollywood, and in fact is restricted on virtually every side street along the "hot zone" (Sunset Boulevard from Fairfax to Doheny). There are small pockets of metered street parking (don't count on finding one of those spaces), which is fine as long as you feed the meter every half hour or hour until 10 PM. Signage indicating the restrictions is usually clear but is naturally harder to pick up at night. Paying $5 to $10, and at some venues even $15, for valet parking is often the easiest way to go.

Bars

As at so many other nightspots in this neck of the woods, the popularity and clientele of **Bar Marmont** (✉ 8171 Sunset Blvd., West Hollywood ☎ 323/650–0575) bulged—and changed—after word got out it was a favorite of celebrities. The bar is adjacent to the inimitable hotel, Chateau Marmont. The **Beauty Bar** (✉ 1638 Cahuenga Blvd., Hollywood ☎ 323/464–7676) offers manicures and makeovers along with perfect martinis, but the hotties who flock to this retro salon-bar (the little sister of the Beauty Bars in N.Y.C. and San Fran) don't really need the cosmetic care—this is where the edgier beautiful people hang.

Fodor's Choice   The **Downtown L.A. Standard** (✉ 550 S. Flower St., Downtown ☎ 213/
★ 892–8080) has a groovy lounge with pink sofas and DJs, as well as an
all-white restaurant that looks like something out of *2001: A Space
Odyssey*. But it's the rooftop bar, with an amazing view of the city's illuminated skyscrapers, a heated swimming pool, and private, podlike
water-bed tents, that's worth waiting in line to get into. And wait you
probably will, especially on weekends and in summer.

★   The **Rainbow Bar & Grill** (✉ 9015 Sunset Blvd., West Hollywood ☎ 310/
278–4232), in the heart of the Strip and next door to the legendary Roxy,
is a landmark in its own right as *the* drinking spot of the '80s hair-metal
scene—and it still attracts a music-industry crowd.

Want women to come to your new hangout? Give 'em what they love.
That's the premise behind **Star Shoes** (✉ 6364 Hollywood Blvd., Hollywood ☎ 323/462–7827), the vintage-shoe store and bar from the people behind the equally kitschy and conceptual Beauty Bar. Of course,
the place attracts both sexes with its stiff drinks and DJ music ranging
from funky to rocking. But it's the cool shoe displays that make it a step
above the rest.

★ **Tiki Ti** (✉ 4427 W. Sunset Blvd., Silver Lake ☎ 323/669–9381) is one of
the most charming drinking huts in the city. You can spend hours just
looking at the Polynesian artifacts strewn around the place, but be careful—time flies in this tiny tropical bar, and the colorful drinks can be so
potent that you may have to stay marooned for a while. The casually hip
★ **Three Clubs** (✉ 1123 N. Vine St., Hollywood ☎ 323/462–6441) is
furtively located in a strip mall, beneath the Bargain Clown Mart discount store. The DJs segue through the many faces and phases of rock-
and-roll and dance music. With dark-wood paneling, lamp-lighted tables,
and even some sofas, you could be in a giant basement rec room from
decades past—no fancy dress required, but fashionable looks suggested.

★   A lovely L.A. tradition is to meet at **Yamashiro** (✉ 1999 N. Sycamore
Ave., Hollywood ☎ 323/466–5125) for cocktails at sunset. In the elegant restaurant, waitresses glide by in kimonos, and entrées can zoom
up to $39; on the terrace, a spectacular hilltop view spreads out before
you. ■ TIP➜ Mandatory valet parking is $3.50, but happy-hour drinks are just
a bit more than that.

Blues

Babe & Ricky's Inn (✉ 4339 Leimert Blvd., Leimert Park ☎ 323/295–
9112) is an old blues favorite. The great jukebox and photo-poster
gallery and the barbecue and brew (or wine) will get you in the mood.
It's closed Tuesday; covers vary from $4 to $10, and for Monday night's
jam, admission will also get you a fried-chicken dinner, served at 10 PM.

B. B. King's Blues Bar (✉ 1000 Universal Center Dr., Universal City
☎ 818/622–5464) is a spacious, three-story venue at Universal CityWalk,
with music nightly (at 8). Cover runs from $5 to $15.

Cabaret, Performance & Variety

Beyond Baroque (✉ 681 Venice Blvd., Venice ☎ 310/822–3006 ⊕ www.
beyondbaroque.org), in the old Venice Town Hall, is a performance space

and bookstore dedicated to the literary arts, with popular poetry and literature readings that have included the likes of Viggo Mortensen.

★ Stoke the old-fashioned burlesque revival at **Forty Deuce** (✉ 5574 Melrose Ave., Hollywood ☎ 323/465–4242), where sultry yet relatively demure strip shows recall another era. The eye candy here is nonstop, but not just on stage—the lounge-bar is one of the most celeb-studded hangouts in town. With seating for 120, **Highways Performance Space** (✉ 1651 18th St., Santa Monica ☎ 310/453–1755 or 310/315–1459) is one of the primary venues for avant-garde, offbeat, and alternative performance-art, theater, dance, and comedy programs—plus, it has two art galleries.

Coffeehouses

★ **Highland Grounds** (✉ 742 N. Highland Ave., Hollywood ☎ 323/466–1507) is one of L.A.'s oldest coffeehouses. It serves meals, plus it has a balcony, a patio, and a selection of beer as good as that of coffee. Nightly entertainment is mostly acoustic.

A good place to take a break from the nonstop party of L.A. is the **Unurban Coffee House** (✉ 3301 Pico Blvd., at Urban Ave., Santa Monica ☎ 310/315–0056). Enjoy a stiff cup of coffee or some luscious chai tea, and hear the music or spoken-word performances on Sunday during the day or on weekend evenings.

Comedy & Magic

The zany performances at the **Acme Comedy Theater** (✉ 135 N. La Brea Ave., Hollywood ☎ 323/525–0202) include improv, sketch comedy, an improvised game show, and an improvised 1940s-style radio drama. A nightly premier comedy showcase, **Comedy Store** (✉ 8433 Sunset Blvd., West Hollywood ☎ 323/656–6225) has been going strong for more than two decades, with three stages (with covers ranging from free to $20). Famous comedians occasionally make unannounced appearances. Look FodorśChoice for top stand-ups and frequent celeb drop-ins at **Laugh Factory** (✉ 8001 ★ Sunset Blvd., West Hollywood ☎ 323/656–1336). The club has shows nightly at 8 PM, plus added shows at 10 and midnight on Friday; the cover is $10 to $12.

Dance Clubs

Though the establishments listed below are predominantly dance clubs as opposed to live-music venues, there is often some overlap. Also, a given club can vary wildly in genre from night to night, or even on the same night. Gay-lesbian and promoter-driven theme nights tend to "float" from venue to venue. Call ahead to make sure you don't end up looking for retro '60s music at an industrial bondage celebration (or vice versa). Covers vary according to the night and the DJs.

The landmark formerly known as the Palace is now the **Avalon** (✉ 1735 N. Vine St., Hollywood ☎ 323/462–3000). The multilevel art-deco building opposite Capitol Records has a fabulous sound system, four bars, and a balcony. Big-name rock and pop concerts hit the stage during the week, but on weekends the place becomes a dance club, with the most popular night the DJ-dominated Avaland. Upstairs, but with a separate entrance, you'll find celeb hub the **Spider Club**, a Moroccan-style room where celebs and their entourages are frequent visitors.

★ As a bar, **Boardner's** (✉ 1652 N. Cherokee Ave., Hollywood ☎ 323/462–9621) has a multidecade history (in the '20s it was a speakeasy), but with the adjoining ballroom, which was added a couple of years ago, it's now a state-of-the-art dance club. DJs may be spinning electronica, funk, or something else depending on the night—at the popular Saturday Goth event "Bar Sinister," patrons must wear black or risk not getting in. The cover here is anywhere from free to $10.

Gabah (✉ 4658 Melrose Ave., Hollywood ☎ 323/664–8913) is Arabic for "jungle," and it's a fitting moniker for a place offering such exotic and diverse music. DJs spin everything from hip-hop to dub to reggae to obscure rarities during the long-running Saturday Chocolate Bar.

Ivar (✉ 6356 Hollywood Blvd., Hollywood ☎ 310/829–1933) has been attracting the model-actor "discover me" set with weekly hip-hop, electronic, and old-school music promotions. VIPs get to hang in a two-level, neon-lighted cylindrical area that looks like something out of *Star Trek,* but for the most part, that A-list set has moved on. Still, expect lines around the block on weekends.

Gay & Lesbian Clubs

Some of the most popular gay and lesbian "clubs" are weekly theme nights at various venues, so read the preceding list of clubs, *LA Weekly* listings, and gay publications such as *Odyssey* in addition to the following recommendations.

The **Factory** (✉ 652 La Peer Dr., West Hollywood ☎ 310/659–4551) churns out dance music for those who like to grind. In the adjoining **Ultra Suede** (✉ 661 N. Robertson Blvd., West Hollywood), there's '80s and '90s pop on Wednesday and Friday. Saturday, the two houses combine for an event called "The Factory." Covers range from $5 to $15. A long-running gay-gal fave, the **Palms** (✉ 8572 Santa Monica Blvd., West Hollywood ☎ 310/652–6188) continues to thrive thanks to great DJs spinning dance tunes Wednesday through Sunday, plus an outdoor patio, pool tables, and occasional live performances.

The Parlour Club (✉ 7702 Santa Monica Blvd., West Hollywood ☎ 310/650–7968) hosts unique music-themed nights, featuring so-bad-they're-good AM radio hits, campy punk rock, Roaring '20s music, and retro pop from Japan, Spain, and France. Most nights are free; live performances usually command a $5 to $10 cover. **Peanuts** (✉ 7969 Santa Monica Blvd., West Hollywood ☎ 323/654–0280) has groovy bordello-esque decor and mixed/gay-theme nights, including the stripper rock-and-roll night called Club Vodka and the campy dance shindig "Velvet."

Jazz

After moving to a bigger space in 2005, **Catalina** (✉ 6725 W. Sunset Blvd., Hollywood ☎ 323/466–2210) is hotter than ever, with top-notch jazz bookings ranging from classic Chicago style to Latin-flavored.

Come to **Jazz Bakery** (✉ 3233 Helms Ave., Culver City ☎ 310/271–9039) for world-class jazz nightly at 8 and 9:30, in a quiet, respectful concert-like setting. The cover is $10 to $25; parking is free.

Latin

The **Conga Room** (⊠ 5364 Wilshire Blvd., Mid-Wilshire ☎ 323/938–1696), which is co-owned by local celebs, including Jimmy Smits, presents Latin music (primarily salsa) and the odd rock or soul show. The tropical interiors and hot music may not soften the blow to your wallet; regular admission is $10 to $20, but VIP treatment costs $30 to $40. The Cuban food at **El Floridita** (⊠ 1253 N. Vine St., Hollywood ☎ 323/871–8612) is anywhere from good to great—and the music (Monday, Friday, and Saturday) is anywhere from very good to through the roof. A frequent guest is ex–New Yorker Johnny Polanco, backed by the sizzling Conjunto Amistad. Even watching some of the paying customers who get up to dance is worth the price of admission (usually $10, or free with dinner).

Rock & Other Live Music

The **House of Blues** (⊠ 8430 Sunset Blvd., West Hollywood ☎ 323/848–5100) is a club that functions like a concert venue, hosting popular jazz, rock, and blues performers such as Etta James, Lou Rawls, Joe Cocker, Cheap Trick, Pete Townshend, and the Commodores. Occasional shows are presented cabaret style and include dinner in the restaurant area upstairs; you can *sort of* see from some of it. Every Sunday there's a gospel brunch.

The **Key Club** (⊠ 9039 Sunset Blvd., West Hollywood ☎ 310/274–5800) is a flashy, multitiered rock club with four bars, presenting current artists of all genres (some on national tours, others local aspirants). After the concerts, there's dancing with DJs spinning techno and house.

The Knitting Factory (⊠ 7021 Hollywood Blvd., Hollywood ☎ 323/463–0204) is the L.A. offshoot of the eponymous downtown N.Y.C. club. The modern, medium-size room seems all the more spacious for its balcony-level seating and sizable stage. Despite its dubious location on Hollywood Boulevard's tourist strip—in the building housing the Galaxy movie theater—it's a great set-up for the arty, big-name performers it presents. There's live music almost every night in the main room and in the smaller Alter-Knit Lounge. Covers are free to $40.

Musician and producer Jon Brion (Fiona Apple, Aimee Mann, et al) shows off his ability to play virtually any instrument or song in the rock lexicon—and beyond—as host of a popular evening of music every Friday at **Largo** (⊠ 432 N. Fairfax Ave., Hollywood ☎ 323/852–1073). Other nights, low-key rock and singer-songwriter fare is offered at this cozy supper club–bar. And when comedy acts come in, about one night a week, it's usually one of the best comedy nights in town, with folks like Margaret Cho. Reservations are required for tables, but bar stools are open.

McCabe's Guitar Shop (⊠ 3101 Pico Blvd., Santa Monica ☎ 310/828–4497, 310/828–4403 concert information) is rootsy-retro-central, where all things earnest and (preferably) acoustic are welcome—chiefly folk, blues, bluegrass, and rock; usually electrified performers will go unplugged (or semi, anyway) to play here. It *is* a guitar shop (so no liquor license), with a room full of folding chairs for concert-style presentations. Make reservations well in advance.

Neighborhoody and relaxed **Silver Lake Lounge** (✉ 2906 Sunset Blvd., Silver Lake ☎ 323/666–2407) draws a mixed collegiate and boho crowd. The club is very unmainstream "cool," the booking policy an adventurous mix of local and touring alt-rockers. Bands play three to five nights a week; covers vary but are low. The hottest bands of tomorrow, surprises from yesteryear, and unclassifiable bands of today perform at **Spaceland** (✉ 1717 Silver Lake Blvd., Silver Lake ☎ 323/661–4380 ⊕ www.clubspaceland.com), which has a bar, jukebox, and pool table. Monday is always free. Spaceland has a nice selection of beers, some food if you're hungry, and a hip but relaxed interior.

★ **Troubadour** (✉ 9081 Santa Monica Blvd., West Hollywood ☎ 310/276–6168), one of the best and most comfortable clubs in town, has weathered the test of time since its '60s debut as a folk club. After surviving the '80s heavy-metal scene, this all-ages, wood-paneled venue has caught a second (third? fourth?) wind by booking hot alternative-rock acts. There's valet parking, but if you don't mind walking up Doheny a block or three, there's usually ample street parking (check the signs carefully). Actor Johnny Depp sold his share of the infamous **Viper Room** (✉ 8852 Sunset Blvd., West Hollywood ☎ 310/358–1880) in 2004, but the place continues to rock with a motley live-music lineup, if a less stellar crowd.

Whisky-A-Go-Go (✉ 8901 Sunset Blvd., West Hollywood ☎ 310/652–4202) is the most famous rock-and-roll club on the Strip, where back in the '60s, Johnny Rivers cut hit singles and the Doors, Love, and the Byrds cut their musical eyeteeth. It's still going strong, with up-and-coming alternative, hard rock, and punk bands. Mondays showcase L.A.'s cutting-edge acts.

SPORTS & THE OUTDOORS

Updated by
Matthew Flynn

From surfing to whale-watching, L.A. has an enviable scope of activities. Given the right weather conditions, it's possible to choose between skiing and a trip to the beach. A word to the wise, though: the air is dry, so no matter where your adventures take you, bring bottled water and lip balm. Also, don't forget sunscreen; even on overcast days the sunburn index can be high.

Beaches

From downtown, the easiest way to hit the coast is by taking the Santa Monica Freeway (Interstate 10) due west. Once you reach the end of the freeway, Interstate 10 runs into Highway 1 (better known as the Pacific Coast Highway, or PCH). Highway 1 continues north to Sonoma County and south to San Diego. MTA buses run from downtown along Pico, Olympic, Santa Monica, Sunset, and Wilshire boulevards westward to the coasts.

Los Angeles County beaches (and state beaches operated by the county) have lifeguards on duty year-round, with expanded forces in summer. Public parking is usually available, though fees can be as much as $8; in some areas, it's possible to find free street and highway parking. Several beaches have improved their parking facilities, and both restrooms and beach access have been brought up to Americans with Disabilities Act standards. Generally, the northernmost beaches are best for surfing, hiking, and fishing, and the wider and sandier southern beaches are better for tanning and relaxing. Almost all are great for swimming, but beware: pollution in Santa Monica Bay sometimes approaches dangerous levels, particularly after storms. Call ahead or check online for **beach conditions** (☎ 310/457–9701 ⊕ www.healthebay.org).

Leo Carrillo State Beach. On the very edge of Ventura County, this narrow beach is better for exploring than for swimming or sunning. On your own or with a ranger, venture down at low tide to examine the tide pools among the rocks. Sequit Point, a promontory dividing the northwest and southeast halves of the beach, creates secret coves, sea tunnels, and boulders on which you can perch and fish. Generally, anglers stick to the northwest end of the beach; experienced surfers brave the rocks to the southeast. Campgrounds are set back from the beach; call ahead to reserve campsites. ⊠ *35000 PCH, Malibu* ☎ *818/880–0350, 800/444–7275 for camping reservations* ☞ *Parking, lifeguard (year-round, except only as needed in winter), restrooms, showers, fire pits.*

Robert H. Meyer Memorial State Beach. Part of Malibu's most beautiful coastal area, this beach is made up of three minibeaches: El Pescador, La Piedra, and El Matador. "El Mat" has a series of caves, Piedra some nifty rock formations, and Pescador a secluded feel, but they all have spectacular views and a fair amount of privacy. You may see the occasional nude sunbather—although in recent years, police have been cracking down. ⊠ *32350, 32700, and 32900 PCH, Malibu* ☎ *818/880–0350* ☞ *Parking, 1 roving lifeguard unit, restrooms.*

Zuma Beach Park. Zuma, 2 mi of white sand usually littered with tanning teenagers, has it all: from fishing and diving to swings for the kids to volleyball courts. Beachgoers looking for quiet or privacy should head elsewhere. The surf is rough and inconsistent. ⊠ *30050 PCH, Malibu* ☎ *310/305–9503* ☞ *Parking, lifeguard (year-round, except only as needed in winter), restrooms, food concessions, playground.*

Malibu Lagoon State Beach/Surfrider Beach. Steady 3- to 5-foot waves make this beach, just west of Malibu Pier, a popular surfing location. The International Surfing Contest is held here in September, and the surf is best around that time. Water runoff from Malibu Canyon forms a natural lagoon 75 yards inland that's a sanctuary for 250 species of birds. Unfortunately, the lagoon is often polluted and algae-filled. If you're leery of going into the water, you can bird-watch, play volleyball, or take a sunset stroll on one of the nature trails. ⊠ *23200 PCH, Malibu* ☎ *310/305–9503* ☞ *Parking, lifeguard (year-round), restrooms, picnicking, visitor center.*

Will Rogers State Beach. This clean, sandy, 3-mi beach, with a dozen volleyball nets, gymnastics equipment, and playground equipment for kids, is an all-around favorite. The surf is gentle, perfect for swimmers and beginning surfers. However, beware after a storm, when untreated water flows from storm drains into the sea. ⊠ *15100 PCH, 2 mi north of Santa*

Monica Pier, Pacific Palisades ☏ *818/880–0350* ☞ *Parking, lifeguard (year-round, except only as needed in winter), restrooms.*

★ **Santa Monica State Beach.** It's the first beach you'll hit after the Santa Monica Freeway (Interstate 10) runs into the PCH, and it's one of L.A.'s best known. Wide and sandy, Santa Monica is *the* place for sunning and socializing: be prepared for a mob scene on summer weekends, when parking becomes an expensive ordeal. Swimming is fine (with the usual poststorm-pollution caveat); for surfing, go elsewhere. For a memorable view, climb up the stairway over the PCH to Palisades Park, at the top of the bluffs. Summer-evening concerts are often held here. ✉ *1642 Promenade, PCH at California Incline, Santa Monica* ☏ *310/305–9503* ☞ *Parking, lifeguard (year-round), restrooms, showers.*

Venice City Beach. The surf and sand of Venice are fine, but the main attraction here is the boardwalk scene. There are also swimming, fishing, surfing, basketball (it's the site of some of L.A.'s most hotly contested pickup games), racquetball, handball, and shuffleboard. You can rent a bike or some in-line skates and hit the Strand bike path. ✉ *West of Pacific Ave., Venice* ☏ *310/577–5700* ☞ *Parking, restrooms, food concessions, showers, playground.*

Sports

The **City of Los Angeles Department of Recreation and Parks** (✉ 200 N. Main St., Suite 1350, 90012 ☏ 888/527–2757 ⊕ www.cityofla.org/rap) has information on city parks. For information on county parks, such as Eaton Canyon and Vasquez Rocks, contact the **Los Angeles County Department of Parks and Recreation** (✉ 433 S. Vermont Ave., 90020 ☏ 213/738–2961 ⊕ http://parks.co.la.ca.us).

Los Angeles is home to some of the greatest franchises in pro basketball and baseball, and the greater L.A. area has two teams in each of those pro sports, as well as hockey, too. For tickets to most sporting events, call **Ticketmaster** (☏ 213/480–3232 ⊕ www.ticketmaster.com), or the venue box office.

Baseball

You can watch the **Dodgers** take on their National League rivals while you munch on pizza, tacos, or a foot-long "Dodger dog" at one of the game's most comfortable ball parks, **Dodger Stadium** (✉ 1000 Elysian Park Ave., exit off Interstate 110, Pasadena Fwy. ☏ 323/224–1448 ticket information ⊕ www.dodgers.com). The **Los Angeles Angels of Anaheim** play at **Edison International Field** (✉ 2000 Gene Autry Way, Anaheim ☏ 714/663–9000 ⊕ www.angelsbaseball.com). Several colleges in the area also have baseball teams worth watching, especially USC, which has been a perennial source of major-league talent.

Basketball

L.A.'s pro basketball teams play at the Staples Center. The **Los Angeles Lakers** (☏ 310/426–5000 ⊕ www.nba.com/lakers) still attract a loyal following that includes celebrity fans like Jack Nicholson, Dyan Cannon, and Leonardo DiCaprio. The 2005 return of head coach Phil Jackson, who led the team to three NBA championships, recharged fans after the 2004 departure of superstar Shaquille O'Neal. L.A.'s "other" team, the much-maligned but newly revitalized **Clippers** (☎ 888/895–8662 ⊕ www.nba.com/clippers), sells tickets that are generally cheaper and easier to get than those for Lakers games. The **Los Angeles Sparks** (☎ 310/426–6031 ⊕ www.wnba.com/sparks) have built a WNBA dynasty around former USC star Lisa Leslie.

Bicycling

For an overview of L.A.–area bike routes, including maps and useful links, check online at **Los Angeles Bike Paths** (⊕ www.labikepaths.com).

★ The most famous bike path in the city, which runs for 22 mi along the ocean from Will Rogers State Beach down to Torrance Beach, is known as the **Strand.** Two-wheelers share the path with joggers, skateboarders, in-line skaters, walkers, and other nonvehicular traffic (although for some stretches, bikes have their own parallel path). The sunny beach scenery is uninterrupted, save for a couple of short city-street detours around the Marina del Rey Harbor and the Redondo Beach Pier. The ride can be done in a long leisurely afternoon. You can rent a bike at one of many shops along the Strand's middle section. Cyclists often refer to the 18⁴/₁₀-mi section south of the Santa Monica Pier as the South Bay Bicycle Trail.

The flat, 3-mi paved path around **Lake Hollywood** is a great place to take in views of the HOLLYWOOD sign. Griffith Park, Malibu Creek State Park, and Topanga State Park are all part of the **Santa Monica Mountains,** which have good mountain-biking paths.

Perry's has two bike-rental locations along the Strand: **Perry's Bike & Skate** (⊠ 2600 Ocean Front Walk, Venice ☎ 310/584–9306), and **Perry's Beach Rentals** (⊠ 2400 Ocean Front Walk, Venice ☎ 310/452–7609). **Spokes 'N Stuff** (⊠ Griffith Park, 4400 Crystal Springs Dr., Los Feliz ☎ 323/653–4099 ⊠ Strand, 1700 Ocean Ave., Santa Monica ☎ 310/395–4748 ⊠ Strand, 4175 Admiralty Way, Marina del Rey ☎ 310/306–3332) has a rental shop behind the ranger station in Griffith Park and two rental places on the Strand.

Fishing

Shore fishing and surf casting are excellent on many of the beaches, and pier fishing is popular because no license is necessary to fish off public piers. The **Fish and Game Department** (☎ 562/342–7100, 562/590–5020 for lake-stocking information) can answer questions about licenses and give advice. The **Santa Monica, Redondo Beach,** and **Malibu** piers have bait-and-tackle shops with everything you'll need.

If you want to break away from the piers, sign up for a boat excursion with one of the local charters, most of which will sell you a fishing license and rent tackle. Most also offer whale-watching excursions. **Del Rey Sport Fishing** (⊠ 13759 Fiji Way, dock 52, Marina del Rey ☎ 310/822–3625) runs excursions for $28 per half day and $40 for three-quarters of a day, with tackle rental another $8. **Redondo Sport Fishing Company** (⊠ 233 N. Harbor Dr., Redondo Beach ☎ 310/372–2111) has half-day charters starting at $27 and three-quarter-day cruises for $39 per person.

Golf

The City Parks and Recreation Department lists seven public 18-hole courses in Los Angeles, and L.A. County runs some good ones, too. **Rancho Park Golf Course** (✉ 10460 W. Pico Blvd., West L.A. ☎ 310/838–7373) is one of the most heavily played links in the country. It's a beautifully designed course, but the towering pines present an obstacle for those who slice or hook. There's a two-level driving range, a 9-hole pitch 'n' putt, a snack bar, and a pro shop where you can rent clubs.

★ If you want a scenic course, you've got it in spades at the county-run, par-71 **Los Verdes Golf Course** (✉ 7000 W. Los Verdes Dr., Rancho Palos Verdes ☎ 310/377–7370). You get a cliff-top view of the ocean—time it right and you can watch the sun set behind Catalina Island.

Griffith Park has two splendid 18-hole courses along with a challenging 9-hole course. **Harding Municipal Golf Course** and **Wilson Municipal Golf Course** (✉ 4730 Crystal Springs Dr., Los Feliz ☎ 323/663–2555) are about 1½ mi inside the park entrance, at Riverside Drive and Los Feliz Boulevard. Bridle paths surround the outer fairways, and the San Gabriel Mountains make a scenic background. The 9-hole **Roosevelt Municipal Golf Course** (✉ 2650 N. Vermont Ave., Los Feliz ☎ 323/665–2011) can be reached through the park's Vermont Avenue entrance.

Hiking

"Nobody Walks in L.A." sang Missing Persons back in the '80s, and it's as true as ever—but Los Angelenos do like to hike. The coast, the Hollywood Hills, and the greater Santa Monica Mountains are all convenient getaways. Remember not to venture deep into the national parks and forests alone—and be sure to bring water and sunblock with you. For information on hiking locations and scheduled outings in Los Angeles, contact the **Sierra Club** (✉ 3435 Wilshire Blvd., Suite 320, Los Angeles 90010 ☎ 213/387–4287 ⊕ www.sierraclub.org).

Fodor'sChoice ★ One of the best places to begin is **Griffith Park** (✉ Ranger station, 4730 Crystal Springs Dr., Los Feliz); pick up a map from the ranger station. Many of the paths in the park are not shaded and can be quite steep. A nice, short hike from Canyon Drive, at the southwest end of the park, takes you to **Bronson Caves,** where the *Batman* television show was filmed. Begin at the Observatory for a 3-mi round-trip hike to the top of **Mt. Hollywood.**

★ For a walk, run, or bike ride, the **Hollywood Reservoir (aka Lake Hollywood) Trail** is probably one of the best spots in all L.A. The 4-mi flat walk around the reservoir provides great views of hillside mansions (including the spread once owned by Madonna, with its controversial striped retaining wall), the HOLLYWOOD sign, and the reservoir itself. The park is open dawn to dusk. To get there, exit U.S. 101 at Barham Boulevard (near Universal City). Look for Lake Hollywood Drive soon on your right and take it, making sure you stay the course through its tricky turns. Park when you see the gate.

Who knows how many of Will Rogers's famed witticisms came to him while he and his wife hiked or rode horses along the **Inspiration Point Trail** from their ranch, now **Will Rogers State Historic Park** (✉ 1501 Will Rogers State Park Rd., Pacific Palisades ☎ 310/454–8212). The point is on a detour off the lovely 2-mi loop, which you pick up right by the riding stables beyond the parking lot ($7 per car). On a clear (or even just semiclear) day, the panorama is one of L.A.'s widest and most "wow" inducing, from the peaks of the San Gabriel Mountains in the distant east to the Oz-like cluster of downtown L.A. skyscrapers to Catalina Island looming off the coast to the southwest. If you're looking for a longer trip, the top of the loop meets up with the 65-mi Backbone Trail, which connects to Topanga State Park.

Surfing

Surfing is the sport that truly symbolizes L.A. and Southern California in general; it has a long cultural history here. If you're not a strong swimmer, though, think twice before jumping in; fighting the surf to where the waves break is a strenuous, sometimes even dangerous, proposition.

A lesson from **Malibu Ocean Sports** (✉ 22935 PCH, across from the pier at Malibu Point ☎ 310/456–6302) will keep you on the sand for at least 45 minutes while you learn the basics. **The Surf Academy** (✉ 302 19th St., Hermosa Beach ☎ 310/372–2790 ⊕ www.surfacademy.org) teaches at El Segundo (Dockweiler) and Manhattan Beach, with lessons starting at $35. You'll find plenty of surf shops with rentals at all the surfing hot spots. Competition keeps prices comparable; most rent long, short, and miniboards (kid-size surfboards) from $18 per day, and wet suits from $8 per day (some give discounts for additional days).

Call the **L.A. County Lifeguards** (☎ 310/457–9701 Malibu, 310/578–0478 Santa Monica, 310/379–8471 Manhattan, Redondo, and Hermosa beaches) for prerecorded surf-conditions hotlines.

Tennis

L.A. Department of Recreation and Parks (✉ 200 N. Main St., Downtown ☎ 213/473–7070 ⊕ www.laparks.org/dos/sports/tennis.htm) has a complete list of the city's more than 75 public tennis courts. Some are always free, others only weekdays; others charge $5 to $8 an hour per court, depending on time of day. Reservations are a must during peak hours at the most popular pay courts; to make them, apply for a reservation card (click on "Permits") at the Web site or call ☎ 323/644–3536.

Whale-Watching

From December to March or April, California gray whales migrate from northern waters to warmer breeding and birthing waters off the coast of Mexico. To get an up-close look at these magnificent animals as they pass close to shore, hop aboard one of the **whale-watching tours** that depart from Long Beach and San Pedro; prices are $9 to $18 per person, and reservations are recommended. ■ TIP➔ **Bring binoculars, dress warmly, and be warned that winter seas can be rough.** Contact any of the expedition companies listed under Fishing, *above*; they all have whale-watching outings, too. Or call one of the following tour operators: **Spirit Cruises** (☎ 310/

548–8080 ⊕ www.spiritdinnercruises.com) or **Long Beach** Sportfishing
(☎ 562/432–8993 ⊕ www.longbeachsportfishing.com).

Yoga

Golden Bridge (✉ 6322 De Longpre Ave., Hollywood ☎ 323/936–4172
⊕ www.goldenbridgeyoga.com) is centered on the teachings of Gurmukh
Khalsa, whose approach to kundalini yoga stresses the mind–body connection (yoga for expectant moms is a specialty).

SHOPPING

By Kristina
Brooks

Think of shopping in L.A. as a sport, and you won't be far off the mark.
To "win," plan ahead to maximize your shopping versus driving time;
keep your eyes peeled for dressed-down celebs; and aim to have fun.
One of the greatest pleasures is shopping alfresco, since even most malls
here are outdoors, with courtyards for people-watching or a chai break.
Although the city is notoriously vast, concentrated shopping areas in
many neighborhoods will provide hours of browsing bang for your parking buck. ■ TIP→ One rule of thumb about business hours: the funkier the
neighborhood, the later the shops open.

Shopping Neighborhoods

The "Golden Triangle" formed by Santa Monica and Wilshire boulevards and Beverly Drive contains, like a pearl, famed **Rodeo Drive.** Consider a tour of Beverly Hills a field trip, since most of the boutiques display
their wares like works of art, and many of the toned, polished shoppers
look air-brushed. Although you may feel cowed by some of the astronomical prices or cooler-than-thou attitudes among salespeople, most
shops present a friendly sales front to the public. Also, a recent influx
of midrange stores has supposedly "democratized" the street. Around
this tourist hot spot, many celebrities sneak into their favorite shops before or after hours or through back entrances. Keep in mind that some
stores are by appointment only. ■ TIP→ There are several well-marked, free
(for two hours) parking lots around the core shopping area.

Century City is L.A.'s errand central, where entertainment executives and
industry types do their serious shopping. In general, it's more affordable than Beverly Hills. Although the Century City Shopping Center has
changed names (to Westfield Shoppingtown Century City), it's the same
mall in quality and substance: everything from large retail favorites like
Macy's and Bloomingdale's to small outdoor carts hawking jewelry and
candles are still here.

Dotted with ethnic enclaves (Olvera Street, Chinatown, Koreatown) and
several large, open-air shopping venues (the Fashion District, the Flower
Mart, Grand Central Market, the Toy District, and the Jewelry District),
downtown L.A. offers an urban shopping experience to counterbalance
the precious atmosphere cultivated by the Westside's boutiques. Check
out Santee Alley, where street vendors hawk trendy clothing—and plenty
of knock-off designer sunglasses and purses. You can also buy materials to make your own fashions in the area's numerous fabric stores; the
most popular of these, Michael Levine, offers free parking with purchase.

The retail-hotel-dining-entertainment complex Hollywood & Highland bills itself as the "epicenter of pop culture." A tall claim perhaps, but
★ it did help upgrade the image of **Hollywood** when TV personality Ryan Seacrest began broadcasting his live show here. Along the boulevard, it's one souvenir store after the next, but a few shops—like Frederick's of Hollywood for lingerie, and Hollywood Magic Shop for special effects and stage illusion—are worth the stroll. Outside of Hollywood, especially along La Brea Avenue and Cahuenga Boulevard near Sunset (the home of the city's biggest and best music store, Amoeba Music), you'll find plenty of trendy, quirky, and hip merchandise to splurge on.

As **Los Feliz and Silver Lake** gentrify, distinct shopping areas are rapidly gelling. Many boutiques are clustered along Vermont Avenue and Hollywood Boulevard in Los Feliz, and Sunset Boulevard in Silver Lake; two of the best are Vermont Avenue's Y-Que (which sells the popular "Free Winona" T-shirts) and Soap Plant/Wacko on Sunset, which sells cool art books and hipster housewares. Eastward down Sunset, you'll find plenty of galleries, vintage shops, and local designers offering one of a kind items.

Melrose Avenue has something of a split personality. From North Highland to Sweetzer, it's a bohemian-punk shopping district, where vintage–resale oasis Wasteland, rock-star clothiers Serious, and even a shop selling bones (called Necromance) attract the alternative set. On upper Melrose Avenue and Melrose Place, the shopping scene is more upscale and design-y; shops include such pricey boutiques as Agent Provocateur, Stella McCartney, and the mecca for celebrity stylists, Fred Segal.

Less frenetic and status-conscious than Beverly Hills, **Santa Monica** is ideal for leisurely shopping. Most shopping activity takes place on and around the 3rd Street Promenade, the strip of 3rd Street between Broadway and Wilshire Boulevard, where hip houses of style like Urban Outfitters are always bustling. Montana Avenue has lots of unique boutiques, especially between 7th and 17th streets; one is Patrick Reid, a saucy little frock shop run by the brother of actress Tara Reid, and another is Jenny Bec's, a creative book and toy store for kids. Parking in Santa Monica is next to impossible on Wednesday, when some streets are blocked for the city's fabulous **Farmers Market.**

West Hollywood is a diverse, terrific shopping destination. You'll find every kind of Angeleno browsing the record stores along Sunset Boulevard, while the well-heeled haunt upscale boutiques like MAC Cosmetics, Kitson, Kate Spade, and Lisa Kline on Robertson Boulevard and between Beverly Boulevard and 3rd Street. The big blue Pacific Design Center, on Melrose at San Vicente Boulevard, is the focal point for the neighborhood's art and interior design–related stores, including many on nearby Beverly Boulevard. At Fairfax and 3rd Street you'll find the historic Farmers Market and the adjacent shopping mecca The Grove.

Malls & Markets

Beverly Center. An extensive collection of upscale shops draws a high-end and international clientele here. There's a terrific view of the city from the eighth-floor terrace and rooftop food court. The **California Welcome Center** (☎ 310/854–7616), on the first floor, provides shopping discounts plus information and tickets for most of L.A.'s attractions. ✉ *8500 Beverly Blvd., bounded by Beverly, La Cienega, and San Vicente Blvds. and 3rd St., between Beverly Hills and West Hollywood* ☎ *310/854–0070* ⊕ *www.beverlycenter.com.*

★ ☺ **Hollywood & Highland.** Dozens of stores, the Kodak Theatre, and a slew of eateries fill this outdoor complex, which is meant to embody cinematic glamour. Sweeping steps lead between floors of designer shops and chain stores. From the upper levels, there's a camera-perfect view of the famous HOLLYWOOD sign. ✉ *Hollywood Blvd. and Highland Ave., Hollywood* ☎ *323/960–2331.*

Rose Bowl Flea Market. The vendors come out on the second Sunday of every month, rain or shine. If you expect bargains, you're in for a shock unless you're an expert haggler. This massive, extremely popular market attracts more than 2,200 vendors looking for top dollar for their antiques, crafts, and new furniture. ✉ *1001 Rosebowl Dr., Pasadena* ☎ *323/560–7469* ⊕ *www.rgcshows.com.*

★ **Third Street Promenade.** Whimsical dinosaur-shaped, ivy-covered fountains and buskers of every stripe set the scene along this pedestrians-only shopping stretch. Stores are mainly the chain variety (Restoration Hardware, Von Dutch, Apple), but movie theaters, bookstores, pubs, and restaurants ensure that every need is covered. ✉ *3rd St. between Broadway and Wilshire Blvd.*

Westfield Century City. Known locally as the Century City Shopping Center, this open-air mall is set among office buildings on what used to be the Twentieth Century Fox studios' back lot. A decent selection of upscale shops (Brooks Brothers, Sigrid Olson) are anchored by Macy's and Bloomingdale's. ✉ *10250 Santa Monica Blvd., Century City* ☎ *310/277–3898.*

LOS ANGELES ESSENTIALS

AIR TRAVEL

The major gateway to L.A. is Los Angeles International Airport (LAX); it's serviced by more than 85 major airlines. Flights in and out of LAX are seldom delayed because of weather and generally run on time. Because of heavy traffic around the airport and difficult parking, however, you should allow plenty of time to arrive at the airport prior to scheduled departure or arrival times. There are three other nearby airports that serve L.A. County; they're smaller and have more limited services, but are worth investigating when booking flights.

🛫 **Bob Hope Airport** (BUR) ✉ 2627 N. Hollywood Way, Burbank ☎ 818/840-8830 ⊕ www.bobhopeairport.com. **Long Beach Airport** (LGB) ✉ 4100 Donald Douglas Dr. ☎ 562/570-2600 ⊕ www.lgb.org. **Los Angeles International Airport** (LAX) ☎ 310/646-5252 ⊕ www.lawa.org. **Ontario International Airport** (ONT) ✉ Airport Dr. and Vineyard Ave. ☎ 909/937-2700 ⊕ www.lawa.org.

🛫 Shuttles **Xpress Shuttle** ☎ 800/427-7483 ⊕ www.expressshuttle.com. **Prime Time** ☎ 800/733-8267 ⊕ www.primetimeshuttle.com. **SuperShuttle** ☎ 323/775-6600, 310/782-6600, or 800/258-3826 ⊕ www.supershuttle.com.

BUS TRAVEL TO AND FROM L.A.

🚌 **Greyhound** ✉ 1716 E. 7th St., Downtown ☎ 213/629-8405 or 800/231-2222 ⊕ www. greyhound.com.

BUS TRAVEL WITHIN L.A.

Inadequate public-transportation systems have been an L.A. problem for decades. That said, many local trips can be made, with time and patience, by bus. In certain cases, it may be your best option; for example, if you're visiting the Getty Center with no prior parking reservation. The Metropolitan Transit Authority DASH (Downtown Area Short Hop) minibuses cover six different circular routes in Hollywood, Mid-Wilshire, and the downtown area. The Santa Monica Municipal Bus Line, also known as the Big Blue Bus, is a pleasant and inexpensive way to move around the Westside, where the MTA lines leave off.

🚌 **California Smart Traveler** ☎ 800/266-6883 ⊕ www.dot.ca.gov/caltrans511. **DASH** ☎ 213/626-4455 or 310/808-2273 ⊕ www.ladottransit.com/dash. **Metropolitan Transit Authority (MTA)** ☎ 213/626-4455 or 800/COMMUTE ⊕ www.mta.net. **Santa Monica Municipal Bus Line** ☎ 310/451-5444 ⊕ www.bigbluebus.com.

CAR RENTAL

In Los Angeles, it's not a question of whether wheels are a hindrance or a convenience: they're a necessity. Major-chain rates in L.A. begin at about $25 a day and $125 a week, plus 8.25% sales tax. Luxury and sport utility vehicles start at approximately $49 a day. Some local rental agencies offer specialty vehicles, from classic cars to Ferraris to the latest Hummer. ⇨ Car Rental *in* Smart Travel Tips for national rental-agency contact information.

🚗 Local Agencies **Beverly Hills Budget Car Rental** ✉ 9815 Wilshire Blvd. ☎ 310/274-9173 or 800/227-7117 ⊕ www.budgetbeverlyhills.com. **Beverly Hills Rent-A-Car** ✉ 9220 S. Sepulveda Blvd., near LAX ☎ 800/479-5996 ⊕ www.bhrentacar.com.

CAR TRAVEL

Finding your way by car in Los Angeles can be a piece of cake or a nightmare. The city may be sprawling and traffic-clogged, but at least it has evolved with the automobile in mind. Streets are wide and parking garages abound, but rush hours (7 AM to 10 AM and 3 PM to 7 PM) can be horribly slow. Keep a good map, such as the *Thomas Guide,* on hand at all times, get clear directions and stick to them. Both KFWB 980 AM and KNX 1070 AM have frequent traffic reports. Los Angeles–area gas prices tend to be among the highest in the nation. For assistance in finding competitively priced stations, consult ⊕ www.losangelesgasprices.com.

EMERGENCIES

In case of emergency, dial 911 for police, fire, or ambulance services. In addition to dozens of smaller community hospitals, L.A. is home to several world-renowned medical centers. Many branches of the Rite Aid and Savon drug-store chains maintain 24-hour pharmacies.

🏥 **UCLA Medical Center** ✉ 10833 Le Conte Ave., Westwood ☎ 310/825-9111 ⊕ www. healthcare.ucla.edu. **Los Angeles County–U.S.C. Medical Center** ✉ 1200 N. State St., Downtown ☎ 323/226-2622 ⊕ www.dhs.co.la.ca.us. **Rite Aid** ☎ 800/748-3243 ⊕ www. riteaid.com. **Savon** ☎ 888/746-7252 ⊕ www.savon.com.

METRO-RAIL TRAVEL

Metro Rail covers a limited area of L.A.'s vast expanse, but what there is, is helpful and frequent. The most useful line for visitors is the underground Red Line, which runs from Union Station downtown through Mid-Wilshire, Hollywood, and Universal City on its way to North Hollywood, stopping at the most popular tourist destinations along the way. The Blue Line runs from Union Station to Long Beach, and the Gold Line, which debuted in 2003, begins at Union Station and heads northeast to Pasadena.

🚹 **Metropolitan Transit Authority (MTA)** ☎ 800/266-6883 or 213/626-4455 ⊕ www.mta.net.

TAXIS

Don't even try to hail a cab on the street in Los Angeles. Instead, phone one of the many taxi companies. The metered rate is $2 per mile, plus a $2 per-fare charge. Taxi rides from LAX have an additional $2.50 surcharge. Be aware that distances between sights in L.A. are vast, so cab fares add up quickly.

🚹 **Beverly Hills Cab** ☎ 800/273-6611. **Checker Cab** ☎ 800/300-5007. **Yellow Cab** ☎ 800/200-1085 or 800/200-0011.

TOURS

BUS & VAN TOURS Casablanca Tours, established in 1980, gives sightseeing tours all around L.A., but its specialty is an insider's look at Hollywood and Beverly Hills; it's available in two- and four-hour versions ($32 to $91). Most tours are in minibuses with a maximum of 14 people; others are in 25-seaters. L.A. Tours and Sightseeing has several tours ($29 to $95), by van and bus, covering various parts of the city, including downtown, Hollywood, and Beverly Hills. The company also operates tours to Disneyland, Universal Studios, Six Flags Magic Mountain, beaches, and stars' homes. Starline Tours of Hollywood ($16 to $90) picks up passengers from area hotels and from Grauman's Chinese Theatre. Universal Studios, Knott's Berry Farm, stars' homes, and Disneyland are some of the sights on this popular tour company's agenda.

🚹 **Casablanca Tours** ☎ 323/461-0156. **L.A. Tours and Sightseeing** ☎ 323/460-6490 ⊕ www.latours.net. **Starline Tours of Hollywood** ☎ 323/463-3333 or 800/959-3131 ⊕ www.starlinetours.com.

WALKING TOURS The Los Angeles Conservancy's walking tours (each about 2½ hours long and costing $10 per person), chiefly cover the downtown area.

🚹 **Los Angeles Conservancy** ☎ 213/623-2489 ⊕ www.laconservancy.org.

TRAIN TRAVEL TO AND FROM L.A.

Union Station in downtown Los Angeles is one of the grande dames of railroad stations, and its meticulous restoration has made it truly shine. As the city's rail hub, it's the place to catch an Amtrak train. Amtrak's luxury *Coast Starlight* travels along the spectacular coastline from Seattle to Los Angeles in just a day and a half (though it's often not quite on time). You can make reservations in advance by phone or at the station.

🚹 **Train Information Amtrak** ☎ 800/872-7245 ⊕ www.amtrak.com. **Union Station** ✉ 800 N. Alameda St. ☎ 213/683-6979.

VISITOR INFORMATION

🔲 **Beverly Hills Conference and Visitors Bureau** ✉ 239 S. Beverly Dr., 90212 ☎ 310/248-1000 or 800/345-2210 ⊕ www.beverlyhillsbehere.com. **Hollywood Chamber of Commerce Info Center** ✉ 7018 Hollywood Blvd., 90028 ☎ 323/469-8311 ⊕ www.hollywoodchamber.net. **L.A. Inc./The Convention and Visitors Bureau** ✉ 333 S. Hope St., 18th fl., Los Angeles 90071 ☎ 213/624-7300 or 800/228-2452 ⊕ www.lacvb.com. **Pasadena Convention & Visitors Bureau** ✉ 171 S. Los Robles Ave., 91101 ☎ 626/795-9311 ⊕ www.pasadenacal.com. **Santa Monica Convention & Visitors Bureau** ✉ 520 Broadway, Suite 250, 90401 ☎ 310/319-6263 or 800/544-5319 ⊕ www.santamonica.com. **Santa Monica Visitors Centers** ✉ 1400 Ocean Ave., 90401 ☎ 310/393-7593 ✉ 395 Santa Monica Pl., 90401 ☎ 310/393-7593. **West Hollywood Convention and Visitors Bureau** ✉ 8687 Melrose Ave., Suite M25, 90069 ☎ 310/289-2525 or 800/368-6020 ⊕ www.visitwesthollywood.com.

The Inland Empire

WORD OF MOUTH

"If you're looking for a skiing vacation, Big Bear gives you the choice of 2 mountains—Snow Summit, which is family-oriented and Bear Mountain, which is dominated by snowboarders."

—Lvk

Updated by
Veronica Hill

FEW PEOPLE THINK OF THE REGION east of Los Angeles as a worthwhile travel destination. But the Inland Empire, an area often overlooked by vacationers because of its tangled freeways and suburban sprawl, does have its charms. No more than a few hours' drive from metropolitan Los Angeles, you can ski a 7,000-foot mountain overlooking a crystal blue lake or go wine tasting at a vineyard swept by ocean breezes. At the heart of this desert and mountain region is Riverside, the birthplace of California's multi-million-dollar navel-orange industry, established in 1875. The tree that started it all still flourishes on Magnolia Avenue. Today the streets of downtown buzz with people on their way to shop for antiques, eat in exciting restaurants, and listen to live jazz. The scene is completely different northeast of Riverside, in the San Bernardino Mountains. There, Wrightwood, Big Bear Lake, and Lake Arrowhead lie amid prime ski country. To the south, in the San Jacinto Mountains just west of Palm Springs, Idyllwild is a popular year-round getaway with romantic bed-and-breakfasts, fashionable boutiques, and cozy restaurants. In the southernmost reaches of the Inland Empire, on the way from Riverside to San Diego, is the wine-growing region around Temecula.

Exploring the Inland Empire

Several major freeways provide access to the Inland Empire. Ontario, Corona, and Temecula line up along Interstate 15, and Interstate 215 and State Route 91 lead to Riverside and San Bernardino. The area's popularity as a bedroom community for Los Angeles has created some nasty freeway congestion, so try to avoid driving during rush hour, usually 6 to 8 AM and 4 to 7 PM.

About the Restaurants

Inland Empire residents no longer have to travel to their big-sister communities of L.A. or Orange County for a good meal. Downtown Riverside is home to some ambitious restaurants, along with the chains you'll find in most areas. The college towns of Claremont and Redlands are great showcases for creative vegetarian cuisine. In Temecula, the choices expand to wine-country cooking, with many vintners showcasing their products alongside California–French dishes. Your options are limited in the smaller mountain communities; typically each town supports a single upscale restaurant, along with fast-food outlets, steak-and-potatoes family spots, and perhaps an Italian or Mexican eatery. Universally, dining out is casual.

About the Hotels

In the San Gabriel and San Bernardino mountains most accommodations are B&Bs or rustic cabins, though Lake Arrowhead offers more luxurious resort lodging. Rates for Big Bear lodgings fluctuate widely, depending on the season. When winter snow brings droves of Angelenos to the mountains for skiing, expect to pay sky-high prices for any kind of room. Most establishments require a two-night stay on weekends. In Riverside, you might enjoy a stay at the landmark Mission Inn, a rambling Spanish-style hotel with elaborate courtyards, fountains, and a mixture of ornate Mission revival–, Spanish baroque–, Renaissance revival–, and Asian-architecture styles. In wine country, lodgings range from chain hotels and motels to golf resorts.

GREAT ITINERARIES

Numbers correspond to the Inland Empire map.

IF YOU HAVE 3 DAYS

If you have only three days to visit the Inland Empire, start your visit in the vineyards surrounding ▣ **Temecula** ⑫ ▶, being sure to sample the champagne flight at Thornton Winery and the highly recommended Castelletto at Mount Palomar. Splurge for the evening at Churon Vineyards, a French château-style B&B that also makes a fine syrah, or stay in a luxurious villa at the new South Coast Winery Resort and Spa. Next morning, hitch a ride on a hot-air balloon for a bird's-eye view of the valley followed by a brunch, and then head to **Corona** ⑥ for a soak in the mud bath at Glen Ivy Hot Springs. That evening, book into the magnificent Mission Inn in ▣ **Riverside** ⑦ and head for dinner. On Day 3 spend the morning taking in the beautiful historic homes of Riverside and **Redlands** ⑧, followed by a leisurely drive into the San Bernardino Mountains for an afternoon of shopping and exploring in the village of ▣ **Lake Arrowhead** ⑨.

IF YOU HAVE 5 DAYS

Follow the three-day itinerary, and on Day 4 continue your exploration of the San Bernardino Mountains by moving on to ▣ **Big Bear Lake** ⑩, a mountain town with a host of fine restaurants, ski resorts, and fishing and hiking opportunities. On your last day, slow the pace with a drive to **Wrightwood** ⑤, a laid-back mountain community bordering the Mojave Desert—it lies at the highest point on the San Andreas Fault.

WHAT IT COSTS					
	$$$$	**$$$**	**$$**	**$**	**¢**
RESTAURANTS	over $30	$23–$30	$16–$22	$10–$15	under $10
HOTELS	over $250	$176–$250	$121–$175	$90–$120	under $90

Restaurant prices are for a main course at dinner, excluding sales tax of 7¾%. Hotel prices are for two people in a standard double room in high season, excluding service charges and 7¾% tax.

Timing

The climate varies greatly depending on what part of the Inland Empire you're visiting. Summer temperatures in the mountains and in Temecula, 20 mi from the coast, usually hover around 80°, though it's not uncommon for Riverside to reach temperatures over 100°. In winter, temperatures in the mountains and in Temecula usually range from 30° to 55°, and in the Riverside area 40° to 60°. Most of the ski resorts open when the first natural snow falls (usually in November) and close in mid-March, when even the best snowmaking equipment can't compete with rising spring temperatures.

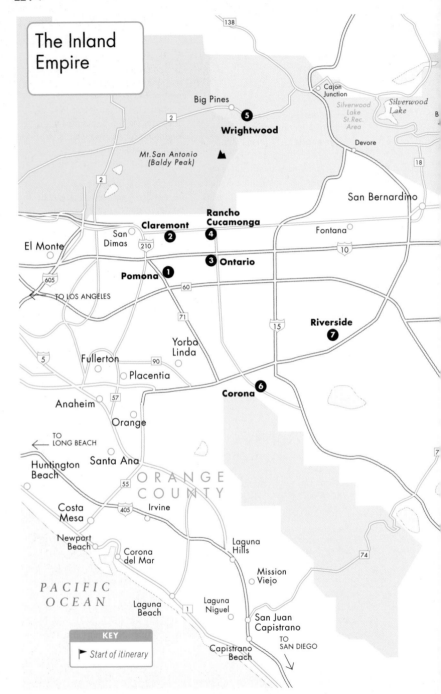

The Inland Empire

138

Cajon
Junction

Silverwood
Lake
St. Rec.
Area

Silverwood
Lake

B

Big Pines

5

Wrightwood

2

Devore

Mt. San Antonio
(Baldy Peak)

18

2

San Bernardino

**Rancho
Cucamonga**

Claremont

San
Dimas

2

4

Fontana

El Monte

210

3 **Ontario**

10

605

3

Pomona **1**

TO LOS ANGELES

60

71

15

Riverside

7

5

Yorba
Linda

Fullerton

90

Placentia

Corona **6**

Anaheim

57

Orange

TO
LONG BEACH

Santa Ana

 O R A N G E

Huntington
Beach

55

C O U N T Y

Costa
Mesa

405

Irvine

Newport
Beach

Corona
del Mar

Laguna
Hills

7

Mission
Viejo

*P A C I F I C
O C E A N*

Laguna
Beach

Laguna
Niguel

74

1

San Juan
Capistrano

TO
SAN DIEGO

Capistrano
Beach

KEY

▶ *Start of itinerary*

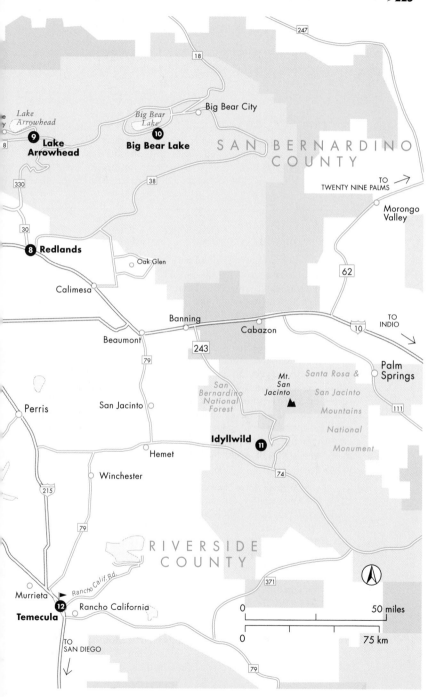

THE WESTERN INLAND EMPIRE

POMONA, CLAREMONT & THE SAN GABRIEL MOUNTAINS

At the foot of the San Gabriel Mountains, the tree-lined communities of Pomona and Claremont are known for their prestigious colleges: California State Polytechnic University–Pomona and the Claremont Colleges. There's not much to do here; the appeal of these towns is simply that they are cute, lively college towns, with pleasant architecture and a few little cafés to kick back in. Turn north into the hills and you'll find Wrightwood, an old-fashioned small town that makes a great base for outdoor adventure.

Pomona

❶ *23 mi north of Anaheim on Hwy. 57; 27 mi east of Pasadena on I–210.*

The green hills of Pomona, dotted with horses and houses, are perhaps best known as the site of the Los Angeles County Fair and of California State Polytechnic University–Pomona. Named for the Roman goddess of fruit, the city was established in 1938 and has a rich citrus-growing heritage. Today, Pomona is becoming better known for its art galleries and antiques stores.

Don't miss the **Kellogg House** (⌧ 3801 W. Temple Ave. ☎ 909/869–2280 ⊕ www.kellogghouse.csupomona.edu ✉ Free ☉ Oct.–June, 1st Sun. of every month, noon–2), which was once the scenic hilltop winter estate of cereal magnate Will Keith Kellogg. The circa-1925 home was designed by Myron Hunt (of Rose Bowl and Huntington Library fame) and has a blend of Islamic, Spanish, and Italian architecture. You can stroll the courtyard and gardens (both open to the public year-round), landscaped by Charles Gibbs Adams of Hearst Castle fame, then head inside for a look at the grand tapestries, hardwood floors, and intricately detailed ceilings.

The classic **Arabian Horse Shows** (⌧ 3801 W. Temple Ave. ☎ 909/869–2224 ✉ $3), started by Kellogg in 1926, are still a tradition on the CSU Pomona campus. More than 85 of the purebreds still call Kellogg's ranch home, and the university offers exhibitions of the equines in English and Western tack every first Sunday at 2 PM. There are also shows at 10:30 AM every Thursday from October through June; tours of the stables are available by appointment only.

Site of the Los Angeles County Fair (ninth-largest in the United States), the **Fairplex** exposition center has a 9,500-seat grandstand, an outdoor exhibit area, and nine exhibit buildings. The venue is the site of open-air markets, antiques shows, and the annual Wines of the World competition. Fairplex houses the **Wally Parks NHRA Motorsports Museum** (☎ 909/622–2133 ⊕ www.nhra.com/museum ✉ $5 ☉ Wed.–Sun. 10–5), dedicated to the history of American motor sports. ⌧ *1101 W.*

IF YOU LIKE

SPORTS & THE OUTDOORS

Those in search of the great outdoors in Southern California invariably make their way to the Inland Empire's mountain ranges. In winter, ski resorts in Wrightwood and Big Bear offer great snow and challenging terrain, along with often crowded conditions. Summer brings opportunities for hiking the Pacific Crest Trail, fishing in streams or lakes such as Silverwood and Big Bear, and camping at thousands of sites peppered through the mountains. If you're going to do any hiking, camping, or fishing, you need a **National Forest Adventure Pass** (☎ 909/382–2622 ⊕ www. fsadventurepass.org), which costs $5 per vehicle per day. Anglers must have a valid license from the **California Department of Fish and Game** (☎ 916/227–2245 ⊕ www. dfg.ca.gov/licensing/index.html), which you can purchase at Kmart, Longs Drugs, Wal-Mart, Big 5 Sporting Goods, and many other stores throughout Riverside County.

WINE TASTING

The Temecula Valley is quickly gaining a reputation as an outstanding wine region. At the area's 20-odd vineyards, most of them along Rancho California Road, you can taste wines made from a wide range of varietals using diverse wine-making styles. Wilson Creek's almond champagne is a crowd pleaser, as is the sauvignon blanc at Maurice Car'rie. Stuart Cellars' 1998 port has received high accolades from international experts. For tried-and-true quality, head for Mount Palomar, which has received dozens of medals for its Castelletto line.

McKinley Ave. ☎ 909/623–3111 ⊕ www.fairplex.com ☉ Call for current show listings and admission prices.

Where to Stay & Eat

$$–$$$ ✕ **Pomona Valley Mining Company.** Perched on a hilltop near an old mining site, this rustic steak-and-seafood restaurant provides a greatview of the city at night. The decor reflects the local mining heritage—authentic gold-rush pieces and 1800s memorabilia hang on the walls, and old lanterns are the centerpiece of each table. The food is well prepared, with a special nod to prime rib, and service is friendly. During June, book early—this is a favorite spot on prom nights. ⊠ 1777 Gillette Rd. ☎ 909/623–3515 ⊕ www.pomonavalleyminingco.com ▤ AE, D, DC, MC, V ☉ No lunch.

$–$$$ ⊞ **Sheraton Suites Fairplex.** County-fair murals and whimsical carousel animals welcome you to this all-suites hotel at the entrance to Pomona's Fairplex. Contemporary in style, rooms are done in neutral tans and blues and have coffeemakers and wet bars. It's about the only lodging in Pomona you should consider staying at, say locals and visitors alike, who rave about its comfort and cleanliness. The Brass Ring restaurant serves California cuisine. Mountain Meadows Golf Course is 1 mi away. ⊠ 601 W. McKinley Ave., 91768 ☎ 888/627–8074 ⊕ www.sheraton.com

247 suites ☼ Restaurant, room service, microwaves, refrigerators, cable TV with movies, in-room data ports, Wi-Fi, pool, gym, outdoor hot tub, sauna, bar, lobby lounge, shop, dry cleaning, laundry service, concierge, business services, meeting rooms, airport shuttle, car rental, some pets allowed (fee) ⊟ AE, D, DC, MC, V.

Claremont

② *4 mi north of Pomona along Gary Ave., then 2 mi east on Foothill Blvd.*

Nicknamed "Oxford in the Orange Belt," the seven Claremont Colleges are among the most prestigious in California. The campuses are all laid out cheek-by-jowl; as you wander from one leafy street to the next, you won't be able to tell where one college ends and the next begins.

In its heyday, Claremont was the home of the Sunkist cooperative movement. Today, Claremont Village harks back to the 1950s with its main street and hot-rod shows. The downtown district is a beautiful place to visit, with citrus- and oak-lined streets and Victorian, Craftsman, and Spanish-colonial buildings. College walking tours, a downtown tour, and historic home tours are conducted throughout the year by **Claremont Heritage** (☎ 909/621–0848). On the first Saturday of each month the organization gives walking tours of the village.

Be prepared for hot and smoggy conditions; the town is not gifted with SoCal's best climate.

NEED A BREAK?

Bert & Rocky's Cream Company. (✉ 242 Yale Ave. ☎ 909/621-0848). This independent ice-cream store is known for its innovative and simply sinful concoctions. There are more than 175 flavors from which to choose. The champagne and merlot sorbets are hot items, as is the Madagascar vanilla ice cream (paired with a chocolate dessert wine from Rancho Cucamonga winery). And yes, the nonalcoholic varieties are just as heavenly.

★ Founded in 1927 by Susanna Bixby Bryant, a wealthy landowner and conservationist, **Rancho Santa Ana Botanical Gardens** is a living museum and research center dedicated to the conservation of more than 2,800 native-California plant species. Meandering trails, set on 86 acres of ponds and greenery, guide visitors past such fragrant specimens as wild lilacs, big berry manzanita, and four-needled piñon. Countless birds also make their homes here. Before you start your tour, pick up a native-bird field guide at the gift shop. ✉ *1500 N. College Ave.* ☎ *909/625–8767* ⊕ *www.rsabg.org* ✑ *$4 donation requested* ☉ *Daily 8–5.*

Where to Eat

$–$$$ ✕ **Cafe Provencal.** If you're in the mood for something fancy, this is the place. Decorated in the style of a French-country kitchen, complete with ceramic plates from Provence and handmade dolls from Marseille, the restaurant is cozy and inviting. The menu is heavy on classic dishes from the French Mediterranean and Italy. ✉ *967 W. Foothill Blvd., Upland* ☎ *909/608–7100* ⊕ *www.cafe-provencal.com* ⊟ *AE, D, DC, V.*

¢–$$ ✕ **Viva Madrid!** More than 40 different tapas are on the menu at this festive old-world restaurant in Claremont Village. Start out with a cool glass of sangria, followed by the signature paella, which comes to your table sizzling in a cast-iron pan. On Wednesday and Thursday nights, you can enjoy live Spanish guitar. You can bring your own wine for a $10 corkage fee. ⊠ *225 Yale Ave.* ☎ *909/624–5500* ⊕ *www.viva-madrid.com* ⊟ *D, MC, V* ⊙ *Closed Mon. No lunch.*

★ $ ✕ **Caffe Allegro.** This romantic spot in downtown Upland resembles an Italian country villa, complete with candles, worn-looking walls, and an ornate wood bar. Locals rave about the chicken marsala, served on a bed of spinach fettuccine. ⊠ *186 N. 2nd Ave., Upland* ☎ *909/949–0805* ⊕ *www.caffeallegro.com* ⊟ *AE, D, MC, V.*

Nightlife

Being a college town, Claremont has lots of bars and cafés, some of which showcase bands. Karaoke and live jazz are popular at the **British Bulldog Pub and Restaurant** (⊠ 1667 N. Mountain Ave., Upland ☎ 909/946–6614). Both college kids and old-timers appreciate the **Buffalo Inn** (⊠ 1814 W. Foothill Blvd., Upland ☎ 909/981–5515), a rustic bar and hamburger joint along historic Route 66. On summer nights, acoustic musicians sing Jim Croce covers on the patio.

Sports & the Outdoors

SKIING The 10,064-foot mountain's real name is Mt. San Antonio, but **Mt. Baldy Ski Resort**—the oldest ski area in Southern California—takes its name from the treeless slopes. It's known for its steep triple-diamond runs, though the facilities could use some updating. The Mt. Baldy base lies at 6,500 feet, and four chairlifts ascend to 8,600 feet. There are 26 runs; the longest is 2,100 vertical feet. Whenever abundant fresh snow falls, there's a danger of avalanche in out-of-bounds areas. Backcountry skiing is available via shuttle in the spring, and there's a kiddie school ($75, including lift ticket and lunch) on weekends for children ages 5 to 12. Winter or summer, you can take a scenic chairlift ride ($10) to the Top of the Notch restaurant, and hiking and mountain-biking trails. ⊠ *From E. Foothill Blvd. about ½ mi north on N. Claremont Blvd., then 3 mi north on Monte Vista Ave. and 7 mi east on Mount Baldy Rd.* ☎ *909/981–3344* ⊕ *www.mtbaldy.com* ⊠ *Full day $45, half day (1–4) $30* ⊙ *Snow season Nov.–Apr., weekdays 8–4:30, weekends 7:30–4:30; summer season May–Oct., weekends 9–4:30.*

WATER PARK **Raging Waters,** a tropical-theme water park in San Dimas (10 mi west of Claremont), has 17 chutes and slides with such names as Neptune's Fury, Thunder Rapids, and Dragon's Den. When you're ready for a break, head over to the sandy beach lagoon and relax, or go to the Tropical Bar for a fruit drink or funnel cake. The Tropical Trading Post sells swimsuits, tanning lotion, and sunglasses. Lockers rent for $4 to $6, inner tubes for $4. For a special treat, rent a cabana ($55 midweek; $65 Friday through Sunday). Check the Web site for online coupons. ⊠ *111 Raging Waters Dr., San Dimas* ☎ *909/802–2200* ⊕ *www.ragingwaters.com* ⊠ *$32* ⊙ *Late June–Aug., daily 10–8; 1st 3 wks of June, daily 10–6; May, weekends 10–6; Sept.–mid-Oct., call for hrs.*

Ontario

❸ *Junction of I–10 and I–15, 6 mi east of Pomona.*

Ontario, in the Cucamonga Valley, has a rich agricultural and industrial heritage. The valley's warm climate once supported vineyards that produced Mediterranean-grape varietals such as grenache, mourvedre, and zinfandel. Today almost all of the vineyards have been replaced by housing tracts and shopping malls. But the Inland Empire's major airport is here, so you may well find yourself passing through Ontario.

Ontario's oldest existing business, **Graber Olive House,** opened in 1894 when, at the urging of family and friends, C. C. Graber bottled his meaty, tree-ripened olives and started selling them; they are still sold throughout the United States. Stop by the gourmet shop for a jar, then have a picnic on the shaded grounds. Free tours are conducted year-round; in fall you can watch workers grade, cure, and can the olives. ✉ *315 E. 4th St.* ☎ *909/983–1761 or 800/996–5483* ⊕ *www.graberolives.com* ✆ *Free* ☉ *Mon.–Sat. 9–5:30, Sun. 9:30–6.*

Where to Stay

$–$$ ⬚ **Ayres Inn & Suites.** This chain offers great value, and is known for its "Ovations" rooms, which have pillow-top mattresses, ergonomic chairs, and oversize desks. It's steps away from Ontario Mills Mall and dozens of restaurants. ✉ *4395 E. Ontario Mills Pkwy., 91764* ☎ *909/987–5940 or 866/999–1111* ⊕ *www.ayreshotels.com* ⤳ *86 rooms, 19 suites* ⌂ *Cable TV with movies, in-room broadband, Wi-Fi, pool, gym, Internet room, airport shuttle, no-smoking rooms* ▭ *AE, D, MC, V* ❙◯❙ *CP.*

★ $–$$ ⬚ **Doubletree Hotel Ontario Airport.** A beautifully landscaped courtyard greets you at this exceptional chain, the only full-service hotel in Ontario. Rooms here are spacious, and decorated in jewel tones and dark wood; the business center has printers, a copier, and laptop hookups as well as a computer with Internet access. The vineyards are only a few miles away. ✉ *222 N. Vineyard Ave., 91764* ☎ *909/937–0900 or 800/222–8733* ⊕ *www.doubletree.com* ⤳ *484 rooms, 22 suites* ⌂ *2 restaurants, room service, refrigerators, cable TV with movies, in-room broadband, Wi-Fi, pool, gym, hot tub, 2 lounges, shop, laundry service, concierge, business services, meeting rooms, airport shuttle, car rental, some pets allowed, no-smoking rooms* ▭ *AE, D, MC, V* ❙◯❙ *CP.*

Shopping

♻ The gargantuan **Ontario Mills Mall** is California's largest, packing in more than 200 outlet stores, a 30-screen movie theater, and the Improv comedy theater. Also in the mall are three entertainment complexes: Dave & Buster's pool hall–restaurant-arcade, Vans Skate Park, and Game-Works video-game center. Dining options include the kid-friendly jungle-theme Rainforest Cafe (complete with animatronic elephants and simulated thunderstorms), the chic Wolfgang Puck Cafe, and a 1,000-seat food court. ✉ *1 Mills Circle, 4th St. and I–15* ☎ *909/484–8300* ⊕ *www.ontariomills.com* ☉ *Mon.–Sat. 10–9:30, Sun. 10–8.*

Rancho Cucamonga

④ *5 mi north of Ontario on I–15.*

Once a thriving wine-making area with more than 50,000 acres of wine grapes, Rancho Cucamonga lost most of its pastoral charm after real-estate developers bought up the land for a megamall and affordable housing. It's now a squeaky-clean planned community, but you can still get a taste of the grape here. At the **Joseph Filippi Winery,** J. P. and Gino Filippi continue the family tradition that was started in 1922. They produce handcrafted wines from cabernet, sangiovese, and zinfandel grapes, among other varieties. You can taste up to four wines for $5, and take the free guided tour that's given at noon, Wednesday through Sunday. ⊠ *12467 Base Line Rd.* ☎ *909/899–5755* ⊕ *www.josephfilippiwinery. com* ⊡ *Free* ☾ *Mon.–Sat. 10–5, Sun. 11–5.*

★ ☺ **Victoria Gardens** feels a lot like downtown Disneyland with its vintage signs, antique lampposts, and colorful California-theme murals along its 12 city blocks. At this shopping, dining, and entertainment complex, such stores as Banana Republic, Abercrombie & Fitch, Williams-Sonoma, and Pottery Barn are flanked by a Macy's, a Robinsons-May, and a 12-screen AMC movie theater. After you're finished shopping, grab an ice cream at the Ben & Jerry's shop and linger in the 1920s-style Town Square, a relaxing little park with fountains, grass, and an old-fashioned trolley ($2 per ride). Restaurants such as the Cheesecake Factory, Lucille's Smokehouse Barbecue, P. F. Chang's China Bistro, and the Yardhouse often have lines out the door. The Victoria Gardens Cultural Center has a library and a 540-seat performing-arts center. ⊠ *12505 N. Main St.* ☎ *909/463–2828 general information, 909/477–2720 Cultural Center* ⊕ *www.victoriagardensie.com* ⊡ *Free* ☾ *Mon.–Sat. 10–9, Sun. 11–7.*

Where to Stay & Eat

★ **$$-$$$** ✕ **The Sycamore Inn.** Flickering gas lamps and a glowing fireplace greet you at this rustic inn. Built in 1921, the restaurant stands on the site of a pre-statehood stagecoach stop; it's one of the oldest buildings in town. The specialty of the house is the rack of Colorado lamb, pan seared and roasted with a mustard–bread crumb crust and a red-wine reduction. The wine list is impressive; by the glass, you can choose from more than 20 vintages from the Central Coast, Napa Valley, and such nearby wineries as Joseph Filippi and Temecula. ⊠ *8318 Foothill Blvd.* ☎ *909/ 982–1104* ⊕ *www.thesycamoreinn.com* ⊟ *AE, D, MC, V* ☾ *No lunch.*

★ **¢** ✕ **Vince's Spaghetti House.** A swooping yellow neon arrow points the way to this boisterous family eatery, open since 1945. The restaurant claims to serve more than 15,000 mi of spaghetti every year. The menu is limited, but reliably good. The *mostaccioli* with meat sauce and the meatball sandwiches are excellent choices. ⊠ *8241 Foothill Blvd.* ☎ *909/ 981–1003* ⊕ *www.vinces-spaghetti.com* ⊟ *AE, D, MC, V.*

$-$$ ▦ **Best Western Heritage Inn.** Along with gorgeous views of the San Gabriel mountains, this hotel provides contemporary rooms and a wine-and-cheese tasting at dusk. In the morning the newspaper is delivered to your door. If you're hungry, head across the parking lot to Mimi's

Cafe, a cheerful eatery known for its breakfast. ⊠ *8179 Spruce Ave.,
91730* ☎ *909/466–1111 or 800/780–7234* 🖷 *909/466–3876* ⊕ *www.
bestwestern.com* ⇥ *116 rooms* ᗒ *Some microwaves, some minibars,
some refrigerators, cable TV with movies, in-room data ports, pool, gym,
outdoor hot tub, dry cleaning, laundry service, business services, meeting room* ⍾⊙⍾ *CP.*

Wrightwood

❺ *39 mi north of Ontario, via I–15, Hwy. 138, and Hwy. 2.*

Wrightwood prides itself on having no stoplights, fast-food restaurants,
or chain stores. What you will find are old-fashioned candy purveyors,
antiques shops, and crafts boutiques. Since Wrightwood has the most
accessible roads of all Southland ski-resort communities (no winding roads
and jaw-dropping cliffs to deal with), it's popular with day-trippers.

An old stone tower at **Big Pines Visitors Center,** part of Angeles National
Forest, marks the highest spot (6,862 feet) along the San Andreas Fault,
the unstable crack in the earth's crust that has caused so many California earthquakes. At the visitor center you can get information on camping, fishing, and hiking in the forest; buy souvenirs; and get the National
Forest Adventure passes ($5 per vehicle day) that allow you access to
the forest. ⊠ *Hwy. 2, 3 mi west of Wrightwood* ☎ *760/249–3504*
⊙ *Daily 8–3.*

Where to Stay & Eat

★ **$–$$$** ✕ **Blue Ridge Inn.** This rustic 1948 lodge has a bar with a huge fireplace,
and a cozy, wood-panel dining room, decorated with flickering lanterns
and 19th-century clocks. The food—surf-and-turf specialties, such as
grilled Malaysian shrimp and prime rib—is probably the best you'll find
in Wrightwood. ⊠ *6060 Park Dr.* ☎ *760/249–3440* ⊟ *AE, MC, V*
⊙ *Closed Mon. No lunch.*

$–$$ ✕ **Evergreen Cafe.** This cozy little coffee shop, adorned with country jars,
striped wallpaper, and little white lights, is a favorite of locals. Break-
fasts, served all day, are hearty and generous. For lunch, try the grilled
chicken sandwich, topped with ortega chilies, tomatoes, jack cheese, onion,
and lettuce. For dinner, try the home-style meat loaf, served with soup
or salad, rice or potato, vegetables, and toasted garlic bread. ⊠ *1269
Evergeen Rd.* ☎ *760/249–6393 or 760/249–4277* ⊟ *MC, V.*

$–$$$ ◫ **Canyon Creek Inn.** Fluffy goose down comforters and soft-as-a-cloud
featherbeds are the showpieces of this tiny boutique inn, which was con-
verted from a cluster of real-estate offices. In addition to those amaz-
ing beds, rooms have rustic pine furniture; lamps with moose on them
provide a tiny bit of whimsy. Midweek ski packages, at $249, include
a two-night stay and two eight-hour lift tickets. ⊠ *6059 Pine St., 92397*
☎ *760/249–4800* ⊕ *www.canyoncreekinn.com* ⇥ *3 rooms* ᗒ *Refrig-
erators, cable TV, in-room DVDs, playground; no room phones, no smok-
ing* ⊟ *AE, D, MC, V.*

$–$$ ◫ **Pines Motel and Cabins.** This property, steps from Wrightwood's village, has plenty of simple charm. Rooms have knotty-pine walls and lodge-
style beds with country quilts. Cabins have living rooms with fireplaces,

kitchens, and separate bedrooms; studio suites have dining areas and entertainment centers. ⊠ *6045 Pine St., 92397* ☎ *760/249–9974* ⟿ *10 rooms, 2 cabins, 2 suites* ⚇ *Picnic area, BBQs, fans, some kitchenettes, some microwaves, some refrigerators, cable TV, playground* ⊟ *AE, D, MC, V.*

⚠ **Table Mountain.** Scenic views of the desert from 7,000 feet make this campground, next to the Big Pines Visitor Center, popular. You can buy firewood at the campground, and there's a restaurant nearby. Reservations must be made at least four days in advance, and no refunds are given in case of bad weather. The sites are drive-in, but despite the presence of cars, remain pretty and secluded. ⚇ *Grills, pit toilets, portable toilets, drinking water, bear boxes, fire pits, picnic tables, public telephone, ranger station* ⟿ *118 sites* ⊠ *22223 Big Pines Hwy.* ☎ *805/ 944–2187 or 877/444–6777* ⊕ *www.reserveusa.com* ⚇ *Reservations essential* ⊡ *$13–$26* ⊟ *AE, D, MC, V* ☉ *May–Nov.*

Sports & the Outdoors

HIKING In April, Wrightwood is a major stopping point for hikers traveling the **Pacific Crest Trail** (⊠ Big Pines Visitors Center, Rte. 2, 3 mi west of Wrightwood ☎ 760/249–3504), which runs 2,600 mi from Mexico to Canada. There's a trailhead near Inspiration Point on Highway 2, 5 mi west of Wrightwood.

SKIING In addition to two mountains, a vertical drop of 8,200 feet, and 220 skiable acres, **Mountain High** (⊠ 24510 Hwy. 2 ☎ 760/249–5808 ⊕ www. mthigh.com ⊡ $48 day pass; $30 night skiing 5–10) has 46 trails for skiing and snowboarding. The Flex ticket allows you to ski in four- or eight-hour blocks, and the Point Ticket lets you choose the number of runs you want to take. Snowboarders flock to Mountain High to test their skills at Faultline Terrain Park. There's regular bus service between the mountains. In 2005 the resort purchased neighboring Ski Sunrise, which was transformed into Mountain High North, complete with a tubing park.

RIVERSIDE AREA

In the late 1700s, Mexican rancheros called this now-suburban region Valle de Paraiso. Citrus-growing here began in 1873, when homesteader Eliza Tibbets planted two navel-orange trees in her yard. The area's biggest draws are the majestic Mission Inn, with its fine restaurants and unique history and architecture, and Glen Ivy Hot Springs.

Corona

❻ *13 mi south of Ontario on I–15.*

Corona's Temescal Canyon is named for the dome-shape mud saunas that the Luiseno Indians built around the artesian hot springs in the early 19th century. Starting in 1860, weary Overland Stage Company passengers stopped to relax in the soothing mineral springs. In 1890 Mr. and Mrs. W. G. Steers turned the springs into a resort whose popularity has yet to fade.

Presidents Herbert Hoover and Ronald Reagan are among the thousands of guests who have soaked their toes at the very relaxing and beautiful **Glen Ivy Hot Springs.** Colorful bougainvillea and birds-of-paradise surround the secluded canyon spa, which offers a full range of facials, manicures, pedicures, body wraps, and massages; some treatments are performed in underground granite spa chambers known collectively as the Grotto, highly recommended by readers. Don't bring your best bikini if you plan to dive into the red clay (brought in daily from a local mine) of Club Mud. Children under 16 are not permitted at the spa except on three family days: Memorial Day, July 4, and Labor Day. ⊠ *25000 Glen Ivy Rd., Glen Ivy* ☎ *951/277–3529* ⊕ *www.glenivy.com* 🔲 *Mon.–Thurs. $35; Fri.–Sun. $48* ☉ *Apr.–Oct., daily 9:30–6; Nov.–Mar., daily 9:30–5.*

Fodor'sChoice
★

★ ☺ Opened as a produce stand in 1974, **Tom's Farms** has grown to include a hamburger stand, furniture showroom, and health-food store. You can still buy produce here, but the big draw is various attractions for the kiddies: a duck pond, a petting zoo, a children's train, and an old-style carousel. Of interest for adults is the wine-and-cheese shop, which has more than 600 varieties of wine, including many from nearby Temecula Valley; wine tasting ($1 for three samples) takes place daily 11 to 6. On weekends there's a country fair with children's crafts, face painting, a free magic show, and snack booths. ⊠ *23900 Temescal Canyon Rd.* ☎ *951/277–4422* ⊕ *www.tomsfarms.com* 🔲 *Free* ☉ *Daily 8–8.*

Where to Stay & Eat

★ $$–$$$$ ✕ **Napa 29.** A cellar with more than 220 wines from California's Napa Valley and Central Coast is the main draw at this stylish restaurant and specialty-foods shop. Dark wood and white tablecloths are the backdrop for stellar California cuisine, such as cold smoked buffalo and macadamia-crusted sea bass with chardonnay sauce. Live jazz is performed on Thursday, Friday, and Saturday nights. ⊠ *280 Teller St., Suite 130* ☎ *951/273–0529* ⊕ *www.napa29.com* 🟰 *AE, MC, V* ☉ *Closed Mon. No lunch.*

$$ 🏨 **Country Suites By Ayres at Corona West.** This ranch-style hotel, with its leather couches, wrought-iron light fixtures, and courtyard adobe fireplace, harks back to the days of Spanish California. Some rooms have fireplaces. If you feel so inclined, you can mingle with fellow guests over beer, cheese, and crackers during the 5 to 7 PM "social hour." ⊠ *1900 W. Frontage Rd., 92882* ☎ *951/738–9113 or 800/676–1363* ⊕ *www. countrysuites.com/coronawest.htm* 🛏 *114 rooms* ⌂ *Room service, microwaves, refrigerators, cable TV, in-room broadband, Wi-Fi, pool, gym, hot tub, meeting rooms* 🟰 *AE, D, MC, V* ¶◯¶ *BP.*

Riverside

❼ *14 mi north of Corona on Route 91, 34 mi from Anaheim on Route 91.*

By 1882 Riverside was home to more than half of California's citrus groves, making it the state's wealthiest city per capita in 1895. The prosperity produced a downtown area of magnificent architecture, which is well preserved today. Main Street's pedestrian strip is lined with antiques and gift stores, art galleries, salons, and the UCR/California Museum of Photography.

Fodor'sChoice ★ The crown jewel of Riverside is the **Mission Inn,** a remarkable Spanish-revival hotel whose elaborate turrets, clock tower, mission bells, and flying buttresses rise above downtown. The inn was designed in 1902 by Arthur B. Benton and Myron Hunt; the team took its cues from the Spanish missions in San Gabriel and Carmel. You can climb to the top of the Rotunda Wing's five-story spiral stairway, or linger awhile in the Courtyard of the Birds, where a tinkling fountain and shady trees invite meditation. You can also peek inside the St. Francis Chapel, where folks such as Bette Davis, Humphrey Bogart, and Richard and Pat Nixon tied the knot before the Mexican cedar altar. The Presidential Lounge, a dark, wood-panel bar, has been patronized by eight U.S. presidents. ⊠ *3649 Mission Inn Ave.* ☎ *951/784–0300 or 800/843–7755* 🖷 *951/683–1342* ⊕ *www.missioninn.com.*

Fodor'sChoice ★ The Mission Inn also has a luxurious spa, **Kelly's Spa,** a 6,000-square-foot poolside retreat. Warm-tone woods, hand-painted frescoes, Venetian chandeliers, and barrel-vaulted ceilings set the scene for this tranquil Tuscan-style escape, which has six treatment rooms and two private villas. The villas, which run $249 for a half day and $399 for a full day, have outdoor teak rain showers and marble-encased aromatherapy baths, as well as flat-screen TVs. After a round in the eucalyptus-infused steam room, you can grab your white cashmere robe and indulge in your choice of facials, massages, and body polishes. Guests ages 14 to 18 must be accompanied by a parent, and must wear swimsuits during treatments. ⊠ *3649 Mission Inn Ave.* ☎ *951/341–6725 or 800/440–5910* ⊕ *www.kellysspa.com* ⊙ *Daily 7:30 AM–8:30 PM.*

California Citrus State Historic Park. A celebration of California's citrus-growing history, this Victorian-style park occupies 377 well-kept acres of working citrus groves. The grounds, developed in 1880, are perfect for a leisurely afternoon picnic. Work off your lunch on the 2-mi interpretive trail, or check out the park's Craftsman-style bungalows, Victorian banister house, or museum and gift shop. Guided tours are conducted Saturday at 10 AM and by request. On Friday from June through August, free concerts present the bluegrass and jazz of 1900–1930. ⊠ *1879 Jackson St.* ☎ *951/780–6222* ⊕ *www.parks.ca.gov* 🎟 *Free* ⊙ *Wed. and Sat. 10–4.*

Riverside celebrates its juicy raison d'être each April at the **Orange Blossom Festival** (☎ 888/748–7733). The **National Orange Show,** held in May, includes orange-crate label exhibits, orange-packing demonstrations, and other citrus-related fun.

Where to Stay & Eat

$–$$$ ✕ **Mario's Place.** The clientele is as beautiful as the food at this intimate
Fodor'sChoice ★ jazz and supper club. The northern Italian cuisine is first-rate, as are the bands that perform Friday and Saturday at 10 PM. Try the pear-and-Gorgonzola wood-fired pizza, followed by the caramelized banana napoleon

(made with hazelnut phyllo, vanilla mascarpone, and coffee sauce). ✉ *3646 Mission Inn Ave.* ☎ *951/684–7755* ⊕ *www.mariosplace.com* ⊟ *AE, D, MC, V* ⊘ *No lunch Sat.–Thurs.*

¢ ✕ **Simple Simon's.** Expect to wait in line at this little sandwich shop on the pedestrian-only shopping strip outside the Mission Inn. Traditional salads, soups, and sandwiches on house-baked breads are served; stand-out specialties include the chicken-apple sausage sandwich and the roast lamb sandwich topped with grilled eggplant, red peppers, and tomato-fennel-olive sauce. ✉ *3636 Main St.* ☎ *951/369–6030* ⊟ *No credit cards* ⊘ *Closed Sun. No dinner.*

$$$ ✕▢ **Mission Inn.** This grand Spanish colonial–era hotel was designated
Fodor'sChoice a National Historic Landmark in 1977. Most standard rooms have an
★ early–Spanish California look, with Mission-style artwork and dark wooden headboards. Dining is a rewarding experience, whether you choose the grand Duane's Steakhouse ($$–$$$$), famed for its maple-leaf duck breast and osso buco; Las Campanas ($–$$), where Mexican-style *carnitas* (shredded pork) are served in a pool of *mole negro* (a savory chili-and-chocolate-based sauce); or the Mission Inn Restaurant ($–$$), where you can relax next to a bubbling fountain on the Spanish patio. ■ TIP→ **Sunday brunch here is excellent, though pricey, say locals.** ✉ *3649 Mission Inn Ave.* ☎ *951/784–0300 or 800/843–7755* 🖷 *951/683–1342* ⊕ *www.missioninn.com* ↝ *211 rooms, 28 suites* ⚴ *3 restaurants, café, room service, minibars, cable TV with movies and video games, in-room broadband, Wi-Fi, pool, gym, massage, spa, steam room, 2 lounges, shop, dry cleaning, laundry service, business services, meeting rooms, airport shuttle, no-smoking rooms* ⊟ *AE, D, DC, MC, V.*

Nightlife & the Arts

NIGHTLIFE Savor tapas and sangria at **Cafe Sevilla** (✉ 3252 Mission Inn Ave. ☎ 951/778–0611) while enjoying live flamenco, salsa, and rumba music on weeknights. Dance lessons are offered Tuesday and Thursday nights. On weekend nights, the restaurant plays host to a Latin-Euro Top 40 dance club.

Shopping

Some fine boutiques, antiques stores, and specialty shops line pedestrian-only Main Street between 6th and 10th streets. British-theme **Farthings** (✉ 3653 Main St. ☎ 951/784–3111), which specializes in seasonal gifts and garden art, also has a nice line of upscale stationery and wrapping paper. You can buy Mission Inn souvenirs at **Inn-credible Gift Corner** (✉ 3668 Main St. ☎ 951/788–8090). The three-story **Mission Galleria** (✉ 3700 Main St. ☎ 951/276–8000) is an antiques mall specializing in vintage furniture, with a café downstairs. **Tiggy-Winkles Gift Shoppe** (✉ Main and 7th Sts. ☎ 951/683–0221) carries all things Curious George and Beatrix Potter, as well as designer jewelry, porcelain knick-knacks, potpourri, and soap. The incense-scented **Dragonmarsh** (✉ 3744 Main St. ☎ 951/276–1116) has Renaissance-style jewelry, candles, crystal balls, and swords.

Sports & the Outdoors

Golf enthusiasts have eight courses to choose from around Riverside. **Riverside Golf Club** (✉ 1011 N. Orange St. ☎ 951/682–3748) is an 18-

hole, par-72 public course with a full-service restaurant and bar. Greens fee: $25–$37. The Harold Heers and Jimmy Powell course at **Indian Hills Golf Club** (✉ 5700 Club House Dr. ☎ 951/360–2090 ⊕ www. indianhillsgolf.com) is a scenic 18-hole, par-70 championship course. Greens fee: $24–$48.

Redlands

❽ *15 mi northeast of Riverside via I–215 north and I–10 east.*

Redlands lies at the center of what once was the largest navel-orange-producing region in the world. The town's main artery, Orange Street, is lined with fancy boutiques, trendy restaurants, and antiques shops. Orange groves are still plentiful throughout the area. You can glimpse Redlands' origins in several fine examples of California Victorian residential architecture.

In 1897 Cornelia A. Hill built **Kimberly Crest House and Gardens** to mimic the châteaux of France's Loire Valley. Surrounded by orange groves, lily ponds, and terraced Italian gardens, the mansion has a French-revival parlor, a mahogany staircase, a glass mosaic fireplace, and a bubbling fountain in the form of Venus rising from the sea. In 1905 the property was purchased by Alfred and Helen Kimberly, founders of the Kimberly-Clark Paper Company. Their daughter, Mary, lived in the house until 1979. Almost all of the home's 22 rooms are in original condition. Guided tours begin at 1 and run every 30 minutes; the last tour is at 3:30. ✉ *1325 Prospect Dr.* ☎ *909/792–2111* ⊕ *www.kimberlycrest. org* ✉ *$7* ☉ *Sept.–July, Thurs.–Sun. 1–4.*

To learn more about Southern California's shaky history, head to the ☺ **San Bernardino County Museum,** where you can watch a working seismometer or check out a display about the San Andreas Fault. Specializing in the natural and regional history of Southern California, the museum is big on birds, eggs, dinosaurs, and mammals. Afterward, go for a light lunch at the Garden Cafe, open Tuesday through Sunday 11 to 2. ✉ *2024 Orange Tree La.* ☎ *909/307–2669* ⊕ *www.sbcounty.gov/ museum* ✉ *$6* ☉ *Tues.–Sun. 9–5.*

After the Franciscan Fathers of Mission San Gabriel built it in 1830, the **Asistencia Mission de San Gabriel** functioned as a mission only for a few years. In 1834 it became part of a Spanish-colonial rancho; later the mission served as a school and a factory and was finally purchased by the county, which restored it in 1937. The landscaped courtyard contains an old Spanish mission bell; one building holds a small museum. ✉ *26930 Barton Rd.* ☎ *909/793–5402* ✉ *$1* ☉ *Tues.–Sat. 10–3.*

Where to Eat

$$–$$$$ ✕ **Joe Greensleeves.** Housed in the 19th-century brick Board of Trade building, this classic restaurant is homey and inviting. Wood-grilled steaks, chicken, and fish take up most of the menu, which leans toward Italian, but adventurous eaters may enjoy the mallard duck or the elk chops. ✉ *220 N. Orange St.* ☎ *909/792–6969* ▭ *AE, D, DC, MC, V.*

$–$$$ ✕ **Citrone.** This hip and casual downtown bistro has won *Wine Specta-*
Fodor'sChoice   *tor* awards continually since 1998. More than 600 wines are served here,
★   which complement such light California fare as the Citrone Stack (lay-
ered roasted red peppers, red onion, grilled tomato, potato, mush-
rooms, and buffalo mozzarella), or the signature pizza, topped with feta
cheese, onions, and sliced apples. Don't miss the Citrone martini, made
with premium vodka and fresh-squeezed lemons. ⊠ *328 Orange St.*
☎ *909/793–6635* ▤ *AE, MC, V.*

¢–$ ✕ **Royal Falconer.** This stately British-theme pub is a great spot to enjoy
a pint and a traditional English meal of shepherd's pie, fish-and-chips,
or bangers-and-mash. There are 20 beers on tap and 30 by the bottle.
The upstairs game room has pool tables and dartboards. ⊠ *106 Or-
ange St.* ☎ *909/307–8913* ▤ *AE, MC, V* ☽ *Daily 11–10.*

The Arts

Redlands Bowl, a 6,000-seat outdoor amphitheater in juniper-shaded Smi-
ley Park, is the scene of ballet, opera, and symphony performances as
well as jazz and folk concerts. On Tuesday and Friday nights, June through
August, free performances take place at 8:15. ⊠ *Eureka St. at Redlands
Blvd.* ☎ *909/793–7316* ⊕ *www.redlandsbowl.org* ✉ *Free.*

SAN BERNARDINO MOUNTAINS

The twin resorts of Lake Arrowhead and the always sunny Big Bear are
the recreational center of this area; though the two are geographically
close, they're distinct in appeal, smaller, but similar to Lake Tahoe, say
visitors. Lake Arrowhead, with its cool mountain air, trail-threaded
woods, and brilliant lake, draws a summertime crowd—a well-heeled
one, if the prices in its shops and restaurants are any indication. Big Bear's
ski and snowboarding slopes, cross-country trails, and cheerful lodges
come alive in winter. Even if you're not interested in the resorts them-
selves, the Rim of the World Scenic Byway (Highway 18), which con-
nects the two at an elevation of 8,000 feet, is a magnificent drive.

Lake Arrowhead

❾ *37 mi northeast of Riverside via I–215 north to Hwy. 330 north to Hwy.
18 west.*

Lake Arrowhead Village is an alpine community with offices, shops, out-
let stores, and eateries that descend the hill to the lake. Outside the vil-
lage, access to the lake and its beaches is limited to area residents and
their guests. You can take a 45-minute cruise on the *Arrowhead Queen,*
operated daily by **LeRoy Sports** (☎ 909/336–6992) from the waterfront
marina in Lake Arrowhead Village. Tickets are available on a first-come,
first-served basis and cost $12. Call for departure times.

★ ☾ If you're in the mood to skate, head over to **Ice Castle,** where you may
catch a glimpse of Olympic gold-medalist Michelle Kwan, who regu-
larly trains on its International-size rink. Skate rentals cost $2 per per-
son. ⊠ *410 Burnt Mill Rd.* ☎ *909/337–5283* ⊕ *www.icecastle.us* ✉ *$8*
☽ *Tues. and Fri. 7:30 PM–9 PM, Sat. 2:30–4:30, Sun. 11–1.*

Where to Stay & Eat

★ **$$–$$$** ✕ **Casual Elegance.** This intimate house with a fireplace is a couple of miles outside Arrowhead Village. Featured menu items change weekly, but the steaks and seafood are first-rate. ☒ *26848 Hwy. 189, Blue Jay* ☎ *909/337–8932* 🖃 *AE, D, DC, MC, V* ⊘ *Closed Mon. and Tues. No lunch.*

★ **$–$$** ✕ **The Chef's Inn & Tavern.** This romantic lakefront restaurant, which survived Cedar Glen's devastating 2003 wildfires, is a favorite of locals. Once a mountain bordello, the historic building is decorated in the Victorian style with antiques and has a lower-level saloon. Standout dishes such as the chateaubriand and German sausage platter are accompanied by soup, salad, and dessert. ☒ *29020 Oak Terr., Cedar Glen* ☎ *909/ 336–4488* 🖃 *AE, MC, V.*

¢–$ ✕ **Belgian Waffle Works.** This waterfront eatery, just steps from the Arrowhead Queen, is quaint and homey, with country decor and beautiful views of the lake. Don't miss their namesake waffles, crisp on the outside and moist on the inside, topped with fresh berries and cream. Lunch is also delicious, with choices ranging from basic burgers to tuna melts and salads. The restaurant gets crowded during lunch on the weekend, so get there early to snag a table with a view. ☒ *28200 Hwy. 189, Bldg. E140, Lake Arrowhead* ☎ *909/337–5222* 🖃 *AE, D, MC, V.*

★ **$$$** ✕🖭 **Lake Arrowhead Resort and Spa.** This lakeside lodge started a $12-million renovation in 2006. Most rooms have water or forest views. The on-premises Village Bay Spa offers facials, massages, and other body treatments. In June 2006, the resort welcomed acclaimed chef Randal St. Clair of the famed Galileo restaurant at the Observatory in Sydney. His BIN189 restaurant, with its granite-and-pine decor and private wine-tasting room, serves up an eclectic menu of international specialties such as loin of venison or scallop and white-asparagus risotto. ☒ *27984 Hwy. 189, Lake Arrowhead Village 92352* ☎ *909/336–1511 or 800/800–6792* 🖷 *909/336–1378* ⊕ *www.lakearrowheadresort.com* ➡ *177 rooms, 4 suites, 3 condos* ⚎ *Restaurant, room service, cable TV with movies, in-room data ports, Wi-Fi, pool, health club, spa, beach, bar, children's programs (ages 4–12), meeting rooms, no-smoking rooms* 🖃 *AE, D, DC, MC, V.*

$$–$$$ 🖭 **Fleur de Lac European Inn.** This elegant 1915 home, decorated like a French château, offers style, comfort, and a great location just steps from the village. Each room has an antique carved-wood bed with luxury linens, whirlpool bath, and private balcony. In the Great Room you can sit by the massive granite fireplace and enjoy a glass of Fleur de Lac's signature red wine. If you're lucky, the breakfast menu may include crème brûlée French toast. Bringing children to the inn is politely discouraged. ☒ *285 Hwy. 173, just outside Lake Arrowhead Village, 92352* ☎ *909/ 336–4612* ⊕ *www.fleurdelac.com* ➡ *5 rooms* ⚎ *In-room hot tubs, cable TV, in-room VCRs, health club, spa, meeting room; no kids, no smoking* 🖃 *MC, V* ⦿ *BP.*

¢–$$$ 🖭 **Bracken Fern Manor.** For a unique—albeit spooky—evening, head to this "haunted" English Tudor–style hotel. Mobster Bugsy Siegel opened the property in 1929 as a brothel and private gambling resort; today it's a certified historic landmark, which was completely restored in

1993. Each of the rooms, decorated in florals and English and Belgian antiques, are named for the aspiring actresses who once entertained here. In summer, wine and hors d'oeuvres are offered in the wine cellar, just steps from the secret tunnel used by gangsters in the hotel's heyday. A separate cottage, which sleeps four, includes a fireplace, TV/VCR, kitchenette and garden patio with barbecue and Jacuzzi. ✉ *815 Arrowhead Villas Rd., Lake Arrowhead Village, 92352* ☎ *888/244–5612 or 909/ 337–8557* ⊕ *www.brackenfernmanor.com* ⇄ *10 rooms* ♨ *Hot tub, some cable TV, some in-room VCRs, some fireplaces; no smoking* ⊟ *D, MC, V* ⏧ *BP.*

Sports & the Outdoors

Waterskiing and wakeboarding lessons are available on Lake Arrowhead in summer at **McKenzie Waterski School** (☎☎ 909/337–3814 ⊕ www. mckenzieskischool.com).

Lovely **Lake Gregory** was formed by a dam constructed in 1938. Because the summer water temperature is often quite warm (rare for lakes at this altitude), this is the best swimming lake in the area. It's open in summer only, and there's a nominal charge to swim. You can fish, go on the waterslides, and rent rowboats at Lake Gregory Village. ✉ *24171 Lake Dr. off Rim of World Hwy.* ☎ *909/338–2233.*

Big Bear Lake

🔟 *24 mi east of Lake Arrowhead on Hwy. 18, Rim of the World Hwy.*

The town of Big Bear Lake, on the lake's south shore, has a classic Western-Alpine style; you'll spot the occasional chaletlike building here. Big Bear City, at the east end of Big Bear Lake, has restaurants, motels, and a small airport. From May through October, the paddle wheeler *Big Bear Queen* departs daily at noon, 2, and 4 from **Big Bear Marina** (✉ 500 Paine Rd., Big Bear Lake ☎ 909/866–3218 ⊕ www.bigbearmarina.com) for 90-minute tours of the lake; the cost is $14; $18.50 for dinner cruises.

☺ Kids will enjoy a cruise on the **Time Bandit Pirate Ship,** which is a small-scale replica of a 17th-century English galleon. The ship, which was featured in Terry Gilliam's 1981 movie, *Time Bandits,* is also the centerpiece attraction at the annual Big Bear Pirate Faire, which kicked off this year in June. During the event, Captain John's Harbor in Fawnskin is transformed into a 17th-century Buccaneer Village, complete with ship-to-shore pirate battles, a treasure hunt, and cold grog. ☎ *909/878–4040* ⊕ *www.800bigbear.com/timebandit.html* 🎫 *$15* ⏰ *Tours weekdays at 2, weekends at noon, 2, and 4.*

☺ **Moonridge Animal Park,** a rescue and rehabilitation center, specializes in animals native to the San Bernardino Mountains. Among its residents are black bears, bald eagles, coyote, beavers, and bobcats. You can catch an educational presentation at noon and feeding tour at 3. ✉ *43285 Goldmine Dr.* ☎ *909/584–1171* ⊕ *www.moonridgezoo.org* 🎫 *$5* ⏰ *May–Sept., daily 10–5; Oct.–Apr., daily 10–4.*

☺ Take a ride down a twisting bobsled course in winter, or beat the summer heat on a dual waterslide at **Alpine Slide at Magic Mountain.** Miniature golf and go-carts add to the fun. ⊠ *800 Wildrose La., ¼ mi west of Big Bear Village* ☎ *909/866–4626* ⊕ *www.alpineslidebigbear.com* 🎟 *$4 single rides, $20 day pass* ☉ *Daily 10–6.*

🐣 **Big Bear Discovery Center.** Operated by the forest service, this nature cen-

Fodor'sChoice ter is the place to sign up for a canoe ride through Grout Bay, or natu-

★ ralist-led Discovery Tours, including visits to bald eagle–nesting grounds, wildflower fields, and historic gold mines. The popular Bald Eagle Tours, which run January through March, take you to the winter nesting grounds of these magnificent birds. The center also has rotating flora and fauna exhibits, and a nature-oriented gift shop. ⊠ *North Shore Dr., Hwy. 38 between Fawnskin and Stanfield Cutoff* ☎ *909/866–3437* ⊕ *www.bigbeardiscoverycenter.com* 🎟 *Free* ☉ *June–Aug., daily 8–6; Sept.–May, daily 8–4:30.*

Where to Stay & Eat

$$–$$$ ✕**Evergreen International.** This rustic-style steak house has sweeping views of Big Bear Lake. In winter you can stay warm in the comfortable dining room, which has dark paneling and exposed beams; in summer head out to the deck to enjoy a glass of wine while you watch the sun set. Lunch and dinner choices include grilled chicken topped with passion-fruit sauce, pepper-crusted ahi tuna, or prime rib with king crab legs. ⊠ *40771 Lakeview Dr.* ☎ *909/878–5588* 🖃 *MC, V.*

$$–$$$ ✕**The Iron Squirrel.** Dark-wood paneling, colorful oil paintings, and black booths with crisp white tablecloths set the scene at this cozy French country eatery, known for its Veal Normandie (veal scaloppine sautéed with apples, calvados, and cream) and duck à l'orange. Fresh fish, grilled meats, pastas, and salads round out the menu. ⊠ *646 Pine Knot Blvd.* ☎ *909/ 866–9121* 🖃 *AE, MC, V* ☉ *No lunch.*

$$–$$$ ✕**Madlon's.** The menu at this gingerbread-style cottage includes sophisticated dishes such as lamb chops with Gorgonzola butter, cream of jalapeño soup, and Asian black-peppercorn filet mignon. Reservations are essential on weekends. ⊠ *829 W. Big Bear Blvd., Big Bear City* ☎ *909/ 585–3762* 🖃 *D, DC, MC, V* ☉ *Closed Mon. No lunch.*

$–$$$ ✕**Mandoline Bistro.** Locals looking to impress out-of-town guests make reservations at this Cal-fusion restaurant, known for its flavorful combinations of Mexican, Thai, Asian, and Island cuisine. The mountain-chic bistro, accented with stark black and white linens and antler chandeliers, serves up fusion cuisine like tempura avocados with raspberry remoulade, roasted duck salad with sweet walnuts and Gorgonzola cheese or Caribbean salmon with sticky rice and grilled bananas. ⊠ *40701 Village Dr.* ☎ *909/866–4200* 🖃 *AE, MC, V.*

★ $$–$$$ 🏠 **Apples Bed & Breakfast Inn.** Despite its location on a busy road to the ski lifts, the Apples Inn feels remote and peaceful, thanks to the surrounding pine trees. The colorful rooms have names such as Golden Delicious, Royal Gala, and Sweet Bough; all have gas fireplaces, and four have Jacuzzis. A common room has a wood-burning stove, baby grand piano, game table, and library loft. A full breakfast, afternoon refreshments, and evening dessert are included. ⊠ *42430 Moonridge Rd., 92315* ☎ *909/866–0903* ⊕ *www.applesbedandbreakfast.com* 🛏 *13 rooms* ♨ *Some in-room hot tubs, cable TV, in-room DVDs, in-room VCRs,*

Wi-Fi, outdoor hot tub, paddle tennis, volleyball, meeting room; no a/c, no room phones, no smoking ⊟ *AE, D, MC, V* ⃝ *BP.*

$$–$$$ ▣ **Gold Mountain Manor.** This restored log mansion, originally built in 1928, has a wide porch under wooden eaves and an Adirondack-style swingset on the lawn. Each room has its own theme; the Clark Gable room, for example, contains the old Franklin stove that once graced Gable's and Carole Lombard's honeymoon suite. All rooms have fireplaces and log beds original to the house. The common area has a TV, a VCR, and a collection of videos. Afternoon hors d'oeuvres and wine are included. ⊠ *1117 Anita Ave., off North Shore Dr., Big Bear City 92314* ☎ *909/585–6997 or 800/509–2604* 🖷 *909/585–0327* ⊕ *www.goldmountainmanor.com* ⇲ *4 rooms, 3 suites* ⬡ *Some in-room hot tubs, no-smoking rooms; no a/c, no room phones, no room TVs* ⊟ *AE, D, MC, V* ⃝ *BP.*

$$–$$$ ▣ **Northwoods Resort.** A giant log cabin with the amenities of a resort, Northwoods has a lobby that resembles a 1930s hunting lodge: canoes, antlers, fishing poles, and a grand stone fireplace all decorate the walls. Rooms are large but cozy; some have fireplaces and whirlpool tubs. Stillwells Restaurant, next to the lobby, serves hearty American fare. Ski packages are available. ⊠ *40650 Village Dr., 92315* ☎ *909/866–3121 or 800/866–3121* 🖷 *909/878–2122* ⊕ *www.northwoodsresort.com* ⇲ *138 rooms, 9 suites* ⬡ *2 restaurants, room service, some in-room hot tubs, cable TV with movies and video games, in-room data ports, Wi-Fi, pool, gym, outdoor hot tub, sauna, bar, concierge, meeting rooms, no-smoking rooms* ⊟ *AE, D, DC, MC, V.*

¢–$$$ ▣ **Robinhood Resort.** Across the street from the Pine Knot Marina, this family-oriented motel has rooms with fireplaces and some with whirlpool tubs or kitchenettes. Also available are several condos just feet from Snow Summit ski resort and deluxe spa rooms with in-room hot tubs, DVD players, and fireplaces. ⊠ *40797 Lakeview Dr., 92315* ☎ *909/866–4643 or 800/990–9956* 🖷 *909/866–4645* ⊕ *www.robinhoodresort.info* ⇲ *50 rooms, 8 condos* ⬡ *Restaurant, some in-room hot tubs, some kitchenettes, cable TV with movies, in-room VCRs, outdoor hot tub, bar, no-smoking rooms; no a/c in some rooms* ⊟ *AE, D, MC, V.*

Sports & the Outdoors

★ You don't have to be a mountain biker to enjoy Bear Mountain's **Scenic Sky Chair.** The lift takes you to the mountain's 8,400-foot peak, where you can lunch at View Haus (¢), a casual outdoor restaurant with breathtaking views of the lake and San Gorgonio mountain. Fare includes barbecued-chicken sandwiches, hot dogs, and burgers, along with cold beer and wine. ⊠ *43101 Goldmine Dr.* ☎ *909/866–5766* ⊕ *www. bigbearmountainresorts.com* ⊴ *$10 round-trip* ⊘ *Mid-June–early Sept., daily 9–4; early Sept.–mid-June, weekends, call for hrs.*

Looking for adventure? For $35, you can ride a horse through the snow-covered forest at **Baldwin Lake Stables** (☎ 909/585–6482 ⊕ www. baldwinlakestables.com). If you want to get out on the lake for a day, stop at **Big Bear Parasail and Water Sports** (⊠ 439 Pine Knot Ave., Big Bear Lake ☎ 909/866–4359) for waterskiing, tubing, and parasailing.

Jet Ski, water-ski, fishing boat, and equipment rentals are available from **Big Bear Marina** (⊠ Paine Rd. ☎ 909/866–3218). **Pine Knot Land-**

ing (✉ 439 Pine Knot ☎ 909/866–2628) rents fishing boats and sells bait, ice, and snacks.

SKIING **Big Bear Mountain Resorts** is Southern California's largest winter resort.
★ Here you can board more than 200 freestyle terrain features at Bear Mountain's massive snowboard terrain park, then shuttle 1 mi down the road to Snow Summit for its open skiing terrain and special area designed for kids. The megaresort offers 430 skiable acres, 55 runs, and 23 chairlifts, including four high-speed quads. An all-day lift ticket includes admission and shuttle rides at both resorts. On busy winter weekends and holidays it's best to reserve tickets before heading to either mountain. ✉ *Big Bear, 43101 Goldmine Dr., off Moonridge Rd.* ✉ *Snow Summit, 880 Summit Blvd., off Big Bear Blvd.* ☎ *909/866–5766* ⊕ *www.bigbearmountainresorts.com* 🎟 *$49; $62 peak season.*

THE SOUTHERN INLAND EMPIRE
THE SAN JACINTO MOUNTAINS & TEMECULA VALLEY

Life is quieter in the southern portion of the Inland Empire than it is to the north. In this corner of Riverside County, small towns such as Idyllwild and Temecula are oases of the good life for locals and visitors alike.

Idyllwild

⑪ *85 mi south of Big Bear Lake via Hwys. 18, 330, and 30, then I–10 east to Hwy. 243 south; 51 mi southeast of Rte. 60 east and Hwy. 243 south.*

Famous as a serene hideaway and artists' colony, the low-key and relaxed community of Idyllwild also has great rock climbing, hiking, and shopping. On weekends and by appointment May through November, Atipahato Lodge's **Idyllwild Tours** (☎ 951/659–2201 🎟 $10) operates narrated shuttle rides through the town's most scenic locations, including the Cahuilla Indian pictograph site, Idyllwild Arts Academy, and the famous rock-climbing area of Humber Park. On summer weekends, hitch a ride with **The Hay Dude Ranch** (☎ 951/659–0383 or 951/763–2473 ⊕ www.hayduderanch.com), with its $35 trail rides or occasional $20 horse-drawn carriage tours of downtown Idyllwild.

At the **Idyllwild Nature Center,** you can learn about the area's Native American history, try your hand at astronomy, and listen to traditional storytellers. Outside there are 3 mi of hiking trails, plus picnic areas. Native-plant lectures and wildflower walks are offered every Memorial Day weekend during the center's Wildflower Show. ✉ *25225 Hwy. 243* ☎ *951/659–3850* ⊕ *www.idyllwildnaturecenter.net* 🎟 *$2* ☉ *May–Sept., Thurs.–Sun. 9–4:30; Oct.–Apr., Fri.–Sun. 9–4.*

Where to Stay & Eat
★ **$–$$$** ✕ **Restaurant Gastrognome.** Elegant and dimly lighted, with wood paneling and an often-glowing fireplace, "The Gnome" is where locals go

for a romantic dinner with great food, a full bar, and nice ambience. The French onion soup is a standout appetizer; the calamari amandine and Southwest grilled pork are excellent entrées. The crème brûlée makes for a sweet finale. ☒ *54381 Ridgeview Dr.* ☏ *951/659–5055* ⊕ *www.gastrognome.com* ☰ *MC, V* ☺ *No lunch Mon.*

¢ ✕ **Oma's European Bakery and Restaurant.** Three generations of the Solleveld family run this breakfast and lunch spot, tempting early birds with hot *roerei* (a scramble of eggs, onions, and tomatoes) and cinnamon rolls. For lunch, don't miss the Black Forest ham on black bread with German *butterkase* (jack) cheese, or Oma's wurst platter, stacked high with three European links, red cabbage, or sauerkraut, and German potatoes. ☒ *54241 Ridgeview Dr.* ☏ *951/659–2979* ⊕ *www. omabakery.com* ☰ *MC, V* ☺ *No dinner.*

★ $$–$$$ ▦ **Strawberry Creek Inn.** This charming B&B nestled among the pines consistently draws raves from readers. Each room boasts Aveda bath products and fluffy white robes. Many rooms have wood-burning fireplaces. In the morning don't miss the inn's famous German-style French toast, topped with sliced Granny Smith apples, cinnamon sugar, and smoked bratwurst. The cottage is a nice honeymoon spot, equipped with a full kitchen, microwave, fireplace, and deck. ☒ *26370 Hwy. 243* ☏ *951/659–3202 or 800/262–8969* ⊕ *www.strawberrycreekinn.com* ⤶ *9 rooms, 1 cottage* ⌂ *Some refrigerators, some in-room VCRs, Wi-Fi* ☰ *D, MC, V* ⍰ *BP.*

¢–$$ ▦ **Atipahato Lodge.** Perfect for nature lovers, this woodsy retreat is on 5 acres of hilltop that overlook the San Jacinto Wilderness. Each room has pine-paneled walls, a vaulted ceiling, and a balcony. Each of two luxury cabins includes a fireplace, Jacuzzi, full kitchen, private deck, CD stereo, cable TV, and VCR. While you're here, check out the nature trail, which passes a springtime stream and waterfall and the Native American Nature Center. ☒ *25525 Hwy. 243, 92549* ☏ *888/ 400–0071* 🖷 *951/966–9822* ⊕ *www.atipahatolodge.com* ⤶ *18 rooms, 2 cabins* ⌂ *Some in-room hot tubs, kitchenettes, some microwaves, refrigerators, some in-room VCRs, meeting rooms; no a/c in some rooms* ☰ *AE, D, MC, V.*

¢–$$ ▦ **Cedar Street Inn and Spa.** This Victorian-style inn, made from two converted 1930s homes, offers suites within walking distance of the village and hiking trails. Most rooms have knotty-pine walls and are decorated with antiques and quilts. If you're on a budget, the cozy Attic Room, accessed by a spiral staircase, is a good choice for its views of the trees. The inn also rents out cabins; the Hobbit House comes with its own Jacuzzi, wet bar, and sauna. The new on-site massage studio has Swedish, deep-tissue, and sacred-stone massages starting at $95 for one hour. ☒ *25880 Cedar St., 92549* ☏ *951/659–4789* 🖷 *951/659–1049* ⊕ *www. cedarstreetinn.com* ⤶ *9 suites, 3 cabins* ⌂ *Refrigerators, cable TV with movies, some in-room VCRs, massage, Internet room, meeting rooms; no a/c* ☰ *D, MC, V.*

Sports & the Outdoors

FISHING **Lake Fulmor** (☒ Hwy. 243, 10 mi north of Idyllwild ☏ 951/659–2117) is stocked with rainbow trout, largemouth bass, catfish, and bluegill. To fish here you'll need a California fishing license and a National Forest Adventure Pass ($5 per vehicle per day). Adventure Passes are available at the **Idyllwild Ranger Station** (✉ Pine Crest Ave. off Hwy. 243 ☎ 951/659–2117).

HIKING Hike the 2.6-mi Ernie Maxwell Scenic Trail at **Humber Park** (✉ At top of Fern Valley Rd. ☎ 951/659–2117). Along the way you'll have views of Little Tahquitz Creek, Marion Mountain, and Suicide Rock. A permit is not required to hike this trail. The **Pacific Crest Trail** is accessible at Highway 74 1 mi east of Highway 371, or via the Fuller Ridge Trail at Black Mountain Road 15 mi north of Idyllwild. Permits ($5 per day) are required for camping and day hikes in San Jacinto Wilderness. They are available through the **Idyllwild Ranger Station** (✉ Pine Crest Ave. off Hwy. 243 ☎ 951/659–2117).

Temecula

▶ ⑫ *43 mi south of Riverside on I–15; 60 mi north of San Diego on I–15; 90 mi southeast of Los Angeles via I–10 and I–15.*

In the mood for wine and romance but can't make it to northern California? Temecula, with its rolling green vineyards, comfy country inns, and first-rate restaurants, makes a fine alternative to Napa Valley. There are 20 wineries in the Temecula Valley, with still more being built. The name Temecula comes from a Luiseno Indian word meaning "where the sun shines through the mist"—ideal conditions for wine growing. Intense afternoon sun and cool nighttime temperatures, complemented by ocean breezes that flow through the Rainbow and Santa Margarita gaps in the coastal range, help grapevines flourish in the area's granitic soil. The Temecula Valley is known for chardonnay, merlot, and sauvignon blanc, but in recent years there has been a trend toward viognier, syrah, and pinot gris varietals. Most wineries charge a small fee ($2 to $6) for a tasting of several wines. For a map of the area's wineries, visit ⊕ www.temeculawines.org.

Temecula is more than just vineyards and tasting rooms. For a bit of old-fashioned fun, head to historic **Old Town Temecula** (✉ Front St. between Rancho California Rd. and Hwy. 79 ☎ 951/694–6412), a turn-of-the-20th-century cluster of storefronts and boardwalks that holds more than 640 antiques stores, boutiques, and art galleries. This is where special events such as the Rod Run, Frontier Days Rodeo, and Fall Car Cruise take place. A farmers' market is held here every Saturday from 8 to noon.

☾ If you have the kids along, check out the **Imagination Workshop,** the fictional 7,500-square-foot home of Professor Phineas T. Pennypickle, PhD. This elaborately decorated children's center is filled with secret passageways, machines, wacky contraptions, and time-travel inventions, making it an imaginative way to spend the afternoon. ✉ *42081 Main St.* ☎ *951/308–6370 or 951/308–6476* ⊕ *www.pennypickles.org* ✆ *$4.50* ☾ *Tues.–Sat. 10–5.*

In September check out the annual **Temecula Valley International Film Festival** (☎ 951/699–6267 ⊕ www.tviff.com), which has honored celebs including the late Ray Charles, Carl Reiner, and Michael York. The event also is host to film-industry workshops, panel discussions, and seminars, all open to the public. Temecula holds its annual **Balloon and Wine Festival** (☎ 951/676–6713) each June. The spectacular event includes 50 hot-air balloons, a gourmet food court, a wine-tasting garden, and live music.

Most of the Temecula wineries are close to each other on Rancho California Road. If you plan to visit several wineries (and taste a lot of wine), catch the **Grapeline Wine Country Shuttle** (✉ 29909 Corte Castille ☎ 951/693–5463 or 888/894–6379 ⊕ www.gogrape.com ✆ $38), which operates weekends and some holidays. Private shuttles are available daily. The Cabernet Picnic Tour, at $75 ($85 Saturday), includes transportation, a wine-making demonstration, free tastings at four wineries, and a gourmet picnic lunch catered by Allie's at Callaway.

Baily Vineyard & Winery has grown to include an 8,000-square-foot wine-making facility with 50,000 gallons of wine tanks. Most folks come here for their two noteworthy restaurants, Carol's and Baily's. In the tasting room, browse the gourmet gift shop before sampling the cabernet, Riesling, and muscat blanc. ✉ *33440 La Serena Way* ☎ *909/676–9463* ⊕ *www.baily.com* ✆ *Free; $5 tastings* ☉ *Sun.–Fri. 11–5, Sat. 10–5.*

Established in 1969, **Callaway Coastal Vineyards** is well known for chardonnays and merlots by winemaker Art Villarreal. Complimentary tours are offered weekdays at 11, 1, and 3, and on weekends 11 to 4 on the hour. You are welcome to picnic in the arbor or dine alfresco at the vineyard-view **Allie's** (☎ 951/694–0560), which serves California–Mediterranean fare. ✉ *32720 Rancho California Rd.* ☎ *951/676–4001* ⊕ *www.callawaywinery.com* ✆ *Free; $5 tastings* ☉ *Daily 10:30–5.*

Bringing a bit of French-country elegance to Temecula, **Churon Winery** welcomes you to its tasting room via a winding stone staircase. Try winemaker Marshall Stuart's cabernet sauvignon, viognier, chenin blanc, and syrah at the large, dark-wood bar, which has ample seating and doubles as a fine art gallery. A deli offers gourmet items that you can take outside to the gorgeous patio. ✉ *33233 Rancho California Rd.* ☎ *951/694–9070* ⊕ *www.innatchuronwinery.com* ✆ *Free; $6 tastings* ☉ *Daily 10–5.*

Falkner Winery's big Western-style barn with its wraparound deck overlooking the vineyards is a great spot to enjoy Temecula's cool ocean breezes. Falkner has garnered great word-of-mouth, especially for their red Tuscan Amante. Winemaker Steve Hagata is also known for his viognier, chardonnay, and Riesling. Packaged snacks, along with a huge variety of gourmet gifts, are available in the shop. Tours are given at 11 AM on weekends. ✉ *40620 Calle Contento Rd.* ☎ *951/676–8231* ⊕ *www.falknerwinery.com* ✆ *Free; $6 tastings* ☉ *10–5 daily.*

Producing consistently delicious sparkling wines, cabernet sauvignons, and gewürztraminers, William Filsinger of **Filsinger Vineyards & Winery** carries on the wine-making traditions of his mother's family, which owned a winery in Germany. His son Eric has joined up as assistant winemaker. ✉ *39050 De Portola Rd.* ☎ *909/302–6363* ⊕ *www.filsingerwinery.com* ✆ *Free* ☉ *Fri. 11–4, weekends 10–5, Mon.–Thurs. by appointment.*

With Mediterranean varietals grown on 11 acres of vineyards in Temecula and in the nearby Cucamonga Valley, **Hart Winery** makes dry reds and the fortified dessert wine Italian Aleatico, named for the rare grape from which it comes. The purple tasting room is decked out with ribbons and medals won by the winery. ✉ *41300 Avenida Biona* ☎ *909/ 676–6300* 💳 *Free* 🕙 *Daily 9–4:30.*

Don't be surprised to come upon a barbecue or equestrian event at **Keyways Vineyard & Winery,** which has an Old West feel. In the tasting room decorated with lanterns and antiques, you can listen to country music while sampling tasty reds such as the zinfandel or Cabernet Franc. ✉ *37338 DePortola Rd.* ☎ *909/302–7888* ⊕ *www.keywayswinery1. com* 💳 *Free* 🕙 *Daily 10–5.*

Maurice Car'rie Vineyard & Winery, housed in an 1800s-style farmhouse, is one of the few Temecula wineries that offers complimentary tastings. Winemaker Gus Vizgirda works with 16 different varietals, producing wines such as a light and fruity pineapple-flavored sparkling wine. The wines are fairly sweet, but readers rave about the whites. On your way out, stop by the gourmet shop for a chunk of homemade sourdough-and-Brie bread. ✉ *34225 Rancho California Rd.* ☎ *951/676–1711* ⊕ *www.mauricecarriewinery.com* 💳 *Free* 🕙 *Daily 10–5.*

Perched on a hilltop, **Miramonte Winery** is Temecula's hippest, thanks to the vision of owner Cane Vanderhoof, who replanted the vineyard in almost 100% syrah grapes. Listen to Spanish-guitar recordings while sampling the Opulente meritage, a supple sauvignon blanc, or the smooth Cinsault rosé. On Friday and Saturday nights from 5 to 8, the winery turns into a hot spot with signature wines ($6 to $8), gourmet meals ($8 to $10), live flamenco music, and dancing that spills out into the vineyards. You can take a wine-tasting class or view film classics such as *Casablanca* on monthly movie nights ($15). ✉ *33410 Rancho California Rd.* ☎ *951/506–5500* ⊕ *www.miramontewinery.com* 💳 *Free; $7 tastings* 🕙 *Tastings daily 10–5.*

★ **Mount Palomar Winery** is generally considered to produce the best wines in Temecula. Winemaker Etienne Cowper trained under Jed Steele of Kendall-Jackson and Villa Mt. Eden fame, and with Andre Tchelistcheff, a mentor of Robert Mondavi and creator (at Beaulieu Vineyards in the 1930s) of California's first world-class cabernets. Mount Palomar was the first winery to introduce sangiovese grapes to Temecula, and the variety has proven perfectly suited to the region's soil and climate. In a Spanish colonial–style building, the tasting room offers must-tries such as red meritage, white cortese, and a cream sherry to die for. If you want to picnic on the grounds, stop by the deli for top-notch potato salad and Italian-style sandwiches. ✉ *33820 Rancho California Rd.* ☎ *951/ 676–5047* ⊕ *www.mountpalomar.com* 💳 *Free; $5 tastings* 🕙 *Daily 10–4.*

Palumbo Family Vineyards & Winery occupies a converted garage, but there's something charming about the place. Grab a glass of the Bordeaux-style blend, Tre Fratelli, and enjoy a chat with the owners on the little white deck outside. For $75 per person, Palumbo—who is a chef as well as a winemaker—will prepare a private dinner for 2 to 10 guests; dishes might include a petit filet mignon with a sauce of *cambazola* (a soft blue cheese), with truffle-oil mashed potatoes and baby broccoli with beurre noisette. Palumbo pours and discusses the wine. ⊠ *40150 Barksdale Circle* ☎ *909/676–7900* ⊗ *Weekends 10–5, weekdays by appointment.*

★ Lush gardens and 350 acres of vineyards welcome you onto **Ponte Family Estates,** a rustic winery that's a hot spot for tour groups. In the open-beamed tasting room, you can sample six different varietals, including cabernet, syrah (recommended by readers), viognier, and chardonnay. The open-air marketplace sells artisan ceramics, specialty foods, and wine country gift baskets. Around lunchtime, the winery's Smokehouse Cafe buzzes with guests who come for the wood-fired Vineyard Pizza, topped with rose muscat grapes, fresh rosemary, red onion, and aged fontina cheese, or the bacon-wrapped grilled barbecue meat loaf served with rustic fried potato wedges. ⊠ *35053 Rancho California Rd.* ☎ *951/694–8855* ⊕ *www.pontewinery.com* ☒ *Free; $8 tastings* ⊗ *Daily 10–5.*

Temecula's best-kept secret, stellar **Santa Margarita Winery** produces the best cabs in the area. They also make a good sauvignon blanc and chardonnay. The small, unassuming winery isn't shown on most maps, but you'll be glad you found it. Owner Barret Bird is a friendly, salt-of-the-earth soul who really knows his wine, and tastings are free. ⊠ *33490 Madera de Playa, off Calle Contento Rd.* ☎ *909/676–4431* ☒ *Free* ⊗ *Weekends 11–4:30.*

FodorśChoice A rambling French Mediterranean–style stone building houses **Thornton** ★ **Winery,** a producer best known for its sparkling wine. You can taste wine-maker Don Reha's outstanding brut reserve and cuvée rouge at a table in the lounge, or along with some food at Café Champagne. Readers rave about the pinot blanc. On the weekend, take a free tour of the grounds and the wine cave. Summer smooth-jazz concerts (admission is charged) and elaborate winemaker dinners ($80 to $90) make this a fun place to spend an evening. Tastings here—$9 for four tastes; $12 for all four champagnes; $15 for reserve wines plus two champagnes and two reds—are pricier than at other area wineries. ⊠ *32575 Rancho California Rd.* ☎ *951/699–0099* ⊕ *www.thorntonwine.com* ☒ *Free* ⊗ *Daily 10–5.*

A small stream winds through flower gardens and vineyards at peaceful, parklike **Wilson Creek Winery & Vineyard.** In the huge tasting room you'll find a little bit of heaven in the "Decadencia" chocolate port and the almond Oh-My-Gosh sparkling wine, much loved by Fodor's readers. ⊠ *35960 Rancho California Rd.* ☎ *951/699–9463* ⊕ *www. wilsoncreekwinery.com* ☒ *Free; $7 tastings* ⊗ *Daily 10–5.*

Where to Stay & Eat

$$–$$$$ ✕ **Café Champagne.** The spacious patio, with its bubbling fountain,
FodorśChoice flowering trellises, and views of Thornton Winery's vineyards, is the per-
★ fect place to lunch on a sunny day. Inside, the dining room is decked out in French-country style, and the kitchen turns out such dishes as crispy roast duck breast drizzled with ginger-lavender honey sauce. The eclectic menu is complemented by a reasonably priced wine list featuring Italian, French, and California wines—including, of course, Thornton sparklers. Sunday brunch is accompanied by live accordion and violin

music. ⊠ *32575 Rancho California Rd.* ☎ *951/699–0088* ⊕ *www. thorntonwine.com/cafe.html* ▭ *AE, D, MC, V.*

★ ¢ ✕ **Carol's.** Gray stone walls and a shining suit of armor welcome you to this genteel lunch spot beside the tasting room at Baily Vineyard & Winery. Wine-friendly dishes such as chicken and smoked gouda on a croissant, and a vineyard salad with cabernet-citrus vinaigrette, often include produce from the garden outside. ⊠ *33440 La Serena Way* ☎ *951/ 676–9243* ▭ *AE, MC, V* ⊙ *Closed Mon. and Tues.*

$$$ ✕▦ **Temecula Creek Inn.** If you want the relaxation of the wine country and the challenge of hitting the links on a championship golf course, this is the place for you. Each room has a private patio or balcony over-looking the course and is decorated in soothing earth tones with a southwestern theme. The on-site restaurant, Temet Grill ($$–$$$) serves regional fare and local wines. Try the seared buffalo tenderloin with brandied green-peppercorn sauce or the herbed seared chicken breast with sundried tomato and sweet vermouth jus. ⊠ *44501 Rainbow Canyon Rd., 92592* ☎ *951/694–1000 or 800/962–7335* ⊕ *www. temeculacreekinn.com* ⊅ *120 rooms, 10 suites* ⚘ *Restaurant, café, minibars, refrigerators, cable TV, some in-room broadband, in-room data ports, 27-hole golf course, pool, gym, hot tub, lounge, meeting rooms* ▭ *AE, D, MC, V.*

★ $$$–$$$$ ▦ **South Coast Winery Resort and Spa.** Temecula's wine community recently added this luxurious resort. Locals and readers highly recommend its vineyard villas, which are spacious, and have marble bathrooms, private patios, and flickering fireplaces. Readers particularly appreciate that there are no common walls between the villas, making their stay quieter than at most resorts. The spa has 13 treatment rooms, featuring such services as Merlot Masks and Grapeseed Body Scrubs. The on-site Vineyard Rose Restaurant serves up Asian, European, and Southwest cuisine. ⊠ *34843 Rancho California Rd.* ☎ *951/587–9463* ⊕ *www. wineresort.com* ⊅ *76 villas* ⚘ *Restaurant, minibars, in-room safes, Wi-Fi, 2 outdoor hot tubs, pool, spa, massage, parking (free); no smoking* ▭ *AE, MC, V.*

★ $$–$$$ ▦ **Inn at Churon Winery.** You'll feel like royalty when you stay at this château-style winery perched on a hill overlooking manicured gardens and vineyards. Butter-yellow hallways lead to a library nook, where you can relax over a cup of coffee by the fire. Rooms are decorated with French antiques and outfitted with gas-burning fireplaces and marble hot tubs. Each evening a private wine reception is held in the tasting room, with crusty homemade pizza for nibbling. ⊠ *33233 Rancho California Rd., 92591* ☎ *951/694–9070* ⊕ *www.innatchuronwinery. com* ⊅ *16 rooms, 6 suites* ⚘ *Dining room, grocery, picnic area, in-room hot tubs, cable TV, in-room data ports, meeting rooms; no smoking* ▭ *AE, D, DC, MC, V* ⑽ *BP.*

Shopping

While you're shopping in Old Town, stop by the **Temecula Olive Oil Company** tasting room for a sample of its extra-virgin olive oils, bath products, and Mission, Ascalano, and Italian olives. ⊠ *42030 Main St., Suite H* ☎ *866/654–8396* ⊙ *Daily 9–5.*

Sports & the Outdoors

GOLF Temecula has seven championship golf courses cooled by the valley's ocean breezes. **Redhawk Golf Club** (⊠ 45100 Redhawk Pkwy. ☎ 951/302–3850 ⊕ www.redhawkgolfcourse.com) has an 18-hole championship course designed by Ron Fream. For a special treat, head to the **Temecula Creek Inn Golf Resort** (⊠ 44501 Rainbow Canyon Rd. ☎ 951/676–2405 ⊕ www.temeculacreekinn.com), whose 27-hole course was designed by Ted Robinson and Dick Rossen.

HOT-AIR BALLOONING If you're in the mood to swoop or float above Temecula's green vineyards and country estates, sign up for a trip with **California Dreamin' Balloon & Biplane Rides** (☎ 800/373–3359 ⊕ www.californiadreamin.com). Balloon trips depart from the company's vineyards at 5:30 AM; the $158 per-person fee includes champagne, coffee, a pastry breakfast, and a souvenir photo.

THE INLAND EMPIRE ESSENTIALS

To research prices, get advice from other travelers, and book travel arrangements, visit www.fodors.com.

AIR TRAVEL

Aero Mexico, Alaska, America West, American, Continental, Delta, Frontier, Hawaiian, JetBlue, Lineas Aereas Azteca, Northwest, Southwest, United, and United Express serve Ontario International Airport. ⇨ Air Travel *in* Smart Travel Tips A to Z for airline phone numbers.

🛪 **Ontario International Airport** ⊠ Airport Dr., Archibald Ave. exit off I-10, Ontario ⊕ www.lawa.org ☎ 866/456–3900 or 909/937–2700.

BUS TRAVEL

Greyhound serves Claremont, Corona, Fontana, Moreno Valley, Perris, Riverside, San Bernardino, and Temecula. Most stations are open daily during business hours; some are open 24 hours.

The Foothill Transit Bus Line serves Pomona, Claremont, and Montclair, with stops at Cal Poly and the Fairplex. Riverside Transit Authority (RTA) serves Riverside and some outlying communities, as does OmniTrans.

🛪 **Foothill Transit** ☎ 800/743–3463 ⊕ www.foothilltransit.org. **Greyhound** ☎ 800/231–2222 ⊕ www.greyhound.com. **OmniTrans** ☎ 800/966–6428 ⊕ www.omnitrans.org. **Riverside Transit Authority** ☎ 800/800–7821 ⊕ www.rrta.com.

CAR TRAVEL

Avoid Highway 91 if possible; it's almost always backed up from Corona through Orange County.

🛪 **California Highway Patrol 24-hour road info** ☎ 800/427–7623 ⊕ www.dot.ca.gov/hq/roadinfo.

EMERGENCIES

In an emergency dial 911.

🛪 **Parkview Community Hospital** ⊠ 3865 Jackson St., Riverside ☎ 951/688–2211. **Rancho Springs Medical Center** ⊠ 25500 Medical Center Dr., Murrieta ☎ 909/696–

6000. **Riverside Community Hospital** ✉ 4445 Magnolia Ave., Riverside ☎ 951/788–3000. **St. Bernardine Medical Center** ✉ 2101 N. Waterman Ave., San Bernardino ☎ 909/883–8711. **San Bernardine County Sheriff** ☎ 909/955–2444.

TRAIN TRAVEL

■ TIP→ **Many locals use the Metrolink to get around, which is clean and quick, and generally a much nicer way to travel than by bus.**

Metrolink has several Inland Empire stations on its Inter-County, San Bernardino, and Riverside rail lines. The Riverside Line connects downtown Riverside, Pedley, East Ontario, and downtown Pomona with City of Industry and with Union Station in Los Angeles. The Inter-County Rail Line connects San Bernardino, downtown Riverside, Riverside La Sierra, and West Corona with San Juan Capistrano and Orange County. Metrolink's busiest train, the San Bernardino Line, connects Pomona, Claremont, Montclair, and San Bernardino with the San Gabriel Valley and downtown Los Angeles. Bus service extends the reach of train service, to spots including Ontario Airport, the Claremont Colleges, and the Fairplex at Pomona. You can buy tickets and passes at the ticket vending machine at each station, or by telephone. A recorded message announces Metrolink schedules 24 hours a day.

🚆 **Metrolink** ☎ 800/371-5465 ⊕ www.metrolinktrains.com.

VISITOR INFORMATION

🚆 **Big Bear Lake Resort Association** ✉ 630 Bartlett Rd., Big Bear Lake 92315 ☎ 909/866-7000 or 800/424-4232 🖷 909/866-5671 ⊕ www.bigbearinfo.com. **Claremont Chamber of Commerce** ✉ 205 Yale Ave., Claremont 91711 ☎ 909/624-1681 ⊕ www.claremontchamber.org. **Corona Chamber of Commerce** ✉ 904 E. 6th St., Corona 92879 ☎ 951/737-3350 ⊕ www.coronachamber.org. **Idyllwild Chamber of Commerce** ✉ 54295 Village Center Dr., Box 304, Idyllwild 92549 ☎ 951/659-3259 or 888/659-3259 ⊕ www.idyllwild.com. **Lake Arrowhead Communities Chamber of Commerce** ✉ 28200 Hwy. 189, Bldg. F, Suite 290, Box 219, Lake Arrowhead 92352 ☎ 909/337-3715 🖷 909/336-1548 ⊕ www.lakearrowhead.com. **Ontario Convention & Visitors Authority** ✉ 2000 Convention Center Way, Ontario 91764 ☎ 909/937-3000 ⊕ www.ontariocc.com. **Pomona Chamber of Commerce** ✉ 401 S. Main St., #210, Pomona 91769 ☎ 909/622-1256 ⊕ www.pomonachamber.org. **Redlands Chamber of Commerce** ✉ 1 E. Redlands Blvd., Redlands 92373 ☎ 909/793-2546 ⊕ www.redlandschamber.org. **Riverside Convention and Visitors Bureau** ✉ 3750 University Ave., #175, Riverside 92501 ☎ 888/748-7733 or 951/222-4700 ⊕ www.riversidecb.com. **Temecula Valley Chamber of Commerce** ✉ 26790 Ynez Ct., Temecula 92591 ☎ 951/676-5090 ⊕ www.temecula.org. **Wrightwood Chamber of Commerce** ✉ Box 416, Wrightwood 92397 ☎ 760/249-4320, 760/249-6822 for recorded information ⊕ www.wrightwoodcalif.com.

Palm Springs &
the Southern Desert

WITH JOSHUA TREE NATIONAL PARK

WORD OF MOUTH

"We toured California for 2 weeks and Joshua Tree National Park was our favorite. Absolutely stunning land. Rent a 4-wheel drive and go off-roading, or better yet, camp overnight. We got out and took hiking trails. Don't miss this place if you're visiting Palm Springs!"

—Jill2

"The Palm Springs Aerial Tramway is the longest span of any gondola in the world and only the second spinning gondola in the world. Most of all it is a great way to see the whole valley and the mountains beyond. A not to be missed attraction."

—Blane

Updated by
Bobbi Zane

IMAGINE THE DESERT HERE AS THE BOTTOM OF A VAST SEA. Many millions of years ago, that's what it was. By 10 million years ago, the waters had receded and the climate was hospitable to prehistoric mastodons, zebras, and camels. As recently as 10,000 years ago, the Colorado River still spilled into this basin intermittently, and around AD 700 Lake Cahuilla formed. The first human inhabitants of record were the Agua Caliente, part of the Cahuilla people, who settled in and around the Coachella Valley (the northwestern portion of the Colorado Desert, between the San Jacinto and Little San Bernardino mountain ranges) about 1,000 years ago. Lake Cahuilla dried up about 300 years ago, but by then the Agua Caliente had discovered the area's hot springs and were making use of their healing properties during winter visits to the desert. The springs became a tourist attraction in 1871, when the tribe built a bathhouse (on a site near the current Spa Resort Casino in Palm Springs) to serve passengers on a pioneer stage highway. The Agua Caliente still own about 32,000 acres of desert, 6,700 of which lie within the city limits of Palm Springs.

In the last half of the 19th century, farmers established a date-growing industry at the southern end of the Coachella Valley. By 1900 word had spread about the manifold health benefits of the area's dry climate, inspiring the gentry of the northern United States to winter under the warm desert sun. In the mid-1900s, farmers southeast of the Coachella had transformed the barren Imperial Valley—home of the broad, brackish Salton Sea—into rich fields of tomatoes, corn, and grain. The Anza-Borrego Desert, which stretches from the southern end of the Coachella Valley nearly to the Mexican border, was then a mostly unpopulated desert outpost occupied by a few hardy homesteaders and visited in winter by a few adventurous campers. Growth hit the Coachella Valley in the 1970s, when developers began to construct the fabulous golf courses, country clubs, and residential communities that would draw celebrities, tycoons, and politicians. Communities sprang up south and east of what is now Palm Springs, creating a sprawl of tract houses and strip malls and forcing nature lovers to push farther south into the sparsely settled Anza-Borrego Desert and the Imperial Valley.

Exploring the Southern Desert

The desert resort cities of the Coachella Valley—Palm Springs, Cathedral City, Rancho Mirage, Palm Desert, Indian Wells, La Quinta, and Indio—are strung out along Highway 111, with Palm Springs at the northwestern end of this strip and Indio at the southeastern end. North of Palm Springs, between Interstate 10 and Highway 62, is Desert Hot Springs. Northeast of Palm Springs, the towns of the Morongo Valley lie along Twentynine Palms Highway (Highway 62), which leads to Joshua Tree National Park. Head south on Highway 86 from Indio to reach Anza-Borrego State Park and the Salton Sea. All of the area's attractions are easy day trips from Palm Springs.

About the Restaurants

Long a culinary wasteland, the desert now supports many trendy restaurants. Italian cuisine remains popular, but you can now dine at restaurants that serve fare from Thai to Indian to Brazilian, from seafood to vegetarian, and from classic French to contemporary Californian. You can find Mexican food everywhere; in the smaller communities it may be your best choice. Dining throughout the region is casual. Many restaurants that were traditionally closed in summer (the off-season) are now open on a limited basis and offer deep discounts during this time; hours vary, so call ahead.

About the Hotels

You can stay in the desert for as little as $40–or spend more than $1,000 a night. Rates vary widely by season: hotel prices are frequently 50% less in summer than in winter and early spring. January through May prices soar, and accommodations can be difficult to secure, so reserve as far ahead as you can. In any season it pays to inquire about hotel and resort packages that include extras such as golf or spa services. Some desert hotels add an optional–and sometimes not advertised–resort fee of $10 to $25 to the daily rate; covered by the fee may be parking, spa admission, use of high-speed Internet connections, daily newspaper, and airport shuttle service.

Palm Springs has a growing number of small boutique hotels and bed-and-breakfasts that have historical character and offer good value; they are listed separately below. Discounts are sometimes given for extended stays. Year-round, budget lodgings are most easily found in Palm Springs and in the less glamorous towns of Cathedral City, Indio, Borrego Springs, El Centro, and in the Morongo Valley towns along Twentynine Palms Highway.

WHAT IT COSTS				
	$$$$	**$$$**	**$$**	**$**	**¢**
RESTAURANTS	over $30	$23–$30	$16–$22	$10–$15	under $10
HOTELS	over $250	$176–$250	$121–$175	$90–$120	under $90

Restaurant prices are for a main course at dinner, excluding sales tax of 7¼%. Hotel prices are for two people in a standard double room in high season, excluding service charges and 9%–13.5% tax.

Timing

Because Palm Springs and the surrounding desert average 350 sunny days a year, you are almost assured a chance to get in a round or two of golf or some lounging by the pool whenever you visit. During the season (January through May), as everybody calls it, the desert weather is at its best, with daytime temperatures ranging between 70°F and 90°F. This is the time when you're most likely to see colorful displays of wildflowers and when most of the golf and tennis tournaments take place. The fall months are nearly as lovely, with the added bonus of being less crowded and less expensive. In summer, daytime temperatures may rise above 110°F, though evenings cool to the mid-70s. Some attractions and restaurants, particularly those in the Borrego Springs area, close during this period.

GREAT ITINERARIES

Numbers correspond to the Palm Springs and Southern Desert maps.

IF YOU HAVE 1 DAY

If you've just slipped into the desert for a day, focus your activities around ► **Palm Springs** ❶–❿. Get an early-morning scenic overview by taking the **Palm Springs Aerial Tramway** ❶ to the top of Mt. San Jacinto. In the afternoon head for Palm Canyon Drive, where you can have lunch and pick up tickets for an evening performance of the Fabulous Palm Springs Follies (better still, make reservations before your visit). You can also visit **Palm Desert** ⓭, the trendiest of the desert cities, for a walk through the canyons and hillsides of the Living Desert Zoo and Gardens and a preshow dinner at a restaurant on El Paseo.

IF YOU HAVE 3 DAYS

▣ **Palm Springs** ❶–❿ ► makes a good base for exploring the area. On your first day head to the **Palm Springs Aerial Tramway** ❶ in the morning and have lunch at a sidewalk café on Palm Canyon Drive. Spend the afternoon browsing through the Uptown District shops or (unless it's the height of summer) hiking through the **Indian Canyons** ❿. On Day 2 take an early-morning drive to **Twentynine Palms** ⓭ and Joshua Tree National Park, where you can explore the terrain, crawl through the entrance to Hidden Valley, and stop by the Oasis Visitor Center. Have a picnic lunch in the park or head back to El Paseo, in **Palm Desert** ⓭, for a midafternoon bite before exploring the chic shopping area. On the third morning take in the **Palm Springs Art Museum** ❹. In the afternoon

pamper yourself at a spa, then have dinner and take in a performance of the Fabulous Palm Springs Follies.

IF YOU HAVE 5 DAYS

If you have five days to spend in the desert, you'll have time to explore beyond the immediate ▣ **Palm Springs** ❶–❿ ► area. On your first day take in a sweeping view of the Coachella Valley from the top of the **Palm Springs Aerial Tramway** ❶ in the morning, and stroll along Palm Canyon Drive in the afternoon. On the second morning visit the **Palm Springs Art Museum** ❹. Then grab a picnic lunch and head out to **Indian Canyons** ❿, where you can eat by a waterfall. By evening you'll be ready to live it up at one of the desert's nightspots. Spend Days 3 and 4 at Joshua Tree National Park. You can camp in the park or stay at a B&B in ▣ **Twentynine Palms** ⓭, just outside the park. In the evening, be sure to gaze at the stars. On Day 5 get an early start and complete your drive through the park so you can arrive back in the Palm Springs area for lunch. Check into a spa for the afternoon, and catch the Fabulous Palm Springs Follies on your last night.

Alternatively, you can spend Days 3 and 4 in quiet ▣ **Borrego Springs** ⓴, exploring the wonders of Anza-Borrego Desert State Park and the **Salton Sea** ㉑. On the fifth morning drive to **Palm Desert** ⓭ to visit the Living Desert Zoo and Gardens, have lunch on El Paseo, do some shopping, and head back to your hotel for one last dip in the pool.

5

THE DESERT RESORTS
INCLUDING PALM SPRINGS

Around the desert resorts, privacy is the watchword. Celebrities flock to the desert from Los Angeles, and many communities are walled and guarded. Still, you might spot Hollywood stars, sports personalities, politicians, and other high-profile types in restaurants, out on the town, or on a golf course. For the most part, the desert's social, sports, shopping, and entertainment scenes center on Palm Springs and Palm Desert.

Palm Springs

90 mi southeast of Los Angeles on I–10.

▶ A major tourist destination since the late 19th century, Palm Springs had already caught Hollywood's eye by the time of the Great Depression. It was an ideal hideaway: celebrities could slip into town, play a few sets of tennis, lounge around the pool, attend a party or two, and, unless things got out of hand, remain safely beyond the reach of gossip columnists. But it took a pair of tennis-playing celebrities to put Palm Springs on the map. In the 1930s actors Charlie Farrell and Ralph Bellamy bought 200 acres of land for $30 an acre and opened the Palm Springs Racquet Club, which soon listed Ginger Rogers, Humphrey Bogart, and Clark Gable among its members.

During its slow, steady growth period from the 1930s to 1970s, the Palm Springs area drew some of the world's most famous architects to design homes for the rich and famous. The collected works, inspired by the mountains and desert sands and notable for the use of glass and indoor–outdoor space, became known as Palm Springs Modernism. The city lost some of its luster in the 1970s as the wealthy moved to newer down-valley communities. But Palm Springs reinvented itself in the 1990s, restoring the bright and airy old houses and hotels, and cultivating a welcoming atmosphere for well-heeled gay visitors.

You'll find reminders of the city's glamorous past in its unique architecture and renovated hotels; change and progress are evidenced by trendy restaurants and upscale shops. Formerly exclusive Palm Canyon Drive is now a lively avenue filled with coffeehouses, outdoor cafés, and bars.

■ TIP➔ **Note: Tahquitz Canyon Way marks the division between north and south on major streets (e.g., North and South Palm Canyon Drive).**

★ ☾ ❶ A trip on the **Palm Springs Aerial Tramway** provides a 360-degree view of the desert through the picture windows of rotating tram cars. The 2½-mi ascent through Chino Canyon, the steepest vertical cable ride in the United States, brings you to an elevation of 8,516 feet in less than 20 minutes. On clear days, which are common, the view stretches 75 mi—from the peak of Mt. San Gorgonio in the north, to the Salton Sea in the southeast. At the top, a bit below the summit of Mt. San Jacinto, are several diversions. Mountain Station has an observation deck, a restaurant, a cocktail lounge, apparel and gift shops, picnic facilities, and a theater

IF YOU LIKE

DESERT WILDLIFE

The southern desert is a land of fascinating geology and wildlife. Explore the terrain at ground level at the Living Desert Zoo and Gardens. Other great places to learn about the natural history of the desert are Indian Canyons, Joshua Tree National Park, Anza-Borrego State Park, and along the shores of the Salton Sea.

NIGHTLIFE & THE ARTS

Nightlife is concentrated—and abundant—in the Palm Springs resort communities. Options include a good jazz bar, a clutch of retro shows and glamorous clubs, several dance clubs, and hotel entertainment. The Fabulous Palm Springs Follies—a vaudeville-style revue starring retired professional performers—is a must-see for most visitors. Arts festivals occur on a regular basis, especially in winter and spring. The "Desert Guide" section of *Palm Springs Life* magazine (available at most hotels and visitor information centers) has nightlife listings, as does the "Weekender" pullout in the Friday edition of the *Desert Sun* newspaper. The gay scene is covered in the *Bottom Line* and in the *Gay Guide to Palm Springs*, published by the Desert Gay Tourism Guild.

SPORTS & THE OUTDOORS

The Palm Springs area has more than 100 golf courses, many of which are familiar to fans of the sport as the sites of championship and celebrity tournaments seen on television. You can tee off where the pros play at PGA West, Mission Hills North, and La Quinta, all of which have instructors ready to help you finesse your swing. Even Borrego Springs and El Centro have golf courses.

The desert holds a world of athletic opportunities for nongolfers, too. With almost 30,000 public and private pools in the region, swimming and sunning are a daily ritual. More than 35 mi of bike trails crisscross the mostly flat Palm Springs area alone. Indian Canyons, Mount San Jacinto State Park, Living Desert Zoo and Gardens, Joshua Tree National Park, Anza-Borrego State Park, and Big Morongo Canyon Preserve have scenic hiking trails. The Salton Sea attracts many migratory birds, especially in winter. Some of the best rock-climbing highways in the world are in Joshua Tree National Park.

Whatever your sport, avoid outdoor activities midday during the hot season (roughly May through October). Any time of the year, take precautions against the sun, such as wearing a hat and using sunscreen. Always drink plenty of water—at least a gallon of water per day (more if you are exercising)—to prevent dehydration.

SHOPPING

Designer boutiques, antiques shops, art galleries, vintage resale palaces, and a huge upmarket discount mall lure dedicated shoppers to the desert. Popular shopping venues include the Thursday-night Palm Springs Village Fest; El Paseo, in Palm Desert; Desert Hills Factory Stores, in Cabazon; and the consignment and resale shops in many desert communities.

5

that screens a worthwhile 22-minute film on the history of the tramway. Take advantage of free guided and self-guided nature walks, or if there's snow on the ground, rent skis, snowshoes, or snow tubes (inner tubes or similar contraptions for sliding down hills). ■ TIP→ **Ride-and-dine packages are available in late afternoon. The tram is a popular attraction; to avoid a two-hour or longer wait, arrive before the first car leaves.** ⊠ *1 Tramway Rd.* ☎ *760/325–1391 or 888/515–8726* ⊕ *www.pstramway.com* ✉ *$22; ride-and-dine package $34* ☉ *Tram cars depart at least every 30 min from 10 AM weekdays and 8 AM weekends; last car up leaves at 8 PM, last car down leaves Mountain Station at 9:45 PM.*

OFF THE BEATEN PATH

MOUNT SAN JACINTO STATE PARK – The park, accessible by hiking or via the Palm Springs Aerial Tramway, has primitive camping and picnic areas and 54 mi of hiking trails. The Nordic Ski Center rents cross-country ski equipment. You must get a free permit before coming for day or overnight wilderness hiking. ⊠ *Mountain Station* ☎ *951/659–2607* ⊕ *www.sanjac.statepark.org* ✉ *$20 camping.*

② Stop at the **Palm Springs Visitor Information Center,** near the Tramway, for information on sights to see and things to do in the area. ⊠ *2901 N. Palm Canyon Dr.* ☎ *760/778–8418 or 800/347–7746* ⊕ *www.palm-springs.org* ☉ *Weekdays 9–5.*

❸ A stroll down shop-lined Palm Canyon Drive will take you past the **Palm Springs Starwalk** (✉ Palm Canyon Dr. around Tahquitz Canyon Way, and Tahquitz Canyon Way between Palm Canyon and Indian Canyon Drs.), whose nearly 200 bronze stars are embedded in the sidewalk (à la the Hollywood Walk of Fame). Most of the names, all with a Palm Springs connection, are ones you'll recognize (such as Elvis Presley, Marilyn Monroe, Lauren Bacall, and Liberace). Others are local celebrities.

★ ❹ The **Palm Springs Art Museum** and its grounds hold several wide-ranging collections of contemporary and traditional art, including several striking sculpture courts and a modern-art gallery with works by such artists as Alberto Giacometti, Henry Moore, and Helen Frankenthaler. The permanent collection has a selection of studio art glass by Dale Chihuly and William Morris. You'll find sculpture by Frederic Remington and Charles Russell alongside a collection of handcrafted furniture by actor George Montgomery in the Western Art collection. Contemporary Native American artists Allen Houser, Arlo Namingha, and Fritz Scholder have sculpture on display in the Contemporary American Indian Collection. The Annenberg Theater presents plays, concerts, lectures, operas, and other cultural events. ✉ *101 Museum Dr.* ☎ *760/325–7186* ⊕ *www.psmuseum.org* 🎫 *$12.50 Oct.–May, $3 June–Sept.; free Thurs. 4–8 during Village Fest* ☉ *Oct.–May, Tues., Wed., and Fri.–Sun. 10–5, Thurs. noon–8; June–Sept., Wed. and Fri.–Sun. 10–5, Thurs. noon–8.*

❺ Three small museums at the **Village Green Heritage Center** illustrate pioneer life in Palm Springs. The **Agua Caliente Cultural Museum** (free) is devoted to the culture and history of the Cahuilla tribe. The **McCallum Adobe** ($2) holds the collection of the Palm Springs Historical Society. **Rudy's General Store Museum** (95¢) is a re-creation of a 1930s general store. ✉ *221 S. Palm Canyon Dr.* ☎ *760/327–2156* 🎫 *95¢* ☉ *Call for hrs.*

❻ Ranger-led tours of **Tahquitz Canyon** take you into a secluded canyon on the Agua Caliente Reservation. Within the canyon are a spectacular 60-foot waterfall, rock art, ancient irrigation systems, and native wildlife and plants. Tours are conducted several times daily; participants must be able to navigate 100 steep steps. A visitor center at the canyon entrance shows a video tour, displays artifacts, and sells maps. ✉ *500 W. Mesquite Ave.* ☎ *760/416–7044* ⊕ *www.tahquitzcanyon.com* 🎫 *$12.50* ☉ *Daily 7:30–5.*

❼ Four-acre **Moorten Botanical Garden** nurtures more than 3,000 plant varieties in settings that simulate their original environments. Native American artifacts, rock, and crystal are exhibited. ✉ *1701 S. Palm Canyon Dr.* ☎ *760/327–6555* 🎫 *$2.50* ☉ *Mon., Tues., and Thurs.–Sat. 9–4:30, Sun. 10–4.*

🧒 ❽ The **Palm Springs Air Museum** showcases 26 World War II aircraft, including a B-17 Flying Fortress bomber, a P-51 Mustang, a Lockheed P-38, and a Grumman TBF Avenger. Cool exhibits include a Grumman Goose into which kids can crawl, model warships, and a Pearl Harbor diorama. ⊠ *745 N. Gene Autry Trail* ☎ *760/778–6262* ⊕ *www.air-museum.org* ☎ *$10* ⊗ *Daily 10–5.*

☺ ❾ For a break from the desert heat, head to **Knott's Soak City.** You'll find 1950s-theme ambience complete with Woodies (antique station wagons from the 1950s), 13 waterslides, a huge wave pool, an arcade, and other fun family attractions. ⊠ *1500 S. Gene Autry Trail* ☎ *760/327–0499* ⊕ *www.knotts.com* ☎ *$27, $15 after 3* PM ⊗ *Mid-May–early Sept., daily; early Sept.–Oct., weekends; hrs 10–varying closing times.*

☺ ❿ The **Indian Canyons** are the ancestral home of the Agua Caliente, part of the Cahuilla people. You can see remnants of their ancient life, including rock art, house pits and foundations, irrigation ditches, bedrock mortars, pictographs, and stone houses and shelters built atop high cliff walls. Short, easy walks through the canyons reveal palm oases, waterfalls, and spring wildflowers. Tree-shaded picnic areas are abundant. The attraction includes three canyons open for touring: Palm Canyon, noted for its stand of Washingtonia palms; Murray Canyon, home of Peninsula bighorn sheep and a herd of wild ponies; and Andreas Canyon, where a stand of fan palms contrasts with sharp rock formations. Ranger-led hikes to Palm and Andreas canyons are offered daily for an additional charge. The trading post at the entrance to Palm Canyon has hiking maps and refreshments, as well as Native American art, jewelry, and weavings. ⊠ *38520 S. Palm Canyon Dr.* ☎ *800/790–3398* ⊕ *www.indian-canyons.com* ☎ *$8* ⊗ *Daily 8–5.*

Where to Eat

★ $$$–$$$$ ✕ **Le Vallauris.** Le Vallauris, in the historic Roberson House, is popular with ladies who lunch, all of whom get a hug from the maitre'd. The menu changes daily, and each day it's handwritten on a white board. Lunch entrées may include perfectly rare tuna niçoise salad, or grilled whitefish with Dijon mustard sauce. Dinner might bring roasted quail with orange sauce or rack of lamb. Service is beyond attentive. The restaurant has a lovely tree-shaded garden. On cool winter evenings, request a table by the fireplace. ⊠ *385 W. Tahquitz Canyon Way* ☎ *760/325–5059* ⌞ *Reservations essential* ☰ *AE, D, DC, MC, V* ⊗ *No lunch Wed.–Sat. in July and Aug.*

$$–$$$$ ✕ **Copley's on Palm Canyon.** Chef Manion Copley is cooking up the most innovative cuisine in the desert, drawing fans region-wide. Start with such appetizers as roasted beet and warm goat cheese salad or perfectly grilled charred prawns and scallops. Oh My Lobster Pot Pie is the biggest hit on the entrée menu. And save room for Copley's sweet and savory servings of herb ice cream. The rustic, casual eatery is in a hacienda that was once owned by Cary Grant. Service is pleasant and friendly. ⊠ *621 N. Palm Canyon Dr.* ☎ *760/327–9555* ☰ *AE, D, DC, MC, V* ⊗ *Closed Mon. No lunch.*

$$–$$$$ ✕ **Europa.** Housed inside the Villa Royale Inn, this restaurant provides both indoor and garden dining–and artfully prepared cuisine. Popular menu items include rack of lamb with tapenade of dates and olives, duck confit with Grand Marnier, and salmon in parchment with wild mushrooms. ⊠ *1620 Indian Trail* ☎ *760/327–2314* ☰ *AE, D, DC, MC, V* ⊗ *Closed Mon. No lunch.*

$$–$$$$ ✕ **St. James at the Vineyard.** A colorful interior, an outdoor terrace with street views, and a bubbling modern fountain all help to set a playful mood at this hot spot for dining and sipping cocktails. The eclectic menu roams the world; entrées range from bouillabaisse Burmese to veal shank osso buco. Some vegetarian items are available. Service can be rushed on weekend nights in high season. ⊠ *265 S. Palm Canyon Dr.* ☏ *760/320–8041* ⌔ *Reservations essential* ▤ *AE, D, DC, MC, V* ⊘ *No lunch.*

$–$$$ ✕ **Edgardo's Cafe Veracruz.** For a sampling of Maya and Aztec flavors, try some of the unusual items on Edgardo's menu, such as soup made with *nopales* (cactus) and roast pork wrapped in banana leaves. The menu also has more familiar items, such as tamales and enchiladas. ⊠ *787 N. Palm Canyon Dr.* ☏ *760/320–3558* ⌔ *Reservations essential* ▤ *AE, D, MC, V* ⊘ *Closed Wed.*

$–$$ ✕ **El Mirasol.** This local favorite storefront café serves up a traditional Mexican menu including tastefully prepared *pollo en mole poblano* (chicken in a red mole sauce), carne asado, and shrimp in garlic tomatillo. There's also a selection of vegetarian items. ⊠ *140 E. Palm Canyon Dr.* ☏ *760/323–0721* ⌔ *Reservations not accepted* ▤ *AE, MC, V.*

$–$$ ✕ **Marchbox Vintage Pizza Bistro.** The name says pizza, but this bistro offers much more: you'll find interesting salads topped with sweet and tangy calamari or grilled tuna, and a selection of sandwiches with fillings like crab cakes or portobello mushrooms. The pizzas are made just about any way you'd like—even with fresh berries and mascarpone for dessert. The bistro has an upstairs location in Marcado Plaza, and overlooks the nightly action on Palm Canyon Drive. ⊠ *155 S. Palm Canyon Dr.* ☏ *760/778–6000* ▤ *AE, D, DC, MC, V* ⊘ *No lunch.*

$–$$ ✕ **Wang's in the Desert.** Locals flock to Wang's for its lovely Asian setting, complete with koi pond, indoor garden, and original art on the walls. The menu's well-chosen selection of Chinese and Asian-influence entrées ranges from kung pao chicken to tangerine shrimp. ⊠ *424 S. Indian Canyon Dr.* ☏ *760/325–9264* ▤ *AE, D, DC, MC, V* ⊘ *No lunch.*

¢ ✕ **Peabody's Café Bar & Coffee.** The place to go for a cup of joe and people-watching, Peabody's has been a Palm Canyon Drive institution for years. By day Peabody's serves lunch, including salads and hot and cold sandwiches. By night the place becomes a popular bar (open until 2 AM Thursday through Saturday). ⊠ *134 S. Palm Canyon Dr.* ☏ *760/322–1877* ▤ *AE, D, DC, MC, V* ⊘ *No dinner.*

¢ ✕ **Tyler's.** Join the lineup at this casual spot in the heart of town, then snag one of the umbrella-shaded picnic tables outside. Locals go for bite-size burgers, fries, and lemonade. The menu also lists veggie burgers, BLTs, and root-beer floats. ⊠ *149 S. Indian Canyon Dr.* ☏ *760/325–2990* ▤ *No credit cards* ⊘ *Closed Sun.*

Where to Stay

HOTELS & RESORTS

★ **$$$$** ▣ **The Parker Palm Springs.** Le Parker Meridien has been transformed into a cacophony of color, flashing lights, and over-the-top contemporary art, assembled by New York designer Jonathan Adler. No longer the stately hotel it once was, the Parker is now the hottest hotel in the desert, appealing to a hip, young clientele. When you arrive, a greeter will whisk you to your room to complete registration; the stroll takes you through a luscious desert garden. Guests will find relaxation around the pools, if nowhere else—pulsating music fills the air throughout the resort. Rooms have textured sisal floor coverings, exotic woven fabrics in bright reds and browns, and leather seating. All have private balconies or patios (with hammocks) that are secluded behind tall shrubs. The clubby restaurant, Mister Parker's ($$$$), will delight any well-heeled carnivore. ⊠ *4200 E. Palm Canyon Dr., 92264* ☎ *760/770–5000 or 800/543–4300* 🖷 *760/324–2188* ⊕ *www.theparkerpalmsprings.com* ⇖ *133 rooms, 12 suites* ⚭ *2 restaurants, snack bar, room service, in-room safes, minibars, cable TV with movies, in-room DVDs, in-room data ports, Wi-Fi, golf privileges, 4 tennis courts, 2 pools, 2 indoor pools, fitness classes, gym, 2 indoor hot tubs, 1 outdoor hot tub, sauna, hair salon, massage, spa, steam room, bicycles, croquet, lawn bowling, bar, lobby lounge, shop, babysitting, dry cleaning, laundry service, concierge, business services, meeting room, helipad, free parking, no-smoking rooms* ⊟ *AE, D, DC, MC, V.*

★ **$$$$**   **Smoke Tree Ranch.** A world apart from Palm Springs' pulsating urban village, the area's most exclusive resort occupies 400 pristine desert acres, surrounded by mountains and quiet desert vistas. A laid-back genteel retreat since the mid-1930s for some of the world's foremost families, including Walt Disney, it still provides a quietly luxurious experience reminiscent of the Old West. A collection of simple cottages is spread among manicured desert gardens and shaded by smoke trees. A large rambling ranch house, with gleaming paneled walls and picture windows, holds a dining room where three meals are served daily. Tradition prevails in a dress code at dinner and the perfect service. ⊠ *1800 S. Sunrise Way, 92264* ☎ *760/327–1221 or 800/787–3922* 🖷 *760/327–9490* ⊕ *www.smoketreeranch.com* ⇖ *56 cottages* ⚭ *Dining room, some microwaves, minibars, refrigerators, cable TV, golf privileges, 9 tennis courts, pro shop, pool, fitness classes, exercise equipment, outdoor hot tub, massage, bicycles, basketball, billiards, croquet, hiking, horseback riding, horseshoes, lawn bowling, bar, library, babysitting, children's programs (ages 5–12), playground, laundry facilities, meeting rooms, free parking, some pets allowed; no smoking* ⊟ *D, MC, V* ☾ *Closed mid-Apr. to late Oct.* �†○† *BP, FAP.*

$$$–$$$$ **Palm Springs Hilton Resort.** This venerable hotel across the street from the tented Spa Casino has aged gracefully. Rooms, decorated in soft desert colors, are both spacious and spare. All have private balconies or patios, some overlooking the hotel's lushly landscaped pool area. ⊠ *400 E. Tahquitz Canyon Way, 92262* ☎ *760/320–6868 or 800/522–6900* 🖷 *760/320–2126* ⊕ *www.hiltonpalmsprings.com* ⇖ *260 rooms, 71 suites* ⚭ *Restaurant, café, room service, microwaves, refrigerators, cable TV, in-room broadband, golf privileges, pool, gym, 2 outdoor hot tubs, massage, 2 bars, children's programs (ages 4–16; summer only), concierge, business services, meeting rooms, airport shuttle, some pets allowed, no-smoking rooms* ⊟ *AE, D, DC, MC, V.*

$$$ **Spa Resort Casino.** Part of a complex that includes a spa and a casino across the street, this hotel, owned and operated by the Agua Caliente, is adjacent to a mineral-water spring used by generations of Native Americans. (The spa uses the healing mineral waters in treatments that draw locals on a regular basis.) Until 2003 the hotel was a bit dowdy, but a renovation brought modern rooms and public areas up-to-date with soothing desert colors and added amenities. ⊠ *100 N. Indian Canyon Dr., 92262* ☎ *760/325–1461 or 888/999–1995* 🖷 *760/325–3344* ⊕ *www.sparesortcasino.com* 🛏 *215 rooms, 5 suites* ♨ *2 restaurants, room service, refrigerators, cable TV with movies, broadband, in-room data ports, 2 pools, fitness classes, gym, hair salon, 1 outdoor hot tub, sauna, spa, steam room, 2 bars, casino, laundry service, concierge, meeting room, no-smoking rooms* ▤ *AE, D, MC, V.*

$$–$$$ 🏨 **Hyatt Regency Suites.** An enormous metal sculpture suspended from the ceiling dominates this hotel's six-story asymmetrical atrium lobby. One- and two-bedroom suites have private balconies and two TVs. Suites in the back have views of the pool and mountains. There's free underground parking, and you have golf privileges at Rancho Mirage Country Club and four other area courses. ⊠ *285 N. Palm Canyon Dr., 92262* ☎ *760/322–9000 or 800/633–7313* 🖷 *760/969–6005* ⊕ *www.palmsprings.hyatt.com* 🛏 *192 suites* ♨ *3 restaurants, room service, in-room safes, minibars, cable TV with movies, in-room broadband, in-room data ports, golf privileges, putting green, pool, gym, outdoor hot tub, bar, dry cleaning, laundry service, concierge, babysitting, business services, meeting room, airport shuttle, no-smoking rooms* ▤ *AE, D, DC, MC, V.*

$$–$$$ 🏨 **Wyndham Palm Springs.** The main appeal of this hotel is its location adjacent to the Palm Springs Convention Center. The terra-cotta Spanish colonial–style building surrounds the largest swimming pool in Palm Springs. Because most customers are here on business, the vibe is more serious than at most other desert establishments. ⊠ *888 E. Tahquitz Canyon Way, 92262* ☎ *760/322–6000 or 800/822–4200* 🖷 *760/322–5351* ⊕ *www.wyndham.com* 🛏 *252 rooms, 158 suites* ♨ *Restaurant, cable TV with movies, in-room broadband, in-room data ports, Web TV, golf privileges, pool, health club, hair salon, 2 outdoor hot tubs, massage, sauna, spa, 2 bars, dry cleaning, laundry service, business services, meeting room, airport shuttle, some pets allowed, no-smoking rooms* ▤ *AE, D, MC, V.*

¢–$$ 🏨 **Vagabond Inn.** Rooms are smallish at this centrally located motel, but they're clean, comfortable, and a good value. Continental breakfast is included in the price. ⊠ *1699 S. Palm Canyon Dr., 92264* ☎ *760/325–7211 or 800/522–1555* 🖷 *760/322–9269* ⊕ *www.vagabondinn.com* 🛏 *117 rooms* ♨ *In-room data ports, pool, outdoor hot tub, some pets allowed (fee), no-smoking rooms* ▤ *AE, D, DC, MC, V* ⦿ *CP.*

SMALL HOTELS &
BED-AND-
BREAKFASTS
★ **$$$$**

🏨 **Orbit In Oasis.** Step back to 1957 at this hip inn, which has rooms appointed with mid-century furnishings by such designers as Eames, Noguchi, and Breuer. Some rooms have private patios; all have a few Melmac dishes tucked here and there. There's an outside shower, cruiser bikes, books, games, and videos available for guest use. A lively atmosphere prevails poolside, where a complimentary breakfast is served daily. ⊠ *Oasis: 562 W. Arenas Rd., 92262* ☎ *760/323–3585 or 877/996–7248* 🖷 *760/323–3599* ⊕ *www.orbitin.com* 🛏 *9 rooms* ♨ *Some kitchenettes, cable TV with movies, in-room broadband, in-room data* *ports, Wi-Fi, saltwater pool, outdoor hot tub, massage, spa, bicycles, library, free parking, no-smoking rooms* ☰ *AE, D, MC, V* ⧍⧍ *CP.*

★ **$$$$** ⌸ **Willows Historic Palm Springs Inn.** This luxurious hillside B&B is within walking distance of many village attractions. An opulent Mediterranean-style mansion built in the 1920s, it has gleaming hardwood and slate floors, stone fireplaces, fresco ceilings, hand-painted tiles, iron balconies, antiques throughout, and a 50-foot waterfall that splashes into a pool outside the dining room. There's even a private hillside garden planted with native flora, which has one of the best views in the area. Guest rooms are decorated to recall the movies of Hollywood's golden era. ✉ *412 W. Tahquitz Canyon Way, 92262* ☎ *760/320–0771 or 800/966–9597* 🖷 *760/320–0780* ⊕ *www.thewillowspalmsprings. com* ⤷ *8 rooms* ⋄ *Cable TV, in-room data ports, pool, outdoor hot tub; no smoking* ☰ *AE, D, DC, MC, V* ⧍⧍ *BP.*

★ **$$$–$$$$** ⌸ **Movie Colony Hotel.** The rooms in this classy, intimate hotel, designed in 1935 by Albert Frey, are elegantly appointed with soft desert colors accented by bright reds and yellows; many features, including tiny showers, are authentic to the period. A convivial atmosphere prevails in late afternoons as guests share experiences during the wine hour and again over morning coffee and a sumptuous continental breakfast served in the flower-decked courtyard. ✉ *726 N. Indian Canyon Dr., 92262* ☎ *760/320–6340 or 760/953–5700* 🖷 *760/320–1640* ⊕ *www. moviecolonyhotel.com* ⤷ *16 rooms, 3 suites* ⋄ *Refrigerators, cable TV, in-room DVDs, some in-room broadband, in-room data ports, some in-room Wi-Fi, pool, outdoor hot tub, massage, bicycles, lobby lounge* ☰*AE, MC, V* ⧍⧍ *CP.*

$$$ ⌸ **Calla Lily Inn.** This tranquil palm-shaded oasis one block from Palm Canyon Drive has spacious rooms decorated in a vaguely tropical style. Furnishings are contemporary wicker, and an image of a calla lily adorns every room. Rooms surround the pool. ✉ *350 S. Belardo Rd., 92262* ☎ *760/323–3654 or 888/888–5787* 🖷 *760/323–4964* ⊕ *www. callalilypalmsprings.com* ⤷ *9 rooms* ⋄ *Refrigerators, cable TV, in-room DVD, in-room VCRs, in-room broadband, in-room Wi-Fi, pool, outdoor hot tub, massage, free parking, no-smoking rooms* ☰ *MC, V.*

$$–$$$ ⌸ **East Canyon Resort & Spa.** This classy resort, which serves a primarily gay clientele, is the only one in the desert with an in-house spa. Large rooms, each individually decorated, surround a sparkling pool; they have carefully coordinated dark colors, and ample bathrooms. The vibe here is social, presided over by the resort's gracious hosts. ✉ *288 E. Camino Monte Vista, 92262* ☎ *760/320–1928 or 877/324–6835* 🖷 *760/320– 0599* ⊕ *www.eastcanyonps.com* ⤷ *15 rooms, 1 suite* ⋄ *Refrigerators, cable TV with movies, in-room DVDs, in-room data ports, Wi-Fi, pool, outdoor hot tub, massage, spa, steam room, library, recreation room, concierge, no-smoking rooms* ☰ *AE, MC, V* ⧍⧍ *CP.*

$$–$$$ ⌸ **Casitas Laquita.** This collection of Spanish-style bungalows occupying more than an acre caters mainly to lesbians. Rooms, decorated with a southwestern theme, have handcrafted furnishings; many have fireplaces. The innkeepers regularly host informal social activities. ✉ *450 E. Palm Canyon Dr., 92264* ☎ *760/416–9999 or 877/203–3410* 🖷 *760/ 416–5415* ⊕ *www.casitaslaquita.com* ⤷ *15 rooms* ⋄ *Kitchenettes,* *cable TV, in-room data ports, Wi-Fi, pool, massage, no-smoking rooms* ⊟ *MC, V* ⏹ *CP.*

¢–$$$ 🏠 **Casa Cody.** The service is personal and gracious at this large, Western-style B&B a few steps from the Palm Springs Art Museum. Spacious studios and one- and two-bedroom suites are furnished simply. Some have fireplaces, and most have kitchens. The homey rooms are in four buildings surrounding courtyards lushly landscaped with bougainvillea and citrus trees. There are also two adobe cottages, one of which was the desert home of opera singer Lawrence Tibbett. ✉ *175 S. Cahuilla Rd., 92262* ☎ *760/320–9346 or 800/231–2639* 🖷 *760/325–8610* ⊕ *www.casacody.com* 🛏 *16 rooms, 7 suites, 2 cottages* ♿ *Some kitchens, refrigerators, in-room data ports, 2 pools, outdoor hot tub, some pets allowed (fee), no-smoking rooms* ⊟ *AE, D, MC, V* ⏹ *CP.*

Nightlife & the Arts

NIGHTLIFE Next to the Plaza Theatre, **Blue Guitar** (✉ 120 S. Palm Canyon Dr. ☎ 760/327–1549), owned by jazz artists Kal David and Lauri Bono, presents jazz and blues. **Hair of the Dog English Pub** (✉ 238 N. Palm Canyon Dr. ☎ 760/323–9890) is a friendly bar popular with a young crowd that likes to tip back English ales and ciders. **Zelda's** (✉ 169 N. Indian Canyon Dr. ☎ 760/325–2375) has two rooms, one featuring Latin sounds and another with Top 40 dance music and a male dance revue. It's closed Sunday through Tuesday.

Casino Morongo (✉ Cabazon off-ramp, Interstate 10 ☎ 951/849–3080), about 20 minutes west of Palm Springs, has 2,000 slot machines. The classy **Spa Resort Casino** (✉ 401 E. Amado Rd. ☎ 888/999–1995) holds 1,000 slot machines, blackjack tables, a high-limit room, four restaurants, two bars, and a lounge with entertainment.

GAY & LESBIAN **Heaven Dance Haus** (✉ 611 S. Palm Canyon Dr. ☎ 760/416–0950) is a multitier dance club catering to a mixed gay clientele. **Hunter's Video Bar** (✉ 302 E. Arenas Rd. ☎ 760/323–0700) is a popular bar with dancing that draws a young crowd. **Toucans** (✉ 2100 N. Palm Canyon Dr. ☎ 760/416–7584), a friendly place with a tropical jungle in a rain-forest setting, serves festive drinks.

In late March, when the world's finest female golfers hit the links for the Annual LPGA Kraft Nabisco Championship in Rancho Mirage, thousands of lesbians converge on Palm Springs for a four-day party popularly known as **Dinah Shore Weekend—Palm Springs** (⊕ www.clubskirts.com). The **White Party** (☎ 323/944–0051 for tickets), held on Easter weekend, draws tens of thousands of gay men from around the country to the Palm Springs area for a round of parties and gala events.

THE ARTS At the Palm Springs Art Museum, the **Annenberg Theater** (✉ 101 Museum Dr. ☎ 760/325–4490 ⊕ www.psmuseum.org) is the site of Broadway shows, opera, lectures, Sunday-afternoon chamber concerts, and other events. ■ TIP➔ In mid-January the **Palm Springs International Film Festival** (☎ 760/322–2930 or 800/898–7256 ⊕ www.psfilmfest.org) brings stars and more than 150 feature films from 25 countries, plus panel discussions, short films, and documentaries, to the McCallum and other venues.

The Spanish-style **Historic Plaza Theatre** (⊠ 128 S. Palm Canyon Dr. ☎ 760/327–0225) opened in 1936 with a glittering premiere of the MGM film *Camille*. In the '40s and '50s, it presented some of Hollywood's biggest stars, including Bob Hope, Bing Crosby, and Frank Sinatra. Today it plays host to the hottest ticket in the desert, the **Fabulous Palm Springs Follies** (⊕ www.palmspringsfollies.com), which mounts 10 sell-out performances each week, November through May. The vaudeville-style revue, about half of which focuses on World War II nostalgia, stars extravagantly costumed, retired (but very fit) showgirls, singers, and dancers. Tickets are $39 to $85. In addition to the follies, the theater is home to a January film festival and is favored by fans of old-time radio even in the off-season.

Cirque Dreams (⊠ Palm Springs Pavilion Theater ☎ 760/778–5715 ⊕ www.pspavilion.com) delights audiences from November through May. Contortionists, acrobats, and strongmen perform in a huge white big-top set in a parking lot across the street from the Palm Springs Art Museum. Tickets are $50 to $64. The theater presents reviews during the summer.

Sports & the Outdoors

BICYCLING **Big Wheel Tours** (☎ 760/779–1837 ⊕ www.bwbtours.com) rents cruisers and mountain bikes in Palm Springs and offers road tours to La Quinta Loop and the San Andreas fault. Off-road tours are also available. The company will pick up and deliver at area hotels. **Palm Springs Recreation Division** (⊠ 401 S. Pavilion Way ☎ 760/323–8272 ☉ Weekdays 7:30–6) can provide you with maps of city bike trails.

GOLF Palm Springs is host to more than 100 golf tournaments annually. The Palm Springs Desert Resorts Convention and Visitors Bureau **Events Hotline** (☎ 760/770–1992) lists dates and locations. **Palm Springs TeeTimes** (☎ 760/324–5012) can match golfers with courses and arrange tee times. If you know which course you want to play, you can book tee times online (⊕ www.palmspringsteetimes.com).

Tahquitz Creek Palm Springs Golf Resort (⊠ 1885 Golf Club Dr. ☎ 760/328–1005 ⊕ www.tahquitzcreek.com) has two 18-hole, par-72 courses and a 50-space driving range. Greens fees, including cart, run $70–$90, depending on the course and day of the week. **Tommy Jacobs' Bel Air Greens Country Club** (⊠ 1001 S. El Cielo Rd. ☎ 760/322–6062) has a 9-hole executive course. Greens fees are $15 ($10 for replay).

SPAS Taking the waters at the **Spa Resort Casino** (⊠ 100 N. Indian Canyon Dr. ☎ 760/778–1772 ⊕ www.sparesortcasino.com) is an indulgent pleasure. You can spend a full day enjoying a five-step, wet-and-dry treatment program that includes a mineral bath, steam, sauna, and eucalyptus inhalation. The program allows you to take fitness classes and use the gym and, for an extra charge, add massage or body treatments. The rate is $40 for a full day, less if you combine it with a treatment.

TENNIS **Demuth Park** (⊠ 4375 Mesquite Ave. ☎ No phone) has four lighted courts. **Ruth Hardy Park** (⊠ Tamarisk Rd. and Avenida Caballeros ☎ No phone) has eight lighted courts.

Shopping

The main **North Palm Canyon Drive shopping district** (✉ Between Alejo and Ramon Rds.) is the commercial core of Palm Springs. Anchoring the center of the drive is the Palm Springs Mall, with about 35 boutiques.

★ Every Thursday night, the **Village Fest** (✉ Palm Canyon Dr. between Tahquitz Canyon Way and Baristo Rd. ☎ 760/778–8415 ⊕ www.palm-springs.org) fills the drive with street musicians, a farmers' market, and stalls with food, crafts, art, and antiques. It's a great place for celebrity spotting.

Extending north of the main shopping area, the **Uptown Heritage Galleries & Antiques District** (✉ N. Palm Canyon Dr. between Amado Rd. and Tachevah Dr. ☎ 760/778–8415 ⊕ www.palm-springs.org) is a collection of consignment and secondhand shops, galleries, and restaurants whose theme is decidedly retro. Many shops and galleries offer mid-century modern furniture and decorator items, and others carry consignment clothing and estate jewelry. First Friday on North Palm Canyon is a monthly festival of shopping, food, and entertainment.

East Palm Canyon Drive can be a source of great bargains. **Estate Sale Co.** (✉ 4185 E. Palm Canyon Dr. ☎ 760/321–7628) is the biggest consignment store in the desert, with a warehouse of furniture, fine art, china and crystal, accessories, jewelry, movie memorabilia, and exercise equipment. Prices are set to keep merchandise moving. It's closed Monday and Tuesday.

At the Cabazon exit of I–10, **Hadley's Fruit Orchards** (✉ 48–980 Seminole Dr., Cabazon ☎ 951/849–5255 ⊕ www.hadleyfruitorchards.com) sells dried fruit, nuts, date shakes, and wines.

Cathedral City

⓫ *2 mi southeast of Palm Springs on Hwy. 111.*

One of the fastest-growing communities in the desert, Cathedral City is more residential than tourist oriented. However, the city has a number of good restaurants and entertainment venues with moderate prices.

Pickford Salon, a small museum inside the Mary Pickford Theater, showcases the life of the famed actress. On display is a selection of personal items contributed by family members, including her 1976 Oscar for contributions to the film industry, a gown she wore in the 1927 film *Dorothy Vernon of Haddon Hall,* and dinnerware from Pickfair. One of the two biographical video presentations was produced by Mary herself. ✉ *36–850 Pickfair St.* ☎ *760/328–7100* ⊠ *Free* ☉ *Daily 10:30 AM–midnight.*

☾ At **Boomers Camelot Park** you can play miniature golf, drive bumper boats, swing in the batting cages, test your skill in an arcade, and play video games. ✉ *67–700 E. Palm Canyon Dr.* ☎ *760/770–7522* ⊠ *$5–$7 per activity* ☉ *Mon.–Thurs. 11–10, Fri.–Sun. 11–11.*

Where to Stay & Eat

★ **$–$$$** ✕ **Oceans.** This bistro tucked into the back corner of a shopping center serves a surprising selection of beautifully prepared seafood. Start with

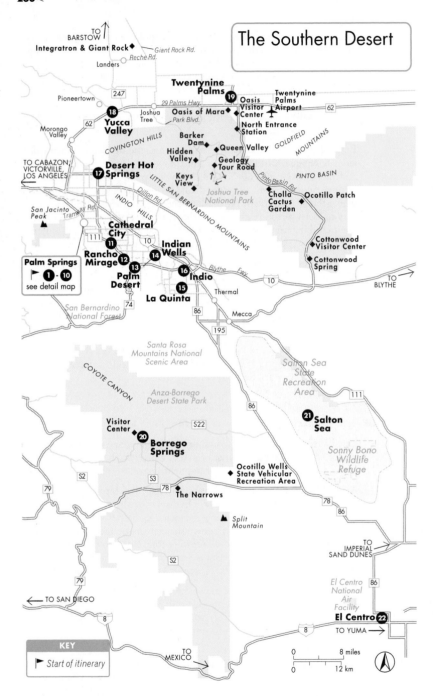

The Southern Desert

TO BARSTOW

Integratron & Giant Rock ◆ — Giant Rock Rd.

Landers — Reche Rd.

Pioneertown — 247

Twentynine Palms ⑲ Oasis Visitor Center — Twentynine Palms Airport — 62

29 Palms Hwy.

Joshua Tree — Park Blvd. — **Oasis of Mara** ◆

⑱ **Yucca Valley** — North Entrance Station ◆

62 — COVINGTON HILLS — Barker Dam ◆ — Queen Valley ◆ — GOLDFIELD MOUNTAINS

Morongo Valley

TO CABAZON, VICTORVILLE, LOS ANGELES — ⑰ **Desert Hot Springs** — Hidden Valley ◆ — Geology Tour Road ◆ — PINTO BASIN

LITTLE SAN BERNARDINO MOUNTAINS — Keys View ◆

Dillon Rd. — *Joshua Tree National Park* — Cholla Cactus Garden ◆ — Ocotillo Patch ◆ — Pinto Basin Rd.

San Jacinto Peak ▲ — INDIO HILLS

Tramway Rd.

Cathedral City ⑪ — 10

111 — **Indian Wells** ⑭ — Cottonwood Visitor Center ◆

Rancho Mirage ⑫ ⑬ — Blythe Fwy. — Cottonwood Spring ◆

Palm Springs ► ❶ - ❿ see detail map — **Palm Desert** ⑯ **Indio** — 10 — TO BLYTHE

74 — **La Quinta** ⑮ — Thermal

San Bernardino National Forest — 86 — Mecca

195

Santa Rosa Mountains National Scenic Area — *Salton Sea State Recreation Area*

COYOTE CANYON — 86 — 111

Anza-Borrego Desert State Park — ㉑ **Salton Sea**

S22

Visitor Center ⑳ **Borrego Springs** — *Sonny Bono Wildlife Refuge*

S2 — S3 — 78 — Ocotillo Wells State Vehicular Recreation Area ◆

79 — ◆ **The Narrows** — 78 — 86

▲ Split Mountain

S2 — TO IMPERIAL SAND DUNES

79 — ← TO SAN DIEGO — *El Centro National Air Facility* — 86

8 — **El Centro** ㉒

TO MEXICO — 8 — TO YUMA →

0 — 8 miles
0 — 12 km

KEY
► *Start of itinerary*

Mussels Oceans, a bowl of tender bivalves in a creamy anisette broth. Entrées include perfectly grilled ahi tuna, blackened catfish with Cajun seasonings, and lobster ravioli with saffron cream sauce. ⊠ *Canyon Plaza S, 67–555 E. Palm Canyon Dr.* ☎ *760/324–1554* ⌖ *Reservations essential* ⊟ *AE, D, DC, MC, V* ⊗ *Closed Sun. No lunch Sat.*

¢–$$$$ ▦ **Comfort Suites.** This chain motel is about as close as you can get to Rancho Mirage without paying sky-high prices. Public areas are spacious, modern, and attractively appointed. Some accommodations here are cramped, even though most are one- or two-bedroom suites. Noise can be a problem, because the motel is on busy Highway 111. ⊠ *69–151 E. Palm Canyon Dr., 92234* ☎ *760/324–5939 or 800/862–5085* 🖷 *760/324–3034* ⟿ *21 rooms, 77 suites* ⌂ *Some kitchens, microwaves, refrigerators, cable TV, in-room data ports, pool, outdoor hot tub, laundry facilities, meeting room, free parking, some pets allowed (fee)* ⊟ *AE, D, DC, MC, V* ⎆ *CP.*

Nightlife

The **Desert IMAX Theater** (⊠ Hwy. 111 at Cathedral Canyon Dr. ☎ 760/324–7333), the only IMAX theater in the region, screens such films as *Alaska: Spirit of the Wild* and *Lewis & Clark: Great Journey West.*

Desert Hot Springs

🔟 *9 mi north of Palm Springs on Gene Autry Trail*

Desert Hot Springs' famous hot mineral waters, thought by some to have curative powers, bubble up at temperatures of 90°F to 148°F and flow into the wells of more than 40 hotel spas.

Where to Stay

$$$–$$$$ ▦ **Two Bunch Palms Resort & Spa.** This legendary resort and spa has made a comeback after a long period of neglect. The legendary desert retreat of gangster Al Capone now shines again with manicured landscaping, sparkling ponds, and nicely appointed rooms, many with private patios holding hot tubs. Although the lovely hillside setting and the opportunity to soak in natural hot springs are the main attractions, the resort also has a pleasant dining room (for guests only), a spa that offers a wide-range of treatments, and the level of privacy and pampering that continues to draw celebrities. ⊠ *67–425 Two Bunch Palms Trail, 92240* ☎ *760/329–8791 or 800/472–4334* 🖷 *760/564–5718* ⊕ *www.twobunchpalms.com* ⟿ *35 rooms, 15 suites* ⌂ *Dining room, fans, some in-room hot tubs, minibars, refrigerators, cable TV with movies, in-room broadband, Wi-Fi, 2 tennis courts, fitness classes, gym, hair salon, 12 outdoor hot tubs, Japanese baths, massage, spa, steam room, shop, dry cleaning, meeting rooms; no kids, no-smoking* ⊟ *AE, D, DC, MC, V.*

$$–$$$ ▦ **The Spring.** This laid-back inn, tucked into a hillside with a lovely desert view, caters to guests seeking quiet and personal service. Simply furnished rooms have modern decor; most open onto the pool and colorful flower gardens. In addition to the typical wraps, scrubs, and massages, the inn's spa menu offers cranial dreamwork, body–mind integrative therapy, and lymphatic massage. ⊠ *12699 Reposo Way, 92240* ☎ *760/251–6700 or 877/200–2110* 🖷 *760/251–6701* ⊕ *www.the-spring.com* ⟿ *12 rooms*

♨ *Picnic area, fans, some kitchenettes, microwaves, refrigerators, no room TVs, no in-room phones, pool, 2 outdoor hot tubs, spa, shop; no kids, no smoking* ☰ *AE, D, DC, MC, V.*

Rancho Mirage

⑫ *4 mi southeast of Cathedral City on Hwy. 111.*

Much of the scenery in exclusive Rancho Mirage is concealed behind the walls of gated communities and country clubs. The rich and famous live in estates and patronize elegant resorts and expensive restaurants. The city's golf courses host many high-profile tournaments. When the excesses of the luxe life become too much, the area's residents can check themselves into the Betty Ford Center, the famous drug-and-alcohol rehab center.

You'll find some of the swankiest resorts in the desert here, plus great golf, and plenty of peace and quiet.

⊙ The **Children's Discovery Museum of the Desert** contains instructive hands-on exhibits—a miniature rock-climbing area, a magnetic sculpture wall, make-it-and-take-it-apart projects, a rope maze—and an area for toddlers. ⊠ *71–701 Gerald Ford Dr.* ☏ *760/321–0602* ⊕ *www.cdmod.org* ☞ *$6* ⊙ *Jan.–April Mon.–Sat. 10–5, Sun, noon–5; May–Dec. Tues.–Sat. 10–5, Sun. noon–5.*

Where to Stay & Eat

$$–$$$ ✕ **Shame on the Moon.** Old-fashioned ambience complete with big booths, friendly service, an eclectic menu, and modest prices make this one of the most popular restaurants in the desert. Entrées include baked salmon with a horseradish crust, grilled flank steak with peanut teriyaki, and wild mushroom ravioli. Portions leave you plenty to take home. ⊠ *69–950 Frank Sinatra Dr.* ☏ *760/324–5515* ⚭ *Reservations essential* ☰ *AE, MC, V* ⊙ *No lunch.*

$–$$$ ✕ **Las Casuelas Nuevas.** Hundreds of artifacts from Guadalajara, Mexico, lend festive charm to this casual restaurant, which has an expansive garden patio. Tamales and shellfish dishes are among the specialties. The margaritas will make you wish you'd brought your cha-cha heels. ⊠ *70–050 Hwy. 111* ☏ *760/328–8844* ⚭ *Reservations essential* ☰ *AE, D, DC, MC, V.*

$$$$ ▦ **Lodge at Rancho Mirage.** The most secluded and the quietest resort in the desert, the Lodge frequently hosts politicians and celebrities. Originally a Ritz-Carlton, this hilltop hotel, perched high above the Coachella Valley, is being transformed into a casually elegant destination as rooms are redecorated with lots of chrome, glass, mirrors, and bright primary colors in stark contrast to the gold fabrics and crystal that remains in public areas from its days as the Ritz. Spacious rooms have mountain, pool or valley views; Frette linens; and private balconies or patios. Service is thoughtful and impeccable. ⊠ *68–900 Frank Sinatra Dr., 92270* ☏ *760/321–8282 or 877/770–7025* ☐ *760/321–6928* ⊕ *www.ranchomirage. rockresorts.com* ⇋ *219 rooms, 21 suites* ♨ *3 restaurants, room service, in-room safes, minibars, cable TV, in-room broadband, in-room data ports, golf privileges, putting green, 8 tennis courts, pool, gym, outdoor* *hot tub, spa, basketball, croquet, hiking, lawn bowling, volleyball, 2 bars, shops, laundry service, concierge, business services, meeting room, car rental, some pets allowed (fee); no smoking ⊟ AE, D, DC, MC, V.*

☾ **$$$$** ⊞ **Westin Mission Hills Resort.** A sprawling resort on 360 acres, the Westin is surrounded by fairways, putting greens, and a collection of time-share accommodations. Rooms, in two-story buildings amid patios and fountains, have a stylish Arts-and-Crafts look with sleek dark mahogany furnishings accented with sand-color upholstery and crisp white linens. All have private patios or balconies. Paths and creeks meander through the complex, and a lagoon-style swimming pool is encircled with a waterslide several stories high. ✉ *71333 Dinah Shore Dr., 92270* ☏ *760/328–5955 or 800/544–0287* 📠 *760/770–2199* ∰ *www.westin.com* ⇆ *472 rooms, 30 suites* ♨ *2 restaurants, 3 snack bars, room service, in-room safes, minibars, some refrigerators, cable TV with movies and video games, in-room broadband, in-room data ports, 2 18-hole golf courses, 7 tennis courts, pro shop, 4 pools, health club, hair salon, 4 outdoor hot tubs, spa, steam room, croquet, shuffleboard, volleyball, bar, recreation room, children's programs (ages 4–12), playground, business services, convention center, some pets allowed (fee), no-smoking rooms ⊟ AE, D, DC, MC, V.*

¢ ⊞ **Motel 6.** This motel may be bare-bones, but it puts you in tony Rancho Mirage, right in the shadow of the Lodge at Rancho Mirage up the hill. Kids stay free, and you can help yourself to free morning coffee. ✉ *69570 Hwy. 111, 92270* ☏ *760/324–8475 or 800/466–8356* 📠 *760/328–0864* ∰ *www.motel6.com* ⇆ *101 rooms* ♨ *Cable TV, in-room data ports, pool, outdoor hot tub, some pets allowed, no-smoking rooms ⊟ AE, D, DC, MC, V.*

Nightlife

The elegant and surprisingly quiet **Agua Caliente Casino** (✉ 32–250 Bob Hope Dr. ☏ 760/321–2000) contains 1,000 slot machines, 48 table games, a 1,000-seat bingo room, a high-limit room, and even a no-smoking area. The Cahuilla Showroom presents such headliners as the Smothers Brothers and Carrot Top as well as live boxing, and there are three restaurants and a food court.

Sports & the Outdoors

The best female golfers in the world compete in the LPGA **Kraft Nabisco Championship** (✉ Mission Hills Country Club ☏ 760/324–4546 ∰ www. kraftnabiscochampionship.com) held in late March.

★ Of the two golf courses at the **Westin Mission Hills Resort Golf Club** (✉ 71–501 Dinah Shore Dr. ☏ 760/328–3198 ∰ www.troongolf.com), the 18-hole, par-70 Pete Dye course is especially noteworthy. The club plays host to a number of major tournaments, is a member of the Troon Golf Institute, and has several teaching facilities, including the Westin Mission Hills Resort Golf Academy and the Golf Digest Golf School. Greens fees are $145 during peak season, including a mandatory cart; off-season promotional packages sometimes run as low as $60.

Shopping

The **River at Rancho Mirage** (✉ 71–800 Hwy. 111 ☏ 760/341–2711) is a shopping/dining/entertainment complex with a collection of 20 high-end shops. Bang & Olufsen, Borders Books & Music, Tulip Hill Winery tasting room, and other shops front a faux river with cascading waterfalls. The complex includes a 12-screen cinema, an outdoor amphitheater, and seven restaurants.

Palm Desert

❸ *2 mi southeast of Rancho Mirage on Hwy. 111.*

Palm Desert is a thriving retail and business community, with some of the desert's most popular restaurants, private and public golf courses, and premium shopping.

★ West of and parallel to Highway 111, **El Paseo** (⊠ Between Monterey and Portola Aves. ☎ 877/735-7273 ⊕ www.elpaseo.com) is a mile-long Mediterranean-style avenue with fountains and courtyards, French and Italian fashion boutiques, shoe salons, jewelry stores, children's shops, 28 restaurants, and nearly 30 art galleries. The pretty strip is a pleasant place to stroll, window-shop, people-watch, and exercise your credit cards. Each January, the **Palm Desert Golf Cart Parade** (☎ 760/346-6111 ⊕ www.golfcartparade.com) celebrates golf with a procession of 100 carts disguised as floats buzzing up and down El Paseo.

Come eyeball to eyeball with wolves, coyotes, mountain lions, cheetahs, bighorn sheep, golden eagles, warthogs, and owls at the **Living Desert Zoo and Gardens.** Easy to challenging scenic trails traverse 1,200 acres of desert preserve populated with plants of the Mojave, Colorado, and Sonoran deserts in 11 habitats. But in recent years, the zoo has expanded its vision to Africa. A family of reticulated giraffes moved into the park in 2002. At the 3-acre African Wa TuTu village, there's a traditional marketplace as well as camels, leopards, hyenas, and other African animals. Children can pet African domestic animals, including goats and guinea fowl, in a petting kraal. Gecko Gulch Children's Play Land has crawl-through underground tunnels and climb-on snake sculptures. Yet another exhibit demonstrates the path of the San Andreas Fault across the Coachella Valley. The Tennity Amphitheater stages daily wildlife shows, and "Wildlights," an evening light show, takes place during the winter holidays. ■ TIP→ **A garden center sells native desert flora, much of which is unavailable elsewhere.** ⊠ *47–900 Portola Ave.* ☎ *760/346-5694* ⊕ *www. livingdesert.org* 🎟 *$8.75 mid-June–Aug.; $12 Sept.–mid-June* ☉ *Mid-June–Aug., daily 8–1:30; Sept.–mid-June, daily 9–5.*

The **Santa Rosa Mountains/San Jacinto National Monument**, administered by the Bureau of Land Management, protects Peninsula bighorn sheep and other wildlife on 272,000 acres of desert habitat. For an introduction to the site, stop by the visitor center—staffed by knowledgeable volunteers—for a look at exhibits illustrating the natural history of the desert. A landscaped garden displays native plants and frames a sweeping view. ⊠ *51–500 Hwy. 74* ☎ *760/862-9984* ⊕ *www.ca.blm.gov/palmsprings* 🎟 *Free* ☉ *Daily 9–4.*

Where to Stay & Eat

$$$$ ✕ **Picanha.** Carnivores flock to this bright and airy Brazilian grill and bar as much for the show as for the meat. The servers, booted and bloused to resemble gauchos, move among tables passing chunks of skewered grilled meat that they cut to order for guests. You can order beef, pork, chicken, sausage, or lamb. A salad buffet, consisting of 30 items, is also popular in this all-you-can-eat restaurant. The restaurant also serves Brazilian cocktails, plus South American beers and wine. ⊠ *73–399 El Paseo* ☎ *760/674–3434* ▭ *AE, MC, V* ☉ *No lunch.*

★ **$$$–$$$$** ✕ **Cuistot.** Once hidden in an El Paseo courtyard, Cuistot is now easy to find. In late 2003 chef-owner Bernard Dervieux opened his new restaurant in a big, bright, airy reproduction of a French farmhouse on El Paseo's west end. The menu lists rabbit bourguignon with mushrooms and pancetta, along with such signature dishes as skillet-roasted veal chop with mushrooms and roasted garlic, fresh Dover sole with hazelnut-lemon sauce, and handmade vegetable ravioli with white truffle oil. ⊠ *72–595 El Paseo* ☎ *760/340–1000* ⌂ *Reservations essential* ▭ *AE, D, MC, V* ☉ *Closed Mon. and July and Aug. No lunch Sun.*

$$–$$$$ ✕ **Jillian's.** Husband-and-wife team Jay and June Trubee are the stars behind this trendy restaurant. Antiques and art fill the space, and the nighttime sky sets the mood in the center courtyard. Try the monumental appetizer called Tower of Crab (layers of crab, tomatoes, avocados, and brioche) and main dishes such as salmon baked in parchment and fettuccine with lobster. Save room for the Hawaiian cheesecake with macadamia-nut crust. Men will feel more comfortable wearing jackets, and shorts are not allowed. ⊠ *74–155 El Paseo* ☎ *760/776–8242* ⌂ *Reservations essential* ▭ *AE, DC, MC, V* ☉ *Closed Sun. and mid-June–Oct. No lunch.*

★ **$–$$$$** ✕ **Palmie.** Its humble location in the back of a shopping center gives nary a hint of the subtle creations prepared at this gem of a French restaurant. The two-cheese soufflé is one of several mouthwatering appetizers. Equally impressive are the duck *cassoulet,* duck fillets served with pear slices in red wine, and Palmie's signature dish: a perfectly crafted fish stew in a thin yet rich butter-cream broth. ⊠ *44–491 Town Center Way* ☎ *760/341–3200* ▭ *AE, DC, MC, V* ☉ *Closed Sun. No lunch.*

$$–$$$ ✕ **Café des Beaux Arts.** This café brings a little bit of Paris to the desert, with sidewalk dining, colorful flower boxes, and a bistro menu of French and Californian favorites, such as a broiled portobello mushroom with duck confit served with a sherry sauce, and ravioli stuffed with lobster. Leisurely dining is encouraged, which allows more time to savor the well-chosen French and domestic wines. ⊠ *73–640 El Paseo* ☎ *760/346–0669* ▭ *AE, D, DC, MC, V* ☉ *Closed July and Aug.*

¢–$$$ ✕ **Daily Grill.** This combination upscale coffee shop and bar serves good salads (the niçoise is particularly scrumptious), a fine gazpacho, zesty pasta dishes, and various blue-plate specials. The sidewalk terrace invites people-watching, and the weekend brunches are festive. ⊠ *73–061 El Paseo* ☎ *760/779–9911* ▭ *AE, D, DC, MC, V.*

¢–$ ✕ **Native Foods.** Despite what the menu implies, you'll find no meat at this brightly lighted, contemporary, totally vegan restaurant. The Bali surf burger contains tempeh, lettuce, tomato, plus other fixings, but no meat. Same story with Spike's BBQ, made with soy "chicken," barbecue sauce, and caramelized onions. ⊠ *73–890 El Paseo* ☎ *760/836–9396* ▭ *AE, MC, V* ☉ *Closed Sun.*

$$$$ ▣ **J. W. Marriott's Desert Springs Resort and Spa.** This sprawling convention-oriented hotel set on 450 landscaped acres has a dramatic U-shape design. The building wraps around the desert's largest private lake, into which an indoor, stair-stepped waterfall flows. Rooms have lake or Santa Rosa Mountains views, balconies, and oversize bathrooms. It's a long walk from the lobby to the rooms; if you're driving, you might want to request a room close to the parking lot. ⊠ *74–855 Country Club Dr., 92260* ☎ *760/341–2211 or 800/331–3112* 📠 *760/341–1872* ⊕ *www. desertspringsresort.com* ↗ *833 rooms, 51 suites* ♧ *13 restaurants, snack bar, in-room safes, minibars, cable TV with movies, in-room broadband, in-room data ports, driving range, 2 18-hole golf courses, putting green, 20 tennis courts, 3 pools, health club, hair salon, 4 outdoor hot tubs, spa, basketball, croquet, volleyball, 2 bars, nightclub, shop, children's programs (ages 4–12), laundry service, business services, convention center, car rental, no-smoking rooms* ⊟ *AE, D, DC, MC, V.*

$–$$$ ▣ **Mojave.** This tranquil inn, just steps from busy El Paseo, is a 1940s motel that's been transformed into a retro urban oasis. Rooms surround a landscaped courtyard, where a small stream and pond are shaded by mature trees bearing oranges and grapefruit. Large rooms are furnished with reproductions of 1940s chairs, armoires, and tables. Minibars come stocked with bottles of Nehi sodas, and there's a video library of vintage films. All rooms have outdoor sitting areas appointed with director's chairs. In-room spa services are available. ⊠ *73–721 Shadow Mountain Dr., 92260* ☎ *760/346–6121 or 866/846–8358* 📠 *760/674–9072* ⊕ *www.hotelmojave.com* ↗ *22 rooms, 2 suites* ♧ *Some kitchens, minibars, cable TV, in-room VCRs, in-room broadband, in-room data ports, pool, outdoor hot tub, massage, meeting room, no-smoking rooms* ⊟ *AE, D, DC, MC, V* ¶◎ *CP.*

The Arts

McCallum Theatre (⊠ 73–000 Fred Waring Dr. ☎ 760/340–2787 ⊕ www. mccallumtheatre.com), the principal cultural venue in the desert, presents film, classical and popular music, opera, ballet, and theater.

Sports & the Outdoors

BALLOONING **Fantasy Balloon Flights** (⊠ 74–181 Parosella St. ☎ 760/568–0997 ⊕ www. fantasyballoonflights.com) operates sunrise excursions over the southern end of the Coachella Valley. Flights ($160) run from an hour to an hour and a half, followed by a traditional champagne toast.

BICYCLING **Big Wheel Bike Tours** (☎ 760/779–1837 ⊕ www.bwbtours.com) delivers rental mountain, three-speed, and tandem bikes to area hotels. The company also conducts full- and half-day escorted on- and off-road bike tours throughout the area, starting at about $75 per person.

GOLF **Desert Willow Golf Resort** (⊠ 38–500 Portola Ave. ☎ 760/346–7060 ⊕ www.desertwillow.com) is one of the newest golf resorts in the desert. A public course managed by the City of Palm Desert, it has two challenging 18-hole links. Greens fees are $175, including cart.

Shopping

In addition to El Paseo's other shopping treasures, check out **Gardens on El Paseo** (⊠ El Paseo at San Pablo Ave. ☎ 760/862–1990 ⊕ www.

thegardensonelpaseo.com), a shopping center anchored by Saks Fifth Avenue and populated by such mainstream retailers as Brooks Brothers, Ann Taylor, Williams-Sonoma, Tommy Bahama's Emporium, and Pacifica Seafood Restaurant.

Indian Wells

⑭ *5 mi east of Palm Desert on Hwy. 111.*

For the most part a quiet residential community, Indian Wells is the site of golf and tennis tournaments throughout the year, including the Pacific Life Open tennis tournament. Most dining and shopping venues are inside the two huge hotels that dominate the resort scene.

Where to Stay

★ **$$$$** 🏨 **Hyatt Grand Champions Resort.** This stark white resort on 34 acres is one of the grandest in the desert. Standard rooms, large even by local standards, come with furnished patios or balconies and separate living and sleeping areas; they're decorated in warm desert golds and greens. Private villas have secluded garden courtyards with outdoor whirlpool tubs, living rooms with fireplaces, dining rooms—and private butlers who attend to your every whim. The pool area is a kind of garden water park, surrounded by palms and private cabanas. Despite all of its resorty trappings, the Hyatt actually caters to business travelers, not vacationers. ✉ *44–600 Indian Wells La., 92210* ☎ *760/341–1000 or 800/552–4386* 🖷 *760/568–2236* ⊕ *www.grandchampions.hyatt.com* ⇨ *426 rooms, 54 suites* ♨ *4 restaurants, room service, in-room safes, minibars, cable TV with movies, in-room broadband, in-room data ports, Wi-Fi, driving range, 2 18-hole golf courses, putting green, 3 tennis courts, pro shop, 7 pools, health club, hair salon, 3 outdoor hot tubs, massage, sauna, spa, steam room, bicycles, 2 bars, shop, children's programs (ages 3–12), dry cleaning, laundry service, business services, Internet room, meeting rooms, convention center, car rental, no-smoking rooms* ⊟ *AE, D, DC, MC, V.*

$$$$ 🏨 **Renaissance Esmeralda Resort and Spa.** The centerpiece of this luxurious Mediterranean-style resort is an eight-story atrium lobby with a fountain whose water flows through a rivulet in the floor into cascading pools and outside to lakes surrounding the property. Given its size, the hotel is surprisingly intimate. Spacious guest rooms are decorated in soft sunset colors and equipped with sitting areas, balconies, and marble vanities in the bathrooms. One of the resort's pools has a sandy beach. ✉ *44–400 Indian Wells La., 92210* ☎ *760/773–4444 or 800/214–5540* 🖷 *760/773–9308* ⊕ *www.marriothotels.com* ⇨ *538 rooms, 22 suites* ♨ *5 restaurants, room service, in-room safes, minibars, cable TV with movies and video games, in-room broadband, in-room data ports, 2 18-hole golf courses, putting green, 2 tennis courts, pro shop, 3 pools, wading pool, gym, hair salon, 2 outdoor hot tubs, massage, sauna, spa, steam room, bicycles, basketball, volleyball, bar, shop, babysitting, children's programs (ages 5–12), laundry facilities, laundry service, concierge, business services, Internet room, meeting rooms, car rental, free parking, no-smoking rooms* ⊟ *AE, D, DC, MC, V.*

Sports & the Outdoors

GOLF   Next door to the Hyatt Grand Champions Resort, the **Golf Resort at Indian Wells** (⊠ 44–500 Indian Wells La. ☎ 760/346–4653) has two 18-hole Ted Robinson–designed championship courses: the 6,500-yard West Course and the 6,700-yard East Course. A public course, it has been named one of the country's top 10 resorts by *Golf Magazine*. Monday through Thursday greens fees are $125; Friday through Sunday they're $135 (fees may be deeply discounted in summer). The resort also offers instruction through the Indian Wells Golf School.

TENNIS   The **Pacific Life Open** (☎ 800/999–1585 for tickets ⊕ www.pacificlifeopen. com) tennis tournament draws 200 of the world's top players to the Indian Wells Tennis Garden for two weeks in March. With more than 16,000 seats, the stadium is the second largest in the nation.

La Quinta

⑮ *4 mi south of Indian Wells via Washington St.*

The desert became a Hollywood hideout in the 1920s, when La Quinta Hotel (now La Quinta Resort) opened, introducing the Coachella Valley's first golf course. The opening of Old Town La Quinta in 2004 changed the once-quiet atmosphere of this community. A popular attraction, the complex holds popular dining spots, shops, and galleries.

Where to Stay & Eat

$$–$$$$ ✕ **Arnold Palmer's.** From the photos on the walls to the trophy-filled display cases to the putting green for diners awaiting a table, Arnie's image fills this restaurant, surrounded by verdant greens and colorful gardens. The menu lists an array of steaks and chops, including an 18-ounce cowboy bone-in rib eye and barbecued baby back ribs. A few seafood dishes, including halibut and vegetable stir-fry and pasta with lobster, salmon, and shrimp in dill cream sauce, round out the selections. ⊠ *78–164 Ave. 52* ☎ *760/771–4653* ⌂ *Reservations essential* ⊟ *AE, D, MC, V* ☉ *No lunch.*

$–$$$$ ✕ **Hog's Breath Inn.** Clint Eastwood watches over this replica of his Hog's Breath restaurant in Carmel, his presence felt in the larger-than-life photos that fill the walls of its bright dining room. The menu lists a large selection of American comfort food ranging from hanger steak to beef brisket. ⊠ *78–065 Main St.* ☎ *760/564–5556 or 866/464–7888* ⊟ *AE, D, DC, MC, V.*

$$$$ ▥ **La Quinta Resort and Club.** Opened in 1926 (and now a member of
Fodor'sChoice   the Waldorf-Astoria Collection), the desert's oldest resort is a lush green
★   oasis. Broad expanses of lawn separate the adobe casitas that house some rooms; other rooms are in newer two-story units surrounding individual swimming pools and hot tubs amid brilliant gardens. Fireplaces, stocked refrigerators, and fruit-laden orange trees contribute to a luxurious ambience. A premium is placed on privacy, which accounts for La Quinta's continuing popularity with Hollywood celebrities. You can play on the championship golf courses either at La Quinta or at the adjacent PGA West. ⊠ *49–499 Eisenhower Dr., 92253* ☎ *760/564–4111 or 800/598–3828* ⊜ *760/564–5718* ⊕ *www.laquintaresort.com* ⤴ *640*

rooms, 244 suites ♨ 7 restaurants, room service, some in-room safes, minibars, refrigerators, cable TV with movies and video games, in-room data ports, 2 18-hole golf courses, golf privileges, putting green, 23 tennis courts, 41 pools, gym, hair salon, 53 outdoor hot tubs, spa, croquet, volleyball, shops, babysitting, children's programs (ages 4–16), concierge, business services, meeting rooms, car rental, no-smoking rooms ▤ AE, D, DC, MC, V.

The Arts

La Quinta Arts Festival (☎ 760/564–1244 ⊕ www.lqaf.com), normally held the third weekend in March, showcases painting, sculpture, photography, drawing, and printmaking. The show is accompanied by entertainment and food.

Sports & the Outdoors

★ **PGA West** (⊠ 49–499 Eisenhower Dr. ☎ 760/564–7170, 760/564–5729 for tee times ⊕ www.pgawest.com) operates three 18-hole, par-72 championship courses and provides instruction and golf clinics. Greens fees (which include a mandatory cart) range from $50 on weekdays in summer to $235 on weekends in February and March. Bookings are accepted 30 days in advance, but prices are lower when you book close to the date you need.

Indio

⑯ *5 mi east of Indian Wells on Hwy. 111.*

Indio is the home of the date shake, which is exactly what it sounds like: a delicious, extremely thick milk shake made with dates. The city and surrounding countryside generate 95% of the dates grown and harvested in the United States. If you take a hot-air balloon ride, you will likely drift over the tops of date palm trees.

Displays at the **Coachella Valley Museum and Cultural Center,** in a former farmhouse, explain how dates are harvested and how the desert is irrigated for date farming. On the grounds you'll find a smithy and an old sawmill. ⊠ 82–616 Miles Ave. ☎ 760/342–6651 ☒ Free ☉ Sept.–June, Wed.–Sat. 10–4, Sun. 1–4.

You can buy a date shake and take a walking tour of the 175-acre palm arboretum and orchard at **Oasis Date Gardens.** On the tour you learn how dates are pollinated, grown, sorted, stored, and packed for shipping. ⊠ 59–111 Hwy. 111, Thermal ☎ 800/827–8017 ⊕ www.oasisdategardens.com ☒ Free ☉ Walking tours daily 10:30 and 2:30.

🖰 Indio celebrates its raison d'être each February at the **National Date Festival and Riverside County Fair.** The midmonth festivities include an Arabian Nights pageant, camel and ostrich races, and exhibits of local dates. Admission includes camel rides. ⊠ Riverside County Fairgrounds, 46–350 Arabia St. ☎ 800/811–3247 ⊕ www.datefest.org ☒ $7.

Where to Stay & Eat

$–$$ ✕ **Ciro's Ristorante and Pizzeria.** This popular casual restaurant has been serving pizza and pasta since the 1970s. The menu lists some unusual pizzas, such as cashew with three cheeses. Daily pasta specials vary but might include red- or white-clam sauce or scallops with parsley and red wine. ☒ 81–963 Hwy. 111 ☎ 760/347–6503 ⊕ www.cirospasta.com ▤ AE, D, MC, V ⊘ No lunch Sun.

♨ **$$** ▥ **Fantasy Springs Resort Casino.** Opened in early 2005, this family-oriented resort casino, operated by the Cabazon Band of Mission Indians, is the tallest building in the Coachella Valley, affording mountain views from most rooms and the rooftop bar. Rooms are appointed in dark-wood Arts-and-Crafts style. Many have balconies overlooking the pool area, which has not only a free-form pool with a sandy beach at one end but also fountains and waterfalls adjacent to a grassy area where families can picnic. The casino provides Las Vegas–style gaming. ☒ 84–245 Indio Springs Pkwy., 92203 ☎ 760/342–5000 or 800/827–2946 ☐ 760/238–5616 ⊕ www.fantasyspringsresort.com ⇌ 240 rooms, 11 suites ↺ 4 restaurants, café, coffee shop, picnic area, room service, in-room safes, cable TV with movies and video games, some in-room DVDs, in-room broadband, golf privileges, pool, wading pool, gym, 2 outdoor hot tubs, massage, billiards, bowling, 5 bars, sports bar, casino, video game room, shops, babysitting, dry cleaning, laundry service, concierge, meeting rooms, free parking, no-smoking rooms ▤ AE, D, MC, V.

Sports & the Outdoors

The **Eldorado Polo Club** (☒ 50–950 Madison St. ☎ 760/342–2223), known as the winter polo capital of the West, is the site of many polo events. You can pack a picnic and watch practice matches for free during the week.

ALONG TWENTYNINE PALMS HIGHWAY
INCLUDING JOSHUA TREE NATIONAL PARK

The towns of Yucca Valley and Twentynine Palms punctuate Twentynine Palms Highway (Highway 62)—the northern highway from the desert resorts to Joshua Tree National Park—and provide lodging and other visitor services to park goers. Flanked by Twentynine Palms Highway on the north and Interstate 10 on the south, the park protects some of the southern desert's most interesting and beautiful scenery. A visit to the park provides a glimpse of the rigors of desert life in the Little San Bernardino Mountains. You can see the park highlights in a half day or take a daylong expedition into the backcountry.

Yucca Valley

⓲ *30 mi northeast of Palm Springs on Hwy. 62, Twentynine Palms Hwy.*

One of the fastest-growing cities in the high desert, Yucca Valley is emerging as a bedroom community for people who work as far away as Ontario, 85 mi to the west. In this sprawling suburb you can shop for necessities, get your car serviced, and chow down at the fast-food outlets. For some fun, head a few miles north to Pioneertown.

The **Hi-Desert Nature Museum** has a small live animal display containing creatures that make their homes in Joshua Tree, including scorpions, snakes, ground squirrels, and chuckawallas, a type of lizard. There's also a collection of rocks, minerals, and fossils from the Paleozoic era, a Native American collection, and a children's room. ⊠ *57–116 Twentynine Palms Hwy.* ☎ *760/369–7212* ⊕ *www.yucca-valley.org* ✉ *Free* ☉ *Tues.–Sun. 10–5.*

In 1946 Roy Rogers, Gene Autry, and Russ Hayden built **Pioneertown** (⊠ 4 mi north of Yucca Valley on Pioneertown Rd. ⊕ www.pioneertown. com), an 1880s-style Wild West movie set complete with hitching posts, saloon, and an OK Corral. Today 250 people call the place home, even as film crews continue shooting. You can stroll past wooden and adobe storefronts and feel like you're back in the Old West. The new owners of Pappy & Harriet's have started building an outdoor concert venue for about 500 people and have started booking popular bands and singers. Gunfights are staged April through November, Saturday at 1 and 2 and Sunday at 2:30.

Where to Stay & Eat

$–$$ ✕ **Pappy & Harriet's Pioneertown Palace.** Smack in the middle of a Western-movie-set town is this Western-movie-set saloon where you can have dinner, dance to live country-and-western music, or just relax with a drink at the bar. The food ranges from Tex-Mex to Santa Maria barbecue to steak and burgers—no surprises but plenty of fun. ■ TIP→ **Pappy & Harriet's may be in the middle of nowhere, but you'll need reservations for dinner on weekends.** ⊠ *53688 Pioneertown Rd., Pioneertown* ☎ *760/ 365–5956* ⊕ *www.pappyandharriets.com* 🖃 *AE, D, MC, V* ☉ *No lunch Mon.–Wed.*

¢–$ ✕ **Edchada's.** Rock climbers who spend their days in Joshua Tree National Park swear by the margaritas at this Mexican restaurant, which also has a location in Twentynine Palms. Specialties include climber-size portions of fajitas, carnitas, seafood enchiladas, and fish tacos. ⊠ *56–805 Twentynine Palms Hwy., Yucca Valley* ☎ *760/365–7655* 🖃 *AE, D, MC, V* ⊠ *73–502 Twentynine Palms Hwy., Twentynine Palms* ☎ *760/367– 2131* 🖃 *AE, D, MC, V.*

$–$$ 🏨 **Rimrock Ranch Cabins.** The quiet beauty of the surrounding desert attracts Hollywood writers, artists, and musicians to these four circa-1940s housekeeping cabins. Owners Szu and Dusty Wakeman have restored the cabins to their original condition, complete with knotty-pine paneling, vintage Wedgwood stoves, artisan tiles, and antique furnishings. Special touches include outdoor fireplaces and espresso machines in the fully equipped kitchens. The grounds include a stargazing deck, campfire pit, and a deep-pit barbecue. ⊠ *53688 Pioneertown Rd., Pioneertown 92268* ☎ *760/228–1297* 🖷 *818/557–6383* ⊕ *www. pappyandharriets.com* ➥ *4 cabins* ᐰ *Kitchens, in-room VCRs, pool, massage, some pets allowed; no room phones, no room TVs, no smoking* 🖃 *AE, MC, V.*

¢ 🏨 **Pioneertown Motel.** Built in 1946 as a bunkhouse for Western film stars shooting in Pioneertown, this motel sticks close to its roots. Each room, from the Cowboy Room to the Twilight Zone Room, has a theme that matches its name. For example, the Flower Room is all about buds and blooms. Hiking trails outside the motel lead into the desert. Bring your horse—there are corrals for visiting animals. ✉ *5040 Curtis Rd., Pioneertown 92268* ☎ *760/365–4879* 🖷 *760/365–3127* ⊕ *www.pioneertownmotel.com* ⇌ *20 rooms* △ *Some kitchenettes, microwaves, refrigerators, some pets allowed (fee); no a/c in some rooms, no room phones, no TV in some rooms* ▭ *AE, D, MC, V.*

Twentynine Palms

❶❾ *24 mi east of Yucca Valley on Hwy. 62, Twentynine Palms Hwy.*

The main gateway town to Joshua Tree National Park, Twentynine Palms is also the location of the U.S. Marine Air Ground Task Force Training Center. You can find services, supplies, and lodgings in town. The history and current life of Twentynine Palms is depicted in **Oasis of Murals**, a collection of 20 murals painted on the sides of buildings. If you drive around town, you can't miss them, but you can also pick up a free map from the **Action Council for 29 Palms** (✉ 6455B Mesquite Ave. ☎ 760/361–2286 ⊕ www.oasisofmurals.com).

☾ The area's big draw, however, is **Joshua Tree National Park,** whose main
Fodor'sChoice   entrance is 2 mi south of Twentynine Palms. In part because it's so close
★   to Los Angeles and San Diego, this 794,000-acre expanse of complex, ruggedly beautiful desert scenery receives more than a million visitors each year. Its boulder-strewn mountains, natural cactus gardens, and lush oases shaded by tall fan palms mark the meeting place of the Mojave (high) and Colorado (low) deserts. This is prime hiking, rock-climbing, and exploring country, where coyotes, desert pack rats, and exotic plants such as the white yucca, red-tipped ocotillo, and cholla cactus reside. Extensive stands of Joshua trees (they're actually shrubs, not trees) give the park its name. The plants reminded early white settlers of the biblical Joshua, with their thick, stubby branches representing his arms raised toward heaven. You can see portions of the park in a half-day excursion from Palm Springs or the other desert resort cities. A full-day driving tour allows time for a nature walk or two and stops at many of the 50 wayside exhibits, which provide insight into Joshua Tree's geology and rich vegetation.

The elevation in some areas of the park exceeds 4,000 feet, and light snowfalls and cold, strong north winds are common in winter. There are no services within the park and little water, so you should carry a gallon of water per person per day. Use sunscreen liberally any time of the year.

To get oriented, head to the **Oasis Visitor Center** (✉ Utah Trail, ½ mi south of Hwy. 62 ☎ 760/367–5500), about 3 mi north of the north entrance to the park. It has many free and inexpensive brochures, books, posters, and maps as well as several educational exhibits. Rangers are on hand to answer questions. Walk ½ mi from the visitor center to the **Oasis of Mara.** Inhabited by Native Americans and later by prospectors and homesteaders, the oasis provides a home for birds, small mammals, and other wildlife.

Heading south from the visitor center, you can drive west on Park Boulevard to take in several scenic valleys, a dam, and an old ranch, or you can head southwest on Pinto Basin Road for a stunning desert drive through Pinto Basin.

On the Park Boulevard side, you can hike the ¼-mi **Skull Rock Trail** (⊠ Jumbo Rocks Campground, just beyond loop E), which passes through boulder piles, desert washes, and a rocky valley. About 10 mi from the North Entrance Station, **Geology Tour Road** (⊠ South of Queen Valley) is an 18-mi dirt road with 18 stops, recommended only for four-wheel-drive vehicles. The road winds through some of the park's most fascinating landscapes. Alternatively, you can drive east to west through **Queen Valley** (⊠ Barker Dam Rd.) to see stands of Joshua trees that are particularly alluring in spring, when they display large creamy white blossoms. **Hidden Valley,** a boulder-strewn area, was once a cattle rustlers' hideout. You'll understand why the bandits chose this spot when you crawl between the big rocks. On the Saturday night closest to each full moon the Andromda Astronomical Society hosts a stargazing party here; visit ⊕ www.nps.gov/jotr/ for dates and times. A 1¹⁄₁₀-mi loop trail leads from Hidden Valley to **Barker Dam.** Built around 1900 by ranchers and miners to hold water for cattle and mining operations, the dam now serves the same purpose for wildlife.

Near Hidden Valley you can take the 90-minute guided **Keys–Desert Queen Ranch walking tour.** This ranger-led tour explores the homestead created by Joshua Tree pioneers William and Frances Keys and provides a glimpse of the 60 years the couple spent raising a family and working the land under extreme desert conditions. Bill Keys dug wells by hand and installed an irrigation system to water his vegetable gardens, fruit orchards, and wheat and alfalfa fields. The ranch has been restored to look much as it did when he died in 1969—the missus succumbed years earlier. The house, schoolhouse, store, and workshop still stand; the orchard has been replanted; and the grounds are full of old trucks, cars, and mining equipment. ⊠ *Off Park Blvd., 2 mi north of intersection with western end of Barker Dam Rd.* ☎ *760/367–5555* ✍ *$5* ☉ *Oct.–May, daily at 10 and 1.*

Survey all of Hidden Valley from **Keys View** (⊠ Keys View Rd., 21 mi south of west entrance), the most dramatic overlook in Joshua Tree National Park. At 5,185 feet, the spot has a view across the desert to Mt. San Jacinto near Palm Springs, and, on clear days, as far south as the Salton Sea. Sunrise and sunset are magical times, when the light throws rocks and trees into high relief before (or after) bathing the hills in brilliant shades of red, orange, and gold. A fairly strenuous 4-mi round-trip hike on **Lost Horse Mine Trail** (⊠ Parking area 1¼ mi east of Keys View Rd.) takes you along a former mining road to a well-preserved stamp mill, which was used to crush rock mined from the nearby mountain in search of gold. The operation was one of the most successful around, and the mine's cyanide settling tanks and stone buildings are the area's best preserved. Allow about four hours for the hike. From the mill area, a short but steep 10-minute climb takes you to the top of a 5,278-foot mountain.

If, on the other hand, you head east on Pinto Basin Road, you'll get to **Cholla Cactus Gardens** (✉ Pinto Basin Rd., 10 mi southeast of junction with Park Blvd.). Here you can see a stand of Bigelow cholla, sometimes called the jumping cholla because its hooked spines seem to jump at you as you walk past. The chollas are best seen and photographed in late afternoon, when their backlighted, spiky stalks stand out against a colorful sky. The **Ocotillo Patch** (✉ Pinto Basin Rd., about 3 mi east of Cholla Cactus Gardens) has a roadside exhibit on the dramatic display made by the red-tipped succulent after even the shortest rain shower.

Follow Pinto Basin Road south toward **Cottonwood Visitor Center** (✉ Pinto Basin Rd., 32 mi southeast of North Entrance Station ☎ No phone), which has a small museum, picnic tables, drinking water, and restrooms. (If you're coming on Interstate 10 you enter at this end of the park.) A 1-mi trail leads from the visitor center to the **Cottonwood Spring Oasis**. Noted for its abundant birdlife, the palm-shaded oasis was an important water stop for prospectors, miners, and teamsters traveling between the small town of Mecca (to the southwest) and mines to the north. You can see the remains of an *arrastra*, a primitive type of gold mill, near the oasis, as well as the concrete ruins of two gold mines. Bighorn sheep frequent this area in winter. ✉ *74–485 National Park Dr., Twentynine Palms* ☎ *760/367–5500* ⊕ *www.nps.gov/jotr* ☞ *$15 per vehicle, $5 per person on foot or bike, $5–$10 per night camping fee* ☉ *Daily 24 hrs; visitor centers daily 8–5.*

⚠ There are no restaurants inside Joshua Tree, so you have to bring your own lunch. Picnic areas within the park are equipped with just the basics—picnic tables, fire pits, and primitive restrooms. Only those near the entrances have water. There are picnic areas at the Cottonwood Spring Visitor Center and in Hidden Valley, as well as at Live Oak Springs, on Park Boulevard east of Jumbo Rocks.

Where to Stay & Eat

¢ ✕ **Park Rock Café.** If you're on your way to the national park on Highway 62, stop in the town of Joshua Tree (not to be confused with the park) to fill up on a hearty breakfast bagel sandwich and order a bag lunch to take with you. The café creates some hearty sandwiches such as roast beef with Philly cheese or chicken Parmesan. Outside dining is pleasant here. ✉ *6554 Park Blvd., Joshua Tree* ☎ *760/366–3622* ▭ *MC, V* ☉ *No dinner Sun.–Thurs.*

¢–$$ ✕▭ **29 Palms Inn.** The funky 29 Palms is the lodging closest to the entrance to Joshua Tree National Park. The collection of adobe and wood-frame cottages is scattered over 70 acres of grounds that are popular with birds and bird-watchers year-round. Innkeeper Jane Smith's warm, personal service more than makes up for the cottages' rustic qualities. Ranging from pasta to seafood, the contemporary fare at the inn's convivial restaurant ($$–$$$) is more sophisticated than its Old West appearance might suggest. ✉ *73–950 Inn Ave., 92277* ☎ *760/367–3505* 🖷 *760/367–4425* ⊕ *www.29palmsinn.com* ☞ *18 rooms, 5 suites* △ *Restaurant, pool, hot tub, some pets allowed (fee); no a/c, no room phones, no smoking* ▭ *AE, D, DC, MC, V* ⑪ *CP.*

★ **$$** ▦ **Roughley Manor.** To the wealthy pioneer who erected the stone mansion now occupied by this B&B, expense was no object. A 50-foot-long planked maple floor is the pride of the great room, the carpentry on the walls throughout is intricate, and huge stone fireplaces warm the house on the rare cold night. Original fixtures still gleam in the bathrooms, and bedrooms hold pencil and canopy beds and some fireplaces. The innkeepers serve afternoon tea and evening dessert. An acre of gardens shaded by Washingtonia palms surrounds the house. ⊠ *74–744 Joe Davis Rd., 92277* ☎ *760/367–3238* 🖷 *760/367–6261* ⊕ *www.roughleymanor. com* 🛏 *2 suites, 7 cottages* ♿ *Some kitchens, microwaves, refrigerators, pool, outdoor hot tub, some pets allowed; no room phones, no smoking* ⊟ *DC, MC, V* ⏇ *BP.*

★**¢–$** ▦ **Best Western Garden Inn & Suites.** This bright complex has smartly furnished rooms, some of which have coffeemakers and hot tubs. ⊠ *71–487 Twentynine Palms Hwy., 92277* ☎ *760/367–9141* 🖷 *760/367–2584* ⊕ *www.bestwestern.com* 🛏 *72 rooms, 12 suites* ♿ *Some kitchenettes, microwaves, refrigerators, cable TV, in-room broadband, Wi-Fi, in-room data ports, pool, outdoor hot tub, laundry facilities, free parking, no-smoking rooms* ⊟ *AE, D, DC, MC, V* ⏇ *CP.*

⚠ **Cottonwood Campground.** In spring this campground is surrounded by some of the desert's finest wildflowers. Joshua Tree National Park's southernmost campground, Cottonwood is often the last to fill up. Reservations are not accepted. ⊠ *Pinto Basin Rd., 32 mi south of North Entrance Station* ☎ *760/367–5500* ⊕ *www.nps.gov/jotr* 🖃 *$10* ♿ *Flush toilets, dump station, fire pits, picnic tables, ranger station* 🛏 *62 sites, 3 group sites.*

⚠ **Hidden Valley Campground.** This campground is most popular with rock climbers, who make their way up valley rock formations that have names like the Blob, Old Woman, and Chimney Rock. RVs are permitted, but there are no hookups. Reservations are not accepted. ⊠ *Off Park Blvd., 20 mi southwest of Oasis of Mara* ☎ *760/367–5500* ⊕ *www. nps.gov/jotr* 🖃 *$5* ♿ *Pit toilets, fire pits, picnic tables* 🛏 *39 sites.*

Sports & the Outdoors

Joshua Tree Rock Climbing School offers several programs, from introductory classes to multiday programs for experienced climbers. All equipment is provided. Beginning classes are limited to six people age 13 or older. 🖙 *HCR Box 3034, Joshua Tree 92252* ☎ *760/366–4745 or 800/ 890–4745* ⊕ *www.joshuatreerockclimbing.com* 🖃 *$110 for beginner class.*

Vertical Adventures Climbing School trains about 1,000 climbers each year in Joshua Tree National Park. Classes meet at a designated location in the park. All equipment is provided. ☎ *800/514–8785* ⊕ *www. verticaladventures.com* 🖃 *$105 per person for one-day class* ⊘ *Closed July and Aug.*

ANZA-BORREGO DESERT

Largely uninhabited, the Anza-Borrego Desert is popular with those who love solitude, silence, space, starry nights, light, and sweeping vistas. The desert lies south of the Palm Springs area, stretching along the western shore of the Salton Sea down to Interstate 8 along the Mexican border. Isolated from the rest of California by mile-high mountains to the north and west, most of this desert falls within the borders of Anza-Borrego Desert State Park, which at more than 600,000 acres is the largest state park in the contiguous United States. This is a place where you can escape the cares of the human world.

For thousands of years Native Americans of the Cahuilla and Kumeyaay people inhabited this area, spending their winters on the warm desert floor and their summers in the mountains. The first Europeans—a party led by Spanish explorer Juan Baptiste de Anza—crossed this desert in 1776. Anza, for whom the desert is named, made the trip through here twice. Roadside signs along highways 86, 78, and S2 mark the route of the Anza expedition, which spent Christmas Eve 1776 in what is now Anza-Borrego Desert State Park. Seventy-five years later thousands of immigrants on their way to the goldfields up north crossed the desert on the Southern Immigrant Trail, remnants of which remain along Highway S2. Permanent settlers arrived early in the 20th century, and by the 1930s the first adobe resort cottage had been built.

Borrego Springs

② *59 mi south of Indio via Hwys. 86 and S22.*

The permanent population of Borrego Springs, set squarely in the middle of Anza-Borrego Desert State Park, hovers around 2,500. Long a quiet town, it's emerging as a laid-back destination for desert lovers. September through June, when temperatures stay in the 80s and 90s, you can engage in outdoor activities such as hiking, nature study, golf, tennis, horseback riding, and mountain biking. If winter rains cooperate, Borrego Springs puts on some of the best wildflower displays in the low desert. In some years the desert floor is carpeted with color: yellow dandelions and sunflowers, pink primrose, purple sand verbena, and blue phacelia. The bloom generally runs from late February through April. For current information on wildflowers around Borrego Springs, call ☎ 760/767–4684.

★ One of the richest living natural-history museums in the nation, **Anza-Borrego Desert State Park** is a vast, nearly uninhabited wilderness where you can step through a field of wildflowers, cool off in a palm-shaded oasis, count zillions of stars in the black night sky, and listen to coyotes howl at dusk. The landscape, largely undisturbed by humans, reveals a rich natural history. There's evidence of a vast inland sea in the piles of oyster beds near Split Mountain and of the power of natural forces such as earthquakes and flash floods. In addition, recent scientific work has confirmed that the Borrego Badlands, with more than 6,000 meters of exposed fossil-bearing sediments is likely the richest such deposit in North America, telling the story of 7 million years of climate change, upheaval, and prehistoric animals. They've found evidence of saber-tooth cats, flamingos, zebras, and the largest flying bird in the Northern Hemisphere beneath the now parched sand. Today the desert's most treasured inhabitants are the herds of elusive and endangered native bighorn sheep, or *borego,* for which the park is named. Among the strange desert plants you may observe are the gnarly elephant trees. As these are endangered, rangers don't encourage visitors to seek out the secluded grove at Fish Creek, but there are a few examples at the visitor center garden. After a wet winter you can see a short-lived but stunning display of cacti, succulents, and desert wildflowers in bloom.

Anza-Borrego Desert State Park is unusually accessible to visitors. Admission to the park is free, and few areas are off-limits. Unlike most parks in the country, Anza-Borrego lets you camp anywhere; just follow the trails and pitch a tent wherever you like. There are more than 500 mi of dirt roads, two huge wilderness areas, and 110 mi of riding and hiking trails. Many of the park's sites can be seen from paved roads, but some require driving on dirt roads, for which rangers recommend you use a four-wheel-drive vehicle. When you do leave the pavement, carry the appropriate supplies: a cell phone (which may be unreliable in some areas), a shovel and other tools, flares, blankets, and plenty of water. The canyons are susceptible to flash flooding, so inquire about weather conditions (even on sunny days) before entering.

To get oriented and obtain information on weather and wildlife conditions, stop by the **Visitors Information Center.** Designed to keep cool during the desert's blazing hot summers, the center is built underground, beneath a demonstration desert garden. A nature trail here takes you through a garden containing examples of most of the native flora and a little pupfish pond. ⊠ *200 Palm Canyon Dr., Hwy. S22* ☎ *760/767–5311, 760/767–4684 wildflower hotline* ⊕ *www.anzaborrego.statepark. org* ☉ *June–Sept., weekends and holidays 9–5; Oct.–May, daily 9–5.*

At **Borrego Palm Canyon** (⊠ Palm Canyon Dr., Hwy. S22, about 1 mi west of the Visitors Information Center), a 1½-mi trail leads to one of the few native palm groves in North America. There are more than 1,000 native fan palms in the grove, and a stream and waterfall greet you at trail's end. The moderate hike is the most popular in the park.

Yaqui Well Nature Trail (⊠ Hwy. 78, across from Tamarisk Campground) takes you along a path to a desert water hole where birds and wildlife are abundant. It's also a good place to look for wildflowers in spring.

Coyote Canyon (⊠ Off DiGiorgio Rd., 4½ mi north of Borrego Springs) has a year-round stream and lush plant life. Portions of the canyon road follow a section of the old Anza Trail. The canyon is closed between June 15 and September 15 to allow native bighorn sheep undisturbed use of the water. The dirt road that gives access to the canyon may be sandy enough to require a four-wheel-drive vehicle.

The late-afternoon view of the Borrego badlands from **Font's Point** (⊠ Off Borrego Salton Seaway, Hwy. S22, 13 mi east of Borrego Springs) is one of the most breathtaking views seen in the desert, especially when the setting sun casts a golden glow on the eroded mountain slopes. The road from the Font's Point turnoff can be rough enough to make using a four-wheel-drive vehicle advisable; inquire about its condition at the visitor center before starting out. Even if you can't make it out on the paved road, you can see some of the view from the highway.

Narrows Earth Trail (⊠ Off Hwy. 78, 13 mi west of Borrego Springs) is a short walk off the road east of Tamarisk Grove campground. Along the way you can see evidence of the many geologic processes involved in forming the canyons of the desert, such as a contact zone between two earthquake faults, and sedimentary layers of metamorphic and igneous rock.

Geology students from all over the world visit the Fish Creek area of Anza-Borrego to explore a canyon known as **Split Mountain** (⊠ Split Mountain Rd., 9 mi south of Hwy. 78 at Ocotillo Wells). The narrow gorge with 600-foot walls was formed by an ancient stream. Fossils in this area indicate that a sea once covered the desert floor.

The easy, mostly flat **Pictograph/Smuggler's Canyon Trail** (⊠ Blair Valley, Hwy. S2, 6 mi southeast of Hwy. 78 at Scissors Crossing intersection) traverses a boulder-strewn trail. At the end is a collection of rocks covered with muted red and yellow pictographs painted within the last hundred years or so by Native Americans. Walk about ½ mi beyond the pictures to reach Smuggler's Canyon, where an overlook provides views of the Vallecito Valley. The hike is 2 to 3 mi round-trip.

Just a few steps off the paved road, **Carrizo Badlands Overlook** (⊠ Off Hwy. S2, 40 mi south of Scissors Crossing [intersection of Hwys. S2 and 78]) offers a view of eroded and twisted sedimentary rock that obscures the fossils of the mastodons, saber-tooths, zebras, and camels that roamed this region a million years ago. The route to the overlook through Earthquake Valley and Blair Valley parallels the Southern Emigrant Trail.

Where to Stay & Eat

$$-$$$$ ✕ **Krazy Coyote Bar & Grill.** Dine inside in the cozy bar or outside by the pool at this restaurant at the Palms at Indianhead. Either way you'll hear Bing Crosby and Peggy Lee softly crooning '50s songs in the background as you enjoy a well-prepared seared ahi, spicy Santa Fe crab cakes, or sesame-garlic grilled pork tenderloin. Be warned that summer hours vary. ⊠ 2220 Hoberg Rd. ☎ 760/767–7788 ▤ AE, D, DC, MC, V ☉ No lunch.

¢-$$ ✕ **Bernard's.** In a single large room with a wall of windows, chef-owner Bernard offers casual dining with an Alsatian flavor. Try sauerkraut Alsatian style, daily regional preparations of duck, and roast leg of lamb. ⊠ 501 Palm Canyon Dr. ☎ 760/767–5666 ▤ AE, D, MC, V ☉ Closed Sun.

★ $$$$ ✕▦ **La Casa del Zorro.** This serene resort owned by San Diego's prominent Copley family pampers guests with spectacular desert scenery, luxurious accommodations, and gracious service. A few hundred yards away from your room is a quiet desert garden, where you can walk and find yourself surrounded by ocotillo and cholla. Accommodations range from ample standard rooms to private casitas with their own pools or private outdoor hot tubs. The elegant restaurant ($$$–$$$$) has excellent service, fireside dining, and a good Sunday brunch. La Casa schedules wine, music, and astronomy weekends throughout the year. In summer, prices are deeply discounted. ⊠ 3845 Yaqui Pass Rd., 92004

☎ 760/767–5323 or 800/824–1884 🖶 760/767–5963 ⊕ *www. lacasadelzorro.com* ⇨ *48 rooms, 12 suites, 19 1- to 4-bedroom casitas* ♨ *2 restaurants, room service, BBQs, fans, some in-room hot tubs, microwaves, minibars, cable TV with movies, some in-room DVD/VCR, in-room broadband, in-room data ports, Wi-Fi, putting green, 6 tennis courts, 5 pools, fitness classes, health club, hair salon, 3 outdoor hot tubs, massage, bicycles, archery, boccie, croquet, hiking, horseback riding, horseshoes, Ping-Pong, shuffleboard, volleyball, lounge, children's programs (ages 7–12), concierge, business services, meeting room, free parking, no-smoking rooms* ☰ *AE, D, MC, V.*

$$–$$$ 🏨 **Borrego Valley Inn.** Desert gardens of mesquite, ocotillo, and creosote surround adobe Southwestern-style buildings. Spacious rooms with plenty of light are decorated with Native American–designed fabrics and hold original art. Furnishings include lodgepole-pine beds with down comforters and serape-stripe bedspreads, walk-in showers with garden views, and double futons facing corner fireplaces. Every room opens out to its own enclosed garden with chaises, chairs, and table. Friendly innkeepers serve a tasty continental breakfast, and you can enjoy the courtyard desert garden while dining. ✉ *405 Palm Canyon Dr., 92004* ☎ *760/767–0311 or 800/333–5810* 🖶 *760/767–0900* ⊕ *www. borregovalleyinn.com* ⇨ *14 rooms, 1 suite* ♨ *Some kitchenettes, microwaves, refrigerators, cable TV, in-room data ports, Wi-Fi, 2 pools, 2 outdoor hot tubs; no smoking* ☰ *D, MC, V* ⭐ *CP.*

¢–$$$ 🏨 **Borrego Springs Resort and Country Club.** This quiet resort offers good value when compared with other Borrego Springs lodgings. Large rooms in a collection of two-story buildings surrounding the swimming pool are nicely kept and appointed with simple oak furnishings. All have shaded balconies or patios. In spring desert gardens surrounding the property show a colorful bloom. The Borrego Springs Country Club restaurant on-site is open daily except Monday for lunch and dinner. ✉ *1112 Tilting T Dr., 92004* ☎ *760/767–5700 or 888/826–7734* 🖶 *760/767–5710* ⊕ *www.borregospringsresort.com* ⇨ *66 rooms, 34 suites* ♨ *2 restaurants, some kitchenettes, microwaves, refrigerators, cable TV, in-room data ports, 3 9-hole golf courses, putting green, 6 tennis courts, 2 pools, gym, outdoor hot tub, bar, laundry facilities, meeting room, free parking, some pets allowed (fee), no-smoking rooms* ☰ *AE, D, MC, V.*

¢–$$$ 🏨 **Palm Canyon Resort.** One of the largest properties around, Palm Canyon Resort includes a hotel a quarter mile from the park visitor center and an RV park with 130 spaces. Western-style rooms with balconies or patios were undergoing renovation in summer 2006. ✉ *221 Palm Canyon Dr., 92004* ☎ *760/767–5341 or 800/242–0044* 🖶 *760/767–4073* ⊕ *www.pcresort.com* ⇨ *60 rooms, 1 suite* ♨ *Restaurant, minibars, refrigerators, cable TV with movies, in-room VCRs, in-room broadband, in-room data ports, some Wi-Fi, pool, gym, outdoor hot tub, bar, library, shop, laundry facilities, meeting room, no-smoking rooms* ☰ *AE, D, MC, V.*

🏕 **Borrego Palm Canyon.** This pleasant campground is near the Borrego Palm Canyon trailhead. There are two sections: one for recreational vehicles with hookups and another without hookups, designed for tent campers. Tent sites have ramadas (rock walls with thatched roofs) for shade. ⊠ *Palm Canyon Dr., Hwy. S22, about 1 mi west of Visitors Information Center* ☎ *760/767–5311, 800/444–7275 for reservations* ⊕ *www.reserveamerica.com* ⚐ *$15–29* ⚲ *Flush toilets, full hookups, drinking water, showers, fire pits, picnic tables, public telephone* ⚑ *52 RV sites, 65 tent sites.*

⚠ **Tamarisk Grove.** Campsites are tucked under the shade of sprawling tamarisk trees at this campground across the road from the 1½-mi Yaqui Well Nature Trail. There are no hookups, but the sites can hold RVs up to 21 feet. ⊠ *Yaqui Pass Rd., 13 mi west of Borrego Springs* ☎ *760/767–5311, 800/444–7275 for reservations* ⊕ *www.reserveamerica. com* ⚐ *$15–$20* ⚲ *Flush toilets, drinking water, showers, fire pits, picnic tables* ⚑ *27 sites.*

Sports & the Outdoors

The 27 holes of golf at **Borrego Springs Resort and Country Club** (⊠ 1112 Tilting T Dr. ☎ 760/767–3330 ⊕ www.borregospringsresort.com) are open to the public. Three 9-hole courses, with natural desert landscaping and mature date palms, can be played individually or in any combination. Greens fees are $65 to $75, depending on the course and the day of the week, and include a cart. **Roadrunner Club** (⊠ 1010 Palm Canyon Dr. ☎ 760/767–5374 ⊕ www.roadrunnerclub.com) has an 18-hole golf course. Greens fees are $20, and carts are $14.

You can select from a variety of equine encounters at **Smoketree Institute and Ranch** (☎ 760/767–5850), which gives desert horseback rides on Arabian or quarter horses, pony rides for kids, and a nonriding human/horse communication experience similar to horse-whispering.

IMPERIAL VALLEY

FROM THE SALTON SEA TO THE MEXICAN BORDER

Imperial County lies between the Colorado River, to the east, and the Anza-Borrego Desert, to the west. The area is both a great desert and one of the richest agricultural regions in the world, producing primarily winter vegetables, grains, and cattle. The briny Salton Sea, California's largest lake, occupies a large portion of Imperial County. The sea is a vast inland water-recreation area, and El Centro is the commercial and business heart of the valley. This is stereotypical desert, complete with miles and miles of sand dunes, an average annual rainfall of less than 1 inch, and summer temperatures soaring above 100°F.

Salton Sea

★ *30 mi southeast of Indio via Hwy. 86 on western shore and via Hwy. 111 on eastern shore; 29 mi east of Borrego Springs via Hwy. S22.*

The Salton Sea, barely 100 years old, is the product of both natural and artificial forces. The sea occupies the Salton Basin, a remnant of prehistoric Lake Cahuilla. Over the centuries the Colorado River flooded the basin and the water drained into the Gulf of California. In 1905 a flood once again filled the Salton Basin. Because the exit to the gulf was now blocked by sediment, the floodwaters remained in the basin. The resulting body of water was trapped 228 feet below sea level, creating a saline lake about 35 mi long and 15 mi wide, with a surface area of nearly 380 square mi. The lake has no real inflow, so over the years evaporation has made it 25% saltier than the ocean, creating a rare and splendid habitat for birds and fish. Lying along the Pacific Flyway, the sea supports 400 species of birds. Four sport fish inhabit the Salton Sea: corvina, sargo, Gulf croaker, and tilapia. Fishing, boating, camping, and bird-watching are popular activities year-round. Despite earlier development failures along the banks of the sea, a new housing boom is beginning to emerge along its western shore. Just the same, sea's future remains uncertain.

On the north shore of the sea, the huge **Salton Sea State Recreation Area** draws thousands each year to its playgrounds, hiking trails, fishing spots, boat launches, and swimming areas. The Headquarters Visitor Center contains exhibits and shows a short film on the history of the Salton Sea. Summer is the best time for fishing here. ⊠ *100–225 State Park Rd., North Shore* ☎ *760/393–3052* ⊕ *www.parks.ca.gov* ☜ *$6* ☽ *Park daily 8–sunset, visitor center Oct.–Apr., daily 8–sunset, May–Sept., weekends only.*

The 1,785-acre **Sonny Bono National Wildlife Refuge,** on the Pacific Flyway, is a wonderful spot for viewing migratory birds. You might see eared grebes, burrowing owls, great blue herons, ospreys, yellow-footed gulls, white and brown pelicans, and snow geese heading south from Canada. Facilities include a visitor center with bird displays, self-guided trails, observation platforms, and interpretive exhibits. Fishing and waterfowl hunting are permitted in season in designated areas. ⊠ *906 W. Sinclair Rd., Calipatria* ☎ *760/348–5278* ⊕ *www.fws.gov/saltonsea* ☜ *Free* ☽ *Daily sunrise–sunset. Visitor center weekdays 7–3:30.*

Sports & the Outdoors

At the Salton Sea all sorts of water sports are popular. You can waterski, kayak, and canoe, or fish from the shore, from a boat, and from the jetty at Varner Harbor. Swimming is permitted at beaches anywhere along the shoreline, but be warned that the water is brackish. You can launch your boat at **Varner Harbor** (⊠ 100–225 State Park Rd., North Shore ☎ 760/393–3052, 800/444–7275 for reservations), where a ramp and five docks are available. The fee is $6.

Camping

△ **New Camp.** Near park headquarters, New Camp is designed for tent campers. Sites have shaded ramadas and paved parking stalls. It's a short walk from here to the Varner Harbor boat-launching area and the park's prime fishing spots. ♿ *Flush toilets, drinking water, showers, fire pits, picnic tables* ⊅ *25 sites* ⊠ *100–225 State Park Rd., North Shore* ☎ *760/393–3052, 800/444–7275 for reservations* ⊕ *www.parks.ca.gov* ☜ *$12–$18.*

△ **Salton Sea State Recreation Area Headquarters.** This tree-shaded parking area for RVs is right on the sand, just steps from the beach. It's adjacent to New Camp. ♿ *Flush toilets, full hookups, dump station, drinking water, showers, fire pits, picnic tables, play area* ⊅ *15 sites*

⊠ *100–225 State Park Rd., North Shore* ☎ *760/393–3052, 800/444–7275 for reservations* ⊕ *www.parks.ca.gov* ⊠ *$18–$23.*

El Centro

② *28 mi south of Salton Sea on Hwy. 86.*

Bisected by Interstate 8, El Centro lies close to the Mexican border at the southern end of the Imperial Valley. Primarily a commercial and business community, it occupies some of the richest farmland in California, with more than a half million acres in cultivation. Year-round the region produces bumper crops of lettuce, carrots, sugar beets, seed, and grain. There's not much to see in the area, but the town is one of the only real rest stops on Interstate 8.

Naval Air Facility El Centro, the winter home of the Blue Angels aerobatic team, opens each March for a huge air show with stunt flying, displays of antique and experimental aircraft, and a food fest ($5). ⊠ *Bennett Rd.* ☎ *760/339–2519* ⊕ *www.nafec.navy.mil* ⊠ *Free.*

Where to Stay & Eat

¢ ✕🏨 **Barbara Worth Golf Resort and Convention Center.** Taking its name from the 1911 Harold Bell Wright book *The Winning of Barbara Worth,* about turning the desert into farmland by irrigation, this resort is a green spot in the desert. Low-lying buildings overlooking the golf course house pleasant rooms with exterior entrances. The dining room ($–$$$) has a Polynesian look, but the kitchen is American. Evenings at the karaoke bar can be lively. ⊠ *2050 Country Club Dr., Holtville 92250* ☎ *760/356–2806 or 800/356–3806* ⊠ *760/356–4653* ⊕ *www.bwresort.com* ⇗ *104 rooms* ⚘ *Restaurant, room service, some in-room safes, microwaves, refrigerators, cable TV, in-room data ports, driving range, 18-hole golf course, putting green, 2 pools, gym, hot tub, lounge, meeting rooms, no-smoking rooms* ⊟ *AE, D, DC, MC, V.*

$ 🏨 **Best Western John Jay Inn.** The federalist architecture of this three-story motel stands out in the desert environment, and the traditional theme is carried into the well-appointed rooms. Suites have coffeemakers, microwaves, and minibars, and a complimentary continental breakfast is available each morning. ⊠ *2352 S. 4th St., 92243* ☎ *760/337–8677* ⊠ *760/337–8693* ⊕ *www.bestwestern.com* ⇗ *50 rooms, 8 suites* ⚘ *Some microwaves, some minibars, some refrigerators, cable TV, in-room broadband, in-room data ports, pool, gym, outdoor hot tub, laundry facilities, no-smoking rooms* ⊟ *AE, D, DC, MC, V* ⍣ *CP.*

PALM SPRINGS & THE SOUTHERN DESERT ESSENTIALS

To research prices, get advice from other travelers, and book travel arrangements, visit ⊕ *www.fodors.com.*

AIRPORTS & TRANSFERS

Palm Springs International Airport is the major airport serving California's southern desert. Alaska, America West, American, Continental,

Delta, and United airlines all fly to Palm Springs year-round. The airport is about 2 mi from downtown Palm Springs. SkyWest/Delta Connection serves Imperial County Airport. A Valley Cabousine has taxis serving the Palm Springs airport. ⇨ Air Travel *in* Smart Travel Tips for airline phone numbers.

🛈 **Imperial County Airport** ☎ 760/355-7944. **Palm Springs International Airport** ☎ 760/318-3800 ⊕ www.palmspringsairport.com. **A Valley Cabousine** ☎ 760/340-5845.

BUS TRAVEL

Greyhound provides service to the El Centro and Palm Springs depots. Imperial County Transit provides bus service for the El Centro and Salton Sea communities. SunBus, operated by the SunLine Transit Agency, serves the entire Coachella Valley, from Desert Hot Springs to Mecca.

🛈 **Greyhound** ☎ 800/231-2222 ⊕ www.greyhound.com. **El Centro Depot** ✉ 460 State St. ☎ 760/352-6363. **Palm Springs Depot** ✉ 311 N. Indian Canyon Dr. ☎ 760/325-9557. **Imperial County Transit** ✉ 792 E. Ross Rd. ☎ 800/804-3050. **SunLine Transit** ☎ 760/343-3456 or 800/347-8628 ⊕ www.sunline.org.

CAR TRAVEL

The desert resort communities occupy a 20-mi stretch between Interstate 10, to the east, and Palm Canyon Drive (Highway 111), to the west. The area is about a two-hour drive east of Los Angeles and a three-hour drive northeast of San Diego. It can take twice as long to make the trip from Los Angeles to the desert on winter weekends because of heavy traffic. From Los Angeles take the San Bernardino Freeway (Interstate 10) east to Highway 111. From San Diego Interstate 15 heading north connects with the Pomona Freeway (Highway 60), leading to the San Bernardino Freeway (Interstate 10) east. If you're coming from the Riverside area, you can also take Highway 74 (Palms to Pines Highway) east.

To reach Borrego Springs from Los Angeles, take Interstate 10 east past the desert resorts area to Highway 86 south, and follow it to the Borrego Salton Seaway (Highway S22). Drive west on S22 to Borrego Springs. You can reach the Borrego area from San Diego via Interstate 8 to Highway 79 through Cuyamaca State Park. This will take you to Highway 78 in Julian, which you follow east to Yaqui Pass Road (S3) into Borrego Springs.

The Imperial Valley lies south of S22 on Highway 86. Salton Sea attractions are on the south and east sides of the sea. El Centro is about a two-hour drive east of San Diego via Interstate 8.

EMERGENCIES

In the event of an emergency, dial 911.

In the desert you should play it safe by being prepared and taking a few simple safety precautions. Always travel with a companion, especially if you are not familiar with the area. Let someone know about your trip, destination, and estimated time and date of return. Carry a cell phone as a precaution, but know that reception in the desert can be spotty at best. Before setting out, make sure that your vehicle is in good condition. Carry a jack, tools, and tow rope or chain. Fill up your tank whenever you see a gas pump—it can be miles between service stations. Stay on main roads: if you drive even a few feet off the pavement, you could get stuck in sand. Plus, venturing off-road is illegal in many areas. When driving, watch out for wild burros, horses, and range cattle. They roam free throughout much of the desert and have the right-of-way.

Drink at least 1 gallon of water per day, preferably more (3 gallons if you plan on hiking or engaging in other strenuous activity), even if you don't feel thirsty. Dress in layered clothing and wear comfortable, sturdy shoes and a hat. Keep snacks, sunscreen, and a first-aid kit on hand. If you suddenly have a headache or feel dizzy or nauseated, you could be suffering from dehydration. Get out of the sun immediately and drink plenty of water. Dampen your clothing to lower your body temperature.

Avoid canyons during rainstorms. Floodwaters can quickly fill up dry riverbeds and cover or wash away roads. Never place your hands or feet where you can't see them. Rattlesnakes, scorpions, and black widow spiders may be hiding there.

🚹 Hospitals **Borrego Medical Center** ✉ 4343 Yaqui Pass Rd., Borrego Springs ☎ 760/767-5051. **Desert Regional Medical Center** ✉ 1150 N. Indian Canyon Dr., Palm Springs ☎ 760/323-6511. **El Centro Regional Medical Center** ✉ 1415 Ross Ave., El Centro ☎ 760/339-7100.

TAXIS

A Valley Cabousine serves Palm Desert and goes to the Palm Springs airport. Mirage Taxi serves the Coachella Valley and the Los Angeles and Ontario International airports. Fares in the Coachella Valley run about $2.25 per mile and up to $290 one-way to LAX. Yellow Cab of El Centro serves the Imperial Valley. Service within the El Centro city limits is $5 per trip.

🚹 Taxi Companies **A Valley Cabousine** ☎ 760/340-5845. **Mirage Taxi** ☎ 760/322-2008. **Yellow Cab of El Centro** ☎ 760/352-3100.

TOURS

Desert Adventures takes to the wilds with two- to four-hour Jeep tours ($69 to $159) on private land along the canyons of the San Andreas earthquake fault. Departures are from Palm Springs and La Quinta; hotel pickups are available. Elite Land Tours gives three- to five-hour treks led by knowledgeable guides, who take you to the San Andreas Fault, Joshua Tree National Park, Indian Canyons, Pioneertown, Old Indian Pueblo in Desert Hot Springs, and the Salton Sea. Tours include hotel pickup, lunch, snacks, and beverages.

Three thousand windmills churn mightily on the slopes surrounding Palm Springs, generating electricity used by Southern California residents. Each windmill stands more than 150 feet high. EV Adventures conducts 1½-hour tours among the giant rotors, towers, and blades in what NASA declares is one of the most consistently windy places on earth. Palm Springs Celebrity Tours conducts 2½-hour tours that cover Palm Springs–area history, points of interest, and celebrity homes. Trail Discovery–Desert

Safari Guides conducts tours of various lengths through the Indian Canyons, moonlight hiking in the Palm Springs area, and daytime excursions to Joshua Tree National Park. Transportation from most area hotels is included.

Desert Adventures ✉ 67-555 E. Palm Canyon Dr., Cathedral City ☎ 760/324-5337 ⊕ www.red-jeep.com. **Elite Land Tours** ✉ 555 S. Sunrise Way, Suite 200, Palm Springs ☎ 760/318-1200 ⊕ www.elitelandtours.com. **EV Adventures** ✉ 62-950 20th Ave., North Palm Springs ☎ 760/251-1997 ⊕ www.windmilltours.com. **Palm Springs Celebrity Tours** ✉ 4751 E. Palm Canyon Dr., Palm Springs ☎ 760/770-2700 ⊕ www.celebrity-tours. com. **Trail Discovery-Desert Safari Guides** ☎ 760/325-4453 or 888/324-4453.

TRAIN TRAVEL

The Amtrak *Sunset Limited*, which runs between Florida and Los Angeles, stops in Palm Springs and Indio.

Amtrak ☎ 800/872-7245 ⊕ www.amtrakcalifornia.com.

VISITOR INFORMATION

Borrego Springs Chamber of Commerce ✉ 786 Palm Canyon Dr., 92004-0420 ☎ 760/ 767-5555 or 800/559-5524 ⊕ www.borregosprings.org. **El Centro Chamber of Commerce & Visitors Bureau** ✉ 1095 S. 4th St., 92243 ☎ 760/352-3681 ⊕ www. elcentrochamber.com. **Joshua Tree National Park** ✉ 74-485 National Park Dr., Twentynine Palms 92277 ☎ 760/367-5500 ⊕ www.nps.gov/jotr. **Palm Springs Desert Resorts Authority** ✉ 70-100 Hwy. 111, Rancho Mirage 92270 ☎ 760/770-9000 or 800/ 967-3767 ⊕ www.palmspringsusa.com. **Palm Springs Visitor Information Centers** ✉ 2901 N. Palm Canyon Dr., 92262 ☎ 800/347-7746 ⊕ www.palm-springs.org.

5

The Mojave Desert & Death Valley

WITH THE OWENS VALLEY

WORD OF MOUTH

"Death Valley National Park is one of the most unique experiences of a lifetime. I have spent a lot of time exploring and showing-off this treasure to friends and family. I have even spent Christmas at the Furnace Creek Ranch and saw Santa arrive in a buckboard wagon pulled by mules! Nature's miracles really put on a show from one end of the park to the other!"

—Sunnyd

Updated by
Veronica Hill

DUST AND DESOLATION, tumbleweeds and rattlesnakes, barren land-scapes—these are the bleak images that come to mind when most people hear the word *desert*. But east of the Sierra Nevada, where the land quickly flattens and the rain seldom falls, the desert is anything but a wasteland. The topography here is extreme; whereas Death Valley drops to almost 300 feet below sea level and contains the lowest (and hottest) spot in the Western Hemisphere, the Mojave Desert, which lies to the south, has elevations ranging from 3,000 to 5,000 feet. These remote regions (which are known, respectively, as low desert and high desert) possess a singular beauty found nowhere else in California: there are vast open spaces populated with spiky Joshua trees, undulating sand dunes, faulted mountains, and dramatic rock formations. Owens Valley is where the desert meets the mountains; its 80-mi width separates the depths of Death Valley from Mt. Whitney, the highest mountain in the continental United States. Exploring the wonders of Death Valley in the morning and then heading to the Sierra to cool off in the afternoon is an amazing study in contrasts.

Exploring the Mojave Desert & Death Valley

6

Be sure to stop in Death Valley National Park, with its miles of dunes, crusted salt flats, and jagged canyons. A drive east takes you to the Mojave National Preserve, 1.4 million acres of sand, scrub, volcanic cinder cones, and rock-strewn mountains. The eastern Mojave stretches to the Arizona border at the Colorado River—a popular place for swimming and water sports. ⚠ **You may spot fossils at some of the archaeological sites in the desert. If you do, leave them where they are; it's against the law to remove them.**

About the Restaurants

Throughout the desert and the eastern Sierra, dining is a fairly simple affair. Owens Valley is home to many mom-and-pop eateries, as well as a few fast-food chains. The restaurants in Death Valley range from coffee shops to upscale cafés. In the Mojave there are chain establishments in Ridgecrest, Victorville, and Barstow, as well as some ethnic eateries.

About the Hotels

Hotel chains and roadside motels make up most of the lodging options in the desert. The tourist season runs through the summer months, from late May through September, when many travelers are heading out of California on Interstate 15. Reservations are never a problem: you're almost always guaranteed a room. But if your plans take you to the most luxurious resort in the entire desert—the Furnace Creek Inn, in Death Valley—be sure to book in advance for the winter season. This hottest of spots is busiest during the cooler months. For a true American experience, visit one of the many historic Route 66 motels along the "Mother Road," which travels through the heart of the Mojave Desert along Interstate 40 and Interstate 15.

WHAT IT COSTS				
$$$$	**$$$**	**$$**	**$**	**¢**
RESTAURANTS over $30	$23–$30	$16–$22	$10–$15	under $10
HOTELS over $250	$176–$250	$121–$175	$90–$120	under $90

Restaurant prices are for a main course at dinner, excluding sales tax of 7¾%. Hotel prices are for two people in a standard double room in high season, excluding service charges and 7¼% tax.

Timing

Spring and fall are the best seasons to tour the desert and Owens Valley. Winters are generally mild, but summers can be cruel. If you're on a budget, keep in mind that room rates drop as the temperatures rise. Early morning is the best time to visit sights and avoid crowds, but some museums and visitor centers don't open until 10. If you schedule your town arrivals for late afternoon, you can drop by the visitor centers just before closing hours to line up an itinerary for the next day. Plan indoor activities for midday during hotter months. ⚠ **Because relatively few people visit the desert, many attractions have limited hours of access:** for instance, Petroglyph Canyon tours are given only on weekends in fall and spring, and the Calico Early Man Archaeological Site does not offer tours Monday and Tuesday. Summer is the best time to visit the Ancient Bristlecone Pine Forest, near Big Pine; in winter, snowpack may prohibit vehicles from entering the area.

THE WESTERN MOJAVE

Stretching from the town of Ridgecrest to the base of the San Gabriel Mountains, the western Mojave is a varied landscape of ancient Native American petroglyphs, tufa towers, and hillsides covered in bright-orange poppies.

Palmdale

 60 mi north of Los Angeles on Hwy. 14.

Before calling itself the aerospace capital of the world, the desert town of Palmdale was an agricultural community. Swiss and German descendants, moving west from Nebraska, first settled here in 1886. Most residents made their living as farmers, growing alfalfa, pears, and apples. After World War II, with the creation of Edwards Air Force Base and U.S. Air Force Plant 42, the area turned into a center for aerospace and defense, with such big companies as McDonnell Douglas, Rockwell, Northrop, and Lockheed establishing factories here. Today, it's one of the fastest-growing cities in Southern California.

Antelope Valley Indian Museum has more than 2,500 items on display, including pieces from California, southwestern, and Great Basin tribes. The unusual Swiss chalet–style building, built in 1928, clings to the rocky hillside of Piute Butte and is listed on the National Register of Historic Places. At this writing, the museum was closed for renovations; it is ex-

GREAT ITINERARIES

Numbers correspond to the Death Valley & Owens Valley map and the Mojave Desert map.

IF YOU HAVE 3 DAYS

Start in **Death Valley National Park** ⑭–㉗ ▶. Stop for lunch at **Stovepipe Wells Village** ㉑; then spend the rest of the afternoon at **Scotty's Castle** ㉒ and **Ubehebe Crater** ㉓. Stay the night in 🏨 **Furnace Creek Village** ⑮ and explore the southern half of the park on Day 3. Be sure not to miss the vivid desert colors of **Artists Palette** ⑯, the Western Hemisphere's lowest spot, at **Badwater** ⑱, or the stunning panorama from **Dante's View** ⑲.

IF YOU HAVE 7 DAYS

Spend two days exploring the many wonders of 🏨 **Death Valley National Park** ⑭–㉗ ▶. On your third day, head out of the park to 🏨 **Ridgecrest** ④ for a hike through Red Rock Canyon, Fossil Falls, or Trona Pinnacles Natural National Landmark. If you're visiting on a spring or fall weekend, make advance arrangements at the Maturango Museum to tour Petroglyph Canyons. The next morning continue south to **Lancaster** ② to see Antelope Valley

Poppy Reserve, where poppies cover the hillsides as far as the eye can see. Move on to **Palmdale** ① and its Antelope Valley Indian Museum, then drive to Pearblossom to pick up some ceramic tiles at St. Andrew's Abbey. Return to Palmdale for dinner and a night's rest. On the morning of Day 5, after a stop at Big Pines Visitor Center, at the highest point on the San Andreas Fault, venture north on Interstate 15 into Route 66 country. In **Victorville** ⑤, the California Route 66 Museum tells the story of one of America's most famous roads. Heading for 🏨 **Barstow** ⑥, get another hit of Route 66 nostalgia at Casa del Desierto Harvey House, site of the Route 66 Mother Road Museum and Gift Shop. Explore the Barstow area, including Desert Discovery Center, Calico Ghost Town, and Rainbow Basin National Natural Landmark, on Day 6. The next morning, drive to **Mojave National Preserve** ⑨ to see Kelso Dunes and to tour Mitchell Caverns (in Providence Mountains State Recreation Area). If time and road conditions permit, drive through Afton Canyon on your way back to Barstow.

pected to reopen in fall 2007. ✉ *Ave. M between 150th and 170th Sts. E, 17 mi east of Antelope Valley Freeway, Hwy. 14* ☎ *661/942–0662* ⊕ *www.avim.parks.ca.gov* 💲 *$2* ☉ *Mid-Sept.–mid-June, weekends 11–4; tours Tues.–Thurs. by appointment.*

A mile from the San Andreas Fault, the namesake of the **Devil's Punchbowl Natural Area** is a natural bowl-shape depression in the earth, framed by 300-foot rock walls. At the bottom is a stream, which you can reach via a 1-mi hike; at the top an interpretive center has displays of native flora and fauna, including live animals such as snakes, lizards, and birds of prey. ✉ *28000 Devil's Punchbowl Rd., south of Hwy. 138, Pearblossom* ☎ *661/944–2743* 💲 *Free* ☉ *Daily 8–4.*

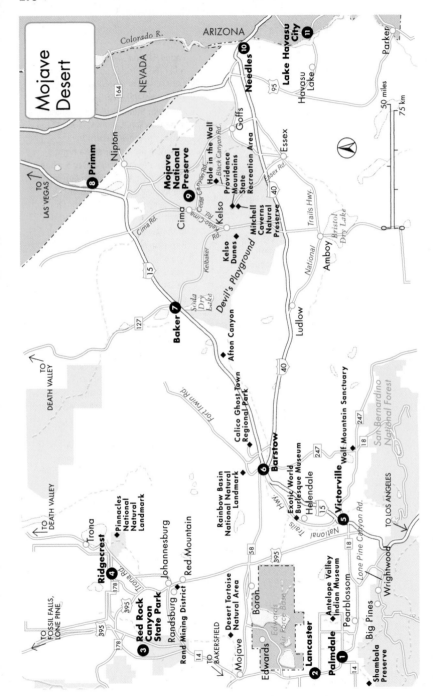

DESERT SURVIVAL TIPS

Believe everything you've ever heard about desert heat: it can be brutal. You need sunglasses, sunblock, a hat, clothing that blocks the sun's rays and the wind, and plenty of water. Because this region is vast–about as big as Ohio–and the weather is unpredictable, you'll also need to make careful driving plans. Facilities such as gas stations and supermarkets are few, so be sure to fill your gas tank whenever you can and check your vehicle's fluids and tire pressure frequently. Shut off your car's air-conditioning on steep grades to avoid engine overheating. At the start of each day load the car with three gallons of water per person, plus additional radiator water, and a cooler stocked with extra food. Be sure to bring reliable maps; signage can be limited and, in some places, nonexistent. It's a good idea to have a compass and a cell phone (though the signal may fade in remote areas). A pair of binoculars can also come in handy, and don't forget your camera–you're likely to come across things you've never seen before.

The Benedictine monastery **St. Andrew's Abbey** stands on 760 acres of lush greenery and natural springs. A big draw here is the property's ceramics studio, established in 1969; St. Andrew's Ceramics sells handmade tile saints, angels, and plaques designed by Father Maur van Doorslaer, a monk from Sint Andries in Brugges, Belgium, whose work is collected across the United States and Canada. Don't miss the abbey's fall festival, where you can sample tasty dishes and enjoy entertainment that includes singing nuns and dancing monks. ⊠ *31101 N. Valyermo Rd., south of Hwy. 138, Valyermo* ☎ *888/454–5411, 661/944–1047 for ceramics studio* ⊕ *www.saintsandangels.org* ☐ *Free* ☉ *Weekdays 9–11:30 and 1:30–4, weekends 9:30–11:45 and 1:30–4:30.*

Adventure-seekers will enjoy flying over the scenic San Gabriel mountain pines, across the jagged San Andreas fault, and over the sandy soil of El Mirage Dry Lake at **Great Western Soaring School,** the only place near Los Angeles that offers sailplane rides (no engines!). You'll be accompanied by an FAA-certified instructor, who will teach you the basics of airspeed control, straight flight, and turns before letting you handle the craft on your own. Basic flights range from $96 to $176. Advance reservations are required. ⊠ *32810 165th St. E, Llano* ☎ *661/944–9449* ⊕ *www.greatwesternsoaring.com* ☉ *Thurs.–Mon. 10–6.*

You can take ultralight (very small two-seater planes that can be flown without a pilot's license) lessons at the **Brian Ranch Airport,** which offers 15-minute ($30), half-hour ($50), and hourlong ($85) rides across the Mojave. The airport is also known for its annual "World's Smallest Air Show" every Memorial Day weekend, which draws aviation enthusiasts from around the country. ⊠ *34180 Largo Vista Rd., Llano* ☎ *661/261–3216* ⊕ *www.brianranch.com.*

The closest you'll get to an African safari near Los Angeles is **Shambala Preserve,** an 80-acre wildlife preserve run by actress Tippi Hedren. Afternoon safaris, held twice a month by advanced reservation only, get you up to one foot away from 70 rescued wild cats and an African elephant. ⊠ *6867 Soledad Canyon, Acton* ☎ *661/268–0380* ⊕ *www. shambala.org* 🖃 *$35.*

Where to Stay

$$–$$$ 🏨 **Residence Inn Palmdale.** Accommodations here range from studios to one-bedroom suites, all with full kitchens, sitting areas, and sleeper sofas. Some suites have fireplaces. Sip your complimentary in-room coffee while reading the free newspaper that's delivered to your room weekdays. There's complimentary hot breakfast daily, and you can have dinner delivered from several local restaurants. The staff will even do your grocery shopping for you. ⊠ *514 W. Ave. P, 93551* ☎ *661/947–4204 or 800/331–3131* ⊕ *www.marriott.com* ⟳ *90 suites* ⌂ *Kitchens, refrigerators, cable TV with movies, in-room VCRs, in-room broadband, Wi-Fi, tennis court, indoor pool, gym, hot tub, dry cleaning, laundry facilities, laundry service, concierge, business services, meeting room, car rental* ⊟ *AE, D, DC, MC, V* ⍓ *BP.*

¢–$$ 🏨 **Best Western John Jay Inn & Suites.** Antique furnishings decorate the rooms and suites at this full-service hotel. Each room has a large desk with ergonomic chair. Suites have balconies, fireplaces, wet bars, and Jacuzzis. Buffet breakfast and a *USA Today* newspaper is included in your room rate. ⊠ *600 W. Palmdale Blvd., 93551* ☎ *661/575–9322* 🖷 *661/575–9495* ⊕ *www.bestwestern.com* ⟳ *45 rooms, 18 suites* ⌂ *Some in-room hot tubs, microwaves, refrigerators, cable TV with movies, in-room broadband, Wi-Fi, pool, gym, sauna, laundry service, business services, meeting room, no-smoking rooms* ⊟ *AE, D, DC, MC, V* ⍓ *CP.*

Lancaster

❷ *8 mi north of Palmdale via Hwy. 14.*

Lancaster was founded in 1876, when the Southern Pacific Railroad arrived. Before that it was inhabited by Native American tribes: Kawarisu, Kitanemuk, Serrano, Tataviam, and Chemehuevi. Descendants of some of these tribes still live in the surrounding mountains. Points of interest around Lancaster are far from the downtown area, some in neighboring communities.

★ California's state flower, the California poppy, can be spotted just about anywhere in the state, but the densest concentration is in the **Antelope Valley Poppy Reserve.** Seven miles of trails lead you through 1,745 acres of hills carpeted with poppies and other wildflowers as far as the eye can see. Peak blooming time is usually March through May, though you're free to hike the grounds year-round. The visitor center has books and information about the reserve and other desert areas. Many trails are wheelchair- and stroller-accessible. ⊠ *Ave. I between 110th and 170th Sts. W* ☎ *661/724–1180 or 661/942–0662* ⊕ *www.parks.ca.gov* 🖃 *$5 per vehicle, $2 Jun.–Feb.* ☾ *Visitor center mid-Mar.–mid-May, daily 9–5.*

Thirteen species of wild cats, from the weasel-size jaguarundi to leopards, tigers, and jaguars, inhabit the **Exotic Feline Breeding Compound & Feline Conservation Center.** You can see the cats (behind barrier fences) in the park-like public zoo and research center. The center's biggest achievement has been the successful breeding of the rare Amur leopard, whose native habitat is remote border areas between Russia and China. ⊠ *Off Mojave-Tropico Rd., Rosamond, 4½ mi west of Hwy. 14 via Rosamond Blvd., 10 mi north of Lancaster* ☎ *661/256–3793, 661/256–3332 for recorded information* ⊕ *www.cathouse-fcc.org* ⊠ *$3* ☉ *Thurs.–Tues. 10–4.*

Closed for many years following the September 11 terrorist attacks, the **Air Flight Test Center Museum at Edwards Air Force Base** has reopened to the public, complete with a new parking facility and free shuttle service to the museum. Considered the birthplace of supersonic flight, Edwards Air Force Base has been the world's premiere flight-testing and flight-research center since the World War II era. It was here that the sound barrier was broken on October 14, 1947. The museum displays the rich history of the base and of USAF flight testing and has a dozen airplanes on exhibit, from the first F-16B to the giant B-52D bomber. ■ TIP➔ To visit, you must clear a security screening by providing your full name, social-security number or driver's license number, and date and place of birth at least one week in advance. Ninety-minute walking tours are generally open to the public on the first and third Friday of each month, though security alerts may affect this schedule, so you should always reconfirm. Tours include a visit to the NASA Dryden Flight Research Center, a presentation at the Air Force Flight Test Center Museum, and a windshield tour of the Edwards Air Force Base flightline. Every October, the base puts on a spectacular Open House and Air Show featuring its high-flying Thunderbirds. ⊠ *Edwards Air Force Base, Edwards 93524* ☎ *661/277–3512* ⊕ *www.edwards.af.mil/trip/index.html* ⊠ *Free* ☉ *1st and 3rd Fri. of each month, tours every 90 min. from 9:30–3.*

A winery in the middle of the desert? Only in California could you find a place like **Antelope Valley Winery and Buffalo Company.** Industry scoffing hasn't stopped Cecil W. McLester, a graduate of UC Davis's renowned wine-making and viticulture program, from crafting a decent batch of wines, including the award-winning AV Burgundy (a house red) and Paloma Blanca (a Riesling-style blend of French Colombard, chenin blanc, and muscat grapes). The winery is also home to the Antelope Valley Buffalo Company, a producer of fine buffalo steaks, patties, and jerky, made from its roaming herd in the Leona Valley. ⊠ *42041 20th St. W, Lancaster* ☎ *661/722–0145* ⊕ *www.avwinery.com* ⊠ *First two samples free; $6–$10 for additional samples* ☉ *Daily 11–6.*

OFF THE
BEATEN
PATH

DESERT TORTOISE NATURAL AREA – Between mid-March and mid-June, this natural habitat of the elusive desert tortoise blazes with desert candles, primroses, lupine, and other wildflowers. Get there bright and early to spot the state reptile, while it grazes on fresh flowers and grass shoots. It's also a great spot to see desert kit fox, red-tailed hawks, cactus wrens, and Mojave rattlesnakes. ⊠ *8 mi northeast of California City via Randsburg Mojave Rd.* ☎ *951/683–3872* ⊕ *www.tortoise-tracks.org* ⊠ *Free* ☉ *Daily.*

6

Where to Stay & Eat

$–$$ ✕ **Downtown Bistro and Café.** This romantic little restaurant, tucked in an old downtown strip mall, is the locals' favorite for leisurely lunches with friends. The garden-inspired decor is complete with a lot of indoor trees and a bubbling fountain. Standout dishes include garlic chicken or salmon with cream sauce. This is also a great spot to sample locally made Antelope Valley wines and buffalo steaks. ⊠ *858 West Lancaster Blvd., Lancaster* ☎ *661/948–2253* ⊟ *AE, MC, V.*

$$ ✕⊡ **Essex House Hotel and Convention Center.** The Essex House is the most popular hotel in the Lancaster–Palmdale area. Rooms are modern and clean, decorated in mauve, tan, and yellow floral patterns. Amenities include a 14,000-square-foot health club with a racquetball court, and Wi-Fi in all rooms. There are plenty of dining and drinking options on-site: breakfast, lunch, and dinner are served at JJ's Cafe and Dinner House, and you can grab a beer and play pool in the Pub, which serves up a British-style happy hour with imported and domestic beers. Complimentary cookies are served daily in the lobby, and complimentary hors d'oevres are weekday evenings in the Pub. ⊠ *44916 N. 10th St. W, Lancaster* ☎ *661/948–0961 or 800/843–7739* ☒ *661/945–3821* ⊕ *www. essexhouse-hotel.com* ⇆ *146 rooms, 83 kitchenette suites* ⅋ *Restaurant, pub, room service, cable TV, Wi-Fi, pool, gym, business services, convention center* ⊟ *AE, D, DC, MC, V.*

Red Rock Canyon State Park

❸ *48 mi north of Lancaster via Hwy. 14; 17 mi west of U.S. 395 via Red Rock–Randsburg Rd.*

A geological feast for the eyes with its layers of pink, white, red, and brown rock, Red Rock Canyon State Park is also a region of fascinating biological diversity—the ecosystems of the Sierra Nevada, the Mojave Desert, and the Basin Range all converge here. Entering the park from the south on Red Rock–Randsburg Road, you pass through a steep-walled gorge to a wide bowl tinted pink by volcanic ash. Native Americans known as the Old People lived here some 20,000 years ago; later, Mojave Indians roamed the land for centuries. Gold-rush fever hit the region in the mid-1800s, and you can still see remains of mining operations in the park. In the 20th century, Hollywood invaded the canyon, shooting westerns, TV shows, commercials, music videos, and movies such as *Jurassic Park* here. Be sure to check out the Red Cliffs Preserve on Highway 14, across from the entrance to the Red Rock campground. ⊠ *Ranger station: Abbott Dr. off Hwy. 14* ☎ *661/942–0662* ⊕ *www. parks.ca.gov* ⌸ *$5* ⊙ *Visitor center daily 10–4.*

Camping

⚠ **Red Rock Canyon State Park.** Open year-round, the park's campground is in the colorful cliff region of the southern El Paso Mountains, where there are lots of hiking trails. Spring and fall book quickly, so be sure to arrive early to get a spot. The drive-in sites are remote and beautiful, with wonderful views of the cliffs. ⅋ *Pit toilets, drinking water, fire pits, picnic tables* ⇆ *50 sites* ⊠ *Off Hwy. 14, 30 mi southwest of Ridgecrest* ☎ *661/942–0662* ⚏ *Reservations not accepted* ⌸ *$12.*

Ridgecrest

❹ *28 mi northeast of Red Rock Canyon State Park via Hwy. 14; 77 mi south of Lone Pine via U.S. 395.*

A military town that serves the U.S. Naval Weapons Center to its north, Ridgecrest has dozens of stores, restaurants, and hotels. It's a good base for exploring the northwestern Mojave, because it's the last big city you'll hit along U.S. 395 before you enter the desert.

The **Maturango Museum,** which also serves as a visitor information center, has pamphlets and books about the region. Small but informative exhibits detail the natural and cultural history of the northern Mojave. The museum runs wildflower tours in March and April. ⊠ *100 E. Las Flores Ave.* ☎ *760/375–6900* 🖷 *760/375–0479* ⊕ *www.maturango.org* 🖃 *$4* ⊘ *Daily 10–5.*

Fodor'sChoice
★

Guided tours conducted by the Maturango Museum are the only way to see **Petroglyph Canyons,** among the desert's most amazing spectacles. The two canyons, commonly called Big Petroglyph and Little Petroglyph, are in the Coso Mountain range on the million-acre U.S. Naval Weapons Center at China Lake. Each of the canyons holds a superlative concentration of ancient rock art, the largest of its kind in the Northern Hemisphere. Thousands of well-preserved images of animals and humans—some more than 16,000 years old—are scratched or pecked into dark basaltic rocks. The tour takes you through 3 mi of sandy washes and boulders, so wear comfortable walking shoes. ⚠ **At an elevation of 5,000 feet weather conditions can be quite extreme, so dress in layers and bring plenty of drinking water (none is available at the site) and snacks.** Children under 10 are not allowed on the tour. The military requires everyone to produce a valid driver's license, social-security number, passport, and vehicle registration before the trip (nondrivers must provide a birth certificate). ⊠ *Tours depart from Maturango Museum* ☎ *760/375–6900* ⊕ *www.maturango.org* 🖃 *$35* ⊘ *Tours Feb.–June and Sept. or Oct.–early Dec.; call for tour times.*

6

Rounded up by the Bureau of Land Management on public lands throughout the Southwest, the animals at the **Wild Horse and Burro Corrals** are available for adoption. You can bring along an apple or carrot to feed the horses, but the burros are usually too wild to approach. Individual and group tours are available. ⊠ *Off Hwy. 178, 3 mi east of Ridgecrest* ☎ *760/384–5430 or 866/468–7826* ⊕ *www.wildhorseandburro.blm.gov* 🖃 *Free* ⊘ *Weekdays 7:30–4.*

It's worth the effort (especially for sci-fi buffs, who will recognize the landscape from the film *Star Trek V*) to seek out **Trona Pinnacles National Natural Landmark.** These fantastic-looking formations of calcium carbonate, known as tufa, were formed underwater along fault lines in the bed of what is now Searles Dry Lake. A ½-mi trail winds around this surreal landscape of more than 500 spires, some of which stand as tall as 140 feet. Wear sturdy shoes—tufa cuts like coral. The best road to the area can be impassable after a rainstorm. ⊠ *5 mi south of Hwy. 178,*

18 mi east of Ridgecrest ☎ *760/384–5400 Ridgecrest BLM office* ⊕ *www.blm.gov/ca/ridgecrest/trona.html.*

Named for Dr. Darwin French, who explored this desert wilderness in 1860, the 80-foot **Darwin Falls** are a unique sight in the arid, unforgiving desert. The falls plunge over a rocky landscape, accented with trees and moss, into a cool pool that you can swim in. The falls are 1 mi west of Panamint Springs on Highway 190. Exit south on the signed dirt road and travel 2½ mi to the parking area. The only facilities near here are at Panamint Springs Resorts, which has a restaurant.

NEED A BREAK?

After driving through the hot desert, you'll surely appreciate a cold one at **Indian Wells Brewing Company** (⊠ 2565 N. Hwy. 14, Inyokern, 2 mi west of Hwy. 395 ☎ 760/377–5989 ⊕ www.mojave-red.com ⊙ Daily 10–5), where master brewer Rick Lovett lovingly crafts his Desert Pale Ale, Eastern Sierra Lager, Mojave Gold, and Sidewinder Missile Ales. If you have the kids along, grab a six-pack of his specialty root beer, black cherry, orange or cream sodas. The large gift shop carries bottled beer to go, as well as beef jerky, beer-infused barbecue sauces, and souvenirs.

Where to Stay & Eat

$$ ✕⬚ **Carriage Inn.** All the rooms at this large hotel are roomy and well-kept, but the poolside cabanas are a bit more cozy. The hotel has a long list of amenities, some of which are definitely not standard: a mister cools off sunbathers during the hot summer months. Café Potpourri serves a mix of American, Italian, and southwestern specials. Charlie's Pub & Grill ($) serves burgers and sandwiches, which go nicely with the custom home-brewed ale from Indian Wells Valley Brewery. ⊠ *901 N. China Lake Blvd.* ☎ *760/446–7910 or 800/772–8527* 🖷 *760/446–6408* ⊕ *www.carriageinn.biz* ↩ *152 rooms, 8 suites, 2 cabanas* ⌂ *2 restaurants, café, room service, cable TV with video games, in-room data ports, Wi-Fi, pool, gym, hot tub, sauna, bar, meeting room* ⊟ *AE, D, DC, MC, V* ⦿| *MAP.*

$ ✕⬚ **Heritage Inn and Suites.** This well-appointed and popular establishment is geared to business travelers, but the staff is equally attentive to tourists' concerns. Victoria's Restaurant ($$), with an American-casual menu, is a favorite fine-dining spot for locals. ⊠ *1050 N. Norma St.* ☎ *760/446–6543 or 800/843–0693* 🖷 *760/446–2884* ⊕ *www.heritageinnsuites.com* ↩ *82 rooms, 42 suites* ⌂ *Restaurant, room service, microwaves, refrigerators, cable TV with movies, in-room data ports, pool, gym, hot tub, bar, laundry facilities, business services, meeting room, shuttle service* ⊟ *AE, D, DC, MC, V* ⦿| *BP.*

EN ROUTE
★ ☕

The towns of Randsburg, Red Mountain, and Johannesburg make up the **Rand Mining District** (⊠ U.S. 395, 20 mi south of Ridgecrest), which first boomed with the discovery of gold in the Rand Mountains in 1895. Rich tungsten ore, used in World War I to make steel alloy, was discovered in 1907, and silver was found in 1919. The boom has gone bust, but the area still has a few residents, a dozen antiques shops, and plenty of character. Johannesburg is overlooked by an archetypal Old West cemetery in the hills above town.

THE EASTERN MOJAVE

Like the western Mojave, the east has plenty of flat, open land dotted with Joshua trees and rock-strewn mountains. It also has more greenery and regular stretches of cool weather. Much of this area is uninhabited, so be cautious when driving the back roads, where towns and services are few and far between.

Victorville

⑤ *87 mi south of Ridgecrest on U.S. 395. Turn east onto Bear Valley road and travel 2 mi to town center.*

At the southwest corner of the Mojave is the sprawling town of Victorville, a town rich in Route 66 heritage. Victorville was named for Santa Fe Railroad pioneer Jacob Nash Victor, who drove the first locomotive through the Cajon Pass here in 1885. Once home to Native Americans, the town later became a rest stop for Mormons and missionaries. In 1941 George Air Force Base (which now serves as an airport and storage area), brought scores of military families to the area, many of which have stayed on to raise families of their own. February is one of the best times to visit, when the city holds its annual Roy Rogers and Dale Evans Western Film Festival and Adelanto Grand Prix, the largest motorcycle and quad off-road event in the country.

Fans of the Mother Road can visit the **California Route 66 Museum,** whose exhibits chronicle the history of America's most famous highway. At the museum you can pick up a book that details a self-guided tour of the old Sagebrush Route from Oro Grande to Helendale. The road passes Route 66 icons such as Potapov's Gas and Service Station (where the words BILL'S SERVICE are still legible) and the once-rowdy Sagebrush Inn, now a private residence. ⊠ *16825 D St., Rte. 66* ☎ *760/951–0436* ⊕ *www.califrt66museum.org* ⌕ *Free* ☉ *Thurs.–Mon. 10–4.*

The California high desert's only zoo, the small-scale **Hesperia Zoo** houses animals that have retired from or are still working in the entertainment industry. Among the residents are a lion, a tiger, and a baboon; performing-animal shows are sometimes held. You can visit Cinema Safari on a regularly scheduled tour or by appointment. ⊠ *19038 Willow St., Hesperia* ☎ *760/948–9430* ⌕ *$6* ☉ *Tours weekends at 10.*

OFF THE
BEATEN
PATH

WOLF MOUNTAIN SANCTUARY – Apache Indian Tonya "Littlewolf" Carloni founded this desert sanctuary in 1980. Today it's a refuge for a dozen injured or abused wolves, including the rare buffalo wolf, the white arctic tundra wolf, and the Alaskan timber wolf. The most famous resident is Apache Moon, a McKenzie timber wolf "ambassador" who visits local schools. ⊠ *7520 Fairlane St., Lucerne Valley* ☎ *760/248–7818* ⊕ *www.wolfmountain.com* ⌕ *$10* ☉ *By appointment.*

Where to Stay & Eat

¢–$ ✕ **Emma Jean's Hollandburger Cafe.** This circa-1940s diner sits right on U.S. Historic Route 66 and is favored by locals for its generous portions and old-fashioned home cooking. Try the biscuits and gravy, chicken-fried steak, or the famous Trucker's Sandwich, chock-full of roast beef, bacon, chilies, and cheese. ⊠ *17143 D St.* ☎ *760/243–9938* ⊟ *AE, MC, V* ⊘ *Closed Sun. No dinner.*

$–$$ ▥ **La Quinta Inn and Suites Victorville.** If you're looking for a clean and comfortable hotel with reasonable prices, this is a good choice. Rooms are modern, decorated in rich earth tones with floral bedspreads and cherry-color furniture. ⊠ *12000 Mariposa Rd., Hesperia 92345* ☎ *760/949–9900* ⊕ *www.lq.com* ➟ *53 rooms, 22 suites* ⚘ *Microwaves, refrigerators, cable TV, in-room broadband, pool, gym, some hot tubs, sauna, laundry service, business services* ⊟ *AE, D, DC, MC, V* ⍩⍝ *CP.*

⚠ **Mojave Narrows Regional Park.** In one of the few spots where the Mojave River flows above ground, this park has two lakes surrounded by cottonwoods and cattails. You'll find fishing, rowboat rentals, a bait shop, equestrian paths, and a wheelchair-accessible trail. The campsites cluster by the lake amid grass and trees. ■ TIP→ **The park is also home to the annual Huck Finn Jubilee (visit ⊕ www.huckfinn.com for more info), a festive, down-home event with live bluegrass music, trout fishing, cow-chip throwing contests and southern grub that draws thousands every Fathers Day Weekend.** ⚘ *Grills, flush toilets, full hookups, dump station, drinking water, showers, fire pits, picnic tables, electricity, public telephone, play area* ➟ *87 sites, 37 with hookups* ⊠ *18000 Yates Rd.* ☎ *760/245–2226* ▨ *$15–$20 camping, $5 day-use.*

Barstow

❻ *32 mi northeast of Victorville on I–15.*

In 1886, when a subsidiary of the Atchison, Topeka, and Santa Fe Railway began construction of a depot and hotel here, Barstow was born. Today outlet stores, chain restaurants, and motels define the landscape, though old-time neon signs light up the town's main street.

When the sun sets in the Mojave, check out a bit of surviving Americana at the **Skyline Drive-In Theatre,** where you can watch the latest Hollywood flicks among the Joshua trees and starry night sky in good old-fashioned stereo FM sound. ⊠ *31175 Old Hwy. 58, Barstow* ☎ *760/256–3333* ▨ *$6* ⊘ *Shows daily at 7:30.*

The **California Welcome Center** has exhibits about desert ecology, wildflowers, and wildlife, as well as general visitor information for the state of California. ⊠ *2796 Tanger Way* ☎ *760/253–4782* ⊕ *www.visitcwc.com* ⊘ *Daily 9–6.*

★ The earliest-known Americans fashioned the artifacts buried in the walls and floors of the pits at **Calico Early Man Archaeological Site.** Nearly 12,000 stone tools—used for scraping, cutting, and gouging—have been excavated here. The apparent age of some of these items (said to be as much as 200,000 years old) contradicts the dominant archaeological theory that humans populated North America only 13,000 years ago. Noted archaeologist Louis Leakey was so impressed with the Calico site that he became its director in 1963 and served in that capacity until his death in 1972. His old camp is now a visitor center and museum. The only way into the site is by guided tour (call ahead, as scheduled tours sometimes don't take place). ⊠ *Off I–15, Minneola Rd. exit, 15 mi northeast of Barstow* ☎ *760/254–2248* ⊕ *www.blm.gov/ca/Barstow/calico* ☒ *Donation requested* ⊙ *Visitor center Wed. 12:30–4:30, Thurs.–Sun. 9–4:30; tours Wed. 1:30 and 3:30, Thurs.–Sun. 9:30, 11:30, 1:30, and 3:30.*

ⓒ
Calico Ghost Town was once a wild and wealthy mining town. In 1881 prospectors found a rich deposit of silver in the area, and by 1886 more than $85 million worth of silver, gold, and other precious metals had been harvested from the surrounding hills. Once the price of silver fell, though, the town slipped into decline. Many buildings here are authentic, but the restoration has created a theme-park version of the 1880s. You can stroll the wooden sidewalks of Main Street, browse shops filled with western goods, roam the tunnels of Maggie's Mine, and take a ride on the Calico-Odessa Railroad. Festivals in March, May, October, and November celebrate Calico's Wild West theme. ⊠ *Ghost Town Rd., 3 mi north of I–15, 5 mi east of Barstow* ☎ *760/254–2122* ⊕ *www.calicotown.com* ☒ *$6* ⊙ *Daily 9–5.*

A Spanish-named spot meaning "house of the desert," the **Casa Del Desierto Harvey House** was one of many hotel and restaurant depots opened by Santa Fe railroad guru Fred Harvey in the early 20th century. The location where Judy Garland's film *The Harvey Girls* was shot, the building is now completely restored. Inside the Casa Del Desierto is the Route 66 Mother Road Museum and Gift Shop. ⊠ *681 N. 1st Ave.* ☎ *760/255–1890* ⊕ *www.route66museum.org* ☒ *Free* ⊙ *Fri.–Sun. 11–4. Guided tours by appointment.*

ⓒ Stop by the **Desert Discovery Center** to see exhibits of fossils, plants, and local animals. The main attraction here is Old Woman, the second-largest iron meteorite ever found in the United States. It was discovered in 1976 about 50 mi from Barstow in the Old Woman Mountains. The center also has visitor information for the Mojave Desert. ⊠ *831 Barstow Rd.* ☎ *760/252–6060* ⊕ *www.discoverytrails.org* ☒ *Free* ⊙ *Tues.–Sat. 11–4.*

One of the world's largest natural Native American art galleries, **Inscription Canyon,** north of Barstow in the Black Mountains, has nearly 10,000 petroglyphs and pictographs of bighorn sheep and other Mojave wildlife. ⊠ *EF373, off Copper City Rd., 10 mi west of Fort Irwin Rd.* ☎ *760/252–6000.*

★ So many science-fiction movies set on Mars have been filmed at **Rainbow Basin National Natural Landmark,** 8 mi north of Barstow, that you may feel like you're visiting the red planet. Huge slabs of red, orange, white, and green stone tilt at crazy angles like ships about to capsize; hike the washes, and you'll likely see the fossilized remains of creatures (such as mastodons and dog-bears), which roamed the basin up to 16 million years ago. You can camp here, at Owl Canyon Campground, on the east side of Rainbow Basin. Part of the drive to the basin is on dirt roads. ⊠ *Fossil Bed Rd., 3 mi west of Fort Irwin Rd.* ☎ *760/252–6000* ⊕ *www.blm.gov/ca/Barstow/basin.html.*

6

If you're a railroad buff, then you'll love the **Western American Rail Museum.** It houses memorabilia from Barstow's early railroad days, as well as interactive and historic displays on railroad history. Be sure to check out the old locomotives and cabooses for a truly nostalgic experience. ⊠ *685 N. 1st St.* ☎ *760/256–9276* ⊕ *www.barstowrailmuseum.org* ⊠ *Free* ⊗ *Fri.–Sun. 11–4.*

If you've seen Jodie Foster's movie *Contact,* about intelligent signals from outer space, then you'll probably enjoy visiting the **Goldstone Deep Space Communications Complex** on the Fort Irwin Military Base near Barstow. By appointment, the staff offers guided tours of the 53-square-mi complex, including its large antennas, which search for signs of otherworldly life. Start out at the Goldstone Museum, with its exhibits dedicated to current missions, past missions, and Deep Space Network history, or take the kids into the hands-on room for a lesson about the universe. ⊠ *35 mi north of Barstow on Ft. Irwin Military Base* ☎ *760/255–8687 or 760/255–8688* ⊕ *http://deepspace.jpl.nasa.gov/dsn/features/goldstonetours.html* ⊠ *Free* ⊗ *Guided tours by appointment only.*

Where to Stay & Eat

★ **$–$$$$** ✕ **Idle Spurs Steakhouse.** Since the 1950s this roadside ranch has been a Barstow dining staple. Covered in cacti outside and Christmas lights inside, it's a colorful, cheerful place with a big wooden bar. The menu features prime cuts of meat, ribs, and lobster, and there's a great microbrew list. ⊠ *690 Hwy. 58* ☎ *760/256–8888* ⊕ *www.idlespurssteakhouse. com* ⊟ *AE, D, MC, V.*

★ **¢–$** ✕ **Bagdad Café.** Tourists from all over the world flock to the site where the 1988 film of the same name was shot. Built in the 1940s, this Route 66 eatery serves a home-style menu of burgers, chicken-fried steak, and seafood. An old Airstream trailer from the movie sits outside the café. ⊠ *46548 National Trails Hwy., Newberry Springs* ☎ *760/257–3101* ⊕ *www.bagdadcafeusa.com* ⊟ *AE, MC, V.*

¢–$ ✕ **Peggy Sue's 50s Diner.** Checkerboard floors and life-size versions of Elvis and Marilyn Monroe greet you at this funky little coffee shop and pizza parlor in the middle of the Mojave. Outside, kids can play by the duck pond before heading in to spin a tune on the jukebox or order from the soda fountain. The fare is basic American, heavy on the fries, onion rings, burgers, or pork chops. ⊠ *35654 Yermo Rd., Yermo* ☎ *760/254–3370* ⊟ *AE, D, MC, V.*

¢–$ ✕ **Slash X Ranch Cafe.** If you have a craving for cold beer, burgers, and chili-cheese fries, look no further than this Wild West watering hole, a Barstow favorite since 1954. Named for the cattle ranch that preceded it, the café lures a mix of visitors and locals, who relish its rowdy atmosphere, hearty portions, and friendly service. Shuffleboard tables and horseshoe pits add to the fun. ⊠ *28040 Barstow Rd.* ☎ *760/252–1197* ⊕ *www.slashxranchcafe.com* ⊟ *AE, D, MC, V.*

¢–$ 🛏 **Ramada Inn.** Though this large property is slightly more expensive than others lining Main Street, it also has more amenities (which is why it tends to attract business travelers). The modern rooms have a desert theme and are decorated in browns and pinks that evoke the surrounding landscape. ⊠ *1511 E. Main St.* ☎ *760/256–5673* 🖷 *760/256–*

5917 ⊕ *www.ramada.com* ⤶ *148 rooms* ⚏ *Restaurant, room service, cable TV with movies, some in-room broadband, in-room data ports, Wi-Fi, pool, hot tub, laundry service, meeting room, some pets allowed (fee), no-smoking rooms* ▭ *AE, D, DC, MC, V.*

⚠ **Calico Ghost Town Regional Park.** This dusty, flat campsite with views of the ghost town provides an authentic Wild West atmosphere. In addition to the campsites, you have six cabins ($28) and bunkhouse accommodations ($5 per person, with a 12-person minimum) to choose from. There's a two-night minimum during Calico Ghost Town festival weekends. ⚏ *Grills, flush toilets, full hookups, partial hookups, dump station, drinking water, showers, fire pits, picnic tables, electricity, public telephone, general store* ⤶ *250 sites, 104 with hookups* ⊠ *Ghost Town Rd., 3 mi north of I–15, 5 mi east of Barstow* ☎ *760/254–2122 or 800/862–2542* ⊕ *www.calicotown.com* ⧉ *$18–$22* ▭ *D, MC, V.*

EN
ROUTE

Because of its colorful, steep walls, **Afton Canyon** (⊠ Off Afton Canyon Rd., 36 mi northeast of Barstow via I–15) is often called the Grand Canyon of the Mojave. It was carved over thousands of years by the rushing waters of the Mojave River, which makes one of its few aboveground appearances here. Where you find water in the desert you'll also find trees, grasses, and wildlife, so the canyon has attracted people for a long time: Native Americans and, later, settlers following the Mojave Trail from the Colorado River to the Pacific Ocean set up camp here. Now you can, too, at a 22-site campground amid high-desert cliffs and a mesquite thicket. The dirt road that leads to the canyon is ungraded in spots, so you are best off driving it in an all-terrain vehicle. Check with the **Mojave Desert Information Center** (☎ 760/733–4040 ⊕ www.nps.gov/moja), in Baker, about road conditions before you head in.

Baker

❼ *63 mi northeast of Barstow on I–15; 84 mi south of Death Valley Junction via Hwy. 127.*

The small town of Baker is Death Valley's gateway to the western Mojave. There are several gas stations and restaurants (most of them fast-food outlets), a few motels, and one general store (which has the distinction of selling the most winning Lotto tickets in California).

▥ TIP→ **While you're driving through the Mojave, tune in to the Highway Stations (98.1 FM near Barstow, 98.9 FM near Essex, and 99.7 FM near Baker) for the latest Mojave traffic and weather. The stations cover 40,000 square mi of the desert, making it an important source of information on the area.** Traffic can be especially troublesome Friday through Sunday, when scores of harried Angelenos head to Las Vegas for a bit of R&R.

You can't help but notice Baker's 134-foot-tall **thermometer** (⊠ 72157 Baker Blvd.), whose height in feet pays homage to the record-high U.S. temperature: 134°F, recorded in Death Valley on July 10, 1913. The Baker thermometer marks the location of the National Park Service's **Mojave Desert Information Center** (☎ 760/733–4040 ⊕ www.nps.gov/moja ☉ Daily 9–5), where you can browse the bookstore, pick up maps, and buy souvenir posters and postcards. The center also has visitor information for Mojave National Preserve, Death Valley, and other Mojave attractions.

Where to Eat

¢–$ ✕ **The Mad Greek.** This whimsical, over-the-top place somehow manages to fuse the cultures of ancient Athens, Los Angeles, and the Mojave Desert. Deep-blue ceramic tiles adorn the walls, and neoclassical statues pose amid the tables. The food ranges from traditional Greek (gyros, kebabs, strong coffee) to classic American (hot dogs and ice-cream sundaes). ⊠ *72112 Baker Blvd., at I–15* ☎ *760/733–4354* ▭ *AE, D, DC, MC, V.*

Primm, NV

❽ *52 mi northeast of Baker, via I–15; 118 mi east of Death Valley, via Hwy. 160 and I–15; 114 mi north of Barstow, via I–15.*

Amid the rugged beauty of the Mojave's landscapes, this bustling mecca for gamblers and theme-park lovers has sprung up on the border between California and southern Nevada. The casino resorts here are the first to greet you on the lonely stretch of road connecting Los Angeles with Las Vegas—and increasingly, visitors are simply stopping and spending their gambling vacations here.

One of Primm's greatest claims to fame is its 24-hour **Bonnie and Clyde Gangster Exhibit.** Here, you'll find the bullet-riddled Ford car in which the 1930s duo perished in a hailstorm of gunfire in Louisiana on May 3, 1934. There are also other Bonnie and Clyde memorabilia, such as newspaper clippings and items owned by the couple, and a restored 1931 armored Lincoln belonging to gangsters Al Capone and Dutch Schultz. The exhibits are free to view in the rotunda connecting Primm Valley Resort and Casino with the Fashion Outlet Mall. ⊠ *32100 Las Vegas Blvd. S* ☎ *702/874–1400 Ext. 7073, 888/424–6898 for Fashion Outlet Mall* ⊕ *www.fashionoutletlasvegas.com.*

Though there are plenty of family-friendly activities in Primm (such as shopping at the mall, hitting the waterslide at Whiskey Pete's, or the amusement park at Buffalo Bill's), guests under 21 are not allowed on the casino floors, and children under 13 may not be left unattended. Each of the casinos has a video arcade, which may provide some solace for the teenage set.

Where to Stay & Eat

¢–$$ ✕▥ **Buffalo Bill's Resort and Casino.** Decorated in the style of a western frontier town, this hotel is the biggest and most popular in Primm. Its buffalo-shape swimming pool and a large amusement park—which features several roller coasters and other rides—make the property a hit with families. The casino itself is enormous (46,000 square feet), and rooms here are bright and cheery and decorated with lodge-style furniture. Among the resort's several restaurants, Batelli's Italiano Restaurante and Oyster Bar ($–$$$) is a favorite; chef Fernando Batelli serves up his signature cioppino (a hearty seafood stew) and other Italian favorites with brio. ⊠ *31700 Las Vegas Blvd. S, 89019* ☎ *702/386–7867 or 800/386–7867, 702/837–0022 for Batelli's* ⊕ *www.primmvalleyresorts.com*

↗ *1,193 rooms, 49 suites* ⚄ *8 restaurants, coffee shop, food court, ice-cream parlor, pizzeria, some in-room hot tubs, some kitchenettes, some minibars, some refrigerators, cable TV with movies, in-room data ports, pool, outdoor hot tub, 2 bars, lounge, casino, video game room, shop, concierge, no-smoking rooms* ▤ *AE, D, DC, MC, V.*

¢–$$ ✕▣ **Primm Valley Resort and Casino.** This elegant resort, which evokes a 1930s country club, is conveniently near the Primm Valley Conference Center. Rooms are decorated in warm tones, with dark-wood furniture. If you feel like splurging, check into one of the 640-square-foot Jacuzzi suites. GP's ($–$$$), one of the on-site restaurants, is the fanciest in town, and popular for its aged prime rib and veal cordon bleu. ✉ *31900 Las Vegas Blvd. S, 89019* ☎ *702/386–7867 or 800/386–7867* ⊕ *www.primmvalleyresorts.com* ↗ *592 rooms, 31 suites* ⚄ *3 restaurants, café, food court, ice-cream parlor, pizzeria, snack bar, room service, some in-room hot tubs, some kitchenettes, some minibars, some refrigerators, cable TV with movies, in-room data ports, pool, outdoor hot tub, 2 bars, piano bar, casino, video game room, shops, meeting rooms, convention center, no-smoking rooms, Internet* ▤ *AE, D, DC, MC, V.*

¢–$$ ✕▣ **Whiskey Pete's Hotel and Casino.** Opened in 1977, this castle-inspired property is the oldest of the three casinos in Primm. Rooms are decorated in mahogany and have Spanish tile floors; each of the 725-square-foot Jacuzzi suites has a four-person hot tub in the living room and a full bar. If you're visiting in summer, the tropical-theme pool with its shade trees and waterslide is a cool retreat. The Silver Spur Steakhouse ($–$$) serves excellent prime rib and chateaubriand. ✉ *100 W. Primm Blvd., 89019* ☎ *702/386–7867 or 800/386–7867* ⊕ *www.primmvalleyresorts.com* ↗ *765 rooms, 12 suites* ⚄ *4 restaurants, coffee shop, room service, some in-room hot tubs, some kitchenettes, some microwaves, some minibars, some refrigerators, cable TV with movies, in-room data ports, pool, gym, outdoor hot tub, 2 bars, casino, comedy club, video game room, shops, no-smoking rooms* ▤ *AE, D, DC, MC, V.*

Mojave National Preserve

❾ *Between I–15 and I–40, roughly east of Baker and Ludlow to the California/Nevada border.*

The 1.4 million acres of the Mojave National Preserve hold a surprising abundance of plant and animal life—especially considering their elevation (nearly 8,000 feet in some areas). There are traces of human history here as well, including abandoned army posts and vestiges of mining and ranching towns. The town of Cima still has a small functioning store.

Created millions of years ago by volcanic activity, **Hole in the Wall** formed when gases were trapped between layers of deposited ash, rock, and lava; the gas bubbles left holes in the solidified material. The area was named by Bob Hollimon, a member of the Butch Cassidy gang, because it reminded him of his former hideout in Wyoming. To hike the canyon, you first must make your way down Rings Trail, a narrow 200-foot vertical chute. To make the rather strenuous descent you must grasp a series of metal rings embedded in the rock. The trail drops you into Banshee Canyon, where you are surrounded by steep, pockmarked walls and small caverns. You can explore the length of the canyon, but climbing the walls is not recommended, as the rock is soft and crumbles easily. Keep your eyes open for native lizards such as the chuckwalla. The Hole in the Wall ranger station has docents who can answer questions about the area. ⊠ *Black Canyon Rd., 9 mi north of Mitchell Caverns* ☎ *760/928–2572 or 760/733–4040* ⊕ *www.nps.gov/moja* ☉ *Weekends 10–2.*

As you enter the preserve from the south, you'll pass miles of open scrub brush, Joshua trees, and beautiful red-black cinder cones before encountering the **Kelso Dunes** (⊠ Kelbaker Rd., 90 mi east of I–15 and 14 mi north of I–40 ☎ 760/928–2572, 760/733–4040, or 760/252–6100 ⊕ www.nps.gov/moja). These perfect, pristine slopes of gold-white sand cover 70 square mi, often reaching heights of 500 to 600 feet. You can reach them via a ½-mi walk from the main parking area. When you reach the top of a dune, kick a little bit of sand down the lee side and listen to the sand "sing." North of the dunes, in the town of Kelso, is the Mission revival–style **Kelso Depot Information Center,** flanked by three swaying palm trees. The building, which dates to 1923, is the main stopping point for Mojave National Preserve. The Depot's Beanery restaurant will reopen in 2007 with the same historic menu that refueled weary passengers and rail workers. Primitive campsites are available at no charge near the dunes' main parking area.

The National Park Service administers most of the Mojave preserve, but **Providence Mountains State Recreation Area** is under the jurisdiction of the California Department of Parks. The visitor center has views of mountain peaks, dunes, buttes, crags, and desert valleys. At **Mitchell Caverns Natural Preserve** (🎫 $4) you have a rare opportunity to see all three types of cave formations—dripstone, flowstone, and erratics—in one place. The year-round 65°F temperature provides a break from the desert heat. Tours, the only way to see the caverns, are given weekdays at 1:30 and weekends at 10, 1:30, and 3. Arrive a half-hour before tour time to secure a spot. Between late May and early September, tours are given only on weekends at 1:30. ⊠ *Essex Rd., 16 mi north of I–40* ☎ *760/ 928–2586* ⊕ *www.parks.ca.gov* ☉ *Visitor center May–Sept., Fri. and Sat. 9–4.*

Camping

⚠ **Hole-in-the-Wall Campground.** At a cool 4,500 feet above sea level, backed by volcanic-rock formations, this is a fine place to spend a quiet night, and to use as a base for hiking. The campground is near the Hole in the Wall ranger station. ♿ *Pit toilets, dump station, drinking water, fire pits, picnic tables* ⇆ *35 RV/trailer sites, 2 walk-in tent sites* ⊠ *Black Canyon Rd. north of Essex* ☎ *760/928–2572 or 760/733–4040* ⊕ *www. nps.gov/moja* ▭ *No credit cards* ⚠ *Reservations not accepted* 🎫 *$12.*

Needles

🔟 *I–40, 150 mi east of Barstow.*

On Route 66 and the Colorado River, Needles is a good base for exploring many desert attractions, including Mojave National Preserve.

Founded in 1883, the town of Needles, named for the jagged mountain peaks that overlook the city, served as a stop along the Santa Fe Railroad. One of its crown jewels was the elegant El Garces Harvey House Train Depot, which is being restored. Today, Needles is a thriving community and a popular getaway for California residents who want to enjoy the river a little closer to home.

Don't miss the historic 1908 **El Garces Harvey House Train Depot** (✉ 900 Front St. ☎ 760/326–5678), one of the many restaurant-boarding-houses built by the Fred Harvey company. Renovations on the property will keep it closed to tours until mid–2008, but the exterior is still worth a look.

Mystic Maze (✉ Park Moabi Rd., off I–40 11 mi southeast of Needles ☎ 760/326–5678) is an unexplained geological site of spiritual significance to Pipa Aha Macav (Fort Mojave) Indians. The maze consists of several rows of rocks and mounds of dirt in different patterns.

Fodor'sChoice ★

In 1941, after the construction of Parker Dam, President Franklin D. Roosevelt set aside **Havasu National Wildlife Refuge,** a 24-mi stretch of land along the Colorado River between Needles and Lake Havasu City. Best seen by boat, this beautiful waterway is punctuated with isolated coves, sandy beaches, and Topock Marsh, a favorite nesting site of herons, egrets, and other waterbirds. You can see wonderful petroglyphs on the rocky red canyon cliffs of Topock Gorge. The park has 11 access points, including boat launches at Catfish Paradise, Five Mile Landing, and Pintail Slough. There's camping below Castle Rock. ✉ *3 mi southeast of Needles off I–40* ☎ *760/326–3853* ⊕ *www.fws.gov/ southwest/refuges/Arizona/havasu.*

Moabi Regional Park, on the banks of the Colorado River, is a good place for swimming, boating, picnicking, horseback riding, and fishing. Bass, bluegill, and trout are plentiful in the river. There are 600 campsites with full amenities, including RV hookups, laundry and showers, and grills. ✉ *11 mi southeast of Needles on Park Moabi Rd.* ☎ *760/326–3831* ⊕ *www.moabi.com* 🖼 *$6 day-use, $12–$35 camping.*

Where to Stay & Eat

¢–$$ ✕ **Mudshark Pizza and Pasta.** There are slim pickin's in Needles when it comes to good grub, which is all the more reason to check out this satellite location of the popular Lake Havasu restaurant. The restaurant is clean and simple, with vibrant hand-painted scenes of Route 66 and the Colorado River on the walls. Try the Mudshark Special Pizza, which has pepperoni, onions, black olives, mushrooms, sausage, and fresh-chopped garlic, or the Burnt Butter Linguini tossed with fried Mizithra and Parmesan cheeses. It all goes down great with a mug of cold lager or ale, handcrafted at the restaurant's brewery in Havasu. ✉ *819 Broadway, Needles* ☎ *760/326–9191* ⊕ *www.mudsharkbrewingco.com* 🖃 *AE, D, MC, V.*

¢–$$ 🏨 **Best Western Colorado River Inn.** The country-western style rooms at this reliable chain are spartan, but they're decorated in rich colors. The property is right off Interstate 40. Expect the standard Best Western amenities, including free local calls and complimentary coffee in the lobby each morning. ⊠ 2371 Needles Hwy., 92363 🕿 760/326–4552 or 800/780–7234 ⊕ www.bestwestern.com ⬓ 63 rooms ♢ Some microwaves, some refrigerators, cable TV with movies, some in-room broadband, in-room data ports, Wi-Fi, indoor pool, hot tub, sauna, laundry facilities, some pets allowed, no-smoking rooms ⊟ AE, DC, MC, V.

¢ 🖭 **Fender's River Road Resort.** This funky little 1960s-era motel is one of the best-kept secrets in Needles. The rooms are clean and well kept, many decorated with such whimsical accents as fish and stars. On a calm section of the Colorado River, this resort caters to families with a grassy play area shaded with trees and a picnic area. Camping is $25 to $40 a night. ⊠ 3396 Needles Hwy, 92363 🕿 760/326–3423 ⊕ www.fendersriverroadresort.com ⬓ 10 rooms, 27 campsites with full hookups ♢ Picnic area, BBQs, kitchens, refrigerators, beach, dock, boating, fishing, recreation room, playground, laundry facilities ⊟ D, MC, V.

⚠ **Needles Marina Park.** This "luxury" campground sits along the glassy waters of the Colorado River and is just a 30-minute boat ride from Topock Gorge or a 1½-hour ride from London Bridge on Lake Havasu. A recreation room, Jacuzzi, and 18-hole golf course are at your disposal. The resort has its own boat ramp and slips. ♢ Grills, pool, flush toilets, full hookups, drinking water, guest laundry, showers, picnic tables, electricity, public telephone, general store, play area ⬓ 194 sites with hookups ⊠ River Rd. off Broadway 🕿 760/326–2197 ⊕ www.needlesmarinapark.com ⊟ MC, V ⊞ $30–$32.

Lake Havasu City, AZ

⓫ Hwy. 95, 43 mi southeast of Needles in Arizona.

In summer Angelenos throng to Lake Havasu. This wide spot in the Colorado River, which has backed up behind Parker Dam, is accessed from its eastern shore in Arizona. Here you can swim; zip around on a Jet Ski; paddle a kayak; fish for trout, bass, or bluegill; or boat beneath the London Bridge, one of the desert's oddest sights. During sunset the views are breathtaking.

Once home to the Mohave Indians, this riverfront community (which means "blue water") was settled in the 1930s with the construction of Parker Dam. But what really put this town on the map was the piece-by-piece reconstruction in 1971 of **London Bridge** by town founder Robert P. McCulloch. Today the circa-1831 bridge, designed by John Rennie, connects the city to a small island and is the center of a town including numerous restaurants, hotels, RV parks, and a reconstructed English village. 🕿 928/855–4115 ⊕ www.havasuchamber.com ⊠ Free ☉ Daily 24 hrs.

★ ♨

Where to Stay & Eat

★ $–$$$ ✕ **Shugrue's.** This lakefront restaurant, a favorite of locals and tourists, serves up beautiful views of London Bridge and the English Village. Heavy on fresh seafood, steak, and lobster, the restaurant is also known for such specials as Bombay chicken and shrimp, served with spicy yogurt sauce and mango chutney. ⊠ 1425 McCulloch Blvd. 🕿 928/453–1400 ⊕ www.shugrues.com ⊟ AE, D, DC, V.

$$–$$$$ ✕⊞ **Nautical Inn Resort and Conference Center.** This riverfront property, completely remodeled in 2002, has views of Lake Havasu and the nearby mountain ranges. The modern water-view rooms all have oversize patios or balconies. You can rent water-sports equipment and dock your boat outside the hotel. There's an 18-hole golf course next door, and the hotel arranges golf packages with three other local courses. You can dine on the waterfront at Captain's Table ($–$$), which serves such American fare as London broil and grilled halibut, or enjoy a drink at sunset at the Naked Turtle Beach Bar or Hard Shell Cafe. ✉ *1000 McCullough Blvd., 86403* ☎ *928/855–2141 or 800/892–2141* ⊕ *www.nauticalinn. com* ⇔ *76 rooms, 63 suites* ⌂ *Restaurant, some kitchenettes, microwaves, refrigerators, cable TV, in-room data ports, pool, lake, hot tub, beach, dock, boating, jet skiing, marina, parasailing, fishing, hiking, bar, shop, laundry service, meeting rooms* ☰ *AE, D, MC, V.*

Sports & the Outdoors

☾ Docked at the London Bridge, **_The Dixie Bell_** (☎ 928/453–6776 ⌑ $13) offers a leisurely way to spend an afternoon. The two-story, old-fashioned paddle-wheel boat, with air-conditioning and a cocktail lounge, takes guests on a one-hour narrated tour around the island. Tours are given daily at 11:30, 1, and 2:30. **London Bridge Watercraft Tours & Rentals** (✉ 141 Swanson Ave. ☎ 928/453–8883 ⊕ www.havasuwatercraftrentals. com) is the place to rent personal watercraft such as Jet Skis and Sea Doos for a day or to join a 50-mi personal-watercraft adventure through Topock Gorge.

DEATH VALLEY

Anglo-Americans first learned of the existence of Death Valley in 1849, when wayward travelers looking for a shortcut to the California goldfields stumbled into the area and were temporarily stranded. By 1873, borax, the so-called white gold of the desert, was found in the valley, and 20-mule teams hauled it out from 1883 to 1889.

The topography of Death Valley is a geology lesson in itself. Some 200 million years ago, seas covered the area, depositing layers of sediment and fossils. Between 35 million and 5 million years ago, faults in the earth's crust and volcanic activity pushed and folded the ground, causing mountain ranges to rise and the valley floor to drop. The valley was then filled periodically by lakes, which eroded the surrounding rocks into fantastic formations and deposited the salts that now cover the floor of the basin. The area has 14 square mi of sand dunes; 200 square mi of crusty salt flats; and hills, mountains, and canyons of many colors. If you have a four-wheel-drive vehicle, bring it—many of Death Valley's most spectacular canyons are reachable only in a 4x4. ■ TIP→ **The desert appears quite barren most of the year, but if you visit in April or May, expect a wonderful treat. More than 1,000 species of plants and trees thrive here, 21 of which (including the yellow Panamint daisy and the blue-flowered Death Valley sage) are unique to the valley.** Many annual plants lie dormant as seeds for all but a few months of the year, when spring rains trigger a bloom. At higher elevations you will find piñon, juniper, and bristlecone

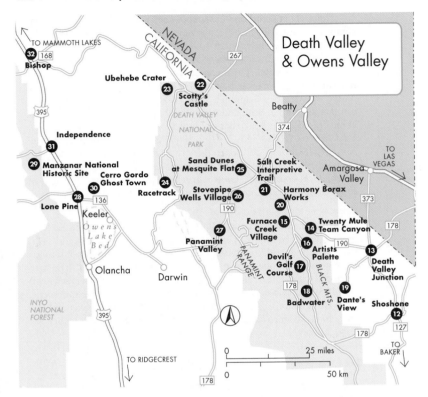

pine. Wildlife, such as bighorn sheep, spend most of their time in rugged, secluded canyons and upper ridges. You may see coyotes lazing in the shade at lower elevations, and the smaller desert fox is a regular sight among the sand dunes.

Shoshone

12 *Hwy. 127, 202 mi north of Ridgecrest, via U.S. 395, Rte. 58, and I–15.*

Shoshone started as a mining town where prospectors lived in small caves dynamited out of the rock. The caves, named Dublin Gulch, were carved into the caliche soil by miners during the 1920s and have an eerie, Egyptian feel. You are free to explore the cells, with their stone walls, sleeping platforms, and metal chimneys, but do so at your own risk. The area, dotted with tamarisk trees and date palms, is home to a natural warm-springs pool fed by an underwater river that's a nice spot to take a dip. It is named for the Shoshone Indians who once lived here.

Visit the **Shoshone Museum** to see a complete woolly mammoth skeleton that was excavated nearby. The museum also houses antiques, minerals, and other items related to the history of Death Valley, including an interesting display about the female prospectors who settled here.

✉ *Hwy. 127* ☎ *760/852–4524*
⊕ *www.deathvalleychamber.org*
🎫 *Free* ☉ *Daily 8–4.*

LAST CHANCE TO CHECK E-MAIL

Shoshone's **Charles Brown General Store** is a popular stop on the way into Death Valley National Park, as is its Internet café and coffee shop, C'est Si Bon. ✉ *Hwy. 127* ☎ *760/852–4242 general store, 760/852–4307 Internet café.*

Where to Stay & Eat

$–$$ ✕ **Crowbar Café & Saloon.** Housed in an old wooden building where antique photos adorn the walls and mining equipment stands in the corners, the fun and friendly Crowbar serves enormous helpings of regional dishes such as steak and taco salads. The chatty spot is popular with European travelers, and is famous for its home-baked fruit pies and frosty beers. ✉ *Hwy. 127* ☎ *760/852–4180* ▭ *AE, D, MC, V.*

¢–$ ▢ **Shoshone Inn.** Built in 1956, the rustic Shoshone Inn is the only motel in town. Rooms are simple and bright, with Southwest accents, but the big draw here is the warm spring-fed swimming pool built into the foothills. A market, café, gas station, and museum are all within walking distance. ✉ *Hwy. 127* 🖃 *Box 67, 92384* ☎ *760/852–4335* 🖶 *760/852–4250* ⊕ *www.shoshonevillage.com* ⇆ *10 rooms, 6 kitchenettes* ⌂ *Some kitchenettes, cable TV, laundry facilities, some pets allowed; no a/c, no smoking* ▭ *AE, D, MC, V.*

Death Valley Junction

⑬ *30 mi north of Shosone on Hwy. 127.*

With the exception of the opera house and hotel, Death Valley Junction has little to offer, but it's a fine place to stop and stretch your legs. There are no services here.

Marta Becket's Amargosa Opera House is an unexpected novelty in the desert. An artist and dancer from New York, Becket first visited the former railway town of Amargosa while on tour in 1964. Three years later she returned to town and bought a boarded-up theater that sat amid a group of run-down mock–Spanish colonial buildings. To compensate for the sparse audiences in the early days, Becket painted a Renaissance-era Spanish crowd on the walls and ceiling, turning the theater into a trompe l'oeil masterpiece. Now in her late 70s, Becket performs her blend of ballet, mime, and 19th-century melodrama to sellout crowds. After the show you can meet her in the adjacent gallery, where she sells her paintings and autographs her books. There are no performances May through September. Note that Becket injured herself in early 2006, but is expected to recover in time for the 2007 season. Reservations are required. ✉ *Hwy. 127* ☎ *760/852–4441* ⊕ *www.amargosaoperahouse. com* 🎫 *$15* ☉ *Oct.–mid-May, Sat. 8:15.*

Where to Stay

¢ ▢ **Opera House Hotel.** The Pacific Coast Borax Company built this hotel in 1923 to serve railroad passengers; it's now listed on the National Register of Historic Places. Rooms have one or two double beds, and are furnished with antiques and adorned with murals. It's nothing fancy, but it does a swift business: if you're planning a winter visit, make your reservations at least two months in advance. ☒ *Hwy. 127* ☏ *760/852–4441* 🖷 *760/852–4138* ⊕ *www.amargosaoperahouse.com* ⇄ *14 rooms* △ *No room phones, no room TVs* ⊟ *AE, MC, V.*

Death Valley National Park

☛ *105 mi west of Lone Pine on Hwys. 136 and 190, to Furnace Creek.*

Fodor'sChoice

★

With more than 3.3 million acres (5,200 square mi), Death Valley National Park is America's largest national park outside Wrangell–St. Elias, Alaska. The Panamint Range parallels Death Valley to the west; the Amargosa Range, to the east. Minerals and ores in the rock here have tinted the mountains and canyons all shades of green, yellow, brown, white, and black. Of course, Death Valley is hot: the park's record high temperature (and the record high for the entire United States), recorded in 1913, was 134°F. Seeing nature at its most extreme is precisely what attracts many people; there are more visitors to Death Valley in July and August than in December and January. Despite its popularity, Death Valley is still an empty and lonely place. Although some sights appear in clusters, others require extensive travel. The 54-mi trip from Furnace Creek to Scotty's Castle, for example, can take two hours or more.

The park entrance fee is $20 per vehicle and $10 for those entering on foot, bus, bike, or motorcycle. Admission, valid for seven consecutive days, is collected at the park's entrance stations and at the visitor center at Furnace Creek. ⛭ *Box 579, Death Valley 92328* ☏ *760/786–3200* ⊕ *www.nps.gov/deva.*

⑭ A drive in colorful **Twenty Mule Team Canyon** delivers quite a few thrills. The canyon was named for the 20-mule teams that between 1883 and 1889 carried 10-ton loads of borax through the burning desert. At places along the loop road off Highway 190, the soft rock walls reach high on both sides, making it seem like you're on an amusement-park ride. Remains of prospectors' tunnels are visible here, along with some brilliant rock formations. You can park and walk in places. ☒ *20 Mule Team Rd. off Hwy. 190, 4 mi south of Furnace Creek, 20 mi west of Death Valley Junction* ⛒ *Trailers not permitted.*

⑮ **Furnace Creek Village** is a center of activity amid the sprawling quiet of Death Valley. Covered with tropical landscaping, it has jogging and bicycle paths, golf, tennis, a general store, and—rare for these parts—a few different dining options. The exhibits and artifacts at **Furnace Creek Visitor Center and Museum** (☏ *760/786–3200* ⊕ *www.nps.gov/deva*) provide a broad overview of how Death Valley formed; you can pick up maps at the bookstore run by the Death Valley Natural History Association. This is also the place to sign up for ranger-led walks or check out a live presentation about the valley's cultural and natural history. **Furnace Creek Ranch** (*see* Where to Stay, *below*) conducts guided horseback, carriage, and hayrides that traverse trails with views of the surrounding mountains, where multicolor volcanic rock and alluvial fans make a dramatic backdrop for date palms and other vegetation.

✉ *4 mi north of Twenty Mule Team Canyon on Hwy. 190, 54 mi south of Scotty's Castle, 25 mi southeast of Stovepipe Wells Village on Hwy. 190.*

★ ⓰ **Artists Palette,** so called for the brilliant colors of its volcanic deposits, is one of the most magnificent sights in Death Valley. Artists Drive, the approach to the area, is one-way heading north off Badwater Road, so if you're visiting Badwater, it saves time to come here on the way back. The drive winds through foothills of sedimentary and volcanic rocks. Within the palette, the huge expanses of Death Valley are replaced by intimate, small-scale natural beauty. It's a quiet, lonely drive. ✉ *11 mi south of Furnace Creek off Badwater Rd.*

⓱ At **Devil's Golf Course** thousands of miniature salt pinnacles carved into surreal shapes by the desert wind dot the landscape. The salt was pushed up to the earth's surface by pressure created as underground salt- and water-bearing gravel crystallized. In some spots, perfectly round holes descend into the ground (hence the name of this site). Nothing grows in this barren landscape. ✉ *Badwater Rd., 13 mi south of Furnace Creek. Turn right onto dirt road and drive 1 mi.*

⓲ Reaching **Badwater,** you'll see a shallow pool containing mostly sodium chloride—the pool is saltier than the sea—in an expanse of desolate salt flats. It's a sharp contrast to the expansive canyons and elevations nearby. At 282 feet below sea level, Badwater is the lowest spot on land in the Western Hemisphere—and also one of the hottest. The legend of its name is that an early surveyor noticed his mule wouldn't drink from the pool and wrote "badwater" on his map. ✉ *Badwater Rd., 19 mi south of Furnace Creek.*

★ ⓳ **Dante's View** is more than 5,000 feet up in the Black Mountains. In the dry desert air you can see across most of 110-mi-wide Death Valley. The view is astounding: you can see the highest and lowest spots in the contiguous United States from the same vantage point. The tiny blackish patch far below is Badwater, at 282 feet below sea level; on the western horizon is Mt. Whitney, which rises to 14,496 feet. It's one of the most extraordinary sights anywhere in California. ✉ *Dante's View Rd. off Hwy. 190, 35 mi from Badwater, 20 mi south of Twenty Mule Team Canyon.*

⓴ From the **Harmony Borax Works,** Death Valley's mule teams hauled borax to the railroad town of Mojave, 165 mi away. The teams plied the route until 1889, when the railroad finally arrived in Zabriskie. Constructed in 1883, one of the oldest buildings in Death Valley houses the **Borax Museum** (✉ Hwy. 190, 2 mi south of borax works 🎫 Free). Originally a miners' bunkhouse, the building once stood in Twenty Mule Team Canyon. Now it displays mining machinery and historical exhibits. The adjacent structure is the original mule-team barn. ✉ *Harmony Borax Works Rd., west of Hwy. 190, 2 mi north of Furnace Creek* ☉ *Daily 9–4:30.*

On Highway 190, south of its junction with Scotty's Castle Road and 14 mi north of the town of Furnace Creek, is a 1-mi gravel road that ㉑ leads to the **Salt Creek Interpretive Trail.** The trail, a ½-mi boardwalk circuit, loops through a spring-fed wash. The nearby hills are brown and gray, but the floor of the wash is alive with aquatic plants such as

6

pickerelweed and salt grass. The stream and ponds here are among the few places in the park to see the rare pupfish, the only native fish species in Death Valley. The tiny fish are shy and hard to see, so you'll have to be a little sneaky or stand quietly and wait for them to appear. Animals such as bobcats, fox, coyotes, and snakes visit the spring, and you may also see ravens, common snipes, killdeer, and great blue herons. ⊠ *Off Hwy. 190, 14 mi north of Furnace Creek.*

★ ☺ ㉒ **Scotty's Castle** is an odd apparition rising out of a canyon. This Moorish-style mansion, begun in 1924 and never completed, takes its name from Walter Scott, better known as Death Valley Scotty. An ex-cowboy, prospector, and performer in Buffalo Bill's Wild West Show, Scotty always told people the castle was his, financed by gold from a secret mine. In reality, there was no mine, and the house belonged to a Chicago millionaire named Albert Johnson (advised by doctors to spend time in a warm, dry climate), whom Scott had finagled into investing in the fictitious mine. The house functioned for a while as a hotel—guests included Bette Davis and Norman Rockwell—and still contains works of art, imported carpets, handmade European furniture, and a tremendous pipe organ. Costumed rangers re-create life at the castle circa 1939. ■ TIP→ **Try to arrive for the first tour of the day to avoid a wait.** ⊠ *Scotty's Castle Rd., 53 mi north of Salt Creek Interpretive Trail on Hwy. 267* ☎ *760/786–2392* ⊕ *www.nps.gov/deva* � *$11* ☉ *Daily 8:30–5, tours daily 9–5.*

NEED A BREAK?

At **Xanterra Concessions** (☎ 760/786–2325), outside the castle, you can refuel on a steak, roast beef, or turkey sandwich for around $5. The snack bar is open 8:30 to 5:30, and there are picnic areas on the castle grounds where you can kick back with your refreshments.

㉓ The impressive **Ubehebe Crater**, 500 feet deep and ½ mi across, is the result of underground steam and gas explosions that occurred about 3,000 years ago. Its volcanic ash spreads out over most of the area, and the cinders lie as deep as 150 feet, near the crater's rim. You'll get superb views of the valley from here, and you can take a fairly easy hike around the west side of the rim to Little Hebe Crater, one of a smaller cluster of craters to the south and west. It's always windy here, so hold on to your hat. ⊠ *8 mi northwest of Scotty's Castle on N. Death Valley Hwy.*

★ ㉔ Although reaching the **Racetrack** involves a 27-mi journey over rough and almost nonexistent dirt road, the trip is well worth the reward. Where else in the world do rocks move on their own? This phenomenon has baffled scientists for years. Is it some sort of magnetic field? No one has actually seen the rocks in motion, but theory has it that when it rains, the hard-packed lakebed becomes slippery enough that gusty winds push the rocks along—sometimes for several hundred yards. When the mud dries, a telltale trail remains. The trek to the Racetrack can be made in a passenger vehicle, but high clearance is suggested. ⊠ *From Ubehebe Crater, west 27 mi on dirt rd.*

㉕ Made up of minute pieces of quartz and other rock, the **Sand Dunes at Mesquite Flat** are ever-changing products of the wind—rippled hills with curving crests and a sun-bleached hue. The dunes are the most photographed destination in the park, and you can see them at their best at sunrise and sunset. There are no trails; you can roam where you please. Keep your eyes open for animal tracks—you may even spot a fox or coyote roaming the dunes. ⚠ **Bring plenty of water, and remember where you parked your car: it's easy to become disoriented in this ocean of sand. If you lose your bearings, simply climb to the top of a dune and scan the horizon for the parking lot.** ✉ *19 mi north of Hwy. 190, northeast of Stovepipe Wells Village.*

❷❻ **Stovepipe Wells Village** was the first resort in Death Valley. The tiny town, which dates to 1926, takes its name from the stovepipe that an early prospector left to indicate where he found water. The area contains a motel, a restaurant, a grocery store, campgrounds, and a landing strip. The multicolor walls of **Mosaic Canyon** (✉ Off Hwy. 190, on a 3-mi gravel road immediately southwest of Stovepipe Wells Village) are extremely close together in spots. A ¾-mi hike will give you a good sense of the area. If weather permits, it's rewarding to continue into the canyon for a few more miles. Be prepared to clamber over larger boulders. ✉ *2 mi from Sand Dunes; 77 mi east of Lone Pine on Hwy. 190.*

❷❼ The **Panamint Valley,** west of the forbidding Panamint Range, is a great place to stop if you're arriving late in the day and don't want to drive over the winding mountain roads into Death Valley after dark. The views here are spectacular. From Highway 178 south of Highway 190, turn north on Wildrose Canyon Road and east onto the dirt track leading to the **Charcoal Kilns** (✉ 9 mi east of Hwy. 178). The drive will take about a half hour, but it's worth it. Ten stone kilns, each 30 feet high and 25 feet wide, stand as if on parade in a line up a mountain. The kilns, built by Chinese laborers in 1879, were used to burn wood from piñon pines to turn it into charcoal. The charcoal was then transported over the mountains into Death Valley, where it was used to extract lead and silver from the ore mined there. If you hike nearby Wildrose Peak, you will be rewarded with terrific views of the kilns, with Death Valley's phenomenal colors as a backdrop. ✉ *31 mi southwest of Stovepipe; 51 mi southeast of Lone Pine on Hwy. 190.*

Where to Stay & Eat

$$$$ ✕🏨 **Furnace Creek Inn.** Built in 1927, this adobe-brick-and-stone lodge
Fodor'sChoice   is nestled in one of the park's greenest oases. A warm mineral stream
★   gurgles across the property, and its 85°F waters feed into a swimming pool. The rooms are decorated in earth tones, with old-style furnishings. The top-notch Furnace Creek Inn Dining Room ($$$) serves desert-theme dishes such as rattlesnake empanadas and crispy cactus, as well as less exotic fare such as cumin-lime shrimp, lamb, and New York strip steak. Afternoon tea has been a tradition since 1927. The inn is closed mid-May through mid-October. ✉ *Furnace Creek Village, Hwy. 190, 92328* ☎ *760/786–2361* 📠 *760/786–2514* ⇔ *66 rooms* ↳ *Restaurant, room service, some refrigerators, cable TV with video games, in-room data ports, 4 tennis courts, pool, hot tubs, massage, sauna, bar, shop, meeting rooms* 🖃 *AE, D, DC, MC, V.*

6

$–$$$ ✕⊞ **Furnace Creek Ranch.** Originally crew headquarters for the Pacific Coast Borax Company, the four buildings here have motel-type rooms that are good for families. Readers say rooms are clean and spacious with an added bonus of being recently refurbished, whereas others complain they are a bit overpriced. The best ones overlook the green lawns of the resort and the surrounding mountains. The property is adjacent to a golf course with its own team of pros, and also has a general store and a campground. The family-style Wrangler Steak House ($$$) and 49er Café ($) serve American fare in simple surroundings. ⊠ *Furnace Creek Village, 92328* ☎ *760/786–2345* 🖷 *760/786–9945* ⊕ *www. furnacecreekresort.com* ⮐ *224 rooms* ⚹ *Restaurant, coffee shop, grocery, some refrigerators, cable TV with movies, in-room data ports, golf course, 4 tennis courts, pro shop, pool, horseback riding, bar, shop, playground, laundry facilities; no smoking* ▭ *AE, D, DC, MC, V.*

¢–$ ✕⊞ **Stovepipe Wells Village.** If you prefer quiet nights and an unfettered view of the night sky and nearby sand dunes, this property is for you. No telephones break the silence here, and only the deluxe rooms have televisions. Readers say the rooms are clean but dated—some to the point of "shabby"—but the resort does have a nice pool and is close to the dunes. The Toll Road Restaurant ($–$$$) serves American breakfast, lunch, and dinner favorites, from omelets and sandwiches to burgers and steaks. RV campsites with full hookups ($22) are available on a first-come, first-served basis. ⊠ *Stovepipe Wells Village, Hwy. 190, 92328* ☎ *760/786–2387* 🖷 *760/786–2389* ⊕ *www.stovepipewells.com* ⮐ *83 rooms* ⚹ *Restaurant, some refrigerators, pool, bar, shop, airstrip; no room phones, no TV in some rooms* ▭ *AE, D, MC, V.*

⚠ **Sunset Campground.** This campground is a gravel-and-asphalt RV city. Hookups are not available, but you can walk across the street to the showers, laundry facilities, and swimming pool at Furnace Creek Ranch. Many of Sunset's denizens are senior citizens who migrate to Death Valley each winter to play golf and tennis or just to enjoy the mild, dry climate. ⚹ *Flush toilets, dump station, drinking water, ranger station, play area* ⮐ *1,000 sites* ⊠ *1 mi north of Furnace Creek Village* ☎ *760/786– 2331* ⊕ *www.nps.gov/deva* ⚹ *Reservations not accepted* ▭ *No credit cards* ⊘ *Mid-Oct.–mid-Apr.* 🗒 *$12.*

Sports & the Outdoors

BIRD-WATCHING   Approximately 250 bird species have been identified in Death Valley. The best place to see the park's birds is along the Salt Creek Interpretive Trail, where you can spot ravens, common snipes, killdeer, spotted sandpipers, and great blue herons. Along the fairways at Furnace Creek Golf Club, you can see kingfishers, peregrine falcons, hawks, Canada geese, yellow warblers, and the occasional golden eagle—just remember to stay off the greens.

GOLF   At **Furnace Creek Golf Club,** the lowest golf course in the world, you can opt to play 9 or 18 holes. The club rents clubs and carts, and greens fees are reduced if you're a guest of Furnace Creek Ranch or Furnace Creek Inn. In winter, reservations are essential. Stay and Play packages, which include accommodations for two, a day of golfing and cart rental, start at $80 for the ranch and $166 for the Inn. ⊠ *Furnace Creek Vil-*

lage ☎ *760/786–2301* ✉ *$55* ⊙ *Tee times daily sunrise–sundown; pro shop daily 7–5.*

HIKING Hiking trails and routes abound throughout Death Valley National Park, though few are maintained by the Park Service. Try the 2-mi round-trip Keane Wonder Mine Trail, with spectacular views of the valley; the winding 4-mi round-trip Mosaic Canyon Trail, between smoothly polished walls of a narrow canyon; or Natural Bridge Canyon Trail, an easy half-mile round-trip to a bridge formation. Plan to take your walks before or after midday (when the sun is hottest). Be sure to carry plenty of water, wear protective clothing, and be wary of tarantulas, black widows, scorpions, snakes, and other potentially dangerous creatures. Some of the best trails are unmarked; ask locals for directions.

OWENS VALLEY

ALONG U.S. 395 EAST OF THE SIERRA NEVADA

Lying in the shadow of the eastern Sierra Nevada, the Owens Valley stretches along U.S. 395 from the Mono–Inyo county line, in the north, to the town of Olancha, in the south. This stretch of highway is dotted with tiny towns, some containing only a minimart and a gas station. If you're traveling from Yosemite National Park to Death Valley National Park or are headed from Lake Tahoe or Mammoth to the desert, U.S. 395 is your corridor.

6

Lone Pine

28 *30 mi west of Panamint Valley via Hwy. 190*

Mt. Whitney towers majestically over this tiny community, which supplied nearby gold- and silver-mining outposts in the 1860s. In more recent decades—especially the 1950s and '60s—the town has been touched by Hollywood glamour: more than 300 movies, TV shows, and commercials have been filmed here. The Lone Pine Film Festival now takes place here every October.

Drop by the Lone Pine Visitor Center for a map of the **Alabama Hills** and take a drive up Whitney Portal Road (turn west at the light) to this wonderland of granite boulders. Erosion has worn the rocks smooth; some have been chiseled to leave arches and other formations. The hills have become a popular location for rock climbing. There are three campgrounds among the rocks, each with a stream for fishing. ⊠ *Whitney Portal Rd., 4½ mi west of Lone Pine.*

★ Straddling the border of Sequoia National Park and Inyo National Forest–John Muir Wilderness, **Mt. Whitney** (14,496 feet) is the highest mountain in the continental United States. A favorite game for travelers passing through Lone Pine is trying to guess which peak is Mt. Whitney. Almost no one gets it right because Mt. Whitney is hidden behind other mountains. There is no road that ascends the peak, but you can catch a glimpse of the mountain by driving curvy Whitney Portal Road west from Lone Pine into the mountains. The pavement ends at the trailhead to the top of the mountain, which is also the start of the 211-mi John Muir Trail from Mt. Whitney to Yosemite National Park. At the portal, a restaurant (known for its pancakes) and a small store mostly cater to hikers and campers staying at Whitney Portal Campground. You can see a waterfall from the parking lot and go fishing in a small trout pond. The portal area is closed from mid-October to early May; the road closes when snow conditions require.

Where to Stay & Eat

$–$$$ ✕ **Seasons Restaurant.** This inviting, country-style diner serves all kinds of upscale American fare. For a special treat, try the medallions of Cervena venison, smothered in port wine, dried cranberries, and toasted walnuts; finish with the Baileys Irish Cream cheesecake or the lemon crème brûlée for dessert. Children's items include a mini–sirloin steak. ⊠ *206 S. Main St.* ☎ *760/876–8927* ⊟ *AE, D, MC, V* ⊘ *Closed Sun. No lunch.*

¢–$ ✕ **Mt. Whitney Restaurant.** A boisterous family-friendly restaurant with a game room and 50-inch television, this place is especially popular during *Monday Night Football.* The best burgers in town are here—you can choose from the usual beef or branch out with ostrich, venison, or buffalo burgers. There's a gift shop on the premises. ⊠ *227 S. Main St.* ☎ *760/876–5751* ⊟ *D, MC, V.*

¢–$$ ⌂ **Dow Villa Motel and Hotel.** John Wayne slept here, and you can, too. Built in 1923 to cater to the film industry, Dow Villa is in the center of Lone Pine. Some rooms have views of the mountains; both buildings are within walking distance of just about everything in town. There are in-room coffeemakers and whirlpool tubs, though some of the guest rooms share bathrooms. Pets are allowed only in smoking rooms. Many units have an Old West feel, and are decorated with antique furniture and pictures of John Wayne or Mt. Whitney. ⊠ *310 S. Main St., 93545* ☎ *760/876–5521 or 800/824–9317* 🖷 *760/876–5643* ⊕ *www.dowvillamotel.com* ⇆ *91 rooms* ♻ *Refrigerators, cable TV, in-room VCRs, some in-room broadband, in-room data ports, pool, hot tub, no-smoking rooms* ⊟ *AE, D, DC, MC, V.*

🏕 **Whitney Portal.** The campsites here are spread beneath towering pines and adjacent to a small pond. The campground can accommodate tents or RVs up to 16 feet. The camp is popular with hikers, so it's best to reserve a spot in advance. The property has a store and café that are open in summer. ♻ *Flush toilets, drinking water, showers, fire grates, picnic tables, public telephone* ⇆ *43 sites* ⊠ *Whitney Portal Rd., 13 mi west of Lone Pine* ☎ *760/867–6200 or 877/444–6777* 🖷 *760/876–6202* ⊕ *www.reserveusa.com* ⚠ *Reservations essential* ⊟ *AE, D, MC, V* ⊘ *Early May–mid-Oct.* ⊡ *$16.*

Manzanar National Historic Site

㉙ *U.S. 395, 11 mi north of Lone Pine.*

A reminder of an ugly episode in U.S. history, the remnants of the Manzanar War Relocation Center have been designated the Manzanar National Historic Site. This is where some 10,000 Japanese-Americans were confined behind barbed-wire fences between 1942 and 1945. Manzanar was the first of 10 such internment camps erected by the federal government following Japan's attack on Pearl Harbor in 1941. In the name of national security, American citizens of Japanese descent were forcibly relocated to these camps, many of them losing their homes, businesses, and most of their possessions in the process. Today not much remains of Manzanar but a guard post, the auditorium, and some concrete foundations. But you can stop at the entrance station, pick up a brochure, and drive the one-way dirt road past the ruins to a small cemetery, where a monument stands as a reminder of what took place here. Signs mark where structures such as the barracks, a hospital, school, and fire station once stood. An 8,000-square-foot interpretive center also opened in April 2004, with exhibits and a 15-minute film. ⌂ *Manzanar Information, c/o Superintendent: Death Valley National Park, Death Valley 92398* ☎ *760/878–2932* ⊕ *www.nps.gov/manz* ✉ *Free.*

Cerro Gordo Ghost Town

★ ㉚ *20 mi east of Lone Pine.*

Discovered by Mexican miner Pablo Flores in 1865, Cerro Gordo was California's biggest producer of silver and lead, raking in almost $13 million before it shut down in 1959. Today, it's a ghost town, home to many original buildings, including the circa-1871 American Hotel; the fully restored 1904 bunkhouse; the 1868 Belshaw House; a bullet-riddled saloon; and Union Mine and General Store, which now serves as a museum and outlook point over the majestic Sierra mountains and Owens Dry Lake. The privately owned ghost town offers overnight accommodations in the Belshaw House for $150 per night, billing itself as the only "bed and cook-your-own-breakfast ghost town in the world." Larger groups can stay in the bunkhouse for $300 per night, which includes catered meals in the American Hotel for an extra charge. The Sarsaparilla Saloon inside the hotel serves up its own Cerro Gordo Freighting Company Root Beer, bottled in nearby Indian Wells (proceeds go back to restoring and maintaining the ghost town). You'll have to time your visit for summer, as its 8,300-foot elevation means that the steep road into the town is impassable in winter. A four-wheel-drive vehicle is recommended at all times. A day pass is $5 per person, which includes a tour if arranged in advance. Guests are forbidden to take artifacts from the area or explore nearby mines. ⌂ *Box 221, Keeler 93530* ☎ *760/876–5030* ⊕ *www.cerrogordo.us.*

Independence

㉛ *U.S. 395, 5 mi north of Manzanar National Historic Site.*

Named for a military outpost that was established near here in 1862, Independence is small and sleepy. But the town has some wonderful historic buildings and is certainly worth a stop on your way from the Sierra Nevada to Death Valley.

As you approach Independence from the north, you'll pass the **Mt. Whitney Fish Hatchery,** a delightful place for a family picnic. Bring some dimes for the machines filled with fish food; the hatchery's lakes are full of hefty, always-hungry breeder trout. Built in 1915, the hatchery was one of the first trout farms in California, and today it produces fish that stock lakes throughout the state. ⊠ *Fish Hatchery Rd., 1 mi north of Independence* ☏ *760/878–2272* ⊡ *Free* ⊙ *Daily 8–5.*

The **Eastern California Museum** provides a glimpse of Inyo County's history. Highlights include a fine collection of Paiute and Shoshone Indian basketry and a yard full of agricultural implements used by early area miners and farmers. ⊠ *155 N. Grant St.* ☏ *760/878–0364* ⊕ *www.inyocounty.us/ecmuseum* ⊡ *Donation suggested* ⊙ *Wed.–Mon. 10–4.*

Where to Stay

¢ ▥ **Winnedumah Hotel Bed & Breakfast.** This 1927 B&B has the best—and most famous—digs in town: celebrities such as Roy Rogers, John Wayne, and Bing Crosby all stayed here while filming nearby. Outfitted in an eclectic mix of Wild West chic and modern bric-a-brac, the rooms are simple yet comfortable. There are also hostel rooms. Breakfast is usually a hearty affair of bacon, eggs, waffles, and fresh fruit. ⊠ *211 N. Edwards St.* ☏ *760/878–2040* 🖷 *760/878–2833* ⊕ *www.winnedumah.com* ⊅ *24 rooms, 14 with bath* ⚬ *Some pets allowed (fee); no phones in some rooms, no room TVs, no smoking* ⊟ *AE, D, DC, MC, V* ⦿ *BP.*

EN
ROUTE
★ ⊙

Traveling north from Independence on U.S. 395, turn onto Highway 168 and follow the signs 31 mi to the **Ancient Bristlecone Pine Forest.** Here you can see some of the oldest living trees on earth, some of which date back more than 40 centuries. These rare, gnarled pines in the White Mountains can grow only in harsh, frigid conditions above 9,000 feet. At the **Schulman Grove Visitor Center** (☏ 760/873–2500 ⊕ www.fs.fed.us/r5/inyo/about), open from 8 to 4:30 weekdays, late May through October, you can learn about the bristlecone and take a walk to the 4,700-year-old Methuselah tree. Admission to the forest is $3.

Bishop

③② *U.S. 395, 43 mi north of Independence.*

One of the biggest towns along U.S. 395, Bishop has views of the Sierra Nevada and the White and Inyo mountains. First settled by the Northern Paiute Indians, the area was named in 1861 for cattle rancher Samuel Bishop, who established a camp here. Paiute and Shoshone people reside on four reservations in the area.

One of Bishop's biggest draws is its **Mule Days Celebration** each Memorial Day weekend. More than 40,000 tourists and RVers pack into this lazy town for the longest nonmotorized parade in the world, mule races, a rodeo, and good old-fashioned country-and-western concerts. ☏ *760/872–4263* ⊕ *www.muledays.org.*

⊙ The **Laws Railroad Museum** is a complex of historic buildings and train cars from the Carson and Colorado Railroad Company, which set up a narrow-gauge railroad yard here in 1883. Among the exhibits are a self-propelled car from the Death Valley Railroad and a full village of rescued buildings, including a post office, an 1883 train depot, the 1909

North Inyo Schoolhouse, and a restored 1900 ranch house. ☒ *U.S. 6, 3 mi north of U.S. 395* ☎ *760/873–5950* ⊕ *www.lawsmuseum.org* ◷ *$5 suggested donation* ◷ *Daily 10–4.*

Where to Stay & Eat

★ ¢–$$$ ✕ **Whiskey Creek.** Since 1924, this Wild West–style saloon, restaurant, and gift shop has been serving crisp salads, warm soups, and juicy barbecued steaks to locals and tourists. Warm days are perfect for sitting on the shaded deck and enjoying one of the many available microbrews. ☒ *524 N. Main St.* ☎ *760/873–7174* ▤ *AE, MC, V.*

¢ ✕ **Erick Schat's Bakkery.** A popular stop for motorists traveling to and from Mammoth Lakes, this shop is chock-full of delicious pastries, cookies, rolls, and other baked goods. But the biggest draw here is the sheepherder bread, a hand-shaped and stone hearth–baked sourdough that was introduced during the gold rush by immigrant Basque sheepherders in 1907. In addition to the bakery, Schat's has a gift shop and a sandwich bar. ☒ *763 N. Main St.* ☎ *760/873–7156* ⊕ *www.erickschatsbakery.com* ▤ *AE, MC, V.*

$–$$ ▨ **Best Western Creekside Inn.** One of the nicest spots to stay in Bishop, this clean and comfortable mountain-style hotel is a good base from which to explore the town or go skiing and trout fishing nearby. Rooms are elegantly furnished with cherrywood armoires and beds; the ranch-style lobby has a wonderfully large brick hearth. In summer you can sit on the patio near a trickling creek. ☒ *725 N. Main St.* ☎ *760/872–3044 or 800/273–3550* ⊕ *www.bestwestern.com* ⇨ *89 rooms* ♿ *Some kitchenettes, cable TV, in-room data ports, Wi-Fi, pool, hot tub; no smoking* ▤ *AE, MC, V* ⦂◯⦂ *CP.*

Sports & the Outdoors

Sierra Mountain Center (☒ 174 W. Line St. ☎ 760/873–8526 ⊕ www.sierramountaincenter.com) provides instruction and guided hiking, skiing, snowshoe, rock-climbing, and mountain-biking trips for all levels of expertise.

FISHING The Owens Valley is trout country; its glistening alpine lakes and streams are brimming with feisty rainbow, brown, brook, and golden trout. Popular spots include Owens River, the Owens River gorge, and Pleasant Valley Reservoir. Although you can fish year-round here, some fishing is catch-and-release. Bishop is the site of fishing derbies throughout the year, including the popular Blake Jones Blind Bogey Trout Derby, in March. Whether you want to take a fly-fishing class or a guided wade trip, **Brock's Flyfishing Specialists and Tackle Experts** (☒ 100 N. Main St. ☎ 760/872–3581 or 888/619–3581 ⊕ www.brocksflyfish.com) is a valuable resource.

HORSE PACKING The **Rock Creek Pack Station** (✉ Box 248, 93516 ☎ 760/935–4493 in summer, 760/872–8331 in winter ⊕ www.rockcreekpackstation.com) outfit runs 3- to 24-day horse-packing trips in the High Sierra, including Mt. Whitney, Yosemite National Park, and other parts of the John Muir Wilderness. One expedition tracks wild mustangs through Inyo National Forest; another is an old-fashioned horse drive between the Owens Valley and the High Sierra.

THE MOJAVE ESSENTIALS

To research prices, get advice from other travelers, and book travel arrangements, visit ⊕ www.fodors.com.

AIRPORTS & TRANSFERS

Inyokern Airport, near Ridgecrest, is served by United Express from Los Angeles. McCarran International Airport, in Las Vegas, Nevada, served by dozens of major airlines, is about as close to Furnace Creek, in Death Valley National Park, as Inyokern Airport is. Needles Airport serves small, private planes, as does Furnace Creek's 3,000-foot airstrip in Death Valley. ⇨ Air Travel *in* Smart Travel Tips A to Z for airline phone numbers.

🚩 **Inyokern Airport** ⊠ Inyokern Rd., Hwy. 178, 9 mi west of Ridgecrest, Inyokern ☎ 760/377-5844 ⊕ www.inyokernairport.com. **McCarran International Airport** ⊠ 5757 Wayne Newton Blvd., Las Vegas, NV ☎ 702/261-5733 ⊕ www.mccarran.com. **Needles Airport** ⊠ 711 Airport Rd., Needles ☎ 760/326-5263.

BUS TRAVEL

Greyhound serves Baker, Barstow, Ridgecrest, and Victorville, but traveling by bus to the Mojave Desert is neither convenient nor cheap. There's no scheduled bus service to Death Valley National Park or within Owens Valley. Victor Valley Transit serves Victorville, Hesperia, Phelan, Adelanto, and other nearby areas.

🚩 **Greyhound** ☎ 800/231-2222 ⊕ www.greyhound.com. **Victor Valley Transit** ☎ 760/948-3030 ⊕ www.vvta.org.

CAR RENTAL

In the Owens Valley, reliable regional car-rental agencies include Eastern Sierra Motors and U-Save Auto Rentals. The major national agencies serve the larger cities of the Mojave Desert: Barstow has Hertz and Avis offices, and Victorville has Avis, Budget, and Enterprise offices. ⇨ Car Rental *in* Smart Travel Tips A to Z for national rental-agency phone numbers.

🚩 **Local Agencies** **Eastern Sierra Motors** ⊠ 1440 N. U.S. 6, Bishop ☎ 760/873-4291 or 877/503-6257 ⊕ www.easternsierramotorsinc.com. **U-Save Auto Rentals** ⊠ 1075 Main St., Bishop ☎ 800/207-2681 ⊕ www.usavemammothbishop.com.

CAR TRAVEL

Much of the desert can be seen from the comfort of an air-conditioned car, though you need not despair if you're without air-conditioning—just avoid driving in the middle of the day and in the middle of summer. You can approach Death Valley from the west or the southeast. Whether you've come south from Bishop or north from Ridgecrest, head east from U.S. 395 on Highway 190 or 178. To enter Death Valley from the southeast, take Highway 127 north from Interstate 15 in Baker and link up with Highway 178, which travels west into the valley and then cuts north toward Highway 190 at Furnace Creek.

The Mojave is shaped like a giant L, with one leg jutting north toward the Owens Valley and the other extending east toward California's borders with Nevada and Arizona. The major north–south route through the western Mojave is U.S. 395, which intersects with Interstate 15 between Cajon Pass and Victorville. U.S. 395 travels north into the Owens Valley, passing such dusty little stops as Lone Pine, Independence, Big Pine, and Bishop. Farther west, Highway 14 runs north–south between Inyokern (near Ridgecrest) and Palmdale. Two major east–west routes travel through the Mojave: to the north, Interstate 15 between Barstow and Las Vegas, Nevada; to the south, Interstate 40 between Barstow and Needles. At the intersection of the two interstates, in Barstow, Interstate 15 veers south toward Victorville and Los Angeles, and Interstate 40 gives way to Highway 58 toward Bakersfield.

California Highway Patrol 24-hour road info ☎ 800/427-7623 ⊕ www.dot.ca.gov/hq/roadinfo.

EMERGENCIES

In an emergency dial 911.

Emergencies can arise easily in the desert, but you can go a long way toward avoiding them if you take a few simple safety precautions. Never travel alone. Always take a companion, especially if you're not familiar with the area. Let someone know your trip route, destination, and estimated time and date of return. Before setting out, make sure your vehicle is in good condition. Carry a jack, tools, and tow rope or chain. Fill up your tank whenever you see a gas pump—it might be many miles before you see another service station. Stay on main roads: if you drive even a few feet off the pavement, you can get stuck in sand (and besides, venturing off-road is illegal in many areas). When driving, watch out for wild burros, horses, and range cattle. They roam freely throughout much of the desert and have the right-of-way.

Drink at least a gallon of water a day (three gallons if you're hiking or otherwise exerting yourself), even if you don't feel thirsty. Dress in layered clothing and wear comfortable, sturdy shoes and a hat. Keep snacks, sunscreen, and a first-aid kit on hand. If you suddenly have a headache or feel dizzy or nauseous, you could be suffering from dehydration. Get out of the sun immediately and drink plenty of water. Dampen your clothing to lower your body temperature.

Do not enter mine tunnels or shafts. The structures may be unstable, and there may be hidden dangers such as pockets of bad air. Avoid canyons during rainstorms. Floodwaters can quickly fill up dry riverbeds and cover or wash away roads. Never place your hands or feet where you can't see them. Rattlesnakes, scorpions, and black widow spiders may be hiding there.

BLM Rangers ☎ 760/255-8700. **Community Hospital** ✉ Barstow ☎ 760/256-1761. **Northern Inyo Hospital** ✉ 150 Pioneer La., Bishop ☎ 760/873-5811. **San Bernardino County Sheriff** ☎ 760/256-1796 in Barstow, 760/733-4448 in Baker.

TOURS

The Mojave Group of the Sierra Club regularly organizes field trips to interesting spots such as Red Mountain, Silverwood Lake, and the San Gabriel Mountains. The San Gorgonio Sierra Club chapter also conducts desert excursions.

Sierra Club ✉ 3345 Wilshire Blvd., Suite 508, Los Angeles 90010 ☎ 213/387-4287, 909/686-6112 for San Gorgonio chapter ⊕ www.sierraclub.com.

TRAIN TRAVEL

Amtrak makes stops in Victorville, Barstow, and Needles, but the stations are not staffed and do not have phone numbers, so you'll have to purchase your tickets in advance and handle your own baggage. You can travel west to connect with the *Coast Starlight* in Los Angeles or the *San Diegan* in Fullerton. The *Southwest Chief* stops twice a day at the above cities on its route from Los Angeles to Chicago and back. The Barstow station is served daily by Amtrak California motor coaches that travel between San Joaquin, Bakersfield, and Las Vegas.

Amtrak ☎ 800/872-7245 ⊕ www.amtrakcalifornia.com.

VISITOR INFORMATION

Barstow Area Chamber of Commerce and Visitors Bureau ⊠ 681 N. 1st Ave., Barstow 92311 ☎ 760/256-8617 ⊕ www.barstowchamber.com. **Big Pine Chamber of Commerce** ⊠ 128 S. Main St., Big Pine 93513 ☎ 760/938-2114. **Bishop Chamber of Commerce** ⊠ 690 N. Main St., Bishop 93514 ☎ 760/873-8405 ⊕ www.bishopvisitor.com. **Bureau of Land Management** ⊠ California Desert District Office, 6221 Box Springs Blvd., Riverside 92507 ☎ 909/697-5200 ⊕ www.ca.blm.gov. **California Welcome Center** ⊠ 2796 Tanger Way, Barstow 92311 ☎ 760/253-4782 ⊕ www.barstowchamber.com. **Death Valley Chamber of Commerce** ⊠ 118 Hwy. 127, Shoshone 92384 ☎ 760/852-4524 ⊕ www.deathvalleychamber.org. **Death Valley National Park** ⊠ Visitor Center at Furnace Creek, Death Valley 92328 ☎ 760/786-2331 ⊕ www.nps.gov/deva. **Death Valley Natural History Association** ⊠ Box 188, Death Valley 92328 ☎ 800/478-8564. **Desert Discovery Center** ⊠ 831 Barstow Rd., Barstow 92311 ☎ 760/252-6060. **Independence Chamber of Commerce** ⊠ 139 N. Edwards, Independence 93526 ☎ 760/878-0084 ⊕ www.countyofinyo.org. **Lone Pine Chamber of Commerce** ⊠ 126 S. Main St., Lone Pine 93545 ☎ 760/876-4444 or 877/253-8981 ⊕ www.lonepinechamber.org. **Needles Chamber of Commerce** ⊠ 100 G St., Needles 92363 ☎ 760/326-2050 ⊕ www.needleschamber.com. **Ridgecrest Area Convention and Visitors Bureau** ⊠ 100 W. California Ave., Ridgecrest 93555 ☎ 760/375-8202 or 800/847-4830 ⊕ www.visitdeserts.com. **San Bernardino County Regional Parks Department** ⊠ 777 E. Rialto Ave., San Bernardino 92415 ☎ 909/387-2594 ⊕ www.co.san-bernardino.ca.us/parks. **Victorville Chamber of Commerce** ⊠ 14174 Green Tree Blvd., Victorville 92393 ☎ 760/245-6506 ⊕ www.vvchamber.com.

The Southern Sierra

WITH SEQUOIA, KINGS CANYON
& YOSEMITE NATIONAL PARKS

WORD OF MOUTH

"[Yosemite National Park] is a garden of eden!! I love it and have been here many times. The Waterfalls are FABULOUS! The meadow is green and breathtaking! When the sun hits it just right . . . you will never forget this beauty. Wish my backyard was a paradise like this!"

—Jim Holseth

Updated by
Reed Parsell

VAST GRANITE PEAKS AND GIANT SEQUOIAS are among the mind-boggling natural wonders of the Southern Sierra, many of which are protected in three national parks. Endowed with glacially carved valleys, deep canyons, and towering peaks and trees, Kings Canyon and Sequoia national parks abut each other and are easy to visit together. Yosemite, the state's most famous national park, is renowned for its staggering U-shape valleys and mile-high walls of granite formed during the Ice Age. Outside the parks, pristine lakes, superb skiing, rolling hills, and small towns complete the picture of the Southern Sierra.

Exploring the Southern Sierra

For the full Sierra experience, explore the national forests as well as the national parks. Stop at any of the ranger stations near the forests' borders and pick up information on lesser-known sights and attractions. Spend a few nights in the small towns outside the parks. If, however, you're tight on time and want to focus on the attractions that make the region famous, then stay in the parks themselves instead of the gateway towns in the foothills or the Central Valley; you won't want to lose time shuttling back and forth.

Yosemite Valley is the primary destination for many visitors. Because the valley is 7 mi long and mostly less than 1 mi wide, you can visit its attractions in whatever order you choose and return to your favorites at different times of the day. Famous for plunging canyons and the world's largest trees, Kings Canyon and Sequoia are more spread out and don't pack the same instant wallop that Yosemite Valley does, but they're no less gratifying, and you'll encounter fewer people.

About the Restaurants

Towns in the Sierra Nevada are small, but they usually have at least one diner or restaurant. In the national parks, snack bars, coffee shops, and cafeterias are not expensive. The three fanciest lodgings within Yosemite National Park are prime dining spots, with hefty price tags to match. With few exceptions, which are noted, dress is casual at the restaurants listed in this chapter.

When you're traveling in the area, expect to spend a lot of time in the car, so pick up snacks and drinks to keep with you, and keep the gas tank full—especially in winter, when roads sometimes close because of heavy snow (having tire chains or four-wheel drive in winter is also strongly recommended). Stop at a grocery store and fill the ice chest before you set out so you'll be able to explore the national parks without searching for food when you get hungry. With picnic supplies on hand you can enjoy a meal under giant trees; just be certain to leave no food or trash behind.

About the Hotels

Towns are few and far between in the Southern Sierra. Whenever possible, book lodging reservations in advance—especially in summer—or plan to camp out. If you don't, you may find yourself driving long distances to find a place to sleep.

GREAT ITINERARIES

Numbers correspond to the Sequoia & Kings Canyon National Parks, Yosemite National Park, and Southern Sierra maps.

IF YOU HAVE 3 DAYS

If your time is limited, explore Yosemite National Park. Use the Big Oak Flat Entrance on Highway 120, and head east toward ⊞ **Yosemite Valley** ⑬ – ㉓ ⯈. Once you reach the valley floor, traffic is diverted onto a one-way loop road. Continue east, following the signs to day-use parking, and ride the shuttle to **Yosemite Village** ⑬ and the Valley Visitor Center. Loop back west for a short hike near **Yosemite Falls** ⑭, the highest waterfall in North America. Hop back in the car and continue west for a valley view of famous **El Capitan** ⑮. Double back onto Southside Drive en route to Highway 41 southbound, stopping at misty **Bridalveil Fall** ⑰; then follow Highway 41/Wawona Road south 14 mi to the Chinquapin junction and make a left turn onto Glacier Point Road. From **Glacier Point** ㉒ (road closed in winter) you'll get a phenomenal bird's-eye view of the entire valley. If you want to avoid the busloads of tourists, stop at **Sentinel Dome** ㉓ instead.

On Day 2, head south again on Highway 41/Wawona Road and visit the **Mariposa Grove of Big Trees** ㉕ at the southern end of the park. Afterward tour the Pioneer Yosemite History Center. Head back to Yosemite Valley on Wawona Road, and stop at the mouth of the tunnel on Highway 41, just before you drop into the valley, for one of the park's most famous and spectacular views. Plan to watch the sunset on **Half Dome** ㉑ from Sentinel Bridge, and take in a ranger-led program in the early evening. On the third day, have breakfast near the Valley Visitor Center before hiking to Vernal Fall or Nevada Fall.

IF YOU HAVE 5 DAYS

On your first day, stop briefly at the **Foothills Visitor Center** ③ ⯈ in Sequoia National Park to pick up park information and tickets to **Crystal Cave** ⑤. After visiting the cave, stop to explore the museum at **Giant Forest** ④ and the park's other sights; if you're fit, be sure to climb Moro Rock. Spend the night in ⊞ **Grant Grove** ⑩ or ⊞ **Wuksachi Village** ⑦. On Day 2, explore the sights in Grant Grove, then (if you've started early) drive east along Kings Canyon Highway (Highway 180) to **Cedar Grove** ⑪. After lunch, double back on Highway 180, continuing west out of the park to Fresno, where you'll turn north onto Highway 41 toward Yosemite National Park. (It will take you three to four hours to reach the park.) Spend the night just south of the park in ⊞ Oakhurst or just inside the south entrance gate at ⊞ **Wawona** ㉔.

On your third morning, visit the Pioneer Yosemite History Center, and wander beneath the giant sequoias at the nearby **Mariposa Grove of Big Trees** ㉕. From here, head to ⊞ **Yosemite Valley** ⑬ – ㉓, where you should stay the next two nights. Stop just past the tunnel on Highway 41 to take in the dramatic view of **Half Dome** ㉑. Dedicate Day 4 to exploring the valley. On your last day, pack a picnic and drive 55 mi east on Tioga Road to Tuolumne Meadows, the largest subalpine meadow in the Sierra.

7

Other than the Ahwahnee and Wawona hotels in Yosemite, most accommodations inside Sequoia, Kings Canyon, and Yosemite national parks can best be described as "no frills"—think basic motels or rustic cabins, many of which have no electricity or indoor plumbing. In Sequoia and Kings Canyon, lodging rates remain the same throughout the year. In winter, only some lodgings in Grant Grove remain open. Rates in Yosemite are pricey except during the off-peak season, from November through March.

If you'd like assistance booking your lodgings, try the following agencies: **DNC Parks & Resorts at Yosemite** (☎ 559/252–4848 ⊕ www.yosemitepark.com). **Kings Canyon Lodging** (☎ 559/335–5500 or 866/522–6966 ⊕ www.sequoia-kingscanyon.com). **Mammoth Lakes Visitors Bureau Lodging Referral** (☎ 760/934–2712 or 888/466–2666 ⊕ www.visitmammoth.com). **Mammoth Reservations** (☎ 800/223–3032 ⊕ www.mammothreservations.com). **Sequoia Lodging** (☎ 559/253–2199 or 888/252–5757 ⊕ www.visitsequoia.com). **Three Rivers Reservation Center** (☎ 866/561–0410 or 559/561–0410 ⊕ www.rescentre.com).

WHAT IT COSTS					
	$$$$	**$$$**	**$$**	**$**	**¢**
RESTAURANTS	over $30	$23–$30	$16–$22	$10–$15	under $10
HOTELS	over $250	$176–$250	$121–$175	$90–$120	under $90

Restaurant prices are for a main course at dinner, excluding sales tax of 7¼%. Hotel prices are for two people in a standard double room in high season, excluding service charges and 9%–10% tax.

About the Campgrounds

In the national parks you can camp only in designated areas, but in the national forests you can pitch a tent anywhere you want, so long as there are no signs specifically prohibiting camping in that area. Always know and obey fire regulations; you can find out what they are in a specific area by checking with forest-service rangers, either by telephone or at any of the ranger stations just inside park boundaries.

Except for Lodgepole and Dorst in Sequoia, all sites at the **campgrounds** (☎ 559/565–3341 ⊕ www.nps.gov/seki) near each of the major tourist centers in Sequoia and Kings Canyon parks are assigned on a first-come, first-served basis; on weekends in July and August they are often filled by Friday early afternoon. Lodgepole, Potwisha, and Azalea campsites stay open all year, but Lodgepole is not plowed, and camping is limited to snow-tenting or recreational vehicles in plowed parking lots. Other campgrounds in Sequoia and Kings Canyon are open from whenever the snow melts until late September or early October.

If you plan to camp in the backcountry in Sequoia or Kings Canyon national parks, your group must have a backcountry camping permit, which costs $15 for hikers or $30 for stock users (horseback riders, etc.). One permit covers a group of up to 15 people. Availability of permits depends on trailhead quotas. Advance reservations are accepted by mail or fax beginning March 1 and must be made at least three weeks in advance. Without a reservation, you may still get a permit on a first-come, first-served basis starting at 1 PM the day before you plan to hike. Whether you reserve or not, permits must be picked up in person from the permit-issuing station nearest your trailhead. For more information on backcountry camping or travel with pack animals, call the **Wilderness Permit Office** (☎ 559/565–3766 ⊕ www.nps.gov/seki).

Most of Yosemite's 14 campgrounds are in Yosemite Valley and along the Tioga Road. Glacier Point and Wawona have one each. Several campgrounds operate on a first-come, first-served basis year-round (some 400 of the park's sites remain open year-round), whereas some take reservations in high season; in summer, reservations are strongly recommended, if not required. It's sometimes possible to get a campsite on arrival by stopping at the campground reservations office in Yosemite Valley, but this is a risky strategy. **Yosemite Campground Reservations** (☎ 301/722–1257 or 800/436–7275 ⊕ http://reservations.nps.gov) handles all bookings for the reservable campgrounds within the park. During the last two weeks of each month, beginning on the 15th, you can reserve a site up to five months in advance. **DNC Parks & Resorts at Yosemite** (☎ 559/252–4848 ⊕ www.yosemitepark.com) handles reservations for the tent-cabins at Curry Village and for the camping shelters at Housekeeping Camp. If you want to overnight in Yosemite's backcountry, you'll need a wilderness permit. They're free, but it's best to reserve one in advance for $5. You can request a reservation between 24 weeks and two days ahead, but making a request doesn't guarantee a reservation. For more information, contact the **Wilderness Permit Office** (☎ 209/372–0740 permit office, 209/372–0200 general inquiries ⊕ www.nps.gov/yose).

RVs and trailers are permitted in most national park campgrounds, though space is scarce at some. The length limit is 40 feet for RVs and 35 feet for trailers, but the park service recommends that trailers be no longer than 22 feet. Disposal stations are available in the main camping areas.

About the Bears

The Sierra Nevada is home to thousands of bears, and if you plan on camping, you should take all necessary precautions to keep yourself—and the bears—safe. Bears that acquire a taste for human food can become very aggressive and destructive and often must eventually be destroyed by rangers. The national parks' campgrounds and some campgrounds outside the parks provide food-storage boxes that can keep bears from pilfering your edibles (portable canisters for backpackers can be rented in most park stores). It's imperative that you move all food, coolers, and items with a scent (including toiletries, toothpaste, chewing gum, and air fresheners) from your car (including the trunk) to the storage box at your campsite. If you don't, a bear may break into your car by literally peeling off the door or ripping open the trunk, or it may ransack your tent. The familiar tactic of hanging your food from high tree limbs is not an effective deterrent, as bears can easily scale trees. In the Southern Sierra, bear canisters are the only effective and proven method for preventing bears from getting human food. Whether hiking or camping, it's important to respect the landscape and wildlife around you. For detailed information about responsible outdoor recreation, visit the Web site of the **Leave No Trace Center for Outdoor Ethics** (☏ 303/442–8222 or 800/332–4100 ⊕ www.lnt.org).

Timing

Summer is by far the busiest season for all the parks, though things never get as hectic at Sequoia and Kings Canyon as they do at Yosemite. During extremely busy periods, such as July 4, you may experience delays at the entrance gates. If you can make it here only when school is out, try to visit midweek. In winter, heavy snows occasionally cause road closures, and tire chains or four-wheel drive may be required on roads that remain open; trails in the backcountry and in wilderness areas aren't accessible (except on cross-country skis). To avoid these problems, visit between mid-April and late May, or early September to mid-October, when the parks are less busy and the weather usually is hospitable.

The falls at Yosemite are at their most spectacular in May and June. By the end of summer some will have dried up. They begin flowing again in late fall with the first storms, and in winter they may be hung with ice, a dramatic sight. "Spring" wildflowers can bloom late into the summer as you rise in elevation. Snow on the floor of Yosemite Valley is rarely deep, so you can often camp there even in winter (January highs are in the mid-40s, lows in the mid-20s). Tioga Road is usually closed from late October through May or June. Unless you ski or snowshoe in, you can't get to Tuolumne Meadows then. The road from the turnoff for Badger Pass to Glacier Point is not cleared in winter, but it's groomed for cross-country skiing, a 10-mi trek one-way.

SEQUOIA & KINGS CANYON

Naturalist John Muir declared in the early 20th century that the beauty of Sequoia and Kings Canyon national parks easily rivaled that of Yosemite; he described the sequoia trees here as "the most beautiful and majestic on Earth." The largest living things on the planet, *Sequoiadendron giganteum* trees are not as tall as the coast redwoods (*Sequoia sempervirens*), but they're more massive and, on average, older. Exhibits at the visitor centers explain why they can live so long and grow so big, as well as the special relationship between these trees and fire (their thick, fibrous bark helps protect them from flames and insects, and their seeds can't germinate until they first explode out of a burning pinecone).

A little more than 1.5 million people visit Sequoia and Kings Canyon annually, wandering trails through groves and meadows or tackling the rugged backcountry. The topography of the two parks runs the gamut from chaparral, at an elevation of 1,500 feet, to the giant sequoia belt, at 5,000 to 7,500 feet, to the towering peaks of the Great Western Divide and the Sierra crest. Mt. Whitney, the highest point in the contiguous United States, at 14,494 feet, is the crown jewel of the parks' less-crowded eastern side (the border between Sequoia National Park and John Muir Wilderness runs right through the summit of Mt. Whitney). You cannot access Mt. Whitney from Sequoia's western side; you must circumnavigate the Sierra range via a 10-hour, nearly 400-mi drive outside the park (⇨ Chapter 6, The Mojave Desert & Death Valley, *for Mt. Whitney*).

Sequoia and Kings Canyon national parks share their administration and are connected by the Generals Highway (Highway 198). Kings Canyon Highway (Highway 180) runs east from Grant Grove to Cedar Grove. The entrance fee to Sequoia and Kings Canyon (good for admission to both for seven consecutive days) is $20 per vehicle, or $10 per person for those who don't arrive by car. An information-packed quarterly newspaper and a map are handed out at the parks' entrances.

Three Rivers

❶ *200 mi north of Los Angeles via I–5 to Hwy. 99 to Hwy. 198; 8 mi south of Ash Mountain/Foothills entrance to Sequoia National Park on Hwy. 198.*

In the foothills of the Sierra along the Kaweah River, this sparsely populated, serpentine hamlet serves as the parks' main gateway town. Its livelihood depends largely on tourism from the national parks, courtesy of two markets, a few service stations, banks, a post office, and several lodgings, which are good spots to find a room when park accommodations are full.

Where to Stay & Eat

$–$$$$ ✕ **Gateway Restaurant and Lodge.** The patio of this raucous roadhouse overlooks the roaring Kaweah River as it plunges out of the high country, and though the food is nothing special, the location makes up for it. Standouts include baby back ribs and eggplant parmigiana; there's also a cocktail lounge, and guest rooms are available for overnight visitors. Breakfast isn't served weekdays; dinner reservations are essential on weekends. ✉ *45978 Sierra Dr.* ☎ *559/561–4133* ▭ *AE, D, MC, V.*

¢ ✕ **We Three Bakery.** This popular-with-the-locals, friendly spot packs lunches for trips into the nearby national parks. Also open for breakfast. ✉ *43370 Sierra Dr.* ☎ *559/561–4761* ▭ *MC, V.*

$–$$ ⌂ **Buckeye Tree Lodge.** Every room at this two-story motel has a patio facing a sun-dappled grassy lawn, right on the banks of the Kaweah River. Accommodations are simple and well kept, and the lodge sits a mere quarter mile from the park gate. Book well in advance for the summer. The jointly owned Sequoia Village Inn, across the highway, was extensively renovated in 2006 and is another good option (☎ *559/561–3652*). ✉ *46000 Sierra Dr., Hwy. 198, 93271* ☎ *559/561–5900* ⊕ *www.buckeyetree.com* ⤳ *11 rooms, 1 cottage* ⌂ *BBQs, cable TV, in-room VCRs, Wi-Fi, pool, fishing, hiking, some pets allowed (fee), no-smoking rooms* ▭ *AE, D, DC, MC, V* ▯◎▮ *CP.*

$–$$ ⌂ **Lazy J Ranch Motel.** Surrounded by 12 acres of green lawns and a split-rail fence, the Lazy J is a modest, well-kept compound of freestanding cottages near the banks of the Kaweah River. A few hundred feet off Highway 198, it's also very quiet and has an inviting pool as its centerpiece. Some rooms have gas fireplaces; all have coffeemakers. ✉ *39625 Sierra Dr., Hwy. 198, 93271* ☎ *559/561–4449 or 888/315–2378*

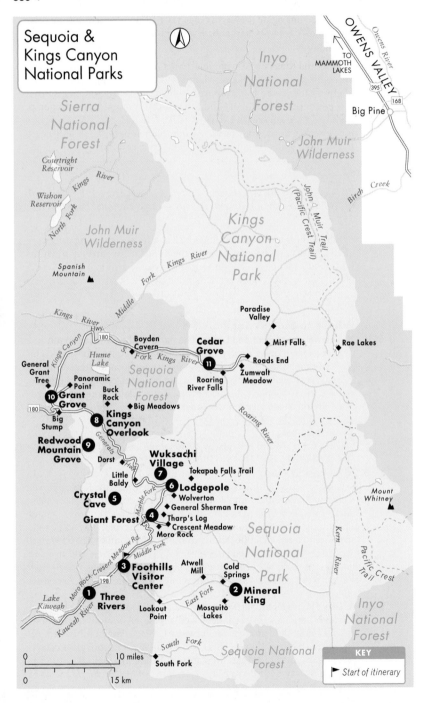

Sequoia & Kings Canyon National Parks

Sierra National Forest

Inyo National Forest

OWENS VALLEY

Owens River

TO MAMMOTH LAKES

395

168

Big Pine

Courtright Reservoir

Kings River

Wishon Reservoir

North Fork

John Muir Wilderness

Spanish Mountain

Middle Fork Kings River

Kings Canyon National Park

John Muir Trail (Pacific Crest Trail)

Birch Creek

Kings River

Kings Canyon Hwy.

180

Boyden Cavern

S. Fork Kings River

Cedar Grove

11

Paradise Valley

Mist Falls

Rae Lakes

Roads End

Hume Lake

Sequoia National Forest

Zumwalt Meadow

General Grant Tree

Panoramic Point

Buck Rock

Roaring River Falls

Roaring River

10 Grant Grove

180

Big Stump

8 Kings Canyon Overlook

Big Meadows

9 Redwood Mountain Grove

Dorst

Generals Hwy.

Little Baldy

7 Wuksachi Village

Tokapah Falls Trail

Mount Whitney

5 Crystal Cave

Marble Fork

6 Lodgepole

Wolverton

General Sherman Tree

Pacific Crest Trail

Giant Forest

4

Tharp's Log

Crescent Meadow

Moro Rock

Sequoia National Park

Kern River

Moro Rock-Crescent Meadow Rd.

3 Foothills Visitor Center

Middle Fork

Atwell Mill

Cold Springs

2 Mineral King

Lake Kaweah

198

1 Three Rivers

Lookout Point

East Fork

Mosquito Lakes

Inyo National Forest

Kaweah River

South Fork

Sequoia National Forest

South Fork

| 0 | 10 miles |
| 0 | 15 km |

KEY

► Start of itinerary

🗑 559/561–4889 ⊕ *www.bvilazyj.com* ➥ *11 rooms, 7 cottages ⎕ Picnic area, BBQs, some kitchens, refrigerators, cable TV, in-room VCRs, pool, fishing, playground, laundry facilities, some pets allowed (fee), no-smoking rooms* ⊟ *AE, D, DC, MC, V* ¦◎¦ *CP.*

$ ▥ **Sequoia Motel.** An old-fashioned, single-story, mom-and-pop motel, the Sequoia stands out with such extra touches as country-style quilts and mismatched Americana furnishings that lend a retro charm to the meticulously clean rooms. There are also one- and two-bedroom cottages with full kitchens. ⊠ *43000 Sierra Dr., Hwy. 198, Box 145, 93271* 🖀 *559/561–4453* 🗑 *559/561–1625* ⊕ *www.sequoiamotel.com* ➥ *11 rooms, 3 cottages ⎕ BBQs, some kitchens, cable TV, some in-room VCRs, Wi-Fi, pool, laundry facilities; no room phones, no smoking* ⊟ *AE, D, MC, V.*

Sports & the Outdoors

Contact the **Sequoia Natural History Association** (⍟ HCR 89, Box 10, 93271 🖀 559/565–3759 ⊕ www.sequoiahistory.org) for information on bird-watching in the Southern Sierra.

Kaweah White Water Adventures (🖀 559/561–1000 or 800/229–8658 ⊕ www.kaweah-whitewater.com) guides two-hour and full-day rafting trips in spring and early summer, with some Class III rapids; longer trips may include some Class IV.

For hourly horseback rides or riding lessons, contact **Wood 'n' Horse Training Stables** (🖀 559/561–4268 ⊠ 42846 N. Fork Dr.).

Mineral King

❷ *25 mi east of Three Rivers via Hwy. 198 and Mineral King Rd.*

Incorporated into Sequoia National Park in 1978, the Mineral King area is accessible from late May or early June through October (depending on snowmelt) by a narrow, twisting, steep road (trailers and RVs are prohibited) off Highway 198, several miles outside the park entrance. This exciting drive (budget 90 minutes each way) leads to an alpine valley, where there are two campgrounds and a ranger station. Facilities are limited, but some supplies are available. Many backpackers use this as a trailhead, and fine day-hiking trails lead from here as well.

Where to Stay

☾ ¢–**$$$$** ▥ **Silver City Mountain Resort.** High on the Mineral King Road, this resort provides an excellent alternative to the crowded properties at the parks' lower elevations. Lodgings range from modern Swiss-style chalets to traditional rustic alpine cabins with woodstoves and central bathing facilities. There's a small general store, a bakery serving homemade pies, and a modestly priced restaurant on-site, though the latter serves Thursday through Monday only. Some cabins share a central shower and bath. ⊠ *Mineral King Rd., 20 mi east of Hwy. 198, 93271* 🖀 *559/561–3223 or 805/528—2730, 805/4613223 off-season* ⊕ *www.silvercityresort.com* ➥ *13 units, 5 with shared baths ⎕ Restaurant, BBQs, kitchens, some refrigerators, some in-room data ports, fishing, hiking, horseshoes, Ping-Pong, playground; no a/c, no phones*

7

in some rooms, no room TVs, no smoking ⊟ *MC, V* ⊗ *Closed mid-Oct.–Memorial Day weekend.*

⚠ **Atwell Mill Campground.** Set at 6,650 feet, this tents-only campground is just south of the Western Divide. There are telephones and a general store ½ mi away at the Silver City Resort. Reservations are not accepted. ⊠ *Mineral King Rd., 20 mi east of Hwy. 198* ☏ *559/565–3341* 🏷 *$12* ⤴ *23 sites* ♨ *Pit toilets, drinking water, showers, bear boxes, fire grates, picnic tables* ⊗ *Closed Nov.–Apr.*

Lodgepole & Giant Forest Area

16–27 mi northeast of the Foothills Visitor Center on Generals Hwy.

To see Sequoia National Park from the south, take Generals Highway, which begins at the park's Ash Mountain–Foothills entrance (and in mid-2006 was in need of resurfacing). Before you venture into the park, it's ▶ ❸ helpful to stop at the **Foothills Visitor Center** for information and tickets to Crystal Cave. ⊠ *Generals Hwy.* ☏ *559/565–3135* 🏷 *Free* ⊗ *Daily 8–4:30, 8–6 in summer.*

★ ❹ A 50-minute drive from Foothills, **Giant Forest** is known for its trails through a series of sequoia groves. You can get the best views of the big trees from the park's meadows, where flowers burst into bloom by June or July. The outstanding exhibits at the **Giant Forest Museum** trace the ecology of the giant sequoia. The **Big Trees Trail,** a ¾-mi paved trail, is easy to reach from the museum and circles a beautiful meadow. ⊠ *Generals Hwy., 16 mi northeast of Foothills Visitor Center* ☏ *559/565–4480 museum* ⊗ *Museum: late May–mid-June, daily 8–5; mid-June–early Sept., daily 8–6; early Sept.–late May, daily 9–4:30.*

The **Moro Rock–Crescent Meadow Road** is a 3-mi spur road (closed in winter) that begins immediately south of the Giant Forest Museum and leads to Crescent Meadow, passing several landmarks along the way. The **Auto Log** is a wide fallen tree that visitors used to be able to drive their cars on. The road also leads to the **Tunnel Log,** which is exactly that: a tunnel through a fallen sequoia tree. If your vehicle is short enough—7 feet 9 inches or less—you might be allowed to drive through. (There is no standing drive-through Sequoia tree in the park. There used to be one in Yosemite, but it fell in 1969.) John Muir called **Crescent Meadow** the "gem of the Sierra"—brilliant wildflowers bloom here by midsummer; and a nearly 2-mi trail loops around the meadow. A 1½-mi round-trip trail that begins at Crescent Meadow leads to **Tharp's Log,** named for Hale Tharp, who built a pioneer cabin (still standing) out of a fire-hollowed sequoia.

★ **Moro Rock,** an immense granite monolith, stands along Moro Rock–Crescent Meadow Road, rising 6,725 feet above sea level, right from the edge of the Giant Forest. About 350 steps lead to the top courtesy of a cleverly constructed stairway that is on the National Register of Historic Places. The view from the top is stunning. To the southwest you look more than 4,000 vertical feet down the Kaweah River to Three Rivers, Lake Kaweah, and—on clear days, which are very rare due to smog—the Central Valley and the Coast Range. To the east stand the jagged peaks of the High Sierra.

The most famous sequoia in the Giant Forest area is the **General Sherman Tree** (✉ 1 mi north of Giant Forest, off Generals Hwy.) Benches allow you to sit and contemplate the tree's immensity: weighing in at 2.7 million pounds, it has the greatest volume of any living thing in the world and each year grows the equivalent weight of a normally proportioned 60-foot tree. The first major branch is 130 feet above the ground. The paved **Congress Trail**, a popular 2-mi hike, starts at the General Sherman Tree and loops through the heart of the Giant Forest, passing groups of trees known as the House and Senate and individual trees called the President and McKinley.

★ ☾ ❺ Discovered in 1918 by two park employees, **Crystal Cave** is the best known of Sequoia's many caverns. Its interior, which was formed from limestone that metamorphosed into marble, is decorated with stalactites and stalagmites of various shapes, sizes, and colors. To visit the cave, you must first stop at the Foothills or Lodgepole Visitor Center to buy tickets; they are not sold at the cave. A narrow, twisting 7-mi road off the Generals Highway leads you 2.2 mi south of the old Giant Forest Village. From the parking area it's a 15-minute hike down a steep path to the cave's entrance. It's cool inside—48°F—so bring a sweater. ✉ *Crystal Cave Rd., off Generals Hwy.* ☎ *559/565–3759* ⊕ *www.sequoiahistory. org* ✑ *$11* ☾ *May–mid-Nov., call for tour times.*

❻ **Lodgepole** sits in a canyon on the Marble Fork of the Kaweah River. Lodgepole pines, rather than sequoias, grow here because the U-shape canyon funnels in air from the high country that is too cold for the big trees. This area has a campground and a post office open year-round. A snack bar, market and deli, public laundry, and showers are open in the late spring and summer only. The **Lodgepole Visitor Center** (also seasonal) has extensive exhibits, a small theater where you can watch an orientation slide show, and a first-aid center. You can buy tickets for the Crystal Cave, get advice from park rangers, purchase maps and books, and pick up wilderness permits. The **Tokopah Falls Trail** is an easy and rewarding 3½-mi round-trip hike from the Lodgepole Campground up the Marble Fork of the Kaweah River. The walk to the 1,200-foot falls, which flow down granite cliffs, is the closest you can get to the high country without substantial wear and tear on your hiking boots. Trail maps are available at the Lodgepole Visitor Center. Bring insect repellent in summer; the mosquitoes can be ferocious. ✉ *Generals Hwy., 5 mi north of Giant Forest Museum* ☎ *559/565–4436* ✑ *Free* ☾ *Visitor center mid-Apr.–mid-June, daily 9–4:30; mid-June–early Sept., daily 8–6; early Sept.–mid-Apr., weekends 9–4:30.*

❼ The dining and lodging facilities at **Wuksachi Village** (✉ Generals Hwy., 6 mi north of Lodgepole) have replaced the antiquated facilities of the old Giant Forest Village, most of which has been demolished. These are the nicest facilities in the area. There's also a gift shop.

Where to Stay & Eat

★ **$–$$$$** ✕ **Wuksachi Village Dining Room.** In the high-ceiling dining room at Sequoia's only upscale restaurant, huge windows run the length of the room, providing a view of the surrounding wilderness. The dinner menu offers everything from sandwiches and burgers to steaks and pasta, but has only salads for vegetarians. Breakfast and lunch are also served. ⊠ *Wuksachi Village* ☎ *559/565–4070* ⌣ *Reservations essential* ▭ *AE, D, DC, MC, V.*

★ $$–$$$ ⌂ **Wuksachi Village Lodge.** These cedar-and-stone lodge buildings, which blend with the landscape, house comfortable rooms with modern amenities. The village is 7,200 feet above sea level; many of the rooms have spectacular views. ⊠ *Wuksachi Village* ☎ *559/565–4070 front desk, 559/253–2199, 888/252–5757 reservations* ☎ *559/456–0542* ⊕ *www.visitsequoia.com* ⌲ *102 rooms* ⌂ *Restaurant, fans, refrigerators, cable TV, in-room data ports, hiking, cross-country skiing, ski storage, bar, meeting room; no a/c, no smoking* ▭ *AE, D, DC, MC, V.*

⚠ **Lodgepole Campground.** The largest Lodgepole-area campground is also the noisiest, though things do quiet down at night. Restrooms are nearby. Lodgepole and Dorst (a mile or so to the west) are the two campgrounds within Sequoia that accept reservations (essential up to five months in advance for stays between mid-May and mid-October). ⊠ *Off Generals Hwy. beyond Lodgepole Village* ☎ *559/565–3341 Ext. 2 information, 800/365–2267 reservations* ⊕ *http://reservations.nps.gov* ⌲ *$18* ⌲ *214 sites (tent and RV)* ⌂ *Flush toilets, dump station (summer only), drinking water, guest laundry (summer only), showers (summer only), bear boxes, fire grates, picnic tables, public telephone, general store.*

Sports & the Outdoors

Hiking and backpacking are the top outdoor activities in Sequoia National Park. In winter you can cross-country ski, snowshoe, and sled, and in summer mule rides are available. The visitor centers have information on trail conditions, ranger-guided hikes, and snowshoe walks. Conditions permitting, you can rent winter-sports equipment at **Wuksachi Village Lodge** (☎ 559/565–4070).

Sequoia National Forest

15–20 mi northwest of Lodgepole on Generals Hwy.

Though you may not even notice the change, on your way to Grant Grove the Generals Highway leaves Sequoia National Park and passes through a section of Sequoia National Forest.

❽ **Kings Canyon Overlook,** a turnout on the north side of the Generals Highway, has tree-obstructed views across the canyon of mountain peaks and the backcountry. If you drive to Cedar Grove (about one hour east of Grant Grove on Highway 180, open summer only) along the south fork, you will see these spectacular canyons at much closer range.

★ ❾ The **Redwood Mountain Grove** is the largest grove of sequoias in the world. As you enter Kings Canyon on the Generals Highway, several paved turnouts allow you to look out over the grove (and into the smog of the Central Valley). The grove itself is accessible only on foot or horseback.

Where to Stay

$$–$$$ 🏨 **Montecito-Sequoia Lodge.** A summer-camp atmosphere prevails all year long at this family-oriented resort just south of Kings Canyon National Park. Specializing in all-inclusive vacations, it offers everything from skiing and snowboarding in winter to sailing and horseback riding in summer. From mid-June to early September there's normally a six-night minimum, but you can book a one-night stay on Saturday. Note: prices are per-person, and include all meals plus a soup and dessert bar. ⊠ *Generals Hwy., 11 mi south of Grant Grove* ☎ *559/565–3388, 800/ 227–9900 reservations* 📠 *650/967–0540* ⊕ *www.mslodge.com* ↘ *32 rooms, 13 cabins* ♿ *Dining room, snack bar, BBQs, tennis court, pool, lake, boating, water-skiing, fishing, bicycles, archery, hiking, horseback riding, volleyball, cross-country skiing, ice-skating, children's programs (ages 2–18); no a/c, no room phones, no room TVs* 🚭 *AE, D, MC, V* ⏐◎⏐ *FAP.*

$$ 🏨 **Stony Creek.** Sitting at 6,800 feet among the peaceful pines, summer-only Stony Creek is on national forest land between Giant Forest and Grant Grove. Expect motel-style accommodations in the woods. A restaurant is adjacent to the lodge. ⊠ *Generals Hwy.* ⌖ *Sequoia Kings Canyon Park Services Co., 5755 E. Kings Canyon Rd., Suite 101, Fresno 93727* ☎ *559/565–3909 or 866/522–6966* 📠 *559/452–1353* ⊕ *www.sequoia-kingscanyon.com* ↘ *11 rooms* ♿ *Restaurant, cable TV, in-room data ports, Internet room; no a/c, no smoking* 🚭 *AE, D, MC, V* ⊙ *Closed Sept.–late May* ⏐◎⏐ *CP.*

Grant Grove

➓   *27 mi north of Lodgepole via Generals Hwy. to Kings Canyon Hwy.*

Kings Canyon's most developed area was designated General Grant National Park (the forerunner of Kings Canyon National Park) in 1890. This is another entry point to the national parks, and the **Kings Canyon Visitor Center** is the best place to gather information about the park's three major resources: sequoias, the High Sierra, and Kings Canyon itself. Exhibits about conservation efforts are especially well-done. ⊠ *Kings Canyon Hwy., Grant Grove Village* ☎ *559/565–4307* ⌖ *Free* ⊙ *May–mid-June and early Sept.–Oct., daily 8–8; mid-June–early Sept., daily 8–8; Nov.–Apr., daily 9–4:30.*

The visitor center is part of compact and often crowded **Grant Grove Village,** which also contains a grocery store, gift shop, campgrounds, a restaurant that has family dining, overnight lodging, and a post office. A walk along 1-mi **Big Stump Trail,** which starts near the park entrance, graphically demonstrates the toll heavy logging takes on wilderness. The **General Grant Tree Trail,** a paved ⅓-mi path, winds past the General Grant, an enormous, 2,000-year-old sequoia, the world's third-largest, which President Calvin Coolidge designated "the nation's Christmas tree." The **Gamlin Cabin,** an 1867 pioneer cabin, is listed on the National Register of Historic Places. Also within Grant Grove is the **Fallen Monarch,** a huge, toppled sequoia whose hollow core has served as a saloon and horse stable, among other things.

Where to Stay

$–$$ ⊡ **John Muir Lodge.** This modern, timber-sided lodge is nestled in a wooded area near Grant Grove Village. The 24 rooms and six suites all have queen beds and private baths, and there's a comfortable lobby with low-pile carpeting and a stone fireplace where you can play cards and board games. The inexpensive, family-style Grant Grove Restaurant is a three-minute walk away. Though it's little more than a good motel, this is the best place to stay in Grant Grove. ⊠ *Kings Canyon Hwy., ¼ mi north of Grant Grove Village* ⓓ *Sequoia Kings Canyon Park Services Co., 5755 E. Kings Canyon Rd., Suite 101, Fresno 93727* ☎ *559/335–5500 or 866/522–6966* 🖶 *559/335–5507* ⊕ *www.sequoia-kingscanyon.com* ⇗ *24 rooms, 6 suites* ⚘ *Meeting room; no a/c, no room TVs* ⊟ *AE, D, MC, V.*

⚠ **Azalea Campground.** One of three campgrounds in the Grant Grove area (the others are Sunset and Crystal Springs, both open May through September only), Azalea is open year-round. It sits at 6,500 feet amid giant sequoias, yet is close to restaurants, stores, and other facilities. Some sites at Azalea are wheelchair accessible. The campground can accommodate RVs up to 30 feet. Though it costs $18 May to mid-October—and reservations are not accepted—it's free the rest of the year. ⊠ *Kings Canyon Hwy., ¼ mi north of Grant Grove Village* ☎ *559/565–3341* 🗑 *$18* ⇗ *113 sites (tent or RV)* ⚘ *Flush toilets, drinking water, showers, bear boxes, fire grates, picnic tables, public telephone, general store.*

Sports & the Outdoors

The primary activities in Kings Canyon are hiking and backpacking. Bicycling is discouraged, because the only paved roads outside village areas are the Kings Canyon and Generals highways, both winding mountain roads with heavy traffic. Horseback riding is an enjoyable alternative in summer. Winter snows turn the park into a playground for cross-country skiers and snowshoers, and there are dedicated areas for sledding. Check with the visitor center for conditions and trail maps.

HORSEBACK RIDING **Grant Grove Stables** (⊠ Grant Grove Village ☎ 559/335–9292 mid-June–Sept., 559/594–9307 Oct.–mid-June) is the stable to choose if you want a short ride; for overnight trips, head to Cedar Grove (below).

EN ROUTE ★ The spectacular 30-mi, hourlong descent along **Kings Canyon Highway** runs along the south fork of the Kings River. It cuts through dry hills covered with yuccas that bloom in summer and passes the scars where large groves of sequoias were felled at the beginning of the 20th century. There are amazing views into the deepest gorge in the United States—deeper even than the Grand Canyon—and up the canyons to the High Sierra, which remain snowcapped until midsummer, a thrilling sight. It takes about an hour from Grant Grove to Roads End, where you can hike or camp. Built by convict labor in the 1930s, the road (usually closed from mid-October through mid-May) clings to some dramatic cliffs along the way: watch out for falling rocks, and though it may be difficult at times, keep your eye on the road.

Cedar Grove

⓫ *31 mi east of Grant Grove on Kings Canyon Hwy.*

Named for the incense cedars that grow in the area, Cedar Grove is in a valley that snakes along the south fork of the Kings River. **Cedar Grove Village** (⊠ East end of Kings Canyon Hwy. ☎ 559/565–3793 visitor center) has campgrounds, lodgings, a small visitor center, a snack bar, a cafeteria, a convenience market, and a gift shop, but it's open only April to November, depending on snowfall.

About 4½ mi southeast of Cedar Grove Village, short trails circle grassy **Zumwalt Meadow,** which is surrounded by towering granite walls. Trails from Zumwalt Meadow lead to the base of **Roaring River Falls,** which run hardest in spring and early summer.

Where to Stay & Eat

$–$$ ✕⊡ **Cedar Grove Lodge.** Although accommodations are close to the road, this lodge manages to deliver peace and quiet. Book far in advance—the lodge has only 21 rooms. Each has two queen-size beds, and three have kitchenettes and patios. You can order trout, hamburgers, hot dogs, and sandwiches at the snack bar (¢–$) and take them to one of the picnic tables along the river's edge. ⊠ *Kings Canyon Hwy.* ✑ *Sequoia Kings Canyon Park Services Co., 5755 E. Kings Canyon Rd., Suite 101, Fresno 93727* ☎ *559/335–5500 or 866/522–6966* 🖷 *559/335–5507* ⊕ *www.sequoia-kingscanyon.com* ⟿ *21 rooms* ⚘ *Snack bar, some kitchenettes, hiking, laundry facilities; no room phones, no room TVs, no smoking* ▭ *AE, D, MC, V* ☉ *Closed mid-Oct.–mid-May.*

Sports & the Outdoors

For horseback rides and overnight pack trips into the wilderness, call **Cedar Grove Pack Station** (⊠ Cedar Grove Village ☎ 559/565–3464 mid-June–Sept., 559/337–2314 Oct.–mid-June).

SOUTH OF YOSEMITE
FROM OAKHURST TO EL PORTAL

Several gateway towns to the south and west of Yosemite National Park, most within an hour's drive of Yosemite Valley, have food, lodging, and other services. Highway 140 heads east from the San Joaquin Valley to El Portal and Yosemite's west entrance. Highway 41 heads north from Fresno to Oakhurst and Fish Camp to Yosemite's south entrance.

Oakhurst

40 mi north of Fresno and 23 mi south of Yosemite National Park's south entrance on Hwy. 41.

Motels, restaurants, gas stations, and small businesses line both sides of Highway 41 as it cuts through Oakhurst. This is the last sizeable community before Yosemite and a good spot to find provisions. There are two major grocery stores near the intersection of highways 41 and 49.

Three miles north of town, then 6 mi east, honky-tonky Bass Lake is a popular spot in summer with motorboaters, jet-skiers, and families looking to cool off in the reservoir.

Where to Stay & Eat

$$$$ × **Erna's Elderberry House.** Austrian-born Erna Kubin, the grande dame
Fodor'sChoice   of Château du Sureau, has created a culinary oasis, stunning for its un-
★   derstated elegance, gorgeous setting, and impeccable service. Red walls and dark beams accent the dining room's high ceilings, and arched windows reflect the glow of candles. The seasonal six-course prix-fixe dinner can be paired with superb wines, a must-do for oenophiles. When the waitstaff places all the plates on the table in perfect synchronicity, you know this will be a meal to remember. Pre-meal drinks are served in the former wine cellar. ⊠ *48688 Victoria La.* ☎ *559/683–6800* ⌒ *Reservations essential* ⊟ *AE, D, MC, V* ☉ *No lunch Mon.–Sat.*

¢–$$ × **Yosemite Fork Mountain House.** Bypass Oakhurst's greasy spoons and instead head to this family restaurant, 3 mi north of the Highway 49/ Highway 41 intersection, with open-beam ceiling and a canoe in the rafters. Portions are huge. Expect standard American fare: bacon and eggs at breakfast, sandwiches at lunch, and pastas and steaks at dinner. ⊠ *Hwy. 41 at Bass Lake turnoff* ☎ *559/683–5191* ⌒ *Reservations not accepted* ⊟ *D, MC, V.*

$$$$ ⊞ **Château du Sureau.** This romantic inn, adjacent to Erna's Elderberry
Fodor'sChoice   House, is straight out of a children's book. From the moment you drive
★   through the wrought-iron gates and up to the fairy-tale castle, you feel pampered. Every room is impeccably styled with European antiques, sumptuous fabrics, fresh-cut flowers, and oversize soaking tubs. After falling asleep by the glow of a crackling fire amid feather-light goose-down pillows and Italian linens, awaken to a hearty European breakfast in the dining room, then relax with a game of chess in the grand salon beneath an exquisite ceiling mural—or play chess on the giant board off the impeccably landscaped garden trail. Cable TV is available by request only. In 2006, the château added a stunning spa. ⊠ *48688 Victoria La., Box 577, 93644* ☎ *559/683–6860* 🖷 *559/683–0800* ⊕ *www.elderberryhouse. com* ⇆ *10 rooms, 1 villa* ⌒ *Restaurant, some in-room hot tubs, in-room data ports, Wi-Fi, golf privileges, pool, pond, spa, boccie, bar, shop, laundry service; no kids under 12, no smoking* ⊟ *AE, MC, V* ⌸ *BP.*

★ **$–$$$$**   ⊞ **Homestead Cottages.** If you're looking for peace and quiet, this is the place. Serenity is the order of the day at this secluded getaway in Ahwahnee, 6 mi west of Oakhurst. On 160 acres of rolling hills that once held a Miwok village, these cottages have gas fireplaces, living rooms, fully equipped kitchens, and queen-size beds; the largest sleeps six. The cottages, hand-built by the owners out of real adobe bricks, are stocked with soft robes, oversize towels, and paperback books. ⊠ *41110 Rd. 600, 2½ mi off Hwy. 49, Ahwahnee 93601* ☎ *559/683–0495 or 800/ 483–0495* 🖷 *559/683–8165* ⊕ *www.homesteadcottages.com* ⇆ *5 cottages, 1 loft* ⌒ *BBQs, kitchens, cable TV, hiking; no room phones, no smoking* ⊟ *AE, D, MC, V.*

⌾ **¢–$$**   ⊞ **Best Western Yosemite Gateway Inn.** Oakhurst's best motel has carefully tended landscaping and rooms with attractive dark-wood American colonial–style furniture and slightly kitsch hand-painted wall murals of Yosemite. Kids love choosing between the two pools. ✉ *40530 Hwy. 41, 93644* ☎ *559/683–2378 or 800/545–5462* 📠 *559/683–3813* 🌐 *www.yosemitegatewayinn.com* 🛏 *121 rooms, 16 suites* ᕕ *Restaurant, microwaves, refrigerators, cable TV, in-room broadband, 2 pools (1 indoor), exercise equipment, hot tub, bar, playground, laundry facilities, no-smoking rooms* ▤ *AE, D, MC, V.*

Sports & the Outdoors

Bass Lake Water Sports and Marina (✉ Bass Lake Reservoir ☎ 559/642–3565), 3 mi north and 6 mi east of Oakhurst, rents ski boats, patio boats, and fishing boats. In summer, the noisy reservoir gets packed shortly after it opens at 8 AM. There's also a restaurant and snack bar.

Fish Camp

⑫ *57 mi north of Fresno and 4 mi south of Yosemite National Park's south entrance*

As you climb in elevation along Highway 41 northbound, you see nothing but trees until you get to the small settlement of Fish Camp, where there's a post office and general store, but no gasoline (for gas, head 10 mi north to Wawona, in the park, or 17 mi south to Oakhurst).

The **Yosemite Mountain Sugar Pine Railroad** has a narrow-gauge steam engine that chugs through the forest. It follows 4 mi of the route the Madera Sugar Pine Lumber Company cut through the forest in 1899 to harvest timber. The steam train runs daily May through September, and weekends and Wednesday in April and October; call for schedules. Other times, Jenny railcars—open-air cars powered by Ford Model A engines—operate every half hour, 9:30 AM to 3 PM. On Saturday (and Wednesday in summer), the Moonlight Special dinner excursion (reservations essential) includes a picnic with toe-tappin' music by the Sugar Pine Singers, followed by a sunset steam-train ride. ✉ *56001 Hwy. 41* ☎ *559/683–7273* 🌐 *www.ymsprr.com* 🎫 *$16; Moonlight Special $44* 🕐 *Mar.–Oct., daily.*

Where to Stay & Eat

$$$$ ✕🏠 **Tenaya Lodge.** One of the region's largest hotels, the Tenaya Lodge is ideal for people who enjoy wilderness treks by day but prefer creature comforts at night. The hulking prefab buildings and giant parking lot look out of place in the woods, but inside, the rooms have all the amenities of a modern, full-service hotel. The ample regular rooms are decorated in pleasant earth tones, deluxe rooms have minibars and other extras, and the suites have balconies. Off-season rates can be as low as $100. The Sierra Restaurant ($$–$$$$), with its high ceilings and giant fireplace, serves continental cuisine. The more casual Jackalopes Bar and Grill ($–$$) has burgers, salads, and sandwiches. ✉ *1122 Hwy. 41* 📪 *Box 159, 93623* ☎ *559/683–6555 or 888/514–2167* 📠 *559/683–0249* 🌐 *www.tenayalodge.com* 🛏 *244 rooms, 6 suites* ᕕ *2 restaurants, snack bar, room service, some minibars, cable TV with movies and video games, in-room data ports, Wi-Fi, indoor pool, health club, hot tub, mountain bikes, hiking, bar, recreation room, babysitting, children's programs (ages 5–12), playground,* *laundry service, concierge, business services, meeting room; no smoking* ⊟ *AE, D, DC, MC, V.*

★ **$–$$$** ✕⊞ **Narrow Gauge Inn.** All of the rooms at this well-tended, family-owned property have balconies (some shared) and great views of the surrounding woods and mountains. For maximum atmosphere, book a room overlooking the brook; for quiet, choose a lower-level room on the edge of the forest. All are comfortably furnished with old-fashioned accents and railroad memorabilia. Reserve way ahead. The restaurant ($–$$$; open Apr.–Oct., Wed.–Sun.), which is festooned with moose, bison, and other wildlife trophies, specializes in steaks and American fare, and merits a special trip. ⊠ *48571 Hwy. 41, 93623* ☎ *559/683–7720 or 888/644–9050* 🖷 *559/683–2139* ⊕ *www.narrowgaugeinn.com* ⤳ *26 rooms, 1 suite* ⚘ *Restaurant, cable TV, in-room data ports, Wi-Fi, pool, hot tub, bar, some pets allowed (fee); no a/c in some rooms, no smoking* ⊟ *D, MC, V* ⦿| *CP.*

El Portal

14 mi west of Yosemite Valley on Hwy. 140.

The market in town is a good place to pick up provisions before you get to Yosemite. There's also a post office and a gas station, but not much else.

Where to Stay

$$–$$$ ⊞ **Yosemite View Lodge.** The Yosemite View Lodge's motel-like design aesthetic is ameliorated by its location right on the banks of the boulder-strewn Merced River and its proximity to the park entrance 2 mi east. Many rooms have whirlpool baths, fireplaces, kitchenettes, and balconies or decks. The motel complex is on the public bus route to the park, near fishing and river rafting. Ask for a river-view room. The lodge's sister property, the Cedar Lodge, sits 6 mi farther west and has similar-looking, less expensive rooms without river views. ⊠ *11136 Hwy. 140, 95318* ☎ *209/379–2681 or 888/742–4371* 🖷 *209/379–2704* ⊕ *www.yosemiteresorts.us* ⤳ *335 rooms* ⚘ *Restaurant, pizzeria, some in-room hot tubs, some kitchenettes, cable TV, 2 pools (1 indoor), bar, laundry facilities, meeting room, gift shop, some pets allowed (fee), no-smoking rooms* ⊟ *AE, MC, V.*

YOSEMITE NATIONAL PARK

▶ Of Yosemite's 1,189 square mi of parkland, 94.5% is undeveloped wilderness, most of it accessible only on foot or horseback. The western boundary dips as low as 2,000 feet in the chaparral-covered foothills; the eastern boundary rises to 13,000 feet at points along the Sierra crest.

Yosemite is so large you can think of it as five different parks. Yosemite Valley, famous for waterfalls and cliffs, and Wawona, where the giant sequoias stand, are open all year. Hetch Hetchy, home of less-used backcountry trails, closes after the first big snow and reopens in May or June. The subalpine high country, Tuolumne Meadows, is open for summer hiking and camping; in winter it's accessible only by cross-country skis or snowshoes. Badger Pass Ski Area is open in winter only. The fee to visit Yosemite National Park (good for seven days) is $20 per car, $10 per person if you don't arrive in a car. Within park boundaries, you can buy gasoline only in Wawona and Crane Flat, not the valley.

On entering the park, you'll receive a small glossy magazine with general information about the park, and a free monthly newspaper, *Yosemite Today,* which lists locations and times for ranger-led nature walks. Make it a point to read at least the newspaper for up-to-date visitors' information.

Yosemite Valley

214 mi east of San Francisco via I–80 to I–580 to I–205 to Hwy. 120; 330 mi northeast of Los Angeles via I–5 to Hwy. 99 to Hwy. 41.

> ### GUIDED EXCURSIONS
>
> The best way to see the Southern Sierra is on foot. For top-notch guided day-hiking or multiday treks into the national parks or the Ansel Adams Wilderness and surrounding areas, contact **Southern Yosemite Mountain Guides** (✉ 621 Highland Ave., Santa Cruz, CA 95060 ☎ 831/459–8735 or 800/231–4575 ⊕ www.symg.com), one of the Sierra's premier guide services. In addition to excellent interpretation, they provide all necessary equipment (including tents and bags), permits, guides, and food. On some trips, mules carry your gear, freeing you to walk unencumbered by a backpack. They also conduct fly-fishing, rock-climbing, and custom trips.

Yosemite Valley has been so extravagantly praised (John Muir described it as "a revelation in landscape") and so beautifully photographed (by Ansel Adams, who said, "I knew my destiny when I first experienced Yosemite") that you may wonder if the reality can possibly measure up. For almost everyone it does. It's a true reminder of what *breathtaking* really means. The Miwok, the last of several Native American people to inhabit the Yosemite area (they were forced out by gold miners in 1851), named the valley Ahwahnee, which is thought to mean "the place of the gaping mouth."

It's important to remember a few things when visiting the valley. The roads at the eastern end of the valley are closed to private cars, but a free shuttle bus runs about every 15 minutes from the village (7 AM–10 PM May–September and approximately 9 AM–8:30 PM the rest of the year). Directions to the day-use parking lot, near the intersection of Sentinel and Northside drives, can be found on the back of *Yosemite Today,* along with a shuttle-bus map and current schedule. Bears are a huge problem in Yosemite; be sure to read pamphlets on the subject or speak with a ranger, and take proper precautions while in the park.

⓭ The center of activity in Yosemite Valley is **Yosemite Village,** which contains restaurants, stores, a post office, and a clinic; the Ahwahnee Hotel and Yosemite Lodge are nearby. You can get your bearings, pick up maps and books, and obtain information from park rangers at the village's **Valley Visitor Center;** the center's new exhibit hall is scheduled for completion in 2007. At the **Wilderness Center** you can find out everything you need to know about such backcountry activities as hiking and camping. The **Yosemite Museum** has a Native American cultural exhibit, with displays about the Miwok and Paiute people who lived in the region; there's a re-created Ahwahneechee village behind it. The **Ansel Adams Gallery** shows works of the master photographer and sells prints and camera equipment. ☒ *Off Northside Dr.* ☎ *209/372–0200 visitor center, 209/372–4413 gallery* ☉ *Visitor center fall–spring, daily 9–5; summer, daily 8–6.*

Yosemite Valley is famed for its waterfalls, and the mightiest of them all is **Yosemite Falls,** the highest waterfall in North America and the sixth-highest in the world. The upper fall (1,430 feet), the middle cascades (675 feet), and the lower fall (320 feet) combine for a total drop of 2,425 feet. In spring and early summer, when the falls run their hardest, you can hear them thunder all across the valley. Peak flow is in May. (Be warned, though, that the falls slow to a trickle in winter.) The Upper Yosemite Fall Trail, a strenuous 3½-mi climb rising 2,700 feet, takes you above the top of the falls. It starts at Camp 4, formerly known as Sunnyside Campground. You cannot park at the falls, and the adjacent Yosemite Lodge parking is for lodge guests only (rangers will ticket illegally parked vehicles); park in the day-use area and ride the shuttle.

Yosemite Valley's waterfalls tumble past magnificent geological scenery. **El Capitan,** rising 3,593 feet above the valley, is the largest exposed granite monolith in the world, almost twice the height of the Rock of Gibraltar.

At 1,612 feet, **Ribbon Fall** is the highest single fall in North America. It's also the first waterfall in the valley to dry up; the rainwater and melted snow that create the slender fall evaporate quickly at this height.

Bridalveil Fall, a filmy fall of 620 feet that is often diverted as much as 20 feet one way or the other by the breeze, is the first view of Yosemite Valley for those who arrive via Wawona Road. Native Americans called the fall Pohono ("spirit of the puffing wind"). A ¼-mi trail leads to the base of the fall from the parking lot off the intersection of Southside Drive and Wawona Road.

As you venture through the valley amid Yosemite's natural wonders, stop at the **Happy Isles Nature Center** to see ecology exhibits and find books for children. ☒ *½ mi east of Curry Village* ☎ *209/372–0631 or 209/372–0200* ☉ *Mid-May–Oct., daily 10–4.*

Fern-covered black rocks frame **Vernal Fall** (317 feet), and rainbows play in the spray at its base. The hike from the Happy Isles Nature Center to the bridge at the base of Vernal Fall is less than 1 mi long, on a mostly paved trail, and only lightly strenuous. It's another steep (and often wet) ¾ mi up the Mist Trail—which is open only from late spring to early fall—to the top of Vernal Fall. Allow two to four hours for the 3-mi round-trip hike. In winter the Mist Trail freezes with black ice; be sure to take the signed detour to the top of the fall.

Nevada Fall (594 feet) is the first major fall as the Merced River plunges out of the high country toward the eastern end of Yosemite Valley. A strenuous 2-mi section of the Mist Trail leads from Vernal Fall to the

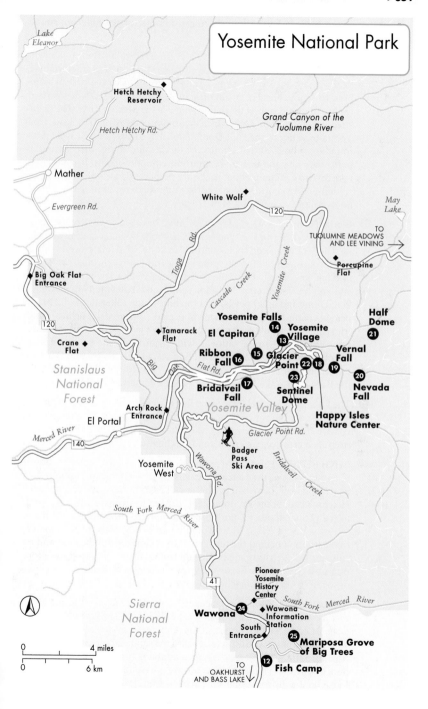

Yosemite National Park

Lake Eleanor

Hetch Hetchy Reservoir

Grand Canyon of the Tuolumne River

Hetch Hetchy Rd.

Mather

Evergreen Rd.

White Wolf

120

May Lake

TO TUOLUMNE MEADOWS AND LEE VINING →

Tioga Rd.

Cascade Creek

Yosemite Creek

Porcupine Flat

Big Oak Flat Entrance

120

Crane Flat

Tamarack Flat

Stanislaus National Forest

Big Oak Flat Rd.

Yosemite Falls
El Capitan

14 **Yosemite Village**
13

15 **Glacier Point**

Ribbon Fall 16

22 18 19

Half Dome
21

Vernal Fall

20 **Nevada Fall**

17 23

Bridalveil Fall

Sentinel Dome

Happy Isles Nature Center

Yosemite Valley

Arch Rock Entrance

El Portal

Merced River

140

Glacier Point Rd.

Bridalveil Creek

Yosemite West

Badger Pass Ski Area

Wawona Rd.

South Fork Merced River

Sierra National Forest

41

Pioneer Yosemite History Center

South Fork Merced River

Wawona 24

Wawona Information Station

South Entrance

25 **Mariposa Grove of Big Trees**

12 **Fish Camp**

TO OAKHURST AND BASS LAKE ↓

0 _____ 4 miles
0 _____ 6 km

top of Nevada Fall. Allow six to eight hours for the full 7-mi round-trip hike.

★ ㉑ Astounding **Half Dome** rises 4,733 feet from the valley floor to a height 8,842 feet above sea level. The west side of the dome is fractured vertically and cut away to form a 2,000-foot cliff. For the best pictures, head to Sentinel Bridge late in the day, just before sunset, when you can capture the reflection of the mighty dome in the Merced River. The highly strenuous **John Muir Trail**, which incorporates the Mist Trail, leads from Yosemite Valley to the Half Dome Trail. The views from the top are astounding. Allow 10 to 12 hours for the 16¾-mi round-trip; start early in the morning and beware of afternoon thunderstorms. If you plan to take this hike, inquire about necessary preparations at one of the ranger stations; more injuries occur here than anywhere else in the park. There's no overnight camping on Half Dome.

㉒ **Glacier Point** yields what may be the most spectacular vista of the valley and the High Sierra that you can get without hiking, especially at sunset. Glacier Point Road splits off from Wawona Road (Highway 41) about 23 mi southwest of the valley; then it's a 16-mi drive through the woods into higher country. From the parking area walk a few hundred yards, and you'll be able to see Nevada, Vernal, and Yosemite Falls as well as Half Dome and other peaks. You can hike to the valley floor (3,214 feet below) via the Panorama or Four-Mile trails. To avoid a grueling round-trip, catch a ride to Glacier Point on one of the three daily **hikers' buses** (☎ 209/372–1240 reservations), which run from late spring through October; the cost is $20 one-way, $38 round-trip. Reservations are essential. In winter, Glacier Point Road is closed beyond the turnoff for the Badger Pass Ski Area, making Glacier Point inaccessible.

Fodor'sChoice
★

㉓ The view from **Sentinel Dome** is similar to that from Glacier Point, except you can't see the valley floor. A 1.1-mi path begins at a parking lot on Glacier Point Road a few miles below Glacier Point. The trail is long and steep enough to keep the crowds and tour buses away, but not overly rugged.

OFF THE
BEATEN
PATH

HETCH HETCHY RESERVOIR – Supplier of water and hydroelectric power to San Francisco, the Hetch Hetchy is about 40 mi from Yosemite Valley via Big Oak Flat Road to Highway 120 to Evergreen Road to Hetch Hetchy Road. Some say John Muir died of heartbreak when the gates to the O'Shaughnessy Dam closed and flooded the valley beneath 300 feet of water in 1913. Muir would be thrilled to learn of the momentum gathering behind the movement to decommission the dam and restore the valley to its original splendor (for more on the restoration effort, pick up a copy of *The Battle Over Hetch Hetchy,* by Robert W. Righter, or log on to ⊕ www.hetchhetchy.org).

TUOLUMNE MEADOWS – Spectacularly scenic Tioga Road is the only route to Tuolumne Meadows, which sits at 8,575 feet in altitude about 55 mi from Yosemite Valley. The largest subalpine meadow in the Sierra, it bursts with late-summer wildflowers; it's also the trailhead for many backpack trips into the High Sierra. The area contains campgrounds, a gas station, a store (with limited and expensive provisions), stables, a tent-cabin lodge, and a visitor center that is open from late June until early September from 9 to 5. Tioga Road (Highway 120) stays open until the first big snow of the year, usually about mid-October.

Where to Stay & Eat

★ **$$–$$$** ✕ **Mountain Room Restaurant.** Though remarkably good, the food becomes secondary when you see Yosemite Falls through this dining room's wall of windows. Almost every table has a view of the falls. Grilled trout and salmon, steak, pasta, and several children's dishes are on the menu. ✉ *Yosemite Lodge off Northside Dr.* ☎ *209/372–1281* ⌕ *Reservations essential* ▭ *AE, D, DC, MC, V* ⊗ *No lunch.*

$$$$ ✕▣ **Ahwahnee Hotel & Dining Room.** This grand 1920s-era mountain lodge,
Fodor'sChoice designated a National Historic Landmark, is constructed of rocks and
★ sugar-pine logs. Some of the amenities found in a luxury hotel, including turn-down service and guest bathrobes, are standard here. The Dining Room ($$$–$$$$; jacket required, reservations essential), which has a 34-foot-tall beamed ceiling, full-length windows, and wrought-iron chandeliers, is by far the most impressive restaurant in the park, and one of the most beautiful rooms in California. Specialties include sautéed salmon, roast duckling, and prime rib. ✉ *Ahwahnee Rd. north of Northside Dr., 95389* ⌖ *Yosemite Reservations, 5410 E. Home Ave., Fresno 93727* ☎ *559/252–4848 lodging reservations, 209/372–1489 restaurant* ⊕ *www.yosemitepark.com* ⟿ *99 rooms, 4 suites, 24 cottages* ⌕ *Restaurant, refrigerators, cable TV, in-room data ports, Wi-Fi, tennis court, pool, lounge, concierge; no a/c in some rooms, no smoking* ▭ *AE, D, DC, MC, V.*

★ ♺ ✕▣ **Evergreen Lodge.** It feels like summer camp at the Evergreen, where
**$–$$$$** you can ditch the valley's hordes for a cozy cabin in the woods 8 mi from Hetch Hetchy. The perfect blend of rustic charm and modern comfort, cabins have sumptuous beds, comfy armchairs, candy-cane-stripe pull-out sofas, 3- by 4-foot topographic wall maps, and such retro-fun details as tree-stump end tables. The terrific roadhouse-style restaurant (¢–$$$) serves everything from buffalo burgers and rib eyes to rainbow trout and pastas. After dinner, shoot pool in the rough-hewn-wood bar, melt s'mores, attend a lecture or film, or play Scrabble by the fire in the barnlike recreation center. ✉ *33160 Evergreen Rd., 25 mi east of Groveland, 23 mi north of Yosemite Valley, Groveland 95321* ☎ *209/379–2606 or 800/935–6343* ⧫ *209/391–2390* ⊕ *www.evergreenlodge.com* ⟿ *66 cabins* ⌕ *Restaurant, snack bar, fans, refrigerators, Wi-Fi, pool, massage, fishing, bicycles, badminton, basketball, billiards, boccie, hiking, horseback riding, horseshoes, Ping-Pong, bar, recreation room, children's programs (ages 5–12), playground, Internet room, meeting room; no a/c, no room phones, no room TVs, no smoking* ▭ *AE, D, DC, MC, V* ⊗ *Closed Jan. and weekdays in Feb.*

$–$$ ✕▣ **Yosemite Lodge.** This lodge near Yosemite Falls, which dates from 1915, once housed the U.S. Army cavalry. Today it looks like a 1950s motel-resort complex, with several brown-and-white buildings that blend in with the landscape. Rooms have two double beds, and larger rooms have dressing areas and balconies. A few have views of the falls. Of the lodge's eating places, the Mountain Room Restaurant ($$–$$$) is the most formal. The cafeteria-style Food Court (¢–$) serves three meals a day and offers salads, soups, sandwiches, pastas, and roasted meats.

⊠ *Off Northside Dr., 95389* ⬚ *Yosemite Reservations, 5410 E. Home Ave., Fresno 93727* ☎ *559/252–4848* 🖷 *559/456–0542* ⊕ *www. yosemitepark.com* ⥱ *239 rooms* ⚭ *Restaurant, cafeteria, fans, in-room data ports, Wi-Fi, pool, bicycles, bar, no-smoking rooms; no a/c* ▤ *AE, D, DC, MC, V.*

¢–$ ▦ **Curry Village.** Opened in 1899 as a place where travelers could enjoy the beauty of Yosemite for a modest price, Curry Village has plain accommodations: standard motel rooms, cabins, and tent cabins. The tent cabins are a step up from camping, with rough wood frames, canvas walls, and roofs; linens and blankets are provided. Some have heat. Most of the cabins share shower and toilet facilities. ⊠ *South side of Southside Dr., 95389* ⬚ *Yosemite Reservations, 5410 E. Home Ave., Fresno 93727* ☎ *209/372–8333 front desk, 559/252–4848 reservations* 🖷 *559/456–0542* ⊕ *www.yosemitepark.com* ⥱ *19 rooms; 182 cabins, 102 with bath; 427 tent cabins* ⚭ *Cafeteria, pizzeria, pool, bicycles, ice-skating, no-smoking rooms; no a/c, no room phones, no room TVs* ▤ *AE, D, DC, MC, V.*

¢ ▦ **Housekeeping Camp.** Set along the Merced River, these three-sided concrete units with canvas roofs may look a bit rustic, but they're good for travelers with RVs or those without a tent who want to camp. You can cook here on gas stoves rented from the front desk, or you can use the fire pits. Toilets and showers are in a central building, and there's a camp store for provisions. ⊠ *North side of Southside Dr., near Curry Village* ⬚ *Yosemite Reservations, 5410 E. Home Ave., Fresno 93727* ☎ *209/ 372–8338, 559/252–4848 reservations* 🖷 *559/456–0542* ⊕ *www. yosemitepark.com* ⥱ *226 units* ⚭ *Picnic area, beach, laundry facilities; no a/c, no room phones, no room TVs* ▤ *AE, D, DC, MC, V* ☉ *Closed early Oct.–late Apr.*

⛺ **Camp 4.** Formerly known as Sunnyside Walk-In, this is the only valley campground available on a first-come, first-served basis and the only one west of Yosemite Lodge. Open year-round, it's a favorite for rock climbers and solo campers, so it fills quickly and is typically sold out by 9 AM every day from spring through fall. ⊠ *Base of Yosemite Falls Trail, near Yosemite Lodge* ☎ *209/372–0265* ⊕ *www.nps.gov/yose* 🖷 *209/372– 0371* ⬚ *$5* ⥱ *35 sites* ⚭ *Flush toilets, drinking water, showers, bear boxes, fire grates, picnic tables, public telephone, ranger station.*

⛺ **Tuolumne Meadows.** In a wooded area at 8,600 feet, just south of its namesake meadow, this campground is one of the most spectacular and sought-after campgrounds in Yosemite. Hot showers can be used at the Tuolumne Meadows Lodge, though only at certain strictly regulated times. Half the sites are first-come, first-served, so arrive early or make reservations. The campground is open July through September. ⊠ *Hwy. 120, 46 mi east of Big Oak Flat entrance station* ☎ *209/372–0265 or 800/ 436–7275* 🖷 *209/372–0371* ⊕ *http://reservations.nps.gov* ⬚ *$18* ⥱ *314 sites (tent or RV)* ⚭ *Flush toilets, dump station, drinking water, bear boxes, fire grates, picnic tables, public telephone, general store, ranger station.*

Sports & the Outdoors

BICYCLING You can explore the 12 mi of dedicated bicycle paths in Yosemite Valley or, if you don't mind traffic, ride the park's 196 mi of paved roads. **Yosemite Lodge** (☎ 209/372–1208) rents bicycles all year for $7.50 an hour or $24.50 per day. Rental bikes for the same prices are available at **Curry Village** (☎ 209/372–8319) from April through October. Baby jogger strollers and bikes with child trailers are also available.

HIKING Yosemite's 840 mi of hiking trails range from short strolls to rugged multiday treks. The park's visitor centers have trail maps and information, and rangers will recommend easy trails to get you acclimated to the altitude. The staff at the **Wilderness Center** (⊠ Yosemite Village, near Ansel Adams Gallery ⌂ Yosemite Wilderness Reservations, Box 545, Yosemite 95389 ☎ 209/372–0740 ⊕ www.nps.gov/yose/wilderness) provides free wilderness permits, which are required for overnight camping (reservations are available for $5 per person and are highly recommended for popular trailheads from May through September and on weekends). They also provide maps and advice to hikers heading into the backcountry.

Yosemite Mountaineering School (☎ 209/372–8344 ⊕ www.yosemitepark. com), at the Curry Village Mountain Shop and other satellite locations, has guided half- and full-day treks, conducts rock-climbing and backpacking classes, and can design customized hikes for you.

HORSEBACK RIDING For a few months starting in July, **Tuolumne Meadows Stables** (☎ 209/372–8427 ⊕ www.yosemitepark.com) runs two-, four-, and eight-hour trips, costing $53 to $96, and High Sierra four- to six-day camping treks on mules beginning at $625. You can tour the valley and the start of the high country on two-hour, four-hour, and all-day rides at **Yosemite Valley Stables** (⊠ Near Curry Village ☎ 209/372–8348 ⊕ www. yosemitepark.com). You must reserve in advance.

ICE-SKATING The outdoor **ice-skating rink** (⊠ South side of Southside Dr., Curry Village ☎ 209/372–8319) is open from Thanksgiving through April, afternoons and evenings, with morning sessions on the weekends. Admission is $10.75, including skate rental.

SKIING California's first ski resort, **Badger Pass Ski Area** has nine downhill runs, 90 mi of groomed cross-country trails, and two excellent ski schools. Free shuttle buses from Yosemite Valley operate in ski season (December through early April, weather permitting). Lift tickets are $38, downhill equipment rents for $24, and snowboard rental is $35. The gentle slopes of Badger Pass make **Yosemite Ski School** (☎ 209/372–8430) an ideal spot for children and beginners to learn downhill skiing or snowboarding. The highlight of Yosemite's cross-country skiing center is a 21-mi loop from Badger Pass to Glacier Point. You can rent cross-country skis for $17 per day at the **Cross-Country Ski School** (☎ 209/372–8444), which also rents snowshoes ($15 per day), telemarking equipment ($21.50), and skate-skis ($19.50). ⊠ *Badger Pass Rd., off Glacier Point Rd., 18 mi from Yosemite Valley* ☎ 209/372–8430 ⌂ *10 trails on 85 acres, rated 35% beginner, 50% intermediate, 15% advanced. Longest run* $3/10$ *mi, base 7,200', summit, 8,000'. Lifts: 5.*

Yosemite Mountaineering School (⊠ Badger Pass Ski Area ☎ 209/372–8344 ⊕ www.yosemitepark.com) conducts snowshoeing, cross-country skiing, telemarking, and skate-skiing classes.

Wawona

24 *25 mi south of Yosemite Valley and 16 mi north of Fish Camp on Hwy. 41.*

The historic buildings in **Pioneer Yosemite History Center** were moved to Wawona from their original sites in the park. You can take a self-guided tour around their exteriors at any time, day or night. Wednesday through Sunday (hours sometimes vary; call ahead) in summer, costumed docents re-create 19th-century Yosemite life in a blacksmith's shop, a jail, and other buildings. At the nearby information center, you can ask about schedules of ranger-led walks and horse-drawn stage rides (alternatively, check *Yosemite Today*). ⊠ *Hwy. 41* ☎ *209/375–9531 or 209/ 379–2646* ☞ *Free* ☉ *Grounds daily 24 hrs. Buildings mid-June–early Sept., Wed. 2–5, Thurs.–Sun. 10–1 and 2–5. Information center late May–early Sept., daily 8:30–4:30.*

25 **Mariposa Grove of Big Trees,** Yosemite's largest grove of giant sequoias, can be visited on foot—trails all lead uphill—or, in summer, on one-hour tram rides (reservations essential). The Grizzly Giant, the oldest tree here, is estimated to be 2,700 years old. In summer, a free shuttle connects Wawona to the Mariposa Grove between 9 and 6 (the last shuttle leaves Wawona at 4:30, the grove at 6). If the road to the grove is closed, which happens when Yosemite is crowded (or when there's been heavy snow), park in Wawona and take the free shuttle, which makes pickups near the gas station. You can also walk, snowshoe, or ski in, a worthwhile effort when the woods fall silent under a mantle of white. ⊠ *Off Hwy. 41, 2 mi north of south entrance* ☎ *209/375–1621 or 209/375–6551* ☞ *Free; tram tour $11* ☉ *Tram May–Oct., daily 9–5; shuttle late May–early Sept., daily 9–6.*

Where to Stay & Eat

$$-$$$ ✕▦ **Wawona Hotel and Dining Room.** This 1879 National Historic Landmark sits at Yosemite's southern end, near the Mariposa Grove of Big Trees. It's an old-fashioned New England–style estate, with whitewashed buildings, wraparound verandas, and pleasant, no-frills rooms decorated with period pieces (many share a bath; inquire when you book). In the romantic, candlelighted dining room ($$–$$$), the smoky corn-trout soup hits the spot on cold winter nights. (The dining room is closed January through March, except holidays; call for hours.) Afterward, you can visit the cozy Victorian parlor, which has a fireplace, board games, and a pianist who plays ragtime most evenings. ⊠ *Hwy. 41* ⎘ *Yosemite Reservations, 5410 E. Home Ave., Fresno 93727* ☎ *559/252–4848 lodging reservations, 209/375–1425 dining reservations* ☎ *559/456–0542* ⊕ *www.yosemitepark.com* ⤳ *104 rooms, 52 with bath* ⚑ *Restaurant, 9-hole golf course, putting green, tennis court, pool, horseback riding, bar; no a/c, no room phones, no room TVs, no smoking* ▭ *AE, D, DC, MC, V* ☉ *Closed Jan. and Feb.*

⚠ **Wawona.** Near the Mariposa Grove, just downstream from a popular fishing spot, this year-round campground (reservations essential May through September) has larger, less closely packed sites than campgrounds in the valley, plus they're right by the river. The downside is that it's an hour's drive to the valley's major attractions. ✉ *Hwy. 41, 1 mi north of Wawona* ☎ *209/372–0265 or 800/436–7275* 🖶 *209/372– 0371* ⊕ *http://reservations.nps.gov* ✉ *$18* ⇆ *93 sites (tent or RV)* ♿ *Flush toilets, dump station, drinking water, bear boxes, fire grates, picnic tables, ranger station, swimming (river).*

Sports & the Outdoors

Wawona Stables (☎ 209/375–6502) has several rides, starting at $51 reservations essential.

MAMMOTH AREA

A jewel in the vast eastern Sierra Nevada, the Mammoth Lakes area lies just east of the Sierra crest, on the back side of Yosemite and the Ansel Adams Wilderness. It's a place of rugged beauty, where giant sawtooth mountains drop into the vast deserts of the Great Basin. In winter, 11,053-foot-high Mammoth Mountain provides the finest skiing and snowboarding in California—sometimes as late as June or even July. Once the snows melt, Mammoth transforms itself into a warm-weather playground, with fishing, mountain biking, golfing, hiking, and horseback riding. Nine deep-blue lakes are spread through the Mammoth Lakes Basin, and another 100 lakes dot the surrounding countryside. Crater-pocked Mammoth Mountain hasn't had a major eruption for 50,000 years, but the region is alive with hot springs, mud pots, fumaroles, and steam vents.

7

Mammoth Lakes

㉖ *30 mi south of eastern edge of Yosemite National Park on U.S. 395.*

Much of the architecture in the ordinary hub town of Mammoth Lakes (elevation 7,800 feet) is of the faux-alpine variety. You'll find mostly basic dining and lodging options here, but that's changing. International real-estate developers have recently joined forces with Mammoth Mountain Ski Area and are working hard to transform the once sleepy town into a chic ski destination. In fall 2007 a new Westin hotel is slated to open, and both Ritz-Carlton and Four Seasons have projects in the works. The new Mammoth Mountain Village (*below*) is the epicenter of all the recent development. Winter is high season at Mammoth; in summer room rates plummet. Highway 203 heads west from U.S. 395, becoming Main Street as it passes through the town of Mammoth Lakes, and later Minaret Road (which makes a right turn) as it continues west to the Mammoth Mountain ski area and Devils Postpile National Monument.

The lakes of the **Mammoth Lakes Basin,** reached by Lake Mary Road off Highway 203 southwest of town, are popular for fishing and boating in summer. First comes Twin Lakes, at the far end of which is Twin Falls, where water cascades 300 feet over a shelf of volcanic rock. Also popular are Lake Mary, the largest lake in the basin; Lake Mamie; and Lake George. Horseshoe Lake is the only lake in which you can swim.

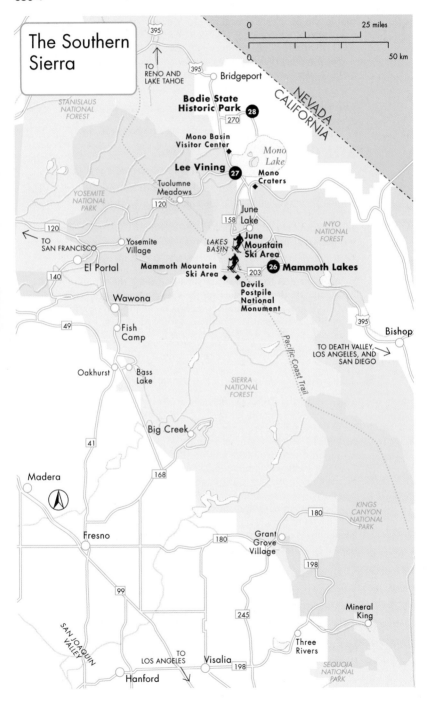

The Southern Sierra

395
TO RENO AND LAKE TAHOE
395
Bridgeport

STANISLAUS NATIONAL FOREST

NEVADA
CALIFORNIA

0   25 miles
0   50 km

Bodie State Historic Park 28
270

Mono Basin Visitor Center

Mono Lake

Lee Vining 27
Mono Craters

Tuolumne Meadows
120

YOSEMITE NATIONAL PARK

June Lake
158

INYO NATIONAL FOREST

120
TO SAN FRANCISCO

Yosemite Village

LAKES BASIN

June Mountain Ski Area

El Portal
140

Mammoth Mountain Ski Area

203 26 **Mammoth Lakes**

Devils Postpile National Monument

Wawona

49

Fish Camp

Pacific Coast Trail

395
Bishop

TO DEATH VALLEY, LOS ANGELES, AND SAN DIEGO

Oakhurst
Bass Lake

SIERRA NATIONAL FOREST

Big Creek

41

168

Madera

KINGS CANYON NATIONAL PARK

180

Fresno

180
Grant Grove Village

198

99

245

Mineral King

SAN JOAQUIN VALLEY

TO LOS ANGELES
Visalia
198

Three Rivers

Hanford

SEQUOIA NATIONAL PARK

The glacial-carved sawtooth spires of the Minarets, the remains of an ancient lava flow, are best viewed from the **Minaret Vista,** off Highway 203 west of Mammoth Lakes.

Even if you don't ski, ride the **Panorama Gondola** to see Mammoth Mountain, the aptly named dormant volcano that gives Mammoth Lakes its name. Gondolas serve skiers in winter and mountain bikers and sightseers in summer. The high-speed, eight-passenger gondolas whisk you from the chalet to the summit, where you can read about the area's volcanic history and take in top-of-the-world views. Standing high above the tree line atop this dormant volcano, you can look west 150 mi across the state to the Coastal Range; to the east are the highest peaks of Nevada and the Great Basin beyond. You won't find a better view of the Sierra High Country without climbing. Remember, though, that the air is thin at the 11,053-foot summit; carry water, and don't overexert yourself. The boarding area is at the Main Lodge. ⊠ *Off Hwy. 203* ☎ *760/934–2571 Ext. 2400 information, Ext. 3850 gondola station* 🕿 *$16 in summer* ☉ *July 4–Oct., daily 9–4:30; Nov.–July 3, daily 8:30–4.*

The overwhelming popularity of Mammoth Mountain has generated a real-estate boom, and a huge new complex of shops, restaurants, and luxury accommodations, called the **Village at Mammoth,** has become the town's tourist center. Parking can be tricky in mid-winter. There's a lot across the street on Minaret Road; pay attention to time limits.

DEVILS POSTPILE NATIONAL MONUMENT – An easy 10-minute walk from the Devils Postpile National Monument ranger station takes you to a geologic formation of smooth, vertical basalt columns sculpted by volcanic and glacial forces. A short but steep trail winds to the top of the 60-foot-high rocky cliff, where you'll find a bird's-eye view of the columns. A 2-mi hike past the Postpile leads to the monument's second scenic wonder, **Rainbow Falls,** where a branch of the San Joaquin River plunges more than 100 feet over a lava ledge. When the water hits the pool below, sunlight turns the mist into a spray of color. Walk down a bit from the top of the falls for the best view.

Devils Postpile National Monument is only accessible in summer and fall. To get here, you must take the shuttle bus from the Adventure Center at the Mammoth Mountain Main Lodge gondola building. The shuttle begins operation as soon as the road is cleared of snow—usually in June, but sometimes as late as July. The shuttle departs approximately every 20 to 30 minutes, generally from 7 AM to 7 PM, with the last ride out of Red's Valley at 7:30. The shuttle stops running by the end of September, but you can drive to the falls until October 31 or the first significant snowfall. Scenic picnic spots dot the bank of the San Joaquin River. ⊠ *Hwy. 203, 13 mi west of Mammoth Lakes* ☎ *760/ 934–2289, 760/924–5502 shuttle-bus information* ⊕ *www.nps.gov/ depo* 🕿 *$7 per person, not to exceed $20 per carload* ☉ *Shuttle mid-June–mid-Sept., daily.*

HOT CREEK GEOLOGICALSITE/HOT CREEK FISH HATCHERY – Forged by an ancient volcanic eruption, the Hot Creek GeologicalSite is a landscape of boiling hot springs, fumaroles, and occasional geysers about 10 mi

OFF THE BEATEN PATH

southeast of the town of Mammoth Lakes. You can soak in hot springs (at your own risk, bathing suits mandatory) or look down from the parking area into the canyon to view the steaming volcanic features, a very cool sight indeed. Fly-fishing for trout is popular upstream from the springs. En route to the geologic site is the outdoor Hot Creek Fish Hatchery, the breeding ponds for many of the fish (typically 3 to 5 million annually) with which the state stocks eastern Sierra lakes and rivers. In recent years, budget cuts have drastically reduced these numbers, but locals have formed foundations to keep the hatchery going. For more details, take the worthwhile self-guided tour. ⊠ *Hot Creek Hatchery Rd. east of U.S. 395* ☎ *760/924–5500 for geological site, 760/934–2664 for hatchery* 🖥 *Free* ☉ *Site daily sunrise–sunset; hatchery June–Oct., daily 8–4, depending on snowfall.*

Where to Stay & Eat

★ $$$–$$$$ ✕ **Restaurant LuLu.** LuLu imports the sunny, sensual, and assertive flavors of Provençal cooking—think olive tapenade, aioli, and lemony vinaigrettes—to Mammoth Lakes. An outpost of the famous San Francisco restaurant, the formula remains the same here: small plates of southern French cooking served family-style in a sexy dining room packed with bon vivants. Stand-outs include rotisseried meats, succulent roasted mussels, homemade gnocchi, and a fantastic wine list, with 50 vintages available in 2-ounce pours. The only drawback is price: many ingredients are imported at great expense, but if you can swing it, it's worth every penny. The waiters wear jeans so you can, too. ⊠ *Village at Mammoth, 1111 Forest Trail, Unit 201* ☎ *760/924–8781* ♢ *Reservations essential* ☰ *AE, D, MC, V.*

★ $$–$$$$ ✕ **Restaurant at Convict Lake.** Tucked in a tiny valley ringed by mile-high peaks, Convict Lake sits in one of the most spectacular spots in the eastern Sierra. Thank heaven the food lives up to the view. The chef's specialties include beef Wellington, rack of lamb, and pan-seared local trout, all beautifully prepared. The woodsy room is long on charm, with a vaulted knotty-pine ceiling and a copper-chimney fireplace that roars on cold nights. Service is so good that if you forget your glasses, the waiter will provide a pair. The wine list is exceptional for its reasonably priced European and California varietals. ⊠ *2 mi off U.S. 395, 4 mi south of Mammoth Lakes* ☎ *760/934–3803* ♢ *Reservations essential* ☰ *AE, D, MC, V* ☉ *No lunch early Sept.–July 4.*

$$$ ✕ **Nevados.** Nevados is a perennial favorite. Hearty specialties include rack of lamb, New York steak, and pistachio-crusted elk, as well as tuna sashimi and other good seafood dishes. For $46, the three-course prix-fixe is a great choice. There's nothing cutting-edge about the menu, but the quality is consistent, a major accomplishment in this tourist town and the reason it's been going strong since 1978. The atmosphere is convivial and welcoming—if a bit loud—and the 30-seat bar is a fun spot for cocktails and appetizers. Book a week in advance. ⊠ *Main St. and Minaret Rd.* ☎ *760/934–4466* ♢ *Reservations essential* ☰ *AE, MC, V* ☉ *No lunch; call ahead for May and June hours.*

☾ ¢–$$ ✕ **Berger's.** Don't even think about coming to this bustling restaurant unless you're hungry. Berger's is known, appropriately enough, for its burgers and sandwiches, and everything comes in mountainous portions.

At lunch try the sourdough patty melt, at dinner the beef ribs. The seasoned french fries are delicious. ⊠ *Minaret Rd. near Canyon Blvd.* ☏ *760/934–6622* ▭ *MC, V* ◷ *Closed 2 wks in May and 4–6 wks in Oct.–Nov.*

¢–$　✕ **Side Door Café.** Half wine bar, half café, this is a laid-back spot for an easy lunch or a long, lingering afternoon. The café serves grilled panini sandwiches, sweet and savory crepes, and espresso. At the wine bar, order cheese plates and charcuterie platters, designed to pair with the 25 wines available by the glass. If you're lucky, a winemaker will show up and hold court at the bar. ⊠ *Village at Mammoth, 1111 Forest Trail, Unit 229* ☏ *760/934–5200* ▭ *AE, D, MC, V.*

☺ ¢–$　✕ **The Stove.** A longtime family favorite for down-to-earth, folksy cooking, the Stove is the kind of place you take the family to fill up before a long car ride. The omelets, pancakes, huevos rancheros, and meat loaf won't win any awards, but they're tasty. The room is cute, with gingham curtains and pinewood booths, and service is friendly. Dinners are fine for unfussy eaters, but breakfasts and lunch are best. ⊠ *644 Old Mammoth Rd.* ☏ *760/934–2821* ⌂ *No reservations* ▭ *AE, MC, V.*

$$$$　✕▦ **Double Eagle Resort and Spa.** You won't find a better spa retreat in the eastern Sierra than the Double Eagle. Dwarfed by towering, craggy peaks, the resort is in a spectacularly beautiful spot along a creek, near June Lake, 20 minutes north of Mammoth Lakes. Accommodations are in comfortable knotty-pine two-bedroom cabins that sleep up to six, or in cabin suites with efficiency kitchens; all come fully equipped with modern amenities. If you don't want to cook (the nearest grocery is in Mammoth), the Eagles Landing Restaurant ($–$$$) serves three meals a day, but the quality is erratic. For good food, you'll have to drive. Spa services and treatments are available for nonguests by reservation. ⊠ *5587 Hwy. 158, Box 736, June Lake 93529* ☏ *760/648–7004 or 877/648–7004* 🖷 *760/648–7014* ⊕ *www.doubleeagleresort.com* ⇆ *16 2-bedroom cabins, 16 cabin suites, 1 3-bedroom cabin* ⌂ *Restaurant, café, BBQs, some kitchens, microwaves, refrigerators, cable TV, in-room VCRs, in-room data ports, indoor pool, fitness classes, health club, hair salon, 3 hot tubs, spa, steam room, boating (nearby), fishing, hiking, horseback riding (nearby), volleyball, cross-country skiing (nearby), downhill skiing (nearby), ice-skating, bar, shop, some pets allowed (fee); no a/c, no smoking* ▭ *AE, D, MC, V.*

$$–$$$$　✕▦ **Tamarack Lodge Resort & Lakefront Restaurant.** Tucked away on the
Fodor'sChoice　edge of the John Muir Wilderness Area, where cross-country ski trails
★　loop through the woods, this original 1924 lodge looks like something out of a snow globe. Rooms in the charming main lodge have spartan furnishings, and in old-fashioned style, some share a bathroom. For more privacy, opt for one of the cabins, which range from rustic to downright cushy; many have fireplaces, kitchens, or wood-burning stoves. In warm months, fishing, canoeing, hiking, and mountain biking are right outside. The small and romantic Lakefront Restaurant ($$–$$$) serves outstanding contemporary French-inspired dinners, with an emphasis on game, in a candlelit dining room. Reservations are essential. ⊠ *Lake Mary Rd. off Hwy. 203* 🖃 *Box 69, 93546* ☏ *760/934–2442 or 800/626–6684* 🖷 *760/934–2281* ⊕ *www.tamaracklodge.com* ⇆ *11 rooms,*

29 cabins ⌂ Restaurant, fans, some kitchens, some kitchenettes, lake, boating, fishing, hiking, cross-country skiing, ski shop, lobby lounge; no a/c, no room TVs, no smoking ▭ AE, MC, V.

$$$$ ▦ **Village at Mammoth.** At the epicenter of Mammoth's burgeoning dining and nightlife scene, this cluster of four-story timber-and-stone condo buildings nods to Alpine style, with exposed timbers and peaked roofs. Units have gas fireplaces, kitchens or kitchenettes, daily maid service, high-speed Internet access, DVD player, slate-tile bathroom floors, and comfortable furnishings. The decor is a bit sterile, but there are high-end details like granite counters. And you won't have to drive anywhere: the buildings are connected by a ground-floor pedestrian mall, with shops, restaurants, bars, and—best of all—a gondola (November through mid-April only) that whisks you right from the Village to the mountain. ⊠ *100 Canyon Blvd.* ⌖ *Box 3459, 93546* ☎ *760 934–1982 or 800/626–6684* ⎙ *760/934–1494* ⊕ *www.mammothmountain.com* ⇆ *277 units ⌂ Some kitchens, some kitchenettes, cable TV, in-room broadband, in-room data ports, pool, gym, 3 outdoor hot tubs, downhill skiing, ski storage, laundry facilities, free parking; no a/c, no smoking ▭ AE, MC, V.*

$$$–$$$$ ▦ **Juniper Springs Lodge.** Tops for slope-side comfort, these condominium-style units have full kitchens and ski-in, ski-out access to the mountain. Extras include fireplaces, balconies, and stereos with CD players; the heated outdoor pool—surrounded by a heated deck—is open year-round. If you like to be near nightlife, you'll do better at the Village, but if you don't mind having to drive to go out for the evening, this is a great spot. In summer hardly anyone stays here, and rates are a steal. Skiers: the lifts on this side of the mountain close in mid-April; for springtime ski-in, ski-out access, stay at the Mammoth Mountain Inn. ⊠ *4000 Meridian Blvd.* ⌖ *Box 2129, 93546* ☎ *760/924–1102 or 800/626–6684* ⎙ *760/924–8152* ⊕ *www.mammothmountain.com* ⇆ *10 studios, 99 1-bedrooms, 92 2-bedrooms, 5 3-bedrooms ⌂ Restaurant, café, room service, fans, kitchens, microwaves, refrigerators, cable TV, in-room VCRs, in-room broadband, in-room data ports, 18-hole golf course, pool, exercise equipment, 3 outdoor hot tubs, mountain bikes, downhill skiing, ski shop, ski storage, bar, laundry service, concierge, meeting rooms; no a/c, no smoking ▭ AE, MC, V.*

$$–$$$$ ▦ **Mammoth Mountain Inn.** If you want to be within walking distance of the Mammoth Mountain Main Lodge, this is the place. In winter, check your skis with the concierge, pick them up in the morning, and head directly to the lifts. In summer the proximity to the gondola means you can hike and mountain bike to your heart's delight. The accommodations, which vary in size, include standard hotel rooms and condo units; the latter have kitchenettes, and many have lofts. The inn has licensed on-site child care in winter. ⊠ *Minaret Rd., 4 mi west of Mammoth Lakes* ⌖ *Box 353, 93546* ☎ *760/934–2581 or 800/626–6684* ⎙ *760/934–0701* ⊕ *www.mammothmountain.com* ⇆ *124 rooms, 91 condos ⌂ 2 restaurants, fans, some kitchenettes, some microwaves, some refrigerators, cable TV, in-room broadband, some in-room data ports, Wi-Fi, hot tub, hiking, downhill skiing, ski storage, bar, video game room, shop, babysitting, playground, laundry facilities, meeting room; no a/c, no smoking ▭ AE, MC, V.*

$$–$$$ 🏨 **Holiday Inn Mammoth Lakes.** In a town known for Carter-era condo units, this stands out as being the only modern, midprice hotel, with fresh looking decor. Rooms and public areas are sparkling clean, and extras include voice mail, irons, microwaves, and refrigerators. Families enjoy the special "kids' suites," which have bunk beds and video games. There's also a year-round indoor pool. The place looks decidedly pre-fab and the maids spray too much air freshener, but for up-to-date amenities and services, you'll be hard pressed to find better in this price range. ✉ *3236 Main St., 93546* ☎ *760/924–1234 or 866/924–1234* 🖷 *760/934–3626* ⊕ *www.holidayatmammoth.com* 🛏 *71 rooms, 3 suites* ⚅ *Cafeteria, microwaves, refrigerators, some kitchenettes, cable TV, in-room data ports, Wi-Fi, indoor pool, exercise equipment, hot tub, billiards, Ping-Pong, bar, laundry facilities, meeting room; no smoking* 🚍 *AE, D, DC, MC, V.*

$–$$$ 🏨 **Convict Lake Resort.** The lake on which this resort stands (about 10 minutes south of Mammoth Lakes) was named for an 1871 gunfight between local vigilantes and six escaped prisoners. Cabins range from rustic to modern, and come with fully equipped kitchens (including coffeemakers and premium coffee). The least fancy feel like upgraded fishing cabins; the nicest have Jacuzzi tubs and other creature comforts. Regardless of what room you book, the valley here is so drop-dead gorgeous, chances are you'll want to spend all your time outdoors. ✉ *2 mi off U.S. 395* ⬡ *Box 204, 93546* ☎ *760/934–3800 or 800/992–2260* ⊕ *www.convictlakeresort.com* 🛏 *29 cabins* ⚅ *Restaurant, some in-room hot tubs, kitchens, some microwaves, cable TV, in-room VCRs, lake, boating, fishing, bicycles, horseback riding, shop, Internet room, some pets allowed (fee); no a/c, no room phones* 🚍 *AE, D, MC, V.*

$–$$ ✕🏨 **Alpenhof Lodge.** The owners of the Alpenhof lucked out when developers built the fancy-schmancy Village at Mammoth right across the street from their mom-and-pop motel. The place remains a simple, mid-budget motel, with basic comforts and a few niceties like attractive pine furniture. Rooms are dark and the foam pillows thin, but the damask bedspreads are pretty and the low-pile carpeting clean, and best of all you can walk to restaurants and shops. Downstairs there's a lively, fun pub; if you want quiet, request a room that's not above it. Petra's, an excellent small-plates restaurant ($$–$$$), adjoins the motel. Some rooms have fireplaces and kitchens. In winter, the Village Gondola is across the street, a major plus for skiers. ✉ *6080 Minaret Rd., Box 1157, 93546* ☎ *760/934–6330 or 800/828–0371* 🖷 *760/ 934–7614* ⊕ *www.alpenhof-lodge.com* 🛏 *54 rooms, 3 cabins* ⚅ *Restaurant, some kitchens, some microwaves, some refrigerators, cable TV, pool, hot tub, bar, pub, recreation room, laundry facilities; no a/c, no smoking* 🚍 *AE, D, MC, V.*

🏕 **Convict Lake Campground.** Ten minutes south of Mammoth, this campground, near the Convict Lake Resort, is run by the U.S. Forest Service. It's open May to October, and sites are available on a first-come, first-served basis. They're extremely popular. One look at the scenery and you'll understand why. ✉ *2 mi off U.S. 395* ☎ *760/924–5500* ⊕ *www.fs.fed.us/r5/inyo* 🖾 *$16* 🛏 *88 campsites* ⚅ *Flush toilets, dump station, drinking water, showers, fire pits, general store.*

⚠ **Lake Mary Campground.** There are few sites as beautiful as this lake-side campground at 8,900 feet, open June to September. If it's full, which it often is, try the adjacent Coldwater campground. You can catch trout in taurmaline Lake Mary, the biggest in the region. There's a general store nearby. ⊠ *Lake Mary Loop Dr. off Hwy. 203* ☎ *760/924–5500* 🖥 *760/924–5537* ⊕ *www.fs.fed.us/r5/inyo* 🗺 *$16* 🛏 *48 sites (tent or RV)* ♿ *Flush toilets, drinking water, fire grates, picnic tables.*

Nightlife & the Arts

The summertime **Mammoth Lakes Jazz Jubilee** (☎ 760/934–2478 or 800/367–6572 ⊕ www.mammothjazz.org) is hosted by the local Temple of Folly Jazz Band and takes place in 10 venues, most with dance floors. For one long weekend every summer, Mammoth Lakes holds **Blue-sapalooza and Festival of Beers** (☎ 760/934–0606 or 800/367–6572 ⊕ www.mammothconcert.com), a blues-and-beer festival—with emphasis on the beer. Concerts occur throughout the year on Mammoth Mountain; contact **Mammoth Mountain Music** (☎ 760/934–0606 ⊕ www.mammothconcert.com) for listings.

The Village at Mammoth hosts events and has several rockin' bars and clubs. Sip mai tais at the tiki bar at **Lakanuki Lounge** (⊠ 6201 Minaret Rd. ☎ 760/934–7447); Thursday is karaoke night. You can sometimes sing karaoke after 10 PM at **Shogun** (⊠ 452 Old Mammoth Rd. ☎ 760/934–3970), Mammoth's only Japanese restaurant; call ahead. The bar at **Whiskey Creek** (⊠ Main St. and Minaret Rd. ☎ 760/934–2555) plays host to musicians on weekends winter and summer, and on Wednesday nights there's a DJ.

Sports & the Outdoors

For information on winter conditions around Mammoth, call the **Snow Report** (☎ 760/934–7669 or 888/766–9778). The **U.S. Forest Service ranger station** (☎ 760/924–5500) can provide general information year-round.

BICYCLING **Mammoth Mountain Bike Park** (⊠ Mammoth Mountain Ski Area ☎ 760/934–3706 ⊕ www.mammothmountain.com) opens when the snow melts, usually by July, with 70-plus mi of single-track trails—from mellow to super-challenging. Chairlifts and shuttles provide trail access, and rentals are available. Various shops around town also rent bikes and provide trail maps, if you don't want to ascend the mountain.

FISHING Crowley Lake is the top trout-fishing spot in the area; Convict Lake, June Lake, and the lakes of the Mammoth Basin are other prime spots. One of the best trout rivers is the San Joaquin, near Devils Postpile. Hot Creek, a designated Wild Trout Stream, is renowned for fly-fishing (catch and release only). The fishing season runs from the last Saturday in April until the end of October. To maximize your time on the water, get tips from local anglers, or better yet, book a guided fishing trip with **Sierra Drifters Guide Service** (☎ 760/935–4250 ⊕ www.sierradrifters.com).

Kittredge Sports (⊠ 3218 Main St., at Forest Trail ☎ 760/934–7566 ⊕ www.kittredgesports.com) rents rods and reels and also conducts guided trips.

GOLF Because it's nestled right up against the forest, you might see deer and bears on the fairways on the picture-perfect 18-hole **Sierra Star Golf Course** (✉ 2001 Sierra Star Pkwy. ☎ 760/924–2200 ⊕ www.mammothmountain. com), California's highest-elevation golf course (take it slow!). Greens fees run $80 to $125.

The 9-hole course at **Snowcreek Resort** (✉ Old Mammoth Rd. ☎ 760/934–6633 ⊕ www.snowcreekresort.com) sits in a meadow with drop-dead-gorgeous, wide-open vistas of the mountains. Nine-hole play costs $30 and includes a cart; 18 holes run $50.

HIKING Hiking in Mammoth is stellar, especially along the trails that wind through the pristine alpine scenery around the Lakes Basin. Carry lots of water; remember, you're above 8,000-foot elevation, and the air is thin. Stop at the **U.S. Forest Service ranger station** (✉ Hwy. 203 ☎ 760/924–5500 ⊕ www.fs.fed.us/r5/inyo), on your right just before the town of Mammoth Lakes, for a Mammoth area trail map and permits for back-packing in wilderness areas.

HORSEBACK RIDING Stables around Mammoth are typically open from June through September. **Mammoth Lakes Pack Outfit** (✉ Lake Mary Rd., between Twin Lakes and Lake Mary ☎ 760/934–2434 or 888/475–8747 ⊕ www. mammothpack.com) runs day and overnight horseback trips, or will shuttle you to the high country. **McGee Creek Pack Station** (☎ 760/935–4324 or 800/854–7407 ⊕ www.mcgeecreekpackstation.com) customizes pack trips or will shuttle you to camp alone. Operated by the folks at McGee Creek, **Sierra Meadows Ranch** (✉ Sherwin Creek Rd. off Old Mammoth Rd. ☎ 760/934–6161) conducts horseback and wagon rides that range from one-hour to all-day excursions.

HOT-AIR BALLOONING The balloons of **Mammoth Balloon Adventures** (☎ 760/937–8787 ⊕ www. mammothballoonadventures.com) glide over the countryside in the morning from spring until fall, weather permitting.

SKIING **June Mountain Ski Area.** In their rush to Mammoth Mountain, most people overlook June Mountain, a compact, low-key resort 20 mi north of Mammoth. Snowboarders especially dig it. Three freestyle terrain areas are for both skiers and boarders, including a huge 16-foot-wall super pipe. Best of all, there's rarely a line for the lifts—if you want to avoid the crowds but must ski on a weekend, this is the place. And in a storm, June is better protected from wind and blowing snow than Mammoth Mountain. (If it starts to storm, you can use your Mammoth ticket at June.) Expect all the usual services, including a rental-and-repair shop, ski school, and sports shop, but the food quality is way better at Mammoth. Lift tickets run $53, with discounts for multiple days. ✉ *Off June Lake Loop, Hwy. 158, June Lake* ☎ *760/648–7733 or 888/586–3686* ⊕ *www.junemountain.com* ☞ *35 trails on 500 acres, rated 35% beginner, 45% intermediate, 20% advanced. Longest run 2½ mi, base 7,510', summit 10,174'. Lifts: 7.*

Fodor'sChoice **Mammoth Mountain Ski Area.** If you ski only one mountain in California, ★ make it Mammoth. One of the West's largest and best resorts, Mammoth has more than 3,500 acres of skiable terrain and a 3,100-foot vertical drop. The views from the 11,053-foot summit are some of the most stunning in the Sierra. Below, you'll find a 6½-mi-wide swath of groomed boulevards and canyons, as well as pockets of tree-skiing and a dozen vast bowls. Snowboarders are everywhere on the slopes; there are three outstanding freestyle terrain parks of varying technical difficulty, with jumps, rails, tabletops, and giant superpipes, (this is the location of several international snowboarding competitions). Mammoth's season begins in November and often lingers until July 4. Lift tickets cost $61. Lessons and equipment are available, and there's a children's ski and snowboard school. Mammoth runs four free shuttle-bus routes around town and to the ski area, and the Village Gondola runs from the Village complex to Canyon Lodge. However, only overnight guests are allowed to park at the Village for more than a few hours, so if you want to ride the gondola to the mountain, take a shuttle bus to the Village. ⌧ *Minaret Rd. west of Mammoth Lakes* ☎ *760/934–2571 or 800/626–6684, 760/934–0687 shuttle* ☞ *150 trails on 3,500 acres, rated 30% beginner, 40% intermediate, 30% advanced. Longest run 3 mi, base 7,953', summit 11,053'. Lifts: 27, including 9 high-speed and 2 gondolas.*

Trails at **Tamarack Cross Country Ski Center** (⌧ Lake Mary Rd. off Hwy. 203 ☎ 760/934–5293 or 760/934–2442 ⊕ www.tamaracklodge.com), adjacent to Tamarack Lodge, meander around several lakes. Rentals are available.

Mammoth Sporting Goods (⌧ 1 Sierra Center Mall, Old Mammoth Rd. ☎ 760/934–3239 ⊕ www.mammothsportinggoods.com) rents good skis for intermediates, and sells equipment, clothing, and accessories. Advanced skiers should rent from **Kittredge Sports** (⌧ 3218 Main St. ☎ 760/934–7566 ⊕ www.kittredgesports.com).

★ When the U.S. Ski Team visits Mammoth and needs their boots adjusted, they head to **Footloose** (⌧ 3043 Main St. ☎ 760/934–2400 ⊕ www. footloosesports.com), the best place in town—and possibly all California—for ski-boot rentals and sales, as well as custom insoles (ask for Kevin or Corty).

SNOWMOBILING   **Mammoth Snowmobile Adventures** (⌧ Mammoth Mountain Main Lodge ☎ 760/934–9645 or 800/626–6684 ⊕ www.mammothmountain.com) conducts guided tours along wooded trails.

EAST OF YOSEMITE NATIONAL PARK
FROM LEE VINING TO BRIDGEPORT

The area to the east of Yosemite National Park includes some ruggedly handsome, albeit desolate, terrain, most notably around Mono Lake. The area is best visited by car, as distances are great and public transportation is limited. U.S. 395 is the main north–south road on the eastern side of the Sierra Nevada, at the western edge of the Great Basin. It's one of California's most stunningly beautiful highways; plan to snap pictures at roadside pullouts. Because it's hard to judge distances in the vast landscape, drive with your lights on, even in daytime.

Lee Vining

27 *20 mi east of Tuolumne Meadows via Hwy. 120 to U.S. 395; 30 mi north of Mammoth Lakes on U.S. 395.*

Tiny Lee Vining is known primarily as the eastern gateway to Yosemite National Park (summer only) and the location of vast and desolate Mono Lake. Pick up supplies at the general store year-round, or stop here for lunch or dinner before or after a drive through the high country. In winter the town is all but deserted, except for the ice climbers who come to scale frozen waterfalls. You can meet these hearty souls at Nicely's restaurant, where the climbers congregate for breakfast around 8 AM on winter mornings. (If you want to try your hand at the sport, contact **Sierra Mountain Guides** (☎ 760/648–1122 or 877/423–2546 ⊕ www.themountainguide.com).

★ Eerie tufa towers—calcium carbonate formations that often resemble castle turrets—rise from impressive **Mono Lake.** Since the 1940s, the city of Los Angeles has diverted water from streams that feed the lake, lowering its water level and exposing the tufa. Court victories by environmentalists in the 1990s forced a reduction of the diversions, and the lake has since risen about 9 feet. From April through August, millions of migratory birds nest in and around Mono Lake. The best place to view the tufa is at the south end of the lake along the mile-long **South Tufa Trail.** To reach it, drive 5 mi south from Lee Vining on U.S. 395, then 5 mi east on Highway 120. There's a $3 fee. You can swim (or float) in the salty water at Navy Beach near the South Tufa Trail or take a kayak or canoe trip for close-up views of the tufa (check with rangers for boating restrictions during bird-nesting season). You can rent kayaks in Mammoth Lakes. The **Scenic Area Visitor Center** (⊠ U.S. 395 ☎ 760/647–3044 ⊕ www.monolake.org) is open daily from June through September, (Sunday through Thursday 8 to 5, Friday and Saturday 8 to 7), and the rest of the year Thursday through Monday 9–4. Rangers and naturalists lead walking tours of the tufa daily in summer and on weekends (sometimes on cross-country skis) in winter.

Where to Stay & Eat

★ **$–$$$** ✕ **Mono Inn at Mono Lake.** It's worth the 30-minute drive from Mammoth Lakes to get to this updated 1922 roadhouse. Impeccably decorated with Stickley furniture and contemporary crafts, the dining room has drop-dead 180-degree views of Mono Lake through big picture windows. During a full moon, the glow on the water is magical. The adeptly prepared menu leans toward comfort foods, with an occasional flourish; dishes include braised lamb shank, flat-iron steak with homemade french fries, and duck confit. There's also a good burger. The lovely owner, Sarah Adams, is Ansel Adams' granddaughter, and the master photographer's work adorns the walls. ⊠ *U.S. 395, north of Lee Vining* ☎ *760/647–6581* ⌕ *Reservations essential* ⊟ *AE, D, MC, V* ☉ *Closed Nov.–Mar. No lunch.*

★ **$–$$** ✕ **Tioga Gas Mart & Whoa Nelli Deli.** Near the eastern entrance to Yosemite, Whoa Nelli serves some of Mono County's better food, with lobster taquitos, barbecued ribs, gourmet pizzas, Angus roast-beef sandwiches, and herb-crusted pork tenderloin with berry glaze. But what makes it special is that it's in a gas station—possibly the only one in America where you can order cocktails—and outside there's a full-size trapeze where you can take lessons (by reservation). A few years ago, before word got out, the food was better; now they're resting on their laurels, but it's still a wacky spot, well worth a visit. ⊠ *Hwy. 120 and U.S. 395* ☎ *760/647–1088* ☰ *AE, MC, V* ⊘ *Closed mid-Nov.–mid-Apr.*

¢–$ ✕ **Nicely's.** Old photographs of local attractions decorate the walls of this vintage-1965 diner. The country cooking ain't fancy—think blueberry pancakes for breakfast and chicken-fried steak for dinner—but it's a good spot for families with kids and unfussy eaters looking for a square meal, the kind of place where the waitress walks up with a pot of coffee and asks, "Ya want a warm-up, hon?" ⊠ *U.S. 395 and 4th St.* ☎ *760/647–6477* ☰ *MC, V* ⊘ *Closed Tues. and Wed. in winter.*

$ ▣ **Tioga Lodge.** A fun alternative to Lee Vining's plain-Jane motels, the lodge centers around a 19th-century building that has been by turns a store, a saloon, a tollbooth, and a boardinghouse. Surrounding the rustic lodge are modest, attached, weathered-wooden cottages, tucked beneath towering cottonwoods on a grassy hillside. The proud owners have given the place much-needed TLC, and the simple, country-cute rooms have cozy furnishings that—thank heaven—manage not to be tacky. Alas, cottages are a bit close to the road, but the views of Mono Lake can't be beat. Be sure to ask about summer boat tours. ⊠ *U.S. 395* ⌂ *Box 580, 93541* ☎ *760/647–6423 or 888/647–6423* 🖷 *760/647–6074* ⊕ *www.tiogalodge.com* ⇆ *13 rooms* ⌂ *Restaurant, boating; no a/c, no room phones, no room TVs, no smoking* ☰ *AE, D, MC, V* ⊘ *Closed Nov.–Mar.*

▐ EN ROUTE ★   Heading south from Lee Vining, U.S. 395 intersects the **June Lake Loop** (⊠ Hwy. 158 West). This gorgeously scenic 17-mi drive follows an old glacial canyon past Grant, June, Gull, and other lakes before reconnecting with U.S. 395 on its way to Mammoth Lakes. The loop is especially colorful in fall.

Bodie State Historic Park

❷❽ *23 mi northeast of Lee Vining via U.S. 395 to Hwy. 270 (last 3 mi are unpaved).*

Old shacks and shops, abandoned mine shafts, a Methodist church, the mining village of Rattlesnake Gulch, and the remains of a small Chinatown are among the sights at fascinating **Bodie Ghost Town.** The town, at an elevation of 8,200 feet, boomed from about 1878 to 1881, as gold prospectors, having worked the best of the western Sierra mines, headed to the high desert on the eastern slopes. Bodie was a mean place—the booze flowed freely, shootings were commonplace, and licentiousness reigned. Evidence of the town's wild past survives today at an excellent museum, and you can tour an old stamp mill (where ore was stamped into fine powder to extract gold and silver) and a ridge that contains many mine sites. No food, drink, or lodging is available in Bodie, and the nearest picnic area is a half mile away. Though the park stays open in winter, snow may close Highway 270. Still, it's a

FodorśChoice ★

fantastic time to visit: rent cross-country skis in Mammoth Lakes, drive north, ski in, and have the park to yourself. ⊠ *Museum: Main and Green Sts.* ☎ *760/647–6445* ⊕ *www.bodie.net or www.parks.ca. gov* ☞ *Park $3; museum free* ☉ *Park: late May–early Sept., daily 8–7; early Sept.–late May, daily 8–4. Museum: late May–early Sept., daily 9–6; early Sept.–late May, hrs vary.*

EN ROUTE

Historic **Bridgeport** lies within striking distance of a myriad of alpine lakes and streams and both forks of the Walker River, making it a prime spot for fishing. It's also the gateway to Bodie State Historic Park, and the only supply center for miles around. The scenery is spectacular, with craggy, snow-capped peaks lording above vast open prairie lands. Gas prices are likewise spectacular; fuel up in Bishop, Mammoth Lakes, or ideally Carson City, Nevada. In winter much of Bridgeport shuts for the season.

SOUTHERN SIERRA ESSENTIALS

To research prices, get advice from other travelers, and book travel arrangements, visit www.fodors.com.

Transportation

BY AIR

Fresno Yosemite International Airport (FYI) is the nearest airport to Sequoia and Kings Canyon national parks. Alaska, Allegiant, American, America West, Continental, Delta, Frontier, Hawaiian, Horizon, Mexicana, Northwest, United Express, and US Airways fly here. The closest major airport to Mammoth Lakes is in Reno (though there are tentative plans to expand the Mammoth-Yosemite Airport, which currently only serves charter flights, commercial service to Mammoth is slated to begin December 2007). ➪ the Lake Tahoe chapter for details on the Reno airport.

🖪 **Fresno Yosemite International Airport** ⊠ 5175 E. Clinton Ave., Fresno ☎ 559/621–4500 or 559/498–4095 ⊕ www.flyfresno.org.

BY BUS

Greyhound serves Fresno, Merced, and Visalia from many California cities. VIA Adventures runs five daily buses from Merced to Yosemite Valley; buses also depart daily from Mariposa. The 2½-hour ride from Merced costs $20 round-trip, which includes admission to the park.

🖪 **Greyhound** ☎ 800/231-2222 ⊕ www.greyhound.com. **VIA Adventures** ☎ 888/727-5287 or 209/384-1315 ⊕ www.via-adventures.com.

BY CAR

From San Francisco, Interstate 80 and Interstate 580 are the fastest routes toward the central Sierra Nevada, but avoid driving these routes during weekday rush hours. Through the Central Valley, Interstate 5 and Highway 99 are the fastest north–south routes, but the latter is narrower and has heavy farm-truck traffic. To get to Kings Canyon, plan on a six-hour drive. Two major routes, Highways 180 and 198, intersect with Highway 99 (Highway 180 is closed east of Grant Grove in winter). To get to Yosemite, plan on driving four to five hours. Enter the park either on Highway 140, which is the best route in inclement weather, or on Highway 120, which is the fastest route when the roads are clear. To get to Mammoth Lakes in summer and early fall (or whenever snows aren't blocking Tioga Road), you can travel via Highway 120 (to U.S. 395 south) through the Yosemite high country; the quickest route in winter is Interstate 80 to U.S. 50 to Highway 207 (Kingsbury Grade) to U.S. 395 south; either route takes six to seven hours.

Keep your tank full, especially in winter. Distances between gas stations can be long, and there's no fuel available in Yosemite Valley, Sequoia, or Kings Canyon. If you're traveling from October through April, rain on the coast can mean heavy snow in the mountains. Carry tire chains, and know how to put them on (on Interstate 80 and U.S. 50 you can pay a chain installer $20 to do it for you, but on other routes you'll have to do it yourself). Alternatively, you can rent a four-wheel-drive vehicle with snow tires. Always check road conditions before you leave. Traffic in national parks in summer can be heavy, and there are sometimes travel restrictions.

🚗 **California Road Conditions** ☎ 800/427-7623 ⊕ www.dot.ca.gov/hq/roadinfo. **Sequoia–Kings Canyon Road and Weather Information** ☎ 559/565-3341. **Yosemite Area Road and Weather Conditions** ☎ 209/372-0200.

CAR RENTALS The car-rental outlets closest to the Southern Sierra are at Fresno Yosemite International Airport, where the national chains have outlets. If you're traveling to Mammoth Lakes and the eastern Sierra in winter, the closest agencies are in Reno. *See* Car Rental *in* Smart Travel Tips for national rental-agency phone numbers.

Contacts & Resources

EMERGENCIES

In an emergency dial 911.

🚑 Emergency Services **Mammoth Hospital** ✉ 85 Sierra Park Rd., Mammoth Lakes ☎ 760/934-3311 ⊕ www.mammothhospital.com. **Yosemite Medical Clinic** ✉ Ahwahnee Rd. north of Northside Dr. ☎ 209/372-4637.

TOUR OPTIONS

San Francisco's California Parlor Car Tours serves Yosemite with one-day and overnight trips as well as some rail-bus combinations, though the latter are logistically inconvenient from San Francisco. DNC Parks & Resorts at Yosemite operates guided bus tours of the Yosemite Valley floor daily year-round, plus seasonal tours of Glacier Point and the Mariposa Grove of Big Trees. The company's Grand Tour ($60), offered between June and October, weather permitting, covers the park's highlights.

🚗 **California Parlor Car Tours** ✉ 1255 Post St., #1011, San Francisco 94109 ☎ 415/474-7500 or 800/227-4250 ⊕ www.calpartours.com. **DNC Parks & Resorts at Yosemite** ✉ Box 578, Yosemite National Park 95389 ☎ 209/372-1240 7 or fewer days in advance, 559/252-4848 more than 7 days in advance ⊕ www.yosemitepark.com.

VISITOR INFORMATION

🚌 **Bridgeport Chamber of Commerce** ✆ Box 541, Bridgeport 93517 ☎ 760/932-7500 ⊕ www.bridgeportcalifornia.com. **DNC Parks & Resorts at Yosemite** ✆ Box 578, Yosemite National Park 95389 ☎ 209/372-1000 ⊕ www.yosemitepark.com. **Lee Vining Chamber of Commerce** ✆ Box 29, Lee Vining 93541 ☎ 760/647-6629 ⊕ www.monolake.org/chamber. **Mammoth Lakes Visitors Bureau** ✉ Along Hwy. 203, Main St., near Sawmill Cutoff Rd., Box 48, Mammoth Lakes 93546 ☎ 760/934-2712 or 888/466-2666 ⊕ www.visitmammoth.com. **Mono Lake** ✆ Box 49, Lee Vining 93541 ☎ 760/647-3044 ⊕ www.monolake.org. **Sequoia-Kings Canyon National Park** ✉ Three Rivers, 93271 ☎ 559/565-3341 or 559/565-3134 ⊕ www.nps.gov/seki. **Yosemite National Park** ✆ Information Office, Box 577, Yosemite National Park 95389 ☎ 209/372-0200 or 209/372-0264 ⊕ www.nps.gov/yose. **Yosemite Sierra Visitors Bureau** ✉ 41969 Hwy. 41, Box 1998, Oakhurst 93644 ☎ 559/683-4636 ⊕ www.yosemitethisyear.com.

The Central Valley

WORD OF MOUTH

"A trip through the Forestiere Underground Gardens is a near-magical experience. The tunnels, the exotic trees, the grottoes—it's amazing to think someone actually lived here."

—marie606

8

Updated by
Reed Parsell

AMONG THE WORLD'S MOST FERTILE working lands, the Central Valley is important due to the scale of its food production but, to be brutally honest, it lacks substantial appeal for visitors. For most people, the Central Valley is simply a place to pass through on the way to greater attractions in the north, south, or east. For those willing to invest a little effort, however, California's heartland can be surprisingly rewarding.

The agriculturally rich area is home to a diversity of wildlife. Many telephone posts are crowned by a hawk or kestrel hunting the land below. Vineyards, especially in the northern valley around Lodi, and almond orchards whose white blossoms make February a brighter month are pleasant sights out motorists' windows. In the towns, historical societies display artifacts of the valley's eccentric past; concert halls and restored theaters showcase samplings of contemporary culture; and museums provide a blend of both. Restaurants can be very good, whether they be fancy or mom-and-pop. Country-music enthusiasts will find a lot to appreciate on the radio and on stages, especially in the Bakersfield area. Summer nights spent at one of the valley's minor-league baseball parks—Fresno, Modesto, Stockton, and Bakersfield have teams—can be a relaxing experience. Whether on back roads or main streets, people are not only friendly but proud to help outsiders explore the Central Valley.

The valley's history of being passed over dates back hundreds of years. Until the mid-19th century, the area was a desert. Gold discoveries, starting in the 1850s, sparked the birth of some towns; the arrival of the railroad in following decades spurred the development of others. But it was the coming of water, courtesy of private dams and, in the 1930s, the Central Valley Project, that transformed this land into the country's most vital agricultural region.

As soon as irrigation gave potential to the valley's open acres, the area became a magnet for farmers, ranchers, developers, World War II refugees, and immigrants from places as diverse as Portugal, China, Armenia, and Laos. Today refugees from the state's big cities come in search of cheaper real estate, safer neighborhoods, and more space. With development has come some unsightly sprawl, air pollution, and pressure on crucial water supplies. Nevertheless, the region's cultural diversity and agricultural roots have woven a textured social fabric that has been chronicled by some of the country's finest writers, including Fresno native William Saroyan, Stockton native Maxine Hong Kingston, and *Grapes of Wrath* author John Steinbeck.

Just as these authors found inspiration in a place you cannot view while speeding down the highway, you must invest time and footwork to appreciate the Central Valley. The rewards can be surprising, relaxing . . . even poetic.

Exploring the Central Valley

The 225-mi Central Valley cuts through Kern, Tulare, Kings, Fresno, Madera, Merced, Stanislaus, and San Joaquin counties. It's bounded on the east by the mighty Sierra Nevada and on the west by the smaller coastal ranges. Interstate 5 runs south–north through the valley, as does Highway 99.

About the Restaurants

Fast-food places and chain restaurants dominate valley highways, but away from the main drag, independent and family-owned eateries will awaken your taste buds. Many bistros and fine restaurants take advantage of the local produce and locally raised meats that are the cornerstone of California cuisine. Even simple restaurants produce hearty, tasty fare that often reflects the valley's ethnic mix. Some of the nation's best Mexican restaurants call the valley home. Chinese, Italian, Armenian, and Basque restaurants also are abundant; many serve massive, many-course meals. Although dress at most valley eateries is casual, you won't feel out of place in jacket and tie or cocktail dress at some of the finer establishments.

About the Hotels

The Central Valley has many chain motels and hotels, but independently owned hotels and bed-and-breakfasts also can be found. There's a large selection of upscale lodgings, Victorian-style B&Bs, and places that are simply utilitarian but clean and comfortable.

WHAT IT COSTS				
$$$$	**$$$**	**$$**	**$**	**¢**
RESTAURANTS over $30	$23–$30	$16–$22	$10–$15	under $10
HOTELS over $250	$176–$250	$121–$175	$90–$120	under $90

Restaurant prices are for a main course at dinner, excluding sales tax of 7%–10% (depending on location). Hotel prices are for two people in a standard double room in high season, excluding service charges and 8%–13% tax.

Timing

Spring, when wildflowers are in bloom and the scent of fruit blossoms is in the air, and fall, when the air is brisk and leaves turn red and gold, are the best times to visit. Many of the valley's biggest festivals take place during these seasons. (If you suffer from allergies, though, beware of spring, when stone-fruit trees blossom.) Summer, when temperatures often top 100°F, can be oppressive. June through August, though, are great months to visit area water parks and lakes or to take in the museums, where air-conditioning provides a reprieve from the heat. Many attractions close in winter, which can get cold and dreary. Thick, ground-hugging fog, called tule fog by locals, is a common driving hazard November through February.

SOUTHERN CENTRAL VALLEY

BAKERSFIELD & KERNVILLE

When gold was discovered in Kern County in the 1860s, settlers flocked to the southern end of the Central Valley. Black gold—oil—is now the area's most valuable commodity; the county provides 64% of Califor-

GREAT ITINERARIES

Numbers correspond to the Central Valley and Fresno Area maps.

IF YOU HAVE 1 DAY

Touring the Fresno area is a good strategy if you have only a day to spend in the valley. **Roeding Park 6** ⚑ has a striking tropical rain forest within Chaffee Zoological Gardens; the park's Playland and Storyland are great stops if you're traveling with children. Don't miss the **Forestiere Underground Gardens 12**, on Shaw Avenue. In springtime take the self-guided **Blossom Trail** driving tour through orchards, vineyards, and fields. Along the trail in Reedley is the Mennonite Quilt Center. Depending on your mood and the weather, you can spend part of the afternoon at Wild Water Adventures or visit the **Fresno Metropolitan Museum 7**, whose highlights include an exhibit about author William Saroyan.

IF YOU HAVE 3 DAYS

Start your trip through the Central Valley in **Bakersfield 1** ⚑, with a visit to the Kern County Museum.

Drive north on Highway 99 and west on Highway 122 to drive to **Colonel Allensworth State Historic Park 3**, which is on the site of a now-deserted town founded by African-Americans in 1908. Continue north on Highway 34 to 🖼 **Hanford 5** and stroll around Courthouse Square and China Alley. The next morning proceed to 🖼 **Fresno 6 – 13** via highways 43 and 99 north and spend the day there, as in the one-day itinerary above. In the evening take in a show at Roger Rocka's or the Tower Theatre, both in Fresno's Tower District. On Day 3 continue up Highway 99 and stop off at the Castle Air Museum, north of **Merced 14** in Atwater. **Modesto 15** is a good place to stop for lunch. In the afternoon, choose from a rafting trip on the Stanislaus River near **Oakdale 16**, an hour or two of art appreciation at the Haggin Museum in **Stockton 17**, and a tour of the wineries around **Lodi 18**. Lodi is a pleasant place to overnight.

nia's oil production. Kern is also among the country's five most productive agricultural counties. From the flat plains around Bakersfield, the landscape grows gently hilly and then graduates to mountains as it nears Kernville, which lies in the Kern River valley.

Bakersfield

⚑ **1** *110 mi north of Los Angeles on I–5 and Hwy. 99; 110 mi west of Ridgecrest via Hwy. 14 south and Hwy. 58 west.*

Bakersfield's founder, Colonel Thomas Baker, arrived with the discovery of gold in the nearby Kern River valley in 1851. Now Kern County's biggest city (it has a population of 279,000, which includes the largest Basque community in the United States), Bakersfield probably is best known as Nashville West, a country-music haven and hometown of performers Buck Owens (who died in 2006) and Merle

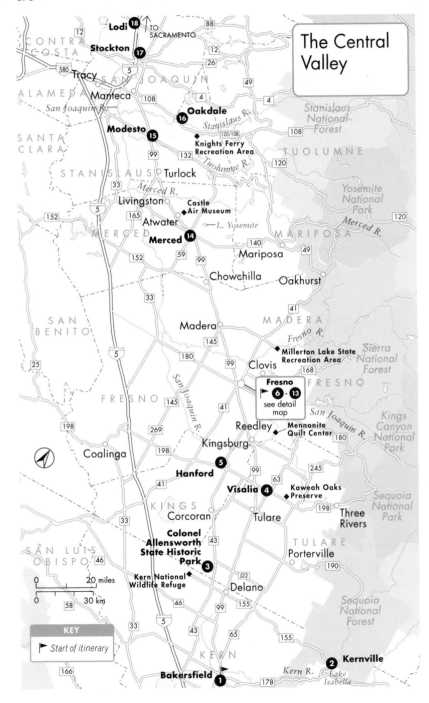

The Central Valley

TO SACRAMENTO

Lodi **18**
Stockton **17**
Tracy

CONTRA COSTA

12
88
12
26
580
5

ALAMEDA
Manteca
108
4
4
San Joaquin R.
SAN JOAQUIN

Stanislaus National Forest

SANTA CLARA

Modesto **15**
Oakdale **16**
Knights Ferry Recreation Area
Stanislaus R.
120/108
108
TUOLUMNE

STANISLAUS
Turlock
99
132
Tuolumne R.
120

33
Merced R.
Livingston
165
Atwater
Castle Air Museum
L. Yosemite
120
MARIPOSA
Merced R.

Yosemite National Park

MERCED
Merced **14**
152
59
99
140
Mariposa
49

Chowchilla
Oakhurst
33
41

SAN BENITO

Madera
MADERA
Fresno R.
145
180
99
Millerton Lake State Recreation Area
Clovis
168
Sierra National Forest

25
FRESNO
145
41
Fresno **6** - **13**
see detail map
San Joaquin R.
FRESNO

198
269
198
Reedley
Mennonite Quilt Center
180
Kings Canyon National Park

Kingsburg
San Joaquin R.
5

Hanford **5**
99
245
Coalinga
41
Visalia **4**
63
Kaweah Oaks Preserve
KINGS
Corcoran
Tulare
198
Three Rivers
Sequoia National Park

Colonel Allensworth State Historic Park
33
43
TULARE
Porterville
190

SAN LUIS OBISPO
46
Kern National Wildlife Refuge
3
J22
Delano
0 — 20 miles
0 — 30 km
58
46
99
155
Sequoia National Forest

33
5
43
65
155
KERN

166
Bakersfield **1**
178
Kern R.
Kernville **2**
Lake Isabella

KEY
► Start of itinerary

Haggard. It also has its own symphony orchestra and two good museums.

★ ☺ The **Kern County Museum and Lori Brock Children's Discovery Center** form one of the Central Valley's top museum complexes. The indoor-outdoor Kern County Museum is set up as an open-air, walk-through historic village with more than 55 restored or re-created buildings dating from the 1860s to the 1940s. "Black Gold: The Oil Experience," a permanent exhibit, shows how oil is created, discovered, extracted, and transformed for various uses. The Children's Discovery Center has hands-on displays and an indoor playground. ⊠ *3801 Chester Ave.* ☎ *661/852–5000* ⊕ *www.kcmuseum.org* ⊡ *$8* ☽ *Mon.–Sat. 10–5, Sun. noon–5.*

★ ☺ At the **California Living Museum,** a combination zoo, botanical garden, and natural-history museum, the emphasis is on zoo. All animal and plant species displayed are native to the state. Within the reptile house lives every species of rattlesnake found in California. The landscaped grounds—in the hills about a 20-minute drive northeast of Bakersfield—also shelter captive bald eagles, tortoises, coyotes, black bears, and foxes. ⊠ *10500 Alfred Harrell Hwy., Hwy. 178 east, then 3½ mi northwest on Alfred Harrell Hwy.* ☎ *661/872–2256* ⊕ *www.calmzoo.org* ⊡ *$6.50* ☽ *Daily 9–5.*

Where to Stay & Eat

$–$$$ ✕ **Uricchio's Trattoria.** This downtown restaurant draws everyone from office workers to oil barons—all attracted by the tasty food and casual atmosphere. *Panini* (Italian pressed sandwiches, served at lunch only), pasta, and Italian-style chicken dishes dominate the menu; the chicken piccata outsells all other offerings. ⊠ *1400 17th St.* ☎ *661/326–8870* ▤ *AE, D, DC, MC, V* ☽ *Closed Sun. No lunch Sat.*

$–$$ ✕ **Woolgrower's Restaurant.** Thick lamb chops, roast lamb, oxtail stew, and shrimp scampi have made this spot popular with locals. All meals are served family-style, so you might share your table with diners you don't know. Meals include vegetables and a potato or rice dish. ⊠ *620 E. 19th St.* ☎ *661/327–9584* ▤ *AE, D, MC, V* ☽ *Closed Sun.*

$ ✕ **Jake's Tex Mex Cafe.** Don't let the cafeteria-style service fool you; this is probably the best lunch place in Bakersfield. The chicken burritos and the chili fries (with meaty chili ladled on top) are superb. For dessert, try the Texas sheet cake or the homemade chocolate-chip cookies. It's open for dinner, too. ⊠ *1710 Oak St.* ☎ *661/322–6380* ⌦ *Reservations not accepted* ▤ *AE, D, MC, V* ☽ *Closed Sun.*

$–$$$ ▥ **Four Points by Sheraton.** Fountains, lush lawns, and exotic plants provide a spectacular setting for this hotel. Occupying 7.5 acres in Bakersfield's business district, it's a mile west of Highway 99. The large rooms come equipped with coffeemakers, irons, hair dryers, and DSL connections. The pool is just shy of Olympic size. ⊠ *5101 California Ave., 93309* ☎ *661/325–9700 or 800/368–7764* ⊟ *661/323–3508* ⊕ *www.fourpoints.com* ⇆ *198 rooms* ⌂ *Cable TV, in-room data ports, pool, gym, hot tub, meeting rooms, airport shuttle, no-smoking rooms* ▤ *AE, D, DC, MC, V.*

¢ ▥ **Quality Inn.** Near downtown in a relatively quiet location off Highway 99, this two-story motel offers good value. Most rooms have king-

8

or queen-size beds, and all have HBO. Some have refrigerators and a patio or a balcony overlooking the heated pool. Complimentary coffee is available all day. ⊠ *1011 Oak St., 93304* ☎ *661/325–0772 or 877/ 424–6423* 🖷 *661/325–4646* ⊕ *www.qualityinn.com* ↪ *89 rooms* ♨ *Some refrigerators, cable TV, Wi-Fi, pool, gym, hot tub, laundry facilities* ⊟ *AE, D, DC, MC, V* ⍩ *BP.*

Nightlife & the Arts

The **Bakersfield Symphony Orchestra** (⊠ 1328 34th St., Suite A ☎ 661/ 323–7928 ⊕ www.bakersfieldsymphony.org) performs classical-music concerts at the convention center from October through May.

Buck Owens' Crystal Palace (⊠ 2800 Buck Owens Blvd. ☎ 661/328–7560 ⊕ www.buckowens.com) is a combination nightclub, restaurant, and showcase of country-music memorabilia. Country-and-western singers perform here, as Owens did countless times before his death in March 2006. A dance floor beckons customers who can still twirl after sampling the menu of steaks, burgers, nachos, and gooey desserts. Entertainment is free on most weeknights; on Friday and Saturday nights, there's a cover charge (usually $6 to $12) for some of the more well-known entertainers.

Sports & the Outdoors

CAR RACING   At **Bakersfield Speedway** (⊠ 5001 N. Chester Ave. ☎ 661/393–3373 ⊕ www.bakersfieldspeedway.com), stock and sprint cars race around a ⅓-mi clay oval track. **Mesa Marin Raceway** (⊠ 11000 Kern Canyon Rd. ☎ 661/397–7333 ⊕ www.mesamarin.com) presents high-speed stock-car, Craftsman Truck, and NASCAR racing on a ½-mi paved oval course.

SKATING   The free skate park at **Beach Park** (⊠ Oak and 21st Sts. ☉ Daily 5 AM–10 PM) has good street skating as well as a relaxing grassy area.

Shopping

Many antiques shops are on 18th and 19th streets between H and R streets, and on H Street between Union and California avenues. **Central Park Antique Mall** (⊠ 701 19th St. ☎ 661/633–1143) has a huge selection. **Great American Antiques** (⊠ 625 19th St. ☎ 661/322–1776) is full of treasures.

Dewar's Candy Shop (⊠ 1120 Eye St. ☎ 661/322–0933) was founded in 1909 and has been owned by the Dewar family ever since. The handdipped chocolate cherries are delicious; so are the Dewar's Chews, a mouthwatering taffy concoction available in peanut butter, peppermint, caramel, and almond flavors. There's also an old-fashioned soda fountain. Dewar's has a second shop in Hollywood.

Kernville

❷ *50 mi from Bakersfield, northeast on Hwy. 178 and north on Hwy. 155.*

The wild and scenic Kern River, which flows through Kernville en route from Mt. Whitney to Bakersfield, delivers some of the most exciting whitewater rafting in the state. Kernville (population 1,700) rests in a mountain valley on both banks of the river and also at the northern tip of Lake Isabella (a dammed portion of the river used as a reservoir and for recreation). By far the most scenic town described in this chapter, Kernville has lodgings, restaurants, and antiques shops. The main streets are lined with Old West–style buildings, reflecting Kernville's heritage as a rough-and-tumble gold-mining town once known as Whiskey Flat. (Present-day Kernville dates from the 1950s, when it was moved upriver to make room for Lake Isabella.) The road from Bakersfield includes stretches where the rushing river is on one side and granite cliffs are on the other.

Where to Stay & Eat

$–$$ ✕ **That's Italian.** For northern Italian cuisine in a typical trattoria, this is the spot. Try the braised lamb shanks in a Chianti wine sauce or the linguine with clams, mussels, calamari, and shrimp in a white-wine clam sauce. ⊠ *9 Big Blue Rd.* ☎ *760/376–6020* ⊟ *AE, D, MC, V.*

$$–$$$$ 🏨 **Whispering Pines Lodge.** Perched on the banks of the Kern River, this 8-acre property gives you a variety of overnight options. Units are motel-style or in duplex bungalows and all have fireplaces, coffeemakers, and king-size beds. Some have full kitchens, queen-size sleepers, and whirlpool tubs. ⊠ *13745 Sierra Way, 93238* ☎ *760/376–3733 or 877/ 241–4100* 🖷 *760/376–6513* ⊕ *www.kernvalley.com/whisperingpines* ➲ *17 rooms* ⚐ *Some kitchenettes, refrigerators, cable TV, pool* ⊟ *AE, D, MC, V* ⊺◉⊺ *BP.*

Sports & the Outdoors

BOATING &
WINDSURFING
The Lower Kern River, which extends from Lake Isabella to Bakersfield and beyond, is open for fishing year-round. Catches include rainbow trout, catfish, smallmouth bass, crappie, and bluegill. Lake Isabella is popular with anglers, water-skiers, sailors, and windsurfers. Its shoreline marinas have boats for rent, bait and tackle, and moorings. **North Fork Marina** (☎ 760/376–1812) is in Wofford Heights, on the lake's north shore. **French Gulch Marina** (☎ 760/379–8774) is near the dam on Lake Isabella's west shore.

WHITE-WATER
RAFTING
The three sections of the Kern River—known as the Lower Kern, Upper Kern, and the Forks—add up to nearly 50 mi of white water, ranging from Class I (easy) to Class V (expert). The Lower and Upper Kern are the most popular and accessible sections. Organized trips can last from one hour (for as little as $20) to more than two days. Rafting season usually runs from late spring until the end of summer. **Kern River Tours** (☎ 800/844–7238 ⊕ www.kernrivertours.com) leads several rafting tours from half-day trips to three days of navigating Class V rapids, and also arranges for mountain-bike trips.

Mountain & River Adventures (☎760/376–6553 or 800/861–6553 ⊕www. mtnriver.com) gives calm-water kayaking tours as well as white-water rafting trips. Half-day Class II and III white-water rafting trips are emphasized at **Sierra South** (☎ 760/376–3745 or 800/457–2082 ⊕ www. sierrasouth.com), which also offers kayaking classes and calm-water excursions.

8

MID-CENTRAL VALLEY
FROM VISALIA TO FRESNO

The Mid-Central Valley extends over three counties—Tulare, Kings, and Fresno. Historic Hanford and bustling Visalia are off the tourist-traffic radar but have their charms. From Visalia, Highway 198 winds east 35 mi to Generals Highway, which passes through Sequoia and Kings Canyon national parks. Highway 180 snakes east 55 mi to Sequoia and Kings Canyon. From Fresno, Highway 41 leads north 95 mi to Yosemite National Park.

Colonel Allensworth State Historic Park

★ ❸ *45 mi north of Bakersfield on Hwy. 43.*

A former slave who became the country's highest-ranking black military officer of his time founded Allensworth—the only California town settled, governed, and financed by African-Americans—in 1908. After enjoying early prosperity, the town was plagued by hardships and eventually was deserted. Its rebuilt buildings reflect the few years in which it thrived. Festivities each October commemorate the town's rededication. ⊠ *4129 Palmer Ave.* ☎ *661/849–3433* ⊕ *www.cal-parks.ca.gov* ⊡ *$4 per car* ☉ *Daily sunrise–sunset, visitor center open on request, buildings open by appointment.*

OFF THE BEATEN PATH

KERN NATIONAL WILDLIFE REFUGE – Snowy egrets, peregrine falcons, warblers, dozens of types of ducks, and other birds inhabit the marshes and wetlands here from November through April. Follow the 6½-mi loop drive (pick up maps at the entrance) to find good viewing spots, but beware that waterfowl hunting is allowed Wednesday and Saturday, October through January. ⊠ *10811 Corcoran Rd., 18 mi west of Delano on Hwy. 155, Garces Hwy.; from Allensworth take Hwy. 43 south to Hwy. 155 west* ☎ *661/725–2767* ⊕ *www.natureali.org/KNWR.htm* ⊡ *Free* ☉ *Daily sunrise–sunset.*

Visalia

❹ *40 mi north of Colonel Allensworth State Historic Park on Hwy. 99 and east on Hwy. 198; 75 mi north of Bakersfield via Hwy. 99 north and Hwy. 198 east.*

Visalia's combination of a reliable agricultural economy and civic pride has yielded perhaps the most vibrant downtown in the Central Valley. A clear day's view of the Sierra from Main Street is spectacular, if sadly rare, and even Sunday night can find the streets busy with pedestrians. Founded in 1852, the town contains many historic homes; ask for a free guide at the **visitor center** (⊠ 220 N. Santa Fe St., 93921 ☎ 559/734–5876 ☉ Mon. 10–5, Tues.–Fri. 8:30–5).

The **Chinese Cultural Center,** housed in a pagoda-style building, mounts exhibits about Asian art and culture. ⊠ *500 S. Akers Rd., at Hwy. 198* ☎ *559/625–4545* ⊡ *Free* ☉ *Wed.–Sun. 11–6.*

In oak-shaded **Mooney Grove Park** you can picnic alongside duck ponds, rent a boat for a ride around the lagoon, and view a replica of the famous *End of the Trail* statue. The original, designed by James Earl Fraser for the 1915 Panama-Pacific International Exposition, is now in the Cowboy Hall of Fame in Oklahoma. ⊠ *27000 S. Mooney Blvd., 5 mi south of downtown* ☎ *559/733–6291* 🖀 *$6 per car, free in winter, dates vary* ☉ *Late May–early Sept., weekdays 8–7, weekends 8 AM–9 PM; early Sept.–Oct. and Mar.–late May, Mon., Thurs., and Fri. 8–5, weekends 8–7; Nov.–Feb., Thurs.–Mon. 8–5.*

The indoor-outdoor **Tulare County Museum** contains several re-created environments from the pioneer era. Also on display are Yokuts tribal artifacts (basketry, arrowheads, clamshell-necklace currency) as well as saddles, guns, dolls, quilts, and gowns. ⊠ *Mooney Grove Park, 27000 S. Mooney Blvd., 5 mi south of downtown* ☎ *559/733–6616* 🖀 *Free with park entrance fee of $6* ☉ *Weekdays 10–4, weekends 1–4.*

Trails at the 324-acre **Kaweah Oaks Preserve,** a wildlife sanctuary off the main road to Sequoia National Park, lead past oak, sycamore, cottonwood, and willow trees. Among the 125 bird species you might spot are hawks, hummingbirds, and great blue herons. Lizards, coyotes, and cottontails also live here. ⊠ *Follow Hwy. 198 for 7 mi east of Visalia, turn north on Rd. 182, and proceed ½ mi to gate on left side* ☎ *559/738–0211* ⊕ *www.sequoiariverlands.org* 🖀 *Free* ☉ *Daily sunrise–sunset.*

Where to Stay & Eat

$$–$$$$ ✕ **The Vintage Press.** Built in 1966, the Vintage Press is the best restaurant in the Central Valley. Cut-glass doors and bar fixtures decorate the artfully designed rooms. The California–continental cuisine includes dishes such as crispy veal sweetbreads with a port-wine sauce, and a bacon-wrapped filet mignon stuffed with mushrooms. The chocolate Grand Marnier cake is a standout among the homemade desserts and ice creams. The wine list has more than 900 selections. ⊠ *216 N. Willis St.* ☎ *559/733–3033* ▤ *AE, DC, MC, V.*

Fodor'sChoice
★

$–$$$ ✕ **Café 225.** This downtown favorite combines high ceilings and warm yellow walls with soft chatter and butcher-papered tables to create an elegance that's relaxed enough for kids. The basic menu of pastas and grilled items is highlighted with unusual treats, such as *scusami* (calzone with melting Gorgonzola and tomato, basil, and garlic). ⊠ *225 W. Main St.* ☎ *559/733–2967* ▤ *AE, D, DC, MC, V* ☉ *Closed Sun.*

¢–$$$ ✕ **Henry Salazar's.** Traditional Mexican food with a contemporary twist is served at this restaurant that uses fresh ingredients from local farms. Bring your appetite if you expect to finish the Burrito Fantastico, a large flour tortilla stuffed with your choice of meat, beans, and chili sauce, and smothered with melted Monterey Jack cheese. Another signature dish is grilled salmon with lemon-butter sauce. Colorfully painted walls, soft reflections from candles in wall niches, and color-coordinated tablecloths and napkins make the atmosphere cozy and restful. ⊠ *123 W. Main St.* ☎ *559/741–7060* ▤ *AE, D, MC, V.*

$ 🛏 **Ben Maddox House.** Housed in a building dating to 1876, this homey B&B offers the best of all worlds: plush beds, a cool swimming pool, and excellent service remind you you're on vacation; private bathrooms and dining tables on the sunny porch make the surroundings homey and comfortable. The Water Tower Room has its own sitting area, and all rooms have wireless Internet access. ⊠ *601 N. Encina St., 93291* ☎ *559/739–0721 or 800/401–9800* 🖷 *559/625–0420* ⊕ *www.benmaddoxhouse.com* ➷ *5 rooms* ⚭ *Cable TV, in-room data ports, Wi-Fi, pool; no smoking* ⊟ *AE, D, MC, V* ⦿⦿ *BP.*

$ ⊡ **The Spalding House.** This restored colonial revival B&B is decked out with antiques, Oriental rugs, handcrafted woodwork, and glass doors. The house, built in 1901, has suites with separate sitting rooms and private baths. The quiet neighborhood, also home to the Ben Maddox House, offers a place for one of life's simple pleasures: an evening walk on lovely, tree-lined streets. ⊠ *631 N. Encina St., 93291* ☎ *559/739–7877* 🖷 *559/625–0902* ⊕ *www.thespaldinghouse.com* ➷ *3 suites* ⚭ *No room phones, no room TVs, no smoking* ⊟ *AE, MC, V* ⦿⦿ *BP.*

Hanford

★ ❺ *20 mi west of Visalia on Hwy. 198; 43 mi north of Colonel Allensworth State Historic Park on Hwy. 43.*

Founded in 1877 as a Southern Pacific Railroad stop, Hanford had one of California's largest Chinatowns—the Chinese came to help build the railroads and stayed on to farm. You can take a self-guided walking tour with the help of a free brochure, or take a driving tour in a restored 1930s Studebaker fire truck ($35 for up to 15 people) through the **Hanford Visitor Agency** (☎ 559/582–5024 ⊕ www.visithanford.com). One tour explores the restored buildings of Courthouse Square, whose art-deco Hanford Auditorium is a visual standout; another heads to narrow China Alley. If you have specific interests, a tour can also be designed for you.

The **Hanford Carnegie Museum** displays fashions, furnishings, toys, and military artifacts that tell the region's story. The living-history museum is inside the former Carnegie Library, a Romanesque building dating from 1905. ⊠ *109 E. 8th St.* ☎ *559/584–1367* ▨ *$2* ⊙ *Wed.–Sat. 10–2.*

A first-floor museum in the 1893 **Taoist Temple** displays photos, furnishings, and kitchenware from Hanford's once-bustling Chinatown. The second-floor temple, largely unchanged for a century, contains altars, carvings, and ceremonial staves. You can visit as part of a guided tour at noon on the first Saturday of the month, or by appointment. ⊠ *12 China Alley* ☎ *559/582–4508* ▨ *Free; donations welcome.*

Where to Stay & Eat

$$–$$$ ✕ **The Purple Potato.** With the recent closing of Imperial Dynasty, this modern, colorful restaurant has become what locals say is the best restaurant in town. The broad menu, which includes steaks, pasta, and poultry, draws raves for its shrimp scampi and pan-seared scallops. The wine list is extensive. ⊠ *A few blocks west of downtown, 601 W. 7th St.* ☎ *559/587–4568* ⊟ *AE, D, MC, V* ⊙ *No lunch weekends.*

¢–$ ✕ **La Fiesta.** Mexican-American families, farmworkers, and farmers all eat here, polishing off traditional Mexican dishes such as enchiladas and tacos. The Fiesta Special—for two or more—includes nachos, garlic shrimp, shrimp in a spicy red sauce, clams, and two pieces of top sirloin. ⊠ *106 N. Green St.* ☎ *559/583–8775* ▭ *AE, D, MC, V.*

★ ¢-$$ 🏠 **Irwin Street Inn.** This inn is one of the few lodgings in the valley that warrants a detour. Four tree-shaded, restored Victorian homes have been converted into spacious accommodations with comfortable rooms and suites. Most have antique armoires, dark-wood detailing, lead-glass windows, and four-poster beds; bathrooms have old-fashioned tubs, brass fixtures, and marble basins. ⊠ *522 N. Irwin St., 93230* ☎ *559/583–8000 or 866/583–7378* 📠 *559/583–8793* ⤺ *24 rooms, 3 suites* 🏃 *Restaurant, pool* ▭ *AE, D, DC, MC, V* ⦿ *CP.*

Nightlife & the Arts

The restored Moorish Castilian–style **Hanford Fox Theatre** (⊠ 326 N. Irwin St. ☎ 559/584–7823 ⊕ www.foxhanford.com) was built as a movie palace in 1929. The 1,000-seat venue is now host to a variety of live performances, including jazz, country, pop, and comedy.

Fresno

35 mi north of Hanford via Hwys. 43 and 99 north.

Sprawling Fresno, with more than 450,000 people, is the center of the richest agricultural county in the United States. Cotton, grapes, and tomatoes are among the major crops; poultry and milk are also important. One of the city's most important products, Pulitzer Prize–winning playwright and novelist William Saroyan (*The Time of Your Life, The Human Comedy*), was born here in 1908. About 75 ethnic groups, including Armenians, Laotians, and Indians, call Fresno home. The city has a burgeoning arts scene, several public parks, and an abundance of low-price restaurants serving tasty food. The Tower District—with its chic restaurants, coffeehouses, and boutiques—is the trendy spot.

☁ ⊳ ❻ Tree-shaded **Roeding Park** is a place of respite on hot summer days; it has picnic areas, playgrounds, tennis courts, horseshoe pits, and a zoo. The most striking exhibit at **Chaffee Zoological Gardens** (☎ 559/498–2671 ⊕ www.chaffeezoo.org 🎟 $7 🕐 Feb.–Oct., daily 9–4; Nov.–Jan., daily 10–3) is the tropical rain forest, where you'll encounter exotic birds along the paths and bridges. Elsewhere you'll find tigers, grizzly bears, sea lions, tule elk, camels, elephants, and hooting siamangs. Also here are a high-tech reptile house and a petting zoo. A train, little race cars, paddleboats, and other rides for kids are among the amusements that operate March through November at **Playland** (☎ 559/233–3980 🕐 Wed.–Fri. 11–5, weekends 10–6). Children can explore attractions with fairy-tale themes at **Storyland** (☎ 559/264–2235 🕐 Weekdays 11–5, weekends 10–6), which is also open March through November. ⊠ *Olive and Belmont Aves.* ☎ *559/498–1551* 🎟 *$1 per vehicle park entrance; Playland rides require tokens; $4 for Storyland.*

☁ ❼ The **Fresno Metropolitan Museum,** which was extensively renovated in 2006, mounts art, history, and hands-on science exhibits, many of them quite innovative. The William Saroyan History Gallery presents a riveting in-

troduction in words and pictures to the author's life and times. ✉ *1515 Van Ness Ave.* ☎ *559/441–1444* ⊕ *www.fresnomet.org* 🎟 *$8, $1 Thurs. nights after 5* ◷ *Tues., Wed., and Fri.–Sun. 11–5, Thurs. 11–8.*

8 The **Legion of Valor Museum** is a real find for military history buffs of all ages. It has German bayonets and daggers, a Japanese Namby pistol, a Gatling gun, and an extensive collection of Japanese, German, and American uniforms. The staff is extremely enthusiastic. ✉ *2425 Fresno St.* ☎ *559/498–0510* ⊕ *www.legionofvalor.com/museum.php* 🎟 *Free* ◷ *Mon.–Sat. 10–3.*

9 Inside a restored 1889 Victorian, the **Meux Home Museum** displays furnishings typical of early Fresno. Guided tours proceed from the front parlor to the backyard carriage house. ✉ *Tulare and R Sts.* ☎ *559/233–8007* ⊕ *www.meux.mus.ca.us* 🎟 *$5* ◷ *Fri.–Sun. noon–3:30.*

10 The **Fresno Art Museum** exhibits American, Mexican, and French art; highlights of the permanent collection include pre-Columbian works and graphic art from the postimpressionist period. The 152-seat Bonner Auditorium is the site of lectures, films, and concerts. ✉ *Radio Park, 2233 N. 1st St.* ☎ *559/441–4221* ⊕ *www.fresnoartmuseum.org* 🎟 *$4; free Tues.* ◷ *Tues., Wed., and Fri.–Sun. 11–5, Thurs. 11–8.*

★ ⓫ **Woodward Park,** which consists of 300 acres of jogging trails, picnic areas, and playgrounds in the northern reaches of the city, is especially pretty in the spring, when plum and cherry trees, magnolias, and camellias bloom. Outdoor concerts take place in summer. The **Shinzen Friendship Garden** has a teahouse, a koi pond, arched bridges, a waterfall, and Japanese art. ⊠ *Audubon Dr. and Friant Rd.* ☎ *559/621–2900* 💲 *$3 per car Feb.–Oct.; additional $3 for Shinzen Garden* ☉ *Apr.–Oct., daily 7 AM–10 PM; Nov.–Mar., daily 7–7.*

★ ☾ ⓬ Sicilian immigrant Baldasare Forestiere spent four decades (1906–46) carving out the **Forestiere Underground Gardens,** a subterranean realm of rooms, tunnels, grottoes, alcoves, and arched passageways that extends for more than 10 acres beneath busy, mall-pocked Shaw Avenue. Only a fraction of Forestiere's prodigious output is on view, but you can tour his underground living quarters, including bedrooms (one with a fireplace), the kitchen, living room, and bath, as well as a fishpond and an aquarium. Skylights allow exotic full-grown fruit trees, including one that bears seven kinds of citrus as a result of grafting, to flourish more than 20 feet belowground. Reservations are recommended. ⊠ *5021 W. Shaw Ave., 2 blocks east of Hwy. 99* ☎ *559/271–0734* ⊕ *www. undergroundgardens.com* 💲 *$10* ☉ *Tours weekends at noon and 2. Call for other tour times.*

⓭ The drive along palm-lined Kearney Boulevard is one of the best reasons to visit the **Kearney Mansion Museum,** which stands in shaded 225-acre **Kearney Park.** The century-old home of M. Theo Kearney, Fresno's onetime "raisin king," is accessible only by taking a guided 45-minute tour. ⊠ *7160 W. Kearney Blvd., 6 mi west of Fresno* ☎ *559/441–0862* 💲 *Museum $5, park entrance $4, waived for museum visitors* ☉ *Park 7 AM–10 PM; museum tours Fri.–Sun. at 1, 2, and 3.*

8

OFF THE
BEATEN
PATH

BLOSSOM TRAIL – This 62-mi self-guided driving tour takes in Fresno-area orchards, citrus groves, and vineyards during spring blossom season. Pick up a route map at the **Fresno City & County Convention and Visitors Bureau** (⊠ 848 M St., Fresno 93721 ☎ 559/233–0836 or 800/788–0836 ⊕ www.fresnocvb.org). The route passes through small towns and past rivers, lakes, and canals. The most colorful and aromatic time to go is from late February to mid-March, when almond, plum, apple, orange, lemon, apricot, and peach blossoms shower the landscape with shades of white, pink, and red. Directional and crop identification signs mark the trail. Allow at least two to three hours for the tour.

Along the Blossom Trail, roughly halfway between Fresno and Visalia, the colorful handiwork of local quilters is on display at the **Mennonite Quilt Center** (⊠ 1012 G St. [take Manning Ave. exit off Hwy. 99 and head east 12 mi] Reedley ☎ 559/638–3560). The center is open weekdays 10 to 5 and Saturday 10 to 4, but try to visit on Monday (except holidays) between 8 and noon, when two dozen quilters stitch, patch, and chat over coffee. Prime viewing time—with the largest number of quilts—is in February and March, before the center's early-April auction. Ask a docent to take you to the locked upstairs room, where most of the quilts hang; she'll explain the fine points of patterns such as the Log Cabin Romance, the Dahlia, and the Snowball-Star. Admission is free.

Where to Stay & Eat

$–$$$ ✕ **Tahoe Joe's.** This restaurant is known for its steaks—rib eye, strip, or filet mignon. Other selections include the slow-roasted prime rib, center-cut pork chops, and chicken breast served with a whiskey peppercorn sauce. The baked potato that accompanies almost every dish is loaded tableside with your choice of butter, sour cream, chives, and bacon bits. Tahoe Joe's has two Fresno locations. ⊠ *7006 N. Cedar Ave.* ☎ *559/299–9740* ⌲ *Reservations not accepted* ⊟ *AE, D, MC, V* ⊠ *2700 W. Shaw Ave.* ☎ *559/277–8028* ⌲ *Reservations not accepted* ⊟ *AE, D, MC, V* ⊗ *No lunch.*

$–$$ ✕ **La Rocca's Ristorante Italiano.** The sauces that top these pasta and meat dishes will make your taste buds sing. The rich tomato sauce, which comes with or without meat, is fresh and tangy. The marsala sauce—served on either chicken or veal—is rich but not overpowering. Typical red-sauce dishes such as spaghetti, rigatoni, and lasagna are offered here, but you'll also be happily surprised with more adventurous offerings such as the bowtie pasta with cream, peas, bacon, tomato sauce, and olive oil. Pizzas also are served. ⊠ *6735 N. 1st St.* ☎ *559/431–1278* ⊟ *AE, MC, V* ⊗ *No lunch weekends.*

$ ✕ **Irene's.** Downtown workers pack this Tower District restaurant at lunchtime. Handmade, half-pound burgers are the most popular, and most filling, items on the menu. Other popular dishes include the smoked ham and melted Swiss cheese sandwich served on a hard roll, and fresh salads. For breakfast, homemade granola, huge buttermilk pancakes, and the Denver omelet (with ham, onions, and green peppers) will fill up even those with the most hearty appetites. ⊠ *747 E. Olive Ave.* ☎ *559/237–9919* ⊟ *AE, D, MC, V.*

$$ ▥ **Piccadilly Inn Shaw.** This two-story property has 7½ attractively landscaped acres and a big swimming pool. The sizeable rooms have king- and queen-size beds, robes, ironing boards, and coffeemakers; some have fireplaces and wireless Internet access. ⊠ *2305 W. Shaw Ave., 93711* ☎ *559/226–3850* ⊟ *559/226–2448* ⊕ *www.piccadillyinn.com/west-shaw* ⇗ *194 rooms, 5 suites* ⌂ *Restaurant, some microwaves, refrigerators, cable TV, in-room data ports, Wi-Fi, pool, gym, hot tub, laundry facilities, laundry service, business services, meeting rooms, no-smoking rooms* ⊟ *AE, D, DC, MC, V.*

¢–$ ▥ **La Quinta Inn.** Rooms are ample at this basic three-story motel near downtown. Most rooms have large desks that prove helpful for business travelers. ⊠ *2926 Tulare St., 93721* ☎ *559/442–1110 or 866/725–1661* ⊟ *559/237–0415* ⇗ *129 rooms* ⌂ *Some microwaves, some refrigerators, cable TV, in-room data ports, pool, gym, no-smoking rooms* ⊟ *AE, D, DC, MC, V* ◎ *CP.*

Nightlife & the Arts

The **Fresno Philharmonic Orchestra** (☎ 559/261–0600 ⊕ www.fresnophil. org) performs classical concerts (sometimes pops) on weekends, usually at the **William Saroyan Theatre** (⊠ 700 M St.), from September through June. **Roger Rocka's Dinner Theater** (⊠ 1226 N. Wishon Ave. ☎ 559/266–

9494 or 800/371–4747 ⊕ www.rogerrockas.com), in the Tower District, stages six Broadway-style musicals a year. The **Tower Theatre for the Performing Arts** (⊠ 815 E. Olive Ave. ☎ 559/485–9050 ⊕ www.towertheatrefresno.org) has given its name to the trendy Tower District of theaters, clubs, restaurants, and cafés. The restored 1930s art-deco movie house presents theater, ballet, concerts, and other cultural events year-round.

Sports & the Outdoors

Kings River Expeditions (⊠ 211 N. Van Ness Ave. ☎ 559/233–4881 or 800/846–3674 ⊕ www.kingsriver.com) arranges one- and two-day white-water rafting trips on the Kings River. **Wild Water Adventures** (⊠ 11413 E. Shaw Ave., Clovis ☎ 559/299–9453 or 800/564–9453 ⊕ www.wildwater.net ⊡ $23, $16 after 4 PM), a 52-acre water-theme park about 10 mi east of Fresno, is open from late May to early September.

Shopping

Old Town Clovis (⊠ Upper Clovis Ave., Clovis) is an area of restored brick buildings with numerous antiques shops and art galleries (along with restaurants and saloons). Be warned, though: not much here is open on Sunday. Head east on Fresno's Herndon Avenue about 10 mi, and then turn right onto Clovis Avenue.

NORTH CENTRAL VALLEY
FROM MERCED TO LODI

8

The northern section of the valley cuts through Merced, Madera, Stanislaus, and San Joaquin counties, from the flat, abundantly fertile terrain between Merced and Modesto north to the edges of the Sacramento River delta and the fringes of the Gold Country. If you're heading to Yosemite National Park from northern California, chances are you'll pass through (or very near) at least one of these gateway cities.

Merced

 50 mi north of Fresno on Hwy. 99.

Thanks to a branch of the University of California opening in 2005 and an aggressive community redevelopment plan, the downtown of county seat Merced is coming back to life. The transformation is not yet complete, but there are promising signs: a brewpub, several boutiques, a multiplex, the restoration of numerous historic buildings, and foot traffic won back from outlying strip malls.

Even if you don't go inside, be sure to swing by the **Merced County Courthouse Museum.** The three-story former courthouse, built in 1875, is a striking example of Victorian Italianate style. The upper two floors are a museum of early Merced history. Highlights include ornate restored courtrooms and an 1870 Chinese temple with carved redwood altars. *⊠ 21st and N Sts. ☎ 209/723–2401 ⊕ www.mercedmuseum.org ⊡ Free ⊙ Wed.–Sun. 1–4.*

The **Merced Multicultural Arts Center** displays paintings, sculpture, and photography. The Big Valley Arts & Culture Festival, which celebrates the area's ethnic diversity and children's creativity, is held here in late September or early October. ⊠ *645 W. Main St.* ☎ *209/388–1090* ⊕ *www.artsmerced.org* ☑ *Free* ☉ *Weekdays 9–5, Sat. 10–2.*

OFF THE BEATEN PATH

MILLERTON LAKE STATE RECREATION AREA – This lake at the top of Friant Dam is a great place for boating, fishing, camping, and summertime swimming. The lake and its surrounding hills are wintering grounds for bald eagles, and boat tours are available to view the birds between December and February. ⊠ *5290 Millerton Rd., 20 mi northeast of Fresno via Hwy. 41 and Hwy. 145, Friant* ☎ *559/822–2225, 559/822–2332 for tour information* ☑ *$7 per car* ☉ *Daily Oct.–Mar., 6 AM–6 PM; Apr.–Sept., 6 AM–10 PM.*

Where to Stay & Eat

$$–$$$ ✕ **The Branding Iron.** Beef is what this restaurant is all about. It's a favorite among farmers and ranchers looking for a place to refuel as they travel through cattle country. Try the juicy cut of prime rib paired with potato and Parmesan-cheese bread. California cattle brands decorate the walls, and when the weather is nice, cooling breezes refresh diners on the outdoor patio. ⊠ *640 W. 16th St.* ☎ *209/722–1822* ⊕ *www. thebrandingiron-merced.com* ☰ *AE, MC, V* ☉ *No lunch weekends.*

★ **$–$$$** ✕ **DeAngelo's.** This restaurant isn't just the best in Merced—it's one of the best in the Central Valley. Chef Vincent DeAngelo, a graduate of the Culinary Institute of America, brings his considerable skill to everything from basic ravioli to calamari steak topped with two prawns. Half the restaurant is occupied by a new bar-bistro with its own menu, which includes brick-oven pizza. The delicious crusty bread comes from the Golden Sheath bakery, in Watsonville. ⊠ *350 W. Main St.* ☎ *209/383–3020* ⊕ *www.deangelosrestaurant.com* ☰ *AE, D, MC, V* ☉ *No lunch weekends.*

¢–$ ✕ **Main Street Café.** This bright downtown café dishes up tasty breakfast and lunch fare. Sandwiches (try "The Chicago"—beef is topped with onion, roasted red pepper, garlic, mayonnaise, provolone, and pepperoncini) are served with tasty side salads. You can also get pastries, along with espresso or cappuccino. ⊠*460 W. Main St.* ☎*209/725–1702* ☰*AE, MC, V* ☉ *Closed Sun. No dinner.*

$–$$ ▦ **Hooper House Bear Creek Inn.** This 1931 neocolonial home stands regally at the corner of M Street. The immaculately landscaped 1½-acre property has fruit trees and grapevines, and the house is appointed in well-chosen antiques and big, soft beds. Breakfast (which can be served in your room) is hearty and imaginative, featuring locally grown foods such as fried sweet potatoes and black walnuts. Across the street is a walking–bicycling trail that runs for a few miles beside the creek. ⊠ *575 W. N. Bear Creek Dr., at M St., 95348* ☎ *209/723–3991* ☎ *209/723–7123* ⊕ *www.hooperhouse.com* ⇔ *3 rooms, 1 suite, 1 cottage* ⚹ *Cable TV, in-room data ports, no-smoking rooms* ☰ *AE, D, MC, V* ⊗ *BP.*

Sports & the Outdoors

At **Lake Yosemite Regional Park** (⊠ N. Lake Rd. off Yosemite Ave., 5 mi northeast of Merced ☎ 209/385–7426 ☑ $6 per car late May–early

Sept.), you can boat, swim, windsurf, water-ski, and fish on a 387-acre reservoir. Paddleboat rentals and picnic areas are available.

EN
ROUTE

Heading north on Highway 99 from Merced, stop at the outdoor **Castle Air Museum**, adjacent to the former Castle Air Force Base (now Castle Airport). You can stroll among fighter planes and other historic military aircraft. The 47 restored vintage war birds include the B-25 Mitchell medium-range bomber (best known for the Jimmy Doolittle raid on Tokyo after the attack on Pearl Harbor) and the speedy SR-71 Blackbird, used for reconnaissance over Vietnam and Libya. ☒ *Santa Fe Ave. and Buhach Rd., 6 mi north of Merced, take Buhach Rd. exit off Hwy. 99 in Atwater and follow signs, Atwater* ☏ *209/723–2178* ⊕ *www.elite.net/castle-air* ☒ *$8* ☾ *Apr.–Sept., daily 9–5; Oct.–Mar., Wed.–Mon. 10–4.*

Modesto

⑮ *38 mi north of Merced on Hwy. 99.*

Modesto, a gateway to Yosemite and the southern reaches of the Gold Country, was founded in 1870 to serve the Central Pacific Railroad. The frontier town was originally to be named Ralston, after a railroad baron, but as the story goes, he modestly declined—thus the name Modesto. The Stanislaus County seat, a tree-lined city of 180,000, is perhaps best known as the site of the annual Modesto Invitational Track Meet and Relays and birthplace of film producer-director George Lucas, creator of the *Star Wars* film series.

The **Modesto Arch** (☒ 9th and I Sts.) bears the city's motto: WATER, WEALTH, CONTENTMENT, HEALTH. The prosperity that water brought to Modesto has attracted people from all over the world. The city holds a well-attended **International Heritage Festival** (☏ 209/521–3852) in early October that celebrates the cultures, crafts, and cuisines of many nationalities. You can witness the everyday abundance of the Modesto area at the **Blue Diamond Growers Store** (☒ 4800 Sisk Rd. ☏ 209/545–3222), which offers free samples, shows a film about almond growing, and sells many roasts and flavors of almonds, as well as other nuts.

★ A rancher and banker built the 1883 **McHenry Mansion**, the city's sole surviving original Victorian home. The Italianate-style mansion has been decorated to reflect Modesto life in the late 19th century. Its period-appropriate wallpaper is especially impressive. ☒ *15th and I Sts.* ☏ *209/577–5341* ⊕ *www.mchenrymuseum.org* ☒ *Free* ☾ *Sun.–Thurs. 12:30–4.*

The **McHenry Museum of Arts** is a jumbled repository of early Modesto and Stanislaus County memorabilia, including re-creations of an old-time dentist's office, a blacksmith's shop, a one-room schoolhouse, an extensive doll collection, and a general store stocked with period goods such as hair crimpers and corsets. ☒ *14th and I Sts.* ☏ *209/577–5366* ☒ *Free* ☾ *Tues.–Sun. noon–4.*

8

Where to Stay & Eat

$$–$$$$ ✕ **Hazel's Elegant Dining.** Hazel's is *the* special-occasion restaurant in Modesto. The seven-course dinners include continental entrées served with appetizer, soup, salad, pasta, and dessert. Members of the Gallo family, which owns much vineyard land in the Central Valley, eat here often, perhaps because the wine cellar's offerings are so comprehensive. ⊠ *431 12th St.* ☎ *209/578–3463* ⊕ *www.hazelsmodesto.com* ▤ *AE, D, DC, MC, V* ⊗ *Closed Sun. and Mon. No lunch Sat.*

$$–$$$ ✕ **Tresetti's World Caffe.** An intimate setting with white tablecloths and contemporary art draws diners to this eatery—part wineshop (with 500-plus selections), part restaurant—with a seasonally changing menu. For a small supplemental fee, the staff will uncork any wine you select from the shop. The Cajun-style crab cakes, served year-round, are outstanding. ⊠ *927 11th St.* ☎ *209/572–2990* ⊕ *www.tresetti.com* ▤ *AE, D, DC, MC, V* ⊗ *Closed Sun.*

$–$$ ✕ **St. Stan's.** Modesto's renowned microbrewery makes St. Stan's beers. The 14 on tap include the delicious Whistle Stop pale ale and Red Sky ale. The restaurant is casual and serves good corned-beef sandwiches loaded with sauerkraut as well as a tasty beer-sausage nibbler. ⊠ *821 L St.* ☎ *209/524–2337* ▤ *AE, MC, V* ⊗ *Closed Sun.*

$$–$$$ ▦ **Doubletree Hotel.** Modesto's largest hotel rises 15 stories over the downtown area. Each room has a coffeemaker, hair dryer, iron, and desk. The convention center is adjacent, and St. Stan's brewpub is across the street. ⊠ *1150 9th St., 95354* ☎ *209/526–6000 or 800/222–8733* ▧ *209/526–6096* ⊕ *www.doubletree.com* ⇥ *258 rooms* ⌂ *Café, room service, pool, gym, hair salon, hot tub, sauna, nightclub, laundry service, meeting rooms, airport shuttle, no-smoking rooms* ▤ *AE, D, DC, MC, V.*

¢ ▦ **Best Western Town House Lodge.** The downtown location is the primary draw for this hotel. The county's historical library is across the street, and the McHenry Mansion and the McHenry Museum are nearby. All rooms come equipped with a coffeemaker, hair dryer, and iron. ⊠ *909 16th St., 95354* ☎ *209/524–7261 or 800/772–7261* ▧ *209/579–9546* ⊕ *www.bestwestern.com* ⇥ *59 rooms* ⌂ *Microwaves, refrigerators, cable TV, Wi-Fi, pool, hot tub, free parking, no-smoking rooms* ▤ *AE, D, DC, MC, V* ⑩ *CP.*

Oakdale

⑯ *15 mi northeast of Modesto on Hwy. 108.*

Oakdale is a bit off the beaten path from Modesto. You can sample the wares at **Oakdale Cheese & Specialties** (⊠ *10040 Hwy. 120* ☎ *209/848–3139* ⊕ *www.oakdalecheese.com*), which has tastings (try the aged Gouda) and cheese-making tours. There's a picnic area and a petting zoo.

If you're in Oakdale—home of a Hershey's chocolate factory—the third weekend in May, check out the **Oakdale Chocolate Festival** (☎ *209/847–2244* ⊠ *$4*), which attracts 50,000 to 60,000 people each year. The event's main attraction is Chocolate Avenue, where vendors proffer cakes, cookies, ice cream, fudge, and cheesecake.

★ ☺ The featured attraction at the **Knights Ferry Recreation Area** is the 355-foot-long Knights Ferry covered bridge. The beautiful and haunting structure, built in 1863, crosses the Stanislaus River near the ruins of an old gristmill. The park has picnic and barbecue areas along the riverbanks, as well as three campgrounds accessible only by boat. You can hike, fish, canoe, and raft on 4 mi of rapids. ⊠ *Corps of Engineers Park, 17968 Covered Bridge Rd., Knights Ferry, 12 mi east of Oakdale via Hwy. 108* ☎ *209/881–3517* ◻ *Free* ☉ *Daily dawn–dusk.*

Sports & the Outdoors

Rafting on the Stanislaus River is a popular activity near Oakdale. **River Journey** (⊠ 14842 Orange Blossom Rd. ☎ 209/847–4671 or 800/292–2938 ⊕ www.riverjourney.com) will take you out for a few hours of fun. To satisfy your white-water or flat-water cravings, contact **Sunshine River Adventures** (☎ 209/848–4800 or 800/829–7238 ⊕ www.raftadventure.com).

Stockton

🔟 *29 mi north of Modesto on Hwy. 99.*

California's first inland port—connected since 1933 to San Francisco via a 60-mi-long deepwater channel—is wedged between Interstate 5 and Highway 99, on the eastern end of the Sacramento River delta. Stockton, founded during the gold rush as a way station for miners traveling from San Francisco to the Mother Lode and now a city of 261,000, is where many of the valley's agricultural products begin their journey to other parts of the world. If you're here in late April, don't miss the **Stockton Asparagus Festival** (☎ 209/644–3740 ⊕ www.asparagusfest.com), at the Downtown Stockton Waterfront. The highlight of the festival is the food; organizers try to prove that almost any dish can be made with asparagus. A car show, kids' activity area, and musical entertainment also are part of the event.

★ The **Haggin Museum,** in pretty Victory Park, has one of the Central Valley's finest art collections. Highlights include landscapes by Albert Bierstadt and Thomas Moran, a still life by Paul Gauguin, a Native American gallery, and an Egyptian mummy. ⊠ *1201 N. Pershing Ave.* ☎ *209/940–6300* ⊕ *www.hagginmuseum.org* ◻ *$5* ☉ *Wed.–Sun. 1:30–5.*

Where to Stay & Eat

$$$–$$$$ ✕ **Le Bistro.** This upscale restaurant serves fairly standard continental fare—rack of lamb, fillet of sole, sautéed shrimp, soufflé Grand Marnier—but you can count on high-quality ingredients and presentation with a flourish. ⊠ *Marina Center Mall, 3121 W. Benjamin Holt Dr., off I–5, behind Lyon's* ☎ *209/951–0885* ⊕ *www.lebistrostockton.com* ▭ *AE, D, DC, MC, V* ☉ *No lunch weekends.*

¢–$ ✕ **On Lock Sam.** This Stockton landmark (it's been operating since 1898) is in a modern pagoda-style building with framed Chinese prints on the walls, a garden outside one window, and a sparkling bar area. One touch of old-time Chinatown remains: a few booths have curtains that can be drawn for complete privacy. The Cantonese food is among the best in the valley. ⊠ *333 S. Sutter St.* ☎ *209/466–4561* ▭ *AE, D, MC, V.*

8

$–$$ La Quinta Inn. Close to downtown and near many upscale restaurants, this is a good choice for business and pleasure travelers. The spacious and quiet rooms have large desks and televisions; if you're feeling active, you can get free passes to a nearby gym. ⊠ *2710 W. March La., 95219* ☎ *209/952–7800 or 866/725–1661* ⊟ *209/472–0732* ⊕ *www. laquinta.com* ⏎ *151 rooms* ⓓ *Cable TV with movies, in-room data ports, Wi-Fi, pool, laundry service, meeting rooms, no-smoking rooms* ⊟ *AE, D, DC, MC, V.*

¢   Best Western Stockton Inn. Four miles from downtown, this large motel is conveniently situated off Highway 99. The central courtyard with a pool and lounge chairs is a big plus on hot days. Most rooms are spacious. ⊠ *4219 Waterloo Rd., 95215* ☎ *209/931–3131 or 888/829– 0092* ⊟ *209/931–0423* ⊕ *www.bestwesterncalifornia.com* ⏎ *136 rooms, 5 suites* ⓓ *Restaurant, microwaves, refrigerators, cable TV, in-room data ports, Wi-Fi, pool, wading pool, hot tub, bar, laundry service, meeting room, no-smoking rooms* ⊟ *AE, D, DC, MC, V.*

Sports & the Outdoors

Several companies rent houseboats (of various sizes, usually for three, four, or seven days) on the Sacramento River delta waterways near Stockton. Herman & Helen's Marina (⊠ 15135 W. 8 Mile Rd. ☎ 209/ 951–4634) rents houseboats with hot tubs and fireplaces. **Paradise Point Marina** (⊠ 8095 Rio Blanco Rd. ☎ 209/952–1000) rents a variety of watercraft, including patio boats.

Lodi

🔞   *13 mi north of Stockton and 34 mi south of Sacramento on Hwy. 99.*

Founded on agriculture, Lodi was once the watermelon capital of the country. Today it's surrounded by fields of asparagus, pumpkins, beans, safflowers, sunflowers, kiwis, melons, squashes, peaches, and cherries. It also has become a wine-grape capital of sorts, producing zinfandel, merlot, cabernet sauvignon, chardonnay, and sauvignon blanc grapes. For years California wineries have built their reputations on the juice of grapes grown around Lodi. Now the area that includes Lodi, Lockeford, and Woodbridge is a wine destination in itself, boasting about 40 wineries, many offering tours and tastings. Lodi still retains an old rural charm. You can stroll downtown or visit a wildlife refuge, all the while benefiting from a Sacramento River delta breeze that keeps this microclimate cooler in summer than anyplace else in the area.

☾   The 65-acre **Micke Grove Park and Zoo,** an oak-shaded county park 5 mi north of Stockton off—Highway 99, includes a Japanese garden, picnic areas, a golf course, and an agricultural museum with a collection of 94 tractors. Geckos and frogs, black-and-white ruffed lemurs, and hissing cockroaches found only on the African island of Madagascar inhabit "An Island Lost in Time," an exhibit at the **Micke Grove Zoo** (☎ 209/953–8840 ⊕ www.mgzoo.com ⊠ $2 ☾ Daily 10–5). California sea lions bask on rocks much as they do off the coast of San Francisco in the "Islands Close to Home" exhibit, another highlight of this compact facility. Most rides and diversions at Micke Grove's **Funder-**

woods Playland (☎ 209/368–1092 ☉ Weekdays 11:30–6, weekends 10:30–6), a family-oriented amusement park, are geared to children. ⊠ *11793 N. Micke Grove Rd.* ☎ *209/331–7400* 🅿 *Parking $3 weekdays, $5 weekends and holidays.*

Stop by the **Lodi Wine & Visitor Center** (⊠ 2545 W. Turner Rd. ☎ 209/ 365–0621) to see exhibits on Lodi's viticultural history, pick up a map of area wineries, and even buy wine. One of the standout wineries in the area is **Jessie's Grove** (⊠ 1973 W. Turner Rd. ☎ 209/368–0880 ⊕ www. jgwinery.com ☉ Fri.–Sun. 11–4), a wooded horse ranch and vineyard that has been in the same family since 1863. In addition to producing outstanding old-vine zinfandels, it presents blues concerts on various Saturdays June through October. At the **Woodbridge Winery** (⊠5950 E. Woodbridge Rd., Acampo ☎ 209/369–5861 ⊕ www.woodbridgewines.com ☉ Tues.–Sun. 10:30–4:30), you can take a free 30-minute tour of the vineyard and aging room. At its homey facility, kid-friendly **Phillips Farms Michael-David Winery** (⊠ 4580 W. Hwy. 12 ☎ 209/368–7384 ⊕ www. lodivineyards.com) offers tastings from its affordable Michael-David vineyard. You can also cut flowers from the garden, pet the animals, eat breakfast or lunch at the café, and buy Phillips' and other local produce. **Vino Piazza** (⊠ 12470 Locke Rd., Lockeford ☎ 209/727–9770) is a sort of wine co-op housed in the old Lockeford Winery building, where 13 vineyards operate tasting rooms. If you don't have time to see the vineyards themselves, this is a good way to sample the area's many wines.

Where to Stay & Eat

$$–$$$$ ✕ **Rosewood Bar & Grill.** In downtown Lodi, Rosewood offers fine dining without formality. Operated by the folks at Wine & Roses Hotel and Restaurant, this low-key spot serves American fare with a twist, such as meat loaf wrapped in bacon, and daily seafood specials. The bar has a full-service menu, and live music on Friday and Saturday. ⊠*28 S. School St.* ☎ *209/369–0470* ⊕ *www.rosewoodbarandgrill.com* ▤ *AE, D, DC, MC, V* ☉ *No lunch.*

$–$$$ ✕ **Habanero Hots.** If your mouth can handle the heat promised by the restaurant's name, try the tamales. If you want to take it easy on your taste buds, stick with the rest of the menu. ⊠ *1024 E. Victor Rd.* ☎ *209/369–3791* ▤ *AE, MC, V.*

¢ ✕ **Angelo's.** Authentic Mexican dishes such as chili verde, steak ranchero, and all-meat chimichangas draw locals to this downtown eatery. The service is friendly and quick, and the atmosphere is casual. ⊠*28 N. School St.* ☎ *209/366–2728* ▤ *AE, DC, MC, V.*

★ $$–$$$$ ✕▣ **Wine & Roses Hotel and Restaurant.** Set on 7 acres amid a tapestry of informal gardens, this hotel has cultivated a sense of refinement typically associated with Napa or Carmel. Rooms are decorated in rich earth tones, and linens are imported from Italy. Some rooms have fireplaces; all have coffeemakers, irons, and hair dryers. Some of the bathrooms even have TVs. The restaurant ($$–$$$$) is *the* place to eat in Lodi. The Sunday buffet champagne brunch includes ham, prime rib, and made-to-order crepes and omelets. Afterward, consider heading to the spa for a facial or herbal body scrub. ⊠ *2505 W. Turner Rd., 95242* ☎ *209/ 334–6988* 🖷 *209/371–6049* ⊕ *www.winerose.com* ⇗ *47 rooms, 4* *suites ॐ Restaurant, room service, refrigerators, cable TV, in-room data ports, Wi-Fi, spa, bar, laundry service, no-smoking rooms ⊟ AE, D, DC, MC, V* ⏺ *CP.*

$$–$$$ ▦ **The Inn at Locke House.** Built in 1865, this B&B was a pioneer family's home and is on the National Register of Historic Places. Airy rooms with garden views are filled with Locke family antique furnishings, and all have fireplaces and private bathrooms. The centerpiece of the Water Tower Suite is a queen canopy bed; it also has a deck and a private sitting room at the top of the tower. Refreshments are served in the parlor, where there's also an old pump organ. ⊠ *19960 N. Elliott Rd., Lockeford 95237* ☎ *209/727–5715* 🖶 *209/727–0873* ⊕ *www. theinnatlockehouse.com* ➔ *4 rooms, 1 suite ॐ Library, no-smoking rooms; no room TVs ⊟ AE, D, DC, MC, V* ⏺ *BP.*

¢ ▦ **Lodi Comfort Inn.** This downtown motel has quiet rooms with contemporary furnishings and blow dryers in the bathrooms. It's easily accessible from Highway 99. Muffins, waffles, bagels, juice, and coffee make up the complimentary breakfast. ⊠ *118 N. Cherokee La.* ☎ *209/ 367–4848 or 877/424–6423* 🖶 *209/367–4898* ⊕ *www.comfortinn. com* ➔ *55 rooms ॐ Microwaves, refrigerators, cable TV, in-room data ports, Wi-Fi, pool, hot tub, laundry facilities, laundry service ⊟ AE, D, DC, MC, V* ⏺ *CP.*

Sports & the Outdoors

Even locals need respite from the heat of Central Valley summers, and **Lodi Lake Park** (⊠ 1101 W. Turner Rd. ☎ 209/333–6742 ◫ $5) is where they find it. The banks, shaded by grand old elms and oaks, are much cooler than other spots in town. Swimming, bird-watching, and picnicking are possibilities, as is renting a kayak, canoe, or pedal boat ($2 to $4 per half hour, Tuesday through Sunday, late May through early September only).

THE CENTRAL VALLEY ESSENTIALS

To research prices, get advice from other travelers, and book travel arrangements, visit www.fodors.com.

Transportation

BY AIR

Fresno Yosemite International Airport is serviced by Alaska, Allegiant, America West, American and American Eagle, Continental, Delta, Hawaiian, Horizon, Northwest, Skywest, United, and United Express. Kern County Airport at Meadows Field is serviced by America West Express, Continental, and United Express. United Express flies from San Francisco to Modesto City Airport and from Los Angeles to Visalia Municipal Airport. ⇨ Air Travel *in* Smart Travel Tips A to Z for airline phone numbers.

🛈 **Fresno Yosemite International Airport** ⊠ 4995 E. Clinton Way, Fresno ☎ 559/ 621–4500 ⊕ www.fresno.gov/flyfresno. **Kern County Airport at Meadows Field** ⊠ 1401 Skyway Dr., Bakersfield ☎ 661/391–1800 ⊕ www.meadowsfield.com. **Modesto City Airport** ⊠ 617 Airport Way, Modesto ☎ 209/577–5319 ⊕ www.modairport.com.

Visalia Municipal Airport ✉ 9501 W. Airport Dr., Visalia ☎ 559/713-4201 ⊕ www.flyvisalia.com.

BY BUS

Greyhound provides service between major valley cities. Orange Belt Stages provides bus service, including Amtrak connections, to many valley locations, including Bakersfield, Fresno, Hanford, Modesto, Merced, and Stockton.

🖪 **Greyhound** ☎ 800/231-2222 ⊕ www.greyhound.com. **Orange Belt Stages** ☎ 800/266-7433 ⊕ www.orangebelt.com.

BY CAR

To reach the Central Valley from Los Angeles, follow Interstate 5 north; Highway 99 veers north about 15 mi after entering the valley. To drive to the valley from San Francisco, take Interstate 80 east to Interstate 580 and then Interstate 580 east to Interstate 5, which leads south into the valley (several roads from Interstate 5 head east to Highway 99); or continue east on Interstate 580 to Interstate 205, which leads to Interstate 5 north to Stockton or (via Highway 120) east to Highway 99 at Manteca.

Highway 99 is the main route between the valley's major cities and towns. Interstate 5 runs roughly parallel to it to the west but misses the major population centers; its main use is for quick access from San Francisco or Los Angeles. Major roads that connect Interstate 5 with Highway 99 are Highways 58 (to Bakersfield), 198 (to Hanford and Visalia), 152 (to Chowchilla, via Los Banos), 140 (to Merced), 132 (to Modesto), and 120 (to Manteca). For road conditions, call the California Department of Transportation hotline.

🖪 **California Department of Transportation** ☎ 800/266-6883 or 916/445-1534.

CAR RENTAL Avis, Budget, Dollar, Enterprise, Hertz, and National rent cars at Fresno Yosemite International Airport. Avis, Budget, Hertz, and National rent cars at Kern County Airport at Meadows Field. Avis, Enterprise, and Hertz rent cars at Modesto City Airport. Enterprise is represented at Visalia Municipal Airport. ⇨ Car Rental *in* Smart Travel Tips A to Z for national rental-agency phone numbers.

BY TRAIN

Amtrak's daily *San Joaquin* travels among Bakersfield, San Jose, and Oakland, stopping in Hanford, Fresno, Madera, Merced, Modesto, and Stockton. Amtrak Thruway bus service connects Bakersfield with Los Angeles.

🖪 **Amtrak** ☎ 800/872-7245 ⊕ www.amtrakcalifornia.com.

Contacts & Resources

EMERGENCIES

In an emergency dial 911.

🖪 Hospitals **Bakersfield Memorial Hospital** ✉ 420 34th St., Bakersfield ☎ 661/327-4647. **St. Joseph's Medical Center** ✉ 1800 N. California St., Stockton ☎ 209/943-2000. **University Medical Center** ✉ 445 S. Cedar Ave., Fresno ☎ 559/459-4000.

TOUR OPTIONS

Central Valley Tours provides general and customized tours of the Fresno area and the valley, with special emphasis on the fruit harvests and Blossom Trail.

🗊 **Central Valley Tours** 🕾 559/276-4479 ⊕ www.angelfire.com/poetry/inc/valleytours. html.

VISITOR INFORMATION

🗊 **Fresno City & County Convention and Visitors Bureau** ✉ 848 M St., Fresno 93721 🕾 559/233-0836 or 800/788-0836 ⊕ www.fresnocvb.org. **Greater Bakersfield Convention & Visitors Bureau** ✉ 515 Truxton Ave., Bakersfield 93301 🕾 661/325-5051 or 866/425-7353 ⊕ www.bakersfieldcvb.org. **Hanford Visitor Agency** ✉ 200 Santa Fe Ave., Suite D, Hanford 93230 🕾 559/582-5024 ⊕ www.visithanford.com. **Kern County Board of Trade** ✉ 2101 Oak St., Bakersfield 93301 🕾 661/861-2367 or 800/500-5376 ⊕ www.co.kern.ca.us. **Lodi Conference and Visitors Bureau** ✉ 2545 W. Turner Dr., Lodi 95242 🕾 209/365-1195 or 800/798-1810 ⊕ www.visitlodi.com. **Merced Conference and Visitors Bureau** ✉ 710 W. 16th St., Merced 95340 🕾 209/384-2791 ⊕ www.yosemite-gateway.org. **Modesto Convention and Visitors Bureau** ✉ 1150 9th St., Suite C, Modesto 95353 🕾 209/526-5588 or 888/640-8467 ⊕ www.visitmodesto.com. **Stockton Visitors Bureau** ✉ 46 W. Fremont St., Stockton 95202 🕾 209/937-5089 ⊕ www.visitstockton.org. **Visalia Chamber of Commerce and Visitors Bureau** ✉ 220 N. Santa Fe St., Visalia 93291 🕾 559/734-5876 ⊕ www.cvbvisalia.com.

The Central Coast

WORD OF MOUTH

"The Channel Islands are my favorite place to visit in southern California. Just getting there is an adventure by ferry from either Oxnard, Ventura, or Santa Barbara. You're likely to see schools of dolphins, sea lions, whales and numerous birds. The islands are uninhabited except for the park rangers and campers and are natural and a haven for wildlife. There is excellent snorkeling, kayaking (lots of caves!) and hiking. I visit every year."

—Ann

"The drive from Cambria to Carmel is one of the most spectacular things one ever can experience. Many people enjoy stopping frequently and hiking or, in my case, taking photos. So I would not plan on blasting up Highway 1."

—youngtom2910

Updated by
Cheryl
Crabtree &
Constance
Jones

THE COASTLINE BETWEEN SANTA BARBARA AND CARMEL, a distance of about 200 mi, is one of the most popular drives in California. Except for a few smallish cities—Ventura and Santa Barbara, in the south, and San Luis Obispo, in the north—the area is sparsely populated. The countryside's few inhabitants relish their isolation at the sharp edge of land and sea. Around Santa Barbara, Ventura, and Oxnard, Southern California peters out in long, sandy beaches. To the north the shoreline gradually rises into hills dotted with cattle, and by the time you reach Big Sur, the Santa Lucia Mountains drop down to the Pacific with dizzying grandeur.

Sunny, well-scrubbed Santa Barbara, 95 mi north of Los Angeles, is the link between northern and Southern California. Santa Barbara's Spanish-Mexican heritage is reflected in the architectural style of the mission, courthouse, and many homes and public buildings. Inland from the Pacific a burgeoning Central Coast wine region stretches 100 mi from Santa Ynez north to Paso Robles; the 230-plus wineries here have earned reputations for high-quality vintages that rival those of northern California. Visual artists create and sell their works in towns such as Ojai and Cambria. The town of Solvang, where restaurants serve Scandinavian fare and windmills line the streets, is a European outpost in this otherwise quintessentially Californian landscape.

Exploring the Central Coast

Driving is the easiest way to experience the Central Coast, which extends from Ventura County in the south to the Big Sur coastline in the north. A car gives you the flexibility to stop at scenic vista points along Highway 1, take detours through wine country, and drive to rural lakes and mountains. Avoid driving on Highway 101 during weekday commuter hours, especially from Ventura and the Santa Ynez Valley to Santa Barbara in the morning, and returning to those destinations in the late afternoon to early evening. The freeway traffic can also slow to a snail's pace on late Sunday afternoon as travelers head back to Los Angeles after a weekend getaway. Traveling north through Ventura County to San Luis Obispo (note that from just south of Ventura up to San Luis Obispo, U.S. 101 and Highway 1 are the same road), you can feast your eyes on the rolling hills, peaceful valleys, and rugged mountains that stretch for miles along the shore. Especially in summer, you'll need to make reservations for a visit to Hearst San Simeon State Historical Monument (home to Hearst Castle) well before you depart for the coast. In summer and on foggy days the traffic on windy, two-lane Highway 1 can seem to move at a snail's pace from Cambria to Big Sur. Moving slowly, though, will give you the chance to enjoy the breathtaking views.

About the Restaurants

The cuisine in Ventura and Santa Barbara is every bit as eclectic as it is in California's bigger cities. Fresh seafood is a standout, whether it's prepared simply in wharf-side hangouts or incorporated into sophisticated bistro menus. If you're after good, cheap food with an international flavor, follow the locals to Milpas Street, on the eastern edge of Santa Bar-

GREAT ITINERARIES

Numbers correspond to the Ventura & Santa Barbara Counties, Santa Barbara, and San Luiso Obispo County & Big Sur maps.

IF YOU HAVE 3 DAYS

Start your trip in ▶ 🖼 **Santa Barbara ④–⑲**, where you can tour the **Santa Barbara County Courthouse ⑪** and **Mission Santa Barbara ⑮**. In the afternoon explore **Stearns Wharf ⑦** and other waterfront sights, and stroll State Street if you like to shop, or have some fun at the **Santa Barbara Zoo ⑰**. The next day, drive up to 🖼 **San Luis Obispo ㉖** and visit Mission San Luis Obispo de Tolosa and the nearby County Historical Museum. Pausing north of town to poke your head into the kitschy Madonna Inn, drive to **Morro Bay ㉗** to stroll the Embarcadero and see Morro Rock. Stop at Montaña de Oro State Park for a late-afternoon hike and spend the evening in 🖼 San Luis Obispo. In the morning, driving north through **Cambria ㉙** to **San Simeon ㉚** for a tour of Hearst San Simeon State Historical Monument. Next, head for the Big Sur coastline, where you can have a sunset dinner at Nepenthe and spend the night in or near Pfeiffer Big Sur State Park in 🖼 **Central Big Sur ㉜**.

IF YOU HAVE 7 DAYS

Get your tour off to a natural start in ▶ 🖼 **Ventura ①**, on a morning cruise to **Channel Islands National Park ②**. In the afternoon, take Highway 33 east to see **Ojai ③**. On Day 2, drive to 🖼 **Santa Barbara ④–⑲** and get a feel for the city's architecture, history, and vegetation at the **Santa Barbara County Courthouse ⑪**, **Mission**

Santa Barbara ⑭, and the **Santa Barbara Botanic Garden ⑯**. Have dinner in **Montecito ⑲** and explore the Coast Village Road shopping district. It's a short walk south from here to the shore to catch the sunset before or after you eat. The next day take it easy with a visit to **Stearns Wharf ⑦**, a walk or bike along East Beach, and a prowl through **Andree Clark Bird Refuge ⑱**. Have dinner on State Street and check out the area's shops and clubs. Day 4 starts with a drive up U.S. 101 to Highway 246 west to reach La Purisima Mission State Historic Park in **Lompoc ㉓**. Spend the afternoon in Santa Barbara wine country, stopping at wineries in Santa Ynez and Los Olivos. Another option is to browse the shops in Danish **Solvang ㉒**, where there are plenty of places to choose from for dinner. In the morning continue north through **Morro Bay ㉗** to **Cambria ㉙**, a good place for lunch, and take an afternoon tour of Hearst San Simeon State Historical Monument. After a night in 🖼 **San Simeon ㉚**, head for the Big Sur coast on Day 6. Observe the glories of Los Padres National Forest up close by hiking one of the many trails in the Ventana Wilderness. Overnight at one of the spots around Pfeiffer Big Sur State Park in 🖼 **Central Big Sur ㉜**, and on your last day watch the waves break on Pfeiffer Beach, one of the few places in the area where you can actually set foot on the shore. If you're here on a weekend (or on Wednesday April through October), tour Point Sur State Historic Park.

9

bara's downtown. Dining attire on the Central Coast is generally casual, though slightly dressy casual wear is the custom at pricier restaurants.

The Central Coast, from Solvang to Big Sur, is far enough off the interstate to ensure that nearly every restaurant or café has its own personality—from chic to down-home and funky. A "foodie" renaissance has overtaken the Santa Ynez Valley, San Luis Obispo, Cambria, and Paso Robles, spawning dozens of new restaurants touting nouveau cuisine made with fresh organic produce and meats. There aren't many restaurants between Hearst San Simeon State Historical Monument and Big Sur.

About the Hotels

Santa Barbara's numerous hotels and bed-and-breakfasts—despite rates that range from pricey to downright shocking—attract thousands of patrons year-round. Air-conditioning is a rarity at coastal lodgings from Pismo Beach to Big Sur, because the sea breeze cools the air. Many moderately priced hotels and motels—most of them just decent places to hang your hat—can be found between San Luis Obispo and San Simeon. Big Sur has only a few lodgings, but even its budget accommodations have character.

Budget-conscious travelers will find more affordable options in Carpinteria, Ventura, and Oxnard, a short drive south of Santa Barbara along the coast, or inland, in smaller towns such as Paso Robles. If possible, visit sometime between October and March, when many Central Coast lodgings offer reduced rates and promotional packages. Otherwise, try for midweek specials. Wherever you stay, be sure to make reservations for the summer and holiday weekends (especially Memorial Day, Labor Day, and Thanksgiving) well ahead of time. It's not unusual for all coastal accommodations (meaning every single one) to fill completely during these busy times. It's also common for hotels to require minimum stays on holidays and some weekends, especially in summer, and to double their rates during festivals and other events.

Hot Spots (☎ 805/564–1637 or 800/793–7666 ⊕ www.hotspotsusa. com) provides room reservations and tourist information for destinations in Ventura, Santa Barbara, and San Luis Obispo counties.

WHAT IT COSTS				
	$$$$	**$$$**	**$$**	**$**	**¢**
RESTAURANTS	over $30	$23–$30	$16–$22	$10–$15	under $10
HOTELS	over $250	$176–$250	$121–$175	$90–$120	under $90

Restaurant prices are for a main course at dinner, excluding sales tax of 7¼%–7¾% (depending on location). Hotel prices are for two people in a standard double room in high season, excluding service charges and 9%–10% tax.

Timing

The Central Coast is hospitable most of the year. Santa Barbara and Ventura are pleasant year-round. Fog often rolls in north of Pismo Beach in summer; you'll need a jacket, especially after sunset, close to the shore. The rains usually come from December through March. Hotel rooms

IF YOU LIKE

MISSIONS

Six important California missions established by Franciscan friars are within the Central Coast region. San Miguel (closed to the public because of earthquake damage in 2003) is one of California's best-preserved missions. La Purisima is the most fully restored; Mission Santa Barbara is perhaps the most beautiful in the state; and Mission San Luis Obispo de Tolosa has a fine museum with many Chumash Indian artifacts. Mission Santa Inés is known for its serene gardens and restored artworks, and Mission San Buenaventura has 250-year-old paintings and a statuary.

WINERIES

Hundreds of vineyards and wineries dot the hillsides from Paso Robles to San Luis Obispo, through the scenic Edna Valley and south to northern Santa Barbara County. The wineries offer much of the variety of northern California's Napa and Sonoma valleys—without the glitz and crowds. Since the early 1980s the region has steadily increased production and developed an international reputation for high-quality wines, most notably pinot noir, chardonnay, and zinfandel. Today there are nearly 200 wineries. They tend to be small, but most have tasting rooms (some have tours), and you'll often meet the winemakers themselves. There are maps and brochures at the visitor centers in Solvang, San Luis Obispo, and Santa Barbara, or you can contact the wine associations of Paso Robles, San Luis Obispo, and Santa Barbara. Many tasting rooms, hotels, and motels also keep a supply of wine-touring maps for visitors

fill up in summer, but from April to early June and in the early fall the weather is almost as fine and the pace is less hectic. And remember that hotels offer considerable discounts in winter.

9

VENTURA COUNTY
WITH CHANNEL ISLANDS NATIONAL PARK

Ventura County was first settled by the Chumash Indians. Spanish missionaries were the first Europeans to arrive, followed by Americans and other Europeans, who established bustling towns, transportation networks, and highly productive farms. Since the 1920s, though, agriculture has been steadily replaced as the area's main industry—first by the oil business, and more recently, by tourism.

Ventura

➤ ❶ *60 mi north of Los Angeles on U.S. 101.*

Like Los Angeles, the city of Ventura enjoys gorgeous weather and sun-kissed beaches—but without the smog and congestion. The miles of beautiful beach attract both athletes—bodysurfers and boogie-boarders, runners and bikers—and those who'd rather doze beneath a rented umbrella all day. Ventura Harbor is home to the Channel Islands National Park Visitor Center and myriad fishing boats, restaurants, and water-activity centers where you can rent boats and take harbor cruises. Foodies can get their fix here, too; dozens of upscale cafés and wine and tapas bars have opened in recent years. Ventura is also a magnet for arts and antiques buffs who come to browse the dozens of galleries and shops in the downtown area. You can pick up an antiques guide downtown at the **visitor center** (✉ 89 S. California St., #C ☎ 805/648–2075 or 800/ 333–2989 ⊕ www.ventura-usa.com) run by the Ventura Visitors and Convention Bureau.

More than three millennia of human history in the Ventura region is charted in the archaeological exhibits at the small **Albinger Archaeological Museum.** Some of the relics on display date back to 1600 BC. ✉ 113 E. Main St. ☎ 805/648–5823 ☜ Free ☉ June–Aug., Wed.–Sun. 10–4; Sept.–May, Wed.–Fri. 10–2, weekends 10–4.

Lunker largemouth bass, rainbow trout, crappie, red-ears, and channel catfish live in the waters at **Lake Casitas Recreation Area,** an impoundment of the Ventura River. The lake is one of the country's best bass-fishing areas, and anglers come from all over the United States to test their luck. The park, nestled below the Santa Ynez Mountains' Laguna Ridge, is also a beautiful spot for pitching a tent or having a picnic. The Lake Casitas Water Adventure, which has two water playgrounds and a lazy river for tubing and floating, is a great place to take kids in summer ($10 for an all-day pass; $5 from 5 to 7 PM). The park is 13 mi northwest of Ventura. ✉ Hwy. 33 ☎ 805/649–2233, 805/649–1122 for campground reservations ⊕ www.lakecasitas.info ☜ $8 per vehicle, $7 per boat ☉ Daily.

The ninth of the 21 California missions, **Mission San Buenaventura** burned to the ground in the 1790s. It was rebuilt and rededicated in 1809. A self-guided tour takes you through a small museum, a quiet courtyard, and a chapel with 250-year-old paintings. ✉ 211 E. Main St. ☎ 805/ 643–4318 ⊕ www.sanbuenaventuramission.org ☜ $1 ☉ Weekdays 10–5, Sat. 9–5, Sun. 10–4.

OFF THE BEATEN PATH

FILLMORE – Visiting the tiny, well-preserved downtown of Fillmore, east of Santa Paula on Highway 126, is like entering turn-of-the-20th-century California. If you're here on a weekend, hop aboard the **Fillmore & Western Railway** (✉ 351 Santa Clara Ave. ☎ 805/524–2546 or 800/773–8724 ⊕ www.fwry.com). The vintage trains travel on century-old restored tracks to Santa Paula and back (the ride usually takes 2½ hours).

CHANNEL ISLANDS HARBOR – If you continue south 5 mi along Harbor Boulevard, you eventually connect with this classic Southern California–style harbor, the fifth largest for small-craft recreation in the state. Concerts, boat shows, fireworks displays, art festivals, and other events take place here year-round. At the **Ventura County Maritime Museum** (☎ 805/984–6260) within the harbor, you can learn everything you ever wanted to know about the shipping and whaling history of the Channel Islands. You can rent bikes, paddleboats, and electric boats to tour the harbor. A visitor center, adjacent to the Maritime Museum, can help

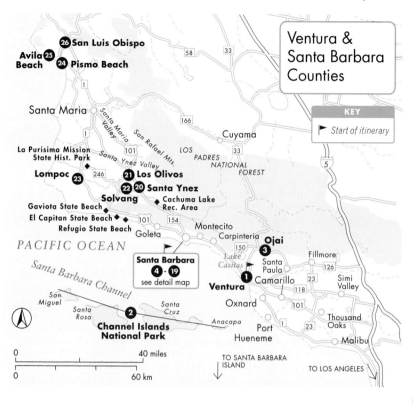

Ventura &
Santa Barbara
Counties

KEY

► *Start of itinerary*

San Luis Obispo 26

Avila 25
Beach Pismo Beach 24

Santa Maria

Santa Maria Valley

San Rafael Mts.

La Purisima Mission
State Hist. Park

Lompoc 23

LOS PADRES NATIONAL FOREST

Cuyama

58   33

166

Santa Ynez Valley

Los Olivos 21
Santa Ynez 20
Solvang 22

Gaviota State Beach
El Capitan State Beach
Refugio State Beach

Goleta

Montecito

PACIFIC OCEAN

Santa Barbara
4 · 19
see detail map

Carpinteria Ojai 3

Lake
Casitas

Santa
Paula

Fillmore

Ventura 1 Camarillo

Oxnard

Santa Barbara Channel

San
Miguel Santa
Rosa

Santa
Cruz

Anacapa

Channel Islands
National Park 2

Port
Hueneme

Simi
Valley

Thousand
Oaks

Malibu

0 ———— 40 miles

0 ———— 60 km

TO SANTA BARBARA
ISLAND

TO LOS ANGELES

you get oriented. ✉ *2741 S. Victoria Ave., Suite F* ☎ *805/985–4852*
⊕ *www.channelislandsharbor.org* ✉ *Free.*

HERITAGE SQUARE – Driving east toward U.S. 101, stop in downtown Oxnard and take a stroll along Heritage Square to see more than a dozen late-19th-century homes and other buildings, many with manicured gardens and courtyards. Docent-led tours allow you to see the gracious interiors. ✉ *715 S. A St.* ☎ *805/483–7960* ✉ *$2* ⊙ *Guided tours Sat. 10–2.*

Where to Stay & Eat

$$–$$$ ✕ **Jonathan's at Peirano's.** The main dining room here has a gazebo where you can eat surrounded by plants and local art. The menu has dishes from Spain, Portugal, France, Italy, Greece, and Morocco. Standouts are the Basque-style chicken, the *penne checca* pasta, and the halibut with almonds. The owners also run an evening tapas bar next door, which serves exotic martinis. ✉ *204 E. Main St.* ☎ *805/648–4853* ▭ *AE, D, DC, MC, V* ⊙ *Closed Mon. No lunch Sun.*

$–$$$ ✕ **71 Palm Restaurant.** This elegant restaurant occupies a 1910 house, and it still has touches that make it feel like a home: lace curtains, wood floors, a dining patio for good weather, and a fireplace that's often crackling in winter. A standout appetizer is the homemade country pâté with cornichons; for dinner, try the grilled salmon on a potato pancake, or the New Zealand rack of lamb Provençal. ⊠ *71 N. Palm St.* ☎ *805/653–7222* ⊟ *AE, D, DC, MC, V* ⊗ *Closed Sun. No lunch Sat.*

¢–$ ✕ **Andria's Seafood.** At this casual, family-oriented restaurant in Ventura Harbor, the specialties are fresh fish-and-chips—said to rival England's best—and homemade clam chowder. After placing your order at the counter, you can sit outside on the patio with a view of the harbor and marina. ⊠ *1449 Spinnaker Dr., Suite A* ☎ *805/654–0546* ⊟ *MC, V.*

¢ ✕ **Christy's.** You can get breakfast all day—don't miss the breakfast burrito—at this cozy, nautical-theme locals' hangout in the harbor, across the water from the Channel Islands. It also serves burgers, sandwiches, and soup. ⊠ *1559 Spinnaker Dr.* ☎ *805/642–3116* ⊟ *D, MC, V.*

$–$$$ ⬚ **The Brakey House.** Built circa 1890, this three-story Victorian sits on a steep hillside near the courthouse in the heart of the historic district. All seven individually themed rooms have private entrances, DVD players, pillow-top queen beds, and private baths; three have whirlpool tubs. When you rise for a traditional Bavarian breakfast in the breakfast room, you can also feast your eyes on a view of the ocean and offshore islands. ⊠ *411 Poli St., 93001* ☎ *805/643–3600* ⬚ *805/653–7329* ⊕ *www.brakeyhouse.com* ↪ *7 rooms* ⌂ *Cable TV, in-room DVDs, outdoor hot tub, Internet room, some pets allowed; no a/c in some rooms* ⊟ *AE, D, MC, V* ⊚ *BP.*

$–$$ ⬚ **Clocktower Inn.** In the heart of downtown, this motel-style inn is next to Mission San Buenaventura, the Historical Museum, and the area's many boutique shops. Rooms are done up in soft southwestern colors, and many have private patios, fireplaces, carved headboards, desks, leather chairs, and armoires. Continental breakfast and access to a fitness studio are complimentary. ⊠ *181 E. Santa Clara, 93001* ☎ *805/652–0141 or 800/727–1027* ⬚ *805/643–1432* ⊕ *www.clocktowerinn.com* ↪ *50 rooms* ⌂ *Restaurant, room service, cable TV with movies, in-room broadband, meeting room, no-smoking rooms* ⊟ *AE, D, DC, MC, V* ⊚ *CP.*

Sports & the Outdoors

The most popular outdoor activities in Ventura are beach-going and whale-watching. California gray whales migrate offshore through the Santa Barbara Channel from late December through March; giant blue and humpback whales feed here from mid-June through September. In fact, the channel is teeming with marine life year-round, so tours include more than just whale sightings. A cruise through the Santa Barbara Channel with **Island Packers** (⊠ 1691 Spinnaker Dr., Ventura Harbor ☎ 805/642–1393 ⊕ www.islandpackers.com) will give you the chance to spot dolphins and seals—and sometimes even whales—throughout the year.

Channel Islands National Park

❷ *In Santa Barbara Channel southwest of Ventura and Oxnard; accessible from Ventura, Santa Barbara, Camarillo, and Oxnard.*

Fodor'sChoice
★

Often referred to as North America's Galapagos, this park includes five of the eight Channel Islands and the nautical mile of ocean that surrounds them. The Channel Islands range in size from 1-square-mi Santa Barbara to 96-square-mi Santa Cruz. Together they form a magnificent nature preserve, home of wildlife unique to the islands, such as the island scrub-jay, the island fox, and the Anacapa deer mouse. Plant species, such as the Santa Rosa Torrey pine and the island oak, have also evolved differently from their counterparts on the mainland. It all adds up to a living laboratory not unlike the one naturalist Charles Darwin discovered off the coast of Ecuador more than 150 years ago.

The channel waters are also teeming with life, including dolphins, whales, seals, sea lions, and seabirds. If you visit East Anacapa in spring or summer, you'll walk through a nesting area of western gulls. If you're lucky enough to get to windswept San Miguel, you might have a chance to see as many as 30,000 pinnipeds (seals and sea lions) camped out on the beach. If you're a kayaker, you can paddle close to the seals (as long as you don't disturb them); if you're a diver or snorkeler you can explore some of the world's richest kelp forests. Even traveling on an excursion boat gives you a chance to view sea lions, brown pelicans, and spouting whales.

★ Whether or not you plan to visit the islands, you should definitely stop by the **Channel Islands National Park Robert J. Lagomarsino Visitor Center.** The center has a museum, a bookstore, a three-story observation tower with telescopes, and island exhibits. There's a tide pool where you can see a brilliant orange garibaldi, sea stars clinging to rocks, and anemones waving their colorful, spiny tentacles. There are also full-size reproductions of a male northern elephant seal and the pygmy mammoth skeleton unearthed on Santa Rosa Island in 1994. On weekends and holidays at 11 and 3, rangers lead various free public programs describing park resources; they can also provide you with a detailed map and trip-planning packet, if you want to visit the actual islands. ✉ *1901 Spinnaker Dr., Ventura* ☎ *805/658–5730* ⊕ *www.nps.gov/chis* ⌷ *Free* ☉ *Daily 8:30–5.*

You can get to the Channel Islands with **Island Packers** (✉ 1691 Spinnaker Dr., Suite 105B, Ventura ☎ 805/642–1393 ⊕ www.islandpackers. com), which sails from Ventura and Oxnard. Boats in the fleet travel to Anacapa and Santa Cruz daily in summer, less frequently the rest of the year. Their two 64-foot high-speed catamarans zip over to Santa Cruz Island, with stops at Anacapa Island, almost daily. Both catamarans run on environmentally friendly biodiesel fuel. Island Packers also visits the other islands three or four times a month (most frequently in spring, summer, and fall) and provides transportation for campers. **Truth Aquatics** (✉ 301 W. Cabrillo Blvd., Santa Barbara ☎ 805/962–1127 ⊕ www. truthaquatics.com) departs from the Santa Barbara Harbor for single- and multiday hiking, scuba, and camping excursions to Santa Cruz, Santa Rosa, and San Miguel islands. **Channel Islands Aviation** (✉ 305 Durley Ave., Camarillo ☎ 805/987–1301 ⊕ www.flycia.com) provides charter flights from Camarillo Airport, about 10 mi east of Oxnard, to an airstrip on Santa Rosa. It will also pick up groups of six or more at Santa Barbara Airport. Day trips are usually from 9:30 to 4.

Although most people think of it as an island, **Anacapa** actually comprises three narrow islets. The tips of these volcanic formations nearly touch, but they are inaccessible from one another except by boat. All three islets have towering cliffs, isolated sea caves, and natural bridges;

9

Arch Rock, on East Anacapa, is one of the best-known symbols of Channel Islands National Park. Wildlife viewing is the reason most people come to East Anacapa, particularly in summer when seagull chicks are newly hatched and sea lions and seals lounge on the beaches. The compact **museum** on East Anacapa tells the history of the island, and houses the original lead-crystal Fresnel lens from the island's lighthouse (circa 1937). If you come in summer, you can also learn about the nearby kelp forests by asking questions of underwater rangers, who communicate via microphone and camera. The sessions take place Tuesday, Wednesday, and Thursday afternoons at 2 and are broadcast live to the visitor center. Depending on the season and the number of desirable species lurking about there, a limited number of boats travel to Frenchy's Cove, at West Anacapa, where there are pristine tide pools. The rest of West Anacapa is closed to protect nesting brown pelicans. Trips to Middle Anacapa Island require a ranger escort.

Five miles west of Anacapa, 96-square-mi **Santa Cruz** is the largest of the Channel Islands. The National Park Service manages the easternmost 25% of the island; the rest is owned by the Nature Conservancy, which requires a permit to land. When your boat drops you off on the 70 mi of craggy coastline, you'll find two rugged mountain ranges with peaks soaring to 2,500 feet and deep canyons traversed by streams. This landscape is the habitat of a remarkable variety of flora and fauna—more than 600 types of plants, 140 kinds of land birds, 11 mammal species, 5 varieties of reptiles, and 3 amphibian species. Bird-watchers may want to look for the endemic scrub-jay, found nowhere else in the world.

The largest and deepest known sea cave in the world, **Painted Cave** lies along the northwest coastline of Santa Cruz Island. Named for the colorful lichen and algae that cover its walls, Painted Cave is nearly ¼ mi long and 100 feet wide. In spring a waterfall cascades over the entrance. Kayakers may encounter seals or sea lions cruising alongside their boats inside the cave.

Remnants of a dozen Chumash villages can be seen on the island. The largest of these villages, at the eastern end of the island, occupied the area now called **Scorpion Ranch.** The Chumash mined extensive chert deposits on the island for tools to produce shell-bead money, which they traded with people on the mainland. Remnants of the early-1900s ranching era can also be seen in the restored historic buildings, equipment, and adobe ovens that produced bread for the entire island.

Between Santa Cruz and San Miguel islands, **Santa Rosa** is the second largest of the Channel Islands. The island has a relatively low profile, broken by a central mountain range rising to 1,589 feet. The coastal areas range from broad sandy beaches to sheer cliffs. The island is the home of about 500 species of plants, including the rare Torrey pine. Three unusual mammals—the endemic island fox, spotted skunk, and deer mouse—are among those that make their home here. On Santa Rosa Island you can see **Vail and Vickers,** a ranch where sheep and cattle were raised from 1901 to 1998. The westernmost of the Channel Islands, **San**

Miguel is frequently battered by storms sweeping across the Pacific. The 15-square-mi island's wild, windswept landscape is lush with vegetation. Point Bennett, at the western tip, offers one of the world's most spectacular wildlife displays when more than 30,000 pinnipeds hit the beach. Explorer Juan Rodríguez Cabrillo was the first European to visit this island; he claimed it for Spain in 1542. Legend holds that Cabrillo died on one of the Channel Islands. No one knows where he's buried, but there's a memorial to him on a bluff above Cuyler Harbor.

At about 1 square mi, **Santa Barbara** is the smallest of the Channel Islands. It's also the southernmost island in the chain, separated from the others by nearly 35 mi. Roughly triangular in shape, its steep cliffs are topped by twin peaks. The island was visited in 1602 by explorer Sebastian Vizcaino, who named it in honor of St. Barbara. Come in spring to see a brilliant display of yellow coreopsis. The cliffs here offer a perfect nesting spot for the Xantus's murrelet, a rare seabird. With exhibits on the region's natural history, the small Santa Barbara Island **museum** is a great place to learn about the wildlife on and around the Channel Islands.

Camping

Camping is the best way to experience the natural beauty and isolation of Channel Islands National Park. Unrestricted by tour schedules, you'll have plenty of time to explore mountain trails, snorkel in the kelp forests, or kayak into sea caves. There are five campgrounds, on East Anacapa, Santa Cruz (near Scorpion Ranch), Santa Rosa, San Miguel, and Santa Barbara islands. Campsites are primitive, with no water (except on Santa Rosa and Santa Cruz) or electricity; enclosed camp stoves must be used. Campfires are not allowed on the islands except in a ring at Scorpion Beach, and then only at certain times between December and mid-May. You must carry all your gear and pack out all trash. Campers must arrange transportation to the islands before reserving a campsite (and yes, this information is checked by park personnel). You can get specifics on each campground and reserve a campsite ($15 per night) by contacting the **National Park Service Reservation System** (☎ 800/365–2267 ⊕ http://reservations.nps.gov) up to five months in advance.

Sports & the Outdoors

Because private vehicles are not allowed on the islands, hiking is the only way to explore them. Terrain on most islands ranges from flat to moderately hilly. Santa Cruz has the most options, from a ½-mi stroll to the historic Scorpion Ranch House to a strenuous 8-mi off-trail climb up an 1,808-foot peak. Naturalist-led day trips and overnight camping trips are available year-round through the three official park concessionaires: Island Packers, Truth Aquatics, and Channel Islands Aviation. Several other outfits also arrange sailing, diving, and kayak excursions around the islands but do not land; contact the Channel Islands National Park Visitor Center for more information. There are no services (including public phones, and cell-phone reception is dicey) on the islands—you have to bring all your own food, water (except on Santa Cruz and Santa Rosa), and supplies.

Ojai

③ *15 mi north of Ventura, U.S. 101 to Hwy. 33.*

The Ojai Valley, which director Frank Capra used as a backdrop for his 1936 film *Lost Horizon,* sizzles in the summer when temperatures routinely reach 90°F. The acres of orange and avocado groves here evoke postcard images of agricultural Southern California from decades ago. This is a lush, slow-moving place, where many artists and celebrities have sought refuge from life in the fast lane. The town can be easily explored on foot; you can also hop on the **Ojai Valley Trolley** (⊕ www.ojaitrolley. com 🖘 50¢), which rides on two routes around Ojai and neighboring Miramonte (between 7:15 and 5:40 on weekdays, 9 and 5 on weekends). If you tell the driver you're a visitor, you'll get an informal guided tour. Maps and tourist information are available at the **visitor center** (⊠ 150 W. Ojai Ave. ☎ 805/646–8126 ⊕ www.ojaichamber.org ⊗ Mon. and Wed.–Fri. 9:30–4:30, weekends 10–4).

The work of local artists is displayed in the Spanish-style shopping arcade along **Ojai Avenue** (Highway 150). Organic and specialty growers sell their produce on Sunday from 10 to 2 (9 to 1 in summer) at the farmers' market behind the arcade. The **Ojai Center for the Arts** (⊠ 113 S. Montgomery St. ☎ 805/646–0117) exhibits artwork and presents theater and dance performances. The **Ojai Valley Museum** (⊠ 130 W. Ojai Ave. ☎ 805/640–1390) has exhibits on the valley's history and many Native American artifacts. The 18-mi **Ojai Valley Trail** (⊠ Parallel to Hwy. 33, from Soule Park in Ojai to ocean in Ventura ☎ 805/654–3951 ⊕ www.ojaichamber.org) is open to pedestrians, bikers, joggers, equestrians, and nonmotorized vehicles. You can access it anywhere along its route.

Where to Stay & Eat

★ **$$$** ✕ **The Ranch House.** This elegant, yet laid-back eatery—said to be the best in town—has been around for decades, attracting celebrities like Paul Newman. Main dishes such as rack of venison in a red-wine and juniper-berry sauce, and grilled diver scallops with snow crab and béchamel sauce are not to be missed. The verdant patio is a wonderful place to have Sunday brunch. ⊠ *500 S. Lomita Ave.* ☎ *805/646–2360* ⊟ *AE, D, DC, MC, V* ⊗ *Closed Mon. No lunch.*

$$–$$$ ✕ **Suzanne's Cuisine.** Peppered filet mignon, linguine with steamed clams, and grilled salmon with caramelized-citrus glaze are among the offerings at this European-style restaurant. Game, seafood, and vegetarian dishes dominate the dinner menu, and salads and soups star at lunchtime. All the breads and desserts are made on the premises. ⊠ *502 W. Ojai Ave.* ☎ *805/640–1961* ⊟ *MC, V* ⊗ *Closed Tues. and 1st 2 wks in Jan.*

¢–$$ ✕ **Azu.** Delectable tapas, a full bar, slick furnishings, and piped jazz music lure diners to this popular, artsy European bistro. You can also order soups, salads, and traditional bistro fare such as veal shanks, roast duck, and cassoulet. Save room for the homemade gelato. Live music is sometimes performed after 9 PM, and breakfast is served on weekends. ⊠ *457 E. Ojai Ave.* ☎ *805/640–7987* ⊟ *AE, D, MC, V.*

¢–$ ✕ **Ojai Café Emporium.** Best known for healthful, California-style salads such as the Topa Topa (greens with roasted chicken, kidney beans, corn chips, and taco seasoning), this casual downtown eatery across from the art center also offers standout make-your-own sandwiches, home-style fish cakes, and fresh fish and pasta entrées. The cheery dining rooms and outdoor patio are open for breakfast, lunch, and dinner. ✉ *108 S. Montgomery St.* ☎ *805/646–2723* ▭ *AE, MC, V* ⊘ *No dinner Sun. and Mon.*

★ $$$$ ⊞ **Ojai Valley Inn & Spa.** This outdoorsy, golf-oriented resort and spa is set on beautifully landscaped grounds, with hillside views in nearly all directions. Nearby is the inn's 800-acre ranch, where you can take riding lessons and go on guided trail rides. In 2005 the resort completed a $70 million renovation. Two restaurants, a ballroom, and 100 guest rooms were added; all existing rooms and suites were refurbished to reflect the Spanish-colonial architecture of the original 1923 resort. If you're a history buff, ask for a room in the original 80-year-old adobe building. The four restaurants tout "Ojai regional cuisine," which incorporates locally grown produce and fresh seasonal meats and seafood. ✉ *905 Country Club Rd., 93023* ☎ *805/646–1111 or 800/422–6524* 🖷 *805/646–7969* ⊕ *www.ojairesort.com* 🛏 *305 rooms, 60 suites* ♿ *4 restaurants, minibars, cable TV with movies, in-room broadband, Wi-Fi, 18-hole golf course, 4 tennis courts, 3 pools, spa, hiking, horseback riding, bar, pub, children's programs (ages 5–12), convention center, some pets allowed (fee); no smoking* ▭ *AE, D, DC, MC, V.*

$$–$$$ ⊞ **Oaks at Ojai.** Rejuvenation is the name of the game at this comfortable spa resort. You can work out all day or just lounge by the pool. The fitness package is a great value and includes lodging, use of the spa facilities, a choice of 18 daily exercise classes, hikes, and fitness activities, and 3 nutritionally balanced, low-calorie meals a day, plus snacks and beverages. Nonguests can eat here, too, but it's mainly for the fitness-conscious. Cell-phone use is not allowed in public areas. Guests under age 16 are not recommended. ✉ *122 E. Ojai Ave., 93023* ☎ *805/646–5573 or 800/753–6257* 🖷 *805/640–1504* ⊕ *www.oaksspa.com* 🛏 *46 rooms* ♿ *Dining room, pool, gym, hair salon, hot tub, massage, sauna, spa; no smoking* ▭ *AE, D, MC, V* ⊙⏐ *FAP* ☞ *2-night minimum stay.*

$–$$ ⊞ **The Blue Iguana Inn & Cottages.** Artists run this southwestern-style hotel, and their work (which is for sale) decorates the rooms. The small, cozy main inn is about 2 mi west of downtown. Its sister property, the Emerald Iguana Inn, consists of eight more art-nouveau cottages closer to downtown Ojai. Suites and cottages all have kitchenettes. ✉ *11794 N. Ventura Ave., Hwy. 33, 93023* ☎ *805/646–5277* ⊕ *www.blueiguanainn.com* 🛏 *4 rooms, 7 suites, 8 cottages* ♿ *Some kitchenettes, some microwaves, refrigerators, cable TV, some in-room VCRs, Wi-Fi, pool, hot tub, massage, some pets allowed (fee); no smoking* ▭ *AE, D, DC, MC, V.*

The Arts

On Wednesday evenings in summer, all-American music played by the Ojai Band draws crowds to **Libbey Park** (✉ Ojai Ave. ☎ 805/640–2560 🎟 Free) in downtown Ojai. Since 1947, the **Ojai Music Festival** (☎ 805/646–2094 ⊕ www.ojaifestival.org) has attracted internationally known progressive and traditional musicians for outdoor concerts in Libbey Park for a weekend in late May or early June.

SANTA BARBARA

27 mi northwest of Ventura and 29 mi west of Ojai on U.S. 101.

Santa Barbara has long been an oasis for Los Angelenos seeking respite from hectic big-city life. The attractions begin at the ocean and end in the foothills of the Santa Ynez Mountains. A few miles up the coast—but still very much a part of Santa Barbara—is the exclusive residential district of Hope Ranch. Santa Barbara is on a jog in the coastline, so the ocean is actually to the south, instead of the west; for this reason, directions can be confusing. "Up" the coast toward San Francisco is west, "down" toward Los Angeles is east, and the mountains are north. A car is handy but not essential if you're planning to stay in town. The beaches and downtown are easily explored by bicycle or on foot. You can also hop aboard one of the electric shuttles that cruise the downtown and waterfront every 8 to 15 minutes (25¢ each way) and connect with local buses such as Line 22, which goes to major visitor sights (⊕ www.sbmtd.gov). Visit **Santa Barbara Car Free** (⊕ www.santabarbaracarfree.org) for bike route and walking-tour maps and car-free vacation packages with substantial lodging discounts. A motorized San Francisco–style cable car operated by **Santa Barbara Trolley Co.** (☎ 805/965–0353 ⊕ www.sbtrolley.com) makes 90-minute runs from 10 to 4 past major hotels, shopping areas, and attractions. Get off whenever you like, and pick up another trolley when you're ready to move on (they come every 45 minutes). The trolley departs from and returns to Stearns Wharf. The fare is $18 for the day.

From the Ocean to the Mountains

Santa Barbara's waterfront is beautiful, with palm-studded promenades and plenty of sand. In the few miles between the beaches and the hills are downtown, the old mission, and the botanic gardens. For maps and visitor information, drop by the **Santa Barbara Chamber of Commerce Visitor Information Center** (✉ 1 Garden St., at Cabrillo Blvd. ☎ 805/965–3021 ⊕ www.sbchamber.org).

> A GOOD
> TOUR

Start your tour at the west end of Cabrillo Boulevard, with a stroll around **Santa Barbara Harbor** ▶. You can take a ½-mi walk along the breakwater that protects the harbor, check out the tackle-and-bait shops, or hire a boat. At the base of the breakwater, stop in at the **Outdoors Santa Barbara Visitor Center** 4 and the **Santa Barbara Maritime Museum** 5; they're in the same building. For a cultural interlude walk three blocks up Castillo Street from the harbor to the **Carriage and Western Art Museum** 6. Return to Cabrillo Boulevard, the main drag fronting the harbor, and stroll east along **West Beach** to **Stearns Wharf** 7, where the **Ty Warner Sea Center** 8 is a major attraction.

 To explore downtown, walk up **State Street** (it starts at Stearns Wharf) from the harbor and turn left on Montecito Street, then walk one block to the corner of Chapala Street for a look at the **Moreton Bay Fig Tree.** Planted in 1874 and transplanted to its present location in 1877, this tree is so huge it reputedly can provide shade for 1,000 people. Return

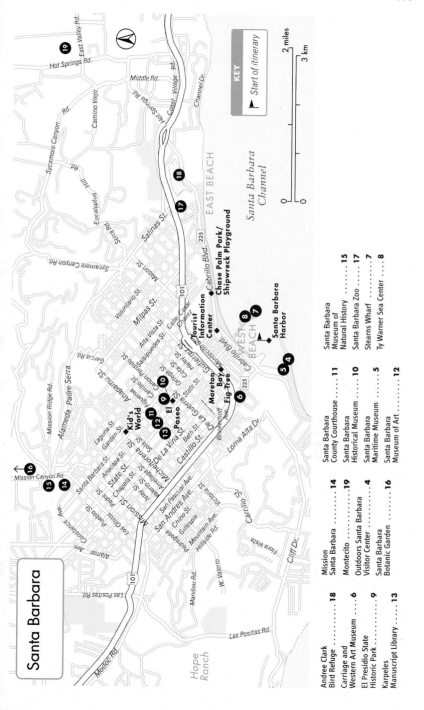

Santa Barbara

Andree Clark
Bird Refuge **18**

Carriage and
Western Art Museum **6**

El Presidio State
Historic Park **9**

Karpeles
Manuscript Library **13**

Mission
Santa Barbara **14**

Montecito **19**

Outdoors Santa Barbara
Visitor Center **4**

Santa Barbara
Botanic Garden **16**

Santa Barbara
County Courthouse **11**

Santa Barbara
Historical Museum **10**

Santa Barbara
Maritime Museum **5**

Santa Barbara
Museum of Art **12**

Santa Barbara
Museum of
Natural History **15**

Santa Barbara Zoo **17**

Stearns Wharf **7**

Ty Warner Sea Center **8**

KEY

▲ *Start of itinerary*

to State Street and continue northwest (away from the harbor) past **El Paseo**, a handsome shopping arcade built around an old adobe home. Make a right at East Canon Perdido Street to reach **El Presidio State Historic Park** ⑨. From here turn right on Santa Barbara Street and right onto De La Guerra Street to reach the entrance of the **Santa Barbara Historical Museum** ⑩. Now make a right onto Anacapa Street and walk three blocks to the **Santa Barbara County Courthouse** ⑪, at Anapamu Street. On the next block of Anapamu Street (at State Street) stands the **Santa Barbara Museum of Art** ⑫, and one block farther is the **Karpeles Manuscript Library** ⑬.

To see the sights of the foothills, hop into your car and take State Street northwest (away from the water) to Los Olivos Street. Turn right, and you'll soon see **Mission Santa Barbara** ⑭. From the mission you can walk the block north to the **Santa Barbara Museum of Natural History** ⑮. You'll probably want to drive the 1½ mi north (via Mission Canyon Road) to the **Santa Barbara Botanic Garden** ⑯. Once you've seen the flora, check out the fauna by heading back toward the ocean via Alameda Padre Serra, Montecito Street, and then Milpas Street to Ninos Drive and the **Santa Barbara Zoo** ⑰. More creatures await at the **Andree Clark Bird Refuge** ⑱, which is adjacent to the zoo. For a drive through a lush enclave of estates, head up into the hills to the Upper Village of **Montecito** ⑲.

TIMING   You could spend an entire day on the harborfront, or devote only two or three hours to it if you drive and stop only briefly at the various attractions. Set aside an hour each for the art and natural-history museums and for the botanic gardens. A spin through the zoo takes about an hour. Add plenty of time if you're a shopper—the stores and galleries around State Street may sidetrack you for hours.

What to See

⑱ **Andree Clark Bird Refuge.** This peaceful lagoon and gardens sits north of East Beach. Bike trails and footpaths, punctuated by signs identifying native and migratory birds, skirt the lagoon. ⊠ *1400 E. Cabrillo Blvd.* ✉ *Free.*

⑥ **Carriage and Western Art Museum.** The country's largest collection of old horse-drawn vehicles—painstakingly restored—is exhibited here. Everything from polished hearses to police buggies to old stagecoaches and circus vehicles is on display. In August the Old Spanish Days Fiesta borrows many of the vehicles for a jaunt about town. This is one of the city's true hidden gems, a wonderful place to help history come alive—especially for children. ⊠ *129 Castillo St.* ☎ *805/962-2353* ⊕ *www. carriagemuseum.org* ✉ *Free* ⊙ *Daily 9–3.*

★ ⑨ **El Presidio State Historic Park.** Founded in 1782, El Presidio was one of four military strongholds established by the Spanish along the coast of California. The park encompasses much of the original site in the heart of downtown. El Cuartel, the adobe guardhouse, is the oldest building in Santa Barbara and the second oldest in California. ⊠ *123 E. Canon Perdido St.* ☎ *805/965-0093* ⊕ *www.sbthp.org* ✉ *$3* ⊙ *Daily 10:30–4:30.*

13 **Karpeles Manuscript Library.** Ancient political tracts and old Disney cartoons are among the holdings at this facility, which also houses one of the world's largest privately owned collections of rare manuscripts. Fifty display cases contain a sampling of the archive's million-plus documents. ⊠ *21 W. Anapamu St.* ☎ *805/962–5322* ⊕ *www.karpeles. com* 🖂 *Free* ⊙ *Daily 10–4.*

14 **Mission Santa Barbara.** Widely referred to as the "Queen of Missions," Fodor'sChoice this is one of the most beautiful and frequently photographed buildings ★ in coastal California. The architecture, which was originally built in 1786, evolved from adobe-brick buildings with thatch roofs to more permanent edifices as its population burgeoned. An earthquake in 1812 destroyed the third church built on the site. Its replacement, the present structure, is still a functioning Catholic church. The building is surrounded by cacti, palms, and other succulents. ⊠ *2201 Laguna St.* ☎ *805/682–4149* ⊕ *www.sbmission.org* 🖂 *$4* ⊙ *Daily 9–5.*

19 **Montecito.** Since the late 1800s the tree-studded hills and valleys of this town have attracted the rich and famous (Hollywood icons, business tycoons, "dot-commers" who divested before the crash, and "old-money" families who installed themselves here years ago). Shady roads wind through the community, which consists mostly of gated estates. Swank boutiques line Coast Village Road, where well-heeled residents such as Oprah Winfrey and John Cleese sometimes browse for truffle oil, picture frames, and designer sweats. Residents also hang out in the Upper Village, a chic shopping area with restaurants and cafés at the intersection of San Ysidro and East Valley roads. Montecito is just about 3 mi east of Santa Barbara.

Fodor'sChoice The 37-acre Montecito estate called **Lotusland** (☎ 805/969–9990 ★ ⊕www.lotusland.org 🖂$20) once belonged to Polish opera singer Ganna Walska. Many of the exotic trees and other subtropical flora were planted in 1882 by horticulturist R. Kinton Stevens. On the two-hour guided tour (the only option for visiting), you'll see an outdoor theater, a topiary garden, a huge collection of rare cycads (an unusual plant genus that has been around since the time of the dinosaurs), and a lotus pond. Tours are conducted mid-February through mid-November, Wednesday through Saturday at 10 and 1:30. Reservations are required. Children under 10 are not allowed, except on family tours, offered on Thursday and the second Saturday of each month.

4 **Outdoors Santa Barbara Visitor Center.** The small office provides maps and other information about Channel Islands National Park, Channel Islands National Marine Sanctuary, and Los Padres National Forest. The same building houses the Santa Barbara Maritime Museum. ⊠ *113 Harbor Way* ☎ *805/884–1475* ⊕ *www.outdoorsb.noaa.gov* 🖂 *Free* ⊙ *Daily 11–5; in summer on Sat. until 7.*

16 **Santa Barbara Botanic Garden.** Scenic trails meander through the garden's 78 acres of native plants. The Mission Dam, built in 1806, stands just beyond the redwood grove and above the restored aqueduct that once carried water to Mission Santa Barbara. An ethnobotanical display demonstrates how Native Americans used plants to create baskets, clothing, and structures. ✉ *1212 Mission Canyon Rd.* ☎ *805/682–4726* ⊕ *www.sbbg.org* ✒ *$7* ⊙ *Mar.–Oct., daily 9–6; Nov.–Feb., daily 9–5. Guided tours daily at 2; additional tour on weekends at 11.*

★ ⓫ **Santa Barbara County Courthouse.** Hand-painted tiles and a spiral staircase infuse the courthouse with the grandeur of a Moorish palace. This magnificent building was completed in 1929, part of a rebuilding process after a 1925 earthquake destroyed many downtown structures. At the time Santa Barbara was also in the midst of a cultural awakening, and the trend was toward an architectural style appropriate to the area's climate and history. The result is the harmonious Mediterranean–Spanish look of much of the downtown area, especially the municipal buildings. An elevator rises to an arched observation area in the courthouse tower that provides a panoramic view of the city. The murals in the ceremonial chambers on the courthouse's second floor were painted by an artist who did backdrops for some of Cecil B. DeMille's films. ✉ *1100 block of Anacapa St.* ☎ *805/962–6464* ⊕ *www.santabarbaracourthouse.org* ⊙ *Weekdays 8–4:45, weekends 10–4:30. Free guided tours Mon., Tues., and Fri. at 10:30, Mon.–Sat. at 2.*

NEED A BREAK? Both children and adults can enjoy themselves at **Kids' World** (✉ Garden St. at Micheltorena St.), a public playground with a complex, castle-shape maze of fanciful climbing structures, slides, and tunnels built by Santa Barbara parents.

⓾ **Santa Barbara Historical Museum.** The historical society's museum exhibits decorative and fine arts, furniture, costumes, and documents from the town's past. Adjacent to it is the Gledhill Library, a collection of books, photographs, maps, and manuscripts. ✉ *136 E. De La Guerra St.* ☎ *805/ 966–1601* ⊕ *www.santabarbaramuseum.com* ✒ *Museum by donation; library $2–$5 per hr for research* ⊙ *Museum Tues.–Sat. 10–5, Sun. noon–5; library Tues.–Fri. 10–4, 1st Sat. of month 10–1. Free guided tours Wed. and weekends at 1:30.*

❺ **Santa Barbara Maritime Museum.** California's seafaring history is the focus at this museum. High-tech, hands-on exhibits, such as a sportfishing activity that lets you catch a "big one," make this a fun stop for families. ✉ *113 Harbor Way* ☎ *805/962–8404* ⊕ *www.sbmm.org* ✒ *$6* ⊙ *June–Aug., 10–6 daily; Sept.–May, 10–5 daily.*

⓬ **Santa Barbara Museum of Art.** The highlights of this museum's permanent collection include ancient sculpture, Asian art, impressionist paintings, contemporary Latin American art, and American works in several media. ✉ *1130 State St.* ☎ *805/963–4364* ⊕ *www.sbmuseart.org* ✒ *$9, free on Sun.* ⊙ *Tues.–Sun. 11–5. Free guided tours Tues.–Sun. at noon and 1.*

⓯ **Santa Barbara Museum of Natural History.** The gigantic skeleton of a blue whale greets you at the entrance of this complex. The major draws include the planetarium, space lab, and a gem and mineral display. A room of dioramas illustrates Chumash Indian history and culture. Startlingly alive-looking stuffed specimens, complete with nests and eggs, roost in the bird diversity room. Many exhibits have interactive components. Outdoors you can stroll on nature trails that wind through the serene oak-studded grounds. Admission is free on the third Sunday of each month. ⊠ *2559 Puesta del Sol Rd.* ☎ *805/682–4711* ⊕ *www.sbnature.org* ⊠ *$8* ⊙ *Daily 10–5.*

🖐 **⑰ Santa Barbara Zoo.** The grounds of this smallish zoo are so gorgeous people book their weddings here long in advance. The palm-studded lawns on a hilltop overlooking the beach are perfect spots for family picnics. The natural settings of the zoo shelter elephants, gorillas, exotic birds, and big cats such as the rare snow leopard, a thick-furred, high-altitude dweller from Asia. For small children, there's a scenic railroad and barnyard petting zoo. ⊠ *500 Niños Dr.* ☎ *805/962–5339* ⊕ *www. santabarbarazoo.org* ⊠ *$10; parking $3* ⊙ *Daily 10–5.*

NEED A BREAK? The antique carousel, large playground with a nautical theme, picnic areas, and snack bar make the scenic waterfront **Chase Palm Park and Ship-wreck Playground** (⊠ Cabrillo Blvd. between Garden St. and Calle Cesar 🖐 Chavez) a favorite destination for kids and parents.

❼ Stearns Wharf. Built in 1872, historic Stearns Wharf is Santa Barbara's most visited landmark. Expansive views of the mountains, cityscape, and harbor unfold from every vantage point on the three-block-long pier. Although it's a nice walk from the Cabrillo Boulevard parking areas, you can also park on the pier and then wander through the shops or stop for a meal at one of the wharf's restaurants. ⊠ *Cabrillo Blvd. at foot of State St.* ☎ *805/897–2683 or 805/564–5531.*

🖐 **❽ Ty Warner Sea Center.** A branch of the Santa Barbara Museum of Natural History, the Sea Center specializes in Santa Barbara Channel marine life and conservation. In 2005 it reopened in a new, $6.5 million facility bearing the name of Ty Warner, Beanie Baby mogul and local resident, whose hefty donation helped the center complete the final stages of construction. The new Sea Center is small compared to aquariums in Monterey and Long Beach, but it's a fascinating, hands-on marine science laboratory that lets you participate in experiments, projects, and exhibits, including touch tanks. Haul up and analyze water samples, learn to identify marine mammals, and check out amazing creatures in the tide-pool lab and animal nursery. The two-story glass walls open to stunning ocean, mountain, and city views. ⊠ *211 Stearns Wharf* ☎ *805/962–2526* ⊕ *www.sbnature.org* ⊠ *$7* ⊙ *Daily 10–5.*

Where to Stay & Eat

$$$$
Fodor's Choice
★
✕ **Wine Cask.** Seared peppercorn ahi tuna and grilled filet mignon are among the most popular entrées at this slick restaurant, which has a beautiful wooden interior and Santa Barbara's most extensive wine list. In fine weather, couples seek out the romantic outdoor patio. ⊠ *813 Anacapa St.* ☎ *805/ 966–9463* ⚲ *Reservations essential* ☰ *AE, DC, MC, V.*

$$$–$$$$ ✕ **Bouchon.** This upscale restaurant showcases fine local wines, produce, and such regional specialties as bluefin tuna and organic pork chops. The mood is intimate and the wine selection huge. ⊠ *9 W. Victoria St.* ☎ *805/730–1160* ☰ *AE, DC, MC, V* ⊙ *No lunch.*

$$–$$$ ✕ **Olio e Limone.** Sophisticated Italian cuisine (with an emphasis on Sicily) is served at this restaurant near the Arlington Center for the Performing Arts. The juicy veal chop is a popular dish, but surprises abound here; be sure to try unusual dishes such as ribbon pasta with quail and sausage in a mushroom ragout, duck ravioli, or swordfish with Sicilian ratatouille. Tables are placed a bit close together, so this may not be the best spot for intimate conversations. ⊠ *17 W. Victoria St.* 🕾 *805/899–2699* ⊟ *AE, D, DC, MC, V.*

$$–$$$ ✕ **Palace Grill.** Mardi Gras energy, team-style service, lively music, and great food have made the Palace a Santa Barbara icon. Acclaimed for its Cajun and creole dishes such as blackened redfish and jambalaya with dirty rice, the Palace also serves Caribbean fare, including a delicious coconut-shrimp dish. If you're spice-phobic, you can choose pasta, soft-shell crab, or filet mignon. Be prepared to wait as long as 45 minutes for a table on Friday and Saturday night, when reservations are taken for a 5:30 seating only. ⊠ *8 E. Cota St.* 🕾 *805/963–5000* ⊟ *AE, MC, V.*

$–$$$ ✕ **Arigato Sushi.** You might have to wait 45 minutes for a table at this trendy, two-story restaurant and sushi bar—locals line up early for the hip, casual atmosphere and wildly creative combination rolls. Fans of authentic Japanese food sometimes disagree about the quality of the seafood, but all dishes are fresh and artfully presented. The menu includes traditional dishes as well as innovative creations such as sushi pizza on seaweed and Hawaiian sashimi salad. ⊠ *1225 State St.* 🕾 *805/965–6074* ⚠ *Reservations not accepted* ⊟ *AE, MC, V* ☾ *No lunch.*

$–$$$ ✕ **Roy.** Owner-chef Leroy Gandy serves a $25 fixed-price dinner—a real bargain—that includes a small salad, fresh soup, homemade organic bread, and a selection from a rotating list of contemporary American main courses. If you're lucky, the entrée choices might include grilled local fish with a mandarin beurre blanc, or bacon-wrapped filet mignon. You can also choose from an à la carte menu of inexpensive appetizers and entrées, plus local wines. Half a block from State Street in the heart of downtown, Roy is a favorite spot for late-night dining (it's open until midnight and has a full bar). ⊠ *7 W. Carrillo St.* 🕾 *805/966–5636* ⊟ *AE, D, DC, MC, V* ☾ *No lunch.*

$–$$ ✕ **Brophy Bros.** The outdoor tables at this casual harborside restaurant have perfect views of the marina and mountains. The staff serves enormous, exceptionally fresh fish dishes—don't miss the seafood salad and chowder—and provides you with a pager if there's a long wait for a table. You can stroll along the waterfront until the beep lets you know your table's ready. This place is hugely popular; so it can be crowded and loud, especially on weekend evenings. ⊠ *119 Harbor Way* 🕾 *805/966–4418* ⊟ *AE, MC, V.*

¢–$ ✕ **The Taj Cafe.** Traditional village-style Indian cooking and exotic decor—fabrics, curtains, and artwork are all imported from the East—make for a deliciously different dining experience here. The chef uses organic spices to create a host of lean, healthful dishes, such as tandoori entrées, curries, masalas, vegetarian dishes, and Frankies (Bombay-style burritos). Can't decide? Try the Taj Special, with samples of various tandoori dishes, or one of the many combination plates. ⊠ *905 State St.* 🕾 *805/564–8280* ⊟ *AE, D, MC, V.*

★ ¢ ✕ **La Super-Rica.** Praised by Julia Child, this food stand with a patio on the east side of town serves some of the spiciest and most authentic Mexican dishes between Los Angeles and San Francisco. Fans drive for miles to fill up on the soft tacos served with yummy spicy or mild sauces and legendary beans. Three daily specials are offered each day. Portions are on the small side; order several dishes and share. ⊠ *622 N. Milpas St., at Alphonse St.* ☏ *805/963–4940* ▤ *No credit cards.*

★ **$$$$** ✕▥ **Four Seasons Biltmore Santa Barbara.** Surrounded by lush, perfectly manicured gardens and across from the beach, Santa Barbara's grande dame has long been a favorite for quiet, California-style luxury. The sumptuous 10,000-square-foot spa, which includes 10 treatment rooms, a pool, and gardens, is an oasis for rejuvenation. Dining is upscale casual at the ocean-view Bella Vista Restaurant ($$$–$$$$), where the seasonal California-contemporary menu changes monthly. ⊠ *1260 Channel Dr., 93108* ☏ *805/969–2261 or 800/332–3442* ⊟ *805/565–8323* ⊕ *www. fourseasons.com* ⇲ *178 rooms, 17 suites, 12 cottages* ⌕ *Restaurant, room service, minibars, cable TV, in-room DVDs, in-room broadband, Wi-Fi, putting green, 3 tennis courts, pool, health club, hot tub, spa, croquet, bar, babysitting, children's programs (ages 5–12), concierge, business services, meeting rooms, some pets allowed; no smoking* ▤ *AE, D, DC, MC, V.*

$$$$ ✕▥ **Hotel Andalucia.** The city's first full-service downtown hotel opened in late 2004. Everything within the tony interior reflects Andalusian hacienda style, from Spanish tiles and gold–red colors to wrought-iron chandeliers and arched doorways. Rooms are on the small side, but include such homey touches as fresh flowers and candles. Ride up to the sixth-floor rooftop terrace—which has a pool, hot tub, and outdoor fireplace—for exotic drinks at El Cielo, a hip bar with some of the best views in Santa Barbara. The hotel's sophisticated 31 West restaurant ($$–$$$) draws discerning diners from all over Southern California. Don't look out the window, though; the Greyhound station across the street will draw you back to reality. ⊠ *31 W. Carrillo St., 93101* ☏ *805/884–0300 or 877/468–3515* ⊟ *805/884–8153* ⊕ *www.andaluciasb.com* ⇲ *77 rooms, 20 suites* ⌕ *Restaurant, in-room safes, minibars, in-room DVDs, in-room broadband, Wi-Fi, pool, hot tub, bar, lobby lounge, laundry service, concierge, meeting rooms, some pets allowed; no smoking* ▤ *AE, D, DC, MC, V.*

★ **$$$$** ✕▥ **San Ysidro Ranch.** At this romantic hideaway in the Montecito foothills—where John and Jackie Kennedy spent their honeymoon and Oprah sends her out-of town guests—guest cottages are scattered among groves of orange trees and flower beds. All have down comforters and fireplaces; most have private outdoor spas, and one has its own pool. Seventeen miles of hiking trails crisscross 500 acres of open space surrounding the property. The Stonehouse Restaurant ($$–$$$$) and Plow & Angel Bistro ($–$$$) are Santa Barbara institutions. At this writing, the property was undergoing a major renovation; the project was scheduled to be completed by early 2007. ⊠ *900 San Ysidro La., Montecito 93108* ☏ *805/565–1700 or 800/368–6788* ⊟ *805/565–1995* ⊕ *www. sanysidroranch.com* ⇲ *40 cottages* ⌕ *2 restaurants, room service, refrigerators, cable TV, in-room DVDs, in-room broadband, Wi-Fi, pool, gym, massage, bar, some pets allowed (fee); no smoking* ▤ *AE, DC, MC, V* ⌕ *2-day minimum stay on weekends, 3 days on holiday weekends.*

$$$$ **Inn of the Spanish Garden.** A half block from the Presidio in the heart of downtown, this elegant Spanish–Mediterranean retreat celebrates Santa Barbara style, from tile floors, wrought-iron balconies, and exotic plants to original art by famed local plein air artists. The luxury rooms have private balconies or patios, fireplaces, Frette linens, and deep soaking tubs. In the evening, you can order a glass of wine and relax in the candlelighted courtyard. This inn is a good choice if you want to park your car for most of your stay and walk to theaters, restaurants, and shuttle buses. ✉ *915 Garden St., 93101* ☎ *805/564–4700 or 866/564–4700* 🖷 *805/564–4701* 🌐 *www.spanishgardeninn.com* *23 rooms* *Fans, minibars, cable TV with movies, in-room VCRs, in-room broadband, Wi-Fi, pool, gym, massage, wine bar, laundry service, concierge, business services, meeting rooms, free parking; no smoking* 💳 *AE, D, DC, MC, V* 🍽 *CP.*

★ **$$$–$$$$** **Simpson House Inn.** If you're a fan of traditional B&Bs, this property, with its beautifully appointed Victorian main house and acre of lush gardens, is for you. If privacy and luxury are your priority, choose one of the elegant cottages or a room in the century-old barn; each has a wood-burning fireplace, luxurious bedding, and state-of-the-art electronics (several even have whirlpool baths). In-room massages and other spa services are available. Room rates include use of a downtown athletic club. ✉ *121 E. Arrellaga St., 93101* ☎ *805/963–7067 or 800/676–1280* 🖷 *805/564–4811* 🌐 *www.simpsonhouseinn.com* *11 rooms, 4 cottages* *Some in-room hot tubs, some refrigerators, cable TV, in-room DVDs, Wi-Fi, bicycles, croquet; no smoking* 💳 *AE, D, MC, V* ☞ *2-night minimum stay on weekends* 🍽 *BP.*

$–$$ **Franciscan Inn.** Part of this Spanish–Mediterranean motel, a block from the harbor and West Beach, dates back to the 1920s. The friendly staff and range of cheery, spacious country-theme rooms, from singles to mini- and family suites, make this a good choice for families. ✉ *109 Bath St., 93101* ☎ *805/963–8845* 🖷 *805/564–3295* 🌐 *www.franciscaninn.com* *48 rooms, 5 suites* *Some kitchens, some kitchenettes, some microwaves, some refrigerators, cable TV with movies, in-room VCRs, in-room data ports, pool, hot tub, laundry facilities, no-smoking rooms* 💳 *AE, DC, MC, V* 🍽 *CP.*

¢–$ **Motel 6 Santa Barbara Beach.** A half block from East Beach amid fancier hotels sits this basic but comfortable motel, which was the first Motel 6 in existence. It's an incredible bargain for the location and fills quickly; book months in advance if possible. Kids 17 and under stay free. Two sister properties in Carpinteria, 12 mi south of Santa Barbara and 1 mi from the beach, offer equally comfortable rooms at even lower rates. ✉ *443 Corona Del Mar Dr., 93103* ☎ *805/564–1392 or 800/466–8356* 🖷 *805/963–4687* 🌐 *www.motel6.com* *51 rooms* *Some microwaves, some refrigerators, cable TV with movies, in-room data ports, pool, some pets allowed, no-smoking rooms* 💳 *AE, D, DC, MC, V.*

Nightlife & the Arts

Most major hotels present entertainment nightly during the summer season and on weekends all year. Much of the town's bar, club, and live music scene centers around lower State Street (between the 300 and 800 blocks). The thriving arts district, with theaters, restaurants, and cafés, starts around the 900 block of State Street and continues north to the Arlington Center for the Performing Arts, in the 1300 block. Santa Barbara supports a professional symphony and a chamber orchestra. The proximity to the University of Califorina at Santa Barbara assures an endless stream of visiting artists and performers. To see what's scheduled around town, pick up a copy of the free weekly *Santa Barbara Independent* newspaper.

NIGHTLIFE Rich leather couches, a crackling fire in chilly weather, a cigar balcony, and pool tables draw a fancy Gen-X crowd to **Blue Agave** (✉ 20 E. Cota St. ☎ 805/899–4694) for good food and designer martinis. All types of people hang out at **Darghan's** (✉ 18 E. Ortega St. ☎ 805/568–0702), a lively pub with four pool tables, a great selection of draft beer and Irish whiskeys, and a full menu of traditional Irish dishes. The **James Joyce** (✉ 513 State St. ☎ 805/962–2688), which sometimes plays host to folk and rock performers, is a good place to have a few beers and while away an evening.

Call ahead to reserve an outdoor table at **Indochine** (✉ 434 State St. ☎ 805/ 962–0154), a sleek Thai-style nightclub filled with Southeast Asian furniture and art, open Tuesday through Saturday nights. **Joe's Cafe** (✉ 536 State St. ☎ 805/966–4638), where steins of beer accompany hearty bar food, is a fun, if occasionally rowdy, collegiate scene. The bartenders at **Left at Albuquerque** (✉ 803 State St. ☎ 805/564–5040) pour 141 types of tequila, making the southwestern-style bar one of Santa Barbara's less sedate nightspots. Smooth martinis, and balconies overlooking State Street, attract a crowd of varying ages to **Rocks** (✉ 801 State St. ☎ 805/ 884–1190). **SOhO** (✉ 1221 State St. ☎ 805/962–7776), a hip restaurant and bar, presents weeknight jazz; on weekends, the mood livens with good blues and rock.

This is closed but should reopen fall 2006. A slick sports bar attached to an upscale steak house owned by the maker of Lucky Brand Dungarees, **Lucky's** (✉ 1279 Coast Village Rd., Montecito ☎ 805/565–7540) attracts a flock of hip, fashionably dressed patrons hoping to see and be seen.

THE ARTS **Arlington Center for the Performing Arts** (✉ 1317 State St. ☎ 805/963– 4408), a Moorish-style auditorium, is the home of the Santa Barbara Symphony. **Center Stage Theatre** (✉ 700 block of State St., 2nd fl. of Paseo Nuevo ☎ 805/963–0408) presents plays, music, dance, and readings. **Ensemble Theatre Company** (✉ 914 Santa Barbara St. ☎ 805/962–8606) stages plays by authors ranging from Henrik Ibsen to David Mamet. The **Lobero Theatre** (✉ 33 E. Canon Perdido St. ☎ 805/963–0761), a state landmark, hosts community theater groups and touring professionals. In Montecito, the **Music Academy of the West** (✉ 1070 Fairway Rd. ☎ 805/969–4726) showcases orchestral, chamber, and operatic works every summer.

Sports & the Outdoors

BEACHES Santa Barbara's beaches don't have the big surf of the shoreline farther south, but they also don't have the crowds. You can usually find a solitary spot to swim or sunbathe. In June and July, fog often hugs the coast until about noon. The wide swath of sand at the east end of Cabrillo Boulevard on the harbor front is a great spot for people-watching. **East Beach** (✉ 1118 Cabrillo Blvd. ☎ 805/897–2680) has sand volleyball courts, summertime lifeguard and sports competitions, and arts-and-crafts shows on Sunday and holidays. You can use showers, a weight room, and lockers (bring your own towel) and rent umbrellas and boogie boards at the Cabrillo Bathhouse. Next door, there's an elaborate jungle-gym play area for kids. The usually gentle surf at **Arroyo Burro County Beach** (✉ Cliff Dr. at Las Positas Rd.) makes it ideal for families with young children.

BICYCLING The level, two-lane, 3-mi **Cabrillo Bike Lane** passes the Santa Barbara Zoo, the Andree Clark Bird Refuge, beaches, and the harbor. There are restaurants along the way, and you can stop for a picnic along the palm-lined path looking out on the Pacific. **Wheel Fun Rentals** (✉ 22 State St. ☎ 805/ 966–2282) has bikes, quadricycles, and skates.

BOATS & CHARTERS **Adventours Outdoor Excursions** (✉ 726 Reddick Ave. ☎ 805/899–2929) arranges everything from kayak to mountain-bike excursions. **Santa Barbara Sailing Center** (✉ Santa Barbara Harbor launching ramp ☎ 805/ 962–2826 or 800/350–9090) offers sailing instruction, rents and charters sailboats, and organizes dinner and sunset champagne cruises, island excursions, and whale-watching trips. **Sea Landing** (✉ Cabrillo Blvd. at Bath St. and the breakwater in the Santa Barbara Harbor ☎ 805/882–0088 or 888/779–4253) operates surface and deep-sea fishing charters year-round. From Sea Landing, the *Condor Express* (☎ 805/963–3564), a 75-foot high-speed catamaran, whisks up to 149 passengers toward the Channel Islands on dinner cruises, whale-watching excursions, and pelagic-bird trips. **Truth Aquatics** (☎ 805/962–1127) departs from Sea Landing in the Santa Barbara Harbor to ferry passengers to Channel Islands National Park. Their three dive boats also take scuba divers on single- and multiday trips. **Captain Don's** (✉ Stearns Wharf ☎ 805/969–5217) operates whale-watching and harbor cruises aboard the 90-foot *Rachel G.*

GOLF Robert Trent Jones Jr. designed the stunning par-71 **Rancho San Marcos Golf Course** (✉ 12½ mi north of Santa Barbara on Hwy. 154 ☎ 805/ 683–6334). Greens fees range from $65 to $85 and include a golf cart and driving range time. Like Pebble Beach, the 18-hole, par-72 **Sandpiper Golf Club** (✉ 14 mi north of downtown on Hwy. 101, 7925 Hollister Ave. ☎ 805/968—1541) sits on the ocean bluffs and combines stunning views with a challenging game. Greens fees are $119–$139; an optional cart is $16. **Santa Barbara Golf Club** (✉ Las Positas Rd. and McCaw Ave. ☎ 805/687–7087) has an 18-hole, par 70 course. The greens fees are $33–$43; an optional cart costs $13 per person.

TENNIS Many hotels in Santa Barbara have courts. The **City of Santa Barbara Parks and Recreation Department** (☎ 805/564–5418) operates public courts with lighted play until 9 PM weekdays. You can purchase day permits ($5) at the courts, or call the department. **Las Positas Municipal Courts** (✉ 1002 Las Positas Rd.) has six lighted hard courts open daily. The 12 hard courts at the **Municipal Tennis Center** (✉ 1414 Park Pl., near Salinas St. and U.S.

101) include an enclosed stadium court and three lighted courts open daily. **Pershing Park** (⊠ 100 Castillo St., near Cabrillo Blvd.) has eight lighted courts available for public play after 5 PM weekdays and all day on weekends and Santa Barbara City College holidays.

Shopping

SHOPPING AREAS **State Street,** roughly between Cabrillo Boulevard and Sola Street, is the commercial hub of Santa Barbara and a shopper's paradise. Chic malls, quirky storefronts, antiques emporia, elegant boutiques, and funky thrift shops abound here. **Paseo Nuevo** (⊠ 700 and 800 blocks of State St.), an open-air mall anchored by chains such as Nordstrom and Macy's, also contains a few local institutions such as the children's clothier This Little Piggy. You can do your shopping on foot or by a battery-powered trolley (25¢) that runs between the waterfront and the 1300 block.

Shops, art galleries, and studios share the courtyard and gardens of **El Paseo** (⊠ Canon Perdido St. between State and Anacapa Sts.), an historic arcade. Antiques and gift shops are clustered in restored Victorian buildings on **Brinkerhoff Avenue** (⊠ 2 blocks west of State St. at West Cota St.). Serious antiques hunters can head a few miles south of Santa Barbara to the beach town of **Summerland,** which is full of shops and markets.

CLOTHING The complete line of **Big Dog Sportswear** (⊠ 6 E. Yanonali St. ☎ 805/963–8728) is sold at the Santa Barbara–based company's flagship store. **Channel Islands Surfboards** (⊠ 36 Anacapa St. ☎ 805/966–7213) stocks the latest in California beachwear, sandals, and accessories. **Territory Ahead** (⊠ Main store: 515 State St. ⊠ Outlet store: 400 State St. ☎ 805/962–5558), a high-quality outdoorsy catalog company, sells fashionably rugged clothing for men and women. **Pierre Lafond–Wendy Foster** (⊠ 833 State St. ☎ 805/966–2276) is a casual-chic clothing store for women.

EN ROUTE If you choose to drive north via U.S. 101 without detouring to the Solvang/Santa Ynez area, you will drive right past some good beaches. In succession from east to west, **El Capitan, Gaviota, and Refugio state beaches** all have campsites, picnic tables, and fire rings. If you'd like to encounter nature without roughing it, you can try "comfort camping" at **El Capitan Canyon** (⊠ 11560 Calle Real, north side of El Capitan State Beach exit ☎ 800/248–6274). The safari tents and cedar cabins here have fresh linens and creature comforts.

SANTA BARBARA COUNTY
INCLUDING SOLVANG

Residents refer to the glorious 30-mi stretch of coastline from Carpinteria to Gaviota as the South Coast. The Santa Ynez Mountains divide the county geographically; U.S. 101 passes through a mountain tunnel leading inland. Northern Santa Barbara County used to be known for its sprawling ranches and strawberry and broccoli fields. Today its 70-plus wineries and 18,000 acres of vineyards dominate the landscape from the Santa Ynez Valley, in the south, to Santa Maria in the north.

The hit film *Sideways* was filmed almost entirely in the North County–wine country; when the movie won Golden Globe and Oscar awards in 2005, it sparked national and international interest in visits to the region. **The Santa Barbara Conference & Visitors Bureau** (☎ 805/966–9222 or 800/676–1266 ⊕ www.santabarbaraca.com) created a detailed map highlighting film location spots. Maps are readily available at hotels and visitor centers throughout the region.

Santa Ynez

❷ *31 mi north of Goleta via Hwy. 154.*

Founded in 1882, the tiny town of Santa Ynez still has many of its original frontier buildings. You can walk through the three-block downtown area in just a few minutes, shop for antiques, and hang around the old-time saloon. At some of the eponymous valley's best restaurants, you just might bump into one of the many celebrities who own nearby ranches. Just south of Santa Ynez on the Chumash Indian reservation lies the sprawling, Las Vegas–style **Chumash Casino Resort** (⊠ 3400 E. Hwy. 246 ☎ 877/248–6274). The casino has 2,000 slot machines, and the property includes three restaurants, a spa, and an upscale hotel ($$–$$$$) that was completed in 2004.

OFF THE
BEATEN
PATH

★

SAN MARCOS PASS – A former stagecoach route, Highway 154 winds its spectacular way southeast from Santa Ynez through the Los Padres National Forest. Eight miles from Santa Ynez, **Cachuma Lake Recreation Area** (⊠ Hwy. 154 ☎ 805/686–5054 ⊕ www.sbparks.com) centers around a jewel of an artificial lake. Hiking, fishing, and boating are popular here, and there are eagle- and wildlife-watching excursions aboard the *Osprey,* a 48-foot cruiser. The lively, one-of-a-kind **Cold Spring Tavern** (⊠ 5995 Stagecoach Rd., off Hwy. 154 ☎ 805/967–0066), near Cachuma Lake, has been serving travelers since stagecoach days. Part biker hangout and part romantic country hideaway, the tavern specializes in game dishes, such as rabbit and venison, along with such American standards as ribs, steak, and great chili. The tavern serves lunch and dinner daily, plus breakfast on weekends.

Where to Stay & Eat

★ $–$$$ ╳ **Trattoria Grappolo.** Authentic Italian fare, an open kitchen, and festive, family-style seating make this trattoria equally popular with celebrities from Hollywood and ranchers from the Santa Ynez Valley. Italian favorites on the extensive menu range from thin-crust pizza to homemade ravioli, risottos, and seafood linguine to grilled lamb chops in red-wine sauce. The noise level tends to rise in the evening, so this isn't the best spot for a romantic getaway. ⊠ *3687-C Sagunto St.* ☎ *805/688–6899* ▤ *AE, MC, V* ⊗ *No lunch Mon.*

$$$$ ▥ **Santa Ynez Inn.** This posh two-story Victorian inn in downtown Santa Ynez was built from scratch in 2002. The owners have furnished all the rooms with authentic historical pieces. The inn caters to a discerning crowd with the finest amenities—Frette linens, thermostatically controlled heat and air-conditioning, DVD/CD entertainment systems, and custom-made bathrobes. Most rooms have gas fireplaces, double steam showers, and whirlpool tubs. Rates include a phenomenal evening

wine and hors d'oeuvres hour and a full breakfast. The Santa Ynez Inn Wine Cellar, about 50 yards from the main building, is open to the public for wine tasting Thursday through Monday 10 to 4. ⊠ *3627 Sagunto St., 93460* ☎ *805/688–5588 or 800/643–5774* 🖶 *805/686–4294* ⊕ *www.santaynezinn.com* ⇆ *14 rooms* ↻ *Some in-room hot tubs, in-room broadband, Wi-Fi, gym, hot tub, massage, library, laundry service, concierge, meeting rooms; no smoking* ⊟ *AE, D, MC, V* †○† *BP.*

Sports & the Outdoors

The scenic rides operated by **Windhaven Glider** (⊠ Santa Ynez Airport, Hwy. 246 ☎ 805/688–2517) cost between $95 and $185 and last up to 30 minutes.

Los Olivos

㉑ *4 mi north of Santa Ynez on Hwy. 154.*

This pretty village in the Santa Ynez Valley was once on the Spanish-built El Camino Real (Royal Highway) and later a stop on major stagecoach and rail routes. It's so sleepy today, though, that TV's *Return to Mayberry* was filmed here. A row of tasting rooms, art galleries, antiques stores, and country markets lines Grand Avenue. At **Los Olivos Tasting Room & Wine Shop** (⊠ 2905 Grand Ave. ☎ 805/688–7406 ⊕ www.losolivoswines.com), you can sample locally produced wines and pick up winery maps. Historic Heather Cottage, originally an early-1900s doctor's office, houses the **Daniel Gehrs Tasting Room** (⊠ 2939 Grand Ave. ☎ 800/275–8138 ⊕ www.dgwines.com). Here you can sample Gehrs's various varietals, produced in limited small-lot quantities.

Firestone Vineyard (⊠ 5000 Zaca Station Rd. ☎ 805/688–3940 ⊕ www.firestonewine.com) has been around since 1972. It has daily tours, grassy picnic areas, and hiking trails in the hills overlooking the valley; the views are fantastic.

Where to Stay & Eat

$$–$$$$
Fodor's Choice
★

✕ **Brothers Restaurant at Mattei's Tavern.** In the stagecoach days, Mattei's Tavern provided wayfarers with hearty meals and warm beds. Chef-owners and brothers Matt and Jeff Nichols renovated the 1886 building, and while retaining the original character, transformed it into one of the best restaurants in the valley. The casual, unpretentious dining rooms with their red-velvet wallpaper and historic photos reflect the rich history of the tavern. The menu changes every few weeks but often includes house favorites such as foie gras with spiced apples, prime rib, and salmon, and the locally famous jalapeño corn bread. There's also a full bar and an array of vintages from the custom-built cedar wine cellar. ⊠ *2350 Railway Ave.* ☎ *805/688–4820* ⟳ *Reservations essential* ⊟ *AE, MC, V* ⊘ *No lunch.*

$–$$$
✕ **Los Olivos Cafe.** Site of the scene in *Sideways* where the four main characters dine together and share a few bottles of wine, this down-to-earth restaurant not only provided the setting but served the actors real food from their existing menu during filming. Part wine store and part social hub for locals, the café focuses on wine-friendly fish, pasta, and meat dishes made from local bounty, plus salads, pizzas, and burgers. Don't

9

miss the homemade muffuletta and tapenade. Other house favorites include an artisan cheese plate, baked Brie with honey-roasted hazelnuts, and braised pot roast with whipped potatoes. ☒ *2879 Grand Ave.* ☎ *805/688–7265* ☰ *AE, D, MC, V.*

$$$–$$$$　✕🅸 **The Ballard Inn.** Set among orchards and vineyards in the tiny town of Ballard, 2 mi south of Los Olivos, this inn makes an elegant wine-country escape. Rooms are furnished with antiques and original art. Seven rooms have wood-burning fireplaces; the inn provides room phones and TVs on request. The inn's tasting room serves boutique wines Friday through Sunday. At the Ballard Inn Restaurant ($$–$$$), which serves dinner Wednesday through Sunday, owner-chef Budi Kazali creates sumptuous French–Asian dishes in one of the area's most romantic dining rooms. ☒ *2436 Baseline Ave., Ballard 93463* ☎ *805/688–7770 or 800/638–2466* 🖷 *805/688–9560* ⊕ *www.ballardinn.com* 🖙 *15 rooms* ♿ *Restaurant, in-room data ports, bicycles; no room phones* ☰ *AE, MC, V* ⦿ *BP.*

$$$$　🅸 **Fess Parker's Wine Country Inn and Spa.** This luxury inn includes an elegant, tree-shaded French country–style main building and an equally attractive annex across the street with a pool and a hot tub. The spacious accommodations have fireplaces, seating areas, and wet bars. Wine Cask Los Olivos ($$$–$$$$), run by the same folks who own the landmark Wine Cask Restaurant in Santa Barbara, is one of the hotel's main draws. They also operate Intermezzo, a classy wine bar with late-night dining and live music. ☒ *2860 Grand Ave., 93441* ☎ *805/688– 7788 or 800/446–2455* 🖷 *805/688–1942* ⊕ *www.fessparker.com* 🖙 *20 rooms, 1 suite* ♿ *Restaurant, cable TV, Wi-Fi, pool, gym, hot tub, spa, meeting rooms, some pets allowed; no smoking* ☰ *AE, DC, MC, V* ⦿ *BP.*

Solvang

🌙 ㉒　*5 mi south of Los Olivos on Alamo Pintado Rd.; Hwy. 246, 3 mi east of U.S. 101.*

You'll know you've reached the town of Solvang when the architecture suddenly changes to half-timber buildings and windmills. This town was settled in 1911 by a group of Danish educators (the flatlands and rolling green hills reminded them of home), and even today, more than two-thirds of the residents are of Danish descent. Although it's attracted tourists for decades, in recent years it has become more sophisticated, with galleries, upscale restaurants, and wine-tasting rooms. Most shops are locally owned; the city has a new ordinance prohibiting chain stores. A good way to get your bearings is to park your car in one of the many free public lots and stroll around town. Stop in at one of the visitor centers—at 2nd Street and Copenhagen Drive, or Mission Drive (Highway 246) at 5th Street—for maps and helpful advice on what to see and do. Don't forget to stock up on Danish pastries from the town's excellent bakeries before you leave.

Often called the "Hidden Gem" of the missions, **Mission Santa Inés** (☒ 1760 Mission Dr. ☎ 805/688–4815, ⊕ www.missionsantaines.org ☉ Daily 9–5 🎟 $3) has an impressive collection of paintings, statuary, vestments, and Chumash and Spanish artifacts in a serene blufftop setting. Take a self-guided tour through the museum, sanctuary, and tranquil gardens.

Housed in an 1884 adobe, the **Rideau Vineyard** (⊠ 1562 Alamo Pintado Rd. ☎ 805/688–0717 ⊕ www.rideauvineyard.com) tasting room provides simultaneous blasts from the area's ranching past and from its hand-harvested, Rhone-varietal wine-making present.

Just outside Solvang is the **Alma Rosa Winery** (⊠ 7250 Santa Rosa Rd. ☎ 805/688–9090 ⊕ www.almarosawinery.com). Owners Richard and Thekla Sanford helped put Santa Barbara County on the international wine map with a 1989 pinot noir. Recently the Sanfords started a new winery, Alma Rosa, with wines made from grapes grown on their 100-plus-acre certified organic vineyards in the Santa Rita Hills. You can taste the current releases at one of the most environmentally sensitive tasting rooms and picnic areas in the valley. All their vineyards are certified organic, and the pinot noirs and chardonnays are exceptional.

Where to Stay & Eat

$$–$$$$ ✕ **The Hitching Post.** You'll find everything from grilled artichokes to ostrich at this casual eatery just outside of Solvang, but most people come for what is said to be the best Santa Maria–style barbecue in the state. The oak used in the barbecue imparts a wonderful smoky taste. Be sure to try a glass of owner-chef-winemaker Frank Ostini's signature High-liner Pinot Noir, a star in the 2004 film *Sideways*. ⊠ *406 E. Hwy. 246* ☎ *805/688–0676* ▭ *AE, MC, V* ☽ *No lunch.*

$–$$ ✕ **Bit O' Denmark.** Perhaps the most authentic Danish eatery in Solvang, this restaurant (the oldest food establishment in Solvang), occupies an old-beam building that was a church until 1929. Two specialties of the house are the *Frikadeller* (meatballs with pickled red cabbage, potatoes, and thick brown gravy) and the *Medisterpølse* (Danish beef and pork sausage with cabbage). ⊠ *473 Alisal Rd.* ☎ *805/688–5426* ▭ *AE, D, MC, V.*

★ $$$$ ▥ **Alisal Guest Ranch and Resort.** Since 1946 this 10,000-acre ranch has been popular with celebrities and plain folk alike. There are lots of activities to choose from here: horseback riding, golf, fishing, sailing in the 100-acre spring-fed lake—although you can also just lounge by the pool. The ranch-style rooms and suites come with garden views, covered porches, high-beam ceilings, and wood-burning fireplaces, with touches of Spanish tile and fine Western art. A jacket is required at the nightly dinners (which are included in your room rate). ⊠ *1054 Alisal Rd., 93463* ☎ *805/688–6411 or 800/425–4725* ▤ *805/688–2510* ⊕ *www.alisal.com* ⊅ *36 rooms, 37 suites* ♨ *Restaurant, room service, refrigerators, 2 18-hole golf courses, 7 tennis courts, pool, gym, bicycles, billiards, croquet, hiking, horseback riding, Ping-Pong, shuffleboard, volleyball, bar, babysitting, children's programs (ages 6 and up), Internet room; no a/c, no room TVs* ▭ *AE, DC, MC, V* ⏍ *MAP.*

$$$–$$$$ ▥ **Petersen Village Inn.** Like most of Solvang's buildings, this upscale country inn wouldn't seem out of place in a small European village. The canopy beds here are plush, the bathrooms small but sparkling. Rates include a complete French-theme dinner for two in the guests-only Café Provence—prepared by Swiss chef Erminio Dal-Fuoco—and a European buffet breakfast. ⊠ *1576 Mission Dr., 93463* ☎ *805/688–3121 or 800/ 321–8985* ▤ *805/688–5732* ⊕ *www.peterseninn.com* ⊅ *39 rooms, 1 suite* ♨ *Dining room, cable TV with movies, Wi-Fi, meeting rooms; no smoking* ▭ *AE, MC, V* ⏍ *MAP.*

9

$$–$$$ ▦ **Solvang Gardens Lodge.** Lush gardens with fountains and waterfalls, friendly staff, and cheery English-country-theme rooms with antiques make for a peaceful retreat just a few blocks—but worlds away—from Solvang's main tourist area. Rooms range from basic to elegant; each has unique character and furnishings, and many have marble showers and baths. ⊠ *293 Alisal Rd., 93463* ☎ *805/688–4404 or 888/688–4404* ⊕ *www.solvanggardens.com* ⟿ *16 rooms, 8 suites* ⌂ *Some in-room hot tubs, some refrigerators, some kitchens, some kitchenettes, some microwaves, cable TV with movies, Wi-Fi, massage, Internet room, meeting room; no room phones, no smoking* ☰ *AE, MC, V* ¶⊙¶ *CP.*

¢–$$ ▦ **Best Western King Fredric Inn.** Rooms at this comfortable and central motel are fairly spacious. If you want to stay right in Solvang and don't want to spend a fortune, this is a good bet. ⊠ *1617 Copenhagen Dr., 93463* ☎ *805/688–5515 or 800/549–9955* 🖷 *805/688–1600* ⊕ *www.bwkingfrederik.com* ⟿ *44 rooms, 1 suite* ⌂ *Some refrigerators, cable TV with movies, in-room data ports, Wi-Fi, pool, hot tub, no-smoking rooms* ☰ *AE, D, DC, MC, V* ¶⊙¶ *CP.*

The Arts

PCPA Theaterfest (☎ 805/922–8313 ⊕ www.pcpa.org), the Pacific Conservatory of the Performing Arts, presents contemporary and classic plays as well as musicals in theaters in Solvang and Santa Maria. Summer events in Solvang are held in the open-air Festival Theatre, on 2nd Street off Copenhagen Drive.

Lompoc

㉓ *20 mi west of Solvang on Hwy. 246.*

Known as the flower-seed capital of the world, Lompoc is blanketed with vast fields of brightly colored flowers that bloom from May through August. For five days around the last weekend of June, the **Lompoc Valley Flower Festival** (☎ 805/735–8511 ⊕ www.flowerfestival.org) brings a parade, carnival, and crafts show to town.

☾ At **La Purisima Mission State Historic Park** you can see Mission La Purisima Concepción, the most fully restored mission in the state. Founded in 1787, it stands in a stark and still remote location and powerfully evokes the lives of California's Spanish settlers. Docents lead tours every afternoon, and displays illustrate the secular and religious activities that were part of mission life. From March through October the mission holds special events, including crafts demonstrations by costumed docents. ⊠ *2295 Purisima Rd., off Hwy. 246* ☎ *805/733–3713, 805/7331303 tour info* ⊕ *www.lapurisimamission.org* 🎟 *$4 per vehicle* ☉ *Daily 9–5; tour daily at 1.*

SAN LUIS OBISPO COUNTY
FROM PISMO BEACH TO SAN SIMEON

San Luis Obispo County's pristine landscapes and abundant wildlife areas, especially those around Morro Bay and Montaña de Oro State Park, have long attracted nature lovers. In the south, Pismo Beach and other coastal towns have great sand and surf; inland, a booming wine region stretches from the Edna and Arroyo Grande Valleys in the south to Paso Robles in the north. With historical attractions, a photogenic downtown, and busy shops and restaurants, the college town of San Luis Obispo is at the heart of the county.

Pismo Beach

㉔ *U.S. 101/Hwy. 1, about 40 mi north of Lompoc.*

About 20 mi of sandy shoreline—nicknamed the "Bakersfield Riviera" for the throngs of vacationers who come here from the Central Valley—begins at the town of Pismo Beach. The southern end of town runs along sand dunes, some of which are open to cars and off-road vehicles; sheltered by the dunes, a grove of eucalyptus trees attracts thousands of migrating monarch butterflies November through February. A long, broad beach fronts the center of town, where a municipal pier extends into the sea at the foot of shop-lined Pomeroy Street. To the north, hotels and homes perch atop chalky oceanfront cliffs.

Fewer than 10,000 people live in this quintessential surfer haven, but Pismo Beach has a slew of hotels and restaurants with great views of the Pacific Ocean. Still, rooms can sometimes be hard to come by. Each Father's Day weekend the Pismo Beach Classic, one of the West Coast's largest classic-car and street-rod shows, overrruns the town. A Dixieland jazz festival in February also draws crowds.

EN ROUTE ★ ☾ The spectacular **Guadalupe-Nipomo Dunes Preserve** stretches 18 mi along the coast south of Pismo Beach. It's the largest and most ecologically diverse dune system in the state, and a habitat for more than 200 species of birds as well as sea otters, black bears, bobcats, coyotes, and deer. The 1,500-foot Mussel Rock is the highest beach dune in the western states. As many as 20 movies have been filmed here, including Cecil B. DeMille's 1923 silent *The Ten Commandments*. The main entrances to the dunes are at Oso Flaco Lake (about 13 mi south of Pismo Beach on U.S. 101/Highway 1, then 3 mi west on Oso Flaco Road) and at the far west end of Highway 166 (Main Street) in Guadalupe. At the **Dunes Center** (✉ 1055 Guadalupe St., 1 mi north of Hwy. 166 ☎ 805/343–2455 ⊕ www.dunescenter.org ☉ Tues.–Sun. 10–4), you can get nature information and view an exhibit about *The Ten Commandments* movie set, which weather and archaeologists are slowly unearthing near Guadalupe Beach. Parking at Oso Flaco Lake is $5 per vehicle.

Where to Stay & Eat

$–$$$$ ✕ **Cracked Crab.** This traditional New England–style crab shack imports fresh seafood daily from Australia, Alaska, and the East Coast. Fish is line-caught, much of the produce is organic, and everything is made from scratch. For a real treat, don a bib and chow through a bucket of steamed shellfish with Cajun sausage, potatoes, and corn on the cob, all dumped right onto your table. The menu changes daily. ✉ *751 Price St.* ☎ *805/773–2722* ⚭ *Reservations not accepted* ⊟ *AE, D, MC, V.*

$$–$$$ ✕ **Giuseppe's Cucina Italiana.** The classic flavors of southern Italy are highlighted at this lively, warm downtown spot. Most recipes originate

San Luis
Obispo County
& Big Sur

from Bari, a seaport on the Adriatic; the menu includes breads and pizzas baked in the wood-burning oven, hearty dishes such as osso buco and lamb, and homemade pastas. The wait for a table can be long at peak dinner hours, but sometimes an accordion player gets the crowd singing. Next door, their bakery sells take-out selections. ⊠ *891 Price St.* ☎ *805/773–2870* ⌕ *Reservations not accepted* ▤ *AE, D, MC, V* ⊘ *No lunch weekends.*

¢ ✕ **Splash Café.** Folks line up all the way down the block for clam chowder served in a sourdough bread bowl at this wildly popular seafood stand. You can also order beach food such as fresh steamed clams, burgers, and fried calamari at the counter (no table service)—and nearly everything on the menu is $6 or less. The grimy, cramped, but cheery hole-in-a-wall, a favorite with locals and savvy visitors, is open daily for lunch and dinner, but closes early on weekday evenings during low season. ⊠ *197 Pomeroy St.* ☎ *805/773–4653* ▤ *AE, D, MC, V.*

$$$–$$$$ ✕▤ **Sea Venture Resort.** The bright, homey rooms at this hotel all have fireplaces and featherbeds; most have balconies with private hot tubs, and some have beautiful ocean views. A breakfast basket is delivered to your room in the morning, and the elegant Sea Venture Restaurant ($$–$$$, no lunch weekdays)—with sweeping ocean vistas from the third floor—features fresh seafood and local wines. ⊠ *100 Ocean View Ave.,*

93449 ☎ 805/773–4994 or 800/662–5545 🖷 805/773–0924 ⊕ www. seaventure.com ⇆ 50 rooms ⚲ Restaurant, fans, minibars, refrigerators, in-room VCRs, in-room broadband, hot tubs, spa, bicycles, meeting rooms; no a/c, no smoking ⊟ AE, D, DC, MC, V ⊺◎⊦ CP.

$$$$ 🖭 **Pismo Lighthouse Suites.** Each of the well-appointed two-room, two-bath suites at this oceanfront resort has a private balcony or patio. Some suites are suitable for couples, others for families, and all have crisp nautical-style furnishings. Ask for a corner oceanfront suite for the best views. On the central sport court you can play a variety of games, including chess on a life-size board. ⊠ 2411 Price St., 93449 ☎ 805/773–2411 or 800/245–2411 🖷 805/773–1508 ⊕ www.pismolighthousesuites. com ⇆ 70 suites ⚲ Microwaves, refrigerators, cable TV with movies and video games, in-room data ports, in-room broadband, putting green, pool, gym, badminton, Ping-Pong, laundry facilities, meeting rooms; no smoking ⊟ AE, D, DC, MC, V ⊺◎⊦ CP.

$$$–$$$$ 🖭 **The Cliffs at Shell Beach.** Perched dramatically on an oceanfront cliff, this resort is surrounded by lawns and palm trees; the pool, with a cascading fountain, overlooks the sea. The rooms are modern, with Spanish marble bathrooms (some are quite small; some have hot tubs), and the ones facing the beach have wonderful views from their balconies. All visiting dogs receive a bed, two dishes, and bottled water, and the concierge can arrange dog-walking services. ⊠ 2757 Shell Beach Rd., 93449 ☎ 805/773–5000 or 800/826–7827 🖷 805/773–0764 ⊕ www. cliffsresort.com ⇆ 142 rooms, 23 suites ⚲ Restaurant, room service, cable TV with movies, Wi-Fi, pool, gym, indoor hot tub, outdoor hot tub, sauna, spa, badminton, volleyball, bar, dry cleaning, laundry facilities, concierge, business services, Internet room, meeting rooms, some pets allowed; no smoking ⊟ AE, D, DC, MC, V.

$–$$ 🖭 **Shell Beach Inn.** Just 2½ blocks from the beach, this basic but cozy motor court is a great bargain for the area. Along with a 2005 room remodel, the property upgraded its name from "motel" to "inn." Choose from king, queen, or two-bedded rooms; all have European country–style furnishings and floral details painted on the walls and ceilings. ⊠ 653 Shell Beach Rd., 93449 ☎ 805/773–4373 or 800/549–4727 🖷 805/773–6208 ⊕ www.shellbeachmotel.com ⇆ 10 rooms ⚲ Microwaves, refrigerators, cable TV with movies, in-room data ports, pool, some pets allowed (fee); no a/c ⊟ AE, DC, MC, V.

Avila Beach

㉕ 4 mi north of Pismo Beach on U.S. 101/Hwy. 1.

Because the village of Avila Beach and the sandy, covefront shoreline for which it's named face south into the Pacific Ocean, they get more sun and less fog than any other stretch of coast in the area. It can be bright and warm here while, just beyond the surrounding hills, communities shiver under the marine layer. With its fortuitous climate and protected waters, Avila's public beach draws plenty of sunbathers and families; weekends are very busy. Demolished in 1998 to clean up extensive oil seepage from a Unocal tank farm, downtown Avila Beach has sprung back to life. The seaside promenade has been fully restored and shops and hotels have quickly popped up; with mixed results the town has tried to recreate its former offbeat character. For real local color, head to the far end of the cove and watch the commercial fishing boats offload their catch on the old Port San Luis wharf. A few seafood shacks and fish markets do business on the pier while sea lions congregate below.

Where to Stay & Eat

$–$$$$ ✕ **Olde Port Inn.** Locals swear by this old-fashioned fish house at the end of the Port San Luis Pier. Ask for today's fresh catch, or go for the *cioppino* (spicy tomato-based seafood stew) or fish tacos; simplicity is the key to a decent meal here. You can't beat the views, whether you're looking out over the ocean or through the Plexiglas surface of your table into the waters below. ⊠ *End of 3rd pier* ☎ *805/595–2515* ▤ *AE, MC, V.*

$$–$$$$ ✕▣ **Sycamore Mineral Springs Resort.** This wellness resort's hot mineral springs bubble up into private outdoor tubs on an oak and sycamore-forest hillside. Whether or not you stay here, it's worth coming for a soak—even though the grounds are well within earshot of a busy road. Each room or suite has its own private balcony with a hot tub; about half have mineral water piped in. New owners have gradually been up-grading furnishings and amenities since taking over in 2003; insist on a renovated room. The spa offers everything from massages and skin care to yoga classes and a variety of integrative healing arts. Creative spa and California cuisine is served in the romantic Gardens of Avila restaurant ($–$$$). ⊠ *1215 Avila Beach Dr., San Luis Obispo 93405* ☎ *805/595–7302 or 800/234–5831* ▤ *805/595–4007* ⊕ *www.sycamoresprings.com* ☞ *26 rooms, 50 suites* ⌂ *Restaurant, room service, in-room hot tubs, some microwaves, some refrigerators, cable TV with movies, some in-room VCRs, in-room broadband, Wi-Fi, pool, outdoor hot tubs, spa; no smoking* ▤ *AE, D, DC, MC, V.*

$$–$$$$ ▣ **Avila Village Inn.** Opened in 2005, this small, adult-oriented hotel embraces Craftsman style in its wood-and-stone architecture and in custom furnishings such as faux-Tiffany lampshades. Rooms are decked out with comforts: down bedding, robes, fireplaces, flat-screen TVs; most have hot tubs—some on private creek-side balconies. The staff delivers breakfast each morning and pours local wines in the guests-only cocktail lounge. ⊠ *6655 Bay Laurel Dr., 93424* ☎ *800/454–0840 or 805/627–1810* ⊕ *www.avilavillageinn.com* ☞ *26 rooms, 4 suites* ⌂ *Refrigerators, cable TV, in-room DVDs, in-room broadband, gym, lounge, meeting rooms* ▤ *AE, D, DC, M, V* ❑ *CP.*

San Luis Obispo

㉖ *8 mi north of Avila Beach on U.S. 101/Hwy. 1.*

About halfway between San Francisco and Los Angeles, San Luis Obispo—nicknamed SLO—spreads out below gentle hills and rocky extinct volcanoes. Its main appeal lies in its architecturally diverse and commercially lively downtown, especially several blocks of Higuera Street. The pedestrian-friendly district bustles with shoppers, restaurant-goers, and students from California Polytechnic State University, known as Cal Poly. On Thursday from 6 PM to 9 PM a farmers' market fills Higuera Street with local produce, entertainment, and food stalls. SLO is less a vacation destination than a pleasant stopover along Highway 1; it's a nice place to stay while touring the wine country south of town.

★ Special events often take place on sun-dappled Mission Plaza in front of **Mission San Luis Obispo de Tolosa,** established in 1772. Its small museum exhibits artifacts of the Chumash Indians and early Spanish settlers, and docents sometimes lead tours of the church and grounds. ✉ 751 Palm St. ☎ 805/543–6850 ⊕ www.missionsanluisobispo.org 🎫 $2 suggested donation ☉ Apr.–Oct., daily 9–5; late Oct.–Mar., daily 9–4.

Ⓒ Across the street from the old Spanish mission, **San Luis Obispo County Historical Museum** presents rotating exhibits on various aspects of county history—such as Native American life, California ranchos, and the impact of railroads. A separate children's room has theme activities where kids can earn prizes. ✉ 696 Monterey St. ☎ 805/543–0638 ⊕ www. slochs.org 🎫 Free ☉ Wed.–Sun. 10–4.

San Luis Obispo is the commercial center of **Edna Valley/Arroyo Grande Valley wine country,** whose appellations stretch east–west from San Luis Obispo toward the coast and toward Lake Lopez in the inland mountains. Many of the 20 or so wineries line Highway 227 and connecting roads. The region is best known for chardonnay and pinot noir, although many wineries experiment with other varietals and blends. Wine-touring maps are readily available around town; note that many wineries charge a small tasting fee and most tasting rooms close at 5.

For sweeping views of the Edna Valley while you sample estate-grown chardonnay, go to the modern tasting bar at **Edna Valley Vineyard** (✉ 2585 Biddle Ranch Rd. ☎ 805/544–5855 ⊕ www.ednavalley.com). A refurbished 1909 schoolhouse serves as tasting room for **Baileyana Winery** (✉ 5828 Orcutt Rd. ☎ 805/269–8200 ⊕ www.baileyana.com), which produces concentrated chardonnays, pinot noirs, and syrahs.

Best-known for its pinot noir- and syrah-based reds, **Domaine Alfred** (✉ 7525 Orcutt Rd. ☎ 805/541–9463 ⊕ www.domainealfred.com) grows most of its grapes in the Edna Valley's oldest vineyard, which the winery bought in 1994. An ecofriendly winery built from straw bales, **Claiborne & Churchill** (✉ 2649 Carpenter Canyon Rd. ☎ 805/544–4066 ⊕ www.claibornechurchill.com) makes small lots of exceptional Alsatian-style wines such as dry Riesling and Gewürztraminer.

While touring Edna Valley wine country, be sure to stop at **Old Edna** (✉ Hwy. 227 at Price Canyon Rd. ☎ 805/544–8062 ⊕ www.oldedna. com), a peaceful, 2-acre site that once was the town of Edna. Browse for gifts and antiques, pick up sandwiches at the gourmet deli, and stroll along Old Edna Lane.

Where to Stay & Eat

★ $$–$$$$ ✕ **The Park Restaurant.** This is one of the most sophisticated restaurants in the county. Chef-owner Meghan Loring presents food that she describes as "refined rustic." The always evolving menu relies on seasonal ingredients sourced from local producers. You might find sweet pea-asparagus soup with mint cream, or organic rib eye with panko-fried shitakes. The well-crafted wine and beer list includes local and international selections. Service is skillful in the spare, white-tablecloth dining room and on the tree-rimmed patio. ⊠ *1819 Osos St.* ☎ *805/545–0000* ⊟ *AE, MC, V* ⊘ *Closed Mon. No lunch.*

$–$$$ ✕ **Buona Tavola.** Homemade pasta with river shrimp in a creamy tomato sauce and porcini-mushroom risotto are among the northern Italian dishes served at this casual spot. Daily fresh fish and salad specials and an impressive wine list attract a steady stream of regulars. In good weather you can dine on the flower-filled patio. The Paso Robles branch is equally enjoyable. ⊠ *1037 Monterey St.* ☎ *805/545–8000* ⊠ *943 Spring St., Paso Robles* ☎ *805/237–0600* ⊟ *AE, D, MC, V* ⊘ *No lunch weekends.*

$–$$$ ✕ **Novo Restaurant and Bakery.** In the colorful dining room or on the large creek-side deck, this animated downtown eatery will take you on a culinary world tour. The salads, small plates, and entrées come from nearly every continent. The wine and beer list also covers the globe—and includes local favorites. Many of the decadent desserts are baked at the restaurant's sister property in Cambria, the French Corner Bakery. ⊠ *726 Higuera St.* ☎ *805/543–3986* ⊟ *MC, V.*

★ ¢–$$ ✕ **Big Sky Café.** A popular gathering spot three meals a day, this quintessentially Californian, family-friendly (and sometimes noisy) café turns local and organically grown ingredients into global dishes. Spicy Portuguese piri-piri chicken, Thai catfish, New Mexican *pozole* (hominy stew): just pick your continent. Vegetarians have lots to choose from. ⊠ *1121 Broad St.* ☎ *805/545–5401* ⌂ *Reservations not accepted* ⊟ *AE, MC, V.*

¢–$$ ✕ **Mo's Smokehouse BBQ.** Barbecue joints abound on the Central Coast, but this one excels. A variety of southern-style sauces seasons tender hickory-smoked ribs and shredded meat sandwiches; sides such as baked beans, cole slaw, homemade potato chips, and garlic bread extend the pleasure. ⊠ *970 Higera St.* ☎ *805/544–6193* ⊟ *AE, MC, V.*

$$–$$$ ▦ **Garden Street Inn.** From this fully restored 1887 Italianate–Queen Anne, the only lodging in downtown SLO, you can walk to many restaurants and attractions. The individually decorated rooms, each with private bath, are filled with antiques; some have stained-glass windows, fireplaces, and decks. Each evening, wine and hors d'oeuvres are served in the intimate dining room; there's also a lavish homemade breakfast when you rise. ⊠ *1212 Garden St., 93401* ☎ *805/545–9802 or 800/488–2045* ⊟ *805/545–9403* ⊕ *www.gardenstreetinn.com* ⇨ *9 rooms, 4 suites* ⌂ *In-room data ports, library; no TV in some rooms, no smoking* ⊟ *AE, D, MC, V* ❙◎❙ *BP.*

$$–$$$ ▦ **Petit Soleil.** A cobblestone courtyard, country-French custom furnishings, and Gallic music piped through the halls evoke a Provençal mood at this cheery inn on upper Monterey Street's motel row. With extensive experience in luxury lodging, the owners are serious about the details: The individually themed rooms, sprinkled with lavender water, have CD players and L'Occitane bath products. Rates include wine and appetizers at cocktail hour and a full homemade breakfast in the sun-filled patio or dining room. ⊠ *1473 Monterey St., 93401* ☎ *805/549–0321 or 800/676–1588* ⊟ *805/549–0383* ⊕ *www.petitsoleilslo.com* ⇨ *15 rooms, 1 suite* ⌂ *Fans, cable TV, Wi-Fi, business services, meeting room; no a/c, no smoking* ⊟ *AE, MC, V* ❙◎❙ *BP.*

¢–$$$ ▦ **Peach Tree Inn.** Extra touches such as rose gardens, a porch with rockers, and flower-filled vases turn this modest, family-run motel into a relaxing creek-side haven. Four rooms have king and sofa beds with private patios overlooking the creek. You can use the refrigerator and microwave in the sunny breakfast room, and snacks are available all day and evening. ⊠ *2001 Monterey St., 93401* ☎ *805/543–3170 or 800/227–6396* 🖷 *805/543–7673* ⊕ *www.peachtreeinn.com* ⌁ *37 rooms* ⌂ *Cable TV, in-room VCRs, in-room broadband, Wi-Fi; no smoking* ⊟ *AE, D, DC, MC, V* ⍰ *CP.*

Nightlife & the Arts

NIGHTLIFE The club scene in this college town is centered on Higuera Street off Monterey Street. The **Frog and Peach** (⊠ 728 Higuera St. ☎ 805/595–3764) is a decent spot to nurse an English beer and listen to live music. **Linnaea's Cafe** (⊠ 1110 Garden St. ☎ 805/541–5888), a mellow java joint, sometimes holds poetry readings, as well as blues, jazz, and folk music performances. Chicago-style **Mother's Tavern** (⊠ 725 Higuera St. ☎ 805/541–8733) draws crowds with good pub food and live entertainment in a turn-of-the-20th-century setting (complete with antique U.S. flags and a wall-mounted moose head).

THE ARTS The **Performing Arts Center** (⊠ 1 Grand Ave. ☎ 805/756–7222 for information, 805/756–2787 for tickets outside CA, 888/233–2787 for tickets in CA ⊕ www.pacslo.org) at Cal Poly hosts live theater, dance, and music performances by artists from around the world. The **San Luis Obispo Mozart Festival** (☎ 805/781–3008 ⊕ www.mozartfestival.com) takes place in late July and early August. Not all the music is Mozart; you'll also hear Haydn and other composers. **San Luis Obispo Art Center** (⊠ 1010 Broad St., at Mission Plaza ☎ 805/543–8562 ⊕ www.sloartcenter.org ⊙ Closed Tues. early Sept.–late May) displays and sells a mix of traditional work and cutting-edge arts and crafts by Central Coast artists.

Sports & the Outdoors

A hilly greenbelt with vast amounts of open space and extensive hiking trails surrounds the city of San Luis Obispo. For information on trailheads, call the city **Parks and Recreation Department** (☎ 805/781–7300 ⊕ www.slocity.org/parksandrecreation) or visit its Web site to download a trail map.

EN
ROUTE
Instead of continuing north on Highway 1 from San Luis Obispo to Morro Bay, consider taking Los Osos Valley Road (off Madonna Road, south of downtown) past farms and ranches to dramatic **Montaña de Oro State Park** (⊠ 7 mi south of Los Osos on Pecho Rd. ☎ 805/528–0513 or 805/772–7434 ⊕ www.parks.ca.gov). The park has miles of nature trails along rocky shoreline, wild beaches, and hills overlooking some of California's most spectacular scenery. Check out the tide pools, watch the waves roll into the bluffs, and picnic in the eucalyptus groves.

Morro Bay

❷ *14 mi north of San Luis Obispo on Hwy. 1.*

Commercial fishermen slog around Morro Bay in galoshes, and beat-up fishing boats bob in the bay's protected waters. At the mouth of Morro Bay, which is both a state and national estuary, stands 576-foot-high **Morro Rock** (⊠ Northern end of Embarcadero) one of nine such small volcanic peaks, or morros, in the area. A short walk leads to a break-water, with the harbor on one side and the crashing waves of the Pacific on the other. You may not climb the rock, where endangered falcons and other birds nest. Sea lions and otters often play in the water at the foot of the peak. The center of the action on land is the **Embarcadero** (✉ On waterfront from Beach St. to Tidelands Park), where vacationers pour in and out of souvenir shops and seafood restaurants. From here, you can get out on the bay in a kayak or tour boat.

★ ☺ South of downtown Morro Bay, interactive exhibits at the spiffy **Morro Bay State Park Museum of Natural History** teach kids and adults about the natural environment—both in the Morro Bay estuary and on the rest of the planet. ✉ *State Park Rd.* ☎ *805/772–2694* ⊕ *www.slostateparks. com/morro_bay* ⊐ *$2* ☼ *Daily 10–5.*

Where to Stay & Eat

$$-$$$$ ✕ **Windows on the Water.** From giant picture windows at this second-floor spot, watch the sun set over the water. Fresh fish and other dishes based on local ingredients emerge from the wood-fired oven in the open kitchen; a variety of oysters on the half shell beckon from the raw bar. About 20 of the wines on the extensive, mostly California list are poured by the glass. Service is uneven and can be amateurish for the setting. ✉ *699 Embarcadero* ☎ *805/772–0677* ⊟ *AE, D, DC, MC, V* ☼ *No lunch.*

$-$$$ ✕ **Dorn's Original Breakers Cafe.** This seafood restaurant overlooking the harbor has satisfied Morro Bay appetites since 1948. In addition to excellent, straight-ahead fish dishes such as petrale sole or calamari steaks sautéed in butter and wine, Dorn's serves breakfast. ✉ *801 Market Ave.* ☎ *805/772–4415* ⊟ *D, MC, V.*

★ ¢ ✕ **Taco Temple.** The devout stand in line at this family-run diner that serves some of the freshest food around. Seafood anchors a menu of dishes—salmon burritos, superb fish tacos with mango salsa—hailing from somewhere between California and Mexico. Desserts get rave reviews, too. Make an effort to find this gem tucked away in the corner of a supermarket parking lot north of downtown—it's on the frontage road parallel to Highway 1, just north of the Highway 41 junction. A renovation and expansion are planned; call ahead to be sure they're open. ✉ *2680 Main St., at Elena* ☎ *805/772–4965* ⌫ *No reservations* ⊟ *No credit cards* ☼ *Closed Tues.*

$$-$$$$ ▦ **Ascot Suites.** A hop and a skip from the Embarcadero, this hotel wins loyal guests with its high-end conveniences. There are large jetted tubs in most bathrooms, well-stocked wet bars, and gas fireplaces. A complimentary breakfast basket arrives at your door each morning. ✉ *260 Morro Bay Blvd., 93442* ☎ *805/772–4437 or 800/887–6454* ⊟ *805/ 772–8860* ⊕ *www.ascotinn.com* ⌫ *32 units* ⌂ *Minibars, refrigerators, cable TV, in-room VCRs, pool, hot tub, massage, concierge, meeting room; no smoking* ⊟ *AE, D, DC, MC, V* ⊖* CP.*

$$-$$$$ ▦ **The Inn at Morro Bay.** Surrounded by eucalyptus trees on the edge of Morro Bay, the inn abuts a heron rookery and Morro Bay State Park. It's a beautiful setting, even though the birds can cause a din (and make a mess of parked cars). The contemporary-style rooms—many with fireplaces, private decks with spa tubs, and bay views—could use sprucing up, but you are likely to spend your time elsewhere: take a massage

at the on-site wellness center, play a round (fee) at the golf course across the road, or peddle through the state park on a complimentary bicycle. ⊠ *60 State Park Rd., 93442* ☎ *805/772–5651 or 800/321–9566* 🖷 *805/772–4779* ⊕ *www.innatmorrobay.com* ⮌ *97 rooms, 1 cottage* ⚲ *2 restaurants, room service, refrigerators, cable TV with movies, in-room broadband, pool, spa, mountain bikes, bar, dry cleaning, laundry service, meeting room; no smoking* ⊟ *AE, D, DC, MC, V.*

$–$$ 🏨 **Embarcadero Inn.** The rooms at this waterfront hotel are cheery and welcoming, and many have fireplaces. All are decorated with old maritime photographs and have balconies facing the sea. You can borrow binoculars and videos for free. ⊠ *456 Embarcadero, 93442* ☎ *805/772–2700 or 800/292–7625* 🖷 *805/772–1060* ⊕ *www.embarcaderoinn. com* ⮌ *29 rooms, 4 suites* ⚲ *Some microwaves, refrigerators, cable TV with movies, in-room VCRs, Wi-Fi, 2 hot tubs, no-smoking rooms* ⊟ *AE, D, DC, MC, V* ⫢⊙⫣ *CP.*

¢–$$ 🏨 **Bayfront Inn.** Nautical murals decorate this small, pet-friendly motel facing Morro Rock. Rooms are plain but comfortable. Amenities include coffeemakers and free HBO for you, and morning treats for your pet. ⊠ *1150 Embarcadero, 93442* ☎ *805/772–5607 or 800/799–5607* ⊕ *http://bayfront-inn.com* ⮌ *16 rooms* ⚲ *Restaurant, fans, refrigerators, cable TV with movies, pool, hot tub, some pets allowed (fee); no smoking* ⊟ *AE, D, MC, V* ⫢⊙⫣ *CP.*

Sports & the Outdoors

Kayak Horizons (⊠ 551 Embarcadero ☎ 805/772–6444 ⊕ www. kayakhorizons.com) rents kayaks and gives lessons and guided tours. **Sub-Sea Tours** (⊠ 699 Embarcadero ☎ 805/772–9463) operates glass-bottom boat and catamaran cruises, and has kayak and canoe rentals and lessons. **Virg's Sport Fishing** (⊠ 1215 Embarcadero ☎ 805/772–1222 ⊕ www. virgs.com) conducts deep-sea fishing and whale-watching trips.

Paso Robles

㉘ *30 mi north of San Luis Obispo on U.S. 101; 25 mi northwest of Morro Bay via Hwy. 41 and U.S. 101.*

In the 1860s tourists began flocking to this dusty ranching outpost to "take the cure" in a luxurious bathhouse fed by underground mineral hot springs. An Old West town, complete with opera house, emerged; grand Victorian homes went up, followed in the 20th century by Craftsman bungalows. A 2003 earthquake demolished or weakened several beloved downtown buildings, but historically faithful reconstruction has proceeded rapidly.

Today the wine industry booms and mile upon mile of vineyards envelops Paso Robles; golfers play the four local courses and spandex-clad bicyclists race along the winding back roads. A mix of down-home and up-market restaurants, bars, antiques stores, and little shops fills the streets around oak-shaded City Park, where special events of all kinds—custom car shows, an olive festival, Friday night summer concerts—take place on many weekends. Still, Paso (as the locals call it) more or less remains cowboy country: each year in late July and early August, the city throws the two-week California Mid-State Fair, complete with live-stock auctions, carnival rides, and corn dogs.

Take a look back at California's rural heritage at the **Paso Robles Pioneer Museum.** Displays of historical ranching paraphernalia, horse-drawn vehicles, hot springs artifacts, and photos evoke the town's old days; a one-room schoolhouse is part of the complex. ⊠ *2010 Riverside Ave.* ☎ *805/239–4556* ⊕ *www.pasoroblespioneermuseum.org* ۞ *Thurs.–Sun. 1–4.*

The lakeside **River Oaks Hot Springs & Spa,** on 240 hilly acres near the intersection of U.S. 101 and Highway 46E, is a great place to relax before and after wine tasting or festival-going. Soak in a private indoor or outdoor hot tub fed by natural mineral springs, or indulge in a massage or facial. ⊠ *3725 Buena Vista Dr.* ☎ *805/238–4600* ⊕ *www. pasohotsprings.com* ⊜ *Hot tubs $12 per person per hr* ۞ *Sun.–Thurs. 9–9; Fri. and Sat. 9–10.*

In **Paso Robles wine country,** nearly 100 wineries and 26,000 vineyard acres pepper the wooded hills west of U.S. 101 and blanket the flatter, more open land on the east side. The region's brutally hot summer days and cool nights yield stellar grapes that make noteworthy wines, particularly robust reds such as cabernet sauvignon, merlot, zinfandel, and Rhône varietals such as syrah. An abundance of exquisite whites also comes out of Paso, including chardonnay and Rhône varietals such as viognier. Small-town friendliness prevails at most wineries, especially smaller ones, which tend to treat visitors like neighbors. Pick up a regional wine-touring map at lodgings, wineries, and attractions around town. Most tasting rooms close at 5 PM; many charge a small fee.

Most of the local wineries pour at the **Paso Robles Wine Festival,** held mid-May in City Park. The outdoor tasting—the largest such California event—includes live bands and diverse food vendors. Winery open-houses and winemaker dinners round out the weekend. ⊠ *City Park, Spring St. between 10th and 12th Sts.* ☎ *805/239–8463* ⊕ *www. pasowine.com* ⊜ *$50; $15 for designated driver.*

Small but swank **Justin Vineyards & Winery** (⊠ 11680 Chimney Rock Rd. ☎ 805/238–6932 or 800/726–0049 ⊕ www.justinwine.com) makes Bordeaux-style blends at the western end of Paso Robles wine country. This reader favorite offers winery, vineyard, and barrel-tasting tours ($10 to $50). In the tasting room there's a deli bar; a tiny high-end restaurant is also part of the complex. Tucked in the far-west hills of Paso Robles, **Tablas Creek Vineyard** (⊠ 9339 Adelaida Rd. ☎ 805/237–1231 ⊕ www.tablascreek.com) makes some of the area's finest wine by blending organically grown, hand-harvested Rhône varietals such as syrah, grenache, roussanne, and viognier. Tours include a chance to graft your own grapevine. While touring the idyllic west side of Paso Robles, take ★ a break from wine by stopping at **Willow Creek Olive Ranch** (⊠ 8530 Vineyard Dr. ☎ 805/227–0186 ⊕ www.pasolivo.com). Find out how they make their Tuscan-style Pasolivo olive oils on a high-tech Italian press, and taste the widely acclaimed results.

In southeastern Paso Robles–wine country, **Wild Horse Winery & Vineyards** (⊠ 1437 Wild Horse Winery Ct., Templeton ☎ 805/434–2541 ⊕ www.

wildhorsewinery.com) was a pioneer Central Coast producer. You can try delicious, well-priced pinot noir, chardonnay, and merlot in their simple tasting room. As they say around Paso Robles, it takes a lot of beer to make good wine, and to meet that need the locals turn to **Firestone Walker Fine Ales** (⊠1400 Ramada Dr. ☎805/238–2556 ⊕www.firestonewalker. com). In the brewery's taproom, sample medal-winning craft beers such as Double Barrel Ale. They close at 7 PM. Even if you don't drink wine, stop at **Eberle Winery** (⊠Hwy. 46E, 3½ mi east of U.S. 101 ☎805/238–9607 ⊕www.eberlewinery.com) for a fascinating tour of the huge wine caves beneath the east-side Paso Robles vineyard. Gary Eberle, one of Paso wine's founding fathers, is obsessed with cabernet sauvignon.

For an aerial view of vineyards, ranches, and mountains, make an advance reservation with **Let's Go Ballooning!** Flights carrying up to four passengers launch at sunrise and last about an hour. ⊠ *Paso Robles Airport, 4912 Wing Way* ☎*805/458–1530* ⊕*www.sloballoon.com* 🖃*$189 per person* ⊗ *Daily.*

Where to Stay & Eat

$$–$$$$ ✕**McPhee's Grill.** The grain silos across the street and the floral oilcloths on the tables belie the sophisticated cuisine at this casual chop house. Housed in an 1860s building in the tiny cow town of Templeton (just south of Paso Robles), the restaurant serves creative, contemporary versions of traditional Western fare—such as oak-grilled filet mignon and cedar-planked salmon. House-label wines, made especially for McPhee's, are quite good. ⊠ *416 Main St., Templeton* ☎ *805/434–3204* 🖃 *AE, D, MC, V.*

★ $$–$$$ ✕**Bistro Laurent.** Owner-chef Laurent Grangien has created a handsome, welcoming French bistro in an 1890s brick building across from City Park. He focuses on traditional dishes such as osso buco, cassoulet, rack of lamb, goat-cheese tart, and onion soup, but always offers a few updated dishes as daily specials. Wines come from around the world. Le Petit Marcel, a tiny nook next door to the main restaurant, is open just for lunch Monday through Saturday. ⊠ *1202 Pine St.* ☎ *805/226–8191* 🖃 *MC, V* ⊗ *Closed Sun. No lunch.*

$$–$$$ ✕**Villa Creek.** With a firm nod to the Southwest, chef Tom Fundero conjures distinctly modern magic with locally and sustainably grown ingredients. The seasonal menu has included butternut-squash enchiladas and braised rabbit with mole negro, but you might also find duck breast with sweet-potato latkes. Central Coast wines dominate the list, with a smattering of Spanish and French selections. All brick and bare wood, the dining room can get loud when winemakers start passing their bottles from table to table, but it's always festive. For lighter appetites or wallets, the bar serves smaller plates—not to mention a killer margarita. ⊠ *1144 Pine St.* ☎ *805/238–3000* 🖃 *AE, D, MC, V* ⊗ *No lunch Sun.–Mon.*

¢   ✕**Joe's Place.** You might have to wait for a seat at the counter or several tables in this snug diner, but locals insist it serves the best breakfast in town. Joe is famous for his biscuits with sausage gravy and for his spicy sauces; zesty *chilaquiles* (a casserole-like dish made with tortillas strips, cheese, and other ingredients) are on the menu along with omelets and epic hash-browns. For lunch there are hefty burritos, sandwiches, and burgers. ⊠ *608 12th St.* ☎ *805/238–5637* 🖃 *MC, V* ⊗ *No dinner.*

9

$$$$ 🏨 **Villa Toscana.** Smack in the middle of the Martin & Weyrich vineyard, this exclusive Tuscan-style villa opened in 2002. The eight ultraposh suites with wood-beam ceilings have custom linens, huge baths with oversize whirlpool tubs, spacious sitting areas, and patios or balconies overlooking the vineyard. You can arrange for spa treatments in your suite. Start the day with an elaborate breakfast, and wind down in the afternoon with wine and hors d'oeuvres. The mood can be somewhat stiff at this pricey cocoon. ⊠ *4230 Buena Vista Rd., 93446* ☎ *805/238–5600* 🖷 *805/238–5605* ⊕ *www.myvillatoscana.com* 🛏 *8 suites, 1 apartment* ♿ *Dining room, in-room hot tubs, microwaves, refrigerators, cable TV with movies, in-room DVDs, in-room broadband, pool, massage, lounge; no smoking* ▤ *AE, D, DC, MC, V* ⧄ *BP.*

$$$–$$$$ 🏨 **Summerwood Inn.** Verdant gardens and vineyards envelop Summerwood Winery's elegant, friendly B&B in tranquillity. Four-poster and sleigh beds, lace and floral fabrics, thick robes, and nightly turn-down service bring comfort to the individually designed rooms. All have gas fireplaces and balconies or decks with vineyard views; some have vaulted ceilings or jetted tubs. Order what you like for breakfast and sip Summerwood wines in the evening. ⊠ *2130 Arbor Rd., 1 mi west of U.S. 101 at Hwy. 46W and Arbor Rd., 93446* ☎ *805/227–1111* 🖷 *805/227–1112* ⊕ *www.summerwoodwine.com* 🛏 *9 rooms* ♿ *Cable TV; no smoking* ▤ *AE, DC, MC, V* ⧄ *BP.*

$–$$$ 🏨 **Paso Robles Inn.** On the site of a luxurious old spa hotel by the same name, the inn is built around a lush, shady garden with a hot mineral pool. Most rooms have seen better days; accommodations are nicer in the building that opened in 2006. The water is still the reason to stay here, and each deluxe room (new and old) has a spring-fed hot tub in its bathroom or on its balcony. Have breakfast in the circular 1940s coffee shop, and on weekends dance with the ranchers in the Cattlemen's Lounge. ⊠ *1103 Spring St., 93446* ☎ *805/238–2660 or 800/676–1713* 🖷 *805/238–4707* ⊕ *www.pasoroblesinn.com* 🛏 *92 rooms, 6 suites* ♿ *Restaurant, coffee shop, some in-room hot tubs, some microwaves, refrigerators, cable TV with movies, in-room broadband, Wi-Fi, pool, hot tub, bar, meeting rooms, no-smoking rooms* ▤ *AE, D, DC, MC, V.*

¢–$ 🏨 **Adelaide Inn.** Family-owned and -managed, this clean, friendly oasis

Fodor's Choice with meticulous landscaping offers spacious rooms and everything you

★ need: coffeemaker, iron, hair dryer, and peace and quiet. In the lobby, complimentary muffins and newspapers are set out in the morning; cookies come out in the afternoon. The motel has been around for decades, but nearly half the rooms were built in 2005. It's a tremendous value, so it books out weeks or even months in advance. A short walk from the fairgrounds, the Adelaide is tucked behind a conglomeration of gas stations and fast-food outlets just west of the U.S. 101 and Highway 46E interchange. ⊠ *1215 Ysabel Ave., 93446* ☎ *805/238–2770 or 800/549–7276* 🖷 *805/238–3497* ⊕ *www.adelaideinn.com* 🛏 *109 rooms* ♿ *Refrigerators, cable TV with movies, in-room broadband, miniature golf, putting green, pool, hot tub, laundry facilities, laundry service, business services, no-smoking rooms* ▤ *AE, D, DC, MC, V* ⧄ *CP.*

Cambria

㉙ *28 mi west of Paso Robles on Hwy. 46; 20 mi north of Morro Bay on Hwy. 1.*

Cambria, set on piney hills above the sea, was settled by Welsh miners in the 1890s. In the 1970s, the gorgeous, isolated setting attracted artists and other independent types; the town now caters to tourists, but it still bears the unmistakable imprint of its bohemian past. Both of Cambria's downtowns, the original East Village and the newer West Village, are packed with art and craft galleries, antiques shops, cafés, restaurants, and B&Bs. Late-Victorian homes stand along side streets, and the hills are filled with redwood-and-glass residences. Lined with low-key motels, **Moonstone Beach Drive** runs along a bluff above the ocean. The boardwalk that winds along the beach side of the drive makes a great walk. **Leffingwell's Landing** (✉ North end of Moonstone Beach Dr. ☎ 805/927–2070), a state picnic ground, is a good place for examining tidal pools and watching otters as they frolic in the surf.

Arthur Beal (aka Captain Nit Wit, Der Tinkerpaw) spent 51 years building **Nit Wit Ridge,** a home with terraced rock gardens. For building materials, he used all kinds of collected junk: beer cans, rocks, abalone shells, car parts, TV antennas—you name it. The site, above Cambria's West Village, is a State Historic Landmark. You can drive by and peek in; better yet, call ahead for a guided tour of the house and grounds. ✉ *881 Hillcrest Dr.* ☎ *805/927–2690* 💰 *$10* ☉ *Daily by appointment.*

Where to Stay & Eat

$$–$$$$ ╳ **The Sea Chest.** By far the best seafood place in town—readers give it a big thumbs-up—this Moonstone Beach restaurant fills soon after it opens at 5:30. Those in the know grab seats at the oyster bar, where they can take in spectacular sunsets while watching the chefs broil fresh halibut and steam garlicky clams. If you can't get there early, play some cribbage or checkers while you wait for a table. ✉ *6216 Moonstone Beach Dr.* ☎ *805/927–4514* ♣ *Reservations not accepted* ▭ *No credit cards* ☉ *Closed Tues. mid-Sept.–Apr. No lunch.*

$$–$$$ ╳ **The Black Cat.** Jazz wafts through the several small rooms of this intimate East Village bistro where leopard-print cushions line the banquettes. Start with an order of the fried olives stuffed with gorgonzola, accompanied by a glass from the eclectic list of local and imported wines. On the daily-changing, always exciting menu, you might find braised short ribs with goat-cheese polenta or duck breast with dried-cherry couscous. ✉ *1602 Main St.* ☎ *805/927–1600* ♣ *Reservations essential* ▭ *AE, D, DC, MC, V* ☉ *Closed Tues. and Wed. No lunch.*

$–$$$ ╳ **Robin's.** A truly multiethnic and vegetarian-friendly dining experience awaits you at this East Village cottage filled with country antiques. At dinner, choose from lobster enchiladas, Brazilian-style pork tenderloin, Thai red tofu curry, and more; lunchtime's extensive salad and sandwich menu embraces burgers and tempeh alike. Unless it's raining, ask for a table on the secluded (and heated) garden patio. ✉ *4095 Burton Dr.* ☎ *805/927–5007* ▭ *MC, V.*

9

¢ ✕ **French Corner Bakery.** Place your order at the counter and then sit outside to watch the passing East Village scene (if the fog has rolled in, take a seat in the tiny deli). The rich aroma of coffee and fresh breakfast pastries makes mouths water in the morning; for lunch, try a quiche with flaky crust or a sandwich on house-baked bread. ⊠ *2214 Main St.* ☎ *805/927–8227* ⌦ *No reservations* ⊘ *No dinner.*

$$–$$$$ ▦ **Cambria Pines Lodge.** With lots of recreational facilities and a range of accommodations—from basic state park–style cabins to motel-style standard rooms to large fireplace suites—this 25-acre retreat up the hill from the East Village is a good choice for families. Walls can be thin in buildings dating as far back as the 1940s; a separate cluster of luxury suites and rooms opened in 2006. The lodge is always busy: its extensive gardens are popular with wedding parties, groups and conferences are big business, and bands play light rock, folk, and jazz in the lounge. ⊠ *2905 Burton Dr. 93428* ☎ *805/927–4200* 🖷 *805/927–4016* ⊕ *www. cambriapineslodge.com* ⌦ *72 rooms, 19 cabins, 62 suites* ⌂ *Restaurant, room service, some microwaves, some refrigerators, cable TV with movies, some in-room VCRs, in-room broadband, Web TV, indoor pool, exercise equipment, hot tub, sauna, spa, volleyball, bar, lounge, concierge, meeting rooms, some pets allowed; no smoking* ▤ *AE, D, DC, MC, V.*

$$–$$$$ ▦ **Fog Catcher Inn.** The landscaped gardens and 10 faux-thatched and timbered buildings here evoke an English-country village. Fireplaces and robes cozy up rooms decorated in floral chintz with country-style wood furniture; most have ocean views. ⊠ *6400 Moonstone Beach Dr., 93428* ☎ *805/927–1400 or 800/425–4121* 🖷 *805/927–0204* ⊕ *www. fogcatcherinn.com* ⌦ *51 rooms, 9 suites* ⌂ *Minibars, refrigerators, microwaves, cable TV, in-room broadband, pool, hot tub, some pets allowed; no smoking* ▤ *AE, D, DC, MC, V* ◉ *CP.*

★ $$–$$$$ ▦ **Moonstone Landing.** Friendly staff, lots of amenities, and reasonable rates make this up-to-date motel a top pick with readers who like to stay right on Moonstone Beach. All rooms have Mission-style furnishings, DVD players, fireplaces, and Internet access. From their balconies or patios, a few of the deluxe rooms, which have marble whirlpool tubs and showers, offer some of the best views in Cambria. ⊠ *6240 Moonstone Beach Dr., 93428* ☎ *805/927–0012 or 800/830–4540* 🖷 *805/927– 0014* ⊕ *www.moonstonelanding.com* ⌦ *29 rooms* ⌂ *Microwaves, refrigerators, cable TV with movies, in-room DVDs, hot tubs; no smoking* ▤ *AE, D, MC, V* ◉ *CP.*

$$–$$$ ▦ **J. Patrick House.** Monterey pines and flower gardens surround this Irish-theme inn, which sits on a hilltop above Cambria's East Village. All rooms—one in the main log house, along with a sunny dining room and parlor, and seven in a separate carriage house—have traditional country furnishings, wood-burning fireplaces, private baths, and window seats. The full vegetarian breakfast always includes a hot entrée such as eggs Florentine or French toast. ⊠ *2990 Burton Dr., 93428* ☎ *805/927–3812 or 800/341–5258* ⊕ *www.jpatrickhouse.com* ⌦ *8 rooms* ⌂ *Concierge; no room phones, no room TVs, no smoking* ▤ *D, DC, MC, V* ◉ *BP.*

¢–$$ ▦ **Bluebird Inn.** This sweet motel in Cambria's East Village sits amid beautiful gardens along Santa Rosa Creek. Rooms include simply furnished doubles and nicer creek-side suites with patios, fireplaces, and refrigerators. The Bluebird isn't the fanciest place, but if you don't require beach-side accommodations, it's a bargain. ⊠ *1880 Main St., 93428* ☎ *805/927–4634 or 800/552–5434* 🖷 *805/927–5215* ⊕ *www.bluebirdmotel.com* ⤵ *37 rooms* ♨ *Some refrigerators, cable TV, some in-room VCRs, Wi-Fi, no-smoking rooms* ▤ *AE, D, MC, V.*

San Simeon

㉚ *Hwy. 1, 9 mi north of Cambria and 65 mi south of Big Sur.*

Whalers founded San Simeon in the 1850s but had virtually abandoned the town by the time Senator George Hearst reestablished it 20 years later. Hearst bought up most of the surrounding ranch land, built a 1,000-foot wharf, and turned San Simeon into a bustling port. His son, William Randolph Hearst, further developed the area during the construction of Hearst Castle. Today the town, 4 mi south of the entrance to Hearst San Simeon State Historical Monument, is basically a strip of gift shops and mediocre motels along Highway 1.

★ At **Hearst San Simeon State Historical Monument,** sits in solitary splendor atop La Cuesta Encantada (the Enchanted Hill). Its buildings and gardens spread over 127 acres that were the heart of newspaper magnate William Randolph Hearst's 250,000-acre ranch. Hearst devoted nearly 30 years and about $10 million to building this elaborate estate. He commissioned renowned architect Julia Morgan—who also designed buildings at the University of California at Berkeley—but he was very much involved with the final product, a hodgepodge of Italian, Spanish, Moorish, and French styles. The 115-room main building and three huge "cottages" are connected by terraces and staircases and surrounded by pools, gardens, and statuary. In its heyday the castle was a playground for Hearst and his guests, many of whom were Hollywood celebrities. Construction began in 1919 and was never officially completed. Work was halted in 1947 when Hearst had to leave San Simeon because of failing health. The Hearst family presented the property to the State of California in 1958.

Access to the castle is through the large visitor center at the foot of the hill, which contains a collection of Hearst memorabilia and a giant-screen theater that shows a 40-minute film giving a sanitized version of Hearst's life and of the castle's construction. Buses from the visitor center zigzag up the hillside to the neoclassical extravaganza, where guides conduct four different daytime tours of various parts of the main house and grounds. Tour No. 1 (which includes the movie) provides a good overview of the highlights; the others focus on particular parts of the estate. Daytime tours take about two hours. In spring and fall, docents in period costume portray Hearst's guests and staff for the slightly longer evening tour, which begins at sunset. All tours include a ½-mi walk and between 150 and 400 stairs. Reservations for the tours, which can be made up to eight weeks in advance, are necessary. ⊠ *San Simeon State Park, 750 Hearst Castle Rd.* ☎ *805/927–2020 or 800/444–4445* ⊕ *www.hearstcastle.com* 🎫 *Daytime tours $24, evening tours $30* ☉ *Tours daily 8:20–3:20, later in summer; additional tours take place most Fri. and Sat. evenings Mar.–May and Sept.–Dec.* ▤ *AE, D, MC, V.*

9

A large and growing colony (at last count 14,000 members) of elephant seals gathers every year at **Piedras Blancas Elephant Seal Rookery,** on the beaches near Piedras Blancas Lighthouse. The huge males with their pendulous, trunklike noses typically start appearing on shore in late November, and the females begin to arrive in December to give birth—most babies are born in the last two weeks of January. The newborn pups spend about four weeks nursing before their mothers head out to sea, leaving them on their own; the "weaners" leave the rookery when they are about 3 ½ months old. The seals return once or twice in the spring and summer months to molt or rest, but not en masse as in winter. You can watch them from a boardwalk along the bluffs just a few feet above the beach; do not attempt to approach them, as they are wild animals. Docents are often on hand to give background information and statistics. The rookery is just south of Piedras Blancas Lighthouse (4½ mi north of Hearst San Simeon State Historical Monument); the nonprofit Friends of the Elephant Seal runs a small visitor center and gift shop at their San Simeon office. ⊠ *Friends of the Elephant Seal, 250 San Simeon Ave., Suite 3, 93452* ☎ *805/924–1628* ⊕ *www.elephantseal.org* ✆ *Free* ☉ *Daily.*

Where to Stay

$$–$$$$ 🏨 **Best Western Cavalier Oceanfront Resort.** Reasonable rates, an oceanfront location, evening bonfires, and well-equipped rooms—some with wood-burning fireplaces and private patios—make this motel by far the best choice in San Simeon. ⊠ *9415 Hearst Dr., 93452* ☎ *805/927–4688 or 800/826–8168* 🖷 *805/927–6472* ⊕ *www.cavalierresort.com* ⤵ *90 rooms* ⌂ *2 restaurants, minibars, refrigerators, cable TV with movies, in-room DVDs, Wi-Fi, 2 pools, gym, hot tub, shop, laundry facilities, meeting rooms, some pets allowed; no smoking* ▤ *AE, D, DC, MC, V.*

BIG SUR COASTLINE

Long a retreat of artists and writers, Big Sur is a place of ancient forests and rugged shoreline, stretching 90 mi from San Simeon to Carmel. Residents have protected it from overdevelopment, and much of the region lies within several state parks and the more than 165,000-acre Ventana Wilderness, itself part of the Los Padres National Forest.

Southern Big Sur

③①   *Hwy. 1 from San Simeon to Julia Pfeiffer Burns State Park.*

This especially rugged stretch of oceanfront is a rocky world of mountains, cliffs, and beaches. One of California's most spectacular drives, **Fodor'sChoice**   **Highway 1** snakes up the coast north of San Simeon. Numerous pull-
★   outs along the way offer tremendous views and photo ops. On some of the beaches, huge elephant seals lounge nonchalantly, seemingly oblivious to the attention of rubberneckers—but keep your distance. In rainy seasons, the southern Big Sur portion of Highway 1 is regularly shut down by mudslides. Contact **CalTrans** (☎ 800/427–7623 ⊕ www.dot. ca.gov) for road conditions.

In Los Padres National Forest just north of the town of Gorda is **Jade Cove** (⊠ Hwy. 1, 34 mi north of San Simeon), a well-known jade-hunting spot. Rock hunting is allowed on the beach, but you may not remove anything from the walls of the cliffs.

Julia Pfeiffer Burns State Park provides some fine hiking, from an easy ½-mi stroll with marvelous coastal views to a strenuous 6-mi trek through the redwoods. The big attraction here, an 80-foot waterfall that drops into the ocean, gets crowded in summer; still, it's an astounding place to sit and contemplate nature. Migrating whales, as well as harbor seals and sea lions, can sometimes be spotted not far from shore. ⊠ *Hwy. 1, 53 mi north of San Simeon, 15 mi north of Lucia* ☎ *831/667–2315* ⊕ *www.parks.ca.gov* 🖼 *$5* ☉ *Daily sunrise–sunset.*

Where to Stay & Eat

$$–$$$ ✕🏠 **Ragged Point Inn.** At this clifftop resort—the only inn and restaurant for miles around—glass walls in most rooms open to awesome, unobstructed ocean views. Though not especially luxurious, some rooms have spa tubs, kitchenettes, and fireplaces. The restaurant ($$–$$$) is a good place to fill up on standard American fare—sandwiches, salads, pastas, and main courses—before or after the long, winding Highway 1 drive. Even if you're just passing by, stop to stretch your legs on the 14 acres of lush gardens above the sea; you can pick up souvenirs, a burger, or an espresso to go. ⊠ *19019 Hwy. 1, 20 mi north of San Simeon, Ragged Point 93452* ☎ *805/927–4502, 805/927–5708 restaurant* ⊕ *www.raggedpointinn.com* 🍴 *Restaurant, picnic area, snack bar, some kitchenettes, cable TV, Wi-Fi, shops, laundry facilities; no room phones, no smoking* 🖃 *AE, D, DC, MC, V.*

$$–$$$ 🏠 **Treebones Resort.** Perched on a hilltop, surrounded by national forest and stunning, unobstructed ocean views, this yurt resort opened in 2004. The yurts here—circular structures of heavy-duty fabric, on individual platforms with decks—are designed for upscale camping. Each has one or two queen beds with patchwork quilts, wicker furniture, and pine floors. Electricity and hot and cold running water come to you, but you have to walk to squeaky-clean bathhouse and restroom facilities. The sunny main lodge, where breakfast and dinner (not included) are served, has a big fireplace, games, and a well-stocked sundries and gift shop. Younger children have difficulty on the steep paths between buildings. ⊠ *71895 Hwy. 1, Willow Creek Rd., 32 mi north of San Simeon, 1 mi north of Gorda, Big Sur 93920* ☎ *877/424–4787* ⊕ *www.treebonesresort.com* 🛏 *16 yurts* 🍴 *Grocery, pool, spa, shop, laundry facilities, Internet room, some pets allowed (fee)* 🖃 *AE, MC, V* ⬤ *CP.*

Central Big Sur

㉜ *Hwy. 1, from Partington Cove to Bixby Bridge.*

The countercultural spirit of Big Sur—which instead of a conventional town is a loose string of coast-hugging properties along Highway 1—is alive and well today. Its few residents include the very wealthy, the enthusiastically outdoorsy, and the thoroughly evolved: since the 1960s the Esalen Institute, a center for alternative education and East–West philosophical study, has attracted seekers of higher consciousness and devotees of the property's hot springs. Today, posh and rustic resorts hidden among the redwoods cater to visitors drawn from near and far by the extraordinary scenery and serene isolation.

Through a hole in one of the gigantic boulders at secluded **Pfeiffer Beach,** you can watch the waves break first on the sea side and then on the beach side. Keep a sharp eye out for the unsigned road to the beach: it is the only ungated paved road branching west of Highway 1 between the post office and Pfeiffer Big Sur State Park. The 2-mi, one-lane road descends sharply. ⊠ *Off Hwy. 1, 1 mi south of Pfeiffer Big Sur State Park* ☜ *$5 per vehicle, day use.*

Among the many hiking trails at **Pfeiffer Big Sur State Park** ($8 per vehicle for day use) a short route through a redwood-filled valley leads to a waterfall. You can double back or continue on the more difficult trail along the valley wall for views over miles of treetops to the sea. Stop in at the Big Sur Station visitor center, off Highway 1, less than ½ mi south of the park entrance, for information about the entire area; it's open 8–4:30. ⊠ *47225 Hwy. 1* ☎ *831/667–2315* ⊕ *www.parks.ca.gov* ☉ *Daily dawn–dusk.*

★ **Point Sur State Historic Park** is the site of an 1889 lighthouse that still stands watch from atop a large volcanic rock. Four lighthouse keepers lived here with their families until 1974, when the light station became automated. Their homes and working spaces are open to the public only on 2½- to 3-hour ranger-led tours. Considerable walking, including up two stairways, is involved. Strollers are not allowed; you'll have to carry small children in a backpack. ⊠ *Hwy. 1, 7 mi north of Pfeiffer Big Sur State Park* ☎ *831/625–4419* ⊕ *www.parks.ca.gov* ☜ *$8* ☉ *Tours generally Nov.–Mar., Sat. at 10 and 2, Sun. at 10; Apr.–Oct., Wed. and Sat. at 10 and 2, Sun. at 10; call to confirm.*

The graceful arc of **Bixby Creek Bridge** (⊠ Hwy. 1, 6 mi north of Point Sur State Historic Park, 13 mi south of Carmel) is a photographer's dream. Built in 1932, it spans a deep canyon, more than 100 feet wide at the bottom. From the parking area on the north side you can admire the view or walk across the 550-foot span.

Where to Stay & Eat

$$–$$$$ ✕ **Nepenthe.** It may be that no other restaurant between San Francisco and Los Angeles has a better coastal view; no wonder Orson Welles and Rita Hayworth once owned the place. The food and drink are overpriced but good; there are burgers, sandwiches, and salads for lunch, and fresh fish and hormone-free steaks for dinner. For the real show, settle on the terraced deck in the late afternoon, order a glass from the extensive wine list, and watch the sun slip into the Pacific Ocean. The less expensive, outdoor Café Kevah serves breakfast and lunch. ⊠ *Hwy. 1, 2½ mi south of Big Sur Station* ☎ *831/667–2345* ▤ *AE, MC, V.*

$–$$$ ✕ **Big Sur Roadhouse.** In their colorful, well-executed California Latin–fusion fare. Crispy striped bass atop a pillow of carrot-coconut puree, tangy-smoky barbecue chicken breast beneath a julienne of jicama and cilantro: the zesty, balanced flavors wake up your mouth. Emphasizing new-world vintages, the wine list is gently priced. The chocolate-caramel layer cake may bring tears to your eyes. ✉ *Hwy. 1, 1 mi north of Pfeiffer Big Sur State Park* ☎ *831/667–2264* ⊘ *Closed Tues. No lunch.*

$$$$ ✕▥ **Post Ranch Inn.** This luxurious retreat, designed exclusively for adult
Fodor'sChoice getaways, has remarkably environmentally conscious architecture. The
★ redwood guesthouses, all of which have views of the sea or the mountains, blend almost invisibly into a wooded cliff 1,200 feet above the ocean. Each unit has its own fireplace, stereo, private deck, and massage table. On-site activities include everything from yoga to star-gazing. The inn's restaurant, Sierra Mar ($$$$), serves cutting-edge American food at lunch and dinner, including a stellar four-course prix-fixe menu. ✉ *Hwy. 1, 1½ mi south of Pfeiffer Big Sur State Park, 93920* ☎ *831/667–2200 or 800/527–2200* ▤ *831/667–2824* ⊕ *www.postranchinn.com* ⇱ *30 units* ⌂ *Restaurant, in-room hot tubs, refrigerators, 2 pools, gym, spa, bar, library, Internet room; no room TVs, no smoking* ▭ *AE, MC, V* ⎪◯⎪ *BP.*

$$$$ ✕▥ **Ventana Inn & Spa.** Hundreds of celebrities, from Oprah Winfrey
Fodor'sChoice to Sir Anthony Hopkins, have escaped to Ventana, a romantic resort
★ on 243 tranquil acres 1,200 feet above the Pacific. The activities here are purposely limited. You can sunbathe (there is a clothing-optional deck and pool), walk or ride horses in the nearby hills, or pamper yourself with mind-and-body treatments at the Allegria Spa or in your own private quarters. All rooms have walls of natural wood and cool tile floors; some have private hot tubs on their patios. The inn's Cielo restaurant ($$$–$$$$) showcases fine California cuisine and wine. ✉ *Hwy. 1, almost 1 mi south of Pfeiffer Big Sur State Park, 93920* ☎ *831/667–2331 or 800/628–6500* ▤ *831/667–0573* ⊕ *www.ventanainn.com* ⇱ *25 rooms, 31 suites, 3 houses* ⌂ *Restaurant, in-room DVDs, in-room broadband, Wi-Fi, 2 pools, gym, 2 Japanese baths, sauna, spa, bar, library; no smoking* ▭ *AE, D, DC, MC, V* ☞ *2-night minimum stay on weekends and holidays; children allowed only in houses* ⎪◯⎪ *BP.*

$–$$$ ✕▥ **Deetjen's Big Sur Inn.** This historic 1930s Norwegian-style property
is endearingly rustic and charming, especially if you're willing to go with a camplike flow. The room doors lock only from the inside, and your neighbors can often be heard through the walls—if you plan to bring children, you must reserve an entire building. Still, Deetjen's is a special place. Its village of cabins is nestled in the redwoods, and many of the very individual rooms have their own fireplaces. The candlelighted, creaky-floored restaurant ($$–$$$) in the main house serves roast duck, steak, and rack of lamb for dinner and wonderfully light and flavorful pancakes for breakfast. ✉ *Hwy. 1, 3½ mi south of Pfeiffer Big Sur State Park, 93920* ☎ *831/667–2377* ▤ *831/667–0466* ⊕ *www.deetjens.com* ⇱ *20 rooms, 15 with bath* ⌂ *Restaurant; no room phones, no room TVs, no smoking* ▭ *MC, V.*

$–$$ ▥ **Glen Oaks Motel.** At this appealingly retro cluster of adobe-and-redwood buildings in the heart of Big Sur, you can choose between simple yet comfortable motel-style rooms and frontier-style cottages in the woods. All are decorated with photos of Big Sur; the cottages have gas fireplaces. ✉ *Hwy. 1, 1 mi north of Pfeiffer Big Sur State Park, 93920* ☎ *831/667–2105* ▤ *831/667–1105* ⊕ *www.glenoaksbigsur.com* ⇱ *15 rooms, 2 cottages* ⌂ *No room phones, no room TVs, no smoking* ▭ *No credit cards.*

⚠ **Pfeiffer Big Sur State Park.** Redwood trees tower over this large campground. It's often crowded in summer, so reserve a site or a tent cabin

9

as far ahead as possible. There are no hookups, but the park has Wi-Fi. ♿ *Flush toilets, dump station, drinking water, guest laundry, showers, fire grates, fire pits, picnic tables, food service, public telephone, Wi-Fi, general store, ranger station* 🚫 *218 sites* ✉ *47225 Hwy. 1* ☏ *800/444–7275 for reservations* ⊕ *www.parks.ca.gov* 💳 *$15–$20.*

CENTRAL COAST ESSENTIALS

To research prices, get advice from other travelers, and book travel arrangements, visit www.fodors.com.

Transportation

BY AIR

America West Express, American Eagle, Delta/Delta Connection, Horizon Air, and United Express fly to Santa Barbara Municipal Airport, 12 mi from downtown. American Eagle, Mesa/America West, and Skywest/United Express provide service to San Luis Obispo County Regional Airport, 3 mi from downtown San Luis Obispo. ⇨ Air Travel *in* Smart Travel Tips A to Z for airline phone numbers.

🛈 **San Luis Obispo County Regional Airport** ✉ 903–5 Airport Dr., San Luis Obispo ☏ 805/781–5205 ⊕ www.sloairport.com. **Santa Barbara Municipal Airport** ✉ 500 Fowler Rd., Santa Barbara ☏ 805/683–4011 ⊕ www.flysba.com.

AIRPORT TRANSFERS Santa Barbara Airbus shuttles travelers between Santa Barbara and Los Angeles for $46 one-way and $86 round-trip (slight discount with 24-hour notice, larger discount for groups of six or more). The Santa Barbara Metropolitan Transit District Bus 11 ($1.25) runs every 30 minutes from the airport to the downtown transit center. A taxi between the airport and the hotel district runs $18 to $25.

🛈 **Santa Barbara Airbus** ☏ 805/964–7759 or 800/733–6354, 800/423–1618 in CA ⊕ www.sbairbus.com. **Santa Barbara Metropolitan Transit District** ☏ 805/683–3702 or 805/963–3364 ⊕ www.sbmtd.gov.

BY BUS

Greyhound provides service from San Francisco and Los Angeles to San Luis Obispo, Ventura, and Santa Barbara. From Monterey and Carmel, Monterey-Salinas Transit operates buses to Big Sur between May and mid-October. From San Luis Obispo, Central Coast Transit runs buses around Santa Maria and out to the coast. Santa Barbara Metropolitan Transit District provides local service. The State Street and Waterfront shuttles cover their respective sections of Santa Barbara during the day. South Coast Area Transit buses serve the entire Ventura County region.

🛈 **Central Coast Transit** ☏ 805/781–4472 ⊕ www.slorta.org. **Greyhound** ☏ 800/231–2222 ⊕ www.greyhound.com. **Monterey-Salinas Transit** ☏ 888/678–2871 ⊕ www.mst.org. **San Luis Obispo Transit** ☏ 805/781–4472 ⊕ www.slorta.org. **Santa Barbara Metropolitan Transit District** ☏ 805/683–3702 or 805/963–3364 ⊕ www.sbmtd.gov. **South Coast Area Transit** ☏ 805/643–3158 for Oxnard and Ventura ⊕ www.scat.org.

BY CAR

Highway 1 and U.S. 101 run north–south and more or less parallel along the Central Coast, with Highway 1 hugging the coast and U.S. 101 running inland. The most dramatic section of the Central Coast is the 70 mi between Big Sur and San Simeon. Don't expect to make good time along here: the road is narrow and twisting with a single lane in each direction, making it difficult to pass the many lumbering RVs. In fog or rain the drive can be downright nerve-racking; in wet seasons mudslides can close portions of the road. Once you start south from Carmel, there is no route east from Highway 1 until Highway 46 heads inland from Cambria to connect with U.S. 101. At Morro Bay, Highway 1 turns inland for 13 mi and connects with U.S. 101 at San Luis Obispo. From here south to Pismo Beach the two highways run concurrently. South of Pismo Beach to Las Cruces the roads separate, then run together all the way to Oxnard. Along any stretch where they are separate, U.S. 101 is the quicker route.

U.S. 101 and Highway 1 will get you to the Central Coast from Los Angeles and San Francisco. If you are coming from the east, you can take Highway 46 west from Interstate 5 in the Central Valley (near Bakersfield) to U.S. 101 at Paso Robles, where it continues to the coast, intersecting Highway 1 a few miles south of Cambria. Highway 33 heads south from Interstate 5 at Bakersfield to Ojai. About 60 mi north of Ojai, Highway 166 leaves Highway 33, traveling due west through the Sierra Madre to Santa Maria at U.S. 101 and continuing west to Highway 1 at Guadalupe. South of Carpinteria, Highway 150 winds from Highway 1/U.S. 101 through sparsely populated hills to Ojai. From Highway 1/U.S. 101 at Ventura, Highway 33 leads to Ojai and the Los Padres National Forest. South of Ventura, Highway 126 runs east from Highway 1/U.S. 101 to Interstate 5.

🚗 **Caltrans** ☎ 800/427-7623 ⊕ www.dot.ca.gov/hq/roadinfo.

CAR RENTAL Most major car-rental companies have offices in San Luis Obispo, Santa Barbara, and Ventura. ⇨ Car Rental *in* Smart Travel Tips A to Z for national rental-agency phone numbers.

BY TRAIN

The Amtrak *Coast Starlight,* which runs between Los Angeles and Seattle via Oakland, stops in Paso Robles, San Luis Obispo, Santa Barbara, and Oxnard. Amtrak runs several *Pacific Surfliner* trains daily between San Luis Obispo, Santa Barbara, Los Angeles, and San Diego. Metrolink Regional Rail Service trains connect Ventura and Oxnard with Los Angeles and points between.

🚆 **Amtrak** ☎ 800/872-7245, 805/963-1015 in Santa Barbara, 805/541-0505 in San Luis Obispo ⊕ www.amtrakcalifornia.com. **Metrolink** ☎ 800/371-5465 within service area, 213/347-2800 ⊕ www.metrolinktrains.com.

EMERGENCIES

In case of emergency dial 911.

🚑 **Big Sur Health Center** ⊠ Hwy. 1¼ mi south of River Inn, Big Sur ☎ 831/667-2580 is open weekdays 10-5. **Cottage Hospital** ⊠ Pueblo and Bath Sts., Santa Barbara ☎ 805/682-7111, 805/569-7210 for emergency. **Sierra Vista Regional Medical Center** ⊠ 1010 Murray Ave., San Luis Obispo ☎ 805/546-7600.

TOUR OPTIONS

Cloud Climbers Jeep and Wine Tours offers four types of daily tours: wine tasting, mountain, sunset, and a discovery tour for families. These trips to the Santa Barbara/Santa Ynez mountains and wine country are conducted in open-air, six-passenger jeeps. Fares range from $79 to $99 per adult. The company also arranges biking, horseback riding, and trap-shooting tours by appointment. Central Coast Wine Tours' 15-passenger vans can take you on a scheduled trip to wineries in the Edna Valley, Paso Robles, or to Hearst Castle. Fares for wine tours are $50, with pick-ups in San Luis Obispo, Morro Bay, Pismo Beach, and Cambria. The Hearst Castle tour costs $60. Wine Adventures operates customized Santa Barbara County tours and narrated North County wine-country tours in 25-passenger minicoaches. Fares for the wine tours are $95 per person. The Grapeline Wine Country Shuttle leads daily wine and vineyard picnic tours with flexible itineraries in Paso Robles wine country; they stop at most Paso Robles hotels, and can pick up in Templeton, Cambria, and San Luis Obispo with advance reservations. Fares range from $38 to $85, depending on pickup location and tour choice.

Spencer's Limousine & Tours offers customized tours of the city of Santa Barbara and wine country via sedan, limousine, van, or minibus. A four-hour basic tour with at least four participants costs about $50 per person. Sultan's Limousine Service has a fleet of super stretches; each can take up to eight passengers on Paso Robles and Edna Valley–Arroyo Grande wine tours and tours of the San Luis Obispo County coast. Hiring a limo for a four-hour wine country tour typically costs $360 to $410 with tip.

🚙 **Central Coast Wine Tours** ☎ 866/717-2298. **Cloud Climbers Jeep and Wine Tours** ☎ 805/965-6654 ⊕ www.ccjeeps.com. **The Grapeline Wine Country Shuttle** ☎ 805/239-4747 or 888/894-6379 ⊕ pasorobles.gogrape.com. **Spencer's Limousine & Tours** ✉ Santa Barbara ☎ 805/884-9700 ⊕ www.spencerslimo.com. **Sultan's Limousine Service** ✉ Paso Robles ☎ 805/466-3167 ⊕ www.sultanslimo.com. **Wine Adventures** ✉ 3463 State St., #228, Santa Barbara ☎ 805/965-9463 ⊕ www.welovewines.com.

VISITOR INFORMATION

🚹 **Big Sur Chamber of Commerce** ☎ 831/667-2100 ⊕ www.bigsurcalifornia.org. **Cambria Chamber of Commerce** ☎ 805/927-3624 ⊕ www.cambriachamber.org. **Central Coast Tourism Council** ✉ Box 1435, San Juan Bautista 95045 ☎ 831/902-7275 ⊕ www.centralcoast-tourism.com. **Ojai Valley Chamber of Commerce** ☎ 805/646-8126 ⊕ www.ojaichamber.org. **Paso Robles Wine Country Alliance** ✉ 744 Oak St. ☎ 805/239-8463 ⊕ www.pasowine.com. **Paso Robles Visitors and Conference Bureau** ✉ 1225 Park St. ☎ 805/238-0506 ⊕ www.pasorobleschamber.com. **San Luis Obispo Chamber of Commerce** ✉ 1039 Chorro St. ☎ 805/781-2777 ⊕ www.visitslo.com. **San Luis Obispo County Visitors and Conference Bureau** ✉ 811 El Capitan Way #200 ☎ 805/541-8000 or 800/634-1414 ⊕ www.sanluisobispocounty.com. **San Luis Obispo Vintners Association** ☎ 805/541-5868 ⊕ www.slowine.com. **Santa Barbara Conference and Visitors Bureau** ✉ 1601 Anacapa St. ☎ 805/966-9222 or 800/927-4688 ⊕ www.santabarbaraca.com. **Santa Barbara County Vintners' Association** ☎ 805/688-0881 or 800/218-0881 ⊕ www.sbcountywines.com. **Santa Ynez Valley Visitors Association** ☎ 800/742-2843 ⊕ www.syvva.com. **Solvang Conference & Visitors Bureau** ✉ 1511 Mission Dr. ☎ 805/688-6144 or 800/468-6765 ⊕ www.solvangusa.com. **Ventura Visitors and Convention Bureau** ✉ 89 S. California St., #C ☎ 805/648-2075 or 800/483-6214 ⊕ www.ventura-usa.com.

Monterey Bay Area

FROM CARMEL TO SANTA CRUZ

WORD OF MOUTH

"The Monterey Bay Aquarium is a great experience for young kids and adults. Venues for the sea creatures are very well done. It is quite a fun and an educational experience. I suggest going early in the day to avoid the lines. Either way, it's well worth the wait."

—Tom

"The beauty of Point Lobos State Reserve was so stunning, I could not believe it. Here you have a mix of tall cliffs, crashing waves, gorgeous wild flowers, abundant wild life (seals, sea otters, deer), and sheltered emerald-green coves with white sandy beaches."

—Birder

Updated by
Constance
Jones

IN THE GOOD LIFE OF MONTEREY BAY'S coast-side towns, in the pleasures of its luxurious resorts, and in the vitality of its resplendent marine habitat, this piece of California shows off its natural appeal. The abundance is nothing new: an abiding current of plenty runs through the many histories of the region. Military buffs see it in centuries' worth of battles for control of the rich territory. John Steinbeck saw it in the success of a community built on the elbow grease of farm laborers in the Salinas Valley and fishermen along Cannery Row. Biologists see it in the ocean's potential as a more sustainable source of food.

It's easy to see the Monterey Peninsula's diverse cultural and maritime heritage. Cannery Row, the former center of Monterey's once-thriving sardine industry, has been reborn as a tourist attraction with shops, restaurants, hotels, and the Monterey Bay Aquarium. Downtown Carmel-by-the-Sea and Monterey are walks through history. Santa Cruz shows its colors along an old-time beach boardwalk and municipal wharf. The bay itself is protected by the Monterey Bay National Marine Sanctuary, the nation's largest undersea canyon—bigger and deeper than the Grand Canyon. And of course, the backdrop of natural beauty is still everywhere to be seen.

Exploring Monterey Bay

The individual charms of its towns complement Monterey Bay's natural beauty. On the Monterey Peninsula, at the southern end of the bay, are Carmel-by-the-Sea, Pacific Grove, and Monterey; Santa Cruz sits at the northern tip of the crescent. In between, Highway 1 cruises along the coastline, passing windswept beaches piled high with sand dunes. Along the route are wetlands, artichoke and strawberry fields, and workaday towns such as Castroville and Watsonville.

About the Restaurants

Between San Francisco and Los Angeles, some of the finest dining to be found is around Monterey Bay. The surrounding waters are full of fish, wild game roams the foothills, and the inland valleys are some of the most fertile in the country—local chefs draw on this bounty for their fresh, truly California cuisine. Except at beachside stands and inexpensive eateries, where anything goes, casual but neat dress is the norm. Only a few places require more formal attire.

About the Hotels

Monterey-area accommodations range from no-frills motels to luxurious hotels. Many of the area's small inns and bed-and-breakfasts pamper the traveler in grand style. Pacific Grove, amply endowed with ornate Victorian houses, has quietly turned itself into the region's B&B capital; Carmel also has charming inns in residential areas. Truly lavish resorts, with everything from featherbeds to heated floors, cluster in exclusive Pebble Beach and pastoral Carmel Valley. ⚠ **Many of the fancier accommodations are not suitable for children, so if you're traveling with kids, be sure to ask before you book.**

Around Monterey Bay high season runs April through October. Rates in winter, especially at the larger hotels, may drop by 50% or more, and B&Bs often offer midweek specials in the off-season. However, special

GREAT ITINERARIES

Numbers correspond to the Monterey Bay and Monterey maps.

Life around Monterey Bay is focused on the water, but the area is chock-full of other diversions as well. In Carmel-by-the-Sea you can shop until you drop, and when the summer and weekend hordes descend, you can slip off to enjoy the coast. Fans of Victorian architecture will want to search out the many fine examples in Pacific Grove. If you have an interest in California history and historic preservation, the place to start is Monterey, with its adobe buildings along the downtown Path of History. Poke around in the antiques shops of Capitola and Soquel, and check out the rinky-dink fun at the Santa Cruz Beach Boardwalk.

IF YOU HAVE 3 DAYS

Start in ► ⛶ **Carmel-by-the-Sea** ❶ to visit Carmel Mission and Tor House (if it's open). Leave yourself plenty of time to browse the shops of Ocean Avenue, then stroll over to Scenic Road and spend time on Carmel Beach before dinner. On the following morning, take a hike at Point Lobos State Reserve for some great views, then motor up **17-Mile Drive** ❸. That afternoon visit a few of the buildings in the state historic park in ⛶ **Monterey** ❺–❷⓿. Spend your final day along Cannery Row and **Fisherman's Wharf** ❼. Don't miss the **Monterey Bay Aquarium** ❷⓿. Catch the sunset from the bustling wharf or slip into the serene bar at the Monterey Plaza Hotel and Spa.

IF YOU HAVE 5 DAYS

Spend your first day and second morning following the itinerary above, but instead of continuing to Monterey on your second afternoon, explore the shoreline and Victorian houses of ⛶ **Pacific Grove** ❹. Start Day 3 at the **Monterey Bay Aquarium** ❷⓿ and enjoy the afternoon either relaxing on the waterfront in ⛶ **Monterey** ❺–❷⓿ or getting a glimpse of the city's fascinating past at Monterey State Historic Park. The next morning, take a whale-watching or other cruise from **Fisherman's Wharf** ❼. Head up Highway 1 in the afternoon, stopping in **Capitola** ❷❹ to stretch your legs and grab an ice-cream cone. Wander downtown ⛶ **Santa Cruz** ❷❺ in the evening, and start Day 5 with a stroll along West Cliff Drive. While away the rest of the day on Santa Cruz Beach Boardwalk and Santa Cruz Municipal Wharf, or try a surfing lesson.

events throughout the year can fill lodgings far in advance. Whatever the month, even the simplest of the area's lodgings are expensive, and most properties require a two-night stay on weekends.

Bed and Breakfast Innkeepers of Santa Cruz County (☎ 831/688–0444 ⊕ www.santacruzbnb.com), an association of innkeepers, can help you find a B&B. **Monterey County Conventions and Visitors Bureau Visitor Services** (☎ 888/221–1010 ⊕ www.montereyinfo.org) operates a lodging referral line and publishes an informational brochure with discount coupons that are good at restaurants, attractions, and shops. **Monterey**

Peninsula Reservations (☎ 888/655–3424 ⊕ www.monterey-reservations. com) will assist you in booking lodgings.

WHAT IT COSTS				
$$$$	**$$$**	**$$**	**$**	**¢**
RESTAURANTS over $30	$23–$30	$16–$22	$10–$15	under $10
HOTELS over $250	$176–$250	$121–$175	$90–$120	under $90

Restaurant prices are for a main course at dinner, excluding sales tax of 7½%–8¼% (depending on location). Hotel prices are for two people in a standard double room in high season, excluding service charges and 10%–10½% tax.

Timing

Summer is peak season; mild weather brings in big crowds. In this coastal region, a cool breeze generally blows and fog often rolls in from offshore; you will frequently need a sweater or windbreaker. Off-season, from November through April, fewer people visit and the mood is mellower. Rainfall is heaviest in January and February, but autumn through spring days are more often crystal-clear than they are in summer.

CARMEL & PACIFIC GROVE

If you want to see small towns and spectacular vistas, be sure to visit the stretch of coast between Big Sur and Monterey. Each of the communities here is distinct, and you'll see everything from thatch-roof cottages to palatial estates, rolling hills to craggy cliffs.

Carmel-by-the-Sea

▶ ❶ *26 mi north of Big Sur on Hwy. 1.*

Although the community has grown quickly through the years and its population quadruples with tourists on weekends and in summer, Carmel-by-the-Sea, commonly referred to as Carmel, retains its identity as a quaint village. Self-consciously charming, the town is populated by many celebrities, major and minor, and has more than its share of quirky ordinances. For instance, women wearing high heels do not have the right to pursue legal action if they trip and fall on the cobblestone streets; drivers who hit a tree and leave the scene are charged with hit-and-run; live music is banned in local watering holes; and ice-cream parlors are not allowed to sell cones—only cups—because children might drop them, leaving unsightly puddles on the pretty streets. Buildings still have no street numbers (street names are written on discreet white posts) and consequently no mail delivery (if you really want to see the locals, go to the post office). Artists started this community, and their legacy is evident in the numerous galleries. Wandering the side streets off Ocean Avenue, where you can poke into hidden courtyards and stop at cafés for tea and crumpets, is a pleasure. For a look past the shops and into the town's colorful history, the **Carmel Heritage Society** (⊠ Lincoln St. at 6th Ave. ☎ 831/624–4447 ⊕ www.carmelheritage.org) leads 1½-hour walking tours most Saturdays at 9:30 AM.

IF YOU LIKE

FINE DINING

In California you can eat well, and around Monterey Bay you can eat very, very well. Thanks to the abundance of local produce, meats, seafood, and wine, the best cuisine here is that which doesn't stray too far from home. Monterey and Carmel fairly burst at the seams with such restaurants, with Monterey's Montrio Bistro—a temple of California cuisine—leading the pack. Carmel's restaurants are guided by their worldly chefs, most notably the inventive Walter Manske at intimate L'Auberge Carmel. And although Santa Cruz is not famed for its restaurants, the county is famous for its organic farmers; the best place to taste the fruits of their labor is at Theo's in Soquel, which specializes in seasonal American dishes.

GREAT GOLF

Since the opening of the Del Monte Golf Course in 1897, golf has been an integral part of the Monterey Peninsula's social and recreational scene. Pebble Beach's championship courses host prestigious tournaments, and though the greens fees at these courses can run well over $200,

elsewhere on the peninsula you'll find less expensive—but still challenging and scenic—options. Many hotels will help with golf reservations or have golf packages; inquire when you book your room.

WHALE-WATCHING

On their annual migration between the Bering Sea and Baja California, thousands of gray whales pass close by the Monterey coast. They are sometimes visible through binoculars from shore, but a whale-watching cruise is the best way to get a close look at these magnificent mammals. The migration south takes place from December through March. January is prime viewing time. The migration north occurs from March through June. In addition, some 2,000 blue whales and 600 humpbacks pass the coast and are easily spotted in late summer and early fall. Smaller numbers of minke whales, orcas, sperm whales, and fin whales have been sighted in mid-August. Even if no whales surface, bay cruises from Monterey and Moss Landing almost always encounter other enchanting sea creatures, such as sea otters, sea lions, and porpoises.

10

Downtown Carmel's chief lure is shopping, especially along its main street, **Ocean Avenue,** between Junipero Avenue and Camino Real; the architecture here is a mishmash of ersatz Tudor, Mediterranean, and other styles. **Carmel Plaza** (⊠ Ocean and Junipero Aves. ☎ 831/624–0138 ⊕ www.carmelplaza.com), in the east end of the village proper, holds more than 50 shops and restaurants.

Long before it became a shopping and browsing destination, Carmel was an important religious center during the establishment of Spanish California. That heritage is preserved in the Mission San Carlos Borroméo del Rio Carmelo, more commonly known as the **Carmel Mission.** Founded in 1771, it served as headquarters for the mission system in California under Father Junípero Serra. Adjoining the stone church is

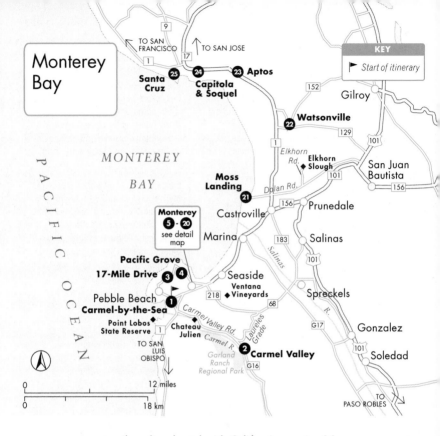

Monterey Bay

KEY

► Start of itinerary

TO SAN FRANCISCO
TO SAN JOSE

Santa Cruz **25**
Capitola & Soquel **24**
Aptos **23**
Gilroy **152**

Watsonville **22**
129
101

Elkhorn Rd.
Elkhorn Slough ◆
San Juan Bautista
101
156

MONTEREY

BAY

Moss Landing **21**
Dolan Rd.
156
Prunedale
Castroville
Marina
Salinas **101**
183

Monterey **5** · **20**
see detail map

Seaside
Ventana Vineyards ◆
218
68
Spreckels

Pacific Grove
17-Mile Drive **3** **4**
1
Pebble Beach
Carmel-by-the-Sea **1**
Carmel Valley Rd.
Point Lobos State Reserve ◆
1
Chateau Julien ◆
Carmel R.
Carmel Valley **2**
Gonzalez
G17

TO SAN LUIS OBISPO
Garland Ranch Regional Park
G16
Soledad
101

PACIFIC OCEAN

0 ___ 12 miles
0 ___ 18 km

TO PASO ROBLES

a tranquil garden planted with California poppies. Museum rooms at the mission include an early kitchen, Serra's spartan sleeping quarters, and the first college library in California. ⊠ *3080 Rio Rd., at Lasuen Dr.* ☎ *831/624–3600* ⊕ *www.carmelmission.org* ⊠ *$5* ⊘ *Weekdays 9:30–5, weekends 10:30–5.*

Scattered throughout the pines in Carmel by-the-Sea are houses and cottages originally built for the writers, artists, and photographers who discovered the area decades ago. Among the most impressive dwellings is **Tor House,** a stone cottage built in 1919 by poet Robinson Jeffers on a craggy knoll overlooking the sea. Portraits, books, and unusual art objects fill the low-ceiling rooms. The highlight of the small estate is Hawk Tower, a detached edifice set with stones from the Carmel coastline—as well as one from the Great Wall of China. The docents who lead tours (six people maximum) are well informed about the poet's work and life. Reservations for tours are recommended. ⊠ *26304 Ocean View Ave.* ☎ *831/624–1813* ⊕ *www.torhouse.org* ⊠ *$7* ☞ *No children under 12* ⊘ *Tours on the hr Fri. and Sat. 10–3.*

Carmel-by-the-Sea's greatest attraction is its rugged coastline, with pine and cypress forests and countless inlets. **Carmel Beach** (⊠ End of Ocean Ave.), an easy walk from downtown shops, has sparkling white sands and magnificent sunsets. **Carmel River State Beach** stretches for 106 acres along Carmel Bay. The sugar-white beach is adjacent to a bird sanctuary, where you might spot pelicans, kingfishers, hawks, and sandpipers. ⊠ *Off Scenic Rd. south of Carmel Beach* ☎ *831/624–4909 or 831/649–2836* ⊕ *www.cal-parks.ca.gov* ⌷ *Parking $8* ☉ *Apr.–Oct., daily 9–7; Nov.–Mar., daily 9–5.*

★ **Point Lobos State Reserve,** a 350-acre headland harboring a wealth of marine life, lies a few miles south of Carmel. The best way to explore the reserve is to walk along one of its many trails. The Cypress Grove Trail leads through a forest of Monterey cypress (one of only two natural groves remaining), which clings to the rocks above an emerald-green cove. Sea Lion Point Trail is a good place to view sea lions. From those and other trails you may also spot otters, harbor seals, and (in winter and spring) migrating whales. An additional 750 acres of the reserve is an undersea marine park open to qualified scuba divers. ■ TIP→ **Arrive early (or in late afternoon) to avoid crowds; the parking lots fill up.** No pets are allowed. ⊠ *Hwy. 1* ☎ *831/624–4909, 831/624–8413 for scuba-diving reservations* ⊕ *www.pointlobos.org* ⌷ *$8 per vehicle* ☉ *Apr.–Oct., daily 9–7; Nov.–Mar., daily 9–4:30.*

Where to Stay & Eat

★ **$$$–$$$$** ✕ **Casanova.** Built in a former home, this cozy restaurant inspires European-style celebration and romance—chairs are painted in all colors, accordions hang from the walls, and tiny party lights dance along the low ceilings. All entrées include antipasti and your choice of appetizers, which all but mandate you to sit back and enjoy a long meal. The food consists of delectable seasonal dishes from southern France and northern Italy. Private dining and a special menu are offered at Van Gogh's Table, a special table imported from France's Auberge Ravoux, the artist's final residence. ⊠ *5th Ave. between San Carlos and Mission Sts.* ☎ *831/625–0501* ⌷ *Reservations essential* ⊟ *AE, MC, V.*

$$–$$$$ ✕ **Anton and Michel.** Carefully prepared European cuisine is the draw at this airy restaurant. The rack of lamb is carved at the table, the duck prosciutto is cured in-house, and the desserts are set aflame before your eyes. In summer, you (and your dog!) can have lunch served in the courtyard; inside, the dining room looks onto a lighted fountain. ⊠ *Mission St. and 7th Ave.* ☎ *831/624–2406* ⌷ *Reservations essential* ⊟ *AE, D, DC, MC, V.*

★ **$$–$$$$** ✕ **Bouchée.** Prepared by a chef whose pedigree includes six years at L.A.'s storied Patina, the food here presents an innovative take on local ingredients—a Reuben sandwich is made with veal sweetbreads and ravioli is stuffed with parsnip and served with crispy pancetta. With its copper bar, the dining room feels more urban than most of Carmel; perhaps this is why Bouchée is the "cool" place in town to dine. The stellar wine list sources the selection at adjoining Bouchée Wine Merchant. ⊠ *Mission St. between Ocean and 7th Aves.* ☎ *831/626–7880* ⌷ *Reservations essential* ⊟ *AE, MC, V* ☉ *Closed Mon. No lunch.*

$$–$$$$ ✕ **Grasing's Coastal Cuisine.** Chef Kurt Grasing's contemporary adaptations of European-provincial and American cooking include artichoke lasagna in a roasted tomato sauce. Since he opened his chop house around

10

the corner, this restaurant has come to focus on fish and vegetarian dishes (though red meat and poultry still appear daily). ⊠ *6th Ave. and Mission St.* ☎ *831/624–6562* ⌖ *Reservations essential* ▤ *AE, D, DC, MC, V.*

$$–$$$ ✕ **Flying Fish.** Simple in appearance yet bold with its flavors, this Japanese–California seafood restaurant has quickly established itself as one of Carmel's most inventive eateries. Among the best entrées is the almond-crusted sea bass served with Chinese cabbage and rock shrimp stir-fry. The warm, wood-lined dining room is broken up into very private booths. For the entrance, go down the steps near the gates to Carmel Plaza. ⊠ *Mission St. between Ocean and 7th Aves.* ☎ *831/625–1962* ▤ *AE, D, MC, V* ⊘ *Closed Tues. No lunch.*

$$–$$$ ✕ **L'Escargot.** Chef-owner Kericos Loutas personally sees to each plate of food served at this romantic and mercifully unpretentious French restaurant. Take his recommendation and order the duck confit in puff pastry or the bone-in steak in truffle butter; or, if you can't decide, choose the three-course prix-fixe dinner. Service is warm and attentive. ⊠ *Mission St. between 4th and 5th Aves.* ☎ *831/620–1942* ⌖ *Reservations essential* ▤ *AE, DC, MC, V* ⊘ *Closed Tues. No lunch.*

$–$$$ ✕ **Bahama Billy's.** The energy is electric at this always-bustling Caribbean bar and restaurant. An excellent and diverse menu combined with a lively crowd makes it a prime spot for fun and good eating in Carmel. Particularly good is the ahi tuna, which is rolled in Jamaican jerk seasoning, seared, and served with aioli. Because Billy's is outside the area covered by the town's strict zoning laws, there's often live music in the bar. ⊠ *Barnyard Shopping Center, Hwy. 1 and Carmel Valley Rd.* ☎ *831/626–0430* ⌖ *Reservations essential* ▤ *AE, D, MC, V.*

$–$$$ ✕ **Lugano Swiss Bistro.** Fondue is the centerpiece here. The house specialty is a version made with Gruyère, Emmentaler, and Appenzeller. Rotisserie-broiled meats are also popular, and include rosemary chicken, plum-basted duck, and fennel pork loin. Ask for a table in the back room, which contains a hand-painted street scene of Lugano. ⊠ *Barnyard Shopping Center, Hwy. 1 and Carmel Valley Rd.* ☎ *831/626–3779* ▤ *AE, DC, MC, V.*

$–$$ ✕ **The Cottage Restaurant.** If you're looking for the best breakfast in Carmel, this is the place: the menu offers six different preparations of eggs Benedict, and all kinds of sweet and savory crepes. Sandwiches and homemade soups are served at lunch, and there are dinner specials on weekends, but you'll have the best meals here in the morning. ⊠ *Lincoln St. between Ocean and 7th Aves.* ☎ *831/625–6260* ▤ *MC, V* ⊘ *No dinner Sun.–Wed.*

¢–$ ✕ **Tuck Box.** This bright little restaurant is in a cottage right out of a fairy tale, complete with a stone fireplace that's lighted on rainy days. Handmade scones are the house specialty, and are good for breakfast or afternoon tea. ⊠ *Dolores St. between Ocean and 7th Aves.* ☎ *831/624–6365* ▤ *No credit cards* ⊘ *No dinner.*

$$$$ ✕▥ **L'Auberge Carmel.** Stepping through the doors of this elegant inn is
Fodor'sChoice like being transported to a little European village. The rooms are lux-
★ urious yet understated, with Italian sheets and huge, classic soaking tubs; sitting in the sun-soaked brick courtyard makes you feel like a movie star. ■ TIP➔ **To eat and sleep here is a weekend in itself, but even those staying elsewhere should consider splurging on the intimate restaurant ($$$$).** The single, prix-fixe tasting menu consists of endless courses, each one a mar-

vel imagined by chef Walter Manske. The deconstructed lobster taco, for example, consists of a tortilla strip balanced atop a tiny glass of clear tomato and cilantro essence, a cube of lobster, and a shot of lime ice drenched in fine tequila. ☒ *Monte Verde at 7th Ave., 93921* ☎ *831/ 624–8578* 🖷 *831/626–1018* ⊕ *www.laubergecarmel.com* ⇗ *20 rooms* ☖ *Restaurant, room service, in-room safes, minibars, cable TV with movies, in-room DVDs, lobby lounge, concierge; no smoking* ▭ *AE, D, MC, V* ⦿ *CP.*

$$$$ ✕⊡ **Park Hyatt Carmel Highlands Inn.** High on a hill overlooking the Pacific, this place has superb views. Accommodations include king rooms with fireplaces, suites with personal Jacuzzis, and full town houses with all the perks. The excellent prix-fixe menus at the inn's Pacific's Edge restaurant ($$$$; jackets recommended) blend French and California cuisine; the sommelier helps choose the perfect wines. ☒ *120 Highlands Dr., 93921* ☎ *831/620–1234 or 800/682–4811, 831/622–5445 for restaurant* 🖷 *831/626–1574* ⊕ *highlandsinn.hyatt.com* ⇗ *48 rooms, 105 suites* ☖ *2 restaurants, room service, in-room safes, some in-room hot tubs, some kitchenettes, refrigerators, cable TV with movies, some in-room VCRs, in-room data ports, Wi-Fi, pool, gym, 3 hot tubs, bicycles, 3 lounges, babysitting, laundry service, concierge, business services, meeting rooms; no a/c, no smoking* ▭ *AE, D, DC, MC, V.*

$$$$ ⊡ **Tickle Pink Inn.** Atop a towering cliff, this inn has views of the Big Sur coastline, which you can contemplate from your private balcony. After falling asleep to the sound of surf crashing below, you'll wake to a continental breakfast and the morning paper in bed. If you prefer the company of fellow travelers, breakfast is also served buffet-style in the lounge, as is complimentary wine and cheese in the afternoon. Many rooms have wood-burning fireplaces, and there are six luxurious spa suites. ☒ *155 Highlands Dr., 93923* ☎ *831/624–1244 or 800/635–4774* 🖷 *831/626–9516* ⊕ *www.ticklepink.com* ⇗ *24 rooms, 11 suites* ☖ *Room service, some in-room hot tubs, refrigerators, cable TV, in-room VCRs, in-room data ports, outdoor hot tub, concierge; no a/c, no smoking* ▭ *AE, DC, MC, V* ⦿ *CP.*

★ $$$$ ⊡ **Tradewinds Inn.** Its sleek decor inspired by the South Seas, this converted motel encircles a courtyard with waterfalls, a meditation garden, and a fire pit. Each room has a tabletop fountain and orchids, to complement antique and custom furniture from Bali and China. Some private balconies afford a view of the bay or the mountains. The chic boutique hotel, owned by the same family since it opened in 1959, is on a quiet downtown side street. ☒ *Mission St. at 3rd Ave., 93921* ☎ *831/624–2776 or 800/624–6665* 🖷 *831/624–0634* ⊕ *www.carmeltradewinds. com* ⇗ *26 rooms, 2 suites* ☖ *In-room safes, some in-room hot tubs, refrigerators, cable TV, in-room data ports, Wi-Fi, massage, concierge, business services, meeting room, some pets allowed (fee); no a/c, no smoking* ▭ *AE, MC, V* ⦿ *CP.*

$$$–$$$$ ⊡ **La Playa Hotel.** Norwegian artist Christopher Jorgensen built this property's original structure in 1902 for his bride, a member of the Ghirardelli-chocolate clan. The property has since undergone many additions and now resembles a Mediterranean estate. Rooms are small but comfortable, with furnishings in muted colors; some have views of gardens or the ocean. You can also opt for a cottage; most have full kitchens

10

and wood-burning fireplaces, and all have patios or terraces. ✉ *Camino Real at 8th Ave., 93921* 🕾 *831/624–6476 or 800/582–8900* 🖶 *831/624–7966* ⊕ *www.laplayahotel.com* 🛏 *73 rooms, 2 suites, 5 cottages* ⚬ *Restaurant, refrigerators, cable TV, Wi-Fi, pool, massage, bar, laundry service, business services, meeting rooms; no a/c, no smoking* ☰ *AE, DC, MC, V.*

\$\$\$–\$\$\$\$ 🏨 **Tally Ho Inn.** This inn is nearly all suites, many of which have fireplaces and floor-to-ceiling glass walls that open onto ocean-view patios. The motif is reproduction old world and can lean heavily toward the floral, but all rooms have spa tubs and marble bathrooms. Evening aperitifs are served in the English garden courtyard, where a fire blazes on chilly nights. ✉ *Monte Verde St. and 6th Ave., 93921* 🕾 *831/624–2232 or 877/482–5594* 🖶 *831/624–2661* ⊕ *www.tallyho-inn.com* 🛏 *1 room, 11 suites* ⚬ *Some fans, some refrigerators, Wi-Fi, laundry service; no a/c, no TV in some rooms, no smoking* ☰ *AE, D, DC, MC, V* ⦿ *CP.*

\$\$–\$\$\$\$ 🏨 **Cypress Inn.** The decorating style here is luxurious but refreshingly simple. Rather than chintz and antiques, there are wrought-iron bed frames, wooden armoires, and rattan armchairs. Some rooms have fireplaces, some hot tubs, and one (Room 215) even has its own sunny veranda that looks out on the ocean. The in-town location makes walking to area attractions easy, and pet owners will be pleased to hear that in the spirit of the dog-loving owner, movie star Doris Day, animal companions are always welcome. ✉ *Lincoln St. and 7th Ave., Box Y, 93921* 🕾 *831/624–3871 or 800/443–7443* 🖶 *831/624–8216* ⊕ *www.cypress-inn.com* 🛏 *39 rooms, 5 suites* ⚬ *Fans, some in-room hot tubs, cable TV, in-room data ports, gym, bar, laundry service, concierge, some pets allowed (fee); no a/c in some rooms, no smoking* ☰ *AE, D, DC, MC, V* ⦿ *CP.*

\$\$–\$\$\$\$ 🏨 **Pine Inn.** A favorite with generations of Carmel-by-the-Sea visitors, the Pine Inn has Victorian-style furnishings, complete with grandfather clock, padded fabric wall panels, antique tapestries, and marble tabletops. Only four blocks from the beach, the property includes a brick courtyard of specialty shops and a modern Italian restaurant. ✉ *Ocean Ave. and Monte Verde St., 93921* 🕾 *831/624–3851 or 800/228–3851* 🖶 *831/624–3030* ⊕ *www.pine-inn.com* 🛏 *43 rooms, 6 suites* ⚬ *Restaurant, fans, some refrigerators, cable TV, Wi-Fi, bar, laundry service, meeting room; no a/c, no smoking* ☰ *AE, D, DC, MC, V.*

\$–\$\$\$\$ 🏨 **Mission Ranch.** The property at Mission Ranch is gorgeous and includes a sprawling sheep pasture, bird-filled wetlands, and a sweeping view of the ocean. The ranch is nicely decorated but low-key, with a 19th-century farmhouse as the central building. Other accommodations include rooms in a converted barn, and several cottages, many with fireplaces. Though the ranch belongs to movie star Clint Eastwood, relaxation, not celebrity, is the focus here. ✉ *26270 Dolores St., 93923* 🕾 *831/624–6436 or 800/538–8221* 🖶 *831/626–4163* ⊕ *www.missionranchcarmel.com* 🛏 *31 rooms* ⚬ *Restaurant, fans, some in-room hot tubs, some refrigerators, cable TV, in-room data ports, 6 tennis courts, pro shop, gym, piano bar, meeting rooms; no a/c, no smoking* ☰ *AE, MC, V* ⦿ *CP.*

★ **\$\$–\$\$\$** 🏨 **Cobblestone Inn.** Stones from the Carmel River cover the exterior walls of this English-style country inn; inside, the work of local painters is on display. Guest rooms have stone fireplaces, busily patterned wallpaper and fabrics, and thick quilts on the beds. Antiques in the cozy sitting room, and afternoon wine and hors d'oeuvres, contribute to the homey feel. ⊠ *Junipero Ave., between 7th and 8th Aves., 93921* ☎ *831/625–5222 or 800/833–8836* 🖷 *831/625–0478* ⊕ *www.cobblestoneinncarmel. com* ⇆ *22 rooms, 2 suites* ⚬ *Refrigerators, cable TV, in-room data ports, bicycles; no a/c, no smoking* ▭ *AE, DC, MC, V* ⦿⎮ *BP.*

$–$$ 🏠 **Lobos Lodge.** The white-stucco motel units here are set amid cypress, oaks, and pines on the edge of the business district. All accommodations have fireplaces, and some have private patios. ⊠ *Monte Verde St. and Ocean Ave., 93921* ☎ *831/624–3874* 🖷 *831/624–0135* ⊕ *www. loboslodge.com* ⇆ *28 rooms, 2 suites* ⚬ *Fans, refrigerators, cable TV, in-room data ports, no-smoking rooms; no a/c* ▭ *AE, MC, V* ⦿⎮ *CP.*

$–$$ 🏠 **Sea View Inn.** In a residential area a few hundred feet from the beach, this restored 1905 home has a double parlor with two fireplaces, Oriental rugs, canopy beds, and a spacious front porch. Rooms are individually done in cheery colors and country patterns; taller guests might feel cramped in those tucked up under the eaves. Afternoon tea and evening wine and cheese are offered daily. Because of the fragile furnishings and quiet atmosphere, families with kids will likely be more comfortable elsewhere. ⊠ *Camino Real between 11th and 12th Aves., 93921* ☎ *831/ 624–8778* 🖷 *831/625–5901* ⊕ *www.seaviewinncarmel.com* ⇆ *8 rooms, 6 with private bath* ⚬ *No a/c, no room phones, no room TVs, no smoking* ▭ *AE, MC, V* ⦿⎮ *CP.*

The Arts

Carmel Bach Festival (☎ 831/624–2046 ⊕ www.bachfestival.org) has presented the works of Johann Sebastian Bach and his contemporaries in concerts and recitals since 1935. The festival runs for three weeks, starting mid-July. **Monterey County Symphony** (☎ 831/624–8511 ⊕ www. montereysymphony.org) performs classical concerts from October through May at the Sunset Center.

The **Pacific Repertory Theater** (☎ 831/622–0700 ⊕ www.pacrep.org) puts on the Carmel Shakespeare Festival from August through October and performs contemporary dramas and comedies at several area venues from February through July. **Sunset Center** (⊠ San Carlos St. at 9th Ave. ☎ 831/624–3996 ⊕ www.sunsetcenter.org), which presents concerts, lectures, and headline acts, is the Monterey Bay area's top venue for the performing arts.

Shopping

ART GALLERIES **Carmel Art Association** (⊠ Dolores St. between 5th and 6th Aves. ☎ 831/ 624–6176 ⊕ www.carmelart.org) exhibits the paintings, sculptures, and prints of local artists. **Galerie Plein Aire** (⊠ Dolores St. between 5th and 6th Aves. ☎ 831/625–5686 ⊕ www.galeriepleinaire.com) showcases oil paintings by a group of seven local artists. **Masterpiece Gallery** (⊠ Dolores St. and 6th Ave. ☎ 831/624–2163 ⊕ www.masterpiecegallerycarmel. com) shows early-California-impressionist art. Run by the family of the late Edward Weston, **Weston Gallery** (⊠ 6th Ave. between Dolores and Lincoln Sts. ☎ 831/624–4453 ⊕ www.westongallery.com) is hands-down the best photography gallery around, with contemporary color photography complemented by classic black-and-whites.

10

SPECIALTY SHOPS **Bittner** (✉ Ocean Ave. between Mission and San Carlos Sts. ☎ 831/626–8828) has a fine selection of collectible and vintage pens from around the world. **Intima** (✉ Mission St. between Ocean and 7th Aves. ☎ 831/625–0599) is the place to find European lingerie that ranges from lacy to racy. **Jan de Luz** (✉ Dolores St. between Ocean and 7th Aves. ☎ 831/622–7621) monograms and embroiders fine linens (including bathrobes) while you wait. **Madrigal** (✉ Carmel Plaza and Mission St. ☎ 831/624–3477) carries sportswear, sweaters, and accessories for women. **Mischievous Rabbit** (✉ Lincoln Ave. between 7th and Ocean Aves. ☎ 831/624–6854) sells toys, nursery accessories, books, music boxes, china, and children's clothing, and specializes in Beatrix Potter items.

Carmel Valley

❷ *10 mi east of Carmel, Hwy. 1 to Carmel Valley Rd.*

Carmel Valley Road, which heads inland from Highway 1 south of Carmel-by-the-Sea, is the main thoroughfare through this valley, a secluded enclave of horse ranchers and other well-heeled residents who prefer the area's sunny climate to the fog and wind on the coast. Once thick with dairy farms, the valley has recently proved itself as a venerable wine appellation. Tiny Carmel Valley Village, about 13 mi southeast of Carmel-by-the-Sea via Carmel Valley Road, has several crafts shops and art galleries, as well as tasting rooms for numerous local wineries. At **Bernardus Tasting Room,** you can sample many of the wines—including older vintages and reserves—from the nearby Bernardus Winery and Vineyard. ✉ *5 W. Carmel Valley Rd.* ☎ *800/223–2533* ⊕ *www.bernardus.com* ☉ *Daily 11–5.*

Garland Ranch Regional Park (✉ Carmel Valley Rd., 9 mi east of Carmel-by-the-Sea ☎ 831/659–4488) has hiking trails across nearly 4,500 acres of property that includes meadows, forested hillsides, and creeks. The extensive **Château Julien** winery, recognized internationally for its chardonnays and merlots, gives weekday tours at 10:30 and 2:30 and weekends at 12:30 and 2:30, all by appointment. The tasting room is open daily. ✉ *8940 Carmel Valley Rd.* ☎ *831/624–2600* ⊕ *www.chateaujulien.com* ☉ *Weekdays 8–5, weekends 11–5.*

Where to Stay & Eat

$$–$$$$ ✕ **Will's Fargo.** On the main street of Carmel Valley Village since the 1920s, this restaurant calls itself a "dressed-up saloon." Steerhorns and gilt-frame paintings adorn the walls of the Victorian-style dining room; you can also eat on the patios. The menu is mainly steaks, including a 24-ounce porterhouse. ✉ *16 E. Carmel Valley Rd.* ☎ *831/659–2774* ▭ *AE, DC, MC, V.*

$–$$ ✕ **Café Rustica.** Italian-inspired country cooking is the focus at this lively roadhouse. Specialties include roasted meats, pastas, and thin-crust pizzas from the wood-fired oven. Because of the tile floors, it can get quite noisy inside; opt for a table outside if you want a quieter meal. ✉ *10 Delfino Pl.* ☎ *831/659–4444* ⚠ *Reservations essential* ▭ *MC, V* ☉ *Closed Wed.*

¢ ✕ **Wagon Wheel Coffee Shop.** This local hangout decorated with wagon wheels, cowboy hats, and lassos serves up terrific hearty breakfasts, including date-walnut-cinnamon French toast and a plate of trout and eggs. The lunch menu includes a dozen different burgers and other sandwiches. ⊠ *Valley Hill Center, Carmel Valley Rd. next to Quail Lodge* ☎ *831/ 624–8878* ▭ *No credit cards* ⊗ *No dinner.*

$$$$
Fodor'sChoice
★

×▦ **Bernardus Lodge.** Even before you check-in at this luxury spa resort, the valet hands you a glass of chardonnay. Spacious guest rooms have vaulted ceilings, featherbeds, fireplaces, patios, and bathtubs for two. The restaurant, Marinus ($$$$; jacket recommended), is perhaps the best in the Monterey Bay area, with a menu that changes daily to highlight local meats and produce. Reserve the chef's table in the main kitchen and you can talk to the chef as he prepares your meal. ⊠ *415 Carmel Valley Rd., 93924* ☎ *831/659–3131 or 888/648–9463* ⊟ *831/659–3529* ⊕ *www.bernardus. com* ⇴ *54 rooms, 3 suites* ⌕ *2 restaurants, room service, in-room safes, minibars, refrigerators, cable TV with movies, in-room DVDs, Wi-Fi, 2 tennis courts, pool, gym, hair salon, hot tub, sauna, spa, steam room, croquet, lawn bowling, bar, lobby lounge, laundry service, concierge, Internet room, meeting room; no smoking* ▭ *AE, DC, MC, V.*

★ $$$$

×▦ **Quail Lodge.** What began as the Carmel Valley Country Club—a hangout for Frank Sinatra, among others—is now a private golf club and resort in the valley's west side. Winding around swimming pools and putting greens, the buildings' exteriors recall the old days, but indoors the luxury is totally updated with a cool, modern feel: plasma TVs swing out from the walls, the toiletries include giant tea bags to infuse your bath with herbs, and each room has a window seat overlooking a private patio. The Covey at Quail Lodge ($$$–$$$$; jacket recommended) serves contemporary California cuisine in a romantic lakeside dining room. ⊠ *8205 Valley Greens Dr., 93923* ☎ *831/624–1581 or 800/538–9516* ⊟ *831/624–3726* ⊕ *www.quaillodge.com* ⇴ *83 rooms, 14 suites* ⌕ *2 restaurants, room service, in-room safes, minibars, refrigerators, cable TV with movies and video games, in-room data ports, Wi-Fi, 18-hole golf course, putting green, 4 tennis courts, pro shop, 2 pools, gym, hot tub, spa, steam room, bicycles, hiking, lawn bowling, 2 bars, babysitting, laundry service, concierge, business services, Internet room, meeting rooms, no-smoking rooms* ▭ *AE, DC, MC, V.*

$$$$
Fodor'sChoice
★

▦ **Stonepine Estate Resort.** Set on 330 pastoral acres, this former estate of the Crocker banking family has been converted to a luxurious inn. The oak-paneled main château holds eight elegantly furnished rooms and suites, and a dining room for guests (although with advance reservations, it's also possible for nonguests to dine here). The property's "cottages" are equally opulent, each with its own luxurious identity (the Hermes House has four fireplaces and a 27-foot-high living room ceiling). Fresh flowers, afternoon tea, and evening champagne are offered daily. This is a quiet property, best suited to couples traveling without children. ⊠ *150 E. Carmel Valley Rd., 93924* ☎ *831/659–2245* ⊟ *831/ 659–5160* ⊕ *www.stonepinecalifornia.com* ⇴ *3 rooms, 9 suites, 3 cottages* ⌕ *Dining room, room service, fans, some in-room safes, in-room hot tubs, some minibars, cable TV, in-room DVDs/VCRs, in-room data ports, Wi-Fi, 9-hole golf course, 2 tennis courts, 2 pools, gym, massage, mountain bikes, archery, croquet, hiking, horseback riding, library, piano, recreation room, laundry service, concierge, Internet room; no a/c, no smoking* ▭ *AE, MC, V* ⧉ *BP.*

10

$$$ ⊡ **Carmel Valley Lodge.** This small inn has rooms surrounding a garden patio, and separate one- and two-bedroom cottages with fireplaces and full kitchens. Open-beam ceilings, Shaker-style furnishings, and plaid easy chairs give the rooms a casual, almost rustic air. ⊠ *8 Ford Rd., at Carmel Valley Rd., 93924* ☎ *831/659–2261 or 800/641–4646* 🖷 *831/ 659–4558* ⊕ *www.valleylodge.com* ⤳ *19 rooms, 4 suites, 8 cottages* ⚘ *Fans, some kitchenettes, refrigerators, cable TV, in-room VCRs, in-room data ports, Wi-Fi, pool, exercise equipment, hot tub, sauna, horseshoes, Ping-Pong, Internet room, meeting rooms, some pets allowed (fee), no-smoking rooms; no a/c* ⊟ *AE, MC, V* ⎅◎⎅ *CP.*

The Arts

The **Magic Circle Center** (⊠ 8 El Caminito ☎ 831/659–1108) presents three comedies, two dramas, and a music series annually in an intimate 60-seat theater. **Hidden Valley Performing Arts Institute** (⊠ Carmel Valley Road at Ford Rd. ☎ 831/659–3115) gives classes for promising young musicians and holds a year-round series of classical and jazz concerts by students, masters, and the Monterey Peninsula Choral Society.

Sports & the Outdoors

The **Golf Club at Quail Lodge** (⊠ 8000 Valley Greens Dr. ☎ 831/624– 2770) incorporates several lakes into its course. Depending on the season and day of the week, greens fees range from $115 to $140 for guests and $125 to $175 for nonguests, including cart rental. **Rancho Cañada Golf Club** (⊠ 4860 Carmel Valley Rd., 1 mi east of Hwy. 1 ☎ 831/624– 0111) is a public course with 36 holes, some of them overlooking the Carmel River. Fees range from $35 to $80, plus $34 for cart rental, depending on course and tee time.

17-Mile Drive

★ ❸ *Off North San Antonio Rd. in Carmel-by-the-Sea or off Sunset Dr. in Pacific Grove.*

Primordial nature resides in quiet harmony with palatial late-20th-century estates along 17-Mile Drive, which winds through an 8,400-acre microcosm of the Monterey coastal landscape. Dotting the drive are rare Monterey cypress, trees so gnarled and twisted that Robert Louis Stevenson described them as "ghosts fleeing before the wind." Some sightseers balk at the $8.75-per-car fee collected at the gates—this is the only private toll road west of the Mississippi—but most find the drive well worth the price. An alternative is to grab a bike: ■ TIP→ **cyclists tour for free, as do those with confirmed lunch or dinner reservations at one of the hotels.**

You can take in views of the impeccable greens at **Pebble Beach Golf Links** (⊠ 17-Mile Dr. near Lodge at Pebble Beach ☎ 800/654–9300 ⊕ www. pebblebeach.com) over a drink or lunch at the Lodge at Pebble Beach. The ocean plays a major role in the 18th hole of the famed links. Each winter the course is the main site of the AT&T Pebble Beach Pro-Am (formerly the Bing Crosby Pro-Am), where show business celebrities and golf pros team up for one of the nation's most glamorous tournaments.

Many of the stately homes along 17-Mile Drive reflect the classic Monterey or Spanish Mission style typical of the region. A standout is the

Crocker Marble Palace, about a mile south of the Lone Cypress (⇨ *below*). It's a private waterfront estate inspired by a Byzantine castle, easily identifiable by its dozens of marble arches.

The most-photographed tree along 17-Mile Drive is the weather-sculpted **Lone Cypress,** which grows out of a precipitous outcropping above the waves about 1½ mi up the road from Pebble Beach Golf Links. You can stop for a view of the Lone Cypress at a parking area, but you can't walk out to the tree. Sea creatures and birds—as well as some very friendly ground squirrels—make use of **Seal Rock,** the largest of a group of islands about 2 mi north of Lone Cypress.

Bird Rock, the largest of several islands at the southern end of the Monterey Country Club's golf course, teems with harbor seals, sea lions, cormorants, and pelicans.

Where to Stay & Eat

$$$$ ✕🏠 **Inn at Spanish Bay.** This resort sprawls across a breathtaking stretch of shoreline, and has lush, 600-square-foot rooms. Peppoli's restaurant ($$–$$$), which serves Tuscan cuisine, overlooks the coast and the golf links; Roy's Restaurant ($$–$$$$) serves more casual and innovative Euro–Asian fare. When you stay here, you're also allowed privileges at the Lodge at Pebble Beach, which is under the same management. ⊠ *2700 17-Mile Dr., Pebble Beach 93953* ☎ *831/647–7500 or 800/ 654–9300* 🖷 *831/644–7960* ⊕ *www.pebblebeach.com* ➷ *252 rooms, 17 suites* ⌂ *3 restaurants, room service, minibars, refrigerators, cable TV with movies, in-room VCRs, in-room broadband, in-room data ports, 18-hole golf course, 8 tennis courts, pro shop, pool, fitness classes, health club, hot tub, sauna, steam room, beach, bicycles, bar, lobby lounge, laundry service, concierge, business services, Internet room, meeting rooms; no a/c, no smoking* ▤ *AE, D, DC, MC, V.*

★ **$$$$** ✕🏠 **Lodge at Pebble Beach.** All rooms have fireplaces and many have wonderful ocean views at this circa 1919 resort. The golf course, tennis club, and equestrian center are posh. Overlooking the 18th green, the intimate Club XIX restaurant ($$$$; jackets recommended) serves expertly prepared French cuisine. When staying here, you also have privileges at the Inn at Spanish Bay. ⊠ *1700 17-Mile Dr., Pebble Beach 93953* ☎ *831/624–3811 or 800/654–9300* 🖷 *831/644–7960* ⊕ *www. pebblebeach.com* ➷ *142 rooms, 19 suites* ⌂ *3 restaurants, coffee shop, some in-room hot tubs, minibars, refrigerators, cable TV with movies and video games, some in-room DVDs/VCRs, in-room broadband, in-room data ports, 18-hole golf course, 12 tennis courts, pro shop, pool, gym, health club, sauna, spa, beach, bicycles, horseback riding, 2 bars, lobby lounge, laundry service, concierge, business services, Internet room, meeting rooms, some pets allowed; no a/c, no smoking* ▤ *AE, D, DC, MC, V.*

★ **$$$$** 🏠 **Casa Palmero.** This exclusive spa resort evokes a stately Mediterranean villa. Rooms are decorated with sumptuous fabrics and fine art; each has a wood-burning fireplace and heated floor, and some have private outdoor patios with in-ground Jacuzzis. Complimentary cocktail service is offered each evening in the main hall and library. The spa is state-

10

of-the-art, and you have use of all facilities at the Lodge at Pebble Beach and the Inn at Spanish Bay. ✉ *1518 Cypress Dr., Pebble Beach 93953* ☎ *831/622–6650 or 800/654–9300* 🖷 *831/622–6655* 🌐 *www. pebblebeach.com* ⬎ *21 rooms, 3 suites* ⚸ *Room service, some in-room hot tubs, minibars, refrigerators, cable TV with movies and video games, in-room VCRs, in-room data ports, 18-hole golf course, pool, spa, bicycles, billiards, lounge, laundry service, concierge, meeting rooms; no a/c, no smoking* ☰ *AE, D, DC, MC, V.*

Sports & the Outdoors

GOLF The **Links at Spanish Bay** (✉ 17-Mile Dr., north end ☎ 831/624–3811, 831/624–6611, or 800/654–9300), which hugs a choice stretch of shoreline, is designed in the rugged manner of a traditional Scottish course, with sand dunes and coastal marshes interspersed among the greens. Greens fees are $240, plus $25 per person for cart rental (cart included for resort guests); nonguests can reserve tee times up to two months in advance.

Pebble Beach Golf Links (✉ 17-Mile Dr. near Lodge at Pebble Beach ☎ 831/624–3811, 831/624–6611, or 800/654–9300) attracts golfers from around the world, despite greens fees of $450, plus $25 per person for an optional cart (complimentary cart for guests of the Pebble Beach and Spanish Bay resorts). Nonguests can reserve a tee time only one day in advance on a space-available basis (up to a year for groups); resort guests can reserve up to 18 months in advance.

Peter Hay (✉ 17-Mile Dr. ☎ 831/625–8518 or 831/624–6611), a 9-hole, par-3 course, charges $20 per person, no reservations necessary. **Poppy Hills** (✉ 3200 Lopez Rd., at 17-Mile Dr. ☎ 831/625–2035), a splendid 18-hole course designed in 1986 by Robert Trent Jones Jr., has greens fees of $130–$160; an optional cart costs $32. Individuals may reserve up to one month in advance, groups up to a year.

Spyglass Hill (✉ Stevenson Dr. and Spyglass Hill Rd. ☎ 831/624–3811, 831/624–6611, or 800/654–9300) is among the most challenging Pebble Beach courses. With the first 5 holes bordering on the Pacific and the other 18 reaching deep into the Del Monte Forest, the views offer some consolation. Greens fees are $300, and an optional cart costs $25 (the cart is complimentary for resort guests). Reservations are essential and may be made up to one month in advance (18 months for guests).

HORSEBACK The **Pebble Beach Equestrian Center** (✉ Portola Rd. and Alva La. ☎ 831/
RIDING 624–2756) offers guided trail rides along the beach and through 26 mi of bridle trails in the Del Monte Forest. Rates are $47–$110 per rider.

Pacific Grove

❹ *3 mi north of Carmel-by-the-Sea on Hwy. 68.*

This picturesque town, which began as a summer retreat for church groups more than a century ago, recalls its prim and proper Victorian heritage in its host of tiny board-and-batten cottages and stately mansions. However, long before the church groups flocked here the area received thousands of annual pilgrims—in the form of bright orange-and-black monarch butterflies. They still come, migrating south from Canada and the Pacific Northwest to take residence in pine and eucalyptus groves from October through March. In Butterfly Town USA, as Pacific Grove is known, the sight of a mass of butterflies hanging from the branches like a long, fluttering veil is unforgettable.

A prime way to enjoy Pacific Grove is to walk or bicycle the 3 mi of city-owned shoreline along Ocean View Boulevard, a cliff-top area landscaped with native plants and dotted with benches meant for sitting and gazing at the sea. You can spot many types of birds here, including colonies of web-foot cormorants crowding the massive rocks rising out of the surf.

Among the Victorians of note is the **Pryor House** (⊠ 429 Ocean View Blvd.), a massive, shingled, private residence with a leaded- and beveled-glass doorway. **Green Gables** (⊠ 5th St. and Ocean View Blvd. ☎ 831/375–2095 ⊕ www.greengablesinnpg.com), a romantic Swiss Gothic–style mansion with peaked gables and stained-glass windows, is a B&B.

🐚 The view of the coast is gorgeous from **Lovers Point Park** (☎ 831/648–5730), on Ocean View Boulevard midway along the waterfront. The park's sheltered beach has a children's pool and picnic area, and the main lawn has a sandy volleyball court and snack bar. At the 1855-

🐚 vintage **Point Pinos Lighthouse,** the oldest continuously operating lighthouse on the West Coast, you can learn about the lighting and foghorn operations and wander through a small museum containing U.S. Coast Guard memorabilia. ⊠ *Lighthouse Ave. off Asilomar Blvd.* ☎ *831/648–5716* ⊕ *www.pgmuseum.org* 🎫 *$2* ☉ *June–Sept., 11:30–5 daily; Oct.–May, Thurs.–Mon. 1–4.*

Asilomar State Beach (☎ 831/372–4076 ⊕ www.parks.ca.gov), a beautiful coastal area, is on Sunset Drive between Point Pinos and the Del Monte Forest in Pacific Grove. The 100 acres of dunes, tidal pools, and pocket-size beaches form one of the region's richest areas for marine life—including surfers, who migrate here most winter mornings.

Where to Stay & Eat

$$–$$$$ ✕ **Old Bath House.** This romantic converted bathhouse overlooks the water at Lovers Point. The menu makes the most of local produce and seafood (such as Monterey Bay shrimp) and specializes in game meats. There's also a less expensive menu for late-afternoon diners. ⊠ *620 Ocean View Blvd.* ☎ *831/375–5195* ⊟ *AE, D, DC, MC, V* ☉ *No lunch.*

$$$ ✕ **Robert's White House.** The culinary experience of chef-owner Robert Kincaid (the man behind Fresh Cream, in Monterey), which stretches from California to Europe and Japan, is reflected in the menu, which might include shrimp cake with pineapple-rum and dill sauces or poussin (young hen) with chicken mousse and brandied orange sauce. You can order à la carte or try the three-course, prix-fixe menus ($37). The restaurant itself, housed in a stately Victorian downtown, is an elegant showcase for sophisticated cuisine. ⊠ *649 Lighthouse Ave.* ☎ *831/375–9626* ⊟ *MC, V* ☉ *Closed Mon. No lunch.*

$–$$$ ✕ **Fandango.** The menu here is mostly Mediterranean and southern French, with such dishes as calves' liver and onions and paella served in a skillet. The decor follows suit: stone walls and country furniture give the restaurant the earthy feel of a European farmhouse. This is where

10

locals come when they want to have a big dinner with friends, drink wine, have fun, and generally feel at home. ⊠ *223 17th St.* ☎ *831/372–3456* ⊟ *AE, D, DC, MC, V.*

$–$$$ ✕ **Red House Café.** When it's nice out, sun pours through the big windows of this cozy restaurant and across tables on the porch; when fog rolls in, the fireplace is lighted. The American menu is simple but selective, including grilled lamb fillets atop mashed potatoes for dinner and a huge Dungeness crab cake over salad for lunch. Breakfast on weekends is a local favorite. ⊠ *662 Lighthouse Ave.* ☎ *831/643–1060* ⊟ *AE, D, DC, MC, V* ⊗ *Closed Mon.*

$–$$ ✕ **Fifi's Café.** Candlelight and music fill this small bistro known for its generous wine pours and French cuisine. The menu ranges from escargot to petrale sole piccata to steak frites; lunch and the early-bird dinner (until 6 PM) are an exceptional value. ⊠ *1188 Forest Ave.* ☎ *831/372–5325* ⩗ *Reservations essential* ⊟ *AE, D, DC, MC, V.*

$–$$ ✕ **Fishwife.** Fresh fish with a Latin accent makes this a favorite of locals for lunch or a casual dinner. Standards are the sea garden salads topped with your choice of fish and the fried seafood plates with fresh veggies. Large appetites appreciate the fisherman's bowls, which feature fresh fish served with rice, black beans, spicy cabbage, salsa, vegetables, and crispy tortilla strips. ⊠ *1996½ Sunset Dr., at Asilomar Blvd.* ☎ *831/375–7107* ⊟ *AE, D, MC, V.*

★ $–$$ ✕ **Passion Fish.** South American artwork and artifacts decorate the room, and Latin and Asian flavors infuse the dishes at Passion Fish. Chef Ted Wolters shops at local farmers' markets several times a week to find the best produce, fish, and meat available, then pairs it with creative sauces. The ever-changing menu might include crispy squid with spicy orange-cilantro vinaigrette. ⊠ *701 Lighthouse Ave.* ☎ *831/655–3311* ⊟ *AE, D, MC, V* ⊗ *No lunch.*

$–$$ ✕ **Taste Café and Bistro.** A favorite of locals, Taste serves hearty European-inspired food in a casual, airy room with high ceilings and an open kitchen. Meats, such as grilled marinated rabbit, roasted half chicken, and filet mignon, are the focus. ⊠ *1199 Forest Ave.* ☎ *831/655–0324* ⊟ *AE, MC, V* ⊗ *Closed Mon.*

¢–$$ ✕ **Peppers Mexicali Cafe.** A local favorite, this cheerful white-walled storefront serves traditional dishes from Mexico and Latin America, with an emphasis on fresh seafood. Excellent red and green salsas are made throughout the day, and there's a large selection of beers. ⊠ *170 Forest Ave.* ☎ *831/373–6892* ⊟ *AE, D, DC, MC, V* ⊗ *Closed Tues. No lunch Sun.*

$$$–$$$$ ▦ **Martine Inn.** The glassed-in parlor and many guest rooms at this 1899 Mediterranean-style villa have stunning ocean views. The inn is furnished with exquisite antiques, and the owner's collection of classic race cars is on display in the patio area. In the rooms, thoughtful details such as robes, rocking chairs, and nightly turn-down combine in luxuriant comfort. Lavish breakfasts—and winemaker dinners of up to 12 courses—are served on lace-clad tables set with china, crystal, and silver. Because of the fragility of the antiques, the inn is not suitable for children. ⊠ *255 Ocean View Blvd., 93950* ☎ *831/373–3388 or 800/852–5588* ⎙ *831/373–3896* ⊕ *www.martineinn.com* ➥ *24 rooms* ♿ *Some fans, refrigerators, in-room broadband, Wi-Fi, hot tub, billiards,*

library, Internet room, meeting rooms; no a/c, no room TVs, no smoking 🖿 D, MC, V ⦿ BP.

$$–$$$$ ⬚ **The Inn at 213 Seventeen Mile Drive.** Set in a residential area just past
town, this carefully restored 1920s Craftsman-style home and cottage
are surrounded by gardens and redwood, cypress, and eucalyptus trees.
Spacious, well-appointed rooms have simple, homey furnishings. The
innkeepers offer complimentary wine and hors d'oeuvres in the evening
and tea and snacks throughout the day. ✉ *213 17-Mile Dr., 93950* ☎ *831/
642–9514 or 800/526–5666* 🖷 *831/642–9546* ⊕ *www.innat17.com*
⤵ *14 rooms* 🜄 *Some fans, cable TV, in-room data ports, Wi-Fi, hot
tub; no a/c, no smoking* 🖿 *AE, MC, V* ⦿ *BP.*

$–$$$$ ⬚ **Lighthouse Lodge and Suites.** Near the tip of the peninsula, this com-
plex straddles Lighthouse Avenue—the lodge is on one side, the all-suites
facility on the other. Suites have fireplaces and whirlpool tubs. Standard
rooms are simple, but they're decently sized and much less expensive.
▪ TIP➔ **With daily afternoon barbecues, this is a woodsy alternative to down-
town Pacific Grove's B&B scene.** ✉ *1150 and 1249 Lighthouse Ave., 93950*
☎ *831/655–2111 or 800/858–1249* 🖷 *831/655–4922* ⊕ *www.lhls.
com* ⤵ *64 rooms, 31 suites* 🜄 *Fans, microwaves, minibars, refrigera-
tors, cable TV with movies, in-room data ports, Wi-Fi, pool, hot tub,
meeting rooms, some pets allowed (fee); no a/c, no smoking* 🖿 *AE, D,
DC, MC, V* ⦿ *BP.*

$$–$$$ ⬚ **Gosby House Inn.** Though in the town center, this turreted butter-yel-
low Queen Anne Victorian has an informal feel. Florals, ruffles, and lace
make the rooms rather country-grandma; the two most private rooms,
which have fireplaces, balconies, and whirlpool tubs, are in the rear car-
riage house. Homemade cookies, sodas, and evening wine and hors d'oeu-
vres are complimentary. Buffet breakfast is served in the parlor or
garden. ✉ *643 Lighthouse Ave., 93950* ☎ *831/375–1287 or 800/527–
8828* 🖷 *831/655–9621* ⊕ *www.gosbyhouseinn.com* ⤵ *22 rooms, 20
with bath* 🜄 *Some fans, some in-room hot tubs, some refrigerators, some
cable TV, some in-room VCRs, in-room data ports; no a/c, no TV in
some rooms, no smoking* 🖿 *AE, DC, MC, V* ⦿ *BP.*

★ **$–$$$** ⬚ **Green Gables Inn.** Stained-glass windows and ornate interior details com-
pete with spectacular ocean views at this Queen Anne–style mansion, built
by a businessman for his mistress in 1888. Rooms in a carriage house perched
on a hill out back are larger, have more modern amenities, and afford more
privacy, but rooms in the main house have more charm. Afternoon wine
and cheese are served in the parlor. ✉ *301 Ocean View Blvd., 93950* ☎ *831/
375–2095 or 800/722–1774* 🖷 *831/375–5437* ⊕ *www.greengablesinnpg.
com* ⤵ *7 rooms, 3 with bath; 4 suites* 🜄 *Some in-room hot tubs, some
cable TV, some in-room VCRs, some in-room data ports, bicycles; no a/c,
no smoking* 🖿 *AE, D, DC, MC, V* ⦿ *BP.*

Sports & the Outdoors

GOLF Greens fees at the 18-hole **Pacific Grove Municipal Golf Links** (✉ 77 Asilomar Blvd. ☎ 831/648–5777 ⊕ www.ci.pg.ca.us/golf) run between $35
and $40 (you can play 9 holes for $20–$23), with an after-2 PM twi-
light rate of $20. Optional carts cost $30 ($18 for 9 holes). The course
has spectacular ocean views on its back 9. Tee times may be reserved
up to seven days in advance.

TENNIS   The municipal **Morris Dill Tennis Courts** (✉ 515 Junipero St. ☎ 831/648–5729) are available for public play for a small hourly fee. The pro shop here rents rackets and offers lessons.

MONTEREY

Early in the 20th century Carmel Martin, the first mayor of the city of Monterey, saw a bright future for his town: "Monterey Bay is the one place where people can live without being disturbed by manufacturing and big factories. I am certain that the day is coming when this will be the most desirable place in the whole state of California." It seems that Mayor Martin was not far off the mark.

Historic Monterey

2 mi southeast of Pacific Grove via Lighthouse Ave.; 2 mi north of Carmel-by-the-Sea via Hwy. 1.

What to See

❶❾ A Taste of Monterey. Without driving the back roads, you can taste the wines of 40 area vintners. Purchase a few bottles and pick up a map and guide to the county's wineries and vineyards. ✉ *700 Cannery Row, Suite KK* ☎ *831/646–5446 or 888/646–5446* ⊕ *www.tastemonterey.com* ⊗ *Daily 11–6.*

❾ California's First Theatre. This adobe began its life in 1846 as a saloon and lodging house for sailors. Four years later stage curtains were fashioned from army blankets, and some U.S. officers staged plays to the light of whale oil lamps. As of this writing, the building is undergoing restoration and is open only rarely. ✉ *Monterey State Historic Park, Scott and Pacific Sts.* ☎ *831/649–7118* 🎫 *Free* ⊗ *Call for hrs.*

Cannery Row. When John Steinbeck published the novel *Cannery Row* in 1945, he immortalized a place of rough-edged working people. The waterfront street once was crowded with sardine canneries processing, at their peak, nearly 200,000 tons of the smelly silver fish a year. During the mid-1940s, however, the sardines disappeared from the bay, causing the canneries to close. Through the years the old tin-roof canneries have been converted into restaurants, art galleries, and malls with shops selling T-shirts, fudge, and plastic sea otters. Recent tourist development along the row has been more tasteful, however, and includes several stylish inns and hotels. ✉ *Cannery Row, between Prescott and David Aves.* ⊕ *www.canneryrow.com* 🎫 *Free* ⊗ *Daily.*

❿ Casa Soberanes. A classic low-ceiling adobe structure built in 1842, this was once a Custom House guard's residence. Exhibits at the house survey life in Monterey from the era of Mexican rule to the present. The building is open only during the free 45-minute tours, but feel free to stop at the peaceful rear garden with a lovely rose-covered arbor and sitting benches. ✉ *Monterey State Historic Park, 336 Pacific St.* ☎ *831/649–7118* 🎫 *Free* ⊗ *Tours Mon. and Fri. at 11:30; Sat. at noon.*

⓮ Colton Hall. A convention of delegates met in 1849 to draft the first state constitution at California's equivalent of Independence Hall. The stone

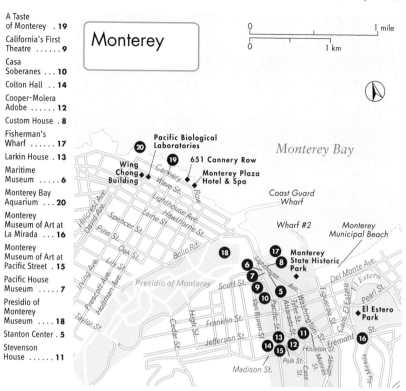

building, which has served as a school, a courthouse, and the county seat, is a city-run museum furnished as it was during the constitutional convention. The extensive grounds outside the hall surround the Old Monterey Jail. ⊠ *500 block of Pacific St., between Madison and Jefferson Sts.* ☎ *831/646–5640* ⊠ *Free* ☉ *Mon.–Sat. 10–noon and 1–4, Sun. 11–noon and 1–3.*

⑫ Cooper-Molera Adobe. The restored 2-acre complex includes a house dating from the 1820s, a visitor center, a bookstore, and a large garden enclosed by a high adobe wall. The mostly Victorian-era antiques and memorabilia that fill the house provide a glimpse into the life of a prosperous early sea merchant's family. The building is open only during organized 45-minute tours, which leave from the Cooper Museum Store. ⊠ *Monterey State Historic Park, Polk and Munras Sts.* ☎ *831/649–7118* ⊠ *Free* ☉ *Tours Mon., Wed., Fri., Sat. at 3.*

⑧ Custom House. This adobe structure built by the Mexican government in 1827—now California's oldest standing public building—was the first stop for sea traders whose goods were subject to duties. At the beginning of the Mexican-American War, in 1846, Commodore John Sloat raised the American flag over the building and claimed California for the United States. The house's lower floor displays cargo from a 19th-

10

century trading ship. ⊠ *Monterey State Historic Park, 1 Custom House Plaza, across from Fisherman's Wharf* ☎ *831/649–2909* ⊡ *Free* ☉ *Thurs.–Mon., 10–3.*

⓱ Fisherman's Wharf. The mournful barking of sea lions provides a steady sound track all along Monterey's waterfront, but the best way to actually view the whiskered marine mammals is to walk along one of the two piers across from Custom House Plaza. Fisherman's Wharf is lined with souvenir shops, seafood restaurants, and whale-watching tour boats. It's undeniably touristy, but still a lively and entertaining place. Up the harbor to the right is Wharf No. 2, a working municipal pier where you can see fishing boats unloading their catches to one side, and fishermen casting their lines into the water on the other. The pier has a couple of low-key restaurants, from whose seats lucky customers may spot otters and harbor seals. ⊠ *At end of Calle Principal* ☎ *831/373–0600* ⊕ *www.montereywharf.com.*

⓭ Larkin House. A veranda encircles the second floor of this architecturally significant two-story adobe built in 1835, whose design bears witness to the Mexican and New England influences on the Monterey style. The rooms are furnished with period antiques, many of them brought from New Hampshire by the building's namesake, Thomas O. Larkin, an early California statesman. The building is open only during organized 45-minute tours. ⊠ *Monterey State Historic Park, 510 Calle Principal, between Jefferson and Pacific Sts.* ☎ *831/649–7118* ⊡ *Free* ☉ *Tours Wed. and Sat. at 2.*

❻ Maritime Museum of Monterey. Maintained by the Monterey History and Art Association, this collection of maritime artifacts belonged to Allen Knight, who was Carmel-by-the-Sea's mayor from 1950 to 1952. Highlights are a collection of outstanding scrimshaw, including fully jointed pocket knives and a toy guillotine, and a lively movie from 1943 chronicling a day in the life of the cannery that used to stand where the aquarium is. The jewel in the museum's crown is the enormous, multi-faceted Fresnel lens from the lighthouse at Point Sur Light Station. ⊠ *Stanton Center, 5 Custom House Plaza* ☎ *831/372–2608* ⊕ *www.montereyhistory.org* ⊡ *$8* ☉ *Thurs.–Tues. 10–5.*

⓴ Monterey Bay Aquarium. The minute you hand over your ticket at this extraordinary aquarium you're surrounded by sea creatures; right at the entrance, you can see dozens of them swimming in a three-story-tall, sunlit kelp forest tank. The beauty of the exhibits here is that they are all designed to give a sense of what it's like to be in the water with the animals—sardines swim around your head in a circular tank, and jellyfish drift in and out of view in dramatically lighted spaces that suggest the ocean depths. A petting pool gives you a hands-on experience with bat rays, and the million-gallon "Outer Bay" tank shows the vast variety of creatures (from sharks to placid-looking turtles) that live in the eastern Pacific. The only drawback to the experience is that it must be shared with the throngs of people that crowd the place daily; most think it's worth it. ⊠ *886 Cannery Row* ☎ *831/648–4888, 800/756–3737 in CA for advance tickets* ⊕ *www.montereybayaquarium.org* ⊡ *$19.95* ☉ *Late May–early Sept., daily 9:30–6; early Sept.–late May, daily 10–6.*

Fodor'sChoice
★

⑯ Monterey Museum of Art at La Mirada. Asian and European antiques fill this 19th-century adobe house. A newer 10,000-square-foot gallery space, designed by Charles Moore, houses Asian and California regional art. Outdoors are magnificent rose and rhododendron gardens. A single fee covers admission to the La Mirada and Pacific Street facilities of the Monterey Museum of Art. ✉ *720 Via Mirada, at Fremont St.* ☎ *831/372–3689* ⊕ *www.montereyart.org* ✎ *$5* ☉ *Wed.–Sat. 11–5, Sun. 1–4.*

⑮ Monterey Museum of Art at Pacific Street. Photographs by Ansel Adams and Edward Weston, as well as works by other artists who have spent time on the peninsula, are on display here. There's also a colorful collection of international folk art; the pieces range from Kentucky hearth brooms to Tibetan prayer wheels. A single fee covers admission to the Pacific Street and La Mirada facilities of the Monterey Museum of Art. ✉ *559 Pacific St., across from Colton Hall* ☎ *831/372–5477* ⊕ *www.montereyart.org* ✎ *$5* ☉ *Wed.–Sat. 11–5, Sun. 1–4.*

Monterey State Historic Park. You can glimpse Monterey's early history in the well-preserved adobe buildings scattered along several city blocks. Far from being a hermetic period museum, the park facilities are an integral part of the day-to-day business life of the town—within some of the buildings are a store, a theater, and government offices. At some of the historic houses, the gardens (open daily 10 to 4) are worthy sights themselves. Departing from the Pacific House Museum, guided 45-minute walking tours of Old Monterey take place Monday and Friday at 10:30 AM and Wednesday at noon. ✉ *20 Custom House Plaza* ☎ *831/649–7118* ⊕ *www.parks.ca.gov* ✎ *Free* ☉ *Call for hrs.*

❼ Pacific House Museum. Once a hotel and saloon, this visitor center and museum now commemorates early-California life with gold-rush relics and photographs of old Monterey. The upper floor displays Native American artifacts, including gorgeous baskets and pottery. ✉ *Monterey State Historic Park, 10 Custom House Plaza* ☎ *831/649–7118* ✎ *Free* ☉ *Fri.–Mon. and Wed. 10–3.*

⑱ Presidio of Monterey Museum. This spot has been significant for centuries as a town, a fort, and the site of several battles, including the skirmish in which the pirate Hipoleto Bruchard conquered the Spanish garrison that stood here. Its first incarnation was as a Native American village for the Rumsien tribe; then it became known as the landing site for explorer Sebastien Vizcaíno in 1602, and father of the California missions, Father Serra, in 1770. The indoor museum tells the stories; the outdoor sites are marked with plaques. ✉ *Corporal Ewing Rd., Presidio of Monterey* ☎ *831/646–3456* ⊕ *www.monterey.org/museum/pom* ✎ *Free* ☉ *Mon. 10–1, Thurs.–Sat. 10–4, Sun. 1–4.*

❺ Stanton Center. This is the place to go to load up on maps and area information. Especially worthwhile are the brochures on self-guided walking tours of historic Monterey and Cannery Row; admission to most sites along the walks is free, and most are open daily. The Maritime Museum of Monterey is in the Stanton Center; you can also view a free 20-minute film about Old Monterey. ✉ *5 Custom House Plaza* ☎ *831/372–2608* ⊕ *www.montereyhistory.org* ✎ *Free* ☉ *Thurs.–Sat. 10–4, Sun. 1–4.*

10

⑪ Stevenson House. This house was named in honor of author Robert Louis Stevenson, who boarded here briefly in a tiny upstairs room. Items from his family's estate furnish Stevenson's room; period-decorated chambers elsewhere in the house include a gallery of the author's memorabilia and a children's nursery stocked with Victorian toys and games. The building is open only during the free 45-minute tours. ⊠ *Monterey State Historic Park, 530 Houston St.* ☎ *831/649–7118* ⊡ *Free* ⊙ *Tours Mon. and Fri. at 2, Sat. at 10:30.*

Where to Stay & Eat

$$$$ ✕ **Fresh Cream.** For years this dining room with a view of glittering Heritage Harbor has provided one of the most refined dining experiences in Monterey. The wine list is carefully chosen, the service is attentive yet restrained, and everything carries an air of luxury. The menu centers around imaginative variations on classic French cuisine, such as lobster and prawns with white corn bisque. Though there's no requirement for dress, men will feel more comfortable in a jacket. ⊠ *99 Pacific St., Suite 100C* ☎ *831/375–9798* ⚏ *Reservations essential* ▭ *AE, D, DC, MC, V* ⊙ *No lunch.*

$–$$$$ ✕ **Monterey's Fish House.** Casual yet stylish, and removed from the hubbub of the wharf, this always-packed seafood restaurant attracts locals and frequent visitors to the city. If the dining room is full, you can wait at the bar and savor deliciously plump oysters on the half shell. The bartenders and waitstaff will gladly advise you on the perfect wine to go with your poached, blackened, or oak-grilled seafood. ⊠ *2114 Del Monte Ave.* ☎ *831/373–4647* ▭ *AE, D, DC, MC, V* ⊙ *No lunch weekends.*

$$–$$$ ✕ **Montrio Bistro.** This quirky, converted firehouse, with its rawhide
FodorśChoice walls and iron indoor trellises, has a wonderfully sophisticated menu.
★ Chef Tony Baker uses organic produce and meats to create imaginative dishes that reflect local agriculture, such as baby artichoke risotto and whole stuffed quail with savory French toast and apple-blackberry reduction. Likewise, the wine list draws primarily on California, and many come from the Monterey area. ⊠ *414 Calle Principal* ☎ *831/648–8880* ⚏ *Reservations essential* ▭ *AE, D, DC, MC, V* ⊙ *No lunch.*

$–$$$ ✕ **Stokes Restaurant & Bar.** This 1833 adobe building glows with well-being, its many fireplaces, booths, and banquettes bringing coziness to the numerous intimate dining rooms. Regional ingredients handled with Mediterranean techniques combine in dishes such as Monterey Bay sardines escabeche and pork shoulder with celery root gratin. Small plates are a specialty, and wines come from all over the world. ⊠ *500 Hartnell St.* ☎ *831/373–1110* ▭ *AE, D, DC, MC, V* ⊙ *No lunch weekends.*

$–$$$ ✕ **Tarpy's Roadhouse.** Fun, dressed-up American favorites—a little something for everyone—are served in this renovated early-1900s stone farmhouse several miles outside town. The kitchen cranks out everything from Cajun-spiced prawns to meat loaf with marsala-mushroom gravy to grilled ribs and steaks. Eat indoors by a fireplace or outdoors in the courtyard. ⊠ *2999 Monterey–Salinas Hwy., Hwy. 68* ☎ *831/647–1444* ▭ *AE, D, DC, MC, V.*

¢–$ ✕ **Old Monterey Café.** Breakfast here gets constant local raves. Its fame rests on such familiar favorites in many incarnations: a dozen kinds of omelets, and pancakes from blueberry to cinnamon-raisin-pecan. The lunch and dinner menus have good soups, salads, and sandwiches, and this is a great place to relax with an afternoon cappuccino. ⊠ *489 Alvarado St.* ☎ *831/646–1021* ⌕ *Reservations not accepted* ▭ *AE, D, MC, V.*

¢–$ ✕ **Thai Bistro.** This cheery mom-and-pop restaurant serves excellent, authentic Thai cuisine from family recipes. Though technically just over the city line in Pacific Grove, it's within walking distance of Cannery Row and the Monterey Bay Aquarium. ⊠ *159 Central Ave., Pacific Grove* ☎ *831/372–8700* ▭ *AE, D, MC, V.*

¢ ✕ **Café Noir.** Attached to the lobby of Monterey's art-house cinema, this café shows work by local artists. Eat a light lunch, drink coffee, or choose a pot of tea from the extensive selection. Menu items include simple sandwiches, hummus, and green salads. Most patrons bring their laptops for the free Wi-Fi, and most tables are shared. Close to downtown bars, it's open until midnight on weekends and 10 PM otherwise. ⊠ *365 Calle Principal* ☎ *831/649–6647* ▭ *No credit cards.*

$$$$ 🏨 **Old Monterey Inn.** This three-story manor house was the home of Mon-
Fodor'sChoice terey's first mayor, and today it remains a private enclave within walk-
★ ing distance of downtown. Lush gardens are shaded by huge old trees and bordered by a creek. Rooms are individually decorated with tasteful antiques; many have fireplaces, and all have featherbeds. Those with private entrances have split doors; you can open the top half to let in cool air and the sound of birds. In the spa room, indulge in a massage or wrap in front of the fireplace. The extensive breakfast is delivered to the rooms, and wine, cheese, and cookies are served each afternoon in the parlor. ⊠ *500 Martin St., 93940* ☎ *831/375–8284 or 800/350–2344* 🖷 *831/375–6730* ⊕ *www.oldmontereyinn.com* ⇆ *6 rooms, 3 suites, 1 cottage* ⌕ *Some in-room hot tubs, cable TV, in-room VCRs, in-room broadband, in-room data ports, hot tub, concierge; no a/c, no smoking* ▭ *MC, V* ⍾⃝ *BP.*

$$$–$$$$ 🏨 **Hotel Pacific.** A few blocks from the historic Old Monterey, this modern hotel has a cool, adobe style. Two greenery-filled courtyards have a fountain and hot tub. Rooms—all of them junior suites—are updated Spanish colonial, with featherbeds, hardwood floors, fireplaces, and balconies or patios. The rates include afternoon tea, fruit, and cheese. ⊠ *300 Pacific St., 93940* ☎ *831/373–5700 or 800/554–5542* 🖷 *831/373–6921* ⊕ *www.hotelpacific.com* ⇆ *105 rooms* ⌕ *Some fans, minibars, cable TV with movies, in-room VCRs, in-room broadband, in-room data ports, 2 hot tubs, meeting rooms; no a/c, no smoking* ▭ *AE, D, DC, MC, V* ⍾⃝ *CP.*

★ $$$–$$$$ 🏨 **Monterey Plaza Hotel and Spa.** This full-service hotel commands a waterfront location on Cannery Row, where you can see frolicking sea otters from the wide outdoor patio and many room balconies. The architecture blends early California and Mediterranean styles, and also echoes elements of the old cannery design. Meticulously maintained, the property offers both simple and luxurious accommodations. On the top floor, the spa offers a full array of treatments, perfect after a workout in the rooftop fitness center. ⊠ *400 Cannery Row, 93940* ☎ *831/646–1700 or 800/368–2468* 🖷 *831/646–0285* ⊕ *www.montereyplazahotel.com* ⇆ *280 rooms, 10 suites* ⌕ *2 restaurants, room service, fans, minibars, cable TV with movies, some in-room DVDs, in-room data ports,*

10

health club, spa, laundry service, concierge, business services, Internet room, meeting rooms; no a/c, no smoking ▭ *AE, D, DC, MC, V.*

$$$–$$$$ 🏨 **Spindrift Inn.** This boutique hotel on Cannery Row, under the same management as the Hotel Pacific and the Monterey Bay Inn, has beach access and a rooftop garden that overlooks the water. Designed with traditional American style, spacious rooms have sitting areas, hardwood floors, fireplaces, and down comforters, among other pleasures. This is an adults-only property. ⊠ *652 Cannery Row, 93940* ☎ *831/646–8900 or 800/841–1879* 🖷 *831/646–5342* ⊕ *www.spindriftinn. com* ➲ *42 rooms* ⌂ *Minibars, refrigerators, cable TV, in-room VCRs, in-room broadband, in-room data ports, Wi-Fi, concierge; no a/c, no smoking* ▭ *AE, D, DC, MC, V* ⦿ *CP.*

$–$$$$ 🏨 **The Beach Resort.** The rooms here may be nondescript, but this Best Western hotel has a great waterfront location about 2 mi north of town that affords views of the bay and the city skyline. Amenities are surprisingly ample. The grounds are pleasantly landscaped, and there's a large pool with a sunbathing area. ⊠ *2600 Sand Dunes Dr., 93940* ☎ *831/394–3321 or 800/242–8627* 🖷 *831/393–1912* ⊕ *www.montereybeachresort.com* ➲ *196 rooms* ⌂ *Restaurant, room service, in-room safes, refrigerators, cable TV with movies, in-room data ports, Wi-Fi, pool, exercise equipment, hot tub, beach, lounge, shop, dry cleaning, business services, meeting rooms, some pets allowed (fee); no smoking* ▭ *AE, D, DC, MC, V.*

★ $–$$$ 🏨 **Monterey Bay Lodge.** Location (on the edge of Monterey's El Estero Park) and superior amenities give this cheerful facility an edge over other motels in town. Lots of greenery, indoors and out, views over El Estero Lake, and a secluded courtyard with a heated pool are other pluses. ⊠ *55 Camino Aguajito, 93940* ☎ *831/372–8057 or 800/558–1900* 🖷 *831/655–2933* ⊕ *www.montereybaylodge.com* ➲ *43 rooms, 2 suites* ⌂ *Restaurant, in-room safes, refrigerators, cable TV with movies and video games, some in-room VCRs, in-room data ports, in-room broadband, Wi-Fi, pool, hot tub, some pets allowed (fee), no-smoking rooms* ▭ *AE, D, DC, MC, V.*

$–$$ 🏨 **Quality Inn Monterey.** This attractive motel has a friendly, country-inn feeling. Rooms are light and airy, some have fireplaces—and the price is right. ⊠ *1058 Munras Ave., 93940* ☎ *831/372–3381* 🖷 *831/372–4687* ⊕ *www.qualityinnmonterey.com* ➲ *55 rooms* ⌂ *Microwaves, refrigerators, cable TV, in-room VCRs, some in-room data ports, in-room broadband, indoor pool, hot tub, sauna; no smoking* ▭ *AE, D, DC, MC, V* ⦿ *CP.*

Nightlife & the Arts

NIGHTLIFE **Planet Gemini** (⊠ 625 Cannery Row ☎ 831/373–1449 ⊕ www. planetgemini.com) presents comedy shows on weekends and dancing to a DJ or live music most nights. An Italian restaurant with a big bar area, **Cibo** (⊠ 301 Alvarado St. ☎ 831/649–8151 ⊕ www.cibo.com) brings live jazz, Latin, soul, and more to downtown Tuesday through Sunday. Loungey **Monterey Live** (⊠ 414 Alvarado St. ☎ 831/646–1415 ⊕ www.montereylive.net), in the heart of downtown, presents jazz, rock, and comedy acts, including some big names, nightly. **Sly McFly's** (⊠ 700-A Cannery Row ☎ 831/372–3225 ⊕ www.slymcflys.com), a straight-ahead bar, has live blues or classic rock every night.

THE ARTS **Dixieland Monterey** (☎831/633–5053 or 888/349–6879 ⊕www.dixieland-monterey.com), held on the first full weekend of March, presents traditional jazz bands at waterfront venues on the harbor. The **Monterey Bay Blues Festival** (☎831/394–2652 ⊕www.montereyblues.com) draws blues fans to the Monterey Fairgrounds the last weekend in June. The **Monterey Jazz Festival** (☎831/373–3366 ⊕ www.montereyjazzfestival.org), the world's oldest, attracts jazz and blues greats from around the world to the Monterey Fairgrounds on the third full weekend of September.

★

Near Cannery Row, **Barbary Coast Theater** (⊠ 320 Hoffman ☎831/655–4992) performs vaudeville acts and spoofy comedy-melodramas. Audience participation is encouraged. **Monterey Bay Theatrefest** (☎831/622–0700) presents free outdoor performances at Custom House Plaza on weekend afternoons and evenings from late June to mid-July. The **Bruce Ariss Wharf Theater** (⊠ One Fisherman's Wharf ☎831/649–2332) focuses on American musicals past and present.

Sports & the Outdoors

Throughout most of the year, the Monterey Bay area is a haven for those who love tennis, golf, surfing, fishing, biking, hiking, scuba diving, and kayaking. In the rainy winter months, when the waves grow larger, adventurous surfers flock to the water. The **Monterey Bay National Marine Sanctuary** (☎ 831/647–4201 ⊕ http://montereybay.noaa.gov), home to mammals, seabirds, fishes, invertebrates, and plants, encompasses a 276-mi shoreline and 5,322 square mi of ocean. Ringed by beaches and campgrounds, it's a place for kayaking, whale-watching, scuba diving, and other water sports.

BICYCLING For bicycle and surrey rentals, visit **Bay Bikes** (⊠585 Cannery Row ☎831/655–2453). **Adventures by the Sea, Inc.** (⊠ 299 Cannery Row ☎ 831/372–1807 or 831/648–7236 ⊕ www.adventuresbythesea.com) rents tandem and standard bicycles.

FISHING **Randy's Fishing Trips** (⊠ 66 Fisherman's Wharf ☎ 831/372–7440 or 800/251–7440) has been operating under the same skippers since 1958.

GOLF Greens fees at the 18-hole **Del Monte Golf Course** (⊠1300 Sylvan Rd. ☎831/373–2700) are $105, plus $25 per person for an optional cart. The $25 twilight special (plus cart rental) begins two hours before sunset.

KAYAKING **Monterey Bay Kayaks** (⊠ 693 Del Monte Ave. ☎ 831/373–5357, 800/649–5357 in CA ⊕www.montereybaykayaks.com) rents equipment and conducts classes and natural-history tours.

SCUBA DIVING Monterey Bay waters never warm to the temperatures of their Southern California counterparts (the warmest they get is low 60s), but that's one reason why the marine life here is among the world's most diverse. The staff at **Aquarius Dive Shop** (⊠ 2040 Del Monte Ave. ☎ 831/375–1933, diving conditions 831/657–1020 ⊕ www.aquariusdivers.com) gives diving lessons and tours, and rents equipment. Their scuba-conditions information line is updated daily.

WALKING From Custom House Plaza, you can walk along the coast in either direction on the 29-mi-long **Monterey Bay Coastal Trail** (☎831/372–3196 ⊕)

10

for spectacular views of the sea. It runs all the way from north of Monterey to Pacific Grove, with sections continuing around Pebble Beach.

WHALE-
WATCHING

★

Monterey Bay Whale Watch (✉ 84 Fisherman's Wharf ☎ 831/375–4658 ⊕ www.montereybaywhalewatch.com), which operates out of Sam's Fishing at Fisherman's Wharf, gives three-to-five-hour tours led by marine biologists. **Monterey Whale Watching** (✉ 96 Fisherman's Wharf #1 ☎ 831/372–2203 or 800/200–2203) provides shorter, somewhat less expensive tours on large, 75-foot boats.

Shopping

Stroll among the many boutiques along Alvarado Street. **Old Monterey Book Co.** (✉ 136 Bonifacio Pl., off Alvarado St. ☎ 831/372–3111) specializes in antiquarian books and prints. For new books, try **Bay Books & Coffeehouse** (✉ 316 Alvarado St. ☎ 831/375–0277)

Antiques and reproductions of 1850s merchandise—linens, crockery, preserves, soaps, etc.—are available at **The Boston Store** (✉ Monterey State Historic Park, 1 Custom House Plaza, across from Fisherman's Wharf ☎ 831/649–3364). Bargain hunters can sometimes find little treasures at the **Cannery Row Antique Mall** (✉ 471 Wave St. ☎ 831/655–0264), which houses 150 local vendors under one roof. Historical Society–operated, **The Pickett Fence** (✉ Monterey State Historic Park, 1 Custom House Plaza, across from Fisherman's Wharf ☎ 831/649–3364) sells high-end garden accessories and furnishings.

AROUND THE BAY

As Highway 1 follows the curve of the bay between Monterey and Santa Cruz, it passes through a rich agricultural zone. Opening right onto the bay, where the Salinas and Pajaro rivers drain into the Pacific, a broad valley brings together fertile soil, an ideal climate, and a good water supply to create optimum growing conditions for crops such as strawberries, artichokes, lettuce, and broccoli. Several beautiful beaches line this part of the coast.

Moss Landing

㉑ *17 mi north of Monterey on Hwy. 1.*

Moss Landing is not much more than a couple blocks of cafés and antiques shops plus a busy fishing port, but therein lies its charm. It's a fine place to stop for lunch and get a dose of nature. In the **Elkhorn Slough at the National Estuarine Research Reserve** (✉ 1700 Elkhorn Rd., Watsonville ☎ 831/728–2822 ⊕ www.elkhornslough.org ☑ $2.50 ☉ Wed.–Sun. 9–5), 1,400 acres of tidal flats and salt marshes form a complex environment that supports some 300 species of birds. A walk or a kayak trip along the meandering waterways and wetlands can reveal hawks, white-tailed kites, owls, herons, and egrets. Sea otters, sharks, rays, and many other animals also live or visit here. On weekends guided walks from the visitor center to the heron rookery begin at 10 and 1. Although the reserve lies across the town line in Watsonville, you reach its entrance through Moss Landing.

★

SALINAS & JOHN STEINBECK'S LEGACY

Salinas (17 mi east of Monterey), a hard-working city surrounded by vegetable fields, honors the memory and literary legacy of John Steinbeck, its most well-known native, at the modern **National Steinbeck Center** (⊠ 1 Main St., 17 mi east of Monterey via Hwy. 68, Salinas ☎ 831/796-3833 ⊕ www. steinbeck.org ⊠ $11 ⊙ Daily 10–5). Exhibits document the life of the Pulitzer and Nobel prize-winner and the history of the local communities that inspired Steinbeck novels such as *The Grapes of Wrath.* Highlights include reproductions of the green pickup-camper from *Travels with Charley* and of the bunkroom from *Of Mice and Men;* you can watch actors read from Steinbeck's books on video screens throughout the museum. The museum is the centerpiece of the revival of Old Town Salinas, where handsome turn-of-the-20th-century stone buildings have been renovated and filled with shops and restaurants. Two blocks from the National Steinbeck Center is the author's Victorian birthplace, **Steinbeck House** (⊠ 132 Central Ave. ☎ 831/424-2735). It operates as a lunch spot Monday through Saturday and displays some Steinbeck memorabilia.

Aboard a 27-foot pontoon boat operated by **Elkhorn Slough Safari** (⊠ Moss Landing Harbor ☎ 831/633-5555 ⊕ www.elkhornslough.com), a naturalist leads an up-close look at wetlands denizens. Advance reservations are required for the two-hour tours ($28). **Sanctuary Cruises** (⊠ "A" Dock ☎ 831/643-0128) offers four–five-hour whale-watching trips ($42) on Monterey Bay, some on catamarans and others on boats powered by bio-diesel. **Tom's Sportfishing** (⊠ Moss Landing Harbor ☎ 831/633-2564 ⊕ www.tomssportfishing.com) takes anglers out onto Monterey Bay ($60 to $65). Depending on the season, king salmon, albacore, or halibut may be the quarry.

Where to Eat

$-$$ ✕ **Phil's Fish Market & Eatery.** Exquisitely fresh, simply prepared seafood (try the cioppino) is on the menu at this warehouselike restaurant on the harbor; all kinds of glistening fish are on offer at the market in the front. ■ TIP→ **Phil's Snack Shack, a tiny sandwich-and-smoothie joint, serves quicker meals at the north end of town.** ⊠ *7600 Sandholdt Rd.* ☎ *831/633-2152* ▤ *MC, V.*

Watsonville

22 *7 mi north of Moss Landing on Hwy. 1.*

If ever a city was built on strawberries, Watsonville is it. Produce has long driven the economy here, and this is where the county fair takes place each September. One feature of the Santa Cruz County Fairgrounds is the **Agricultural History Project,** which preserves the history of farming in the Pajaro Valley. In the Codiga Center and Museum you can examine antique tractors and milking machines, peruse an exhibit

SAN JUAN BAUTISTA

About as close to early-19th-century California as you can get, San Juan Bautista (15 mi east of Watsonville on Hwy. 156) has been protected from development since 1933, when much of it became a state park. Small antiques shops and restaurants occupy the Old West and art-deco buildings that line 3rd Street.

The wide green plaza of San Juan Bautista State Historic Park is ringed by 18th- and 19th-century buildings, many of them open to the public. The cemetery of the long, low, colonnaded mission church contains the unmarked graves of more than 4,300 Native American converts. Nearby is an adobe home furnished with Spanish-colonial antiques, a hotel frozen in the 1860s, a blacksmith shop, a stable, a pioneer cabin, and a jailhouse. The first Saturday of each month, costumed volunteers engage in quilting bees, tortilla making, and other frontier activities.

on the era when Watsonville was the "frozen food capitol of the West," and watch experts restore farm implements and vehicles. ✉ *2601 E. Lake Ave.* ☎ *831/724–5898* ⊕ *www.aghistoryproject.org* ✆ *Free* ☉ *Thurs.–Sun. noon–4.*

Every Memorial Day weekend, aerial performers execute elaborate aerobatics at the **Watsonville Fly-in & Air Show.** More than 300 classic, experimental, and military aircraft are on display; concerts and other events fill three days. ✉ *Watsonville Municipal Airport, 100 Aviation Way* ☎ *831/763–5600* ⊕ *www.watsonvilleflyin.org* ✆ *$15.*

Aptos

23 *7 mi north of Watsonville on Hwy. 1.*

Backed by a redwood forest and facing the sea, downtown Aptos—known as Aptos Village—is a place of wooden walkways and false-fronted shops. Antiques dealers cluster along Trout Gulch Road, off Soquel Drive east of Highway 1. Sandstone bluffs tower above **Seacliff State Beach** (✉ 201 State Park Dr. ☎ 831/685–6440 ⊕ www.parks.ca.gov), a favorite of locals. You can fish off the pier, which leads out to a sunken World War I tanker ship built of concrete.

Where to Stay & Eat

★ **$–$$$** ✕ **Bittersweet Bistro.** A large old tavern with cathedral ceilings houses this popular bistro, where chef-owner Thomas Vinolus draws culinary inspiration from the Mediterranean. The menu changes seasonally, but regular highlights include the pan-seared sand dabs (a species of flounder), seafood puttanesca (pasta with a spicy sauce of garlic, tomatoes, anchovies, and olives), and grilled lamb tenderloin. The decadent chocolate desserts are not to be missed. You can order many of the entrées in small or regular portions. Lunch is available to go from the express counter. ✉ *787 Rio Del Mar Blvd.* ☎ *831/662–9799* ▭ *AE, MC, V.*

☺ **$$$$** ⌂ **Seascape Resort.** On a bluff overlooking Monterey Bay, Seascape is a full-fledged resort that makes it easy to unwind. The spacious suites sleep from two to six people; each has a kitchenette and fireplace, and many have ocean-view patios with barbecue grills. Treat yourself to an in-room manicure, facial, or massage. ⊠ *1 Seascape Resort Dr., 95003* ☎ *831/688-6800 or 800/929-7727* 📠 *831/685-0615* ⊕ *www.seascaperesort.com* 🛏 *285 suites* ⚐ *Restaurant, room service, some kitchens, some kitchenettes, cable TV with movies and video games, some in-room DVDs, in-room data ports, Wi-Fi, golf privileges, 3 pools, health club, 3 hot tubs, spa, beach, children's programs (ages 5–10), laundry service, business services, Internet room, meeting room, convention center; no a/c, no smoking* 🖃 *AE, D, DC, MC, V.*

★ **$$$** ⌂ **Historic Sand Rock Farm.** On the site of a former winery, this century-old Arts-and-Crafts–inspired farmhouse, surrounded by 10 acres of forest and meadow, has been beautifully restored and modernized. There are comfortable, spacious rooms here, and sumptuous breakfasts are served. Most rooms have their own Jacuzzi tubs; if yours doesn't, there's also a large outdoor hot tub. ⊠ *6901 Freedom Blvd., 95003* ☎ *831/688-8005* 📠 *831/688-8025* ⊕ *www.sandrockfarm.com* 🛏 *3 rooms, 2 suites* ⚐ *Fans, some in-room hot tubs, cable TV, in-room VCRs, in-room broadband, Wi-Fi, outdoor hot tub; no a/c, no smoking* 🖃 *D, DC, MC, V* ❑ *BP.*

Capitola & Soquel

㉔ *4 mi northwest of Aptos on Hwy. 1.*

On the National Register of Historic places as California's first seaside resort, the village of Capitola has been in a holiday mood since the late 1800s. Its walkable downtown is jam-packed with casual eateries, surf shops, and ice-cream parlors. Inland, across Highway 1, antiques shops line Soquel Drive in the town of Soquel. Wineries dot the Santa Cruz Mountains beyond.

New Brighton State Beach (⊠ 1500 State Park Dr. ☎ 831/464–6330), once the site of a Chinese fishing village, is now a popular surfing and camping spot. Its Pacific Migrations Visitor Center, opened in 2006, traces the history of Chinese and other people who settled around Monterey Bay, as well as the migratory patterns of the area's wildlife, such as monarch butterflies and gray whales.

Where to Stay & Eat

$–$$$$ ✕ **Shadowbrook.** To get to this romantic spot overlooking Soquel Creek, you can take a cable car or walk the stairs down a steep, fern-lined bank beside a running waterfall. Dining room options include the rooftop Redwood Room, the wood-paneled Wine Cellar, and the airy, glass-enclosed Garden Room. Prime rib and grilled seafood are the stars of the simple menu. A cheaper menu of light entrées is available in the lounge. Champagne brunch is served on Sunday. ⊠ *1750 Wharf Rd.* ☎ *831/475–1571 or 800/975–1511* 🖃 *AE, D, DC, MC, V* ☽ *No lunch.*

★ **$$–$$$** ✕ **Theo's.** Theo's is on a quiet side street in a residential neighborhood. It serves mainly three- and five-course prix-fixe dinners; seasonal standouts

10

include duck with garden vegetables and currants, as well as rack of lamb with ratatouille. Much of the produce comes from the ¾-acre organic garden behind the restaurant (where you can stroll between courses); the rest comes from area farmers and ranchers. Service is gracious and attentive, and the wine list has won awards from *Wine Spectator* 14 years in a row. ⊠ *3101 N. Main St., Soquel* ☎ *831/462–3657* ⚫ *Reservations essential* ▭ *AE, MC, V* ⊙ *Closed Sun. and Mon. No lunch.*

¢–$ ✕ **Gayle's Bakery & Rosticceria.** Whether you're in the mood for an orange-olallieberry muffin, a chicken-satay salad, or tri-tip on garlic toast, this bakery-cum-deli's varied menu is likely to satisfy. Munch your chocolate macaroon on the shady patio or dig into the daily blue-plate dinner amid the whirl inside. ⊠ *504 Bay Ave.* ☎ *831/462–1200* ▭ *AE, MC, V.*

$$$–$$$$ ▦ **Capitola Venetian Motel.** Brightly painted Venetian Court, a funky 1923 cluster of garden apartments, is a landmark on Capitola's waterfront. The complex's pseudo-Mediterranean style extends next door, to this old (but well-maintained and up-to-date) motel on the beach. Popular with families, it offers studios to three-bedroom units with kitchen. Ocean-view rooms have balconies, and some rooms have fireplaces. ⊠ *1500 Wharf Rd., 95010* ☎ *831/476–6471 or 800/332–2780* ⌨ *805/475–3897* ⊕ *www.capitolavenetian.com* ⇥ *19 units* ⚫ *Kitchens, cable TV, in-room data ports, beach* ▭ *D, MC, V.*

$$$–$$$$ ▦ **Inn at Depot Hill.** This inventively designed B&B in a former rail depot sees itself as a link to the era of luxury train travel. Each double room or suite, complete with fireplace and featherbeds, is inspired by a different destination—Italy's Portofino, France's Côte d'Azur, Japan's Kyoto. One suite is decorated like a Pullman car for a railroad baron. Some accommodations have private patios with hot tubs. This is a great place for an adults-only weekend. ⊠ *250 Monterey Ave. 95010* ☎ *831/ 462–3376 or 800/572–2632* ⌨ *831/462–3697* ⊕ *www.innatdepothill. com* ⇥ *8 rooms, 4 suites* ⚫ *Fans, cable TV, in-room VCRs, in-room data ports, hot tub; no a/c, no smoking* ▭ *AE, D, MC, V.*

SANTA CRUZ

The big city on this stretch of the California coast, Santa Cruz (pop. 55,000) is less manicured than Carmel or Monterey. Long known for its surfing and its amusement-filled beach boardwalk, the town is a mix of grand Victorian-era homes and rinky-dink motels. The opening of the University of California campus in the 1960s swung the town sharply to the left, and the counterculture more or less lives on here. At the same time, the revitalized downtown and an insane real-estate market reflect the city's proximity to Silicon Valley and to a growing wine country in the surrounding mountains.

The Waterfront, Downtown & the University

㉕ *5 mi west of Capitola on Hwy. 1; 48 mi north of Monterey on Hwy. 1.*

The sleepy small-town personality of Santa Cruz changed forever in 1965, when a new University of California campus opened on a redwood-studded hillside above town. Tie-dye, yoga, and social progressivism arrived with the students and faculty, many of whom settled here permanently.

In 1989 another radical event—the 7.1 Loma Prieta earthquake—wreaked havoc on downtown, which reinvented itself during reconstruction. Today, a lively mix of families, vacationers, students, surfers, and time-warp victims makes Santa Cruz hum.

What to See

Santa Cruz has been a seaside resort since the mid-19th century. Along one end of the broad, south-facing beach, the **Santa Cruz Beach Boardwalk** has entertained holiday-makers for almost as long. Its Looff carousel and classic wooden Giant Dipper roller coaster, both dating from the early 1900s, are surrounded by high-tech thrill rides and easygoing kiddie rides with ocean views. Video and arcade games, a mini-golf course, and a laser-tag arena pack one gigantic building. You have to pay to play, but you can wander the entire boardwalk for free while sampling delicacies such as corn dogs and chowder fries. ✉ *Along Beach St.* ☎ *831/423–5590 or 831/426–7433* ⊕ *www.beachboardwalk.com* ✉ *$26.95, day pass for unlimited rides* ☺ *Late May–early Sept., daily; early Sept.–late May, weekends only, weather permitting, call for hrs.*

Jutting half a mile into the ocean near one end of the Santa Cruz Beach Boardwalk, the **Santa Cruz Municipal Wharf** (✉ Beach St. at Pacific Ave. ☎ 831/420–6025 ⊕ www.santacruzwharf.com) is topped with seafood restaurants; souvenir shops; and outfitters offering bay cruises, fishing trips, and boat rentals. A salty soundtrack drifts up from under the wharf, where barking sea lions lounge in heaps on crossbeams.

West Cliff Drive winds along the top of an oceanfront bluff from the municipal wharf to Natural Bridges State Beach. It's a spectacular drive, but it's much more fun to walk, blade, or bike the paved path that parallels the road. Groups of surfers bob and swoosh in Santa Cruz Harbor at several points near the foot of the bluff, especially at a break known as Steamer Lane. Named for a surfer who died here in 1965, nearby Mark Abbott Memorial Lighthouse stands at Point Santa Cruz, the cliff's major promontory. From here you can watch pinnipeds hang out, sunbathe, and frolic on Seal Rock.

★ The **Santa Cruz Surfing Museum,** on the ground floor of Mark Abbott Memorial Lighthouse, traces local surfing history back to the early 20th century. Historical photographs show old-time surfers, and a display of boards includes rarities such as a heavy redwood plank predating the fiberglass era and the remains of a modern board chomped by a great white shark. ✉ *701 W. Cliff Dr.* ☎ *831/420–6289* ⊕ *www.santacruzsurfingmuseum.org* ✉ *Free* ☺ *Wed.–Mon. noon–4.*

At the end of West Cliff Drive lies **Natural Bridges State Beach,** a stretch of soft sand edged with tidepools and sea-sculpted rock bridges. ■ TIP➔ **From October to early March a colony of monarch butterflies roosts in a eucalyptus grove.** ✉ *2531 W. Cliff Dr.* ☎ *831/423–4609* ⊕ *www.parks.ca.gov* ✉ *Parking $3* ☺ *Park daily 8 AM–sunset. Visitor center Oct.–Feb., daily 10–4; Mar.–Sept., weekends 10–4.*

Seymour Marine Discovery Center, part of Long Marine Laboratory at UCSC's Institute of Marine Sciences, looks more like a research facility than like a slick aquarium. Interactive exhibits demonstrate how sci-

10

entists study the ocean, and the aquarium displays creatures of particular interest to marine biologists. The 87-foot blue whale skeleton is the world's largest. ⊠ *100 Shaffer Rd., off Delaware St. west of Natural Bridges State Beach* ☎ *831/459–3800* ⊕ *www2.ucsc.edu/seymour-center* 🔄 *$6* ⊘ *Tues.–Sat. 10–5, Sun. noon–5.*

In the Cultural Preserve of **Wilder Ranch State Park** you can visit the homes, barns, workshops, and bunkhouse of a 19th-century dairy farm. Nature has reclaimed most of the ranch land, and native plants and wildlife have returned to the 7,000 acres of forest, grassland, canyons, estuaries, and beaches. Hike, bike, or ride horseback on miles of ocean-view trails. ⊠ *Hwy. 1, 1 mi north of Santa Cruz* ☎ *831/426–0505 Interpretive Center, 831/423–9703 trail information* ⊕ *www.parks.ca.gov* 🔄 *Parking $6* ⊘ *8 AM–sunset.*

When you've had your fill of the city's beaches and waters, take a stroll in downtown Santa Cruz, especially on **Pacific Avenue** between Laurel and Water streets. Vintage boutiques and mountain sports stores, sushi bars and Mexican restaurants, day spas and nightclubs keep the main drag and the surrounding streets hopping mid-morning until late evening. On the northern fringes of downtown, **Santa Cruz Mission State Historic Park** preserves the site of California's 12th Spanish Mission, built in the 1790s and destroyed by an earthquake in 1857. A museum in a restored 1791 adobe and a half-scale replica of the mission church are part of the complex. ⊠ *144 School St.* ☎ *831/425–5849* ⊕ *www.parks.ca. gov* 🔄 *Free* ⊘ *Thurs.–Sun. 10–4.*

Hokey tourist trap or genuine scientific enigma? Since 1940, curious throngs baffled by the **Mystery Spot** have made it one of the most visited attractions in Santa Cruz. The laws of gravity and physics don't appear to apply in this tiny patch of redwood forest, where balls roll uphill and people stand on a slant. ⊠ *465 Mystery Spot Rd.* ☎ *831/423–8897* ⊕ *www.mysteryspot.com* 🔄 *$5, plus $5 parking* ⊘ *Late May–early Sept. daily 9–7, early Sept.–late May daily 9–5.*

The modern 2,000-acre campus of the **University of California at Santa Cruz** nestles in the forested hills above town. Its sylvan setting, sweeping ocean vistas, and redwood architecture make the university worth a visit. Campus tours, offered several times daily (reserve in advance), offer a glimpse of college life and campus highlights. They run about an hour and 45 minutes and combine moderate walking with shuttle transport. Half a mile beyond the main campus entrance, the **UCSC Arboretum** (⊠ *1156 High St.* ☎ *831/427–2998* 🔄 *Free* ⊘ *Daily 9–5*) is a stellar collection of gardens arranged by geography. A walking path leads through areas dedicated to the plants of California, Australia, New Zealand, and South Africa. ⊠ *Main entrance at Bay and High Sts.* ☎ *831/459–0111* ⊕ *www.ucsc.edu.*

OFF THE
BEATEN
PATH
★

SANTA CRUZ MOUNTAINS – Highway 9 heads northeast from Santa Cruz into hills densely timbered with massive coastal redwoods. The road winds through the lush San Lorenzo Valley, past hamlets consisting of a few cafés, antiques shops, and old-style tourist cabins. Here, residents of the hunting-and-fishing persuasion coexist with hardcore flower-power survivors and wannabes. Along Highway 9 and its side roads are about a dozen **wineries,** most notably Bonny Doon Vineyard, Organic Wineworks, and David Bruce Winery. ■ TIP→ **The Santa Cruz Mountains Winegrowers Association distributes a wine-touring map at many lodgings and attractions around Santa Cruz.**

On your way into **Felton** (⊠ Hwy. 9, 7 mi north of Santa Cruz ☎ 831/ 335–9000), stop at the tiny, brick-red Bigfoot Discovery Museum, then take a walk in Henry Cowell Redwoods State Park. Off Graham Hill Road in town are a covered bridge and Roaring Camp, where you can take a vintage train to Bear Mountain or down the San Lorenzo Gorge to Santa Cruz Beach. **Ben Lomond** (⊠ Hwy. 9, 3 mi north of Felton ☎ 831/ 336–4521 ⊕ www.ben-lomond-ca.org) has the rough-hewn Henfling's Tavern, which presents a broad spectrum of live American and international music, and the kitschy chalet-style Tyrolean Inn, a Bavarian restaurant (no lunch) offering German beer and music. For its over-the-top architecture alone, the supposedly haunted **Brookdale Lodge** (⊠ 11570 Hwy. 9, Brookdale ☎ 831/338–6433 ⊕ www.brookdalelodge.com), a few miles north of Ben Lomond, is worth a stop. A natural brook runs through the multilevel 1920s dining room (no lunch), and the lounge presents serious rock and blues acts.

In **Boulder Creek** (⊠ Hwy. 9, 2 mi north of Brookdale ☎ 831/338– 7099), buildings from the 1880s–1920s line the main street; pick up the walking-tour pamphlet, available at many local businesses, to learn more. Boulder Creek is the gateway to **Big Basin Redwoods State Park** (⊠ Hwy. 236, Big Basin Way, 9 mi northwest of Boulder Creek, Boulder Creek ☎ 831/338–8860 ⊕ www.parks.ca.gov). In California's oldest state park (established 1902), more than 80 mi of hiking trails thread through redwood groves and past waterfalls.

Where to Stay & Eat

$–$$$ ✗ **Gabriella Café.** The work of local artists hangs on the walls of this petite, romantic café in a tile-roof cottage. Featuring organic produce from area farms, the seasonal Italian menu has offered steamed mussels, braised lamb shank, and grilled portobello mushrooms. ⊠ *910 Cedar St.* ☎ *831/457–1677* ▤ *AE, MC, V.*

★ $–$$ ✗ **O'mei.** This is Chinese food like you've never had it. Imagine red-oil dumplings stuffed with pork and vegetables, oolong-smoked chicken wok-cooked with crimini mushrooms and rosemary, impossibly fluffy fried potatoes topped with house-cured bacon and black date sauce. Service in the tasteful west side dining room is excellent; you can also order take-out. ⊠ *2316 Mission St.* ☎ *831/425–8458* ▤ *AE, D, DC, MC, V* ⊗ *No lunch weekends.*

$–$$ ✗ **Soif.** Wine reigns at this sleek bistro and wineshop that takes its name from the French word for thirst. The lengthy list includes selections from near and far, dozens of which you can order by the taste or glass. Infused with the tastes of the Mediterranean, small plates and mains are served at the copper-top bar, the big communal table, and private tables. A jazz combo or solo pianist play some evenings. ⊠ *105 Walnut Ave.* ☎ *831/423–2020* ▤ *AE, MC, V* ⊗ *No lunch.*

10

¢–$$ ✗ **Seabright Brewery.** Great burgers, big salads, and stellar house-made microbrews make this a favorite hangout in the youthful Seabright neighborhood east of downtown. Sit outside on the large patio or inside at a comfortable, spacious booth; both are popular with families. ✉ *519 Seabright Ave.* ☎ *831/426–2739* ▤ *AE, MC, V.*

¢ ✗ **Zachary's.** This noisy café filled with students and families defines the funky essence of Santa Cruz. It also dishes up great breakfasts: stay simple with sourdough pancakes, or go for the "Mike's Mess"—eggs scrambled with bacon, mushrooms, and home fries, then topped with sour cream, melted cheese, and fresh tomatoes. ⚠ **If you arrive after 9 AM, expect a long wait for a table; lunch is a shade calmer, but closing time is 2 PM.** ✉ *819 Pacific Ave.* ☎ *831/427–0646* ⬟ *Reservations not accepted* ▤ *MC, V* ⊘ *Closed Mon. No dinner.*

$$$$ 🏠 **Pleasure Point Inn.** Tucked in a residential neighborhood at the east end of town, this modern Mediterranean-style B&B sits right across the street from the ocean and a popular surfing beach (where surfing lessons are available). The rooms are handsomely furnished and include such deluxe amenities as wireless Internet access and dimmer switches; some rooms have fireplaces. You have use of the large rooftop sundeck and hot tub, which overlook the Pacific. Because this is a popular romantic getaway spot, it's best not to bring kids. ✉ *2–3665 E. Cliff Dr., 95062* ☎ *831/475–4657 or 877/557–2567* ⊞ *831/479–1347* ⊕ *www.pleasurepointinn.com* ⌇ *4 rooms* ⬟ *Fans, in-room safes, some in-room hot tubs, minibars, refrigerators, cable TV, in-room data ports, hot tub, beach; no a/c, no smoking* ▤ *MC, V* ⦿ *CP.*

$$$–$$$$ 🏠 **Babbling Brook Inn.** Though it's smack in the middle of Santa Cruz, this B&B has lush gardens, a running stream, and tall trees that make you feel like you're in a secluded wood. All rooms have fireplaces (though a few are electric) and featherbeds; most have private patios. Complimentary wine, cheese, and fresh-baked cookies are available in the afternoon. ✉ *1025 Laurel St., 95060* ☎ *831/427–2437 or 800/866–1131* ⊞ *831/427–2457* ⊕ *www.babblingbrookinn.com* ⌇ *11 rooms, 2 suites* ⬟ *Some in-room hot tubs, cable TV, in-room VCRs; no a/c, no smoking* ▤ *AE, D, DC, MC, V* ⦿ *BP.*

$$$–$$$$ 🏠 **Chaminade.** A full-on renovation in 2005 sharpened this hilltop resort's look and enhanced its amenities. Secluded on 300 acres of redwood and eucalyptus forest, the mission-style complex commands expansive views of Monterey Bay. Guest rooms are furnished in a modern Spanish style, with dark wood, deep colors, and patterned fabrics; some have private patios or decks. The spa employs all-natural products in its complete menu of body and beauty treatments. ✉ *1 Chaminade La., 95065* ☎ *800/283–6569* ⊞ *831/476–4798* ⊕ *www.chaminade.com* ⌇ *112 rooms, 44 suites* ⬟ *3 restaurants, in-room safes, some refrigerators, cable TV with movies, in-room broadband, 4 tennis courts, pool, gym, 2 outdoor hot tubs, sauna, spa, steam room, badminton, basketball, billiards, croquet, hiking, Ping-Pong, volleyball, bar, lounge, shops, dry cleaning, laundry service, business services, meeting rooms, airport shuttle, no-smoking rooms* ▤ *AE, D, DC, MC, V.*

$$–$$$$ 🏠 **Sea & Sand Inn.** The main appeal of this aging motel perched on a waterfront bluff is its location: every room has an ocean view, and the boardwalk is just down the street. Blond-wood furniture and floral fab-

rics create a vaguely country look; some rooms have private hot tubs or fireplaces. A few studios and suites include kitchenettes. The staff is friendly and the landscaping tidy, but the parking lot, fronting a busy road, is tight. ⊠ *201 W. Cliff Dr., 95060* ☎ *831/427–3400* 🖷 *831/466–9882* ⊕ *www.santacruzmotels.com* 🛏 *15 rooms* ♨ *Some in-room hot tubs, some kitchenettes, room TVs, some in-room VCRs, Wi-Fi, no-smoking rooms* 🖃 *AE, MC, V* ❙❍❙ *CP.*

$$$ 🖫 **Cliff Crest.** You'll receive the warmest of welcomes from hosts Adriana and Constantin, owners of this 1887 Queen Anne, which is crammed with historical photographs, antiques from around the world, and artwork by Adriana. Choose one of the highly individual rooms (some with fireplace, all with four-poster bed and private bath) and come down the creaky stairs to the solarium for a different breakfast each morning. If your taste in B&Bs runs more to the very homey and slightly wacky than to frills and fussiness, you'll enjoy a stay at this house between the beach and downtown. ⊠ *407 Cliff St., 95060* ☎ *831/427–2609 or 831/252–1057* 🖷 *831/427–2710* ⊕ *www.cliffcrestinn.com* 🛏 *5 rooms* ♨ *Room TVs, Wi-Fi; no a/c, no smoking* 🖃 *AE, D, MC, V* ❙❍❙ *BP.*

Nightlife & the Arts

NIGHTLIFE Dance with the crowds at **The Catalyst** (⊠ 1011 Pacific Ave. ☎ 831/423–1338 ⊕ www.catalystclub.com), a huge, grimy downtown club that has regularly featured big names, from Neil Young to Nirvana to Ice T. Renowned in the international jazz community, and drawing performers such as Herbie Hancock, Pat Metheny, and Charlie Hunter, the ★ nonprofit **Kuumbwa Jazz Center** (⊠ 320–2 Cedar St. ☎ 831/427–2227 ⊕ www.kuumbwajazz.org) bops with live music most nights; "Jazz and Dinner" Thursday include a meal with the show. Blues, salsa, reggae, funk: you name it, **Moe's Alley** (⊠ 1535 Commercial Way ☎ 831/479–1854 ⊕ www.moesalley.com) has it all, six nights a week.

THE ARTS Each August, the **Cabrillo Festival of Contemporary Music** (☎ 831/426–6966, 831/420–5260 box office ⊕ www.cabrillomusic.org) brings some of the world's finest artists to the Santa Cruz Civic Auditorium to play ground-breaking symphonic music, including major world premieres. Using period and reproduction instruments, the **Santa Cruz Baroque Festival** (☎ 831/457–9693 ⊕ www.scbaroque.org) presents a wide range of classical music at various venues throughout the year. As the name suggests, the focus is on 17th- and 18th-century composers such as Bach and Handel. **Shakespeare Santa Cruz** (⊠ Performing Arts Complex, University of California at Santa Cruz ☎ 831/459–2121 ⊕ www.shakespearesantacruz.org) stages a six-week Shakespeare festival in July and August that may also include the occasional modern dramatic performance. Most performances are outdoors under the redwoods. A holiday program is also performed in December.

Sports & the Outdoors

BICYCLING Park the car and rent a beach cruiser at **Bike Shop Santa Cruz** (⊠ 1325 Mission St. ☎ 831/454–0909). Mountain bikers should head to **Another Bike Shop** (⊠ 2361 Mission St. ☎ 831/427–2232 ⊕ www.anotherbikeshop.com) for tips on the best trails around and a look at cutting-edge gear made and tested locally.

10

BOATS &
CHARTERS
Chardonnay Sailing Charters (☎ 831/423–1213 ⊕ www.chardonnay.com) cruises Monterey Bay year-round on a variety of trips, such as whale-watching, astronomy, and winemaker sails. The 70-foot *Chardonnay II* leaves from the yacht harbor in Santa Cruz. Food and drink are served on many of their cruises. Reservations are essential. **Original Stagnaro Fishing Trips** (✉ June–Aug., Santa Cruz Municipal Wharf; Sept.–May, Santa Cruz West Harbor ☎ 831/427–2334) operates salmon-, albacore-, and rock-cod-fishing expeditions; the fees ($45 to $70) include bait. The company also runs whale-watching cruises ($32) December through April and May through Nov.

SURFING
Surfers gather for spectacular waves and sunsets at **Pleasure Point** (✉ E. Cliff and Pleasure Point Drs.). **Steamer Lane,** near the lighthouse on West Cliff Drive, has a decent break. The area plays host to several competitions in summer.

Find out what all the fun is about at **Club-Ed Surf School and Camps** (✉ Cowell Beach, at Coast Santa Cruz Hotel ☎ 831/464–0177 or 800/287–7873 ⊕ www.club-ed.com). Your first private or group lesson ($85 and up) includes all equipment. The most welcoming place in town to buy or rent surf gear is **Paradise Surf Shop** (✉ 3961 Portola Dr. ☎ 831/462–3880 ⊕ www.paradisesurf.com). The shop is owned by local amateur longboarder Sally Smith and run by women who aim to help everyone feel comfortable on the water. **Cowell's Beach Surf Shop** (✉ 30 Front St. ☎ 831/427–2355) sells bikinis, rents surfboards and wet suits, and offers lessons.

MONTEREY BAY–AREA ESSENTIALS

To research prices, get advice from other travelers, and book travel arrangements, visit www.fodors.com.

AIR TRAVEL

Monterey Peninsula Airport is 3 mi east of downtown Monterey (take Olmstead Road off Highway 68). It's served by America West, American, American Eagle, United, and United Express. ⇨ Air Travel *in* Smart Travel Tips A to Z for airline phone numbers. Taxi service to downtown runs about $9 to $10; to Carmel the fare is $16 to $25. To and from Mineta San Jose International Airport and San Francisco International Airport, Monterey Airbus starts at $30 and the Santa Cruz Airporter runs $40 to $50.

🚖 **Carmel Taxi** ☎ 831/624–3885. **Monterey Airbus** ☎ 831/373–7777 ⊕ www.montereyairbus.com. **Monterey Airport Taxi** ☎ 831/626–3385. **Monterey Peninsula Airport** ✉ 200 Fred Kane Dr., Monterey ☎ 831/648–7000 ⊕ www.montereyairport.com. **Santa Cruz Airporter** ☎ 800/497–4997. **Yellow Checker Cabs** ☎ 831/646–1234.

BUS TRAVEL

Greyhound serves Santa Cruz and Monterey from San Francisco three or four times daily. The trips take about 3 and 4½ hours, respectively. Monterey-Salinas Transit provides frequent service between the peninsula's towns and many major sightseeing spots and shopping areas. The base fare is $2, with an additional $2 for each zone you travel into. A day pass costs \$4.50 to \$9, depending on how many zones you'll be traveling through. Monterey-Salinas Transit also runs the WAVE shuttle, which links major attractions on the Monterey waterfront. The free shuttle operates late May through early September, daily from 9 to 6:30.

Greyhound ☎ 800/231-2222 ⊕ www.greyhound.com. **Monterey-Salinas Transit** ☎ 831/899-2555 or 888/678-2871 ⊕ www.mst.org.

CAR TRAVEL

Most of the major car-rental agencies have locations in downtown Santa Cruz and at the Monterey Airport. ⇨ Car Rental *in* Smart Travel Tips A to Z for national car-rental agency phone numbers. Parking is especially difficult in Carmel-by-the-Sea and in the heavily touristed areas of Monterey.

Two-lane Highway 1 runs south–north along the coast, linking the towns of Carmel-by-the-Sea, Monterey, and Santa Cruz. The freeway, U.S. 101, lies to the east, roughly parallel to Highway 1. The two roads are connected by Highway 68 from Pacific Grove to Prunedale; Highway 152 from Watsonville to Gilroy; and Highway 17 from Santa Cruz to San Jose. Highway 17 crosses the redwood-filled Santa Cruz Mountains; △ traffic near Santa Cruz can crawl to a standstill.

The drive south from San Francisco to Monterey can be made comfortably in three hours or less. The most scenic way is to follow Highway 1 down the coast past flower, pumpkin, and artichoke fields and small seaside communities. Unless you drive on sunny weekends when locals are heading for the beach, the two-lane coast highway may take no longer than the freeway. A sometimes faster route is Interstate 280 south from San Francisco to Highway 17, north of San Jose. A third option is to follow U.S. 101 south through San Jose to Prunedale and then take Highway 156 west to Highway 1 south into Monterey.

From Los Angeles the drive to Monterey can be made in five to six hours by heading north on U.S. 101 to Prunedale and then west on Highway 68. The spectacular but slow alternative is to take U.S. 101 to San Luis Obispo and then follow the hairpin turns of Highway 1 up the coast. Allow about three extra hours if you take this route.

10

EMERGENCIES

In the event of an emergency, dial 911. The Monterey Bay Dental Society provides dentist referrals throughout the area. The Monterey County Medical Society and the Santa Cruz County Medical Society can refer you to a doctor in Monterey and Santa Cruz counties, respectively. There are 24-hour Walgreens pharmacies in Seaside, about 4 mi northeast of Monterey via Highway 1, and in Freedom, on the eastern edge of Watsonville.

Hospitals **Community Hospital of Monterey Peninsula** ✉ 23625 Holman Hwy., Monterey ☎ 831/624-5311 ⊕ www.chomp.org. **Dominican Hospital** ✉ 1555 Soquel Dr., Santa Cruz ☎ 831/462-7700 ⊕ www.dominicanhospital.org.

Pharmacies **Walgreens** ✉ 1055 Fremont Blvd., Seaside ☎ 831/393-9231. **Walgreens** ✉ 1810 Freedom Blvd., Freedom ☎ 831/768-0183.

🔗 Referrals **Monterey Bay Dental Society** ☎ 831/658-0168 ⊕ http://mbdsdentists. com. **Monterey County Medical Society** ☎ 831/455-1008 ⊕ www.montereymedicine. org. **Santa Cruz County Medical Society** ☎ 831/479-7226 ⊕ www.cruzmed.org.

TOUR OPTIONS

California Parlor Car Tours operates motor-coach tours from San Francisco that include one or two days in Monterey and Carmel. Ag Venture Tours runs wine-tasting, sightseeing, and agricultural tours in the Monterey, Salinas, Carmel Valley, and Santa Cruz areas.

🔗 **Ag Venture Tours** ☎ 831/643-9463 ⊕ www.agventuretours.com. **California Parlor Car Tours** ☎ 415/474-7500 or 800/227-4250 ⊕ www.calpartours.com.

TRAIN TRAVEL

Amtrak's *Coast Starlight* runs between Los Angeles, Oakland, and Seattle. From the train station in Salinas, connecting Amtrak Thruway buses serve Monterey and Carmel-by-the-Sea; from San Jose, connecting buses serve Santa Cruz.

🔗 **Amtrak** ☎ 800/872-7245 ⊕ www.amtrakcalifornia.com. **Salinas Amtrak Station** ✉ 11 Station Pl., Salinas ☎ 831/422-7458. **San Jose Amtrak Station** ✉ 65 Cahill St., San Jose ☎ 408/287-7462.

VISITOR INFORMATION

🔗 **Aptos Chamber of Commerce** ✉ 7605-A Old Dominion Ct., Aptos 95003 ☎ 831/688-1467 ⊕ www.aptoschamber.com. **Capitola-Soquel Chamber of Commerce** ✉ 716-G Capitola Ave., Capitola 95010 ☎ 831/475-6522 ⊕ www.capitolachamber.com. **Carmel Chamber of Commerce** ✉ San Carlos between 5th and 6th, Carmel 93921 ☎ 831/624-2522 or 800/550-4333 ⊕ www.carmelcalifornia.org. **Monterey County Convention & Visitors Bureau** ☎ 888/221-1010 ⊕ www.montereyinfo.org. **Monterey County Vintners and Growers Association** ☎ 831/375-9400 ⊕ www.montereywines.org. **Monterey Peninsula Visitors and Convention Bureau** ✉ 462 Webster St., #4, Monterey 93940 ☎ 831/372-9323 ⊕ www.monterey.com. **Moss Landing Chamber of Commerce** ✉ Box 41, Moss Landing 95039 ☎ 831/633-4501 ⊕ www.mosslandingchamber.com. **Pajaro Valley Chamber of Commerce** ✉ 444 Main St., Watsonville 95076 ☎ 831/724-3900 ⊕ www.pajarovalleychamber.com. **Salinas Valley Chamber of Commerce** ✉ 119 E. Alisal St., Salinas 93901 ☎ 831/424-7611 ⊕ www.salinaschamber.com. **Santa Cruz County Conference and Visitors Council** ✉ 1211 Ocean St., Santa Cruz 95060 ☎ 831/425-1234 or 800/833-3494 ⊕ www.scccvc.org. **Santa Cruz Chamber of Commerce** ✉ 1519 Pacific Ave., Santa Cruz 95060 ☎ 831/426-4900 ⊕ www.santacruzchamber.org. **Santa Cruz Mountain Winegrowers Association** ✉ 7605-A Old Dominion Ct., Aptos 95003 ☎ 831/685-8463 ⊕ www.scmwa.com.

The Peninsula & South Bay

SOUTH OF SAN FRANCISCO

WORD OF MOUTH

"I never knew that San Jose had such a great little Egyptian Museum! And the architecture of the Park (replicas of Egyptian temples) is very impressive. My family and I stumbled across this treasure and want to go back. A must see!"

—Lisa

"I love the Tech Museum of Innovation. I guess I am just a kid at heart!"

—jcorrea

Updated by
Lisa M.
Hamilton

TWO PARALLEL WORLDS LIE SOUTH OF SAN FRANCISCO. The fog-shrouded San Mateo County coast is dotted with a few small towns, but mostly the world here is undeveloped—with green hills to the east and a rugged coastline to the west. Half Moon Bay, Pescadero, and the other towns here are no more than a few blocks long, just enough room for a couple of bed-and-breakfasts, restaurants, and local shops. As you wind your way from one to the other, past artichoke fields and stunning beaches, you'll find that the pace of life is slower here than in the rest of the Bay Area.

Over the Santa Cruz Mountains from the coast, the Inland Peninsula pulses with prosperity and creative energy. Many visitors to the Bay Area associate the region from Santa Clara County to San Francisco with traffic congestion and suburban sprawl, but a closer look at the Peninsula reveals redwood forests and grassy hills where mountain lions still roam. Stanford University's bucolic campus is wonderful to visit, as are the wooded former country estates built by 19th-century mining and transportation "bonanza kings"—early adopters who realized the area's potential long before the "dot-com" boom.

Farther south is the heart of Silicon Valley, the birthplace of the tiny electronic chips and circuits that support the information age. Although from the highways this region appears to be comprised entirely of office parks, shopping centers, and high-rises, the South Bay in fact contains many old-fashioned neighborhoods and quiet, tree-lined parks. There are diverse towns such as Santa Clara, with its 200-year-old mission; Saratoga, with its fine antiques stores and posh restaurants; and San Jose—the third-largest city on the West Coast—with its flourishing downtown center and a growing ribbon of urban green connecting the city from north to south.

Exploring the Peninsula & South Bay

You'll need a car to get around. The stretch of Highway 1 that leads north from the Monterey Bay area passes through a sparsely populated landscape punctuated by a few small towns. By contrast, the Inland Peninsula and South Bay is a tangle of freeways. Public transportation can get you far here, but if you're in a car, it's best to avoid driving during rush hour.

About the Restaurants

Gone are the days when Peninsula and South Bay food lovers had to drive to San Francisco for an exceptional meal. Today some of the country's greatest chefs have recognized the area's appeal, opening trendy bistros and eateries, especially in San Jose's revitalized downtown. All along the coast as well as in more progressive inland communities like Palo Alto and Saratoga, the best chefs follow the farm-to-table ideals that guide northern California's best restaurants. Dining in the South Bay might be a little less formal than in San Francisco—and a little less expensive—but that doesn't mean you won't need reservations. Along the coast, however, restaurants are almost all casual, and unless otherwise noted, you can generally walk in without waiting for a table.

GREAT ITINERARIES

11

Numbers correspond to the Peninsula & South Bay and Downtown San Jose maps.

IF YOU HAVE 1 DAY

Spend your morning in **Palo Alto ❼ ▶**, taking a look around town and a tour of Stanford University. In the afternoon head for 🖼 **San Jose ⓫–㉒** and the **Tech Museum of Innovation ⓯**, the **Rosicrucian Egyptian Museum ⓳**, and the **Winchester Mystery House ㉑**. Depending on your taste, have an evening of symphony, ballet, or theater at San Jose's Center for Performing Arts.

IF YOU HAVE 3 DAYS

Spend your first day on the coast, noodling around **Año Nuevo State Reserve ❷ ▶**, **Pescadero State Beach ❸**, **Half Moon Bay ❹**, and **Moss Beach ❺**. After overnighting in a Half Moon Bay B&B, drive Route 92 through the countryside to Interstate 280 and head south to **Woodside ❻**, where you can tour Filoli (except Monday November through January). Drive south on Interstate 280 to the Sand Hill Road exit and take that route to the central campus of Stanford University. Take an afternoon tour of the university and its Iris and B. Gerald Cantor Center for Visual Arts, then have dinner in 🖼 **Palo Alto ❼**. On your third day stop in **Santa Clara ❽** to see Mission Santa Clara de Asis, or if you have kids in tow, you might want to treat them to a morning at Paramount's Great America. Devote your afternoon to 🖼 **San Jose ⓫–㉒** and its attractions, then take a sunset drive to **Saratoga ❿**.

About the Hotels

Along the coastal peninsula, accommodations tend to have homegrown character and cater to San Franciscans and weekend visitors here for a romantic getaway. Because of the weekend demand on the coast you'd be wise to make reservations as far in advance as possible. Inland Peninsula and South Bay lodgings generally attract business travelers—most are chain motels and hotels, though a handful of B&Bs have popped up in recent years. During the week, when business conventions are in full swing, many of these hotels are fully booked up to two weeks in advance. However, some are nearly empty on weekends—this is when rates plummet and package deals abound.

WHAT IT COSTS					
	$$$$	**$$$**	**$$**	**$**	**¢**
RESTAURANTS	over $30	$23–$30	$16–$22	$10–$15	under $10
HOTELS	over $250	$176–$250	$121–$175	$90–$120	under $90

Restaurant prices are for a main course at dinner, excluding sales tax of 8¼% (depending on location). Hotel prices are for two people in a standard double room in high season, excluding service charges and 10% tax.

Timing

The hills that separate the Santa Clara Valley from the coast keep summertime fog from blowing into the Inland Peninsula and South Bay. This means that there are usually drastic variations in temperature between the coast and the inland area from April through October. In July you can expect foggy weather and temperatures in the mid-60s along the coastline, whereas just inland the days are sunny, with temperatures in the mid-80s. The rainy season runs from about November through March, and temperatures are generally constant across the region; daytime highs are ordinarily in the 50s and 60s.

THE COASTAL PENINSULA
UP HIGHWAY 1 FROM AÑO NUEVO TO MOSS BEACH

The coastal towns between Santa Cruz and San Francisco were founded in the late 18th century by Spanish explorer Gaspar de Portola. For the following two centuries they were primarily agricultural, supplying food first for the missions and later for the American vegetable market. Artichokes and other cool-weather crops still grow in coastal fields, but these days the big attraction here is the beaches. The shoreline is nearly all public and varies widely from long, sandy stretches to tidepool-covered flats. State park signs will lead to paved parking lots, but you can often also just stop where other cars are parked by the highway and find a footpath to the water. Drive north from Santa Cruz (⇨ Chapter 10) to San Francisco along scenic Highway 1, hugging the twists and turns of the coast, or venture 11 mi inland at Half Moon Bay, over hilly Route 92 to San Mateo.

Big Basin Redwoods State Park

❶ *17 mi north of Santa Cruz on Hwy. 1.*

California's oldest state park is the best place to see old-growth redwoods without going north of San Francisco (and it's far less crowded than Muir Woods and other famous spots). The parkland ranges from sea level up to 2,000 feet in elevation, which means the landscape changes often, from dark redwood groves to oak pastures that are deep green in winter and bleached nearly white in summer. The mountain setting also makes for countless waterfalls, most visible during the winter rains. The visitor's center is inland, at park headquarters in Boulder Creek. Staffing is spotty, but there's always park information and camping check-in available at a self-service kiosk.

Coming from the coast, you'll access the park at **Waddell Creek** (Highway 1, 17 mi north of Santa Cruz), where a confluence of waterways pour out of the redwoods and into the ocean. A short walk on the Marsh Trail leads to the **Rancho Del Oso Nature Center** (☎ 831/427–2288 ☻ Weekends noon–4), which has natural-history exhibits and is the meeting point for free ranger-led nature walks, every Saturday at 1. Moun-

IF YOU LIKE

BEACHES

The main draw of coastal San Mateo County is its beaches. From Montara to Pescadero the strands accessible from Highway 1 are surprisingly uncrowded. Fog and cool weather may keep many people out of the water for large portions of the year, but the unspoiled beauty and wildlife make these beaches a treasure of the Bay Area. Some standouts are San Gregorio and Pomponio for strolling and sunbathing; windy Waddell Creek for windsurfing and kite-surfing; and Fitzgerald Marine Preserve for tide pooling. Then again, since nearly three-quarters of the county (70%) is open space, there's enough beach that you can usually find a good one by simply pulling over wherever you see a patch of sand.

HISTORIC HOMESTEADS

The communities of the Peninsula and South Bay have worked hard to preserve their parklands and turn-of-the-20th-century homesteads. In Woodside, Filoli stands as one of the great California country houses that remain intact. The Winchester Mystery House, in San Jose, may be the best-known site, but look beyond the tales of ghosts to see the sprawling farmhouse it once was. You can also visit former vineyards and historic homes in the Santa Cruz Mountains, notably Villa Montalvo and the Mountain Winery in Saratoga.

tain bikers, horseback riders, and hikers can take the nearly level Canyon Road (a dirt fire road) back up the creek and into the woods. Hikers looking for solitude might consider a more strenuous, uphill climb on Clark Connection to Westridge Trail, which rewards hard work with spectacular views of the ocean. Those who don't want to go anywhere can just stay on the windswept beach, where the main attraction is watching kite surfers get huge air on the windy shoreline waves. ⌧ *21600 Big Basin Way Boulder Creek* ☎ *831/338–8860* ⌧ *$6 parking fee.*

EN ROUTE Not your average farm stand, **Swanton Berry Farm** (⌧ 12 ½ mi north of Santa Cruz ☎ 831/469–8804 ☉ Sept.–Apr. daily 8–5, May–Aug., daily 8–8), a locally legendary organic farm, offers seasonal delicacies including chocolate-dipped strawberries, strawberry cheesecake, and artichoke soup. There are indoor picnic tables here, as well as a modest but interesting museum covering topics such as native people, local agriculture, the United Farm Workers, and the history of the strawberry. Jams, pies, and pick-your-own berries are for sale.

Año Nuevo State Reserve

★ ☺ ▶ ❷ *21 mi north of Santa Cruz on Hwy. 1.*

At the height of mating season, upward of 4,000 elephant seals congregate at Año Nuevo, the world's only approachable mainland rookery. The seals are both vocal and spectacularly big (especially the males, which can weigh up to 2 ½ tons), and some are in residence year-round. An easy, 1 ½ -hour round-trip walk takes you to the dunes, from which you can look down onto the animals lounging on the shoreline. Note that during mating season (mid-December through March), visitors may do the hike only as part of a 2 ½-hour guided tour, for which reservations must be made well in advance. The area's visitor center has a fascinating film about the seals and some natural-history exhibits (including a sea otter's pelt that you can touch). ⊠ *Hwy. 1, 13 mi south of Pescadero* ☎ *650/879–2025, 800/444–4445 for tour reservations* ⊡ *$4, parking $6* ⊘ *Tours leave every 15 min, daily 8:45–3.*

Pescadero

12 mi north of Año Nuevo State Reserve on Hwy. 1.

As you walk down Stage Road, Pescadero's main street, it's hard to believe you're only 30 minutes from Silicon Valley. If you could block out the throngs of weekend cyclists, the downtown area could almost serve as the backdrop for a western movie. (In fact, with few changes, Duarte's Tavern could fill in as the requisite saloon.) This is a good place to stop for a bite or to browse for antiques. The real attractions, though, are the spectacular beaches and hiking in the area.

❸ If a quarantine is not in effect (watch for signs), from November through April you can look for mussels amid tidal pools and rocky outcroppings at **Pescadero State Beach,** then roast them at the barbecue pits. Any time of year is good for exploring the beach, the north side of which has several secluded spots along sandstone cliffs. Across U.S. 101, the **Pescadero Marsh Natural Preserve** has hiking trails that cover 600 acres of marshland. Early spring and fall are the best times to come, when there are lots of migrating birds and other wildlife to see. ⊠ *14½ mi south of Half Moon Bay on Hwy. 1* ☎ *650/879–2170* ⊡ *Free, parking $5* ⊘ *Daily 8 AM–sunset.*

Goat cheese goes from pasture to product at **Harley Farms,** a short drive inland from Pescadero's main street. Every Saturday at 1 PM, the owners give a tour (reservations essential, $20) that allows guests to see cheese being made, learn about the pastures, and even milk the goats. If you miss the tour, stop by anyway to purchase cheese and other goat milk products at the store, see goats in the field, and chat with the friendly owners. ⊠ *205 North St.* ☎ *650/879–0480.*

Where to Eat

¢–$$$ ✕ **Duarte's Tavern.** Though it has been noted by national press, this 19th-century roadhouse continues to serve simple American fare with a modest, hometown attitude. The restaurant's bar, for instance, is a great place to sip a whiskey; but it's also the local liquor store, which means some locals take their orders to go. The dining room is no frills, but offers a solid menu based on locally grown vegetables and fresh fish. House specialties include abalone ($40), artichoke soup, and old-fashioned berry pie à la mode (which *Life* magazine once named best in the United States). ⊠ *202 Stage Rd.* ☎ *650/879–0464* ⊕ *www.duartestavern.com* ⊟ *AE, MC, V.*

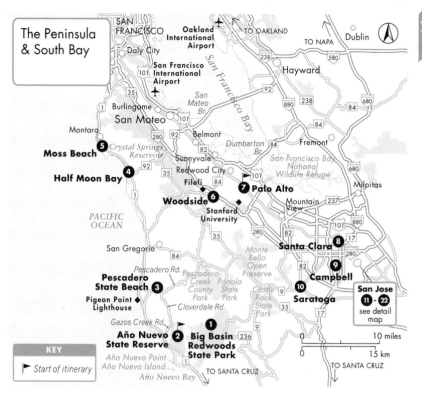

The Peninsula & South Bay

¢–$$$$ 🔲 **Costanoa.** Nearly everything about this ecolodge is geared to the great outdoors, but there's nothing rustic about it. After hiking trails through the adjoining 30,000 acres of state park land, you can get a facial or unwind in one of numerous saunas. This is a great place for families, as there is lots of space to run around and many organized activities, such as naturalist-led hikes and guided stargazing. Lodging options include tidy, comfortable rooms in the wood-walled lodge (some with fireplaces), cabins with window seats, and platform tents that have down bedding, heated mattress pads, and doors that lock. If you genuinely want to camp, pitch-your-own tent and RV spaces are available, and have access to the saunas. ⊠ *2001 Rossi Rd., 94060* ☎ *650/879–1100 or 877/262–7848* 🖷 *650/879–2225* ⊕ *www.costanoa.com* ⬎ *38 rooms, 83 bungalows, 12 cabins, 1 suite* ⚒ *Restaurant, BBQs, fans, some in-room data ports, Wi-Fi, some refrigerators, outdoor hot tubs, massage, saunas, spa, mountain bikes, hiking, horseback riding, shop, babysitting, children's programs (ages 5–12), concierge, business services, meeting rooms; no a/c in some rooms, no phones in some rooms, no room TVs* ▭ *AE, D, MC, V* ⦿ *CP.*

$$$ 🔲 **Pescadero Creek Inn.** Set along a tree-lined creek, this modest inn is wonderfully quiet, except for the springtime chorus of frogs. Innkeepers Ken and Penny Donnelly serve a breakfast made with ingredients

from local organic farms or their own gardens. The private, lush yard has many places to sit and relax, including a hammock set between two redwoods that looks down onto the creek. Rooms are small but comfy, and all but one has a claw-foot tub for deep soaking. All the rooms in the house open onto a living room with a fireplace; if privacy is important, splurge on the cottage, which is detached and has its own fireplace. (Because of close quarters, families traveling with children under seven must stay in the cottage.) ⊠ *393 Stage Rd., 94060* ☎ *650/879–1898 or 888/307–1898* 🖷 *650/726–3031* ⊕ *www.pescaderocreekinn.com* 🗗 *3 rooms, 1 cottage* ♻ *No-smoking rooms; no room phones, no room TVs* ▭ *D, MC, V* ❘⊙❘ *BP.*

Half Moon Bay

❹ *16 mi north of Pescadero on Hwy. 1.*

It may be the largest and most visited of the coastal communities, but Half Moon Bay is still by all measures a small town. Looking from the highway you'd hardly even know it was there. Turn onto Main Street, though, and you'll find five blocks of galleries, shops, and cafés, many of which occupy renovated 19th-century buildings. Traditionally this was an agricultural center for local growers of artichokes and other coastal crops, but in recent years it has become a haven for Bay Area retirees. The town comes to life on the third weekend in October, when 250,000 people gather for the **Half Moon Bay Art and Pumpkin Festival** (☎ 650/726–9652).

The 4-mi stretch of **Half Moon Bay State Beach** (⊠ Hwy. 1, west of Main St. ☎ 650/726–8819) is perfect for long walks, kite flying, and picnic lunches, though the 50°F water and dangerous currents make swimming inadvisable. There are three access points, one in Half Moon Bay and two south of town off the highway. To find them, look for road signs that have a picture of footsteps.

Where to Stay & Eat

$$–$$$$ ✕ **Cetrella.** This is the coast at its most dressed up. The restaurant is all polished wood and pressed tablecloths, and hits every gourmet mark—adventurous wine list, sumptuous cheese course, and live jazz Thursday through Saturday. The creative menu (which changes daily) pairs regional produce and fish with choice imported ingredients, like tangy Italian *Burrata di Bufala* cheese. What results is sophisticated but not stuffy, for instance the Catalonian Shellfish stew, which has a tomato, almond, and saffron broth and comes with a lobster cracker and extra napkins. The café has a smaller and cheaper but no less delectable menu. ⊠ *845 Main St.* ☎ *650/726–4090* ⊕ *www.cetrella.com* ▭ *AE, MC, V.*

★ **$$–$$$** ✕ **Pasta Moon.** As one of the best restaurants on the coast between San Francisco and Monterey, Pasta Moon boasts a friendly, laid-back staff and fun, jovial crowd. Local produce flavors the seasonal menu, which includes such highlights as wood-fired-oven pizzas and grilled quail. Though the dining room can get slightly noisy on weekend nights, the food is worth it. ⊠ *315 Main St.* ☎ *650/726–5125* ⊕ *www.pastamoon. com* ▭ *AE, D, DC, MC, V.*

¢–$$ ✕ **Sushi Main Street.** A Japanese surfer and a Californian designer are the creative minds behind this unusual restaurant. The menu's backbone is classic Japanese, but inventive twists abound—such as sushi rolls that incorporate papaya, artichokes, and jalapeños. The dining room is anchored by a standard sushi bar, but is surrounded by Balinese wood carvings. Above the tables hang heavy wooden lamps that cast down soft light for an intimate, sophisticated feeling. Prices here are markedly lower than at most Japanese restaurants in the city. ⊠ *696 Mill St.* ☎ *650/726–6336* ⊕ *www.sushimainst.com* ▭ *AE, MC, V* ⊗ *No lunch Sun.*

$$$$ ✕🏠 **The Ritz-Carlton.** With its enormous and elegantly decorated rooms, secluded oceanfront property, and a staff that waits on guests hand and foot, this golf and spa resort defines opulence. Attention to detail is remarkable, right down to the silver service, china, and 300-thread-count Egyptian cotton sheets. During cocktail hour, view the ocean from the plush conservatory bar, or from under a heavy blanket on an Adirondack chair on the lawn. The main restaurant, Navio ($$$–$$$$), is suitably decadent, with a kitchen that turns local fish and produce into dishes like foie gras with vichyssoise, and slow-cooked sea trout with Moroccan sauce. ⊠ *1 Miramontes Point Rd., 94019* ☎ *650/712–7000 or 800/241–3333* 🖶 *650/712–7070* ⊕ *www.ritzcarlton.com* ⇗ *261 rooms, 22 suites* ⇘ *2 restaurants, room service, in-room safes, some in-room hot tubs, cable TV with movies and video games, some in-room DVDs, in-room broadband, in-room data ports, 2 18-hole golf courses, 6 tennis courts, fitness classes, health club, hair salon, 2 hot tubs, massage, sauna, spa, steam room, bicycles, 2 bars, shops, babysitting, children's programs (ages 4–12), dry cleaning, laundry service, concierge, concierge floor, business services, Internet rooms, meeting rooms, airport shuttle, some pets allowed (fee), no-smoking rooms* ▭ *AE, D, DC, MC, V.*

$$–$$$$ 🏠 **Mill Rose Inn.** Just off Main Street, this B&B is nothing if not flowery. Roses, sweet peas, daisies, and trees heavy with blossoms just about climb over each other for room in the exuberantly colored garden and courtyard. Faux wisteria blooms year-round over the gazebo housing a hot tub. The rooms follow suit, with different colors, patterns, and frills everywhere one looks (beware, minimalists). Extras include fireplaces, cocoa, fruit baskets, and decanters of sherry in each room. Room rates include champagne breakfast and afternoon snacks. ⊠ *615 Mill St., 94019* ☎ *650/726–8750 or 800/900–7673* 🖶 *650/726–3031* ⊕ *www. millroseinn.com* ⇗ *4 rooms, 2 suites* ⇘ *Some in-room hot tubs, refrigerators, cable TV, in-room VCRs, in-room broadband, Wi-Fi, hot tub, massage, meeting room; no a/c, no smoking* ▭ *AE, D, DC, MC, V* ⧄⧉ *BP.*

★ **$$–$$$$** 🏠 **Old Thyme Inn.** The owners of this 1898 Princess Anne Victorian love herbs and flowers. If you have a green thumb of your own, this is the place for you. The gardens alongside the house burst with blossoms year-round, guest rooms are filled with fragrant bouquets, and each room is named after an herb and decorated in its colors. Down comforters and luxury linens make the beds here especially wonderful. ⊠ *779 Main St., 94019* ☎ *650/726–1616 or 800/720–4277* 🖶 *650/726–6394* ⊕ *www. oldthymeinn.com* ⇗ *7 rooms* ⇘ *Some in-room hot tubs, cable TV, in-room VCRs, in-room data ports, Wi-Fi, concierge; no a/c, no smoking* ▭ *AE, D, MC, V* ⧄⧉ *BP.*

Nightlife & the Arts

Every week's musical peak comes Sunday afternoon at the **Bach Dancing and Dynamite Society** (⊠ 311 Mirada, at Miramar Beach ☎ 650/726–4143), which brings in top-notch local jazz and world music bands, as well as classical performers. Concerts have the informal feel of a club but the seating of a concert, making for a party atmosphere with good acoustics. All concerts begin at 4:30 PM, and you can buy your tickets at the door.

Sports

The Bike Works (⊠ 20 Stone Pine Ctr. ☎ 650/726–6708) rents bikes and can provide information on organized rides up and down the coast. If you prefer to go it alone, try the 3-mi bike trail that leads from Kelly Avenue in Half Moon Bay to Mirada Road in Miramar.

Moss Beach

⑤ *7 mi north of Half Moon Bay on Hwy. 1; 20 mi south of San Francisco on Hwy. 1.*

Moss Beach was a busy outpost during Prohibition, when regular shipments of liquid contraband from Canada were unloaded at the secluded beach and hauled off to San Francisco. The town stayed under the radar out of necessity, with only one local hotel and bar (now the Distillery) where Bay Area politicians and gangsters could go for a drink while waiting for their shipments. Today, although it has grown into a cheerful surfing town with charming inns and restaurants, it is still all but invisible from the highway—a good hideaway for those allergic to crowds.

★ The biggest Moss Beach attraction is the **Fitzgerald Marine Reserve** (⊠ California and North Lake Sts. ☎ 650/728–3584), a 3-mi stretch of bluffs and tide pools. Since the reserve was protected in 1969, scientists have discovered 25 new aquatic species here; depending on the tide, you'll most likely find shells, anemones, or starfish.

Just off the coast at Moss Beach is **Mavericks.** When there's a big swell, it's one of the biggest surfing breaks in the world. Waves here have reportedly reached 60 feet in height, and surfers get towed out to them by Jet Skis. The break is a mile offshore, so seeing it from the coast can be tough and requires a challenging hike. The intrepid can get photocopied directions at the Distillery restaurant, then drive 3 mi south for the trail out of **Pillar Point Harbor.** Even if you're not hunting for waves, the harbor is a nice place to wander, with its laid-back restaurants and waters full of fishing boats and sea lions.

Built in 1928 after two horrible shipwrecks on the point, the **Point Montara Lighthouse** still has its original light keeper's quarters from the late 1800s. Gray whales pass this point during their migration from November through April, so bring your binoculars. Visiting hours coincide with morning and afternoon check-in and check-out times at the adjoining youth hostel ($18 to $21 dorm beds, $51 private room). ⊠ *16th St. at Hwy. 1, Montara* ☎ *650/728–7177* ☉ *Daily 8 AM–sunset.*

Where to Stay & Eat

$$$–$$$$ ✕ **The Distillery.** Story has it that this Prohibition-era restaurant still harbors the ghost of a 1930s adulteress, who appears from time to time. In its modern incarnation, the upstairs restaurant is candlelighted and has a good surf-and-turf menu. Things are more casual (and less expensive) at the self-service lunch spot and bar on the deck downstairs. On chilly afternoons couples can cuddle under heavy woolen blankets on swinging benches and sip wine while watching the fog roll in. ✉ *140 Beach Way* ☎ *650/728–5595* ⊕ *www.mossbeachdistillery.com* ▭ *D, DC, MC, V.*

★ **$–$$$** ✕ **Cafe Gibraltar.** Chef-owner Jose Luiz Ugalde is a master of creative dishes, particularly the sweet and spicy (many sauces contain fruits such as apricots and currants). The flavors here are unexpected—calamari baked with cinnamon, Catalan-style pork in grape leaves—and the atmosphere is sensual, with peach walls lighted by flickering candles and booths draped with curtains and lined with pillows. Two miles south of Moss Beach on the east side of the highway, it's a bit hard to find, but worth the hunt. At signs for Pillar Point Harbor, turn inland onto Capistrano, then right onto Alhambra. ✉ *425 Ave. Alhambra, at Palma Ave., El Granada* ☎ *650/560–9039* ⊕ *www.cafegibraltar.com* ▭ *AE, MC, V* ⊘ *Closed Mon. No lunch.*

¢–$ ✕ **Three-Zero Cafe.** This busy restaurant at the tiny Half Moon Bay Airport is a local favorite, especially for weekend breakfasts. The food is standard—eggs and pancakes for breakfast, burgers and panini for lunch—but reliably good. Get a window table, and as you eat, watch two-seater planes take off and land on the runway 20 feet away. ✉ *Hwy. 1, 2 mi south of Moss Beach, El Granada* ☎ *650/728–1411* ⊕ *www.3-zero.com* ▭ *MC, V* ⊘ *No dinner.*

$$$ ▦ **Seal Cove Inn.** Travel writer Karen Brown has written guidebooks to inns all over the world, and this is what she has created at home. Her inn is modern but charming and warm, with all windows looking onto flower gardens and toward cypress trees that border the marine reserve. Rooms have antique bed frames and writing desks, plush mattresses, lounge chairs, and fireplaces. Upstairs rooms have cathedral ceilings and balconies. ✉ *221 Cypress Ave., 94038* ☎ *650/728–4114 or 800/995–9987* 🖷 *650/728–4116* ⊕ *www.sealcoveinn.com* ⟿ *8 rooms, 2 suites* ♨ *Minibars, refrigerators, in-room VCRs, Wi-Fi, meeting room; no a/c* ▭ *AE, D, MC, V* ℺ *BP.*

$$–$$$ ▦ **The Goose and Turrets.** Artifacts from the international travels of innkeepers Raymond and Emily Hoche-Mong fill the shelves of this inn 8 mi north of Half Moon Bay. A full home-cooked breakfast, afternoon goodies, and homemade chocolate truffles are sure to make anyone feel at home. Some rooms have fireplaces. ✉ *835 George St., Montara 94037* ☎ *650/728–5451* 🖷 *650/728–0141* ⊕ *goose.montara.com* ⟿ *5 rooms* ♨ *Wi-Fi, boccie, piano; no a/c, no smoking* ▭ *AE, D, DC, MC, V* ℺ *BP.*

THE INLAND PENINSULA

Much of your first impression of the Inland Peninsula will depend on where and when you enter. Take the 30-mi stretch of U.S. 101 from San Francisco along the eastern side of the Peninsula, and you'll see office complex after shopping center after corporate tower—and you'll likely get caught in horrific morning and evening commuter traffic. On the west side, however, the less crowded Interstate 280 takes you past soul-soothing hills, lakes, and reservoirs.

Woodside

6 *31 mi south of San Francisco via I–280.*

West of Palo Alto, Woodside is a tiny rustic town where weekend warriors stock up on espresso and picnic fare before charging off on their mountain bikes. Blink once and you're past the town center. The main draw here is the wealth of surrounding lush parks and preserves.

★ One of the few great country houses in California that remains intact is **Filoli.** Built between 1915 and 1917 for wealthy San Franciscan William B. Bourn II, it was designed by Willis Polk in a Georgian-revival style, with redbrick walls and a tile roof. The name is Bourn's acronym for "fight, love, live." Alongside the house are 16 acres of formal gardens, which include a sunken garden and a teahouse in the Italian Renaissance style. Guided tours leave several times daily (reservations essential) but during open hours you can tour yourself around at any time. (Note that while the park is open until 3:30, you must arrive before 2:30 to be admitted.) From June through September Filoli is the site of a series of Sunday afternoon jazz concerts, and in December the mansion is festively decorated for a series of holiday events including afternoon teas and Christmas concerts. ⊠ *Cañada Rd. near Edgewood Rd.* ☎ *650/364–8300* ⊕ *www.filoli.org* ⌲ *$12* ⊙ *Mid-Feb.–Oct., Tues.–Sat. 10–3:30, Sun. 11–3:30.*

Where to Eat

$–$$$ ✕ **Woodside Bakery and Café.** The bakery section of this bustling spot is perfect for a cup of hot cocoa and a fresh-baked pastry; the café area in the courtyard is equally pleasant for a glass of wine and a meal. Although the café menu focuses mostly on light pastas and wood-fired pizzas, there are also a few more-substantial entrées such as oven-braised lamb shank and baked Dijon chicken. ⊠ *3052 Woodside Rd.* ☎ *650/ 851–0812* ⊟ *AE, MC, V.*

¢–$$$ ✕ **Bucks in Woodside.** This casual restaurant typifies Silicon Valley's unusual approach to corporate culture. The walls may be decorated with giant plastic alligators and Elvis paintings, but the guy in bike shorts at the next table may well be a high-power tech executive. The menu is a grab bag of crowd pleasers: soups, sandwiches, burgers, and salads. For breakfast there's a "U-do-it" omelet in addition to standard choices. ⊠ *3062 Woodside Rd.* ☎ *650/851–8010* ⊕ *www.buckswoodside.com* ⊟ *AE, D, MC, V.*

Palo Alto

7 *34 mi south of San Francisco via I–280 or U.S. 101.*

Palo Alto's main attraction is the pastoral campus of Stanford University, which encompasses 8,200 acres of grassy hills. The university also serves as an emblem of the city's dual personality: at once cutting-edge techno-savvy and outspoken California liberal. A wander up and down University Avenue and its surrounding side streets will reveal myriad restaurants as well as attractions such as the 1920s-style Stanford Theatre.

Stanford University was former California governor Leland Stanford's horse-breeding farm, and the land is still known as the Farm. Founded in 1885 and opened in 1891, the university occupies a campus designed by Frederick Law Olmsted. Its unique California Mission—Romanesque sandstone buildings, joined by arcades and topped by red-tile roofs—are mixed with newer buildings in variations on Olmstead's style. The 285-foot Hoover Tower is a landmark and a tourist attraction; an elevator ($2) leads to an observation deck that provides sweeping views. Free one-hour **walking tours** (⊠ Serra St., opposite Hoover Tower ☎ 650/723–2560) of the Stanford campus leave daily at 11 and 3:15 from the visitor center in the front hall of Memorial Auditorium. ⊠ *Galvez St. at Serra St.* ☎ *650/723–2300* ⊕ *www.stanford.edu.*

★ **The Iris and B. Gerald Cantor Center for Visual Arts,** one of the most comprehensive and varied art collections in the Bay Area, includes works from pre-Columbian periods through the modern. Included is the world's largest collection—180 pieces—of Rodin sculptures outside Paris, many of them displayed in the outdoor garden (for a spectacular sight, visit these at night during a full moon). Other highlights include a bronze Buddha from the Ming dynasty, wooden masks and carved figurines from 18th- and 19th-century Africa, paintings by Georgia O'Keeffe, and sculpture by Willem de Kooning and Bay Area artist Robert Arneson. The exceptional café has a menu—mostly organic—and clientele that's savvy but unpretentious. You can sit in the airy dining room or on the sunny terrace overlooking the Rodin garden. ⊠ *328 Lomita Dr. and Museum Way, off Palm Dr. at Stanford University* ☎ *650/723–4177* ⊕ *www. museum.stanford.edu* ⊠ *Free* ⊙ *Wed., Fri.–Sun. 11–5, Thurs. 11–8.*

Tucked into a small, heavily wooded plot is the **Papua New Guinea Sculpture Garden,** filled with tall, ornately carved poles, drums, and stones—all created in the 1990s by 10 artists from Papua New Guinea. Complementing them are plants from Melanesia, including a huge, gorgeous Silk Oak tree. Detailed plaques explain the concept and the works. ⊠ *Santa Teresa St. and Lomita Dr., at Stanford University* ⊠ *Free.*

Two-hour tours of the **Stanford Linear Accelerator Center (SLAC)** reveal the workings of the 2-mi-long electron accelerator, which is used by Stanford University scientists for research into elementary particles. Tours are the only way to see the center, and are given sporadically; call for times and reservations. ⊠ *Sand Hill Rd., 3 mi west of central campus* ☎ *650/926–2204* ⊕ *home.slac.stanford.edu.*

Where to Stay & Eat

★ **$$–$$$$** ✕ **Evvia.** This Greek restaurant is no shish-kebab joint. The dining rooms are decorated in the fashion of a (superbly tasteful) Greek-country house, with copper pots and garlic wreaths lining the mantels. The menu is rustic yet elegant, and ranges from the familiar—roast chicken,

Greek salad—to the adventurous—wood-grilled octopus and cabbage leaves stuffed with spiced buffalo. ✉ *420 Emerson St.* ☎ *650/326–0983* ⊕ *www.evvia.net* ⌕ *Reservations essential* ▭ *AE, D, DC, MC, V* ✆ *No lunch weekends.*

★ **$$–$$$$** ✕ **Flea Street Café.** The staff at this romantic restaurant has been on board for decades and takes great care in preparing and serving its food. Ingredients are selected from farmers that owner Jesse Cool knows personally, and the dishes are fresh and inventive: the winter *fritto misto* (batter-fried vegetables) includes Meyer lemon slices; the spring pork chops come with strawberry rhubarb sauce and smoked cheddar grits. ✉ *3607 Alameda de las Pulgas* ☎ *650/854–1226* ⊕ *www.cooleatz.com* ▭ *AE, MC, V* ✆ *Closed Mon. No lunch.*

$–$$$$ ✕ **Zibibbo.** The menu changes seasonally at this two-story Victorian establishment, where you can sit in a garden, a glassed-in atrium, or a dining room. Even the pickiest diner is likely to find something appealing on the unusually long menu, which includes such creative dishes as crispy saffron rice balls with chorizo, and pork loin with a pomegranate-molasses glaze. Vegetarians will be happy here, too; there are many tempting meat-free choices. ✉ *430 Kipling St.* ☎ *650/328–6722* ⊕ *www. restaurantlulu.com* ▭ *AE, DC, MC, V.*

$$–$$$ ✕ **Tamarine.** Bamboo place mats and paper lamps suggest the cultural roots of the Vietnamese cuisine here, but the menu is hardly traditional. Crab wontons are served in a lemongrass and coconut milk consommé; duck is glazed with *yuzu,* garlic, and orange juice. The tatami-mat interior is stylish, as is the perpetual crowd at the door. ✉ *546 University Ave.* ☎ *650/325–8500* ⊕ *www.tamarinerestaurant.com* ▭ *AE, D, MC, V* ✆ *No lunch weekends.*

$ ✕ **JZ Cool Eatery.** Comfort food favoring local organic ingredients—such as homemade meat loaf topped with caramelized onions—is the focus at this spot in downtown Menlo Park. Touches such as butcher-block tables and potato salad disguise the health-conscious bent; you might just forget the food here is supposed to be good for you. ✉ *827 Santa Cruz Ave., Menlo Park* ☎ *650/325–3665* ▭ *MC, V.*

¢ ✕ **Bay Leaf Café.** This place is about as ecofriendly as you can get. Organic ingredients and vegan cuisine are the fare here, and flavors range from grilled nondairy cheese to spicy tofu masala. The restaurant is calm, bright, and quiet, and is a favorite of South Bay herbivores. An added bonus: free Wi-Fi is available. ✉ *520 Ramona St.* ☎ *650/321–7466* ⊕ *www.thebayleafcafe.com* ▭ *MC, V* ✆ *Closed Mon.*

¢ ✕ **Pasta?** The most expensive pasta dish here—and there are many on the menu—is $9. This is good food, plain and simple, made with fresh seasonal ingredients and presented with care. In addition to such standard pasta dishes as salmon fettuccine, there are always a few lighter selections made without heavy oils, cheese, or salt. Naturally, the place does a brisk business with students. ✉ *326 University Ave.* ☎ *650/328–4585* ▭ *AE, MC, V.*

★ **$$$$** ▱ **Garden Court Hotel.** The outside of this boutique hotel looks like an Italian villa, with columns and arches, a dormer roof, and bougainvillea-draped balconies. Inside, though, the feeling is more modern California, with gauzy bed canopies and colorful walls. Some rooms overlook a lush central courtyard, others have fireplaces or four-poster beds; all suites have private terraces. ✉ *520 Cowper St., 94301* ☎ *650/322–9000 or 800/824–9028* 🖷 *650/324–3609* ⊕ *www.gardencourt.com* ⮌ *50 rooms, 12 suites* ♿ *Restaurant, room service, in-room safes, some in-room hot tubs, minibars, refrigerators, cable TV with movies, in-room broadband, in-room data ports, Wi-Fi, gym, bar, laundry service, concierge, business services, Internet room, meeting rooms, some pets allowed (fee), no-smoking rooms* ▭ *AE, D, DC, MC, V* ◉ *CP.*

$$$$ 🏨 **The Westin Palo Alto.** Though it's near the highway and Stanford Shopping Center (in the interest of its business clientele), this upscale hotel is relatively quiet. The elegant decor is tastefully spare, including clean, white beds and simple, Audubon-inspired framed prints. Outside are several inviting courtyards, cooled by arbors and olive trees. The prices can drop by nearly half on weekends. ✉ *675 El Camino Real, 94301* ☎ *650/321–4422 or 800/937–8461* 🖷 *650/321–5522* ⊕ *www. westin.com* ⮌ *162 rooms, 22 suites* ♿ *Restaurant, room service, cable TV with movies and video games, in-room broadband, in-room data ports, pool, gym, hot tub, massage, bar, dry cleaning, laundry facilities, laundry service, concierge, business services, Internet room, meeting rooms, some pets allowed; no smoking* ▭ *AE, D, DC, MC, V.*

$$–$$$$ 🏨 **Stanford Park Hotel.** The interior of this stately hotel takes its cues from an English hunt club, with antiques, oil paintings, and a forest-green color scheme. The grand lobby is focused around a fireplace surrounded by armchairs, and the formal Duck Club restaurant ($$–$$$$) is decorated with paintings of waterfowl. The warm rooms follow suit, featuring tapestry-print bedspreads and plaid armchairs. The staff is delightful. ✉ *100 El Camino Real, 94025* ☎ *650/322–1234 or 800/368–2468* 🖷 *650/322–0975* ⊕ *www.woodsidehotels.com* ⮌ *155 rooms, 8 suites* ♿ *Restaurant, minibars, cable TV with movies and video games, in-room data ports, Wi-Fi, pool, gym, hot tub, bar, lobby lounge, library, dry cleaning, laundry service, concierge, business services, Internet room, meeting rooms; no smoking* ▭ *AE, D, DC, MC, V.*

$$–$$$ 🏨 **Atherton Inn.** Set in a residential neighborhood, this inn is meant to feel like a home. You can lounge by the fireplace in armchairs or sit among flowers on the patio, and the do-it-yourself kitchen is open 24 hours a day. Rooms are simple but plush, with European down pillows and cherrywood armoires. A bonus for those with physical limitations: this B&B also has an elevator. ✉ *1201 W. Selby La., Redwood City 94061* ☎ *650/474–2777 or 800/603–8105* 🖷 *650/474–0733* ⊕ *www.athertoninn.com* ⮌ *5 rooms* ♿ *Some in-room hot tubs, cable TV, in-room DVDs, piano, in-room broadband, Wi-Fi; no smoking* ▭ *AE, D, DC, MC, V* ◉ *BP.*

¢–$$ 🏨 **Cowper Inn.** This former Victorian home in a quiet residential neighborhood is one of the least-expensive-lodging options around, and it's charming to boot. The cozy parlor has a brick fireplace, a piano, and a big window looking out on tree-lined Cowper Street. Breakfast includes homemade muffins and granola and fresh-squeezed orange juice. ✉ *705 Cowper St., 94301* ☎ *650/327–4475* 🖷 *650/329–1703* ⊕ *www. cowperinn.com* ⮌ *14 rooms, 12 with bath* ♿ *Fans, cable TV, in-room VCRs, Wi-Fi, piano; no a/c, no smoking* ▭ *AE, MC, V* ◉ *CP.*

SOUTH BAY
WEST OF SAN JOSE

To many the South Bay is synonymous with Silicon Valley, the center of high-tech research and the corporate headquarters of such giants as Apple, Sun Microsystems, Oracle, and Hewlett-Packard. But Silicon Valley is more a state of mind than a place—it's an attitude held by the legions of software engineers, programmers, and computerphiles who call the area home. That home is becoming increasingly visitor-friendly; within the sprawl are appealing towns whose histories stretch back centuries, a thriving arts scene, and shops and restaurants to satisfy the most discerning tastes.

Santa Clara

❽ *40 mi south of San Francisco on Hwy. 101.*

Santa Clara has two major attractions at opposite ends of the sightseeing spectrum: Mission Santa Clara de Asis, founded in 1777, and Paramount's Great America, northern California's answer to Disneyland. Although many visitors head straight to the amusement park, Santa Clara has plenty of history and is worthy of a visit—despite its ubiquitous shopping malls and sterile business parks.

Santa Clara University, founded in 1851 by Jesuits, was California's first college. The campus's **de Saisset Art Gallery and Museum** shows a permanent collection that includes California mission artifacts and gold rush–era pieces, California-theme artwork, and contemporary Bay Area art, especially prints. ⊠ *500 El Camino Real* ☎ *408/554–4528* ⊕ *www. scu.edu/desaisset* 🎫 *Free* ⊙ *Tues.–Sun. 11–4.*

In the center of Santa Clara University's campus is the **Mission Santa Clara de Asis,** the first of California's original missions to honor a female saint. In 1926 the mission chapel was destroyed by fire. Roof tiles of the current building, a reproduction of the original, were salvaged from earlier structures, which dated from the 1790s and 1820s. Early adobe walls and a spectacular rose garden with 4,500 roses—many of the varieties classified as antique—remain intact as well. Part of the wooden Memorial Cross, from 1777, is set in front of the church. ⊠ *500 El Camino Real* ☎ *408/554–4023* ⊕ *www.scu.edu/visitors/mission* 🎫 *Free* ⊙ *Self-guided tours daily 1–sundown.*

☾ At the gigantic theme park **Paramount's Great America,** each section recalls a familiar part of North America: Hometown Square, Yukon Territory, Yankee Harbor, or County Fair. Popular attractions include the Drop Zone Stunt Tower and a *Top Gun* movie-theme roller coaster, whose cars travel along the outside of a 360-degree loop track. You can get to the park via Valley Transit Authority, Caltrain, and BART. ⊠ *Great America Pkwy. between U.S. 101 and Rte. 237, 6 mi north of San Jose* ☎ *408/988–1776* ⊕ *www.pgathrills.com* 🎫 *$51.99, parking $10*

✆ *Apr., May, Sept., and Oct. weekends; June–Aug., daily; opens 10 AM, closing times vary* ☱ *AE, D, MC, V.*

The **Carmelite Monastery** is a fine example of Spanish-ecclesiastical architecture. Built in 1917, it's on the grounds of a mission-era ranch crossed by shady walkways and dotted with benches perfect for quiet contemplation. ⊠ *1000 Lincoln St.* ☎ *408/296–8412* ⊕ *members.aol.com/ santaclaracarmel* ☒ *Free* ☉ *Grounds daily 6:30–4:15.*

Skylights cast natural light for viewing the exhibitions in the **Triton Museum of Art.** A permanent collection of 19th- and 20th-century sculpture by Bay Area artists is displayed in the garden, which you can see through a curved-glass wall at the rear of the building. Indoor galleries present excellent, eclectic shows of contemporary Native American work. ⊠ *1505 Warburton Ave.* ☎ *408/247–3754* ⊕ *www.tritonmuseum. org* ☒ *$2 suggested donation* ☉ *Fri.–Wed. 11–5, Thurs. 11–9.*

The **Harris-Lass Historic Museum** is built on Santa Clara's last farmstead. A restored house, summer kitchen, and barn convey what life was like on the farm from the early 1900s through the 1930s. Guided tours take place every half hour until 3:30. ⊠ *1889 Market St.* ☎ *408/249–7905* ☒ *$3* ☉ *Weekends noon–4.*

Where to Stay & Eat

$$–$$$$ ✕ **Birk's.** Silicon Valley's businesspeople come to this sophisticated American grill to unwind. High-tech sensibilities will appreciate the modern open kitchen and streamlined, multilevel dining area—yet the menu is traditional, strong on steaks and chops. An oyster bar adds a lighter element, as do the simply prepared but high-quality organic vegetable dishes such as garlic mashed potatoes and creamed spinach. ⊠ *3955 Freedom Circle, at Hwy. 101 and Great America Pkwy.* ☎ *408/980–6400* ⊕ *www. birksrestaurant.com* ☱ *AE, D, DC, MC, V* ☉ *No lunch weekends.*

$–$$ ✕ **Mio Vicino.** Mio's is a small, bare-bones, checkered-tablecloth Italian bistro in Old Santa Clara. The menu includes a long list of classic and contemporary pastas—and if you don't see what you want on the menu, just ask. The house specialties are shellfish pasta and chicken cannelloni. ⊠ *1290 Benton St.* ☎ *408/241–9414* ⊕ *www.miovicino-santaclara. com* ☱ *MC, V* ☉ *No lunch weekends.*

$–$$$ ⊞ **Embassy Suites.** This upper-end chain hotel attracts Silicon Valley business travelers—but because the rates plummet on the weekends, it's even better suited to families bound for Paramount's Great America. Nearly all the accommodations here are two-room suites, and rates include cooked-to-order breakfasts and evening beverages. ⊠ *2885 Lakeside Dr., 95054* ☎ *408/496–6400 or 800/362–2779* 🖷 *408/988–7529* ⊕ *www.embassy-suites.com* ⤳ *17 rooms, 240 suites* ♿ *Restaurant, room service, refrigerators, cable TV with movies and video games, in-room data ports, Wi-Fi, pool, gym, hot tub, bar, shop, dry cleaning, laundry facilities, laundry service, business services, Internet room, meeting rooms, airport shuttle, no-smoking rooms* ☱ *AE, D, DC, MC, V* ⑩ *BP.*

¢–$ ⊞ **Madison Street Inn.** At this Queen Anne Victorian, complimentary afternoon refreshments and a full breakfast are served on a brick garden patio with a bougainvillea-draped trellis. The inn feels like a private home, with its green-and-red-trimmed facade and individually styled rooms that range from homey to fancy. ✉ *1390 Madison St., 95054* ☎ *408/249–5541* 🖷 *408/249–6676* ⊕ *www.madisonstreetinn.com* ⤴ *5 rooms, 3 with bath, 1 suite* ⚶ *Some fans, some microwaves, some refrigerators, some cable TV with movies, some in-room DVDs, in-room broadband, Wi-Fi, pool, hot tub, sauna, bicycles, library, dry cleaning, laundry service, Internet room, meeting room, some pets allowed (fee); no a/c in some rooms, no TV in some rooms, no smoking* ▭ *AE, D, DC, MC, V* ⏦ *BP.*

Campbell

⑨ *6 mi southwest of Santa Clara on Hwy. 17.*

Buried in the heart of metropolitan Santa Clara County 10 minutes south of San Jose on Highway 17, the town of Campbell has a small-town center with a friendly neighborhood mood. Within a couple of blocks are the city hall, an old fruit cannery that now houses offices, and a handful of galleries, boutiques, and restaurants.

On Campbell's Civic Center Plaza, the Tudor-revival **Ainsley House** gives a glimpse of South Bay life in the 1920s and '30s, when it was owned by the valley's founding canner. The structure was moved in one piece from its previous location a half mile away, after descendants of the owners donated it to the city for preservation. Admission includes access to the Campbell Historical Museum down the street. ✉ *300 Grant St.* ☎ *408/866–2119* 🏷 *$6 for Ainsley House* ⊙ *Guided tours Thurs.–Sun. noon–4; gardens daily sunrise–sunset.*

Committed to exploring themes in Americana, the **Campbell Historical Museum** presents exhibits on life in Silicon Valley in the age before computers. ✉ *51 N. Central Ave.* ☎ *408/866–2119* 🏷 *Museum $2* ⊙ *Thurs.–Sun. noon–4.*

Where to Stay & Eat

¢–$ ✕ **Chez Sovan.** This Cambodian jewel is a departure from the average South Bay restaurant—and a reliable one. The noodle dishes, grilled meats, and curries are all excellently flavored. Specialties of the house are the spring rolls and the rice noodles in tamarind sauce. ✉ *2425 S. Bascom Ave.* ☎ *408/371–7711* ▭ *AE, MC, V.*

¢ ✕ **Orchard Valley Coffee.** At this favorite local hangout, the large-pane front windows open wide on spring and summer days. Despite the propensity of laptops (taking advantage of free Wi-Fi), the café keeps its cozy feel with well-worn pillows and benches you can feel comfortable putting your feet on. The menu includes light meals, salads, soups, and pastries. ✉ *349 E. Campbell Ave.* ☎ *408/374–2115* ▭ *AE, MC, V.*

$–$$ 🛏 **Campbell Inn.** There are plenty of reasons to stay 10 minutes from downtown San Jose at this creek-side inn. You can play tennis, swim in the pool, ride one of the inn's bicycles on a nearby trail, or simply relax in the lobby, which has large, comfortable chairs and a fireplace. Suites have whirlpool tubs and saunas, and all room rates include a complimentary breakfast buffet. ✉ *675 E. Campbell Ave., 95008* ☎ *408/374–4300 or 800/582–4449* 🖷 *408/379–0695* ⊕ *www.campbell-inn.*

com ↪ *85 rooms, 10 suites* ♨ *Some in-room hot tubs, refrigerators, cable TV, Wi-Fi, tennis court, pool, outdoor hot tub, bicycles, airport shuttle, no-smoking rooms* ▭ *AE, D, DC, MC, V* ⑩ *BP.*

Saratoga

❿ *12 mi southwest of Santa Clara on Hwy. 85.*

A 10-mi detour southwest of San Jose's urban core puts you in the heart of Saratoga, at the foot of the Santa Cruz Mountains. Once an artists' colony, the town is now home to many Silicon Valley CEOs, whose mansions dot the hillsides. Spend a slow-paced afternoon exploring Big Basin Way, the ⅓-mi main drag of the Village, as the downtown area is locally known. Here you'll find antiques stores, galleries, spas, and a handful of worthwhile restaurants.

Just up the hill from town, the **Saratoga Historical Museum** has a small but interesting collection of photographs and artifacts pertaining to the history of Saratoga and the surrounding mountains. You can dig through their extensive research files for information on the Ohlone Indians, fruit orchards, and more. ✉ *20450 Saratoga–Los Gatos Rd.* ☎ *408/867–4311* ✑ *Free* ☉ *Fri.–Sun. 1–4.*

★ Built in 1912 by former governor James Phelan, **Villa Montalvo** is a striking white mansion presiding over an expansive lawn. You can picnic on the lawn amidst sculptures or stroll through the gallery, whose changing exhibits feature work by local artists and artists-in-residence. Additional draws are a gift shop and 175-acre park with hiking trails, as well as a summer concert series and year-round literary events. ✉ *15400 Montalvo Rd.* ☎ *408/961–5800* ⊕ *www.villamontalvo.org* ✑ *Free* ☉ *Park Apr.–Sept., Mon.–Thurs. 8–7, Fri.–Sun. 9–5; Oct.–Mar., weekdays 8–5, weekends 9–5. Gallery Wed.–Sat. 1–4, Sun. 10–4.*

★ For a quick driving tour of the hills with their sweeping valley views, drive south out of Saratoga on Big Basin Way, which is **Scenic Highway 9.** The road leads into the Santa Cruz Mountains, all the way to the coast at the city of Santa Cruz. But you can take in some great views about 1½ mi out of town by taking a right on Pierce Road and driving out to the **Mountain Winery.** Built by Paul Masson in 1905 and now listed on the National Register of Historic Places, it's constructed of masonry and oak to resemble a French-country château. The winery still produces wines of several varietals, and has a tasting room (☎ *408/741–2822* ☉ *Wed.–Sun., 1–4).* It also hosts winemaker dinners and a summer concert series. Walking tours are available for free if you call in advance.

Where to Stay & Eat

$$$–$$$$
Fodor's Choice
★

✕ **Sent Sovi.** Chef Josiah Slone picks the best local produce and natural meats, then creates dishes around them that let the ingredients speak for themselves. The French-inspired menu might include porcini mushroom–dusted scallops with freshly shelled peas and lemon-infused beets with pistachios. With copper-panel walls, wooden floors, and candlelight, the dining room is among the most formal in town. Order 48 hours in advance to get the decadent grand tasting menu (from $125 per person), a multicourse feast designed specifically according to your desires. ✉ *14583 Big Basin Way* ☎ *408/867–3110* ⊕ *www.sentsovi.com* ⌁ *Reservations essential* ⊟ *AE, MC, V* ⊘ *Closed Mon. No lunch.*

★ **$–$$$** ✕ **The Basin.** Organic produce, meats, and fresh fish are the starting points for this long, imaginative menu of American cuisine. Aside from a few flights of fancy, familiar favorites—pork and beans, beet salad, spaghetti carbonara—take on a personality all their own. The dim, clubby dining room and bar feels more like Manhattan than small-town California. ✉ *14572 Big Basin Way* ☎ *408/867–1906* ⊕ *www.thebasin.com* ⊟ *AE, DC, MC, V* ⊘ *No lunch.*

$$$–$$$$ ▦ **Inn at Saratoga.** This European-style inn is 20 minutes from San Jose, but its aura of calm makes it feel far from the Silicon Valley buzz. The furnishings are rather lackluster—reminiscent of an upscale motel—but each room's view of a creek makes for a relaxing stay. In the evening wine and hors d'oeuvres are set out in the cozy lobby, and although modern business conveniences are available, they are discreetly hidden. ✉ *20645 4th St., 95070* ☎ *408/867–5020 or 800/543–5020* 🖷 *408/741–0981* ⊕ *www.innatsaratoga.com* ⇥ *41 rooms, 4 suites* ⌂ *Some in-room hot tubs, refrigerators, cable TV, in-room VCRs, in-room broadband, in-room data ports, Wi-Fi, exercise equipment, babysitting, dry cleaning, laundry service, business services, meeting room; no smoking* ⊟ *AE, DC, MC, V* �'◯| *CP.*

$–$$ ▦ **Saratoga Oaks Lodge.** This is the best place to stay in town. The towering namesake trees shade the property and provide a spot for birds to sing. Furnishings are neat and classic, with wooden armoires and steam showers in most rooms. Up the hill in back are several bungalows, the patios of which look onto a soothing fountain. ✉ *14626 Big Basin Way, 95070* ☎ *408/867–3307 or 888/867–3588* 🖷 *408/867–6765* ⊕ *www.saratogaoakslodge.com* ⇥ *15 rooms, 5 suites* ⌂ *Microwaves, refrigerators, cable TV, some in-room DVDs, in-room VCRs, in-room data ports, Wi-Fi; no smoking* ⊟ *AE, D, MC, V* �'◯| *CP.*

SAN JOSE

For years San Jose has played second fiddle to its more celebrated cousin just up the highway, but in truth this city of nearly 1 million people has a lot to offer. The city has nationally recognized art and science museums, and its own ballet and repertory companies. It's also a city of great diversity, for no ethnic group holds the majority here. Residents speak a total of 46 languages, and alongside machines vending the *San Jose Mercury News*, you'll find *Nuevo Mundo* and the *Chinese World Journal*. The city is also one of the safest in the country, with the lowest crime rate for any city of more than 500,000 people.

The diversity extends to San Jose's various neighborhoods. Downtown has wide streets and several parks for enjoying the usually warm weather from March to October. The SoFA (South of First Area) district, along 1st and 2nd streets south of San Carlos Avenue, is the best spot for nightlife, with its numerous music clubs. Japantown, around Jackson and Taylor streets between 4th and 6th streets, has modern shops and restaurants and many historical buildings. Willow Glen (Lincoln Avenue between Willow and Minnesota streets) is a place of boutiques, small cafés, and tree-lined streets—a welcome counter to downtown's urbanity.

Downtown can be easily explored on foot, and Guadalupe River Park, a 3-mi belt of trees and gardens, connects downtown with the Children's Discovery Museum to the south. (A walking tour of downtown San Jose is detailed in a brochure available from the Convention and Visitors Bureau.) A 21-mi light-rail system links downtown to the business district and Paramount's Great America to the north, but you will still need a car to get to such sights as the Egyptian Museum and the Winchester Mystery House.

Downtown San Jose & Vicinity

4 mi east of Santa Clara on Hwy. 82; 55 mi south of San Francisco on Hwy. 101 or I–280.

What to See

⑭ **Cathedral Basilica of St. Joseph.** This Renaissance-style cathedral embodies the idea of resurrection: it is the fifth church of St. Joseph built in San Jose (the fourth on this site). All its predecessors have perished in earthquakes and other natural disasters. The original adobe church began serving the residents of the pueblo of San Jose in 1803. The current and longest-standing incarnation, built in 1877, is a grand cathedral with stained-glass windows and murals. The basilica hosts musical performances by excellent jazz and chorale groups. ⊠ *80 S. Market St.* ☎ *408/283–8100* ⊕ *www.stjosephcathedral.org.*

☾ ⌐ ⑪ **Children's Discovery Museum of San Jose.** You can't miss this angular purple building that seems to rise from the creek across from the convention center. Exhibits here explore the world of how things work, from why water gushes to why springs go *boing.* Everything is hands-on, so kids can blow gigantic bubbles, dress up in old-time clothes, or climb on the oversize animal sculptures outside while tired parents picnic on the lawn. ⊠ *180 Woz Way, at Auzerais St.* ☎ *408/298–5437* ⊕ *www. cdm.org* ⊡ *$7* ⊙ *Tues.–Sat. 10–5, Sun. noon–5.*

⑯ **Fallon House.** San Jose's seventh mayor, Thomas Fallon, built this Victorian mansion in 1855. The house's period-decorated rooms can be viewed on a 90-minute tour that includes the Peralta Adobe and a screening of a video about the two houses. ⊠ *175 W. St. John St.* ☎ *408/993–8300* ⊕ *www.historysanjose.org* ⊡ *Free* ⊙ *Guided tours weekends noon–5, last tour at 3:30.*

☾ ⑫ **Guadalupe River Park.** This downtown park includes the Arena Green, next to the sports arena, with a carousel, children's playground, and artwork honoring five champion figure skaters from the area. The River Park path, which stretches for 3 mi, starts at the Children's Discovery Museum and runs north, ending at the Arena Green. The ranger station at Arena Green (open weekdays 8:30 to 5:30) has interpretive programs, brochures, and maps of the park. ⊠ *345 W. Santa Clara St.* ☎ *408/ 277–5904* ⊕ *www.grpg.org* ⊡ *Free.*

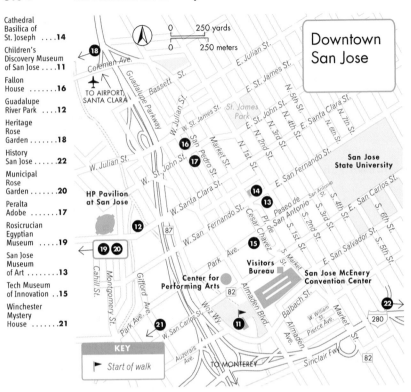

Downtown
San Jose

Heritage Rose Garden. The newer of the city's two rose gardens has won national acclaim for its 5,000 rosebushes and trees. This quiet, 4-acre retreat has ample benches and is alongside the Historic Orchard, which has fruit trees indigenous to the Santa Clara Valley. The garden is northwest of downtown, near the airport. ⊠ *Taylor and Spring Sts.* ☎ *408/ 298–7657* ⊕ *www.heritageroses.us* ✉ *Free* ☉ *Daily dawn–dusk.*

History San Jose. Occupying 25 acres of Kelley Park, this outdoor "museum" highlights the history of San Jose and the Santa Clara Valley. You can see 28 historic and reconstructed buildings, hop an antique trolley, observe letterpress printing, and grab a snack at O'Brien's Ice Cream Parlor. On weekdays admission is free, but the buildings are closed except for the galleries, Pacific Hotel, and the candy store. ⊠ *1650 Senter Rd., at Phelan Ave.* ☎ *408/287–2290* ⊕ *www.historysanjose.org* ✉ *Free* ☉ *Tues.–Sun. noon–5; call for weekend tour times.*

Ira F. Brilliant Center for Beethoven Studies. This museum holds endless scores of music—hand-written by the composer—as well as thousands of books and a 19th-century Viennese fortepiano. In true rock star fashion, there's also a lock of Beethoven's hair. ⊠ *Dr. Martin Luther King Jr. Library One Washington Sq. San Jose* ☎ *408/808–2058* ⌨ *Free* ⊙ *Mon., Tues., and Thurs. 11–6, Wed. 11–8, Fri. 11–5, Sat. 1–5.*

⓴ Municipal Rose Garden. Installed in 1931, the Municipal Rose Garden is one of several outstanding green spaces in the city's urban core—and certainly the most fragrant. West of downtown San Jose you'll find 5½ acres of roses here, with 4,000 shrubs and trees in 189 well-labeled beds, as well as walkways, fountains, and trellises. Some of the neighboring homes in the Rose Garden district date to the time of the city's founding. ⊠ *Naglee and Dana Aves.* ☎ *408/277–2757* ⊕ *www.sjparks.org* ⌨ *Free* ⊙ *Daily 8 AM–sunset.*

⓱ Peralta Adobe. California pepper trees shade the last remaining structure (circa 1797) from the Pueblo de Guadalupe, the original settlement from which the modern city of San Jose was born. This whitewashed, two-room house has been furnished to show what home life was like during the Spanish occupation and the Mexican-rancho era. ⊠ *184 W. St. John St.* ☎ *408/993–8300* ⊕ *www.historysanjose.org* ⌨ *Free* ⊙ *Guided tours weekends noon–5, last tour 3:30.*

Phantom Galleries. Free art abounds in the storefronts of downtown San Jose courtesy of this program. Exhibits rotate bimonthly in empty storefronts beginning at the corner of San Fernando Street and South 1st Street, down to Santa Clara Street. Call to find out about the latest installations. ☎ *408/271–5151* ⊕ *www.populuspresents.com.*

⓳ Rosicrucian Egyptian Museum. Owned by the Rosicrucian Order (a modern-day group devoted to the study of metaphysics for self-improvement), this museum exhibits the West Coast's largest collection of Egyptian and Babylonian antiquities, including mummies, and an underground reproduction of a rock tomb. The planetarium gives related presentations daily. The complex, 3 mi from downtown, is surrounded by a garden filled with palms, papyrus, and other plants recalling ancient Egypt. ⊠ *1342 Naglee Ave., at Park Ave.* ☎ *408/947–3635* ⊕ *www.egyptianmuseum. org* ⌨ *$9* ⊙ *Weekdays 10–5, weekends 11–6.*

★ ⓭ San Jose Museum of Art. Housed in a former post-office building, this museum doesn't attempt to compete with the larger, swankier art museums in San Francisco. Instead, it does its own thing. The permanent collection of paintings, sculpture, photography, and large-scale multimedia installations is solid, with an emphasis on cutting-edge California and Latino artists. The massive Dale Chihuly glass sculpture hanging above the lobby hints at the appreciation for futuristic, high-tech pieces. ⊠ *110 S. Market St.* ☎ *408/294–2787* ⊕ *www.sjmusart.org* ⌨ *Free* ⊙ *Tues.–Sun. 11–5.*

San Jose Institute of Contemporary Art. The best local art in San Jose is at this white-walled gallery, which shows groundbreaking work by Bay Area artists. ⊠ *451 S. 1st St.* ☎ *408/283–8155* ⊕ *www.sjica.org* ⌨ *Free* ⊙ *Tues., Wed., and Fri. 10–5, Thurs. 10–8, Sat. noon–5.*

(C) **⑮ Tech Museum of Innovation.** Designed by renowned architect Ricardo

FodorśChoice Legorreta of Mexico City, this museum of technology is both high-tech

★ and hands-on. Exhibits allow you to create an action movie in a video-editing booth, solve the story behind a crime scene using real forensic techniques, and talk with a roaming robot named Zaza. Another highlight is the 299-seat Hackworth IMAX Dome Theater. ⊠ *201 S. Market St., at Park Ave.* ☎ *408/294–8324* ⊕ *www.thetech.org* ▣ *Museum $10, IMAX $10, combination ticket $16* ☉ *Tues.–Sun., 10–5.*

(C) **㉑ Winchester Mystery House.** Convinced that spirits would harm her if construction on her house ever stopped, the late Sarah Winchester kept carpenters working for 38 years to create this bizarre 160-room labyrinth. Today the 19th-century house (which is on the National Register of Historic Places) is a favorite family attraction, and though the grounds are no longer overgrown, the place retains an air of mystery. You can explore the house on the 65-minute mansion tour or the 50-minute behind-the-scenes tour (these depart every 20–30 minutes); each Friday the 13th there's also a special nighttime flashlight tour. ⊠ *525 S. Winchester Blvd., between Stevens Creek Blvd. and I–280* ☎ *408/247–2101* ⊕ *www. winchestermysteryhouse.com* ▣ *Mansion tour $21.95, behind-the-scenes tour $18.95, combination ticket $26.95* ☉ *Oct. 8–Apr., daily 9–5; May–mid-June., Sun.–Thurs. 9–5, Fri. and Sat. 9–7; mid-June–early Sept., daily 9–7, early Sept.–Oct. 7, Sun.–Thurs. 9–5, Fri. and–Sat., 9–7.*

Where to Stay & Eat

★ **$$$–$$$$** ✗ **Emile's Restaurant.** In a city that's gone through numerous changes, Emile's has remained a solidly popular downtown dining spot for decades. The menu, which focuses on European-influenced California cuisine, is given a slightly decadent edge by Swiss chef-owner Emile Mooser: duck à l'orange is flavored with Grand Marnier; spinach salad comes with scallops and a bacon-honey vinaigrette. Half portions allow you to create your own tasting menu. ⊠ *545 S. 2nd St.* ☎ *408/289–1960* ⊕ *www.emiles. com* ▭ *AE, D, DC, MC, V* ☉ *Closed Sun. and Mon. No lunch.*

$$–$$$$ ✗ **Menara Moroccan Restaurant.** The delicious cumin- and coriander-spice cuisine is only part of what makes dining here an exotic experience. Arched entryways, lazily spinning ceiling fans and a tile fountain all evoke a glamorous Moroccan palace. If sitting on jewel-tone cushions and feasting on lamb with honey, delicately spiced chicken kebabs, or hare with paprika doesn't make you feel like you've traveled to a distant land, then just wait until the belly dancers arrive for their nightly performance. ⊠ *41 E. Gish Rd.* ☎ *408/453–1983* ⊕ *www.menara41. com* ▭ *AE, D, MC, V* ☉ *No lunch.*

$$–$$$$ ✗ **Paolo's.** This Italian restaurant is run by the fourth generation of a family that arrived in California in 1917. Its food, however, is firmly in the 21st century. The seasonal menu might include lamb chops complimented by fig, fennel, and sweet pepper, or duck mousse with essence of truffles; fresh pasta is made daily. Italophiles will love the wine list, which has more than 450 vintages—most of them, naturally, from the mother country. ⊠ *333 W. San Carlos St.* ☎ *408/294–2558* ⊕ *www.paolosrestaurant.com* ▭ *AE, D, DC, MC, V* ☉ *Closed Sun. No lunch Sat.*

11

$$–$$$$ ✕ **7 Restaurant & Lounge.** People come to this flashy restaurant and lounge as much to eat as to feel glamorous at the tight bar and in the high-ceiling, industrial-chic dining room. Case in point: there are only five entrées on the menu. Better to choose from the long list of small plates, share with friends, and get ready to people-watch. Crab cakes served with Napa cabbage slaw and black-bean vinaigrette is a top choice, as is the pasta with prosciutto, asparagus, and smoked mozzarella. ⊠ *754 the Alameda* ☎ *408/280–1644* ⊕ *www.7restaurant.us* ▤ *AE, D, DC, MC, V* ⊘ *Closed Sun. No lunch Sat.*

$–$$$ ✕ **Henry's World-Famous Hi-Life.** Many locals agree this is the best steak house in town. But unlike the shiny new restaurants downtown, this place has character (and grit) instead of glitz, built over 43 years in business. The dining room's decoration is a picket fence running along the wall. There are no menus; dinner selections are written on the wall, and only the prices have changed over the years. You can choose from pork chops, ribs, or chicken, but really, the whole point is to order one of the nine varieties of steak that have made this place "famous." ⊠ *301 W. St. John St.* ☎ *408/295–5414* ⊕ *www.henryshilife.com* ▤ *AE, MC, V* ⊘ *No lunch Sat.–Mon.*

★ **$–$$$** ✕ **71 Saint Peter.** This is among the prettiest restaurants in San Jose: ceramic tile floors, skylights, and rough wood walls give it the feel of an elegant farmhouse. Chef Mark Tabak prepares each dish carefully— you can even watch him do so in the glass-walled kitchen, which takes an unpretentious center stage here. Try the five-part tasting menu, which changes often to reflect the best of local ingredients. In summer, the menu might include a Mission fig strudel with dolce gorgonzola and duck prosciutto, or honey-lavender grilled apricots for dessert. ⊠ *71 N. San Pedro St.* ☎ *408/971–8523* ▤ *AE, D, DC, MC, V* ⊘ *Closed Sun. No lunch Sat.*

★ **¢–$$** ✕ **Citronelle.** If you can endure the distance from downtown (6 mi), you'll find that this Vietnamese restaurant is a jewel in the rough of strip malls. A bouquet of flowers from the owner's garden graces each table, and the sophisticated, seasonal menu is based on natural meats and organic produce. Specialties include the traditional clay-pot catfish and the chef's very own lemongrass pork chop. ⊠ *826 S. Winchester Blvd.* ☎ *408/244–2528* ⊕ *www.citronellemv.com* ▤ *MC, V.*

¢–$ ✕ **Tacqueria la Mordida.** At this authentic tacqueria, choices range from standard burritos to such house creations as Shrimp à la Diabla. Portions are huge across the board. Bright yellow decor, Mexican pop music, and a weekend margarita bar complete the experience. ⊠ *86 N. Market St.* ☎ *408/298–9357* ▤ *MC, V.*

¢ ✕ **Tofoo Com Chay.** This bare-bones vegetarian restaurant is a favorite of college students and local hipsters. There's no table service—order at the counter from a selection of sandwiches and simple entrées—but the food is reliably good, as well as super cheap. ⊠ *388 E. Santa Clara St.* ☎ *408/286–6335* ▤ *No credit cards* ⊘ *Closed Sun.*

¢ ✕ **La Villa.** People come from all over the South Bay to take home the house-made ravioli that made this deli locally famous. You can taste them or any of the other Italian specialties for lunch at tables outside on the street. This is also a good place for picnic supplies such as deli salads, cheese, and sausage. ⊠ *1319 Lincoln Ave.* ☎ *408/295–7851* 🖃 *AE, MC, V* ☙ *Closed Sun. and Mon.*

$$–$$$$ 🏨 **The Fairmont.** This downtown gem is as opulent as its sister property in San Francisco. Get lost in the lavish lobby sofas under dazzling chandeliers, or dip your feet in the 4th-floor pool, which is surrounded by exotic palms. Rooms have every imaginable comfort, from down pillows and custom-designed comforters to oversize bath towels changed twice a day. ⊠ *170 S. Market St., 95113* ☎ *408/998–1900 or 800/257–7544* 🖷 *408/287–1648* ⊕ *www.fairmont.com* ⇗ *718 rooms, 77 suites* ♨ *3 restaurants, room service, some in-room safes, minibars, cable TV with movies, in-room broadband, in-room data ports, Wi-Fi, pool, health club, hair salon, massage, steam room, sauna, bar, lobby lounge, dry cleaning, laundry service, concierge, business services, Internet room, meeting rooms, some pets allowed (fee); no-smoking* 🖃 *AE, D, DC, MC, V.*

$$–$$$$ 🏨 **Hotel Montgomery.** *Wall Street Journal* meets *Wallpaper* magazine is the
Fodor$Choice   feel at this boutique hotel. It's the hippest place to stay in San Jose—evi-
   ★   dent even as you enter the lobby through an outdoor lounge complete with martinis, boccie courts, and either hip-hop or soul music playing at all times. The rooms are stylish, with an emphasis on texture rather than bright color: faux-fur throw pillows, woven wool blankets, leather headboards, and even leather-texture wallpaper. The restaurant, Paragon ($–$$$), has low lighting and a thriving cocktail bar. But for all the hipness, no congeniality is sacrificed. The staff is young and friendly, and little perks like the CD lending library give the hotel a welcoming vibe. ⊠ *211 S. 1st St., 95113* ☎ *408/282–8800 or 866/823–0530* 🖷 *408/282–8850* ⊕ *www. montgomeryhotelsj.com* ⇗ *80 rooms, 6 suites* ♨ *Restaurant, room service, in-room safes, minibars, refrigerators, cable TV with movies, in-room broadband, in-room data ports, Wi-Fi, exercise equipment, boccie, bar, dry cleaning, laundry service, concierge, business services, Internet room, meeting rooms, no-smoking floors* 🖃 *AE, DC, MC, V.*

★ **$–$$$**   🏨 **Hotel De Anza.** This lushly appointed art-deco hotel has hand-painted ceilings, a warm coral-and-green color scheme, and an enclosed terrace with towering palms and dramatic fountains. Business travelers will appreciate the many amenities, including a full-service business center and personal voice-mail services—not to mention the fireside lounge, where jazz bands often play. ⊠ *233 W. Santa Clara St., 95113* ☎ *408/ 286–1000 or 800/843–3700* 🖷 *408/286–0500* ⊕ *www.hoteldeanza.com* ⇗ *90 rooms, 10 suites* ♨ *Restaurant, some in-room hot tubs, minibars, refrigerators, cable TV with movies, in-room VCRs, in-room broadband, in-room data ports, Wi-Fi, exercise equipment, bar, dry cleaning, laundry service, concierge, business services, Internet room, no-smoking floors* 🖃 *AE, D, DC, MC, V.*

Nightlife & the Arts

NIGHTLIFE   **Agenda** (⊠ 399 S. 1st St. ☎ 408/380–3042) is one of the most popular nightspots downtown, with a restaurant on the main floor, a bar upstairs, and a nightclub on the bottom floor.

In the burgeoning SoFA district, there are several dance clubs as well as trendy **South Firstt Billiards** (⊠ 420 S. 1st St. ☎ 408/294–7800).

THE ARTS The **Center for Performing Arts** (✉ 255 Almaden Blvd. ☎ 408/277–3900) is the city's main performance venue. **American Musical Theatre of San Jose** (☎ 408/453–7108) presents a half-dozen musicals per year. **Ballet San Jose Silicon Valley** (☎ 408/288–2800) performs from October through April. **San Jose Repertory Theatre** (✉ 101 Paseo de San Antonio ☎ 408/367–7255) occupies a contemporary four-story, 528-seat theater, dubbed the Blue Box because of its angular blue exterior. **City Lights Theater Co.** (✉ 529 S. 2nd St. ☎ 408/295–4200) presents progressive and traditional programs in an intimate 99-seat theater.

The 17,496-seat **HP Pavilion at San Jose** (✉ Santa Clara St. at Autumn St. ☎ 408/287–9200), looks like a giant hothouse, with its glass entrance, shining metal armor, and skylight ceiling. The building is known locally as the Shark Tank (because it's home to the National Hockey League's **San Jose Sharks**), but the arena also hosts rock concerts and other major events.

Sports & the Outdoors

GOLF **San Jose Municipal Golf Course** (✉ 1560 Oakland Rd. ☎ 408/441–4653) is an 18-hole course. Greens fees are $34 on weekdays and $48 on weekends. Cart rental is $25 extra. **Cinnabar Hills Golf Club** (✉ 23600 McKean Rd. ☎ 408/323–5200) is a 27-hole course. Greens fees are $80 on weekdays and $100 on weekends until 2 PM; late-afternoon fees are considerably lower.

THE PENINSULA & SOUTH BAY ESSENTIALS

To research prices, get advice from other travelers, and book travel arrangements, visit www.fodors.com.

Transportation

BY AIR
All the major airlines serve San Francisco International Airport, and most of them fly to San Jose International Airport. ⇨ Air Travel *in* Smart Travel Tips A to Z for airline and airport phone numbers.

AIRPORT South & East Bay Airport Shuttle can transport you between the air-
TRANSFERS port and Saratoga, Palo Alto, and other destinations.
🛈 **South & East Bay Airport Shuttle** ☎ 408/225–4444 or 800/548–4664.

BY BUS
SamTrans buses travel to Moss Beach and Half Moon Bay from the Daly City BART (Bay Area Rapid Transit) station. Another bus connects Half Moon Bay with Pescadero. Each trip takes approximately one hour. Call for schedules, because departures are infrequent. The Valley Transportation Authority (VTA) shuttle links downtown San Jose to the Cal-Train station, across from the Arena Green, every 20 minutes during morning and evening commute hours.
🛈 **SamTrans** ☎ 800/660–4287 ⊕ www.samtrans.org. **VTA Shuttle** ☎ 408/321–2300 or 800/894–9908 ⊕ www.vta.org.

BY CAR

Public transportation to coastal areas is limited, so it's best to drive. To get to Moss Beach or Half Moon Bay, take Highway 1, also known as the Coast Highway, south along the length of the San Mateo coast. When coastal traffic is heavy, especially on summer weekends, you can also reach Half Moon Bay via Interstate 280, the Junipero Serra Freeway; follow it south as far as Route 92, where you can turn west toward the coast. To get to Pescadero, drive south 16 mi on Highway 1 from Half Moon Bay. For Año Nuevo continue south on Highway 1 another 12 mi.

By car the most pleasant route down the Inland Peninsula to Palo Alto, Woodside, Santa Clara, and San Jose is Interstate 280, which passes along Crystal Springs Reservoir. U.S. 101, also known as the Bayshore Freeway, is more direct but also more congested. To avoid the often-heavy commuter traffic on Highway 101, use Interstate 280 during rush hours.

To reach Saratoga take Interstate 280 south to Highway 85 and follow Highway 85 south toward Gilroy. Exit on Saratoga–Sunnyvale Road, go south, and follow the signs to the Village—about 2½ mi. Signs will also direct you to Hakone Gardens, Villa Montalvo, and on concert nights, the Mountain Winery.

CAR RENTAL   You can rent a car at the San Jose airport from any of the many major agencies. Specialty Rentals offers standard cars and luxury vehicles; it has an office in Palo Alto and will deliver a car to you anywhere on the Peninsula or at the airport. ⇨ Car Rental *in* Smart Travel Tips A to Z for national rental-agency phone numbers.

🚗 Local Agencies **Specialty Rentals** ☎ 650/856–9100 or 800/400–8412.

BY TRAIN

CalTrain runs from 4th and Townsend streets in San Francisco to Palo Alto ($5.25 each way); from there take the free Marguerite shuttle bus to the Stanford campus and the Palo Alto area. Buses run about every 15 minutes from 6 AM to 7:45 PM and are timed to connect with trains and public transit buses.

CalTrain service continues south of Palo Alto to Santa Clara's Railroad and Franklin streets stop, near Santa Clara University ($5.50 one-way), and to San Jose's Rod Diridon station ($5.50 one-way). The trip to Santa Clara takes approximately 1¼ hours; to San Jose, it's about 1½ hours.

Valley Transportation Authority buses run efficiently throughout the Santa Clara Valley, although not as frequently as you might like. Operators can help you plan routes.

In San Jose, light-rail trains run 24 hours a day and serve most major attractions, shopping malls, historic sites, and downtown. Trains run every 10 minutes weekdays from 6 AM to 8 PM and vary during weekends and late-night hours from every 15 minutes to once an hour. Tickets are valid for two hours; they cost $1.75 one-way or $5.25 for a day pass. Buy tickets at vending machines in any transit station. For more information call or visit the Downtown Customer Service Center.

🚆 **CalTrain** ☎ 800/660–4287 ⊕ www.caltrain.com. **Downtown Customer Service Center** Light Rail ✉ 2 N. 1st St., San Jose ☎ 408/321–2300. **Marguerite Shuttle**

☎ 650/723-9362. **Valley Transportation Authority** ☎ 408/321-2300 or 800/894-9908 ⊕ www.vta.org.

Contacts & Resources

EMERGENCIES

In an emergency dial 911.

🏥 Hospitals **San Jose Medical Center** ✉ 675 E. Santa Clara St., San Jose ☎ 408/998-3212. **Stanford Hospital** ✉ 300 Pasteur Dr., Palo Alto ☎ 650/723-4000.

VISITOR INFORMATION

🏛 **California State Parks** ☎ 800/777-0369. **Half Moon Bay Chamber of Commerce** ✉ 520 Kelly Ave., Half Moon Bay 94019 ☎ 650/726-8380 ⊕ www.halfmoonbaychamber. org. **Palo Alto Chamber of Commerce** ✉ 122 Hamilton Ave., Palo Alto 94301 ☎ 650/324-3121 ⊕www.paloaltochamber.com. **San Jose Convention and Visitors Bureau** ✉408 Almaden Blvd., 3rd fl., San Jose 95110 ☎ 800/726-5673, 408/295-2265, or 408/295-9600 ⊕ www.sanjose.org. **Santa Clara Chamber of Commerce and Convention and Visitors Bureau** ✉ 1850 Warburton Ave., Santa Clara 95050 ☎ 408/244-9660, 408/244-8244 ⊕ www.santaclarachamber.org. **Saratoga Chamber of Commerce** ✉ 14485 Big Basin Way, Saratoga 95070 ☎ 408/867-0753 ⊕ www.saratogachamber.org. **Woodside Town Hall** ✉ 2955 Woodside Rd., Woodside 94062 ☎ 650/851-6790 ⊕ www. woodsidetown.org.

San Francisco

WITH SAUSALITO & BERKELEY

WORD OF MOUTH

"A walk across the Golden Gate Bridge is an unforgettable experience. I live here and am thrilled every time I drive across. The views are unsurpassed."

–philip bewley

"Visit the ferry building, walk downtown and admire the beautiful architecture, and stroll across the Golden Gate Bridge. Skip the rest unless you want the complete touristy things. The Golden Gate may be touristy, but at least you get to SEE San Francisco because the view (not to mention the bridge itself) is amazing. You can see so much from the vista points there. San Francisco is about art, food, and whatever you may find on the streets."

–suz11

IN ITS FIRST LIFE San Francisco was little more than a small, well-situated settlement. Founded by Spaniards in 1776, it was prized for its natural harbor, so commodious that "all the navies of the world might fit inside it," as one visitor wrote. Around 1849 the discovery of gold at John Sutter's sawmill in the nearby Sierra foothills transformed the sleepy little settlement into a city of 30,000. Millions of dollars' worth of gold was panned and blasted out of the hills, the impetus for the development of a western Wall Street. Fueled by the 1859 discovery of a fabulously rich vein of silver in Virginia City, Nevada, San Francisco became the West Coast's cultural fulcrum and major transportation hub, and its population soared to 342,000. In 1869 the transcontinental railway was completed, linking the once-isolated western capital to the east. San Francisco had become a major city of the United States.

Loose, tolerant, and even *licentious* are words used to describe San Francisco. Bohemian communities thrive here. As early as the 1860s the Barbary Coast—a collection of taverns, whorehouses, and gambling joints along Pacific Avenue close to the waterfront—was famous, or infamous. North Beach, the city's Little Italy, became the home of the Beat movement in the 1950s (Herb Caen, the city's best-known columnist, coined the term *beatnik*). Lawrence Ferlinghetti's City Lights, a bookstore and publishing house that still stands on Columbus Avenue, brought out, among other titles, Allen Ginsberg's *Howl* and *Kaddish*. In the 1960s the Free Speech movement began at the University of California at Berkeley, and Stanford's David Harris, who went to prison for defying the draft, numbered among the nation's most famous student leaders. The Haight-Ashbury district became synonymous with hippiedom, giving rise to such legendary bands as Jefferson Airplane and the Grateful Dead. Southwest of the Haight is the onetime Irish neighborhood known as the Castro, which during the 1970s became identified with gay and lesbian liberation.

Technically speaking, it's only California's fourth-largest city, behind Los Angeles, San Diego, and nearby San Jose. But that statistic is misleading: the Bay Area, extending from the bedroom communities north of Oakland and Berkeley south through the peninsula and the San Jose area, is really one continuous megacity, with San Francisco as its heart.

EXPLORING SAN FRANCISCO

Updated by
Denise M. Leto

YOU COULD LIVE IN SAN FRANCISCO a month and ask no greater entertainment than walking through it," wrote Inez Hayes Irwin, author of *The Californiacs,* an effusive 1921 homage to the state of California and the City by the Bay. Follow in her footsteps and you'll find her claim as true today: simply wandering on foot is the best way to experience this diverse metropolis.

Snuggled on a 46½-square-mi tip of land between San Francisco Bay and the Pacific Ocean, San Francisco is a relatively small city of about 750,000 residents. San Franciscans cherish the city, partly for the same reasons so many visitors do: the proximity of the bay and its pleasures, rows of Victorian homes clinging precariously to the hillsides, the sun setting behind the Golden Gate Bridge. Longtime locals know the city's attraction goes much deeper, from the diversity of its neighborhoods and residents to the city's progressive free spirit. Take all these things together and you'll begin to understand why, despite the dizzying cost of living here, many San Franciscans can't imagine calling anyplace else home.

San Francisco's charms are great and small. You wouldn't want to miss Golden Gate Park, the Palace of Fine Arts, the Golden Gate Bridge, or a cable-car ride over Nob Hill. But a walk down the Filbert Steps or through Macondray Lane or an hour gazing at murals in the Mission or the thundering Pacific from the cliffs of Lincoln Park can be equally inspiring.

Numbers in the text correspond to numbers in the margin and on the neighborhood maps.

Union Square Area

The Union Square area bristles with big-city bravado. The city's finest department stores (including Bloomingdale's, as of fall 2006) do business, along with such exclusive emporiums as Tiffany & Co., Prada, and Coach, and such big-name franchises as Niketown, the Original Levi's Store, Apple Store, Virgin Megastore, and the two new (as of Christmas 2005) much hyped H&M outposts. Visitors lay their heads at several dozen hotels within a three-block walk of the square, and the downtown theater district and many fine arts galleries are nearby.

What to See

❂ ➋ **Cable-car terminus.** San Francisco's signature red cable cars were declared National Landmarks in 1964. Two of the three operating lines begin and end their runs at Powell and Market streets. The more dramatic Powell–Hyde line crosses Nob Hill and continues up Russian Hill before a white-knuckle descent down steep Hyde Street to Victorian Park, across from the Buena Vista Café and near the Maritime Museum and the Hyde Street Pier; Fisherman's Wharf is a few blocks away. The Powell–Mason line also climbs up Nob Hill, then winds through North Beach to Fisherman's Wharf. Buy tickets ($5 one-way) onboard. If it's just the experience of riding a cable car you're after, board the less-busy California line at Van Ness Avenue and ride it down to the Hyatt Regency hotel. ✉ *Powell and Market Sts., Union Sq.*

➌ **Geary Theater.** The American Conservatory Theater (ACT), one of North America's leading repertory companies, uses the 1,035-seat Geary as its main venue. Built in 1910, the theater has a serious neoclassic design lightened by colorful carved terra-cotta columns depicting a cornucopia of fruits. Damaged heavily in the 1989 earthquake, the Geary has been completely restored to gilded splendor. ✉ *415 Geary St., box office at 405 Geary St., Union Sq.* ☎ *415/749–2228.*

➐ **Hallidie Building.** Named for cable-car inventor Andrew S. Hallidie, this 1918 structure is best viewed from across the street. Willis Polk's revolutionary glass-curtain wall—believed to be the world's first such facade—hangs a foot beyond the reinforced concrete of the frame. The reflecting glass, decorative exterior fire escapes that appear to be metal

GREAT ITINERARIES

IF YOU HAVE 3 DAYS

Spend your first morning checking out Fisherman's Wharf and Pier 39. Jump a cable car (the Powell–Hyde line is the most dramatic) at the wharf and take in sweeping views of the bay as you rattle your way to Union Square. Charming Maiden Lane is worth a look.

On the second day, begin with a walk on the Golden Gate Bridge, then explore North Beach, the Italian quarter, filled with tempting food, Beat-era landmarks, and reminders of the city's bawdy past. Move on to labyrinthine Chinatown.

Begin your third day by taking a ferry from Pier 41 to the infamous Alcatraz prison. Spend the rest of the day in whichever neighborhood most appeals to you: the Haight, the epicenter of 1960s counterculture, whose streets are lined with excellent music and bookshops and cool vintage-clothing stores; colorful, gay-friendly Castro, brimming with shops and cafés; or the mural-filled Mission District, a neighborhood of twentysomething hipsters and working-class Latino families. Simple Mission Dolores,

built in 1776, is San Francisco's oldest standing structure.

IF YOU HAVE 5 DAYS

Follow the three-day itinerary above, and on the morning of your fourth day walk up Telegraph Hill to Coit Tower; you'll be rewarded with breathtaking views of the bay and the city's tightly stacked homes. Head for the Marina neighborhood, and if you love chocolate, stop at Ghirardelli Square, which includes a shopping center and the tempting Ghirardelli Chocolate Factory. Make a beeline for the end of the Marina and the stunning Palace of Fine Arts. Don't miss the Palace's hands-on science museum, the Exploratorium. In the afternoon join in-line skaters, joggers, and walkers in picnic-perfect Golden Gate Park—more than 1,000 acres of greenery stretching from the Haight to the Pacific.

On Day 5, explore one of the neighborhoods you missed on Day 3, and in the afternoon take the ferry to Sausalito or head to the East Bay to explore formerly radical, still-offbeat Berkeley.

balconies, and Venetian–Gothic cornice are worth noting. ⊠ *130 Sutter St., between Kearny and Montgomery Sts., Union Sq.*

8 **Hammersmith Building.** Glass walls and a colorful design distinguish this compact four-story Beaux-Arts-style structure, built in 1907. Strips of blue-gray marble adorn the lavender and pink facade, and the lovely awning is studded with faux jewels. The Foundation for Architectural Heritage once described the building as a "commercial jewel box," and indeed, it was designed for use as a jewelry store. ⊠ *301 Sutter St., at Grant Ave., Union Sq.*

6 **Maiden Lane.** Known as Morton Street in the raffish Barbary Coast era, this former red-light district reported at least one murder a week during the late 19th century. After the 1906 fire destroyed the brothels, the street emerged as Maiden Lane, and it has since become a chic pedestrian mall stretching two blocks, between Stockton and Kearny streets.

With its circular interior ramp and skylights, the handsome brick 1948 structure at **140 Maiden Lane,** the only Frank Lloyd Wright building in San Francisco, is said to have been his model for the Guggenheim Museum in New York. **Xanadu Tribal Arts** (☎ 415/392–9999), a gallery showcasing Baltic, Latin-American, and African folk art, occupies space at 140 Maiden Lane. ⊠ *Between Stockton and Kearny Sts., Union Sq.*

❾ Ruth Asawa's Fantasy Fountain. Local artist Ruth Asawa's sculpture, a wonderland of real and mythical creatures, honors the city's hills, bridges, and architecture. Children and friends helped Asawa shape the hundreds of tiny figures from baker's clay; these were assembled on 41 large panels from which molds were made for the bronze casting. ⊠ *In front of Grand Hyatt at 345 Stockton St., Union Sq.*

▶ **❶ San Francisco Visitor Information Center.** A multilingual staff operates this facility below the cable-car terminus. Staffers answer questions and provide maps and pamphlets. You can also pick up discount coupons and hotel brochures here. ⊠ *Hallidie Plaza, lower level, Powell and Market Sts., Union Sq.* ☎ *415/391–2000 or 415/283–0177* ⊕ *www.sfvisitor. org* ⊙ *Weekdays 9–5, Sat. 9–3; also Sun. 9–3 May–Oct.*

❺ Union Square. The heart of San Francisco's downtown since 1850, the 2½-acre square offers respite with an open-air stage and central plaza, a café, gardens, a visitor information booth, and a front-row seat to the cable-car tracks. Four sculptures by the artist R. M. Fischer preside over the space, which fills daily with a familiar kaleidoscope of characters: office workers sunning and brown-bagging, street musicians, the occasional preacher, kids chasing pigeons, and a fair number of homeless people. The square takes its name from the violent pro-union demonstrations staged here before the Civil War. At center stage, Robert Ingersoll Aitken's *Victory Monument* commemorates Commodore George Dewey's victory over the Spanish fleet at Manila in 1898. The 97-foot Corinthian column, topped by a bronze figure symbolizing naval conquest, was dedicated by Theodore Roosevelt in 1903 and withstood the 1906 earthquake. ⊠ *Bordered by Powell, Stockton, Post, and Geary Sts., Union Sq.*

❹ Westin St. Francis Hotel. The second-oldest hotel in the city, established in 1904, was conceived by railroad baron and financier Charles Crocker and his associates as a hostelry for their millionaire friends. After the hotel was ravaged by the 1906 fire, a larger, more luxurious Italian Renaissance–style residence was opened in 1907. The hotel's checkered past includes the ill-fated 1921 bash in the suite of the silent-film comedian Fatty Arbuckle, at which a woman became ill and later died. In 1975 Sara Jane Moore, standing among a crowd outside the hotel, attempted to shoot then-president Gerald Ford. One of the best views in the city is from the glass elevators here—and best of all, it's free. ⊠ *335 Powell St., at Geary St., Union Sq.* ☎ *415/397–7000* ⊕ *www. westinstfrancis.com.*

IF YOU LIKE

THE BAY

The bay provides a stunning backdrop to a visit here. San Franciscans often gravitate toward spaces with views of the water, especially the shoreline promenades of the Embarcadero and Marina, lounges such as the Top of the Mark, and parks that cling precariously to the hillsides. On a sunny day, simply hopping the ferry to Oakland or Sausalito and enjoying a beer among commuters is an inexpensive but exquisite pleasure.

THE HILLS

Driving the hills in San Francisco is like riding a roller coaster, as you creep up on the crest of a hill where you can't see the street coming up to greet your front tires until the very last second. If the gradient of streets on Russian Hill, Nob Hill, and Potrero Hill intimidates you, a cab ride down California Street or a cable-car ride down Hyde Street can be just as hair-raising, and you'll be free to enjoy those dazzling bay views to boot.

HIDDEN LANES & STAIRWAYS

San Francisco is full of hidden garden lanes and alleyways, as well as stairways that trace the hills between rows of homes. Macondray Lane, on Russian Hill, is a gem, worth seeking out for its lovely gardens. Also on Russian Hill, the Vallejo Steps stretch two taxing blocks from Jones Street to Mason Street. In the middle cascades Ina Coolbrith Park, whose manicured grounds and wide-open views make this one of the most popular stairway walks in the city.

GREEN SPACES

San Francisco is an outdoor-person's dream. Golden Gate Park, with more than 1,000 acres of trails and fields, is especially popular with cyclists and in-line skaters. Less famous but equally accessible is the Presidio, with almost 1,500 acres of hilly, wooded trails and breathtaking views of the bay and the Pacific. This former military base at the foot of the Golden Gate Bridge is the city's secret forest, the easiest place in San Francisco to forget you're in a big city.

CAFÉS

To experience life in San Francisco the way the locals do, while away a few hours in its cafés. The city has hundreds, each a microcosm of its neighborhood. And there's more on tap than caffeine—here you can sample some of the city's famous gastronomic fare on the (relative) cheap, without having to make a reservation weeks in advance.

SoMa & the Embarcadero

SoMa—as the region South of Market Street is known—is less a neighborhood than it is a sprawling area of wide, traffic-heavy boulevards lined with office high-rises, pricey live-work lofts, and major commercial ventures. SoMa was once known as South of the Slot (read: the Wrong Side of the Tracks) in reference to the cable-car slot that ran up Market Street. Industry took over much of the area when the 1906 earthquake collapsed most of the homes into their quicksand bases. Huge sections of the then-industrial neighborhood were razed in the 1960s,

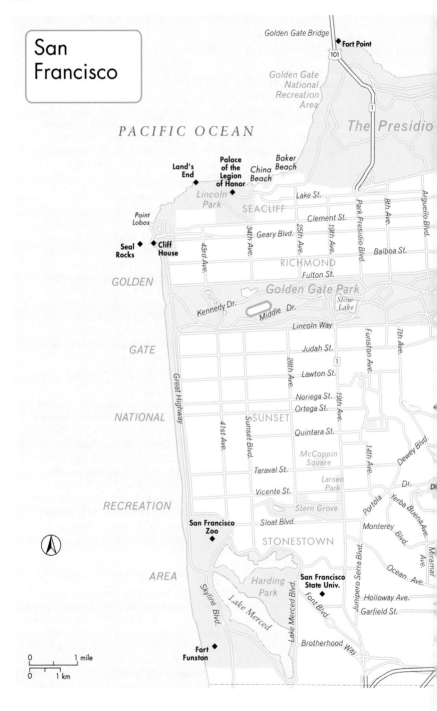

San
Francisco

PACIFIC OCEAN

Golden Gate Bridge

Fort Point

101

Golden Gate
National
Recreation
Area

The Presidio

Land's
End

Palace
of the
Legion
of Honor

Baker
Beach

China
Beach

Lincoln
Park

SEACLIFF

Lake St.

Park Presidio Blvd.

8th Ave.

Arguello Blvd.

Point
Lobos

Clement St.

Geary Blvd.

34th Ave.

25th Ave.

19th Ave.

Balboa St.

Seal
Rocks

Cliff
House

43rd Ave.

RICHMOND

Fulton St.

GOLDEN

Golden Gate Park

Stow
Lake

Kennedy Dr.

Middle Dr.

Lincoln Way

7th Ave.

GATE

Judah St.

Funston Ave.

28th Ave.

Lawton St.

1

Noriega St.

19th Ave.

NATIONAL

41st Ave.

Sunset Blvd.

SUNSET

Ortega St.

Quintara St.

14th Ave.

Dewey Blvd.

McCoppin
Square

Taraval St.

Larsen
Park

Vicente St.

RECREATION

Stern Grove

Portola

Yerba Buena Ave.

Monterey

Miramar

San Francisco
Zoo

Sloat Blvd.

STONESTOWN

Junipero Serra Blvd.

Blvd.

Ave.

Ocean Ave.

AREA

Harding
Park

San Francisco
State Univ.

Holloway Ave.

Skyline Blvd.

Lake Merced

Lake Merced Blvd.

Font Blvd.

Garfield St.

Fort
Funston

Brotherhood Way

0   1 mile

0   1 km

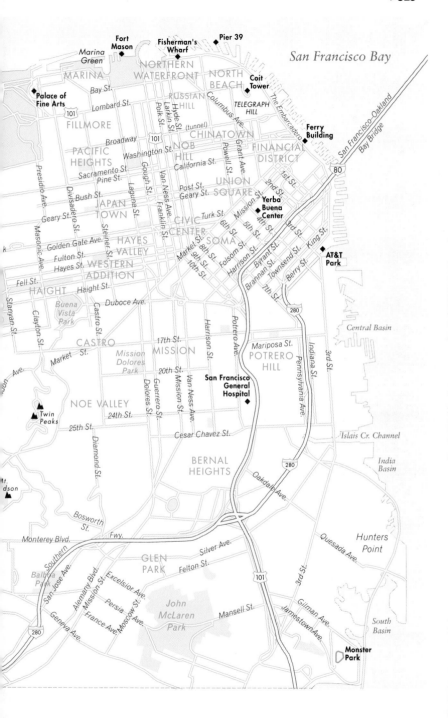

In & Around Downtown San Francisco

Chestnut St.
Lombard St.
Chestnut St.
Lombard St.
Greenwich St.
Filbert St.

Tattoo Art Museum

Wedding Houses

RUSSIAN HILL

NORTH BEACH

Gree
Vallejo

Powell-Hyde Cable Car
Powell-Mason Cable Car

Broadway Tunnel
Broadway
Pacific Ave.

Jackson St.
Washington St.
Clay St.
Sacramento St.

Lafayette Park

NOB HILL

CHINATOWN

California St.
California Street Cable Car

Pine St.
Bush St.
Sutter St.
Post St.

Waverl
Pl.

Chinatown Gate

UNION SQUARE

St. Mary's Cathedral

Geary Blvd.
O'Farrell St.
Geary St.
O'Farrell St.

TENDERLOIN

Union Square

Maiden Ln.

Yerba Buena Garden

Jefferson Square

Ellis St.
Eddy St.
Turk St.

Visitor Information Center

Powell St. BART

Yerba Buena Lane

Golden Gate Ave.

HAYES VALLEY

McAllister St.
Grove St.
Hayes St.

CIVIC CENTER

City Hall
Civic Center BART

Fulton St.

United Nations Plaza

Market St.

Mission St.
Howard St.

SOUTH OF MARKET (SOMA)

KEY
- BART stop
- Start of walk

0 ——————— 1/2 mile
0 ——————— 500 meters

San Francisco Bay

TO FISHERMAN'S WHARF

Levi Strauss Headquarters

Coit Tower

TELEGRAPH HILL

Pier 23
Pier 19
Pier 17
Pier 15
Pier 9
Pier 7
Pier 5
Pier 3
Pier 1

The Embarcadero
Front St.
Battery St.
Sansome St.
Montgomery St.
Davis St.
Drumm St.
Hotaling Pl.

23

Transamerica Pyramid

22

FINANCIAL DISTRICT

Clay St

17

Embarcadero Center

21 Halleck St.

Front St.
Davis St.

Justin Herman Plaza

18

Audiffred Building

Embarcadero BART

19 20

Montgomery St. BART

16

14

10

1

New Montgomery St.
2nd St.
1st St.
Fremont St.
Beale St.
Main St.
Spear St.
Steuart St.

Howard St.
Folsom St.
Harrison St.
Hawthorne St.
Folsom St.
80
Bryant St.
Brannan St.

SOUTH BEACH

TO AT&T PARK

Townsend St.

A GOOD WALK

Set aside an hour to scope out the stores and sites in and around Union Square. If you're a shopper, you can easily spend the day here.

Begin three blocks south of Union Square at the **San Francisco Visitor Information Center** ❶ ►, on the lower level of Hallidie Plaza at Powell and Market streets. Up the escalators on the east side of the plaza, where Powell dead-ends into Market, lies the **cable-car terminus** ❷ for two of the city's three lines. Head north on Powell from the terminus to Geary Street, make a left, and walk west 1½ blocks into the theater district for a peek at the **Geary Theater** ❸. Backtrack on the north side of Geary Street, where the sturdy and stately **Westin St. Francis Hotel** ❹ dominates Powell between Geary and Post streets. **Union Square** ❺ is across Powell from the hotel's main entrance.

From the square head south on Stockton Street to O'Farrell Street for the Virgin Megastore; the Original

Levi's Store is north. Walk back toward Union Square past Geary Street and make a right on **Maiden Lane** ❻, a two-block alley directly across Stockton from Union Square that runs east parallel to Geary. When the lane ends at Kearny Street, turn left, walk 1½ blocks to Sutter Street, make a right, and walk a half block to the **Hallidie Building** ❼. After viewing this historic building, reverse direction and head west 1½ blocks up Sutter to the fanciful Beaux-Arts-style **Hammersmith Building** ❽, on the southwest corner of Sutter Street and Grant Avenue. In the middle of the next block, at 450 Sutter, stands a glorious 1928 art-deco skyscraper, a masterpiece of terra-cotta and other detailing; handsome Maya-inspired designs adorn its exterior and interior surfaces. From here, backtrack a half block east to Stockton Street and take a right. In front of the Grand Hyatt hotel sits **Ruth Asawa's Fantasy Fountain** ❾. Union Square is a half block south on Stockton.

and alternative artists and the gay leather crowd set up shop. The neighborhood lost many artists to the far reaches of SoMa and to the Mission District when urban renewal finally began in earnest in the 1970s; still more fled when the dot-com heyday sent prices here skyrocketing and changed the face of SoMa forever. For visitors, SoMa holds one or two points of interest—SFMOMA and the Yerba Buena Gardens top the list—and these are conveniently close together. Along the waterfront from south of Market to North Beach stretches the Embarcadero, where the only don't-miss site is the fabulous Ferry Building.

What to See

❶❹ **California Historical Society.** The society, founded in 1871, administers a vast repository of Californiana—500,000 photographs, 150,000 manuscripts, thousands of books, periodicals, and paintings, as well as gold-rush paraphernalia. ⊠ *678 Mission St., SoMa* ☎ *415/357–1848* ⊕ *www.californiahistoricalsociety.org* ✆ *$3, free 1st Tues. of month* ☉ *Wed.–Sat. noon–4:30; galleries close between exhibitions.*

12

15 Cartoon Art Museum. Krazy Kat, Zippy the Pinhead, Batman, and other colorful cartoon icons greet you at the Cartoon Art Museum, established with an endowment from cartoonist-icon Charles M. Schulz. The museum's strength is its changing exhibits, which explore such topics as America from the perspective of international political cartoons, and the output of women and African-American cartoonists. ⊠ *655 Mission St., SoMa* ☎ *415/227–8666* ⊕ *www.cartoonart.org* ✉ *$6, pay what you wish 1st Tues. of month* ☉ *Tues.–Sun. 11–5.*

20 Contemporary Jewish Museum. Exhibits at this small museum (previously known as the Jewish Museum San Francisco) survey Jewish art, history, and culture. In lieu of a static collection, the museum relies on a series of temporary exhibitions that often include political themes. These can be controversial, even within the Jewish community, and offer insight to anyone interested in contemporary Jewish life. Call ahead before visiting; the museum sometimes closes between exhibits. In 2007 the museum plans to move into state-of-the-art, Daniel Libeskind–designed quarters south of Market, on Mission Street between 3rd and 4th streets. ⊠ *121 Steuart St., Embarcadero* ☎ *415/591–8800* ⊕ *www.jmsf.org* ✉ *$5, free 3rd Mon. of month* ☉ *Sun.–Thurs. noon–6.*

17 Embarcadero Center. John Portman designed this five-block complex built during the 1970s and early 1980s. Shops and restaurants abound on the first three levels; there's ample office space on the floors above. Louise Nevelson's 54-foot-tall black-steel sculpture, *Sky Tree,* stands guard over Building 3 and is one of 19 artworks throughout the center. ⊠ *Clay St., between Battery St. and Embarcadero* ☎ *415/772–0734* ⊕ *www.embarcaderocenter.com.*

18 Ferry Building. Renovated in 2003, the Ferry Building is the jewel of the

Fodor's Choice ★ Embarcadero. The beacon of the port area, erected in 1896, has a 230-foot clock tower modeled after the campanile of the cathedral in Seville, Spain. On the morning of April 18, 1906, the four great clock faces on the tower, powered by the swinging of a 14-foot pendulum, stopped at 5:17—the moment the great earthquake struck—and stayed still for 12 months. Today San Franciscans flock to the street-level gourmet Market Hall, stocking up on supplies from local favorites such as Acme Bread, Scharffen Berger Chocolate, and Cowgirl Creamery; lucky diners claim a coveted table at Slanted Door, the city's beloved high-end Vietnamese restaurant. The waterfront promenade extends from the piers on the north side of the building south to the Bay Bridge, and ferries behind the building sail to Sausalito, Larkspur, Tiburon, and the East Bay. ⊠ *Embarcadero at foot of Market St., Embarcadero.*

12 Metreon. Child's play meets the 21st century at this high-tech mall, adored by gearheads and teenage boys obsessed with tabletop games. A 15-screen multiplex, retail shops such as PlayStation and Sony Style, and outposts of some of the city's favorite restaurants are all part of the complex. Even with Sony's sale of the Metreon in 2006, in all likelihood it will remain a mall with a legion of teenage fans and a good place to pick up lunch for a picnic in the Yerba Buena Gardens, right outside. ⊠ *101 4th St., between Mission and Howard Sts., SoMa* ☎ *800/638–7366* ⊕ *www.metreon.com.*

A GOOD WALK

Allow a solid two hours for this walk, more if you visit the museums and galleries. SFMOMA and MoAD merit about two hours each; the Center for the Arts and the Cartoon Art Museum, 45 minutes each.

The **San Francisco Museum of Modern Art** (SFMOMA) ⑩ ➤ dominates a half block of 3rd Street between Howard and Mission streets. Use the crosswalk near SFMOMA's entrance to head across 3rd Street into Yerba Buena Gardens. To your right after you've walked a few steps, a sidewalk leads to the main entrance of the **Yerba Buena Center for the Arts** ⑪. Straight ahead is the East Garden of Yerba Buena Gardens, and beyond that, on the 4th Street side of the block, is the **Metreon** ⑫ entertainment, retail, and restaurant complex. A second-level walkway in the southern portion of the East Garden, above the Martin Luther King Jr. waterfall, arches over Howard Street, leading to the main (south) entrance to Moscone Convention Center and the **Rooftop@Yerba Buena Gardens** ⑬ facilities.

Exit the rooftop, head north up 4th Street to Mission Street and walk east on Mission (toward SFMOMA) past the monolithic San Francisco Marriott, also known as the "jukebox" Marriott because of its exterior design. Just before St.

Patrick's Catholic Church turn left onto the pedestrian walkway Yerba Buena Lane past a water course, shops and restaurants to the plaza on Market Street at the foot of Grant Avenue. The Mexican Museum and the Contemporary Jewish Museum are to open on this block in late 2007. Head east on Market Street past Lotta's Fountain and then walk south on 3rd Street to Mission Street; a half block east on Mission is the headquarters of the **California Historical Society** ⑭. Across the street and a few steps farther east is the **Cartoon Art Museum** ⑮.

Continue east on Mission Street, turn left onto New Montgomery Street, and continue to Market Street and the **Palace Hotel** ⑯. Enter via the Market Street entrance, checking out the Pied Piper Bar, Garden Court restaurant, and main lobby. Exit via the lobby onto New Montgomery Street and make a left, which will bring you back to Market Street. Turn right and head toward the waterfront. Toward the end of Market a three-tier pedestrian mall connects the five buildings of the **Embarcadero Center** ⑰ office-retail complex. Across the busy Embarcadero roadway from the plaza stands the port's trademark, the **Ferry Building** ⑱.

❻ **Palace Hotel.** The city's oldest hotel, a Sheraton property, opened in 1875. Fire destroyed the original Palace after the 1906 earthquake, despite the hotel's 28,000-gallon reservoir fed by four artesian wells; the current building dates from 1909. President Warren Harding died at the Palace while still in office in 1923, and the body of King Kalakaua of Hawaii spent a night here after he died in San Francisco in 1891. The managers play up this ghoulish past with talk of a haunted guest room. **San Francisco City Guides** (☎ 415/557–4266 ⊙ Tours Tues. and Sat. at 10 AM, Thurs. at 2 PM) offers free guided tours of the Palace Hotel's grand interior. ⊠ *2 New Montgomery St., SoMa* ☎ *415/512–1111* ⊕ *www.sfpalace.com.*

19 Rincon Center. The only reason to visit what is basically a modern office building is the striking Works Project Administration mural by Anton Refregier in the lobby of the streamline moderne–style former post office on the building's Mission Street side. The 27 panels depict California life from the days when Native Americans were the state's sole inhabitants through World War I. A sheer five-story column of water resembling a mini-rainstorm is the centerpiece of the indoor arcade around the corner from the mural. ⊠ *Bordered by Steuart, Spear, Mission, and Howard Sts., SoMa.*

13 Rooftop@Yerba Buena Gardens. Fun is the order of the day among these brightly colored concrete and corrugated-metal buildings atop Moscone Convention Center South. The historic **Looff carousel** ($2 for two rides) twirls daily 11 to 6. South of the carousel is **Zeum** (☎ 415/777–2800 ⊕ www.zeum.org), a high-tech, interactive arts-and-technology center ($7) geared to children ages eight and over. Kids can make Claymation videos, work in a computer lab, and view exhibits and performances. Zeum is open 11 to 5 Tuesday through Sunday in summer and Wednesday through Sunday in winter. Also part of the rooftop complex are gardens, an ice-skating rink, and a bowling alley. ⊠ *4th St. between Howard and Folsom Sts., SoMa.*

10 San Francisco Museum of Modern Art (SFMOMA). Mario Botta designed the striking SFMOMA facility, completed in early 1995, which consists of a sienna brick facade and a central tower of alternating bands of black and white stone. Inside, natural light from the tower floods the central atrium and some of the museum's galleries. Works by Henri Matisse, Pablo Picasso, Georgia O'Keeffe, Frida Kahlo, Jackson Pollock, and Andy Warhol form the heart of the diverse permanent collection, which art enthusiasts claim isn't the world-class collection it should be. The photography holdings are unusually strong, and the media arts and architecture and design collections are appropriately cutting-edge for this high-tech area. ⊠ *151 3rd St., SoMa* ☎ *415/357–4000* ⊕ *www.sfmoma.org* ☺ *$12.50, free 1st Tues. of month, ½ price Thurs. 6–9* ⊙ *Labor Day–Memorial Day, Fri.–Tues. 11–5:45, Thurs. 11–8:45; Memorial Day–Labor Day, Fri.–Tues. 10–5:45, Thurs. 10–8:45; call for hrs for special exhibits.*

Fodor'sChoice ★

11 Yerba Buena Center for the Arts. The dance, music, theater, visual arts, films, and videos presented at this facility in Yerba Buena Gardens range from the community-based to the international and lean toward the cutting edge. ⊠ *701 Mission St., SoMa* ☎ *415/978–2787* ⊕ *www. ybca.org* ☺ *Galleries $6, free 1st Tues. of month* ⊙ *Galleries and box office Tues., Wed., and Fri.–Sun. noon–5; Thurs. noon–8.*

Heart of the Barbary Coast

It was on Montgomery Street, in the Financial District, that Sam Brannan proclaimed the historic gold discovery that took place at Sutter's

Mill on January 24, 1848. The gold rush brought streams of people from across America and Europe, transforming the onetime frontier town into a cosmopolitan city almost overnight. Other fortune seekers, including saloon keepers, gamblers, and prostitutes, all flocked to the so-called Barbary Coast (now Jackson Square and the Financial District). Since then the red-light establishments have edged upward to the Broadway strip of North Beach, and Jackson Square evolved into a sedate district of refurbished brick buildings decades ago.

What to See

㉓ Jackson Square. Here was the heart of the Barbary Coast of the Gay '90s. Although most of the red-light district was destroyed in the 1906 fire, old redbrick buildings and narrow alleys recall the romance and rowdiness of the early days. Some of the city's earliest business buildings, survivors of the 1906 quake, still stand in Jackson Square, between Montgomery and Sansome streets.

Restored 19th-century brick buildings line Hotaling Place, which connects Washington and Jackson streets. The lane is named for the head of the **A. P. Hotaling Company whiskey distillery** (⊠ 451 Jackson St., at Hotaling Pl.), which was the largest liquor repository on the West Coast in its day. The Italianate Hotaling building reveals little of its infamous past, but a plaque on the side of the structure repeats a famous query about its surviving the quake: IF, AS THEY SAY, GOD SPANKED THE TOWN FOR BEING OVER FRISKY, WHY DID HE BURN THE CHURCHES DOWN AND SAVE HOTALING'S WHISKEY?

㉔ San Francisco Brewing Company. Built in 1907, this pub looks like a museum piece from the Barbary Coast days. An old upright piano sits in the corner under the original stained-glass windows. Take a seat at the mahogany bar, where you can look down at the white-tile spittoon. An adjacent room holds the handmade copper brewing kettle used to produce a dozen beers—with names such as Pony Express—by means of old-fashioned gravity-flow methods. ⊠ *155 Columbus Ave., North Beach* ☎ *415/434–3344* ⊕ *www.sfbrewing.com* ⊙ *Mon.–Sat. 11:30–1 AM, Sun. noon–1 AM.*

㉒ Transamerica Pyramid. It's neither owned by Transamerica nor is it a pyramid, this 853-foot-tall obelisk, the most photographed of the city's highrises. Designed by William Pereira and Associates in 1972 and excoriated in the design stages as "the world's largest architectural folly," the icon when unveiled was quickly hailed as a masterpiece and today is probably the city's most recognized structure after the Golden Gate Bridge. ⊠ *600 Montgomery St., Financial District* ⊕ *www.tapyramid.com.*

㉑ Wells Fargo Bank History Museum. There were no formal banks in San Francisco during the early years of the gold rush, and miners often entrusted their gold dust to saloon keepers. In 1852 Wells Fargo opened its first bank in the city, and the company soon established banking offices in the mother-lode camps throughout California. Stagecoaches and Pony Express riders connected points around the burgeoning state, where the population boomed from 15,000 to 200,000 between 1848 and 1852. The showpiece is the red Concord stagecoach, the likes of

A GOOD WALK

While wandering through Chinatown's streets and alleys, don't forget to look up. Above street level, many older structures—mostly brick buildings that replaced rickety wooden ones destroyed during the 1906 earthquake—have ornate balconies and cornices. The architecture on the 900 block of Grant Avenue (at Washington Street) and Waverly Place (west of and parallel to Grant Avenue between Sacramento and Washington streets) is particularly noteworthy.

Allow at least two hours to see Chinatown. Brief stops will suffice at the cultural center and temples.

Enter Chinatown through the green-tile **Chinatown Gate** ㉕ ▶, on Grant Avenue at Bush Street. Shops selling souvenirs, jewelry, and home furnishings line Grant north past the gate. Continue on Grant to Clay Street and turn right. A half block down on your left is **Portsmouth Square** ㉖. A walkway on the eastern edge of the park leads over Kearny Street to the 3rd floor of the Holiday Inn, where you find the **Chinese Culture Center** ㉗.

Backtrack on the walkway to Portsmouth Square and head west up Washington Street a half block to the **Old Chinese Telephone Exchange** ㉘ (now the Bank of Canton), and then continue west on Washington Street. Cross Grant Avenue and look for Waverly Place a half block up on the left. One of the best examples of this alley's traditional architecture is the **Tin How Temple** ㉙. After visiting Waverly Place and Tin How, walk back to Washington Street. Several herb shops do business in this area. Two worth checking out are Superior Trading Company, at No. 839, and the Great China Herb Co., at No. 857.

Across Washington Street from Superior is Ross Alley. Head north on Ross toward Jackson Street, stopping along the way to watch the bakers at the **Golden Gate Fortune Cookie Factory** ㉚. Turn right on Jackson. When you get to Grant Avenue, don't cross it. For some of Chinatown's best pastries, turn left and stop by No. 1029, the Golden Gate Bakery, where the moon cakes are delicious. The markets in the 1100 block of Grant Avenue carry intriguing delicacies, such as braised pig noses and ears, eels, and all manner of live game birds and fish.

Head west on Pacific Avenue to Stockton Street, turn left, and walk south past Stockton Street's markets. At Clay Street make a right and head halfway up the hill to the **Chinese Historical Society of America Museum and Learning Center** ㉛. Return to Stockton Street and make a right; a few doors down is the **Kong Chow Temple** ㉜, and next door is the elaborate **Chinese Six Companies** building.

which carried passengers from St. Joseph, Missouri, to San Francisco in three weeks during the 1850s. ✉ *420 Montgomery St., Financial District* ☎ *415/396–2619* 🖾 *Free* ⊙ *Weekdays 9–5.*

Chinatown

Not for nothing is Chinatown the number two tourist draw after Fisherman's Wharf: few regions so pleasurably assault all five of your senses. Pungent smells waft out of restaurants, fish markets, and produce stands. Good-luck banners of crimson and gold hang beside dragon-entwined lampposts, pagoda roofs, and street signs with Chinese calligraphy. Honking cars chime in with shoppers bargaining loudly in Cantonese or Mandarin. Add to this the sight of millions of Chinese-theme goods spilling out of the shops along Grant Avenue, and you get an idea of what Chinatown is all about.

What to See

▶ **㉕ Chinatown Gate.** Stone lions flank the base of the pagoda-topped gate. The male lion's right front paw rests playfully on a ball; the female's left front paw tickles a cub lying on its back. The lions and the glazed clay dragons atop the largest of the gate's three pagodas symbolize, among other things, wealth and prosperity. The fish whose mouths wrap tightly around the crest of this pagoda also symbolize prosperity. The four Chinese characters immediately beneath the pagoda represent the philosophy of Sun Yat-sen (1866–1925), the leader who unified China in the early 20th century. The vertical characters under the left pagoda read "peace" and "trust," the ones under the right pagoda "respect" and "love." ✉ *Grant Ave. at Bush St., Chinatown.*

㉛ Chinese Historical Society of America Museum and Learning Center. This airy, light-filled gallery has displays about the Chinese-American experience from 19th-century agriculture to 21st-century food and fashion trends, including a poignant collection of racist games and toys. A separate room hosts rotating exhibits by contemporary Chinese-American artists; another describes the building's time as the Chinatown YWCA, which served as a meeting place and residence for Chinese women in need of social services. ✉ *965 Clay St., Chinatown* ☎ *415/391–1188* ⊕ *www.chsa.org* 🖾 *$3, free 1st Thurs. of month* ⊙ *Tues.–Fri. noon–5, weekends noon–4.*

㉗ Chinese Culture Center. The San Francisco Redevelopment Commission agreed to let **Holiday Inn** build in Chinatown if the chain provided room for a Chinese culture center. Inside the center are the works of Chinese and Chinese-American artists as well as traveling exhibits relating to Chinese culture. Walking tours ($12; make reservations a week ahead) of historic points in Chinatown begin here most days at 10 AM. ✉ *Holiday Inn, 750 Kearny St., 3rd fl., Chinatown* ☎ *415/986–1822* ⊕ *www. c-c-c.org* 🖾 *Free* ⊙ *Tues.–Sat. 10–4.*

㉚ Golden Gate Fortune Cookie Factory. Walk down Ross Alley and you'll chance upon this tiny cookie factory. The workers sit at circular motorized griddles and wait for dollops of batter to drop onto a tiny metal plate, which rotates into an oven. A few moments later out comes a cookie that's pliable and ready for folding. It's easy to peek in for a moment, and hard to leave without a few free samples. A bagful of cookies costs $2 or $3; personalized fortunes are also available. You can also purchase the cookies "fortuneless" in their waferlike unfolded state. ✉ *56 Ross Alley, west of and parallel to Grant Ave. between Washington and Jackson Sts., Chinatown* ☎ *415/781–3956* ▣ *Free* ◷ *Daily 9–8.*

㉜ Kong Chow Temple. The god to whom the members of this temple pray represents honesty and trust. Take the elevator up to the fourth floor, where incense fills the air. You can show respect by placing a dollar or two in the donation box and by leaving your camera in its case. Amid the statuary, flowers, and richly colored altars, a couple of plaques announce that MRS. HARRY S. TRUMAN CAME TO THIS TEMPLE IN JUNE 1948 FOR A PREDICTION ON THE OUTCOME OF THE ELECTION . . . THIS FORTUNE CAME TRUE. The temple's balcony has a good view of Chinatown. ✉ *855 Stockton St., Chinatown* ☎ *No phone* ▣ *Free* ◷ *Mon.–Sat. 9–4.*

㉘ Old Chinese Telephone Exchange. Most of Chinatown burned down after the 1906 earthquake, and this building—today the Bank of Canton— set the style for the new Chinatown. The intricate three-tier pagoda was built in 1909. The exchange's operators were renowned for their prodigious memories, about which the San Francisco Chamber of Commerce boasted in 1914: "These girls respond all day with hardly a mistake to calls that are given (in English or one of five Chinese dialects) by the name of the subscriber instead of by his number—a mental feat that would be practically impossible to most high-schooled American misses." ✉ *Bank of Canton, 743 Washington St., Chinatown.*

㉖ Portsmouth Square. Captain John B. Montgomery landed a block from here (the bay came up this far) in a ship called the *Portsmouth* and raised the American flag in 1846, claiming the area from Mexico. The square—a former potato patch—was the plaza for Yerba Buena, the Mexican settlement that was renamed San Francisco. Robert Louis Stevenson, the author of *Treasure Island,* lived on the edge of Chinatown in the late 19th century and often visited the square. Bruce Porter designed the bronze galleon that sits atop a 9-foot-tall granite shaft in the square's northwestern corner in honor of the writer. By noon dozens of men huddle around Chinese chess tables, engaged in not-always-legal competition. ✉ *Bordered by Walter Lum Pl. and Kearny, Washington, and Clay Sts., Chinatown.*

★ ㉙ Tin How Temple. Duck into the inconspicuous doorway, climb three flights of stairs, and be assaulted by the aroma of incense in this tiny, altar-filled room. Day Ju, one of the first three Chinese to arrive in San Francisco, dedicated this temple to the Queen of the Heavens and the Goddess of the Seven Seas in 1852. In the temple's entryway, elderly ladies can often be seen preparing "money" to be burned as offerings to various Buddhist gods or as funds for ancestors to use in the afterlife. The gold-leaf wood carving suspended from the ceiling depicts the north and east sides of the sea, which Tin How and other gods protect. Tin How presides over the middle back of the temple, flanked by one red and one green lesser god. ✉ *125 Waverly Pl., Chinatown* ☎ *No phone* ▣ *Free, donations accepted* ◷ *Daily 9–4.*

North Beach & Telegraph Hill

San Francisco novelist Herbert Gold calls North Beach "the longest-running, most glorious American bohemian operetta outside Greenwich Village." Indeed, to anyone who's spent some time in its eccentric old bars and cafés or wandered the neighborhood, North Beach evokes everything from the Barbary Coast days to the no-less-rowdy beatnik era. Italian bakeries appear frozen in time, homages to Jack Kerouac and Allen Ginsberg pop up everywhere, and the modern equivalent of the Barbary Coast's "houses of ill repute," strip joints, do business on Broadway. North Beach is the most densely populated district in the city—and among the most cosmopolitan.

What to See

★ ③③ **City Lights Bookstore.** Designated a city landmark, the hangout of Beat-era writers—Allen Ginsberg and Lawrence Ferlinghetti among them—remains a vital part of San Francisco's literary scene. Still leftist at heart, the store has a replica of a revolutionary mural destroyed in Chiapas, Mexico, by military forces. The bookstore draws a loyal following for its excellent selection of poetry and other literature (including works from its own publishing house). ⊠ *261 Columbus Ave., North Beach* ☎ *415/362–8193* ⊕ *www.citylights.com* ⊙ *Daily 10 AM–midnight.*

③⑦ **Coit Tower.** Whether you think it resembles a fire hose or something more, ahem, adult, this 210-foot tower, indeed a monument to the city's firefighters, is among San Francisco's most distinctive skyline sights. During the early days of the gold rush, so the story goes, Lillie Hitchcock Coit was said to have deserted a wedding party and chased down the street after her favorite engine, Knickerbocker No. 5, while clad in her bridesmaid finery. She was soon made an honorary member of the Knickerbocker Company. Lillie died in 1929 at the age of 86, leaving the city $125,000 to "expend in an appropriate manner . . . to the beauty of San Francisco." Inside the tower, 19 Depression-era murals depict economic and political life in California. ⊠ *Telegraph Hill Blvd. at Greenwich St. or Lombard St., North Beach* ☎ *415/362–0808* ⊡ *Free; elevator to top $3.75* ⊙ *Daily 10–6.*

FodorśChoice ★

③④ **St. Francis of Assisi Church.** The 1860 building stands on the site of the frame parish church that served the Catholic community during the gold rush. Its solid terra-cotta facade complements the many brightly colored restaurants and cafés nearby. ⊠ *610 Vallejo St., North Beach* ☎ *415/983–0405* ⊕ *www.shrinesf.org* ⊙ *Daily 11–5.*

③⑤ **Saints Peter and Paul Catholic Church.** Camera-toting visitors focus their lenses on the Romanesque splendor of what's often called the Italian Cathedral. Completed in 1924, the church has Disneyesque stone-white towers that are local landmarks. Following their 1954 City Hall wedding, Marilyn Monroe and Joe DiMaggio had their wedding photos snapped here. ⊠ *666 Filbert St., at Washington Sq., North Beach* ☎ *415/421–0809.*

③⑥ **Telegraph Hill.** The name comes from one of the hill's earliest functions—in 1853 it became the location of the first Morse code signal station. Hill residents have some of the best views in the city, as well as the most difficult ascents to their aeries (the flower-lined steps flanking parts of the hill make the climb more than tolerable for visitors, though). The hill rises from the east end of Lombard Street to a height of 284 feet and is capped by Coit Tower. ⊠ *Bordered by Lombard, Filbert, Kearny, and Sansome Sts., North Beach.*

12

Nob Hill & Russian Hill

Topped with some of the city's most elegant hotels, Gothic Grace Cathedral, and private blue-blood clubs, Nob Hill was officially dubbed during the 1870s when "the Big Four"—Charles Crocker, Leland Stanford, Mark Hopkins, and Collis Huntington, who were involved in the construction of the transcontinental railroad—built their hilltop estates. The hill itself was called Snob Hill, a term that survives to this day. The 1906 earthquake and fire destroyed all the palatial mansions, except for portions of the Flood brownstone. A few blocks north of Nob Hill, the old San Francisco families of Russian Hill were joined during the 1890s by bohemian artists and writers that included Charles Norris, George Sterling, and Maynard Dixon. Essentially a tony residential neighborhood of spiffy pieds-à-terre, Victorian flats, Edwardian cottages, and boxlike condos, Russian Hill also has some of the city's loveliest stairway walks, hidden garden ways, and steepest streets–not to mention those bay views.

What to See

★ ☺ ㊷ **Cable Car Museum.** San Francisco once had more than a dozen cable-car barns and powerhouses. The only survivor, this 1907 redbrick structure, has photographs, old cable cars (including one to sit in), signposts, ticketing machines, and other memorabilia dating from 1873 document the history of these moving landmarks. The massive powerhouse wheels that move the entire cable-car system steal the show. A 15-minute video describes how it all works or you can opt to read the detailed placards. ⊠ *1201 Mason St., at Washington St., Nob Hill* ☎ *415/474–1887* ⊕ *www.cablecarmuseum.com* ⊡ *Free* ☉ *Oct.–Mar., daily 10–5; Apr.–Sept., daily 10–6.*

㊵ **Fairmont San Francisco.** The hotel's dazzling opening was delayed a year by the 1906 quake, but since then the marble palace has been host to presidents, royalty, and movie stars. Things have changed since its early days, however: on the eve of World War I you could get a room for as low as $2.50 per night, meals included. Nowadays, prices go as high as $8,000, which buys a night in the eight-room, Persian art–filled penthouse suite that was showcased regularly in the 1980s TV series *Hotel*. ⊠ *950 Mason St., Nob Hill* ☎ *415/772–5000* ⊕ *www.fairmont.com.*

㊽ **Feusier House.** Octagonal houses were once thought to make the best use of space and enhance the physical and mental well-being of their occupants. A brief mid-19th-century craze inspired the construction of several in San Francisco. Only the Feusier House, built in 1857, and the Octagon House remain standing. ⊠ *1067 Green St., Russian Hill.*

⌐ ㊳ **Grace Cathedral.** The seat of the Episcopal Church in San Francisco, this soaring Gothic structure, erected on the site of Charles Crocker's man-

A GOOD WALK

This tour covers a lot of ground, much of it steep. If you're in reasonably good shape, you can complete this walk in 3½ to 4 hours, including 30-minute stops at Grace Cathedral and the Cable Car Museum. Add time for gazing at the bay from Ina Coolbrith Park or enjoying tea or a cocktail at one of Nob Hill's grand hotels.

Start off at California and Taylor streets at the majestic ▶ **Grace Cathedral** ㊳. From the cathedral walk east (toward Mason Street and downtown) on California Street to the exclusive **Pacific Union Club** ㊴. Across Mason Street from the club is the lush **Fairmont San Francisco** ㊵, with its kitchy tiki Tonga Room bar. Directly across California Street is the **Inter-Continental Mark Hopkins** ㊶, beloved for the panoramic views from its Top of the Mark lounge. Walk north on Mason street to the **Cable Car Museum** ㊷.

From the Cable Car Museum, you'll be leaving Nob Hill for Russian Hill. Continue four blocks north on Mason Street to Vallejo Street, turn west, and start climbing the steps that lead to the multilevel **Ina**

Coolbrith Park ㊸. At the top, the Flag House, one of several brown-shingle prequake buildings in this area, is to your left at Taylor Street. Cross Taylor Street and ascend the Vellejo steps; the view east takes in downtown and the Bay Bridge. Down and to your left is Florence Place, an enclave of large 1920s stucco homes, and down a bit farther on your right is brick Russian Hill Place, with a row of 1915 Mediterranean town houses designed by Willis Polk. After reemerging on Vallejo Street from the alleys, descend the steps to street level and walk north (right) on Jones Street one short block to Green Street. Head west (left) halfway down the block to the octagonal **Feusier House** ㊹. Turn north (right) on Leavenworth Street and duck east (right) onto **Macondray Lane** ㊺; the lovely part begins a block later across Jones. Backtrack to Leavenworth and head north (to the right) to the bottom of **Lombard Street** ㊻, the "Crookedest Street in the World." Continue north one block on Leavenworth and then east one block on Chestnut Street to the **San Francisco Art Institute** ㊼.

sion, took 53 years to build. The gilded bronze doors at the east entrance were taken from casts of Lorenzo Ghiberti's Gates of Paradise, which are on the baptistery in Florence, Italy. A black-and-bronze stone sculpture of St. Francis by Beniamino Bufano greets you as you enter. The 35-foot-wide labyrinth, a large, purplish rug, is a replica of the 13th-century stone maze on the floor of the Chartres cathedral. ✉ *1100 California St., at Taylor St., Nob Hill* ☎ *415/749–6300* ⊕ *www.gracecathedral.org* ☉ *Weekdays 7–6, Sat. 8–5:30, Sun. 7–7.*

㊸ **Ina Coolbrith Park.** Beloved for its meditative setting and spectacular bay views, this spot is unusual because it's vertical—that is, rather than being one open space, it's composed of a series of terraces up a very steep hill. A poet, Oakland librarian, and niece of Mormon prophet Joseph Smith,

Ina Coolbrith (1842–1928) introduced Jack London and Isadora Duncan to the world of books. For years she entertained literary greats in her Macondray Lane home near the park. ⊠ *Vallejo St. between Mason and Taylor Sts., Russian Hill.*

46 Lombard Street. The block-long "Crookedest Street in the World" makes eight switchbacks down the east face of Russian Hill between Hyde and Leavenworth streets. Residents bemoan the traffic jam outside their front doors, and occasionally the city attempts to discourage drivers by posting a traffic cop near the top of the hill. If no one is standing guard, join the line of cars waiting to drive down the steep hill, or avoid the whole morass and walk down the steps on either side of Lombard. ⊠ *Lombard St. between Hyde and Leavenworth Sts., Russian Hill.*

Fodor'sChoice ★

45 Macondray Lane. Enter this "secret garden" under a lovely wooden trellis and proceed down a quiet cobbled pedestrian lane lined with Edwardian cottages and flowering plants and trees. Watch your step—the cobblestones are quite uneven in spots. A flight of steep wooden stairs at the end of the lane leads to Taylor Street—on the way down you can't miss the bay views. If you've read any of Armistead Maupin's *Tales of the City* or sequels, you may find the lane vaguely familiar. It's the thinly disguised setting for part of the series' action. ⊠ *Between Jones and Taylor Sts. and Union and Green Sts. Russian Hill.*

41 Inter-Continental Mark Hopkins Hotel. Built on the ashes of railroad tycoon Mark Hopkins's grand estate (constructed at his wife's urging; Hopkins himself preferred to live frugally), this 19-story hotel went up in 1926. A combination of French-château and Spanish-Renaissance architecture, with noteworthy terra-cotta detailing, it has hosted statesmen, royalty, and Hollywood celebrities. The 11-room penthouse was turned into a glass-walled cocktail lounge in 1939: the Top of the Mark is remembered fondly by thousands of World War II veterans who jammed the lounge before leaving for overseas duty. With its 360-degree views, the lounge is a wonderful spot for a nighttime drink. ⊠ *999 California St., at Mason St., Nob Hill* ☎ *415/392–3434* ⊕ *www.markhopkins.net.*

39 Pacific Union Club. The former home of silver baron James Flood cost a whopping $1.5 million in 1886, when even a stylish Victorian like the Haas-Lilienthal House cost less than $20,000. All that cash did buy some structural stability. The Flood residence was the only Nob Hill mansion to survive the 1906 earthquake and fire. The Pacific Union Club, a bastion of the wealthy and powerful, purchased the house in 1907 and commissioned Willis Polk to redesign it; the architect added the semicircular wings and 3rd floor. The club itself is closed to the public. ⊠ *1000 California St., Nob Hill.*

47 San Francisco Art Institute. A Moorish-tile fountain in a tree-shaded courtyard draws the eye as soon as you enter the institute. The highlight of a visit is Mexican master Diego Rivera's *Making of a Fresco Showing the Building of a City* (1931), in the student gallery to your immediate left inside the entrance. Rivera himself is in the fresco—his back is to the viewer—and he's surrounded by his assistants. The older portions of the Art Institute were erected in 1926. Ansel Adams created the school's fine-arts photography department in 1946, and school directors established the country's first fine-arts film program. The **Walter & McBean Galleries** (☎ 415/749–4563 ⊙ Tues.–Sat. 11–6) exhibit the often provocative works of established artists. ⊠ *800 Chestnut St., North Beach* ☎ *415/771–7020* ⊕ *www.sanfranciscoart.edu* ⊠ *Galleries free* ⊙ *Student gallery daily 8:30–8:30.*

Pacific Heights & Japantown

Pacific Heights defines San Francisco's most expensive and dramatic real estate. Grand Victorians line the streets, mansions and town houses are often priced in the millions, and there are magnificent views from almost any point in the neighborhood. Japantown, or Nihonmachi, is centered on the southern slope of Pacific Heights, north of Geary Boulevard between Fillmore and Laguna streets. Around 1860 a wave of Japanese immigrants arrived in San Francisco, which they called Soko. By the 1930s they had opened shops, markets, meeting halls, and restaurants and established Shinto and Buddhist temples.

What to See

48 Alta Plaza Park. Landscape architect John McLaren, who also created Golden Gate Park, designed Alta Plaza in 1910, modeling its terracing on the Grand Casino in Monte Carlo, Monaco. From the top you can see Marin to the north, downtown to the east, Twin Peaks to the south, and Golden Gate Park to the west. ⊠ *Bordered by Clay, Steiner, Jackson, and Scott Sts., Pacific Heights.*

52 Franklin Street buildings. What at first looks like a stone facade on the **Golden Gate Church** (⊠ 1901 Franklin St., Pacific Heights) is actually redwood painted white. A Georgian-style residence built in the early 1900s for a coffee merchant sits at 1735 Franklin. On the northeast corner of Franklin and California streets is a **Christian Science church**; built in the Tuscan-revival style, it's noteworthy for its terra-cotta detailing. The **Coleman House** (⊠ 1701 Franklin St., Pacific Heights) is an impressive twin-turreted Queen Anne mansion that was built for a gold-rush mining and lumber baron. Don't miss the large, brilliant-purple stained-glass window on the house's north side. ⊠ *Franklin St. between Washington and California Sts., Pacific Heights.*

51 Haas-Lilienthal House. A small display of photographs on the bottom floor of this elaborate, gray 1886 Queen Anne house, which cost a mere $18,500 to build, makes clear that it was modest compared with some of the giants that fell victim to the 1906 earthquake and fire. The Foundation for San Francisco's Architectural Heritage operates the home, whose carefully kept rooms provide an intriguing glimpse into late-19th-century life. Volunteers conduct one-hour house tours three days a week and informative two-hour walking tours ($8) of the Civic Center, Broadway, and Union Street areas on Saturday afternoons, and of the eastern portion of Pacific Heights on Sunday afternoons. ⊠ *2007 Franklin St., between Washington and Jackson Sts., Pacific Heights* ☎ *415/441–3004* ⊕ *www.sfheritage.org* ⊠ *Entry $8* ⊙ *1-hr tour Wed. and Sat. noon–3, Sun. 11–4, 2-hr tour Sun. at 12:30.*

12

55 **Japan Center.** The noted American architect Minoru Yamasaki created this 5-acre complex, which opened in 1968. Architecturally the development hasn't aged well, and its Peace Plaza, where seasonal festivals are held, is an unwelcoming sea of cement. The Japan Center includes the shop- and restaurant-filled Kintetsu and Kinokuniya buildings; the excellent Kabuki Springs & Spa; the Radisson Miyako hotel; and a multiplex cinema. Five major components of the center were put up for sale in 2006 as Japantown prepared to celebrate its centennial. Between the Miyako Mall and Kintetsu Building are the five-tier, 100-foot-tall **Peace Pagoda** and the Peace Plaza. ⊠ *Bordered by Geary Blvd. and Fillmore, Post, and Laguna Sts., Japantown* ☎ *415/922–6776.*

54 **Japan Center Mall.** The buildings lining this open-air mall are of the shoji school of architecture. Seating in this area can be found on local artist Ruth Asawa's twin origami-style fountains, which sit in the middle of the mall; they're squat circular structures made of fieldstone, with three levels for sitting and a brick floor. ⊠ *Buchanan St. between Post and Sutter Sts., Japantown* ☎ *No phone.*

★ **56** **Kabuki Springs & Spa.** Japantown's house of tranquility offers a treatment regimen that includes facials, salt scrubs, and mud and seaweed wraps. You can take your massage in a private room with a bath or in a curtained-off area. The communal baths ($16 before 5 PM, $20 after 5 and all weekend) contain hot and cold tubs, a large Japanese-style bath, a sauna, a steam room, and showers. ⊠ *1750 Geary Blvd., Japantown* ☎ *415/922–6000* ⊕ *www.kabukisprings.com* ⊙ *Daily 10–10.*

53 **Noteworthy Victorians.** Two **Italianate Victorians** (⊠ 1818 and 1834 California St., Pacific Heights) stand out on the 1800 block of California. A block farther is the Victorian-era **Atherton House** (⊠ 1990 California St., Pacific Heights), whose mildly daffy design incorporates Queen Anne, Stick-Eastlake, and other architectural elements. Many claim the house—now apartments—is haunted by the ghosts of its 19th-century residents, who regularly whisper, glow, and generally cause a mild fuss. The oft-photographed **Laguna Street Victorians,** on the west side of the 1800 block of Laguna Street, cost between $2,000 and $2,600 when they were built in the 1870s. ⊠ *California St. between Franklin and Octavia Sts., and Laguna St. between Pine and Bush Sts., Pacific Heights.*

50 **Spreckels Mansion.** Shrouded behind tall juniper hedges at the corner of lovely winding, brick Octavia Street, overlooking Lafayette Park, the estate was built for sugar heir Adolph Spreckels and his wife, Alma. Mrs. Spreckels was so pleased with her house that she commissioned George Applegarth to design the Legion of Honor. Alma Spreckels was the model for the bronze figure atop the Victory Monument in Union Square. Today the house belongs to prolific romance novelist Danielle Steele. ⊠ *2080 Washington St., at Octavia St., Pacific Heights.*

49 **Whittier Mansion.** With a Spanish-tile roof and scrolled bay windows on all four sides, this was one of the most elegant 19th-century houses in the state. An anomaly in a town that lost most of its grand mansions to the 1906 quake, the Whittier Mansion was built so solidly that only a chimney toppled over during the disaster. ⊠ *2090 Jackson St., Pacific Heights.*

Civic Center

The Civic Center—the Beaux-Arts complex between McAllister and Grove streets and Franklin and Hyde streets that includes City Hall, the War Memorial Opera House, the Veterans Building, and the old public library, now home of the Asian Art Museum and Cultural Center—is a product of the "City Beautiful" movement of the early 20th century. City Hall, completed in 1915 and renovated in 1999, is the centerpiece.

What to See

★ ⑤⑧ **Asian Art Museum.** One of the largest collections of Asian art in the world is housed within this museum's monumental, imposing exterior. More than 15,000 sculptures, paintings, and ceramics from 40 countries, illustrating major periods of Asian art, are stored here, with about 2,500 pieces on display. Highlights of Buddhism in Southeast Asia and early China include a large, jewel-encrusted, 19th-century Burmese Buddha seated on a throne and exquisitely painted and clothed rod puppets from Java. ✉ *200 Larkin St., between McAllister and Fulton Sts., Civic Center* ☎ *415/581–3500* ⊕ *www.asianart.org* ✑ *$10, free 1st Tues. of month; tea ceremony $20 (includes museum)* ☉ *Tues., Wed., and Fri.–Sun. 10–5, Thurs. 10–9.*

⑤⑨ **City Hall.** This masterpiece of granite and marble was modeled after St. Peter's cathedral in Rome. City Hall's bronze and gold-leaf dome dominates the area. The classical influences of Paris-trained architect Arthur Brown Jr., who also designed Coit Tower and the War Memorial Opera House, can be seen throughout the structure. The palatial interior, full of grand arches and with a sweeping central staircase, is impressive. Some noteworthy events that have taken place here include the hosing—down the central staircase—of civil-rights and freedom-of-speech protesters (1960) and the murders of Mayor George Moscone and openly gay supervisor Harvey Milk (1978). In spring 2004 thousands of gay and lesbian couples responded to Mayor Gavin Newsom's decision to issue marriage licenses to same-sex partners, turning City Hall into the site of raucous celebration and joyful nuptials for a month before the state Supreme Court ordered the practice stopped. Inside City Hall you can view pieces from the yet-to-be-relocated **Museum of the City of San Francisco** (⊕ www.sfmuseum.org), including historical items, maps, photographs, and the enormous head of the *Goddess of Progress* statue, which crowned the original City Hall building when it crumbled during the 1906 earthquake. ✉ *Bordered by Van Ness Ave. and Polk, Grove, and McAllister Sts., Civic Center* ☎ *415/554–6023* ⊕ *www.ci. sf.ca.us/cityhall* ✑ *Free* ☉ *Weekdays 8–8, Sat. noon–4.*

⑤⑦ **United Nations Plaza.** Brick pillars listing various nations and the dates of their admittance into the United Nations line the plaza, and its floor is inscribed with the goals and philosophy of the United Nations charter. ✉ *Fulton St. between Hyde and Market Sts., Civic Center.*

⑥⓪ **War Memorial Opera House.** All the old opera houses were destroyed in the 1906 quake, but lusty support for opera continued. The San Francisco Opera didn't have a permanent home until the War Memorial Opera House was inaugurated in 1932 with a performance of *Tosca*. Modeled after its European counterparts, the building has a vaulted and coffered ceiling, marble foyer, two balconies, and a huge silver art-deco chandelier that resembles a sunburst. ⊠ *301 Van Ness Ave., Civic Center* ☎ *415/621–6600* ⊕ *www.sfwmpac.org.*

The Northern Waterfront

For the sights, sounds, and smells of the sea, hop the Powell–Hyde cable car from Union Square and take it to the end of the line. The views as you descend Hyde Street toward the bay are breathtaking—tiny sailboats bob in the whitecaps, Alcatraz hovers ominously in the distance, and the Marin Headlands form a rugged backdrop to the Golden Gate Bridge. Once you reach sea level at the cable-car turnaround, Aquatic Park and the National Maritime Museum are immediately to the west, and the commercial attractions of the Fisherman's Wharf area are to the east. Bring good walking shoes and a jacket or sweater for midafternoon breezes or foggy mists.

What to See

★ **Alcatraz Island.** The boat ride to the island is brief (15 minutes) but affords beautiful views of the city, Marin County, and the East Bay. The audio tour, highly recommended, includes observations of guards and prisoners about life in one of America's most notorious penal colonies. A separate ranger-led tour surveys the island's ecology. Plan your schedule to allow at least three hours for the visit and boat rides combined. Reservations, even in the off-season, are strongly recommended. ⊠ *Pier 41, Fisherman's Wharf* ☎ *415/773–1188 boat schedules and information, 415/705–5555, 800/426–8687 credit-card ticket orders, 415/705–1042 park information* ⊠ *$11.50; $16 with audio tour; $23.50 evening tour, including audio* ☉ *Ferry departures every 30–45 mins Sept.–late May, daily 9:30–2:15, 4:20 for evening tour Thurs.–Mon. only; late May–Aug., daily 9:30–4:15, 6:30 and 7:30 for evening tour* ⊕ *www.parksconservancy.org/visit/alcatraz.php.*

63 **The Cannery at Del Monte Square.** The three-story structure was built in 1894 to house what became the Del Monte Fruit and Vegetable Cannery. Today it contains shops, art galleries, a comedy club (the Green Room), and some unusual restaurants, all geared toward tourists. ⊠ *2801 Leavenworth St., Fisherman's Wharf* ☎ *415/771–3112* ⊕ *www.delmontesquare.com.*

64 **Fisherman's Wharf.** Ships creak at their moorings; seagulls cry out for a handout. By midafternoon the fishing fleet is back to port. The chaotic streets of the wharf have numerous seafood restaurants, among them sidewalk stands where shrimp and crab cocktails are sold in disposable containers. T-shirts and sweats, gold chains galore, redwood furniture, acres of artwork, and generally amusing street artists also beckon to visitors.

Most of the entertainment at the wharf is schlocky and overpriced, with one notable exception: the splendid **Musée Mécanique** (☎ 415/346–2000 ☉ Memorial Day–Labor Day, daily 10–8; rest of yr, weekdays 11–7, weekends 10–8), a time-warped arcade with antique mechanical contrivances, including peep shows and nickelodeons. Some favorites are the giant and rather creepy "Laughing Sal," an arm-wrestling machine, and

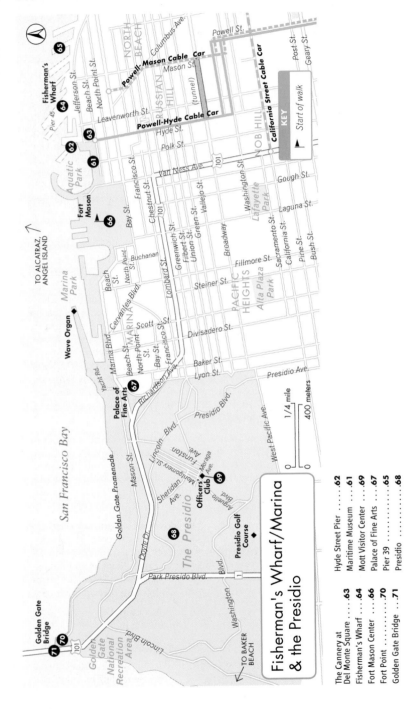

Fisherman's Wharf/Marina & the Presidio

mechanical fortune-telling figures that speak from their curtained boxes. Admission is free, but you'll need quarters to bring the machines to life.

The USS *Pampanito* (⊠ Pier 45, Fisherman's Wharf ☎ 415/775–1943 ☉ Oct.–Memorial Day, Sun.–Thurs. 9–6, Fri. and Sat. 9–8; Memorial Day–Sept., Thurs.–Tues. 9–8, Wed. 9–6) provides an intriguing if mildly claustrophobic glimpse into life on a submarine during World War II. Admission is $9; the family pass is a great deal at $20 for two adults and up to four kids. ⊠ *Jefferson St. between Leavenworth St. and Pier 39, Fisherman's Wharf.*

12

❻❷ Hyde Street Pier. Cotton candy and souvenirs are all well and good, but if you want to get to the heart of the wharf—boats—there's no better place to do it than this pier, by far one of the wharf area's best bargains. Depending on the time of day, you might see boatbuilders at work or children manning a ship as folks did in the early 1900s. Don't pass up the centerpiece collection of historic vessels, part of the **San Francisco Maritime National Historic Park,** all of which can be boarded. Across the street from the pier and almost a museum in itself, the San Francisco Maritime National Historic Park's **Visitor Center** (⊠ Jefferson St., at Hyde St. ☎ 415/447–5000 ☉ Memorial Day–mid-Oct., daily 9:30–7; mid-Oct.–Memorial Day, daily 9:30–5) is an engaging and relatively quick stop. ⊠ *Hyde and Jefferson Sts., Fisherman's Wharf* ☎ *415/561–7100* ⊕ *www.nps.gov/safr* ☑ *Ships $5* ☉ *Daily 9:30–5.*

❻❶ Maritime Museum. Part of the **San Francisco Maritime National Historical Park,** the museum has three floors that exhibit intricate ship models, beautifully restored figureheads, photographs of life at sea, and other artifacts chronicling the maritime history of San Francisco and the West Coast. ⚠ **At this writing, the ship-shaped structure is expected to be closed for extensive renovations until 2009.** ⊠ *Aquatic Park foot of Polk St., Fisherman's Wharf* ☎ *415/561–7100* ⊕ *www.nps.gov/safr* ☑ *Donation suggested* ☉ *Daily 10–5.*

❻❺ Pier 39. The city's most popular waterfront attraction draws millions of visitors each year, who come to browse through its vertiginous array of shops and concessions hawking every conceivable form of souvenir. You may feel as if the many millions are there at once—the pier can be quite crowded, and the numerous street performers may leave you feeling more harassed than entertained. Brilliant colors enliven the double-decker **San Francisco Carousel** (☑ $2 per ride), decorated with images of such city landmarks as the Golden Gate Bridge and Lombard Street. At **Aquarium of the Bay** (☎ 415/623–5300 or 888/732–3483 ⊕ www. aquariumofthebay.com ☑ $12.95), moving walkways transport you through a space surrounded on three sides by water filled with indigenous San Francisco Bay marine life. The aquarium is open June through September daily 9 to 8, otherwise weekdays 10 to 6, weekends 10 to 7. ⊠ *Beach St. at Embarcadero, Fisherman's Wharf* ⊕ *www.pier39.com.*

The Marina & the Presidio

The Marina district was a coveted place to live until the 1989 earthquake, when the area's homes suffered the worst damage in the city—

A GOOD TOUR

Though you can visit the sights below using public transportation, this is the place to use your car if you have one. You might even consider renting one for a day to cover the area, as well as Lincoln Park, Golden Gate Park, and the western shoreline.

The time it takes to see this area varies greatly, depending on whether you take public transportation or drive. If you drive, plan to spend at least three hours, not including a walk across the Golden Gate Bridge or hikes along the shoreline—each of which takes a few hours. With or without kids, you could easily pass two hours at the Exploratorium.

Start at **Fort Mason Center** 🅖🅖 ▶, whose entrance for automobiles is off Marina Boulevard at Buchanan Street. If you're coming by bus, take Bus 30-Stockton heading north (and later west); get off at Chestnut and Laguna streets and walk north three blocks to the pedestrian entrance at Marina Boulevard and Laguna. To get from Fort Mason to the **Palace of Fine Arts** 🅖 by car, make a right on Marina Boulevard. The road curves past a small marina and the Marina Green. Turn left at Divisadero Street, right on North Point Street, left on Baker Street, and right on Bay Street, which passes the palace's lagoon and dead-ends at the Lyon Street parking lot. Part of the palace complex is the **Exploratorium,** a hands-on science museum. (If you're walking from Fort Mason to the palace, the directions are easier: Follow Marina Boulevard to Scott Street. Cross to the south side of the street—away from the water—and continue past Divisadero Street to

Baker Street; turn left; the palace lagoon is on your right. To take Muni, walk back to Chestnut and Laguna streets and take Bus 30-Stockton continuing west; get off at North Point and Broderick streets and walk west on North Point.)

The least confusing way to drive to the **Presidio** 🅖🅖 from the palace is to exit from the south end of the Lyon Street parking lot and head east (left) on Bay Street. Turn right (south) onto Baker Street, and right (west) on Francisco Street, taking it across Richardson Avenue to Lyon Street. Turn south (left) on Lyon and right (west) on Lombard Street, and go through the main gate to Presidio Boulevard. Turn right on Lincoln Boulevard and left on Funston Avenue to Moraga Avenue and the Presidio's **Mott Visitor Center** 🅖🅖 at the Officers' Club. (To take the bus to the Presidio, walk north from the palace to Lombard Street and catch Bus 28 heading west; it stops on Lincoln near the visitor center.)

From the visitor center head back up Funston Avenue and turn left on Lincoln Boulevard. Lincoln winds through the Presidio past a large cemetery and some vista points. After a couple of miles is a parking lot marked FORT POINT on the right. Park and follow the signs leading to **Fort Point** 🅖🅖, walking downhill through a lightly wooded area. To walk the short distance to the **Golden Gate Bridge** 🅖🅖, follow the signs from the Fort Point parking lot; to drive across the bridge, continue on Lincoln Boulevard a bit and watch for the turnoff on the right. Bus 28 serves stops fairly near these last two attractions; ask the driver to call them out.

largely because the Marina is built on landfill. Many home owners and renters fled in search of more-solid ground, but young professionals quickly replaced them, changing the tenor of this formerly low-key neighborhood. The number of upscale coffee emporiums skyrocketed, a bank became a Williams-Sonoma, and the local grocer gave way to a Pottery Barn. West of the Marina is the sprawling Presidio, a former military base. The Presidio has superb views and the best hiking and biking areas in San Francisco.

What to See

★ ☺ **Exploratorium.** The curious of all ages flock to this fascinating "museum of science, art, and human perception." The more than 650 exhibits focus on sea and insect life, computers, electricity, patterns and light, language, the weather, and much more. Reservations are required to crawl through the pitch-black, touchy-feely Tactile Dome, a 15-minute adventure. ⊠ *3601 Lyon St., at Marina Blvd., Marina* ☎ *415/561–0360 general information, 415/561–0362 Tactile Dome reservations* ⊕ *www. exploratorium.edu* ✆ *$13, free 1st Wed. of month; Tactile Dome $3 extra* ☉ *Tues.–Sun. 10–5.*

▶ ⑥⑥ **Fort Mason Center.** Originally a depot for the shipment of supplies to the Pacific during World War II, the fort was converted into a cultural center in 1977. Here you'll find the vegetarian restaurant Greens and shops, galleries, and performance spaces, most of which are closed Monday. There's also plentiful free parking—a rarity in the city.

The **Museo Italo-Americano** (⊠ Bldg. C ☎ 415/673–2200 ☉ Wed.–Sun. noon–4; noon–7 1st Wed. of month) mounts impressive exhibits of Italian and Italian-American paintings, sculpture, etchings, and photographs. Admission is $3; free on the first Wednesday of the month. At the free **SFMOMA Artists Gallery** (⊠ Bldg. A ☎ 415/441–4777) you can rent or buy what you see. It's open Tuesday through Saturday 11:30–5:30, until 7:30 the first Wednesday of the month. ⊠ *Buchanan St. and Marina Blvd., Marina* ☎ *415/979–3010 event information* ⊕ *www.fortmason.org.*

☺ ⑦⓪ **Fort Point.** Designed to mount 126 cannons with a range of up to 2 mi, the fort was constructed between 1853 and 1861 to protect San Francisco from sea attack during the Civil War—but it was never used for that purpose. It was, however, used as a coastal-defense-fortification post during World War II, when soldiers stood watch here. This National Historic Site is a museum filled with military memorabilia. On days when Fort Point is staffed, guided tours and cannon drills take place. ⊠ *Marine Dr. off Lincoln Blvd., Presidio* ☎ *415/556–1693* ⊕ *www. nps.gov/fopo* ✆ *Free* ☉ *Fri.–Sun. 10–5.*

★ ⑦① **Golden Gate Bridge.** The suspension bridge that connects San Francisco with Marin County has long wowed sightseers with its simple but powerful art-deco design. Completed in 1937 after four years of construction, the 2-mi span and its 750-foot towers were built to withstand winds of more than 100 mph. The east walkway yields a glimpse of the San Francisco skyline and the bay islands, and the view west takes in the wild hills of the Marin Headlands, the curving coast south to Land's

End, and the majestic Pacific Ocean. A vista point on the Marin side affords a spectacular city panorama. ⊠ *Lincoln Blvd. near Doyle Dr. and Fort Point, Presidio* ☎ *415/921–5858* ⊕ *www.goldengatebridge. org* ☉ *Pedestrians Apr.–Oct., daily 5 AM–9 PM; Nov.–May, daily 6 AM–6 PM. Bicyclists daily 24 hrs.*

69 Mott Visitor Center. Tucked away in the Presidio's Mission-style Officers' Club, the William P. Mott Jr. Visitor Center dispenses maps, brochures, and schedules for guided walking and bicycle tours, along with information about the Presidio's past, present, and future. History boards tell the story of the Presidio, from military outpost to self-sustaining park. ⊠ *50 Moraga Ave., Presidio* ☎ *415/561–4323* ☉ *Daily 9–5.*

67 Palace of Fine Arts. At first glance this stunning, rosy rococo palace
FodorsChoice seems to be from another world, and indeed, it's the sole survivor of
★ the many tinted-plaster structures (a temporary classical city of sorts) built for the 1915 Panama-Pacific International Exposition, the world's fair that celebrated San Francisco's recovery from the 1906 earthquake and fire. Bernard Maybeck designed this faux Roman-classic beauty, which was reconstructed in concrete and reopened in 1967. The massive columns, great rotunda (dedicated to the glory of Greek culture), and swan-filled lagoon have been used in countless fashion layouts and films. ⊠ *Baker and Beach Sts., Marina* ☎ *415/561–0364 palace tours* ⊕ *www.exploratorium.edu/palace* ⊿ *Free* ☉ *Daily 24 hrs.*

68 Presidio. Part of the **Golden Gate National Recreation Area,** the Presidio was a military post for more than 200 years. Don Juan Bautista de Anza and a band of Spanish settlers first claimed the area in 1776. It became a Mexican garrison in 1822 when Mexico gained its independence from Spain; U.S. troops forcibly occupied the Presidio in 1846. The U.S. Sixth Army was stationed here until October 1994, when the coveted space was transferred into civilian hands. Today, after much controversy, the area is being transformed into a self-sustaining national park with a combination of public, commercial, and residential projects. ⊠ *Between Marina and Lincoln Park, Presidio* ⊕ *www.nps.gov/prsf.*

Golden Gate Park

William Hammond Hall conceived one of the nation's great city parks and began in 1870 to put into action his plan for a natural reserve with no reminders of urban life. John McLaren finished Hall's work during his tenure as park superintendent, from 1890 to 1943, to complete the transformation of 1,000 desolate brush- and sand-covered acres into a rolling, landscaped oasis. Urban reality now encroaches on all sides, but the park remains a great getaway. The fog can sweep into the park with amazing speed; always bring a sweatshirt or jacket.

Because the park is so large, a car comes in handy if you're going to tour it from one end to the other—though you'll still do a fair amount of walking. Weekends and holidays from June to mid-December, the Golden Gate Park Free Shuttle runs every 15 minutes between 15 stops in the park; visit ⊕ www.goldengateparkconcourse.org for information. Muni serves the park. Buses 5–Fulton and 21–Hayes stop along its

A GOOD WALK

You can easily spend an entire day in Golden Gate Park. The **Conservatory of Flowers** ❷ ► is the first stop on this walk. Less than a block away at the intersection of Middle and Bowling Green drives is a sign for the National AIDS Memorial Grove. Before you enter the grove, follow the curve of Bowling Green Drive to the left, past the Bowling Green to the Children's Playground.

Reverse direction on Bowling Green Drive and enter the **National AIDS Memorial Grove** ❸, a sunken meadow that stretches west along Middle Drive East. At the end of the wheelchair-access ramp make a left to view the Circle of Friends; then continue west along the graded paths to another circle with a poem by Thom Gunn. Exit north from this circle. As you're standing in the circle looking at the poem, the staircase to take is on your left. At the top of the staircase make a left and continue west on Middle Drive East.

A hundred feet shy of the 9th Avenue and Lincoln Way entrance to Golden Gate Park is the main entrance to **Strybing Arboretum & Botanical Gardens** ❹. Take the first right after the bookstore. Follow the path as it winds north and west. Take the second right and look for signs for the Fragrance and Biblical gardens.

Backtrack from the gardens to the path you started on and make a right. As the path continues to wind north and west, you'll see a large fountain to the left. Just before you get to the fountain, make a right and head toward the duck pond. A wooden footbridge on the pond's left side crosses the water. Stay to the right on the path, heading

toward the exit gate. Just before the gate, continue to the right to the Primitive Garden. Take the looped boardwalk past ferns, gingko, cycads, conifers, moss, and other plants. At the end of the loop, make a left and then a right, exiting via the Eugene L. Friend gate. Go straight ahead on the crosswalk to the blacktop path on the other side. Make a right, walk about 100 feet, and make a left on Tea Garden Drive. A few hundred feet east of here is the entrance to the **Japanese Tea Garden** ❺.

Tour the garden, exiting near the gate you entered. Make a left toward the huge **de Young Museum** ❻. A crosswalk leads south to the Music Concourse, with its gnarled trees, century-old fountains and sculptures, and the Golden Gate Bandshell. Turn left at the closest of the fountains and head east toward the bronze sculpture of Francis Scott Key.

Turn left at the statue and proceed north through two underpasses. Make an immediate left as you exit the second underpass, cross 10th Avenue, and make a right on John F. Kennedy Drive. After approximately ¼ mi the Rose Garden is on your right. Continue west to the first stop sign. To the left is a sign for **Stow Lake** ❼. Follow the road past the log cabin to the boathouse.

From Stow Lake it's the equivalent of 30 long blocks on John F. Kennedy Drive to the western end of the park and the ocean. Along the way, you pass meadows, the Portals of the Past, the buffalo paddock, and a 9-hole golf course. Your goal is the **Dutch Windmill** ❽ and adjoining garden.

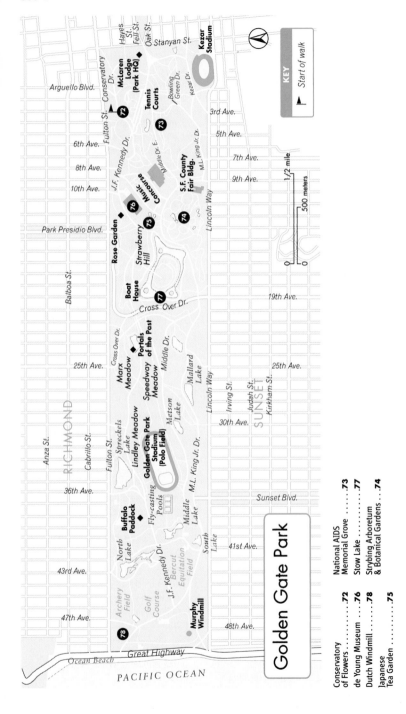

Golden Gate Park

KEY

▲ Start of walk

PACIFIC OCEAN

Ocean Beach

Great Highway

northern edge, and the N–Judah light-rail car stops a block south of the park between Stanyan Street and 9th Avenue, then two blocks south and the rest of the way west.

What to See

(72) **Conservatory of Flowers.** Many first-time visitors gasp in awe when they see this gorgeous, white-framed glass structure, and locals will tell you that its effect isn't much dimmed over time. Built in the late 1870s, the oldest building in the park is the last remaining wood-frame Victorian conservatory in the country. It's also a copy of the conservatory in the Royal Botanical Gardens in Kew, England, with a spectacular, 14-ton glass dome atop its perch. The gardens in front of the conservatory are planted seasonally, with the flowers often fashioned like billboards depicting the Golden Gate Bridge or other city sights. ✉ *John F. Kennedy Dr. at Conservatory Dr., Golden Gate Park* ☎ *415/666–7001* 🌐 *www.conservatoryofflowers.org* 🎫 *$5* 🕘 *Tues.–Sun. 9–4:30.*

★ (76) **de Young Museum.** After suffering irreparable damage in the 1989 Loma Prieta earthquake, the de Young, founded in 1895, was demolished and rebuilt. It seems that everyone in town has a strong opinion about the new museum, unveiled in 2005. The building itself has almost overshadowed the de Young's respected collection which includes paintings by Winslow Homer, Edward Hopper, Georgia O'Keeffe, Diego Rivera, Willem de Kooning, Mark Rothko, and many others. The ninth-story observation room, ringed by floor-to-ceiling windows and home to a full wall-size photo of the city from the air, is worth the price of admission alone. ✉ *50 Tea Garden Dr.* ☎ *415/863–3330* 🌐 *www.thinker.org/deyoung* 🎫 *$10, free 1st Tues. of month* 🕘 *Tues.–Sun. 9:30–5, Fri. 9:30–8:45.*

(78) **Dutch Windmill.** If you venture far enough west in the park, you'll be greeted by the odd sight of these two windmills, one carefully restored, the other in disrepair, both chained down to prevent windmilling. The restored 1902 Dutch Windmill once pumped 20,000 gallons of well water per hour to the reservoir on Strawberry Hill. If you find yourself on this end of the park, the windmills merit a peek, but on their own they're not worth a trip this far west. ✉ *John F. Kennedy Dr. between 47th Ave. and the Great Hwy., Golden Gate Park.*

★ (75) **Japanese Tea Garden.** A peaceful 4-acre landscape of small ponds, streams, waterfalls, stone bridges, Japanese sculptures, *mumsai* (bonsai) trees, perfect miniature pagodas, and some nearly vertical wooden "humpback" bridges, the tea garden was created for the 1894 Mid-Winter Exposition. Go in the spring if you can (March is particularly beautiful), when the cherry blossoms are in bloom. ✉ *Tea Garden Dr. off John F. Kennedy Dr., Golden Gate Park* ☎ *415/752–4227* 🎫 *$3.50* 🕘 *Mar.–Sept., daily 9–6; Oct.–Feb., daily 9–5.*

(73) **National AIDS Memorial Grove.** San Francisco has lost many residents, gay and straight, to AIDS. This 15-acre grove, started in the early 1990s by people with AIDS and their families and friends, was conceived as a living memorial to those the disease has claimed. Coast live oaks, Monterey pines, coast redwoods, and other trees flank the grove, which is anchored at its east end by the stone Circle of Friends. ✉ *Middle Dr.*

E, west of tennis courts, Golden Gate Park ☎ *415/750–8340* ⊕ *www. aidsmemorial.org.*

🐤 **❼ Stow Lake.** One of the most photogenic spots in Golden Gate Park, this placid body of water surrounds Strawberry Hill. Cross one of the bridges—the 19th-century stone bridge on the southwest side of the lake is lovely—and ascend the hill, where a waterfall cascades from the top and panoramic views ease the short hike up here. Just to the left of the waterfall sits the elaborate Chinese Pavilion, a gift from the city of Taipei. ⊠ *Off John F. Kennedy Dr., ½ mi west of 10th Ave., Golden Gate Park* ☎ *415/752–0347 bike rental, 415/668–6699 surrey and bike rental* ☉ *Boat rentals daily 10–4, surrey and bike rentals weekdays 9–dusk, weekends 10–dusk.*

❼ Strybing Arboretum & Botanical Gardens. One of the best picnic spots in a very picnic-friendly park, the 55-acre arboretum specializes in plants from areas with climates similar to that of the Bay Area, such as the west coast of Australia, South Africa, and the Mediterranean; more than 8,000 plant and tree varieties bloom in gardens throughout the grounds. Maps are available at the main and Eugene L. Friend entrances. ⊠ *Enter park at 9th Ave. at Lincoln Way, Golden Gate Park* ☎ *415/661–1316* ⊕ *www.strybing.org* ⊠ *Free* ☉ *Weekdays 8–4:30, weekends 10–5* ☞ *Tours from bookstore weekdays at 1:30, weekends at 10:20 and 1:30; tours from Friend Gate Wed., Fri., and Sun. at 2.*

The Western Shoreline

From Land's End in Lincoln Park you have some of the best views of the Golden Gate (the name was given to the opening of San Francisco Bay long before the bridge was built) and the Marin Headlands. From the historic Cliff House south to the sprawling San Francisco Zoo, the Great Highway and Ocean Beach run along the western edge of the city. The wind is often strong along the shoreline, summer fog can blanket the ocean beaches, and the water is cold and usually too rough for swimming. Carry a jacket and bring binoculars.

What to See

❽ Cliff House. Three buildings have occupied this site since 1863, and the current incarnation includes two restaurants and a gift shop. The vistas, which include offshore Seal Rock (the barking marine mammals there are actually sea lions), can be 30 mi or more on a clear day or less than a mile on foggy days. The upstairs Bistro is more casual, whereas downstairs is the fancier and pricier Sutro's. Both places appropriately emphasize seafood dishes, and though they're both fairly expensive, the grand views are priceless. To the north of the Cliff House are the ruins of the glass-roof **Sutro Baths.** ⊠ *1090 Point Lobos Ave., Lincoln Park* ☎ *415/386–3330* ⊕ *www.cliffhouse.com* ⊠ *Free* ☉ *Weekdays 9 AM– 9:30 PM, weekends 9 AM–10 PM.*

❽ Legion of Honor. Spectacularly situated on cliffs overlooking the ocean, the Golden Gate Bridge, and the Marin Headlands, this landmark building is a fine repository of European art. A pyramidal glass skylight in the entrance court illuminates the lower-level galleries, which exhibit prints

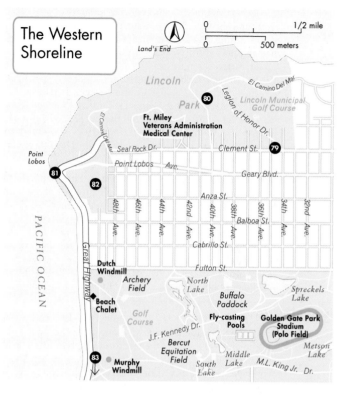

and drawings, English and European porcelain, and ancient Assyrian, Greek, Roman, and Egyptian art. The 20-plus galleries on the upper level display the permanent collection of European art (paintings, sculpture, decorative arts, tapestries) from the 14th century to the present day. The noteworthy Auguste Rodin collection includes two galleries devoted to the master and a third with works by Rodin and other 19th-century sculptors. ⊠ *34th Ave. at Clement St., Lincoln Park* ☎ *415/863–3330* ⊕ *www.thinker.org* ⊠ *$10, $2 off with Muni transfer, free Tues.* ☾ *Tues.–Sun. 9:30–5.*

79 **Lincoln Park.** While many of the city's green spaces are gentle and welcoming, Lincoln Park is wild, a 275-acre park with windswept cliffs and sweeping views. The most dramatic trail leads out to **Land's End**; it starts west of the Legion of Honor, at the end of El Camino del Mar. On the tamer side, large Monterey cypresses line the fairways at Lincoln Park's 18-hole golf course, near the Legion of Honor. ⊠ *Entrance at 34th Ave. at Clement St., Lincoln Park.*

☾ **83** **San Francisco Zoo.** More than 1,000 birds and animals—252 species altogether—reside here. Among the more than 130 endangered species are the snow leopard, Sumatran tiger, jaguar, and grizzly bear. African Kikuyu grass carpets the circular outer area of **Gorilla World**, one of the largest and most natural gorilla habitats of any zoo in the world. Trees and shrubs create communal play areas. Ten species of rare monkeys—including colobus monkeys, white ruffed lemurs, and macaques—live and play at the two-tier **Primate Discovery Center,** which contains 23 interactive learning exhibits on the ground level. The **Feline Conservation Center,** a natural setting for rare cats, plays a key role in the zoo's efforts to encourage breeding among endangered felines. ✉ *Sloat Blvd. and 47th Ave., Sunset, Muni L–Taraval streetcar from downtown* ☎ *415/753–7080* ⊕ *www.sfzoo.org* ✉ *$11, $1 off with Muni transfer, free 1st Wed. of month* ☉ *Daily 10–5. Children's zoo Memorial Day–Labor Day, daily 10:30–4:30; Labor Day–Memorial Day, weekdays 11–4, weekends 10:30–4:30.*

🔵 **Sutro Heights Park.** Crows and other large birds battle the heady breezes at this cliff-top park on what were the grounds of the home of Adolph Sutro, an eccentric mining engineer and former San Francisco mayor. Monterey cypresses and Canary Island palms dot this cliff-top park, and photos on placards depict what you would have seen before the house burned down in 1896. All that remains of the main house is its foundation. San Francisco City Guides (☎ 415/557–4266) runs a free Saturday tour of the park that starts at 2 (meet at the lion statue at 48th and Point Lobos avenues). ✉ *Point Lobos and 48th Aves., Lincoln Park.*

Mission District

The sunny Mission District wins out in San Francisco's system of microclimates—it's always the last to succumb to fog. The Mission has a number of distinct personalities: it's the Latino neighborhood, where working-class folks raise their families and where gangs occasionally clash; it's the hipster hood, where tattooed and pierced twenty- and thirtysomethings hold court in the coolest cafés and bars in town; it's the city's culinary epicenter, whose concentration of destination restaurants and affordable ethnic cuisine draws diners from all over town (and the Bay Area); and it's the artists' quarter, where murals adorn literally blocks of walls. Still quite scruffy in patches, the Mission can be intimidating to visitors, especially at night, when it's at its liveliest. If you're concerned, stick to the area bordered by Mission, Dolores, 16th, and 20th streets—where everything is happening anyway.

What to See

🔵 **Galería de la Raza/Studio 24.** San Francisco's premier showcase for contemporary Latino art, the gallery exhibits the works of local and international artists. Next door is the nonprofit Studio 24, which sells prints and paintings by Chicano artists as well as folk art, mainly from Mexico. ✉ *2857 24th St., at Bryant St., Mission* ☎ *415/826–8009* ⊕ *www. galeriadelaraza.org* ☉ *Gallery Wed.–Sat. noon–6, Studio 24 daily noon–6.*

★ 🔵 **Mission Dolores.** Two churches stand side-by-side at this mission, including the small adobe **Mission San Francisco de Asís,** the oldest standing structure in San Francisco. Completed in 1791, it's the sixth of the 21 California missions founded by Father Junípero Serra in the 18th and early 19th centuries. The tiny chapel includes frescoes and a hand-painted wooden altar; some artifacts were brought from Mexico by mule

The Mission District/ Noe Valley

in the late 18th century. ⊠ *Dolores and 16th Sts., Mission* ☎ *415/621–8203* ⊕ *www.sfmuseum.org/hist5/misdolor.html* ✉ *$3 donation, audio tour $7* ⊘ *Daily 9–4.*

⑱ Precita Eyes Mural Arts and Visitors Center. The nonprofit arts organization sponsors guided walks of the Mission District's murals. Most tours start with a 45-minute slide presentation. The bike and walking trips, which take between one and three hours, pass several dozen murals. May is Mural Awareness Month, with visits to murals-in-progress and presentations by artists. You can pick up a map of 24th Street's murals at the center. ⊠ *2981 24th St., Mission* ☎ *415/285–2287* ⊕ *www.precitaeyes.org* ✉ *Center free, tours $10–$12* ⊘ *Center weekdays 10–5, Sat. 10–4, Sun. noon–4; walks weekends at 11 and 1:30 or by appointment.*

The Castro & the Haight

The Castro district—the social, cultural, and political center of the gay and lesbian community in San Francisco—is one of the liveliest and most welcoming neighborhoods in the city, especially on weekends. On Saturday and Sunday, the streets teem with folks out shopping, pushing political causes, heading to art films, and lingering in bars and cafés.

Young people looking for an affordable spot in which they could live according to new precepts began moving into the big old Victorians in the Haight in the late 1950s and early 1960s. By 1966 the Haight had become a hot spot for rock bands, including the Grateful Dead, Jefferson Airplane, and Janis Joplin. The Haight's famous political spirit survives today alongside some of the finest Victorian-lined streets in the city.

What to See

★ **⑱ Castro Theatre.** There are worse ways to while away an afternoon than catching a flick at this gorgeous, 1,500-seat art-deco theater; opened in 1922, it's the grandest of San Francisco's few remaining movie palaces. The neon marquee, standing at the top of the Castro strip, is the neighborhood's great landmark. Janet Gaynor, who in 1927 won the first Oscar for best actress, worked as an usher here. The Castro's elaborate Spanish baroque interior is fairly well preserved. The crowd can be enthusiastic and vocal, talking back to the screen as loudly as it talks to them. ⊠ *429 Castro St., Castro* ☎ *415/621–6120.*

⑨⓪ Haight-Ashbury intersection. Despite the Gap that today holds court on one of its quadrants, this famed corner was once the center of 1960s counterculture. Among the folks who hung out in or near the Haight during the late 1960s were writers Richard Brautigan, Allen Ginsberg, Ken Kesey, and Gary Snyder; anarchist Abbie Hoffman; rock performers Marty Balin, Jerry Garcia, Janis Joplin, and Grace Slick; LSD champion Timothy Leary; and filmmaker Kenneth Anger.

⛳ **⑱ Harvey Milk Plaza.** An 18-foot-long rainbow flag, a gay icon, flies above this plaza named for the man who electrified the city in 1977 by being elected to its Board of Supervisors as an openly gay candidate. The liberal Milk hadn't served a full year of his term before he and Mayor George Moscone, also a liberal, were shot in November 1978 at City Hall by

12

A GOOD WALK

Allot 60 to 90 minutes to visit the Castro district. Allow additional time for browsing and a coffee break, and set aside an extra hour to hike Corona Heights and visit the Randall Museum. The distance covered in the Haight is only several blocks, and although there are shops aplenty and other amusements, an hour or so should be enough.

Begin at **Harvey Milk Plaza** 87 ⚑ on the southwest corner of 17th and Market streets; it's outside the south entrance to the Castro Street Muni station (K, L, and M streetcars stop here). Across Castro Street from the plaza is the neighborhood's landmark, the **Castro Theatre** 88. Many shops line Castro Street between 17th and 19th streets, 18th between Sanchez and Eureka streets, and Market Street heading east toward downtown. After exploring the shops, get ready for a strenuous walk. For an unforgettable vista, continue north on Castro Street two blocks to 16th Street, turn left, and head up the steep hill to Flint Street. Turn right on Flint and follow the trail on the left (just past the tennis courts) up the hill. The beige buildings on the

left contain the **Randall Museum** 89 for children. Turn right up the dirt path, which soon loops back up Corona Heights. At the top you're treated to an all-encompassing view of the city.

Now continue north to walk the Haight Street tour. Follow the trail down the other side of Corona Heights to a grassy field. The gate to the field is at the intersection of Roosevelt Way and Museum Way. Turn right on Roosevelt (head down the hill) and cross Roosevelt at Park Hill Terrace. Walk up Park Hill to Buena Vista Avenue, turn left, and follow the road as it loops west and south around Buena Vista Park to Central Avenue. Head down Central two blocks to Haight Street and make a left.

Continue west to the fabled **Haight-Ashbury intersection** 90. A motley contingent of folks attired in retro fashions and often sporting hippie-long hair hangs here. One block south of Haight and Ashbury (at 710 Ashbury) is the Grateful Dead house, the pad that Jerry Garcia and band inhabited in the 1960s. The stores along Haight Street up to Shrader Street are worth checking out.

Dan White, a conservative ex-supervisor. Milk's assassination shocked the gay community, which became infuriated when the infamous "Twinkie defense"—that junk food had led to diminished mental capacity—resulted in a manslaughter verdict for White. During the so-called White Night Riot of May 21, 1979, gays and their sympathizers stormed City Hall, torching its lobby and several police cars. ⊠ *Southwest corner of Castro and Market Sts., Castro.*

🖐 89 **Randall Museum.** In addition to a greenhouse, woodworking and ceramics studios, and a theater, the museum has an educational animal room with birds, lizards, snakes, spiders, and other creatures that cannot be released to the wild because of injury or other problems. Spread over 16 acres of public land, the museum sits beneath a hill variously known

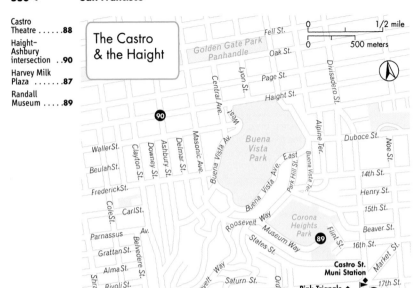

The Castro & the Haight

KEY
▶ Start of walk

TO TWIN PEAKS

TO NOE VALLEY

as Red Rock, Museum Hill, and, correctly, Corona Heights. ✉ *199 Museum Way, off Roosevelt Way, Castro* ☎ *415/554–9600* ⊕ *www. randallmuseum.org* ☐ *Free* ☉ *Tues.–Sat. 10–5.*

WHERE TO EAT

Updated by
Sharon Silva

SINCE THE CITY'S EARLIEST DAYS, food lovers have flocked to San Francisco—a place where diversity rules and trends are set. Nearly every ethnic cuisine is represented—from Afghan to Indian to Vietnamese. And although locals have long headed to the Mission District for Latin food, to Chinatown and the Richmond District for Asian food, and to North Beach for Italian food, they also know that every part of the city offers dining experiences beyond the neighborhood tradition.

WHAT IT COSTS				
$$$$	**$$$**	**$$**	**$**	**¢**
AT DINNER over $30	$23–$30	$15–$22	$10–$14	under $10

Prices are per person for a main course. The final tab will include tax of 8.5%.

Union Square

Contemporary

$$$–$$$$ ✕ **Postrio.** Gone are the days when Postrio was *the* destination. Yet there's still a chance of seeing a celebrity or two here, including the owner, superchef Wolfgang Puck, who periodically commutes north from Los Angeles. And the three-level bar and dining area, connected by copper handrails and dressed up with museum-quality paintings, is as stunning as ever. The seasonal dinner menus, which deliver California cuisine with Mediterranean and Asian accents, rely heavily on specialty ingredients, such as house-smoked salmon, squab, foie gras, and locally grown vegetables. ⊠ *545 Post St., Union Sq.* ☎ *415/776–7825* ⌁ *Reservations essential* ⊟ *AE, D, DC, MC, V.*

French

★ **$$$$**   ✕ **Fleur de Lys.** The creative cooking of chef-owner Hubert Keller has brought every conceivable culinary award to this romantic spot. His three-, four-, and five-course prix-fixe menus (each course with many choices) include plenty of foie gras, squab, lobster, and truffles to satisfy palates geared to fancy—and, some would insist, too fussy—French food. The dining room, with its dramatic tented ceiling of 900 yards of draped and swathed fabric, is an ideal setting for the food. In keeping with Gallic tradition, French-born Keller typically stops by each table at the end of the evening, much like a chef in a small restaurant in France. ⊠ *777 Sutter St., Union Sq.* ☎ *415/673–7779* ⌁ *Reservations essential* ⟁ *Jacket required* ⊟ *AE, D, DC, MC, V* ⊗ *Closed Sun. No lunch.*

Mediterranean

¢–$$ ✕ **Cortez.** Young, well-dressed hipsters with just-cashed paychecks clog this bright, modern space in the Hotel Adagio, where they graze their way through small plates—and run up big bills. The menu changes regularly, with ahi tuna tartare, crab cakes with tarragon aioli, croque madame crowned with a fried quail egg, lamb with mint puree, and port-poached foie gras terrine among the typical picks. ⊠ *Hotel Adagio, 550 Geary St., Union Sq.* ☎ *415/292–6360* ⊟ *AE, MC, V* ⊗ *No lunch.*

Seafood

$$$$ ✕ **Farallon.** Sculpted jellyfish lamps, kelp-covered columns, and sea-
Fodor'sChoice   urchin chandeliers give this swanky Pat Kuleto–designed restaurant a
★   decidedly quirky look. But there's nothing quirky about chef Mark Franz's impeccable seafood, which reels in serious diners from coast to coast. The menu changes daily, but steamed Prince Edward Island mussels with saffron broth, prosciutto-wrapped striped bass with fingerling potatoes, sage-roasted golden trout, and skate wing with trumpet mushrooms circulate in and out regularly. ⊠ *450 Post St., Union Sq.* ☎ *415/ 956–6969* ⊟ *AE, D, DC, MC, V* ⊗ *No lunch Sun. or Mon.*

Vietnamese

$$–$$$$ ✕ **Le Colonial.** This is Vietnamese food served up in a French-colonial time machine: stamped tin ceiling, period photographs, slow-moving fans, and tropical plants. Local blue bloods come for the sea bass steamed in banana leaves, tiger prawns in coconut curry, and lamb chops with grilled

Where to Eat In &
Around Downtown
San Francisco

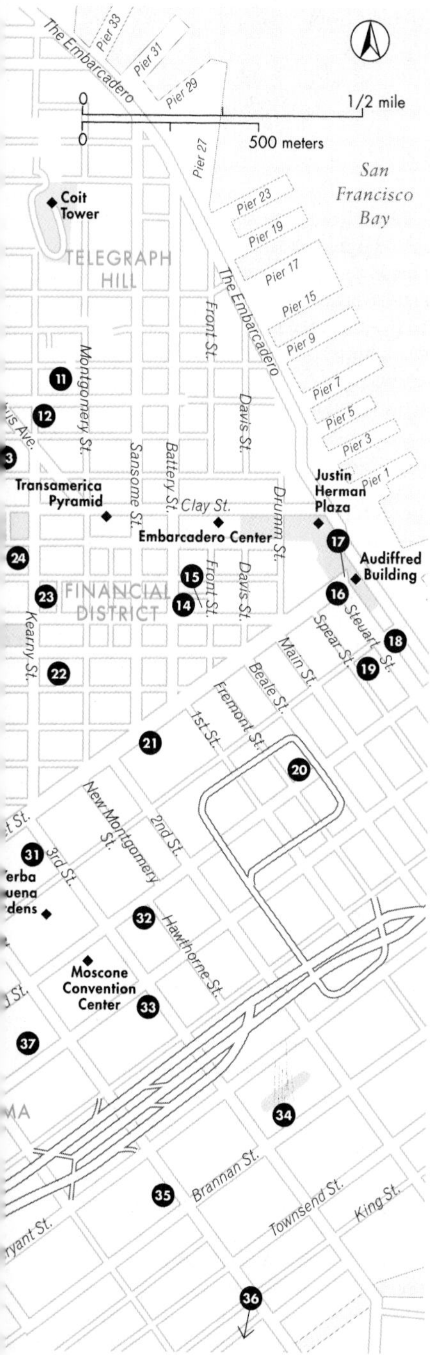

The Embarcadero
Pier 33
Pier 31
Pier 29

0 ____ 1/2 mile
0 ____ 500 meters

Pier 27

San Francisco Bay

◆ **Coit Tower**

TELEGRAPH HILL

Pier 23
Pier 19
Pier 17
Pier 15
Pier 9
Pier 7
Pier 5
Pier 3
Pier 1

The Embarcadero
Front St.

Montgomery St.
Davis St.
Battery St.
Sansome St.

⑪
⑫
③
◆ **Transamerica Pyramid**
Clay St.
◆ **Embarcadero Center**

Justin Herman Plaza
⑰
◆ **Audiffred Building**

②④
②③ **FINANCIAL DISTRICT**
⑮
⑭
⑯
Front St.
Davis St.
Drumm St.

Kearny St.
②②
Main St.
Beale St.
Spear St.
Steuart St.
⑱
⑲

1st St.
②①
Fremont St.
②⓪

New Montgomery St.
2nd St.
③①
Yerba Buena Gardens ◆
③②
Hawthorne St.

◆ **Moscone Convention Center**
③③

③⑦

SOMA

Brannan St.
③⑤
Townsend St.
King St.

③④

③⑥

eggplant salad. They also like to pick from among the big selection of fried or fresh appetizer rolls, filled with everything from lemongrass beef to Dungeness crab. ⊠ *20 Cosmo Pl., Union Sq.* ☎ *415/931–3600* ⌕ *Reservations essential* ▤ *AE, MC, V* ☽ *No lunch.*

SoMa & the Embarcadero

American

★ **$$–$$$**   ✕ **Town Hall.** Chefs Mitchell and Steven Rosenthal, who have long headed up the kitchen at Wolfgang Puck's popular Postrio, are also the brains behind this primary way station for the city's powerbrokers and their acolytes. The fare is new American—roasted veal meatballs, slow-roasted duck with gingersnap gravy; tasso (Cajun cured pork)-and-peanut-crusted pork chops; cedar-planked salmon; butterscotch-and-chocolate *pots de crème*—and the converted-warehouse space, with dark-wood floors, exposed brick walls, white wainscoting, and contemporary art, comfortably blends old with new. ⊠ *342 Howard St., SoMa* ☎ *415/908–3900* ▤ *AE, MC, V* ⌕ *Reservations essential* ☽ *No lunch weekends.*

Contemporary

★ **$$$$**   ✕ **Boulevard.** Two of San Francisco's top restaurant talents—chef Nancy Oakes and designer Pat Kuleto—are responsible for this high-profile, high-priced eatery in the magnificent 1889 Audiffred Building, a Parisian look-alike that was one of the few downtown structures to survive the 1906 earthquake. Oakes's menu, with its nod to the French kitchen, is seasonally in flux, but you can count on her signature juxtapositioning of classy fare—such as pork tenderloin stuffed with chanterelles and truffles—with comfort food, such as wood-oven-roasted rack of lamb. Portions are generous; save room (and calories) for one of the dynamite desserts. ⊠ *1 Mission St., Embarcadero* ☎ *415/543–6084* ⌕ *Reservations essential* ▤ *AE, D, DC, MC, V* ☽ *No lunch weekends.*

$$–$$$$ ✕ **Bacar.** Here, secreted inside an understated brick-and-glass exterior, is one of the city's most wine-savvy restaurants. Serious oenophiles will be giddy with the lists alone: the by-the-glass options run pages, while wines by the bottle require a hefty book. The food menu is far smaller—and nicely unfussy—with a long list of raw-bar options and appetizers, such as wok-roasted mussels, wild boar rillettes, and sumac-spiced lamb riblets. There are fewer mains. The trilevel dining room allows for a mix of vantage points for returning diners who like variety. ⊠ *448 Brannan St., SoMa* ☎ *415/904–4100* ▤ *AE, D, DC, MC, V* ☽ *No lunch.*

$$–$$$$ ✕ **One Market.** A giant among American chefs, Bradley Ogden boasts an enviable mini-restaurant chain that stretches from Marin County to San Diego, with stops in between. This large space, with floor-to-ceiling windows that look out at the Ferry Building and bay, is his popular San Francisco outpost. The two-tier dining room seats 170—many of them suits brokering deals—and serves a seasonal and surprisingly homey menu that might include a rib eye with red wine butter, herb-marinated roast chicken, braised beef cheeks with celery-root puree, and pumpkin tart with ginger ice cream. Service can be inexplicably slow, ruffling the dealmakers and the rest of us. ⊠ *1 Market St., Embarcadero*

12

☎ 415/777–5577 ⚅ *Reservations essential* ⊟ *AE, DC, MC, V* ☺ *Closed Sun. No lunch Sat.*

$$$ ✕ **Hawthorne Lane.** Even early on a Monday night you can't get a table in this big, decade-old restaurant. The place is divided into two rooms: the first, with a beautiful oval cherrywood bar, comfy upholstered booths, and well-spaced tables, has a lively ambience; the second is a more formal, light-flooded dining room. Yellowtail sashimi salad with fleur de sel, Chinese roast duck with green onion buns, and wild mushroom and prosciutto pizza are among the typical offerings on the seasonal menu. The bread basket, full of house-made chive biscuits, bread sticks, and flat bread, is the best in town. ⊠ *22 Hawthorne St., SoMa* ☎ *415/777–9779* ⚅ *Reservations essential* ⊟ *AE, D, DC, MC, V* ☺ *No lunch weekends.*

French

$–$$ ✕ **Fringale.** This quintessential bistro is a bright beacon on an otherwise ordinary street. The founders have gone on to other enterprises, but the new owner, a long-time employee, has kept the regulars happy with traditional French Basque fare, including frisée *aux lardons* (with crisp bacon cubes and a poached egg), foie gras terrine, duck confit with lentils, steak with *pommes frites* (french fries), and dense almond cake with custard cream. ⊠ *570 4th St., SoMa* ☎ *415/543–0573* ⊟ *AE, MC, V* ☺ *Closed Sun. No lunch Mon. or Sat.*

Indian

★ ℭ ¢–$ ✕ **Chaat Café.** This no-frills spot (part of a mini chain) trades in cheap, tasty, homey Indian snacks—*chaat*—such as *pani puri* (small, hollow bread puffs you fill with seasoned potatoes and chickpeas) and chicken and fish *pakora* (fritters). You'll also find thin, chewy nan (flat bread) served alongside simple fish, lamb, chicken, and vegetable curries and used for wraps, including one filled with tandoori lamb, onions, and cilantro. ⊠ *320 3rd St., SoMa* ☎ *415/979–9946* ⚅ *Reservations not accepted* ⊟ *MC, V.*

Mediterranean

★ $$–$$$ ✕ **LuLu.** In its early years, LuLu was a magnet for dot-commers, who jammed the place every night. Nowadays many of the same uncomplicated dishes—fritto misto of artichokes, fennel, and lemon slices; mussels roasted in an iron skillet; wood-oven-roasted poultry, meats, and shellfish; a small selection of pizzas and pastas—fuel a more mixed clientele. There is a well-supplied raw bar, and main-course specials include a rotisserie-cooked main course that changes daily. ⊠ *816 Folsom St., SoMa* ☎ *415/495–5775* ⊟ *AE, D, DC, MC, V.*

Vietnamese

★ $$–$$$ ✕ **Slanted Door.** If you're looking for homey Vietnamese food—or a homey setting—don't stop here. Celebrated chef-owner Charles Phan is the master of the upmarket, Western-accented Vietnamese menu and serves it in a big space that suits his well-heeled customers: sleek wooden tables and chairs, white marble floors, a cocktail lounge and bar, and an enviable bay view. Among his popular dishes are green papaya salad, wood-oven-roasted whole fish with ginger sauce, and shaking beef (tender beef cubes with garlic and onion). Alas, the crush of fame has also brought some ragged service. ⊠ *Ferry Bldg., Embarcadero at Market St., Embarcadero* ☏ *415/861–8032* ⌖ *Reservations essential* ▭ *AE, MC, V.*

Financial District

Chinese

☾ ¢–$ ✕ **Yank Sing.** This is the granddaddy of the city's teahouses. It opened in a plain-Jane storefront in Chinatown in 1959 but left its Cantonese neighbors behind for the high-rises of the Financial District by the 1970s. This brightly decorated location on quiet Stevenson Street (there's also a big, brassy branch in the Rincon Center) serves some of San Francisco's best dim sum to office workers—bosses and clerks alike—on weekdays and to big, boisterous families on weekends. ⊠ *49 Stevenson St., Financial District* ☏ *415/541–4949* ▭ *AE, DC, MC, V* ☾ *No dinner.*

French

★ $$–$$$ ✕ **Jeanty at Jack's.** Chef Philippe Jeanty, who made a name for himself in the wine country (first at Domaine Chandon and then at his Bistro Jeanty and Père Jeanty), oversees this brass-and-wood, three-story brasserie in the former Jack's restaurant, a San Francisco destination for steaks and chops since 1864. The food today is as French as the chef, with cassoulet, *steak frites*, rabbit terrine, steak tartare, and coq au vin among the offerings. ⊠ *615 Sacramento St., Financial District* ☏ *415/693–0941* ▭ *AE, MC, V* ☾ *No lunch Sat. and Sun.*

Japanese

$$–$$$$ ✕ **Kyo-ya.** This showplace in the Palace Hotel, a favorite of visiting Japanese businessmen, replicates the refined experience of dining in a first-class restaurant in Japan. A *kyo-ya* is a nonspecialized restaurant that serves a wide range of food. Here, the range is spectacular, encompassing tempura, one-pot dishes, deep-fried and grilled meats, and impeccably fresh sushi. ⊠ *Palace Hotel, 2 New Montgomery St., at Market St., Financial District* ☏ *415/546–5000* ▭ *AE, D, DC, MC, V* ☾ *Closed Sun. and Mon. No lunch Sat.*

Seafood

★ $$$$ ✕ **Aqua.** Quietly elegant, heavily mirrored, and playing mostly to a society crowd, this spot is among the city's most lauded seafood restaurants—and among the most expensive. The kitchen, known for using exquisite ingredients and classic techniques, assembles beautiful preparations that are seriously fancy but not too fussy: tuna tartare with Moroccan spices, Alaskan black cod with bacon, yellowfin tuna with chanterelles and olives. ⊠ *252 California St., Financial District* ☏ *415/956–9662* ⌖ *Reservations essential* ▭ *AE, D, DC, MC, V* ☾ *No lunch weekends.*

$$–$$$$ ✕ **Tadich Grill.** Locations and owners have changed more than once since this old-timer started as a coffee stand on the waterfront in 1849, but the crowds keep coming. Generations of regulars advise that simple sautés and panfries are the best choices, or cioppino during crab season (October to May), Pacific halibut in season (January to May), and old-fashioned house-made tartar sauce anytime. ⊠ *240 California St., Financial District* ☏ *415/391–2373* ⌖ *Reservations not accepted* ▭ *MC, V* ☾ *Closed Sun.*

Spanish

$$–$$$ ✗ **B44.** Going to restaurant-lined Belden Place is like visiting your favorite candy store: there are just too many choices. But this spare, modern Spanish restaurant, which draws locals and visitors alike with its Catalan tapas and paellas, won't disappoint. The open kitchen sends out appealing small plates: white anchovies with pears and Idiazábal cheese, sherry-scented fish cheeks, warm octopus with tiny potatoes, blood sausage with white beans. The paellas, individually served in an iron skillet, bring together inviting combinations such as chicken, rabbit, and mushrooms or mixed seafood with squid ink. ⊠ *44 Belden Pl., Financial District* ☎ *415/986–6287* ▭ *AE, MC, V* ☺ *Closed Sun. No lunch Sat.*

Chinatown

Chinese

☾ **¢–$$$** ✗ **Great Eastern.** Don't be tempted to order a Szechuan or Beijing dish here or you'll leave unhappy. This is a Cantonese restaurant, and that means fresh, simply prepared seafood, quickly cooked vegetables and meats, clear soups, and no fiery chilies. Tanks filled with crabs, black bass, catfish, shrimp, and other creatures of fresh water and saltwater occupy a corner of the street-level main dining room. Look to them for your meal, but check prices, as swimming seafood isn't cheap. ⊠ *649 Jackson St., Chinatown* ☎ *415/986–2550* ▭ *AE, MC, V.*

☾ **¢–$$$** ✗ **R&G Lounge.** The name conjures up an image of a dark bar with a cigarette-smoking piano player, but the restaurant is actually as bright as a new penny. The classy upstairs space (entrance on Commercial Street) is a favorite stop for Chinese businessmen on expense accounts. The street-level space on Kearny is a comfortable spot to wait for a table to open. A menu with photographs helps you pick from the many wonderful, sometimes pricey, always authentic dishes—such as salt-and-pepper Dungeness crab. ⊠ *631 Kearny St., Chinatown* ☎ *415/982–7877 or 415/982–3811* ▭ *AE, D, DC, MC, V.*

North Beach

Afghan

★ **$–$$** ✗ **Helmand.** Don't be put off by Helmand's address on a rather scruffy block of Broadway. Inside is a world away, with authentic Afghan cooking served in a setting of white table linens and Afghan carpets. Highlights include *aushak* (leek-filled ravioli served with yogurt and ground beef), pumpkin with yogurt-and-garlic sauce, and any of the lamb dishes, in particular the kebab strewn with yellow split peas and served on Afghan flat bread. ⊠ *430 Broadway, North Beach* ☎ *415/362–0641* ▭ *AE, MC, V* ☺ *No lunch weekends.*

Contemporary

$$–$$$$ ✗ **Moose's.** Owners Ed Moose and his wife, Mary Etta, are legendary in San Francisco and beyond, so local and national politicians and media types are as common here as they are on Capitol Hill. Indeed, one local pundit calls Moose's "San Francisco's living room." The regularly changing menu is sophisticated without being fancy, with offerings such as pheasant with house-made pheasant sausage, pan-seared duck breast with brussels sprouts, and warm French pear tart with almond ice cream. The comfortable surroundings come with a view of Washington Square. ⊠ *1652 Stockton St., North Beach* ☎ *415/989–7800* ⚱ *Reservations essential* ⊟ *AE, D, DC, MC, V* ⊗ *No lunch Mon.–Wed.*

Italian

★ ☾ **$–$$$** ✕ **Tommaso's.** This is the site of San Francisco's first wood-fired pizza oven, installed in the 1930s when the restaurant opened. The oven is still here, and the restaurant, with its coat hooks, boothlike dining nooks, and communal table running the length of the basement dining room, has changed little since those early days. The pizzas' delightfully chewy crusts, creamy mozzarella, and full-bodied house-made sauce—for sale in jars, too—have kept legions of happy eaters returning for decades. Pair one of the hearty pies with a salad of grilled sweet peppers or of broccoli dressed in lemon juice and olive oil. ⊠ *1042 Kearny St.* ☎ *415/398–9696* ⊟ *AE, D, DC, MC, V* ⊗ *Closed Mon. No lunch.*

☾ **$–$$** ✕ **L'Osteria del Forno.** A staff chattering in Italian and seductive aromas
Fodor'sChoice drifting from the open kitchen make customers who pass through the
★ door of this modest storefront feel as if they've stumbled into a homey trattoria in Italy. The kitchen produces small plates of simply cooked vegetables, a few pastas, a roast of the day, creamy polenta, and thin-crust pizzas—including a memorable "white" pie topped with porcini mushrooms and mozzarella. At lunch try one of North Beach's best focaccia sandwiches. ⊠ *519 Columbus Ave., North Beach* ☎ *415/982–1124* ⚱ *Reservations not accepted* ⊟ *No credit cards* ⊗ *Closed Tues.*

Nob Hill & Russian Hill

French

$$$$ ✕ **Masa's.** Although the toque has been passed to several chefs since the
Fodor'sChoice death of founding chef Masa Kobayashi, the two-decade-old restaurant,
★ with its chocolate-brown walls, white fabric ceiling, and red-silk-shaded lanterns, is still one of the country's most celebrated food temples. Chef Gregory Short, who worked alongside Thomas Keller at the famed French Laundry for seven years, is at the helm these days, and his tasting menus of four, six, and nine courses are pleasing diners and critics alike. All menus are laced with fancy ingredients—truffles, foie gras, squab—and priced accordingly ($79–$120). ⊠ *Hotel Vintage Court, 648 Bush St., Nob Hill* ☎ *415/989–7154* ⚱ *Reservations essential* ⬜ *Jacket required* ⊟ *AE, D, DC, MC, V* ⊗ *Closed Sun. and Mon. No lunch.*

Italian

★ **$–$$** ✕ **Antica Trattoria.** The dining room—pale walls, dark-wood floors, a partial view of the kitchen—reflects a strong sense of restraint. The same no-nonsense quality characterizes the food of owner-chef Ruggero Gadaldi. A small, regularly shifting menu delivers archetypal Italian dishes such as crostini with chicken-liver pâté, *pappardelle* (wide flat noodles) with wild boar, braised duck with porcini, and *tagliata di manzo* (beef fillet slices) with arugula. The Italian wine list is fairly priced, the genial service is polished but not stiff, and the under $20 prix-fixe menu (before 6:30) is a boon to fatigued pocketbooks. ✉ *2400 Polk St., Russian Hill* ☏ *415/928–5797* 🚃 *DC, MC, V* ⊘ *Closed Mon. No lunch.*

Van Ness/Polk

Italian

★ **$$$–$$$$** ✕ **Acquerello.** Sometimes you need to pamper yourself, and this is a great place to do it. For years, devotees of chef-owner Suzette Gresham's Italian cooking have been swooning over what emerges from her kitchen: lobster *panzerotti* (raviolilike stuffed pasta); *pappardelle* with rabbit ragù; parsnip gnocchi with wild boar ragù, grilled dorade over baby fennel; veal loin roasted with herbs. Co-owner Giancarlo Paterlini oversees the service and the list of Italian wines, both of them superb. ✉ *1722 Sacramento St., Van Ness/Polk* ☏ *415/567–5432* 🚃 *AE, D, MC, V* ⊘ *Closed Sun. and Mon. No lunch.*

Seafood

¢–$$ ✕ **Swan Oyster Depot.** Here is old San Francisco at its best. Half fish market and half diner, this small, slim seafood operation, open since 1912, has no tables, only a narrow marble counter with about a dozen and a half stools. Most people come in to buy perfectly fresh salmon, halibut, crabs, and the like to take home. Everyone else hops onto one of the rickety stools to enjoy a bowl of clam chowder—the only hot food served—a dozen oysters, half a cracked crab, a big shrimp salad, or a smaller shrimp cocktail. ✉ *1517 Polk St., Van Ness/Polk* ☏ *415/673–1101* 🚃 *No credit cards* ⊘ *Closed Sun. No dinner.*

FodorsChoice ★

Lower Pacific Heights & Japantown

Contemporary

$$$ ✕ **Quince.** This is no place for someone living paycheck to paycheck. In one of San Francisco's most fashionable residential neighborhoods, the small, smart eatery caters to folks with fat pocketbooks who plan ahead: tables are booked weeks in advance. Michael Tusk, who has cooked at the legendary Chez Panisse and Oliveto, oversees the kitchen. The menu, which changes daily and marries French, Italian, and American traditions, includes such inviting—and delicious—dishes as fresh pasta with scallops, duck breast and leg confit, wild nettle *sformato* (Italian-style custard), and more. ✉ *1701 Octavia St., Lower Pacific Heights* ☏ *415/775–8500* ⌚ *Reservations essential* 🚃 *AE, MC, V* ⊘ *Closed Mon. No lunch.*

FodorsChoice ★

★ ¢–$ ✕ **Chez Nous.** The concept here is Spanish tapas, although the small dishes—duck-leg confit, baked goat cheese with oven-roasted tomatoes, french fries and aioli spiked with *harissa* sauce—cross borders into other cuisines. Grilled asparagus sprinkled with lemon zest, lamb rib chops seasoned with lavender sea salt, and sautéed spinach tossed with raisins and pine nuts are among the other choices. The stylish yet casual and noisy dining room has wood floors, zinc-topped tables, and blue walls. ✉ *1911 Fillmore St., Lower Pacific Heights* ☏ *415/441–8044* ⌚ *Reservations not accepted* 🚃 *MC, V.*

Italian

$$–$$$ ✕ **Vivande Porta Via.** The secret of how this quarter-century-old Italian delicatessen-restaurant, operated by well-known chef and cookbook author Carlo Middione, has outlasted many of its competitors is simple: authentic, carefully made trattoria dishes served by an engaged staff. The regularly changing menu includes prosciutto with figs, steamed mussels with saffron, *risi e bisi* (rice with peas, pancetta, and grated cheese), and pork chops with *mostarda di frutta* (slightly spicy preserved fruits in simple syrup and mustard oil). ✉ *2125 Fillmore St., Lower Pacific Heights* ☎ *415/346–4430* ▤ *AE, D, DC, MC, V.*

Japanese

$–$$$ ✕ **Maki.** *Wappa-meshi,* rice topped with meat or fish—chicken, eel, salmon, or salmon eggs, among other items—and steamed in a bamboo basket, is the specialty at this small restaurant featuring refined Kansai (Kyoto) cuisine. The sashimi; braised yams, daikon, and pork; sukiyaki; and freshwater eel on rice in a lacquer box are also first-rate. Everything is served on beautiful tableware, from the smallest *sunomono* (salad) to a big lunchtime *donburi* (rice with a topping). Maki stocks an impressive assortment of sakes, which it serves in exquisite decanters. ✉ *Japan Center, Kinokuniya Bldg., 1825 Post St., Japantown* ☎ *415/921–5215* ▤ *MC, V* ☺ *Closed Mon.*

☾ **¢–$$** ✕ **Mifune.** Thin brown soba and thick white udon are the stars at this North American outpost of an Osaka-based noodle empire. A line regularly snakes out the door, but the house-made noodles, served both hot and cold and with more than a score of toppings, are worth the wait. Seating is at wooden tables, where diners can be heard slurping down big bowls of such traditional Japanese combinations as fish-cake-crowned udon, *nabeyaki udon* (wheat noodles topped with tempura, chicken, and fish cake), and *tenzaru* (cold noodles and hot tempura with gingery dipping sauce) served on lacquered trays. ✉ *Japan Center, Kintetsu Bldg., 1737 Post St., Japantown* ☎ *415/922–0337* ⚑ *Reservations not accepted* ▤ *AE, D, DC, MC, V.*

Civic Center/Hayes Valley

Contemporary

$$$–$$$$ ✕ **Jardinière.** A special anniversary? An important business dinner? A tax refund? Any one of these is a good reason to head to Jardinière. The restaurant takes its name from its chef-owner, Traci Des Jardins, and the sophisticated interior, with its eye-catching oval atrium and curving staircase, is the work of famed designer Pat Kuleto. The equally sophisticated menu changes daily but regularly includes such high-style plates as potato gnocchi with Dungeness crab and New York steak with roasted vegetables and creamed nettles. Cheese snobs will appreciate the glassed-in cheese-aging chamber in the rear of the restaurant. ✉ *300 Grove St., Hayes Valley* ☎ *415/861–5555* ⚑ *Reservations essential* ▤ *AE, DC, MC, V* ☺ *No lunch.*

Fodor'sChoice ★

German

¢–$$ ✕ **Suppenküche.** Nobody goes hungry—and no beer drinker goes thirsty—at this lively, hip outpost of simple German cooking in the trendy Hayes

Valley corridor. Strangers sit down together at unfinished pine tables when the room gets crowded, which it regularly does. The food—bratwurst and red cabbage, potato pancakes with house-made applesauce, meat loaf, sauerbraten, schnitzel, strudel—is tasty and easy on the pocketbook, and the brews are first-rate. ⊠ *601 Hayes St., Hayes Valley* ☎ *415/252– 9289* ▭ *AE, MC, V* ✆ *No lunch.*

Mediterranean

$$–$$$
FodorsChoice
★

✕ **Zuni Café.** Owner-chef Judy Rodgers is a national star, and after one bite of her whole roast chicken and Tuscan bread salad for two, you'll be applauding, too. A rabbit warren of rooms on the second level includes a balcony overlooking the main dining room. At the long copper bar, trays of briny-fresh oysters on the half shell are dispensed along with cocktails and wine. The southern French–Italian menu changes daily (though the signature chicken never leaves) but may include house-cured anchovies with Parmigiano-Reggiano, a salad of persimmons with prosciutto and candied walnuts, and stuffed quail. ⊠ *1658 Market St., Hayes Valley* ☎ *415/ 552–2522* ⚐ *Reservations essential* ▭ *AE, MC, V* ✆ *Closed Mon.*

Fisherman's Wharf

French

$$$$
FodorsChoice
★

✕ **Gary Danko.** Be prepared to wait your turn for a table behind chef Gary Danko's legion of loyal fans, who typically keep the reservation book chock-full here. The cost of a meal ($59–$81) is pegged to the number of courses, from three to five. The menu, which changes seasonally, may include risotto with lobster and rock shrimp, Moroccan squab with orange-cumin carrots, and quail stuffed with wild mushrooms and foie gras. The wine list is the size of a small-town phone book, and the banquette-lined room is as high class as the food. ⊠ *800 N. Point St., Fisherman's Wharf* ☎ *415/749–2060* ⚐ *Reservations essential* ▭ *D, DC, MC, V* ✆ *No lunch.*

Seafood

♻ **$–$$$**

✕ **McCormick & Kuleto's.** Here is a visitor's dream come true: a fabulous view of the bay from every seat in the house, an Old San Francisco atmosphere, and dozens of varieties of fish and shellfish prepared in scores of international ways. But not everything is rosy at this seafood emporium, part of a nationwide chain. The food suffers from ups and downs, so stick with the simple preparations such as oysters on the half shell and grilled fish. ⊠ *Ghirardelli Sq. at Beach and Larkin Sts., Fisherman's Wharf* ☎ *415/929–1730* ▭ *AE, D, DC, MC, V.*

Cow Hollow/Marina

French

¢–$$

✕ **Isa.** A tiny storefront dining room, a talented chef, and a heated, candlelit patio—Isa has all the trappings of a great night out whether it's the first date or the fiftieth. The menu of French-inspired tapas changes seasonally but regularly offers such crowd-pleasers as seared foie gras, pan-roasted chicken with herbs secreted under the crispy skin, and potato-wrapped sea bass. Portions are petite, so hearty appetites will run up a good-size tab, and service is sometimes sluggish. The wine list, smartly crafted and including plenty of by-the-glass choices, complements the food. ⊠ *3324 Steiner St., Marina* ☎ *415/567–9588* ▭ *MC, V* ⊘ *Closed Sun. No lunch.*

Italian

★ **$–$$** ╳ **A-16.** Marina residents gravitate to this lively trattoria, named for the autostrada that winds through Italy's sunny south. The kitchen serves the food of Naples and surrounding Campania, including house-cured meats (wild boar salami, fennel salami) and crisp-crusted pizzas, including a classic Neapolitan Margherita (mozzarella, tomato, and basil). Among the regularly changing mains are pork loin with pine nuts and golden raisins and a combo of lamb riblets and lamb sausage. ⊠ *2355 Chestnut St., Marina* ☎ *415/771–2216* ᐃ *Reservations essential* ▭ *AE, MC, V* ⊘ *No lunch Sat.–Tues.*

Mediterranean

$$$–$$$$ ╳ **PlumpJack Café.** This clubby dining room takes its name from an opera (Plump Jack is Queen Elizabeth's name for Falstaff in *Henry IV*) composed by oil tycoon and music lover Gordon Getty, a close friend of the restaurant's founder, San Francisco mayor Gavin Newsom. The high-class clientele comes to eat a seasonal menu that spans the Mediterranean and includes such tempting plates as a trio of foie gras—brûléed, truffled, and seared—on a single plate, chanterelle-crusted salmon, and lamb osso buco. ⊠ *3127 Fillmore St., Cow Hollow* ☎ *415/463–4755* ▭ *AE, DC, MC, V* ⊘ *No lunch weekends.*

The Mission

Contemporary

☾ **$$–$$$** ╳ **Foreign Cinema.** Here, "dinner and a movie" can happen in the same place. In this hip, loftlike space you can not only sit down to oysters on the half shell, curried chicken with gypsy peppers, or steak with Argentine salsa but also watch film classics such as Stanley Kubrick's *Dr. Strangelove* projected on the wall in the large inner courtyard. ⊠ *2534 Mission St., Mission* ☎ *415/648–7600* ▭ *AE, MC, V* ⊘ *No lunch.*

¢–$ ╳ **Andalu.** You can feast on some two dozen globe-circling small plates here, from tuna-tartare-filled miniature tacos and cambozola cheese fondue to curly polenta fries and hangar steak with *romesco* sauce and fries. Average appetites should plan on two plates per person. The equally global wine list has some 60 offerings by the glass, tempting curious palates. The good-looking bilevel north Mission dining room has a sky-blue ceiling and aquamarine-and-black tables. ⊠ *3198 16th St., Mission* ☎ *415/621–2211* ▭ *AE, MC, V* ⊘ *No lunch.*

French

$$–$$$ ╳ **Chez Papa.** France arrived on Potrero Hill with Chez Papa, which delivers food, waiters, and charm that would be right at home in Provence. The modest corner restaurant, with big windows overlooking the street, caters to a lively crowd. Small plates include mussels in wine, grilled lamb with rosemary salt on ratatouille, and beef tartare; lamb daube, grilled salmon, and shellfish stew are among the big plates. ⊠ *1401 18th St., Potrero Hill* ☎ *415/255–0387* ᐃ *Reservations essential* ▭ *AE, DC, MC, V* ⊘ *No lunch Sun.*

Italian

$$ ✕ **Delfina.** "Irresistible"—that's how its countless diehard fans describe
Fodor'sChoice Delfina. That wild enthusiasm has made patience the critical virtue for
★ anyone wanting a reservation here. The interior is comfortable, with hardwood floors, aluminum-top tables, a tile bar, and a casual, friendly atmosphere. The menu changes daily, but among the usual offerings are salt cod *mantecato* (whipped with olive oil) with fennel flat bread; grilled fresh sardine crostini; chicken and pancetta *agnolotti* (stuffed pasta); and roast chicken with trumpet mushrooms. ⊠ *3621 18th St., Mission* ☎ *415/552–4055* ⌢ *Reservations essential* ▤ *MC, V* ⊘ *No lunch.*

Latin

¢–$ ✕ **Charanga.** It's hard to resist the tropical vibe that weaves its way through this animated tapas depot, with its eclectic mix of Caribbean-inspired flavors: *picadillo* (Cuban-style minced beef) studded with green olives and raisins, *patatas bravas* (twice-fried potatoes with roast-tomato sauce), sautéed shrimp and calamari seasoned with chilies and ginger and served with coconut rice. The dining room, with walls of exposed brick and soothing green, is small and friendly, so grab—or make—some friends, order a pitcher of sangria or a round of margaritas, and enjoy yourselves. ⊠ *2351 Mission St., Mission* ☎ *415/282–1813* ⌢ *Reservations not accepted* ▤ *AE, D, MC, V* ⊘ *Closed Sun. and Mon. No lunch.*

The Castro & the Haight

American-Casual

☾ **¢–$$** ✕ **Chow.** Wildly popular and consciously unpretentious, this penny-pinchers' magnet serves honest fare—pizzas from the wood-fired oven, thick
Fodor'sChoice burgers of grass-fed beef, spaghetti with meatballs, roast chicken and mashed
★ potatoes, soup-and-sandwich specials—made with the best local ingredients. The savvy try to leave room for an order of the ginger cake with caramel sauce. Because reservations are restricted to large parties, folks hoping to snag seats usually surround the doorway. ⊠ *215 Church St., Castro* ☎ *415/552–2469* ⌢ *Reservations not accepted* ▤ *MC, V.*

Contemporary

$$ ✕ **2223 Restaurant.** Slip into the smart, sophisticated 2223—the address became the name when the owners couldn't come up with a better one—whether you want a martini and bruschetta in the cozy bar or a full-fledged meal in the dining room. The menu changes seasonally, with lamb spring rolls with sweet chili dipping sauce, double-cut pork chops with chayote squash, and a luscious sour cherry bread pudding among the possible cool-weather offerings. The popular Sunday brunch delivers old favorites with contemporary style. ⊠ *2223 Market St., Castro* ☎ *415/431–0692* ▤ *AE, DC, MC, V* ⊘ *No lunch Mon.–Sat.*

Indian

¢–$$ ✕ **Indian Oven.** This cozy Victorian storefront with dining on two floors never lacks for customers, who travel here from all over the city. Many come for the tandoori specialties—chicken, lamb, breads—but *saag paneer* (spinach with Indian cheese) and *bengan bartha* (roasted eggplant with onions and spices) are also excellent. ⊠ *233 Fillmore St., Lower Haight* ☎ *415/626–1628* ⊟ *AE, D, DC, MC, V* ☺ *No lunch.*

Thai

★ ¢–$$ ✕ **Thep Phanom.** Long ago, local food critics and restaurant goers alike began singing the praises of Thep Phanom—and the tune hasn't stopped, except for an occasional sour note on rising prices. Duck is deliciously prepared in several ways—atop a mound of spinach, in a fragrant curry, minced for salad. Seafood (in various guises) is another specialty, along with warm eggplant salad, stuffed chicken wings, spicy beef salad, fried quail, and rich Thai curries. ⊠ *400 Waller St., Lower Haight* ☎ *415/ 431–2526* ⊟ *AE, D, DC, MC, V* ☺ *No lunch.*

Richmond District

Chinese

☾ ¢–$$$ ✕ **Parc Hong Kong Restaurant.** This tablecloth Cantonese restaurant is typically filled with big groups of Chinese happily eating their way through dozens of dishes—the sort of scene that guarantees the food is authentic. The kitchen is especially celebrated for its seafood, which is plucked straight from tanks and can be a costly indulgence. Chefs here keep up with whatever is hot in Hong Kong eateries, so check the specials menu and ask the generally genial—but often rushed—waiters what's new. A good midday dim sum is available. ⊠ *5322 Geary Blvd., Richmond* ☎ *415/668–8998* ⊟ *AE, D, DC, MC, V.*

Japanese

★ ¢–$$ ✕ **Kabuto A&S.** Master chef Sachio Kojima flashes his knives before an admiring crowd, which can't get enough of his buttery yellowfin tuna or golden sea urchin on pads of pearly rice. In addition to serving fine sushi and sashimi, the restaurant also offers small, cooked plates in its cozy, 20-seat dining room and at the dozen-seat sushi bar. Don't overlook the excellent selection of sakes, each one rated for dryness and labeled with its place of origin. ⊠ *5121 Geary Blvd., Richmond* ☎ *415/ 752–5652* ⊟ *MC, V* ☺ *Closed Wed.*

Vietnamese

☾ ¢–$$ ✕ **Le Soleil.** A renovation—new paint, new furnishings—has delivered some much-needed sparkle to this Clement Street institution. It has long featured dishes from every part of Vietnam, such as raw-beef salad, shaking beef (tender beef cubes in a vinegary sauce), chicken and fresh basil, or prawns simmered in a clay pot. Occasionally both the kitchen and the waiters stumble, but everyone from grandmothers to college students keeps coming back. A large aquarium of tropical fish adds to the tranquil mood. ⊠ *133 Clement St., Inner Richmond* ☎ *415/668–4848* ⊟ *AE, MC, V.*

Sunset District

American-Casual

☾ ¢–$$ ✕ **Park Chow.** Here you'll find just what your appetite ordered after a morning or afternoon in Golden Gate Park. In the mood for spaghetti and meatballs? That's here. Prefer Thai noodles with rock shrimp and chicken? That's also here. Or what about a big American burger, a pizza from the wood-burning oven, a BLT, roast chicken and mashed potatoes, or an order of iron-skillet mussels? They're all here, too, along with fresh-fruit cobbler and ginger cake with pumpkin ice cream. ✉ *1240 9th Ave., Inner Sunset* ☎ *415/665–9912* ⌲ *Reservations not accepted* ▤ *MC, V.*

12

WHERE TO STAY

Updated by
Andy Moore

Few U.S. cities can rival San Francisco's variety in lodging. Its plush hotels rank among the world's finest; its renovated buildings house small hostelries with European flair; its grand Victorian-era homes serve as bed-and-breakfasts; and its private residences rent rooms, apartments, and cottages. You can even find accommodations in boats bobbing on the bay, but the popular chain hotels and motels found in most American cities are here, too. The city's hilly topography and diversity of neighborhoods contribute to each property's unique sense of place, and you may feel like a kid in a candy store as you go about choosing which of the approximately 32,000 rooms here will be your home-away-from-home.

WHAT IT COSTS					
	$$$$	$$$	$$	$	¢
FOR 2 PEOPLE	over $250	$200–$250	$150–$199	$90–$149	under $90

Prices are for two people in a standard double room in high season, excluding 14% tax.

Union Square/Downtown

★ **$$$$** 🏨 **Campton Place.** Highly attentive service is the hallmark of this small, top-tier hotel behind a simple brownstone facade. The pampering—from unpacking assistance to nightly turndown—begins the moment the doormen greet you outside the marble lobby. Many rooms are small-ish, but all are elegant in a contemporary Italian style, with light earth tones and handsome pearwood paneling and cabinetry. Bathrooms have deep soaking tubs, and double-paned windows keep city noises out (a plus in this active neighborhood). The Campton Place Restaurant is famed for its lavish breakfasts and Mediterranean-inspired dinners, and the hotel's lounge is popular at cocktail time with the downtown crowd. ✉ *340 Stockton St., Union Sq., 94108* ☎ *415/781–5555 or 800/235–4300* 🖷 *415/955–5536* ⊕ *www.camptonplace.com* ⇥ *101 rooms, 9 suites* ⌂ *Restaurant, room service, in-room safes, minibars, cable TV with movies and video games, in-room data ports, exercise equipment, gym, bar, lobby lounge, dry cleaning, laundry service, concierge, business services, meeting room, parking (fee), some pets allowed (fee), no-smoking floors* ▤ *AE, DC, MC, V.*

$$$$ 🏨 **Clift.** Behind a stately, beige brick facade lies this "hotel as art" showplace, as conceived by entrepreneur Ian Schrager and artist-designer Philippe Starck. The cavernous lobby contains groupings of whimsical art objects meant to encourage a surreal mood. Spacious rooms with

Where to Stay
In & Around
Downtown
San Francisco

high ceilings, in shades of ivory, gray, and lavender, have blond-wood and see-through orange acrylic furniture, plus two huge mirrors on otherwise empty walls. ⊠ *495 Geary St., Union Sq., 94102* ☎ *415/775–4700 or 800/652–5438* ⊟ *415/441–4621* ⊕ *www.clifthotel.com* ⇨ *337 rooms, 26 suites* ⚐ *Restaurant, room service, in-room safes, minibars, cable TV with movies, in-room VCRs, in-room data ports, Wi-Fi, gym, bar, lobby lounge, babysitting, dry cleaning, laundry service, concierge, business services, Internet room, meeting rooms, parking (fee), some pets allowed (fee), no-smoking floors* ▤ *AE, D, DC, MC, V.*

$$$–$$$$
Fodor'sChoice
★
Hotel Monaco. A cheery 1910 Beaux-Arts facade and snappily dressed doormen welcome you into the plush lobby, with its French inglenook fireplace and vaulted ceiling with murals of World War I–era planes and hot-air balloons. Rooms are full of flair, with vivid stripes and colors, Chinese-inspired armoires, canopy beds, and high-back upholstered chairs. Outer rooms have bay-window seats overlooking the bustling theater district. If you didn't bring a pet, request a "companion goldfish." Guests have cheered the hotel's staff for its "amazing service" and "attention to detail." ⊠ *501 Geary St., Union Sq., 94102* ☎ *415/292–0100* ⊟ *415/292–0111* ⊕ *www.monaco-sf.com* ⇨ *181 rooms, 20 suites* ⚐ *Restaurant, café, room service, in-room fax, in-room safes, some in-room hot tubs, minibars, cable TV with movies and video games, some in-room VCRs, in-room data ports, Wi-Fi, gym, hot tub, massage, sauna, spa, steam room, bar, babysitting, dry cleaning, laundry service, concierge, business services, Internet room, meeting rooms, convention center, parking (fee), some pets allowed, no-smoking floors* ▤ *AE, D, DC, MC, V.*

★ **$$–$$$$**
Hotel Nikko. The vast marble lobby of this Japan Airlines–owned hotel is airy and serene, and its rooms are among the most handsome in the city. Look for gold drapes; wheat-color wall coverings; furniture with clean, elegant lines; and ingenious window shades that screen the sun while allowing views of the city. The excellent, complimentary fifth-floor fitness facility has traditional *ofuros* (Japanese soaking tubs), a *kamaburo* (Japanese sauna), and a glass-enclosed rooftop pool and whirlpool. Restaurant Anzu serves prime-beef dishes and sushi, and a multilingual staff provides attentive, sincere service throughout the hotel. ⊠ *222 Mason St., Union Sq., 94102* ☎ *415/394–1111 or 800/645–5687* ⊟ *415/341–1106* ⊕ *www.hotelnikkosf.com* ⇨ *516 rooms, 16 suites* ⚐ *Restaurant, room service, some in-room faxes, minibars, refrigerators, cable TV with movies and video games, in-room data ports, some Wi-Fi, indoor pool, gym, hair salon, Japanese baths, massage, sauna, bar, lobby lounge, babysitting, dry cleaning, laundry service, concierge, concierge floor, business services, Internet room, meeting rooms, car rental, parking (fee), some pets allowed (fee), no-smoking floors* ▤ *AE, D, DC, MC, V.*

$$–$$$$
Prescott Hotel. Although not as famous as many other hotels in the area, this relatively small establishment provides extremely personalized service, which one guest described as making "you feel welcomed at every point of your stay." It also offers reservations at the ever-popular Postrio, the Wolfgang Puck restaurant attached to its lobby. Rooms, which are filled with cherrywood furniture, are handsomely decorated in dark autumn colors and have bathrooms with marble-top sinks. ⊠ *545 Post St., Union Sq., 94102* ☎ *415/563–0303* ⊟ *415/563–6831* ⊕ *www.*

prescotthotel.com ⊐ *132 rooms, 33 suites* ⌂ *Restaurant, room service, in-room faxes, in-room safes, minibars, cable TV with movies and video games, some in-room VCRs, in-room data ports, Wi-Fi, gym, bar, concierge, concierge floor, business services, Internet room, meeting rooms, parking (fee), some pets allowed, no-smoking floors* ▭ *AE, D, DC, MC, V.*

★ **$$–$$$** **Hotel Adagio.** The gracious, Spanish-colonial facade of this 16-story, theater-row hotel complements its chic, modern interior. Walnut furniture, bronze light fixtures, and brown and deep-orange hues dominate the spacious rooms, half of which have city views—and two penthouse suites have terraces looking out on the neighborhood. The airy, light-filled lobby lounge gives way to the plush Cortez restaurant, where Mediterranean-inspired cuisine is served beneath colorful, glowing sculptures. ⊠ *550 Geary St., Union Sq., 94102* ☎ *415/775–5000 or 800/228–8830* ☐ *415/775–9388* ⊕ *www.thehoteladagio.com* ⊐ *169 rooms, 2 suites* ⌂ *Restaurant, room service, fans, in-room safes, minibars, refrigerators, room TVs with movies and video games, in-room data ports, Wi-Fi, gym, bar, lounge, babysitting, dry cleaning, laundry service, business services, Internet room, meeting rooms, parking (fee), no-smoking floors; no a/c* ▭ *AE, D, DC, MC, V.*

$–$$$ **Hotel Rex.** Literary and artistic creativity are celebrated at this styl-
Fodor'sChoice ish place named after writer Kenneth Rexroth. Shelves of antiquarian
★ books line the 1920s-style lobby lounge, where the proprietors often host book readings and roundtable discussions. Although the spacious rooms evoke the spirit of 1920s salon society with muted checkered bedspreads, striped carpets, and restored period furnishings, they also have modern touches such as CD players, and complimentary Aveda hair and skin products. ⊠ *562 Sutter St., Union Sq., 94102* ☎ *415/433–4434 or 800/433–4434* ☐ *415/433–3695* ⊕ *www.thehotelrex.com* ⊐ *92 rooms, 2 suites* ⌂ *Café, room service, minibars, refrigerators, cable TV with movies, bar, lobby lounge, dry cleaning, laundry service, concierge, business services, Internet, Wi-Fi, meeting rooms, parking (fee), no smoking* ▭ *AE, D, DC, MC, V.*

★ **$–$$** **Hotel Beresford Arms.** Surrounded by fancy molding and 10-foot-tall windows, the red-carpeted lobby of this ornate brick Victorian shows why the building is on the National Register of Historic Places. Rooms with dark-wood antique-reproduction furniture vary in size and setup: junior suites have sitting areas and either a wet bar or kitchenette, and full suites have two queen beds, a Murphy bed, and a kitchen. All suites have a bidet in the bathroom. ⊠ *701 Post St., Union Sq., 94109* ☎ *415/ 673–2600 or 800/533–6533* ☐ *415/929–1535* ⊕ *www.beresford.com* ⊐ *83 rooms, 12 suites* ⌂ *Fans, some in-room hot tubs, some kitchens, some kitchenettes, minibars, some microwaves, refrigerators, cable TV, in-room VCRs, in-room data ports, Wi-Fi, dry cleaning, laundry service, concierge, business services, Internet room, parking (fee), some pets allowed, no-smoking floors; no a/c* ▭ *AE, D, DC, MC, V* ⦿ *CP.*

¢–$ **Grant Plaza Hotel.** Amazingly low room rates make this hotel a find
Fodor'sChoice for budget travelers wanting views of the striking architecture and fas-
★ cinating street life of Chinatown. Small, modern rooms are sparkling clean, with newer, slightly more expensive digs on the top floor and quieter quarters in the back. Even if you're not on the top floor, take the

elevator up anyway to view two large, beautiful stained-glass windows. ⊠ *465 Grant Ave., Chinatown, 94108* ☎ *415/434–3883 or 800/472–6899* 🖷 *415/434–3886* ⊕ *www.grantplaza.com* ⇗ *71 rooms, 1 suite* ⏱ *Some fans, some in-room VCRs, in-room data ports, Wi-Fi, business services, Internet room, parking (fee), no-smoking rooms; no a/c* ▤ *AE, D, DC, MC, V.*

Financial District

$$$$ ▦ **Mandarin Oriental.** Two towers connected by glass-enclosed sky
Fodor'sChoice bridges compose the top 11 floors of San Francisco's third-tallest build-
★ ing. There are spectacular panoramas from every room, and windows open so you can hear the "ding ding" of the cable cars some 40 floors below. The Mandarin Rooms have extradeep tubs next to picture windows so you can literally and figuratively soak up what one guest called "unbelievable views from the Golden Gate to the Bay Bridge and everything in between." All rooms have Egyptian-cotton sheets, two kinds of robes (terry and waffle-weave), and terry slippers. ⊠ *222 Sansome St., Financial District, 94104* ☎ *415/276–9888* 🖷 *415/433–0289* ⊕ *www.mandarinoriental.com* ⇗ *154 rooms, 4 suites* ⏱ *Restaurant, room service, in-room safes, some in-room hot tubs, some kitchenettes, minibars, cable TV with movies and video games, some in-room VCRs, in-room data ports, Wi-Fi, gym, massage, lobby lounge, piano, babysitting, dry cleaning, laundry service, concierge, business services, Internet room, meeting rooms, parking (fee), some pets allowed (fee), no-smoking rooms* ▤ *AE, D, DC, MC, V.*

★ **$$–$$$$** ▦ **Hyatt Regency.** The 20-story gray concrete structure, at the foot of Market Street, is the focal point of the Embarcadero Center, where more than 100 shops and restaurants cater to the Financial District. The spectacular 17-story atrium lobby (listed by Guinness World Records as the largest hotel lobby in the world) is a marvel, with sprawling trees, a shimmering stream, and a huge fountain. Glass elevators whisk you up to Equinox, the city's only revolving rooftop restaurant. Rooms—all with city or bay views, and some with bay-view balconies—have an attractive, contemporary look, with light-color walls and carpets, handsome cherry furniture, and ergonomic desk chairs. ⊠ *5 Embarcadero Center, Embarcadero, 94111* ☎ *415/788–1234 or 800/233–1234* 🖷 *415/398–2567* ⊕ *http://sanfranciscoregency.hyatt.com* ⇗ *776 rooms, 29 suites* ⏱ *2 restaurants, café, dining room, room service, in-room safes, minibars, cable TV with movies, in-room data ports, Wi-Fi, gym, 2 bars, lobby lounge, dry cleaning, laundry service, concierge, business services, meeting rooms, convention center, car rental, parking (fee), no-smoking floors* ▤ *AE, D, DC, MC, V.*

SoMa

$$$$ ▦ **Four Seasons Hotel San Francisco.** On floors 5 through 17 of a skyscraper,
Fodor'sChoice this luxurious hotel is sandwiched between multimillion-dollar condos,
★ elite shops, and a premier sports-and-fitness complex—and while you're here, you can indulge in a little surreptitious celebrity-hunting for the likes of Matt Damon and Renée Zellweger. Elegant rooms with contemporary artwork and fine linens have floor-to-ceiling windows overlooking

Yerba Buena Gardens, the bay, or the city. All have deep soaking tubs and glass-enclosed showers. Take the elevator to the vast Sports Club/ LA, where you have free use of the junior Olympic pool, full-size indoor basketball court, and the rest of the magnificent facilities, classes, and spa services. ⊠ *757 Market St., SoMa, 94103* ☎ *415/633–3000 or 800/ 332–3442* 🖶 *415/633–3009* ⊕ *www.fourseasons.com/sanfrancisco* 🛏 *222 rooms, 55 suites* 🍴 *Restaurant, room service, in-room safes, minibars, cable TV with movies and video games, some in-room VCRs, inroom data ports, Wi-Fi, indoor pool, health club, sauna, spa, steam room, basketball, volleyball, bar, dry cleaning, laundry service, concierge, business services, Internet room, meeting rooms, parking (fee), some pets allowed, no-smoking floors* 🚪 *AE, D, DC, MC, V.*

★ **\$\$\$\$** 🖼 **Hotel Palomar.** The top five floors of the green-tiled and turreted 1908 Pacific Place Building provide a luxurious oasis above the busiest part of town. A softly lighted lounge area with plush sofas gives way to the Fifth Floor restaurant, which serves modern French cuisine. Rooms have muted leopard-pattern carpeting, drapes with bold navy-and-cream stripes, and sleek furniture echoing a 1930s moderne sensibility. Sparkling bathrooms provide a "tub menu" with various herbal and botanical infusions to tempt adventurous bathers. In-room spa services are arranged through Equilibrium Spa. ⊠ *12 4th St., SoMa, 94103* ☎ *415/ 348–1111* 🖶 *415/348–0302* ⊕ *www.hotelpalomar.com* 🛏 *185 rooms, 13 suites* 🍴 *Restaurant, room service, in-room fax, in-room safes, some in-room hot tubs, minibars, cable TV with movies and video games, some in-room VCRs, in-room data ports, gym, massage, bar, lounge, babysitting, dry cleaning, laundry service, concierge, business services, Internet room, meeting rooms, parking (fee), some pets allowed (fee), no-smoking floors* 🚪 *AE, D, DC, MC, V.*

\$\$\$\$ 🖼 **Palace Hotel.** This landmark hotel was the world's largest and most
Fodor'sChoice luxurious when it opened in 1875. Completely rebuilt after the earth-
★ quake and fire of 1906, the splendid hotel has a stunning entryway and the fabulous belle-epoque Garden Court restaurant, with its graceful chandeliers and stained-glass domed ceiling. Rooms, with twice-daily maid service and nightly turndown, have 14-foot ceilings, traditional mahogany furnishings, and marble bathrooms. ⊠ *2 New Montgomery St., SoMa, 94105* ☎ *415/512–1111 or 800/325–3589* 🖶 *415/543–0671* ⊕ *www. sfpalace.com* 🛏 *518 rooms, 34 suites* 🍴 *3 restaurants, room service, in-room safes, some in-room hot tubs, refrigerators, cable TV with movies and video games, in-room data ports, Wi-Fi, indoor pool, gym, hot tub, sauna, spa, steam room, bar, dry cleaning, laundry service, concierge, business services, meeting rooms, parking (fee), no-smoking floors* 🚪 *AE, D, DC, MC, V.*

★ **\$\$–\$\$\$\$** 🖼 **Harbor Court.** The exemplary service of the friendly staff earns high marks for this cozy hotel overlooking the Embarcadero and within shouting distance of the Bay Bridge. Guest rooms are smallish but have double sets of soundproof windows and include nice touches such as wall-mounted 27-inch flat-screen TVs, brightly colored throw pillows on beds with 320-thread-count sheets, and tub-showers with curved shower curtain rods for more elbow room. The hotel provides free use of the adjacent YMCA and free weekday limo service within the Financial District. ⊠ *165 Steuart St., SoMa, 94105* ☎ *415/882–1300* 🖶 *415/ 882–1313* ⊕ *www.harborcourthotel.com* ⮐ *130 rooms, 1 suite* ⚬ *In-room fax, minibars, room TVs with movies and video games, in-room data ports, Wi-Fi, bar, dry cleaning, laundry service, concierge, business services, Internet room, meeting room, parking (fee), some pets allowed, no-smoking rooms* ⊟ *AE, D, DC, MC, V.*

Nob Hill

★ **$$$$** 🏨 **Fairmont San Francisco.** The history of the hotel, which commands the top of Nob Hill like a European palace, includes triumph over the 1906 earthquake and the creation of the United Nations Charter here in 1945. Architect Julia Morgan's 1907 lobby design includes alabaster walls and gilt-embellished ceilings supported by Corinthian columns. Gracious rooms, done in pale color schemes, have high ceilings, fine dark-wood furniture, colorful Chinese porcelain lamps, and marble bathrooms. Rooms in the Tower are generally larger and have better views. An array of amenities and services (including free chicken soup if you're under the weather) keeps loyal (and royal) guests coming back. ⊠ *950 Mason St., Nob Hill, 94108* ☎ *415/772–5000* 🖶 *415/772–5013* ⊕ *www. fairmont.com* ⮐ *526 rooms, 65 suites* ⚬ *2 restaurants, room service, in-room safes, minibars, cable TV with movies and video games, in-room data ports, Wi-Fi, health club, hair salon, spa, steam room, 2 bars, lobby lounge, lounge, shops, babysitting, dry cleaning, laundry service, concierge, business services, Internet room, meeting rooms, convention center, car rental, parking (fee), some pets allowed (fee), no-smoking floors* ⊟ *AE, D, DC, MC, V.*

★ **$$$$** 🏨 **The Huntington Hotel.** The venerable ivy-covered hotel has provided gracious personal service to everyone from Bogart and Bacall to Picasso and Pavarotti. Rooms and suites, many of which have great views of Grace Cathedral, the bay, or the city skyline, are large because they used to be apartments. Most rooms have wet bars; all have large antique desks. The elegant Nob Hill Spa complex has panoramic city views, numerous spa services, and spa cuisine served by white-jacketed waiters around an indoor pool with a fireplace lounge area. ⊠ *1075 California St., Nob Hill, 94108* ☎ *415/474–5400 or 800/227–4683* 🖶 *415/474–6227* ⊕ *www.huntingtonhotel.com* ⮐ *100 rooms, 35 suites* ⚬ *Restaurant, room service, in-room safes, some in-room hot tubs, some kitchenettes, minibars, some refrigerators, cable TV with movies, Wi-Fi, indoor pool, gym, hot tub, massage, sauna, spa, steam room, bar, piano, dry cleaning, laundry service, concierge, business services, meeting rooms, parking (fee), no-smoking floors* ⊟ *AE, D, DC, MC, V.*

$$$$ 🏨 **The Stanford Court.** Formerly a Ritz Carlton, this beautiful hotel is now part of Marriott's Renaissance portfolio. Beyond the Ionic columns of the neoclassic facade, crystal chandeliers illuminate Georgian antiques and museum-quality 18th- and 19th-century paintings in the lobby. All rooms have featherbeds with 300-thread-count Egyptian cotton Frette sheets and down comforters. Afternoon tea in the Lobby Lounge—overlooking the beautifully landscaped garden courtyard—is a San Francisco institution. ⊠ *905 California St., Nob Hill, 94108* ☎ *415/989–3500* 🖶 *415/986–8195* ⊕ *www.stanfordcourt.com* ⮐ *384 rooms, 9 suites*

♝ *Restaurant, room service, cable TV with movies and video games, in-room data ports, Wi-Fi, exercise equipment, gym, bar, lobby lounge, piano, shop, babysitting, dry cleaning, laundry service, concierge, business services, Internet room, meeting rooms, convention center, parking (fee), some pets allowed, no-smoking floors* = *AE, D, DC, MC, V.*

$–$$$ ▣ **Executive Hotel Vintage Court.** This Napa Valley–inspired hotel two blocks from Union Square has inviting rooms named after California wineries. Some have sunny window seats, and all have large writing desks, dark-wood venetian blinds, and steam heat. Bathrooms are small, some with tub-showers and some with stall showers. The Wine Country theme extends to complimentary local vintages served nightly in front of the fireplace in the chocolate-color lobby, where long couches invite lingering. ✉ *650 Bush St., Nob Hill, 94108* ☎ *415/392–4666* = *415/433–4065* ⊕ *www.executivehotels.net* ↪ *106 rooms, 1 suite* ♝ *Restaurant, minibars, refrigerators, cable TV with movies and video games, in-room data ports, Wi-Fi, bar, dry cleaning, concierge, Internet room, meeting rooms, parking (fee), some pets allowed (fee); no smoking* = *AE, D, DC, MC, V* ➟| *CP.*

Fisherman's Wharf/North Beach

$$–$$$$ ▣ **Argonaut Hotel.** When this four-story brick building was a fruit and vegetable canning complex in 1907, boats docked right up against the building. Today it's a tribute to nautical chic—anchors, ropes, compasses, and a row of cruise-ship deck chairs find their way into the lively lobby decor. Spacious rooms, many of which have a sitting area with a sofa bed, have exposed-brick walls, wood-beamed ceilings, and whitewashed wooden furniture that evokes a beach mood. Suites come with extra-deep whirlpool tubs and telescopes for close-up views of passing ships. ✉ *495 Jefferson St., at Hyde St., Fisherman's Wharf, 94109* ☎ *415/563–0800* = *415/563–2800* ⊕ *www.argonauthotel.com* ↪ *239 rooms, 13 suites* ♝ *Restaurant, room service, in-room safes, some in-room hot tubs, minibars, refrigerators, cable TV with movies and video games, in-room VCRs, in-room data ports, Wi-Fi, gym, bar, lounge, babysitting, dry cleaning, laundry service, concierge, Internet room, meeting rooms, convention center, parking (fee), some pets allowed, no-smoking rooms* = *AE, D, DC, MC, V.*

FodorsChoice
★

★ **$$–$$$** ▣ **Radisson Hotel Fisherman's Wharf.** Directly facing Alcatraz, this city block–size hotel and shopping area at Fisherman's Wharf has vast, clear views of the bay. Contemporary rooms, most of which have water vistas, are decorated with cherrywood furniture and black-and-tan-stripe drapes. About half the rooms (those with king-size beds) let you adjust the firmness of each side of the bed individually. A landscaped courtyard and heated pool are in the center of the hotel complex, which provides the closest accommodations to Pier 39 and the bay cruise docks. ✉ *250 Beach St., Fisherman's Wharf, 94133* ☎ *415/392–6700* = *415/986–7853* ⊕ *www.radisson.com/sanfranciscoca_wharf* ↪ *355 rooms* ♝ *In-room safes, some refrigerators, cable TV with movies and video games, in-room data ports, Wi-Fi, pool, gym, dry cleaning, laundry service, concierge, business services, meeting rooms, parking (fee), no-smoking rooms* = *AE, D, DC, MC, V.*

$$ ▦ **Hotel Bohème.** This small hotel in historic North Beach takes you back in time with cast-iron beds, large mirrored armoires, and memorabilia recalling the Beat generation. Allen Ginsberg stayed here many times and could be seen in his later years sitting in a window, tapping away on his laptop computer. Screenwriters from Francis Ford Coppola's nearby American Zoetrope studio stay here often, as do poets and other artists. Rooms have a bistro table, two chairs, and tropical-style mosquito netting over the bed; bathrooms have cheerful yellow tiles and tiny showers. Rooms in the rear are quieter, especially on weekends. ⊠ *444 Columbus Ave., North Beach, 94133* ☎ *415/433–9111* 🖷 *415/362–6292* ⊕ *www.hotelboheme.com* ⤵ *15 rooms* ⚘ *Fans, cable TV, in-room data ports, concierge; no a/c, no smoking* ▭ *AE, D, DC, MC, V.*

¢ ▦ **San Remo Hotel.** A few blocks from Fisherman's Wharf, this three-story 1906 Italianate Victorian was once home to longshoremen and Beat poets. A narrow stairway from the street leads to the front desk and labyrinthine hallways. Rooms are small but charming, with lace curtains, forest-green-painted wood floors, brass beds, and other antique furnishings. About a third of the rooms have sinks, and all rooms share scrupulously clean black-and-white-tile shower and toilet facilities with pull-chain toilets. ⊠ *2237 Mason St., North Beach, 94133* ☎ *415/776–8688 or 800/352–7366* 🖷 *415/776–2811* ⊕ *www.sanremohotel.com* ⤵ *64 rooms with shared baths, 1 suite* ⚘ *Fans, laundry facilities, Internet room, parking (fee); no a/c, no room phones, no room TVs, no smoking* ▭ *AE, MC, V.*

FodorsChoice
★

Cow Hollow

$$–$$$$ ▦ **Union Street Inn.** With the help of precious family antiques and unique artwork, innkeepers Jane Bertorelli and David Coyle (who was a chef for the Duke and Duchess of Bedford) turned this green-and-cream 1902 Edwardian into a delightful B&B. Equipped with candles, fresh flowers, wineglasses, and fine linens, rooms are popular with honeymooners and romantics. The Carriage House, with its whirlpool tub, is set off from the main house by an old-fashioned English garden with lemon trees. ⊠ *2229 Union St., Cow Hollow, 94123* ☎ *415/346–0424* 🖷 *415/922–8046* ⊕ *www.unionstreetinn.com* ⤵ *6 rooms* ⚘ *Cable TV, Wi-Fi, parking (fee); no a/c, no smoking* ▭ *AE, MC, V* ⓞ *BP.*

FodorsChoice
★

★ **$** ▦ **Cow Hollow Motor Inn and Suites.** Rooms at this large, family-owned and -run modern motel are more spacious than average, with sitting-dining areas, dark-wood traditional furniture, and wallpaper with muted yellow, brown, and green patterns. Some rooms have views of the Golden Gate Bridge. The huge and lovely suites ($225 to $275), overlooking the eclectic mix of shops, coffeehouses, and neighborhood businesses on Chestnut Street, have one or two bedrooms and baths. They resemble typical San Francisco apartments, with hardwood floors, Oriental rugs, antique furnishings, marble wood-burning fireplaces, big living rooms, and fully equipped kitchens. ⊠ *2190 Lombard St., Marina, 94123* ☎ *415/921–5800* 🖷 *415/922–8515* ⊕ *www.cowhollowmotorinn.com* ⤵ *117 rooms, 12 suites* ⚘ *Restaurant, some kitchens, in-room data ports, free parking; no smoking* ▭ *AE, DC, MC, V.*

Civic Center/Van Ness

$–$$$$ 🖼 **The Archbishop's Mansion.** Everything in this stately 1904 French-château-style mansion is extravagantly romantic, starting with the cavernous common areas, where a chandelier used in the movie *Gone with the Wind* hangs above a Bechstein grand piano once owned by Noël Coward. Guest rooms here are grand, too; they're individually decorated with ornately carved antiques, and many have whirlpool tubs or fireplaces. Have complimentary Continental breakfast served to you in your canopied bed if you wish, then stroll past the famous Victorian "Painted Ladies" homes that share your Alamo Square location. ✉ *1000 Fulton St., Western Addition, 94117* ☎ *415/563–7872 or 800/543–5820* 🖷 *415/885–3193* ⊕ *www.thearchbishopsmansion.com* ⌁ *10 rooms, 5 suites* ⚘ *Dining room, some fans, some in-room hot tubs, cable TV, in-room VCRs, Wi-Fi, piano, dry cleaning, concierge, meeting room, some free parking; no a/c, no smoking* ⊟ *AE, D, MC, V* ⦿*l CP.*

$ 🖼 **Inn at the Opera.** Within a block or so of Davies Symphony Hall and the War Memorial Opera House, this hotel has played host to such music, dance, and opera stars as Luciano Pavarotti and Mikhail Baryshnikov. Beyond the genteel marble-floor lobby, modern and compact standard rooms have dark-wood furnishings, queen-size pillow-top beds with 250-thread-count sheets, and terry robes. ✉ *333 Fulton St., Van Ness/Civic Center, 94102* ☎ *415/863–8400 or 800/325–2708* 🖷 *415/861–0821* ⊕ *www.innattheopera.com* ⌁ *30 rooms, 18 suites* ⚘ *Restaurant, room service, fans, some microwaves, some refrigerators, cable TV, some in-room VCRs, in-room data ports, Wi-Fi, bar, babysitting, dry cleaning, concierge, business services, parking (fee); no a/c, no smoking* ⊟ *AE, DC, MC, V* ⦿*l CP.*

The Airport

★ $$$–$$$$ 🖼 **Hotel Sofitel–San Francisco Bay.** Set on a lagoon in a business park with several big-name corporate headquarters nearby, the hotel, which underwent a major redesign of its common areas in 2005, is a warm, inviting haven within this somewhat sterile area. Parisian lampposts, a métro sign, and a poster-covered kiosk bring an unexpected French theme to the public spaces, and the light, open feeling extends to the luxurious rooms. Done in pale earth tones, accommodations include fine linens and bath products, complimentary turndown service, Evian water, and fresh orchids. Many staff members speak both French and English. ✉ *223 Twin Dolphin Dr., Redwood City 94065* ☎ *650/598–9000* 🖷 *650/598–0459* ⊕ *www.accorhotels.com/sofitel_san_francisco_bay. htm* ⌁ *400 rooms, 21 suites* ⚘ *Restaurant, coffee shop, picnic area, room service, minibars, cable TV with movies and video games, in-room data ports, pool, gym, bar, lobby lounge, piano bar, shop, dry cleaning, laundry service, concierge, business services, Internet room, meeting rooms, airport shuttle, free parking, some pets allowed (fee), no-smoking rooms* ⊟ *AE, DC, MC, V.*

★ $$ 🖼 **Embassy Suites San Francisco Airport, Burlingame.** This pink California Mission–style hostelry is one of the most lavish hotels in the airport area. Set on the bay, with clear views of airplanes flying above distant

San Francisco, the building centers on a nine-story atrium and tropical garden replete with towering palms, bamboo and banana plants, koi-filled ponds, and a waterfall. This is an all-suites property, and each unit has a living room with a work area and a sleeper sofa, a bedroom, and a kitchenette between the two rooms. The suites were renovated in 2005 and all have views of either the bay or a lagoon. ⊠ *150 Anza Blvd., Burlingame 94010* ☎ *650/342–4600* ♨ *650/343–8137* ⊕ *www. embassysuites.com* ↪ *340 suites* ⌂ *Restaurant, kitchenettes, microwaves, refrigerators, cable TV with movies and video games, in-room data ports, indoor pool, gym, hot tub, sauna, bar, dry cleaning, laundry service, concierge, business services, meeting rooms, airport shuttle, free parking, some pets allowed (fee), no-smoking floors; no kids under 18* ⊟ *AE, DC, MC, V* ⊧⊙⊩ *BP.*

NIGHTLIFE & THE ARTS

Updated by John A. Vlahides

From ultrasophisticated piano bars to come-as-you-are dives that reflect the city's gold-rush past, San Francisco has a tremendous variety of evening entertainment. Enjoy a night out at the opera in the Civic Center area or hit the hip SoMa neighborhood for straight-up rock or retro jazz. Except at a few skyline lounges, you're not expected to dress up. Nevertheless, jeans are the exception and stylish dress is the norm at most nightspots.

The Arts

The best guide to arts and entertainment events in San Francisco is the "Datebook" section, printed on pink paper, in the *San Francisco Sunday Chronicle.* Also consult any of the free alternative weeklies.

City Box Office (⊠ 180 Redwood St., Suite 100, off Van Ness Ave. between Golden Gate Ave. and McAllister St., Civic Center ☎ 415/392–4400 ⊕ www.cityboxoffice.com), a charge-by-phone service, offers tickets for many concerts and lectures. You can buy tickets in person at its downtown location. You can charge tickets for everything from jazz concerts to Giants games by phone or online through **Tickets.com** (☎ 415/478–2277 or 800/955–5566 ⊕ tickets.com). Half-price, same-day tickets for many local and touring stage shows go on sale (cash only) at 11 AM Tuesday through Saturday at the **TIX Bay Area** (⊠ Powell St. between Geary and Post Sts., Union Sq. ☎ 415/433–7827 ⊕ www.theatrebayarea. org) booth on Union Square. TIX is also a full-service ticket agency for theater and music events around the Bay Area.

Dance

★ **San Francisco Ballet.** Under artistic director Helgi Tomasson, both classical and contemporary works have won admiring reviews. Tickets and information are available at the **War Memorial Opera House.** ⊠ *War Memorial Opera House, 301 Van Ness Ave., Civic Center* ☎ 415/865–2000 ⊕ *www.sfballet.org.*

Music

★ **San Francisco Opera.** Founded in 1923, this world-renowned company has resided in the Civic Center's War Memorial Opera House since the building's completion, in 1932. Over its split season—September through January and June through July—the opera presents about 70 performances of 10 to 12 operas. Translations are projected above the stage during almost all non-English operas. Long considered a major international company and the most important operatic organization in the United States outside New York, the opera frequently embarks on productions with European opera companies. Ticket prices are about $25 to $195. The full-time box office is at 199 Grove Street, at Van Ness Avenue. ⊠ *War Memorial Opera House, 301 Van Ness Ave., at Grove St., Civic Center* ☎ *415/864–3330 tickets* ⊕ *www.sfopera.com.*

★ **San Francisco Symphony.** One of America's top orchestras, the symphony performs from September through May, with additional summer performances of light classical music and show tunes. Michael Tilson Thomas, who is known for his innovative programming of 20th-century American works (most notably his Grammy Award–winning Mahler cycle), is the music director, and he and his orchestra often perform with soloists of the caliber of Andre Watts, Gil Shaham, and Renée Fleming. Tickets run about $15 to $100. ⊠ *Davies Symphony Hall, 201 Van Ness Ave., at Grove St., Civic Center* ☎ *415/864–6000* ⊕ *www.sfsymphony.org.*

Theater

★ **American Conservatory Theater.** Not long after its founding in the mid-1960s, the city's major nonprofit theater company became one of the nation's leading regional theaters. During its season, which runs from early fall to late spring, ACT presents approximately eight plays, from classics to contemporary works, often in rotating repertory. In December ACT stages a much-loved version of Charles Dickens's *A Christmas Carol.* The **ACT ticket office** (⊠ 405 Geary St., Union Sq. ☎ 415/749–2228) is next door to Geary Theater, the company's home. ⊠ *Geary Theater, 425 Geary St., Union Sq.* ⊕ *www.act-sfbay.org.*

Magic Theatre. Once Sam Shepard's favorite showcase, the Magic presents works by rising American playwrights, such as Matthew Wells, Karen Hartman, and Claire Chafee. ⊠ *Fort Mason, Bldg. D, Laguna St. at Marina Blvd.* ☎ *415/441–8822* ⊕ *www.magictheatre.org.*

Nightlife

For information on who's performing where, check out the "Datebook" insert of the *San Francisco Chronicle,* or consult the free *San Francisco Bay Guardian,* which lists neighborhood, avant-garde, and budget-priced events. The *SF Weekly,* also free, blurbs nightclubs and music venues and is packed with information on arts events around town. Another handy reference is the weekly *Where* magazine, offered free in most major hotel lobbies and at Hallidie Plaza (Market and Powell streets).

Bars

★ **Beach Chalet.** The restaurant-microbrewery, in a historic building filled with Works Project Administration murals from the 1930s, has a stunning view overlooking the Pacific Ocean. ⊠ *1000 Great Hwy., near Martin Luther King Jr. Dr., Golden Gate Park* ☎ *415/386–8439.*

Big 4 Bar. Dark-wood paneling and green leather banquettes lend a solidly masculine feel to the old-guard bar at the Huntington Hotel, where the over-thirty crowd orders Scotch and Irish coffee, not mojitos and cosmopolitans. ⊠ *The Huntington Hotel, 1075 California St., Nob Hill* ☎ *415/474–5400.*

Buena Vista Café. The Buena Vista packs 'em in for its famous Irish coffee, which made its U.S. debut here in 1952. ⊠ *2765 Hyde St., at Beach St., Fisherman's Wharf* ☎ *415/474–5044.*

Carnelian Room. Only birds get a better view of the San Francisco skyline than you will from the 52nd floor of the Bank of America Building. ⊠ *555 California St., at Kearny St., Financial District* ☎ *415/433–7500.*

★ **Eos Restaurant and Wine Bar.** A narrow and dimly lighted space with more than 400 wines by the bottle and 40-plus by the glass offers two different wine flights, one red and one white, every month. ⊠ *901 Cole St., at Carl St., Haight* ☎ *415/566–3063.*

★ **Harry Denton's Starlight Room.** Velvet booths and romantic lighting help re-create the 1950s high life on the 21st floor of the Sir Francis Drake Hotel. ⊠ *Sir Francis Drake Hotel, 450 Powell St., between Post and Sutter Sts., Union Sq.* ☎ *415/395–8595.*

Jade Bar. This narrow trilevel space with floor-to-ceiling windows, a 15-foot waterfall, and stylish sofas and banquettes attracts a near-capacity crowd even midweek. ⊠ *650 Gough St., between McAllister and Fulton Sts., Hayes Valley* ☎ *415/869–1900.*

Laszlo. At this nightspot attached to the Foreign Cinema restaurant, a bilevel design, dim lighting, and candles on each table set the scene for a romantic tête-à-tête over a classy cocktail or single-malt whiskey. ⊠ *2532 Mission St., between 21st and 22nd Sts., Mission* ☎ *415/401–0810* ☽ *Closed Mon.*

Ovation. A crackling fire sets the mood for quiet conversation over cognac at this restaurant-lounge at the Inn at the Opera. ⊠ *Inn at the Opera, 333 Fulton St., near Franklin St., Hayes Valley* ☎ *415/553–8100 or 415/305–8842.*

FodorśChoice **Redwood Room.** Originally opened in 1933 and updated by über-hip designer Philippe Starck in 2001, the Redwood Room at the Clift Hotel
★ is a San Francisco icon. ⊠ *Clift Hotel, 495 Geary St., at Taylor St., Union Sq.* ☎ *415/929–2372 for table reservations, 415/775–4700.*

Ritz-Carlton Lobby Lounge. A harpist plays during high tea (about 1 to 5:15), and a jazz pianist performs in the evening at this ever-so-civilized lobby lounge. ⊠ *600 Stockton St., at California St., Nob Hill* ☎ *415/296–7465.*

Seasons Bar. Discreet staff members in dark suits serve cocktails and salty nibbles while a piano player entertains Tuesday through Saturday evenings. ⊠ *Four Seasons Hotel San Francisco, 757 Market St., between 3rd and 4th Sts., SoMa* ☎ *415/633–3000.*

Specs'. If you're bohemian at heart, you'll groove on this hidden hangout for artists, poets, and heavy-drinking lefties. ⊠ *12 William Saroyan Pl., off Columbus Ave., between Pacific Ave. and Broadway, North Beach* ☎ *415/421–4112.*

Top of the Mark. A famous magazine photograph immortalized this place, on the 19th floor of the Mark Hopkins Inter-Continental, as a hot spot for World War II servicemen on leave or about to ship out. ⊠ *Mark Hopkins Inter-Continental, 999 California St., at Mason St., Nob Hill* ☎ *415/616–6916.*

Tosca Café. This charmer has an Italian flavor, with opera, big-band, and Italian standards on the jukebox, plus an antique espresso machine that's nothing less than a work of art. ✉ *242 Columbus Ave., near Broadway, North Beach* ☎ *415/391–1244.*

★ **Vesuvio Café.** The 2nd-floor balcony of this boho hangout, little altered since its 1960s heyday, is a fine vantage point for watching the colorful Broadway–Columbus intersection. ✉ *255 Columbus Ave., at Broadway, North Beach* ☎ *415/362–3370.*

Cabaret

asiaSF. The entertainment, as well as gracious food service, is provided by "gender illusionists." These gorgeous men don daring dresses and strut in impossibly high heels on top of the bar, which serves as a catwalk. ✉ *201 9th St., at Howard St., SoMa* ☎ *415/255–2742.*

Fodor'sChoice **Club Fugazi.** Its claim to fame is *Beach Blanket Babylon*, a wacky musical send-up of San Francisco moods and mores that has run since 1974 and become the longest-running show of its genre. Order tickets as far ahead as possible. ✉ *678 Green St., at Powell St., North Beach* ☎ *415/421–4222.*

Dance Clubs

DNA Lounge. The sounds change nightly at this venerable dance club, with psychedelic-trance (aka psytrance), deep house, and Gothic music well represented. ✉ *375 11th St., between Harrison and Folsom Sts., SoMa* ☎ *415/626–1409.*

Fodor'sChoice **El Rio.** Acts at this casual spot range from funk and soul DJs on Monday to a world-music dance party on Friday. Bands play on Saturday. ✉ *3158 Mission St., between Cesar Chavez and Valencia Sts., Mission* ☎ *415/282–3325.*

★ **111 Minna Gallery.** A gallery by day and bar and dance club by night, this unpretentious warehouse space is often full of artsy young San Franciscans who prefer it to some of the glitzier dance clubs. Call for details. ✉ *111 Minna St., bordered by Mission and Howard and 2nd and New Montgomery Sts., SoMa* ☎ *415/974–1719.*

Roccapulco. With live music and salsa dancing on Friday and Saturday, this cavernous dance hall and restaurant knows how to bring 'em in. ✉ *3140 Mission St., between Precita and Cesar Chavez Sts., Mission* ☎ *415/648–6611.*

Gay & Lesbian

MEN **Café Flore.** More of a daytime destination, this café attracts a mixed crowd, including poets, students, and fashionistas. ✉ *2298 Market St., at Noe St., Castro* ☎ *415/621–8579.*

The Cinch. The Wild West–theme neighborhood bar has pinball machines, pool tables, and a smoking patio, and it's not the least bit trendy. ✉ *1723 Polk St., between Washington and Clay Sts., Van Ness/Polk* ☎ *415/776–4162.*

Divas. In the rough-and-tumble Tenderloin, around the corner from the Polk Street bars, this is *the* place for trannies (transvestites and transsexuals) and their admirers. ✉ *1081 Post St., at Larkin St., Tenderloin* ☎ *415/928–6006.*

★ **Eagle Tavern.** Bikers are courted with endless drink specials and, increasingly, live rock music at this humongous indoor-outdoor watering hole, one of the few SoMa bars remaining from the days before

AIDS and gentrification. ⊠ *398 12th St., at Harrison St., SoMa* ☎ *415/626–0880.*

★ **Martuni's.** A mixed crowd enjoys cocktails in the semirefined environment of this elegant bar at the intersection of the Castro, the Mission, and Hayes Valley. Variations on the martini are a specialty. ⊠ *4 Valencia St., at Market St., Mission* ☎ *415/241–0205.*

Midnight Sun. One of the Castro's longest-running bars is popular with the polo-shirt-and-khakis crowd and has giant video screens playing episodes of *Will and Grace, The Simpsons, Queer Eye for the Straight Guy,* and other TV shows, as well as musicals and comedy. ⊠ *4067 18th St., at Castro St., Castro* ☎ *415/861–4186.*

The Stud. Nearly four decades after its opening in 1966, this bar is still going strong seven days a week. Each night's music is different—from funk, soul, and hip-hop to 1980s tunes and disco favorites. ⊠ *399 9th St., at Harrison St., SoMa* ☎ *415/252–7883.*

WOMEN **Lexington Club.** According to its slogan, "every night is ladies' night" at ★ this all-girl club geared toward urban alterna-dykes in their twenties and thirties (think piercings and tattoos, not lipstick). ⊠ *3464 19th St., at Lexington St., Mission* ☎ *415/863–2052.*

Jazz

Bruno's. Selling points of this hot spot are the small plates of Southern-style cooking, swanky cocktails and live music performed by local ensembles. ⊠ *2389 Mission St., at 20th St., Mission* ☎ *415/648–7701.*

Café du Nord. You can hear some of the coolest jazz, blues, rock, and alternative sounds in town at this basement bar. ⊠ *2170 Market St., between Church and Sanchez Sts., Castro* ☎ *415/861–5016.*

★ **Jazz at Pearl's.** Dim lighting, plush 1930s supper-club style, and great straight-ahead jazz make it ideal for a romantic evening. Cover is $5 to $10. ⊠ *256 Columbus Ave., at Broadway, North Beach* ☎ *415/291–8255.*

Rock, Pop, Folk & Blues

★ **Bimbo's 365 Club.** The plush main room and adjacent lounge of this club, here since 1951, retain a retro vibe perfect for the "Cocktail Nation" programming that keeps the crowds entertained. ⊠ *1025 Columbus Ave., at Chestnut St., North Beach* ☎ *415/474–0365.*

Fodor'sChoice **Boom Boom Room.** Top-notch blues acts attract old-timers and hipsters ★ alike. ⊠ *1601 Fillmore St., at Geary Blvd., Japantown* ☎ *415/673–8000.*

Fillmore. San Francisco's most famous rock-music hall serves up a varied menu of national and local acts: rock, reggae, grunge, jazz, folk, acid house, and more. ⊠ *1805 Geary Blvd., at Fillmore St., Western Addition* ☎ *415/346–6000.*

Fodor'sChoice **Great American Music Hall.** You can find top-drawer entertainment at this ★ great, eclectic nightclub; acts run the gamut from the best in blues, folk, and jazz to alternative rock and American roots music. ⊠ *859 O'Farrell St., between Polk and Larkin Sts., Tenderloin* ☎ *415/885–0750.*

Last Day Saloon. Rising local bands as well as major acts perform blues, hip-hop, rock, funk, country, or jazz at this club, open since 1973. ⊠ *406 Clement St., between 5th and 6th Aves., Richmond* ☎ *415/387–6343.*

The Saloon. Hard-drinkin' North Beach locals in the know favor this raucous blues and rock spot. ✉ *1232 Grant Ave., near Columbus Ave., North Beach* ☎ *415/989–7666.*

Slim's. National touring acts—mostly classic rock, blues, jazz, and world music—are the main event at this venue, one of SoMa's most popular nightclubs. ✉ *333 11th St., between Harrison and Folsom Sts., SoMa* ☎ *415/522–0333.*

SPORTS & THE OUTDOORS

Updated by John A. Vlahides

Daytime temperatures rarely drop below 50°F, so it's no surprise that visitors and residents alike find plenty of ways to maximize their time outdoors. The captivating views are a major part of the appeal, as are the city's 3,500 acres of parks and open spaces. On the best days, even longtime city dwellers marvel at the sun sparkling on the bay and the cool, crisp air blowing right off the Pacific Ocean.

Baseball

🕐
Fodor'sChoice
★

Home field for the National League's **San Francisco Giants** (✉ SBC Park, 24 Willie Mays Plaza, between 2nd and 3rd Sts., China Basin ☎ 415/972–2000 or 800/734–4268 ⊕ sanfrancisco.giants.mlb.com) is downtown's **AT&T Park. Tickets.com** (☎ 510/762–2255 Baseball Line, 415/478–2277 or 800/955–5566 ⊕ www.tickets.com) sells game tickets over the phone. Its Baseball Line charges a per-ticket fee of $2–$10, plus a per-call processing fee of up to $5.

Football

The **San Francisco 49ers** (✉ Monster Park, 490 Jamestown Ave., Bayview Heights ☎ 415/656–4900 ⊕ www.sf49ers.com) play at **Monster Park** near the San Mateo County border, just north of the airport. Single-game tickets, available via **Ticketmaster** (☎ 415/421–8497 ⊕ www.ticketmaster.com), almost always sell out far in advance. ■ TIP➜ **Locals stubbornly refer to the park by its original name, Candlestick Park. If you ask people on the street how to get to Monster, many won't know (or will pretend not to know) what you're talking about.**

SHOPPING

Shopping Neighborhoods

Updated by Sharron Wood

The Castro/Noe Valley. Often called the gay capital of the world, it's also a major shopping destination for nongay travelers, filled with men's clothing boutiques, home-accessories stores, and various specialty shops.

Chinatown. The intersection of Grant Avenue and Bush Street marks the gateway to 24 blocks of shops, restaurants, and markets. Dominating the exotic cityscape are the sights and smells of food. Racks of Chinese silks, toy trinkets, colorful pottery, baskets, and carved figurines are displayed chockablock on the sidewalks.

Fisherman's Wharf. Sightseers crowd this area and with good reason: Pier 39, the Anchorage, Ghirardelli Square, and the Cannery. Each has shops and restaurants, as well as outdoor entertainment—musicians, mimes, and magicians. Best of all are the wharf's view of the bay and its proximity to cable-car lines.

The Haight. Haight Street is a perennial attraction for visitors, if only to see the sign at Haight and Ashbury streets. These days chain stores such as the Gap and Ben & Jerry's have taken over large storefronts near the famous intersection, but it's still possible to find high-quality vintage clothing, funky shoes, and folk art from around the world in this always-busy neighborhood.

Jackson Square. Elegant Jackson Square, on the northeastern edge of the Financial District, is home to a dozen or so of San Francisco's finest retail antiques dealers, many of which occupy Victorian-era buildings.

North Beach. Although it's sometimes compared to New York City's Greenwich Village, North Beach is only a fraction of the size, clustered tightly around Washington Square and Columbus Avenue. Most of its businesses are small eateries, cafés, and shops selling clothing, antiques, and vintage wares.

Pacific Heights. Pacific Heights residents seeking fine items for their luxurious homes head straight for Fillmore Street between Post Street and Pacific Avenue, and Sacramento Street between Lyon and Maple streets, where private residences alternate with fine clothing and gift shops and housewares stores.

SoMa. High San Francisco rents mean there aren't many discount outlets in the city, but a few do exist in the semi-industrial zone south of Market Street (SoMa). The gift shop of the San Francisco Museum of Modern Art sells handmade jewelry, upscale and offbeat housewares, and other great gift items.

Union Square. Serious shoppers head straight to San Francisco's main shopping area and the site of most department stores, as well as the Virgin Megastore, the Disney Store, Borders Books and Music, and Frette. Nearby are the pricey international boutiques of Tiffany, Yves Saint Laurent, Cartier, Emporio Armani, Gucci, Hermès of Paris, Louis Vuitton, and Gianni Versace.

Malls & Department Stores

The **Crocker Galleria** (⊠ 50 Post St., at Kearny St., Financial District ☏ 415/ 393–1505), a complex of 40 or so mostly upscale shops and restaurants a few blocks east of Union Square, is housed beneath a glass dome.

Embarcadero Center. Four sprawling buildings of shops, restaurants, offices, and a popular art-movie theater—plus the Hyatt Regency hotel—make up the Embarcadero Center, downtown at the end of Market Street. Most of the stores are branches of upscale national chains, such as Ann Taylor, Banana Republic, and Pottery Barn. ⊠ *Clay and Sacramento Sts. between Battery and Drumm Sts.* ☏ *415/772–0734.*

Japan Center. The three-block complex includes an 800-car public garage and three shop-filled buildings. Especially worthwhile are the Kintetsu and Kinokuniya buildings, where shops and showrooms sell bonsai trees, tapes and records, jewelry, antique kimonos, *tansu* (Japanese chests), electronics, and colorful glazed dinnerware and teapots. ⊠ *Bordered by Laguna, Fillmore, and Post Sts. and Geary Blvd.* ☏ *No phone.*

★ **Gump's.** Stocked with large decorative vases, sumptuous housewares that look too luxe for everyday use, and extravagant jewelry, this airy store exudes a museumlike aura. ⊠ *135 Post St., between Grant Ave. and Kearny St., Union Sq.* ☎ *415/982–1616.*

Macy's. Downtown has two behemoth branches of this retailer. One—with entrances on Geary, Stockton, and O'Farrell streets—houses the women's, children's, furniture, and housewares departments. The men's department occupies its own building, across Stockton Street. ⊠ *170 O'Farrell St., at Stockton St., Union Sq.* ☎ *415/397–3333* ⊠ *Men's branch:* ⊠ *50 O'Farrell St., entrance on Stockton St., Union Sq.* ☎ *415/397–3333.*

Neiman Marcus. The surroundings, which include a Philip Johnson–designed checkerboard facade, gilded atrium, and stained-glass skylight, are as high class as the goods showcased in them. The mix includes designer men's and women's clothing and accessories as well as posh household wares. ⊠ *150 Stockton St., at Geary Blvd., Union Sq.* ☎ *415/362–3900.*

★ **Nordstrom.** This service-oriented store specializes in designer fashions, accessories, cosmetics, and, most notably, shoes. The space, with spiral escalators circling a four-story atrium, is stunning. ⊠ *San Francisco Shopping Centre, 865 Market St., between 4th and 5th Sts., Union Sq.* ☎ *415/243–8500.*

San Francisco Shopping Centre. The center, across from the cable-car turnaround at Powell and Market streets, has spiral escalators that wind up through the sunlit atrium. Inside are 65 retailers, including Nordstrom. ⊠ *865 Market St., between 4th and 5th Sts.* ☎ *415/495–5656.*

Saks Fifth Avenue. A central escalator ascends past a series of designer boutiques that display fashions from conservative to trendy. ⊠ *384 Post St., at Powell St., Union Sq.* ☎ *415/986–4300.*

SIDE TRIPS FROM SAN FRANCISCO

Updated by
John A.
Vlahides

One of San Francisco's best assets is its surroundings. To the north is Marin County, where the lively waterfront town of Sausalito has bougainvillea-covered hillsides, an expansive yacht harbor, and an artists' colony. To the east is Berkeley, a colorful university town. Explore a bit beyond the city limits and you're bound to discover what makes the Bay Area such a coveted place to live.

Sausalito

Like much of San Francisco, Sausalito had a raffish reputation before it went upscale. Discovered in 1775 by Spanish explorers and named Sausalito ("Little Willow") for the trees growing around its springs, the town served as a port for whaling ships during the 19th century. By the mid-1800s wealthy San Franciscans were making Sausalito their getaway across the bay. They built lavish Victorian summer homes in the hills, many of which still stand. In 1875 the railroad from the north connected with ferryboats to San Francisco, bringing the merchant and working classes with it. This influx of hardworking, fun-loving folk polarized the town into "wharf rats" and "hill snobs," and the waterfront area grew thick with saloons, gambling dens, and bordellos.

Sausalito developed its bohemian flair in the 1950s and '60s, when a group of artists established an artists' colony and a houseboat community here. Today more than 450 houseboats are docked in Sausalito, which has since also become a major yachting center. The ferry is the best way to get to Sausalito from San Francisco; you get more romance (and less traffic) and disembark in the heart of downtown.

The U.S. Army Corps of Engineers uses the **Bay Model** to reproduce the rise and fall of tides, the flow of currents, and the other physical forces at work on the bay. ⊠ *2100 Bridgeway, at Marinship Way* ☎ *415/332–3870 recorded information, 415/332–3871 operator assistance* ⊕ *www.spn.usace.army.mil/bmvc* ⊠*Free* ☉ *Memorial Day–Labor Day, Tues.–Fri. 9–4, weekends 10–5; Labor Day–Memorial Day, Tues.–Sat. 9–4.*

The **Bay Area Discovery Museum** fills five former military buildings with entertaining and enlightening hands-on exhibits related to science and the arts. Kids and their families can fish from a boat at the indoor wharf, imagine themselves as marine biologists in the Wave Workshop, and play outdoors at Lookout Cove, a 2.5-acre bay-in-miniature made up of scaled-down sea caves, tide pools, and even a re-created shipwreck. From San Francisco take the Alexander Avenue exit from U.S. 101 and follow signs to East Fort Baker. ⊠ *557 McReynolds Rd., at East Fort Baker* ☎ *415/339–3900* ⊕ *www.baykidsmuseum.org* ⊠*$8.50* ☉ *Tues.–Fri. 9–4, weekends 10–5.*

Where to Stay & Eat

★ **$–$$$** ✕ **Poggio.** One of the few restaurants in Sausalito to attract both food-savvy locals and tourists, Poggio serves modern Tuscan cuisine in a handsome, open-walled space that spills onto the street in the style of restaurants on the Italian Riviera. Expect dishes such as grilled lamb chops with roasted eggplant, braised artichokes with polenta, feather-light gnocchi, and pizzas from the open kitchen's wood-fired oven. ⊠ *777 Bridgeway* ☎ *415/332–7771* ⌕ *Reservations essential* ⊟ *AE, D, MC, V.*

★ **$–$$** ✕ **Fish.** For fresh seafood, you can't beat this gleaming dockside fish house a mile north of downtown. Order at the counter, and then grab a seat by the floor-to-ceiling windows or at a picnic table on the pier, overlooking the yachts and fishing boats. Most of the sustainably caught fish is hauled in from the owner's boats, right at the dock outside. Try the ceviche, crab Louis, cioppino, barbecue oysters, or anything fresh that day that's being grilled over the oak-wood fire. ⊠ *350 Harbor Dr.* ☎ *415/331–3474* ⌕ *Reservations not accepted* ⊟ *No credit cards.*

$$$$ ▥ **Casa Madrona.** What began as a small inn with a handful of historic accommodations in a 19th-century landmark house has expanded over the decades to incorporate a variety of lodgings and a full-service spa, all tiered down the hill in the center of town. The design in the original rooms and suites ranges from the cutesiness of what's called the Artist's Loft to elegant Mediterranean motifs. An adjacent three-story building contains newer rooms that are uniformly contemporary, with wet bars, sunken tubs, and bay windows; some have balconies overlooking Richardson Bay. ⊠ *801 Bridgeway, 94965* ☎ *415/332–0502 or 800/567–9524* ▤ *415/332–2537* ⊕ *www.casamadrona.com* ⊅ *56 rooms, 7 suites* ⌂ *Restaurant, minibars, cable TV, some in-room VCRs, in-room* *data ports, hot tub, spa, dry cleaning, laundry service, concierge, Wi-Fi, meeting rooms; no a/c, no smoking* ☰ *AE, D, DC, MC, V.*

$–$$ ⊡ **Hotel Sausalito.** Soft yellow, green, and orange tones create a warm, Mediterranean-like glow at this well-run inn, which feels like a small European hotel, with handmade furniture and tasteful original art and reproductions. The rooms range from small quarters good for budget-minded travelers to commodious suites. ⊠ *16 El Portal, 94965* ☎ *415/332–0700 or 888/442–0700* 🖷 *415/332–8788* ⊕ *www.hotelsausalito. com* ⇨ *14 rooms, 2 suites* ⚭ *Cable TV, in-room VCRs, in-room data ports, Wi-Fi, concierge; no a/c, no smoking* ☰ *AE, DC, MC, V* ⦿ *CP.*

Berkeley

The birthplace of the Free Speech Movement, the radical hub of the 1960s, the home of arguably the nation's top public university, and the city whose government condemned the bombing of Afghanistan—Berkeley is all of those things. The city of 100,000 facing San Francisco across the bay is also culturally diverse, a breeding ground for social trends, a bastion of the counterculture, and an important center for Bay Area writers, artists, and musicians.

The **Berkeley Visitor Information Center** (⊠ University Hall, Room 101, 2200 University Ave., at Oxford St. ☎ 510/642–5215) is the starting point for the free, student-guided tours of the campus, which last 1½ hours and start at 10 on weekdays.

The **University of California, Berkeley Art Museum & Pacific Film Archive** has an interesting collection of works that spans five centuries, with an emphasis on contemporary art. Changing exhibits line the spiral ramps and balcony galleries. Don't miss the museum's series of vibrant paintings by abstract expressionist Hans Hofmann. On the ground floor, the Pacific Film Archive has programs of historic and contemporary films, and the exhibition theater is at 2575 Bancroft Way, near Bowditch Street. ⊠ *2626 Bancroft Way* ☎ *510/642–0808, 510/642–1124 film-program information* ⊕ *www.bampfa.berkeley.edu* 🖅 *$8* ⊙ *Wed. and Fri.–Sun. 11–5, Thurs. 11–7.*

About 13,500 species of plants from all over the world flourish in the 34-acre **University of California Botanical Garden.** Free garden tours are given Thursday, Saturday, and Sunday at 1:30. Benches and shady picnic tables make this a relaxing alternative to the busy main campus. ⊠ *200 Centennial Dr.* ☎ *510/643–2755* ⊕ *botanicalgarden.berkeley.edu* 🖅 *$3, free Thurs.* ⊙ *Memorial Day–Labor Day, Mon. and Tues. 9–5, Wed.–Sun. 9–8; rest of yr, daily 9–5. Closed 1st Tues. of month.*

☾ At the fortresslike **Lawrence Hall of Science,** a dazzling hands-on science center, kids can look at insects under microscopes, solve crimes using chemical forensics, and explore the physics of baseball. ⊠ *Centennial Dr. near Grizzly Peak Blvd.* ☎ *510/642–5132* ⊕ *www. lawrencehallofscience.org* 🖅 *$8.50* ⊙ *Daily 10–5.*

Where to Stay & Eat

$$–$$$$ ✕ **Café Rouge.** You can recover from 4th Street shopping in this spacious two-story bistro, complete with zinc bar, skylights, and festive lanterns.

The short, seasonal menu ranges from the sophisticated, such as rack of lamb and juniper-berry-cured pork chops, to the homey, such as spit-roasted chicken or pork loin, or cheddar-topped burgers. ⊠ *1782 4th St.* ☎ *510/525–1440* ▤ *MC, V* ✸ *No dinner Mon.*

$$–$$$$ ✕ **Chez Panisse Café & Restaurant.** The downstairs portion of Alice Waters's legendary eatery is noted for its formality and personal service. Here, the daily-changing multicourse dinners are prix fixe and pricey ($$$$), although the cost is slightly lower on weekdays. Upstairs, in the informal café, the crowd is livelier, the prices are lower ($$), and the ever-changing menu is à la carte. The food is simpler, too: penne with new potatoes, arugula, and sheep's-milk cheese; and fresh figs with Parmigiano-Reggiano cheese and arugula, for example. ⊠ *1517 Shattuck Ave., north of University Ave.* ☎ *510/548–5525 restaurant, 510/548–5049 café* ⩜ *Reservations essential* ▤ *AE, D, DC, MC, V* ✸ *Closed Sun. No lunch in restaurant.*

FodorsChoice ★

$$–$$$ ✕ **Rivoli.** Italian-inspired dishes using fresh, mostly organic California ingredients star on a menu that changes every three weeks. Typical meals include fresh line-caught fish, pastas, and inventive offerings such as its trademark portobello fritters with aioli. ⊠ *1539 Solano Ave.* ☎ *510/526–2542* ⩜ *Reservations essential* ▤ *AE, D, DC, MC, V* ✸ *No lunch.*

¢–$ ✕ **Bette's Oceanview Diner.** Buttermilk pancakes are just one of the specialties at this 1930s-inspired diner, complete with checkered floors and burgundy booths. The wait for a seat can be long. If you're starving, head to Bette's to Go, next door, for takeout. ⊠ *1807 4th St.* ☎ *510/644–3230* ⩜ *Reservations not accepted* ▤ *MC, V* ✸ *No dinner.*

$$$$ ▦ **Claremont Resort and Spa.** Straddling the Oakland-Berkeley border, the hotel beckons like a gleaming white castle in the hills. Traveling executives come for the guest rooms' business amenities, including T-1 Internet connections, guest e-mail addresses, and oversize desks. The Claremont also shines for leisure travelers, drawing honeymooners and families alike with its luxurious suites, therapeutic massages, and personalized yoga workouts at the on-site spa. ⊠ *41 Tunnel Rd., at Ashby and Domingo Aves., 94705* ☎ *510/843–3000 or 800/323–7500* ☒ *510/843–6629* ⊕ *www.claremontresort.com* ⇶ *262 rooms, 17 suites* ⌂ *2 restaurants, café, in-room safes, some in-room hot tubs, some minibars, some refrigerators, cable TV, in-room VCRs, in-room data ports, 10 tennis courts, 2 pools, health club, hair salon, hot tub, sauna, spa, steam room, 2 bars, children's programs (ages 6 wks–10 yrs), dry cleaning, laundry service, concierge, Internet room, business services, meeting rooms, parking (fee), no-smoking floor* ▤ *AE, D, DC, MC, V.*

FodorsChoice ★

$$ ▦ **Hotel Durant.** Long the mainstay of parents visiting their children at U.C. Berkeley, the hotel is a good option for those who want to be a short walk from campus and from the restaurants and shops of Telegraph Avenue. Rooms, updated in 2006 with new bathrooms and accented with dark wood set against deep jewel tones, are small without feeling cramped. ⊠ *2600 Durant Ave., 94704* ☎ *510/845–8981* ☒ *510/486–8336* ⊕ *www.hoteldurant.com* ⇶ *139 rooms, 5 suites* ⌂ *Restaurant, room service, some refrigerators, cable TV with movies, in-room data ports, sports bar, dry cleaning, laundry service, concierge, business services, meeting rooms, parking (fee), no-smoking floors; no a/c* ▤ *AE, D, DC, MC, V.*

$ ▨ **French Hotel.** The only hotel in north Berkeley, this three-level brick structure has a certain *pensione* feel. Rooms have pastel or brick walls and modern touches such as white wire baskets in lieu of dressers. Balconies make the rooms seem larger than their modest dimensions. ⊠ *1538 Shattuck Ave., 94709* ☎ *510/548–9930* 🖷 *510/548–9930* 🛏 *18 rooms* ⌂ *Café, cable TV with movies, concierge, business services, free parking; no a/c, no smoking* 🖃 *AE, D, MC, V.*

SAN FRANCISCO ESSENTIALS

To research prices, get advice from other travelers, and book travel arrangements, visit www.fodors.com.

AIR TRAVEL

Heavy fog is infamous for causing chronic delays into and out of San Francisco. If you're heading to the East Bay, make every effort to fly into Oakland International Airport, which is easy to navigate and accessible by public transit. Of the major carriers, Alaska, America West, American, Continental, Delta, Southwest, United, and US Airways fly into both Oakland and San Francisco. JetBlue Airways services Oakland. Northwest flies into San Francisco but not Oakland. Midwest Express and Frontier Airlines, two smaller carriers, both fly into San Francisco. ⇨ Air Travel *in* Smart Travel Tips A to Z for airline phone numbers.

AIRPORTS & TRANSFERS

The major gateway to San Francisco is San Francisco International Airport (SFO), off U.S. 101 15 mi south of the city. Oakland International Airport (OAK) is across the bay, not much farther away from downtown San Francisco (via Interstate 880 and Interstate 80), but rush-hour traffic on the Bay Bridge may lengthen travel times considerably.

🛂 Oakland International Airport (OAK) ☎ 510/577–4000 ⊕ www.flyoakland.com. San Francisco International Airport (SFO) ☎ 650/761–0800 ⊕ www.flysfo.com.

TRANSFERS **From San Francisco International Airport:** A taxi ride to downtown costs $35 to $40. Airport shuttles are inexpensive and generally efficient. The SFO Airporter ($14) picks up passengers at baggage claim (lower level) and serves selected downtown hotels. Lorrie's Airport Service and SuperShuttle both stop at the upper-level traffic islands and take you anywhere within the city limits of San Francisco. They charge $14 to $17, depending on your destination. Lorrie's also sells tickets online, at a $2 discount. Shuttles to the East Bay, such as BayPorter Express, also depart from the upper-level traffic islands; expect to pay around $35. You can **take BART directly to downtown San Francisco;** the trip takes about 30 minutes and costs less than $5. Trains leave from the international terminal every 15 minutes on weekdays and every 20 minutes on weekends. Another inexpensive way to get to San Francisco is via two SamTrans buses: No. 292 (55 minutes, $1.25 to $2.50) and the KX (35 minutes, $3.50; only one small carry-on bag permitted). Board the SamTrans buses at the north end of the lower level.

From Oakland International Airport: A taxi to downtown San Francisco costs $35 to $40. BayPorter Express and other shuttles serve major hotels and provide door-to-door service to the East Bay and San Francisco. Marin Door to Door serves Marin County for a flat $50 fee. The best way to get to San Francisco via public transit is to take the AIR BART bus ($2) to the Coliseum/Oakland International Airport BART station (BART fares vary depending on where you're going; the ride to downtown San Francisco costs $3.15).

🚹 **American Airporter** ☏ 415/202-0733 ⊕ americanairporter.com. **BayPorter Express** ☏ 415/467-1800 ⊕ www.bayporter.com. **East Bay Express Airporter** ☏ 510/547-0404. **Lorrie's Airport Service** ☏ 415/334-9000 ⊕ www.sfovan.com. **Marin Door to Door** ☏ 415/457-2717 ⊕ www.marindoortodoor.com. **SamTrans** ☏ 800/660-4287 ⊕ www.samtrans.com. **SFO Airporter** ☏ 877/877-8819 or 650/624-0500 ⊕ www. sfoairporter.com. **South & East Bay Airport Shuttle** ☏ 408/559-9477. **SuperShuttle** ☏ 800/258-3826 or 415/558-8500 ⊕ www.supershuttle.com. **VIP Airport Shuttle** ☏ 800/235-8847, 408/885-1800, or 408/986-6000 ⊕ www.yourairportride.com.

BOAT & FERRY TRAVEL

Blue & Gold Fleet operates a number of lines, including service to Alcatraz ($11.50 to $16), Angel Island ($13), Sausalito ($7.25 one-way), and Tiburon ($7.25 one-way). Tickets are sold at Pier 41 (next to Fisherman's Wharf), where the boats depart (except the ferry to Tiburon, which departs from the Ferry Building). Golden Gate Ferry runs daily to and from Sausalito and Larkspur (each are $6.15 one-way), leaving from Pier 1, behind the San Francisco Ferry Building at the foot of Market Street on the Embarcadero.

🚹 **Blue & Gold Fleet** ☏ 415/705-5555 ⊕ www.blueandgoldfleet.com. **Golden Gate Ferry** ☏ 415/923-2000 ⊕ www.goldengateferry.org.

BUS TRAVEL TO & FROM SAN FRANCISCO

Greyhound, the only long-distance bus company serving San Francisco, operates buses to and from most major cities in the country.

🚹 **Greyhound** ✉ 425 Mission St., between Fremont and 1st Sts., SoMa ☏ 800/231-2222 or 415/495-1569 ⊕ www.greyhound.com.

BUS & TRAIN TRAVEL WITHIN SAN FRANCISCO

BART: Bay Area Rapid Transit (BART) trains, which run until midnight, connect San Francisco with Oakland, Berkeley, Pittsburgh/Bay Point, Richmond, Fremont, Dublin/Pleasanton, and other small cities and towns in between. Within San Francisco, stations are limited to downtown, the Mission, and a couple of outlying neighborhoods. Trains also travel south from San Francisco as far as Millbrae. The BART-SFO Extension Project connects downtown San Francisco to San Francisco International Airport; a ride is $4.95. Intra-city San Francisco fares are $1.25; inter-city fares are $2.15 to 7.45.

Bus: Outside the city, AC Transit serves the East Bay, and Golden Gate Transit serves Marin County.

Caltrain: Caltrain connects San Francisco to Palo Alto, San Jose, Santa Clara, and many smaller cities en route. In San Francisco, trains leave from the main depot, at 4th and King streets, and a rail-side stop at 22nd and Pennsylvania streets. One-way fares are $1.75 to $8, depending on the number of zones through which you travel. Trips last 1 to 1¾ hours.

Muni: The San Francisco Municipal Railway, or Muni, operates light-rail vehicles, the historic F-line streetcars along Fisherman's Wharf and Market Street, trolley buses, and the world-famous cable cars. On buses and streetcars, the fare is $1.25. Exact change is required, and dollar bills are accepted in the fare boxes. For all Muni vehicles other than cable cars, 90-minute transfers are issued free upon request at the time the fare is paid. Transfers are valid for two additional transfers in any direction. Cable cars cost $3 and include no transfers.

🚊 **AC Transit** ☎ 510/839-2882 ⊕ www.actransit.org. **Bay Area Rapid Transit** (BART) ☎ 650/992-2278 ⊕ www.bart.gov. **Caltrain** ☎ 800/660-4287 ⊕ www.caltrain.com. **Golden Gate Transit** ☎ 415/923-2000 ⊕ www.goldengate.org. **San Francisco Caltrain Station** ✉ 700 4th St., at King St. ☎ 800/660-4287. **San Francisco Municipal Railway System** (Muni) ☎ 415/673-6864 ⊕ www.sfmuni.com.

CAR RENTAL

All of the national car-rental companies have offices at the San Francisco and Oakland airports. ⇨ Car Rental *in* Smart Travel Tips A to Z for national rental-agency phone numbers.

CAR TRAVEL

Driving in San Francisco can be a challenge because of the hills, one-way streets, and traffic. Take it easy and, to avoid getting a ticket, remember to curb your wheels when parking on hills—turn wheels away from the curb when facing uphill, toward the curb when facing downhill.

PARKING On certain streets, parking is forbidden during rush hours. Look for the warning signs; illegally parked cars are towed immediately. Downtown parking lots are often full, and most are expensive. Large hotels often have parking available, but it doesn't come cheap; many charge as much as $40 a day for the privilege.

LODGING

The San Francisco Convention and Visitors Bureau publishes a free lodging guide with a map and listings of San Francisco and Bay Area hotels. You can also reserve a room, by phone or via the Internet, at more than 60 bureau-recommended hotels. San Francisco Reservations, in business since 1986, can arrange reservations at more than 200 Bay Area hotels, often at special discounted rates. Hotellocators.com also offers online and phone-in reservations at special rates.

🏨 **Hotellocators.com** 🏠 9 Sumner St., San Francisco 94103 ☎ 800/576-0003 📠 858/581-1730 ⊕ www.hotellocators.com. **San Francisco Convention and Visitors Bureau** ☎ 415/391-2000 general information, 415/283-0177, 888/782-9673 lodging service ⊕ www.sfvisitor.org. **San Francisco Reservations** ☎ 800/677-1500 ⊕ www.hotelres.com.

TAXIS

Taxi service is notoriously bad in San Francisco, and hailing a cab can be frustratingly difficult in some parts of the city, especially on weekends. In a pinch, hotel taxi stands are an option, as is calling for a pickup. But be forewarned: taxi companies frequently don't answer the phone during peak periods. Taxis in San Francisco charge $2.85 for the first

⅕ mi, 45¢ for each additional ⅕ mi, and 45¢ per minute in stalled traffic. There is no charge for additional passengers; there is no surcharge for luggage.

🚖 **City Wide Cab** ☎ 415/920-0700. **DeSoto Cab** ☎ 415/970-1300. **Luxor Cab** ☎ 415/282-4141. **Veteran's Taxicab** ☎ 415/552-1300. **Yellow Cab** ☎ 415/626-2345.

SIGHTSEEING TOURS

BUS & VAN TOURS In addition to bus and van tours of the city, most tour companies run excursions to various Bay Area and northern California destinations, such as Marin County. City tours generally last 3½ hours and cost $38 to $40. Great Pacific Tours conducts city tours in passenger vans (starting at $40). San Francisco Sightseeing (Gray Line), a much larger, corporately owned outfit, operates 42-passenger motor coaches and motorized cable cars ($17 to $57). For about $15 more, either tour operator can supplement a city tour with a bay cruise.

🚌 **Great Pacific Tours** ☎ 415/626-4499 ⊕ www.greatpacifictour.com. **San Francisco Sightseeing** ☎ 415/558-9400 ⊕ www.graylinesanfrancisco.com.

WALKING TOURS The best way to see San Francisco is to hit the streets. Tours of various San Francisco neighborhoods generally cost $15 to $40. Some tours explore culinary themes, such as Chinese food or coffeehouses: lunch and snacks are often included. Others focus on architecture or history.

🚶 Architecture Tours **"Victorian Home Walk"** ☎ 415/252-9485 ⊕ www.victorianwalk.com.
🚶 Culinary Tours **"Chinatown with the Wok Wiz"** ☎ 415/981-8989 ⊕ www.wokwiz.com. **"Javawalk"** ☎ 415/673-9255 ⊕ www.javawalk.com.
🚶 General Interest Tours **City Guides** ☎ 415/557-4266 ⊕ www.sfcityguides.org. **San Francisco Visitor Information Center** ✉ Hallidie Plaza, lower level, Powell and Market Sts., Union Sq. ☎ 415/391-2000, 415/392-0328 TDD ⊕ www.sfvisitor.org.
🚶 Historic Tours **Chinese Culture Center** ☎ 415/986-1822 ⊕ www.c-c-c.org. **Trevor Hailey** ☎ 415/550-8110 ⊕ www.webcastro.com/castrotour.

TRAIN TRAVEL TO & FROM SAN FRANCISCO

Amtrak trains travel to the Bay Area from some cities in California and the United States. The *Coast Starlight* travels north from Los Angeles to Seattle, passing the Bay Area along the way. Amtrak also has several inland routes between San Jose, Oakland, and Sacramento. The *California Zephyr* route travels from Chicago to the Bay Area. San Francisco doesn't have an Amtrak station, but there is one in Emeryville, just over the Bay Bridge, as well as in Oakland. A free shuttle operates between these two stations and the Ferry Building, the Caltrain station, and several other points in downtown San Francisco.

🚆 **Amtrak** ☎ 800/872-7245 ⊕ www.amtrak.com.

VISITOR INFORMATION

🏛 **Berkeley Convention and Visitors Bureau** ✉ 2015 Center St., Berkeley 94704 ☎ 800/847-4823 or 510/549-7040 ⊕ www.berkeleycvb.com. **San Francisco Convention and Visitors Bureau** ☎ 201 3rd St., Suite 900, 94103 ☎ 415/391-2000, 415/392-0328 TDD ⊕ www.sfvisitor.org. **San Francisco Visitor Information Center** ✉ Hallidie Plaza, lower level, Powell and Market Sts., Union Sq. ☎ 415/391-2000, 415/392-0328 TDD ⊕ www.sfvisitor.org.

The Wine Country

WORD OF MOUTH

"My choice to enjoy the 'flavor' of Sonoma County would be Healdsburg or Glen Ellen."

—razzledazzle

"The Russian River Valley region is quite different than Napa and less crowded."

—kemarshall64

"I lived in SF for 10 years, and took many friends to the 'wine country.' As far as destinations go, Sonoma has a very nice square to walk around, and I think the traffic is lighter. Hwy 29 can be a crawl on nice weekend days."

—Toby1

Updated by
Sharron Wood

IN 1862, AFTER AN EXTENSIVE TOUR of the wine-producing areas of Europe, Count Agoston Haraszthy de Mokcsa reported a promising prognosis about his adopted California: "Of all the countries through which I passed, not one possessed the same advantages that are to be found in California. . . . California can produce as noble and generous a wine as any in Europe; more in quantity to the acre, and without repeated failures through frosts, summer rains, hailstorms, or other causes."

The "dormant resources" that the father of California's viticulture saw in the balmy days and cool nights of the temperate Napa and Sonoma valleys have come to fruition today. The wines produced here are praised and savored by connoisseurs throughout the world. The area also continues to be a proving ground for the latest techniques of grape growing and wine making.

Ever more competitive, vintners constantly hone their skills, aided by the scientific expertise of graduates of the nearby University of California at Davis and by the practical knowledge of the grape growers. They experiment with high-density vineyard planting, canopy management (to control the amount of sunlight that reaches the grapes), and organic farming techniques to finely tune the quality of the grapes that will go into the wine.

For many, wine making is a second career. Any would-be winemaker can rent the cumbersome, costly machinery needed to stem and press the grapes. Many say making wine is a good way to turn a large fortune into a small one, but that hasn't deterred the doctors, former college professors, publishing tycoons, entertainers, and others who come here to try their hand at it.

In 1975 Napa Valley had no more than 20 wineries; today there are more than 250, though not all of these have tasting rooms open to the public. In Sonoma County, where the web of vineyards is looser, there are well over 150 wineries, and development is now claiming the cool Carneros region, at the head of the San Francisco Bay, deemed ideal for growing the chardonnay grape. Nowadays many individual grape growers produce their own wines instead of selling their grapes to larger wineries. As a result, smaller "boutique" wineries harvest excellent, reasonably priced wines that have caught the attention of connoisseurs and critics, while the larger wineries consolidate land and expand their varietals.

This state-of-the-art viticulture has also given rise to an equally robust passion for food. Inspired by the creative spirit that produces the region's great wines, nationally and regionally famous chefs have opened restaurants both extravagant and modest, sealing the area's reputation as one of the finest destinations for dining in the nation.

In addition to great food and wine, you'll find a wealth of California history in the Wine Country. The town of Sonoma is filled with remnants of Mexican California and the solid, ivy-covered, brick wineries built by Haraszthy and his followers. Calistoga is a virtual museum of steamboat Gothic architecture, replete with the fretwork and clapboard beloved of gold-rush prospectors and late-19th-century spa goers. A later architectural fantasy, the beautiful art-nouveau mansion of the Beringer brothers, is in St. Helena. Modern architecture is the exception rather than the rule, but one standout exception is the postmodern extravaganza of Clos Pegase winery, in Calistoga.

The area's natural beauty draws a continuous flow of tourists—from the late winter, when the vineyards bloom yellow with wild mustard and mist shrouds the mountains encircling the valleys, to the fall, when the grapes are ripe.

13

Exploring the Wine Country

The Wine Country is composed of two main areas—the Napa Valley and the Sonoma Valley—but also includes the Carneros district, which straddles southern Sonoma and Napa counties. Five major paths cut through both valleys: U.S. 101 and Routes 12 and 121 through Sonoma County, and Route 29 north from Napa. The 25-mi Silverado Trail, which runs parallel to Route 29 north from Napa to Calistoga, is a more scenic, less-crowded route with a number of distinguished wineries.

One of the most important viticultural areas in the Wine Country spreads across southern Sonoma and Napa counties. The Carneros region has a long, cool growing season tempered by maritime breezes and lingering fogs off the San Pablo Bay—optimum slow-growing conditions for pinot noir and chardonnay grapes. So exotic looking are the misty Carneros marshlands that Francis Ford Coppola chose them as the location for scenes of the Mekong Delta in his 1979 movie *Apocalypse Now.* When the sun is shining, however, Carneros looks like a sprawling and scenic expanse of quintessential Wine Country, where wildflower meadows and vineyards stretch toward the horizon.

About the Restaurants

Many star chefs from urban areas throughout the United States have migrated to the Wine Country, drawn by the area's renowned produce and superlative wines—the products of fertile soil and near-perpetual sun during the growing season. As a result of this marriage of imported talent and indigenous bounty, food now rivals wine as the principal attraction of the region. Although excellent cuisine is available throughout the region, the little town of Yountville has become something of an epicurean crossroads. If you don't succeed at getting a much-coveted reservation at Thomas Keller's French Laundry, often described as one of the best restaurants in the country, then the more casual Bistro Jeanty and Bouchon, as well as a host of other restaurants in and around Yountville, are excellent choices.

Such high quality often means high prices, but you can also find appealing, inexpensive eateries. High-end delis serve superb picnic fare, and brunch is a cost-effective strategy at pricey restaurants.

With few exceptions (which are noted in individual restaurant listings), dress is informal. Where reservations are indicated as essential, you may need to make them a week or more ahead. In summer and early fall you may need to book several weeks ahead.

GREAT ITINERARIES

Numbers correspond to the Napa Valley and Sonoma Valley maps.

IF YOU HAVE 2 DAYS

Start at the circa-1857 **Buena Vista Carneros Winery** ㊺ ▶ just outside Sonoma. From there, take Route 12 north to the Trinity Road/Oakville Grade, then take Route 29 north into historic 🅿 **St. Helena** for lunch and the 30-minute tour of **Beringer Vineyards** ㉘. The next day continue north on Route 29 to **Calistoga** for an early-morning balloon ride, an afternoon trip to the mud baths, and a visit to **Clos Pegase** ㉞ before heading back to St. Helena for dinner at Greystone—the beautiful West Coast campus and highly acclaimed restaurant of the **Culinary Institute of America** ㉗.

IF YOU HAVE 4 DAYS

Make your first stop in **Oakville** ▶, where the circa-1880s **Oakville Grocery** ⑫ is indisputably the most popular place for picnic supplies and an espresso. Enjoy the picnic grounds at **Robert Mondavi** ⑭ before touring the winery and tasting the wine. Spend the night in the town of 🅿 **Rutherford** and visit the **Niebaum-Coppola Estate** ⑯, or continue north to 🅿 **St. Helena**. Take a look at the nearby Silverado Museum and visit the shopping complex surrounding the **Freemark Abbey Winery** ㉙. On your third day drive to 🅿 **Calistoga** for a balloon ride before heading north to **Old Faithful Geyser of California** ㊱; then continue on to **Robert Louis Stevenson State Park** ㊳. On the fourth day take Route 29 just north of Calistoga proper, head west on Petrified Forest Road, and then go south on Calistoga Road, which runs into

Route 12. Follow Route 12 southeast to rustic **Glen Ellen** to visit **Jack London State Historic Park** ㊼, then loop back north on Bennett Valley Road to beautiful **Matanzas Creek Winery** ㊻.

IF YOU HAVE 7 DAYS

Begin in the town of **Sonoma** ▶, whose colorful plaza and mission evoke early California's Spanish past. Afterward, head north to 🅿 **Glen Ellen.** Picnic and explore the grounds at **Jack London State Historic Park** ㊼. The next morning visit **Kenwood Vineyards** ㊿ before heading north to visit wineries in 🅿 **Healdsburg**—including **Ferrari-Carano Winery** ㊻. On the third day cross over into Napa Valley—take Mark Springs Road east off U.S. 101's River Road exit and follow the signs on Porter Creek Road to Petrified Forest Road to Route 29. Spend the day in the western-style town of 🅿 **Calistoga**, noted for its mud baths and mineral springs. Wake up early on the fourth day for a balloon ride. Later, bike the Silverado Trail; stop at **Cuvaison** ㉜, **Stag's Leap Wine Cellars** ⑥, and **Clos du Val** ⑤. On Day 5, visit the galleries, shops, and eateries of **St. Helena** before heading to the **Oakville Grocery** ⑫. Spend the night and visit the wineries in 🅿 **Rutherford.** On Day 6, explore nearby **Yountville,** stopping for lunch at one of its many acclaimed restaurants before heading up the hill to the **Hess Collection Winery and Vineyards** ⑧. On your last day, return to the town of Sonoma via the Carneros Highway, moving on to the landmark **Buena Vista Carneros Winery** ㊺ or **Gloria Ferrer Champagne Caves** ㊶.

About the Hotels

Ranging from unique to utterly luxurious, the area's many inns and hotels are usually exquisitely appointed. Most of the bed-and-breakfasts have historic Victorian and Spanish architecture and include a full breakfast highlighting local produce. The newer hotels tend to have a more modern, streamlined aesthetic, and many have state-of-the-art spas with massage treatments or spring-water pools. Numerous hotels and B&Bs have top-quality restaurants on their grounds, and all that don't are still just a short car ride away from gastronomic bliss.

However, all of this comes with a hefty price tag. As the cost of vineyards and grapes has risen, so have lodging rates. Santa Rosa, the largest population center in the area, has the widest selection of moderately priced rooms. Try there if you've failed to reserve in advance or have a limited budget. In general, all accommodations in the area often have lower rates on weeknights, and prices are about 20% lower in winter.

On weekends, two- or even three-night minimum stays are commonly required, especially at smaller inns and B&Bs. If you'd prefer to stay a single night, though, innkeepers are usually more flexible during winter. Many B&Bs book up long in advance of the summer and fall seasons, and they're often not suitable for children.

WHAT IT COSTS					
	$$$$	**$$$**	**$$**	**$**	**¢**
RESTAURANTS	over $30	$23–$30	$15–$22	$10–$14	under $10
HOTELS	over $250	$200–$250	$150–$199	$90–$149	under $90

Restaurant prices are per person for a main course at dinner. Hotel prices are for two people in a standard double room in high season.

Timing

"Crush," the term used to indicate the season when grapes are picked and crushed, usually takes place in September or October, depending on the weather. From September until November the entire Wine Country celebrates its bounty with street fairs and festivals. The Sonoma County Harvest Fair, with its famous grape stomp, is held the first weekend in October. Golf tournaments, wine auctions, and art and food fairs occur throughout the fall.

In season (April through October), Napa Valley draws crowds of tourists, and traffic along Route 29 from St. Helena to Calistoga is often backed up on weekends. The Sonoma Valley, Santa Rosa, and Healdsburg are less crowded. In season and over holiday weekends it's best to book lodging, restaurant, and winery reservations well in advance. Many wineries give tours at specified times and require appointments.

To avoid crowds, visit the Wine Country during the week and get an early start (most wineries open around 9 or 10). Because many wineries close as early as 4 or 4:30—and almost none are open past 5—you'll need to get a reasonably early start if you want to fit in more than one or two, especially if you're going to enjoy the leisurely lunch customary in the Wine Country. Summer is usually hot and dry, and autumn can be even hotter, so pack a sun hat if you go during these times.

THE NAPA VALLEY

With more than 250 wineries, the Napa Valley is the undisputed capital of American wine production. Famed for its unrivaled climate and neat rows of vineyards, the area is made up of small, quirky towns whose Victorian–Gothic architecture—narrow, gingerbread facades and pointed arches—is reminiscent of a distant world. Yountville, in the lower Napa Valley, is compact and redolent of American history yet is also an important culinary hub. St. Helena, in the middle of the valley, is posh, with tony shops and elegant restaurants. Calistoga, near the north border of Napa County, feels a bit like an Old West–frontier town, with wooden-plank storefronts and a more casual feel than many other Wine Country towns.

Napa

46 mi from San Francisco via I–80 east and north, Rte. 37 west, and Rte. 29 north.

Established in 1848 and with a population of about 120,000, Napa is the oldest town as well as the largest city in the valley. It has been undergoing a cultural rebirth that has encompassed the 2001 opening of Copia: The American Center for Wine, Food & the Arts, the sprucing up of the downtown area, and the reopening of the glamorous 1880 Napa Valley Opera House after years of renovations.

The commercial hub for one of the richest wine-producing regions in the world, the city itself is urban and busy. But it's surrounded by some of California's prettiest agricultural lands. Most destinations in both the Napa and Sonoma valleys are easily accessible from here. For those seeking an affordable alternative to the hotels and B&Bs in the heart of the Wine Country, Napa is a good option. But choose lodgings right downtown or on the north side of town near Yountville, because parts of Napa are downright seedy.

★ ❶ **Domaine Carneros** occupies a 138-acre estate dominated by a classic château inspired by Champagne Taittinger's historic Château de la Marquetterie in France. Carved into the hillside beneath the winery, Domaine Carneros's cellars produce sparkling wines reminiscent of the Taittinger style and use only grapes grown locally in the Carneros wine district. Flights of wines (in which small amounts of several different wines are poured) and accompanying cheese plates and caviar can be ordered from tables inside or on the terrace overlooking the vineyards. ✉ *1240 Duhig Rd.* ☎ *707/257–0101* ⊕ *www.domainecarneros.com* ☜ *Tasting $5.50–$14.50, 40-min tour free* ☉ *Daily 10–6; tour daily at 10:15, 11, noon, 1, 2, 3, and 4.*

❷ **Artesa Vineyards & Winery,** formerly called Codorniu Napa, is bunkered into a Carneros hilltop. The Spanish owners now produce primarily still wines under the talented winemaker Don Van Staaveren. With a modern, minimalist look in the tasting room and contemporary sculptures and fountains on the property, this place is a far cry from the many faux French châteaux and rustic Italian-style villas in the region. Two rooms off the tasting room display exhibits on the Carneros region's history and geography, as well as antique wine-making tools. ⊠ *1345 Henry Rd., north off Old Sonoma Rd. and Dealy La.* ☎ *707/224–1668* ⊕ *www.artesawinery.com* ⊠ *Tasting $2 and up, ½-hr tour free* ☉ *Daily 10–5; tour daily at 11 and 2.*

❸ **Copia: The American Center for Wine, Food & the Arts,** named after the goddess of abundance, is a shrine to American food and wine. An enormous variety of food-related art exhibits, video screenings, food and wine tastings, and tours are scheduled daily (pick up a list from the information desk near the front door). The entry fee allows access to the exhibitions, informative tours, gift shop, and a daily wine tasting. One-hour tours of the ever-changing gardens are very popular. Special programs, such as a luncheon exploration of wine and cheese pairings, are fantastic (additional fee required). ⊠ *500 1st St.* ☎ *707/259–1600* ⊕ *www. copia.org* ⊠ *$12.50* ☉ *Wed.–Mon. 10–5.*

FodorśChoice ★

❹ **Luna Vineyards,** the southernmost winery on the Silverado Trail, was established in 1995 by veterans of the Napa wine industry intent on making less-conventional wines, particularly Italian varieties. (Their whites are styled after those from Fruili, the reds after those from Tuscany.) They've planted pinot grigio on the historic property and also produce Sangiovese and merlot. ⊠ *2921 Silverado Trail* ☎ *707/255–2474* ⊕ *www.lunavineyards.com* ⊠ *Tasting $5–$10, tour $5–$10* ☉ *Daily 10–5; tour by appointment.*

❺ **Clos du Val,** founded by French owner Bernard Portet, produces a celebrated reserve cabernet. It also makes zinfandel, pinot noir, and chardonnay. Although the winery itself is austere, the French-style wines age beautifully. Anyone is welcome to try a hand at the boccie-style game of pétanque. ⊠ *5330 Silverado Trail* ☎ *707/259–2200* ⊕ *www.closduval. com* ⊠ *Tasting and tour $5* ☉ *Daily 10–5; tour by appointment.*

❼ Small **Pine Ridge Winery,** in the StagsLeap district, makes estate-bottled wines, including chardonnay, chenin blanc, and merlot, as well as a first-rate cabernet. Tours (by appointment) include barrel tastings in the winery's caves. ⊠ *5901 Silverado Trail* ☎ *707/252–9777* ⊕ *www. pineridgewinery.com* ⊠ *Tasting $10–$20, tour $20* ☉ *Daily 10:30–4:30; tour at 10, noon, and 2.*

❽ The **Hess Collection Winery and Vineyards** is a delightful discovery on Mt. Veeder 9 mi northwest of the city of Napa. (Don't give up; the road leading to the winery is long and winding.) The simple, rustic limestone structure, circa 1903, contains Swiss owner Donald Hess's personal art collection, including mostly large-scale works by such contemporary European and American artists as Robert Motherwell, Francis Bacon, and Frank Stella. Cabernet sauvignon is the real strength here, though Hess also produces some fine chardonnays. The winery and the art collection are open for self-guided tours (free). ⊠ *4411 Redwood Rd., west of Rte. 29* ☎ *707/255–1144* ⊕ *www.hesscollection.com* ⊠ *Tasting $10* ☉ *Daily 10–4.*

FodorśChoice ★

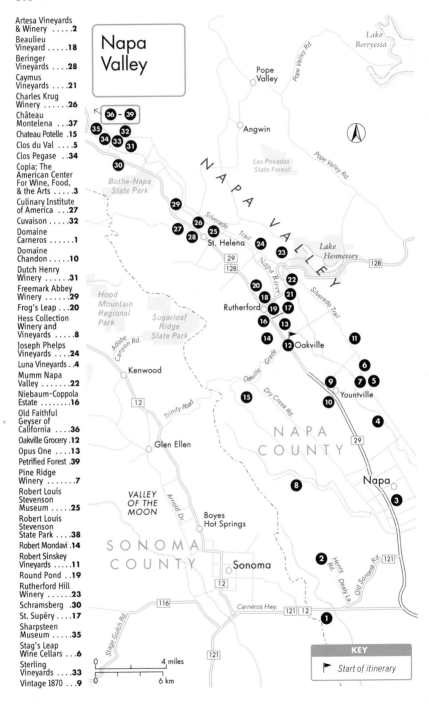

Napa
Valley

KEY

▶ Start of itinerary

Where to Stay & Eat

$$$–$$$$ ✕ **Pilar.** A small, subdued dining room, stylish though not unusually impressive, is one of the hottest dining destinations in downtown Napa, the project of celebrity chef Pilar Sanchez and husband chef Didier Lenders. California cuisine is accented by French and Latin flavors. Rack of lamb is a hearty choice; the lighter steamed mussels with *romesco* (a thick combination of red pepper, tomato, almonds and garlic) sauce and Spanish chorizo hint at Pilar's Spanish and Mexican heritage. California wines line up alongside their continental counterparts on the unusual wine list. ✉ *807 Main St.* ☎ *707/252–4474* 🖃 *AE, D, MC, V* ⊗ *Closed Sun. No lunch weekdays.*

$$–$$$ ✕ **Celadon.** Venture into downtown Napa for chef-owner Greg Cole's creative and enticing "global comfort food." Dishes such as flash-fried calamari with a chipotle-ginger glaze and a Moroccan-inspired lamb shank served with almond couscous make this an ideal place to sample contemporary cuisine accompanied by any of the dozen wines available by the glass. ✉ *500 Main St.* ☎ *707/254–9690* 🖃 *AE, D, DC, MC, V* ⊗ *No lunch weekends.*

$$–$$$ ✕ **Julia's Kitchen.** Named for Julia Child, the restaurant at Copia serves French–California cuisine that relies on the freshest regional ingredients, as well as on the skills of acclaimed chef Victor Scargle. Salad greens and many other vegetables come from Copia's 3½ acres of organic gardens, just outside the door. Grilled quail might be accompanied by frisée and pancetta, and arctic char might be poached in olive oil to wonderfully tender, flaky effect. Diners can watch the chefs at work in the open kitchen. Unusual desserts, such as strawberry mascarpone meringue, show off the talents of the inventive pastry chef. ✉ *500 1st St.* ☎ *707/ 265–5700* 🖃 *AE, MC, V* ⊗ *No lunch Tues. No dinner Mon.–Wed.*

$–$$$ ✕ **Angèle.** Vaulted wood-beam ceilings, dim lights, and candles on every table set a romantic mood at this congenial and cozy French bistro. Classic dishes such as French onion soup and blanquette *de veau* (of veal) are well executed and served by an attentive staff. The charmingly rustic restaurant is housed in the Hatt Building, part of a complex of historic riverside structures in downtown Napa. ✉ *540 Main St.* ☎ *707/ 252–8115* 🖃 *AE, D, DC, MC, V.*

★ **$–$$$** ✕ **Bistro Don Giovanni.** Terra-cotta tile floors and high ceilings surround this lively, festive bistro. The Italian food with a Californian spin is simultaneously inventive and comforting: risotto with squab and radicchio, pizza with pear and prosciutto, and rabbit braised in cabernet. Whole, wood-oven-roasted fish is an unusual specialty. Seats on the covered patio are coveted in fair weather. ✉ *4110 Howard La./Rte. 29* ☎ *707/ 224–3300* 🖃 *AE, D, DC, MC, V.*

$–$$$ ✕ **Boon Fly Cafe.** Part of the Carneros Inn complex, west of downtown Napa, this small spot popular with both inn guests and day-trippers on their way to Napa Valley from San Francisco has a rural charm–meets–industrial chic theme. Outside, rocking chairs and swings occupy the porch of a modern red barn; inside, high ceilings and galvanized steel tabletops set a sleek and stylish mood. The small menu of modern California cuisine includes dishes such as roast organic chicken with sautéed

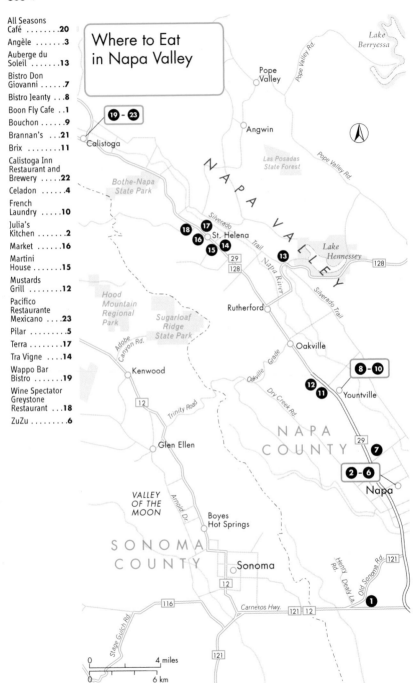

mushrooms and artisanal cheese plates. ☒ *4048 Sonoma Hwy.* ☎ *707/ 299–4872* ⚇ *Reservations not accepted* ▭ *AE, D, MC, V.*

¢–$ ✕ **ZuZu.** Ochre-colored walls, a weathered wood bar, a faded tile floor, and hammered-tin ceiling panels set the tone for a menu composed almost entirely of tapas. These little dishes, so perfect for sharing, and lively Latin jazz on the stereo help make this place a popular spot for festive get-togethers, where diners down *cava* (Spanish sparkling wine) or sangria with dishes such as white anchovies with endive, ratatouille, and salt cod with garlic croutons. They don't take reservations, so expect a wait on weekend nights. ☒ *829 Main St.* ☎ *707/224–8555* ▭ *AE, MC, V* ⊗ *No lunch weekends.*

$$$$ ▦ **Carneros Inn.** Although from the exterior the freestanding cottages
Fodor's Choice at this luxury resort look simple, even spartan, inside, the ethereal beds
★ are piled high with fluffy pillows and covered with Frette linens and pristine white down comforters. High-tech amenities include DVD players, flat-panel TVs, and heated slate bathroom floors, and some fodors.com users rave about the outdoor showers. Each cottage also has a wood-burning fireplace and French doors opening onto a private courtyard with a gas-fired heater. The view from the infinity pool is positively bucolic, and the hilltop dining room serves cocktails and dinner (guests only) overlooking the vineyards. ☒ *4048 Sonoma Hwy., 94559* ☎ *707/299–4900* ⊟ *707/299–4950* ⊕ *www.thecarnerosinn.com* ↝ *76 rooms, 10 suites* ⚅ *2 restaurants, dining room, room service, refrigerators, cable TV, in-room VCRs, in-room data ports, pool, gym, hot tub, spa, bar, dry cleaning, laundry service, concierge, meeting rooms* ▭ *AE, D, DC, MC, V.*

★ $$$$ ▦ **Milliken Creek Inn.** Soft jazz and complimentary port set a romantic mood in the intimate lobby, with its terrace overlooking the Napa River and the inn's lavishly landscaped lawn. The feeling extends to the chic rooms, which replicate the style of British-colonial Asia. Khaki- and cream-color walls surround rattan furniture, hydrotherapy spa tubs, and some of the fluffier beds in the Wine Country. Adirondack chairs and umbrellas are an invitation to lazy afternoons on the lawn in fair weather, and a tiny deck overlooking the river is the spot for massages and private yoga classes. All of the treatment rooms at the serene spa, including one used for popular couples' treatments, have river views. ☒ *1815 Silverado Trail, 94558* ☎ *707/255–1197 or 888/622–5775* ⊕ *www. millikencreekinn.com* ↝ *12 rooms, 7 suites* ⚅ *Minibars, refrigerators, cable TV, in-room VCRs, in-room data ports, spa, dry cleaning, concierge; no kids, no smoking* ▭ *AE, D, DC, MC, V* ⟨◯⟩ *CP.*

$$$–$$$$ ▦ **La Résidence.** Most of these deluxe accommodations, romantic and secluded amid extensive landscaping, are in two buildings: the French Barn and the Mansion, a renovated 1870s Gothic-revival manor house built by a riverboat captain from New Orleans. Towering oaks bathe the entire property in shade. The spacious rooms have floral bedspreads and curtains, period antiques, and fireplaces, and most have double French doors that open onto verandas or patios. In addition to an elegant breakfast, you are treated to a sumptuous spread of appetizers and wine every evening. ☒ *4066 Howard La., 94558* ☎ *707/253–0337*

13

📠 707/253–0382 ⊕ *www.laresidence.com* ⟋ *22 rooms, 1 suite ⟋ Some refrigerators, some cable TV, pool, hot tub; no TV in some rooms, no smoking* ▤ *AE, D, DC, MC, V* ⦿ *BP.*

$$–$$$$ ☒ **Napa River Inn.** A 2½-acre complex includes restaurants, shops, a spa, and this waterfront inn. Accommodations in the 1884 Hatt Building maintain original architectural details, including maple hardwood floors; some rooms have canopy beds, fireplaces, and old-fashioned slipper tubs. Brighter colors dominate in the adjacent Embarcadero building, where some rooms have small balconies and the decor has an understated nautical theme. ⊠ *500 Main St., 94559* ☎ *707/251–8500 or 877/251–8500* 📠 *707/251–8504* ⊕ *www.napariverinn.com* ⟋ *65 rooms, 1 suite ⟋ 2 restaurants, café, patisserie, refrigerators, cable TV with video games, in-room VCRs, in-room data ports, spa, bicycles, wine bar, nightclub, shops, dry cleaning, laundry service, concierge, business services, meeting rooms, some pets allowed (fee), Internet room; no smoking* ▤ *AE, D, MC, V* ⦿ *CP.*

$–$$ ☒ **Chateau Hotel.** Despite a name that evokes a French castle, this is actually just a basic motel. Clean rooms, its location at the entrance to the Napa Valley, the adjacent restaurant, and free stays for children under age 12 are conveniences that make up for the rooms' lack of charm. New conference facilities mean it's a popular place for business travelers. ⊠ *4195 Solano Ave., west of Rte. 29, exit at Trower Ave., 94558* ☎ *707/253–9300, 800/253–6272 in CA* 📠 *707/253–0906* ⊕ *www.napavalleychateauhotel.com* ⟋ *109 rooms, 6 suites ⟋ Some refrigerators, cable TV, pool, hot tub* ▤ *AE, D, DC, MC, V* ⦿ *CP.*

Nightlife & the Arts

In 1995, former telecommunications tycoon and vintner William Jarvis and his wife transformed a historic stone winery building in downtown Napa into the **Jarvis Conservatory,** an excellent venue for baroque ballet and Spanish operetta known as zarzuela. Performances open to the public are held in conjunction with workshops and festivals centered on these two art forms. The conservatory presents opera nights featuring local talent the first Saturday of each month. ⊠ *1711 Main St.* ☎ *707/255–5445* ⊕ *www.jarvisconservatory.com.*

Sports & the Outdoors

BICYCLING Thanks to the long country roads that wind through the region, bicycling is a popular pastime. The Silverado Trail, with its very gently rolling hills, is more scenic than Route 29, which nevertheless tempts some bikers with its pancake-flat aspect. **Napa Valley Bike Tours** (⊠ 6488 Washington St., Yountville ☎ 707/251–8687 or 800/707–2453) rents bikes for $10 to $15 per hour or $30 to $50 per day and will deliver bikes to many hotels in the Napa Valley if you're renting at least two bikes for a full day. One-day winery tours are $115, including lunch and van support.

GOLF The 27 holes at the **Chardonnay Golf Club** (⊠ 2555 Jameson Canyon Rd. ☎ 707/257–1900), which meander through vineyards, can by golfed in three different 18-hole combinations. The greens fee, $55 weekdays and $80 weekends in high season, includes a cart.

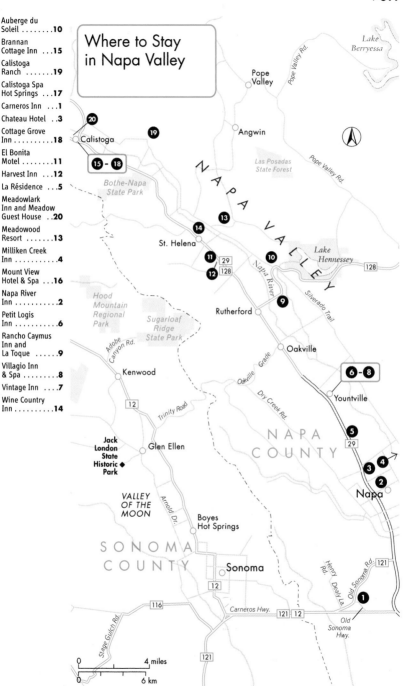

Auberge du
Soleil **10**

Brannan
Cottage Inn . . . **15**

Calistoga
Ranch **19**

Calistoga Spa
Hot Springs . . . **17**

Carneros Inn . . . **1**

Chateau Hotel . . **3**

Cottage Grove
Inn **18**

El Bonita
Motel **11**

Harvest Inn . . . **12**

La Résidence . . **5**

Meadowlark
Inn and Meadow
Guest House . . **20**

Meadowood
Resort **13**

Milliken Creek
Inn **4**

Mount View
Hotel & Spa . . . **16**

Napa River
Inn **2**

Petit Logis
Inn **6**

Rancho Caymus
Inn and
La Toque **9**

Villagio Inn
& Spa **8**

Vintage Inn **7**

Wine Country
Inn **14**

Where to Stay
in Napa Valley

Yountville

13 mi north of the town of Napa on Rte. 29.

Numbers in the margin correspond to numbers on the Napa Valley map.

9 Founded in 1831 by George Calvert Yount, who is credited with planting the first grapevines in the Napa Valley, Yountville has become the valley's boomtown. No other small town in the Wine Country has as many inns, shops, or internationally celebrated restaurants. Particularly popular is **Vintage 1870** (✉ 6525 Washington St. ☎ 707/944–2451), a 26-acre complex of boutiques, restaurants, and fancy-food stores. The vine-covered brick shops, built in 1870, once housed a winery, livery stable, and distillery. The property's original mansion is now the Mexican-style Compadres Bar and Grill. Nearby, the Pacific Blues Café is set in the 1868 train depot built by Samuel Brannan for his privately owned Napa Valley Railroad.

10 French-owned **Domaine Chandon** claims one of Yountville's prime pieces of real estate, on a knoll west of downtown. Tours of the sleek, modern facilities on the beautifully landscaped property are available for free if you forego tasting, but don't; for $20, sample five different varieties of the *méthode champenoise* sparkling wine. Champagne is $9 to $14 per glass, and hors d'oeuvres are available. ✉ *1 California Dr., west of Rte. 29* ☎ *707/944–2280* ⊕ *www.chandon.com* ☉ *May–Oct., Sun.–Thurs. 10–6, Fri. and Sat 10–7; Nov.–Apr., Sun.–Fri. 11–5, Sat. 10–6. Call for tour times.*

6 It was the 1973 cabernet sauvignon produced by **Stag's Leap Wine Cellars** that put the winery—and the California wine industry—on the map by placing first in the famous Paris tasting of 1976. Today, Stag's Leap makes cabernet, as well as chardonnay, sauvignon blanc, white riesling, and merlot. ✉ *5766 Silverado Trail* ☎ *707/265–2441* ⊕ *www.cask23.com* ☒ *Tasting $10–$30, tour $20* ☉ *Daily 10–4:30; tour by appointment.*

11 **Robert Sinskey Vineyards** makes renowned estate-bottled wines, including chardonnay, cabernet, and merlot, but is best known for its pinot noir. The open kitchen in the dramatic tasting room is the site of occasional cooking classes and demos; call ahead for a schedule. ✉ *6320 Silverado Trail* ☎ *707/944–9090* ⊕ *www.robertsinskey.com* ☒ *Tasting $15–$20, tour free* ☉ *Daily 10–4:30; 1-hr tour by appointment.*

Where to Stay & Eat

$$$$
Fodor'sChoice
★

✕ **French Laundry.** An old stone building houses the most acclaimed restaurant in Napa Valley—and, indeed, one of the most highly regarded in the country. The prix-fixe menus ($175), one of which is vegetarian, include seven or nine courses. A full three hours will likely pass before you reach dessert. Chef Thomas Keller doesn't lack for admirers: he's got several James Beard awards under his belt and is renowned of late for launching the New York City destination-restaurant Per Se. Reservations at French Laundry are hard won and not accepted more than two months in advance (call two months ahead to the day). Didn't get a reservation? Call on the day you'd like to dine here to be considered if there's a cancellation. ✉ *6640 Washington St.* ☎ *707/944–2380* ⚐ *Reservations essential* ▭ *AE, MC, V* ⊘ *Closed 1st 2 wks in Jan. No lunch Mon.–Thurs.*

$$–$$$$ ⚔ **Bistro Jeanty.** Philippe Jeanty's menu draws its inspiration from the cooking of his French childhood. His traditional cassoulet will warm those nostalgic for France, and the bistro classic *steak frites* might be served with a decadent béarnaise sauce. The scene here is Gallic through and through, with a small bar and a handful of tables in two crowded, noisy rooms. The best seats are in the back room, near the fireplace. ✉ *6510 Washington St.* ☎ *707/944–0103* ▭ *MC, V.*

$$–$$$$ ⚔ **Brix.** The wall of west-facing windows overlooking vineyards, a garden, and the Mayacamas Mountains augments the spacious dining room's airy feel. Herbs from the garden might end up in such dishes as the chardonnay-steamed mussels perfumed with basil and pastis, or a parsley lemon vinaigrette that dresses a salad of mushrooms and Petit Basque cheese. The wine list showcases Napa wines from both boutique wineries and larger producers. ✉ *7377 St. Helena Hwy./Rte. 29* ☎ *707/944–2749* ▭ *AE, D, DC, MC, V.*

$$–$$$ ⚔ **Bouchon.** The team that brought French Laundry to its current pin-
Fodor'sChoice nacle is behind this place, where everything from the snazzy zinc bar to
★ the black vests on the waiters to the traditional French onion soup could have come straight from a Parisian bistro. *Boudin noir* (blood sausage) with potato puree and leg of lamb with white beans are among the hearty dishes served in the high-ceiling room. Late-night meals are served from a limited menu until 12:45 AM. ✉ *6534 Washington St.* ☎ *707/944–8037* ▭ *AE, MC, V.*

★ **$$–$$$** ⚔ **Mustards Grill.** There's not an ounce of pretension at the first restaurant of owner-chef Cindy Pawlcyn, despite the fact that it's booked solid almost nightly with fans of her hearty cuisine. The menu mixes updated renditions of traditional American dishes such as grilled fish, steak, and lemon meringue pie with innovative choices such as seared ahi tuna on homemade sesame crackers with wasabi crème fraîche. A black-and-white marble tile floor, dark-wood wainscoting, and upbeat artwork set a scene that's casual but refined. ✉ *7399 St. Helena Hwy./Rte. 29, 1 mi north of town* ☎ *707/944–2424* ⚐ *Reservations essential* ▭ *AE, D, DC, MC, V.*

★ **$$$$** ⌂ **Villagio Inn & Spa.** Villalike buildings cluster around fountains that are arranged on the property to evoke a canal. This plush inn in the heart of Yountville offers guest rooms in which streamlined furnishings, subdued color schemes, and high ceilings enhance a sense of spaciousness. Each room has a fireplace and, beyond louvered doors, a balcony or patio. A youthful vibe infuses the pool area, where live music is sometimes played on summer afternoons and automated misters cool sunbathers. The full-service spa has its own pool and whirlpool. Rates include afternoon tea, a bottle of wine, and a generous champagne buffet breakfast. ✉ *6481 Washington St., 94599* ☎ *707/944–8877 or 800/351–1133* ⎙ *707/944–8855* ⊕ *www.villagio.com* ⬐ *86 rooms, 26 suites* ⚐ *Room service, in-room hot tubs, cable TV, in-room VCRs, in-room data ports, 2 tennis courts, pool, outdoor hot tub, spa, bicycles,*

13

boccie, lobby lounge, shops, dry cleaning, laundry service, concierge, business services, meeting rooms; no smoking ⊟ *AE, D, DC, MC, V* ⋈ *CP.*

$$$$ ⊞ **Vintage Inn.** Rooms in this luxurious inn are housed in two-story villas scattered around a lush, landscaped 3½-acre property. French fabrics and plump upholstered chairs outfit spacious, airy guest rooms with vaulted beamed ceilings, all of which have a private patio or balcony, a fireplace, and a whirlpool tub in the bathroom. Some private patios have vineyard views. You're treated to a bottle of wine, a champagne buffet breakfast, and afternoon tea and scones. ⊠ *6541 Washington St., 94599* ☎ *707/944–1112 or 800/351–1133* ⊟ *707/944–1617* ⊕ *www.vintageinn. com* ⇆ *68 rooms, 12 suites* ⌂ *Room service, in-room hot tubs, refrigerators, cable TV, in-room VCRs, in-room data ports, 2 tennis courts, pool, outdoor hot tub, bicycles, lobby lounge, shop, dry cleaning, laundry service, concierge, business services, meeting rooms, some pets allowed (fee), no-smoking rooms* ⊟ *AE, D, DC, MC, V* ⋈ *CP.*

$$ ⊞ **Petit Logis Inn.** Murals and 11-foot-high ceilings infuse a European charm into the rooms of this small, understated one-story inn, which was formerly a row of shops. Though the individually decorated rooms generally recall the 19th century, bathrooms have modern luxuries such as whirlpool baths big enough for two. Breakfast, included in the room rate, is provided by one of two nearby restaurants. The inn's proximity to many of Yountville's best restaurants (within walking distance) is another plus. ⊠ *6527 Yount St., 94599* ☎ *707/944–2332 or 877/944– 2332* ⊟ *707/944–2388* ⊕ *www.petitlogis.com* ⇆ *5 rooms* ⌂ *Refrigerators, cable TV, in-room data ports; no smoking* ⊟ *AE, MC, V* ⋈ *BP.*

Oakville

2 mi west of Yountville on Rte. 29.

Numbers in the margin correspond to numbers on the Napa Valley map.

There are three reasons to visit the town of Oakville: its grocery store, its scenic mountain road, and its magnificent, highly exclusive winery.

⓬ The **Oakville Grocery** (⊠ 7856 St. Helena Hwy./Rte. 29 ☎ 707/944–8802), built in 1881 as a general store, carries a surprisingly wide range of unusual and upscale groceries and prepared foods despite its tiny size. It's a popular place to sit on a bench out front and sip an espresso between winery visits. Along the mountain range that divides Napa and Sonoma, the **Oakville Grade** (⊠ West of Rte. 29) is a twisting half-hour route with breathtaking views of both valleys. Although the surface of the road is good, it can be difficult to negotiate at night, and trucks are advised not to attempt it at any time.

⓭ **Opus One,** the combined venture of California winemaker Robert Mondavi and the late French baron Philippe de Rothschild, is famed for its vast (1,000 barrels side by side on a single floor), semicircular cellar modeled on the Château Mouton Rothschild winery in France. The futuristic building, which appears to be pushing itself out of the earth, is the work of the architects responsible for San Francisco's Transamerica Pyramid. The state-of-the-art facilities produce about 20,000 cases of ultrapremium Bordeaux-style red wine from grapes grown in the estate's vineyards and in the surrounding area. ⊠ *7900 St. Helena Hwy./Rte. 29* ☎ *707/944–9442* ⊕ *www.opusonewinery.com* ⊡ *Tasting $25, tour free* ☼ *Daily 10–4; tasting and tour by appointment.*

⓮ At **Robert Mondavi,** perhaps the best-known winery in the United States, you're encouraged to take the 75- to 90-minute vineyard and winery tour followed by a seated wine tasting. Longer tours ($35 to $65) allow visitors to learn more about the sensory evaluation of wine or the art of making cabernet sauvignon. Afterward, visit the art gallery, or, in summer, stick around for a concert (from jazz to pop and world music). ⊠ *7801 St. Helena Hwy./Rte. 29* ☎ *888/766–6328* ⊕ *www. robertmondaviwinery.com* ⊡ *Tasting $5–$30, tour $20* ☼ *Daily 10–5; tour by appointment.*

★ ⓯ **Chateau Potelle,** an out-of-the-way spot at nearly 2,000 feet on the slopes of Mt. Veeder, produces acclaimed estate zinfandel, chardonnay, and cabernet sauvignon. Jean-Noël and Marketta Fourmeaux were official tasters for the French government before establishing this winery in 1988, which they named for the château in the Champagne region belonging to Jean-Noël's family. The friendly, casual atmosphere and location away from the crowds in the valley below make it an ideal spot for a picnic. ⊠ *3875 Mt. Veeder Rd., 4 mi west of Rte. 29 off Oakville Grade* ☎ *707/255–9440* ⊕ *www.chateaupotelle.com* ⊡ *Tasting $5* ☼ *Mid-Oct.–mid-Apr., daily 11–5; mid-Apr.–mid-Oct., daily 11–6.*

Rutherford

1 mi northwest of Oakville on Rte. 29.

From a fast-moving car, Rutherford is a quick blur of vineyards, a rustic barn or two, and maybe a country store. But don't speed by this tiny hamlet. With its singular microclimate and soil, this is an important viticultural center.

⓳ Five varieties of Italian olives and three types of Spanish olives are grown on 12 acres at **Round Pond.** Within an hour of being handpicked (sometime between October and February), the olives are crushed in the mill on the property to produce pungent, peppery oils that are later blended and sold. Call a day in advance to arrange a tour of the mill followed by an informative tasting, during which you can sample several types of oil, both alone and with Round Pond's own red-wine vinegars and other tasty foods. ⊠ *877 Rutherford Rd.* ☎ *877/963–9364* ⊕ *www. roundpond.com* ⊡ *Tour $20* ☼ *Tour by appointment.*

In the 1970s, filmmaker Francis Ford Coppola bought the old Niebaum property, a part of the world-famous Inglenook estate. He resurrected an early Inglenook-like red with his first bottle of Rubicon, released in ⓰ 1985. Since then, the **Niebaum-Coppola Estate** has consistently received Fodor'sChoice high ratings, and in 1995 Coppola purchased the other half of the Inglenook estate; the ancient, ivy-covered château; and an additional 95 acres. A small museum in the château has displays documenting the history of the Inglenook estates as well as Coppola movie memorabilia, which include Don Corleone's desk and chair from *The Godfather* and costumes from *Bram Stoker's Dracula.* ⊠ *1991 St. Helena Hwy./Rte. 29* ☏ *707/963–9099* ⊕ *www.niebaum-coppola.com* ☕ *Tasting $10, tour $20* ☉ *Daily 10–5; Memorial Day–Labor Day, open until 6 Fri. and Sat.; château tour daily at 10:30, 12:30, and 2:30; vineyard tour daily at 11, weather permitting.*

⑰ Fine sauvignon blancs, merlots, chardonnays, and cabernet sauvignons are among the wines at which **St. Supéry** excels. Although the tasting room is less atmospheric than most, an excellent, free self-guided tour allows you a peek at the barrel and fermentation rooms, as well as a restored home from 1882. ⊠ *8440 St. Helena Hwy. S/Rte. 29* ☏ *707/963–4507* ⊕ *www.stsupery.com* ☕ *Tasting $10–$15, tour $10 (self-guide tour is free)* ☉ *May–Sept., daily 10–5:30; Oct.–Apr., daily 10–5; tour at 1 and 3.*

⑱ **Beaulieu Vineyard** still uses the same wine-making process, from crush to bottle, as it did the day it opened in 1900. The winery's cabernet is a benchmark of the Napa Valley. The Georges de Latour Private Reserve cabernet sauvignon consistently garners high marks from major wine publications. ⊠ *1960 St. Helena Hwy./Rte. 29* ☏ *707/967–5200* ⊕ *www.bvwines.com* ☕ *Tasting $5–$25* ☉ *Daily 10–5.*

⑳ **Frog's Leap** is the perfect place for wine novices to begin their education. The owners, the Williams family, maintain a sense of humor about wine that translates into an entertaining yet informative tour and tasting experience. They also happen to produce some very fine zinfandel, cabernet sauvignon, merlot, and sauvignon blanc. They pride themselves on the sustainability of their operation, and the tour guides can tell you about their organic farming techniques and the 1½ acres of solar panels that provide power to the facilities. ⊠ *8815 Conn Creek Rd.* ☏ *707/963–4704* ⊕ *www.frogsleap.com* ☕ *Tasting and tour free* ☉ *Mon.–Sat. 10–4; tastings and tour by appointment.*

Fodor'sChoice ★

㉑ **Caymus Vineyards** is run by wine master Chuck Wagner, who started making wine on the property in 1972. His family, however, had been farming in the valley since 1906. Today their cabernet is the winery's claim to fame, but their modest production also includes very fine sauvignon blanc and zinfandel. Reserve to taste. ⊠ *8700 Conn Creek Rd.* ☏ *707/963–4204* ⊕ *www.caymus.com* ☕ *Tasting free* ☉ *Sales daily 10–4; tastings by appointment.*

★ **㉒** A joint venture of Mumm—the French champagne house—and Seagram, **Mumm Napa Valley** is considered one of California's premier sparkling-wine producers. Its Napa Brut Prestige and ultrapremium Vintage Reserve are the best known. The excellent tour and comfortable indoor-outdoor tasting room with a view out over the vineyards are two more reasons to visit. A photography gallery contains a permanent exhibit of Ansel Adams photographs as well as rotating exhibits of works by others. ⊠ *8445 Silverado Trail* ☏ *707/967–7700* ⊕ *www. mummnapavalley.com* ☕ *Tasting $5–$14, tour free* ☉ *Daily 10–5; tour daily on the hr 10–3.*

❷❸ The wine at **Rutherford Hill Winery** is aged in French oak barrels stacked in more than 44,000 square feet of caves—the first machine-made cave system to be built in Napa Valley. Tours of the caves can be followed by a picnic in oak, olive, or madrone orchards. ⊠ *200 Rutherford Hill Rd., east of Silverado Trail* ☎ *707/963–7194* ⊕ *www.rutherfordhill.com* 🗏 *Tasting $5–$10, tour $10–$15* ⊙ *Daily 10–5; tour daily at 11:30, 1:30, and 3:30.*

Where to Stay & Eat

★ $$$$ ✕⊞ **Auberge du Soleil.** Earth-tone tile floors, heavy wood furniture, a spare style, and shades of burnt orange and terra-cotta lend the guest rooms at this renowned hotel a slightly Mediterranean feel, and as you lounge on your room's terrace, enjoying the views of the olive-tree-studded slopes dropping off the west, it's not difficult to imagine yourself in the South of France. Bathrooms are truly grand, many of them equipped with whirlpool tubs and spacious showers with multiple shower heads. However, some fodors.com users suggest that at these prices, service could be better. The Auberge du Soleil restaurant has an impressive wine list and serves a menu that relies largely on local produce; the bar serves less expensive fare until 11 PM nightly. ⊠ *180 Rutherford Hill Rd., off Silverado Trail north of Rte. 128, 94573* ☎ *707/963–1211 or 800/348–5406* 🖷 *707/963–8764* ⊕ *www.aubergedusoleil.com* ➥ *18 rooms, 32 suites* ⚫ *2 restaurants, kitchenettes, refrigerators, cable TV with movies, in-room VCRs, in-room data ports, tennis court, pool, gym, hot tub, massage, sauna, spa, bar, concierge, business services, meeting rooms* ⊟ *AE, D, DC, MC, V.*

★ $$$–$$$$ ✕⊞ **Rancho Caymus Inn and La Toque.** California–Spanish in style, this cozy inn has large suites with kitchens and whirlpool baths. Well-chosen details include wrought-iron lamps, tile murals, stoneware basins, and window seats. But even if you don't stay here, come for dinner at the understated La Toque, which gives Yountville's French Laundry its toughest competition for Wine Country diners' haute-cuisine dollars. Reservations are essential, and jackets are preferred for men. Chef-owner Ken Frank's changing prix-fixe menu ($$$$) is loaded with intense flavors; dishes might include seared Sonoma foie gras with dates and roasted boneless quail with winter vegetables. ⊠ *1140 Rutherford Rd., east of Rte. 29, 94573* ☎ *707/963–1777, 800/845–1777 inn, 707/963–9770 restaurant* 🖷 *707/963–5387* ⊕ *www.ranchocaymus.com* ➥ *26 suites* ⚫ *Restaurant, dining room, minibars, refrigerators, cable TV, in-room data ports, wine bar; no smoking* ⊟ *AE, DC, MC, V* ⊙ *Restaurant closed Mon., Tues., and 1st 2 wks in Jan. No lunch* ¶⚪ *CP.*

St. Helena

2 mi northwest of Oakville on Rte. 29.

Numbers in the margin correspond to numbers on the Napa Valley map.

By the time pioneer winemaker Charles Krug planted grapes in St. Helena around 1860, quite a few vineyards already existed in the area. Today the town greets you with its abundant selection of wineries, many of which lie along the route from Yountville to St. Helena, and its wonderful restaurants, including Greystone, on the West Coast campus of the Culinary Institute of America. Many Victorian and false-front buildings dating from the late 19th and early 20th centuries distinguish the downtown area. Arching sycamore trees bow across Main Street (Route 29) to create a pleasant, shady drive.

㉔ Bordeaux blends, Rhône varietals, and a cabernet sauvignon are the specialties at **Joseph Phelps Vineyards.** One of Napa's top wineries, it first hit the mark with Johannisberg Riesling. ✉ *200 Taplin Rd.* ☎ *707/963–2745* ⊕ *www.jpvwines.com* 🍷 *Tasting $5–$10* ⊗ *Tasting and tour by appointment only.*

㉕ For some nonalcoholic sightseeing, visit the **Robert Louis Stevenson Museum** (✉ 1490 Library La. ☎ 707/963–3757 ⊗ Tues.–Sun. noon–4), next door to the public library. Its eponymous memorabilia consists of more than 8,000 artifacts, including first editions, manuscripts, and photographs. The museum is free (donation suggested).

㉖ The first winery founded in the Napa Valley, **Charles Krug Winery** opened in 1861 when Count Haraszthy lent Krug a small cider press. Today the Peter Mondavi family runs it. At this writing, tours have been suspended indefinitely because a major earthquake retrofit project is in the works, but you can still come for tastings. ✉ *2800 N. Main St.* ☎ *707/963–5057* ⊕ *www.charleskrug.com* 🍷 *Tasting $5–$8* ⊗ *Daily 10:30–5.*

★ ㉘ Arguably the most beautiful winery in Napa Valley, the 1876 **Beringer Vineyards** is also the oldest continuously operating property. In 1883 Frederick and Jacob Beringer built the Rhine House Mansion, where tastings are held among pieces of Belgian art-nouveau hand-carved oak and walnut furniture and stained-glass windows. The introductory tour departs every hour. Longer tours and seminars on special topics such as wine-and-cheese pairings occur occasionally. ✉ *2000 Main St./Rte. 29* ☎ *707/963–4812* ⊕ *www.beringer.com* 🍷 *Tasting and tour $10–$35* ⊗ *May 30–Oct. 23, daily 10–6; Oct. 24–May 29, daily 10–5; tour daily every hr 10–4.*

㉗ The West Coast headquarters of the **Culinary Institute of America,** the country's leading school for chefs, are in the **Greystone Winery,** a national historic landmark and, at 117,000 square feet, once the largest stone winery in the world. The campus consists of 30 acres of herb and vegetable gardens, a 15-acre merlot vineyard, and a Mediterranean-inspired restaurant, which is open to the public. Also on the property are a well-stocked culinary store, a quirky corkscrew display, and a culinary library. One-hour cooking demonstrations begin at 1:30 and 3:30 on Monday and Friday, with an extra class at 10:30 on weekend mornings. ✉ *2555 Main St.* ☎ *800/333–9242* ⊕ *www.ciachef.edu* 🍷 *Free, demonstrations $12.50* ⊗ *Restaurant Sun.–Thurs. 11:30–9, Fri. and Sat. 11:30–10; store and museum daily 10–6.*

㉙ **Freemark Abbey Winery** was originally called the Tychson Winery, after Josephine Tychson, the first woman to establish a winery in California. It has long been known for its cabernets, whose grapes come from the fertile Rutherford Bench. A much-touted late-harvest riesling, known as Edelwein Gold, is produced when the climate and conditions allow. ✉ *3022 St. Helena Hwy. N/ Rte. 29* ☎ *707/963–9694* ⊕ *www.freemarkabbey.com* ⊠ *Tasting $5–$10* ☉ *Daily 10–5; tour by appointment.*

Where to Stay & Eat

★ **$$$–$$$$** ✕ **Martini House.** Beautiful and boisterous, St. Helena's hottest new restaurant resides in a converted 1923 Craftsman-style home, where earthy colors (designer Pat Kuleto was inspired by Native American motifs) are made even warmer by the glow of three fireplaces. Woodsy ingredients such as chanterelles or juniper berries might accompany sweetbreads or a hearty grilled pork chop. Inventive salads and delicate desserts such as the blood-orange sorbet demonstrate chef Todd Humphries' range. The patio, where lights sparkle in the trees, is as attractive as the interior. ✉ *1245 Spring St.* ☎ *707/963–2233* ▭ *AE, D, DC, MC, V* ☉ *No lunch Mon.–Thurs.*

$$–$$$ ✕ **Terra.** A romantic, candlelighted restaurant housed in an 1884 fieldstone building, Terra is especially known for its exquisite southern French Fodor'sChoice and northern Italian dishes, some with Asian touches. The duck rillettes ★ with Belgian endive, grilled lobster with saffron risotto, and spaghettini with tripe are memorable. Inventive desserts might include a meyer lemon crème brûlée served with a lemon sablé. Service is exceptionally attentive. ✉ *1345 Railroad Ave.* ☎ *707/963–8931* ◿ *Reservations essential* ▭ *DC, MC, V* ☉ *Closed Tues. and 1st 2 wks in Jan. No lunch.*

$$–$$$ ✕ **Tra Vigne.** A fieldstone building has been transformed into a striking trattoria with a huge wood bar, 25-foot ceilings, and plush banquettes. Homemade mozzarella, dressed with olive oil and vinegar, and a wood-oven-baked pizza with fresh black truffles and garlic cream are preludes to rustic Tuscan specialties such as oak-grilled rabbit with fava beans. The outdoor courtyard in summer and fall is a sun-splashed Mediterranean vision of striped umbrellas and awnings, marble tables, and a whimsical fountain. ✉ *1050 Charter Oak Ave., east of Rte. 29* ☎ *707/963–4444* ▭ *D, DC, MC, V.*

$$–$$$ ✕ **Wine Spectator Greystone Restaurant.** The Culinary Institute of America runs this place in the handsome old Christian Brothers Winery. Century-old stone walls house a cavernous and bustling restaurant, with several cooking stations in full view; on busy nights you might find the hard-at-work chefs more entertaining than your dinner partner. The menu has a Mediterranean spirit and emphasizes locally grown produce. Typical main courses include pan-seared scallops with a white-bean puree and winter-vegetable potpie. ✉ *2555 Main St.* ☎ *707/967–1010* ▭ *AE, D, DC, MC, V.*

$–$$ ✕ **Market.** The fieldstone walls and friendly service would set a homey mood here even if the menu didn't present comfort food's greatest hits, from fried chicken with mashed potatoes to the signature macaroni and cheese. A top-notch team, with experience working at some of San Francisco's finest restaurants, has made this an exceedingly popular spot for casual food that's excellently prepared. ✉ *1347 Main St.* ☎ *707/963–3799* ▭ *AE, MC, V.*

★ **$$$$** ✕⊡ **Meadowood Resort.** Luxurious accommodations are housed in a rambling lodge and several bungalows scattered on a sprawling property at the end of a quiet road off the Silverado Trail. Airy rooms, many with views of the trees through their large windows, have a simple but chic style. Supremely comfortable beds will defy you to rise early enough to indulge in the golf, tennis, hiking, spa treatments, and other activities that are available here. The elegant dining room specializes in California Wine Country cooking, and the Grill, less formal and less pricey, serves pizzas and spa food; at both eateries, call ahead for open hours. ⊠ *900 Meadowood La., 94574* ☎ *707/963–3646 or 800/458–8080* 🖷 *707/963–5863* ⊕ *www.meadowood.com* ⇨ *40 rooms, 45 suites* ⟋ *2 restaurants, room service, refrigerators, cable TV, in-room data ports, 9-hole golf course, 7 tennis courts, 2 pools, health club, hot tub, massage, sauna, steam room, croquet, hiking, bar, concierge, business services, meeting rooms; no smoking* ⊟ *AE, D, DC, MC, V.*

$$$$ ⊡ **Harvest Inn.** Most rooms in this Tudor-esque inn on lushly landscaped grounds have wet bars, antique furnishings, and fireplaces, though some fodors.com users suggest an updating is in order. Some of the rooms are housed in cottages scattered around 8 acres. Pets are allowed in two rooms for a $75 fee. Complimentary breakfast is served in the breakfast room and on the patio overlooking the vineyards, or you can have it delivered to your room. ⊠ *1 Main St., 94574* ☎ *707/ 963–9463 or 800/950–8466* 🖷 *707/963–4402* ⊕ *www.harvestinn.com* ⇨ *51 rooms, 3 suites* ⟋ *Refrigerators, cable TV, in-room VCRs, in-room data ports, 2 pools, 2 hot tubs, spa, bicycles, wine bar, shop, concierge, meeting rooms, some pets allowed (fee)* ⊟ *AE, D, DC, MC, V* ⦿I *CP.*

$$$–$$$$ ⊡ **Wine Country Inn.** A pastoral landscape of hills surrounds this peaceful New England–style retreat. Rooms are filled with comfortable country-style furniture, and many have a wood-burning fireplace, a private hot tub, or a patio or balcony overlooking the vineyards. A hearty country breakfast is served buffet-style in the sun-splashed common room, and wine and appetizers are available in the afternoon. ⊠ *1152 Lodi La., east of Rte. 29, 94574* ☎ *707/963–7077* 🖷 *707/963–9018* ⊕ *www. winecountryinn.com* ⇨ *24 rooms, 5 suites* ⟋ *Refrigerators, pool, hot tub, business services; no room TVs, no smoking* ⊟ *MC, V* ⦿I *BP.*

$–$$$ ⊡ **El Bonita Motel.** Landscaped grounds with picnic tables are some of the pleasant touches at this motel, where rooms vary in style but lean toward a simple country look. Its location right on Route 29 makes it convenient, but light sleepers should ask for rooms farthest from the road. Family-friendly pluses include roll-away beds and cribs for a modest extra charge. ⊠ *195 Main St./Rte. 29, 94574* ☎ *707/963–3216 or 800/541–3284* 🖷 *707/963–8838* ⊕ *www.elbonita.com* ⇨ *37 rooms, 4 suites* ⟋ *Kitchenettes, microwaves, refrigerators, cable TV, in-room data ports, pool, hot tub, sauna, Internet room, business services, some pets allowed (fee); no smoking* ⊟ *AE, D, DC, MC, V* ⦿I *CP.*

Shopping

The **Spice Island Marketplace** (⊠ Culinary Institute of America, 2555 Main St. ☎ 888/424–2433) is the place to shop for all things related to preparing and cooking food, from cookbooks to copper bowls. **Dean &**

Deluca (⊠ 607 St. Helena Hwy. S/Rte. 29 ☎ 707/967–9980), a branch of the famous Manhattan store, is crammed with everything you need in the kitchen—including terrific produce and deli items—as well as a huge wine selection. Many of the cheeses sold here are produced locally. The airy **I. Wolk Gallery** (⊠ 1354 Main St. ☎ 707/963–8800) has works by established and emerging American artists—everything from abstract and contemporary realist paintings to high-quality works on paper and sculpture. Chocolates handmade on the premises are displayed like miniature works of art at **Woodhouse Chocolate** (⊠ 1367 Main St. ☎ 707/963–8413). **On the Vine** (⊠ 1234 Main St. ☎ 707/963–2209) sells wearable art and unique jewelry such as whimsical purses that could easily be mistaken for a bouquet of flowers. Many pieces have a food or wine theme. Italian ceramics, tableware, cutlery, and other high-quality home accessories fill **Vanderbilt & Company** (⊠ 1429 Main St. ☎ 707/963–1010). Bargain hunters delight in designer labels such as Movado and Coach at the small **St. Helena Premier Outlets** (⊠ 3111 St. Helena Hwy. N/Rte. 29 ☎ 707/963–7282) complex, across the street from Freemark Abbey Winery.

Calistoga

3 mi northwest of St. Helena on Rte. 29.

Numbers in the margin correspond to numbers on the Napa Valley map.

In addition to its wineries, Calistoga is noted for its mineral water, hot mineral springs, mud baths, steam baths, and massages. The Calistoga Hot Springs Resort was founded in 1859 by maverick entrepreneur Sam Brannan, whose ambition was to found "the Saratoga of California." He reputedly tripped up the pronunciation of the phrase at a formal banquet—it came out "Calistoga"—and the name stuck.

㉚ Schramsberg, perched on a wooded knoll on the southeast side of Route 29, is one of Napa's oldest wineries, with caves that were dug by Chinese laborers in 1880. Eight distinct sparkling wines come in several price ranges. If you want to taste, you must tour first. ⊠ *1400 Schramsberg Rd.* ☎ *707/942–4558* ⊕ *www.schramsberg.com* ⊒ *Tasting and tour $25* ⊙ *Daily 10–4; tasting and tour by appointment.*

㉛ It's worth taking a slight detour off the main artery to find the family-owned and -operated **Dutch Henry Winery,** where wines are available only on-site or through mail order (they produce only about 5,000 cases annually). Tastings are held in a working winery, where winemakers explain the process. This is a good place to try cabernet sauvignon and merlot. ⊠ *4300 Silverado Trail* ☎ *707/942–5771* ⊕ *www.dutchhenry.com* ⊒ *Tasting $5* ⊙ *Daily 10–5; tasting by appointment.*

㉜ Of the wines produced by **Cuvaison,** 65% are chardonnays, with pinot noir, cabernet sauvignon, and merlot rounding out the choices. Picnic grounds with a view of the valley are shaded by 350-year-old oak trees. ⊠ *4550 Silverado Trail* ☎ *707/942–6266* ⊕ *www.cuvaison.com* ⊒ *Tasting $8–$10, tour $15* ⊙ *Apr.–Nov., daily 10–5; Dec.–Mar., Sun.–Thurs. 11–4, Fri. and Sat. 10–5; tour by appointment.*

13

㉝ **Sterling Vineyards** sits on a hilltop 1 mi south of Calistoga, its pristine white Mediterranean-style buildings reached by an aerial tramway from the valley floor. The view from the tasting room is superb, and the gift shop is one of the best in the valley. ☒ *1111 Dunaweal La., east off Rte. 29* ☎ *707/942–3300* ⊕ *www.sterlingvineyards.com* ☜ *$15, including tramway, self-guided tour, and tasting* ⊘ *Daily 10:30–4:30.*

㉞ Designed by postmodern architect Michael Graves, the **Clos Pegase** winery is a one-of-a-kind "temple to wine and art" packed with unusual art objects from the collection of owner and publishing entrepreneur Jan Shrem, from sculptures made of Italian glass to huge contemporary canvases to a 19th-century courtyard fountain of Bacchus. Cheese and other foods are for sale in the visitor center, ready to take to the shady picnic area. ☒ *1060 Dunaweal La., east off Rte. 29* ☎ *707/942–4981* ⊕ *www.clospegase.com* ☜ *Tasting $5–$10* ⊘ *Daily 10:30–5; tour daily at 11 and 2.*

FodorśChoice
★

㉟ The **Sharpsteen Museum,** in the center of town, has a magnificent diorama of the Calistoga Hot Springs Resort in its heyday. Other permanent and rotating exhibits are dedicated to the region's past, from its prehistory to World War II, and might document the history of the Wappo, the original inhabitants of the area, or typical family life in the 19th century. ☒ *1311 Washington St.* ☎ *707/942–5911* ⊕ *www.sharpsteenmuseum.org* ☜ *$3 donation* ⊘ *Daily 11–4.*

Indian Springs, an old-time spa, has welcomed clients to mud baths, mineral pools, and steam rooms, all supplied with mineral water from its three geysers, since 1871. Today it continues to offer a wide variety of spa treatments and volcanic-ash mud baths and has an Olympic-size mineral-water pool, kept at 90°F to 102°F, depending on the season. The spa rents 16 bungalows ($$$–$$$$) ranging from a studio duplex to a three-bedroom house. Reservations are recommended for spa treatments. ☒ *1712 Lincoln Ave./Rte. 29* ☎ *707/942–4913* ⊕ *www. indianspringscalistoga.com* ⊘ *Daily 9–8.*

☏ **㊱** Many families bring children to Calistoga to see **Old Faithful Geyser of California** blast its 60- to 100-foot tower of steam and vapor about every 45 minutes. One of just three regularly erupting geysers in the world, it's fed by an underground river that's heated by molten magma deep beneath the earth's surface. Picnic facilities are available, and a small exhibit hall explains geothermal processes. ☒ *1299 Tubbs La., 1 mi north of Calistoga* ☎ *707/942–6463* ⊕ *www.oldfaithfulgeyser.com* ☜ *$8* ⊘ *Apr.–Sept., daily 9–6; Oct.–Mar., daily 9–5.*

㊲ **Château Montelena** is a vine-covered stone French château constructed circa 1882 and set amid Chinese-inspired gardens, complete with a man-made lake with gliding swans and islands crowned by Chinese pavilions. Its wines include chardonnays, cabernet sauvignons, and a limited-production riesling. ☒ *1429 Tubbs La.* ☎ *707/942–5105* ⊕ *www.montelena.com* ☜ *Tasting $10–$25, tour $25* ⊘ *Daily 9:30–4; Mar.–Oct., tour at 9:30, 1:30, and by appointment; Nov.–Feb., tour at 2 by appointment.*

🖐 ⑲ **Robert Louis Stevenson State Park** encompasses the summit of **Mount St. Helena.** It was here, in the summer of 1880, in an abandoned bunkhouse of the Silverado Mine, that Stevenson and his bride, Fanny Osbourne, spent their honeymoon. The stay inspired Stevenson's "The Silverado Squatters," and Spyglass Hill in *Treasure Island* is thought to be a portrait of Mount St. Helena. The park's approximately 3,600 acres are mostly undeveloped except for a fire trail leading to the site of the bunkhouse—which is marked with a marble tablet—and to the summit beyond. ✉ *Rte. 29, 7 mi north of Calistoga* ☎ *707/942–4575* ⊕ *www. parks.ca.gov* ✇ *Free* ☾ *Daily sunrise–sunset.*

🖐 ⑳ The **Petrified Forest** contains the remains of the volcanic eruptions of Mount St. Helena 3.4 million years ago. The force of the explosion uprooted the gigantic redwoods, covered them with volcanic ash, and infiltrated the trees with silica and minerals, causing petrifaction. Explore the museum, and then picnic on the grounds. ✉ *4100 Petrified Forest Rd., 5 mi west of Calistoga* ☎ *707/942–6667* ⊕ *www.petrifiedforest.org* ✇ *$6* ☾ *Mid-Apr.–mid-Sept., daily 9–7 mid-Sept.–mid-Apr., daily 9–5.*

Where to Stay & Eat

$$–$$$$ ✕**Brannan's.** Arts and Crafts–style lamps cast a warm glow over the booths and tables at Calistoga's popular spot for hearty dishes. Look for beef tenderloin, served with garlic mashed potatoes, or roast chicken, served with butternut squash risotto. An attractive, well-stocked bar provides a congenial setting for cocktails or for desserts such as chèvre cheesecake with pears and pecans. ✉ *1374 Lincoln Ave.* ☎ *707/942–2233* ▭ *AE, D, MC, V.*

$$–$$$ ✕ **All Seasons Café.** Bistro cuisine takes a California spin in this sun-filled space, where tables topped with flowers sit upon a black-and-white checkerboard floor. The seasonal menu, which includes homemade breads and dessert, might include organic greens, hand-rolled tagliatelle, pan-seared salmon, or braised lamb shank. Attentive service contributes to the welcoming atmosphere. ✉ *1400 Lincoln Ave.* ☎ *707/ 942–9111* ▭ *D, MC, V* ☾ *Call for hours.*

$$–$$$ ✕ **Calistoga Inn Restaurant and Brewery.** A tree-shaded patio on the banks of the Napa River draws diners to a lovely setting where meals might be served with one of the house-made beers. Lunches are light, focusing on soups, salads, and sandwiches, and hearty main courses at dinner include grilled skirt steak with blue-cheese butter and braised lamb shank with tapenade. ✉ *1250 Lincoln Ave.* ☎ *707/942–4101* ▭ *AE, MC, V.*

$–$$$ ✕ **Wappo Bar Bistro.** This colorful restaurant is an adventure in international dining. The menu covers the world, with dishes ranging from tandoori chicken and Thai coconut curry with prawns and vegetables to chiles rellenos and Turkish meze. On warm nights diners vie for seats on the brick patio under the grape arbor. ✉ *1226 S. Washington St.* ☎ *707/942–4712* ▭ *AE, MC, V* ☾ *Closed Tues.*

★ **¢–$$** ✕ **Pacifico Restaurante Mexicano.** At first glance it looks like a Mexican chain restaurant, but be assured that the quality and ingenuity of the food exceed that of the standard franchises. Many choices showcase the regional cuisines of Mexico, such as the sweet and spicy fare of Oaxaca. The chiles rellenos *pacificos* (grilled, cheese-drizzled poblano chilies filled with onions, mushrooms, spinach, and peanuts) make a delicious, inventive dish. Hefty margaritas come in several varieties. ⊠ *1237 Lincoln Ave.* ☎ *707/942–4400* ☰ *MC, V.*

★ **$$$$** ⊞ **Calistoga Ranch.** A sister property of Auberge du Soleil, this posh resort opened in the hills just south of Calistoga in 2004. Spacious cedar-shingle bungalows throughout the sprawling wooded property have outdoor living areas, and even the restaurant, spa, and reception area have outdoor seating areas and fireplaces. Though the service is friendly and cabins are luxurious, with soaking tubs and both indoor and outdoor showers in every room, the overall result still has a casual ranch-like feel rather than the refined sheen of some similarly priced places. ⊠ *580 Lommel Rd., 94515* ☎ *707/254–2820 or 800/942–4220* 🖷 *707/254–2888* ⊕ *www.calistogaranch.com* ⤳ *47 rooms* ⟑ *Restaurant, room service, minibars, refrigerators, cable TV, in-room VCRs, pool, gym, hot tub, sauna, spa, steam room, boccie, hiking, bar, shop, concierge; no smoking* ☰ *AE, D, MC, V.*

★ **$$$–$$$$** ⊞ **Cottage Grove Inn.** Elm trees shade 16 contemporary, individually decorated cottages. Cozy, skylit rooms come with plush furnishings, as well as wood-burning fireplaces, CD players, extradeep two-person whirlpool tubs, and porches with wicker rocking chairs. Spas and restaurants are within walking distance. Rates include afternoon wine and cheese. ⊠ *1711 Lincoln Ave., 94515* ☎ *707/942–8400 or 800/799–2284* 🖷 *707/942–2653* ⊕ *www.cottagegrove.com* ⤳ *16 rooms* ⟑ *In-room safes, minibars, refrigerators, cable TV, in-room VCRs, in-room data ports; no smoking* ☰ *AE, D, DC, MC, V* ⟨O⟩ *CP.*

$$–$$$$ ⊞ **Meadowlark Inn and Meadow Guest House.** Twenty hillside acres just
★ north of downtown Calistoga surround this laid-back and sophisticated inn. Rooms in the main house and guest wing each have their own charms: one has a four-poster bed and opens onto a private garden, and others have a deck with a view of the mountains. Many rooms have fireplaces, and most have whirlpool tubs large enough for two. A spacious two-story guesthouse opens directly onto the clothing-optional pool and sauna area (open to all guests). Guests agree that innkeepers Kurt and Richard are perfectly charming hosts. ⊠ *601 Petrified Forest Rd., 94515* ☎ *707/942–5651 or 800/942–5651* 🖷 *707/942–5023* ⊕ *www.meadowlarkinn.com* ⤳ *5 rooms, 5 suites* ⟑ *Some kitchens, some refrigerators, cable TV, in-room VCRs, pool, hot tub, sauna, some pets allowed, Internet; no smoking* ☰ *AE, MC, V* ⟨O⟩ *BP.*

$$–$$$ ⊞ **Mount View Hotel & Spa.** A National Historic Landmark, the Mount View conjures up Calistoga's 19th-century heyday with its late-Victorian decor. A full-service European spa provides state-of-the-art pampering, and three cottages are each equipped with a private redwood deck, whirlpool tub, and wet bar. The hotel's location on Calistoga's main drag, plus the excellent restaurant and the bar in the same building, mean you won't need to go far if your spa treatment has left you too indolent to drive. ⊠ *1457 Lincoln Ave., 94515* ☎ *707/942–6877 or 800/816–6877* 🖷 *707/942–6904* ⊕ *www.mountviewhotel.com* ⤳ *20 rooms, 12 suites* ⟑ *Restaurant, some refrigerators, cable TV, pool, hot tub, spa, bar, concierge, Internet; no smoking* ☰ *AE, D, MC, V* ⟨O⟩ *CP.*

$–$$ 🏠 **Brannan Cottage Inn.** The pristine Victorian cottage with lacy white fretwork, large windows, and a shady porch is the only one of Sam Brannan's 1860 resort cottages still standing on its original site. Each room has individual touches such as a four-poster bed, a claw-foot tub, or a velvet settee, in keeping with the inn's Greek revival–Victorian style. ✉ *109 Wapoo Ave., 94515* ☎ *707/942–4200* ⊕ *www.brannancottageinn.com* ⤷ *6 rooms* ⚬ *Refrigerators; no TV in some rooms, no smoking* ▤ *AE, MC, V* ◯ *BP.*

$–$$ 🏠 **Calistoga Spa Hot Springs.** Though the rooms are standard motel issue, their well-equipped kitchenettes and the property's four outdoor heated mineral pools make this a popular spot for those who want to enjoy Calistoga's famed waters on a budget. An on-site spa offers mud baths, massage, and other services at reasonable rates, and its location on a quiet side street one block from Calistoga's main drag is another plus. ■ TIP➡ **Fodors.com users suggest staking out a prime lounging spot next to the pools before the day-trippers are admitted each morning.** ✉ *1006 Washington St., 94515* ☎ *707/942–6269* 🖷 *707/942–4214* ⊕ *www.calistogaspa.com* ⤷ *51 rooms, 1 suite* ⚬ *Snack bar, kitchenettes, cable TV, 2 pools, wading pool, fitness classes, gym, outdoor hot tub, massage, spa, laundry facilities, meeting room; no smoking* ▤ *MC, V.*

Sports & the Outdoors

Calistoga Bikeshop (✉ 1318 Lincoln Ave. ☎ 866/942–2453) rents bicycles, including tandem bikes.

Shopping

The **Calistoga Wine Stop** (✉ 1458 Lincoln Ave., No. 2 ☎ 707/942–5556), inside California's second-oldest existing train depot, carries more than 1,000 wines. Handcrafted beeswax candles are for sale at **Hurd Beeswax Candles** (✉ 1255 Lincoln Ave. ☎ 707/963–7211). Unusual tapers twisted into spiral shapes are a specialty.

THE SONOMA VALLEY

Although the Sonoma Valley may not have quite the cachet of the neighboring Napa Valley, wineries here entice with their unpretentious attitude and smaller crowds. Sonoma's landscape seduces, too, its roads gently climbing and descending on their way to wineries hidden from the road by trees. Its name is Miwok for "many moons," but writer Jack London's nickname for the region—Valley of the Moon—is more fitting. The scenic valley, bounded by the Mayacamas Mountains on the east and Sonoma Mountain on the west, extends north from San Pablo Bay nearly 20 mi to the eastern outskirts of Santa Rosa. The varied terrain, soils, and climate (cooler in the south because of the bay influence and hotter toward the north) allow grape growers to raise cool-weather varietals such as chardonnay and pinot noir as well as merlot, cabernet sauvignon, and other heat-seeking vines. The valley is home to dozens of wineries, many of them on or near Route 12, a California Scenic Highway that runs the length of the valley, which is near the Sonoma–Napa county border.

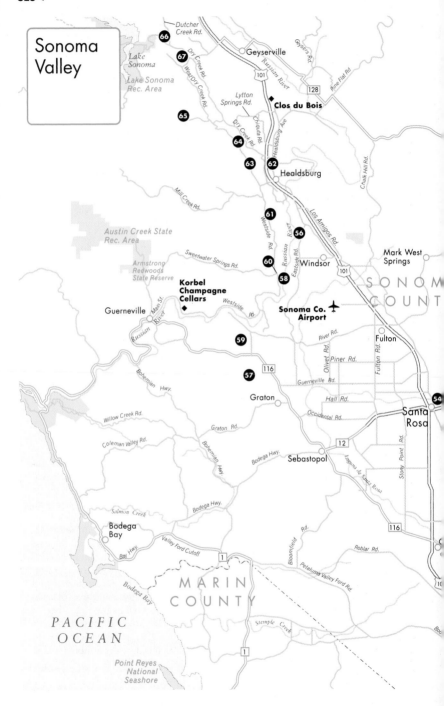

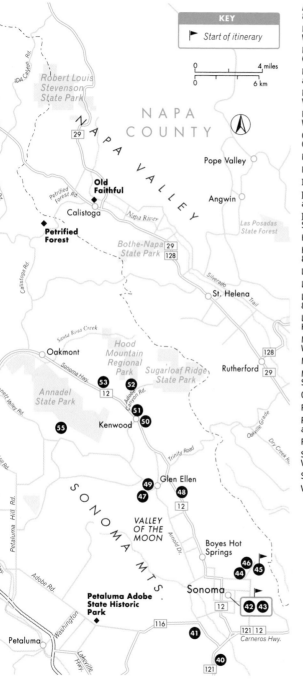

Sonoma

14 mi west of Napa on Rte. 12; 45 mi from San Francisco, north on U.S. 101, east on Rte. 37, and north on Rte. 121/12.

Sonoma is the oldest town in the Wine Country. Its historic town plaza is the site of the last and the northernmost of the 21 missions established by the Franciscan order of Father Junípero Serra. It also includes the largest group of old adobes north of Monterey.

40 On your way into town from the south, you pass through the Carneros wine district, which straddles the southern sections of Sonoma and Napa counties. Sam Sebastiani, of the famous Sebastiani family, and his wife, Vicki, have established their own hilltop winery, **Viansa**, in the Carneros district. Reminiscent of a Tuscan villa, the winery's ocher-color building is surrounded by olive trees and overlooks the valley. The grapes grown here focus on Italian varietals such as Sangiovese, Dolcetto, and Tocai Friulano. The Italian Marketplace on the premises sells sandwiches, salads, and deli foods to complement Viansa's Italian-style wines, as well as a large selection of dinnerware, cookbooks, and condiments. The adjacent Wine Country Visitor Center has brochures and information. Perhaps because of its immensity and location—it's one of the first wineries you'll pass on your way to Sonoma from San Francisco—it tends to be packed with visitors, some of whom arrive by tour bus. ⊠ *25200 Arnold Dr.* ☎ *707/935–4700* ⊕ *www.viansa.com* ⊒ *Tasting $5–$20, tour free* ⊙ *Daily 10–5; tour daily at 11 and 2:15.*

41 The Spanish hacienda–style architecture recalls the native country of the Ferrer family, who make both sparkling and still wines at **Gloria Ferrer Champagne Caves.** The champagne here, all made in the brut style, are aged in a *cava*, or cellar, where several feet of earth maintain a constant temperature. Call the day of your visit after 9:45 to confirm that tours will be conducted as scheduled. ⊠ *23555 Carneros Hwy./Rte. 121* ☎ *707/996–7256* ⊕ *www.gloriaferrer.com* ⊒ *Tasting $2–$3, tour free* ⊙ *Daily 10:30–5:30; tour daily at noon, 2, and 4.*

42 In town, the **Mission San Francisco Solano**, whose chapel and school were used to bring Christianity to the Native Americans, is now a museum with a fine collection of 19th-century watercolors. ⊠ *114 Spain St. E* ☎ *707/938–9560* ⊒ *$2, including Sonoma Barracks on central plaza and Lachryma Montis* ⊙ *Daily 10–5.*

43 A tree-lined driveway leads to **Lachryma Montis,** which General Mariano G. Vallejo, the last Mexican governor of California, built for his large family in 1852; the state purchased the home in 1933. The Victorian–Gothic house, insulated with adobe, represents a blend of Mexican and American cultures. Opulent furnishings, including white-marble fireplaces and a French rosewood piano, are particularly noteworthy. Free tours are occasionally conducted by docents on the weekend; call ahead for a schedule. ⊠ *W. Spain St., near 3rd St. E* ☎ *707/938–9559* ⊒ *$2, tour free* ⊙ *Daily 10–5.*

Originally planted by Franciscans of the Sonoma Mission in 1825, the **44** **Sebastiani Vineyards** were bought by Samuele Sebastiani in 1904. In addition to the regularly scheduled historical tours of the winery, a trolley tour offers an informative glimpse of the vineyards Friday and Saturday at 2. Red wine is king here. ⊠ *389 4th St. E* ☎ *707/938–5532* ⊕ *www.sebastiani.com* 🎫 *Tour $5* ⊗ *Daily 10–5; tour weekdays at 11, 1, and 3, weekends at 11, noon, 1, and 3.*

45 **Buena Vista Carneros Winery** is the oldest continually operating winery in California. It was here, in 1857, that Count Agoston Haraszthy de Mokcsa laid the basis for modern California wine making, bucking the conventional wisdom that vines should be planted on well-watered ground by instead planting on well-drained hillsides. Chinese laborers dug tunnels 100 feet into the hillside, and the limestone they extracted was used to build the main house. The winery, which is surrounded by redwood and eucalyptus trees, has a specialty-foods shop, an art gallery, and picnic areas. The guided tour, which includes a tasting of premium wines, is $15, but the self-guided tour is free. ⊠ *18000 Old Winery Rd., off Napa Rd., follow signs from plaza* ☎ *707/938–1266 or 800/678–8504* ⊕ *www.buenavistawinery.com* 🎫 *Tasting $5–$10, tour $15* ⊗ *Daily 10–5, open until 5:30 weekends June–Oct., tour at 11 and 2.*

46 **Ravenswood,** dug into the mountains like a bunker, is famous for its zinfandel. The merlot should be tasted as well. Tours include barrel tastings of wines in progress in the cellar. ⊠ *18701 Gehricke Rd., off E. Spain St.* ☎ *707/938–1960* ⊕ *www.ravenswood-wine.com* 🎫 *Tasting $5, tour $10* ⊗ *Daily 10–5; tour at 10:30 by appointment.*

Where to Stay & Eat

$$$$ ✕ **Santé.** In the Fairmont Sonoma Mission Inn's formal restaurant, creative fare (on a fixed-price menu) is served in a dining room that's both rustic (wrought-iron chandeliers) and elegant (Frette table linens). Chef Joseph Brown relies as much as possible on local seasonal ingredients, such as cheeses made at nearby Cow Girl Creamery, Sonoma foie gras, or artichokes grown in Half Moon Bay. Main courses could include lobster mushroom risotto or hazelnut-crusted lamb loin with red-pepper confit. ⊠ *Fairmont Sonoma Mission Inn & Spa, 100 Boyes Blvd./Rte. 12, at Boyes Blvd., 2 mi north of Sonoma, Boyes Hot Springs* ☎ *707/ 939–2415* 🖃 *AE, DC, MC, V* ⊗ *No lunch.*

$$–$$$$ ✕ **Harmony Club.** This stylish, urbane restaurant and wine bar has French doors thrown open to Sonoma's main plaza in fair weather and a large fireplace aglow in the evening. Dishes are unusual twists on California cuisine: brie fondue, duck confit with creamy lentils, or pan-roasted quail with grilled tomato polenta, pine nuts, and currants. The extensive wine list includes many choices from the Ledson Winery. Listen to nightly jazz and blues music played on the grand piano. ⊠ *480 1st St. E* ☎ *707/996–9779* 🖃 *AE, D, MC, V* ⊗ *Closed Tues.*

$$–$$$ ✕ **Cafe La Haye.** In a postage-stamp-size kitchen, skillful chefs turn out half a dozen main courses that star on a small but worthwhile menu emphasizing local ingredients. Chicken, beef, pasta, fish, and risotto get deluxe treatment without fuss or fanfare. The offbeat dining room, hung with large, abstract paintings, turns out some of the best food for the price in the Wine Country. ⊠ *140 E. Napa St.* ☎ *707/935–5994* ⊟ *AE, MC, V* ☉ *Closed Sun. and Mon. No lunch.*

$$–$$$ ╳ **LaSalette.** Chef-owner Manny Azevedo, born in the Azores and raised in Sonoma, serves dishes inspired by his native Portugal in this warmly decorated spot a few steps off Sonoma's plaza. Boldly flavored dishes such as prawns with tomato-peanut sauce and coconut rice or salt cod baked with white onions might be followed by a dish of Portuguese rice pudding or a port from the varied list. Crepes are served for breakfast Wednesday through Sunday. ⊠ *452 E. 1st St.* ☎ *707/938–1927* ⊟ *AE, D, MC, V* ☉ *Closed Mon.*

$–$$$ ╳ **The Girl & the Fig.** The popular restaurant was in Glen Ellen before migrating to the Sonoma Hotel, where it has revitalized the historic barroom with cozy banquettes and inventive French-country cuisine. A seasonally changing menu may include something with figs, duck confit with green lentils, steak frites, or Provençale shellfish stew. The wine list is notable for its inclusion of Rhône and other less-common varietals, and the *salon de fromage,* a counter set up in the bar area, sells artisan cheese platters for eating here and cheese by the pound to take home. ⊠ *Sonoma Hotel, Sonoma Plaza, 110 W. Spain St.* ☎ *707/938–3634* ⊟ *AE, D, DC, MC, V.*

$$ ╳ **Meritage.** A fortuitous blend of southern French and northern Italian cuisine is the backbone of this restaurant, where chef Carlo Cavallo works wonders with house-made pastas. The warmly lighted dining room, with its sea of unusual sculpted-glass light fixtures, is more romantic than the lively bar area, where an oyster bar augments the menu's extensive seafood choices. Vegetarians can enjoy a special tasting menu, which can be adapted for vegans. ⊠ *165 Napa St. W* ☎ *707/938–9430* ⊟ *AE, MC, V* ☉ *Closed Tues.*

$–$$ ╳ **Della Santina's.** A longtime favorite with a charming brick patio out back serves the most authentic Italian food in town. Daily fish and veal specials provide an alternative to other classic northern Italian pastas such as linguine with pesto and lasagna Bolognese. Of special note are the roasted meat dishes and, when available, petrale sole and sand dabs. ⊠ *133 E. Napa St.* ☎ *707/935–0576* ⊟ *AE, D, MC, V.*

¢–$$ ╳ **La Casa.** Whitewashed stucco and red tiles evoke old Mexico at this spot around the corner from Sonoma's plaza. There's bar seating, a patio, and an extensive menu of traditional Mexican food: chimichangas and snapper Veracruz (with tomatoes, peppers, onions, and olives) for entrées, sangria for drink, and flan for dessert. The food isn't really the draw here; locals love the casual, festive atmosphere and the margaritas. ⊠ *121 E. Spain St.* ☎ *707/996–3406* ⊟ *AE, D, DC, MC, V.*

$$$$ ▦ **The Fairmont Sonoma Mission Inn & Spa.** California Mission–style architecture combines with the elegance of a European luxury spa at this beautifully landscaped estate. Although not large, standard rooms are supremely comfortable. Some larger rooms have fireplaces and patios or balconies. The real draw is the 43,000-square-foot spa, where you can enjoy a vast array of treatments as well as the warm mineral water that is pumped up from beneath the property to feed the inn's pools. The focus on fitness and rejuvenation extends to a 7,087-yard golf course winding through trees and vineyards, a changing schedule of fitness classes, and guided hiking and biking excursions each morning. ✉ *100 Boyes Blvd./Rte. 12, 2 mi north of Sonoma, Boyes Hot Springs 95476* ☎ *707/938–9000* 🖷 *707/938–4250* ⊕ *www.sonomamissioninn.com* ⇌ *168 rooms, 60 suites* ⚲ *2 restaurants, room service, in-room safes, minibars, refrigerators, cable TV, in-room data ports, 18-hole golf course, pro shop, 3 pools, fitness classes, gym, hair salon, hot tub, sauna, spa, bicycles, 2 bars, shops, babysitting, dry cleaning, laundry service, concierge, business services, meeting rooms; no smoking* ▭ *AE, DC, MC, V.*

$$$$ 🏨 **Ledson Hotel.** The hotel's brickwork and wrought-iron balconies recall an opulent 19th-century home, and its six rooms are lavish in every way. King-size beds, piled high with pillows and silk bedding, sit on beautifully inlaid wooden floors, and all rooms have enormous Jacuzzi tubs. You can enjoy the welcome bottle of wine from the room's balcony, three of which overlook Sonoma's main plaza. ✉ *480 1st St. E, 95476* ☎ *707/ 996–9779* 🖷 *707/996–9776* ⊕ *www.ledsonhotel.com* ⇌ *6 rooms* ⚲ *Restaurant, refrigerators, cable TV, in-room data ports, wine bar, dry cleaning, laundry service; no smoking* ▭ *AE, D, MC, V* ⏐⊙⏐ *BP.*

★ **$$–$$$$**   🏨 **Thistle Dew Inn.** The living room and dining room of this pair of turn-of-the-20th-century Victorian homes half a block from Sonoma Plaza are filled with collector-quality Arts-and-Crafts furnishings and photos of the innkeepers' family. Guest rooms maintain a similar style, with a quilt on every bed. Some rooms have fireplaces; some have whirlpool tubs. Most have private entrances and decks, and rooms in the rear house open onto a garden. Welcome bonuses include a hot tub in the backyard and free use of the inn's bicycles. ✉ *171 W. Spain St., 95476* ☎ *707/938–2909, 800/382–7895 in CA* 🖷 *707/938–2129* ⊕ *www. thistledew.com* ⇌ *4 rooms, 1 suite* ⚲ *In-room data ports, hot tub, bicycles, some pets allowed (fee); no room TVs, no smoking* ▭ *AE, D, MC, V* ⏐⊙⏐ *BP.*

$–$$$ 🏨 **Vineyard Inn.** Built as a roadside motor court in 1941, this inn with red-tile roofs brings a touch of Mexican-village charm to an otherwise lackluster and somewhat noisy location at the junction of two main highways. It's across from two vineyards and is the closest lodging to Infineon Raceway. Rooms have queen- or king- size beds, and continental breakfast is included. ✉ *23000 Arnold Dr., at junction of Rtes. 116 and 121, 95476* ☎ *707/938–2350 or 800/359–4667* 🖷 *707/938–2353* ⊕ *www.sonomavineyardinn.com* ⇌ *19 rooms, 2 suites* ⚲ *Cable TV, in-room data ports, pool; no smoking* ▭ *AE, MC, V* ⏐⊙⏐ *CP.*

$$ 🏨 **El Dorado Hotel.** Light-filled rooms in this remodeled 1843 building strike a spare modern pose, with rectilinear four-poster beds, but the Mexican-tile floors hint at Sonoma's Mission-era past. Renovations completed in 2005 resulted in new high-tech touches like flat-panel TVs. Though its position on Sonoma's Plaza and on top of a bustling restaurant is considered a boon by some, light sleepers might be disturbed by some noise. ✉ *405 1st St. W, 95476* ☎ *707/996–3030 or 800/289–3031* 🖷 *707/996–3148* ⊕ *www.hoteleldorado.com* ⇌ *27 rooms* ⚲ *Restaurant, room service, refrigerators, cable TV, in-room VCRs, in-room data ports, pool, bar, shops, laundry service; no smoking* ▭ *AE, MC, V* ⏐⊙⏐ *CP.*

Where to
Stay & Eat in
Sonoma Valley

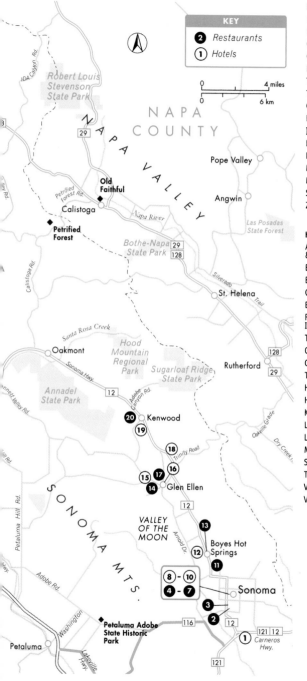

KEY

- **2** Restaurants
- **1** Hotels

0 ——————— 4 miles
0 ——————— 6 km

NAPA COUNTY

NAPA VALLEY

Robert Louis Stevenson State Park

IDA Clayton Rd.

29

Pope Valley

Old Faithful

Angwin

Petrified Forest Rd.

Calistoga

Napa River

Las Posadas State Forest

Petrified Forest

Bothe-Napa State Park

29
128

Silverado Trail

St. Helena

Calistoga Rd.

Santa Rosa Creek

Hood Mountain Regional Park

Oakmont

128

Sonoma Hwy.

Sugarloaf Ridge State Park

Rutherford

29

Annadel State Park

Oakville Grade

12

Adobe Canyon Rd.

Petaluma Hill Rd.

20 **19** Kenwood

Dry Creek

18

Trinity Road

SONOMA

15 **17** **16**

14 Glen Ellen

12

VALLEY OF THE MOON

Arnold Dr.

13

MTS.

12 Boyes Hot Springs

11

Adobe Rd.

8 – **10**

4 – **7**

Sonoma

Washington

3

Petaluma Adobe State Historic Park

116

2

12

Petaluma

121 12

1 Carneros Hwy.

Lakeville Hwy.

121

Nightlife & the Arts

The **Sebastiani Theatre** (✉ 476 1st St. E ☎ 707/996–2020), on historic Sonoma Square, schedules foreign and art films, musical performances, and sometimes quirky theatrical performances.

Shopping

Half-Pint (✉ Sonoma Plaza, 450 1st St. E ☎ 707/938–1722) carries fashionable clothing and accessories for infants and children. Several shops in the four-block **Sonoma Plaza** (✉ Between E. Napa and E. Spain Sts. and 1st St. W and 1st St. E) attract food lovers from miles around. The **Sonoma Cheese Factory and Deli** (✉ Sonoma Plaza, 2 Spain St. ☎ 707/996–1931), run by the same family for four generations, makes Sonoma Jack cheese and the tangy Sonoma Teleme. It has everything you could possibly need for a picnic. **Sign of the Bear** (✉ Sonoma Plaza, 435 1st St. W ☎ 707/996–3722) sells the latest and greatest in kitchenware and cookware, as well as a few Wine Country–themed items, like lazy susans made from wine barrels. At the **Cheesemaker's Daughter** (✉ 127 E. Napa St. ☎ 707/996–4060), half a block from the plaza, proprietor Ditty Vella stocks a fabulous selection of American and European artisanal cheeses.

Glen Ellen

7 mi north of Sonoma on Rte. 12.

Jack London lived in Sonoma Valley for many years. The craggy, quirky, and creek-bisected town of Glen Ellen commemorates him with place-names and nostalgic establishments. In the Jack London Village complex, the **Olive Press** (✉ 14301 Arnold Dr. ☎ 707/939–8900) not only carries many local olive oils, serving bowls, books, and dining accessories but also presses fruit for a number of local growers, usually in the late fall. You can taste a selection of olive oils that have surprisingly different flavors. Built in 1905, the **Jack London Saloon** (✉ 13740 Arnold Dr. ☎ 707/996–3100 ⊕ www.jacklondonlodge.com) is decorated with photos of London and other London memorabilia.

In the hills above Glen Ellen—known as the Valley of the Moon—lies **Jack London State Historic Park.** The author's South Seas artifacts and other personal effects are on view at the House of Happy Walls museum. The ruins of Wolf House, which London designed and which mysteriously burned down just before he was to move in, are close to the House of Happy Walls. Also restored and open to the public are a few farm outbuildings. London is buried on the property. ✉ *2400 London Ranch Rd.* ☎ *707/938–5216* 🅿 *Parking $6* ○ *Park Nov.–Mar., daily 9:30–5; Apr.–Oct., daily 9:30–7. Museum daily 10–5.*

Arrowood Vineyards & Winery is neither as old nor as famous as some of its neighbors, but winemakers and critics are quite familiar with the wines produced here, especially the chardonnays, cabernet sauvignons, and syrahs. The winery's harmonious architecture overlooking the Valley of the Moon earned it an award from the Sonoma Historic Preservation League, and the wine-making equipment is state-of-the-art. A stone fireplace in the tasting room makes this an especially enticing destination in winter. The winery has been owned by Robert Mondavi since

2000, but winemaker Richard Arrowood has stayed on. ✉ *14347 Sonoma Hwy./Rte. 12* ☎ *707/935–2600* ⊕ *www.arrowoodvineyards. com* 🍷 *Tasting $5–$15, tour $15–$25 (includes tasting)* ⊙ *Daily 10–4:30; tour by appointment.*

As you drive along Route 12, you see orchards and rows of vineyards flanked by oak-covered mountain ranges. One of the best-known local

★ ㊾   wineries is **Benziger Family Winery,** situated on a sprawling estate in a bowl with 360-degree sun exposure. Among the first wineries to identify certain vineyard blocks for particularly desirable flavors, Benziger is noted for its merlot, pinot blanc, chardonnay, and fumé blanc. Tram tours through the vineyards cover everything from regional microclimates and geography to a glimpse of the extensive cave system. Tours depart several times a day, weather permitting. ✉ *1883 London Ranch Rd.* ☎ *707/935–3000* ⊕ *www.benziger.com* 🍷 *Tasting $5–$10, tour $10* ⊙ *Daily 10–5.*

Where to Stay & Eat

$$–$$$ ✕ **Glen Ellen Inn Restaurant.** Recommended for romantic evenings, this restaurant adjusts its seafood and pasta offerings according to seasonal availability. Look for braised lamb shank with homemade pasta and seafood risotto. Desserts such as warm pumpkin bread pudding are large enough to share. Seats on the covered patio are more attractive than those inside. ✉ *13670 Arnold Dr.* ☎ *707/996–6409* ▤ *AE, MC, V* ⊙ *No lunch Wed. or Thurs.*

$–$$ ✕ **The Fig Cafe.** Celadon booths, yellow walls, and a sloping high ceiling make the latest in the string of Sondra Bernstein's popular Napa Valley restaurants feel summery and airy even in the middle of winter. Artisanal cheese plates and fried calamari are popular appetizers, and entrées such as braised pot roast and grilled hanger steak tend to be hearty. Don't forget to look on the chalkboard for frequently changing desserts, such as butterscotch pots de crème. The unusual no-corkage-fee policy makes it a great place to drink the wine you just discovered down the road. ✉ *13690 Arnold Dr.* ☎ *707/938–2130* ▤ *AE, D, MC, V* 🪑 *Reservations not accepted* ⊙ *No lunch.*

$$$$ 🛏 **Gaige House Inn.** The elegant comfort of a 19th-century residence is
Fodor'sChoice   enhanced with contemporary, uncluttered furnishings and Asian details
★   at this country inn with gracious service. Eight cottages completed in 2005, the most lavish of the accommodations, have the most pronounced Japanese influence, with 2,500-pound granite soaking tubs overlooking small private gardens and shoji screens hiding a wet bar. Rooms in the main house, some with fireplaces, have their own appeal; one opens onto the pool. The manicured lawn, striped awnings, and magnolias around the pool conjure up genteel refinement in the midst of rustic Glen Ellen. ✉ *13540 Arnold Dr., 95442* ☎ *707/935–0237 or 800/935–0237* 🖷 *707/935–6411* ⊕ *www.gaige.com* ⇆ *12 rooms, 11 suites* ♻ *Some in-room safes, refrigerators, cable TV, in-room data ports, pool, hot tub; no smoking* ▤ *AE, D, DC, MC, V* ⑩ *BP.*

$$–$$$ 🛏 **Glenelly Inn and Cottages.** On a quiet side street a few blocks from the center of sleepy Glen Ellen, this sunny little establishment offers quiet respite from Wine Country crowds. It was built as an inn in 1916, and the rooms, each individually decorated, tend toward a simple country style. Many have four-poster beds and touches such as a wood-burning stove or antique oak dresser; some have whirlpool tubs. All have fluffy down comforters. Breakfast is served in front of the common room's cobblestone fireplace, as are cookies or other snacks in the afternoon. Innkeeper Kristi Hallamore Jeppesen has two children of her own, so this is an unusually kid-friendly inn. ⊠ *5131 Warm Springs Rd., 95442* ☎ *707/996–6720* 🖶 *707/996–5227* ⊕ *www.glenelly.com* 🛏 *8 rooms, 2 suites* ⚘ *Some refrigerators, some in-room VCRs, outdoor hot tub, laundry facilities; no a/c in some rooms, no phones in some rooms, no TV in some rooms, no smoking* ⊟ *AE, D, MC, V* ⏐○⏐ *BP.*

★ **\$–\$\$** 🖼 **Beltane Ranch.** On a slope of the Mayacamas range just a few miles from Glen Ellen, this 1892 ranch house stands in the shade of magnificent oak trees that preexist the building. The charmingly old-fashioned rooms, each individually decorated with lovely antiques, have separate entrances, and some open onto a wraparound balcony ideal for whiling away lazy afternoons. The detached cottage, once the gardener's quarters, has a small sitting room. Formerly a turkey farm, the expansive property is traversed by an 8-mi hiking trail that's popular with guests. ⊠ *11775 Sonoma Hwy./Rte. 12, 95442* ☎ *707/996–6501* ⊕ *www. beltaneranch.com* 🛏 *3 rooms, 3 suites* ⚘ *Tennis court, hiking; no a/c, no room TVs* ⊟ *No credit cards* ⏐○⏐ *BP.*

Kenwood

3 mi north of Glen Ellen on Rte. 12.

Kenwood has a historic train depot and several restaurants and shops that specialize in locally produced goods. Its inns, restaurants, and winding roads nestle in soothing bucolic landscapes.

50 Visitors to **Kunde Estate Winery & Vineyards,** managed by the fourth generation of Kunde-family grape growers and winemakers, arrive at the winery by way of a terrace flanked with a reflecting pool and fountains, where picnickers enjoy the views over the vineyard with a bottle of wine. The tour of the grounds includes its extensive caves, some of which stretch 175 feet below a chardonnay vineyard. Tastings usually include sauvignon blanc, chardonnay, cabernet sauvignon, and zinfandel. ⊠ *10155 Sonoma Hwy./Rte. 12* ☎ *707/833–5501* ⊕ *www.kunde.com* 🍷 *Tasting \$5–\$10, tour free* ☉ *Daily 10:30–4:30, tour hourly Fri.–Sun. 11–3.*

51 The beautifully rustic grounds at **Kenwood Vineyards** complement the tasting room and artistic bottle labels. Although Kenwood produces wine from many varietals, the winery is best known for its Jack London Vineyard reds—pinot noir, zinfandel, merlot, and a unique Artist Series cabernet. Most weekends the winery offers a free food-and-wine pairing, but there are no tours. Free tastings are a boon to those discovering that all those \$10 tasting fees are starting to add up. ⊠ *9592 Sonoma Hwy./Rte. 12* ☎ *707/833–5891* ⊕ *www.kenwoodvineyards. com* 🍷 *Tasting free* ☉ *Daily 10–4:30.*

52 The landscaping and design of **Landmark Vineyards,** established by the heirs of John Deere, are as classical as the winery's wine-making methods. Those methods include two fermentations in French oak barrels and the use of the yeasts present in the skins of the grapes rather than the addition of manufactured yeasts to create the wine. On summer Saturdays visitors can enjoy a free tour of the property in a wagon drawn by two Belgian draft horses, and the bocce ball court is open to visitors year round. ✉ *101 Adobe Canyon Rd., off Sonoma Hwy.* ☎ *707/833–1144 or 800/452–6365* ⊕ *www.landmarkwine.com* ✂ *Tasting $5–$10, tour free* ⊙ *Daily 10–4:30; horse-drawn-wagon vineyard tour Sat. May–Sept.*

❺❸ The outrageously ornate French Normandy castle visible from Route 12 attracts some visitors before they even know that the **Ledson Winery & Vineyards** produces exceptional pinot noirs, merlots, zinfandels, and cabernet francs, as well as a small selection of whites, all available only at the winery and a small number of restaurants. The castle, intended as the Ledson family's opulent home when its construction began in 1989, is now a warren of tasting rooms, special event spaces, and a small market selling gourmet foods. ✉ *7335 Sonoma Hwy./Rte. 12* ☎ *707/537–3810* ⊕ *www.ledson.com* ✂ *Tasting $5, no tour* ⊙ *Daily 10–5.*

Where to Stay & Eat

¢–$$ ✕ **Café Citti.** Opera tunes in the background and a friendly staff (as well as a roaring fire when the weather's cold) keep this no-frills roadside café from feeling too spartan. Order dishes such as roast chicken, pasta, and slabs of tiramisu from the counter and they're delivered to your table. An ample array of prepared salads and sandwiches means they do a brisk business in takeout for picnic packers. ✉ *9049 Sonoma Hwy./Rte. 12* ☎ *707/833–2690* ⊟ *MC, V.*

★ $$$$ ▦ **Kenwood Inn and Spa.** Buildings resembling graceful old haciendas and mature fruit trees shading the courtyards convey the sense that this inn has been here for hundreds of years, even though some of the 30 rooms have been open only since 2003. A swimming pool, Jacuzzis, and saunas pepper three atmospheric courtyards, and you could easily spend an afternoon padding from one to another in your robe and slippers. French doors opening onto terraces or balconies, fluffy featherbeds, and wood-burning fireplaces give the uncommonly spacious guestrooms with tile floors a particularly romantic air. The intimate but well-equipped spa features treatments utilizing vine and grape-seed extracts. ✉ *10400 Sonoma Hwy., 95452* ☎ *707/833–1293* ⊟ *707/833–1247* ⊕ *www.kenwoodinn.com* ➥ *28 rooms, 2 suites* ⚐ *Restaurant, in-room data ports, outdoor pool, 3 hot tubs, sauna, spa, wine bar, laundry service, concierge, meeting room; no room TVs, no smoking.*

ELSEWHERE IN SONOMA COUNTY

At nearly 1,598 square mi, Sonoma is far too large a county to cover in one or two days. The landmass extends from San Pablo Bay south to Mendocino County and from the Mayacamas Mountains on the Napa side west to the Pacific Ocean. Although wineries and restaurants are around almost every bend in the road near Sonoma and Glen Ellen, the western stretches of the county are populated by little more than the occasional ranch.

Within this varied terrain are hills and valleys, rivers, creeks, lakes, and tidal plains that beg to be explored. To be sure, Sonoma offers much more than wine, though the county, with 60,000 acres of vineyards, contributes to the north coast's $4 billion–a–year wine industry. And Sonoma, though less famous than Napa, in fact has more award-winning wines.

In addition to the Sonoma Valley, the major grape-growing appellations include the Alexander and Dry Creek valleys, close to Healdsburg, along with the Russian River Valley to the west of U.S. 101. The last has been gaining an international reputation for its pinot noir, which thrives in the valley climate cooled by the presence of morning and evening fog.

Guerneville, a popular gay and lesbian summer destination, and neighboring Forestville are in the heart of the Russian River Valley. Dozens of small, winding roads and myriad wineries make this region a delight to explore, as do small towns such as Occidental.

After meandering westward for miles, the Russian River arrives at its destination at Jenner, one of several towns on Sonoma's 62 mi of coastline. A number of state beaches offer tide-pooling and fishing. Although less dramatic than the beaches on the far north coast, those along Sonoma's coast offer cooling summer winds. Rustic restaurants and hotels here are more utilitarian than the sophisticated spots so prevalent in the Sonoma and Napa valleys.

Santa Rosa

8 mi northwest of Kenwood on Rte. 12.

Santa Rosa is the Wine Country's largest city and a good bet for moderately priced hotel rooms, especially for those who have not reserved in advance.

54 The **Luther Burbank Home and Gardens** commemorates the great botanist who lived and worked on these grounds and single-handedly developed the modern techniques of hybridization. The 1.6-acre garden shows the results of some of Burbank's experiments to develop spineless cactus, fruit trees, and flowers such as the Shasta daisy. In the music room of his house, a modified Greek-revival structure that was Burbank's home from 1884 to 1906, a dictionary lies open to a page on which the verb "burbank" is defined as "to modify and improve plant life." ⊠ *Santa Rosa and Sonoma Aves.* ☎ *707/524–5445* ⊕ *www.lutherburbank.org* ⊠ *Gardens free, guided tour of house and greenhouse $4* ☉ *Gardens daily 8–dusk; museum and gift shop Apr.–Oct., Tues.–Sun. 10–4; tour Apr.–Oct., Tues.–Sun. 10–3:30.*

★ **55** **Matanzas Creek Winery** specializes in three varietals—sauvignon blanc, merlot, and chardonnay. The visitor center is a far cry from the faux French châteaus and Tuscan villas popular elsewhere in the Wine Country and instead has an understated Japanese aesthetic, with a tranquil fountain and koi pond. Huge windows overlook a vast field of fragrant lavender plants. After you taste the wines, ask for the self-guided garden-tour book before taking a stroll. ⊠ *6097 Bennett Valley Rd.* ☎ *707/ 528–6464 or 800/590–6464* ⊕ *www.matanzascreek.com* ⊠ *Tasting*

$5, tour free ☉ Daily 10–4:30; tour weekdays at 10:30 and 2:30, Sat. at 10:30, by appointment.

Where to Stay & Eat

$$–$$$$ ✕ **John Ash & Co.** Patio seating, views out over vineyards, and a cozy indoor fireplace make this spacious restaurant with an elegant French-country ambience a draw on both summer and winter evenings. The California cuisine incorporates a bit of France, Italy, and even Asia, but the ingredients are largely local: Hog Island oysters come from Tomales Bay, and the goat cheese in the ravioli comes from Laura Chenel, local cheese-maker extraordinaire. Entrées may include Dungeness crab cakes or pan-seared ahi tuna. The wine list is impressive even by Wine Country standards. A café menu offers bites in the bar between meals. ⊠ *4330 Barnes Rd., River Rd. exit west from U.S. 101* ☎ *707/527–7687* ☐ *AE, D, DC, MC, V* ☉ *No lunch in Jan.*

$$ ✕ **Mixx.** This *enoteca* (wine bar) is Italian through and through, from the paintings of Siena on the walls to the personable Italian-speaking servers to the menu featuring bruschetta, housemade ravioli, and *saltimbocca alla Romana* (veal medallions and prosciutto in a red-wine sauce). Even the dramatic hand-carved bar was made in Italy in the 19th century. The frequently changing wine list includes more than a dozen choices by the glass. ⊠ *135 4th St., at Davis St.* ☎ *707/573–1344* ☐ *AE, D, MC, V* ☉ *Closed Sun.*

$$$–$$$$ ▦ **Vintners Inn.** Set on almost 100 acres of vineyards, this French-provincial inn has large rooms, all with a patio or balcony and many with wood-burning fireplaces, and a trellised sundeck. Breakfast is complimentary, and the nearby John Ash & Co. restaurant is tempting for other meals. Guests are often surprised by the tranquil air here, considering how convenient it is to U.S. 101 and downtown Santa Rosa. ⊠ *4350 Barnes Rd., River Rd. exit west from U.S. 101, 95403* ☎ *707/575–7350 or 800/ 421–2584* ▣ *707/575–1426* ⊕ *www.vintnersinn.com* ⤏ *38 rooms, 6 suites* ⌂ *Restaurant, room service, in-room safes, minibars, refrigerators, cable TV, in-room data ports, hot tub, lounge, dry cleaning, laundry service, concierge, business services, meeting room; no smoking* ☐ *AE, D, DC, MC, V* ⏣ *BP.*

¢–$ ▦ **Los Robles Lodge.** Many of the rooms at this bare-bones hotel overlook a pool at the center of the complex. Though they tend to be rather dark, those that are better located catch the sun on their patios, outside sliding-glass doors. Some of the rooms have whirlpool tubs, and pets are permitted in others. ⊠ *1985 Cleveland Ave., Steele La. exit west from U.S. 101, 95401* ☎ *707/545–6330 or 800/255–6330* ▣ *707/ 575–5826* ⤏ *104 rooms* ⌂ *Restaurant, coffee shop, in-room safes, some microwaves, refrigerators, cable TV with movies, in-room data ports, pool, wading pool, gym, hot tub, sauna, bar, laundry facilities, some pets allowed (fee), no-smoking rooms* ☐ *AE, D, DC, MC, V.*

Nightlife & the Arts

The **Luther Burbank Center for the Arts** (⊠ 50 Mark West Springs Rd. ☎ 707/546–3600) presents concerts, plays, and other performances by locally and internationally known artists. For symphony, ballet, and other live theater performances throughout the year, call the **Spreckels Performing Arts Center** (✉ 5409 Snyder La. ☎ 707/588–3400) in Rohnert Park.

Russian River Valley

5 mi northwest of Santa Rosa.

The Russian River flows all the way from Mendocino to the Pacific Ocean, but in terms of wine making, the Russian River Valley is centered on a triangle with points at Healdsburg, Guerneville, and Sebastopol. Tall redwoods shade many of the two-lane roads that access this scenic area, where, thanks to the cooling marine influence, pinot noir and chardonnay are the king and queen of grapes. For a free map of the area, contact **Russian River Wine Road** (📪 Box 46, Healdsburg 95448 ☎ 800/723–6336 ⊕ www.wineroad.com).

56 Of the 225 acres of Russian River Vineyards belonging to **J Vineyards and Winery**, 150 are planted with pinot noir grapes. Since the winemakers here believe that wine should be experienced with food, your tasting fee brings you a flight of four wines, each matched with two bites of hors d'oeuvres. Dry sparkling wines are a specialty. ✉ *11447 Old Redwood Hwy.* ☎ *707/431–3646* 🍷 *Tasting $12* ⊕ *www.jwine.com* ⊙ *Daily 11–5.*

★ **57** Down a one-lane country road from Forestville, **Iron Horse Vineyards** makes sparkling wines as well as estate chardonnays and pinot noirs. Three hundred acres of rolling, vine-covered hills and a rustic outdoor tasting area with a view of Mt. St. Helena seem a world away from the much more developed Napa Valley. Tours are available by appointment on weekdays. ✉ *9786 Ross Station Rd., near Sebastopol* ☎ *707/887–1507* ⊕ *www.ironhorsevineyards.com* 🍷 *Tasting $5, tour free* ⊙ *Daily 10–3:30; tour weekdays at 10.*

58 **Rochioli Vineyards and Winery** claims one of the prettiest picnic sites in the area, with tables overlooking vineyards, which are also visible from the airy little tasting room hung with modern artwork. The winery makes one of the county's best chardonnays but is especially known for its pinot noir. ✉ *6192 Westside Rd.* ☎ *707/433–2305* 🍷 *Tasting free* ⊙ *Feb.–Oct., daily 10–5; Nov.–Jan., daily 11–4.*

59 Fans of pinot noir will surely want to stop at **Hartford Family Winery**, a surprisingly opulent winery off a meandering country road in Forestville. Here grapes from the coolest areas of the Russian River Valley, Sonoma coast, and other regions are turned into single-vineyard pinots, chardonnays, and old-vine zinfandels. ✉ *8075 Martinelli Rd.* ☎ *707/887–1756* ⊕ *www.hartfordwines.com* 🍷 *Tasting free* ⊙ *Daily 10–4:30.*

★ **60** At **Hop Kiln Winery**, you can easily spot the triple towers of the old hop kiln, built in 1905 and now a California state historical landmark. One of the friendliest wineries in the Russian River area, Hop Kiln has a rustic, barnlike tasting room steps away from a duck pond where you can picnic. This is a good place to try light wines such as A Thousand Flowers (a fruity gewürztraminer blend), but be sure to try some of the big-bodied zinfandels and cabernets as well. ✉ *6050 Westside Rd.,*

Healdsburg ☎ *707/433–6491* ⊕ *www.hopkilnwinery.com* 🍷 *Tasting free* ☉ *Daily 10–5.*

61 Known for its relaxed attitude and quirky style, **Roshambo Winery** can seem like a breath of fresh air after visiting more serious-minded wineries. Copiously pierced and tattooed employees pour reasonably priced merlots, chardonnays, and syrahs in the sleek, modern tasting room hung with unusual artwork. The name of the winery is the same as the game—also known as rock paper scissors—once used to settle disputes among the family members who own the property. ✉ *3000 Westside Rd.* ☎ *707/431–2051* ⊕ *www.roshambowinery.com* 🍷 *Tasting $5* ☉ *Daily 10:40–4:30.*

OFF THE
BEATEN
PATH

KORBEL CHAMPAGNE CELLARS – To be called champagne, a wine must be made in the French region of Champagne or it's just sparkling wine. But despite the objections of the French, champagne has entered the lexicon of California winemakers, and many refer to their sparkling wines as champagne. Whatever you call it, Korbel produces a tasty, reasonably priced wine as well as its own brandy, which is distilled on the premises. The wine tour, one of the best in Sonoma County, clearly explains the process of making sparkling wine. The winery's ivy-covered 19th-century buildings and gorgeous rose gardens are a delight in their own right. Call the wineshop at ☎ 707/824–7316 for times of the garden tours, which run mid-April through mid-October. ✉ *13250 River Rd., Guerneville* ☎ *707/824–7000* ⊕ *www.korbel.com* 🍷 *Tasting and tour free* ☉ *Oct.–Apr., daily 9–4:30; May–Sept., daily 9–5; tour Oct.–Apr., daily on the hr 10–3; May–Sept., weekdays every 45 mins 10–3:45, weekends at 10, 11, noon, 12:45, 1:30, 2:15, 3, and 3:45.*

Where to Stay & Eat

★ **$$–$$$$** ✕⬜ **Applewood Inn & Restaurant.** On a knoll in the shelter of towering redwoods, this romantic inn has two distinct types of accommodations. Those in the original Belden House, where cozy chairs around a river-rock fireplace encourage loitering in the lounge area, are comfortable but modest in scale. Most of the 10 rooms in the newer buildings are larger and airier, decorated in sage green and terra-cotta tones that recall a Mediterranean villa. Readers rave about the accommodating service, soothing atmosphere, and the earthy Cal–Italian cuisine served in the cozy restaurant built to recall a French barn. ✉ *13555 Rte. 116, Guerneville 95421* ☎ *707/869–9093 or 800/555–8509* 🖷 *707/869–9170* ⊕ *www.applewoodinn.com* ⤴ *19 rooms* ⛶ *Restaurant, cable TV, in-room data ports, pool, outdoor hot tub; no a/c in some rooms, no smoking* ⊟ *AE, MC, V* ⭐⬤ *BP.*

★ **$$–$$$** ⬜ **The Farmhouse Inn.** This pale yellow 1873 farmhouse and eight adjacent cottages house individually decorated rooms with luxurious touches such as down comforters, whirlpool tubs, and CD players. Most rooms have wood-burning fireplaces and even their own private little sauna, which makes this place especially inviting during the rainy winter months. It's worth leaving your supremely comfortable bed for the sumptuous breakfasts here. The inn's restaurant is one of the most highly regarded in the Wine Country by those in the know. ✉ *7871 River Rd., Forestville 95436* ☎ *707/887–3300 or 800/464–6642* 🖷 *707/*

887–3311 ⊕ *www.farmhouseinn.com* ⤴ *6 rooms, 2 suites* ⟐ *Restaurant, refrigerators, in-room VCRs, pool, sauna, spa, boccie, croquet, concierge, meeting rooms; no smoking* ⊟ *AE, D, DC, MC, V* †⊙| *BP.*

\$\$ ⊞ **Sebastopol Inn.** Simple but stylish rooms in a California-country style are tucked behind an old train station; some have a patio or balcony with views over a wetlands preserve. The offbeat coffeehouse Coffee Catz, on the property, is convenient for light meals. ⊠ *6751 Sebastopol Ave., Sebastopol 95472* ☎ *707/829–2500* 📠 *707/823–1535* ⊕ *www. sebastopolinn.com* ⤴ *29 rooms, 2 suites* ⟐ *Coffee shop, some microwaves, some refrigerators, cable TV, in-room data ports, pool, hot tub, spa, dry cleaning, laundry facilities, laundry service; no smoking* ⊟ *AE, D, DC, MC, V.*

Healdsburg

17 mi north of Santa Rosa on U.S. 101.

The countryside around Dry Creek Valley and Healdsburg is a fantasy of pastoral bliss—beautifully overgrown and in constant repose. Alongside the relatively untrafficked roads, country stores offer just-plucked fruits and vine-ripened tomatoes. Wineries here are barely visible, tucked behind groves of eucalyptus or hidden high on fog-shrouded hills.

Healdsburg itself is centered on a fragrant plaza surrounded by shady trees, upscale antiques shops, spas, and restaurants. A whitewashed bandstand is the venue for free summer concerts, where the music ranges from jazz to bluegrass.

Where to Stay & Eat

\$\$–\$\$\$ ✕ **Barndiva.** One of the hottest new restaurants in Healdsburg (it opened in 2004 to general acclaim) trades in the cozy country style of so many Wine Country spots for a hip nightclub feel. Dance music plays in the background while servers stay busy ferrying inventive (if pricey) specialty cocktails. The food is as stylish as the well-dressed couples cozying up next to one another on the banquette seats: dishes, divided on the menu into "Light Clean," Spicy Passionate," and "Comfort Soothing" categories, are well executed and beautifully presented. During warmer months the beautiful patio more than doubles the number of seats. Service is friendly rather than expert. ⊠ *231 Center St.* ☎ *707/ 431–0100* ⊟ *AE, MC, V* ⊘ *Closed Mon. and Tues.*

\$\$–\$\$\$ ✕ **Bistro Ralph.** Ralph Tingle has discovered a formula for success with his California home-style cuisine, serving up a small menu that changes weekly. Typical dishes include osso buco with saffron risotto and sautéed mahimahi with hedgehog mushrooms. The stark industrial space includes a stunning, gracefully curved wine rack, concrete floors, and a painted brick wall. Take a seat at the bar and chat with the locals, who love this place just as much as out-of-towners do. ⊠ *109 Plaza St., off Healdsburg Ave.* ☎ *707/433–1380* ⊟ *MC, V* ⊘ *Closed Sun.*

\$\$–\$\$\$ ✕ **Zin Restaurant and Wine Bar.** Concrete walls and floors, large canvases on the walls, and servers in jeans and white shirts give the restaurant a casual, industrial, and slightly artsy feel. The American cuisine—such as smoked pork chop with homemade applesauce or the red beans and rice with andouille sausage—is hearty and highly seasoned. True to the restaurant's name, the wine list includes dozens of zinfandels, including half a dozen by the glass. ✉ *344 Center St.* ☎ *707/473–0946* ☰ *AE, DC, MC, V* ⊘ *No lunch weekends.*

$$$$ ✕▣ **Hotel Healdsburg.** Across the street from Healdsburg's tidy town plaza is a spare and sophisticated spot that caters to style-conscious travelers. The attention to detail is striking, from the sleek, modern decor to the Frette bathrobes to the deep bathtubs, and the luxurious beds are some of the most comfortable you'll find anywhere; however, some fodors.com users find that the service doesn't match the luxe surroundings. The attached restaurant, Dry Creek Kitchen, serves celebrity chef Charlie Palmer's cuisine in an elegant and subdued setting. ✉ *25 Matheson St., 95448* ☎ *707/431–2800 or 800/889–7188* 🖷 *707/431–0414* ⊕ *www.hotelhealdsburg.com* ⇶ *45 rooms, 10 suites* ⟁ *Restaurant, room service, refrigerators, cable TV, in-room VCRs, in-room data ports, pool, gym, hot tub, spa, bar, dry cleaning, laundry service, concierge, business services, meeting rooms, some pets allowed (fee), no-smoking rooms* ☰ *AE, DC, MC, V* ⍾ *CP.*

★ **$$$$** ▣ **Hotel Duchamp.** Six identical, freestanding villas are archetypes of spare design, with concrete floors, white walls, and furniture composed strictly of right angles. Luxe lily-white bedding keeps the rooms from feeling spartan, as do CD players loaded with R&B, French love songs, and groovy global dance music. Bathrooms decked out in stainless steel and white tile have showers that could fit four and have just as many showerheads. The four cottages named after artists are larger and less minimalist, with mostly mid-century furniture and quirky, artsy touches. ✉ *421 Foss St.* ☎ *707/431–1300 or 800/431–9341* 🖷 *707/431–1333* ⊕ *www.duchamphotel.com* ⇶ *8 rooms, 2 suites* ⟁ *In-room safes, minibars, refrigerators, cable TV, in-room VCRs, in-room data ports, pool, hot tub, wine bar, some pets allowed (fee); no smoking* ☰ *AE, MC, V* ⍾ *CP.*

★ **$$$–$$$$** ▣ **The Honor Mansion.** Each room is unique at this photogenic 1883 Italianate Victorian. Rooms in the main house preserve a sense of the building's Victorian heritage, whereas the larger suites out back are comparatively understated. Luxurious touches such as lovely antiques and featherbeds are found in every room, and suites have the added advantage of a deck; some even have private outdoor hot tubs. Readers rave about the attentive staff, who coddle you with cookies, cappuccino, and other treats. ✉ *14891 Grove St., 95448* ☎ *707/433–4277 or 800/554–4667* 🖷 *707/431–7173* ⊕ *www.honormansion.com* ⇶ *5 rooms, 8 suites* ⟁ *Refrigerators, cable TV, some in-room VCRs, in-room data ports, putting green, tennis court, pool, hot tub, basketball, boccie, shop* ☰ *AE, MC, V* ⊘ *Closed 1 wk around Christmas* ⍾ *BP.*

$$$–$$$$ ▣ **Madrona Manor.** The oldest continuously operating inn in the area, this 1881 Victorian mansion, surrounded by 8 acres of wooded and landscaped grounds, is straight out of a storybook. Rooms in the splendid three-story mansion, the carriage house, and the two separate cottages are elegant and ornate, with mirrors in gilt frames and paintings covering every wall. Each bed is piled high with silk- and velvet-clad pillows.

Romantic candlelight dinners are served in the formal dining rooms every night (except Monday and Tuesday January through April), and there's jazz on the veranda on Saturday evening from May through July, plus on Friday from August through October. ⊠ *1001 Westside Rd., central Healdsburg exit off U.S. 101, then left on Mill St., 95448* ☎ *707/433–4231 or 800/258–4003* 🖷 *707/433–0703* ⊕ *www.madronamanor.com* ⌨ *17 rooms, 5 suites* ⚐ *Restaurant, in-room data ports, pool, bar, meeting rooms; no room TVs, no smoking* ▤ *MC, V* �📱 *BP.*

$–$$$ 🏠 **Camellia Inn.** Run by the same family for more than 25 years and in a Italianate Victorian constructed in 1869, this colorful B&B is on a quiet residential street just a block from Healdsburg's main square. The parlors downstairs are chockablock with ceramics and other decorative items, while rooms are individually decorated with antiques, such as an impressive mid-19th-century tiger-maple bed from Scotland. Each room has its own charms, such as a gas fireplace or whirlpool tub, and one cozy budget room (with a private bath that's across the hallway) attracts travelers who'd rather spend their money at Healdsburg's pricey restaurants than on lodging. ⊠ *211 North St., 95448* ☎ *707/433–8182 or 800/727–8182* 🖷 *707/433–8130* ⊕ *www.camelliainn.com* ⌨ *8 rooms, 1 suite* ⚐ *Pool; no room TVs, no smoking* ▤ *AE, D, MC, V* �📱 *BP.*

Shopping

Oakville Grocery (⊠ 124 Matheson St. ☎ 707/433–3200) has a bustling Healdsburg branch filled with wine, condiments, and deli items. A terrace with ample seating makes a good place for an impromptu picnic. For a good novel, children's literature, and books on interior design and gardening, head to **Levin & Company** (⊠ 306 Center St. ☎ 707/433–1118), which also stocks a lot of CDs and tapes and has a small art gallery upstairs.

Every Saturday morning from early May through November, Healdsburg locals gather at the open-air **Farmers' Market** (⊠ North Plaza parking lot, North and Vine Sts. ☎ 707/431–1956) to pick up supplies from local producers of vegetables, fruits, flowers, cheeses, and olive oils. An additional market takes place Tuesday 4 to 6:30 PM from June through October on the plaza at Matheson and Center streets.

Dry Creek & Alexander Valleys

On the west side of U.S. 101, Dry Creek Valley remains one of the least-developed appellations in Sonoma. Zinfandel grapes flourish on the benchlands, whereas the gravelly, well-drained soil of the valley floor is better known for chardonnay and, in the north, sauvignon blanc. The wineries in this region tend to be smaller and clustered in bunches.

The Alexander Valley, which lies east of Healdsburg, has a number of family-owned wineries. Most can be found right on Highway 28, which runs through this scenic, diverse region where zinfandel and chardonnay grow particularly well.

62 Giuseppe and Pietro Simi, two brothers from Italy, began growing grapes in Sonoma in 1876, making **Simi Winery**, in the Alexander Valley, one of the oldest in the Wine Country. Though operations are strictly high-tech these days, the winery's tree-studded entrance area and stone buildings recall a more genteel era. Chardonnay is a specialty here, and the cabernet sauvignon is also very good. ☒ *16275 Healdsburg Ave., Dry Creek Rd. exit off U.S. 101* ☎ *707/433–6981* ⊕ *www.simiwinery. com* ☒ *Tasting $5–$10, tour $3* ☉ *Daily 10–5; tours at 11 and 2.*

63 **Dry Creek Vineyard,** where fumé blanc is the flagship wine, also makes a refreshing dry chenin blanc and well-regarded zinfandels. Picnic beneath the flowering magnolias and soaring redwoods. ☒ *3770 Lambert Bridge Rd.* ☎ *707/433–1000* ⊕ *www.drycreekvineyard.com* ☒ *Tasting free–$5* ☉ *Daily 10:30–4:30; tour by appointment.*

64 An unassuming winery in a wood-and-cinder-block barn, **Quivira** produces some of the most interesting wines in Dry Creek Valley. Though it is known for its dangerously drinkable and fruity zinfandel, the intensely flavored syrahs and petite sirahs are also worth checking out. Redwood and olive trees shade the picnic area. ☒ *4900 W. Dry Creek Rd.* ☎ *707/431–8333* ⊕ *www.quivirawine.com* ☒ *Tasting free, tour $15* ☉ *Daily 11–5; tour by appointment weekdays only.*

Housed in a California Mission–style complex in Wine Creek Canyon, **65** **Michel-Schlumberger** produces ultrapremium wines including chardonnay, merlot, and pinot blanc, but its reputation is based on the exquisite cabernet sauvignon. The family of owner Jacques Schlumberger has been making wine in Alsace, France, for more than 400 years. ☒ *4155 Wine Creek Rd.* ☎ *707/433–7427 or 800/447–3060* ⊕ *www. michelschlumberger.com* ☒ *Tasting and tour free* ☉ *Tasting and tour at 11 and 2, by appointment.*

Notable for its wildly opulent Italian-villa-style winery and visitor center, **66** **Ferrari-Carano Winery** produces mostly chardonnays, fumé blancs, syrahs, and cabernet sauvignons. Though whites have traditionally been the specialty here, the reds are now garnering more attention. Tours cover not only the wine-making facilities and underground cellar but also the manicured gardens, where you can see a cork tree and learn about how cork is harvested. ☒ *8761 Dry Creek Rd., Dry Creek Valley* ☎ *707/433–6700* ⊕ *www.ferrari-carano.com* ☒ *Tasting $5–$10, tour free* ☉ *Daily 10–5; tour Mon.–Sat. at 10, by appointment.*

67 **David Coffaro Vineyard and Winery.** David Coffaro himself tends to every aspect of the wine-making process for the 5,000 or so bottles produced here annually, many of which are sold in a futures program (wine can be purchased up to five months before it is even produced). Rather than single-varietal wines, Coffaro crafts unique blends, like the Escuro, made from cabernet, Alvarelhão, petite sirah, and other grapes. Though it is generally open daily 11 to 4, call ahead to ensure someone is available to pour for you. You'll often be treated to a barrel tasting. ☒ *7485 Dry Creek Rd.* ☎ *707/433–9715* ⊕ *www.coffaro.com* ☒ *Tasting free* ☉ *Daily 11–4.*

Where to Stay

$–$$ 🏨 **Best Western Dry Creek Inn.** Continental breakfast is complimentary at this three-story Spanish Mission–style motel, whose lackluster location near U.S. 101 nevertheless means quick access to downtown Healdsburg and other Wine Country locations. Deluxe rooms are slightly more spacious and muted in color than the standard rooms, but both types are kept spotless. A casual family restaurant is next door. ⊠ *198 Dry Creek Rd., Healdsburg 95448* ☎ *707/433–0300 or 800/222–5784* 🖷 *707/433–1129* ⊕ *www.drycreekinn.com* ↶ *103 rooms* ⚒ *Restaurant, refrigerators, cable TV, in-room data ports, pool, gym, hot tub, laundry facilities, some pets allowed (fee), no-smoking rooms* ▤ *AE, D, DC, MC, V* ¶⦿¶ *CP.*

WINE COUNTRY ESSENTIALS

To research prices, get advice from other travelers, and book travel arrangements, visit www.fodors.com.

BUS TRAVEL

Greyhound runs buses from the Transbay Terminal at 1st and Mission streets in San Francisco to Sonoma, Napa, Santa Rosa, and Healdsburg. Sonoma County Transit offers daily bus service to points all over the county. VINE (Valley Intracity Neighborhood Express) provides bus service within the city of Napa and between other Napa Valley towns.

🚍 Bus Lines **Greyhound** ☎ 800/231-2222. **Sonoma County Transit** ☎ 707/576-7433 or 800/345-7433. **VINE** (Valley Intracity Neighborhood Express) ☎ 707/255-7631.

CAR TRAVEL

Although traffic on the two-lane country roads can be heavy during summer and early fall, the best way to get around the sprawling Wine Country is by private car.

From San Francisco, cross the Golden Gate Bridge, and then go north on U.S. 101, east on Route 37, and north and east on Route 121. For Sonoma wineries, head north at Route 12; for Napa, turn left (to the northwest) when Route 121 runs into Route 29.

From Berkeley and other East Bay towns, take Interstate 80 north to Route 37 west to Route 29 north, which will take you directly up the middle of the Napa Valley. To reach Sonoma County, take Route 121 west off Route 29 south of Napa (the city). From points north of the Wine Country, take U.S. 101 south to Geyserville and take Route 128 southeast to Calistoga and Route 29. Most Sonoma County–wine regions are clearly marked and accessible off U.S. 101; to reach the Sonoma Valley, take Route 12 east from Santa Rosa.

LODGING

🏠 **Bed & Breakfast Association of Sonoma Valley** ⊠ 3250 Trinity Rd., Glen Ellen 95442 ☎ 707/938-9513 or 800/969-4667 ⊕ www.sonomabb.com. **The Wine Country Bed and Breakfast Inns of Sonoma County** ☎ 800/946-3268 ⊕ www.winecountryinns.com.

TOURS

Full-day guided tours of the Wine Country usually include lunch and cost about $58 to $83 per person. The guides, some of whom are winery owners themselves, know the area well and may show you some lesser-known cellars. Reservations are usually required.

Gray Line (⊠ Pier 43½ Embarcadero, San Francisco 94133 ☎ 415/434–8687 or 888/428–6937 ⊕ www.graylinesanfrancisco.com) has buses that tour the Wine Country. **Great Pacific Tour Co.** (⊠ 518 Octavia St., Civic Center, San Francisco 94102 ☎ 415/626–4499 ⊕ www.greatpacifictour.com) operates full-day tours of Napa and Sonoma, including a restaurant or picnic lunch, in passenger vans that seat 14. **HMS Travels Food and Wine Trail** (⊠ 707-A 4th St., Santa Rosa 95404 ☎ 707/526–2922 or 800/367–5348 ⊕ www.foodandwinetrails.com) runs customized tours of the Wine Country for six or more people, by appointment only. As the name suggests, the group specializes in chef-led culinary tours of the region. The **Napa Valley Wine Train** (⊠ 1275 McKinstry St., Napa 94559 ☎ 707/253–2111 or 800/427–4124 ⊕ www.winetrain.com) allows you to enjoy lunch, dinner, or weekend brunch on one of several restored 1915–17 Pullman railroad cars that run between Napa and St. Helena. Prices start at around $80 for brunch, and dinners are $95 to $150. Frequency varies according to the season and demand.

HOT-AIR BALLOONING For views of the ocean coast, the Russian River, and San Francisco on a clear day, Sonoma Thunder Above the Wine Country operates out of Santa Rosa. The cost is $195 per person, including a champagne brunch. Balloons Above the Valley is a reliable organization; rides are $210 per person, including a champagne brunch after the flight. Bonaventura Balloon Company schedules flights out of Calistoga or, depending on weather conditions, St. Helena, Oakville, or Rutherford. Flights cost $215 to $237, per person, depending on the breakfast option you choose. Pilots are well versed in Napa Valley lore. Napa Valley Balloons charges $205 per person, including a picnic brunch.

📋 **Balloons Above the Valley** ☎ 707/253-2222, 800/464-6824 in CA ⊕ www.balloonrides.com. **Bonaventura Balloon Company** ☎ 707/944-2822 or 800/359-6272 ⊕ www.bonaventuraballoons.com. **Napa Valley Balloons** ☎ 707/944-0228, 800/253-2224 in CA ⊕ www.napavalleyballoons.com. **Sonoma Thunder Above the Wine Country** ☎ 707/538-7359 or 888/238-6359 ⊕ www.balloontours.com.

VISITOR INFORMATION

📋 **Napa Valley Conference and Visitors Bureau** ⊠ 1310 Napa Town Center, Napa 94559 ☎ 707/226-7459 ⊕ www.napavalley.com. **Sonoma County Tourism Bureau** ⊠ 520 Mendocino Ave., Suite 210, Santa Rosa 95401 ☎ 707/565-5383 or 800/576-6662 ⊕ www.sonomacounty.com. **Sonoma Valley Visitors Bureau** ⊠ 453 1st St. E, Sonoma 95476 ☎ 707/996-1090 ⊕ www.sonomavalley.com.

The North Coast

FROM COASTAL MARIN COUNTY TO REDWOOD NATIONAL PARK

WORD OF MOUTH

"Garberville is a small logging town in the middle of wonderful scenery—it is really the gateway to the best of the north coast redwoods. We drove the Avenue of the Giants, stopped in several groves, and went to Ferndale, where there is some of the most beautiful Victorian houses in northern California."

—janisj

Updated by
Lisa Hamilton

IN MANY WAYS, the spectacular coastline between San Francisco and the Oregon border defies what most people expect of California. The landscape is defined by the Pacific Ocean, but instead of boardwalks and bikinis there are ragged cliffs and pounding waves—and the sunbathers are mostly sea lions. Instead of strip malls and freeways, there are small towns that tuck in around sundown and a single-lane road that follows the fickle shoreline. And that's exactly why this is where many Californians, especially those from the Bay Area, come to escape daily life.

This stretch of coastline between the Golden Gate Bridge and the tiny town of Trinidad, nearly in Oregon, is made up of numerous little worlds, each different from the next. Southerly Marin County's shore is largely protected parkland, famous both for its majestic redwoods and its dirt trails (known as the birthplace of mountain biking). As Highway 1 heads north toward Bodega Bay and on through Sonoma County, the land spreads out into green, rolling pastures and sandy beaches. The coastline turns rocky and dramatic again in Mendocino County, making it the locus for those seeking romance. At Humboldt County the highway heads inland to the redwoods, then returns to the shoreline at the tidal flats surrounding the ports of Eureka and Arcata.

While the towns vary from deluxe spa town to hippie hideaway, they are nearly all reliably sleepy. Most communities have fewer than 1,000 inhabitants, and most main streets are shuttered by 9 PM. Exceptions are Mendocino and Eureka, but even they are loved best by those who want to cozy up in bed rather than paint the town.

About the Restaurants

A few restaurants with national reputations, plus several more of regional note, entertain palates on the North Coast. Even the workaday local spots take advantage of the abundant fresh seafood and locally grown (often organic) vegetables and herbs. Dress is usually informal, though dressy casual is the norm at the pricier establishments. As in many rural areas, plan to dine early: many kitchens close at 8 or 8:30 and virtually no one serves past 9:30.

About the Hotels

Restored Victorians, rustic lodges, country inns, and vintage motels are among the accommodations available along the North Coast. Hardly any have air-conditioning (the ocean breezes make it unnecessary), and many have no phones or TVs. Several towns have only one or two places to spend the night, but some of these lodgings are destinations in themselves. ■ TIP→ **Make summer and weekend bed-and-breakfast reservations as far ahead as possible—rooms at the best inns often sell out months in advance.** Budget accommodations are rare, but in winter you're likely to find reduced rates and nearly empty inns and B&Bs.

	WHAT IT COSTS				
	$$$$	$$$	$$	$	¢
RESTAURANTS	over $30	$23–$30	$16–$22	$10–$15	under $10
HOTELS	over $250	$176–$250	$121–$175	$90–$120	under $90

Restaurant prices are for a main course at dinner, excluding sales tax of 7¼% (depending on location). Hotel prices are for two people in a standard double room in high season, excluding service charges and 8%–10% tax.

Exploring the North Coast

Without a car, it's all but impossible to explore the northern California coast. Highway 1 is a beautiful if sometimes slow and nerve-racking drive. You should stop frequently to appreciate the views, and on many portions of the highway you can't drive faster than 20–40 mph. You can still have a fine trip even if you don't have much time, but be realistic and don't plan to drive too far in one day. The itineraries below proceed north from Marin County, just north of San Francisco.

Timing

The North Coast is a year-round destination, though when you go determines what you will see. The migration of the Pacific gray whales is a wintertime phenomenon, which lasts roughly from mid-December to early April. In July and August views are often obscured by fog. The coastal climate is quite similar to San Francisco's, although winter nights are colder than in the city. If you're seeking warmer days in summer you need only drive inland to Anderson Valley, in Mendocino, or to the redwoods of Humboldt County, to find temperatures often 20 degrees higher.

COASTAL MARIN COUNTY

North over the Golden Gate Bridge from San Francisco lies Marin County, where a collection of hamlets is strung along the coast within an hour's drive of the city. Nearly half of the county, including the majority of the shoreline, is protected parkland encompassing rocky bluffs, beaches, forest, chaparral, and grassland. The beauty of the countryside draws hikers, cyclists, kayakers, families, and urbanites seeking a break from busy streets.

The Marin Headlands

❶ *1 mi north of Golden Gate Bridge on Hwy. 101; first exit north of the bridge.*

The Marin Headlands stretch from the north end of the Golden Gate Bridge to Muir Beach. Part of the Golden Gate National Recreation Area, the headlands are a dramatic stretch of windswept hills that plunge down to the ocean, threaded with scenic roads and trails. Photographers flock to the southern headlands for shots of the city, with the bridge in the foreground and the skyline on the horizon.

GREAT ITINERARIES

Numbers in the text correspond to numbers on the North Coast maps.

IF YOU HAVE 3 DAYS

Some of the finest redwoods in California are found less than 20 mi north of San Francisco in **Muir Woods National Monument** ❷ ▶. After walking through the woods, stop for an early lunch in Point Reyes Station (on the eastern edge of Point Reyes National Seashore) or continue on Highway 1 to **Fort Ross State Historic Park** ❾. Catch the sunset and stay the night in ⌂ **Gualala** ⓫. On Day 2 drive to ⌂ **Mendocino** ⓯. Spend the next day and a half browsing in the many galleries and shops and visiting the historic sites, beaches, and parks of this cliff-side enclave. Return to San Francisco via Highway 1, or the quicker (3½ hours, versus up to 5) and less winding route of Highway 128 east to U.S. 101 south.

IF YOU HAVE 7 DAYS

Early on your first day, walk through **Muir Woods National Monument** ❷ ▶. Then visit **Stinson Beach** ❹ for a walk on the shore and lunch. In springtime and early summer head north on Highway 1 to Bolinas Lagoon, where you can see birds nesting at Audubon Canyon Ranch. At other times of the year (or after you've visited the ranch) continue north on Highway 1 to **Point Reyes National Seashore** ❺.

Tour the reconstructed Miwok village near the visitor center and drive out to Point Reyes Lighthouse. Spend the night in Inverness or one of the other gateway towns. The next day stop at Goat Rock State Beach and **Fort Ross State Historic Park** ❾ on the way to ⌂ **Mendocino** ⓯. On your third morning head toward **Fort Bragg** ⓰ for a visit to the Mendocino Coast Botanical Gardens. If you're in the mood to splurge, continue north to ⌂ **Garberville** ⓱ and spend the night at the Benbow Inn. Otherwise, linger in the Mendocino area and drive on the next morning. On Day 4 continue north through **Humboldt Redwoods State Park** ⓲, including the Avenue of the Giants. Stop for the night in the Victorian village of ⌂ **Ferndale** ⓳ and visit the Ferndale Museum. On Day 5 drive to ⌂ **Eureka** ⓴. Have lunch in the old downtown, visit the shops, and stop in at the Clarke Memorial Museum. Begin Day 6 by driving to Patrick's Point State Park, 5 mi north of Trinidad, to enjoy stunning views of the Pacific from a point high above the surf. Have a late lunch overlooking the harbor in **Trinidad** ㉑ before returning to Eureka for the night. Return to San Francisco on Day 7. The drive back takes six hours on U.S. 101; it's nearly twice as long if you take Highway 1.

The **Marin Headlands Visitor Center** (✉ Fort Barry, Field and Bunker Rds., Bldg. 948 ☎ 415/331–1540 ⊕ www.nps.gov/goga/mahe), open daily 9:30–4:30, has exhibits on headlands history and ecology and posts the latest wildlife sightings. It distributes a map of hiking trails as well as the park newspaper, which lists a calendar of events, including a schedule of guided walks. The bookstore sells a large selection of titles on local and regional flora and fauna, hiking, camping, and history.

The headlands' strategic position at the mouth of the San Francisco Bay made them a logical site for military installations. Today you can explore the crumbling World War II concrete batteries where naval guns protected the approaches from the sea. The now defunct **Nike Missile Site** (⊠ Field Rd., off Bunker Hill Rd. ☎ 415/331–1453) gives you a firsthand view of menacing Hercules missiles and missile-tracking radar. The site is open Wednesday through Friday, 12:30–3:30 (closed in bad weather), with guided walks starting on the hour.

At the end of Conzelman Road is the **Point Bonita Lighthouse,** a restored beauty that is still guiding ships to safety with its original 1855 refractory lens. The steep ½-mi walk from the parking area down to the lighthouse takes you through a rock tunnel and across a suspension bridge. It's open Saturday through Monday 12:30–3:30.

Numerous decommissioned military buildings and properties have been leased out to nonprofit organizations. Among them are the **Headlands Center for the Arts** (⊠ 944 Fort Barry ☎ 415/331-2787 ⊕ www.headlands. org) which hosts artists from around the world. You can see their work at open houses throughout the year, and at the **Project Space** in the main building (⊙ Tues.–Fri., Sun. noon–5) where each month an artist works in a space that's open to the public. The building itself (⊙ weekdays, Sun. 10–5 ☎ free) is a work of art: formerly an army barracks, its interior was creatively renovated by artists including David Ireland and Ann Hamilton. Just down the road another barracks has been made into a popular **youth hostel** (⊠ 941 Fort Barry ☎ 415/331–2777 or 800/909–4776 ⊕ www.norcalhostels.org ☎ Dorm beds $20; private room $60). Accommodations are simple and clean, there's a large kitchen for guests to use, as well as basketball courts and a rec room with Ping-Pong, pool, and foosball.

Muir Woods National Monument

▶ ★ ⊙ ❷ *10 mi northwest of the Marin Headlands off Panoramic Hwy.*

The 550 acres of Muir Woods National Monument contain some of the most majestic redwoods in the world—some nearly 250 feet tall and 1,000 years old. The stand of old-growth *Sequoia sempervirens* became one of the country's first national monuments in 1905; environmental naturalist John Muir, for whom the site was named, declared it "the best tree lover's monument that could be found in all of the forests of the world."

The hiking trails here vary in difficulty and distance. One of the easiest is the 2-mi, wheelchair-accessible **loop trail,** which crosses streams and passes ferns and azaleas, as well as magnificent redwood groves. The most popular are **Bohemian Grove** and the circular formation called **Cathedral Grove,** where crowds of tourists can often be heard oohing and aahing in several languages. If you prefer a little more serenity, consider the challenging **Dipsea Trail,** which climbs west from the forest floor to soothing views of the ocean and the Golden Gate Bridge.

The weather in Muir Woods is usually cool and often wet, so wear warm clothes and shoes appropriate for damp trails. Picnicking and camping aren't allowed, and pets aren't permitted. ■ TIP→ **Parking can be difficult here—the lots are small and the crowds are large—so try to come early in the morning or late in the afternoon.** The small **Muir Woods Visitor Center** has exhibits on redwood trees and the history of Muir Woods, plus a selection of books and gifts; the large gift shop within the park sells all manner of souvenirs.

To get here from the Golden Gate Bridge, take U.S. 101 north to the Mill Valley–Stinson Beach exit and follow Highway 1 north to Panoramic Highway. ⊠ *Muir Woods Rd., 2 mi north of Hwy. 1 via Panoramic Hwy.* ☎ *415/388–2595* ⊕ *www.nps.gov/muwo* ☜ *$3* ☉ *Daily 8 AM–sunset.*

Where to Stay & Eat

$$$ ✕▥ **Pelican Inn.** From its slate roof to its whitewashed plaster walls, this inn looks so Tudor that it's hard to believe it was built in California in the 1970s. Regardless of authenticity, the Pelican *feels* English to the core, with its high half-tester beds draped in heavy fabrics and downstairs pub that has ales and ports. It's particularly lovely on foggy days, when its coziness is highlighted. At dinner in the tavernlike or solarium dining rooms ($–$$$), keep it simple with fish-and-chips, roasted hen, or prime rib, and focus on the well-crafted wine list. ⊠ *10 Pacific Way, at Hwy. 1, Muir Beach 94965* ☎ *415/383–6000* ⊕ *415/383–3424* ⊕ *www. pelicaninn.com* ⊅ *7 rooms* ⇘ *Restaurant, pub, no-smoking rooms; no a/c, no room phones, no room TVs* ⊟ *MC, V* ⍭ *BP.*

Mt. Tamalpais State Park

❸ *6 mi northwest of Muir Woods National Monument on Panoramic Hwy.*

At 2,571 feet, Mt. Tamalpais affords views of the entire Bay Area and the Pacific Ocean. The mountain was sacred to Native Americans, who saw in its profile the silhouette of a sleeping maiden. Within the 6,300-acre park are more than 200 mi of hiking trails, some rugged but many good for easy walking through meadows and forests and along creeks. Locals claim this area is the birthplace of mountain biking, and every day cyclists toil up and whiz down Mt. Tam's winding roads and trails.

The park's major thoroughfare, the Panoramic Highway, snakes its way up from Highway 1 to the **Pantoll Ranger Station** (⊠ 3801 Panoramic Hwy., at Pantoll Rd. ☎ 415/388–2070). Pantoll Road branches off the highway at the station, connecting up with Ridgecrest Boulevard. Along these roads are numerous parking areas, picnic spots, scenic overlooks, and trailheads. Parking is free along the roadside, but there's a fee at the ranger station and other parking lots.

Where to Stay & Eat

★ **$$–$$$$** ✕▥ **Mountain Home Inn.** Next door to 40,000 acres of state and national parks, the inn stands at the foot of Mt. Tamalpais. Its multilevel, airy wooden building nests high up in the trees, with pristine wilderness on one side and an unparalleled view of the bay on the other. Rooms are built for romance, each mixing huge views with some combination of balcony, fireplace, and whirlpool tub. For full-moon nights book far in advance. The on-site wine bar and dining room (closed Monday and

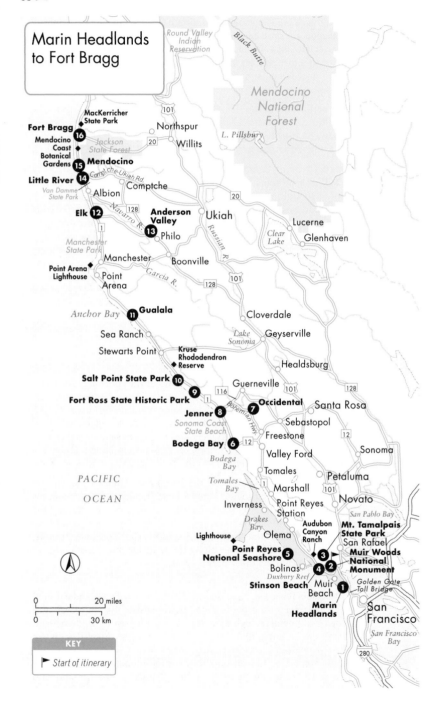

Marin Headlands to Fort Bragg

Fort Bragg **16**
MacKerricher State Park
Northspur
Mendocino Coast Botanical Gardens **15**
Mendocino **15**
Jackson State Forest
101
Willits
20
L. Pillsbury
Mendocino National Forest
Round Valley Indian Reservation
Black Butte

Little River **14**
Albion
Comptche Ukiah Rd.
Comptche
20

Van Damme State Park
Elk **12**
Anderson Valley **13**
Philo
Navarro R.
Ukiah
Russian R.
Lucerne
Glenhaven
Clear Lake

Manchester State Park
Manchester
Boonville
Point Arena Lighthouse
Point Arena
Garcia R.
128
101

Anchor Bay
Gualala **11**
Cloverdale
Sea Ranch
Stewarts Point
Kruse Rhododendron Reserve
Lake Sonoma
Geyserville
Healdsburg
128

Salt Point State Park **10**
Fort Ross State Historic Park **9**
Guerneville
101
Occidental **7**
Santa Rosa
116
Jenner **8**
Bohemian Hwy.
Sonoma Coast State Beach
Sebastopol
Freestone
12
Sonoma

Bodega Bay **6**
12
Valley Ford
Bodega Bay
Tomales
Petaluma
101
Novato

PACIFIC OCEAN

Tomales Bay
Marshall
1
Point Reyes Station
San Pablo Bay

Inverness
Drakes Bay
Olema
Audubon Canyon Ranch
Mt. Tamalpais State Park
San Rafael
Muir Woods National Monument
Lighthouse
Point Reyes National Seashore **5**
Bolinas
Duxbury Reef
Stinson Beach
Muir Beach
1
Golden Gate Toll Bridge

Marin Headlands
San Francisco
San Francisco Bay
280

3
2
4

20 miles
30 km

KEY

⚑ Start of itinerary

Tuesday) serves lunch on the deck and a terrific $38 prix-fixe dinner of American regional cuisine inside by the fire. ⊠ *810 Panoramic Hwy., 94941* ☎ *415/381–9000* 🖷 *415/381–3615* ⊕ *www.mtnhomeinn.com* ↪ *10 rooms* ♨ *Restaurant, Wi-Fi, lounge; no a/c, no room TVs, no smoking* ⊟ *AE, MC, V* ⍾ *BP.*

Stinson Beach

❹ *4 mi west of Mt. Tamalpais State Park on Panoramic Hwy.; 20 mi northwest of Golden Gate Bridge on Hwy. 1.*

Stinson Beach is the most expansive stretch of sand in Marin County. When it's not fogged in, the village clustered by this strand resembles a stereotypical Southern California beach town. On any hot summer weekend every road to Stinson Beach is jam-packed, so factor this into your plans.

Late May through early October, the professional **Shakespeare at Stinson** company performs each Friday, Saturday, and Sunday evening in its outdoor 155-seat theater. Tickets run $25 for adults, $18 for children 16 and under; some Fridays two kids are admitted free with each paying adult. ⊠ *Calle Del Mar and Hwy. 1* ☎ *415/868–1115* ⊕ *www. shakespeareatstinson.org.*

Where to Stay & Eat

$–$$ ✕ **Parkside Cafe.** Most people know the Parkside for its snack bar (¢, cash only) beside the beachfront park, but inside is the best restaurant in Stinson Beach. The food is classic Cal cuisine, with appetizers such as day-boat scallops ceviche and mains such as lamb with goat cheese–stuffed red peppers. Breakfast, a favorite among locals, is served until 2. Eat on the sunny patio or by the fire in the contemporary dining room. ⊠ *43 Arenal Ave.* ☎ *415/868–1272* ⊕ *www.parksidecafe. com* ⊟ *D, MC, V.*

$–$$ ✕ **Sand Dollar.** Old salts have been coming here since 1921, but these days they sip microbrews at a handsome bar or beneath market umbrellas on the heated deck. The American food—panfried sand dabs, pear salad with blue cheese—is good, but the real draw is the lively atmosphere. On sunny afternoons the deck is packed, and on weekends there's live music. ⊠ *3458 Hwy. 1* ☎ *415/868–0434* ⊟ *AE, MC, V.*

¢–$$$ 🏨 **Stinson Beach Motel.** Built in the 1930s, this motel surrounds three courtyards that burst with flowering greenery. Rooms are immaculate, simple, and summery, with freshly painted walls, good mattresses, and some kitchenettes. The motel is conveniently located on the main drag, so it can get loud during the day on busy weekends. Weekday room rates ($85–$125) are a bargain for Marin. ⊠ *3416 Hwy. 1, 94970* ☎ *415/ 868–1712* 🖷 *415/868–1790* ⊕ *www.stinsonbeachmotel.com* ↪ *8 rooms* ♨ *Some kitchenettes, cable TV; no a/c, no room phones* ⊟ *D, MC, V.*

Point Reyes National Seashore

❺ *15 mi north of Stinson Beach on Hwy. 1.*

Fodor's Choice
★

One of the Bay Area's most spectacular treasures and the only national seashore on the West Coast, the 66,500-acre Point Reyes National

Seashore (⊕ www.nps.gov/pore) encompasses secluded beaches, rugged chaparral and grasslands, and dense forest as well as **Point Reyes,** a triangular peninsula that juts into the Pacific. The hills and dramatic cliffs afford hikers, whale-watchers, and solitude seekers magnificent views of the sea.

A few tiny towns along its eastern boundary serve as gateways to the national seashore. **Olema,** a crossroads with a couple of fine restaurants and small inns, is where you'll find the main visitor center. Two miles north on Highway 1 is **Point Reyes Station,** the biggest burg in the area. A mix of upscale, counterculture, and mom-and-pop shops and eateries line several old-timey blocks, and numerous B&Bs lie north of town. On Sir Francis Drake Boulevard, which parallels Highway 1 up the opposite shore of Tomales Bay, **Inverness** overlooks the water from a forested hillside. You can eat and sleep humbly or extravagantly here.

The **Bear Valley Visitor Center** (⊠ Bear Valley Rd. west of Hwy. 1 in Olema ☎ 415/464–5100 ⊙ weekdays 9–5, weekends 8–5), has exhibits about park history and wildlife. Rangers here dispense information about beaches, whale-watching, and hiking trails. The infamous San Andreas Fault runs along the eastern edge of the park and up the center of Tomales Bay; take the short **Earthquake Trail** from the visitor center to see the impact near the epicenter of the 1906 earthquake that devastated San Francisco.

Drive past Inverness on Sir Francis Drake Boulevard to reach the heart of the park: a 20-mi-long road through rolling hills spotted with cattle ranches and dairy farms. There are turnoffs to several beaches along the way; those on the western side compose a 10-mi-long beach that has reliably dramatic surf and gorgeous dunes. At **Drakes Beach** the water is usually calmer (often even swimmable), and there's a visitor center and excellent café (☎ 415/669–1297) that serves hamburgers from beef grown on the surrounding ranches. In late winter and spring, wildlife enthusiasts should make a stop at **Chimney Rock,** just before the lighthouse, and take the short walk to the Elephant Seal Overlook. Even from up on the cliff, the males look enormous as they spar for the resident females.

At the very end of Sir Francis Drake Boulevard (22 mi from the Bear Valley Visitor Center) is the **Point Reyes Lighthouse** (☎ 415/669–1534 ⊙ Thurs.–Mon. 10–4:30, except in very windy weather), which has been in operation since December 1, 1870. Half a mile from the parking lot, 308 steps—the equivalent of 30 stories—lead down to (and back up from) the lighthouse: the view is worth it. On busy whale-watching weekends (late December through mid-April), parking may be restricted and shuttle buses ($5) put in service from Drakes Beach. You don't have to walk down the stairs to have a view of the whales.

Along the park's northernmost finger of land, the 4.7-mi (one-way) **Tomales Point Trail** follows the spine of a ridge through Tule Elk Preserve, providing spectacular ocean views from high bluffs. Expect to see lots of elk, even very close to the trail, but keep your distance from the animals. To reach the fairly easy hiking trail, head north out of Inverness on Sir Francis Drake Boulevard and turn right on Pierce Point Road. Park at the end of the road by the old ranch buildings.

Where to Stay & Eat

$–$$$ ✕ **Station House Cafe.** In good weather hikers fresh from the park fill the adjoining garden for alfresco dining, and on weekends there's not a spare seat on the banquettes in the wide-open dining room. The focus is on traditional American food—fresh popovers hit the table as soon as you arrive—and there's a little of everything on the menu. Grilled salmon, barbecued oysters, and burgers are all predictable hits. The place is also open for breakfast. ✉ *11180 Hwy. 1, Point Reyes Station* ☏ *415/ 663–1515* ▭ *D, MC, V* ☉ *Closed Wed.*

★ **¢–$** ✕ **Tomales Bay Foods.** A renovated hay barn houses this collection of food shops. Watch workers making Cowgirl Creamery cheese, then buy some at a counter that sells exquisite artisanal cheeses from around the world. Tomales Bay Foods showcases local organic fruits and vegetables and premium packaged foods, and the kitchen turns the best ingredients into creative sandwiches, salads, and soups. You can eat at a café table or on the lawn, or take your food to go. The shops are open until 6 PM. ✉ *80 4th St., Point Reyes Station* ☏ *415/663–9335 cheese shop, 415/ 663–8478 deli* ▭ *MC, V* ☉ *Closed Mon. and Tues.*

¢ ✕ **Bovine Bakery.** You can spot this tiny bakery from all the way down Main Street—just look for the line of people streaming out the door. Cyclists get their sugar-fix here courtesy of the delectable pastries; locals come for the excellent coffee (but, as a sign inside states emphatically, no espresso). The best bread in town is available here, but only for early birds— which, in this town, means before noon or so. ✉ *11315 Hwy. 1, Point Reyes Station* ☏ *415/663–9420* ▭ *No credit cards* ☉ *No dinner.*

$$$–$$$$ ✕🏠 **Manka's Inverness Lodge.** Chef-owner Margaret Grade realizes a rustic fantasy in her 1917 hunting lodge and cabins, where mica-shaded lamps cast an amber glow and bearskin rugs warm wide-planked floors. Each detail—featherbeds, deep leather armchairs, huge soaking tubs— bespeaks sensuous indulgence, but this is a private hideout, not a swanky resort. The centerpiece restaurant ($$$$; reservations essential) ranks among California's best. Grade prepares nearly everything over a wood fire with ingredients from within 15 mi, creating boldly flavorful dishes daily according to what comes in from farmers, fishermen, and foragers. Succulent meats reign, but vegetarians can ask for adjustments to the prix-fixe menu. ✉ *30 Calendar Way, at Argyll Way, Inverness 94937* ☏ *415/669–1034* ⊕ *www.mankas.com* ⇒ *8 rooms, 2 suites, 4 cabins* ♨ *Restaurant, some in-room hot tubs, some kitchenettes, piano, Wi-Fi; no a/c, no phones in some rooms, no room TVs, no smoking* ▭ *MC, V* ☉ *No lunch. Restaurant closed Tues. Jan.–mid-Feb., and Wed. year-round. Mon. dinner is for lodge guests only* ❏❘ *BP.*

★ **$$$** ✕🏠 **Olema Inn & Restaurant.** West Marin County is a locus for small-scale, organic farming, and chef Ed Vigil makes that the backbone of his cuisine. Steak from Point Reyes is paired with potatoes from Bolinas; Dungeness crab might come with fiddlehead ferns, fava beans, and wild mushrooms. The food is elegant, the dining room is spare and sophisticated (though casual), and the staff is unpretentious. Come on Monday, locals' night, when there's live music and you can browse a delectable

Fodor'sChoice

small-plates menu. The inn's six rooms ($$–$$$) occupy the floors above and feature sumptuous beds with crisp linens and antique armoires. ⊠ *10000 Sir Francis Drake Blvd., Olema 94950* ☎ *415/663–9559* ⊕ *www.theolemainn.com* ⊟ *AE, MC, V* ☉ *Closed Tues. No lunch weekdays.*

$$$–$$$$ ⊞ **Blackthorne Inn.** There's no other inn quite like the Blackthorne, a combination of whimsy and sophistication tucked on a hill in the woods. The giant tree-house-like structure has spiral staircases, a 3,500-square-foot deck, and a fireman's pole. The solarium was made with timbers from San Francisco wharves, and the outer walls are salvaged doors from a railway station. The best room is aptly named the Eagle's Nest, perched as it is in the glass-sheathed octagonal tower that crowns the inn. ⊠ *266 Vallejo Ave., Inverness Park 94937* ☎ *415/663–8621* ⊕ *www. blackthorneinn.com* ⇆ *3 rooms, 1 suite* ♨ *Dining room, hot tub; no a/c, no room phones, no room TVs, no kids, no smoking* ⊟ *MC, V* ⑩ *BP.*

★ $$–$$$$ ⊞ **Olema Druids Hall.** Built in 1885 as the meeting place for a men's social club called the Druids, this gorgeous, rambling building has been renovated into a place where nothing is just nice; it's deluxe. In winter, rooms are warmed by radiant heat that comes up through the original hardwood floors (marble floors in the bathrooms). The suite has a gourmet kitchen (complete with Viking range and dishwasher), a real log-burning fireplace, and a private deck that leads into the garden's gazebo. The Japanese-influenced cottage has a bedroom made private by Shoji screens and a Jacuzzi bath with double showerheads above. All rooms have down bedding and an emphasis on privacy. ⊠ *9870 Hwy. 1, Olema 94950* ☎ *415/663–8727 or 866/554–4255* 🖷 *415/663–1830* ⊕ *www.olemadruidshall.com* ⇆ *3 rooms, 1 suite, 1 cottage* ♨ *Some in-room hot tubs, some kitchens, cable TV with VCRs, Wi-Fi, massage, babysitting, concierge; no a/c, no smoking* ⊟ *MC, V* ⑩ *BP.*

$$–$$$ ⊞ **Ten Inverness Way.** With its stone fireplace, comfy couches, and window seats, the generous second-floor common room of this low-key inn is an appealing spot to plop down for complimentary wine and cheese or fresh-baked cookies. Upstairs, four rooms under the eaves are snug with patchwork quilts and waffle-weave robes; Room 1 is largest, with skylights and a tub. On the ground floor, a suite with a separate entrance can accommodate three adults or two adults plus two children. The full breakfast, made from scratch using many ingredients grown in the backyard garden, is ample fuel for a day in the great outdoors. ⊠ *10 Inverness Way, 94937* ☎ *415/669–1648* 🖷 *415/669–7403* ⊕ *www. teninvernessway.com* ⇆ *4 rooms, 1 suite* ♨ *1 kitchenette, hot tub, library, shop; no a/c, no room phones, no room TVs* ⊟ *D, MC, V* ⑩ *BP.*

$–$$ ⊞ **Motel Inverness.** This roadside row of rooms has everything a small-town motel should offer: friendly management; spotless, thoughtfully maintained accommodations (some quite small); and extras that add real value. The lodge, a window-lined common room with skylighted cathedral ceiling, has a fireplace, big-screen TV, billiards table, and kitchenette. Sliding glass doors open to a deck overlooking Tomales Bay. For $400, you can have the two-story suite (sleeps four) and its two decks, full kitchen, fireplace, and jetted tub; $500 rents you the ornate Dacha, a three-bedroom Russian-style house on stilts over the bay. ⊠ *12718 Sir*

Francis Drake Blvd., Inverness 94937 ☎ *415/669–1081 or 888/669–6909* 🖷 *415/669–1906* ⊕ *www.motelinverness.com* ⟿ *6 rooms, 2 suites, 1 house* ⚂ *Some kitchens, some kitchenettes, cable TV, billiards; no a/c, no room phones, no smoking* ☰ *MC, V.*

CAMPING Within the Point Reyes National Seashore are four hike-in campgrounds in isolated wilderness areas 3–6½ mi from trailheads. All sites have barbecue pits, picnic tables, pit toilets, and food-storage lockers; the water isn't potable and dogs are not allowed. The fee is $12 per night for up to six people. Reservations are essential spring through fall and can be booked up to three months in advance; to reserve call ☎ 415/663–8054 weekdays between 9 and 2 or inquire in person at the Bear Valley Visitor Center. For detailed information about camping, call the park at ☎ 415/464–5100 or visit ⊕ www.nps.gov/pore.

Sports & the Outdoors

On Tomales Bay, **Blue Waters Kayaking** (✉ 12938 Sir Francis Drake Blvd., Inverness ☎ 415/669–2600 ⊕ www.bwkayak.com) provides guided morning, full-day, sunset, full-moon, and overnight camping paddles. They also rent out kayaks and offer beginner through advanced lessons. **Five Brooks Stables** (✉ 8001 Hwy. 1, Olema ☎ 415/663–1570 ⊕ www.fivebrooks.com) rents horses and equipment. Trails from the stables wind through Point Reyes National Seashore and along the beaches. Group rides run from one to six hours and cost $35–$165 (private rides are more expensive).

THE SONOMA COAST

Heading up through northwestern Marin into Sonoma County, Highway 1 traverses gently rolling pastureland. North of Bodega Bay dramatic shoreline scenery takes over. The road snakes up, down, and around sheer cliffs and steep inclines—some without guardrails—where cows seem to cling precariously. Stunning vistas (or cottony fog) and hairpin turns make this one of the most exhilarating drives north of San Francisco.

Bodega Bay

❻ *34 mi north of Point Reyes National Seashore on Hwy. 1.*

From the busy harbor here, commercial boats pursue fish and Dungeness crab. There's nothing cutesy about this working town without a center—it's just a string of businesses along several miles of Highway 1. But some tourists still come to see where Alfred Hitchcock shot *The Birds* in 1962. The buildings in the movie are gone, but in nearby Bodega you can find Potter Schoolhouse and the Tides Wharf complex, which was a major, if now unrecognizable, location for the movie.

☖ For a closer look at Bodega Bay itself, visit the **Bodega Marine Laboratory** (✉ 2099 Westside Rd. ☎ 707/875–2211 ⚎ suggested donation $2), a 326-acre reserve on Bodega Head. Friday from 2 to 4 PM, docents give free tours and peeks at intertidal invertebrates, such as sea stars and sea anemones.

Where to Stay & Eat

$–$$$ ✕ **Seaweed Café.** Bodega Bay's best restaurant prides itself as a proponent of the Slow Food movement, which focuses on local foods prepared in traditional cooking styles. Here that could mean a simple, perfectly cooked piece of fish from a local fisherman or braised beef tongue and cheeks; no matter what, it's artfully and thoughtfully prepared, with delectable results. The interesting wine list is also local, entirely from Sonoma County. Only the tea bar is based on imports, offering hand-crafted teas from China, Taiwan, and Japan. Brunch is served Friday through Sunday. ⊠ *1580 Eastshore Rd.* ☎ *707/875–2700* ⊕ *www.seaweedcafe.com* ▭ *No credit cards* ☺ *Closed Mon.–Wed. No lunch.*

¢–$$ ✕ **Sandpiper Restaurant.** A local favorite for breakfast, this friendly café on the marina does a good job for a fair price. Peruse the board for the day's fresh catches or order a menu regular such as crab stew or wasabi tuna; clam chowder is the house specialty. There's often live jazz Friday and Saturday evenings. ⊠ *1410 Bay Flat Rd.* ☎ *707/875–2278* ▭ *MC, V.*

$$$–$$$$ ✕☐ **Bodega Bay Lodge & Spa.** Looking out to the ocean across a wetland, a group of shingle-and-river-rock buildings houses Bodega Bay's finest accommodations. Capacious rooms with masculine country-club decor are appointed with high-quality bedding, fireplaces, and patios or balconies; some have vaulted ceilings and jetted tubs. In the health complex, state-of-the-art fitness equipment sparkles and the spa provides a full roster of pampering treatments. The quiet Duck Club restaurant ($$–$$$$), a notch or two above most places in town, hits more than it misses; try the Dungeness crab cakes with tomato-ginger chutney. ⊠ *103 Hwy. 1, 94923* ☎ *707/875–3525 or 800/368–2468* ☐ *707/875–2428* ⊕ *www.bodegabaylodge.com* ⤳ *78 rooms, 5 suites* ⌂ *Restaurant, room service, refrigerators, cable TV with movies, in-room data ports, Wi-Fi, pool, gym, outdoor hot tub, sauna, spa, laundry facilities, concierge, meeting rooms* ▭ *AE, D, DC, MC, V.*

¢–$$ ☐ **Bodega Harbor Inn.** As humble as can be, this is one of the few places on this stretch of the coast where you can get a room for less than $100 a night. Renovated rooms have tile floors and a few antiques; unrenovated rooms are more generic, with wall-to-wall carpeting. All are small and clean. You can also rent an apartment or house nearby for $125–$350. The motel is at the north end of town on a side street off Highway 1, behind Pelican Plaza shopping center. ⊠ *1345 Bodega Ave., 94923* ☎ *707/875–3594* ☐ *707/875–9468* ⊕ *www.bodegaharborinn.com* ⤳ *14 rooms* ⌂ *Cable TV; no a/c, no room phones, no smoking* ▭ *MC, V.*

Sports & the Outdoors

Bodega Bay Sportfishing (⊠ Bay Flat Rd. ☎ 707/875–3344) charters ocean-fishing boats and rents equipment. The operators of the 400-acre **Chanslor Guest Ranch** (⊠ 2660 Hwy. 1 ☎ 707/875–2721 ⊕ www.chanslorranch.com) lead guided horseback rides, some along the beach. At the incredibly scenic oceanfront **Links at Bodega Harbour** (⊠ 21301 Heron Dr. ☎ 707/875–3538 or 800/503–8158 ⊕ www.bodegaharbourgolf.com) you can play an 18-hole Robert Trent Jones–designed course.

Occidental

❼ *14 mi northeast of Bodega Bay on Bohemian Hwy.*

A village surrounded by redwood forests, orchards, and vineyards, Occidental is a former logging hub with a bohemian feel. The 19th-century downtown offers a top-notch B&B, good eats, and a handful of art galleries and crafts and clothing boutiques. To reach Occidental take Highway 12 (Bodega Highway) east 5 mi from Highway 1. Take a left onto Bohemian Highway, where you'll find minuscule Freestone; another 3½ mi and you'll be in Occidental.

A traditional Japanese detoxifying treatment awaits you at **Osmosis–The Enzyme Bath Spa,** the only such facility in America. Your bath is a deep redwood tub of damp cedar shavings and rice bran, naturally heated to 140° by the action of enzymes. Serene attendants bury you up to the neck and during the 20-minute treatment ($75 weekdays, $80 weekends) bring you sips of water and place cool cloths on your forehead. After a shower, lie down and listen to brain-balancing music through headphones or have a massage, perhaps in one of the creek-side pagodas. A stroll through the meditation garden tops off the experience. ⊠ *209 Bohemian Hwy., Freestone* 📞 *707/823–8231* ⊕ *www.osmosis.com* 🖃 *AE, MC, V* ☺ *Daily 9–8.*

Where to Stay & Eat

¢–$$ ✕ **Willow Wood Market Café.** About 5 mi east of Occidental in the village of Graton is one of the best-kept secrets in the Wine Country. Tucked among the market merchandise are a number of tables and a counter where casually dressed locals sit down to order the signature creamy polenta, freshly made soups and salads, dinner plates, and gingerbread cake. ⊠ *9020 Graton Rd., Graton* 📞 *707/522–8372* ⊕ *www.willowwoodgraton. com* ⚑ *Reservations not accepted* 🖃 *MC, V* ☺ *No dinner Sun.*

$$$–$$$$ ▥ **The Inn at Occidental.** Quilts, folk art, and original paintings and
Fodor'sChoice photographs fill this colorful and friendly inn. Some rooms—such as
★ the Cirque du Sonoma Room, with a bright yellow-and-red color scheme—brim with personality and others are more sedate; all are comfortable and have fireplaces. Most guest rooms are spacious and have private decks and jetted tubs. An air of relaxed refinement prevails amid the whimsical antiques and fine Asian rugs in the ground-floor living room, where guests gather for evening hors d'oeuvres and wine. The two-bedroom Sonoma Cottage, which allows pets for an additional fee, goes for $629 a night. ⊠ *3657 Church St., 95465* 📞 *707/874–1047 or 800/522–6324* 🖷 *707/874–1078* ⊕ *www.innatoccidental.com* ⇖ *13 rooms, 3 suites, 1 cottage* ⚐ *1 in-room hot tub, some refrigerators, in-room data ports, Internet room, some pets allowed (fee); no room TVs, no smoking* 🖃 *AE, D, DC, MC, V* ⌷❶ *BP.*

Jenner

❽ *10 mi north of Bodega Bay on Hwy. 1.*

The broad, lazy Russian River empties into the Pacific Ocean at Jenner, a wide spot in the road where houses are sprinkled up a mountainside high above the sea. Facing south, the village looks across the river's mouth to **Goat Rock State Beach,** home to a colony of sea lions for most of the year; pupping season is March through June. The beach, accessed for free off Highway 1 a couple of miles south of town, is open daily from 8 AM to sunset. Bring binoculars and walk north from the parking lot to view the sea lions.

A 10-minute drive up the Russian River Valley via Highway 116, **Duncans Mills** is a restored 19th-century railroad town with a small history museum. A few browsable shops and galleries, a bakery, and a café make it easy to spend an hour or two here; a kayaking outfitter can take you out on the river. In the evening, the Blue Heron Tavern (☎ 707/865–9135), with a popular dinner-only restaurant and a serious lineup of blues, folk, and acoustic artists, is the place to be.

Where to Stay & Eat

$$–$$$$ × **River's End.** A magnificent ocean view makes lunch or an evening here memorable. Come for cocktails and Hog Island oysters on the half shell and hope for a splashy sunset. If you stay for dinner, choose from elaborate entrées such as grilled wild king salmon on cucumber noodles or elk with a red-wine-poached pear and Gorgonzola. The execution may not always justify the prices and the dining room is plain-jane, but just look at that view. Open hours sometimes vary, so call to confirm. River's End also rents out a few ocean-view rooms and cabins ($–$$$). ⊠ *11048 Hwy. 1* ☎ *707/865–2484* ⊕ *www.ilovesunsets.com* ▭ *MC, V* ☺ *Closed Tues. and Wed. No lunch weekdays.*

Fort Ross State Historic Park

☾ ❾ *12 mi north of Jenner on Hwy. 1.*

Fort Ross, established in 1812, became Russia's major outpost in California, meant to produce crops and other supplies for northerly fur-trading operations. The Russians brought Aleut sea-otter hunters down from Alaska. By 1841 the area was depleted of seals and otters, and the Russians sold their post to John Sutter, later of gold-rush fame. After a local Anglo rebellion against the Mexicans, the land fell under U.S. domain, becoming part of California in 1850. The state park service has reconstructed Fort Ross, including its Russian Orthodox chapel, a redwood stockade, the officers' barracks, and a blockhouse. The excellent museum here documents the history of the fort and this part of the North Coast. ⊠ *19005 Hwy. 1* ☎ *707/847–3286* ▧ *$4 per vehicle* ☺ *Daily 10–4:30* ☞ *No dogs allowed past parking lot and picnic area.*

Where to Stay & Eat

¢–$$$$ ×▥ **Timber Cove Inn.** Take a funky 1970s ski lodge, slip it into a weathered redwood-and-glass skin, anchor it to a craggy Sonoma Coast cliff, and you're here. Some guest rooms open onto a gallery suspended from the cross-beam ceiling over the soaring lobby, where a long bar sidles up to a massive rock fireplace. Most rooms offset dated appointments and clunky furniture with ocean views and raw wood flourishes. The best have freestanding fireplaces and big Jacuzzis tucked into tiled corners or placed before sliding-glass doors; the worst have seen better days.

A crew of resident raccoons waddles boldly about, as if they own the place. Picture-windowed and rock-walled, the restaurant ($$–$$$$) is the only one between Jenner and Sea Ranch. ⊠ *21780 Hwy. 1, 3 mi north of Fort Ross State Historic Park, Jenner 95450* ☎ *707/847–3231 or 800/987–8319* 📠 *707/847–3704* ⊕ *www.timbercoveinn.com* ⇨ *50 rooms* ⚐ *Restaurant, in-room hot tubs, cable TV, in-room data ports, hiking, lobby lounge, piano, shop; no a/c, no smoking* ⊟ *AE, MC, V.*

Salt Point State Park

❿ *6 mi north of Fort Ross on Hwy. 1.*

For 5 mi, Highway 1 winds through this park, 6,000 acres of forest washed by the sound of surf pounding on the rocky shore. Hiking trails lead past seals sunning themselves at Gerstle Cove, and through meadows where birds flit through wild brush. Don't miss the unusual *tafonis*—honeycomb patterns in the sandstone caused by centuries of wind and rain erosion—at Fisk Mill Cove in the north end of the park. A five-minute walk uphill from the parking lot leads to a dramatic view of Sentinel Rock, an excellent spot for sunsets. South Gerstle Cove's picnic area overlooks the water. ⊠ *20705 Hwy. 1* ☎ *707/847–3221* 🎫 *$6 per vehicle* ⊗ *Daily sunrise–sunset.*

Adjacent to Salt Point State Park, thousands of rhododendrons bloom in late spring within **Kruse Rhododendron State Reserve.** To reach the peaceful 317-acre evergreen preserve you must drive 4 mi of narrow, unpaved road. ⊠ *Kruse Ranch Rd. off Hwy. 1, north of Fisk Mill Cove* ☎ *707/ 847–3221* 🎫 *Free.*

Where to Stay & Eat

★ **$$$–$$$$** ✕🏨 **Sea Ranch Lodge.** Wide-open vistas and minimalist design keep the focus on nature at this tranquil lodge 8 mi north of Salt Point State Park. Picture windows—some with window seats—overlook trails along the bluff and out to a lofty point. Plank-panel walls and ceilings, goose-down comforters, and robes make large rooms cozy on foggy nights. The noteworthy restaurant ($$–$$$) serves such seasonal fare as wild mushroom risotto with baby leek and fennel confit and braised venison with creamy herbed polenta; there's also a bar menu. A lobby office handles vacation rentals in surrounding Sea Ranch, 10 mi of coastline where architects designed the homes to harmonize with the environment. ⊠ *60 Sea Walk Dr., Sea Ranch 95497* ☎ *707/785–2371 or 800/732–7262* 📠 *707/ 785–2917* ⊕ *www.searanchlodge.com* ⇨ *20 rooms* ⚐ *Restaurant, 18-hole golf course, massage, beach, hiking, bar, lounge, shop, babysitting, concierge, Wi-Fi, business services, meeting rooms, some pets allowed; no TV in some rooms, no smoking* ⊟ *AE, MC, V* ❙❍❙ *BP.*

⚠ **Salt Point State Park Campgrounds.** There are two excellent campsites in the park. Gerstle Cove campground, on the west side of Highway 1, is on a wooded hill with some sites overlooking the ocean. Woodside campground offers more trees and protection from the wind; it's on the east side of Highway 1. Woodside is closed December–March 15. Reservations are accepted March–October. ⊠ *20705 Hwy. 1, 95450* ☎ *800/ 444–7275* ⚐ *Flush toilets, drinking water, fire grates, picnic tables* ⇨ *Gerstle Cove, 30 sites; Woodside, 79 sites* 🎫 *$25.*

THE MENDOCINO COAST

The timber industry gave birth to most of the small towns strung along this stretch of the California coastline. Although tourism now drives the economy, the region has retained much of its old-fashioned charm. The beauty of the coastal landscape, of course, has not changed.

Gualala

⓫ *16 mi north of Salt Point State Park on Hwy. 1.*

This former lumber port on the Gualala River has become a headquarters for exploring the coast. The busiest town between Bodega Bay and Mendocino, it has all the basic services plus a number of galleries and gift shops. Stop by the **Gualala Arts Center** (⊠ 46501 Gualala Rd. ☎ 707/884–1138 ⊕ www.gualalaarts.org ⊘ Weekdays 9–4, weekends noon–4) to see free rotating exhibits of regional art. The third weekend in August the center is the site of Art in the Redwoods, a festival that includes a juried exhibition.

Gualala Point Regional Park (⊠ 1 mi south of Gualala on Hwy. 1 ☎ 707/785–2377 ⊘ Daily 8 AM–sunset) has picnic areas ($5 day-use fee) and is an excellent whale-watching spot December through April.

Where to Stay & Eat

$$$ ✕ **Pangaea.** Some of Gualala's best food is prepared in the artsy jewel-color dining rooms of this little log cabin. The well-traveled chef serves imaginative dishes based on ingredients from local farms and fisheries, such as wild salmon with truffled golden beets, and lamb kebabs with blood oranges and asparagus. Cheeses from Sonoma County and throughout northern California are available for dessert. Intelligent and well priced, the wine list balances local and European selections. ⊠ 39165 Hwy. 1 ☎ 707/884–9669 ⊕ www.pangaeacafe.com ⊟ MC, V ⊘ Closed Mon. and Tues. No lunch.

¢ ✕ **Café LaLa.** Under the clock tower in the Cypress Village shopping center, you can have breakfast or lunch with an ocean view. Along with the standards, choose from bagels stuffed with whatever you want, a long menu of salads, and creative sandwiches. Sip your espresso or chai on the patio. ⊠ 39150 Ocean Dr. ☎ 707/884–1104 ⊟ No credit cards ⊘ No dinner.

★ $–$$$$ ✕⬚ **St. Orres.** Resembling a traditional Russian dacha, with two onion-dome towers, this intriguing lodge stands on 42 acres of redwood forest and meadow scattered with an eclectic collection of cottages. Woodsy to grand, each has different amenities, such as ocean views, fireplaces or woodstoves, saunas, and Jacuzzis. Snug, wood-lined rooms in the main building share large baths. In the tower dining room, a spectacular atrium beneath an onion dome, locally farmed and foraged ingredients appear as garlic flan with black chanterelles, Dijon-crusted rack of lamb, and the like. The prix-fixe menu ($40) includes soup and salad but no appetizer or dessert (available à la carte). ⊠ 36601 Hwy. 1, 3 mi north of Gualala, 95445 ☎ 707/884–3303 ⬚ 707/884–1840 ⊕ www.saintorres.com ⬚ 8 rooms with shared bath, 13 cottages ⬚ Restaurant, some in-room hot tubs, some kitchenettes, some refrigerators, hot tub, *sauna, beach; no room phones, no room TVs, no smoking* ⊟ *MC, V* ⊘ *No lunch* ¡◯¡ *BP.*

$$–$$$ ▦ **Mar Vista Cottages.** The dozen 1930s cottages at Mar Vista have been beautifully restored. Intentionally slim on modern gadgetry (no TV, phone, radio, or even a clock), the thoughtfully appointed and sparkling clean cottages are big on retro charm: windows are hung with embroidered drapes, coffee percolates on a white enamel stove in the full, if diminutive, kitchen, and straw sun hats hang from hooks, ready for your walk down to Fish Rock Beach. Some have wood-burning or gas stoves. Outside, where benches overlook the blustery coastline, you can snip fresh greens from the organic garden for your supper. ⊠ *35101 S. Hwy 1, 5 mi north of Gualala, 95445* ☎ *707/884–3522 or 877/855–3522* 📠 *707/884–4861* ⊕ *www.marvistamendocino.com* ⤳ *8 1-bedroom cottages, 4 2-bedroom cottages* ⟁ *Kitchens, outdoor hot tub, beach; no room phones, no room TVs, no smoking* ⊟ *AE, MC, V.*

$$ ▦ **Seacliff on the Bluff.** Wedged behind a downtown shopping center, it's not much to look at. The interiors are motel standard, but you'll spend your time here staring at the Pacific panorama. Surprising extras ice the cake: take the binoculars out to your balcony or patio; stay in and watch the sunset from your jetted tub; snuggle into a robe and pop that complimentary champagne in front of your gas fireplace. Upstairs rooms have cathedral ceilings. ⊠ *39140 Hwy. 1, 95445* ☎ *707/884–1213 or 800/ 400–5053* 📠 *707/884–1731* ⊕ *www.seacliffmotel.com* ⤳ *16 rooms* ⟁ *Refrigerators, cable TV, Internet room, airport shuttle* ⊟ *MC, V.*

EN ROUTE   For a dramatic view of the surf and, in winter, migrating whales, take the marked road off Highway 1 north of the fishing village of Point Arena to the 115-foot **Point Arena Lighthouse** (☎ 707/882–2777). The lighthouse is open for tours daily from 10 until 3:30, until 4:30 in summer; admission is $5. As you continue north on Highway 1 toward Elk, you'll pass several beaches. Most notable is the one at **Manchester State Park**, 3 mi north of Point Arena, which has 5 mi of sandy, usually empty shoreline and lots of trails through the dunes.

Elk

⓬ *33 mi north of Gualala on Hwy. 1.*

There's not much happening on the streets of this former timber town, but that's exactly why people love it. The beautiful, rocky coastline is the perfect place for romance or a quiet escape.

Where to Stay & Eat

$$$$ ✕▦ **Harbor House.** Constructed in 1916, this redwood Craftsman-style house is as elegant as its location is rugged. Rooms in the main house are decorated with antiques and have gas fireplaces. The newer cottages are luxurious; each has a fireplace and deck, and three have ocean-view claw-foot bathtubs. Room rates include breakfast and a four-course dinner (except on weeknights during January and February, when the rates drop drastically). The ocean-view restaurant ($$$$; reservations essential), which serves California cuisine on a prix-fixe menu, is excellent, but seating for nonguests is limited. ⊠ *5600 S. Hwy. 1, 95432* ☎ *707/*

877–3203 or 800/720-7474 ⊕ *www.theharborhouseinn.com* ⇋ 6 *rooms, 4 cottages* ⚲ *Restaurant; no room phones, no room TVs* ▣ *AE, MC, V* ⦿ *MAP.*

★ **$$–$$$$** ✕▣ **Elk Cove Inn & Spa.** Perched on a bluff above pounding surf and a driftwood-strewn beach, this property has stunning views from most rooms. Spread among four cottages and a grand main house, accommodations are each unique and decorated in soothing tones. Suites have stereos and fireplaces; most have wood-burning stoves. A stone-and-cedar-shingle Arts-and-Crafts–style building houses plush spa suites ($370–$395) with cathedral ceilings. Relax with a massage in the small spa or a cocktail at the bar. 'Zebo restaurant ($$–$$$) fuses California, Southern, and international flavors. ⊠ *6300 S. Hwy. 1, 95432* ☎ *707/877-3321 or 800/275-2967* ⊟ *707/877-1808* ⊕ *www.elkcoveinn.com* ⇋ *7 rooms, 4 suites, 4 cottages* ⚲ *Some in-room hot tubs, some microwaves, some refrigerators, spa, beach, bar; no room TVs* ▣ *AE, D, MC, V* ⦿ *BP.*

Anderson Valley

⑬ *6 mi north of Elk on Hwy. 101, then 22 mi southeast on Hwy. 128.*

At the town of Albion, Highway 128 leads southeast into the Anderson Valley, whose hot summer weather might lure those tired of coastal fog. Most of the first 13 mi wind through dark, majestic redwood forest, then the road opens up to reveal farms and vineyards. While the community here is anchored in ranching, in the past few decades a progressive, gourmet-minded counterculture has taken root and that is what defines most visitors' experience. In the towns of Philo and Boonville you'll find bed-and-breakfasts with classic Victorian style as well as small eateries.

Anderson Valley is best known to outsiders for its wineries. Tasting rooms here are more low-key than in Napa; most are in farmhouses and are more likely to play reggae than classical music. That said, Anderson Valley wineries produce world-class wines, particularly Pinot Noirs and Gewürztraminers, whose grapes thrive in the cool, coastal climate. All the wineries are along Highway 128, mostly in Philo with a few east of Boonville. The following are our favorites and are listed here from west to east.

The valley's oldest winery, **Husch** (⊠ 4400 Hwy. 128 ☎ 800/554-8724 ⊙ Tasting room daily 10–5 winter, 10–6 summer) has a cozy tasting room next to sheep pastures and picnic tables under a grapevine-covered arbor. **Roederer** (⊠ 4501 Hwy. 128 ☎ 707/895-2288 ⊙ Tasting room daily 11–5) pours its famed sparkling wines in a grand tasting room amid vineyards. Look closely on the north side of Highway 128 for a rust-color sign reading LCV, and if the gate is open, drive the winding road through oak forest to **Lazy Creek Vineyards** (⊠ 4741 Hwy. 128 ☎ 707/895-3623). Gregarious owner and chef Josh Chandler offers unique wines, such as his Rosé of Pinot Noir, and has a bountiful rose garden where chickens run loose. White Riesling is the specialty of **Greenwood Ridge Vineyards** (⊠ 5501 Hwy. 128 ☎ 707/895-2002 ⊙ Tasting room daily 10–5), where awards line the walls and you can picnic at tables on a dock in the middle of a pond. Family-run **Navarro** (⊠ 5601 Hwy. 128 ☎ 707/895-3686 ⊙ Tasting room daily 10–5 winter, 10–6 summer) focuses on Alsatian varietals and offers a wide range of wines (pouring up to 15 at a time in the tasting room). The tasting room sells cheese and charcuterie for picnickers, and walking tours of the vineyard and winery are given daily at 10:30 AM.

The aptly named **Navarro River Redwoods State Park** (✉ Hwy. 128, Navarro ☎ 707/937–5804) is great for walks in the second-growth redwood forest and for swimming in the gentle Navarro River. There's also fishing and kayaking in the late winter and spring, when the river is higher. The two campgrounds (one on the river "beach") are quiet and clean.

Where to Stay & Eat

¢–$ ✕ **The Boonville General Store.** The café menu here is nothing surprising, but the exacting attention paid to ingredients elevates each dish above the ordinary. Sandwiches are served on fresh-baked bread, the beet salad comes with roasted pecans and local blue cheese. Even the macaroni and cheese—freshly made—is noteworthy. For breakfast there are granola and pastries, made in-house. ✉ *17810 Farrer La., Boonville* ☎ *707/895–9477* ▤ *MC, V* ✆ *Closed Tues. and Wed. No dinner.*

✕▦ **Boonville Hotel.** Unexpected sophistication is the trademark of this hotel in the center of Boonville. From the street it looks a little rusty, but inside the decor is straight out of Martha Stewart—artful linens, perfectly weathered tiles, walls painted tangerine and lime. Rooms upstairs in the hotel are breezy and bright, and the luxurious bungalow in the garden includes a private porch with hammock. Equally of note is the restaurant ($–$$$), where owner John Schmitt uses local ingredients (including some from his kitchen garden, behind the hotel) to create simple, delicious dishes like braised oxtails with shiitake mushrooms and mashed potatoes, or strawberry rhubarb shortcake. On Thursday you can try a three-course, prix-fixe meal for $30. The restaurant is closed on Tuesday and Wednesday and serves only dinner. ✉ *Hwy. 128, Boonville, 95415* ☎ *707/895–2210* ⊕ *www.boonvillehotel.com* ➥ *8 rooms, 2 suites* ☖ *Fans, some refrigerators, bar, massage, some pets allowed; no a/c, no room phones* ▤ *MC, V.*

$$–$$$ ▦ **The Philo Apple Farm.** Set in an orchard of organic, heirloom apples, the three cottages and one guestroom here are tasteful, spare, and inspired by the surrounding landscape. It all feels very Provençal, from the elegant country linens to the deep soaking tubs and dried flowers adorning the walls. On most weekends the cottages are reserved for people attending the highly respected cooking school here (two of the owners founded the renowned restaurant the French Laundry, in Napa), but midweek there is nearly always a room available. The farm stand, similarly refined, is worth a stop, too. ✉ *18501 Greenwood Rd., Philo, 95466* ☎ *707/895–2461* ⊕ *www.philoapplefarm.com* ➥ *1 room, 3 cottages* ☖ *No a/c, no room phones, no room TVs.* ▤ *MC, V* ❙⊙❙ *CP.*

Little River

⓮ *14 mi north of Elk on Hwy. 1.*

The town of Little River is not much more than a post office and a convenience store; Albion, its neighbor to the south, is even smaller. Along the winding road, though, you'll find numerous inns and restaurants, all of them quiet and focused on the breathtaking ocean.

Van Damme State Park is best known for its beach and for being a prime abalone diving spot. Upland trails lead through lush riparian habitat and the bizarre **Pygmy Forest,** where acidic soil and poor drainage have produced mature cypress and pine trees that are no taller than a person. The visitor center has displays on ocean life and Native American history, and, oddly, Wi-Fi for travelers with laptops. There's a $6 day-use fee. ⊠ *Hwy. 1* ☎ *707/937–4016 for visitor center* ⊕ *www.parks.ca.gov.*

Where to Stay & Eat

$$$ ✕ **Ledford House.** The only thing separating this bluff-top wood-and-glass restaurant from the Pacific Ocean is a great view. Entrées evoke the flavors of southern France and include hearty bistro dishes—stews, cassoulets, and pastas—and large portions of grilled meats and freshly caught fish (though it also is vegetarian friendly.) The long bar, with its unobstructed water view, is a scenic spot for a sunset aperitif. ⊠ *3000 N. Hwy. 1* ☎ *707/937–0282* ⊕ *www.ledfordhouse.com* 🚫 *AE, DC, MC, V* ⊘ *Closed Mon. and Tues. No lunch.*

$$$–$$$$ ✕🖿 **Albion River Inn.** Contemporary New England–style cottages at this inn overlook the dramatic bridge and seascape where the Albion River empties into the Pacific. All but two have decks facing the ocean. Six have spa tubs with ocean views; all have fireplaces. The traditional, homey rooms are filled with antiques; at the glassed-in restaurant ($$–$$$), the grilled meats and fresh seafood are as captivating as the views. ⊠ *3790 N. Hwy. 1, 95410* ☎ *707/937–1919 or 800/479–7944* 🖷 *707/ 937–2604* ⊕ *www.albionriverinn.com* 🛏 *22 rooms* △ *Restaurant, some in-room hot tubs, refrigerators, concierge; no smoking* 🚫 *AE, D, DC, MC, V* ⊘ *No lunch* �◎ *BP.*

★ $$–$$$$ 🖿 **Glendeven Inn.** If Mendocino is the New England village of the West Coast, then Glendeven is the local country manor. The main house was built in 1867 and is surrounded by acres of gardens. Inside are five guest rooms, three with fireplaces. A converted barn holds an art gallery. The 1986 Stevenscroft building, with its high gabled roof, contains four rooms with fireplaces. The carriage-house suite makes for a romantic retreat. La Bella Vista, a two-bedroom house, is the only accommodation appropriate for families. ⊠ *8205 N. Hwy. 1, 95456* ☎ *707/937–0083 or 800/822–4536* 🖷 *707/937–6108* ⊕ *www.glendeven.com* 🛏 *6 rooms, 4 suites, 1 house* △ *Wi-Fi, shop; no room phones, no TV in some rooms* 🚫 *AE, D, MC, V* ◎ *BP.*

Mendocino

🕖 *3 mi north of Little River on Hwy. 1; 153 mi from San Francisco, north on U.S. 101, west on Hwy. 128, and north on Hwy. 1.*

Many of Mendocino's original settlers came from the Northeast and built houses in the New England style. Thanks to the logging boom the town flourished for most of the second half of the 19th century. As the timber industry declined, many residents left, but the town's setting was too beautiful to be ignored. Artists and craftspeople began flocking here in the 1950s, and Elia Kazan chose Mendocino as the backdrop for his 1955 film adaptation of John Steinbeck's *East of Eden,* starring James Dean. As the arts community thrived, restaurants, cafés, and inns started to open. Today, the small downtown area consists almost entirely of places to eat and shop.

The restored **Ford House,** built in 1854, serves as the visitor center for Mendocino Headlands State Park. The house has a scale model of Mendocino as it looked in 1890, when the town had 34 water towers and a 12-seat public outhouse. From the museum, you can head out on a 3-mi trail across the spectacular seaside cliffs that border the town. ⊠ *Main St. west of Lansing St.* ☎ *707/937–5397* ⬚ *Free, $2 donation suggested* ☉ *Daily 11–4.*

An 1861 structure holds the **Kelley House Museum,** whose artifacts include Victorian-era furniture and historical photographs of Mendocino's logging days. ⊠ *45007 Albion St.* ☎ *707/937–5791* ⊕ *mendocinohistory.org* ⬚ *$2* ☉ *June–Sept., daily 1–4; Oct.–May, Fri.–Mon. 1–4.*

The **Mendocino Art Center** (⊠ 45200 Little Lake St. ☎ 707/937–5818 ⊕ www.mendocinoartcenter.org), which has an extensive program of workshops, also mounts rotating exhibits in its galleries and is the home of the Mendocino Theatre Company.

Where to Stay & Eat

$$$–$$$$
Fodor'sChoice
★
✕ **Cafe Beaujolais.** The Victorian cottage that houses this popular restaurant is surrounded by a garden of heirloom and exotic plantings. A commitment to the freshest possible organic, local, and hormone-free ingredients guides the chef here. The menu is eclectic and ever-evolving, but often includes free-range fowl, line-caught fish, and edible flowers. The bakery turns out several delicious varieties of bread from a wood-fired oven. The restaurant typically closes for a month or more in winter. ⊠ *961 Ukiah St.* ☎ *707/937–5614* ⊕ *www.cafebeaujolais. com* ▤ *D, MC, V* ☉ *No lunch.*

$–$$$$
✕ **955 Ukiah Street Restaurant.** A homey, woodsy interior and creative California cuisine make this spot a perennial favorite. Specialties of the house include fresh fish—depending on the catch, weekly offerings change—peppercorn New York steak, and spinach–and–red chard ravioli. When available, flourless chocolate-rum torte is a decadent way to end the evening. ⊠ *955 Ukiah St.* ☎ *707/937–1955* ⊕ *www.955restaurant.com* ▤ *MC, V* ☉ *Closed Mon. and Tues. No lunch.*

$$$$
✕▤ **Stanford Inn by the Sea.** This woodsy yet luxurious family-run property a few minutes south of town feels like the northern California version of an old-time summer resort. Several lodge buildings house guest rooms that range from cozy to chic, many with ocean views, fireplaces, and paintings by local artists. On the spacious, dog-friendly grounds you'll find organic gardens, llamas, and a sandy river beach where you can rent a kayak or canoe and head 8 mi upstream. Yoga classes and in-room massages and body wraps are complemented by the sophisticated vegetarian cuisine at The Ravens restaurant ($$–$$$). Breakfast is vegetarian, too. ⊠ *Comptche-Ukiah Rd. east of Hwy. 1, 95460* ☎ *707/*

14

937–5615 or 800/331–8884 🖷 *707/937–0305* ⊕ *www.stanfordinn. com* ➷ *31 rooms, 10 suites* 🛆 *Restaurant, refrigerators, cable TV with movies, in-room VCRs, in-room data ports, Wi-Fi, indoor pool, hot tub, massage, sauna, beach, bicycles, bar, business services, Internet room, some pets allowed (fee); no smoking* 🖃 *AE, D, DC, MC, V* ⦿ *BP.*

\$\$–\$\$\$\$ ✕🖳 **MacCallum House.** Rosebushes, some planted by the original owner
Fodor'sChoice in the late 1800s, dot the inn's 2 acres in the middle of town. Rooms in
★ the several buildings vary in character: the main house feels genteel, the cottages are bright and honeymoon-y, and the renovated water tower is deluxe—with a living room on the first floor, sauna on the second, and a huge view of the ocean from the bed on the third. Don't miss the outstanding restaurant (\$\$\$–\$\$\$\$; reservations essential), where the chef hand-selects the best local ingredients, even forages some of them himself. Everything from ice cream to mozzarella is prepared daily from scratch. The informal café serves lighter fare. ⊠ *45020 Albion St., 95460* 🕾 *707/937–0289 or 800/609–0492* ⊕ *www.maccallumhouse. com* ➷ *15 rooms, 9 suites, 2 cottages, 1 house* 🛆 *Restaurant, café, cable TV, in-room DVDs, some in-room broadband, in-room data ports, Wi-Fi, outdoor hot tub, massage, bicycles, bar, concierge, Internet room, some pets allowed (fee)* 🖃 *AE, D, MC, V* ⊘ *No lunch* ⦿ *BP.*

\$–\$\$\$ ✕🖳 **Mendocino Hotel & Garden Suites.** From the outside, this hotel's period facade and wide balcony make it look like something out of the Wild West. Inside, though, the stained-glass lamps, polished wood, and Persian rugs are more lumber-baron. Stay in an atmospheric room in the restored 1878 main building or in a larger, modern garden room out back; these rooms have TV and some have a fireplace. The wood-panel restaurant (\$\$\$–\$\$\$\$), fronted by a solarium, serves fine fish entrées and the best deep-dish olallieberry pie in California. ⊠ *45080 Main St., 95460* 🕾 *707/937–0511 or 800/548–0513* 🖷 *707/937–0513* ⊕ *www. mendocinohotel.com* ➷ *45 rooms, 14 with shared bath; 6 suites* 🛆 *Restaurant, room service, cable TV, bar, meeting rooms; no TV in some rooms* 🖃 *AE, MC, V.*

\$\$\$–\$\$\$\$ 🖳 **Brewery Gulch Inn.** This tasteful inn gives a modern twist to the elegance of Mendocino. Furnishings are redwood and leather, beds are plush, and all rooms but two have whirlpool tubs with views. The luxury is in tune with the surrounding nature: large windows frame views of the 10-acre property, bird-filled trees, and winding paths that lead through native plant gardens. An organic farm that's on-site (but out of earshot) provides eggs and other ingredients for the sumptuous breakfast menu. For a special treat, the chef will prepare a multicourse feast to be served in your room. ⊠ *9401 Hwy. 1, 1 mi south of Mendocino, 95460* 🕾 *707/937–4752 or 800/578–4454* 🖷 *707/937–1279* ⊕ *www. brewerygulchinn.com* ➷ *10 rooms* 🛆 *Some in-room hot tubs, cable TV, in-room VCRs, in-room data ports, Wi-Fi, massage, shop, library, concierge, meeting room; no smoking* ⦿ *BP* 🖃 *AE, MC, V.*

\$\$–\$\$\$\$ 🖳 **Alegria.** A pathway from the back porch to Big River Beach makes this the only oceanfront lodging in Mendocino. Each room has something special and unique: beautiful bamboo floors; a woodstove; sunset views from a perfectly positioned window seat. Despite its central location, the property is more private than others in town; it feels like a quiet retreat. The hot tub, surrounded by jasmine vines, is wonderful at night. ☒ *44781 Main St., 95460* ☎ *707/937–5150 or 800/780– 7905* ⊕ *www.oceanfrontmagic.com* ⤶ *7 rooms* ⚲ *Some kitchenettes, some microwaves, refrigerators, cable TV, in-room DVDs, outdoor hot tub, beach* ▤ *AE, MC, V* ⦿*| BP.*

Nightlife & the Arts

Mendocino Theatre Company (☒ Mendocino Art Center, 42500 Little Lake St. ☎ 707/937–4477 ⊕ www.mcn.org/1/mtc) has been around for nearly three decades. Their repertoire ranges all over the contemporary map, including works by David Mamet, Neil Simon, and local playwrights. Performances take place Thursday through Sunday evenings, with some Sunday matinees.

Patterson's Pub (☒ 10485 Lansing St. ☎ 707/937–4782), an Irish-style watering hole, is a friendly gathering place day (there's garden seating) or night, though it becomes boisterous as the evening wears on. Bands entertain on Friday night.

Sports & the Outdoors

Catch-A-Canoe and Bicycles Too (☒ Stanford Inn by the Sea, Comptche-Ukiah Rd., off Hwy. 1 ☎ 707/937–0273) rents kayaks and regular and outrigger canoes as well as mountain and suspension bicycles.

Shopping

Highlight Gallery (☒ 45052 Main St. ☎ 707/937–3132) deals in exquisite handmade wood furniture, particularly from Mendocino County woodworkers. Bath products, pottery, and other items, all with a French Provençal flair, are found at **Sallie Mac** (☒ 10540 Lansing St. ☎ 707/ 937–5357). Musicians come from far away to see the exceptional collection of instruments at **Lark in the Morning** (☒ 45011 Ukiah St. ☎ 707/ 937–5275), which include lutes, ouds, and a rare Chinese pippa. **Gallery Books** (☒ Main and Kasten Sts. ☎ 707/937–2665) is a well-loved, independent bookstore with a separate but adjoining store, **Bookwinkle's,** for children.

Fort Bragg

⑯ *10 mi north of Mendocino on Hwy. 1.*

The commercial center of Mendocino County, Fort Bragg is a working-class town that many feel is the most "authentic" place around; it's certainly less expensive across the board than towns to the south. The declining timber industry has been steadily replaced by booming tourism, but the city maintains a local feel since most people who work at the area hotels and restaurants live here, as do many local artists. A stroll down Franklin Street (one block east of Hwy. 1) takes you past numerous bookstores, antiques shops, and boutiques.

★ The **Mendocino Coast Botanical Gardens** has something for nature lovers in every season. Even in winter, heather and camellias bloom. Along 2 mi of trails with ocean views and observation points for whale-watching is a splendid profusion of flowers. The rhododendrons are at their peak from April through June, and the dahlias are spectacular in August. ✉ *18220 N. Hwy. 1, 1 mi south of Fort Bragg* ☎ *707/964–4352* ⊕ *www.gardenbythesea.org* 🎫 *$7.50* 🕙 *Mar.–Oct., daily 9–5; Nov.–Feb., daily 9–4.*

Back in the 1920s, a fume-spewing gas-powered train car used to shuttle passengers along a rail line dating from the logging days of the 1880s. Nicknamed the **Skunk Train**, it traversed redwood forests inaccessible to automobiles. The reproduction that you can ride today travels the same route, making a 3½-hour round-trip between Fort Bragg and the town of Northspur, 21 mi inland. The schedule varies depending on the season and in summer includes evening barbecue excursions and wine parties. ✉ *Foot of Laurel St., west of Main St.* ☎ *707/964–6371 or 866/457–5865* ⊕ *www.skunktrain.com* 🎫 *$35–$55.*

MacKerricher State Park includes 9 mi of sandy beach and several square miles of dunes. The headland is a good place for whale-watching from December to mid-April. Fishing (at a freshwater lake stocked with trout), canoeing, hiking, jogging, bicycling, beachcombing, camping, and harbor seal–watching at Laguna Point are among the popular activities, many of which are accessible to the mobility-impaired. Rangers lead nature hikes in summer. ✉ *Hwy. 1, 3 mi north of Fort Bragg* ☎ *707/964–9112* 🎫 *Free.*

The ocean is not visible from most of Fort Bragg, but go three blocks west of Main Street and a flat, dirt path leads to wild coastline where you can walk for miles in either direction along the bluffs. The sandy coves in the area you first reach from the road are called **Glass Beach** (✉ *Elm St. and Glass Beach Dr.*) because this used to be the dumping ground for the city. That history is still apparent—in a good way. Look closely at the sand and you'll find the top layer is comprised almost entirely of sea glass, likely more than you've ever seen in one place before.

An unexpected nod to Fort Bragg's rough-and-tumble past is the **Museum in the Triangle Tattoo Parlor** (✉ *356-B N. Main St.* ☎ *707/964–8814* 🕙 *Daily noon–6* 🎫 *Free*). The two-room display shows a ramshackle collection of tattoo memorabilia, including pictures of astonishing tattoos from around the world, early 20th–century Burmese tattooing instruments, and a small shrine to sword-swallowing sideshow king, Captain Don Leslie.

Where to Stay & Eat

$$–$$$ ✕ **Rendezvous Inn.** Applying sophisticated European technique to fresh seasonal ingredients, chef Kim Badenhop turns out a northern California interpretation of country French cooking. To start you might try Dungeness crab bisque finished with brandy, then follow with pheasant pot-au-feu with black chanterelles and glazed fall root vegetables. A sense of well-being prevails in the redwood-panel dining room, where service is never rushed. ✉ *647 N. Main St.* ☎ *707/964–8142 or 800/491-8142* ⊕ *www.rendezvousinn.com* 🟰 *D, MC, V* 🕙 *Closed Mon. and Tues. No lunch.*

¢–$$ ✕ **Mendo Bistro.** Everything on this menu is made from scratch, including the bread, pastas, and charcuterie. Though the chef doesn't tout it, his ingredients are nearly all organic, many of them local. A lingcod with hushpuppy crust is the chef's answer to fish-and-chips, and a wide selection of pastas has something for everyone—or, if not, there's the DIY menu: select your protein (beef, chicken, tofu), method of cooking, and sauce. ⊠ *301 N. Main St.* ☎ *707/964–4974* ▤ *AE, D, DC, MC, V* ⊘ *No lunch.*

¢–$$ ✕ **Piaci.** The seats are stools and your elbows might bang a neighbor's, but nobody seems to mind at this cozy little spot—this is hands down the most popular casual restaurant around. The food is simple, mostly pizza and calzones, but everything is given careful attention and comes out tasty. Alongside the selective list of wines is a distinctive beer list that has been given equal respect; noted are the origin, brewmaster, and alcohol content for each brew. Dogs and their owners are welcome at the tables outside. ⊠ *120 W. Redwood Ave.* ☎ *707/961–1133* ▤ *MC, V* ⊘ *No lunch weekends.*

¢ ✕ **Headlands Coffeehouse.** Eighteen kinds of coffee (plus a good selection of beer and wine), and nightly acoustic music make this the local hangout both day and night. The restaurant is bright and chatty by day, and the casual menu includes panini, soups, and fingerfoods such as samosas. ⊠ *120 E. Laurel St.* ☎ *707/964–1987* ▤ *D, MC, V.*

$$–$$$ ▦ **Weller House Inn.** It's hard to believe that when innkeepers Ted and Eva Kidwell found this house in 1994, it was abandoned and slated for demolition. She is an artist and he a craftsman; together they have hammered and quilted this into the loveliest Victorian in Fort Bragg. Each of the nine guestrooms is colorful and tasteful, with hand-painted ceilings and deep, claw-foot tubs. There's also a stunning redwood-panel ballroom and a water tower (the tallest structure in town), which offers ocean views from its second-floor hot tub and rooftop viewing deck. ⊠ *524 Stewart St., 95437* ☎ *707/964–4415 or 877/893–5537* 🖷 *707/961–1281* ⊕ *www.wellerhouse.com* ↪ *9 rooms* ⌂ *Some microwaves, some refrigerators, hot tub; no room phones, no TV in some rooms, no smoking* ▤ *AE, D, DC, MC, V* ◉| *BP.*

¢–$$ ▦ **Surf and Sand Lodge.** As its name implies, this hotel sits practically right on the beach; pathways lead from the property down to the rock-strewn shore. All rooms are bright and clean, although the six least expensive don't have views. The nicest of the second-story rooms have jetted tubs and fireplaces. ⊠ *1131 N. Main St., 95437* ☎ *707/964–9383 or 800/964–0184* 🖷 *707/964–0314* ⊕ *www.surfsandlodge.com* ↪ *30 rooms* ⌂ *Refrigerators, cable TV, in-room VCRs, beach; no smoking* ▤ *AE, D, MC, V.*

△ **MacKerricher State Park.** The campsites here are in woodsy spots about a quarter mile from the ocean. There are no hookups. Make reservations for summer weekends as early as possible (reservations are taken April–mid-October), unless you want to try your luck getting one of the 25 sites that are available on a first-come, first-served basis each day. ⊠ *Hwy. 1, 3 mi north of Fort Bragg* ☎ *800/444–7275 for reservations* ⌂ *Flush toilets, drinking water, showers, fire pits, picnic tables* ↪ *150 sites* ▭ *$20.*

Nightlife

Caspar Inn (✉ 14957 Caspar Rd. ☎ 707/964–5565) presents DJs or live blues, rock, hip-hop, and alternative rock. If you feel like staying over after a show, there are simple, inexpensive rooms upstairs.

Sports & the Outdoors

All Aboard Adventures (✉ 32400 N. Harbor Dr. ☎ 707/964–1881 ⊕ www.allaboardadventures.com) operates whale-watching trips from December through mid-April, as well as fishing excursions all year. **Ricochet Ridge Ranch** (✉ 24201 N. Hwy. 1 ☎ 707/964–7669 ⊕ www.horse-vacation.com) guides private and group trail rides through redwood forest and on the beach.

REDWOOD COUNTRY
FROM GARBERVILLE TO CRESCENT CITY

From the 1880s into the 1930s, there was a movement for this part of northern California to join with southern Oregon in seceding from their respective governments and forming a new state, called Jefferson. World War II took away the idea's momentum, but a different state of mind lives on in Humboldt County. Here, instead of spas, there are old-time hotels. Instead of wineries, there are breweries. The landscape is primarily thick redwood forest, which gets snow in winter and sizzles in summer while the coast sits covered in fog. Until as late as 1924, there was no road that went north of Willits; the coastal towns were reachable only by sea. That legacy is apparent in the communities here today: Eureka and Arcata are sizeable (both formerly ports), but otherwise towns are tiny and tucked away into the woods, and people have an independent spirit that recalls the original homesteaders.

Garberville

⑰ *67 mi north of Fort Bragg, 204 mi north of San Francisco on U.S. 101.*

Although it's the largest town in the vicinity of Humboldt Redwoods State Park, Garberville hasn't changed much since timber was king. The town is a pleasant place to stop for lunch, pick up picnic provisions, or poke through arts-and-crafts stores. A few miles below Garberville is an elegant Tudor resort, the Benbow Inn. Even if you're not staying there, stop in for a drink or a meal; the architecture and gardens are lovely.

Where to Stay & Eat

¢ ✕ **Woodrose Cafe.** This modest eatery serves basic breakfast items until 1 PM on the weekends and breakfast and healthful lunches every weekday. Dishes include chicken, big salads, burritos, and vegetarian specials. ✉ *911 Redwood Dr.* ☎ *707/923–3191* 🚫 *No credit cards* ⊗ *No dinner.*

$$–$$$$ ✕🏨 **Benbow Inn.** Back in the days of dirt-road travel, this Tudor-style manor resort on the Eel River was a haven of luxury. These days the highway is a bit of an affront to the serenity, but the inn remains a quiet, genteel place to remove oneself from urbanity and simply relax. Even if the furnishings are slightly dated, the feel is still elegant without pre-

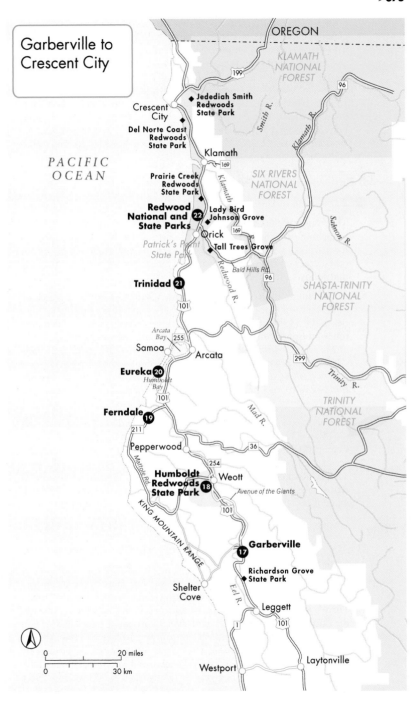

Garberville to
Crescent City

OREGON

KLAMATH
NATIONAL
FOREST

199

96

Jedediah Smith
Redwoods
State Park

Crescent
City

Del Norte Coast
Redwoods
State Park

Klamath

169

*PACIFIC
OCEAN*

Smith R.

Klamath R.

SIX RIVERS
NATIONAL
FOREST

Prairie Creek
Redwoods
State Park

Klamath R.

Salmon R.

**Redwood
National and
State Parks** 22

Lady Bird
Johnson Grove

169

Orick

*Patrick's Point
State Park*

◆ Tall Trees Grove

Redwood R.

Bald Hills Rd.

96

SHASTA-TRINITY
NATIONAL
FOREST

Trinidad 21

101

*Arcata
Bay* 255

Samoa

Arcata

299

Trinity R.

Eureka 20

*Humboldt
Bay*

101

Mad R.

TRINITY
NATIONAL
FOREST

Ferndale 19

211

Pepperwood

36

254

**Humboldt
Redwoods
State Park** 18

Weott

Avenue of the Giants

Mattole Rd.

101

KING MOUNTAIN RANGE

Garberville
17

Richardson Grove
State Park ◆

Shelter
Cove

Eel R.

Leggett

1

101

0   20 miles
0   30 km

Westport

Laytonville

tension. The emphasis here is on relaxation, so bring a good book and claim a chaise on the shady lawn or stroll down to the river for a swim. The wood-panel restaurant ($$$) specializes in locally caught salmon and trout, and in summer serves dinner on the terrace under the stars. ⊠ *445 Lake Benbow Dr., 95542* ☎ *707/923–2124 or 800/355–3301* 🖷 *707/923–2897* ⊕ *www.benbowinn.com* ☞ *43 rooms, 1 cottage* ♨ *Restaurant, some refrigerators, cable TV, some in-room hot tubs, some in-room VCRs, Wi-Fi, pool, hot tub, 9-hole golf course, lake, massage, bicycles, hiking, lounge, meeting rooms; no TV in some rooms, no smoking* ▭ *AE, D, MC, V* ⊗ *Closed early Jan.–late Mar. No lunch mid-Sept.–May.*

Humboldt Redwoods State Park

🖑 ⑱ *20 mi north of Garberville on U.S. 101.*

The **Avenue of the Giants** (Highway 254) traverses the park south–north, branching off U.S. 101 about 7 mi north of Garberville and more or less paralleling that road for 33 mi north to Pepperwood. Some of the tallest trees on the planet tower over the stretch of two-lane blacktop that follows the south fork of the Eel River.

At the **Humboldt Redwoods State Park Visitor Center** you can pick up information about the redwoods, waterways, and recreational activities in the 53,000-acre park. One brochure describes a self-guided auto tour of the park, with short and long hikes into redwood groves. ⊠ *Ave. of the Giants, 2 mi south of Weott* ☎ *707/946–2409 park, 707/946–2263 visitor center* ⊕ *www.humboldtredwoods.org* ☞ *Free; $6 day-use fee for parking and facilities in Williams Grove and Women's Federation Grove* ⊗ *Park daily; visitor center Mar.–Oct., daily 9–5; Nov.–Feb., daily 10–4.*

Reached via a ½-mi trail off Avenue of the Giants is **Founders Grove** (⊠ Hwy. 254, 4 mi north of Humboldt Redwoods State Park Visitor Center). One of the most impressive trees here—the 362-foot-long Dyerville Giant—fell to the ground in 1991; its root base points skyward 35 feet. **Rockefeller Forest** (⊠ Mattole Rd., 6 mi north of Humboldt Redwoods State Park Visitor Center) is the largest remaining coastal redwood forest. It contains 40 of the 100 tallest trees in the world.

Ferndale

 ⑲ *35 mi northwest of Weott, 57 mi northwest of Garberville via U.S. 101 north to Hwy. 211 west.*

Gift shops and ice-cream stores make up a fair share of the businesses here, but at its core, Ferndale miraculously remains a working small town. There's a butcher, a small grocery, a local saloon (the westerly most in the United States), and descendants of the Portuguese and Scandinavian dairy farmers who settled this town continue to farm on the pastures surrounding town. Ferndale is best known for its colorful Victorian architecture, the queen of which is the Gingerbread Mansion, built in 1899. The mansion, now a B&B, gives tours daily noon–4. Many shops carry

a self-guided tour map that shows the town's most interesting historical buildings.

The main building of the **Ferndale Museum** exhibits Victoriana and historical photographs and has a display of an old-style barbershop and
another of Wiyot Indian baskets. In the annex are a horse-drawn buggy,
a re-created blacksmith's shop, and antique farming, fishing, and dairy
equipment. ⊠ *515 Shaw Ave.* ☎ *707/786–4466* ⊕ *www.ferndale-
museum.org* 🖾 *$1* ⊘ *June–Sept., Tues.–Sat. 11–4, Sun. 1–4; Oct.–Dec.
and Feb.–May, Wed.–Sat. 11–4, Sun. 1–4.*

Memorial Day weekend's annual **Kinetic Sculpture Race** has artists and
engineers (and plenty of hacks) building moving sculptures from used
bicycle parts and other scraps, which they race from Arcata to the finish line in Ferndale. Contestants are judged as much on their creativity
as on their ability to cross the finish line, which makes for sculptures
like the past Albino Rhino and a 93-foot-long fish. The **Ferndale Kinetic Museum** (⊠ 580 Main St. ☎ No phone ⊕ www.kineticsculpturerace.
org) has a display of "vehicles, costumes, awards, and bribes" from past
races. The museum is open 10–5 Monday through Friday and 10–4 Sunday. Admission is free but donations are encouraged.

Eel River Delta Tours (⊠ 285 Morgan Slough Rd. ☎ 707/786–4187)
conducts two-hour boat trips that examine the wildlife and history of
the Eel River's estuary and salt marsh.

Where to Stay

$–$$$ 🏠 **Gingerbread Mansion.** This beautifully restored Victorian is dazzling
enough to rival San Francisco's "painted ladies." The exterior has de-
tailed spindlework, turrets, and gables; inside, the guest rooms are dec-
orated in plush, flowery period splendor. Some rooms have views of the
mansion's English garden; one has side-by-side bathtubs. One particu-
larly posh suite is the Veneto, which has hand-painted scenes of Venice
on the walls and ceiling as well as marble floors. ⊠ *400 Berding St.,
off Brown St., 95536* ☎ *707/786–4000 or 800/952–4136* ⊕ *www.
gingerbread-mansion.com* ⤵ *11 rooms, 4 suites* ♻ *No room phones,
no room TVs, no smoking* ⊟ *AE, MC, V* ⌾ *BP.*

Shopping

A sort of general store for visitors, **Golden Gait Mercantile** (⊠ 421 Main
St. ☎ 707/786–4891) sells long johns and penny candy, vintage-style
enamel cookware, and local fruit preserves. With two storefronts in Fer-
ndale and one in Eureka, **The Blacksmith Shop** (⊠ 455 and 491 Main St.
☎ 707/786–4216) celebrates the survival of traditional blacksmithing
arts in the area. The hand-forged works sold here range from flatware
to furniture, and especially nice are the rough-handled chef's knives—
so sharp there are Band-Aids stuffed in behind the display, just in case.
The very air is delectable at **Sweetness and Light** (⊠ 554 Main St. ☎ 707/
786–4403), which makes old-fashioned chocolates. At **Golden Bee Can-
dleworks** (⊠ 451 Main St. ☎ 707/786–4508), products are made ex-
clusively from beeswax and honey produced on a local farm.

Eureka

 *18 mi north of Ferndale, 66 mi north of Garberville on U.S. 101.*

With a population of 26,381, Eureka is the North Coast's largest city. Over the past century, it has gone through several cycles of boom and bust—first with mining and later with timber and fishing—but these days, tourism is becoming a healthy industry. The town's nearly 100 Victorian buildings have caused some to dub it "the Williamsburg of the West." Shops draw people to the renovated downtown, and a walking pier reaches into the harbor.

At the **Eureka Chamber of Commerce** you can pick up maps with self-guided driving tours of Eureka's architecture, and also learn about organized tours. ⊠ *2112 Broadway* ☎ *707/442–3738 or 800/356–6381* ⊕ *www.eurekachamber.com* ⊘ *Weekdays 8:30–5, Sat. 10–4.*

The Native American Wing of the **Clarke Memorial Museum** contains a beautiful collection of northwestern California basketry. Artifacts from Eureka's Victorian, logging, and maritime eras fill the rest of the museum. ⊠ *240 E St.* ☎ *707/443–1947* ⊕ *www.clarkemuseum.org* ✉ *Donations suggested* ⊘ *Tues.–Sat. 11–4.*

The structure that gave **Fort Humboldt State Historic Park** its name was built in response to conflicts between white settlers and Native Americans. It no longer stands, but on its grounds are some reconstructed buildings, fort and logging museums, and old logging locomotives. Demonstrators steam up the machines on the third Saturday of the month, May through September. The park is a good place for a picnic. ⊠ *3431 Fort Ave.* ☎ *707/445–6567 or 707/445–6547* ⊕ *www.parks.ca.gov* ✉ *Free* ⊘ *Daily 8–5, museum and fort 8–4:30.*

Blue Ox Millworks is one of only a handful of woodshops in the country that specialize in Victorian-era architecture, but what makes it truly unique is that it uses antique tools to do the work. The most modern tool here is a 1948 bandsaw. Lucky for curious craftspeople and history buffs, the shop doubles as a dusty historical park. A gregarious host gives an introduction at the entrance, then visitors conduct their own self-guided tour through various work areas where they can watch craftsmen use printing presses, lathes, and even a mill that pares down whole redwood logs into the ornate fixtures for Victorians like those around town. The museum is open but less interesting on Saturday, when the craftspeople generally take the day off. ⊠ *1 X St.* ☎ *707/444–3437, 800/248–4259* ⊕ *www.blueoxmill.com* ✉ *$7.50* ⊘ *Weekdays 9–5, Sat. 9–4.*

Where to Stay & Eat

¢–$$ ✕ **Cafe Waterfront.** This airy local landmark serves a solid basic menu of burgers and steaks, but the real standouts are the daily seafood specials—lingcod, clams, and other treats fresh from the bay across the street. The building, listed on the National Register of Historic Places, was a saloon and brothel until the 1950s. Named after former ladies of the house, two Victorian-style B&B rooms ($$) are available upstairs. Breakfast is served daily. ⊠ *102 F St.* ☎ *707/443–9190* ▤ *MC, V.*

🕐 ¢–$ ✕**Samoa Cookhouse.** For its first 50 years, this cafeteria existed solely to serve the 500 local mill workers their three square meals. In the 1950s it became a restaurant for everyone, but the dining has changed less than you might think. There's still only one menu in the whole building, and even it is superfluous. You take your seat at one of the long, communal tables, and the waiter will bring bottomless, family-style bowls of whatever is being served that meal. For breakfast that means eggs, sausage, biscuits and gravy, and so on. Lunch and dinner have a base of soup, potatoes, salad, and pie, plus daily changing entrées such as pot roast and pork loin. One back room contains a museum commemorating logging culture, but really the whole place is a living tribute to the rough-and-tumble life and hard work that tamed this wild land. Dieters and vegetarians need not apply. ⊠ *Cookhouse Rd.; from U.S. 101 cross Samoa Bridge, turn left onto Samoa Rd., then left 1 block later onto Cookhouse Rd.* ☎ *707/442–1659* ▭ *AE, D, MC, V.*

$$–$$$$ ✕▣**Carter House & Restaurant 301.** According to owner Mark Carter, his staff has been trained always to say "Yes." Whether it's breakfast in bed or an in-room massage, someone here will make sure you get what you want. Richly painted and aglow with wood detailing, rooms blend modern and antique furnishings in two main buildings and several cottages. Eureka's most elegant restaurant ($$$) uses ingredients hand-selected from the farmers' market, local cheese makers and ranchers, and the on-site gardens. Dishes are prepared with a delicate hand and a sensuous imagination—the ever-changing menu has featured sturgeon with house-made mushroom pasta, braised fennel, and white wine sauce. ⊠*301 L St., 95501* ☎ *707/444–8062 or 800/404–1390* ▤ *707/444–8067* ⊕ *www.carterhouse.com* ⇨ *32 rooms, 15 suites* ⚬ *Restaurant, some kitchens, cable TV, in-room VCRs, in-room broadband, massage, shop, laundry service, concierge, meeting rooms; no smoking* ▭ *AE, D, DC, MC, V* ⊘ *No lunch* ▯⦿⊦ *BP.*

FodorsChoice
★

$–$$$ ▣**Abigail's Elegant Victorian Mansion.** Lodging at this 1890 Victorian mansion is not a passive experience. Innkeepers Doug and Lily Vieyra have devoted themselves to honoring this National Historic Landmark (once home to the town's millionaire real estate sultan) by decorating it with authentic, Victorian-era opulence. It seems that every square inch is covered in brocade, antique wallpaper, or old-growth redwood paneling, and from every possible surface hangs a painting with gilt frame, or a historical costume. The Vieyras want their visitors not to just flop into bed, but to pretend they are the current inhabitants—drink tea in the parlor, play croquet on the lawn, select one of hundreds of period movies and watch it while the innkeepers wait on you in the sitting room. If you're ready, don your top hat or corset and embrace what Doug calls his "interactive living history museum." ⊠ *1406 C St., 95501* ☎ *707/ 444–3144* ▤ *707/442–3295* ⊕ *www.eureka-california.com* ⇨ *4 rooms, 2 with shared bath* ⚬ *Tennis court, sauna, bicycles, croquet, laundry service; no smoking* ▭ *MC, V* ▯⦿⊦ *BP.*

Nightlife

Lost Coast Brewery & Cafe (⊠ 617 4th St. ☎ 707/445–4480), a bustling microbrewery, is the best place in town to relax with a pint of ale or porter. Soups, salads, and light meals are served for lunch and dinner.

14

Sports & the Outdoors

Hum-Boats (⊠ A Dock, Woodley Island Marina ☎ 707/444–3048 ⊕ www.humboats.com) provides sailing and kayaking tours, rentals, and lessons.

Shopping

Eureka has several art galleries and numerous antiques stores in the district running from C to I streets between 2nd and 3rd streets. Best for contemporary art is **First Street Gallery** (⊠ 422 1st St. ☎ 707/826–3424), run by Humboldt State University, which showcases sophisticated work by local artists.

Specialty shops in Eureka's Old Town include **Gepetto's** (⊠ 416 2nd St. ☎ 707/443–6255) toy shop and **Flying Tiki Trading** (⊠ 630 2nd St. ☎ 707/441–1234), which stocks a stash of folk art. **Eureka Books** (⊠ 426 2nd St. ☎ 707/444–9593) has an exceptional collection of used books on all topics.

Trinidad

㉑ *21 mi north of Eureka on U.S. 101.*

Trinidad got its name from the Spanish mariners who entered the bay on Trinity Sunday, June 9, 1775. The town became a principal trading post for the mining camps along the Klamath and Trinity rivers. Mining and whaling have faded from the scene, and now Trinidad is a quiet and genuinely charming community with enough sights and activities to entertain visitors.

On a forested plateau almost 200 feet above the surf, **Patrick's Point State Park** (⊠ 5 mi north of Trinidad on U.S. 101 ☎ 707/677–3570 ⊠ $6 per vehicle) has stunning views of the Pacific, great whale- and sea lion–watching in season, picnic areas, bike paths, and hiking trails through old-growth spruce forest. There are also tidal pools at Agate Beach, a re-created Yurok Indian village, and a small museum with natural-history exhibits. Because the park is far from major tourist hubs, there are few visitors (most are local surfers), which leaves the land sublimely quiet. In spruce and alder forest above the ocean, the park's three **campgrounds** (☎ 800/444–7275 ⊠ $19) have all amenities except RV hookups. In summer it's best to reserve in advance.

Together, **Clam Beach County Park and Little River State Beach** (⊠ 6 ½ mi south of Trinidad, on Hwy. 1 ☎ 707/445–7651 ⏲ 5 AM–midnight) make a park that stretches from Trinidad to as far as one can see south. The sandy beach here is exceptionally wide, perfect for kids who need to get out of the car and burn off some energy. It's also the rare sort of beach where vehicles are allowed, so those with 4WD can drive to a perfect fishing spot or tailgate on the sand.

Where to Stay & Eat

$$–$$$ ✕ **Larrupin' Cafe.** Locals consider this restaurant one of the best places to eat on the North Coast. Set in a two-story house on a quiet country road north of town, it's often thronged with people enjoying fresh seafood, Cornish game hen, or mesquite-grilled ribs. The garden setting and candlelight stir thoughts of romance, though service can be rushed. ✉ *1658 Patrick's Point Dr.* ☎ *707/677–0230* ⌂ *Reservations essential* ▬ *No credit cards* ⊙ *Closed Tues. and Wed. in winter, Tues. in summer. No lunch.*

¢–$ ✕ **Katy's Smokehouse.** Purchase delectable picnic fixings at this tiny shop that has been doing things the same way since the 1940s, curing day-boat, line-caught fish with its original smokers. Salmon cured with brown sugar, albacore jerky, and smoked scallops are popular. Buy bread and drinks in town and walk to the waterside for alfresco snacking. Katy's closes at 6 PM. ✉ *740 Edwards St.* ☎ *707/677–0151* ⊕ *www. katyssmokehouse.com* ▬ *MC, V.*

$$$ ⌂ **Turtle Rocks Oceanfront Inn.** This comfortable inn has the best view in Trinidad, and the builders have made the most of it. Each room's private, glassed-in deck overlooks the ocean and rocks where sea lions lie sunning. Interiors are spare and contemporary. The surrounding landscape has been left wild and natural; tucked among the low bushes are sundecks for winter whale-watching and summer catnaps. Patrick's Point State Park is a short walk away. ✉ *3392 Patrick's Point Dr., 4½ mi north of town, 95570* ☎ *707/677–3707* ⊕ *www.turtlerocksinn. com* ⇅ *6 rooms, 1 suite* ⌂ *Cable TV* ▬ *AE, D, MC, V* ⦿ *BP.*

Redwood National & State Parks

☝ ㉒ *Orick entrance 16 mi north of Patrick's Point State Park on U.S. 101.*

After 115 years of intensive logging, this 106,000-acre parcel of towering trees came under government protection in 1968. Redwood National and State Parks encompasses one national and three state parks and is more than 40 mi long. There's no admission fee to the national park, but the state parks charge a $6 day-use fee.

At the **Thomas H. Kuchel Information Center,** open daily 9–5, you can get brochures, advice, and a free permit to drive up the access road to Tall Trees Grove. Whale-watchers will find the deck of the visitor center an excellent observation point, and bird-watchers will enjoy the nearby Freshwater Lagoon, a popular layover for migrating waterfowl. ✉ *Off U.S. 101, Orick* ☎ *707/464–6101 Ext. 5265* ⊕ *www.nps.gov/redw.*

About 3 mi north of Kuchel Information Center, turn east off U.S. 101 onto Bald Hills Road. In a couple of miles you will reach **Lady Bird Johnson Grove,** where a short circular trail leads through splendid redwoods. Continue on Bald Hills Road to Redwood Creek Overlook; the steep, 17-mi road (the last 6 mi are gravel) to **Tall Trees Grove** branches off just beyond. At the grove, a 3-mi round-trip hiking trail leads to the world's tallest redwood, as well as the third- and fifth-tallest ones.

To reach the entrance to **Prairie Creek Redwoods State Park,** leave U.S. 101 at the Newton B. Drury Scenic Parkway. The 10-mi drive through this old-growth redwood forest leads to numerous trailheads that access a 70-mi network of trails; it then rejoins U.S. 101. From the visitor center, a fully accessible trail leads to a meadow grazed by an imposing herd of Roosevelt elk. ✉ *Visitor Center: Newton B. Drury Scenic Pkwy. off U.S. 101* ☎ *707/464–6101 Ext. 5300* ⊙ *Mar.–Oct., daily 9–5; Nov.–Feb., daily 10–4.*

14

U.S. 101 passes through **Del Norte Coast Redwoods State Park** on its way north to Crescent City. Close to the ocean, the immense trees in this cool, often misty area shelter lush undergrowth. Damnation Creek Trail descends a photogenic 1,000 feet through an old-growth forest to the water; expect a strenuous round-trip hike of at least three hours. ⊠ *Crescent City Information Center, 1111 2nd St., Crescent City* ☎ *707/464–6101 Ext. 5064* ⊙ *Daily 9–5.*

THE NORTH COAST ESSENTIALS

To research prices, get advice from other travelers, and book travel arrangements, visit www.fodors.com.

Transportation

BY AIR

The only North Coast airport with commercial air service, Arcata/Eureka Airport (ACV) receives United Express and Alaska Airlines flights from San Francisco. The airport is in McKinleyville, which is 16 mi from Eureka. ⇨ Air Travel *in* Smart Travel Tips for airline phone numbers.

🛂 **Arcata/Eureka Airport** ⊠ 3561 Boeing Ave., McKinleyville ☎ 707/839–5401.

AIRPORT TRANSFERS A taxi costs about $40 and takes roughly 20 minutes. Door-to-door airport shuttle costs $17–$20 to Arcata and Trinidad, $20–$25 to Eureka, and $45/$45 to Ferndale for one/two people.

🛂 **Door to Door Airport Shuttle** ☎ 707/442–9266 or 888/338–5497 ⊕ www.doortodoorairporter.com.

BY BUS

Greyhound buses travel along U.S. 101 from San Francisco to Seattle, with regular stops in Eureka and Arcata. Bus drivers will stop in other towns along the route if you specify your destination when you board. Humboldt Transit Authority connects Eureka, Arcata, and Trinidad.

🛂 **Greyhound** ☎ 800/231–2222 ⊕ www.greyhound.com. **Humboldt Transit Authority** ☎ 707/443–0826 ⊕ www.hta.org.

BY CAR

Although there are excellent services along U.S. 101, long, lonesome stretches separate towns (with their gas stations and mechanics) along Highway 1, and services are even fewer and farther between on the smaller roads. ■ TIP➡ **If you're running low on fuel and see a gas station, stop for a refill.** Driving directly to Mendocino from San Francisco is quicker if, instead of driving up the coast on Highway 1, you take U.S. 101 north to Highway 128 west (from Cloverdale) to Highway 1 north. The quickest way to the far North Coast from the Bay Area is a straight shot up U.S. 101 to its intersection with Highway 1 near Eureka. Weather sometimes forces closure of parts of Highway 1. For information on the condition of roads in northern California, call the Caltrans Highway Information Network's voice-activated system.

🛂 Road Conditions **Caltrans Highway Information Network** ☎ 800/427–7623 ⊕ www.dot.ca.gov/hq/roadinfo.

CAR RENTAL Alamo, Avis, Hertz, and National rent cars at the Arcata/Eureka Airport, but call the reservation desk in advance if your flight will arrive late in the evening—the desks tend to close early, especially on weekends. ⇨ Car Rental *in* Smart Travel Tips for national rental agency phone numbers.

Contacts & Resources

EMERGENCIES

In an emergency dial 911. In state and national parks, park rangers serve as police officers and will help you in any emergency. Bigger towns along the coast have hospitals, but for major medical emergencies you will need to go to San Francisco. Note that cell phones don't work along large swaths of the North Coast.

General Hospital ⊠ 2200 Harrison St., Eureka ☎ 707/445-5111. **Mendocino Coast District Hospital** ⊠ 700 River Dr., Fort Bragg ☎ 707/961-1234. **Palm Drive Hospital** ⊠ 501 Petaluma Ave., Sebastopol ☎ 707/823-8511.

VISITOR INFORMATION

Humboldt County Convention and Visitors Bureau ⊠ 1034 2nd St., Eureka 95501 ☎ 707/443-5097 or 800/346-3482 ⊕ www.redwoodvisitor.org. **Fort Bragg–Mendocino Coast Chamber of Commerce** ⊠ 332 N. Main St., Fort Bragg 95437 ☎ 707/961-6300 or 800/726-2780 ⊕ www.mendocinocoast.com. **Mendocino County Alliance** ⊠ 525 S. Main St., Ukiah 95482 ☎ 707/462-7417 or 866/466-3636 ⊕ www.gomendo.com. **Redwood Empire Association** ⊠ 825 Geary St., Suite 701, San Francisco 94109 ☎ 415/292-5527 or 800/619-2125 ⊕ www.redwoodempire.com. **Sonoma County Tourism Program** ⊠ 520 Mendocino Ave., Suite 210, Santa Rosa 95401 ☎ 707/565-5383 ⊕ www.sonomacounty.com. **West Marin Chamber of Commerce** ☎ 415/663-9232 ⊕ www.pointreyes.org.

14

The Gold Country

WITH SACRAMENTO

WORD OF MOUTH

"The California Caverns were a fantastic experience! Do the rappel, even if you are mildly scared of heights. Very nice tour guide. But there are some tight squeezes, so they retain the right to reject you if you are too big."

—Lorraine

"The smell of the apple pies and pastries at Apple Hill are overwhelmingly good. Great crafts and fun for everyone. A country feel and very friendly. Fun even in the rain!"

—Michelle jacson

Updated by
Reed Parsell

A NEW ERA DAWNED FOR CALIFORNIA when James Marshall turned up a gold nugget in the tailrace of a sawmill he was constructing along the American River. Before January 24, 1848, Mexico and the United States were still wrestling for ownership of what would become the Golden State. With Marshall's discovery the United States tightened its grip on the region, and prospectors from all over the world came to seek their fortunes in the Mother Lode.

As gold fever seized the nation, California's population of 15,000 swelled to 265,000 within three years. The mostly young, mostly male adventurers who arrived in search of gold—the '49ers—became part of a culture that discarded many of the conventions of the eastern states. It was also a violent time. Yankee prospectors chased Mexican miners off their claims, and California's leaders initiated a plan to exterminate the local Native American population. Bounties were paid and private militias were hired to wipe out the Native Americans or sell them into slavery. California was now to be dominated by the Anglo.

15

The boom brought on by the gold rush lasted scarcely 20 years, but it changed California forever. It produced 546 mining towns, of which fewer than 250 remain. The hills of the Gold Country were alive, not only with prospecting and mining but also with business, the arts, gambling, and a fair share of crime. Opera houses went up alongside brothels, and the California State Capitol, in Sacramento, was built with the gold dug out of the hills. A lot of important history was made in Sacramento, the center of commerce during this period. Pony Express riders ended their nearly 2,000-mi journeys in the city in the 1860s. The transcontinental railroad, completed in 1869, was conceived here.

By the 1960s the scars that mining had inflicted on the landscape had largely healed. To promote tourism, locals began restoring vintage structures, historians developed museums, and the state established parks and recreation areas to preserve the memory of this extraordinary episode in American history.

One of California's least expensive destinations, the gold-mining region of the Sierra Nevada foothills is not without its pleasures, natural and cultural. Today you can come to Nevada City, Auburn, Coloma, Sutter Creek, and Columbia not only to relive the past but also to explore art galleries and to stay at inns full of character. Spring brings wildflowers, and in fall the hills are colored by bright red berries and changing leaves. Because it offers a mix of indoor and outdoor activities, the Gold Country is a great place to take the kids.

Exploring the Gold Country

Visiting Old Sacramento's museums is a good way to immerse yourself in history, but the Gold Country's heart lies along Highway 49, which winds the 325-mi north–south length of the historic mining area. The highway, often a twisting, hilly, two-lane road, begs for a convertible with the top down.

About the Restaurants

American, Italian, and Mexican fare are common in the Gold Country, but chefs also prepare ambitious continental, French, and California cuisine. Grass Valley's meat- and vegetable-stuffed *pasties,* introduced by 19th-century gold miners from Cornwall, are one of the region's more unusual treats.

About the Hotels

Full-service hotels, budget motels, small inns, and even a fine hostel can all be found in Sacramento. The main accommodations in the larger towns along Highway 49—among them Placerville, Nevada City, Auburn, and Mariposa—are chain motels and inns. Many Gold Country bed-and-breakfasts occupy former mansions, miners' cabins, and other historic buildings.

WHAT IT COSTS				
$$$$	**$$$**	**$$**	**$**	**¢**
RESTAURANTS over $30	$23–$30	$16–$22	$10–$15	under $10
HOTELS over $250	$176–$250	$121–$175	$90–$120	under $90

Restaurant prices are for a main course at dinner, excluding sales tax of 7%–8% (depending on location). Hotel prices are for two people in a standard double room in high season, excluding service charges and 7%–8% tax.

Timing

The Gold Country is most pleasant in spring, when the wildflowers are in bloom, and in fall. Summers are hot: temperatures of 100°F are common. Sacramento winters tend to be cool with occasionally foggy and/or rainy days. Throughout the year Gold Country towns stage community and ethnic celebrations. In December many towns deck themselves out for Christmas. ■ TIP→ **Sacramento is the site of the annual Jazz Jubilee over Memorial Day weekend and the California State Fair in August and early September.** East of the town of Sutter Creek, flowers bloom on Daffodil Hill in March.

SACRAMENTO & VICINITY

▶ The gateway to the Gold Country, the seat of state government (headed by Governor Arnold Schwarzenegger), and an agricultural hub, the city of Sacramento plays many important contemporary roles. About 2 million people live in the metropolitan area. The continuing influx of newcomers seeking opportunity, sunshine, and lower housing costs than in coastal California has made it one of the nation's fastest-growing regions.

The midtown area, just east of downtown, contains many of the city's best restaurants and quirkiest shops. Midtown is a strange mix of genteel Victorian edifices and cheap-looking apartment buildings, with massive trees, distinctive small shops, and quiet weekend streets making it Sacramento's most interesting neighborhood.

GREAT ITINERARIES

Numbers correspond to the Sacramento and the Gold Country maps.

IF YOU HAVE 1 DAY

Increasing traffic makes a drive from Sacramento to and along Highway 49 potentially long and frustrating. Instead, if you have only one day to spend in the area, stick to ▶ **Sacramento❶** **–❶**. Begin at **Sutter's Fort❶**, and then walk down J Street or take a bus to the **Capitol❶** for a free tour. Its huge park is pleasant for picnics. Next, head to Old Sacramento, perhaps detouring through the vibrant Downtown Plaza mall for a drink in its River City Brewing Co. Explore the **California State Railroad Museum❶**, and, time permitting, take a one-hour river cruise before dining at one of Old Sacramento's many good restaurants.

IF YOU HAVE 5 DAYS

Start your trip in ▶ **Sacramento ❶** **–❶**, where you can visit the **California State Railroad Museum** ❶ and **Sutter's Fort❶** and take a riverboat cruise. On the second day, drive to **Placerville❶** to see Hangtown's Gold Bug Park & Mine and continue to **Sutter Creek ❷❶**. Day 3 starts with a visit to the Amador County Museum, in **Jackson❷**, after which you can head south on Highway 49 and northeast on Highway 4 for lunch in **Murphys❷**. Return to Highway 49 and continue south to Columbia State Historic Park, in **Columbia ❷**. You can relive the 1800s by dining and spending the night at the City Hotel. If you've been itching to pan for gold, do that on the morning of Day 4. Drive back north on Highway 49 to **Coloma❷** and Marshall Gold Discovery State Historic Park, and head to **Auburn❸** to spend the night. On your last day, stop at Empire Mine State Historic Park in **Grass Valley❸** and pay a visit to **Nevada City❸**.

15

Downtown, pedestrian-only K Street Mall has for years struggled to gain momentum but cannot shrug off a persistent homeless problem and a scattering of boarded-up storefronts. Nearby, however, an infusion of upscale, popular restaurants, nightclubs, and breweries is energizing the downtown scene otherwise.

Ten miles west of the city is the college town of Davis, which, like nearby Woodland, is beginning to feel more suburban than agricultural because many Sacramento workers are settling there.

Sacramento also contains more than 2,000 acres of natural and developed parkland. Grand old evergreens, deciduous and fruit-bearing trees (many lawns and even parks are littered with oranges in springtime), and giant palms give it a shady, lush quality.

Exploring Sacramento

Driving 87 mi northeast of San Francisco (Interstate 80 to Highway 99 or Interstate 5) not only brings you to the Golden State's seat of government, but also can take you back in time to the gold-rush days. Wooden sidewalks and horse-drawn carriages on cobblestone streets lend a 19th-century feel to Old Sacramento, a 28-acre district along the Sacramento River waterfront. The museums at the north end hold artifacts of state and national significance, and historic buildings house shops and restaurants. River cruises and train rides are fun family diversions for an hour or two. Call the **Old Sacramento Events Hotline** (☎ 916/558–3912) for information about living-history re-creations and merchant hours.

What to See

❼ California Military Museum. A storefront entrance leads to three floors containing more than 30,000 artifacts—uniforms, weapons, photographs, documents, medals, and flags of all kinds—that trace Californians' roles in the military throughout U.S. history. Recent exhibits have included a study of Native Americans in the U.S. Armed Forces and displays on the post–September 11 wars in Afghanistan and Iraq. ✉ *1119 2nd St.* ☎ *916/442–2883* ⊕ *www.militarymuseum.org* 💲 *$5* ⊗ *Tues.–Fri. 10–4, weekends 10–5.*

NEED A BREAK?

The **River City Brewing Co.** (✉ Downtown Plaza ☎ 916/447–2739) is the best of several breweries that have cropped up in the capital city. The brewery is at the west end of the K Street Mall, between the Capitol and Old Sacramento.

IF YOU LIKE

HISTORIC HOTELS & INNS

The Gold Country abounds in well-preserved examples of gold-rush-era architecture, so why not experience the history up-close by staying at an inn or hotel that dates back to those colorful years? Plenty of old mansions have been converted to inns and B&Bs, and several hotels have been in operation since the gold rush. The very Victorian Imperial Hotel in Amador City opened in 1879, and the stone Murphys Historic Hotel & Lodge in Murphys has served guests such as Mark Twain and Black Bart since 1855. Columbia has the 1856 City Hotel and the 1857 Fallon Hotel, the latter of which was restored by the state of California. In Jamestown, the National Hotel offers an authentic 1859 experience.

SHOPPING

Shoppers visit the Gold Country in search of antiques, collectibles, fine art, quilts, toys, tools, decorative items, and furnishings. Handmade quilts and crafts can be found in Sutter Creek, Jackson, and Amador City. Auburn and Nevada City support many gift boutiques. Sacramento's commuter communities, such as Elk Grove (south), Folsom (east), and Roseville (northeast), are exploding with subdivisions, and with them inevitably come the standard suburban assortment of chain stores and strip malls.

THEATER

For weary miners in search of diversion, theater was a popular form of entertainment in the Gold Country. It still is, and you can take in a show at several venues dating from the era. The Woodland Opera House, opened in 1885, mounts musical theater productions September through July. Nevada City's Nevada Theatre, built in 1865, is the home of the Foothill Theater Company. In Columbia State Historic Park, the Historic Fallon House Theater presents dramas, comedies, and musicals.

15

California Museum for History, Women, and the Arts. California's first lady, Maria Shriver, has taken an active role in having this museum, formerly the California State History Museum, stress women's issues. Though many exhibits use modern technology, there are also scores of archival drawers that you can pull out to see the real artifacts of history and culture—from the California State Constitution to surfing magazines. Board a 1949 cross-country bus to view a video on immigration, visit a Chinese herb shop maintained by a holographic proprietor, or stand on a gubernatorial balcony overlooking a sea of cameras and banners. There's also a café that's open weekdays until 2:30 PM. ⊠ *1020 O St.* ☎ *916/653–7524* ⊕ *www.californiamuseum.org* ⊠ *$5* ☉ *Tues.–Sat. 10–5, Sun. noon–5.*

California State Indian Museum. Among the interesting displays at this well-organized museum is one devoted to Ishi, the last Yahi Indian to emerge from the mountains, in 1911. Ishi provided scientists with insight into the traditions and culture of this group of Native Americans. Arts-and-crafts exhibits, a demonstration village, and an evocative 10-minute video bring to life the multifaceted past and present of California's native peoples. ⊠ *2618 K St.* ☎ *916/324–0971* ⊕ *www.parks.ca.gov* ⊠ *$2* ⊙ *Daily 10–5.*

① California State Railroad Museum. Near what was once the terminus of
FodorsChoice the transcontinental and Sacramento Valley railroads (the actual terminus was at Front and K streets), this 100,000-square-foot museum has 21 locomotives and railroad cars on display along with dozens of other exhibits. You can walk through a post-office car and peer into cubbyholes and canvas mailbags, enter a sleeping car that simulates the swaying on the roadbed and the flashing lights of a passing town at night, or glimpse the inside of the first-class dining car. The museum recently added a compelling permanent display of mannequins dressed in railroad attire and positioned in various work environments. ⊠ *125 I St.* ☎ *916/445–6645* ⊕ *www.csrmf.org* ⊠ *$8* ⊙ *Daily 10–5.*

★ ⑩ Capitol. The Golden State's Capitol was built in 1869. The lacy plasterwork of the 120-foot-high rotunda has the complexity and colors of a Fabergé egg. Underneath the gilded dome are marble floors, glittering chandeliers, monumental staircases, reproductions of 19th-century state offices, and legislative chambers decorated in the style of the 1890s. Guides conduct tours of the building and the 40-acre Capitol Park, which contains a rose garden, an impressive display of camellias (Sacramento's city flower), and the California Vietnam Veterans Memorial. ⊠ *Capitol Mall and 10th St.* ☎ *916/324–0333* ⊕ *www.statecapitolmuseum.com* ⊠ *Free* ⊙ *Daily 9–5; tours hourly 9–4.*

④ Central Pacific Passenger Depot. At this reconstructed 1876 station there's rolling stock to admire, a typical waiting room, and a small restaurant. A steam-powered train departs hourly (weekends April through September, and for special occasions October through December) from the freight depot, south of the passenger depot, making a 40-minute out-and-back trip along the Sacramento riverfront. ⊠ *930 Front St.* ☎ *916/445–6645* ⊠ *$3, free with same-day ticket from California State Railroad Museum; train ride $8 additional* ⊙ *Depot daily 10–4. Train Apr.–Sept. weekends; Oct.–Dec., 1st weekend of month.*

⑧ Crocker Art Museum. The oldest art museum in the American West has a collection of art from Europe, Asia, and California, including *Sunday Morning in the Mines* (1872), a large canvas by Charles Christian Nahl depicting aspects of the original mining industry, and the magnificent *Great Canyon of the Sierra, Yosemite* (1871), by Thomas Hill. The museum's lobby and ballroom retain the original 19th-century woodwork, plaster moldings, and English tiles. ⊠ *216 O St.* ☎ *916/264–5423* ⊕ *www.crockerartmuseum.org* ⊠ *$6* ⊙ *Tues., Wed., and Fri.–Sun. 10–5, Thurs. 10–9.*

③ Discovery Museum History Center. The building that holds this child-oriented museum is a reproduction of the 1854 city hall and waterworks. Interactive history, science, and technology exhibits examine the evolution of everyday life in the Sacramento area. You can pan for gold, examine a Native American thatch hut, or experience the goings-on in the former print shop of the *Sacramento Bee*. The Gold Gallery displays nuggets and veins. ⊠ *101 I St.* ☎ *916/264–7057* ⊕ *www.thediscovery. org* ▱ *$5* ⊙ *July and Aug., daily 10–5; Sept.–June, Tues.–Sun. 10–5.*

⓭ Governor's Mansion. This 15-room house was built in 1877 and used by the state's chief executives from the early 1900s until 1967, when Ronald Reagan vacated it in favor of a newly built home in the more upscale suburbs. Many of the Italianate mansion's interior decorations were ordered from the Huntington, Hopkins & Co. hardware store, one of whose partners, Albert Gallatin, was the original occupant. Each of the seven marble fireplaces has a petticoat mirror that ladies strolled past to see if their slips were showing. The mansion is said to have been one of the first homes in California with an indoor bathroom. ⊠ *1526 H St.* ☎ *916/323–3047* ▱ *$4* ⊙ *Daily 10–5; tours hourly, last one at 4.*

❷ Huntington, Hopkins & Co. Store. This museum is a reproduction of the 1855 hardware store opened by Collis Huntington and Mark Hopkins, two of the Big Four businessmen who established the Central Pacific Railroad. Picks, shovels, gold pans, and other paraphernalia used by miners during the gold rush are on display, along with household hardware and appliances from the 1880s. Some items, such as blue enamelware, wooden toys, gold pans, and oil lamps, are for sale. ⊠ *113 I St.* ☎ *916/ 323–7234* ▱ *Free* ⊙ *Hrs vary.*

⓬ Leland Stanford Mansion. After a 14-year, $22 million renovation, the home of Leland Stanford has reopened as a state historic park. The museum's attractions are both the 19th-century paintings it houses, and the home's general craftsmanship, both indoors and out. Stanford, a railroad baron, California governor, and U.S. senator, had this home built in 1856, with additions in 1862 and the early 1870s. ⊠ *802 N St.* ☎ *916/324–0575* ▱ *$8* ⊙ *Tours daily 10–4; doors close at 5.*

⟳ ❺ Old Sacramento Schoolhouse Museum. Sacramento's first school welcomed students in August 1849 and closed permanently four months later. Five years passed before another public school opened. Today it's a kid-friendly attraction that shows what one-room schoolhouses were like in the California Central Valley and foothills in the late 1800s. ⊠ *Front and L Sts.* ☎ *No phone* ▱ *Free* ⊙ *Mon.–Sat. 10–4, Sun. noon–4.*

❻ Old Sacramento Visitor Information Center. Obtain brochures about nearby attractions, check local restaurant menus, and get advice from the helpful staff here. ⊠ *1101 2nd St., at K St.* ☎ *916/442–7644* ⊕ *www. oldsacramento.com* ⊙ *Daily 10–5.*

★ ⟳ ⓮ Sutter's Fort. Sacramento's earliest Euro–American settlement was founded by German-born Swiss immigrant John Augustus Sutter in 1839. Audio speakers give information at each stop along a self-guided tour that includes a blacksmith's shop, bakery, prison, living quarters, and livestock areas. Costumed docents sometimes reenact fort life, demonstrating crafts, food preparation, and firearms maintenance. ⊠ *2701 L St.* ☎ *916/445–4422* ⊕ *www.parks.ca.gov* ▱ *$4* ⊙ *Daily 10–5.*

⟳ ❾ Towe Auto Museum. With more than 150 vintage automobiles on display, and exhibits ranging from the Hall of Technology to Dreams of Speed

15

and Dreams of Cool, this museum explores automotive history and car culture. A 1920s roadside café and garage exhibit re-creates the early days of motoring. Friendly docents are ready to explain everything. The gift shop sells vintage-car magazines, model kits, and other car-related items. ⊠ *2200 Front St., 1 block off Broadway* ☎ *916/442–6802* ⊕ *www.toweautomuseum.org* ☜ *$7* ☉ *Daily 10–5.*

Where to Stay & Eat

$$–$$$$ ✕ **The Firehouse.** Consistently rated by local publications as among the city's top 10 restaurants, this formal and historic restaurant has a full bar, courtyard seating (its signature attraction), and creative American cooking, such as antelope topped with a blueberry-and-walnut chutney. Visitors who can afford to treat themselves to a fine and leisurely meal can do no better in Old Sacramento. ⊠ *1112 2nd St.* ☎ *916/442–4772* ⊕ *www.firehouseoldsac.com* ▤ *AE, MC, V* ☉ *No lunch weekends.*

★ **$$–$$$** ✕ **Biba.** Owner Biba Caggiano is a nationally recognized authority on Italian cuisine who has appeared on Martha Stewart's TV show. The Capitol crowd flocks here for homemade ravioli, osso buco, grilled pork loin, and veal and rabbit specials. A pianist adds to the upscale ambience nightly. ⊠ *2801 Capitol Ave.* ☎ *916/455–2422* ⊕ *www.biba-restaurant.com* ☟ *Reservations essential* ▤ *AE, DC, MC, V* ☉ *Closed Sun. No lunch Sat.*

$$–$$$ ✕ **Rio City Café.** Contemporary and seasonal Mediterranean and Californian cuisine, and huge floor-to-ceiling windows and an outdoor deck overlooking the river are the attractions of this Old Sacramento restaurant, popular with locals and tourists alike. ⊠ *1110 Front St.* ☎ *916/442–8226* ⊕ *www.riocitycafe.com* ▤ *AE, D, DC, MC, V.*

★ **$$–$$$** ✕ **The Waterboy.** Rural French cooking and California cuisine are the culinary treasures at this upscale yet unfussy midtown restaurant, which features such distinct dishes as chicken potpie, veal sweetbreads, and beet salad. This is where top local restaurateurs go when they want a good meal. ⊠ *2000 Capitol Ave.* ☎ *916/498–9891* ⊕ *www.waterboyrestaurant.com* ▤ *AE, D, DC, MC, V* ☉ *Closed Mon. No lunch weekends.*

¢–$$$ ✕ **The Park Downtown.** Atmosphere is what it's all about at this complex of cutting-edge eateries across from Capitol Park. The upscale Mason's Restaurant specializes in seasonal California cuisine; Ma Jong's Asian Diner has less-expensive fare, some suitable for vegetarians; the indoor-outdoor Park Lounge is a super-modern bar and dance club; and the Park To Go puts a classy spin on breakfasts and lunches for people to take away. ⊠ *1116 15th St.* ☎ *916/492–1960* ⊕ *www.theparkdowntown.com* ▤ *AE, DC, MC, V.*

$–$$ ✕ **Tapa the World.** As the name implies, this cozy midtown bar and restaurant, serves tapas (small plates of meats, seafood, chicken, and veggies shared at the table). One of Sacramento's liveliest yet casual nightspots (it's open until midnight), Tapa presents live Flamenco and Spanish classical guitarists nightly. ⊠ *2115 J St.* ☎ *916/442–4353* ⊕ *www.tapatheworld.com* ▤ *AE, D, DC, MC, V.*

¢–$ ✕ **Ernesto's Mexican Food.** Customers wait up to an hour for a table on Friday and Saturday evenings at this popular midtown restaurant. Fresh ingredients are stressed in the wide selection of entrées, and the margaritas are especially refreshing. **Zocalo** (✉ 1801 Capitol Ave. ☎ 916/441–0303), launched in 2004 by Ernesto's ownership, has a striking indoor-outdoor atmosphere and is a popular launching spot for nights out on the town. Its menu differs slightly from Ernesto's. *✉ 16th and S Sts. ☎ 916/441–5850 ⊕ www.ernestomexicanfood.com ▭ AE, D, DC, MC, V.*

$$$–$$$$ ╳▦ **Sterling Hotel.** This gleaming-white Victorian mansion three blocks from the Capitol has rose-color guest rooms with handsome furniture, including four-poster or canopy beds. Bathrooms are tiled in Italian marble and have Jacuzzi tubs. Restaurant Chanterelle ($–$$$) serves contemporary continental cuisine in its candlelighted dining room and pleasant patio area. *✉ 1300 H St., 95814 ☎ 916/448–1300 or 800/365–7660 ⊟ 916/448–8066 ⊕ www.sterlinghotel.com ⤺ 17 rooms, 2 suites ⚐ Restaurant, room service, in-room data ports, bar, dry cleaning, business services, meeting room, parking (fee), no-smoking rooms ▭ AE, D, DC, MC, V.*

★ $$–$$$$ ▦ **Amber House Bed & Breakfast Inn.** This B&B near the Capitol encompasses two homes. The original house, the Poet's Refuge, is a Craftsman-style home with five bedrooms named for famous writers. The second is an 1897 Dutch colonial–revival home named Musician's Manor. Baths are tiled in Italian marble; some rooms have skylights, fireplaces, patios, and two-person spa tubs, or a combination of some of those features. *✉ 1315 22nd St., 95816 ☎ 916/444–8085 or 800/755–6526 ⊟ 916/552–6529 ⊕ www.amberhouse.com ⤺ 10 rooms ⚐ Cable TV, in-room VCRs, in-room data ports, Wi-Fi, concierge; no smoking ▭ AE, D, DC, MC, V ⦿| BP.*

★ $$–$$$$ ▦ **Hyatt Regency Sacramento.** With a marble-and-glass lobby and luxurious rooms, this hotel across from the Capitol and adjacent to the convention center is arguably Sacramento's finest. The multitiered, glass-dominated hotel has a striking Mediterranean design. The best rooms have Capitol Park views. The service and attention to detail are outstanding. Governor Schwarzenegger, whose family still resides in Southern California, camps out here several nights a week. *✉ 1209 L St., 95814 ☎ 916/443–1234 or 800/633–7313 ⊟ 916/321–3799 ⊕ www.hyatt.com ⤺ 500 rooms, 24 suites ⚐ 2 restaurants, pool, gym, hot tub, bar, dry cleaning, laundry service, concierge, business services, meeting room, car rental, parking (fee) ▭ AE, D, DC, MC, V.*

$–$$$$ ▦ **Radisson Hotel Sacramento.** Mediterranean-style two-story buildings cluster around a large artificial lake on an 18-acre landscaped site a few miles northeast of downtown. Rooms are enlivened with art-deco appointments and furnishings; many have a patio or balcony. The Radisson is more resortlike than other Sacramento-area hotels. *✉ 500 Leisure La., 95815 ☎ 916/922–2020 or 800/333–3333 ⊟ 916/649–9463 ⊕ www.radisson.com/sacramentoca ⤺ 307 rooms, 22 suites ⚐ 2 restaurants, room service, pool, lake, gym, outdoor hot tub, boating, bicycles, bar, convention center ▭ AE, D, DC, MC, V.*

$$–$$$ ▦ **Delta King.** This grand old riverboat, now permanently moored on Old Sacramento's waterfront, once transported passengers between Sacramento and San Francisco. Among many notable design elements

15

are its main staircase, mahogany paneling, and brass fittings. The best of the 43 staterooms, all no-smoking, are on the river side toward the back of the boat. The boat's theater stages high-quality productions. ⊠ *1000 Front St., 95814* ☎ *916/444–5464 or 800/825–5464* 🖷 *916/447–5959* ⊕ *www.deltaking.com* ⇗ *44 rooms* ♿ *Restaurant, lounge, theater, meeting room, parking (fee)* ☰ *AE, D, DC, MC, V* ⍵⍥ *CP.*

$–$$ ⊡ **Holiday Inn Capitol Plaza.** Despite its lack of charm, this high-rise hotel has modern rooms—renovated in 2005—and the best location for visiting Old Sacramento and the Downtown Plaza. It's also within walking distance of the Capitol. ⊠ *300 J St., 95814* ☎ *916/446–0100 or 800/465–4329* 🖷 *916/446–7371* ⊕ *www.holiday-inn.com* ⇗ *362 rooms, 4 suites* ♿ *Restaurant, minibars, cable TV, pool, gym, bar, shop, concierge floor, convention center, no-smoking rooms* ☰ *AE, DC, MC, V.*

¢ ⊡ **Sacramento International Hostel.** This 1885 Victorian mansion has a grand mahogany staircase, a stained-glass atrium, frescoed ceilings, and carved and tiled fireplaces. Dormitory rooms and bedrooms suitable for singles, couples, and families are available, as is a communal kitchen. ⊠ *925 H St., 95814* ☎ *916/443–1691 or 800/909–4776 Ext. 40* 🖷 *916/443–4763* ⊕ *www.norcalhostels.org* ⇗ *70 beds* ♿ *Kitchen; no room TVs* ☰ *MC, V.*

Nightlife & the Arts

Downtown Events Hotline (☎ 916/442–2500 ⊕ www.downtownsac.org) has recorded information about seasonal events in the downtown area.

Nightlife

The **Blue Cue** (⊠ 2730 O St. ☎ 916/442–7208), upstairs from the popular Mexican restaurant Centro, is an eclectic billiard lounge known for its large selection of single-malt scotches. The **Fox and Goose** (⊠ 1001 R St. ☎ 916/443–8825 ⊕ www.foxandgoose.com) is a casual pub with live music (including open-mike Monday), and is a big draw for weekend breakfasts. Traditional pub food (fish-and-chips, Cornish pasties) is served on weekday evenings from 5:30 to 9:30. **Harlow's** (⊠ 2708 J St. ☎ 916/441–4693 ⊕ www.harlows.com) draws a young crowd to its art-deco bar-nightclub for live music after 9. **Streets of London Pub** (⊠ 1804 J St. ☎ 916/498–1388) is a favorite among Anglophiles and stays open until 2 AM every night except Sunday, when it closes an hour earlier.

The Arts

Sacramento Community Center Theater (⊠ 13th and L Sts. ☎ 916/264–5181) holds concerts, Broadway shows, opera, and ballet. The **California Musical Theatre** (⊠ 1419 H St. ☎ 916/557–1999) presents Broadway shows at the Sacramento Community Center Theater and in the huge Music Circus "tent" (now a permanent, thankfully air-conditioned structure) in summer. If you want the really *big* picture, the **Esquire Theater** (⊠ 1211 K St. ☎ 916/443–4629) screens IMAX movies. For art films, visit the funky **Tower Theater** (⊠ 2508 Land Park Dr. ☎ 916/442–4700 ⊕ www.thetowertheatre.com), a few minutes southeast of downtown. The **Crest Theatre** (⊠ 1013 K St. ☎ 916/442–7378 ⊕ www.thecrest.com) is another place to see art films.

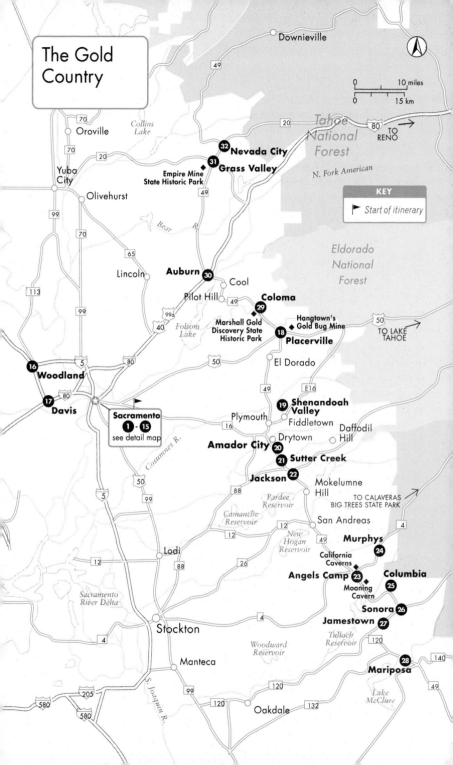

The Gold Country

KEY
▶ *Start of itinerary*

Downieville

Oroville

Yuba City

Olivehurst

Collins Lake

Nevada City 32

Grass Valley 31
Empire Mine
State Historic Park

Tahoe National Forest

TO RENO

N. Fork American

Lincoln

Auburn 30

Cool

Pilot Hill

Bear R.

Folsom Lake

Coloma 29
Marshall Gold
Discovery State
Historic Park

Hangtown's
Gold Bug Mine

Placerville 18

Eldorado National Forest

TO LAKE TAHOE

El Dorado

Woodland 16

Davis 17

Sacramento 1 - 15
see detail map

Shenandoah Valley 19
Fiddletown

Plymouth

Drytown

Daffodil Hill

Amador City 20

Sutter Creek 21

Jackson 22

Mokelumne Hill

Costumnes R.

Pardee Reservoir

Camanche Reservoir

San Andreas

TO CALAVERAS
BIG TREES STATE PARK

New Hogan Reservoir

Lodi

Murphys 24

California Caverns

Angels Camp 23

Moaning Cavern

Columbia 25

Sacramento River Delta

Stockton

Woodward Reservoir

Sonora 26

Jamestown 27

Tulloch Reservoir

Manteca

Mariposa 28

Lake McClure

Oakdale

Shopping

Top local artists and craftspeople exhibit their works at **Artists' Collaborative Gallery** (⊠ 910 15th St. ☎ 916/444–3764). The **Elder Craftsman** (⊠ 130 J St. ☎ 916/264–7762) specializes in items made by local senior citizens. **Gallery of the American West** (⊠ 121 K St. ☎ 916/446–6662) has a large selection of Native American arts and crafts. **Arden Fair Mall** (⊠ Off I–80, northeast of downtown) is Sacramento's largest shopping center. The **Downtown Plaza** and the K Street Mall that leads into it have many shops and restaurants, as well as an outdoor ice-skating rink in winter. Be advised that there are many panhandlers on the prowl along this struggling stretch of downtown.

Woodland

16 *20 mi northwest of Sacramento on I–5.*

Woodland's downtown lies frozen in a quaint and genteel past. In its heyday it was one of the wealthiest cities in California, established in 1861 by gold seekers and entrepreneurs. Once the boom was over, attention turned to the rich surrounding land, and the area became an agricultural gold mine. The legacy of the old land barons lives on in the Victorian homes that line Woodland's wide streets. Many of the houses have been restored and are surrounded by lavish gardens.

More than 300 touring companies, including John Philip Sousa's marching band, and Frank Kirk, the Acrobatic Tramp, appeared at the **Woodland Opera House,** built in 1885 (and rebuilt after it burned in 1892). Now restored, the building is the site of concerts and, September through July, a season of musical theater. Free weekly guided tours reveal old-fashioned stage technology. ⊠ *Main and 2nd Sts.* ☎ *530/666–9617* ⊕ *www.wohtheatre.org* ⊙ *Weekdays 10–5, weekends noon–5, tours Tues. 1–4.*

This 10-room classical-revival home of settler William Byas Gibson was purchased by volunteers and restored as the **Yolo County Historical Museum.** You can see collections of furnishings and artifacts from the 1850s to 1930s. Old trees and an impressive lawn cover the 2½-acre site off Highway 113. ⊠ *512 Gibson Rd.* ☎ *530/666–1045* ⊕ *www.yolo.net/ychm/index.html* 🎫 *$2* ⊙ *Mon. and Tues. 10–4, weekends noon–4.*

Old trucks and farm machinery seem to rumble to life within the shed-like **Heidrick Ag History Center,** where you can see the world's largest collection of antique agricultural equipment. Also here are multimedia exhibits and a gift shop. ⊠ *1962 Hays La.* ☎ *530/666–9700* 🖷 *530/666–9712* ⊕ *www.aghistory.org* 🎫 *$7* ⊙ *Weekdays 10–5, Sat. 10–6, Sun. 10–4.*

Where to Stay & Eat

$$–$$$ ✕ **Morrison's Upstairs.** The Victorian building that houses this restaurant is registered as a State Historic Landmark. Downstairs is a bar, deli, and patio. The top floor, once the attic, is full of nooks and alcoves where you can have your meal. Furnished throughout with polished wood tables that suit the style of the house, Morrison's serves burgers and sandwiches, scampi, Chinese chicken salad, pasta, prime rib, and vegetarian selections. ⊠ *428½ 1st St.* ☎ *530/666–6176* ▤ *AE, D, DC, MC, V.*

$–$$$ ✕ **Tazzina Bistro.** Chef Rebecca Reichardt is attracting regional attention for her creative spin on California cuisine, using French and Creole influences. Seasonal offerings are emphasized, such as roasted beet salad in the spring. ⊠ *614 Main St.* ☎ *530/661–1700* ⊕ *www.tazzinabistro. com* ▤ *AE, MC, V* ☺ *No dinner Sun.*

Davis

🔟 *10 mi west of Sacramento on I–80.*

Though it began as—and still is—a rich agricultural area, Davis doesn't feel like a cow town. It's home to the University of California at Davis, whose students hang at the cafés and bookstores in the central business district, making the city feel a little more cosmopolitan. The city has long enjoyed a progressive, liberal reputation (it's been called "the People's Republic of Davis"), but a rash of new yuppie-stocked subdivisions reflect how Davis is becoming more of a mainstream commuter community, whether residents admit it or not.

The center of action in town is the **Davis Campus of the University of California,** which ranks among the top 25 research universities in the United States. You can take tours of the campus, which depart from Buehler Alumni and Visitors Center. The **Mondavi Center for the Performing Arts,** a strikingly modern glass structure off Interstate 80, offers a busy and varied schedule of performances. ⊠ *1 Shields Ave.* ☎ *530/752–8111* ⊕ *www.ucdavis.edu* ☺ *Tours weekends at 11:30, weekdays by appointment.*

The work by northern California craftspeople displayed at the **Artery,** an artists' cooperative, includes decorative and functional ceramics, glass, wood, jewelry, fiber arts, painting, sculpture, drawing, and photography. ⊠ *207 G St.* ☎ *530/758–8330* ⊕ *www.arteryart.com* ☺ *Mon.–Thurs. and Sat. 10–6, Fri. 10–9, Sun. noon–5.*

Where to Stay & Eat

$–$$$ ✕ **Soga's.** Watercolors by local artists hang on the walls of this elegant restaurant. The California-style menu features various presentations of salmon fillet, swordfish, and veal and also offers vegetable plates. You can eat on the long, covered patio in good weather. ⊠ *217 E St.* ☎ *530/ 757–1733* ⊕ *www.sogasrestaurant.com* ⌂ *Reservations essential* ▤ *AE, D, MC, V* ☺ *Closed Sun. No lunch weekends.*

$–$$ ✕ **Bistro 33.** Sacramento brothers Fred and Matt Haines' latest enterprise has struck a chord with Davis diners, doing great business well into the evenings. Wood-fired pizza and a small but diverse selection of entrées draw big crowds for lunch and dinner in a newly renovated building that has a large, attractively arranged courtyard. Brunch is served on Sunday. ⊠ *226 F St.* ☎ *530/756–4556* ⊕ *www.bistro33.com* ▤ *AE, MC, V.*

$–$$ 🏨 **Aggie Inn.** This hotel, less than a block from the campus, is named for the University of California at Davis "Aggies," the school's team name.

Rooms are clean and basic; convenience is what this place is about. ✉ *245 1st St., 95616* 🕿 *530/756–0352* 🖷 *530/753–5738* ⊕ *www.stayanight. com* 🛏 *25 rooms, 9 suites* ♨ *Some in-room hot tubs, some kitchenettes, outdoor hot tub, sauna, laundry service* ▤ *AE, D, DC, MC, V* ⅋ *CP.*

$–$$ ⊞ **Hallmark Inn.** Two buildings with clean, modern rooms make up this inn, which is five blocks from the University of California campus and is next door to a restaurant. ✉ *110 F St., 95616* 🕿 *530/758–8623 or 800/753–0035* ⊕ *www.hallmarkinn.com* 🛏 *135 rooms* ♨ *Restaurant, some refrigerators, pool, free parking, some no-smoking rooms* ▤ *AE, D, DC, MC, V.*

THE GOLD COUNTRY—SOUTH
HIGHWAY 49 FROM PLACERVILLE TO MARIPOSA

South of its junction with U.S. 50, Highway 49 traces in asphalt the famed Mother Lode. The sleepy former gold-rush towns strung along the road have for the most part been restored and made presentable to visitors with an interest in one of the most frenzied episodes of American history.

Placerville

⑱   *10 mi south of Coloma on Hwy. 49; 44 mi east of Sacramento on U.S. 50.*

It's hard to imagine now, but in 1849 about 4,000 miners staked out every gully and hillside in Placerville, turning the town into a rip-roaring camp of log cabins, tents, and clapboard houses. The area was then known as Hangtown, a graphic allusion to the nature of frontier justice. It took on the name Placerville in 1854 and became an important supply center for the miners. Mark Hopkins, Philip Armour, and John Studebaker were among the industrialists who got their starts here.

★ ☾   Hangtown's Gold Bug Park & Mine, owned by the City of Placerville, centers on a fully lighted mine shaft open for self-guided touring. ■ TIP➡ **The self-guided audio tour is well worth the expense ($1).** A shaded stream runs through the park, and there are picnic facilities. ✉ *North on Bedford Ave., 1 mi off U.S. 50* 🕿 *530/642–5207* ⊕ *www.goldbugpark.org* 🎟 *$4* ⊙ *Tours mid-Apr.–Oct., daily 10–4; Nov.–mid-Apr., weekends noon–4. Gift shop Mar.–Nov., daily 10–4.*

OFF THE BEATEN PATH	**APPLE HILL –** Roadside stands sell fresh produce from more than 50 family farms in this area. During the fall harvest season (from September through December), members of the Apple Hill Growers Association open their orchards and vineyards for apple and berry picking, picnicking, and wine and cider tasting. Many sell baked items and picnic food. ✉ *About 5 mi east of Hwy. 49; take Camino exit from U.S. 50* 🕿 *530/ 644–7692.*

Where to Stay & Eat

$$–$$$$ ✕ **Café Luna.** Tucked into the back of the Creekside Place shopping complex is a small restaurant with about 30 seats inside, plus outdoor tables overlooking a creek. The menu, which changes weekly, encompasses many cuisines, including Indian and Thai. ⊠ *451 Main St.* ☎ *530/642–8669* ⊟ *AE, D, MC, V* ☉ *Closed Mon. and Tues.*

★ **$$–$$$** ✕ **Zachary Jacques.** A few miles south of town, this country French restaurant is worth the extra drive. Appetizers on the seasonal menu might include escargots or mushrooms prepared in several ways, roasted garlic with olive oil served on toast, or spicy lamb sausage. Standard entrées include roast rack of lamb, beef stew, and scallops and shrimp in lime butter. The attached wine bar opens at 4:30. ⊠ *1821 Pleasant Valley Rd., 3 mi east of Diamond Springs* ☎ *530/626–8045* ⊟ *AE, MC, V* ☉ *Closed Mon. and Tues. No lunch.*

¢–$ ✕ **The Cozmic Cafe.** Crowds convene here at any time of day for healthful meals. Portions are big, prices are low, and the ambience is among the most distinctive in Placerville. The eatery is in the 1859 Pearson's Soda Works Building, and extends back into the side of a mountain, into what used to be a mineshaft. ⊠ *594 Main St.* ☎ *530/642–8481* ⊕ *www.thecozmiccafe.com* ⊟ *MC, V.*

$$–$$$ ⌂ **Seasons Bed & Breakfast.** A 10-minute walk from downtown, one of Placerville's oldest homes has been transformed into a lovely and relaxing oasis. The main house, cottages, and gardens are filled with paintings and sculptures. Privacy is treasured here. A suite with a sitting room and stained-glass windows occupies the main house's top floor. One cottage has a little white-picket fence around its own minigarden; another has a two-person shower. ⊠ *2934 Bedford Ave., 95667* ☎ *530/626–4420* ⊕ *www.theseasons.net* ⤳ *3 rooms, 1 suite* ♿ *No-smoking rooms* ⊟ *MC, V* ⎮◎⎮ *BP.*

$–$$ ⌂ **Best Western Placerville Inn.** This motel's serviceable rooms are decorated in the chain's trademark pastels. The pool comes in handy during hot summer months. ⊠ *6850 Green Leaf Dr., near Missouri Flats exit of U.S. 50, 95667* ☎ *530/622–9100 or 800/854–9100* 🖷 *530/622–9376* ⊕ *www.bestwestern.com* ⤳ *105 rooms* ♿ *Cable TV, pool, free parking* ⊟ *AE, D, DC, MC, V.*

Shenandoah Valley

⓳ *20 mi south of Placerville on Shenandoah Rd., east of Hwy. 49.*

The most concentrated Gold Country wine-touring area lies in the hills of the Shenandoah Valley, east of Plymouth. ■ TIP→ **This region is gaining steam as a less-congested alternative to overrun Napa Valley.** Robust Zinfandel is the primary grape grown here, but vineyards also produce other varietals. Most wineries are open on weekend afternoons; several have shaded picnic areas, gift shops, and galleries or museums; all have tasting rooms.

Sobon Estate (⊠ 14430 Shenandoah Rd. ☎ 209/245–6554) operates the Shenandoah Valley Museum, illustrating pioneer life and wine making in the valley. It's open daily from 9:30 to 5. At **Charles Spinetta Winery** (⊠ 12557 Steiner Rd., Plymouth ☎ 209/245–3384 ⊕ www.charlesspinettawinery.com ☉ Mon., Thurs., and Fri. 8–4, weekends 9–5), you can see a wildlife art gallery in addition to tasting the wine.

The gallery at **Shenandoah Vineyards** (✉ 12300 Steiner Rd., Plymouth ☎ 209/245–4455 ☉ Daily 10–5) displays contemporary art, and sells pottery, framed photographs, and souvenirs.

Where to Stay

$$ ▣ **Amador Harvest Inn.** This B&B adjacent to the Deaver Vineyards tasting room occupies a bucolic lakeside spot in the Shenandoah Valley. A contemporary Cape Cod–style structure has homey guest rooms with private baths. Public areas include a living room with fireplace and a music room with a view of the lake. ✉ *12455 Steiner Rd., Plymouth 95669* ☎ *209/245–5512 or 800/217–2304* ▤ *209/245–5250* ⊕ *www.amadorharvestinn.com* ᐅ *4 rooms* ♿ *No room TVs* ▤ *AE, MC, V* ◯ *BP.*

Amador City

⓴ *6 mi south of Plymouth on Hwy. 49.*

The history of tiny Amador City mirrors the boom-bust-boom cycle of many Gold Country towns. With an output of $42 million in gold, its Keystone Mine was one of the most productive in the Mother Lode. After all the gold was extracted, the miners cleared out, and the area suffered. Amador City now derives its wealth from tourists, who come to browse through its antiques and specialty shops, many of them on or just off Highway 49.

Where to Stay & Eat

★ $-$$ ✕▣ **Imperial Hotel.** The whimsically decorated mock-Victorian rooms at this 1879 hotel give a modern twist to the excesses of the era. Antique furnishings include iron-and-brass beds, gingerbread flourishes, and, in one room, art-deco appointments. The two front rooms, which can be noisy, have balconies. The menu at the hotel's fine restaurant ($$$–$$$$) changes quarterly and ranges from country hearty to contemporary eclectic. You can eat in the bright dining room or on the patio, but not on Monday or Tuesday and for lunch only on weekends, when the hotel has a two-night minimum stay. ✉ *Hwy. 49, 95601* ☎ *209/267–9172* ▤ *209/267–9249* ⊕ *www.imperialamador.com* ᐅ *6 rooms* ♿ *Restaurant, bar* ▤ *AE, D, DC, MC, V* ◯ *BP.*

Sutter Creek

★ ⓞ *2 mi south of Amador City on Hwy. 49.*

Sutter Creek is a charming conglomeration of balconied buildings, Victorian homes, and neo–New England structures. The stores along Highway 49 (called Main Street in the town proper) are worth visiting for works by the many local artists and craftspeople. Seek out the **J. Monteverde General Store** (✉ 3 Randolph St.), a typical turn-of-the-20th-century emporium with vintage goods on display (but not for sale), an elaborate antique scale, and a chair-encircled potbellied stove in the corner. Open only weekends 10–3, it closes in January. You can stop by the **Sutter Creek Visitor Center** (✉ 11A Randolph St. ☎ 209/267–1344 or 800/400–0305 ⊕ www.suttercreek.org), also open weekends 10 to 3, for information.

OFF THE BEATEN PATH

DAFFODIL HILL – Each spring a 4-acre hillside east of Sutter Creek erupts in a riot of yellow and gold as 300,000 daffodils burst into bloom. The garden is the work of members of the McLaughlin family, which has owned this site since 1887. Daffodil plantings began in the 1930s. The display usually takes place between mid-March and mid-April. ⊠ *From Main St., Hwy. 49, in Sutter Creek, take Shake Ridge Rd. east 13 mi* ☎ *209/296–7048* ⊕ *www.amadorcountychamber.com* ⊠ *Free* ⊙ *Mid-Mar.–mid-Apr., daily 9–5.*

Where to Stay & Eat

$$–$$$ ✕ **Caffe Via d'Oro.** Tables can be hard to secure at this upscale restaurant, where short ribs, grilled duck breast and pan-seared rainbow trout—all accompanied by seasonal vegetables—are highly recommended by the loyal local patrons. The brick structure dates from the 1860s. ⊠ *36 Main St.* ☎ *209/267–0535* ⊕ *www.caffeviadoro.com* ⊟ *AE, D, MC, V* ⊙ *Closed Mon.–Wed. No lunch.*

¢–$ ✕ **Chatterbox Café.** This classic 1940s luncheonette has only 5 tables and 14 counter stools. Read a vintage newspaper or examine the jazz instruments and Disney memorabilia on the shelves while you wait for your chicken-fried steak, burger, homemade pie, or hot-fudge sundae. The menu is as big as the Chatterbox is small. Beer and wine are available. ⊠ *39 Main St.* ☎ *209/267–5935* ⊟ *AE, D, MC, V* ⊙ *No dinner Wed.–Mon.*

★ **$$–$$$$** ▦ **The Foxes Inn of Sutter Creek.** The rooms in this 1857 white-clapboard house are handsome, with high ceilings, antique beds, and armoires. Five have gas fireplaces. Breakfast is cooked to order and delivered on a silver service to your room or to the gazebo in the garden. ⊠ *77 Main St., 95685* ☎ *209/267–5882 or 800/987–3344* ⊟ *209/267–0712* ⊕ *www.foxesinn.com* ⊶ *5 rooms, 2 suites* ⚘ *Some cable TV, some in-room VCRs; no smoking* ⊟ *D, MC, V* ▯⊙▮ *BP.*

$$ ▦ **Eureka Street Inn.** Original redwood paneling, wainscoting, beams, and cabinets as well as lead- and stained-glass windows lend the Eureka Street Inn a certain coziness. The Craftsman-style bungalow was built in 1914 as a family home. Most rooms have gas-log fireplaces, and wireless Internet is available. ⊠ *55 Eureka St., 95685* ☎ *209/267–5500 or 800/399–2389* ⊕ *www.eurekastreetinn.com* ⊶ *4 rooms* ⚘ *Wi-Fi; no room TVs* ⊟ *AE, D, MC, V* ▯⊙▮ *BP.*

¢–$ ▦ **Sutter Creek Days Inn.** If you're touring the Gold Country on a budget, this hotel is a good choice. The rooms contain coffeemakers, and most have queen-size beds; four rooms are wheelchair accessible. ⊠ *271 Hanford St., 95685* ☎ *209/267–9177* ⊟ *209/267–5303* ⊶ *52 rooms* ⚘ *Cable TV* ⊟ *D, MC, V* ▯⊙▮ *CP.*

Jackson

❷ *8 mi south of Sutter Creek on Hwy. 49.*

Jackson wasn't the Gold Country's rowdiest town, but the party lasted longer here than most anywhere else: "girls' dormitories" (brothels) and nickel slot machines flourished until the mid-1950s. Jackson also had the world's deepest and richest gold mines, the Kennedy and the Arg-

15

onaut, which together produced $70 million in gold. These were deep-rock mines with tunnels extending as much as a mile underground. Most of the miners who worked the lode were of Serbian or Italian origin, and they gave the town a European character that persists to this day. Jackson has pioneer cemeteries whose headstones tell the stories of local Serbian and Italian families. The terraced cemetery on the grounds of the handsome **St. Sava Serbian Orthodox Church** (⊠ 724 N. Main St.) is the most impressive of the town's burial grounds.

The heart of Jackson's historic section is the **National Hotel** (⊠ 2 Water St. ☎ 209/233–0500), which operates an old-time saloon in the lobby. The hotel is especially active on weekends, when people come from miles around to participate in Saturday-night sing-alongs.

The **Amador County Museum,** built in the late 1850s as a private home, provides a colorful take on gold-rush life. Displays include a kitchen with a woodstove, the Amador County bicentennial quilt, and a classroom. A time line recounts the county's checkered past. The museum conducts hourly tours of large-scale working models of the nearby Kennedy Mine. ⊠ 225 Church St. ☎ 209/223–6386 ⊠ Museum free; mine tours $1 ☉ Wed.–Sun. 10–4.

Where to Stay & Eat

¢–$ ✕ **Rosebud's Classic Café.** Art-deco accents and music from the 1930s and 1940s set the mood at this homey café. Charbroiled burgers, freshly baked pies, and espresso coffees round out the lunch menu. Omelets, hotcakes, and many other items are served for breakfast. ⊠ 26 Main St. ☎ 209/223–1035 ⊟ MC, V ☉ Closed Tues. No dinner.

$ ⊡ **Best Western Amador Inn.** Convenience and price are the main attractions of this two-story motel just off the highway. Many rooms have gas fireplaces. If you want an in-room refrigerator and microwave, you'll need to pay $5 extra. ⊠ 200 S. Hwy. 49, 95642 ☎ 209/223–0211 or 800/543–5221 ⊞ 209/223–4836 ⊕ www. bestwestern.com ⋑ 118 rooms ⚲ Restaurant, pool, laundry service ⊟ AE, D, DC, MC, V.

Angels Camp

㉓ 20 mi south of Jackson on Hwy. 49.

Angels Camp is famed chiefly for its May jumping-frog contest, based on Mark Twain's short story "The Celebrated Jumping Frog of Calaveras County." The writer reputedly heard the story of the jumping frog from Ross Coon, proprietor of Angels Hotel, which has been in operation since 1856.

Angels Camp Museum houses gold-rush relics, including photos, rocks, petrified wood, old blacksmith and mining equipment, and a horse-drawn hearse. The carriage house out back holds 31 carriages and an impressive display of mineral specimens. ⊠ 753 S. Main St. ☎ 209/736–2963 ⊠ $2 ☉ Jan. and Feb., weekends 10–3; Mar.–Dec., daily 10–3.

OFF THE BEATEN PATH

CALIFORNIA CAVERN – A ½-mi subterranean trail winds through large chambers and past underground streams and lakes. There aren't many steps to climb, but it's a strenuous walk with some narrow passageways and steep spots. The caverns, at a constant 53°F, contain crystalline formations not found elsewhere, and the 80-minute guided tour explains local history and geology. ⊠ *9 mi east of San Andreas on Mountain Ranch Rd., then about 3 mi on Cave City Rd., follow signs* ☎ *209/736–2708* ⊕ *www.caverntours.com* ☒ *$12.50* ☉ *Daily 10–4.*

MOANING CAVERN – A 235-step spiral staircase leads into this vast cavern. More adventurous sorts can rappel into the chamber—ropes and instruction are provided. Otherwise, the only way inside is via the 45-minute tour, during which you'll see giant (and still growing) stalactites and stalagmites and an archaeological site that holds some of the oldest human remains yet found in America (an unlucky person has fallen into the cavern about once every 130 years for the last 13,000 years). ⊠ *Parrots Ferry Rd., 2 mi south of Vallecito, off Hwy. 4 east of Angels Camp* ☎ *209/736–2708* ⊕ *www.caverntours.com* ☒ *$12.50* ☉ *May–Oct., daily 9–6; Nov.–Apr., weekdays 10–5, weekends 9–5.*

Murphys

㉔ *10 mi northeast of Angels Camp on Hwy. 4.*

Murphys is a well-preserved town of white-picket fences, Victorian houses, and interesting shops that is drawing more and more attention as a Gold Country gem. Horatio Alger and Ulysses S. Grant came through here, staying at Murphys Historic Hotel & Lodge when they, along with many other 19th-century visitors, came to see the giant sequoia groves in nearby Calaveras Big Trees State Park.

The **Kautz Ironstone Winery and Caverns** is ■ TIP→ **worth a visit even if you don't drink wine. Tours take you into underground tunnels cooled by a waterfall from a natural spring and include a performance on a massive automated pipe organ.** The winery schedules concerts during spring and summer in its huge outdoor amphitheater, plus art shows and other events on weekends. On display is a 44-pound specimen of crystalline gold. Visit the deli for lunch. ⊠ *1894 6 Mile Rd.* ☎ *209/728–1251* ⊕ *www. ironstonevineyards.com* ☉ *Daily 10–5; open until 6 in summer.*

OFF THE BEATEN PATH

CALAVERAS BIG TREES STATE PARK – This state park protects hundreds of the largest and rarest living things on the planet—magnificent giant sequoia redwood trees. Some are 3,000 years old, 90 feet around at the base, and 250 feet tall. The park's self-guided walks range from a 200-yard trail to 1-mi and 5-mi (closed in winter) loops through the groves. There are campgrounds and picnic areas; swimming, wading, fishing, and sunbathing on the Stanislaus River are popular in summer. ⊠ *Off Hwy. 4, 15 mi northeast of Murphys, 4 mi northeast of Arnold* ☎ *209/ 795–2334* ☒ *$6 per vehicle, day-use; campsites $20* ☉ *Park daily sunrise–sunset, day-use; visitor center May–Oct., daily 10–4; Nov.–Apr., weekends 11–3.*

15

Where to Stay & Eat

¢–$$$ ✕ **Grounds.** Light Italian entrées, grilled vegetables, chicken, seafood, and steak are the specialties at this bistro and coffee shop. Sandwiches, salads, and homemade soups are served for lunch. The crowd is friendly and the service attentive. ⊠ *402 Main St.* ☎ *209/728–8663* ▤ *MC, V* ☾ *No dinner Mon. and Tues.*

★ $$$–$$$$ ▦ **Dunbar House 1880.** The oversize rooms in this elaborate Italianate-style home have brass beds, down comforters, gas-burning stoves, and claw-foot tubs. Broad wraparound verandas encourage lounging, as do the colorful gardens and large elm trees. The Cedar Room's sun porch has a two-person whirlpool tub, and the Sequoia Room has a two-person whirlpool spa and shower. In the afternoon you are treated to trays of appetizers and wine in your room. ⊠ *271 Jones St., 95247* ☎ *209/728–2897 or 800/692–6006* 🖷 *209/728–1451* ⊕ *www.dunbarhouse. com* ➦ *3 rooms, 2 suites* ♨ *Refrigerators, in-room DVDs* ▤ *AE, MC, V* ⊺◉⊺ *BP.*

¢–$ ▦ **Murphys Historic Hotel & Lodge.** This 1855 stone hotel, whose register has seen the signatures of Mark Twain and the bandit Black Bart, figured in Bret Harte's short story "A Night at Wingdam." Accommodations are in the hotel and a modern motel-style addition. The older rooms are furnished with antiques, many of them large and hand carved. The hotel has a convivial old-time restaurant ($–$$$) and saloon, which can be noisy into the wee hours. ⊠ *457 Main St., 95247* ☎ *209/728–3444 or 800/532–7684* 🖷 *209/728–1590* ⊕ *www.murphyshotel.com* ➦ *29 rooms, 20 with bath* ♨ *Meeting room* ▤ *AE, D, DC, MC, V.*

Columbia

㉕ *14 mi south of Angels Camp via Hwy. 49 to Parrots Ferry Rd.*

Columbia is the gateway for Columbia State Historic Park, which is one of the Gold Country's most visited sites.

☾ **Columbia State Historic Park,** known as the Gem of the Southern Mines,
Fodor'sChoice comes as close to a gold-rush town in its heyday as any site in the Gold
★ Country. You can ride a stagecoach, pan for gold, and watch a blacksmith working at an anvil. Street musicians perform in summer. Restored or reconstructed buildings include a Wells Fargo Express office, a Masonic temple, stores, saloons, two hotels, a firehouse, churches, a school, and a newspaper office. All are staffed to simulate a working 1850s town. The park also includes the **Historic Fallon House Theater,** where a full schedule of entertainment is presented. ⊠ *11175 Washington St.* ☎ *209/532–0150* ⊕ *www.parks.ca.gov* 🎫 *Free* ☾ *Daily 9–5.*

Where to Stay & Eat

$–$$ ✕▦ **City Hotel.** The rooms in this restored 1856 hostelry are furnished with period antiques. Two have balconies overlooking Main Street, and six rooms open onto a second-floor parlor. All the accommodations have private half baths, with showers nearby; robes and slippers are provided. The restaurant ($–$$$; closed Monday), one of the Gold Country's best, serves French-accented California cuisine complemented by a large selection of the state's respected wines. The What Cheer Saloon is right out of a western movie. Combined lodging, dinner, and theater packages are available. ⊠ *22768 Main St., 95310* ☎ *209/532–1479 or 800/ 532–1479* 🖶 *209/532–7027* ⊕ *www.cityhotel.com* 🛏 *10 rooms* ♨ *Restaurant, bar* ⊟ *AE, D, MC, V* ⫾⊙⫾ *CP.*

¢–$$ ☷ **Fallon Hotel.** Restored by the State of California, this 1857 hotel features rooms with antiques and private half baths. (There are separate men's and women's showers.) If you occupy one of the five balcony rooms, you can sit outside with your morning coffee and watch the town wake up. ⊠ *11175 Washington St., 95310* ☎ *209/532–1470* 🖶 *209/532–7027* ⊕ *www.cityhotel.com* 🛏 *14 rooms* ♨ *No room TVs* ⊟ *AE, D, MC, V* ⫾⊙⫾ *CP.*

The Arts

Sierra Repertory Theater Company (☎ 209/532–4644) presents a full season of dramas, comedies, and musicals at the Historic Fallon House Theater and another venue in East Sonora.

15

Sonora

26 *4 mi south of Columbia via Parrots Ferry Rd. to Hwy. 49.*

Miners from Mexico founded Sonora and made it the biggest town in the Mother Lode. Following a period of racial and ethnic strife, the Mexican settlers moved on, and Yankees built the commercial city that is visible today. Sonora's historic downtown section sits atop the Big Bonanza Mine, one of the richest in the state. Another mine, on the site of nearby Sonora High School, yielded 990 pounds of gold in a single week in 1879. Reminders of the gold rush are everywhere in Sonora, in prim Victorian houses, typical Sierra-stone storefronts, and awning-shaded sidewalks. Reality intrudes beyond the town's historic heart, with strip malls, shopping centers, and modern motels.

The **Tuolumne County Museum and History Center** occupies a building that served as a jail until 1951. Restored to an earlier period, it houses a jail museum, vintage firearms and paraphernalia, a case with gold nuggets, a cute exhibit on soapbox derby racing in hilly Sonora, and the libraries of a historical society and a genealogical society. ⊠ *158 W. Bradford St.* ☎ *209/532–1317* ⊕ *www.tchistory.org/museum.html* 🎫 *Free* ⊙ *Daily 10–4.*

Where to Stay & Eat

$–$$ ✕ **Banny's Cafe.** Its pleasant environment and hearty yet refined dishes make Banny's a nice alternative to Sonora's noisier eateries. Try the grilled salmon fillet with scallion rice and ginger-wasabi-soy aioli. ⊠ *83 S. Stewart St.* ☎ *209/533–4709* ⊟ *D, MC, V* ⊙ *No lunch Sun.*

¢ ✕ **Garcia's Taqueria.** This casual, inexpensive eatery serves Mexican and southwestern fare. Vegetarians and vegans are also well served here— a place named after and decorated in the spirit of Grateful Dead legend Jerry Garcia. ⊠ *145 S. Washington St.* ☎ *209/588–1915* ⊟ *No credit cards* ⊙ *Closed Sun.*

$–$$$ ☷ **Barretta Gardens Bed and Breakfast Inn.** This inn is perfect for a romantic getaway. Its elegant Victorian rooms vary in size, but all are furnished with period pieces. The three antiques-filled parlors carry on the Victorian theme. A bakery on the property provides the fresh pastries at breakfast. ⊠ *700 S. Barretta St., 95370* ☎ *209/532–6039 or 800/ 206–3333* 🖷 *209/532–8257* ⊕ *www.barrettagardens.com* ⮎ *5 rooms* △ *Hot tub* ▤ *AE, MC, V* ⦿ *CP.*

$–$$ 🏨 **Best Western Sonora Oaks Motor Hotel.** The standard motel-issue rooms at this East Sonora establishment are clean and roomy; the larger ones have outdoor sitting areas. Suites have fireplaces, whirlpool tubs, and tranquil hillside views. Because the motel is right off Highway 108, the front rooms can be noisy. ⊠ *19551 Hess Ave., 95370* ☎ *209/533– 4400 or 800/532–1944* 🖷 *209/532–1964* ⊕ *www.bestwestern.com* ⮎ *96 rooms, 4 suites* △ *Restaurant, pool, outdoor hot tub, lounge, meeting room* ▤ *AE, D, DC, MC, V.*

Jamestown

㉗ *4 mi south of Sonora on Hwy. 49.*

Compact Jamestown supplies a touristy, superficial view of gold-rush-era life. Shops in brightly colored buildings along Main Street sell antiques and gift items.

The California State Railroad Museum operates **Railtown 1897** at what were the headquarters and general shops of the Sierra Railway from 1897 to 1955. The railroad has appeared in more than 200 movies and television productions, including *Petticoat Junction, The Virginian, High Noon,* and *Unforgiven.* You can view the roundhouse, an air-operated 60-foot turntable, shop rooms, and old locomotives and coaches. Six-mile, 40-minute steam train rides through the countryside operate on weekends during part of the year. ⊠ *5th Ave. and Reservoir Rd., off Hwy. 49* ☎ *209/984–3953* ⊕ *www.csrmf.org* 🖃 *Roundhouse tour $2; train ride $6* ⊘ *Daily 9:30–4:30. Train rides Apr.–Oct., weekends 11–3.*

Where to Stay & Eat

$$ ✕🏨 **National Hotel.** The National has been in business since 1859, and the furnishings—brass beds, regal comforters, and lace curtains—are authentic but not overly embellished. The saloon, which still has its original redwood bar, is a great place to linger. The popular restaurant ($–$$$) serves big lunches: hamburgers and fries, salads, and Italian entrées. More upscale continental cuisine is prepared for dinner (reservations essential). ⊠ *18183 Main St., 95327* ☎ *209/984–3446, 800/894– 3446 in CA* 🖷 *209/984–5620* ⊕ *www.national-hotel.com* ⮎ *9 rooms* △ *Restaurant, in-room VCRs, in-room data ports, bar* ▤ *AE, D, DC, MC, V* ⦿ *CP.*

$$ 🏨 **McCaffrey House Bed and Breakfast Inn.** Remoteness is one of McCaffrey's appeals—it's about 20 mi east of Jamestown on Highway 108 in the mountain community of Twain Harte. Its other draws are lovely furnishings and friendly innkeepers. Each room has a private bath, a black-iron fire stove, and bed quilts that were made in Pennsylvania Amish country. Coffee, tea and snacks are served in the afternoon. ⊠ *23251 Hwy. 108, 95383* ☎ *888/586–0757* 🖷 *209/586–3689* ⊕ *www. mccaffreyhouse.com* ⮎ *8 rooms* △ *Cable TV, in-room VCRs, Wi-Fi* ▤ *AE, MC, V* ⦿ *BP.*

Mariposa

28 *50 mi south of Jamestown on Hwy. 49.*

Mariposa marks the southern end of the Mother Lode. Much of the land in this area was part of a 44,000-acre land grant Colonel John C. Fremont acquired from Mexico before gold was discovered and California became a state.

At the **California State Mining and Mineral Museum,** a glittering 13-pound chunk of crystallized gold makes it clear what the rush was about. Displays include a reproduction of a typical tunnel dug by hard-rock miners, a miniature stamp mill, and a panning and sluicing exhibit. ⊠ *Mariposa County Fairgrounds, Hwy. 49* ☎ *209/742–7625* ⊠ *$3* ☉ *May–Sept., daily 10–6; Oct.–Apr., Wed.–Mon. 10–4.*

Where to Stay & Eat

$–$$$ ✕ **Charles Street Dinner House.** Ever since Ed Uebner moved here from Chicago to become the owner-chef in 1980, Charles Street has been firmly established as the classiest dinner joint in town—plus, it's centrally located. The extensive menu, which won't appeal to vegetarians, includes beef, chicken, pork, lamb, duck, and lobster. ⊠ *Hwy. 140 at 7th St.* ☎ *209/ 966–2366* ☰ *D, MC, V* ☉ *Closed Mon. and Tues. No lunch.*

$ ✕ **Castillo's Mexican Restaurant.** Tasty tacos, enchiladas, chiles rellenos (stuffed, batter-fried, mild chili peppers), and burrito combinations plus chimichangas, fajitas, steak, and seafood are served in a casual storefront a half-block off the main drag. ⊠ *4995 5th St.* ☎ *209/742–4413* ☰ *MC, V.*

$–$$ 🏨 **Little Valley Inn.** Pine paneling, historical photos, and old mining tools recall Mariposa's heritage at this modern B&B. A suite that sleeps five people includes a full kitchen. All rooms have private entrances, baths, and decks. The large grounds include a creek where you can pan for gold. ⊠ *3483 Brooks Rd., off Hwy. 49, 95338* ☎ *209/742–6204 or 800/ 889–5444* 🖷 *209/742–5099* ⊕ *www.littlevalley.com* 🛌 *4 rooms, 1 suite, 1 cabin* ⚏ *Refrigerators, horseshoes; no smoking* ☰ *AE, MC, V* ❢❍❢ *BP.*

¢–$ 🏨 **Mariposa Lodge.** Thoroughly modern and tastefully landscaped, the Mariposa is a solid option for those who want to stay within 30 mi of Yosemite National Park without spending a fortune. ⊠ *5052 Hwy. 140, 95338* ☎ *209/966–3607* ⊕ *www.mariposalodge.com* 🖷 *209/ 742–7038 or 800/966–8819* 🛌 *45 rooms* ⚏ *Pool, outdoor hot tub, no-smoking rooms* ☰ *AE, MC, V.*

THE GOLD COUNTRY—NORTH

HIGHWAY 49 FROM COLOMA TO NEVADA CITY

Highway 49 north of Placerville links the towns of Coloma, Auburn, Grass Valley, and Nevada City. Most are gentrified versions of once-rowdy mining camps, vestiges of which remain in roadside museums, old mining structures, and restored homes now serving as inns.

Coloma

㉙ *8 mi northwest of Placerville on Hwy. 49.*

The California gold rush started in Coloma. "My eye was caught with the glimpse of something shining in the bottom of the ditch," James Marshall recalled. Marshall himself never found any more "color," as gold came to be called.

★ Most of Coloma lies within **Marshall Gold Discovery State Historic Park.** Though crowded with tourists in summer, Coloma hardly resembles the mob scene it was in 1849, when 2,000 prospectors staked out claims along the streambed. The town's population grew to 4,000, supporting seven hotels, three banks, and many stores and businesses. But when reserves of the precious metal dwindled, prospectors left as quickly as they had come. A working reproduction of an 1840s mill lies near the spot where James Marshall first saw gold. A trail leads to a sign marking his discovery. ■ TIP➔ **The museum is not as interesting as the outdoor exhibits.** ⊠ *Hwy. 49* ☎ *530/622–3470* ⊕ *www.parks.ca.gov* ⊠ *$5 per vehicle, day-use* ⊘ *Park daily 8 AM–sunset. Museum daily 10–3.*

Where to Stay

$–$$$$ 🏠 **Coloma Country Inn.** Four of the rooms at this B&B on 2½ acres in the state historic park are inside a restored 1852 Victorian. Two suites, with kitchenettes, are in the carriage house. Appointments include antique double and queen-size beds, handmade quilts, stenciled friezes, and fresh flowers. The owners can direct you to tour operators leading rafting trips on the American River. ⊠ *345 High St., 95613* ☎ *530/622–6919* 🖷 *530/622–1795* ⊕ *www.colomacountryinn.com* ⇴ *4 rooms, 2 suites* ⚭ *Kitchenette* ⊟ *No credit cards* ⊠| *BP.*

Auburn

▶ **㉚** *18 mi northwest of Coloma on Hwy. 49; 34 mi northeast of Sacramento on I–80.*

Auburn is the Gold Country town most accessible to travelers on Interstate 80. An important transportation center during the gold rush, Auburn has a small Old Town district with narrow climbing streets, cobblestone lanes, wooden sidewalks, and many original buildings. ■ TIP➔ **Fresh produce, flowers, baked goods, and gifts are for sale at the farmers' market, held Saturday morning year-round.**

Auburn's standout structure is the **Placer County Courthouse.** The classic gold-dome building houses the Placer County Museum, which documents the area's history—Native American, railroad, agricultural, and mining—from the early 1700s to 1900. ⊠ *101 Maple St.* ☎ *530/889–6500* ⊠ *Free* ⊘ *Daily 10–4.*

The **Bernhard Museum Complex,** whose centerpiece is the former Traveler's Rest Hotel, was built in 1851. A residence and adjacent winery buildings reflect family life in the late Victorian era. The carriage house contains period conveyances. ⊠ *291 Auburn–Folsom Rd.* ☎ *530/889–6500* ⊠ *Free* ⊘ *Tues.–Sun. 11–4.*

The **Gold Country Museum** surveys life in the mines. Exhibits include a walk-through mine tunnel, a gold-panning stream, and a reproduction saloon. ⊠ *1273 High St., off Auburn–Folsom Rd.* ☎ *530/889–6500* ⚐ *Free* ☉ *Tues.–Sun. 11–4.*

Where to Stay & Eat

★ **\$\$–\$\$\$** ✕ **Latitudes.** Delicious multicultural cuisine is served in an 1870 Victorian. The menu (with monthly specials from diverse geographical regions) includes seafood, chicken, beef, and turkey entrées prepared with the appropriate Mexican spices, curries, cheeses, or teriyaki sauce. Vegetarians and vegans have several inventive choices, too. Sunday brunch is deservedly popular. ⊠ *130 Maple St.* ☎ *530/885–9535* ⊕ *www.latitudesrestaurant.com* ⊟ *AE, D, MC, V* ☉ *Closed Mon. and Tues.*

\$\$–\$\$\$ ✕ **Le Bilig French Café.** Simple and elegant cuisine is the goal of the chefs at this country-French café on the outskirts of Auburn. Escargots, coq au vin, and quiche are standard offerings; specials might include salmon in parchment paper. ⊠ *11750 Atwood Rd., off Hwy. 49 near Bel Air Mall* ☎ *530/888–1491* ⊟ *MC, V* ☉ *Closed Mon. and Tues. No lunch.*

¢–\$ ✕ **Awful Annie's.** Big patio umbrellas (and outdoor heaters when necessary) allow patrons to take in the view of the Old Town from this popular spot for breakfast—one specialty is a chili omelet—or lunch. ⊠ *160 Sacramento St.* ☎ *530/888–9857* ⊟ *AE, MC, V* ☉ *No dinner.*

\$–\$\$ 🏨 **Comfort Inn.** The contemporary-style rooms at this well-maintained property are softened with teal and pastel colors. Though it's close to the freeway, the motel is fairly quiet. The expanded continental breakfast includes many choices of baked goods, cereals, fruits, and juices. ⊠ *1875 Auburn Ravine Rd., north of Forest Hill exit of I-80, 95603* ☎ *530/885–1800 or 800/626–1900* 🖷 *530/888–6424* ⭗ *77 rooms, 2 suites* ♧ *In-room data ports, pool, gym, spa, laundry facilities, meeting room, no-smoking floor* ⊟ *AE, D, DC, MC, V* ⦿ *CP.*

\$–\$\$ 🏨 **Holiday Inn.** On a hill above the freeway across from Old Town, this hotel has an imposing columned entrance but a welcoming lobby. Rooms are chain-standard but attractively furnished. All have work areas and coffeemakers. Those nearest the parking lot can be noisy. ⊠ *120 Grass Valley Hwy., 95603* ☎ *530/887–8787 or 800/814–8787* 🖷 *530/887–9824* ⊕ *www.6c.com* ⭗ *96 rooms, 6 suites* ♧ *Restaurant, room service, in-room data ports, pool, gym, spa, bar, business services, convention center* ⊟ *AE, D, DC, MC, V.*

Grass Valley

➌ *24 mi north of Auburn on Hwy. 49.*

More than half of California's total gold production was extracted from mines around Grass Valley, including the Empire Mine, which, along with the North Star Mining Museum, is among the Gold Country's most fascinating attractions. Unlike neighboring Nevada City, urban sprawl surrounds Grass Valley's historic downtown.

In the center of town, on the site of the original, stands a reproduction of the **Lola Montez House** (⊠ 248 Mill St. ☎ 530/273–4667 or 800/655–4667 California only), home of the notorious dancer, singer, and courtesan. Montez, who arrived in Grass Valley in the early 1850s, was no great talent—her popularity among miners derived from her suggestive "spider dance"—but her loves, who reportedly included composer Franz Liszt, were legendary. According to one account, she arrived in California after having been "permanently retired from her job as Bavarian king Ludwig's mistress," literary muse, and political adviser. She apparently pushed too hard for democracy, which contributed to his overthrow and her banishment as a witch—or so the story goes. The Grass Valley/Nevada County Chamber of Commerce is headquartered here.

The landmark **Holbrooke Hotel** (⊠ 212 W. Main St. ☎ 530/273–1353 or 800/933–7077), built in 1851, was host to Lola Montez and Mark Twain as well as Ulysses S. Grant and a stream of other U.S. presidents. Its restaurant-saloon is one of the oldest operating west of the Mississippi.

★ The hard-rock gold mine at **Empire Mine State Historic Park** was one of California's richest. An estimated 5.8 million ounces were extracted from its 367 mi of underground passages between 1850 and 1956. On the 50-minute tours you can walk into a mineshaft, peer into the mine's deeper recesses, and view the owner's "cottage," which has exquisite woodwork. The visitor center has mining exhibits, and a picnic area is nearby. ⊠ *10791 E. Empire St., south of Empire St. exit of Hwy. 49* ☎ *530/273–8522* ⊕ *www.parks.ca.gov* ⊠ *$3* ⊙ *May–Aug., daily 9–6; Sept.–Apr., daily 10–5. Tours May–Aug., daily on the hr 11–4; Sept.–Apr., weekends at 1 (cottage only) and 2 (mine yard only), weather permitting.*

☺ Housed in the former North Star powerhouse, the **North Star Mining Museum** displays the 32-foot-high enclosed Pelton Water Wheel, said to be the largest ever built. It was used to power mining operations and was a forerunner of the modern turbines that generate hydroelectricity. Hands-on displays are geared to children. There's a picnic area nearby. ⊠ *Empire and McCourtney Sts., north of Empire St. exit of Hwy. 49* ☎ *530/273–4255* ⊠ *Donation requested* ⊙ *May–mid-Oct., daily 10–5.*

Where to Stay & Eat

$–$$$ ✕ **Villa Venezia Restaurant.** Pasta and seafood are the specialties served up in a cozy, warm Victorian building with an intimate patio area. Seafood stew is one of the most-ordered entrées. ⊠ *124 Bank St.* ☎ *530/273–3555* ⊟ *AE, D MC, V* ⊙ *No lunch weekends. No dinner Mon.*

¢ ✕ **Cousin Jack Pasties.** Meat- and vegetable-stuffed pasties are a taste of the region's history, having come across the Atlantic with Cornish miners and their families in the mid-19th century. The flaky crusts practically melt in your mouth. A simple food stand, which sometimes closes early on dreary winter days, Jack's is nonetheless a local landmark and dear to its loyal clientele. ⊠ *Auburn and Main Sts.* ☎ *530/272–9230* ⊟ *No credit cards.*

¢–$ ▦ **Holiday Lodge.** This modest hotel is close to many of the town's main attractions, and its staff can help arrange historical tours of Nevada City, Grass Valley, and the small town of Washington. ⊠ *1221 E. Main St., 95945* ☎ *530/273–4406 or 800/742–7125* ⊕ *http://holidaylodge.biz* ⇥ *35 rooms* ⚇ *Pool, sauna, no-smoking rooms* ⊟ *AE, MC, V* ⊙I *CP.*

Nevada City

 4 mi north of Grass Valley on Hwy. 49.

Nevada City, once known as the Queen City of the Northern Mines, is the most appealing of the northern Mother Lode towns. The iron-shutter brick buildings that line the narrow downtown streets contain antiques shops, galleries, bookstores, boutiques, B&Bs, restaurants, and a winery. Horse-drawn carriage tours add to the romance, as do gas street-lamps. At one point in the 1850s Nevada City had a population of nearly 10,000, enough to support much cultural activity.

With its gingerbread-trim bell tower, **Firehouse No. 1** is one of the Gold Country's most distinctive buildings. A museum, it houses gold-rush artifacts and a Chinese joss house (temple). ✉ *214 Main St.* ☎ *530/265–5468* 🖃 *Donation requested* ⊙ *Apr.–Nov., daily 11–4; Dec.–Mar., Thurs.–Sun. 11:30–4.*

The redbrick **Nevada Theatre**, constructed in 1865, is California's oldest theater building. Mark Twain, Emma Nevada, and many other notable people appeared on its stage. Housed in the theater, the **Foothill Theater Company** (☎ *530/265–8587* or *888/730–8587* ⊕ www.nevadatheatre.com) holds theatrical and musical events. Old films are screened here, too. ✉ *401 Broad St.* ☎ *530/265–6161, 530/274–3456 for film show times.*

The **Miners Foundry**, erected in 1856, produced machines for gold mining and logging. The Pelton Water Wheel, a source of power for the mines (the wheel also jump-started the hydroelectric power industry), was invented here. A cavernous building, the foundry is the site of plays, concerts, weddings, receptions, and other events; call for a schedule. ✉ *325 Spring St.* ☎*530/265–5040* ⊕*www.minersfoundry.org* ⊙ *Weekdays 10–4.*

You can watch wine being created while you sip at the **Nevada City Winery,** where the tasting room overlooks the production area. ✉ *Miners Foundry Garage, 321 Spring St.* ☎ *530/265–9463* or *800/203–9463* ⊕*www.ncwinery.com* 🖃*Free* ⊙ *Tastings Mon.–Sat. 11–5, Sun. noon–5.*

Where to Stay & Eat

$$–$$$$ ✕ **Citronee.** Diners pass through an upscale deli—whose pastries and breads are baked on the premises—to the affiliated restaurant in the back. An intimate and romantic atmosphere awaits, with highly regarded fare that includes Maine lobster and leg of venison. ✉ *320 Broad St.* ☎ *530/265–5697* ▭ *AE, MC, V* ⊙ *No lunch weekends. No dinner Mon.–Wed.*

$$–$$$ ✕ **Cirino's.** American–Italian dishes—seafood, pasta, and veal—are served at this informal bar and grill, which typically picks up steam as the clock approaches midnight. The restaurant's handsome bar is of gold-rush vintage. ✉ *309 Broad St.* ☎ *530/265–2246* ▭ *AE, D, MC, V.*

$$–$$$ ✕ **New Moon Cafe.** An attractively lighted room gives diners a cozy feeling, though loyal patrons have been known to complain about the high noise level. Organic flours and free-range meats are used when available. ✉ *203 York St.* ☎ *530/265–6399* ▭ *AE, MC, V* ⊙ *Closed Mon. No lunch weekends.*

$$–$$$ ▦ **Deer Creek Inn.** The main veranda of this 1860 Queen Anne Victorian overlooks a huge lawn that rolls past a rose-covered arbor to the creek below. You can play croquet on the lawn or pan for gold in the creek. All rooms have king- or queen-size beds; some rooms have two-person tubs. Wine service and a full breakfast are included. ✉ *116 Nevada St., 95959* ☎ *530/265–0363 or 800/655–0363* 📠 *530/265–0980* ⊕ *www.deercreekinn.com* ⌁ *5 rooms* ⊟ *AE, MC, V* ⧖❙ *BP.*

★ **$$–$$$** ▦ **Red Castle Historic Lodgings.** A state landmark, this 1857 Gothic-revival mansion stands on a forested hillside overlooking Nevada City, and is a special place for those who appreciate the finer points of Victorian interior design. Its brick exterior is trimmed with white-icicle woodwork. A steep private pathway leads down through the terraced gardens into town. Handsome antique furnishings and Oriental rugs decorate the rooms. ▣ TIP➔ Red Castle features an opulent afternoon tea and morning breakfast buffet that is unparalleled among Gold Country B&Bs. ✉ *109 Prospect St., 95959* ☎ *530/265–5135 or 800/761–4766* ⊕ *www. historic-lodgings.com* ⌁ *4 rooms, 3 suites* ⊟ *MC, V* ⧖❙ *BP.*

$–$$ ▦ **Northern Queen Inn.** Most accommodations at this bright creekside inn are typical motel units, but there are eight two-story chalets and eight rustic cottages with efficiency kitchens and gas-log fireplaces in a secluded wooded area. For a fee, you can ride on the hotel's narrow-gauge railroad, which offers excursions through Maidu Indian homelands and a Chinese cemetery from gold-rush days. ✉ *400 Railroad Ave., Sacramento St. exit off Hwy. 49, 95959* ☎ *530/265–5824 or 800/226–3090* 📠 *530/ 265–3720* ⊕ *www.northernqueeninn.com* ⌁ *70 rooms, 16 suites* ♨ *Restaurant, some kitchenettes, refrigerators, pool, hot tub, convention center* ⊟ *AE, D, DC, MC, V.*

THE GOLD COUNTRY ESSENTIALS

To research prices, get advice from other travelers, and book travel arrangements, visit www.fodors.com.

AIRPORTS & TRANSFERS

Sacramento International Airport is served by Alaska, America West, American, Continental, Delta, Frontier, Horizon Air, Northwest, Southwest, and United. ⇨ Air Travel *in* Smart Travel Tips A to Z for airline phone numbers. A private taxi from the airport to downtown Sacramento is about $20. The cost of the Super Shuttle from the airport to downtown Sacramento is $11. Call in advance to arrange transportation from your hotel to the airport.

🛪 **Sacramento International Airport** ✉ 6900 Airport Blvd., 12 mi northwest of downtown off I-5, Sacramento ☎ 916/874-0700 ⊕ www.sacairports.org. **Super Shuttle** ☎ 800/258-3826.

BOAT TRAVEL

Sacramento's riverfront location enables you to sightsee while getting around by boat. A water taxi run by River Otter Taxi Co. serves the Old Sacramento waterfront during spring and summer, stopping at points near restaurants and other sights. Channel Star Excursions operates the *Spirit of Sacramento,* a riverboat that takes passengers on happy-hour, dinner, lunch, and champagne-brunch cruises in addition to one-hour narrated tours.

✈ Channel Star Excursions ⌧ 110 L St. ☎ 916/552-2933 or 800/433-0263. **River Otter Taxi Co.** ☎ 916/446-7704.

BUS TRAVEL

Getting to and from SIA can be accomplished via taxi, the Super Shuttle, or by Yolo County Public Bus 42, which operates a circular service around SIA, downtown Sacramento, West Sacramento, Davis, and Woodland. Other Gold Country destinations are best reached by private car.

Greyhound serves Sacramento, Davis, Auburn, and Placerville. It's a two-hour trip from San Francisco's Transbay Terminal, at 1st and Mission streets, to the Sacramento station, at 7th and L streets.

Sacramento Regional Transit buses and light-rail vehicles transport passengers in Sacramento. Most buses run from 6 AM to 10 PM, most trains from 5 AM to midnight. A DASH (Downtown Area Shuttle) bus and the No. 30 city bus link Old Sacramento, midtown, and Sutter's Fort. The fare is 50¢ within this area.

✈ Greyhound ☎ 800/231-2222 ⊕ www.greyhound.com. **Sacramento Regional Transit** ☎ 916/321-2877 ⊕ www.sacrt.com. **Yolo County Bus** ☎ 530/666-2837 ⊕ www.yolobus.com.

CAR RENTAL

You can rent a car from any of the major national chains at Sacramento International Airport. ⇨ Car Rental *in* Smart Travel Tips A to Z for national car-rental agency phone numbers.

CAR TRAVEL

Traveling by car is the most convenient way to see the Gold Country. From Sacramento, three highways fan out toward the east, all intersecting with Highway 49: Interstate 80 heads 34 mi northeast to Auburn; U.S. 50 goes east 40 mi to Placerville; and Highway 16 angles southeast 45 mi to Plymouth. Highway 49 is an excellent two-lane road that winds and climbs through the foothills and valleys, linking the principal Gold Country towns.

Sacramento lies at the junction of Interstate 5 and Interstate 80, not quite 90 mi northeast of San Francisco. The 406-mi drive north on Interstate 5 from Los Angeles takes seven to eight hours. Interstate 80 continues northeast through the Gold Country toward Reno, about 136 mi (three hours or so) from Sacramento.

EMERGENCIES

In an emergency dial 911. Each of the following medical facilities has an emergency room open 24 hours a day.

✈ Hospitals Mercy Hospital of Sacramento ⌧ 4001 J St., Sacramento ☎ 916/453-4424. **Sutter General Hospital** ⌧ 2801 L St., Sacramento ☎ 916/733-8900. **Sutter Memorial Hospital** ⌧ 52nd and F Sts., Sacramento ☎ 916/733-1000.

LODGING

A number of organizations can supply information about Gold Country B&Bs and other accommodations.

🚹 **Amador County Innkeepers Association** ☎ 209/267-1710 or 800/726-4667. **Gold Country Inns of Tuolumne County** ☎ 209/533-1845. **Historic Bed & Breakfast Inns of Grass Valley & Nevada City** ☎ 530/477-6634 or 800/250-5808.

TOURS

Gold Prospecting Adventures, LLC, based in Jamestown, arranges gold-panning trips.

🚹 **Gold Prospecting Adventures, LLC** ☎ 209/984-4653 or 800/596-0009 ⊕ www.goldprospecting.com.

TRAIN TRAVEL

Several trains operated by Amtrak stop in Sacramento and Davis. Trains making the 2½-hour trip from Jack London Square, in Oakland, stop in Emeryville (across the bay from San Francisco), Richmond, Martinez, and Davis before reaching Sacramento; some stop in Berkeley and Suisun-Fairfield as well.

🚹 **Amtrak** ☎ 800/872-7245 ⊕ www.amtrakcalifornia.com.

VISITOR INFORMATION

🚹 **Amador County Chamber of Commerce** ✉ 125 Peek St., Jackson 95642 ☎ 209/223-0350 ⊕ www.amadorcountychamber.com. **Davis Chamber of Commerce** ✉ 130 G St., Davis 95616 ☎ 530/756-5160 ⊕ www.davischamber.com. **El Dorado County Chamber of Commerce** ✉ 542 Main St., Placerville 95667 ☎ 530/621-5885 or 800/457-6279 ⊕ www.eldoradocounty.org. **Grass Valley/Nevada County Chamber of Commerce** ✉ 248 Mill St., Grass Valley 95945 ☎ 530/273-4667 or 800/655-4667 ⊕ www.grassvalleychamber.com and www.nevadacitychamber.com. **Mariposa County Visitors Bureau** ✉ 5158 Hwy. 140, Mariposa 95338 ☎ 209/966-7081 or 800/208-2434 ⊕ mariposa.yosemite.net/visitor. **Nevada City Chamber of Commerce** ✉ 132 Main St., Nevada City 95945 ☎ 530/265-2692. **Sacramento Convention and Visitors Bureau** ✉ 1303 J St., Suite 600, Sacramento 95814 ☎ 916/264-7777 ⊕ www.sacramentocvb.org. **Tuolumne County Visitors Bureau** ✉ 542 Stockton St., Sonora 95370 ☎ 209/533-4420 or 800/446-1333 ⊕ www.thegreatunfenced.com. **Woodland Chamber of Commerce** ✉ 307 1st St., Woodland 95695 ☎ 530/662-7327 or 888/843-2636 ⊕ www.woodlandchamber.org.

Lake Tahoe

WITH RENO, NEVADA

WORD OF MOUTH

"Lake Tahoe has lots of great hikes, and water activities range from a paddle boat trip to the Emerald Bay to jet boats along the coast. There are swimming beaches, too. If you've been there skiing, it might be fun to take the ski lift and see how the scenery is different in the summer."

—Vera

Updated by
John A.
Vlahides

STUNNING COBALT-BLUE LAKE TAHOE is the largest alpine lake in North America, famous for its clarity, deep blue water, and surrounding snow-capped peaks. Straddling the state line between California and Nevada, it lies 6,225 feet above sea level in the Sierra Nevada. The border gives this popular resort region a split personality. About half its visitors are intent on low-key sightseeing, hiking, fishing, camping, and boating. The rest head directly for the Nevada side, where bargain dining, big-name entertainment, and the lure of a jackpot draw them into the glittering casinos.

Though Lake Tahoe possesses abundant natural beauty and accessible wilderness, nearby towns are highly developed, and roads around the lake are often congested with traffic. If you prefer solitude, you can escape to the many state parks, national forests, and protected tracts of wilderness that ring the 22-mi-long, 12-mi-wide lake. At a vantage point overlooking Emerald Bay, on a trail in the national forests that ring the basin, or on a sunset cruise on the lake itself, you can forget the hordes and the commercial development. You can even pretend that you're Mark Twain, who found "not fifteen other human beings throughout its wide circumference" when he visited the lake in 1861 and wrote that "the eye never tired of gazing, night or day, calm or storm."

Exploring Lake Tahoe

The typical way to explore the Lake Tahoe area is to drive the 72-mi road that follows the shore through wooded flatlands and past beaches, climbing to vistas on the rugged southwest side of the lake and passing through busy commercial developments and casinos on its northeastern and southeastern edges. Undeveloped Lake Tahoe–Nevada State Park occupies more than half of the Nevada side of Lake Tahoe, stretching along the shore from just north of Zephyr Cove to just south of the upscale community of Incline Village. The California side is more developed, particularly South Lake Tahoe, but there are no garish casino towers, and much wilderness remains immediately outside developed towns.

About the Restaurants

On weekends and in high season, expect a long wait in the more popular restaurants. And expect to pay resort prices almost everywhere. Remember, restaurants see business only 6 out of 12 months. During the "shoulder seasons" (April to May and September to November), some places may close temporarily or limit their hours, so call ahead. Also, check local papers for deals and discounts during this time, especially two-for-one coupons. Many casinos use their restaurants to attract gamblers. Marquees often tout "$8.99 prime rib dinners" or "99¢ breakfast specials." Some of these meal deals, usually found in the coffee shops and buffets, are downright lousy, but at those prices, it's hard to complain. The finer restaurants in casinos deliver pricier food, as well as reasonable service and a bit of atmosphere. A few are exceptionally good. In Reno, two of the city's top restaurants—Harrah's Steakhouse and the White Orchid—bear the standard for old-guard fancy dining, though the most contemporary, foodie-oriented restaurants are not in

GREAT ITINERARIES

Numbers correspond to the Lake Tahoe map.

IF YOU HAVE 3 DAYS

On your first day stop in ⊞ **South Lake Tahoe** ❶ ⚑ and pick up provisions for a picnic lunch. Start in **Pope-Baldwin Recreation Area** ❷ and check out Tallac Historic Site. Head west on Highway 89, stopping at the Lake Tahoe Visitor Center and the **Emerald Bay State Park** ❸ lookout. Have a tailgate picnic at the lookout, or hike down to Vikingsholm, a reproduction of a Viking castle. In the late afternoon explore the trails and mansion at **Sugar Pine Point State Park** ❺; then backtrack on Highway 89 and U.S. 50 for dinner in ⊞ **Stateline** ❸ or in South Lake Tahoe. On Day 2 cruise on the *Tahoe Queen* out of South Lake Tahoe or the MS *Dixie II* out of **Zephyr Cove** ❷ and then ride the Heavenly Gondola at Heavenly Mountain Resort in South Lake Tahoe. Carry a picnic for lunch high above the lake, and (except in snow season) take a walk on one of Heavenly's nature trails. You can try your luck at the Stateline casinos before dinner. Start your third day by heading north on U.S. 50, stopping at Cave Rock and (after turning north on Highway 28) at Sand Harbor Beach. If there's no snow on the ground, tour the Thunderbird Lodge (reservations essential) for a glimpse of life at an old-Tahoe estate just south of **Incline Village** ⑪, or else continue on to **Crystal Bay** ⑩. If you have time, drive to **Tahoe City** ❼ to see the Gatekeeper's Cabin Museum, or make the 45-minute drive down to ⊞ **Reno** ⑭ for dinner and some nightlife.

IF YOU HAVE 5 DAYS

Spend your first morning at **Pope-Baldwin Recreation Area** ❷ ⚑. After a picnic lunch head to the Lake Tahoe Visitor Center and the **Emerald Bay State Park** ❸ lookout. Hike to Vikingsholm or move on to **Sugar Pine Point State Park** ❺. Have dinner in ⊞ **South Lake Tahoe** ❶.

On your second day take a cruise to Emerald Bay or a half-day cruise around the lake; back on land, ride the Heavenly Gondola, and possibly take a hike. Spend the late afternoon or early evening sampling the worldly pleasures of the ⊞ **Stateline** ❸ casinos. On Day 3 visit Cave Rock, and the Thunderbird Lodge (reservations essential) just south of **Incline Village** ⑪, where you can have a late lunch before heading to **Crystal Bay** ⑩ and playing the slots, or to nearby Kings Beach State Recreation Area, where you can spend the late afternoon on the beach. That evening, drive down to ⊞ **Reno** ⑭ for dinner and entertainment. On your fourth day hang out at Sand Harbor Beach. If the high-mountain desert appeals, spend Day 5 in the Great Basin, touring Carson City and Virginia City and the vast expanse of the eastern Sierra. Alternatively, head to **D. L. Bliss State Park** ❹ for a hike; then drive to **Tahoe City** ❼ for lunch and a tour of the Gatekeeper's Cabin Museum. Afterward, visit **Olympic Valley** ❽ and ride the cable car to High Camp at Squaw Valley for a sunset cocktail.

the casinos. Unless otherwise noted, even the most expensive area restaurants welcome customers in casual clothes—not surprising in this year-round vacation spot—but don't expect to be served in most places if you're barefoot, shirtless, or wearing a skimpy bathing suit.

About the Hotels

Quiet inns on the water, suburban-style strip motels, casino hotels, slope-side ski lodges, and house and condo rentals throughout the area constitute the lodging choices at Tahoe. The crowds come in summer and during ski season; reserve as far in advance as possible, especially for holiday periods, when prices skyrocket. Spring and fall give you a little more leeway and lower—sometimes significantly lower—rates.

WHAT IT COSTS				
$$$$	**$$$**	**$$**	**$**	**¢**
RESTAURANTS over $30	$23–$30	$16–$22	$10–$15	under $10
HOTELS over $250	$176–$250	$121–$175	$90–$120	under $90

Restaurant prices are for a main course at dinner, excluding sales tax of 7%–7¼% (depending on location). Hotel prices are for two people in a standard double room in high season, excluding service charges and 9%–12% tax.

Sports & the Outdoors

If you're planning to spend any time outdoors around Lake Tahoe, whether hiking, climbing, or camping, be aware that weather conditions can change quickly in the Sierra: to avoid a life-threatening case of hypothermia, always bring a pocket-size, fold-up rain poncho (available in all sporting-goods stores) to keep you dry. Wear long pants and a hat. Carry plenty of water. Because you'll likely be walking on granite, wear sturdy, closed-toe hiking boots, with soles that grip rock. If you're going into the backcountry, bring a signaling device (such as a mirror), emergency whistle, compass, map, energy bars, and water purifier. When heading out alone, tell someone where you're going and when you're coming back.

If you plan to ski, be aware of resort elevations. In the event of a winter storm, determine the snow level before you choose the resort you'll ski. Often the level can be as high as 7,000 feet, which means rain at some resorts' base areas but snow at others. For storm information, check the **National Weather Service's Web page** (⊕ www.wrh.noaa.gov/rev). If you plan to do any backcountry skiing, check with the **U.S. Forest Service** (☎ 530/587–2158 backcountry recording) for conditions. A shop called the **Backcountry** (☎ 530/581–5861 Tahoe City, 530/582–0909 Truckee ⊕ www.thebackcountry.net), with branches in Tahoe City and Truckee, operates an excellent Web site with current information about how and where to (and where not to) ski, mountain bike, and hike in the backcountry around Tahoe.

If you plan to camp in the backcountry, you'll likely need a wilderness permit, which you can pick up at the **Lake Tahoe Visitor Center** (⊠ Hwy. 89 ☎ 530/543–2600 ⊕ www.fs.fed.us/r5/ltbmu) or at a ranger station at the entrance to any of the national forests. For reservations at camp-

IF YOU LIKE

GAMBLING

Six casinos are clustered on a strip of U.S. 50 in Stateline, and five casinos operate on the north shore. And, of course, in Reno there are more than a dozen major and a dozen minor casinos.

GOLFING

The Tahoe area is nearly as popular with golfers as it is with skiers. More than a dozen superb courses dot the mountains around the lake, with magnificent views, thick pines, fresh, cool air, and lush fairways and greens.

HIKING

There are five national forests in the Tahoe Basin and a half dozen state parks. The main areas for hiking include the Tahoe Rim Trail, a 165-mi path along the ridgelines that now completely rings the lake; Desolation Wilderness, a vast 63,473-acre preserve of granite peaks, glacial valleys, subalpine forests, the Rubicon River, and more than 50 lakes; and the trail systems in D. L. Bliss, Emerald Bay, Sugar Pine Point, and Lake Tahoe–Nevada state parks and near Lake Tahoe Visitor Center. The Pacific Crest Trail, a high-mountain foot trail connecting Mexico to Canada, runs along the Sierra Crest just west of the lake. To the south of Lake Tahoe sits the Mokelumne Wilderness, a whopping 100,848-acre preserve, one of several undeveloped tracts that extend toward Yosemite, which is accessible via the Tahoe-Yosemite Trail, a 186-mi trek.

SKIING & SNOWBOARDING

The mountains around Lake Tahoe are bombarded by blizzards throughout most winters and sometimes in fall and spring; 10- to 12-foot bases are common. Indeed, the Sierra often has the deepest snowpack on the continent, but because of the relatively mild temperatures over the Pacific, falling snow can be very heavy and wet—it's nicknamed Sierra Cement for a reason. The upside is that you can sometimes ski and board as late as July, you probably won't get frostbite, and you'll likely get a tan. Several resorts have backcountry access, most notably Alpine Meadows, Sugar Bowl, and Sierra-at-Tahoe. Snowboarding is permitted at all Tahoe ski areas. Note that the major resorts get extremely crowded on weekends. If you're going to ski on a Saturday, arrive early and quit early. Avoid moving with the masses: eat at 11 AM or 1:30 PM, not noon. Also consider visiting the ski areas with few high-speed lifts or limited lodging and real estate at their bases: Alpine Meadows, Sugar Bowl, Homewood, Mt. Rose, Sierra-at-Tahoe, Diamond Peak, and Kirkwood. Expect traffic when the resorts close. To find out the true ski conditions, talk to waiters and bartenders, most of whom are ski bums.

The Lake Tahoe area is also a great destination for Nordic skiers. You can even cross-country ski on fresh snow right on the lakeshore beaches. "Skinny" (i.e., cross-country) skiing at the resorts can be costly, but you get the benefits of machine grooming and trail preparation. If it's bargain Nordic you're after, take advantage of thousands of acres of public forest and parkland trails.

16

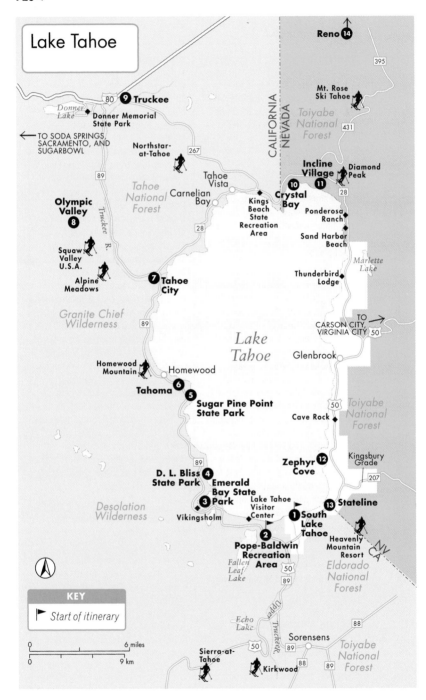

grounds in California state parks, contact **Reserve America** (☎ 800/ 444–7275 ⊕ www.reserveamerica.com).

Timing

Most Lake Tahoe accommodations, restaurants, and even a handful of parks are open year-round, but many visitor centers, mansions, state parks, and beaches are closed from November through May. During those months, multitudes of skiers and other winter-sports enthusiasts are attracted to Tahoe's downhill resorts and cross-country centers, North America's largest concentration of skiing facilities. Ski resorts try to open by Thanksgiving, if only with machine-made snow, and can operate through May or later. During the ski season, Tahoe's population swells on the weekends. If you're able to come midweek, you'll have the resorts and neighboring towns almost to yourself. Bear in mind, though, that Tahoe is a popular wedding and honeymoon destination: on Valentine's Day the chapels become veritable assembly lines.

Unless you want to ski, you'll find that Tahoe is most fun in summer, when it's cooler here than in the scorched Sierra Nevada foothills, the clean mountain air is bracingly crisp, and the surface temperature of Lake Tahoe is an invigorating 65°F to 70°F (compared with 40°F to 50°F in winter). This is also the time, however, when it may seem as if every tourist at the lake—100,000 on peak weekends—is in a car on the main road circling the 72-mi shoreline (especially on Highway 89, just south of Tahoe City; on Highway 28, east of Tahoe City; and on U.S. 50 in South Lake). The crowds increase as the day wears on, so the best strategy for avoiding the crush is to do as much as you can early in the day. The parking lots of the Lake Tahoe Visitor Center, Vikingsholm, and Emerald Bay State Park can be jammed at any time, and the lake's beaches can be packed. September and October, when the throngs have dispersed but the weather is still pleasant, are among the most satisfying—and cheapest—months to visit Lake Tahoe. Christmas week and July 4 are the busiest times, and prices go through the roof; plan accordingly.

CALIFORNIA SIDE

With the exception of Stateline, Nevada—which, aside from its casino-hotel towers, seems almost indistinguishable from South Lake Tahoe, California—the California side is more developed than the Nevada side. Here you can find both commercial enterprises—restaurants, motels, lodges, resorts, residential subdivisions—and public-access facilities, such as historic sites, parks, campgrounds, marinas, and beaches.

South Lake Tahoe

▶ ❶ *50 mi south of Reno on U.S. 395 and U.S. 50; 198 mi northeast of San Francisco on I–80 and U.S. 50.*

The city of South Lake Tahoe's raison d'être is tourism: the casinos of adjacent Stateline, Nevada; the ski slopes at Heavenly Mountain; the beaches, docks, bike trails, and campgrounds all around the south shore; and the backcountry of Eldorado National Forest and Desolation Wilderness. The town itself, however, is disappointingly unattractive, with its mix of cheap motels, strip malls, and low-rise prefab-looking buildings that line both sides of U.S. 50. Though there are lots and lots of places to stay, we haven't recommended many because they're not cream-of-the-crop choices. The small city's saving grace is its convenient location and bevy of services, as well as its gorgeous lake views.

Whether you ski or not, you'll appreciate the impressive view of Lake Tahoe from the **Heavenly Gondola.** Its 138 eight-passenger cars travel from the middle of town 2½ mi up the mountain in 13 minutes. When the weather's fine, you can take one of three hikes around the mountaintop and then have lunch at Adventure Peak Grill. Heavenly also offers day care for children. ⊠ *Downtown* ☎ *775/586–7000 or 800/ 432–8365* ⊕ *www.skiheavenly.com* ⊡ *$24* ☉ *Hrs vary; summer, daily 10–7; winter, daily 9–4.*

At the base of the gonodola, the **Heavenly Village** is the centerpiece of South Lake Tahoe's efforts to reinvent itself and provide a focal point for tourism. Essentially a pedestrian mall, it includes some good shopping, a cinema, an arcade for kids, and the Heavenly Village Outdoor Ice Rink.

Where to Stay & Eat

$$$–$$$$ ✕ **Kalani's.** Fresh-off-the-plane seafood gets flown directly from the Honolulu fish market to Heavenly Village's sexiest (and priciest) restaurant. The sleek, industrial-chic, white-tablecloth dining room is decked out with carved bamboo, sweeping banquettes, a burnt-orange color palette, and modern-glass sculpture, which perfectly complements contemporary Pacific Rim specialties such as the melt-from-the-bone babyback pork ribs with sesame-garlic soy sauce. There's also a good sushi menu with inventive rolls and sashimi combos. ⊠ *1001 Heavenly Village Way, #26* ☎ *530/544–6100* ⊟ *AE, D, MC, V.*

★ **$$$** ✕ **Evan's.** The top choice for high-end dining in South Lake, Evan's contemporary California menu includes such specialties as seared foie gras with curried ice cream and roast pineapple, and venison in a raspberry demi-glace. The 40-seat dining room is intimate, with tables a little close together and decor a bit dated, but the service and food are excellent and merit a special trip. ⊠ *536 Emerald Bay Rd.* ☎ *530/542–1990* ⚱ *Reservations essential* ⊟ *AE, D, MC, V* ☉ *No lunch.*

$$–$$$ ✕ **Café Fiore.** Possibly the most romantic spot in town, this northern Italian restaurant has seven tables in a tiny window-lined cottage. The menu lists a variety of pastas and meat dishes and daily fish specials; sautéed veal dishes are the house specialty. There's nothing groundbreaking about the cooking, but this is a great spot to hold hands by candlelight. Leave the kids at home. Save room for the homemade white-chocolate ice cream. ⊠ *1169 Ski Run Blvd.* ☎ *530/541–2908* ⚱ *Reservations essential* ⊟ *AE, MC, V* ☉ *No lunch.*

¢–$$$ ✕ **Freshies.** When you've had your fill of junk food, come here for delicious, healthful meals. Specialties include seafood and vegetarian dishes, but good grilled meats are always available, such as Hawaiian spare ribs and free-range rib-eye steaks. Keep in mind that Freshies is in a minimall, sometimes gets loud, and may have lots of people wait-

ing for tables, but it's worth it—especially if you snag a spot on the upstairs lake-view deck. ⊠ *3300 Lake Tahoe Blvd.* ☎ *530/542–3630*
⚐ *Reservations not accepted* ☰ *AE, MC, V.*

¢–$$ ✕**Scusa!** The kitchen here turns out big plates of linguine with clam sauce,
veal marsala, and chicken piccata. There's nothing fancy or esoteric about
the menu, just straightforward Italian–American food. Try the excep-
tionally good bread pudding for dessert. ⊠ *1142 Ski Run Blvd.* ☎ *530/
542–0100* ⚐ *Reservations essential* ☰ *AE, MC, V* ☽ *No lunch.*

¢–$ ✕**Orchid's Thai.** If you're hungry for Thai, Orchid's serves good food
at reasonable prices in an attractive dining room with pumpkin-color
walls. It's not fantastic, but it's reliably good, and when every place in
town is booked, this is a great backup. They even take reservations.
⊠ *2180 Lake Tahoe Blvd.* ☎ *530/544–5541* ☰ *AE, D, MC, V* ☽ *No
lunch Sun.*

¢ ✕**Blue Angel Café.** A favorite of locals, who fill the half dozen wooden
tables, the Blue Angel serves everything from frittatas, Benedicts, and house-
made granola at breakfast to beef bourguignon, pasta carbonara, and
chicken curry at lunch and dinner—and best of all, everything costs less
than $14. The cozy room makes the visit feel like you're eating at a friend's
house. The café is open all day, 8 AM to 8 PM. ⊠ *1132 Ski Run Blvd.*
☎ *530/544–6544* ☽ *Call for hrs in May and Nov.* ☰ *MC, V.*

¢ ✕**Red Hut Café.** A vintage-1959 Tahoe diner, all chrome and red plas-
tic, the Red Hut is a tiny place with a dozen counter stools and a dozen
booths. It's a traditional breakfast spot for huge omelets; the banana,
pecan, and coconut waffles; and other tasty vittles. There's another branch
in Stateline, too. ⊠ *2749 U.S. 50* ☎ *530/541–9024* ⚐ *Reservations not
accepted* ☰ *No credit cards* ☽ *No dinner* ⊠ *227 Kingsbury Grade, State-
line, NV* ☎ *775/588–7488.*

$$$–$$$$ ▦ **Black Bear Inn Bed and Breakfast.** South Lake Tahoe's most luxurious
Fodor'sChoice inn feels like one of the great old lodges of the Adirondacks. Its living
★ room has rough-hewn beams, plank floors, cathedral ceilings, Persian
rugs, and even an elk's head over the giant river-rock fireplace. Built in
the 1990s with meticulous attention to detail, the five inn rooms and
three cabins feature 19th-century American antiques, fine art, and fire-
places; cabins also have kitchenettes. Never intrusive, the affable innkeep-
ers provide a sumptuous breakfast in the morning and wine and cheese
in the afternoon. ⊠ *1202 Ski Run Blvd., 96150* ☎ *530/544–4451 or
877/232–7466* ⊕ *www.tahoeblackbear.com* ↝ *5 rooms, 3 cabins*
⚐ *Dining room, some in-room hot tubs, some kitchenettes, cable TV
with movies, in-room VCRs, in-room data ports, Wi-Fi, outdoor hot
tub, ski storage, lounge; no kids under 16, no smoking* ☰ *AE, D, MC,
V* ⑩ *BP.*

★ $$$–$$$$ ▦ **Marriott's Grand Residence and Timber Lodge.** You can't beat the loca-
tion of these two gigantic, modern condominium complexes right at the
base of Heavenly Gondola, smack in the center of town. Though both
are extremely comfortable, Timber Lodge feels more like a family va-
cation resort; Grand Residence is geared to upper-end travelers. Units
vary in size from studios to three bedrooms, and some have amenities
such as stereos, fireplaces, daily maid service, and full kitchens. Ask about
vacation packages. ⊠ *1001 Park Ave., 96150* ☎ *530/542–8400 or*

16

800/627–7468 🖨 *530/524–8410* ⊕ *www.marriott.com* 🛏 *431 condos* ⚉ *Some in-room hot tubs, some kitchens, cable TV, in-room data ports, Wi-Fi, pool, gym, 2 hot tubs, ice-skating, ski shop, ski storage, laundry facilities, laundry service, concierge; no smoking* ⊟ *AE, D, MC, V.*

☾ **\$\$–\$\$\$\$** 🍴 **Lakeland Village Beach and Mountain Resort.** Built in the 1970s, this 19-acre lakefront condominium complex has one- to five-bedroom semidetached town houses, and studios and suites in the lodge building. Each is individually owned and decorated, so there's no uniformity to the furnishings—some are borderline ugly—but all are spacious and come with fireplaces and fully equipped kitchens. Some have decks overlooking the lake, others face the highway; ask when you book. Couples may want to look elsewhere, since the sound insulation isn't the best, but Lakeland is a great place for several families traveling together: the largest unit sleeps 12, and there's lots of room on the grounds for kids to run around and explore. ⊠ *3535 Lake Tahoe Blvd., 96150* ☎ *530/544–1685 or 800/822–5969* 🖨 *530/544–0193* ⊕ *www.lakelandvillage.com* 🛏 *210 units* ⚉ *BBQs, kitchens, cable TV, in-room DVDs, in-room data ports, Wi-Fi, 2 tennis courts, pool, gym, hot tubs (indoor and outdoor), sauna, beach, boating, fishing, ski shop, ski storage, dry cleaning, laundry facilities, meeting rooms* ⊟ *AE, D, MC, V.*

\$–\$\$\$ 🍴 **Sorensen's Resort.** Escape civilization by staying in the Eldorado National Forest, 20 minutes south of town. In a log cabin at this woodsy 165-acre resort, you can lie on a hammock beneath the aspens or sit in a rocker on your own front porch. All but three of the cabins have a kitchen and wood-burning stove or fireplace. Some are close together, and the furnishings aren't fancy (think futons as sofas), but there's a wonderful summer-camp charm about the place that makes it special. There are also three modern homes that sleep six. The resort sits on the edge of the highway, which allows it to stay open in winter—a boon for skiers—but in summer, request a cabin away from the road. ⊠ *14255 Hwy. 88, Hope Valley 96120* ☎ *530/694–2203 or 800/423–9949* ⊕ *www.sorensensresort.com* 🛏 *28 cabins, 2 rooms with shared bath, 4 houses* ⚉ *Restaurant, some fans, some kitchens, some kitchenettes, pond, sauna, boating, fishing, bicycles, croquet, hiking, cross-country skiing, ski shop, ski storage, tobogganing, library, babysitting, children's programs (ages 3–18), playground, some pets allowed; no a/c, no room phones, no room TVs, no smoking* ⊟ *AE, D, MC, V.*

★ **\$\$** 🍴 **Inn by the Lake.** Of all the mid-range lodgings in South Lake, this one is probably the best. Across the road from a beach, the "inn" is essentially a high-end motel, with spacious, spotless rooms and suites decorated in soft, slightly dated color schemes. All rooms have balconies, so you don't feel shut in, and there's lots of light, too. Pricier rooms have lake views (across the road), wet bars, and kitchens. In the afternoon the staff sets out cookies and cider, a nice touch indicative of the better-than-average service you'll find here. ⊠ *3300 Lake Tahoe Blvd., 96150* ☎ *530/542–0330 or 800/877–1466* 🖨 *530/541–6596* ⊕ *www.innbythelake.com* 🛏 *87 rooms, 13 suites* ⚉ *Room service, some in-room hot tubs, some kitchens, some minibars, cable TV with movies and video games, in-room data ports, Wi-Fi, pool, sauna, bicycles, ski storage, dry cleaning, laundry facilities, meeting rooms* ⊟ *AE, D, MC, V* ❧◯ *CP.*

⏚ ¢–$$ ⊞ **Camp Richardson.** An old-fashioned family resort, Camp Richardson is built around a 1920s lodge, with a few dozen cabins and a small inn, all tucked beneath giant pine trees on 80 acres of lakefront land on the southwest shore of Lake Tahoe. The rustic log cabin–style lodge has simple, straightforward accommodations. The cabins (one-week minimum in summer) have lots of space, fireplaces, or woodstoves, and full kitchens; some units sleep eight. The Beachside Inn has more modern amenities and sits right on the lake, but its rooms feel like an ordinary motel. Best of all, the resort sits well off the road and there's tons of space; kids have a blast here. A glass-bottom trimaran makes trips to Emerald Bay directly from the resort. Rates drop significantly in winter, making it a bargain for skiers and off-season travelers. ⊠ *1900 Jameson Beach, 96150* ☎ *530/542–6550 or 800/544–1801* 🖷 *530/541–1802* ⊕ *www.camprichardson.com* ↰ *28 lodge rooms, 47 cabins, 7 inn rooms, 300 campsites* ⚭ *Restaurant, some kitchens, beach, boating, marina, waterskiing, fishing, bicycles, cross-country skiing, sleigh rides; no a/c, no phones in some rooms, no TV in some rooms, no smoking* ▭ *AE, D, MC, V.*

Nightlife

Most of the area's nightlife is concentrated in the casinos across the border in Stateline. If you want to avoid slot machines and blinking lights, you can stay in California and hear live bands every night at **Mc P's Irish Pub & Grill** (⊠ 4093 Lake Tahoe Blvd. ☎ 530/542–4435), also known as the Pub Tahoe. It's right near the Heavenly Gondola.

Sports & the Outdoors

FISHING **Tahoe Sport Fishing** (⊠ Ski Run Marina ☎ 530/541–5448, 800/696–7797 in CA ⊕ www.tahoesportfishing.com) is one of the largest and oldest fishing-charter services on the lake. Morning trips cost $95, afternoon trips $85. They include all necessary gear and bait, and the crew cleans and packages your catch.

GOLF The 18-hole, par-71 **Lake Tahoe Golf Course** (⊠ U.S. 50 between Lake Tahoe Airport and Meyers ☎ 530/577–0788 ⊕ www.laketahoegc.com) has a driving range. Greens fees start at $52; a cart (mandatory Friday to Sunday) costs $23. Twilight rates drop as low as $20.

HIKING The south shore is a great jumping-off point for day treks into nearby Eldorado National Forest and Desolation Wilderness. Hike a couple of miles on the **Pacific Crest Trail** (⊠ Echo Summit, about 12 mi southwest of South Lake Tahoe off U.S. 50 ☎ 916/349–2109 or 888/728–7245 ⊕ www.pcta.org). The Pacific Crest Trail leads into **Desolation Wilderness** (⊠ El Dorado National Forest Information Center ☎ 530/644–6048 ⊕ www.fs.fed.us/r5/eldorado), where you can pick up trails to gorgeous backcountry lakes and mountain peaks (bring a proper topographic map and compass, and carry water and food). Late May through early September, the easiest way to access Desolation Wilderness is via boat taxi ($8.50 one-way) across Echo Lake from **Echo Chalet** (⊠ Echo Lakes Rd. off U.S. 50 near Echo Summit ☎ 530/659–7207 ⊕ www.echochalet.com).

ICE-SKATING If you're here in winter, practice your jumps and turns at the **Heavenly** ☾ **Village Outdoor Ice Rink.** You'll find the rink at the southwestern-most edge of Heavenly Village, near the Raley's supermarket parking lot. ☎ *530/543–1423* ☞ *$10, includes skate rentals* ☉ *Nov.–Mar., daily 10–9, weather permitting.*

KAYAKING **Kayak Tahoe** (✉ Timber Cove Marina; 3411 Lake Tahoe Blvd., behind Best Western Timber Cove Lodge ☎ 530/544–2011 ⊕ www.kayaktahoe. com) has long been teaching people to kayak on Lake Tahoe and the Truckee River. Lessons and excursions (Emerald Bay, Cave Rock, Zephyr Cove) are offered June through September. You can also rent a kayak and paddle solo.

MOUNTAIN With so much national forest land surrounding Lake Tahoe, you may BIKING want to try mountain biking. You can rent both road and mountain bikes and get tips on where to ride from the friendly staff at **Tahoe Sports Ltd.** (✉ 4000 Lake Tahoe Blvd. ☎ 530/542–4000 ⊕ www.tahoesportsltd. com).

SKIING Straddling two states, vast **Heavenly Mountain Resort**—composed of nine Fodor'sChoice peaks, two valleys, and four base-lodge areas, along with the largest snow- ★ making system in the western United States—has terrain for every skier. Beginners can choose wide, well-groomed trails, accessed from the California Lodge or the gondola from downtown South Lake Tahoe; kids have short and gentle runs in the Enchanted Forest area all to themselves. The Sky Express high-speed quad chair whisks intermediate and advanced skiers to the summit for wide cruisers or steep tree-skiing. Mott and Killebrew canyons draw experts to the Nevada side for steep chutes and thick-timber slopes. For snowboarders and tricksters, there are a whopping five terrain parks, including an enormous 22-foot superpipe. The ski school, like everything else at Heavenly, is big and offers everything from learn-to-ski packages to canyon-adventure tours. Call about ski and boarding camps. Skiing lessons are available for children ages 4 and up; there's day care for infants older than six weeks. ✉ *Ski Run Blvd. off Hwy. 89, U.S. 50, Stateline, NV* ☎ *775/586–7000 or 800/432–8365* ⊕ *www.skiheavenly.com* ☞ *91 trails on 4,800 acres, rated 20% beginner, 45% intermediate, 35% expert. Longest run 5½ mi, base 6,540 ft, summit 10,067 ft. Lifts: 30, including 1 aerial tram, 1 gondola, 2 high-speed 6-passenger lifts, and 5 high-speed quads.*

★ Thirty-six miles south of Lake Tahoe, **Kirkwood Ski Resort** is the hardcore skiers' and boarders' favorite south-shore mountain, known for its craggy gulp-and-go chutes, sweeping cornices, steep-aspect glade skiing, and high base elevation. But there's also fantastic terrain for newbies and intermediates down wide-open bowls, through wooded gullies, and along rolling tree-lined trails. Tricksters can show off in the Stomping Grounds terrain park on jumps, wall rides, rails, and a half pipe, all visible from the base area. The mountain gets hammered with more than 500 inches of snow annually, and often has the most in all of North America. If you're into out-of-bounds skiing, check out Expedition Kirkwood, a backcountry-skills program that teaches basic safety awareness. Kirkwood is also the only Tahoe resort to offer Cat-skiing. If you're into cross-country, the resort has 58 mi of superb groomed-track skiing, with skating lanes, instruction, and rentals. Nonskiers can snowshoe, snow-skate, ice-skate, and go dogsledding or snow-tubing. The children's ski school has programs for ages 4 to 12, and there's day care for children 2 to 6 years old. ⊠ *Hwy. 88, 14 mi west of Hwy. 89* ☎ *209/258–6000 downhill, 209/258–7248 cross-country, 209/258–7000 lodging information, 209/258–3000 snow phone* ⌕ *65 trails on 2,300 acres, rated 15% beginner, 50% intermediate, 20% advanced, 15% expert. Longest run 2½ mi, base 7,800 ft, summit 9,800 ft. Lifts: 14, 2 high speed.*

Often overlooked by skiers and boarders rushing to Heavenly or Kirkwood, **Sierra-at-Tahoe** has meticulously groomed intermediate slopes, some of the best tree-skiing in California, and gated backcountry access. Extremely popular with local snowboarders, Sierra also has two terrain parks, including a superpipe with 17-foot walls. For nonskiers there's a snow-tubing hill. Sierra has a low-key atmosphere that's great for families. ⊠ *12 mi from South Lake Tahoe off U.S. 50, near Echo Summit* ☎ *530/659–7453* ⊕ *www.sierraattahoe.com* ⌕ *46 trails on 2,000 acres, rated 24% beginner, 50% intermediate, 25% advanced. Longest run 2½ mi, base 6,640 ft, summit 8,852 ft. Lifts: 11, including 3 high-speed quads.*

At Sorensen's Resort, **Hope Valley Cross Country** (⊠ 14255 Hwy. 88, just east of Hwy. 89, Hope Valley ☎ 530/694–2266 ⊕ www. hopevalleyoutdoors.com) provides instruction and equipment rentals to prepare you for striding and telemarking. The outfit has 36 mi of trails through Eldorado National Forest, 6 of which are groomed.

If you don't want to pay the high cost of rental equipment at the resorts, you'll find reasonable prices and expert advice at **Tahoe Sports Ltd.** (⊠ Downhill: 4000 Lake Tahoe Blvd. ☎ 530/542–4000 ⊕ www. tahoesportsltd.com ⊠ Cross-Country and telemark: South Y Center, Hwy. 89 and U.S. 50 ☎ 530/544–2284). Downhill enthusiasts can get regular and demo-package downhill skis and snowboards, and cross-country skiers can get information on local trails.

Pope-Baldwin Recreation Area

▶ ❷ *5 mi west of South Lake Tahoe on Hwy. 89.*

To the west of downtown South Lake Tahoe, U.S. 50 and Highway 89 come together, forming an intersection nicknamed "the Y." If you head northwest on Highway 89 and follow the lakefront, commercial development gives way to national forests and state parks. One of these is Pope-Baldwin Recreation Area.

The lakeside **Tallac Historic Site** is a pleasant place to take a stroll or have a picnic. Among its attractions are **Pope House,** the magnificently restored 1894 mansion of George S. Pope, who made his money in shipping and lumber and played host to the business and cultural elite of 1920s America. There are two other estates here. One belonged to entrepreneur "Lucky" Baldwin; today it houses the **Baldwin Museum,** a collection of family memorabilia and Washoe Indian artifacts. The other, called the Valhalla, belonged to Walter Heller and is used for community events. The site hosts summertime cultural activities. Docents conduct tours of the Pope House in summers; call for tour times. In winter you can cross-country ski around the site (bring your own equipment). ⊠ *Hwy. 89* ☎ *530/541–5227* ⊕ *www.tahoeheritage.org* 🖾 *Free; Pope House tour $5* ☉ *Grounds daily sunrise–sunset; Pope House and Baldwin Museum late May–mid-June, weekends 11–3; mid-June–early Sept., daily 10–4.*

The U.S. Forest Service operates the **Lake Tahoe Visitor Center,** on Taylor Creek. You can visit the site of a Washoe Indian settlement; walk self-guided trails through meadow, marsh, and forest; and inspect the Stream Profile Chamber, an underground underwater display with windows that afford views right into Taylor Creek (in fall you may see spawning kokanee salmon digging their nests). In summer U.S. Forest Service naturalists organize discovery walks and evening programs (call ahead). ⊠ *Hwy. 89, 3 mi north of junction with U.S. 50* ☎ *530/ 543–2674 June–Oct., 530/543–2600 year-round* ⊕ *www.fs.fed.us/r5/ ltbmu* 🖾 *Free* ☉ *June–late Sept., daily 8–5:30; Memorial Day–mid-June weekends 8–5:30.*

Emerald Bay State Park

❸ *4 mi west of Pope-Baldwin Recreation Area on Hwy. 89.*

Fodor'sChoice
★

Emerald Bay, a 3-mi-long and 1-mi-wide fjordlike inlet on Lake Tahoe's shore, was carved by a massive glacier millions of years ago. Famed for its jewel-like shape and colors, it surrounds Fannette, Tahoe's only island. Highway 89 curves high above the lake through Emerald Bay State Park; from the Emerald Bay lookout, the centerpiece of the park, you can survey the whole scene. This is one of the don't-miss views of Lake Tahoe. Come before the sun drops below the mountains to the west; the light is best in mid- to late mornings, when the bay's colors really pop.

A steep 1-mi-long trail from the lookout leads down to **Vikingsholm,** a 38-room estate completed in 1929. The original owner, Lora Knight, had this precise copy of a 1,200-year-old Viking castle built out of materials native to the area. She furnished it with Scandinavian antiques and hired artisans to build period reproductions. The sod roof sprouts wildflowers each spring. There are picnic tables nearby and a gray-sand beach for strolling. The hike back up is hard (especially if you're not yet acclimated to the elevation), but there are benches and stone culverts to rest on. At the 150-foot peak of Fannette Island are the ruins of a stone structure known as the Tea House, built in 1928 so that Knight's guests could have a place to enjoy afternoon refreshments after a motorboat ride. The island is off-limits from February through June to protect nesting Canada geese. The rest of the year it's open for day-use. ⊠ *Hwy. 89* ☎ *530/541–6498 summer, 530/525–7277 year-round* 🖾 *Day-use parking fee $6, mansion tour $5* ☉ *Late May–mid-June, weekends call for hrs; mid-June–Sept., daily 10–4, call for exact times.*

Sports & the Outdoors

HIKING Leave your car in the parking lot for Eagle Falls picnic area (near Viking-sholm; arrive early for a good spot), and head to **Eagle Falls,** a short but fairly steep walk-up canyon. You'll have a brilliant panorama of Emerald Bay from this spot, near the boundary of Desolation Wilderness. If you want a full-day's hike and you're in good shape, continue 5 mi, past Eagle Lake, to Upper and Middle Velma Lakes (bring a good map).

SWIMMING Hike past Eagle Falls (about 1 mi from the parking lot) to **Eagle Lake,** where you can shed your clothes (bring a suit weekends) and dive into cold, blue, alpine water.

D. L. Bliss State Park

❹ *3 mi north of Emerald Bay State Park on Hwy. 89.*

D. L. Bliss State Park takes its name from Duane LeRoy Bliss, a 19th-century lumber magnate. At one time Bliss owned nearly 75% of Tahoe's lakefront, along with local steamboats, railroads, and banks. The Bliss family donated these 1,200 acres to the state in the 1930s. The park shares 6 mi of shoreline with Emerald Bay State Park. At the north end of Bliss is Rubicon Point, which overlooks one of the lake's deepest spots. Short trails lead to an old lighthouse and Balancing Rock, which weighs 250,000 pounds and balances on a fist of granite. A 4¼-mi trail—one of Tahoe's premier hikes—leads to Vikingsholm and provides stunning lake views. Two white-sand beaches front some of Tahoe's warmest water. ✉ *Hwy. 89* ☎ *530/525-7277* 🏷 *Day-use $6 per vehicle* ⊙ *Late May–Sept., daily sunrise–sunset.*

Camping

⛺ **D. L. Bliss State Park Campground.** In one of California's most beautiful spots, quiet, wooded hills make for blissful family camping near the lake. The campground is open June to September, and reservations are accepted up to seven months in advance. It's expensive for a campground, but the location can't be beat, especially at the beach campsites. Book long in advance. ✉ *Off Hwy. 89, 17 mi south of Tahoe City on lake side* ☎ *916/638-5883 or 800/444-7275* ⊕ *www.reserveamerica. com* 🏷 *$25–$35* ⛺ *168 sites* ♿ *Grills, flush toilets, drinking water, showers, bear boxes, fire pits, picnic tables, public telephone, swimming (beach).*

Sugar Pine Point State Park

★ ❺ *8 mi north of D. L. Bliss State Park on Hwy. 89.*

The main attraction at Sugar Pine Point State Park is **Ehrman Mansion,** a 1903 stone-and-shingle summer home furnished in period style. In its day it was the height of modernity, with a refrigerator, an elevator, and an electric stove (tours leave hourly). Also in the park are a trapper's log cabin from the mid-19th century, a nature preserve with wildlife exhibits, a lighthouse, the start of the 10-mi-long biking trail to Tahoe City, and an extensive system of hiking and cross-country skiing trails. If you're feeling less ambitious, you can relax on the sun-dap-

16

pled lawn behind the mansion and gaze out at the lake. ⊠ *Hwy. 89* ☎ *530/525–7982 mansion in season, 530/525–7232 year-round* 🖅*Day-use $5 per vehicle, mansion tour $5* ☉ *Mansion July–Sept., daily 11–4, call ahead for June hrs.*

Camping

⚠️ **Sugar Pine Point State Park Campground/General Creek Campground.** This beautiful and homey campground on the mountain side of Highway 89 is one of the few public ones to remain open in winter, when it's popular with cross-country skiers. There are no hookups here, and the showers operate from late May to early September only. ⊠ *Hwy. 89, 1 mi south of Tahoma* ☎ *916/638–5883 or 800/444–7275* ⊕ *www.reserveamerica.com* 🖅 *$25* 🛏 *175 sites* ⚐ *Grills, flush toilets, drinking water, showers, bear boxes, fire pits, public telephone.*

Tahoma

❻ *1 mi north of Sugar Pine Point State Park on Hwy. 89; 23 mi south of Truckee on Hwy. 89.*

The quiet west shore offers a glimpse back in time to "Old Tahoe." Tahoma exemplifies life on the lake in its early days, with rustic, lakeside vacation cottages that are far from the blinking lights of South Shore's casinos. In 1960 Tahoma was host of the Olympic Nordic–skiing competitions. Today there's little to do here except stroll by the lake and listen to the wind in the trees, making it a favorite homebase for mellow families and nature buffs.

Where to Stay

★ **$–$$$** 🏠 **Tahoma Meadows B&B Cottages.** It's hard to beat Tahoma Meadows for atmosphere and woodsy charm. Fifteen individually decorated little red cottages sit tucked beneath towering pine trees. Inside, they're cheerful, with fun details like model ships on the shelf and a stuffed bear on the bed; some have claw-foot tubs and fireplaces. Lovingly maintained by kind-hearted, on-site owners with a big white lab and two young kids, the cottages make a great retreat for families and couples. Cottages without kitchens include a delicious family-style breakfast in the cozy, gable-roofed lodge. Down to earth and simple, this is one of Tahoe's best hideaways. ⊠ *6821 W. Lake Blvd., Box 810, 96142* ☎ *530/525–1553 or 866/525–1553* ⊕ *www.tahomameadows.com* 🛏 *15 cabins* ⚐ *Restaurant, some kitchens, cable TV, Wi-Fi, outdoor hot tub, some pets allowed (fee); no a/c, no room phones, no smoking* ☰ *AE, D, MC, V* ✲❘ *BP.*

Sports & the Outdoors

You'll feel as though you're going to ski into the lake when you schuss down the face of **Homewood Mountain Resort**—and you could if you really wanted to, because the mountain rises right off the shoreline. This is the favorite area of locals on a fresh-snow day, because you can find lots of untracked powder. It's also the most protected and least windy Tahoe ski area during a storm; when every other resort's lifts are on wind hold, you can almost always count on Homewood's to be open. There aren't any high-speed chairlifts, but there are rarely any lines, and the ticket prices are some of the cheapest around—and kids 10 and under ski free. It may look small as you drive by, but most of the resort is not visible from the road. In summer, Homewood has **paintball,** Wednesday through Sunday. ✉ *Hwy. 89* ☎ *530/525–2992* ⊕ *www. skihomewood.com* ⟿ *56 trails on 1,260 acres, rated 15% beginner, 50% intermediate, and 35% advanced. Longest run 2 mi, base 6,230 ft, summit 7,880 ft, Lifts: 4 chairlifts, 4 surface lifts.*

Tahoe City

★ ❼ *10 mi north of Sugar Pine Point State Park on Hwy. 89; 14 mi south of Truckee on Hwy. 89.*

Tahoe City is the only lakeside town with a compact downtown area good for strolling and window-shopping. Of the larger towns ringing the lake, it has the most bona fide charm. Stores and restaurants are all within walking distance of the Outlet Gates, enormous Lake Tahoe's only outlet, where water is spilled into the Truckee River to control the surface level of the lake. You can spot giant trout in the river from Fanny Bridge, so-called for the views of the backsides of sightseers leaning over the railing. Here, Highway 89 bears northwest, away from the lake, and parallels the river toward Squaw Valley, Donner Lake, and Truckee. Highway 28 continues northeast around the lake toward Kings Beach and Nevada. Expect traffic as you enter Tahoe City on Hwy 89 and as you leave Tahoe City on Hwy 28.

16

★ The **Gatekeeper's Cabin Museum** preserves a little-known part of the region's history. Between 1910 and 1968 the gatekeeper who lived on this site was responsible for monitoring the level of the lake, using a hand-turned winch system to keep the water at the correct level. That winch system is still used today. The site is also home to a fantastic Native American basket museum that displays 800 baskets from 85 tribes, reason enough to visit. ✉ *130 W. Lake Blvd.* ☎ *530/583–1762* ⊕ *www. northtahoemuseums.org* 🏷 *$3* ⊗ *May–mid-June and Sept., Wed.–Sun. 11–5; mid-June–Aug., daily 11–5; Oct.–April weekends 11–3.*

In the middle of town, the **Watson Cabin Living Museum,** a 1909 log cabin built by Robert M. Watson and his son, is filled with some century-old furnishings and many reproductions. Docents are available to answer questions and will lead tours with advance arrangements. ✉ *560 N. Lake Blvd.* ☎ *530/583–8717 or 530/583–1762* ⊕ *www.northtahoemuseums. org* 🏷 *$2 donation suggested* ⊗ *Late May–June, weekends noon–4; July–early Sept., Wed.–Mon. noon–4.*

Where to Stay & Eat

$$$–$$$$ ✕ **Christy Hill.** Sit near the fireplace in the sparsely decorated, whitewashed dining room or outside on the deck, and take in mesmerizing lake views while dining on solid Euro–Cal preparations of fresh seafood, filet mignon, or Australian lamb loin. Detractors claim the food sometimes lacks oomph, but exceptionally good desserts make up the difference, as do the gracious service and casual vibe. And oh! those lake views. Come early to see the sunset—and you'll understand why the entrée prices are so high. There's also a less expensive café menu served at the wine bar or on the deck. ⊠ *Lakehouse Mall, 115 Grove St.* ☎ *530/583–8551* ⌂ *Reservations essential* ⊟ *AE, MC, V* ⊘ *Closed Mon. No lunch.*

★ **$$–$$$** ✕ **Wolfdale's.** Going strong after 23 years, Wolfdale's consistent, inspired cooking makes it one of the top restaurants on the lake. Seafood is the specialty on the changing menu; the imaginative entrées merge Asian and European cooking (drawing on the chef-owner's training in Japan) and trend toward light and healthful, rather than heavy and overdone. And everything from teriyaki glaze to smoked fish is made in-house. Request a window table, and book early enough to see the lake view from the elegantly sparse dining room. ⊠ *640 N. Lake Blvd.* ☎ *530/583–5700* ⌂ *Reservations essential* ⊟ *MC, V* ⊘ *Closed Tues. No lunch.*

$$ ✕ **Sol y Lago.** It's hard to find imaginative food at Lake Tahoe. Many places serve only the tried-and-true steak-and-seafood menu, especially at factory-style lake-view restaurants where the norm is: the better the view, the worse the food. But Sol y Lago takes big risks with its "Sierra Latino" cuisine (read: Spanish, Portugese, Chilean, Argentinean, and French). Dishes are layered with color and texture, and have a good interplay of spicy, tangy, and sweet flavors. Hard-nosed foodies complain there's too much happening on the plate and that flavors get muddied, but the place deserves praise for ambition, and it's worth a look. Did we mention the killer views? They're some of the best on the lake. Book a window seat. ⊠ *760 N. Lake Blvd., upstairs in Boatworks Mall* ☎ *530/583–0358* ⊟ *AE, D, MC, V* ⊘ *No lunch in spring and fall.*

★ **¢** ✕ **Fire Sign Café.** There's often a wait at the west shore's best spot for breakfast and lunch, but it's worth it. The pastries are made from scratch, the salmon is smoked in-house, the salsa is hand cut, and there's real maple syrup for the many flavors of pancakes and waffles. The eggs Benedict are delicious. ⊠ *1785 W. Lake Blvd.* ☎ *530/583–0871* ⊟ *AE, MC, V* ⌂ *Reservations not accepted* ⊘ *No dinner.*

¢ ✕ **Syd's Bagelry.** For breakfast bagels and pastries, and lunchtime salads and sandwiches, locals head to Syd's, which brews good coffee and provides free Wi-Fi, too. Want the skinny on Tahoe City? Talk to Dean, the affable owner. ⊠ *550 N. Lake Tahoe Blvd.* ☎ *530/583–2666* ⊟ *No credit cards* ⊘ *No dinner.*

★ **$$$–$$$$** ✕⊡ **Sunnyside Restaurant and Lodge.** The views are superb at this pretty little lodge, right on the lake, 3 mi south of Tahoe City. All but four rooms have balconies and locally crafted furnishings; some have river-rock fireplaces and wet bars, and some have pull-out sofas. The lodge is great for couples, but it's not geared toward families. The inviting restaurant ($–$$$) echoes the design of old mahogany Chris Craft speedboats. Alas, there's nothing spectacular about the standard preparations of steak, seafood, and pasta (think fried zucchini, Caesar salad, and prime rib), but the quality is satisfactory, if not special. The bar, however, is a blast, and gets packed with boaters and Bacchanalian revelers. Be forewarned: this is *not* a quiet place on weekends in summer. ⊠ *1850 W. Lake Blvd., Box 5969, 96145* ☎ *530/583–7200 or 800/822–2754* ⊟ *530/583–2551* ⊕ *www.sunnysidetahoe.com* ⇝ *18 rooms, 5 suites* ⌂ *Restaurant, room service, fans, cable TV, in-room VCRs, beach, bar; no a/c, no smoking* ⊟ *AE, MC, V* ⊙⊦ *CP.*

$$–$$$ ⊞ **Cottage Inn.** Avoid the crowds by staying just south of town in one of these charming circa-1938 log cottages under the towering pines on the lake's west shore. Cute as a button, with knotty-pine paneling, lodgepole-pine furniture, and a gas-flame stone fireplace, each unit typifies old-Tahoe style while embracing you with up-to-date comfort. If you're exceptionally tall, you may find some of the sloped ceilings in the upstairs rooms a bit low; ask when you book. There's also a private beach and Wi-Fi in the lobby. ⊠ *1690 W. Lake Blvd., Box 66, 96145* ☎ *530/581–4073 or 800/581–4073* 🖷 *530/581–0226* ⊕ *www. thecottageinn.com* ⟳ *27 rooms* ⚲ *Some in-room hot tubs, cable TV, in-room VCRs, lake, sauna, beach, Wi-Fi; no a/c, no room phones, no kids under 12, no smoking* ⊟ *MC, V* ⦀ *BP.*

$–$$ ⊞ **Tahoe City Travelodge.** There are a lot of shabby motels around Lake Tahoe (especially in South Lake), but this one is a good, solid choice. Rooms are tidy and well maintained, if predictable in their mauve upholstery and blond-wood laminate furniture. The service is sometimes perfunctory, but all in all, this place offers a square deal, with no surprises and no regrets. Best of all, there's a great second-story lake-view deck with a hot tub and a sauna. ⊠ *455 N. Lake Blvd., Box 84, 96145* ☎ *530/583–3766 or 800/578–7878* 🖷 *530/583–8045* ⊕ *www. travelodge.com* ⟳ *47 rooms* ⚲ *Microwaves, refrigerators, cable TV, some in-room VCRs, in-room data ports, pool, hot tub, sauna* ⦀ *CP* ⊟ *AE, D, MC, V.*

¢–$ ⊞ **Mother Nature's Inn.** Smack-dab in the middle of town, this quirky inn is Tahoe City's best bargain. It's actually a two-story motel-style layout of rooms behind a home-furnishings store. The rooms have no views and get little light, but they're surprisingly comfortable and remarkably well decorated. And you can't beat the price. There's no extra charge for additional people staying in the room—a boon for groups traveling on the cheap. ⊠ *551 N. Lake Blvd., Box 7075, 96145* ☎ *530/ 581–4278 or 800/558–4278* 🖷 *530/581–4272* ⊕ *www.mothernaturesinn. com* ⟳ *8 rooms* ⚲ *Refrigerators, cable TV, some pets allowed (fee); no smoking* ⊟ *AE, D, MC, V.*

Sports & the Outdoors

GOLF Golfers use pull carts or caddies at the 9-hole **Tahoe City Golf Course** (⊠Hwy. 28 ☎ 530/583–1516), which opened in 1917. ■ TIP→ **All greens break toward the lake.** Though rates vary by season, the maximum greens fees are $35 for 9 holes, $65 for 18; a power cart costs $18 to $30.

MOUNTAIN **Cyclepaths Mountain Bike Adventures** (⊠ 1785 W. Lake Blvd. ☎ 530/581–
BIKING 1171 or 800/780–2453 ⊕ www.cyclepaths.com) is a combination full-service bike shop and bike-adventure outfitter. It offers instruction in mountain biking, guided tours (from half-day to weeklong excursions), tips for self-guided bike touring, bike repairs, and books and maps on the area.

RIVER RAFTING In summer you can take a self-guided raft trip down a gentle 5-mi
ひ stretch of the Truckee River through **Truckee River Rafting** (☎ 530/583–7238 or 888/584–7238 ⊕ www.truckeeriverrafting.com). They will shuttle you back to your car at the end of your two- to four-hour trip. On a warm day, this makes a great family outing.

16

SKIING ★ The locals' favorite place to ski on the north shore, **Alpine Meadows Ski Area** is also the unofficial telemarking hub of the Sierra. With 495 inches of snow annually, Alpine has some of Tahoe's most reliable conditions. It's usually one of the first areas to open in November and one of the last to close in May or June. Alpine isn't the place for arrogant show-offs; instead, you'll find down-to-earth alpine fetishists. The two peaks here are well suited to intermediate skiers, but for experts there's also an open boundary to the backcountry (take "High Traverse" from the summit). Snowboarders and hot-dog skiers will find a terrain park with a half pipe, superpipe, rails, and tabletops, as well as a boarder-cross course. Alpine is a great place to learn to ski, and the Tahoe Adaptive Ski School here teaches and coaches those with physical and mental disabilities. There's also an area for overnight RV parking. On Saturday, because of the limited parking, there's more acreage per person than at other resorts. Tickets cost only $42, a steal compared to other area resorts. ⊠ *Off Hwy. 89, 6 mi northwest of Tahoe City and 13 mi south of I–80* ☎ *530/583–4232 or 800/441–4423, 530/581–8374 snow phone* ⊕ *www.skialpine.com* ☞ *100 trails on 2,000 acres, rated 25% beginner, 40% intermediate, 35% advanced. Longest run 2½ mi, base 6,835 ft, summit 8,637 ft. Lifts: 12, including 1 high-speed 6-passenger lift and 2 high-speed quads.*

You can rent skis, boards, and snowshoes at **Tahoe Dave's Skis and Boards** (⊠ 620 N. Lake Blvd. ☎ 530/583–0400), which has the area's best selection of downhill rental equipment. If you plan to ski or board the backcountry, you'll find everything from crampons to tranceivers at the **Backcountry** (⊠ 690 N. Lake Blvd. ☎ 530/581–5861 ⊕ www.thebackcountry.net).

Olympic Valley

❽ *7 mi north of Tahoe City via Hwy. 89 to Squaw Valley Rd.; 8½ mi south of Truckee via Hwy. 89 to Squaw Valley Rd.*

Olympic Valley got its name in 1960, when Squaw Valley USA, the ski resort here, hosted the winter Olympics. Snow sports remain the primary activity, but once summer comes, you can hike into the adjacent Granite Chief Wilderness, ride horseback through wildflower-studded alpine meadows, or lie by a swimming pool in one of the Sierra's prettiest valleys.

The centerpiece of Olympic Valley is the **Village at Squaw Valley** (☎ 530/584–1000 or 530/584–6205, 888/805–5022 for condo reservations ⊕ www.thevillageatsquaw.com), a pedestrian mall at the base of several four-story ersatz-Bavarian-style stone-and-timber buildings, where you'll find restaurants, high-end condo rentals, boutiques, and cafés. The village often holds events and festivals. Make it a point to visit **Waxen Moon** (☎ 530/584–6006), a shop where you can make your own candles—a godsend for parents traveling with kids when the weather isn't cooperating. Call or stop by to make reservations, especially during high season.

You can ride the Squaw Valley Cable Car up 2,000 vertical feet to **High Camp,** which at 8,200 feet commands superb views of Lake Tahoe and the surrounding mountains. In summer you can go for a hike, sit by the pool at the High Camp Bath and Tennis Club, or have a cocktail and watch the sunset. In winter you can ski, ice-skate, or snow-tube. There's also a restaurant, lounge, and small Olympic museum. ☒ *Cable Car Bldg., Squaw Valley* ☎ *530/583–6985 cable car, 530/581–7278 High Camp* ⊕ *www.squaw.com* ☒ *Cable car $19; special packages include swimming or skating* ☉ *Daily; call for hrs.*

Where to Stay & Eat

$$$–$$$$

FodorsChoice

★

✕ **PlumpJack Café.** The best restaurant at Olympic Valley is also the finest in the entire Tahoe Basin, the epitome of discreet chic and a must-visit for all serious foodies. The menu changes often, but look for tuna-tartare cones, seared Diver scallops, Sonoma rabbit three ways, or the Liberty duck breast. And rather than complicated, heavy sauces, the chef uses simple reductions to complement a dish. The result: clean, dynamic, bright flavors. The wine list is exceptional for its variety and surprisingly low prices. If not for the view of the craggy mountains through the windows lining the cushy, 60-seat dining room, you might swear you were in San Francisco. ☒ *1920 Squaw Valley Rd.* ☎ *530/583–1576 or 800/323–7666* ⌕ *Reservations essential* ☰ *AE, MC, V.*

$$$

✕ **Graham's of Squaw Valley.** Sit by a floor-to-ceiling river-rock hearth under a knotty-pine peaked ceiling in the intimate dining room in the Christy Inn Lodge. The southern European–inspired menu changes often, but expect such dishes as cassoulet, seafood paella, pheasant ragout with pasta, or a simple grilled rib eye with sautéed onions. The execution can be spotty, but the room is so cozy that most people are willing to overlook the occasional culinary gaffe. You can also stop in at the bar for wine and appetizers by the fire. ☒ *1650 Squaw Valley Rd.* ☎ *530/581–0454* ☰ *MC, V* ⌕ *Reservations essential* ☉ *Closed Mon. No lunch.*

$$–$$$

✕ **Balboa Café.** The top choice for lunch in the Village is also a romantic, if loud, spot for dinner. Aside from having the best burger in the valley, Balboa serves a varied menu of contemporary California cuisine, including steak frites and Cobb salad at lunch, and ahi tuna tartare, Muscovy duck breast, and grilled lamb chops at dinner. The bar is a top choice for cocktails, but occasionally sports fans colonize the place and decible levels go off the charts. ☒ *Village at Squaw Valley, 1995 Squaw Valley Rd.* ☎ *530/583–5850* ⌕ *Reservations essential* ☰ *AE, MC, V.*

$$–$$$

✕ **Mamsake.** The hip and happening spot for sushi at Squaw serves stylized presentations in an industrial-warehouse-like room. Sit at the bar and watch extreme ski movies, many of which were filmed right outside the window. Be patient: service is inconsistent. From 3 PM to 5 PM, you can't beat the afternoon special: a spicy-tuna or salmon handroll and a can of Bud for five bucks. ☒ *The Village at Squaw Valley* ☎ *530/584–0110* ☰ *AE, MC, V.*

$$$$

✕☒ **Resort at Squaw Creek.** Completely redesigned and refurbished in 2005, the rooms at this vast 650-acre resort-within-a-resort look great for the first time since the early 1990s. Done up in warm earth tones, with attractive wooden furnishings and rich fabrics, the resort has been converted into a condo hotel, and most units are kitchen suites. The black-glass-and-concrete behemoth architecture is dated and out of place—more like Scottsdale than the Sierra—but the extensive facilities have all the amenities and services you could possibly want, making it good for large groups and families. In winter the resort operates its own chairlift to the mountain. ⊠ *400 Squaw Creek Rd., 96146* ☎ *530/583-6300 or 800/327-3353* 🖷 *530/581-5407* ⊕ *www.squawcreek.com* ➦ *203 rooms, 200 suites* ♻ *2 restaurants, coffee shop, some kitchens, minibars, cable TV with movies and video games, in-room DVDs, Wi-Fi, 18-hole golf course, 2 tennis courts, 3 pools, health club, hair salon, 4 hot tubs, sauna, spa, cross-country skiing, downhill skiing, ice-skating, ski shop, ski storage, sleigh rides, sports bar, shops, children's programs (ages 4–12), dry cleaning, laundry service, concierge, business services, meeting rooms, free parking* 🖃 *AE, D, MC, V.*

$$$–$$$$ 🏨 **PlumpJack Squaw Valley Inn.** If style and luxury are a must, make Plump-
Fodor'sChoice   Jack your first choice. The two-story, cedar-sided inn sits right next to
★   the cable car, and has a snappy, sophisticated look and laid-back sensibility, perfect for the Bay Area cognoscenti who flock here on weekends. All rooms have sumptuous beds with down comforters, high-end bath amenities, and hooded terry robes to wear on your way to the outdoor hot tubs. The bar is a happening après-ski destination, and the namesake restaurant (*above*) superb. PlumpJack may not have the bells and whistles of big luxury hotels, but the service—personable and attentive—can't be beat. Not all rooms have tubs: if it matters, request one. ⊠ *1920 Squaw Valley Rd., 96146* ☎ *530/583–1576 or 800/323-7666* 🖷 *530/583–1734* ⊕ *www.plumpjack.com* ➦ *56 rooms, 5 suites* ♻ *Restaurant, fans, some in-room hot tubs, minibars, cable TV, in-room DVDs, Wi-Fi, 2 outdoor hot tubs, massage, mountain bikes, basketball, hiking, Ping-Pong, cross-country skiing, downhill skiing, ski storage, bar, shop, babysitting, concierge, meeting rooms, free parking; no a/c* 🖃 *AE, D, MC, V* ⭤ *BP.*

$$$–$$$$ 🏨 **Squaw Valley Lodge.** Ski right to the doors of this all-suites condo complex, which offers many of the amenities of a full-service hotel. The units are individually owned and styled, so there's no uniformity to the decor, but all of them come with down comforters, daily maid service, oversize soaking tubs, and well-stocked kitchens or kitchenettes. There's also an excellent fitness center with plenty of sports-conditioning equipment and Wi-Fi in the lobby. The only drawback is thin walls, so request a quiet room when you book. ⊠ *201 Squaw Peak Rd., 96146* ☎ *530/583–5500 or 800/922–9970* 🖷 *530/583–0326* ⊕ *www.squawvalleylodge.com* ➦ *142 units* ♻ *Some kitchens, some kitchenettes, cable TV, in-room broadband, pool, exercise equipment, 4 indoor hot tubs, 3 outdoor hot tubs, sauna, steam room, downhill skiing, laundry facilities, concierge, Internet room, meeting rooms, free parking* 🖃 *AE, MC, V.*

$$$–$$$$ 🏨 **The Village at Squaw Valley USA.** Right at the base of the slopes at the centerpoint of Olympic Valley, the Village's studios and one-, two-, or three-bedroom condominiums were built in 2000 and still look fresh. Inside they feel generic, like a suburban development does, but each unit comes complete with gas fireplaces, daily maid service, and heated slate-tile bathroom floors. The individually owned units are uniformly decorated with granite counters, wood cabinets, and comfortable furnishings. They're especially appealing to families, since each condo can sleep at least four people. ⊠ *1985 Squaw Valley Rd., 96146* ☎ *530/584–6205 or 888/805–5022* ⊜ *530/584–6290* ⊕ *www.thevillageatsquaw.com* ↜*290 suites* ⚷ *Kitchens, cable TV with movies, in-room DVDs, in-room broadband, in-room data ports, exercise equipment, 2 outdoor hot tubs, billiards, downhill skiing, video game room, shops, laundry facilities, concierge, free parking; no a/c, no smoking* ⊟ *AE, D, MC, V.*

Sports & the Outdoors

GOLF   The **Resort at Squaw Creek Golf Course** (⊠ 400 Squaw Creek Rd. ☎ 530/583–6300 ⊕ www.squawcreek.com), an 18-hole championship course, was designed by Robert Trent Jones Jr. Greens fees range from $50 for afternoon play to $110 for prime time, and include the use of a cart.

HIKING   The Granite Chief Wilderness and the high peaks surrounding Olympic Valley are accessible by foot, but save yourself a 2,000-foot elevation gain by riding the Squaw Valley Cable Car to **High Camp** (☎ 530/583–6985 ⊕ www.squaw.com), where you can begin a trek to Shirley Lake and then head back down-canyon to the valley for a beautiful 4-mi, half-day hike. In late summer, there are full-moon night hikes from High Camp.

HORSEBACK   You can rent a horse or a pony in summer from **Squaw Valley Stables**
RIDING   (⊠ 1525 Squaw Valley Rd. ☎ 530/583–7433), which offers instruction as well as group and private rides.

ICE-SKATING   You can ice-skate year-round at the **Olympic Ice Pavilion** (⊠ High Camp, Squaw Valley ☎ 530/583–6985 or 530/581–7246 ⊕ www.squaw.com). A ride up the mountain and a skating pass costs $24, including skate rental. In summer you can pay $5 extra to swim or sit in the hot tub after you skate. Prices drop after 4 PM in winter.

ROCK CLIMBING   Before you rappel down a granite monolith, you can hone your skills at the **Headwall Climbing Wall** (⊠ Near Village at Squaw Valley ☎ 530/583–7673), at the base of the cable car.

★ ☾   Next to the Olympic Village Lodge, on the far side of the creek, the **Squaw Valley Adventure Center** (☎ 530/583–7673) has a ropes course, a 50-foot tower, a giant swing, and sometimes a bungee-trampoline, a blast for kids.

SKIING   Known for some of the toughest skiing in the Tahoe area, **Squaw Valley**
Fodor'sChoice   **USA** was the centerpiece of the 1960 winter Olympics. Today it's the
★   definitive North Tahoe ski resort and among the top-three megaresorts in California (the other two are Heavenly and Mammoth). Although Squaw has changed significantly since the Olympics, the skiing is still world-class and extends across vast bowls stretched between six peaks. Experts often head directly to the untamed terrain of the infamous KT-22 face, which has bumps, cliffs, and gulp-and-go chutes, or to the nearly vertical Palisades, where many famous Warren Miller extreme-skiing films have been shot. Fret not, beginners and intermediates: you have plenty

16

of wide-open, groomed trails at High Camp (which sits at the *top* of the mountain) and around the more challenging Snow King Peak. Snowboarders and show-off skiers can tear up the two fantastic terrain parks, which include a giant superpipe. Lift prices include night skiing until 9 PM. Tickets for skiers 12 and under cost only $5. ⊠ *Hwy. 89, 5 mi northwest of Tahoe City* ☎ *530/583–6985, 800/545–4350 reservations, 530/583–6955 snow phone* ☞ *100 trails on 4,300 acres, rated 25% beginner, 45% intermediate, 30% advanced. Longest run 3 mi, base 6,200 ft, summit 9,050 ft. Lifts: 31, including a gondola-style funitel, a cable car, 7 high-speed chairs, and 18 fixed-grip chairs.*

If you don't want to pay resort prices, you can rent and tune downhill skis and snowboards at **Tahoe Dave's Skis and Boards** (⊠ Squaw Valley Rd. at Hwy. 89 ☎ 530/583–5665 ⊕ www.tahoedaves.com).

Cross-country skiers will enjoy looping through the valley's giant alpine meadow. The **Resort at Squaw Creek** (⊠ 400 Squaw Creek Rd. ☎ 530/583–6300 ⊕ www.squawcreek.com) rents cross-country equipment and provides trail maps.

SWIMMING There are dramatic views from the pool deck at the **High Camp Bath and Tennis Club** (☎ 530/581–7255 ⊕ www.squaw.com), where you can swim laps or soak in the 25-person hot tub for $26, which includes the cable-car ride; for $3 more you can ice-skate, too, year-round. Prices drop after 5.

TENNIS You'll find two tennis courts at the **Resort at Squaw Creek** (⊠ 400 Squaw Creek Rd. ☎ 530/583–6300 ⊕ www.squawcreek.com), but they're surrounded by a parking lot. **High Camp Bath and Tennis Club** (☎ 530/583–6985) has six summer-only courts on an 8,200-foot ridgeline, but you'll need to bring rackets and balls. Call for reservations and information on lessons and clinics.

Truckee

❾ *13 mi northwest of Kings Beach on Hwy. 267; 14 mi north of Tahoe City on Hwy. 89.*

People are calling it the next Aspen. Formerly a decrepit railroad town in the mountains, Truckee was the only community near the lake where anybody could still afford to buy property in the mid-1990s. Today, prices have skyrocketed, and the town has become Lake Tahoe's gastronomic capital. Around 1863, the town was officially established, and by 1868, it had gone from a stagecoach station to a major stopover for trains bound for the Pacific via the new transcontinental railroad. Freight and passenger trains still stop every day at the depot right in the middle of town. Across from the station, where Old West facades line the main drag, you'll find galleries, tchotchke shops, boutiques, diners, an old-fashioned five-and-dime store, and several remarkably good restaurants. North of the freeway, along Donner Pass Road, there are outlet stores, strip malls, and discount skiwear shops. Because of its location on Interstate 80, Truckee is a favorite stopover for people traveling from the San Francisco Bay Area to the north shore of Lake Tahoe, Reno, and points east.

Stop by the **information booth** (✉ Railroad St. at Commercial Rd.) in the Amtrak depot for a walking-tour map of historic Truckee.

Donner Memorial State Park and Emigrant Trail Museum commemorates the Donner Party, a group of 89 westward-bound pioneers who were trapped in the Sierra in the winter of 1846–47 in snow 22 feet deep. The top of the stone pedestal beneath the monument marks the snow level that year. Only 47 pioneers survived, some by resorting to cannibalism, though none consumed his own kin. (For the full story, pick up a copy of *Ordeal by Hunger*, by George R. Stewart.) The museum's hourly slide show details the Donner Party's plight. Other displays and dioramas relate the history of other settlers and of railroad development through the Sierra. In the park, you can picnic, hike, camp, and go boating, fishing, and waterskiing in summer; winter brings cross-country skiing and snowshoeing on groomed trails. ✉ *Donner Pass Rd., off I–80, 2 mi west of Truckee* ☎ *530/582–7892 museum, 800/444–7275 camping reservations* ⊕ *www.parks.ca.gov* 🖃 *Day-use parking $6* ☉ *Museum daily 9–4, until 5* PM *June–Aug.*

OFF THE
BEATEN
PATH

TAHOE NATIONAL FOREST – Draped along the Sierra Nevada Crest above Lake Tahoe, the national forest offers abundant outdoor recreation: picnicking and camping in summer, and in winter, snowshoeing, skiing, and sledding over some of the deepest snowpack in the West. The **Big Bend Visitor Center** occupies a state historic landmark within the forest, 10 mi west of Donner Summit. This area has been on major cross-country routes for centuries, ever since Native Americans passed through trading acorns and salt for pelts, obsidian, and other materials. Between 1844 and 1860, more than 200,000 emigrants traveled to California along the Emigrant Trail, which passed nearby; you can see rut marks left by wagon wheels scraping the famously hard granite. Later the nation's first transcontinental railroad ran through here (and still does), as do U.S. 40 (the old National Road) and its successor, Interstate 80. Exhibits in the visitor center explore the area's transportation history. There are also occasional exhibits focusing on natural history. Take the Rainbow–Big Bend exit off Interstate 80. ✉ *U.S. 40, Soda Springs* ☎ *530/426–3609 or 530/265–4531* ⊕ *www.fs.fed.us/r5/tahoe/recreation* 🖃 *Free* ☉ *Hrs vary; call ahead.*

Where to Stay & Eat

★ **$$–$$$$** ✕ **Moody's.** The closest thing to a supper club this side of San Francisco, Moody's serves contemporary-Cal cuisine in a sexy dining room with pumpkin-color walls, burgundy velvet banquettes, and art-deco fixtures. The chef-owner's earthy, sure-handed cooking features organically grown ingredients: look for ahi tuna "four ways," house-made charcuterie platters, pan-roasted venison, braised short ribs, and ultrafresh seafood flown in daily. In summer, dine alfresco surrounded by flowers. There's a limited afternoon menu, and Wednesday through Sunday there's live music in the borderline-raucous bar that gets packed with Truckee's bon vivants. ✉ *1007 Bridge St.* ☎ *530/587–8831* 🍴 *Reservations essential* ⊟ *AE, D, MC, V.*

★ **$$$** ✕ **Dragonfly.** Flavors are bold and zingy at this old-town, Cal–Asian spot, where every dish is artfully prepared and stylishly presented—and most importantly, well executed. The bright tones of Southeast Asian cooking inspire most dishes on the changing menu, which you can savor in the bright, contemporary dining room or an outdoor terrace overlooking Main Street and the train depot. Lunch is a bargain, and there are lots of choices for vegetarians. Look for the staircase: the restaurant is on the second floor, not street level. ⊠ *10118 Donner Pass Rd.* ☎ *530/587–0557* ⟁ *Reservations essential* ⊟ *D, MC, V* ⊗ *Closed Tues.*

$$–$$$ ✕ **Cottonwood.** Perched above town on the site of North America's first chairlift, the Cottonwood restaurant is a veritable institution. The bar is decked out with old wooden skis, sleds, skates, and photos of Truckee's early days. In the dining area, the ambitious menu—everything from grilled New York strip steak to vegetarian risotto—sometimes fall flat, but because of the atmosphere and hilltop views, people are willing to put up with the sometimes-lackluster food. On weekends there's live music. ⊠ *Old Brockway Rd., off Hwy. 267, ¼ mi south of downtown* ☎ *530/587–5711* ⟁ *Reservations essential* ⊟ *AE, D, MC, V* ⊗ *No lunch.*

$$–$$$ ✕ **Pianeta.** Right on the main drag of old-town Truckee, this northern Italian trattoria makes good pasta dishes—including homemade ravioli and lasagna Bolognese—and entrées such as double-cut marinated lamb chops with mint pesto, and jumbo-shrimp scampi. Alas, Pianeta suffers from the resort-town curse of inconsistency, but it merits a visit nonetheless. And it's hard to beat the romance of the room: exposed stone walls make you feel as if you're eating inside a Tuscan farmhouse. For a lighter (and less expensive) meal, sit at the bar and order from the extensive list of appetizers. ⊠ *10069 Donner Pass Rd.* ☎ *530/587–4694* ⟁ *Reservations essential* ⊟ *AE, MC, V* ⊗ *No lunch.*

¢ ✕ **Squeeze In.** Meet the locals at Truckee's top choice for breakfast, which serves 57 different omelets; at lunch there are homemade soups and sandwiches. ⊠ *10060 Donner Pass Rd.* ☎ *530/587–9814* ⊟ *No credit cards* ⊗ *No dinner.*

$$$–$$$$ ✕🏠 **Northstar-at-Tahoe Resort.** The area's most complete destination resort is perfect for families, thanks to its many sports activities—from golf and tennis to skiing and snowshoeing—and its concentration of restaurants, shops, recreation facilities, and accommodations (the Village Mall). Lodgings range from hotel rooms to condos to private houses, some with ski-in, ski-out access. The list continues to grow: Northstar has been building lots of new condos as well as a new Ritz-Carlton (due to open in 2009). Whatever lodging you book, you'll receive free lift tickets and on-site shuttle transportation and have complimentary access to the Swim and Racquet Club's swimming pools, outdoor hot tubs, fitness center, and teen center. True North ($–$$$; reservations essential, open winter only) serves contemporary American cooking prepared with organically grown produce and all-natural meats, well worth the drive. ⊠ *Hwy. 267, 6 mi southeast of Truckee, Box 129, 96160* ☎ *530/562–1010 or 800/466–6784* 🖷 *530/562–2215* ⊕ *www.northstarattahoe.com* ⇗ *270 units* ⟁ *6 restaurants, some kitchens, some kitchenettes, some microwaves, cable TV, in-room VCRs, 18-hole golf course, 12 tennis courts, bicycles, horseback riding, cross-country skiing, downhill skiing, ice-skating, ski shop, ski storage, recreation room, video game room, shops, babysitting, children's programs (ages 2–6), laundry facilities, meeting rooms; no a/c in some rooms, no smoking* ⊟ *AE, D, MC, V.*

$$$–$$$$ 🏨 **Cedar House Sport Hotel.** Built in 2006, Cedar House ups the ante for lodging at Tahoe. At first glance, it doesn't look like much, but that's the point: with solid-cedar decks, perforated-steel trim, and recycled-paper countertops, the emphasis is on green. Rooms in the four, two-story satellite buildings are understatedly sexy with monochromatic color schemes and mod-Italian overtones (think chrome and leather). Heated-tile bathroom floors and goose-down duvets with umpteen-thread-count German linens are luxurious extras. Not all rooms have tubs, and some rooms are quite small. Ask about outdoor-sports trips when you book. ✉ *10918 Brockway Rd. 96161* 🕾 *530/582–5655* 🖷 *530/582–5665* ⊕ *www.cedarhousesporthotel.com* ⇨ *36 rooms, 6 suites* ♧ *Refrigerators, some microwaves, cable TV with movies, Wi-Fi, hot tub, bar, meeting room, free parking; no a/c* ⊟ *AE, D, MC, V.*

$–$$ 🏨 **River Street Inn.** On the banks of the Truckee River, this 1885 wood-and-stone inn was at times a boardinghouse and a brothel. Now completely modernized, the uncluttered, comfortable rooms are simply decorated, with attractive, country-style wooden furniture and extras like flat-screen TVs. The cushy beds have top-quality mattresses, down comforters, and high-thread-count sheets. Bathrooms have claw-foot tubs. The affable proprietors are there when you need them, then disappear when you want privacy. ✉ *10009 E. River St., 96161* 🕾 *530/550–9290* 🖷 *530/582–2391* ⊕ *www.riverstreetinntruckee.com* ⇨ *11 rooms* ♧ *Cable TV, Wi-Fi; no a/c, no room phones, no smoking* ⊟*MC, V* ⦿*CP.*

Sports & the Outdoors

GOLF The **Coyote Moon Golf Course** (✉ 10685 Northwoods Blvd. 🕾 530/587–0886 ⊕ www.coyotemoongolf.com) is both challenging and beautiful, with no houses to spoil the view. Fees range from $95 to $150, including cart. **Northstar** (✉ Hwy. 267 🕾 530/562–2490) has open links–style play and tight, tree-lined fairways, including water hazards. Fees range from $55 to $99, including cart. The water hazards at **Old Greenwood** (✉ 12915 Fairway Dr., off the Prosser Village Rd. exit—Exit 190—from I–80; call for specific directions 🕾 530/550–7010 ⊕ www.oldgreenwood.com), north Lake Tahoe's only Jack Nicklaus signature course, are trout streams where you can actually fish. The $100–$170 fee includes a cart.

HORSEBACK RIDING **Northstar Stables** (✉ Hwy. 267 at Northstar Dr. 🕾 530/562–2480 ⊕www.northstarattahoe.com) offers one- and two-hour guided trail rides ($30 and $60), private rides, and half-day and full-day excursions (for experienced riders only). Instruction is provided, ponies are available for tots, and you can even board your own horse here.

MOUNTAIN BIKING In summer you can rent a bike and ride the lifts up the mountain at **Northstar-at-Tahoe** (✉ Hwy. 267 at Northstar Dr. 🕾 530/562–2268 ⊕ www.northstarattahoe.com) for 100 mi of challenging terrain. In 2006 the season was suspended to accommodate on-mountain construction projects; call to verify current times and prices.

SKIING There are several smaller resorts around Truckee, which give you access to the Sierra's slopes for less than half the price of the big resorts. Though you'll sacrifice vertical rise, acreage, and high-speed lifts, you

16

can ski or ride and still have money left over for room and board. These are great places for first-timers and families with kids learning to ski.

Boreal (⊠ Boreal/Castle Peak exit off I–80 ☎ 530/426–3666 ⊕ www. borealski.com) has 380 acres and 500 vertical feet of terrain visible from the freeway; there's also lift-served snow-tubing and night skiing until 9. **Donner Ski Ranch** (⊠ 19320 Donner Pass Rd., Norden ☎ 530/426–3635 ⊕ www.donnerskiranch.com) has 435 acres and 750 vertical feet and sits across from the more challenging Sugar Bowl (*below*). **Soda Springs** (⊠ Soda Springs exit off 1–80, Soda Springs ☎ 530/426–1010 ⊕ www. skisodasprings.com) has 200 acres and 652 vertical feet and lift-served snow-tubing. **Tahoe Donner** (⊠ 11603 Slalom Way ☎ 530/587–9444 ⊕ www.tahoedonner.com) is just north of Truckee and covers 120 acres and 560 vertical feet; the cross-country center includes 68 mi of groomed tracks on 4,800 acres, with night skiing December to February.

Northstar-at-Tahoe may be the best all-around family ski resort at Tahoe. With two tree-lined, northeast-facing, wind-protected bowls, it's the ideal place to ski in a storm. Hot-shot experts unfairly call the mountain "Flat-star," but the meticulous grooming and long cruisers make it an intermediate skier's paradise. Boarders are especially welcome, with an awesome terrain park, including a 400-foot-long superpipe, a half pipe, rails and boxes, and lots of kickers. Experts can ski the steeps and bumps off Lookout Mountain, where there's rarely a line for the high-speed quad. Northstar-at-Tahoe's cross-country center has 28 mi of groomed trails, including double-set tracks and skating lanes. The school has programs for skiers ages four and up, and day care is available for toilet-trained tots. The mountain gets packed on busy weekends— ⇨ the section on skiing in "If You Like," *at the beginning of this chapter,* to find alternatives on busy days—but when there's room on the slopes, Northstar is loads of fun. ⊠ *Hwy. 267, 6 mi southeast of Truckee* ☎ *530/562–1010, 530/562–1330 snow phone* 🖷 *530/562–2215* ⊕ *www. skinorthstar.com* ⌖ *72 trails on 2,420 acres, rated 25% beginner, 50% intermediate, 25% advanced. Longest run 2.9 mi, base 6,400 ft, summit 8,600 ft. Lifts: 17, including a gondola and 5 high-speed quads.*

Opened in 1939 by Walt Disney, **Sugar Bowl** is the oldest—and one of the best—resorts at Tahoe. Atop Donner Summit, it receives an incredible 500 inches of snowfall annually. Four peaks are connected by 1,500 acres of skiable terrain, with everything from gentle groomed corduroy to wide-open bowls to vertical rocky chutes and outstanding tree-skiing. Snowboarders can hit two terrain parks and an 18½-foot superpipe. Because it's more compact than some of the area's megaresorts, there's a certain gentility here that distinguishes Sugar Bowl from its competitors, making this a great place for families and a low-pressure, low-key place to learn to ski. It's not huge, but there's some very challenging terrain (experts: head to the Palisades). There's limited lodging at the base area. This is the closest resort to San Francisco (three hours via Interstate 80). ⊠ *Donner Pass Rd., 3 mi east of Soda Springs/Norden exit off I–80, 10 mi west of Truckee* ☎ *530/426–9000 information and lodging reservations, 530/426–1111 snow phone, 866/843–2695 lodging referral* ⊕ *www.sugarbowl.com* ⌖ *84 trails on 1,500 acres, rated 17%*

beginner, 45% intermediate, 38% advanced. Longest run 3 mi, base 6,883 ft, summit 8,383 ft. Lifts: 12, including 4 high-speed quads.

★ For the ultimate in groomed conditions, head to the nation's largest cross-country ski resort, **Royal Gorge** (⊠ Soda Springs–Norden exit off I–80, Soda Springs ☎ 530/426–3871 ⊕ www.royalgorge.com). It has 197 mi of 18-foot-wide track for all abilities, 88 trails on a whopping 9,172 acres, 2 ski schools, and 10 warming huts. Four trailside cafés, two hotels, and a hot tub and sauna round out the facilities. Since it's right on the Sierra Crest, the views are drop-dead gorgeous, and the resort feels like it goes on forever. If you love to cross-country, don't miss Royal Gorge.

You can save money by renting skis and boards at **Tahoe Dave's** (⊠ 10200 Donner Pass Rd. ☎ 530/582–0900), which has the area's best selection and also repairs and tunes equipment.

Carnelian Bay to Kings Beach

5–10 mi northeast of Tahoe City on Hwy. 28.

The small lakeside commercial districts of Carnelian Bay and Tahoe Vista service the thousand or so locals who live in the area year-round and the thousands more who have summer residences or launch their boats here. Kings Beach, the last town heading east on Highway 28 before the Nevada border, is to Crystal Bay what South Lake Tahoe is to Stateline: a bustling California town full of basic motels and rental condos, restaurants, and shops, used by the hordes of hopefuls who pass through on their way to the casinos.

☺ The 28-acre **Kings Beach State Recreation Area,** one of the largest such areas on the lake, is open year-round. The 700-foot-long sandy beach gets very crowded with people swimming, sunbathing, jet skiing, riding in paddleboats, spiking volleyballs, and tossing Frisbees. If you're going to spend the day, come early enough to snag a table in the picnic area; there's also a good playground. ⊠ N. Lake Blvd., Kings Beach ☎ 530/546–7248 ☝ Free ☉ Daily 24 hrs.

Where to Stay & Eat

★ $$$–$$$$ ✕ **Wild Goose.** Soft leather banquettes and polished mahogany tables complement the gorgeous lake views in this casually elegant 100-seat dining room. Sliding-glass doors open up to a lakeside deck beneath towering pines. Come early to see the sunset. The menu features fine European-inspired contemporary California cuisine; expect resort prices. ⊠ 7320 N. Lake Blvd., Tahoe Vista ☎ 530/546–3640 ☝ Reservations essential ☰ AE, D, MC, V ☉ Closed Mon. No lunch Oct.–May.

$$–$$$ ✕ **Gar Woods Grill and Pier.** The view's the thing at this lakeside stalwart, where you can watch the sun shimmer on the water through the dining room's plate glass windows or from the heated outdoor deck. There are salads and sandwiches at lunch, and steaks and grilled fish at dinner, but the best meal here is Sunday brunch. At all hours in season, the bar gets packed with bacchanalian boaters who pull up to the restaurant's private pier. ⊠ 5000 N. Lake Blvd., Carnelian Bay ☎ 530/546–3366 ☰ AE, MC, V.

$–$$ ✕ **Lanza's.** Lanza's serves good old-fashioned Italian-American food on red-and-white–checked tablecloths in a pine-panel dining room. There's lasagna, manicotti, veal piccata, and eggplant Parmesan, but you can also order your own pasta-and-sauce combination. Leave room for the homemade spumoni. It isn't fancy, but when you're craving spaghetti and meatballs, this is the place. ✉ *7739 N. Lake Blvd., next to Safeway, Kings Beach* ☎ *530/546–2434* ⌦ *Reservations not accepted* ▭ *MC, V* ✆ *No lunch.*

¢–$ ✕ **Log Cabin Caffe.** Almost always hopping, this Kings Beach eatery specializes in hearty breakfast and lunch entrées—five kinds of eggs Benedict, Mexican and smoked-salmon scrambles, omelets, pancakes, and waffles. They also serve sandwiches and freshly baked pastries. Get here early on weekends for the popular brunch, or be prepared to wait. ✉ *8692 N. Lake Blvd., Kings Beach* ☎ *530/546–7109* ▭ *MC, V* ✆ *No dinner.*

★ **$$$–$$$$** ▦ **Shore House.** Every room has a gas fireplace and featherbed at this lakefront B&B in Tahoe Vista. The lovingly tended, knotty-pine-paneled guest rooms beautifully, and simply, capture the woodsy spirit of Tahoe, but without overdoing the pinecone motif. All have private entrances and extra touches such as bathrobes, stereo CD players, and rubber duckies in the bathtubs; many have great views of the water. There's also a private beach. Yes, it's pricey but at how many places can you sip morning coffee while gazing out at the mist rising off the lake? ✉ *7170 N. Lake Blvd., Tahoe Vista 96148* ☎ *530/546–7270 or 800/207–5160* ⊕ *www.shorehouselaketahoe.com* ⇝ *8 rooms, 1 cottage* ♨ *Refrigerators, Wi-Fi, lake, outdoor hot tub, beach; no a/c, no room phones, no room TVs, no smoking* ▭ *D, MC, V* ❙❙ *BP.*

¢–$$ ▦ **Ferrari's Crown Resort.** One of the few remaining family-owned and -operated motels in Kings Beach, Ferrari's has straightforward motel rooms in a resort setting, great for families with kids. Comprised of two, formerly separate vintage-1950s motels, sitting side-by-side right on the lake, Ferrari's is impeccably kept. It's not a fancy-pants place by any stretch, just a plain-old motel, but some of the rooms have awesome views, and for value you can't beat it. Kids love the two pools; adults enjoy the hot tubs. There's also kayak rentals on-site. ✉ *8200 N. Lake Blvd., Kings Beach 96143* ☎ *530/546–3388 or 800/645–2260* ⊟ *530/546–3851* ⊕ *www.tahoecrown.com* ⇝ *71 rooms* ♨ *Some kitchenettes, some refrigerators, cable TV, free in-room broadband, free Wi-Fi, 2 pools, lake, 2 hot tubs, beach, Ping-Pong; no a/c in some rooms, no smoking* ▭ *AE, D, MC, V* ❙❙ *CP.*

¢–$$ ▦ **Rustic Cottages.** These charming clapboard cottages sit clustered beneath tall pine trees across the road from Lake Tahoe and a little beach. Cozy, simple, and well cared for, they offer an inexpensive alternative to a motel. All have patios, and some have fireplaces and kitchens. Kids love Bogie, the black Labrador–Dalmatian who lazes all day on the lodge's front porch (ask to see his one trick). If the cottages are booked, ask about the well-run sister property, Tahoe Vista Lodge and Cabins, just up the road. The service at both is terrific. ✉ *7449 N. Lake Blvd., Box 18, Tahoe Vista 96148* ☎ *530/546–3523 or 888/778–7842* ⊟ *530/546–0146* ⊕ *www.rusticcottages.com* ⇝ *20 cottages* ♨ *Some kitchens, mi-*

crowaves, refrigerators, cable TV, in-room VCRs, some pets allowed (fee); no a/c, no room phones, no smoking ⊟ AE, D, MC, V ⫯◎⫯ CP.

Sports & the Outdoors

SNOWMOBILING **Snowmobiling Unlimited** (⊠ Hwy. 267, 3 mi north of Hwy. 28, Kings Beach ☎ 530/546–4280 ⊕ www.snowmobilingunlimited.com) conducts 1½-, 2-, and 3-hour guided cross-country tours, mostly along the trails in nearby Tahoe National Forest. They provide open-face helmets and mittens, but bring your own goggles or sunglasses.

WINDSURFING Learn to skitter across the blue waters of the lake with one of Tahoe's kindest instructors at **Windsurf North Tahoe** (⊠ 7276 N. Lake Blvd., Tahoe Vista ☎ 530/546–5857 or 800/294–6378 ⊕ www.tahoeholidayhouse. com).

NEVADA SIDE

You don't need a highway sign to know when you've crossed from California into Nevada: the flashing lights and elaborate marquees of casinos announce legal gambling in garish hues.

16

Crystal Bay

🔟 *1 mi east of Kings Beach on Hwy. 28; 30 mi north of South Lake Tahoe via U.S. 50 to Hwy. 28.*

Right at the Nevada border, Crystal Bay has a cluster of casinos that look essentially the same, but have a few minor differences. Plan to stay somewhere else: these casinos tend toward the tacky and none of the lodging merits much attention. The **Cal-Neva Lodge** (⊠ 2 Stateline Rd. ☎ 775/832–4000 ⊕ www.calnevaresort.com) is bisected by the state line. Opened in 1927, this joint has weathered many scandals, the largest involving former owner Frank Sinatra (he lost his gaming license in the 1960s for alleged mob connections). In the words of one fodors. com reader, "The whole place has an old, used-car feel to it . . . Frank must be rolling in his grave." Indeed, the place needs a multi-million-dollar refurbishment, and until it gets one, we can't recommend it for lodging—but the secret tunnel that Frank built so that he could steal away unnoticed to Marilyn Monroe's cabin is definitely worth a look; call for tour times. The **Tahoe Biltmore** (⊠ Hwy. 28 at Stateline Rd. ☎ 775/831–0660 ⊕ www.tahoebiltmore.com) serves its popular $2.49 breakfast special 24 hours a day and has nightly DJs or live bands with dancing. **Jim Kelley's Tahoe Nugget** (⊠ Hwy. 28 at Stateline Rd. ☎ 775/831–0455) serves nearly 100 kinds of beers. The **Crystal Bay Club** (⊠ Hwy. 28 at Stateline Rd. ⊕ www.crystalbaycasino.com ☎ 775/831–0512) has a restaurant with a towering open-truss ceiling that looks like a wooden ship's hull.

Where to Eat

★ **$$–$$$** ✕ **Soule Domain.** Rough-hewn wood beams and a vaulted wood ceiling lend high romance to this cozy 1927 pine-log cabin, tucked beneath tall trees, next to the Tahoe Biltmore. On the eclectic menu, chef-owner Charles Edward Soule IV's specialties include curried cashew chicken, lamb ravioli, rock shrimp with sea scallops, and a vegan sauté, but you'll find the chef's current passion in the always-great roster of nightly specials. Some find it a little pricey, but if you're looking for someplace with a solid menu, where you can hold hands by candlelight, this is it. In winter, request a table near the crackling fireplace. ⊠ *Cove St., ½ block up Stateline Rd. from Hwy. 28* ☎ *530/546–7529* ⚠ *Reservations essential* 🗒 *AE, MC, V* ☉ *No lunch.*

Incline Village

⑪ *3 mi east of Crystal Bay on Hwy. 28.*

Incline Village, Nevada's only privately owned town, dates to the early 1960s, when an Oklahoma developer bought 10,000 acres north of Lake Tahoe. His idea was to sketch out a plan for a town without a central commercial district, hoping to prevent congestion and to preserve the area's natural beauty. One-acre lakeshore lots originally fetched $12,000 to $15,000; today you couldn't buy even the land for less than several million. Check out **Lakeshore Drive,** along which you'll see some of the most expensive real estate in Nevada. The drive is discreetly marked: to find it, start at the Hyatt Hotel and drive westward along the lake.

Fodor'sChoice
★
George Whittell, a San Francisco socialite who once owned 50,000 acres of property along the lake, built the **Thunderbird Lodge** in 1936. You can tour the mansion and the grounds by reservation only, and though it's pricey, it provides a rare glimpse back to a time when only the very wealthy had homes at Tahoe. You can take a bus tour from the Incline Village Visitors Bureau, a 45-passenger catamaran tour from the Hyatt in Incline Village, or a 1950, 21-passenger wooden cruiser from Tahoe Keys Marina in South Lake Tahoe (which includes lunch). ⊠ *5000 Hwy. 28* ☎ *775/832–8750 lodge direct number, 800/468–2463, 775/ 832–1606 reservations, 775/588–1881, 888/867–6394 Tahoe Keys boat, 775/832–1234, 800/553–3288 Hyatt Incline Village boat* ⊕ *www. thunderbirdlodge.org* 🖭 *$25 bus tour, $60–$110 boat tour* ☉ *May–Oct., call for tour times.*

OFF THE BEATEN PATH
LAKE TAHOE–NEVADA STATE PARK – Protecting much of the lake's eastern shore from development, Lake Tahoe–Nevada State Park comprises several sections that stretch from Incline Village to Zephyr Cove. Beaches and trails provide access to a wilder side of the lake, whether you're into cross-country skiing, hiking, or just relaxing at a picnic. The east shore gets less snow and more sun than the west shore, making it a good early or late-season outdoor destination. One of the most likable areas is **Sand Harbor Beach** (⊠ Hwy. 28, 4 mi south of Incline Village ☎ 775/831– 0494). It's so popular that it's sometimes filled to capacity by 11 AM on summer weekends. Stroll the boardwalk and read the information signs for a good lesson in the local ecology.

Where to Stay & Eat

$$–$$$ ✕ **Frederick's.** Copper-top tables lend a chic look to the small dining room at this intimate bistro. The menu consists of a mishmash of European and Asian cooking, mostly prepared using organic produce and free-range meats. Try the braised lamb shank, Parmesan gnocchi, or the deliciously fresh sushi rolls. Ask for a table by the fire. ⊠ *907 Tahoe Blvd.* ☎ *775/832–3007* ⌖ *Reservations essential* ▭ *AE, MC, V* ⊙ *Closed Sun. and Mon. No lunch.*

★ **$$** ╳ **Le Bistro.** Incline Village's hidden gem, Le Bistro serves expertly prepared French-country cuisine in a relaxed, cozy, romantic dining room. The chef-owner makes everything himself, using organically grown ingredients, and changes the menu almost daily. Expect such dishes as pâté de campagne, house-smoked salmon, escargots, and tournedos of beef with red-wine sauce. Try the five-course prix-fixe menu ($42), which can also be paired with wines. Service is gracious and attentive. The restaurant is hard to find; be sure to ask directions when you book. ⊠ *120 Country Club Dr., #29* ☎ *775/831–0800* ⌖ *Reservations essential* ▭ *AE, D, MC, V* ⊙ *Closed Sun. and Mon. No lunch.*

☾ **$–$$** ╳ **Azzara's.** An Italian family restaurant with a light, inviting dining room, Azzara's serves a dozen pasta dishes and many pizzas, as well as chicken, veal, shrimp, and beef. Prices initially seem high—hovering around $20—but once you factor in soup or salad, a vegetable, and olive-oil garlic bread, it's a pretty good value. One fodors.com reader raves: "You gotta try Mrs. Azzara's homemade tiramisu!" We agree. ⊠ *Incline Center Mall, 930 Tahoe Blvd.* ☎ *775/831–0346* ▭ *MC, V* ⊙ *Closed Mon. No lunch.*

$$$$ ╳▦ **Hyatt Regency Lake Tahoe.** Once a dowdy casino hotel, the Hyatt underwent a $60 million renovation between 2001 and 2003 and is now a smart-looking, upmarket, full-service destination resort. On 26 acres of prime lakefront property, the resort has a nice range of luxurious accommodations, from tower-hotel rooms to lakeside cottages. The Lone Eagle Grille ($$–$$$$) serves steaks and seafood in one of the north shore's most handsome lake-view dining rooms. There's also a state-of-the-art, 20,000-square-foot spa. Standard rates are very high, but look for midweek or off-season discounts. We'd like to give the Hyatt a star for its facilities, but the service has been too erratic to earn the hotel special mention this year. Nonetheless, it's worth a visit. ⊠ *Lakeshore and Country Club Drs., 89450* ☎ *775/831–1111 or 888/899–5019* 🖷 *775/831–7508* ⊕ *www.laketahoe.hyatt.com* ⤸ *422 rooms, 28 suites* ⌂ *4 restaurants, café, room service, in-room safes, some kitchenettes, minibars, cable TV with movies and video games, in-room broadband, in-room data ports, Web TV, Wi-Fi, golf privileges, pool, lake, exercise equipment, hair salon, outdoor hot tub, 2 saunas, spa, beach, dock, boating, jet skiing, waterskiing, mountain bikes, volleyball, ski shop, ski storage, 3 bars, lobby lounge, casino, video game room, shop, children's programs (ages 3–12), dry cleaning, laundry service, concierge, concierge floor, business services, Internet room, meeting rooms, no-smoking floor* ▭ *AE, D, MC, V.*

The Arts

★ Fans of the Bard ought not to miss the **Lake Tahoe Shakespeare Festival** (☎ 775/832–1616 or 800/747–4697 ⊕ www.laketahoeshakespeare.com), which is held outdoors at Sand Harbor, with the lake as a stunning backdrop, from mid-July through August.

16

Sports & the Outdoors

Incline Village's **recreation center** (✉ 980 Incline Way ☎ 775/832–1300) has an eight-lane swimming pool and a fitness area, basketball court, game room, and snack bar. Nonresidents pay $13.

GOLF **Incline Championship** (✉ 955 Fairway Blvd. ☎ 775/325–8801 ⊕ www. inclinegolf.com) is an 18-hole, par-72 Robert Trent Jones course with a driving range, both completely renovated between 2002 and 2004. The greens fee of $165 includes an optional cart. **Incline Mountain** (✉ 690 Wilson Way ☎ 775/325–8801 ⊕ www.inclinegolf.com) is an executive (shorter) 18-hole course; par is 58. Greens fees start at $55, including optional cart.

MOUNTAIN You can rent bikes and get helpful tips from **Flume Trail Bikes** (✉ Spooner
BIKING Summit, Hwy. 28, ½ mi north of U.S. 50, Glenbrook ☎ 775/749–5349 or 775/887–8844 ⊕ www.theflumetrail.com), which also operates a bike shuttle to popular trailheads. Ask about the secluded backcountry rental cabins for overnight rides.

SKIING A fun family mood prevails at **Diamond Peak,** which has many special programs and affordable rates. Snowmaking covers 75% of the mountain, and runs are groomed nightly. The ride up the 1-mi Crystal chair rewards you with some of the best views of the lake from any ski area. Diamond Peak is less crowded than the larger areas and provides free shuttles to nearby lodging. It's a great place for beginners and intermediates, and it's appropriately priced for families. However, though there are some steep-aspect black-diamond runs, advanced skiers may find the acreage too limited. For snowboarders there's a half pipe and superpipe. **Diamond Peak Cross-Country** (✉ Off Hwy. 431 ☎ 775/832–1177) has 22 mi of groomed track with skating lanes. The trail system rises from 7,400 feet to 9,100 feet, with endless wilderness to explore. ✉ *1210 Ski Way, off Hwy. 28 to Country Club Dr.* ☎ *775/832–1177 or 800/468–2463* ☞ *29 trails on 655 acres, rated 18% beginner, 46% intermediate, 36% advanced. Longest run 2½ mi, base 6,700 ft, summit 8,540 ft. Lifts: 6, including 2 high-speed quads.*

Ski some of the highest slopes at Tahoe, and take in bird's-eye views of Reno and the Carson Valley at **Mt. Rose Ski Tahoe.** Though more compact than the bigger Tahoe resorts, Mt. Rose has the area's highest base elevation and consequently the driest snow. The mountain has a wide variety of terrain. The most challenging is the Chutes, 200 acres of gulp-and-go advanced-to-expert vertical, opened in the 2004–2005 season. Intermediates can choose steep groomers or mellow, wide-open boulevards. Beginners have their own corner of the mountain, with gentle, nonthreatening, wide slopes. Boarders and tricksters have three terrain parks to choose from, on opposite sides of the mountain, allowing them to follow the sun as it tracks across the resort. Because of its elevation, the mountain gets hit hard in storms; check conditions before heading up during inclement weather or on a windy day. ✉ *Hwy. 431, 11 mi north of Incline Village* ☎ *775/849–0704 or 800/754–7673* ⊕ *www.skirose.com* ☞ *61 trails on 1,200 acres, rated 20% beginner, 30% intermediate, 40% advanced, 10% expert. Longest* run 2½ mi, base 8,260 ft, summit 9,700 ft. Lifts: 6, including 1 high-speed 6-passenger lift.

On the way to Mt. Rose from Incline Village, **Tahoe Meadows** (⊠ Hwy. 431) is the most popular area near the north shore for noncommercial cross-country skiing, sledding, tubing, snowshoeing, and snowmobiling.

You'll find superbly groomed tracks and fabulous views of Lake Tahoe at **Spooner Lake Cross-Country** (⊠ Spooner Summit, Hwy. 28, ½ mi north of U.S. 50, Glenbrook ☎ 775/887–8844 ski phone, 775/749–5349 reservations ⊕ www.spoonerlake.com). It has more than 50 mi of trails on more than 9,000 acres, and two rustic, secluded cabins are available for rent for overnight treks.

EN ROUTE As you head south on Highway 28 toward the south shore, you can take a detour away from the lake (east) on U.S. 50 to reach two interesting towns. After about 10 mi on U.S. 50, take U.S. 395 north for 1 mi to Nevada's capital, **Carson City.** Most of its historic buildings and other attractions, including the Nevada State Museum and the Nevada Railroad Museum, are along U.S. 395, the main street through town. About a 30-minute drive up Highway 342 northeast of Carson City is the fabled mining town of **Virginia City,** one of the largest and most authentic historical mining towns in the West. It's chock-full of mansions, museums, saloons, and, of course, dozens of shops selling everything from amethysts to yucca.

16

Zephyr Cove

⓬ *22 mi south of Incline Village via Hwy. 28 to U.S. 50.*

The largest settlement between Incline Village and the Stateline area is Zephyr Cove, a tiny resort. It has a beach, marina, campground, picnic area, coffee shop in a log lodge, rustic cabins, and nearby riding stables.

★ Nearby **Cave Rock** (⊠ U.S. 50, 4 mi north of Zephyr Cove ☎ 775/831–0494), 75 feet of solid stone at the southern end of Lake Tahoe–Nevada State Park, is the throat of an extinct volcano. Tahoe Tessie, the lake's version of the Loch Ness monster, is reputed to live in a cavern below the impressive outcropping. For the Washoe Indians, this area is a sacred burial site. Cave Rock towers over a parking lot, a lakefront picnic ground, and a boat launch. The views are some of the best on the lake; this is a good spot to stop and take a picture.

Where to Stay & Eat

¢–$ ✕ **Coyote Grill.** Coyote Grill serves delicious fish tacos made with fresh halibut or ahi tuna, sautéed cabbage, and chipotle aioli. There are also sandwiches, burgers, and a full bar, but the best reason to come to this shopping-center restaurant is the tacos. ⊠ *Safeway Shopping Center, 212 Elks Point Dr.* ☎ *775/586–1822* ⚞ *Reservations not accepted* ⊟ *AE, MC, V.*

✆ ▦ ⚠ **Zephyr Cove Resort.** Tucked beneath towering pines at the lake's edge stand 28 cozy, but modern, vacation cabins with peaked knotty-pine ceilings. They're not fancy, but they're immaculate and come in a variety of sizes, some perfect for families. Across U.S. 50, there's a sprawling year-round campground—one of the largest on the lake—that's geared largely toward RVers, but with drive-in and walk-in tent sites, too. The resort has horseback riding, snowmobiling facilities, and a marina with boat rentals, all of which contribute to the summer-camp atmosphere. ⌂ *Restaurant, snack bar, BBQs, some kitchens, some kitchenettes, cable TV, in-room data ports, beach, laundry facilities, flush toilets, full hookups, partial hookups, dump station, drinking water, showers, fire pits, picnic tables, general store; no a/c* ⤶ *175 sites, 28 cabins* ⊠ *U.S. 50, 4 mi north of Stateline* ☎ *775/589–4981* ⊕ *www.zephyrcove.com* ✉ *$27–$53 campsites; $169–$219 cabins* ▭ *AE, D, MC, V.*

Stateline

⑬ *5 mi south of Zephyr Cove on U.S. 50.*

Stateline is the archetypal Nevada border town. Its four high-rise casinos are as vertical and contained as the commercial district of South Lake Tahoe, on the California side, is horizontal and sprawling. And Stateline is as relentlessly indoors oriented as the rest of the lake is focused on the outdoors. This strip is where you'll find the most concentrated action at Lake Tahoe: restaurants (including typical casino buffets), showrooms with famous headliners and razzle-dazzle revues, tower-hotel rooms and suites, and 24-hour casinos.

Where to Stay & Eat

★ **$$–$$$** ✕ **Mirabelle.** The French Alsatian–born chef-owner prepares everything on the menu himself, from puff pastry to chocolate cake to homemade bread. Specialties include an Alsatian onion tart, escargots, and rack of lamb. Leave room for the dessert soufflés. On Monday from April through June, the chef holds cooking classes that culminate with a grand repast in the casual, airy dining room. The only complaint we've gotten from readers had to do with slightly high numbers on the right side of the menu, but good craftsmanship has its price. ⊠ *290 Kingsbury Grade* ☎ *775/586–1007* ▭ *AE, MC, V* ⊘ *Closed Mon. No lunch.*

$$$–$$$$ ✕▣ **Harrah's Tahoe Hotel/Casino.** Harrah's major selling point is that every room has two full bathrooms, each with a television and telephone, a boon if you're traveling with family. Top-name entertainment is presented in the South Shore Room. Among the restaurants, the romantic 16th-floor Summit ($$$$) is a standout, but bring a credit card; there's also a buffet on the 16th floor. A tunnel runs under U.S. 50 to Harveys, which Harrah's now owns. Upper-floor rooms have views of the lake or mountains, but if you really want the view, stay at Harveys instead. ⊠ *U.S. 50 at Stateline Ave., 89449* ☎ *775/588–6611 or 800/427–7247* ⎙ *775/588–6607* ⊕ *www.harrahstahoe.com* ⤶ *470 rooms, 62 suites* ⌂ *7 restaurants, room service, cable TV with movies, in-room broadband, in-room data ports, indoor pool, health club, hair salon, hot tub, casino, showrooms, laundry service, meeting rooms, car rental* ▭ *AE, D, MC, V.*

$$–$$$$ ✕▣ **Harveys Resort Hotel/Casino.** Harveys began as a cabin in 1944, and now it's Tahoe's largest casino-hotel. Premium rooms have custom furnishings, oversize marble baths, minibars, and good lake views. Although it was acquired by Harrah's and has lost some of its cachet, Harveys remains a fine property. At Cabo Wabo ($–$$), an always-hopping Baja-style cantina owned by Sammy Hagar, sip Agave-style Tequila while munching on Mexican and shouting across the table at your date. Harveys Cabaret is the hotel's showroom. ⊠ *U.S. 50 at Stateline Ave., 89449* ☎ *775/588–2411 or 800/648–3361* 🖷 *775/782–4889* ⊕ *www. harrahs.com/our_casinos/hlt* ⬭ *705 rooms, 38 suites* ⟂ *8 restaurants, room service, minibars, cable TV with movies, in-room data ports, Wi-Fi, pool, health club, hair salon, hot tub, spa, casino, showroom, concierge, meeting rooms, car rental* ☰ *AE, D, MC, V.*

$$–$$$$ ▣ **MontBleu.** Formerly Caesar's Tahoe, MontBleu opened in summer 2006, and the tired Roman theme is gone. In its place, you'll find a less garish—though still slightly kitsch—contemporary style. In the guestrooms, the major change has been only the bedding, which has been upgraded to included down comforters. Most rooms have oversize tubs, king beds, two telephones and a view of Lake Tahoe and the surrounding mountains—but many overlook the parking lot's glaring lights. Famous entertainers sometimes perform in the 1,600-seat MontBleu Theater (formerly Circus Maximus). ⊠ *55 U.S. 50, Box 5800, 89449* ☎ *775/588–3515 or 800/648–3353* 🖷 *775/586–2068* ⊕ *www. montbleuresort.com* ⬭ *328 rooms, 112 suites* ⟂ *5 restaurants, coffee shop, room service, cable TV with movies, in-room broadband, Wi-Fi, in-room data ports, Web TV, 4 tennis courts, indoor pool, health club, hair salon, hot tub, sauna, spa, casino, meeting rooms, car rental* ☰ *AE, D, MC, V.*

¢–$$$ ▣ **Lakeside Inn and Casino.** The smallest of the Stateline casinos, the Lakeside has good promotional room rates and simple, attractive accommodations in two-story motel-style buildings away from the casino. Some of the rooms are small and a bit dark, try to request one of the larger, brighter rooms. ⊠ *U.S. 50 at Kingsbury Grade, Box 5640, 89449* ☎ *775/588–7777 or 800/624–7980* 🖷 *775/588–4092* ⊕ *www. lakesideinn.com* ⬭ *115 rooms, 9 suites* ⟂ *Restaurant, in-room data ports, some Wi-Fi, pool, casino* ☰ *AE, D, MC, V.*

Nightlife

Each of the major casinos has its own showroom, including Harrah's **South Shore Room** (☎ 775/588–6611). They feature everything from comedy to magic acts to sexy floor shows to Broadway musicals. If you want to dance to DJ grooves and live bands, check out the scene at MontBleu's **Blu** (⊠ 55 U.S. 50 ☎ 775/588–3515). At Harrah's, you can dance at **Vex** (⊠ U.S. 50 at state line ☎ 775/588–6611). **Harveys Outdoor Summer Concert Series** (☎ 800/427–7247 ⊕ www.harrahs.com) presents outdoor concerts on weekends in summer with headliners such as the Eagles, Alabama, Sammy Hagar, Steve Winwood, and the Wallflowers.

Sports & the Outdoors

One of the south shore's best, **Nevada Beach** (⊠ Elk Point Rd., 3 mi north of Stateline via U.S. 50 ☎ 530/543–2600) has a superwide sandy beach that's great for swimming (most Tahoe beaches are rocky). There are also picnic tables, restrooms, barbecue grills, and a campground beneath

16

towering pines. This is the best place to watch the July 4 or Labor Day fireworks.

On the lake, **Edgewood Tahoe** (✉ U.S. 50 and Lake Pkwy., behind Horizon Casino ☎ 775/588–3566 or 888/881–8659 ⊕ www.edgewood-tahoe.com) is an 18-hole, par-72 course with a driving range. The $200 greens fees include a cart (though you can walk if you wish). You can have breakfast or lunch in the bar, but the best meal at Edgewood is at the lake-view restaurant inside the clubhouse ($$$$; dinner only).

Reno

⑭ *32 mi east of Truckee on I–80; 38 mi northeast of Incline Village via Hwy. 431 and U.S. 395.*

Established in 1859 as a trading station at a bridge over the Truckee River, Reno grew along with the silver mines of nearby Virginia City (starting in 1860), the railroad (railroad officials named the town in 1868), and gambling (legalized in 1931). A sign over the upper end of Virginia Street, proclaims it THE BIGGEST LITTLE CITY IN THE WORLD. Reno is still a gambling town, with most of the casinos crowded into five square blocks downtown. The city has lost significant business to California's Indian casinos over the past few years, which has resulted in cheaper rooms, but mediocre upkeep; there just isn't the money coming into town that there once was. Though parts of downtown are sketchy, things are changing. Several defunct casinos are being converted into condominiums, and downtown is undergoing an urban renewal, sparked by the development of the riverfront, with new shops, boutiques, and nongaming, family-friendly activities like kayaking on the Truckee River, which runs right through downtown. Temperatures year-round in this high-mountain-desert climate are warmer than at Tahoe, though it rarely gets as hot here as in Sacramento and the Central Valley, making strolling around town a pleasure. In recent years, a few excellent restaurants have shown up outside the hotels, but aside from a few notable exceptions, lodging continues to be mediocre (think mirrored surfaces, garish colors, velour upholstery, and so-so service).

Circus Circus (✉ 500 N. Sierra St. ☎ 775/329–0711 or 800/648–5010 ⊕ www.circusreno.com), marked by a neon clown sucking a lollipop, is the best stop for families with children. A midway above the casino floor has clowns, games, fun-house mirrors, and circus acts. **Peppermill** (✉ 2707 S. Virginia St. ☎ 775/826–2121 or 800/648–6992), known for its excellent restaurants, is Reno's most colorful casino, and one of the most lavish, with a 34-screen sports book too. For cocktails, the Fireside Lounge is a blast. **Eldorado** (✉ 345 N. Virginia St. ☎ 775/786–5700 or 800/648–5966 ⊕ www.eldoradoreno.com) is action packed, with tons of slots, good bar-top video poker, and good coffee-shop and food-court fare. **Harrah's** (✉ 219 N. Center St. ☎ 775/786–3232 or 800/648–3773 ⊕ www.harrahs.com) occupies two city blocks, with a sprawling casino and an outdoor promenade; it also has a 29-story Hampton Inn annex. Minimums are low, and service is friendly. **Silver Legacy** (✉ 407 N. Virginia St. ☎ 775/329–4777 or 800/687–8733 ⊕ www.silverlegacyreno.

com) has a Victorian-theme casino with a 120-foot-tall mining rig that mints silver-dollar tokens. The **Downtown River Walk** (⊠ S. Virginia St. and the Truckee River ⊕ www.renoriver.org) has gentrified downtown Reno. Where once there were indigents and homeless people, now there are street performers, art exhibits, shops, a lovely park, and good strolling. At one end, the 2,600-foot-long Truckee River white-water kayaking course runs right through downtown and has become a major attraction for water-sports enthusiasts. On the third Saturday of each month, from 2 to 5, local merchants host a **Wine Walk.** The cost is $15; stop inside the River Walk's shops, galleries, and boutiques, and they'll refill your wine glass. In July look for stellar outdoor art, opera, dance, and kids' performances as part of the monthlong **Artown festival** (⊕ www.renoisartown.com), presented mostly in Winfield Park, along the river.

☺ On the University of Nevada campus, the sleekly designed **Fleischmann Planetarium** has films and astronomy shows, providing a great alternative to the glittering lights of the casinos. ⊠ 1600 N. Virginia St. ☎ 775/784–4811 ⊕ www.planetarium.unr.nevada.edu ⊠ Exhibits free, films and star shows $5 ☉ Weekdays 11–7, weekends 11:30–7.

★ The **Nevada Museum of Art,** the state's largest museum and only accredited art museum, has changing exhibits in a dramatic modern building, a must-see for art aficionados. ⊠ 160 W. Liberty St. ☎ 775/329–3333 ⊕ www.nevadaart.org ⊠ $10 ☉ Tues., Wed., and Fri.–Sun. 10–5, Thurs. 10–8.

☺ More than 220 antique and classic automobiles, including an Elvis Presley Cadillac, are on display at the **National Automobile Museum.** ⊠ Mill and Lake Sts. ☎ 775/333–9300 ⊕ www.automuseum.org ⊠ $9 ☉ Mon.–Sat. 9:30–5:30, Sun. 10–4.

Where to Stay & Eat

$$$$ ✕ **White Orchid.** When high-rollers win big, they head straight for the White Orchid, northern Nevada's fanciest restaurant. Signature dishes on the French–California menu include a succulent elk-and-lobster combination and crab-stuffed prawns. Yes, the frilly rose-pattern upholstered ceiling and fake flowering vines are tired, but the oversize, ivory-color armchairs are wonderfully comfortable, and the solicitous waiters in white dinner jackets make you feel as if you're eating in the first-class dining room aboard a great ocean liner. And you won't find a better wine list anywhere in town. Period. Bring your credit card. ⊠ 2707 S. Virginia St., inside Peppermill Casino ☎ 775/826–2121 ⌲ Reservations essential ⊟ AE, D, MC, V ☉ Closed Mon. and Tues. No lunch.

★ $$$–$$$$ ✕ **LuLou's.** Swank and sexy LuLou's sets the standard for innovative cooking in Reno, with a dynamic, changing menu that draws influences from Europe and Asia. Expect to see anything from foie gras and duck confit to pot stickers and chicken curry, all perfectly prepared. Contemporary artwork adorns the exposed brick walls of the small dining room, making it look more like SoHo than Reno. Foodies: make this your first stop. ⊠ 1470 S. Virginia St. ☎ 775/329–9979 ⌲ Reservations essential ⊟ AE, D, MC, V ☉ Closed Sun. and Mon. No lunch.

★ **$$$** ✕ **4th St. Bistro** For deliciously simple, smart cooking like you'd find in San Francisco, head to this charming little bistro on the outskirts of town. The chef-owner uses sustainably farmed, organic produce and meats in her soulful preparations of dishes like Sonoma duck breast with maple-yam puree. Ochre-color sponge-painted walls lend warmth to the inviting and cheerful white-tablecloth dining room. Prices tend to be high, but you're paying for the top-quality ingredients, all grown by small local farmers. ✉ *3065 W. 4th St.* ☎ *775/323–3200* ⏦ *Reservations essential* ▭ *AE, D, MC, V* ☯ *Closed Sun. and Mon. No lunch.*

$$–$$$ ✕ **Beaujolais Bistro.** Consistently spot-on Beaujolais serves earthy, country-style French food with zero pretention. The understated chef-owner is known for classics like beef bourguignon, roast duck, coq au vin, seafood sausage, and steak frites, all lovingly prepared and seasoned just right. For dessert, try the profiteroles, made with homemade ice cream. They're perfect. The comfortable, airy dining room has exposed brick walls, a parquet floor, and an inviting, casual vibe, making it a good choice for an unfussy meal away from the casinos. ✉ *130 West St.* ☎ *775/323–2227* ⏦ *Reservations essential* ▭ *AE, D, MC, V* ☯ *Closed Mon. No lunch weekends.*

$ ✕ **Chocolate Bar.** If you love chocolate, don't miss this place. Part café, part cocktail bar, this hip little joint a mile from downtown makes killer truffles, chocolate fondue, fabulous fruity cocktails, and of course stellar hot chocolate, served at a small bar or at a dozen or so tables. It's open 10 AM to 11 PM and gets crowded on weekend evenings with twenty- and thirtysomethings. ✉ *475 S. Arlington St.* ☎ *775/337–1122* ▭ *AE, MC, V.*

¢–$ ✕ **Bangkok Cuisine.** If you want to eat well in a pretty dining room but don't want to break the bank, come to this cute little Thai restaurant, where delicious soups, salads, stir-fries, and curries are prepared by a Thai national. ✉ *55 Mt. Rose St.* ☎ *775/322–0299* ▭ *AE, D, MC, V.*

¢–$$$ ✕▦ **Harrah's.** Of the big-name casino hotels in downtown Reno, Harrah's does a good job, with no surprises. The large guest rooms, decorated in blues and mauves, overlook downtown and the entire mountain-ringed valley. The dark and romantic dining room at Harrah's Steak House ($$–$$$$; reservations essential, no lunch weekends) serves excellent prime steaks and seafood that merit a special trip by meat lovers; try the Caesar salad and steak Diane, both prepared tableside by a tuxedoed waiter. ✉ *219 N. Center St., 89501* ☎ *775/786–3232 or 800/648–3773* ⊕ *www.harrahs.com* ⊷ *565 rooms* ⚲ *6 restaurants, room service, 10 bars, in-room safes, some in-room hot tubs, some refrigerators, cable TV with movies and video games, some in-room data ports, pool, health club, casino, video game room, dry cleaning* ▭ *AE, D, MC, V.*

¢–$$$ ✕▦ **Peppermill.** Though the rooms look like the set of *The Tonight Show,* circa 1978, the Peppermill is the place to watch. They're building a new, all-suites tower, slated for completion in late 2007; we've seen a model room, and rest assured that these baroque suites will set a new standard for luxury in Reno. But until then, expect velour and smoky mirrors. The dining options are superior to the other casinos, and include the White Orchid (⇨ review, *above*); Oceana ($$$), an over-the-top seafood restaurant that feels like you're eating inside an aquarium; and Romanza ($$$), with fabulous place settings of Versace china and a planetarium star show. ⊠ *2707 S. Virginia St., 89502* ☎ *775/826–2121 or 800/648–6992* 🖷 *775/826–5205* ⊕ *www.peppermillcasinos.com* ➷ *1,070 rooms, 185 suites* ♨ *7 restaurants, room service, minibars, cable TV with movies, in-room data ports, pool, health club, hair salon, spa, 19 bars, casino, video game room, concierge, meeting rooms* 🗀 *AE, D, MC, V.*

¢–$$ ✕🏨 **Eldorado.** Smack-dab in the middle of glittering downtown sits the Eldorado, an all-suites tower whose rooms overlook the mountains or the lights of the city. La Strada ($–$$; dinner only, closed Wednesday and Thursday) serves great northern Italian cooking in a romantic room; Roxy's ($$–$$$$; dinner only, reservations essential) serves wood-oven-roasted and grilled meats and seafood in an over-the-top, faux-European courtyard. Both restaurants have excellent wine lists. ⊠ *345 N. Virginia St., 89501* ☎ *775/786–5700 or 800/648–5966* 🖷 *702/322–7124* ⊕ *www.eldoradoreno.com* ➷ *836 suites* ♨ *8 restaurants, room service, some in-room hot tubs, cable TV with movies, in-room data ports, Wi-Fi, pool, hot tub, casino, video game room, meeting rooms* 🗀 *AE, D, MC, V.*

¢–$$ ✕🏨 **Siena Hotel Spa Casino.** When it opened with a bang in 2001, the Siena was Reno's most luxurious hotel, breaking the floral-print mold with blond-wood furnishings and top-of-the-line beds dressed with white Egyptian-cotton linens. Alas, service faltered, and we dropped its star. The Ritz it's not, but it's on the upswing. And you won't have to navigate past miles of slots to find the front desk, because the casino is in a self-contained room. The spa merits a special trip, as does Lexie's ($$–$$$$; dinner and Sunday brunch only), which serves terrific steaks and seafood in a sleek, river-view dining room. ⊠ *1 S. Lake St., 89501* ☎ *775/337–6260 or 877/743–6233* 🖷 *775/321–5870* ⊕ *www.sienareno. com* ➷ *193 rooms, 21 suites* ♨ *Restaurant, coffee shop, room service, minibars, refrigerators, cable TV, in-room broadband, in-room data ports, Web TV, Wi-Fi, pool, health club, spa, lounge, wine bar, casino, dry cleaning, laundry service, concierge, business services, Internet room, meeting rooms, airport shuttle* 🗀 *AE, D, MC, V.*

Sports & the Outdoors

If you want to kayak or inner-tube the white-water course through downtown, call **Tahoe Whitewater Tours** (⊠ 400 Island Ave. ☎ 775/787–5000 or 800/442–7237 ⊕ www.gowhitewater.com), which provides guided trips, instruction, and rentals for do-it-yourselfers. They also guide white-water rafting trips outside town.

Rent bicycles as well as kayaks from **Sierra Adventures** (⊠ 254 W. 1st St. ☎ 775/323–8928 or 866/323–8928 ⊕ www.wildsierra.com), which also guides rafting trips.

You can golf 18 holes just 4 mi outside town at **Lake Ridge Golf Course** (⊠ 1218 Golf Club Dr. ☎ 800/815–6966 ⊕ www.lakeridgegolf.com), designed by Robert Trent Jones Sr. The signature 15th hole is set 140 feet above a lake; the green is on an island below. Greens fees range from $45 to $100.

16

LAKE TAHOE ESSENTIALS

To research prices, get advice from other travelers, and book travel arrangements, visit www.fodors.com.

Transportation

BY AIR

Reno–Tahoe International Airport, in Reno, 35 mi northeast of the closest point on the lake, is served by Alaska, Aloha, American, Continental, Delta, Frontier, Horizon, Skywest, Southwest, United, and US Airways. ⇨ Air Travel *in* Smart Travel Tips for airline phone numbers.
🛈 **Reno-Tahoe International Airport** ⊠ U.S. 395, Exit 65B, Reno, NV ☎ 775/328-6400 ⊕ www.renoairport.com.

BY BUS

Greyhound stops in Sacramento, Truckee, and Reno, Nevada. Blue Go runs along U.S. 50 and through the neighborhoods of South Lake Tahoe daily from 6 AM to 12:15 AM; it also operates a 24-hour door-to-door van service to most addresses in South Lake Tahoe and Stateline for $3 per person (reservations essential). Tahoe Area Regional Transit (TART) operates buses along Lake Tahoe's northern and western shores between Tahoma and Incline Village daily from 6:30 to 6:30. They also operate five shuttles daily to Truckee. All buses cost $1.50. In summer TART buses have bike racks; in winter they have ski racks. Free shuttle buses run among the casinos, major ski resorts, and motels of South Lake Tahoe. Tahoe Casino Express runs 11 daily buses between Reno–Tahoe Airport and hotels in Stateline. Reserve online or by telephone.
🛈 **Greyhound** ☎ 800/231-2222 ⊕ www.greyhound.com. **Blue Go** ☎ 530/541-7149 ⊕ www.bluego.org. **Tahoe Area Regional Transit (TART)** ☎ 530/550-1212 or 800/736-6365 ⊕ www.laketahoetransit.com. **Tahoe Casino Express** ☎ 775/325-8944 or 866/898-2463 ⊕ www.southtahoeexpress.com.

BY CAR

Lake Tahoe is 198 mi northeast of San Francisco, a drive of less than four hours in good weather. Avoid the heavy traffic leaving the San Francisco area for Tahoe on Friday afternoon and returning on Sunday afternoon. The major route is Interstate 80, which cuts through the Sierra Nevada about 14 mi north of the lake. From there Highway 89 and Highway 267 reach the west and north shores, respectively. U.S. 50 is the more direct route to the south shore, taking about two hours from Sacramento. From Reno you can get to the north shore by heading south on U.S. 395 for 10 mi, then west on Highway 431 for 25 mi. For the south shore, head south on U.S. 395 through Carson City, and then turn west on U.S. 50 (50 mi total).

The scenic 72-mi highway around the lake is marked Highway 89 on the southwest and west shores, Highway 28 on the north and northeast shores, and U.S. 50 on the east and southeast. Sections of Highway 89 sometimes close during snowy periods in winter, usually at Emerald Bay because of avalanche danger, which makes it impossible to complete the circular drive. Interstate 80, U.S. 50, and U.S. 395 are all-weather highways, but there may be delays as snow is cleared during major storms. (Note that Interstate 80 is a four-lane freeway; U.S. 50 is only two lanes with no center divider.) Carry tire chains from October through May, or rent a four-wheel-drive vehicle (most rental agencies do not allow tire chains to be used on their vehicles; ask when you book).

🔲 **California Highway Patrol** ☎ 530/577–1001 South Lake Tahoe ⊕ www.chp.ca.gov. **Cal-Trans Highway Information Line** ☎ 800/427–7623 ⊕ www.dot.ca.gov/hq/roadinfo. **Nevada Department of Transportation Road Information** ☎ 877/687–6237 ⊕ www.nevadadot.com/traveler/roads. **Nevada Highway Patrol** ☎ 775/687–5300 ⊕ http://dps.nv.gov.

CAR RENTAL   The major car-rental agencies—Hertz, Avis, Budget, National, Thrifty, Enterprise, and Dollar—all have counters at Reno–Tahoe International Airport. Enterprise has an outlet at the Lake Tahoe Airport (in South Lake Tahoe); Avis has one at Embassy Suites in South Lake Tahoe; Hertz has one at Harveys in Stateline; and Dollar has counters at the Reno Hilton and Circus Circus. ⇨ Car Rental *in* Smart Travel Tips A to Z for national car-rental agency phone numbers.

16

BY TRAIN

Amtrak's cross-country rail service makes stops in Truckee and Reno. The *California Zephyr* stops in both towns once daily eastbound (Salt Lake, Denver, and Chicago) and once daily westbound (Sacramento and Oakland). Amtrak also operates several buses daily between Reno and Sacramento to connect with the *Coast Starlight,* which runs south to Southern California and north to Oregon and Washington.

🔲 **Amtrak** ☎ 775/329–8638 or 800/872–7245 ⊕ www.amtrakcalifornia.com.

Contacts & Resources

EMERGENCIES

In an emergency dial 911.

🔲 Hospitals **Barton Memorial Hospital** ✉ 2170 South Ave., South Lake Tahoe ☎ 530/541–3420. **St. Mary's Regional Medical Center** ✉ 235 W. 6th St., Reno, NV ☎ 775/770–3188. **Tahoe Forest Hospital** ✉ 10121 Pine Ave., Truckee ☎ 530/587–6011.

TOUR OPTIONS

Several boats tour Lake Tahoe. The 500-passenger *Tahoe Queen,* a glass-bottom paddle wheeler, makes 2¼-hour sightseeing cruises year-round by reservation and 3-hour dinner–dance cruises April through October from South Lake Tahoe. Fares range from $33 to $61. In winter the boat becomes the only waterborne ski shuttle in the world: $104 covers hotel transfers, a bus transfer from South Lake Tahoe or Stateline to Squaw Valley, lift ticket, and boat transportation back across the lake to South Lake. There's a full bar on board, live music, and an optional dinner. The *Sierra Cloud,* a large 50-passenger catamaran owned by the Hyatt Hotel, cruises the north shore area morning and afternoon, May through September. The fare is $50. The 550-passenger MS *Dixie II,* a stern-wheeler, sails year-round from Zephyr Cove to Emerald Bay on sightseeing, lunch, and dinner cruises. Fares range from $33 to $61.

Also in Zephyr Cove, the *Woodwind II*, a 50-passenger catamaran, sails on regular and champagne cruises April through October. Fares range from $28 to $36. For the same price, the *Woodwind I*, a 30-passenger trimaran, sails from Camp Richardson April through October. Woodwind Cruises also operates half-day round-the-lake cruises aboard the *Safari Rose*, a 76-foot-long wooden motor yacht; $95 includes lunch.

Lake Tahoe Balloons conducts excursions spring through fall over the lake or over the Carson Valley for $225 for hour-long flights (plan four hours total). Soar Minden offers glider rides and instruction over the lake and the Great Basin. Flights cost $105 to $255 and depart from Minden-Tahoe Airport, a municipal facility in Minden, Nevada.

🏁 **Lake Tahoe Balloons** ☎ 530/544-1221 or 800/872-9294 ⊕ www.laketahoeballoons. com. **MS *Dixie II*** ✉ Zephyr Cove Marina, Zephyr Cove ☎ 775/588-3508 ⊕ www. laketahoecruises.com. ***Sierra Cloud*** ✉ Hyatt Regency Lake Tahoe, Incline Village ☎ 775/831-1111. **Soar Minden** ☎ 775/782-7627 or 800/345-7627 ⊕ www.soarminden. com. ***Tahoe Queen*** ✉ Ski Run Marina, off U.S. 50, South Lake Tahoe ☎ 530/541-3364 or 800/238-2463 ⊕ www.laketahoecruises.com. **Woodwind Cruises** ✉ Zephyr Cove Resort, U.S. 50, Zephyr Cove ☎ 775/588-3000.

VISITOR INFORMATION

🏁 **Carson City Chamber of Commerce** ✉ 1900 S. Carson St., Carson City, NV 87901 ☎ 775/882-1565 🖨 775/882-4179 ⊕ www.carsoncitychamber.com. **Lake Tahoe Visitors Authority** ✉ 1156 Ski Run Blvd., South Lake Tahoe 96150 ☎ 530/544-5050 or 800/288-2463 🖨 530/544-2386 ⊕ www.bluelaketahoe.com. **North Lake Tahoe Resort Association** ✎ Box 1757, Tahoe City 96145 ☎ 530/583-3494 or 888/434-1262 🖨 530/581-6904 ⊕ www.tahoefun.org. **Reno-Sparks Convention and Visitors Authority** ✉ 4001 S. Virginia St., Reno, NV 89502 ☎ 775/827-7600 or 800/367-7366 ⊕ www. VisitRenoTahoe.com. **U.S. Forest Service** ☎ 530/587-2158 backcountry recording ⊕ www.fs.fed.us/r5.

The Far North

WITH LAKE SHASTA, MT. SHASTA
& LASSEN VOLCANIC NATIONAL PARK

WORD OF MOUTH

"Lassen Volcanic National park is gorgeous and one of my favorite places. It is quite pretty just for scenic drives, but don't miss Bumpass Hell."

—myst

Updated by
Christine
Vovakes

THE WONDROUS LANDSCAPE of California's northeastern corner, relatively unmarred by development, congestion, and traffic, is the product of volcanic activity. At the southern end of the Cascade Range, Lassen Volcanic National Park is the best place to witness the far north's fascinating geology. Beyond the sulfur vents and bubbling mud pots, the park owes much of its beauty to 10,457-foot Mt. Lassen and 50 wilderness lakes. The most enduring image of the region, though, is Mt. Shasta, whose 14,162-foot snowcapped peak beckons outdoor adventurers of all kinds. There are many versions of Shasta to enjoy—the mountain, the lake, the river, the town, the dam, and the forest—all named after the Native Americans known as the Shatasla, or Sastise, who once inhabited the region.

Its soaring mountain peaks, wild rivers teeming with trout, and almost unlimited recreational possibilities make the far north the perfect destination for sports lovers. You won't find many hot nightspots or cultural enclaves, but you'll find some of the best hiking and fishing in the state. The region offers a glimpse of old California—natural, rugged, and inspiring.

Exploring the Far North

The far north encompasses all of four vast counties—Tehama, Shasta, Siskiyou, and Trinity—as well as parts of Butte, Modoc, and Plumas counties. The area stretches from the valleys east of the Coast Range to the Nevada border and from the almond and olive orchards north of Sacramento to the Oregon border. ■ TIP→ **A car is essential for touring the area unless you arrive by public transportation and plan to stay put in one town or resort.**

About the Restaurants

Redding, the urban center of the far north, has the greatest selection of restaurants. In the smaller towns, cafés and simple eateries are the rule, though trendy, innovative restaurants have been popping up. Dress is always informal.

About the Hotels

Aside from the large chain hotels and motels in Redding and Chico, most accommodations in the far north blend rusticity, simplicity, and coziness. That's just fine with most of the folks who visit, as they spend much of their time outdoors. Wilderness resorts close in fall and reopen after the snow season ends in May.

The far north—especially the mountainous backcountry—is gaining popularity as a tourist destination. For summer holiday weekends make lodging reservations well in advance.

The Web site of the **California Association of Bed & Breakfast Inns** (⊕ www.cabbi.com) lists numerous bed-and-breakfasts in the far north region.

GREAT ITINERARIES

Numbers correspond to the Far North map.

IF YOU HAVE 3 DAYS

From Interstate 5 north of Redding, head northeast on Highways 299 and 89 to **McArthur-Burney Falls Memorial State Park** ⑧ ⌐. To appreciate the falls, take a short stroll to the overlook or hike down for a closer view. Continue north on Highway 89. Long before you arrive in the town of ▦ **Mt. Shasta** ⑦, you will spy the conical peak for which it is named. The central Mt. Shasta exit east leads out of town along Everitt Memorial Highway. Take this scenic drive, which climbs to almost 8,000 feet. The views of the mountain and the valley below are extraordinary. Stay overnight in town. On the second day, head south on Interstate 5 toward **Lake Shasta** ⑤, visible on both sides of the highway. Have a look at Lake Shasta Caverns and the Shasta Dam before heading west on Highway 299 to spend the night in ▦ **Weaverville** ④ or south on Interstate 5 to overnight in ▦ **Redding** ③, where you can stroll across the translucent span of the Sundial Bridge at Turtle Bay Exploration Park. The next day visit Shasta State Historic Park and Weaverville Joss House, on Highway 299.

IF YOU HAVE 5 OR 6 DAYS

Get a glimpse of the far north's heritage in **Red Bluff** ② ⌐ before heading north on Interstate 5 to the town of ▦ **Mt. Shasta** ⑦. On Day 2, drop by the Forest Service ranger station to check on trail conditions on the mountain and to pick up maps. Pack a picnic lunch before taking Everitt Memorial Highway up the mountain. After exploring it, head south on Interstate 5 and spend the night in ▦ **Dunsmuir** ⑥ at the Railroad Park Resort, where most of the accommodations are old cabooses. On your third day take an early morning hike in nearby Castle Crags State Park. Continue south on Interstate 5 to **Lake Shasta** ⑤ and tour Shasta Dam Visitor's Center. Spend the night camping in the area or in ▦ **Redding** ③. On your fourth morning head west on Highway 299, stopping at Shasta State Historic Park on your way to ▦ **Weaverville** ④. Spend the night there or back in Redding. If you will be leaving the area on your fifth day but have a little time, zip north and visit Lake Shasta Caverns. If you're spending the night in Redding and it's between late May and early October, spend the next day and a half exploring **Lassen Volcanic National Park** ⑪. Highway 44 heads east from Redding into the park.

WHAT IT COSTS				
$$$$	**$$$**	**$$**	**$**	**¢**
RESTAURANTS over $30	$23–$30	$16–$22	$10–$15	under $10
HOTELS over $250	$176–$250	$121–$175	$90–$120	under $90

Restaurant prices are for a main course at dinner, excluding sales tax of 7¾% (depending on location). Hotel prices are for two people in a standard double room in high season, excluding service charges and 7¼% tax.

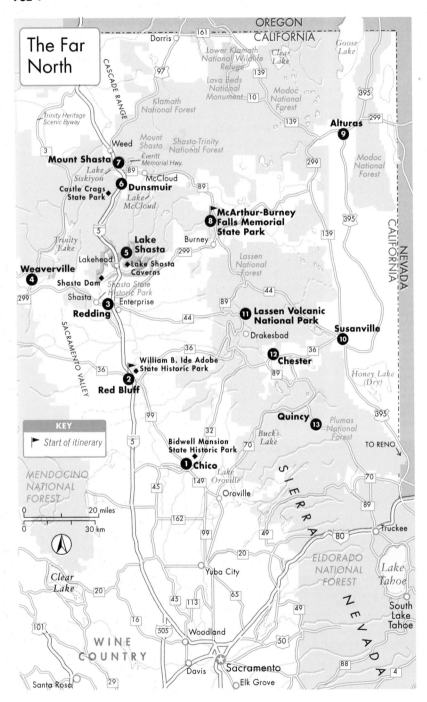

The Far North

OREGON
CALIFORNIA

Dorris · 161

Lower Klamath National Wildlife Refuge

Clear Lake

Goose Lake

97

139

Lava Beds National Monument

10

Modoc National Forest

395

CASCADE RANGE

Klamath National Forest

139

Trinity Heritage Scenic Byway

3

Weed

Mount Shasta

Shasta-Trinity National Forest

299

Modoc National Forest

Alturas
9

299

Mount Shasta **7**
Everitt Memorial Hwy.

89

Lake Siskiyou

Dunsmuir **6**
McCloud

89

Castle Crags State Park ◆

Lake McCloud

395

Lake Shasta **5**

McArthur-Burney Falls Memorial State Park ◆
8

139

Burney

Lassen National Forest

Weaverville
4

Lakehead

Lake Shasta Caverns ◆

Trinity Lake

Shasta Dam ◆

Shasta State Historic Park ◆

44

89

Redding **3**
Shasta · Enterprise

299

44

Lassen Volcanic National Park **11**

Drakesbad ○

Susanville
10

Sacramento Valley

36

William B. Ide Adobe State Historic Park ◆
2

36

12 **Chester**

36

Honey Lake (Dry)

Red Bluff

89

99

32

Quincy
13

Plumas National Forest

395

TO RENO

Buck's Lake

5

Bidwell Mansion State Historic Park ◆

1 ◆ **Chico**

Lake Oroville

70

KEY

▶ Start of itinerary

45

149

Oroville ○

70

89

MENDOCINO NATIONAL FOREST

162

99

49

80

Truckee ○

0   20 miles
0   30 km

S I E R R A

ELDORADO NATIONAL FOREST

Lake Tahoe

Clear Lake

20

Yuba City ○

20

South Lake Tahoe

101

16

45 113

65

49

N E V A D A

29

505

Woodland ○

50

88

4

W I N E
COUNTRY

Santa Rosa ○

Davis ○

Sacramento ☆

Elk Grove ○

Timing

This region attracts more tourists in summer than at any other time of year. Residents of the Sacramento Valley, which is usually dry and scorching during the dog days of summer, tend to flee to the milder climes of the mountains to the north and east. The valley around Redding is mild in winter, whereas snow falls at higher elevations. In winter Mt. Shasta is a great place for downhill and cross-country skiing—and even ice fishing at the area's many high-elevation lakes. Snow closes the roads to some of the region's most awesome sights, including much of Lassen Volcanic National Park, from October until late May. During the off-season many restaurants and museums here have limited hours, sometimes closing for extended periods.

FROM CHICO TO MT. SHASTA
ALONG INTERSTATE 5

The far north is bisected, south to north, by Interstate 5, which winds through historic towns, museums, and state parks. Halfway to the Oregon border is Lake Shasta, a favorite recreation destination, and farther north stands the spectacular snowy peak of Mt. Shasta.

Chico

❶ *180 mi from San Francisco, east on I–80, north on I–505 to I–5, and east on Hwy. 32; 86 mi north of Sacramento on Hwy. 99.*

Chico (which is Spanish for "small") sits just west of Paradise in the Sacramento Valley and offers a welcome break from the monotony of Interstate 5. The Chico campus of California State University, the scores of local artisans, and the area's agriculture (primarily almond orchards) all influence the culture here. Chico's true claim to fame, however, is the popular Sierra Nevada Brewery, which keeps locals and beer drinkers across the country happy with its distinctive microbrews.

★ The sprawling 3,670-acre **Bidwell Park** (✉ River Rd. south of Sacramento St. ☎ 530/896–7800) is a community green space straddling Big Chico Creek, where scenes from *Gone with the Wind* and the 1938 version of *Robin Hood* (starring Errol Flynn) were filmed. It provides the region with a recreational hub, and includes a golf course, swimming areas, and paved biking, hiking, and in-line skating trails. The third-largest city-run park in the country, Bidwell starts as a slender strip downtown and expands eastward toward the Sierra foothills.

★ The renowned **Sierra Nevada Brewing Company,** one of the pioneers of the microbrewery movement, still has a hands-on approach to beer making. You can tour the brew house and see how the beer is produced—from the sorting of hops through fermentation and bottling. You can also visit the gift shop and enjoy a hearty lunch or dinner in the brewpub (it's closed Monday). ✉ *1075 E. 20th St.* ☎ *530/345–2739* ≣ *530/893–9358* ⊕ *www.sierranevada.com* ✆ *Free* ☉ *Tours Sun.–Fri. 2:30, Sat. noon–3 on the ½ hr.*

★ In **Bidwell Mansion State Historic Park** you can take a one-hour tour of approximately 20 of the mansion's rooms. Built between 1865 and 1868 by General John Bidwell, the founder of Chico, the 26-room home was designed by Henry W. Cleaveland, a San Francisco architect. Bidwell and his wife welcomed many distinguished guests to the distinctive pink Italianate mansion, including President Rutherford B. Hayes, naturalist John Muir, suffragist Susan B. Anthony, and General William T. Sherman. ⊠ *525 The Esplanade* ☎ *530/895–6144* ⊡ *$2* ⊗ *Wed.–Fri. noon–5, weekends 10–5, last tour at 4.*

Where to Stay & Eat

$–$$$ ╳ **The Black Crow Grill & Taproom.** Large windows and long, polished bar in one room, and redbrick walls in the other, create a warm atmosphere that draws big dinner crowds to this popular downtown restaurant. Reading the list of wildly inventive "crowtails" will amuse you even if you don't imbibe. Hearty salads, like the smoked tri-tip and the classic Fuji apple with crumbled blue cheese and candied walnuts, are favorites. Steaks and chops share star billing with veggie dishes such as portobello mushroom fettuccine. ⊠ *209 Salem St.* ☎ *530/892–1392* ⊟ *AE, MC, V* ⊗ *No lunch.*

$–$$$ ╳ **Red Tavern.** With its burgundy carpet, white linen tablecloths, and mellow lighting, this is one of Chico's most refined restaurants. The menu, inspired by fresh local produce, changes seasonally. If you're lucky, it might include marinated lamb sirloin with basmati salad and dried fig chutney. There's a great California wine list, and also a full bar. ⊠ *1250 The Esplanade* ☎ *530/894–3463* ⊟ *AE, MC, V* ⊗ *Closed Sun. No lunch.*

¢–$$ ╳ **Kramore Inn.** Crepes—from ham and avocado to crab cannelloni—are this inn's specialty, along with Hungarian mushroom soup. The menu also includes salads, stir-fries, Asian dishes, and pastas. Brunch is Sunday from 9 to 2. ⊠ *1903 Park Ave.* ☎ *530/343–3701* ⊟ *AE, D, MC, V.*

¢ ╳ **Madison Bear Garden.** This downtown favorite two blocks south of the Chico State campus is a great spot for checking out the vibrant college scene while enjoying a delicious burger and a vast selection of brews. ⊠ *316 W. 2nd St.* ☎ *530/891–1639* ⊟ *MC, V.*

★ $$–$$$$ ╳▣ **Hotel Diamond.** Crystal chandeliers, and gleaming wood floors and banisters, elegantly welcome guests into the foyer of this restored gem in downtown Chico near the university. Some rooms are furnished with antiques that reflect the town's historic past. Johnnie's, the hotel's restaurant and bar, provides room service, and is open for lunch and dinner. ⊠ *220 W. 4th St., Chico, 95928* ☎ *530/893–3100 or 866/993–3100* 🖶 *530/893–3103* ⊕ *www.hoteldiamondchico.com* ⬎ *43 rooms, 4 suites* △ *Restaurant, room service, gym* ⊟ *AE, D, DC, MC, V.*

¢–$$ ▣ **Johnson's Country Inn.** Nestled in an almond orchard five minutes from downtown, this Victorian-style farmhouse with a wraparound veranda is a welcome change from motel row. It's full of antique furnishings and modern conveniences. ⊠ *3935 Morehead Ave., 95928* ☎🖶 *530/345–7829 or 866/872–7780* ⊕ *www.chico.com/johnsonsinn* ⬎ *4 rooms* △ *In-room data ports, business services; no room TVs, no smoking* ⊟ *MC, V* ⟡ *BP.*

Shopping

Made in Chico (⊠ 232 Main St. ☎ 530/894–7009) sells locally made goods, including pottery, olives, almonds, and Woof and Poof creations—whimsical home decor items, such as stuffed Santas, elves, animals, and pillows. Beautiful custom-made etched, stained, and beveled glass is created at **Needham Studios** (⊠ 237 Broadway ☎ 530/345–4718). Shop and watch demonstrations of glass blowing at the **Satava Art Glass Studio** (⊠ 819 Wall St. ☎ 530/345–7985).

Red Bluff

▶ ❷ *41 mi north of Chico on Hwy 99.*

Historic Red Bluff is a gateway to Mount Lassen National Park. Established in the mid-19th century as a shipping center and named for the color of its soil, the town is filled with dozens of restored Victorians. It's a great home base for outdoor adventures in the area.

The **Kelly-Griggs House Museum,** a beautifully restored 1880s home, holds an impressive collection of antique furniture, housewares, and clothing arranged as though a refined Victorian-era family were still in residence. A Venetian glass punch bowl sits on the dining room table; in the upstairs parlor costumed mannequins seem eerily frozen in time. *Persephone,* the painting over the fireplace, is by Sarah Brown, daughter of abolitionist John Brown, whose family settled in Red Bluff. Note that the house is undergoing repairs and will be closed until early 2007. ⊠ *311 Washington St.* ☎ *530/527–1129* 🖾 *Donation suggested* ☉ *Thurs.–Sun. 1–3.*

★ **William B. Ide Adobe State Historic Park** is named for the first and only president of the short-lived California Republic of 1846. The Bear Flag Party proclaimed California a sovereign nation, separate from Mexican rule, and the republic existed for 25 days before it was taken over by the United States. The republic's flag has survived, with only minor refinements, as California's state flag. The park's main attraction is an adobe home built in the 1850s and outfitted with period furnishings. There's also a carriage shed, a blacksmith shop, and a small visitor center. Home tours are available on request. ⊠ *21659 Adobe Rd.* ☎ *530/529–8599* ⊕ *www.ideadobe.tehama.k12.ca.us* 🖾 *$4 per vehicle* ☉ *Park and picnic facilities daily sunrise–sunset.*

Where to Stay & Eat

$–$$ ✕ **Crystal Steak & Seafood Co.** On Friday and Saturday, dinner here is served in the Dakota Room, an intimate booth-lined area with a hardwood floor, soft lighting, and prints of classic Old West paintings on the walls. Market-fresh seafood, garlicky scampi, and prime rib are the house specialties; a lunch menu is available in the lounge weekdays. ⊠ *343 S. Main St.* ☎ *530/527–0880* 🝙 *AE, D, MC, V* ☉ *Closed Mon.*

¢ ✕ **Countryside Deli.** Heaping platters of country-fried steak and meat loaf with mashed potatoes and gravy are the draw at this deli. Its old-fashioned soda fountain, lined with red-top swivel seats, is the perfect place to enjoy a hot-fudge sundae or banana split. ⊠ *1007 Main St.* ☎ *530/529–3869* 🝙 *D, MC, V* ☉ *Closed weekends.*

17

¢–$$ ▢ **The Jeter Victorian Inn.** On sunny days, breakfast is served in the garden pavilion outside this 1881 Victorian home. The four guest rooms are elegantly decorated with antiques and period furnishings; two have private baths, and the Imperial Room has a Jacuzzi. A separate cottage is also available. ⊠ *1107 Jefferson St., 96080* ☎ *530/527–7574* ⊕ *www. jetervictorianinn.com* ➷ *4 rooms, 2 with bath; 1 cottage* ⚿ *No room phones, no TV in some rooms, no smoking* ☰ *MC, V* ⎮◎⎮ *BP.*

¢–$ ▢ **Lamplighter Lodge.** Although its name may evoke log cabins, this property is actually a motel on the town's main street. Simple rooms are equipped with mini-refrigerators and microwaves. The pool area is a great place to relax on sweltering summer days, and the Red Rock Cafe next door is open for meals and snacks. ⊠ *210 S. Main St., 96080* ☎ *530/527–1150* ⊕ *www.lamplighterlodge.us* ➷ *50 rooms, 2 suites* ⚿ *Microwaves, refrigerators, pool* ☰ *D, MC, V* ⎮◎⎮ *CP.*

Redding

❸ *32 mi north of Red Bluff on I–5.*

As the largest city in the far north, Redding is an ideal headquarters for exploring the surrounding countryside.

🌀 Curving along the Sacramento River, **Turtle Bay Exploration Park** has a

Fodor'sChoice   museum, an arboretum with walking trails, and lots of interactive ex-

★   hibits for children, including a miniature dam, a gold-panning area, and a seasonal Butterfly House where monarchs emerge from their cocoons. The main draw at the park, however, is the stunning **Sundial Bridge,** a modernist pedestrian footbridge designed by world-renowned Spanish architect Santiago Calatrava. The bridge's architecture consists of a translucent, illuminated span that stretches across the river, and—most strikingly—a soaring white 217-foot needle that casts a slender moving shadow, like a sundial's, over the water and surrounding trees. Watching the sun set over the river from this bridge is a magical experience. The bridge links to the Sacramento River Trail and the park's arboretum and botanical gardens. Access to the bridge and arboretum is free; the fee admits you to both the museum and the botanical gardens. ⊠ *800 Auditorium Dr.* ☎ *530/243–8850* ⊕ *www.turtlebay.org* ✉ *$11* ☾ *Closed Tues. Nov.–Feb.*

Where to Stay & Eat

$–$$$ ✕ **Jack's Grill.** Famous for its 16-ounce steaks, this popular bar and steak house also serves shrimp and chicken. A town favorite, the place is usually jam-packed and noisy. ⊠*1743 California St.* ☎*530/241–9705* ☰*AE, D, MC, V* ☾ *Closed Sun. No lunch.*

¢–$ ✕ **Buz's Crab.** This casual restaurant in central Redding shares space with a bustling seafood market where locals snap up ocean-fresh Dungeness crab in season. The fish-and-chips is a favorite; seafood combos, including Cajun-style selections are also noteworthy. Try the wild salmon or trout charbroiled over mesquite wood. ⊠ *2159 East St.* ☎ *530/243–2120* ☰ *MC, V.*

¢–$ ✕ **Klassique Kafe.** Two sisters run this small, bustling restaurant that caters to locals looking for simple but hearty breakfast and lunch fare. The hot luncheon specials served daily might include butter beans and ham with corn bread, or chicken and dumplings. ⊠ *2427 Athens Ave.* ☎ *530/244–4939* ⊟ *AE, D, MC, V* ☉ *Closed Sat. No dinner.*

★ **$–$$** ✕▥ **The Red Lion.** Adjacent to Interstate 5, and close to Redding's convention center and regional recreation sites, this hotel is a top choice for both business and vacation travelers. Rooms are spacious and comfortable; a large patio surrounded by landscaped grounds is a relaxing spot to enjoy an outdoor meal or snack. There are irons, ironing boards, and hair dryers in the rooms, and video games in the public areas. The hotel's restaurant, 3-Shastas Bar and Grill, is a popular place for locals. ⊠ *1830 Hilltop Dr., Hwy. 44/299 exit from I–5, 96002* ☎ *530/221–8700 or 800/733–5466* 🖷 *530/221–0324* ⊕ *www.redlion.com* ↝ *192 rooms, 2 suites* ♻ *Restaurant, coffee shop, room service, pool, wading pool, gym, hot tub, bar, airport shuttle* ⊟ *AE, D, DC, MC, V.*

Sports & the Outdoors

The **Fly Shop** (⊠ 4140 Churn Creek Rd. ☎ 530/222–3555) sells fishing licenses and has information about guides, conditions, and fishing packages.

Weaverville

❹ *46 mi west of Redding on Hwy. 299, called Main St. in town.*

Weaverville is an enjoyable amalgam of gold-rush history and tourist kitsch. Named after John Weaver, one of three men who built the first cabin here in 1850, the town has an impressive downtown historic district. Weaverville is a popular headquarters for family vacations and biking, hiking, fishing, and gold-panning excursions.

Fodor'sChoice ★ Weaverville's main attraction is the **Weaverville Joss House,** a Taoist temple built in 1874 and called Won Lim Miao ("the temple of the forest beneath the clouds") by Chinese miners. The oldest continuously used Chinese temple in California, it attracts worshippers from around the world. With its golden altar, antique weaponry, and carved wooden canopies, the Joss House is a piece of California history that can best be appreciated on a guided 30-minute tour. The original temple building and many of its furnishings—some of which came from China—were lost to fire in 1873, but members of the local Chinese community soon rebuilt it. ⊠ *Oregon and Main Sts.* ☎ *530/623–5284* 🖾 *Museum free; guided tour $2* ☉ *Wed.–Sun. 10–5; last tour at 4.*

Trinity County Courthouse (⊠ Court and Main Sts.), built in 1856 as a store, office building, and hotel, was converted to county use in 1865. The Apollo Saloon, in the basement, became the county jail. It's the oldest courthouse still in use in California.

★ Trinity County Historical Park houses the **Jake Jackson Memorial Museum,** which has a blacksmith shop, a stamp mill (where ore is crushed) from the 1890s that is still in use, and the original jail cells of the Trinity County Courthouse. ⊠ *508 Main St.* ☎ *530/623–5211* ☉ *May–Oct., daily 10–5; Nov.–Apr., Tues. and Sat. noon–4.*

Where to Stay & Eat

$–$$$ ✕ **La Grange Café.** In two brick buildings dating from the 1850s (they're among the oldest edifices in town), this eatery serves buffalo and other game meats, pasta, fresh fish, and farmers' market vegetables when they're available. There's a full premium bar, and the wine list has 135 vintages. ⊠ *520 Main St.* ☎ *530/623–5325* 🖃 *AE, D, MC, V* ⊘ *Closed Sun. Nov.–Mar.*

¢ ✕ **La Casita.** A traditional selection of Mexican food is on the menu here, including quesadillas (try the version with roasted chili peppers), tostadas, enchiladas, tacos, and tamales. Many dishes are available without meat. Open from late morning through early evening, this casual spot is great for a mid-afternoon snack. ⊠ *252 Main St.* ☎ *530/623– 5797* 🖃 *MC, V.*

¢ 🛏 **Red Hill Motel.** This 1940s-era property is popular with anglers, who appreciate the outdoor fish-cleaning area on the premises. The separate wooden lodgings, painted red and surrounded by pine trees, encircle a grassy knoll. One cozy cabin with full kitchen is good for families; two others have kitchenettes, and the rest have mini-refrigerators and microwaves. ⊠ *Red Hill Rd., 96093* ☎ *530/623–4331* ⊕ *www. redhillresorts.com* ➳ *4 rooms, 6 cabins, 2 duplexes* ⌂ *Some kitchens, some microwaves, some refrigerators, cable TV* 🖃 *AE, D, MC, V.*

Sports & the Outdoors

Below the Lewiston Dam, east of Weaverville on Highway 299, is the **Fly Stretch** of the Trinity River, an excellent fly-fishing area. The **Pine Cove Boat Ramp,** on Lewiston Lake, provides fishing access for those with disabilities—decks here are built over prime trout-fishing waters. Contact the **Weaverville Ranger Station** (⊠ 210 Main St. ☎ 530/623–2121) for maps and information about hiking trails in the Trinity Alps Wilderness.

Shopping

Highland Art Center Gallery (⊠ 691 Main St. ☎ 530/623–5111) showcases and sells painting, photography, fiber arts, ceramics, sculpture, and other handcrafted works produced by local artists and those from surrounding mountain communities.

Lake Shasta Area

12 mi north of Redding on I–5.

★ ❺ Twenty-one types of fish inhabit **Lake Shasta,** including rainbow trout and salmon. The lake region also has the largest nesting population of bald eagles in California. You can rent fishing boats, ski boats, sailboats, canoes, paddleboats, Jet Skis, and windsurfing boards at one of the many marinas and resorts along the 370-mi shoreline.

Stalagmites, stalactites, flowstone deposits, and crystals entice people of all ages to the **Lake Shasta Caverns.** To see this impressive spectacle, you must take the two-hour tour, which includes a catamaran ride across the McCloud arm of Lake Shasta and a bus ride up Grey Rock Mountain to the cavern entrance. The caverns are 58°F year-round, making them a cool retreat on a hot summer day. The most awe-inspiring of the limestone rock formations is the glistening Cathedral Room, which appears to be gilded. During peak summer months (June through August), tours depart every half hour; in April, May, and September it's every hour. A gift shop is open from 8 to 4:30. ✉ *Shasta Caverns Rd. exit off I–5* ☎ *530/238–2341 or 800/795–2283* ⊕ *www. lakeshastacaverns.com* ✉ *$20* ☉ *June–Aug., daily 9–4 with departures every ½ hr; Apr., May, and Sept., daily 9–3 with departures every hr; Oct.–Mar., daily 10–2 with departures every 2 hrs.*

★ **Shasta Dam** is the second-largest concrete dam in the United States (only Grand Coulee in Washington is bigger). On clear days, snowcapped Mt. Shasta glimmers on the horizon above the still waters of its namesake lake. The visitor center has computerized photographic tours of the dam construction, video presentations, fact sheets, and historical displays. Tours of the dam have resumed, with some restrictions. Call for an update. ✉ *16349 Shasta Dam Blvd.* ☎ *530/275–4463* ⊕ *www.usbr.gov/ mp/ncao* ☉ *Visitor center weekdays 8–4:30, weekends 8–5.*

Where to Stay & Eat

$–$$$ ✕ **Tail o' the Whale.** As its name suggests, this restaurant has a nautical theme. You can enjoy a panoramic view of Lake Shasta here while you indulge in charbroiled salmon, prawns with fettuccine in a garlic cream sauce, and prime rib with tempura shrimp. ✉ *10300 Bridge Bay Rd., Bridge Bay exit off I–5* ☎ *530/275–3021* ▭ *D, MC, V.*

△ **Antlers Campground.** On a level bluff above the Sacramento River arm of Lake Shasta, this campground is surrounded by oak and pine forest. Open year-round, it's adjacent to Antlers Boat Ramp, and a nearby marina resort has watercraft rentals, on-water fueling, and a small store. Some campsites are near the lakeshore, but direct access to the water is difficult. Reservations are taken for mid-May through early September only. ♧ *Flush toilets, pit toilets, drinking water, fire pits, picnic tables* ⇨ *59 sites* ✉ *Antlers Rd., 1 mi east of I–5* ☎ *530/275–8113* ▤ *530/ 275–8344* ⊕ *www.reserveusa.com* ✉ *$18–$30* ▭ *AE, D, MC, V.*

Sports & the Outdoors

FISHING **The Fishin' Hole** (✉ 3844 Shasta Dam Blvd., Shasta Lake City ☎ 530/ 275–4123) is a bait-and-tackle shop a couple of miles from the lake. It sells fishing licenses and provides information about conditions.

HOUSEBOATING Houseboats here come in all sizes except small. As a rule, rentals are outfitted with cooking utensils, dishes, and most of the equipment you'll need—all you supply are the food and the linens. When you rent a houseboat, you receive a short course in how to maneuver your launch before you set out. You can fish, swim, sunbathe on the flat roof, or sit on the deck and watch the world go by. The shoreline of Lake Shasta is beautifully ragged, with countless inlets; it's not hard to find privacy. Expect to spend a minimum of $350 a day for a craft that sleeps six. A three-day, two-night minimum is customary. Prices are often lower during the off-season (September through May). The **Shasta Cascade Wonderland Association** (✉ 1699 Hwy. 273, Anderson 96007 ☎ 530/365–7500 or 800/474–2782 ⊕ www.shastacascade.com) provides names of rental companies and prices for Lake Shasta houseboating. **Bridge Bay**

17

Resort (✉ 10300 Bridge Bay Rd., Redding ☎ 800/752–9669) rents houseboats, Jet Skis, fishing boats, and patio boats.

Dunsmuir

❻ *10 mi south of Mt. Shasta on I–5.*

Castle Crags State Park surrounds the town of Dunsmuir, which was named for a 19th-century Scottish coal baron who offered to build a fountain if the town was renamed in his honor. The town's other major attraction is the Railroad Park Resort, where you can spend the night in restored railcars.

★ Named for its 6,000-foot glacier-polished crags, which tower over the Sacramento River, **Castle Crags State Park** offers fishing in Castle Creek, hiking in the backcountry, and a view of Mt. Shasta. The crags draw climbers and hikers from around the world. The 4,350-acre park has 28 mi of hiking trails, including a 2¾-mi access trail to **Castle Crags Wilderness**, part of the **Shasta-Trinity National Forest.** There are excellent trails at lower altitudes, along with picnic areas, restrooms, showers, and campsites. ✉ *15 mi south of Mt. Shasta, Castella/Castle Crags exit off I–5; follow for ¼ mi* ☎ *530/235–2684* 💰 *$6 per vehicle, day-use.*

Where to Stay & Eat

$–$$ ✕ **Café Maddalena.** Café Maddalena serves an adventurous Mediterranean menu with a French influence that draws in diners from nearby mountain communities, and as far away as Redding. Selections change seasonally but always feature offal (such as pickled lamb's tongue and red onion salad), meat and fresh fish entrées, and vegetarian offerings like asparagus cannelloni with Meyer lemon–cream sauce. Wines from Spain, Italy, and France complement the meals. ✉ *5801 Sacramento Ave., Dunsmuir* ☎ *530/235–2725* 🖃 *AE, D, MC, V* ☉ *Closed Mon.–Wed. No lunch.*

☙ $ 🏨 **Railroad Park Resort.** The antique cabooses here were collected over more than three decades and have been converted into cozy motel rooms in honor of Dunsmuir's railroad legacy. The resort has a vaguely *Orient Express*–style dining room and a lounge fashioned from vintage railcars. The landscaped grounds contain a huge steam engine and a restored water tower. There's also an RV park and campground. ✉ *100 Railroad Park Rd., 96025* ☎ *530/235–4440 or 800/974–7245* 🖷 *530/235–4470* ⊕ *www.rrpark.com* 🛏 *23 cabooses, 4 cabins* 🍴 *Restaurant, some kitchenettes, refrigerators, cable TV, pool, hot tub, some pets allowed (fee)* 🖃 *MC, V.*

△ **Castle Crags State Park Campground.** Craggy peaks tower above this campground surrounded by tall evergreens. It's a great base for hiking and rock climbing. The site can accommodate RVs up to 27 feet long. Six environmental sites—with pit toilets, and no parking or running water—in relatively undisturbed areas are for tents only. Reservations are essential late May through early September. 🚻 *Flush toilets, pit toilets, showers, picnic tables* 🛏 *76 sites* ✉ *15 mi south of Mt. Shasta, Castella/Castle Crags exit off I–5* ☎ *530/235–2684* ⊕ *www.parks.ca. gov* 💰 *$15–$20* 🖃 *AE, D, MC, V.*

Mt. Shasta

❼ *34 mi north of Lake Shasta on I–5.*

The crown jewel of the 2.5-million-acre Shasta-Trinity National Forest, Mt. Shasta, a 14,162-foot-high dormant volcano, is a mecca for day hikers. It's especially enticing in spring, when fragrant Shasta lilies and other flowers adorn the rocky slopes. The paved road reaches only as far as the timberline; the final 6,000 feet are a tough climb of rubble, ice, and snow (the summit is perpetually ice packed). Only a hardy few are qualified to make the trek to the top.

The town of Mt. Shasta has real character and some fine restaurants. Lovers of the outdoors and backcountry skiers abound, and they are more than willing to offer advice on the most beautiful spots in the region, which include out-of-the-way swimming holes, dozens of high mountain lakes, and a challenging 18-hole golf course with 360 degrees of spectacular views.

Where to Stay & Eat

★ **$$–$$$** ✕ **Trinity Café.** Once a small home, this cozy restaurant has a bistro feel and a frequently changing dinner menu inspired by seasonal ingredients. The nightly specials might include Dungeness crab gratin with red potatoes, corn, and tarragon crème fraîche, locally caught salmon or trout, or cabernet-braised lamb with toasted couscous. Chef-owner Bill Truby trained in Napa Valley, and brings an extensive knowledge of wine pairings to the menu. ⌧ *622 N. Mt. Shasta Blvd.* ☎ *530/926–6200* ▣ *AE, D, MC, V* ☽ *Closed Sun. and Mon. No lunch.*

$–$$$ ✕ **Michael's Restaurant.** Wood paneling, candlelight, and wildlife prints by local artists create an unpretentious backdrop for favorites such as prime rib and filet mignon, and Italian specialties such as stuffed calamari, scaloppine, and linguine with pesto. ⌧ *313 N. Mt. Shasta Blvd.* ☎ *530/926–5288* ▣ *AE, D, MC, V* ☽ *Closed Sun. and Mon.*

$$ ✕ **Lily's.** This restaurant in a white-clapboard home, framed by a picket fence and arched trellis, serves everything from steaks and pastas to Mexican and vegetarian dishes. Daily specials include prime rib and a fresh fish entrée. The huevos rancheros (sunny-side-up eggs on tortillas in a mildly spicy sauce) or the scrambled eggs with salsa are delicious choices for brunch. ⌧ *1013 S. Mt. Shasta Blvd.* ☎ *530/926–3372* ▣ *AE, D, MC, V.*

¢ ✕ **Seven Suns Coffee and Cafe.** This small coffee shop is a favorite gathering spot for locals. It serves specialty wraps for breakfast and lunch, plus soup and salad selections. Pastries, made daily, include muffins and scones, and blackberry fruit bars in season. ⌧ *1011 S. Mt. Shasta Blvd.* ☎ *530/926–9701* ▣ *AE, D, MC, V.*

★ **$$–$$$** ✕⌂ **Mount Shasta Resort.** Private chalets are nestled among tall pine trees along the shore of Lake Siskiyou, all with gas-log fireplaces and full kitchens. The resort's Highland House Restaurant, above the clubhouse of a spectacular 18-hole golf course, has uninterrupted views of Mt. Shasta. Large steaks and Thai-curry grilled prawns are menu highlights. Take the Central Mount Shasta exit west from Interstate 5, then go south on

17

Old Stage Road. ⊠ *1000 Siskiyou Lake Blvd., 96067* ☎ *530/926–3030 or 800/958–3363* ☐ *530/926–0333* ⊕ *www.mountshastaresort. com* ↪ *65 units* ⟁ *Restaurant, some kitchenettes, some microwaves, some refrigerators, 18-hole golf course, spa, sports bar, meeting room* ⊟ *AE, D, DC, MC, V.*

$ ⊞ **Best Western Tree House Motor Inn.** The clean, standard rooms at this motel less than a mile from downtown Mt. Shasta are decorated with natural-wood furnishings. Some of the nicer ones have vaulted ceilings and mountain views. ⊠ *111 Morgan Way, at I–5 and Lake St., 96067* ☎ *530/926–3101 or 800/545–7164* ☐ *530/926–3542* ⊕ *www. bestwestern.com* ↪ *98 rooms, 5 suites* ⟁ *Restaurant, refrigerators, indoor pool, hot tub* ⊟ *AE, D, DC, MC, V* ⦿⊓ *CP.*

★ ☸ ⛰ **Lake Siskiyou Camp Resort.** On the west side of Lake Siskiyou, the sites on this 250-acre resort sit beneath tall pine trees that filter the light. Group sites, evening movies, and powerboat and kayak rentals make it a great spot for families; there's also a marina, a free boat-launch ramp, and a fishing dock. ⟁ *Flush toilets, full hookups, showers, general store, swimming (lake)* ↪ *200 tent sites, 150 RV sites* ⊠ *4239 W. A. Barr Rd., 3 mi southwest of town of Mt. Shasta* ☎ *530/926–2618 or 888/926–2618* ⊕ *www.lakesis.com* ▭ *$20–$29* ⟑ *Reservations essential* ⊟ *D, MC, V* ⊗ *Apr.–Oct.*

Sports & the Outdoors

GOLF   At 6,100 yards, the **Mount Shasta Resort** golf course isn't long, but it's beautiful and challenging, with narrow, tree-lined fairways and natural alpine terrain. Greens fees range from $30 to $55, depending on the day of the week and the season; carts rent for another $12 to $18, and clubs can be rented, too. ⊠ *1000 Siskiyou Lake Blvd.* ☎ *530/926–3052* ⊕ *www.mountshastaresort.com/golfing.htm.*

HIKING   The **Forest Service Ranger Station** (☎ 530/926–4511 or 530/926–9613) keeps tabs on trail conditions and gives avalanche reports.

MOUNTAIN   **Fifth Season Mountaineering Shop** (⊠ 300 N. Mt. Shasta Blvd. ☎ 530/
CLIMBING   926–3606 or 530/926–5555) rents skiing and climbing equipment and operates a recorded 24-hour climber-skier report. **Shasta Mountain Guides** (☎ 530/926–3117 ⊕ www.shastaguides.com) leads hiking, climbing, and ski-touring groups to the summit of Mt. Shasta.

SKIING   On the southeast flank of Mt. Shasta, **Mt. Shasta Board & Ski Park** has 3
☸   lifts on 425 skiable acres. It's a great place for novices because three-quarters of the trails are for beginning or intermediate skiers. The area's vertical drop is 1,390 feet, with a top elevation of 6,600 feet. The longest of the 31 trails is 1¾ mi. A package for beginners, available through the ski school, includes a lift ticket, ski rental, and a lesson. The school also runs ski and snowboard programs for children. There's night skiing for those who want to see the moon rise as they schuss. The base lodge has a simple café, a ski shop, and a ski-snowboard rental shop. The park's Cross-Country Ski and Snowshoe Center, with 18 mi of trails, is on the same road. ⊠ *Hwy. 89 exit east from I–5, south of Mt. Shasta* ☎ *530/926–8610 or 800/754–7427* ⊕ *www.skipark.com* ⊗ *Winter ski season schedule: Sun.–Tues. 94, Wed.–Sat. 9–9.*

THE BACKCOUNTRY
INCLUDING LASSEN VOLCANIC NATIONAL PARK

East of Interstate 5 the far north's main corridor, dozens of scenic two-lane roads crisscross the wilderness, leading to dramatic mountain peaks and fascinating natural wonders. Small towns settled in the second half of the 19th century seem frozen in time, except that they are well equipped with tourist amenities.

McArthur–Burney Falls Memorial State Park

★ ☾ ⌐ ❽ *Hwy. 89, 52 mi southeast of Mt. Shasta and 41 mi north of Lassen Volcanic National Park.*

Just inside the park's southern boundary, Burney Creek wells up from the ground and divides into two falls that cascade over a 129-foot cliff into a pool below. Countless ribbonlike streams pour from hidden moss-covered crevices; resident bald eagles are frequently seen soaring overhead. You can walk a self-guided nature trail that descends to the foot of the falls, which Theodore Roosevelt—according to legend—called "the eighth wonder of the world." You can also swim at Lake Britton; lounge on the beach; rent motorboats, paddleboats, and canoes; or relax at one of the campsites or picnic areas. The camp store is open from early May to the end of October. ✉ *24898 Hwy. 89, Burney 96013* ☎ *530/335-2777* ✑ *$6 per vehicle, day-use.*

Where to Stay

⛺ **McArthur–Burney Falls Memorial State Park.** Campsites here in the evergreen forests abut Burney Falls, several springs, a half dozen hiking trails, and Lake Britton. Boating and fishing are popular pursuits. Some sites can accommodate 32-foot RVs. Reservations are essential from Memorial Day to Labor Day. ⚐ *Flush toilets, dump station, showers, picnic tables, general store, swimming (lake)* ⇗ *98 RV sites, 24 tent sites* ✉ *McArthur–Burney Falls Memorial State Park, Hwy. 89* ☎ *530/335-2777* ⊕ *www.parks.ca.gov* ✑ *$15–$20* ⊟ *D, MC, V.*

Alturas

❾ *86 mi northeast of McArthur–Burney Falls Memorial State Park on Hwy. 299.*

Alturas is the county seat and largest town in northeastern California's Modoc County. The Dorris family arrived in the area in 1874, built Dorris Bridge over the Pit River, and later opened a small wayside stop for travelers. Today the Alturas area is a land of few people but much rugged natural beauty. Travelers come to see eagles and other wildlife, the Modoc National Forest, and active geothermal areas.

Modoc County Museum exhibits—which include Native American artifacts, firearms, and a steam engine—explore the development of the area from the 15th century through World War II. ✉ *600 S. Main St.* ☎ *530/233-6328* ✑ *$2* ☾ *May–Oct., Tues.–Sat. 10–4.*

Modoc National Forest encompasses 1.6 million acres and protects 300 species of wildlife, including Rocky Mountain elk, wild horses, mule deer, and pronghorn antelope. In spring and fall, watch for migratory waterfowl as they make their way along the Pacific Flyway above the forest. Hiking trails lead to Petroglyph Point, one of the largest panels of rock art in the United States. ⊠ *800 W. 12th St.* ☎ *530/233–5811.*

Established to protect migratory waterfowl, the 6,280-acre **Modoc National Wildlife Refuge** gives refuge to Canada geese, Sand Hill cranes, mallards, teal, wigeon, pintail, white pelicans, cormorants, and snowy egrets. The refuge is open for hiking, bird-watching, and photography, but one area is set aside for hunters. Regulations vary according to season. ⊠ *1½ mi south of Alturas on Hwy. 395* ☎ *530/233–3572* ⊠ *Free* ☉ *Daily dawn–dusk.*

OFF THE
BEATEN
PATH

LAVA BEDS NATIONAL MONUMENT – Thousands of years of volcanic activity created this rugged landscape, which is distinguished by cinder cones, lava flows, spatter cones, pit craters, and more than 400 underground lava tube caves. During the Modoc War (1872–73), Modoc Indians under the leadership of their chief "Captain Jack" Kientopoos took refuge in a natural lava fortress now known as Captain Jack's Stronghold. They managed to hold off U.S. Army forces, which outnumbered them 20 to 1, for five months. ⚠ **When exploring this area, be sure to wear hard-soled boots; other safety gear such as lights and hard hats are available for rent and sale at the Indian Well Visitor Center, at the park's south end.** This is where summer activities such as guided walks, cave tours, and campfire programs depart. ⊠ *Forest Service Rte. 10, 72 mi northwest of Alturas, Hwy. 299 west from Alturas to Hwy. 139, northwest to Forest Service Rte. 97, to Forest Service Rte. 10* ☎ *530/667–2282 Ext. 8113* ⊕ *www.nps.gov/labe* ⊠ *$10 per vehicle; $5 on foot, bicycle, or motorcycle* ☉ *Visitor center late May–early Sept., daily 8–6; early Sept.–late May, daily 8:30–5.*

Where to Stay & Eat

$–$$ ✕ **Brass Rail.** This authentic Basque restaurant offers hearty dinners at fixed prices that include wine, homemade bread, soup, salad, side dishes, coffee, and ice cream. Steak, lamb chops, fried chicken, shrimp, and scallops are among the best entrée selections. A full bar and lounge adjoin the dining area. ⊠ *395 Lakeview Hwy.* ☎ *530/233–2906* ▤ *MC, V* ☉ *Closed Mon. No lunch Sat.*

¢ ▥ **Best Western Trailside Inn.** This is the only motel in town with a swimming pool, a definite plus in summer. It's also centrally located: 2 mi north of Rachael Dorris Park, 3 mi south of Devils Garden, and 5 mi north of Modoc Wildlife Reserve. It's also five blocks south of the Modoc County Museum. ⊠ *343 N. Main St., 96101* ☎ *530/233–4111* ⊟ *530/233–3180* ⊕ *www.bestwesterncalifornia.com/alturas.htm* ⤴ *38 rooms* ⌂ *Some kitchenettes, some microwaves, cable TV, pool, Internet room, some pets allowed* ▤ *AE, D, DC, MC, V.*

¢ ▥ **Hacienda.** In the heart of farm country, this motel is marked with a large 19th-century wagon wheel out front. The spacious, spotless rooms have bright bedspreads and ample natural light from large windows. A gas station, fast-food restaurants, and a supermarket are all within five blocks. ✉ *201 E. 12th St., 96101* ☎ *530/233–3459* ⇱ *18 rooms* ᗕ *Microwaves, refrigerators, cable TV, no-smoking rooms* ▤ *D, MC, V.*

⚠ **Medicine Lake Campground.** One of several small campgrounds on the shores of Medicine Lake, this spot lies at 6,700 feet above sea level, near the western border of Modoc National Forest. Sites can accommodate vehicles up to 22 feet. The lake, 14 mi south of Lava Beds National Monument, is a popular vacation spot with fishing, boating, and waterskiing. ᗕ *Pit toilets, drinking water, fire pits, picnic tables, swimming (lake)* ⇱ *22 sites* ✉ *Off Forest Service Rd. 43N48, Hwy. 139 to County Rd. 97 west to Forest Service Rd. 49, go north 2 mi to Forest Rd. 43N48, follow signs* ☎ *530/667–2246* ⊠ *$7* ᗕ *Reservations not accepted* ▤ *No credit cards* ☉ *July–Oct.*

Susanville

🔟 *104 mi south of Alturas via Rte. 395; 65 mi east of Lassen Volcanic National Park via Hwy. 36.*

Susanville tells the tale of its rich history through murals painted on buildings in the historic uptown area. Established as a trading post in 1854, it's the second-oldest town in the western Great Basin. You can take a self-guided tour around the original buildings and stop for a bite at one of the restaurants now housed within them; or, if you'd rather work up a sweat, you can hit the Bizz Johnson Trail and Eagle Lake recreation areas just outside of town.

Bizz Johnson Trail follows a defunct line of the Southern Pacific Railroad for 25 mi. Known to locals as the Bizz, the trail is open for hikers, walkers, mountain bikers, and horseback riders. It follows the Susan River through a scenic landscape of canyons, bridges, and forests abundant with wildlife. ✉ *Trailhead: 601 Richmond Rd.* ☎ *530/257–0456* ⊕ *www.ca.blm.gov/eaglelake/bizztrail.html* ⊠ *Free.*

Anglers travel great distances to fish the waters of **Eagle Lake,** California's second largest, which is surrounded by high desert to the north and alpine forests to the south. The Eagle Lake trout is prized for its size and fighting ability. The lake is also popular for picnicking, hiking, boating, waterskiing and windsurfing, and bird-watching—ospreys, pelicans, western grebes, and many other waterfowl visit the lake. On land you might see mule deer, small mammals, and even pronghorn antelope. ✉ *20 mi north of Susanville on Eagle Lake Rd.* ☎ *530/257–0456 for Eagle Lake Recreation Area, 530/825–3454 for Eagle Lake Marina* ⊕ *www.reserveusa.com.*

Where to Stay & Eat

¢–$$ ✕ **Josefina's.** Local favorite Josefina's makes its own salsas and tamales. The interior's Aztec accents are a perfect accompaniment to the menu's traditional Mexican fare of *chiles rellenos* (mild, batter-fried chili peppers stuffed with cheese or a cheese-meat mixture), enchiladas, tacos, and fajitas. ✉ *1960 Main St.* ☎ *530/257–9262* ▤ *MC, V.*

★ ¢ ✕ **Grand Cafe.** Walking into this downtown coffee shop, which has been owned and operated by the same family since the 1920s, is like stepping back in time. At the old-fashioned counter, the swiveling seats have hat clips on the back; the booths have their own nickel jukeboxes. Wooden refrigerators are still used here, and if the homemade chili and fruit cobblers are any indication, they work just fine. ⊠ *730 Main St.* ☎ *530/257–4713* ☒ *No credit cards* ⊘ *Closed Sat.–Mon. No dinner.*

¢–$ ⊡ **Best Western Trailside Inn.** This large, modern, business-friendly motel is in the heart of Susanville but only a quick drive from the area's recreational sites. Some rooms have wet bars, and you can enjoy home-style cooking next door at the Black Bear Diner. ⊠ *2785 Main St., 96130* ☎ *530/257–4123* ☒ *530/257–2665* ⊕ *www.bestwesterncalifornia.com* ⤻ *85 rooms* ♻ *Some refrigerators, cable TV, in-room data ports, pool, meeting room, no-smoking rooms* ☒ *AE, D, MC, V* ⍰⍥ *CP.*

¢–$ ⊡ **High Country Inn.** Rooms are spacious in this two-story, colonial-style motel on the east edge of town. Complimentary continental breakfast is provided; more extensive dining is available next door at the Apple Peddler, a 24-hour restaurant. ⊠ *3015 Riverside Dr., 96130* ☎ *530/257–3450* ☒ *530/257–2460* ⊕ *www.high-country-inn.com* ⤻ *66 rooms* ♻ *Microwaves, refrigerators, cable TV, some in-room data ports, Wi-Fi, gym, pool, outdoor hot tub; no smoking* ☒ *AE, D, DC, MC, V* ⍰⍥ *CP.*

△ **Eagle Campground.** One of 11 campgrounds surrounding Eagle Lake, this site nestled among pine trees has a boat ramp. ♻ *Flush toilets, dump station, drinking water, showers, picnic tables* ⤻ *35 tent/RV sites, 14 tent-only sites* ⊠ *County Rd. A-1, 14 mi north of Hwy. 36* ☎ *530/825–3212* ⊕ *www.reserveusa.com* ✉ *$18* △ *Reservations essential* ☒ *AE, D, MC, V* ⊘ *Late May–mid-Oct.*

Lassen Volcanic National Park

⑪ *45 mi east of Redding on Hwy. 44; 48 mi east of Red Bluff on Hwy. 36.*

Fodor'sChoice
★

Lassen Volcanic became a national park in 1916 because of its significance as a volcanic landscape. Several volcanoes—the largest of which is now Lassen Peak—have been active in the area for roughly 600,000 years, and have created an environment full of volcanic wonders including steam vents, mud pots, boiling pools, soaring peaks, and painted dunes. The Lassen Park Road (the continuation of Highway 89 within the park) provides access to these sights, and although it's closed to cars in winter, it's sometimes open to intrepid cross-country skiers and snowshoers. Maps and road guides are available at the Loomis Museum, and at the park headquarters, park entrance, and ranger stations. Also available is the park newspaper, *Peak Experiences,* which gives details on park attractions and facilities.

In 1914 the 10,457-foot Lassen Peak came to life, in the first of 300 eruptions to occur over the next seven years. Molten rock overflowed the crater, and the mountain emitted clouds of smoke and hailstorms of rocks and volcanic cinders. Proof of the volcanic landscape's volatility becomes evident shortly after you enter the park at the **Sulphur Works Thermal Area.** Boardwalks take you over bubbling mud and boiling springs and through sulfur-emitting steam vents. ⊠ *Lassen Park Rd., south end of park.*

The **Lassen Peak Hike** winds 2½ mi to the mountaintop. It's a tough climb—2,000 feet uphill on a steady, steep grade—but the reward is a spectacular view. At the peak you can see into the rim and view the entire park (and much farther, on a clear day). Be sure to bring sunscreen and water. ⊠ *Off Lassen Park Rd., 7 mi north of southwest entrance.*

Along **Bumpass Hell Trail,** a scenic 3-mi round-trip hike to the park's most interesting thermal-spring area, you can view boiling springs, steam vents, and mud pots up close. You'll take a gradual climb of 500 feet to the highest point before you descend 250 feet toward the hissing steam of Bumpass Hell. ⚠ **Near the thermal areas it's important to stay on trails and boardwalks; what appears to be firm ground may be only a thin crust over scalding mud.** ⊠ *Off Lassen Park Rd., 6 mi north of southwest entrance.*

Hot Rock, a 400-ton boulder, tumbled down from the summit during an enormous volcanic surge on May 19, 1915. It was still hot to the touch when locals discovered it nearly two days later. Although cool now, it's still an impressive sight. ⊠ *Lassen Park Rd., north end of park.*

Chaos Jumbles was created 300 years ago when an avalanche from the Chaos Crags lava domes spread hundreds of thousands of rocks, many of them 2 to 3 feet in diameter, over a couple of square miles. *Park Headquarters* ⊠ *Lassen Park Rd., north end of park, 38050 Hwy. 36E, Mineral 96063* ☎ *530/595–4444* ⊕ *www.nps.gov/lavo* ⌨ *$10 per vehicle, $5 on foot or bicycle* ☉ *Park headquarters weekdays 8–4:30.*

Where to Stay

$$$$ ✕⌂ **Drakesbad Guest Ranch.** At an elevation of 5,700 feet, this guest ranch is near Lassen Volcanic National Park's southern border. (It can't be reached from within the park, however; it's accessible only by a dirt road leading out of the town of Chester.) Everything about this more than 100-year-old property is rustic, from the comfortable furnishings, to the propane furnaces, to the kerosene lamps in lieu of electricity. Meals, casual during the day and rather elegant in the evening, are included in the room rate. The waiting list for room reservations can be up to two years long. ⊠ *Chester–Warner Valley Rd., north from Hwy. 36* ⌖ *Booking office: 2150 N. Main St., Suite 5, Red Bluff 96080* ☎ *530/529–1512* 🖶 *530/529–4511* ⊕ *www.drakesbad.com* ⌨ *19 rooms* ⌂ *Dining room, pool, fishing, badminton, horseback riding, horseshoes, Ping-Pong, volleyball* ▭ *D, MC, V* ☉ *Closed early Oct.–early June* ⦿| *FAP.*

¢ ✕⌂ **Lassen Mineral Lodge.** Rooms at this small year-round motel, 9 mi from the southwest entrance to Lassen Volcanic National Park, are reserved well in advance by those who want to explore the park without the hassle of pitching a tent. A restaurant serves breakfast, lunch, and dinner seven days a week from the end of May to the end of October; the lodge is open weekends the rest of the year. You can rent cross-country skis and snowshoes at the lodge's ski shop. There's also a general store. ⊠ *Hwy. 36 E, Mineral 96063* ☎ *530/595–4422* ⊕ *www.minerallodge.com* ⌨ *20 rooms* ⌂ *Restaurant, bar; no a/c, no room phones, no room TVs* ▭ *AE, D, MC, V.*

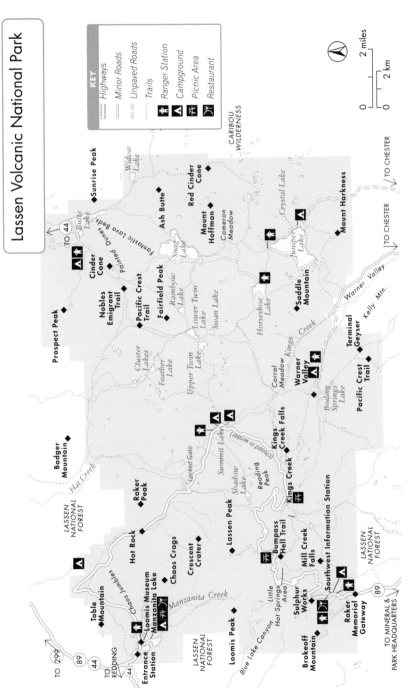

Lassen Volcanic National Park

KEY

Highways
Minor Roads
Unpaved Roads
Trails
Ranger Station
Campground
Picnic Area
Restaurant

2 miles

2 km

CARIBOU
WILDERNESS

TO CHESTER

TO CHESTER

Widow
Lake

Sunrise Peak

Butte
Lake

TO 44

Cinder
Cone

Painted Dunes

Fantastic Lava Beds

Ash Butte

Red Cinder
Cone

Mount
Hoffman

Cameron
Meadow

Crystal Lake

Mount Harkness

Nobles
Emigrant
Trail

Pacific Crest
Trail

Fairfield Peak

Snag
Lake

Rainbow
Lake

Lower Twin
Lake

Swan Lake

Juniper
Lake

Saddle
Mountain

Warner Valley

Kelly Mtn.

Prospect Peak

Cluster
Lakes

Feather
Lake

Upper Twin
Lake

Horseshoe
Lake

Kings

Creek

Coral
Meadow

Warner
Valley

Terminal
Geyser

Pacific Crest
Trail

Boiling
Springs
Lake

Badger
Mountain

Hat Creek

Raker
Peak

Locked Gate

Summit Lake

Shadow
Lake

Reading
Peak

Kings
Creek Falls

Kings Creek

LASSEN
NATIONAL
FOREST

Hot Rock

Chaos Crags

Crescent
Crater

Lassen Peak

(Closed in winter)

Bumpass
Hell Trail

Mill Creek
Falls

Southwest Information Station

LASSEN
NATIONAL
FOREST

Chaos Jumbles

Table
Mountain

Loomis Museum
Manzanita Lake

Manzanita Creek

Little
Hot Springs

Sulphur
Works

Brokeoff
Mountain

Raker
Memorial
Gateway

89

TO 299

89

44

TO
REDDING

44

Entrance
Station

Loomis Peak

LASSEN
NATIONAL
FOREST

Blue Lake Canyon

TO MINERAL &
PARK HEADQUARTERS

🏕 **Manzanita Lake Campground.** The largest of Lassen Volcanic National Park's eight campgrounds is near the northern entrance. It can accommodate vehicles up to 35 feet. A trail near the campground leads east to a crater that now holds Crags Lake. Summer reservations for group campgrounds can be made up to seven months in advance. There is no running water from the end of September until snow closes the campground. ᐲ *Flush toilets, dump station, drinking water, showers, fire pits, picnic tables, boat launch* ⬟ *148 tent/RV sites, no hookups, 31 tent sites* ⬠ *Off Lassen Park Rd., 2 mi east of junction of Hwys. 44 and 89* ☎ *530/595–4444* ⊕ *www.nps.gov/lavo/pphtml/camping.html* ⬟ *$16* ⊟ *D, MC, V* ⊙ *Mid-May–late Oct., depending on snowfall.*

Chester

⑫ *36 mi west of Susanville on Hwy 36.*

The population of this small town on Lake Almanor swells from 2,500 to nearly 5,000 in summer as tourists come to visit. It serves as a gateway to Lassen Volcanic National Park.

Lake Almanor's 52 mi of shoreline lie in the shadow of Mt. Lassen, and are popular with campers, swimmers, water-skiers, and anglers. At an elevation of 4,500 feet, the lake warms to above 70°F for about eight weeks in summer. Information is available at the Chester–Lake Almanor Chamber of Commerce. ⬠ *900 W. Hwy. 36* ☎ *530/258–2426* ⊙ *Mid-May–mid-Oct.*

Lassen Scenic Byway is a 172-mi drive through the forested terrain, volcanic peaks, geothermal springs, and lava fields of Lassen National Forest and Lassen National Park. Along the way you'll pass through five rural communities where refreshments and basic services are available. Park information is available at Almanor Ranger District headquarters. ⬠ *900 W. Hwy. 36* ☎ *530/258–2141* ⬟ *$10 per vehicle within Lassen National Park* ⊙ *Partially inaccessible in winter; call for road conditions.*

Where to Stay & Eat

¢–$ ✕ **Kopper Kettle Cafe.** Locals return again and again to this tidy restaurant that serves savory home-cooked lunch and dinner, and breakfast whenever you've got a hankering for eggs with biscuits and gravy or other morning fare. A junior-senior menu, and beer and wine are available. The patio is open in summer. ⬠ *243 Main St.* ☎ *530/258–2698* ⊟ *MC, V.*

¢–$$ 🏨 **Best Western Rose Quartz Inn.** Down the road from Lake Almanor and close to Lassen Volcanic National Park, this small town inn with its modern "wired" rooms lets you venture into the wilderness and stay in touch with cyberspace. ⬠ *306 Main St., Chester 96020* ☎ *530/258–2002 or 888/571–4885* ᐳ *530/258–3523* ⊕ *www.rosequartzinn.com* ⬟ *50 rooms* ᐲ *Satellite TV, in-room data ports, pool, fitness center, business center* ⊟ *AE, D, MC, V* ⭘ℂ *CP.*

★ ¢–$$ 🏨 **Bidwell House.** This 1901 ranch house sits on 2 acres of cottonwood-studded lawns and gardens, and has views of Lake Almanor and Mt. Lassen. Chairs and swings make the front porch inviting, and there are

17

plenty of puzzles and games in the sunroom. Some rooms have wood-burning stoves, claw-foot or Jacuzzi tubs, hardwood floors, and antiques. A separate cottage, which sleeps six, has a kitchen. The inn's specialties—omelets and blueberry-walnut pancakes—are the stars of the daily full breakfast. ⊠ *1 Main St., 96020* ☎ *530/258–3338* ⊕ *www.bidwellhouse.com* ↩ *14 rooms, 2 with shared bath* ↕ *Cable TV; no a/c, no phones in some rooms, no smoking* ▤ *MC, V* ⑩ *BP.*

Quincy

🔞 *67 mi southwest of Susanville via Hwys. 36 and 89.*

A center for mining and logging in the 1850s, Quincy is nestled against the western slope of the Sierra Nevada. The county seat and largest community in Plumas County, the town is rich in historic buildings that have been the focus of preservation and restoration efforts. The four-story courthouse on Main Street, one of several stops on a self-guided tour, was built in 1921 with marble posts and staircases. The arts are thriving in Quincy, too: catch one of the plays or bluegrass performances at the Town Hall Theatre.

The main recreational attraction in central Plumas County, **Bucks Lake Recreation Area** is 17 mi southwest of Quincy at 5,200 feet. During warm months the lake's 17-mi shoreline, two marinas, and eight campgrounds attract anglers and water-sports enthusiasts. Trails through the tall pines beckon hikers and horseback riders. In winter, much of the area remains open for snowmobiling and cross-country skiing. ⊠ *Bucks Lake Rd.* ☎ *800/326–2247* ⊕ *www.plumascounty.org.*

Plumas County is known for its wide-open spaces, and the 1.2-million-acre **Plumas National Forest,** with its high alpine lakes and crystal-clear woodland streams, is a beautiful example. Hundreds of campsites are maintained in the forest, and picnic areas and hiking trails abound. You can enter the forest from numerous sites along highways 70 and 89. ⊠ *159 Lawrence St.* ☎ *530/283–2050* ☉ *U.S. Forest Service office weekdays 8–4:30.*

The cultural, home arts, and industrial history displays at the **Plumas County Museum** contain artifacts dating to the 1850s. Highlights include collections of Maidu Indian basketry, pioneer weapons, and rooms depicting life in the early days of Plumas County. There's a blacksmith shop and gold-mining cabin, equipment from the early days of logging, a restored buggy, and railroad and mining exhibits. ⊠ *500 Jackson St.* ☎ *530/283–6320* 🎟 *$2* ☉ *Tues.–Sat. 8–5.*

Where to Stay & Eat

$–$$$ ✕ **Moon's.** This restored 1930 building houses a restaurant that serves such delights as honey-almond chicken, eggplant parmigiana, ravioli, and Tuscan pasta. Sauces, salad dressings, pastas, breads, and desserts (be sure to try the chocolate-caramel fudge cake) are all made from scratch. A verdant garden patio adds to Moon's allure. ⊠ *497 Lawrence St.* ☎ *530/283–0765* ▤ *AE, MC, V* ☉ *Closed Mon. No lunch.*

¢–$$ ✕ **Sweet Lorraine's Good Food Good Feelings.** You can choose to eat upstairs by candlelight or in the more casual downstairs bar and dining area. Sweet Lorraine's serves hearty fare such as St. Louis ribs and herb-crusted pork chops, as well as vegetarian selections and lighter items; it also has a good selection of wines. Reservations are recommended. ☒ *384 Main St.* ☎ *530/283–5300* ▭ *MC, V* ⊘ *Closed Sun. No lunch Sat.*

★ **$–$$** ▦ **Ada's Place.** This place is actually four cottages, secluded on a quiet street one block from the county courthouse and downtown Quincy. Each is decorated with a different motif—Ruth's Garden has floral accents, while the serene Hop Sing's (which has lovely wood floors) has Oriental-art details—and each has a private yard or deck and a full kitchen. ☒ *140 Lee Way, Quincy 95971* ☎ *530/283–1954* ⊕ *www.adasplace. com* ⇜ *4 units* ⌂ *Kitchens, cable TV, Wi-Fi; no a/c in two units, no smoking* ▭ *MC, V.*

$–$$ ▦ **Feather Bed.** The quaint romanticism of an 1893 Queen Anne Victorian plus proximity to Quincy's town center are the draws here. Furnishings are antique and the views of the Sierra Nevada spectacular. The five rooms in the main house have claw-foot tubs. Two private guest cottages have fireplaces and outside decks. Classical music plays softly in the morning, and breakfast begins with smoothies made with home-grown blackberries or raspberries. Fresh fruit or baked fruit crunch and home-baked bread or muffins accompany hot entrées. ☒ *542 Jackson St., 95971* ☎ *530/283–0102 or 800/696–8624* ⊕ *www.featherbed-inn.com* ⇜ *5 rooms, 2 cottages* ⌂ *Some cable TV, bicycles, airport shuttle* ▭ *AE, D, DC, MC, V* ⋈ *BP.*

¢ ▦ **Lariat Lodge.** This small, tidy motel 2 mi west of downtown is a quiet haven surrounded by views of the Plumas National Forest. ☒ *2370 E. Main St., 95971* ☎ *530/283–1000 or 800/999–7199* 🖷 *530/283–2164* ⇜ *19 rooms* ⌂ *Some refrigerators, cable TV, pool, no-smoking rooms* ▭ *AE, D, MC, V* ⋈ *CP.*

THE FAR NORTH ESSENTIALS

To research prices, get advice from other travelers, and book travel arrangements, visit www.fodors.com.

AIRPORTS & TRANSFERS
Chico Municipal Airport and Redding Municipal Airport are served by United Express. Horizon Air also uses the airport in Redding. ⇨ Air Travel *in* Smart Travel Tips A to Z for airline phone numbers. There's no shuttle service from either airport, but taxis can be ordered. The approximate cost from the airport to downtown Redding is $25 to $27 and it's $14 to $15 from the Chico airport to downtown.

🛈 **Chico Municipal Airport** ☒ 140 Airpark Blvd., off Cohasset Rd. ☎ 530/345-8828. **Redding Municipal Airport** ☒ Airport Rd. ☎ 530/224-4320. **Taxi Service, Chico** ☎ 530/893-4444 or 530/342-2929. **Taxi Service, Redding** ☎ 530/246-0577 or 530/ 222-1234.

BUS TRAVEL
Greyhound buses travel Interstate 5, serving Chico, Red Bluff, and Redding. Butte County Transit serves Chico, Oroville, and elsewhere. Chico

Area Transit System provides bus service within Chico. The vehicles of the Redding Area Bus Authority operate daily except Sunday within Redding, Anderson, and Shasta Lake. STAGE buses serve Siskiyou County, on weekdays only, from Yreka to Dunsmuir, stopping in Mt. Shasta and other towns, and provide service in Scott Valley, Happy Camp, Hornbrook, Lake Shastina, and the Klamath River area. Lassen Rural Bus serves the Susanville, northeast Lake Almanor, and south and east Lassen County areas, running weekdays except holidays. Lassen Rural Bus connects with Plumas County Transit, which serves the Quincy area, and with Modoc County Sage Stage, which serves the Alturas area.

🚌 **Butte County Transit/Chico Area Transit System** ☎ 530/342-0221 ⊕ www.bcag. org/transit.htm. **Greyhound** ☎ 800/229-9424 ⊕ www.greyhound.com. **Lassen Rural Bus** ☎ 530/252-7433. **Modoc County Sage Stage** ☎ 530/233-3883 or 233-6410. **Plumas County Transit** ☎ 530/283-2538 ⊕ www.susanvillestuff.com/bus.html. **Redding Area Bus Authority** ☎ 530/241-2877 ⊕ www.ci.redding.ca.us. **STAGE** ☎ 530/842-8295 ⊕ www.co.siskiyou.ca.us.

CAMPING

■ **TIP→** Some campgrounds in California's far north get booked as much as a year in advance for the Fourth of July. Although that's not the norm, it's still a good idea to make summer reservations two-three months in advance. You can reserve a site at many of the region's campgrounds through ReserveAmerica and ReserveUSA.

🚩 Campground Reservations **ReserveAmerica** ☎ 800/444-7275 ⊕ www. reserveamerica.com. **ReserveUSA** ☎ 877/444-6777 ⊕ www.reserveusa.com.

CAR RENTAL

Avis and Hertz serve Redding Municipal Airport. Hertz serves Chico Municipal Airport. Enterprise has branches in Chico, Red Bluff, and Redding. ⇨ Car Rental *in* Smart Travel Tips A to Z for national rental-agency phone numbers.

CAR TRAVEL

An automobile is virtually essential for touring the far north unless you arrive by bus, plane, or train and plan to stay put in one town or resort. Interstate 5, an excellent four-lane divided highway, runs up the center of California through Red Bluff and Redding and continues north to Oregon. The other main roads in the area are good two-lane highways that are, with few exceptions, open year-round. Chico is east of Interstate 5 on Highway 32. Lassen Volcanic National Park can be reached by Highway 36 from Red Bluff or (except in winter) Highway 44 from Redding. Highway 299 connects Redding and Alturas. Highway 139 leads from Susanville to Lava Beds National Monument. Highway 89 will take you from Mt. Shasta to Quincy. Highway 36 links Chester and Susanville. If you're traveling through the far north in winter, always carry snow chains in your vehicle. For information on road conditions in northern California, call the Caltrans Highway Information Network's voice-activated system. At the prompt say the route number in which you are interested, and you'll hear a recorded message about current conditions.

🚩 **Caltrans Highway Information Network** ☎ 800/427-7623.

EMERGENCIES

In an emergency dial 911.

🔳Hospitals **Banner-Lassen Medical Center** ✉1800 Spring Ridge Dr., Susanville ☎530/252-2000. **Enloe Medical Center** ✉ 1531 Esplanade, Chico ☎ 530/891-7300. **Mercy Medical Center** ✉ 2175 Rosaline Ave., Redding ☎ 530/225-6000.

TRAIN TRAVEL

Amtrak has stations in Chico, Redding, and Dunsmuir and operates buses that connect to Greyhound service through Redding, Red Bluff, and Chico. 🔳 **Amtrak** ✉ W. 5th and Orange Sts., Chico ✉ 1620 Yuba St., Redding ✉ 5750 Sacramento Ave., Dunsmuir ☎ 800/872-7245 ⊕ www.amtrakcalifornia.com.

VISITOR INFORMATION

🔳 **Alturas Chamber of Commerce** ✉ 522 S. Main St., Alturas 96101 ☎ 530/233-4434 ⊕ www.alturaschamber.org. **Chester–Lake Almanor Chamber of Commerce** ✉ 529 Main St., Chester 96020 ☎530/258-2426 or 800/350-4838 ⊕www.chester-lakealmanor.com. **Chico Chamber of Commerce** ✉ 300 Salem St., Chico 95928 ☎ 530/891-5556 or 800/852-8570 ⊕ www.chicochamber.com. **Lassen County Chamber of Commerce** ✉ 84 N. Lassen St., Susanville 96130 ☎ 530/257-4323 ⊕ lassencountychamber.org. **Plumas County Visitors Bureau** ✉ 550 Crescent St., Quincy 95971 ☎ 530/283-6345 or 800/326-2247 ⊕ www.plumascounty.org. **Quincy Chamber of Commerce** ✉ 464 Main St., Quincy 95971 ☎530/283-0188 ⊕www.quincychamber.com. **Red Bluff–Tehama County Chamber of Commerce** ✉ 100 Main St., Red Bluff 96080 ☎ 530/527-6220 or 800/655-6225 ☎ 530/527-2908 ⊕ www.redbluffchamberofcommerce.com. **Shasta Cascade Wonderland Association** ✉ 1699 Hwy. 273, Anderson 96007 ☎ 530/365-7500 or 800/474-2782 ⊕ www.shastacascade.org. **Siskiyou County Visitors Bureau** ✉ 300 Pine St., Mt. Shasta 96067 ☎ 530/926-3850 or 800/926-4865 ⊕ www.visitsiskiyou.org.

UNDERSTANDING CALIFORNIA

BOUNTIFUL BEAUTY

SOUTHERN CALIFORNIA'S FAMOUS WARM, SUNNY CLIMATE has blessed this corner of the continent with an ever-changing, year-round palette of natural color. It's hard to find a spot anywhere around the globe that produces as spectacular a scene as San Diego does in spring—from the native plant gardens found tucked away in mountain canyons and streambeds to the carpets of wildflowers on the desert floor. You'll have to see it yourself to believe just how alive the deceptively barren desert really is.

Spring debuts in late February or early March. Heavy winter rains always precede the best bloom seasons. And good blooms also bring even more beauty—a bounty of butterflies. A further boon: here in this generally temperate climate, the bloom season lasts nearly all year.

Some drought-tolerant plants rely on fire to germinate, and the years following wildfires generally produce a profusion of plantlife not normally seen. Look for rare western redbud trees erupting into a profusion of crimson flowers, sometimes starting as early as February. Native California lilacs (ceanothus) blanket the hillsides throughout the backcountry with fragrant blue-and-white blossoms starting in May and showing until August.

Native varieties of familiar names show up in the mountain canyons and streambeds. A beautiful white western azalea would be the star in anyone's garden. A pink California rose blooms along streambeds in spring and summer. Throughout the year three varieties of native dogwood show off white blooms and beautiful crimson fall foliage. The Cuyamaca Mountains usually put on a display of fall color as the native oaks turn gold and red. By winter the rare toyon, known as the California Christmas tree, shows off its red berries alongside the roads.

You can get a good introduction to mountain wildflowers by visiting Julian in early May, when the Women's Club puts on its annual Wildflower Show. For more than seven decades members have collected and displayed native plants and flowers from hillsides, meadows, and streambeds surrounding the mountain town. For information on exact dates call the Julian Chamber of Commerce (☎760/765–1857).

Farther east in the Anza-Borrego Desert State Park, the spring wildflower display can be spectacular: carpets of pink, purple, white, and yellow verbena and desert primrose as far as the eye can see. Rocky slopes yield clumps of beavertail cactus topped with showy pink blossoms, clumps of yellow brittlebush tucked among the rocks, and crimson-tip ocotillo trees. For a good introduction to desert vegetation, explore the visitor center demonstration garden, adjacent to the park's underground headquarters.

For a vivid view of both the mountain and desert spring flora, take Interstate 8 east to Route 79, go north to Julian, and then east on Route 78 into Anza-Borrego park.

San Diego County is a leading flower supplier to the nation, with dozens of nurseries turning out poinsettias, ranunculus, bromeliads, orchids, begonias, and other subtropical plants. Many can be seen and visited in the coastal area of the county. In spring, tour the brilliant acres of ranunculus blooms at the Flower Fields at Carlsbad Ranch (Palomar Airport Road, east of I–5, ☎ 760/431–0352, www.theflowerfields.com).

—Bobbi Zane

DISNEY STRATEGIES

ON YOUR MARK, get set . . . a trip to Disneyland Resort gets the adrenaline pumping, but to most enjoy your visit, study these helpful tips. If you're traveling with children, check out the book *Fodor's Disneyland & Southern California with Kids* for more practical advice.

- **Buy entry tickets in advance.** Many nearby hotels sell park admission tickets; you can also buy them through the Disney Web site. If you book a package deal, such as those offered through AAA, tickets are included, too. The lines at the ticket booths can take more than an hour on busy days, so you'll definitely save time by buying in advance.

- **Come midweek.** Weekends, especially in summer, are a mob scene. A winter weekday is often the least crowded time to visit.

- **Plan your times to hit the most popular rides.** If you're at the park when the gates open, make a beeline for the top rides before the crowds reach critical mass. Another good time to avoid lines is in the evening, when the hordes thin out somewhat, and during a parade or other show. Save the quieter attractions for midafternoon.

- **Look into Fastpasses.** These passes allow you to reserve your place in line at some of the most crowded attractions (only one at a time). Distribution machines are posted near the entrances of each attraction. Feed in your park admission ticket, and you'll receive a pass with a printed time frame (generally up to 1 to 1½ hours later) during which you can return to wait in a much shorter line.

- **Plan your meals to avoid peak mealtime crowds.** Start the day with a big breakfast so you won't be too hungry at noon, when restaurants and vendors get swarmed. Wait to have lunch until after 1. If you want to eat at the **Blue Bayou**

in New Orleans Square, it's best to make reservations in person as soon as you get to the park. Another (cheaper) option is to bring your own food. There are areas with picnic tables set up for this. And it's always a good idea to bring water and a few nonmeltable snacks with you.

- **Take a break at a show.** Disneyland is exciting, but it can be exhausting for parents and children alike. Catch a show in the afternoon—it's a great way to get off your feet for a little while, and your kids will probably take a nap. And when it's over, everyone will be refreshed and ready for an evening of fun.

- **Check the daily events schedule.** During parades, fireworks, and other special events, sections of the parks clog with crowds. This can work for you or against you. An event could make it difficult to get around a park—but if you plan ahead, you can take advantage of the distraction to hit popular rides.

—Jennifer Paull

PALM SPRINGS MODERNISM

WITH ONE OF THE LARGEST concentrations of modern architecture in the world, Palm Springs displays a distinctive style, known as Desert or Palm Springs Modernism. Its signature is simple, single-story buildings inspired by vast expanses of desert sand, surrounded by towering mountains, and set against a clear blue sky.

Some of the world's most forward-looking architects designed and constructed buildings around Palm Springs between 1940 and 1970, and modernism, also popular elsewhere in California in the years after World War II, became an ideal fit for desert living, because it minimizes the separation between indoors and outdoors. See-through houses with glass exterior walls are common. Oversize flat roofs provide shade from the sun, and many buildings' sculptural forms reflect nearby landforms. The style is notable for elegant informality, clean lines, and simple landscaping. Emblematic structures in Palm Springs include public buildings, hotels, stores, banks, and private residences.

Most obvious to visitors are three buildings that are part of the Palm Springs Aerial Tramway complex, all built in the 1960s. Albert Frey, a Swiss-born architect whose name is associated with a clutch of historic buildings, designed the soaring A-frame Tramway Gas Station, visually echoing the pointed peaks behind it. Frey also created the glass-walled Valley Station, from which you get your initial view of the Coachella Valley before you board the tram to the Mountain Station, designed by E. Stewart Williams.

Frey, a Palm Springs resident for more than 60 years, also designed the indoor–outdoor City Hall, Fire Station #1, and numerous houses. You can see his second home, perched atop stilts on the hillside above the Desert Museum; it affords a sweeping view of the Coachella Valley through glass walls. The classy Movie Colony Hotel, one of the first buildings Frey designed in the desert, may seem like a typical 1950s motel with rooms surrounding a swimming pool now, but when it was built as the San Jacinto Hotel in 1935, it was years ahead of its time.

Donald Wexler, who honed his vision with Los Angeles architect Richard Neutra, brought new ideas about the use of materials to the desert, where he teamed up with William Cody on a number of projects, including the terminal at the Palm Springs airport. Many of Wexler's buildings have soaring overhanging roofs, designed to provide shade under the blazing desert sun. Wexler also experimented with steel framing back in 1961, but the metal proved too expensive. Seven of his steel-frame houses can be seen in a neighborhood off Indian Canyon and Frances drives.

The Palm Springs Modern Committee is protecting these period structures, occasionally protesting projected demolition projects. The committee also publishes a map and driving guide to 52 historic buildings, which is available for $5 at either of the Palm Springs Visitor Information Centers or at ⊕ www.psmodcom.com.

—Bobbi Zane

WHY IS THERE SO MUCH SNOW?

THE SIERRA NEVADA receive some of the deepest snow anywhere in North America. In winter, houses literally get buried, and home owners have to build tunnels to their front doors (though many install enclosed wooden walkways). In the high country, it's not uncommon for a single big storm to bring 10 feet of snow and for 30 feet of snow to accumulate at the height of the season. In the enormous bowls of Mammoth Mountain, you might ski past a tiny pine that looks like a miniature Christmas tree—until you remember that more than 30 feet of tree is under the snow.

To understand the weather, you have to understand the terrain. The Sierra Nevada are marked by a gentle western rise from sea level to the Sierra crest, which tops out at a whopping 14,494 feet in Sequoia National Park's Mt. Whitney, the highest point in the continental United States. On the eastern side of the crest, at the escarpment, the mountains drop sharply—as much as 5,000 feet—giving way to the Great Basin and the high-mountain deserts of Nevada and Utah.

When winter storms blow in off the Pacific, carrying vast stores of water with them, they race across the relatively flat, 100-mi-wide Central Valley. As they ascend the wall of mountains, though, the decrease in temperature and the increase in pressure on the clouds force them to release their water. Between October and April, that means snow—lots of it. Storms can get hung up on the peaks for days, dumping foot after foot of the stuff. By the time they finally cross over the range and into the Great Basin, there isn't much moisture left for the lower elevations on the eastern side. This is why, if you cross the Sierra eastward on your way to U.S. 395, you'll notice that brightly colored wildflowers and forest-green trees give way to pale-green sagebrush and brown sand as you drop out of the mountains.

The coastal cities and farmlands of the rest of the state depend heavily on the water from the Sierra snowpack. Most of the spring and summer runoff from the melting snows is caught in reservoirs in the foothills and routed to farmlands and cities throughout the state via a complex system of levees and aqueducts, which you'll no doubt see in the foothills and Central Valley, to the west of the range. But much of the water remains in the mountains, forming lakes, most notably giant Lake Tahoe to the north, Mono Lake to the east, and the thousands of little lakes along the Sierra Crest. The lakes are an essential part of the ecosystem, providing water for birds, fish, and plant life.

Sierra Nevada Records:

- On January 4-5, 1982, it snowed 67 inches (5.6 ft.) in 24 hours at Echo Summit. This was the second-largest single-day snowfall in U.S. history.

- The U.S. record for most snow in a month was set at Tamarack; it snowed 390 inches (32.5 ft.) in January 1991.

- Tamarack also holds the U.S. record for greatest snow depth: 451 inches (37.6 ft.), measured on March 11, 1911.

—John A. Vlahides

THE CHUMASH

IN 1542, when Portuguese explorer Juan Rodriguez Cabrillo sailed into the Santa Barbara Channel, he and his party encountered a huge surprise: friendly natives in unusual canoes paddling out to greet them, bearing gifts of beads, animal skins, and food. The welcome party was Chumash Indians, whose homeland stretched from Malibu in the south to what is now San Luis Obispo County in the north, plus the four northern Channel Islands. It would be another 230 years before European settlers came to stay. Still, this was their first encounter with one of North America's most fascinating native cultures.

Ancestors of the Chumash first occupied the Central Coast region some 13,000 years ago. By the time of Cabrillo's visit, the tribe had evolved into a complex culture with an elaborate trading system stretching across much of California. The Channel Island Chumash, in particular, were known for crafting currency out of shell beads, which were exchanged for food, tools, and services. The name Chumash roughly translates as "those who make shell bead money."

Chumash land was abundant in wild game, fish, nuts, seeds, and other natural resources. Tribe members were so successful at hunting, gathering, and storing food that they didn't need to farm or raise domestic animals. This left much time to pursue a rich religious life and create remarkable crafts. As well as being some of the finest basket makers in the world, the Chumash also built swift, light canoes, called *tomols,* that were engineering wonders.

Life changed dramatically for the Chumash in 1769, when Gaspar de Portolá and his land expedition arrived in the area. The Spanish established five missions in Chumash territory, and induced many natives to move to the mission and learn to farm. At the time of initial Spanish contact there were about 20,000 Chumash people, but in the missions many died from European diseases. By the end of the mission system in 1834, fewer than 3,000 Chumash people remained.

In 1901 the U.S. government recognized the Santa Ynez band of Chumash as an official tribal nation and established the Santa Ynez Reservation, which occupies about 75 acres next to the town of Santa Ynez. Today the reservation has about 150 registered tribal members. About 3,000 other people of Chumash descent live elsewhere in the Central Coast region.

You can learn more about Chumash culture and history at a number of Central Coast museums, including Santa Barbara's Museum of Natural History (⊕ www.sbnature.org). For information about modern Chumash life, pop into the Chumash Casino in Santa Ynez, or log on to ⊕www.chumashcasino.com or ⊕ www.SantaYnez Chumash.org.

—Cheryl Crabtree

SKI-PATROL POOCHES

ALL AROUND TAHOE, from bars to ski shops, you'll spot posters of dogs wearing ski-patrol vests riding a chairlift. Stars in their own right, these pooches are the search-and-rescue dogs of Alpine Meadows.

In 1982 an avalanche inundated Alpine's base lodge, destroying a building and a ski lift and killing six people. Search-and-rescue teams brought in a German shepherd named Bridget to help recover the missing from beneath the snow. Though she was unable to help save any victims, she inspired the idea for trained "staff dogs" to be on hand in case of another catastrophe.

Now an integral part of Alpine's safety preparedness, these golden retrievers and chocolate Labradors are the personal pets of ski-patrol employees. Each dog meets exacting standards of obedience and con-

duct and must undergo two years of rigorous training. They must be able to get on and off a ski lift, ride a snowmobile, and keep up with patrollers anywhere on the mountain, including icy cornices, craggy chutes, and steep slopes. Goldens and labs have the right temperament, the right size, and the right fur—long enough to keep them warm but short enough not to get covered in chunky snowballs that weigh them down. They're also able to smell human beings through heavy snow.

You can visit the dogs at the ski patrol hut at the top of the Summit Six, Sherwood, or Lakeview chairlift. And if you've become a fan, you can pick up the poster or patrol-puppy trading cards.

—John A. Vlahides

THE PACIFIC FLYWAY

YOU DON'T NEED WINGS to catch the Pacific Flyway. All it takes is a car, a good map, and high-powered binoculars to follow the flight path of more than 250 bird species that migrate through far northern California and stop at wildlife refuges on their way.

Eagles and hawks make their visits in winter; more than a million waterfowl pass through in fall. Returning migrants such as pelicans, cranes, and songbirds such as the marsh wren and ruby-crowned kinglet arrive in March, just in time to herald the spring; goslings, ducklings, and other newly hatched waterfowl paddle through the wetlands in summer.

February and March are especially good viewing times, when people are scarce but wildlife thrives in the cold climate. Many birds enter their breeding season during

these months, and you can hear their unusual mating calls and witness aerial ballets as vividly plumed males pursue females.

One of the most impressive Pacific Flyway stopovers is on the California–Oregon border: the 46,900-acre Lower Klamath National Wildlife Refuge, established by President Theodore Roosevelt in 1908 as the country's first waterfowl refuge. The area has the largest winter concentration of bald eagles in the lower 48 states. For $3 you can take a 10-mi auto tour through parts of the refuge, where the eagles feed from December through mid-March. (From Interstate 5 north of Mt. Shasta, take the Highway 97 turnoff to Highway 161 and follow the signs.) Even if you're not already an avid bird-watcher, you likely will be after a visit to this special place.

SMART TRAVEL TIPS

There are planners and there are those who, excuse the pun, fly by the seat of their pants. We happily place ourselves among the planners. Our writers and editors try to anticipate all the issues you may face before and during any journey, and then they do their research. This section is the product of their efforts. Use it to get excited about your trip to California, to inform your travel planning, or to guide you on the road should the seat of your pants start to feel threadbare.

AIR TRAVEL

BOOKING

When you book, look for nonstop flights and remember that "direct" flights stop at least once. Try to avoid connecting flights, which require a change of plane. Two airlines may operate a connecting flight jointly, so ask whether your airline operates every segment of the trip; you may find that the carrier you prefer flies you only part of the way. To find more booking tips and to check prices and make online flight reservations, log on to www. fodors.com.

CARRIERS

United, with hubs in San Francisco and Los Angeles, has the greatest number of flights into and within California. But most national and many international airlines fly here.

🛫 Major Airlines **Air Canada** ☎ 888/247-2262 ⊕ www.aircanada.com. **Alaska Airlines** ☎ 800/252-7522 or 206/433-3100 ⊕ www.alaskaair.com. **America West** ☎ 800/235-9292 or 480/693-6701 ⊕ www.americawest.com. **American** ☎ 800/433-7300 ⊕ www.aa.com. **British Airways** ☎ 800/247-9297 ⊕ www.britishairways.com. **Cathay Pacific** ☎ 800/233-2742 ⊕ www.cathaypacific.com. **Continental** ☎ 800/523-3273 ⊕ www.continental.com. **Delta** ☎ 800/221-1212 ⊕ www.delta.com. **Japan Air Lines** ☎ 800/525-3663 ⊕ www.japanair.com. **Northwest/KLM** ☎ 800/225-2525 ⊕ www.nwa.com. **Qantas** ☎ 800/227-4500 ⊕ www.qantas.com. **Southwest Airlines** ☎ 800/435-9792 ⊕ www.southwest.com. **United Airlines** ☎ 800/864-8331 ⊕ www.united.com. **US Airways** ☎ 800/428-4322 ⊕ www.usairways.com.

⚡ Smaller Airlines **American Trans Air** ☎ 800/
435-9282 ⊕ www.ata.com. **Horizon** ☎ 800/547-
9308 ⊕ www.horizonair.com. **JetBlue** ☎ 800/538-
2583 ⊕ www.jetblue.com. **Midwest Airlines**
☎ 800/452-2022 ⊕ www.midwestairlines.com.

CHECK-IN & BOARDING

Double-check your flight times, especially
if you made your reservations far in advance. Airlines change their schedules, and
alerts may not reach you. Always **bring a
government-issued photo I.D. to the airport** (even when it's not required, a passport is best), and **arrive when you need to
and not before.** Check-in usually at least
an hour before domestic flights and two to
three hours for international flights. But
many airlines have more stringent advance
check-in requirements at some busy airports. The TSA estimates the waiting time
for security at most major airports and
publishes the information on its Web site.
Note that if you aren't at the gate at least
10 minutes before your flight is scheduled
to take off (sometimes earlier), you won't
be allowed to board.

Minimize the time spent standing on line.
Buy an e-ticket, check in at an electronic
kiosk, or—even better—check in on your
airline's Web site before you leave home.
These days, most domestic airline tickets
are electronic; international tickets may
be either electronic or paper. Also, pack
light and limit carry-on items to only
the essentials.

You usually pay a surcharge (up to $50) to
get a paper ticket, and its sole advantage is
that it may be easier to endorse over to another airline if your flight is cancelled and
the airline with which you booked can't
accommodate you on another flight. With
an e-ticket, the only thing you receive is an
e-mailed receipt citing your itinerary and
reservation and ticket numbers. Be sure to
carry this with you as you'll need it to get
past security. If you lose you receipt,
though, you can simply print out another
copy or ask the airline to do it for you
at check-in.

Particularly during busy travel seasons and
around holiday periods, if a flight is over-
sold, the gate agent will usually ask for
volunteers and will offer some sort of
compensation if you are willing to take a
different flight. **Know your rights.** If you
are bumped from a flight *involuntarily,* the
airline must give you some kind of compensation if an alternate flight can't be
found within one hour. If your flight is delayed because of something within the airline's control (so bad weather doesn't
count), then the airline has a responsibility
to get you to your destination on the same
day, even if they have to book you on another airline and in an upgraded class if
necessary. Read your airline's Contract of
Carriage; it's usually buried somewhere on
the airline's Web site.

Be prepared to quickly adjust your plans
by programming a few numbers into your
cell: your airline, an airport hotel or two,
your destination hotel, your car service,
and/or your travel agent.

CUTTING COSTS

It's always good to **comparison shop.**
Web sites (a.k.a. consolidators) and travel
agents can have different arrangements
with the airlines and offer different prices
for exactly the same flight and day. Certain Web sites have tracking features that
will e-mail you immediately when good
deals are posted. Other people prefer to
stick with one or two frequent-flier programs, racking up free trips and accumu-
lating perks that can make trips easier. On
some airlines, perks include a special reservations number, early boarding, access to
upgrades, and more roomy economy-class
seating.

Check early and often. Start looking for
cheap fares up to a year in advance, and
keep looking until you see something you
can live with; you never know when a
good deal may pop up. That said, **jump
on the good deals.** Waiting even a few
minutes might mean paying more. For
most people, saving money is more important than flexibility, so the more affordable nonrefundable tickets work. Just
remember that you'll pay dearly (often as
much as $100) if you must change your
travel plans. Check on prices for depar-

tures at different times of the day and to and from alternate airports, and look for departures on Tuesday, Wednesday, and Thursday, typically the cheapest days to travel. Remember to **weigh your options,** though. A cheaper flight might have a long layover rather than being nonstop, or landing at a secondary airport might substantially increase your ground transportation costs.

Note that many airline Web sites—and most ads—show prices *without* taxes and surcharges. Don't buy until you know the full price. Government taxes add up quickly. Also **watch those ticketing fees.** Surcharges are usually added when you buy your ticket anywhere but on an airline's own Web site. (By the way, that includes on the phone–even if you call the airline directly—and for paper tickets regardless of how you book).

Online Consolidators AirlineConsolidator.com ⊕ www.airlineconsolidator.com; for international tickets. Best Fares ⊕ www.bestfares.com; $59.90 annual membership. Cheap Tickets ⊕ www. cheaptickets.com. Expedia ⊕ www.expedia.com. Hotwire ⊕ www.hotwire.com is a discounter. lastminute.com ⊕ www.lastminute.com specializes in last-minute travel; the main site is for the UK, but it has a link to a U.S. site. Luxury Link ⊕ www. luxurylink.com has auctions (surprisingly good deals) as well as offers at the high-end side of travel. Orbitz ⊕ www.orbitz.com. Onetravel.com ⊕ www.onetravel.com. Priceline.com ⊕ www. priceline.com is a discounter that also allows bidding. Travel.com ⊕ www.travel.com allows you to compare its rates with those of other booking engines. Travelocity ⊕ www.travelocity.com charges a booking fee for airline tickets but promises good problem resolution.

ENJOYING THE FLIGHT

Get the seat you want. Avoid those on the aisle directly across from the lavatories. Most frequent fliers say those are even worse than the seats that don't recline (e.g., those in the back row and those in front of a bulkhead). For more legroom, you can request emergency-aisle seats, but only do so if you're capable of moving the 35- to 60-pound airplane exit door—a Federal Aviation Administration requirement

of passengers in these seats. Seats behind a bulkhead also offer more legroom, but they don't have under-seat storage. Often, you can pick a seat when you buy your ticket on an airline's Web site. But it's not always a guarantee, particularly if the airline changes the plane after you book your ticket; check back before you leave. SeatGuru.com has more information about specific seat configurations, which vary by aircraft.

Fewer airlines are providing free food for passengers in economy class. **Don't go hungry.** If you're scheduled to fly during meal times, verify if your airline offers anything to eat; even when it does, be prepared to pay. If you have dietary concerns, request special meals. These can be vegetarian, low-cholesterol, or kosher, for example.

Ask the airline about its children's menus, activities, and fares. On some lines infants and toddlers fly for free if they sit on a parent's lap, and older children fly for half price in their own seats. Also inquire about policies involving car seats; having one may limit where you can sit. While you're at it, ask about seatbelt extenders for car seats. And note that you can't count on a flight attendent to automatically produce an extender; you may have to inquire about it again when you board.

FLYING TIMES

Flying time to California is roughly six hours from New York and four hours from Chicago. Travel from London to Los Angeles or San Francisco takes about 10 hours and from Sydney approximately 14. Flying between San Francisco and Los Angeles takes one hour.

HOW TO COMPLAIN

If your baggage goes astray or your flight goes awry, complain right away. Most carriers require that you **file a claim immediately.** The Aviation Consumer Protection Division of the Department of Transportation publishes *Fly-Rights,* which discusses airlines and consumer issues and is available online. You can also find articles and information on mytravelrights.com, the

Web site of the nonprofit Consumer Travel Rights Center.

🔝 Airline Complaints **Office of Aviation Enforcement and Proceedings** (Aviation Consumer Protection Division) ☎ 202/366-2220 ⊕ airconsumer.ost. dot.gov. **Federal Aviation Administration Consumer Hotline** ☎ 866/835-5322 ⊕ www.faa.gov.

AIRPORTS

The major gateways to California are Los Angeles International Airport (LAX), San Francisco International Airport (SFO), San Diego International Airport (SAN), and San Jose International Airport (SJC).

🔝 Airport Information **Los Angeles International Airport** ☎ 310/646-5252 ⊕ www.lawa.org. **San Diego International Airport** ☎ 619/231-2100 ⊕ www.san.org. **San Francisco International Airport** ☎ 650/761-0800 ⊕ www.flysfo.com. **San Jose International Airport** ☎ 408/277-4759 ⊕ www.sjc.org.

🔝 Airline Security Issues **Transportation Security Administration** ⊕ www.tsa.gov/public has answers for almost every question that might come up.

BIKE TRAVEL

Mountain biking began in California—Marin County, to be exact—and there are plenty of gorgeous places to bike statewide, especially along the coast and in the mountains. Plan accordingly for high-altitude riding in the Sierra Nevada, and avoid the desert regions May through September, when blazing heat presents serious risks. The coastal regions remain cool year-round, making them the ideal places for riding. For specific information on biking in each region of the state, please see the appropriate chapter for ideas.

BIKES IN FLIGHT

Most airlines accommodate bikes as luggage, provided they are dismantled and boxed; check with individual airlines about packing requirements. Some airlines sell bike boxes, which are often free at bike shops, for about $20 (bike bags can be considerably more expensive). International travelers often can substitute a bike for a piece of checked luggage at no charge; otherwise, the cost is about $100. Most U.S. and Canadian airlines charge $40–$80 each way.

BUS TRAVEL

Because of the state's size, traveling by bus in California can be slow. But if you don't want to rent a car and wish to go where the train does not, a bus may be your only option. Greyhound is the major carrier for intermediate and long distances. If you've taken the bus in the past, however, don't assume it still serves your destination. In 2005, service was discontinued in 64 small California cities and towns, so be sure and call ahead. Regional bus service is available in metropolitan areas. Check the specific chapters for the regions you plan to visit. Smoking is prohibited on all buses in California.

🔝 Bus Information **Greyhound** ☎ 800/231-2222 ⊕ www.greyhound.com.

BUSINESS HOURS

Banks in California are typically open from 9 to 4 and are closed most holidays (⇨ Holidays). Smaller shops usually operate from 10 to 6, with larger stores remaining open until 8 or later. Hours vary for museums and historical sites, and many are closed one or more days a week. It's a good idea to check before you visit a tourist site.

CAMERAS & PHOTOGRAPHY

The pounding surf, majestic mountains, sprawling deserts, towering trees, and sparkling beaches—not to mention the cities and towns in between—make California a photographer's dream destination. Bring lots of film (or plenty of digital memory) to capture the special moments of your trip.

The *Kodak Guide to Shooting Great Travel Pictures* (available at bookstores everywhere) is loaded with tips.

🔝 Photo Help **Kodak Information Center** ☎ 800/ 242-2424 ⊕ www.kodak.com.

EQUIPMENT PRECAUTIONS

Don't pack film or equipment in checked luggage, where it is much more susceptible to damage. X-ray machines used to view checked luggage are extremely powerful and therefore are likely to ruin your film. Try to ask for hand inspection of film, which becomes clouded after repeated exposure to airport X-ray machines, and keep videotapes and computer disks away from metal detectors. Always keep film, tape, and computer disks out of the sun. Carry an extra supply of batteries, and be prepared to turn on your camera, camcorder, or laptop to prove to airport security personnel that the device is real.

CAR RENTAL

A car is essential in most parts of California. In compact San Francisco it's better to use public transportation to avoid parking headaches. In sprawling cities such as Los Angeles and San Diego, however, you'll have to take the freeways to get just about anywhere.

Rates statewide begin at around $40 a day and $195 a week. This does not include tax on car rentals, which is 8¼% in Los Angeles, 8½% in San Francisco, and 7¾% in San Diego. You can sometimes get lower rates in San Diego; compare prices by city before you book, and ask about "drop charges" if you plan to return the car in a city other than the one where you rented the vehicle. If you pick up at an airport, there may also be a facility charge of as much as $12 per rental; ask when you book.

Request car seats and extras such as GPS when you book, and make sure that a confirmed reservation guarantees you a car. Agencies sometimes overbook, particularly for busy weekends and holiday periods. Rates are sometimes—but not always— better if you book in advance or reserve through a rental agency's Web site. There are other reasons to book ahead, though: for popular destinations, during busy times of the year, or to ensure that you get a certain type of car (vans, SUVs, exotic sports cars).

CUTTING COSTS

Really weigh your options. Find out if a credit card you carry or organization or frequent-renter program to which you belong has a discount program. And check that such discounts really are the best deal. You can often do better with special weekend or weekly rates offered by a rental

agency. (And even if you only want to rent for five or six days, ask if you can get the weekly rate; it may very well be cheaper than the daily rate for that period of time.).

Price local car-rental companies as well as the majors. Also investigate wholesalers, which don't own fleets but rent in bulk from those that do and often offer better rates (note you must usually pay for such rentals before leaving home). Consider adding a car rental onto your air/hotel vacation package; the cost will often be cheaper than if you had rented the car separately on your own.

When traveling abroad, **look for guaranteed exchange rates,** which protect you against a falling dollar. With your rate locked in, you won't pay more, even if the price goes up in the local currency. (Note to self: Not the best thing if the dollar is surging rather than plunging.)

Beware of hidden charges. Those great rental rates may not be so great when you add in taxes, surcharges, cancellation penalties, taxes, drop-off charges (if you're planning to pick up the car in one city and leave it in another), and surcharges (for being under or over a certain age, for additional drivers, or for driving over state or country borders or out of a specific radius from your point of rental).

Note that airport rental offices often add supplementary surcharges that you may avoid by renting from an agency whose office is just off airport property. Don't buy the tank of gas that's in the car when you rent it unless you plan to do a lot of driving. Avoid hefty refueling fees by filling the tank at a station well away from the rental agency (those nearby are often more expensive) just before you turn in the car.

🚗 Automobile Associations U.S.: **American Automobile Association (AAA)** ☎ 315/797-5000 ⊕ www.aaa.com; most contact with the organization is through state and regional members. **National Automobile Club** ☎ 650/294-7000 ⊕ www.thenac.com; membership is open to California residents only.

🚗 Major Agencies **Alamo** ☎ 800/462-5266 ⊕ www.alamo.com. **Avis** ☎ 800/230-4898 ⊕ www.

avis.com. **Budget** ☎ 800/527-0700 ⊕ www.budget. com. **Hertz** ☎ 800/654-3131 ⊕ www.hertz.com. **National Car Rental** ☎ 800/227-7368 ⊕ www. nationalcar.com.

CONVERTIBLES & SUVS

If you dream of driving down the coast with the top down, or you want to explore the desert landscape not visible from the road, consider renting a specialty vehicle. Agencies that specialize in convertibles and sport-utility vehicles will often arrange airport delivery in larger cities. Unlike most of the major agencies, the following companies guarantee the car class that you book.

🏳 Specialty Car Agencies In San Francisco, **Specialty Rentals** ☎ 800/400-8412 ⊕ www. specialtyrentals.com; in Los Angeles, **Beverly Hills Rent a Car** ☎ 800/479-5996 ⊕ www.bhrentacar. com or **Midway Car Rental** ☎ 800/824-5260 ⊕ www.midwaycarrental.com; in San Diego, **Rent-a-Vette** ☎ 800/627-0808 ⊕ www. sandiegosportscarrental.com.

INSURANCE

Everyone who rents a car wonders about whether the insurance that the rental companies offer is worth the expense. No one—not even us—has a simple answer. It all depends on how much regular insurance you have, how comfortable you are with risk, and whether or not money is an issue.

If you own a car and carry comprehensive car insurance for both collision and liability, your personal auto insurance will probably cover a rental, but read your policy's fine print to be sure. If you don't have auto insurance, then you should probably buy the collision- or loss-damage waiver (CDW or LDW) from the rental company. This eliminates your liability for damage to the car. Some credit cards offer CDW coverage, but it's usually supplemental to your own insurance and rarely covers SUVs, minivans, luxury models and the like. If your coverage is secondary, you may still be liable for loss-of-use costs from the car-rental company (again, read the fine print). But no credit-card insurance is valid unless you use that card for *all* transactions, from reserving to paying the final bill.

You may also be offered supplemental liability coverage; the car-rental company is required to carry a minimal level of liability coverage that covers all renters, but it's rarely enough to cover claims in a really serious accident if you're at fault. Your own auto insurance policy will protect you if you own a car; if you don't, you have to decide if you are willing to take the risk.

U.S. rental companies sell CDWs and LDWs for about $15 to $25 a day; supplemental liability is usually over $10 a day. The car-rental company may offer you all sorts of other policies, but they're rarely worth the cost. Personal accident insurance, which is basic hospitalization coverage, is an especially egregious rip-off if you already have health insurance.

Note that you can decline the insurance from the rental company and purchase it through a third-party provider such as Travel Guard (www.travelguard.com)—$9 per day for $35,000 of coverage. That's sometimes just under half the price of the CDW offered by some car-rental companies. Also, Diners Club offers primary CDW coverage on all rentals reserved and paid for with the card. This means that Diners Club's company—not your own car insurance—pays in case of an accident. It *doesn't* mean your car-insurance company won't raise your rates once it discovers you had an accident.

Some states, including California, have capped the price of the CDW and LDW, but the cap has a floating value, depending on the cost of the vehicle; for those valued at more than $35,000, there's no maximum. Verify the cost of the CDW/LDW at the time you book. Make sure you have enough coverage to pay for the car. If you do not have auto insurance or an umbrella policy that covers damage to third parties, purchasing liability insurance and a CDW or LDW is highly recommended.

Each car-rental company sets its own cap on the insurance it offers. Some agencies may not provide full coverage for their most expensive vehicles. Thus you may rent a car valued at $50,000, but only be able to purchase a CDW or LDW for coverage up to $35,000. The cap varies agency to agency, so as you shop around, ask each agency about its insurance limits, and when you book, **make sure you have enough coverage to pay for the *specific* car that you're renting.**

Rental agencies in California aren't required to include liability insurance in the price of the rental. If you cause an accident, you may expose your assets to litigation. When in doubt about your own policy's coverage, take the liability coverage that the agency offers. If you plan to take the car out of California, ask if the policy is valid in other states or countries. Most car-rental companies won't insure a loss or damage that occurs outside of their coverage area—particularly in Mexico.

REQUIREMENTS & RESTRICTIONS

In California, you must be 21 to rent a car, and rates may be higher if you're under 25. Some agencies will not rent to those under 25; check when you book. Non-U.S. residents must have a license whose text is in the Roman alphabet. Though it need not be entirely written in English, it must have English letters that clearly identify it as a driver's license. An international license is recommended but not required.

CAR TRAVEL

Three major highways—Interstate 5, U.S. 101, and Highway 1—run north–south through California. The main routes into the state from the east are Interstate 15 and Interstate 10 in Southern California and Interstate 80 in northern California.

EMERGENCY SERVICES

Dial 911 to report accidents on the road and to reach police, the California Highway Patrol (CHP), or the fire department. On some rural highways and on most interstates, look for emergency phones on the side of the road.

GASOLINE

Gasoline prices in California vary widely, depending on location, oil company, and whether you buy it at a full-serve or self-serve pump. At this writing regular unleaded gasoline costs about $3 a gallon. It's less expensive to buy fuel in the southern part of the state than in the north. If you're planning to travel near Nevada, you can save a lot by purchasing gas over the border.

Gas stations are plentiful throughout the state. Most stay open late (24 hours along major highways and in big cities), except in rural areas, where Sunday hours are limited and where you may drive long stretches without a chance to refuel.

ROAD CONDITIONS

Rainy weather can make driving along the coast or in the mountains treacherous. Some of the smaller routes over the mountain ranges are prone to flash flooding. When the rains are severe, coastal Highway 1 can quickly become a slippery nightmare, buffeted by strong winds and obstructed by falling debris from the cliffs above. When the weather is particularly bad, Highway 1 may be closed due to mudslides. Drivers should check road and weather conditions before heading out.

Many smaller roads over the Sierra Nevada are closed in winter, and if it's snowing, tire chains may be required on routes that are open, most notably those to Yosemite and Lake Tahoe. From October through April, if it's raining along the coast, it's usually snowing at higher elevations. Do not wait until the highway patrol's chain-control checkpoint to look for chains; you'll be unable to turn around, and will get stuck and have to wait out the storm. Rent a four-wheel-drive vehicle or purchase chains before you get to the mountains. (Chains or cables generally cost $30 to $45, depending on tire size; cables are easier to apply than chains, but chains are more durable.) If you delay and purchase them in the vicinity of the chain-control area, the cost may double. Be aware that most rental-car companies prohibit chain installation on their vehicles. If you choose to risk it and do not tighten them properly, they may snap; insurance will not cover the damage that could result. Uniformed chain installers on Interstate 80 and U.S. 50 will apply them at the checkpoint for $20 or take them off for $10. On smaller roads you are on your own. Always carry extra clothing, blankets, and food when driving to the mountains in the winter, and keep your gas tank full to prevent the fuel line from freezing.

In larger cities the biggest driving hazards are traffic jams. Avoid major urban highways, especially at rush hour.

🚩 Road Conditions **Statewide hotline** ☎ 800//GAS-ROAD or 916/445-1534 ⊕ www.dot.ca. gov/hq/roadinfo.

🚩 Weather Conditions **National Weather Service** ☎ 707/443-6484 northernmost California, 831/656-1725 San Francisco Bay area and central California, 775/673-8100 Reno, Lake Tahoe, and northern Sierra, 805/988-6610 Los Angeles area, 858/675-8700 San Diego area ⊕ www.weather.gov.

ROAD MAPS

You can buy detailed maps in bookstores and gas stations and at some grocery stores and drugstores. For the hands-down best California atlas, with detailed landscape features, a recreation guide, complete GPS grid, and every road in the state, pick up a copy of the **California Road & Recreation Atlas,** by Benchark Maps, available from **Map Link** (☎ 805/692-6777 ⊕ www.maplink.com).

RULES OF THE ROAD

Always strap children under age six or weighing 60 pounds or less into approved child-safety seats; also children up to age six and weighing up to 60 pounds must be placed in booster seats designed to reduce seat-belt injuries. Seat belts are required at all times; tickets can be given for failing to comply. Children must wear seat belts regardless of where they're seated (studies show that children are safest in the rear seats).

Unless otherwise indicated, right turns are allowed at red lights after you've come to a full stop. Left turns between two one-way streets are allowed at red lights after you've come to a full stop. Drivers with a blood-alcohol level higher than 0.08 who are stopped by police are subject to arrest, and police officers can detain those with a level of 0.05 if they appear impaired. California's drunk-driving laws are extremely tough. The licenses of violators may immediately be suspended, and offenders may have to spend the night in jail and pay hefty fines.

The speed limit on many rural highways is 70 mph. In cities, freeway speed limits are between 55 mph and 65 mph. Many city routes have commuter lanes during rush hour, but the rules vary from city to city: in San Francisco, for example, you need three people in a car to use these lanes; in Los Angeles only two. Read the signs. Failure to comply with the rules could cost you more than $300 in fines.

CHILDREN IN CALIFORNIA

California is made to order for traveling with children: youngsters love Disneyland; Legoland, in Carlsbad; the San Diego Zoo; the Monterey Bay Aquarium; San Francisco cable cars; the gold mine in Placerville; Forestiere Underground Gardens in Fresno; and the caverns near Lake Shasta. *Fodor's Around Los Angeles with Kids* and *Fodor's Around San Francisco with Kids* (available in bookstores everywhere) can help you plan your days together.

If you are renting a car, don't forget to arrange for a car seat when you reserve. For general advice about traveling with children, consult *Fodor's FYI: Travel with Your Baby* (available in bookstores everywhere).

FLYING

If your children are two or older, ask about children's airfares. As a general rule, infants under two not occupying a seat fly at greatly reduced fares or even for free. But if you want to guarantee a seat for an infant, you have to pay full fare. Consider flying during off-peak days and times; most airlines will grant an infant a seat without a ticket if there are available seats.

Experts agree that it's a good idea to use safety seats aloft for children weighing less than 40 pounds. Airlines set their own policies: if you use a safety seat, U.S. carriers usually require that the child be ticketed, even if he or she is young enough to ride free, because the seats must be strapped into regular seats. And even if you pay the full adult fare for the seat, it may be worth it, especially on longer trips. Do **check your airline's policy about using safety seats during takeoff and landing.** Safety seats are not allowed everywhere in the plane, so get your seat assignments as early as possible.

When reserving, request children's meals or a freestanding bassinet (not available at all airlines) if you need them. But note that bulkhead seats, where you must sit to use the bassinet, may lack an overhead bin or storage space on the floor.

LODGING

Most hotels in California allow children under a certain age to stay in their parents' room at no extra charge, but others charge for them as extra adults; be sure to find out the cutoff age for children's discounts. If you need a crib, call the hotel directly (not the hotel's reservation center) to confirm availability.

SIGHTS & ATTRACTIONS

Places that are especially appealing to children are indicated by a rubber-duckie icon (🐥) in the margin.

CONSUMER PROTECTION

Whether you're shopping for gifts or purchasing travel services, **pay with a major credit card** whenever possible, so you can cancel payment or get reimbursed if there's a problem (and you can provide documentation). If you're doing business with a particular company for the first time, contact your local Better Business Bureau and the attorney general's offices in your state and (for U.S. businesses) the company's home state as well. Have any complaints been filed? Finally, if you're buying a package or tour, always consider travel insurance that includes default coverage (⇨ Insurance).

📋 BBBs **Council of Better Business Bureaus** ☎ 703/276-0100 ⊕ www.bbb.org.

CUSTOMS & DUTIES

You're always allowed to bring goods of a certain value back home without having to pay any duty or import tax. There's also a limit on the amount of tobacco and liquor you can bring back duty-free, and some countries have separate limits for perfumes; for exact figures, check with your customs department. The values of so-called "duty-free" goods are included in these amounts. When you shop abroad, save all your receipts as customs inspectors may ask to see them as well as the items you purchased. If the total value of your goods is more than the duty-free limit, then you'll have to pay a tax (most often a flat percentage) on the value of everything beyond that limit.

📋 U.S. Information **U.S. Customs and Border Protection** ⊕ www.cbp.gov.

DISABILITIES & ACCESSIBILITY

California is a national leader in making attractions and facilities accessible to people with disabilities.

LODGING

Despite the Americans with Disabilities Act, the definition of accessibility seems to differ from hotel to hotel. Some properties may be accessible by ADA standards for people with mobility problems but not for people with hearing or vision impairments, for example.

If you have mobility problems, ask for the lowest floor on which accessible services are offered. If you have a hearing impairment, check whether the hotel has devices to alert you visually to the ring of the telephone, a knock at the door, and a fire/emergency alarm. Some hotels provide these devices without charge. Discuss your needs with hotel personnel if this equipment isn't available, so that a staff member can personally alert you in the event of an emergency.

If you're bringing a guide dog, get authorization ahead of time and write down the name of the person with whom you spoke.

RESERVATIONS

When discussing accessibility with an operator or reservations agent, ask hard questions. Are there any stairs, inside *or* out? Are there grab bars next to the toilet *and* in the shower/tub? How wide is the doorway to the room? To the bathroom? For the most extensive facilities meeting the latest legal specifications, opt for newer accommodations. If you reserve through a toll-free number, consider also calling the hotel's local number to confirm the information from the central reservations office. Get confirmation in writing when you can.

TRANSPORTATION

Hertz and Avis (⇨ Car Rental) are able to supply cars modified for those with disabilities, but they require one to two days' advance notice. Discounts are available for travelers with disabilities on Amtrak (⇨ Train Travel). On Greyhound (⇨ Bus Travel), your companion can ride free. The U.S. Department of Transportation Aviation Consumer Protection Division's online publication *New Horizons: Information for the Air Traveler with a Disability* offers advice for travellers with a disability, and outlines basic rights. Visit DisabilityInfo.gov for general information.

🔳 Information and Complaints **Aviation Consumer Protection Division** (⇨ Air Travel for airline-related problems; ⊕ airconsumer.ost.dot.gov/publications/horizons.htm for airline travel advice and rights). **Departmental Office of Civil Rights** 🕾 202/366-4648, 202/366-8538 TTY ⊕ www.dotcr.ost.dot.gov. **Disability Rights Section** 🕾 ADA information line 202/514-0301, 800/514-0301, 202/514-0383 TTY, 800/514-0383 TTY ⊕ www.ada.gov. **U.S. Department of Transportation Hotline** 🕾 for disability-related air-travel problems, 800/778-4838 or 800/455-9880 TTY.

TRAVEL AGENCIES

In the United States, the Americans with Disabilities Act requires that travel firms serve the needs of all travelers. Some agencies specialize in working with people with disabilities.

🔳 Travelers with Mobility Problems **Access Adventures/B. Roberts Travel** 🕾 800/444-6540 ⊕ www.brobertstravel.com, run by a former physical-rehabilitation counselor. **Accessible Vans of America** 🕾 877/282-8267, 888/282-8267, 973/808-9709 reservations ⊕ www.accessiblevans.com. **CareVacations** 🕾 780/986-6404 or 877/478-7827

⊕ www.carevacations.com, for group tours and cruise vacations. **Flying Wheels Travel** 🕾 507/451-5005 ⊕ www.flyingwheelstravel.com.

🔳 Travelers with Developmental Disabilities **New Directions** 🕾 805/967-2841 or 888/967-2841 ⊕ www.newdirectionstravel.com. **Sprout** 🕾 212/222-9575 or 888/222-9575 ⊕ www.gosprout.org.

DIVERS' ALERT

Do not fly within 24 hours of scuba diving.

EATING OUT

California has led the pack in bringing natural and organic foods to the forefront of American cooking. Though rooted in European cuisine, California cooking sometimes has strong Asian and Latin influences. Wherever you go, you're likely to find that dishes are made with fresh produce and other local ingredients.

The restaurants we list are the cream of the crop in each price category. Properties indicated by a ✕⌂ are lodging establishments whose restaurant warrants a special trip.

Was the service stellar or not up to snuff? Did the food give you shivers of delight or leave you cold? Did the prices and portions make you happy or sad? Rate restaurants and write your own reviews in Travel Ratings or start a discussion about your favorite places in Travel Talk on www.fodors.com. Your comments might even appear in our books. Yes, you, too, can be a correspondent!

CUTTING COSTS

If you're on a budget, take advantage of the "small plates" craze sweeping California by ordering several appetizer-size portions and having a glass of wine at the bar, rather than having a full meal. Also, better grocery and specialty-food stores have grab-and-go sections, with prepared foods on par with restaurant cooking, perfect for picnicking (remember, it rarely rains between May and October). At resort areas in the off-season (such as Lake Tahoe in October and May, or San Diego in January), you can often find two-for-one dinner specials at upper-end restaurants; check local papers or with visitor bureaus.

MEALTIMES

Unless otherwise noted, the restaurants listed in this guide are open daily for lunch and dinner. Lunch is typically served 11:30–2:30, and dinner service in most restaurants begins at 5:30 and ends at 10. Some restaurants in larger cities stay open until midnight or later, but in smaller towns evening service may end as early as 8.

RESERVATIONS & DRESS

Regardless of where you are, it's a good idea to make a reservation if you can. In some places (Hong Kong, for example), it's expected. We only mention specifically when reservations are essential (there's no other way you'll ever get a table) or when they are not accepted. For popular restaurants, book as far ahead as you can (often 30 days), and reconfirm as soon as you arrive. (Large parties should always call ahead to check the reservations policy.) We mention dress only when men are required to wear a jacket or a jacket and tie.

WINE, BEER & SPIRITS

If you like wine, your trip to California won't be complete unless you sample a few of the local vintages. Throughout the state, most famously in the Napa and Sonoma valleys, you can visit wineries, most of which have tasting rooms and many of which offer tours. The legal drinking age is 21.

ECOTOURISM

When traveling in wilderness areas and parks, remember to tread lightly. Do not drive an SUV through sensitive habitats, and pack out what you pack in. Many remote camping areas do not provide waste disposal. It's a good idea to bring plastic bags to store refuse until you can dispose of it properly. Recycling programs are abundant in California, and trash at many state and national parks is sorted. Look for appropriately labeled garbage containers. Numerous ecotours are available in the state (⇨ Tours & Packages).

GAY & LESBIAN TRAVEL

San Francisco, Los Angeles, West Hollywood, San Diego, and Palm Springs are among the California cities with the most visible lesbian and gay communities. Though it's usually safe to be visibly "out" in many areas, you should always use common sense when in unfamiliar places. Gay bashings still occur in both urban and rural areas. For details about the gay and lesbian scene, consult *Fodor's Gay Guide to the USA* (available in bookstores everywhere).

LOCAL INFORMATION

Many California cities large and small have lesbian and gay publications available in sidewalk racks and at bars, bookstores, and other social spaces; most have extensive events and information listings.

Community Centers **Billy DeFrank Lesbian & Gay Community Center** ⊠ 938 the Alameda, San Jose 95126 🕾 408/293-2429 ⊕ www.defrank.org. **L.A. Gay and Lesbian Center** ⊠ 1625 N. Schrader Blvd., Los Angeles 90028 🕾 323/993-7400 ⊕ www.laglc.org. **Lambda Community Center** ⊠ 1927 L St., Sacramento 95814 🕾 916/442-0185 ⊕ www.lambdasac.org. **Lavender Youth Recreation & Information Center** ⊠ 127 Collingwood St., San Francisco 94114 🕾 415/703-6150 ⊕ www.lyric.org. **Lesbian and Gay Men's Community Center** ⊠ 3909 Centre St., San Diego 92103 🕾 619/692-2077 ⊕ www.thecentersd.org. **Pacific Center for Human Growth** ⊠ 2712 Telegraph Ave., Berkeley 94705 🕾 510/548-8283 ⊕ www.pacificcenter.org. **The Center (San Francisco Lesbian, Gay, Bisexual, Transgender Community Center)** ⊠ 1800 Market St. 🕾 415/865-5555 ⊕ www.sfgaycenter.org.

Local Publications **Bay Area Reporter** 🕾 415/861-5019 ⊕ www.ebar.com. **Bottom Line** 🕾 760/323-0552 ⊕ www.psbottomline.com. **Frontiers** 🕾 323/930-3220 ⊕ www.frontiersnewsmagazine.com. **Mom Guess What!** 🕾 916/441-6397 ⊕ www.mgwnews.com. **Update** 🕾 619/299-0500 ⊕ www.sandiegogaynews.com.

Gay- & Lesbian-Friendly Travel Agencies **Different Roads Travel** 🕾 760/325-6964 or 800/429-8747 ✍ lgernert@tzell.com. **Skylink Travel and Tour/Flying Dutchmen Travel** 🕾 707/546-9888 or 800/225-5759 ; serving lesbian travelers.

INSURANCE

What kind of coverage do you honestly need? Do you even need trip insurance at all? Take a deep breath and read on.

We believe that comprehensive trip insurance is especially valuable if you're booking a very expensive or complicated trip (particularly to an isolated region) or if you're booking far in advance. Who knows what could happen six months down the road? But whether or not you get insurance has more to do with how comfortable you are assuming all that risk yourself.

Comprehensive travel policies typically cover trip-cancellation and interruption, letting you cancel or cut your trip short because of a personal emergency, illness, or, in some cases, acts of terrorism in your destination. Such policies also cover evacuation and medical care. Some also cover you for trip delays because of bad weather or mechanical problems as well as for lost or delayed baggage. Another type of coverage to look for is financial default—that is, when your trip is disrupted because a tour operator, airline, or cruise line goes out of business. Generally you must buy this when you book your trip or shortly thereafter, and it's only available to you if your operator isn't on a list of excluded companies.

If you're going abroad, consider buying medical-only coverage at the very least. Neither Medicare nor some private insurers cover medical expenses anywhere outside of the United States besides Mexico and Canada (including time aboard a cruise ship, even if it leaves from a U.S. port). Medical-only policies typically reimburse you for medical care (excluding that related to pre-existing conditions) and hospitalization abroad and provide for evacuation. You still have to pay the bills and await reimbursement from the insurer, though.

Expect comprehensive travel insurance policies to cost about 4% to 7% of the total price of your trip (it's more like 12% if you're over age 70). A medical-only policy may or may not be cheaper than a comprehensive policy. Always read the fine print of your policy to make sure that you are covered for the risks that are of the most concern to you. Compare several policies to make sure you're getting the best price and range of coverage available.

Just as an aside: You know you can save a bundle on trips to warm-weather destinations by traveling in rainy season. But there's also a chance that a severe storm will disrupt your plans. The solution? Look for hotels and resorts that offer storm/hurricane guarantees. Although they rarely allow refunds, most guarantees do let you rebook later if a storm strikes.

🔲 Insurance Comparison Sites **Insure My Trip. com** ⊕ www.insuremytrip.com. **Square Mouth.com** ⊕ www.quotetravelinsurance.com.

🔲 Comprehensive Travel Insurers **Access America** ☎ 866/807-3982 ⊕ www.accessamerica.com. **CSA Travel Protection** ☎ 800/873-9855 ⊕ www. csatravelprotection.com. **HTH Worldwide** ☎ 610/ 254-8700 or 888/243-2358 ⊕ www.hthworldwide. com. **Travelex Insurance** ☎ 888/457-4602 ⊕ www.travelex-insurance.com. **Travel Guard International** ☎ 715/345-0505 or 800/826-4919 ⊕ www.travelguard.com. **Travel Insured International** ☎ 800/243-3174 ⊕ www.travelinsured.com.

🔲 Medical-Only Insurers **Wallach & Company** ☎ 800/237-6615 or 504/687-3166 ⊕ www.wallach. com. **International Medical Group** ☎ 800/628-4664 ⊕ www.imglobal.com. **International SOS** ☎ 215/942-8000 or 713/521-7611 ⊕ www. internationalsos.com.

FOR INTERNATIONAL TRAVELERS

CAR RENTAL

When picking up a rental car, non-U.S. residents need a reservation voucher for any prepaid reservations that were made in the traveler's home country, a passport, a driver's license, and a travel policy that covers each driver.

CURRENCY

The dollar is the basic unit of U.S. currency. It has 100 cents. Coins are the penny (1¢); the nickel (5¢), dime (10¢), quarter (25¢), and half-dollar (50¢); and the very rare golden $1 coin and even rarer silver $1. Bills are denominated $1, $5, $10, $20, $50, and $100, all mostly green and identical in size; designs and background tints vary. You may come across a $2 bill, but the chances are slim.

CUSTOMS

🔲 **U.S. Customs and Border Protection** ⊕ www.cbp.gov.

DRIVING

Driving in the United States is on the right. Speed limits are posted in miles per hour along roads and highways (usually between 55 mph and 70 mph). Watch for lower limits in small towns and on back roads (usually 30 mph to 40 mph). Most states require front-seat passengers to wear seat belts; many states require children to sit in the back seat and to wear seat belts. In major cities, rush hour is between 7 and 10 AM; afternoon rush hour is between 4 and 7 PM. To encourage carpooling, some freeways have special lanes for so-called high-occupancy vehicles (HOV)—cars carrying more than one passenger—ordinarily marked with a diamond.

Highways are well paved. Interstate highways—limited-access, multilane highways whose numbers are prefixed by "I–"—are the fastest routes. Interstates with three-digit numbers encircle urban areas, which may have other limited-access expressways, freeways, and parkways as well. Tolls may be levied on limited-access highways. So-called U.S. highways and state highways are not necessarily limited-access but may have several lanes.

Gas stations are plentiful. Most stay open late (24 hours along large highways and in big cities), except in rural areas, where Sunday hours are limited and where you may drive long stretches without a refueling opportunity. Along larger highways, roadside stops with rest rooms, fast-food restaurants, and sundries stores are well spaced. State police and tow trucks patrol major highways and lend assistance. If your car breaks down on an interstate, pull onto the shoulder and wait for help, or have your passengers wait while you walk to an emergency phone (available in most states). If you carry a cell phone, dial *55, noting your location on the small green roadside mileage markers.

ELECTRICITY

The U.S. standard is AC, 110 volts/60 cycles. Plugs have two flat pins set parallel to each other.

EMBASSIES

🔲 **Australia** ☎ 202/797-3000 ⊕ www.austemb.org. **Canada** ☎ 202/682-1740 ⊕ www.canadianembassy.org. **United Kingdom** ☎ 202/588-7800 ⊕ www.britainusa.com.

EMERGENCIES

For police, fire, or ambulance dial 911 (0 in rural areas).

HOLIDAYS

Major national holidays are New Year's Day (Jan. 1); Martin Luther King Day (3rd Mon. in Jan.); Presidents' Day (3rd Mon. in Feb.); Memorial Day (last Mon. in May); Independence Day (July 4); Labor Day (1st Mon. in Sept.); Columbus Day (2nd Mon. in Oct.); Thanksgiving Day (4th Thurs. in Nov.); Christmas Eve and Christmas Day (Dec. 24 and 25); and New Year's Eve (Dec. 31).

MAIL

You can buy stamps and aerograms and send letters and parcels in post offices. Stamp-dispensing machines can occasionally be found in airports, bus and train stations, office buildings, drugstores, and the like. U.S. mail boxes are stout, dark blue, steel bins at strategic locations in major cities; pickup schedules are posted inside the bin (pull down the handle to see them). Parcels more than 1 pound must be mailed at a post office or at a private mailing center.

Within the United States, a first-class letter weighing 1 ounce or less costs 39¢, and each additional ounce costs 24¢; postcards cost 24 ¢. A 1-ounce airmail letter to most countries costs 84¢, an airmail postcard costs 75¢; to Canada and Mexico, a 1-ounce letter costs 63¢, a postcard 55¢. An aerogram—a single sheet of lightweight blue paper that folds into its own envelope, stamped for overseas airmail—costs 75¢ regardless of its destination.

To receive mail on the road, have it sent c/o General Delivery at your destination's main post office (use the correct five-digit ZIP code). You must pick up mail in person within 30 days and show a driver's license or passport.

🖫 **DHL** ☏ 800/225-5345 ⊕ www.dhl.com. **Federal Express** ☏ 800/463-3339 ⊕ www.fedex.com. **Mail Boxes, Etc.** (The UPS Store) ☏ 800/789-4623 ⊕ www.mbe.com. **United States Postal Service** ⊕ www.usps.com.

PASSPORTS & VISAS

Visitor visas aren't necessary for citizens of Australia, Canada, the United Kingdom, as well as for most citizens of European Union countries if you're coming for tourism and staying for fewer than 90 days. If you require a visa, the cost is $100 and, depending on where you live, the waiting time can be substantial. Apply for a visa at the U.S. consulate in your place of residence; look at the U.S. State Department's special Visa Web site for further information.

🖫 Visa Information **Destination USA** ⊕ www.unitedstatesvisas.gov.

PHONES

All U.S. telephone numbers consist of a three-digit area code and a seven-digit local number. Within many local calling areas, you dial only the seven-digit number; in others, you must dial "1" first and then the area code. To call between area-code regions, dial "1" then all 10 digits; the same goes for calls to numbers prefixed by "800," "888," "866," and "877"—all toll free. For calls to numbers preceded by "900" you must pay—usually dearly.

For international calls, dial "011" followed by the country code and the local number. For help, dial "0" and ask for an overseas operator. The country code is 61 for Australia, 64 for New Zealand, 44 for the United Kingdom. Calling Canada is the same as calling within the United States. Most phone books list country codes and U.S. area codes. The country code for the United States is 1.

For operator assistance, dial "0." To obtain someone's phone number, call directory assistance at 555–1212 or occasionally 411 (free at many public phones). You can reverse the charges on a long-distance by calling "collect"; dial "0" instead of "1" before the 10-digit number.

At pay phones, instructions often are posted. Usually you insert coins in a slot (usually 25¢–50¢ for local calls) and wait for a steady tone before dialing. When you call long-distance, the operator tells you how much to insert; prepaid phone cards, widely available in various denominations, can be used from any phone. Follow the directions to activate the card (there is usually an access number and then an activation code for the card), then dial your number.

The United States has several GSM (Global System for Mobile Communications) networks, so multiband mobile phones from most countries (except for Japan) work here. Unfortunately, it's almost impossible to buy a pay-as-you-go mobile SIM card in the U.S.—which allows you to avoide roaming charges— without a phone. That said, cell phones with pay-as-you-go plans are available for well under $100. The cheapest ones with decent national coverage are the GoPhone from Cingular and Virgin Mobile, which only offers pay-as-you-go service.

🖫 Cell Phone Contacts **Cingular** ☏ 888/333-6651 ⊕ www.cingular.com. **Virgin Mobile** ☏ No phone ⊕ www.virginmobileusa.com.

LODGING

The lodgings we list are the cream of the crop in each price category. We always list the facilities that are available, but we don't specify whether they cost extra; when pricing accommodations, always ask what's included and what costs extra. Properties marked ✕🏠 are lodging establishments whose restaurants warrant a special trip.

Most hotels and other lodgings require you to give your credit card details before they will confirm your reservation. If you don't feel comfortable e-mailing this information, ask if you can fax it (some places even prefer faxes). However you book, get confirmation in writing and have a copy of it handy when you check in. If you book through an online travel agent, discounter, or wholesaler, you might even want to confirm your reservation with the hotel before leaving home—just to be sure everything was processed correctly.

Be sure you understand the hotel's cancellation policy. Some places allow you to cancel without any kind of penalty—even if you prepaid to secure a discounted rate—if you cancel at least 24 hours in advance. Others require you to cancel a week in advance or penalize you for the cost of one night. Small inns and B&Bs are most likely to require you to cancel far in advance. Most hotels allow children under a certain age to stay in their parents' room at no extra charge, but others charge for them as extra adults; find out the cutoff age for discounts.

Assume that hotels operate on the European Plan (**EP,** no meals) unless we specify that they use the Breakfast Plan (**BP,** with full breakfast), Continental Plan (**CP,** Continental breakfast), Full American Plan (**FAP,** all meals), Modified American Plan (**MAP,** breakfast and dinner) or are **all-inclusive** (all meals and most activities).

Did the resort look as good in real life as it did in the photos? Did you sleep like a baby, or were the walls paper thin? Did you get your money's worth? Rate hotels and write your own reviews in Travel Ratings or start a discussion about your favorite places in Travel Talk on www.fodors.com. Your comments might even appear in our books. Yes, you, too, can be a correspondent!

APARTMENT & HOUSE RENTALS

Hideaways International ☎ 603/430-4433 or 800/843-4433 🖷 603/430-4444 ⊕ www.hideaways.com, annual membership $185. **Interhome** ☎ 954/791-8282 or 800/882-6864 ⊕ www.interhome.us. **Vacation Home Rentals Worldwide** ☎ 201/767-9393 or 800/633-3284 ⊕ www.vhrww.com. **Villas International** ☎ 415/499-9490 or 800/221-2260 ⊕ www.villasintl.com.

BED & BREAKFASTS

Reservation Services Bed & Breakfast.com ☎ 512/322-2710 or 800/462-2632 ⊕ www.bedandbreakfast.com also sends out an online newsletter. **Bed & Breakfast Inns Online** ☎ 615/868-1946 or 800/215-7365 ⊕ www.bbonline.com. **BnB Finder.com** ☎ 212/432-7693 or 888/547-8226 ⊕ www.bnbfinder.com.

CAMPING

California offers numerous camping options, from drive-in family campgrounds with all the amenities to secluded hike-in campsites with no facilities. Some are operated by the state, others are on federal land, and still others are private. Rules vary for each. The most important rule is to always learn and obey local fire regulations; many of California's infamous firestorms are sparked by illegal or improperly extinguished campfires.

You can camp anywhere in a national forest, but in a national park, you must use only specific sites. Whenever possible, book well in advance, especially if your trip will be in summer or on a weekend. Contact the National Parks Reservation Service to reserve a campsite in a national park. ReserveUSA handles reservations for campgrounds administered by the U.S. Forest Service and the Army Corps of Engineers; ReserveAmerica handles reservations for many of the campgrounds in California state parks. On their Web sites you can search for locations, view campground maps, check availability, learn rules and regulations, and find driving directions.

Reservations National Park Reservation Service ☎ 800/436-7275 or 800/365-2267 ⊕ http://reservations.nps.gov. **ReserveAmerica** ☎ 877/444-6777 or 800/444-7275 ⊕ www.reserveamerica.com. **ReserveUSA** ☎ 877/444-6777 ⊕ www.reserveusa.com.

HOME EXCHANGES

With a direct home exchange, you stay in someone else's home while they stay in yours. Some outfits also deal with vacation homes, so you're not actually staying in someone's full-time residence, just their vacant weekend place.

Exchange Clubs HomeLink International ☎ 800/638-3841 ⊕ www.homelink.org; $80 yearly for Web-only membership; $125 with Web access and two directories. **Home Exchange.com** ☎ 800/877-8723 ⊕ www.homeexchange.com; $59.95 for a 1-year online listing. **Intervac U.S.** ☎ 800/756-4663 ⊕ www.intervacus.com; $78.88 for Web-only membership; $126 includes Web access and a catalog.

HOSTELS

Hostels offer barebones lodging at low, low prices—often in shared dorm rooms with shared baths—to people of all ages, though the primary market is young travelers, especially students. Most hostels serve breakfast; dinner and/or shared cooking facilities may also be available. In some hostels, you aren't allowed to be in your room during the day, and there may be a curfew at night. Nevertheless, hostels provide a sense of community, with public rooms where travelers often gather to share stories. Many hostels are affiliated with Hostelling International (HI), an umbrella group of hostel associations with some 4,500 member properties in more than 70 countries. Other hostels are completely independent and may be nothing more than a really cheap hotel.

Membership in any HI association, open to travelers of all ages, allows you to stay in HI-affiliated hostels at member rates. One-year membership is about $28 for adults; hostels charge about $10–$30 per night. Members have priority if the hostel is full; they're also eligible for discounts around the world, even on rail and bus travel in some countries.

🏠 **Hostelling International–USA** ☎ 301/495-1240 ⊕ www.hiusa.org.

HOTELS

Weigh all your options (we can't say this enough). Join "frequent guest" programs. You may get preferential treatment in room choice and/or upgrades in your favorite chains. Check general travel sites and hotel Web sites as not all chains are represented on all travel sites. Always research or inquire about special packages and corporate rates. If you prefer to book by phone, note you can sometimes get a better price if call the hotel's local toll-free number (if one is available) rather than the central reservations number.

If your destination's high season is December through April and you're trying to book, say, in late April, you might save considerably by changing your dates by a week or two. Note, though, that many properties charge peak-season rates for your entire stay even if your travel dates straddle peak and nonpeak seasons. High-end chains catering to businesspeople are often busy only on weekdays and often drop rates dramatically on weekends to fill up rooms. **Ask when rates go down.**

Watch out for hidden costs, including resort fees, energy surcharges, and "convenience" fees for such things as unlimited local phone service you won't use and a free newspaper—possibly written in a language you can't read. Always verify whether local hotel taxes are or are not included in the rates you are quoted, so that you'll know the real price of your stay. In some places, taxes can add 20% or more to your bill. If you're traveling overseas **look for price guarantees,** which protect you against a falling dollar. With your rate locked in, you won't pay more, even if the price goes up in the local currency.

All hotels listed have private bath unless otherwise noted.

Most major hotel chains are represented in California. Make any special needs known when you book your reservation. Guarantee your room with a credit card, or many hotels will automatically cancel your reservations if you don't show up by 4 PM. Always inquire about cancellation policies when you book, and get a confirmation number or the name of the agent with whom you spoke; if you cancel, request a cancellation number. Many hotels, like airlines, overbook. It's best to **reconfirm your reservation directly with the hotel on the morning of your arrival date.**

🏠 Discount Hotel Rooms **Accommodations Express** ☎ 800/444-7666 or 800/277-1064. **Hotels. com** ☎ 800/219-4606 or 800/364-0291 ⊕ www. hotels.com. **Quikbook** ☎ 800/789-9887 ⊕ www.

quikbook.com. **Steigenberger Reservation Service**
☎ 800/223-5652 ⊕ www.srs-worldhotels.com. **Tur-
botrip.com** ☎ 800/473-7829 ⊕ w3.turbotrip.com.

MEDIA

NEWSPAPERS & MAGAZINES

California's major daily newspapers, the
Los Angeles Times, the *San Diego Union-
Tribune,* and the *San Francisco Chronicle,*
maintain up-to-the-minute Web sites. The
state's weekly newspapers are usually the
best source of arts and entertainment information, from what shows are on the
boards to who's playing the clubs. Visit
the Web sites of the *L.A. Weekly,* the *San
Diego Reader,* the *San Francisco Bay
Guardian,* the *San Jose Metro* (MetroAc-
tive), and *SF Weekly* for the latest information on events in your destination.

🔳 Web Sites **L.A. Weekly** ⊕ www.laweekly.com.
Los Angeles Times ⊕ www.latimes.com. **MetroAc-
tive** ⊕ www.metroactive.com. **San Diego Reader**
⊕ www.sdreader.com. **San Diego Union-Tribune**
⊕ www.signonsandiego.com. **San Francisco Bay
Guardian** ⊕ www.sfbayguardian.com. **San Francisco Chronicle** ⊕ www.sfgate.com. **SF Weekly**
⊕ www.sfweekly.com.

MONEY MATTERS

Los Angeles, San Diego, and San Francisco
tend to be expensive cities to visit, and
rates at coastal and desert resorts are almost as high. A day's admission to a
major theme park can run upward of $45
a head, hotel rates average $150 to $250 a
night (though you can find cheaper
places), and dinners at even moderately
priced restaurants often cost $20 to $40
per person. Costs in the Gold Country, the
Far North, and the Death Valley/Mojave
Desert region are considerably less—many
fine Gold Country bed-and-breakfasts
charge around $100 a night, and some
motels in the Far North and the Mojave
charge $50 to $70.

Prices throughout this guide are given
for adults. Substantially reduced fees are
almost always available for children,
students, and senior citizens. For information on taxes, ⇨ Taxes.

ATMS

ATMs are readily available throughout
California. If you withdraw cash from a
bank other than your own, expect to pay a
fee of up to $2.50, plus a fee to your own
bank. If you're going to very remote areas
of the mountains or deserts, take some
extra cash with you or find out ahead of
time if you can pay with credit cards.

CREDIT CARDS

Throughout this guide, the following ab-
breviations are used: **AE,** American Express; **D,** Discover; **DC,** Diners Club; **MC,**
MasterCard; and **V,** Visa.

It's a good idea to inform your credit card
company before you travel, especially if
you're going abroad and don't travel internationally very often. Otherwise, the
credit-card company might put a hold on
your card owing to unusual activity—not
a good thing halfway through your trip.
Record all your credit card numbers—as
well as the phone numbers to call in the if
your cards are lost or stolen—in a safe
place so you're prepared should something
go wrong. Both MasterCard and Visa have
general numbers you can call (collect if
you're abroad) if your card is lost, but
you're better off calling the number of
your issuing bank since MasterCard and
Visa usually just transfer you to your
bank; your bank's number is usually
printed on your card.

🔳 Reporting Lost Cards **American Express**
☎ 800/992-3404 ⊕ www.americanexpress.com.
Diners Club ☎ 800/234-6377 ⊕ www.dinersclub.
com. **Discover** ☎ 800/347-2683 ⊕ www.
discovercard.com. **MasterCard** ☎ 800/622-7747
⊕ www.mastercard.com. **Visa** ☎ 800/847-2911
⊕ www.visa.com.

NATIONAL PARKS

Look into discount passes to save money
on park entrance fees. For $50, the Na-
tional Parks Pass admits you (and any
passengers in your private vehicle) to all
national parks, monuments, and recreation areas, as well as other sites run by
the National Park Service, for a year. (In
parks that charge per person, the pass
admits you, your spouse and children,

and your parents, when you arrive together.) Camping and parking are extra. The $15 Golden Eagle Pass, a hologram you affix to your National Parks Pass, functions as an upgrade, granting entry to all sites run by the NPS, the U.S. Fish and Wildlife Service, the U.S. Forest Service, and the Bureau of Land Management. The upgrade, which expires with the parks pass, is sold by most national-park, Fish-and-Wildlife, and BLM fee stations. A major percentage of the proceeds from pass sales funds National Parks projects.

Both the Golden Age Passport ($10), for U.S. citizens or permanent residents who are 62 and older, and the Golden Access Passport (free), for persons with disabilities, entitle holders (and any passengers in their private vehicles) to lifetime free entry to all national parks, plus 50% off fees for the use of many park facilities and services. (The discount doesn't always apply to companions.) To obtain them, you must show proof of age and of U.S. citizenship or permanent residency—such as a U.S. passport, driver's license, or birth certificate—and, if requesting Golden Access, proof of disability. The Golden Age and Golden Access passes are available only at NPS-run sites that charge an entrance fee. The National Parks Pass is also available by mail and phone and via the Internet.

🖼 **National Park Foundation** ☎ 202/238–4200 or 888/467–2757 (for National Parks Pass info) ⊕ www.nationalparks.org. **National Park Service** ☎ 202/208–6843 ⊕ www.nps.gov. **National Parks Conservation Association** ☎ 202/223–6722 or 800/628–7275 ⊕ www.npca.org.

PACKING

Why do some people travel with a convoy of suitcases the size of large-screen TVs and yet never have a thing to wear? How do others pack a toaster-oven-size duffle with a week's worth of outfits *and* supplies for every possible contingency? We realize that packing is a matter of style—a very personal thing—but there's a lot to be said for traveling light. The tips in this section will help you win the battle of the bulging bag.

Make a list. In a recent Fodor's survey, 29% of respondents said they make lists (and often pack) at least a week before a trip. Lists can be used at least twice—once to pack and once to repack at the end of your trip. You'll also have a record of the contents of your suitcase, just in case it disappears in transit.

Think it through. What's the weather like? Is this a business trip or a cruise or resort vacation? Going abroad? In some places and/or sights, traditions of dress may be more or less conservative than you're used to. As your itinerary comes together, jot activities down and note possible outfits next to each (don't forget those shoes and accessories).

Edit your wardrobe. Plan to wear everything twice (better yet, thrice) and to do laundry along the way. Stick to one basic look—urban chic, sporty casual, etc. Build around one or two neutrals and an accent (e.g., black, white, and olive green). Women can freshen looks by changing scarves or jewelry. For a week's trip, you can look smashing with three bottoms, four or five tops, a sweater, and a jacket you can wear alone or over the sweater.

Be practical. Put comfortable shoes at the top of your list. (Did we need to tell you this?) Pack items that are lightweight, wrinkle resistant, compact, and washable. (Or this?) Stack and then roll your clothes when packing, so they'll wrinkle less. Unless you're on a guided tour or a cruise, select luggage that you can readily carry. Porters, like good butlers, are hard to find these days.

Check weight and size limitations. In the United States you may be charged extra for checked bags weighing more than 50 pounds. Abroad some airlines don't allow you to check bags weighing more than 60 to 70 pounds, or they charge outrageous fees for every pound your luggage is over. Carry-on size limitations can be stringent, too.

Check carry-on restrictions. Research restrictions with the TSA. Rules vary abroad, so check them with your airline if you're traveling overseas on a foreign carrier. Consider packing all but essentials (travel documents, prescription meds, wallet) in checked luggage. This leads to a "pack only what you can afford to lose" approach that might help you streamline.

Lock it up. If you must pack valuables, use TSA-approved locks (about $10) that can be unlocked by all U.S. security personnel.

Tag it. Always put tags on your luggage with some kind of contact information; use your business address if you don't want people to know your home address. Put the same information (and a copy of your itinerary) inside your luggage, too.

Rethink valuables. On U.S. flights, airlines are liable for only about $2,800 per person for bags. On international flights, the liability limit is around $635 per bag. But items like computers, cameras, and jewelry aren't covered, and as gadgetry regularly goes on and of the list of carry-on no-no's, you can't count on keeping things safe by keeping them close. Although comprehensive travel policies may cover luggage, the liability limit is often a pittance. Your home-owner's policy may cover you sufficiently when you travel—or not.

Report problems immediately. If your bags—or things in them—are damaged or go astray, file a written claim with your airline *before you leave the airport.* If the airline is at fault, it may give you money for essentials until your luggage arrives. Most lost bags are found within 48 hours, so alert the airline to your whereabouts for two or three days. If your bag was opened for security reasons in the United States and something is missing, file a claim with the TSA.

WHAT YOU'LL NEED IN CALIFORNIA

When packing for a California vacation, prepare for changes in the weather. Take along sweaters, jackets, and clothes for layering as your best insurance for coping with variations in temperature. Bring along a daypack so you can shed layers midday. Know that San Francisco and other coastal towns can be chilly at any time of the year, especially in summer,

when the fog descends in the afternoon, preceded by strong winds. Even when it's chilly, though, it's smart to bring a bathing suit; many lodgings have heated pools, spas, and saunas. Casual dressing is a hallmark of the California lifestyle, but in the evening men will need a jacket and tie at more formal restaurants, and women will be most comfortable in something dressier than sightseeing garb.

PASSPORTS & VISAS

If you're planning to make a jaunt down to Mexico, be sure to bring along your passport.

We're always surprised at how few Americans have passports—only 25% at this writing. This number is expected to grow in coming years, when it becomes impossible to re-enter the United States from trips to neighboring Canada or Mexico without one. Remember this: A passport verifies both your identity and nationality—a great reason to have one.

U.S. passports are valid for 10 years. You must apply in person if you're getting a passport for the first time; if your previous passport was lost, stolen or damaged; or if your previous passport has expired and was issued more than 15 years ago or when you were under 16. All children under 18 must appear in person to apply for or renew a passport. Both parents must accompany any child under 14 (or send a notarized statement with their permission) and provide proof of their relationship to the child.

There are 13 regional passport offices, as well as 7,000 passport acceptance facilities in post offices, public libraries, and other governmental offices. If you're renewing a passport, you can do so by mail. Forms are available at passport acceptance facilities and online.

The cost to apply for a new passport is $97 for adults, $82 for children under 16; renewals are $67. Allow six weeks to process the paperwork for either a new or renewed passport. For an expediting fee of $60, you can reduce the time to about two weeks. If your trip is less than two weeks away, you can get a passport even more rapidly by going to a passport office with the necessary documentation. Private expediters can get things done in as little as 48 hours but charge hefty fees for their services.

Before your trip, make two copies of your passport's data page (one for someone at home and another for you to carry separately). Or scan the page and e-mail it to someone at home and/or yourself.

🖹 U.S. Passport Information **U.S. Department of State** ☏ 877/487-2778 ⊕ http://travel.state.gov/passport

🖹 U.S. Passport & Visa Expediters **A. Briggs Passport & Visa Expeditors** ☏ 800/806-0581 or 202/464-3000 ⊕ www.abriggs.com. **American Passport Express** ☏ 800/455-5166 or 603/559-9888 ⊕ www.americanpassport.com. **Passport Express** ☏ 800/362-8196 or 401/272-4612 ⊕ www.passportexpress.com. **Travel Document Systems** ☏ 800/874-5100 or 202/638-3800 ⊕ www.traveldocs.com. **Travel the World Visas** ☏ 866/886-8472 or 301/495-7700 ⊕ www.world-visa.com.

SENIOR TRAVEL

To qualify for age-related discounts, mention your senior-citizen status up front when booking hotel reservations (not when checking out) and before you're seated in restaurants (not when paying the bill). Be sure to have identification on hand. When renting a car, ask about promotional car-rental discounts, which can be cheaper than senior-citizen rates.

🖹 Educational Programs **Elderhostel** ☏ 877/426-8056, 978/323-4141 international callers, 877/426-2167 TTY ⊕ www.elderhostel.org.

SMOKING

Smoking is illegal in all California bars and restaurants, except on outdoor patios or in smoking rooms. This law is typically not well enforced and some restaurants and bars do not comply, so take your cues from the locals. Hotels and motels are also decreasing their inventory of smoking rooms; inquire at the time you book your reservation if any are available. In addition, a tax is added to cigarettes sold in California, and prices can be as high as $6 per pack. You might want to bring a carton from home.

SPORTS & THE OUTDOORS

In California you can scale some of North America's highest peaks, hike through sequoia groves or beneath towering redwoods, rappel down boulders in the desert, fish mountain streams, bike undulating coastal hills, sail the icy Pacific, dive in underwater ecopreserves, ski Olympic-class slopes, or golf at some of America's most famous courses. Whatever sport you love, you can do it in California.

FISHING

You'll need a license to fish in California. State residents pay $34.90, but nonresidents are charged $94 for a one-year license or $34.90 for a 10-day license. Residents and nonresidents can purchase a two-day license for $17.60 or a one-day license for $11.30. You can purchase them at outlets, such as sporting-goods stores and bait-and-tackle shops, throughout the state, or from DFG field offices (call for locations). The Web site of the California Department of Fish and Game provides information on fishing zones, licenses, and schedules.

🖹 **Department of Fish and Game; Licensing Dept.** ✉ 3211 S St., Sacramento 95816 ☏ 916/227-2245 ⊕ www.dfg.ca.gov/licensing/fishing/sportfishing.html.

STATE PARKS

California's state parks range from lush coastside recreation areas to ghost towns in the high-mountain deserts of the eastern Sierra Nevada. The extremely useful State Park Web site has a comprehensive list of all them, including facilities lists and campground information.

🖹 **California State Park System** ⌂ Dept. of Parks and Recreation, Box 942896, Sacramento 94296 ☏ 800/777-0369 or 916/653-6995 ⊕ www.parks.ca.gov.

STUDENTS IN CALIFORNIA

🖹 I.D.s & Services **STA Travel** ☏ 212/627-3111, 800/781-4040 24-hr service center ⊕ www.sta.com. **Travel Cuts** ☏ 800/592-2887 in the U.S. ⊕ www.travelcuts.com.

TAXES
Sales tax in California varies from about 7¼% to 8½% and applies to all purchases except for prepackaged food; restaurant food is taxed. Airlines include departure taxes and surcharges in the price of the ticket.

TIME
California is in the Pacific time zone. Pacific daylight time (PDT) is in effect from early April through late October; the rest of the year the clock is set to Pacific standard time (PST). Clocks are set ahead one hour when daylight saving time begins, back one hour when it ends.

TIPPING
At restaurants, a 15% tip is standard for waitstaff; up to 20% may be expected at more expensive establishments. The same goes for taxi drivers, bartenders, and hairdressers. Coat-check operators usually expect $1; bellhops and porters should get $1 to $2 per bag; hotel maids in upscale hotels should get about $2 per day of your stay. A concierge typically receives a tip of $5 to $10, with an additional gratuity for special services or favors.

On package tours, conductors and drivers usually get $1 per person from the group as a whole; check whether this has already been figured into your cost. For local sightseeing tours, you may individually tip the driver-guide 10% to 15% if he or she has been helpful or informative. Ushers in theaters do not expect tips.

TOURS & PACKAGES

GUIDED TOURS
Guided tours are a good option when you don't want to do it all yourself. You travel along with a group (sometimes large, sometimes small), stay in pre-booked hotels, eat with your fellow travelers (sometimes included in the price of your tour, sometimes not), and follow a schedule. But not all guided tours are a "If This is Tuesday, It Must Be Belgium" kind of experience. A knowledgeable guide can take you places that you might never discover on your own, and you may be pushed to see more than you

would have otherwise. Tours aren't for everyone, but they can be just the thing for trips to places where making travel arrangements is difficult or time-consuming (particularly when you don't speak the language). Whenever you book a guided tour, find out what's included and what isn't. A "land-only" tour includes all your travel (by bus, in most cases) in the destination, but not necessarily your flights to or even within it. Also, in most cases, prices in tour brochures don't include fees and taxes. And remember that you'll be expected to tip your guide (in cash) at the end of the tour.

VACATION PACKAGES
Packages *are not* guided tours. Packages combine airfare, accommodations, and perhaps a rental car or other extras (theater tickets, guided excursions, boat trips, reserved entry to popular museums, transit passes), but they let you do your own thing. During busy periods, packages may be your only option because flights and rooms may be otherwise sold out. Packages will definitely save you time. They can also save you money, particularly in peak seasons, but—and this is a really big "but"—you should price each part of the package separately to be sure. And be aware that prices advertised on Web sites and in newspapers rarely include service charges or taxes, which can up your costs by hundreds of dollars.

Note that local tourism boards can provide information about lesser-known and small-niche operators that sell packages to just a few destinations. And don't always assume that you can get the best deal by booking everything yourself. Some packages and cruises are sold only through travel agents.

Each year consumers are stranded or lose their money when packagers—even large ones with excellent reputations—go out of business. How can you protect yourself? First, always pay with a credit card; if you have a problem, your credit-card company may help you resolve it. Second, buy trip insurance that covers default. Third, choose a company that belongs to the United States Tour Operators Association, whose members must set aside funds ($1 million) to cover defaults. Finally choose a company that also participates in the Tour Operator Program of the American Society of Travel Agents (ASTA), which will act as mediator in any disputes. You can also check on the tour operator's reputation among travelers by posting an inquiry on one of the Fodors.com forums.

🖫 Organizations **American Society of Travel Agents (ASTA)** ☎ 703/739-2782 or 800/965-2782 24-hr hotline ⊕ www.astanet.com. **United States Tour Operators Association** (USTOA) ☎ 212/599-6599 ⊕ www.ustoa.com.

TRAIN TRAVEL

Amtrak's *California Zephyr* train from Chicago via Denver terminates in Oakland. The *Pacific Surfliner* connects San Diego and Paso Robles. The *Coast Starlight* train travels between Los Angeles and Seattle. The *Sunset Limited* heads west from Florida through New Orleans and Texas to Los Angeles.

🖫 Train Information **Amtrak** ☎ 800/872-7245 ⊕ www.amtrak.com.

TRAVEL AGENCIES

If you use an agent—brick-and-mortar or virtual—you'll pay a fee for the service. And know that the service you get from some online agents isn't comprehensive. For example Expedia or Travelocity don't search for prices on budget airlines like JetBlue, Southwest, or small foreign carriers. That said, some agents (online or not) *do* have access to fares that are difficult to find otherwise, and the savings can more than make up for any surcharge.

A knowledgeable brick-and-mortar travel agent can be a godsend if you're booking a cruise, a package trip that's not available to you directly, an air pass, or a complicated itinerary including several overseas flights. What's more, travel agents that specialize in a destination may have exclusive access to certain deals and insider information on things such as charter flights. Agents who specialize in types of travelers (senior citizens, gays and lesbians, naturists) or types of trips

(cruises, luxury travel, safaris) can also be invaluable.

A top-notch agent planning your trip to Russia will make sure you get the correct visa application and complete it on time; the one booking your cruise may get you a cabin upgrade or arrange to have bottle of champagne chilling in your cabin when you embark. And complain about the surcharges all you like, but when things don't work out the way you'd hoped, it's nice to have an agent to put things right.

🖫 Agent Resources **American Society of Travel Agents** ☎ 703/739-2782 ⊕ www.travelsense.org. 🖫 Online Agents **Expedia** ⊕ www.expedia.com. **Onetravel.com** ⊕ www.onetravel.com. **Orbitz** ⊕ www.orbitz.com. **Priceline.com** ⊕ www.priceline.com. **Travelocity** ⊕ www.travelocity.com.

VISITOR INFORMATION

For general information about California, contact the California Travel and Tourism Commission. The commission's Web site has travel tips, events calendars, and other resources, and the site will link you—via the Regions icon—to the Web sites of city and regional tourism offices and attractions. For the numbers of regional and city visitor bureaus and chambers of commerce *see* the "Essentials" section at the end of each chapter.

If you're coming to California from overseas, you can check with your home government for official travel advisories and destination information.

🖫 Tourist Information **California Travel and Tourism Commission** ⊠ 980 9th St., Suite 480, Sacramento 95814 ☎ 916/444-4429 information, 800/862-2543 brochures 🖷 916/444-0410 ⊕ www.gocalif.ca.gov.
🖫 Government Advisories **Australian Department of Foreign Affairs and Trade** ☎ 300/139-281 travel advisories, 02/6261-1299 Consular Travel Advice ⊕ www.smartraveller.gov.au. **Consular Affairs Bureau of Canada** ☎ 800/267-6788 or 613/944-6788 ⊕ www.voyage.gc.ca. **New Zealand Ministry of Foreign Affairs and Trade** ☎ 04/439-8000 ⊕ www.mft.govt.nz. **U.K. Foreign and Commonwealth Office** ⊠ Travel Advice Unit, Consular Directorate, Old Admiralty Building, London SW1A 2PA ☎ 0870/606-0290 or 020/7008-1500 ⊕ www.fco.gov.uk/travel.

WEB SITES

We're really proud of our Web site: Fodors.com is a great place to begin any journey. Scan Travel Wire for suggested itineraries, travel deals, restaurant and hotel openings, and other up-to-the-minute info. Check out Booking to research prices and book plane tickets, hotel rooms, rental cars, and vacation packages. Head to Talk for on-the-ground pointers from travelers who frequent our message boards. You can also link to loads of other travel-related resources.

After your trip, be sure to rate the places you visited and share your experiences and travel tips with us and other Fodorites in Travel Ratings and Talk on www.fodors.com.

The California Parks Department site has the lowdown on state-run parks and other recreational areas. A must-visit for outdoors and adventure travel enthusiasts, the Great Outdoor Recreation Page is arranged into easily navigated categories. The site of the Wine Institute, which is based in San Francisco, provides events listings and detailed information about the California wine industry and has links to the home pages of regional wine associations. And if you're fascinated by earthquakes, the U.S. Geological Survey is a must-visit.

🔲 Web Sites **California Parks Department** ⊕ www.parks.ca.gov. **Great Outdoor Recreation Page** ⊕ www.gorp.com. **Wine Institute** ⊕ www. wineinstitute.org. **U.S. Geological Survey** ⊕ www. usgs.gov.

INDEX

NOTES

NOTES

NOTES

ABOUT OUR WRITERS

Native Californian Cheryl Crabtree, who updated the Santa Barbara County and Ventura County portions of the Central Coast chapter, has worked as a freelance writer since 1987. She has contributed to *Fodor's California* since the 2003 edition and has also written for *Fodor's Complete Guide to the National Parks of the West, Resorts & Great Hotels,* and *Touring and Tasting: Great American Wineries.* She currently lives in Santa Barbara with her husband, two sons, and Jack Russell terrier.

When not writing about California travel and the outdoors, North Coast and Peninsula/South Bay updater Lisa M. Hamilton can be found at one of the farms in nearby Marin County. Accounts of her food-related journeys have appeared in *National Geographic Traveler, Gastronomica,* and *Orion.*

Orange County native Veronica Hill, who updated the Mojave Desert/Death Valley and Inland Empire chapters, discovered California at a young age during "Sunday drives" with her family. Now a features editor at the *Daily Press* in Victorville, her articles have also appeared in *US, Rolling Stone, Food & Wine,* and *Seventeen.*

Constance Jones, formerly a Fodor's Senior Editor, pulled up her lifelong New York roots and relocated to California in 2004. Based in Central Coast wine country, she takes off in her very first car whenever she has time to explore another new corner of the state. Jones revised the Monterey Bay chapter and the San Luis Obispo County and Big Sur Coastline portions of the Central Coast chapter; she also wrote the What's Where, Quintessential California, If You Like, and Great Itineraries sections at the front of the book.

Reed Parsell, who updated the Central Valley, Gold Country, and Southern Sierra chapters, writes general-interest stories for *Sacramento magazine* and travel stories for Western newspapers.

California travel expert John A. Vlahides is a longtime contributor to Fodor's and writes about the Golden State for King Features Syndicate, Conde Nast, *San Francisco magazine, Out Traveler,* and *Sunset.* He also discusses travel on international television and radio broadcasts, and his work has appeared on CNN and ABC (Australia). His quick-vacations segment, "One Night Stands with John Vlahides," airs on San Francisco's KRON 4. A French-trained chef and former Clefs d'Or concierge, John spends time away from his desk singing with the San Francisco Symphony, skiing the Sierra Nevada, and touring California on his BMW K-series motorcycle. He updated the Smart Travel Tips, Southern Sierra, and Lake Tahoe chapters of this edition.

A freelance correspondent for the *Sacramento Bee,* Far North updater Christine Vovakes regularly writes news and feature stories about the region. She considers her home turf of 25 years the undiscovered gem of California.

Bobbi Zane, who updated the Palm Springs/Southern Desert chapter, has been living in and visiting the region since her childhood. Her articles on Palm Springs have appeared in the *Orange County Register* and *Westways* magazine. She recently contributed to *Fodor's Complete Guide to the National Parks of the West, Fodor's San Diego,* and *Escape to Nature Without Roughing It.*